3 FREI
of weather info
to 60% on lc

G000144147

Let The Weather Channel® help you pack! Get all the information you need before you leave.

- Current conditions & forecasts for over 900 cities worldwide

- Severe weather information including winter and tropical storm updates

- Wake-up call complete with your local forecast

- Special interest forecasts featuring ski resort, boating and other outdoor conditions

Remove card and see instructions on back.

Plus:

After selecting any additional payment option, you will receive 5 FREE MINUTES of long distance service!

Easy. Convenient. Fast.

It's The Only Phone Card You Will Ever Need!

During your free call, an automated operator will offer you an option to add $10, $20 or $30 to your phone card using any major credit card.

Use your card to:

- Save 20% on comprehensive weather information!
- Save up to 60% on long distance calls to **anywhere** in the U.S., **anytime**!
- Save 20% on other helpful information including lottery, sports, and more!

Domestic long distance service costs $0.25 per minute and all other options cost $0.75 per minute when using your TWC phone card.

Take the worry out of wondering! Carry the power to access all of these essential services with you in your wallet, wherever **Frommer's** may take you!

THE WEATHER CHANNEL ®

No place on Earth has better weather.™

Weather information provided by The Weather Channel. Network Services provided by AT&T. All other services provided by ICN, Ltd. Offer valid only in U.S.

Travel Discount Coupon

This coupon entitles you to special discounts when you book your trip through the

RESERVATION SERVICE

Hotels ◆ Airlines ◆ Car Rentals ◆ Cruises
All Your Travel Needs

Here's what you get: *

◆ A discount of $50 USD on a booking of $1,000** or more for two or more people!

◆ A discount of $25 USD on a booking of $500** or more for one person!

◆ Free membership for three years, and 1,000 free miles on enrollment in the unique Miles-to-Go™ frequent-traveler program. Earn one mile for every dollar spent through the program. Earn free hotel stays starting at 5,000 miles. Earn free roundtrip airline tickets starting at 25,000 miles.

◆ Personal help in planning your own, customized trip.

◆ Fast, confirmed reservations at any property recommended in this guide, subject to availability.***

◆ Special discounts on bookings in the U.S. and around the world.

◆ Low-cost visa and passport service.

◆ Reduced-rate cruise packages.

> Visit our website at http://www.travnet.com/Frommer or call us globally at 201-567-8500, ext. 55. In the U.S., call toll-free at 1-888-940-5000, or fax 201-567-1838. In Canada, call toll-free at 1-800-883-9959, or fax 416-922-6053. In Asia, call 60-3-7191044, or fax 60-3-7185415.

CAL123

Frommer's® 97

California

by Erika Lenkert, Matthew R. Poole, Stephanie Avnet & Elizabeth Hansen

Macmillan • USA

ABOUT THE AUTHORS

A native San Franciscan, **Erika Lenkert** worked for HarperCollins before becoming a freelance writer. She has contributed to dozens of travel guides and is currently seeking her fortune in both San Francisco and Hollywood. Her Siamese cats are along for the ride.

Combining the only three things he's good at—eating, sleeping, and criticizing—**Matthew R. Poole** has found a surprisingly prosperous career as a freelance travel writer. A native Northern Californian and author of nearly a dozen travel guides to California and Hawaii, he's looking forward to retiring at 30 but fears he won't be able to tell the difference. He currently lives in San Francisco and has no intention of writing a novel.

In addition to co-writing chapters 5 through 13 of this book, Erika and Matt author *Frommer's San Francisco.*

A native of Los Angeles and an avid traveler, antique hound, and pop history enthusiast, **Stephanie Avnet** believes that California is best seen from behind the wheel of a red convertible. In addition to writing chapters 14, 15, and 16 for this book, she authors *Frommer's Los Angeles.* Stephanie is currently at work on *Wonderful Weekends from Los Angeles* (Macmillan Travel).

Longtime La Jolla resident **Elizabeth Hansen** is the author of *Frommer's San Diego* as well as *Frommer's Australia from $50 a Day* and *Frommer's New Zealand from $45 a Day.*

MACMILLAN TRAVEL

A Simon & Schuster Macmillan Company
1633 Broadway
New York, NY 10019

Find us online at **http://www.mgr.com/travel** or
on America Online at Keyword: **Frommer's.**

ISBN 0-02-861150-0
ISSN 1044-2146

Editor: Cheryl Farr
Thanks to Phillippe Wamba, Bill Goodwin, Robin Michaelson, Tracy McNamara, and Alicia Scott
Contributors: Lisa Stone-Norman, Andrew Rice, Jim Moore, Mary Herczog, Steve Hochman, Heidi Siegmund Cuda, and John McKinney
Production Editor: John Carroll
Design by Michele Laseau
Digital Cartography by Peter Bogaty, Roberta Stockwell, and Ortelius Design
Maps copyright © by Simon & Schuster, Inc.

SPECIAL SALES

Contents

List of Maps

AN INVITATION TO THE READER

In researching this book, we discovered many wonderful places—hotels, restaurants, shops, and more. We're sure you'll find others. Please tell us about them, so we can share the information with your fellow travelers in upcoming editions. If you were disappointed with a recommendation, we'd love to know that, too. Please write to:

Frommer's California '97
Macmillan Travel
1633 Broadway
New York, NY 10019

AN ADDITIONAL NOTE

Please be advised that travel information is subject to change at any time—and this is especially true of prices. We therefore suggest that you write or call ahead for confirmation when making your travel plans. The authors, editors, and publisher cannot be held responsible for the experiences of readers while traveling. Your safety is important to us, however, so we encourage you to stay alert and be aware of your surroundings. Keep a close eye on cameras, purses, and wallets, all favorite targets of thieves and pickpockets.

WHAT THE SYMBOLS MEAN

✪ Frommer's Favorites

Hotels, restaurants, attractions, and entertainment you should not miss.

⑤ Super-Special Values

Hotels and restaurants that offer great value for your money.

The following abbreviations are used for credit cards:

AE	American Express	EU	Eurocard
CB	Carte Blanche	JCB	Japan Credit Bank
DC	Diners Club	MC	MasterCard
DISC	Discover	V	Visa
ER	enRoute		

Area Code Changes Notice

Please note that a number of area codes in Southern California will be changing during the life of this edition:

- Effective January 25, 1997, portions of Los Angeles County, including Long Beach, are in the new **562** area code. You can dial 310 until July 26, 1997, after which you will have to use 562.
- Effective March 22, 1997, the area code for the desert regions, including the Palm Springs resorts and the desert parks and San Diego's North County beach towns, is scheduled to change to **760.** You will be able to dial 619 until September 27, 1997, after which you will have to use 760.
- Effective June 14, 1997, the eastern portion of Los Angeles County's 818 area code—including Burbank, Glendale, and Pasadena—will change to **626.** You will be able to dial 818 until January 17, 1998, after which you will have to use 626.

These changes have also been noted throughout the text where appropriate.

The Best of California

By Erika Lenkert, Matthew R. Poole,
Stephanie Avnet, and Elizabeth Hansen

1

If ever a state embodied Americana, California does.

Sure, there's famous, fun stuff like Hollywood and the Golden Gate Bridge and miles of beach filled with nubile, tanned surf gods and volleyball goddesses à la *Baywatch.*

But look beyond the headlines. It's not all movie stars, earthquakes, and race riots.

The real California also is Yosemite and Big Sur, whale watching, and the Mojave Desert.

It's small-town pride and commitment, personified by the descendants of gold miners who use their painstakingly restored bed-and-breakfasts to eke the kind of living from the Sierra that eluded most of their ancestors.

And don't picture grizzled miners as whites only—legions of African, Asian, and Hispanic Americans also discovered riches there and elsewhere in the Golden State.

Move over, Ellis Island. Ever since Spain and England laid conflicting claims to the land originally populated by Native Americans and long home to Mexican ranchers, California's history has enjoyed a rainbow hue.

For visitors today, this rich cultural diversity offers literally hundreds of annual celebrations and beautiful monuments to enjoy, from Chinese New Year parades to a chain of 21 beautiful, Spanish-style missions.

Of course, the reigning California tradition is sun worship: Come prepared to enjoy the outdoors. Visitors who aren't content with some of the nation's best white-water rafting and downhill skiing can strap on a snowboard, in-line skates, or a bungee harness for the well-padded thrill of a lifetime.

Then again, other travelers may choose simply—and literally—to feast between gorgeous views of vineyards and sea cliffs.

From white-hatted gourmets of trendy California cuisine to traditional Mexican *cocineras,* amazing cooks serve up the fruits of sea and land with delicious variety and flair.

If you don't like bean sprouts, don't worry—the home-grown Burmese, Italian, Greek, Thai, and Lebanese cuisine is great too, especially when washed down with the state's renowned wines and microbrewed suds.

And California's natural beauty and proud family traditions won't interfere if what you really want is to discover the state's reputation as the bad boy of popular culture.

Megamalls. Movie stars. Mud baths in Calistoga. Tattoo exhibitions and chainsaw jugglers on Venice Beach.

From Castroville's giant plastic artichoke—roughly the size of a Volkswagen bug—to the astonishing opulence of San Simeon, California has kitsch, glitter, and breathtaking self-indulgence to share.

Come and see.

1 The Best of Natural California

- **Año Nuevo State Reserve National Seashore:** Nature enthusiasts come from all over the world to this spot 22 miles north of Santa Cruz to view the elephant seal colony. Pups are born from December to March, and molting follows between April and August. You can also spot sea lions in spring and summer, whales in winter and spring, plus more than 250 bird species. See Chapter 6.
- **Point Reyes:** This extraordinarily scenic stretch of coast and wetlands is one of the best birdwatching spots in California for shore birds, songbirds, and waterfowl, as well as osprey and red-shouldered hawks. There's a rainbow-hued wildflower garden too, and you might catch a glimpse of a whale from the Point Reyes Lighthouse. See Chapter 8.
- **Sonoma Coast State Beaches:** Stretching about 10 miles from Bodega Bay to Jenner, these beaches attract more than 300 species of birds. From December to September, look for osprey. Seal pups can be spotted from March to June, and the gray whale from December to April. See Chapter 8.
- **Redwood National & State Parks:** A wildlife enthusiast's dream. More than 300 bird species and 100 mammals can be seen, many of them year-round. Also watch (or watch out!) for black bears in summer. See Chapter 8.
- **Point Lobos State Reserve:** Take Calif. 1 about 4 miles south of Carmel to view harbor seals, sea lions, and sea otters at play. From December to May gray whales pass by on their migration south. The area is filled with nature walks. See Chapter 12.
- **Cachuma Lake:** Situated on mountainous and scenic Calif. 154, halfway between Solvang and Santa Barbara, is this stunning winter home to dozens of American bald eagles. Loons, white pelicans, and Canadian geese are some of the other migratory birds that call this glassy lake home for part of the year. See Chapter 13.
- **Channel Islands National Park:** This is California in its most natural state. Paddle a kayak into sea caves; camp among indigenous island foxes and sea birds; and swim, snorkel, or scuba dive in tidepools and kelp forests teeming with wildlife. The channel waters are prime for whale watching, and May brings elephant seal mating season, when you'll see them and their sea lion cousins sunbathing on cove beaches. See Chapter 13.
- **Antelope Valley Poppy Reserve:** California's state flower, the poppy, blooms between March and May, carpeting the hillsides in brilliant hues of red, orange, and gold. This reserve, in the high desert near Los Angeles, is one of the poppy's most consistent natural growing sites. The fields extend for miles around—it's not uncommon to see motorists along Calif. 14 pull to the side of the road to marvel at the breathtaking spectacle. From L.A., take I-5 north to Calif. 14; you'll know when you've arrived. See Chapter 16.
- **Joshua Tree National Park:** You'll find awesome rock formations, groves of flowering cacti and stately Joshua trees, ancient Native American petroglyphs, and shifting sand dunes in this desert wonderland—and a brilliant night sky, if you choose to camp here. See Chapter 16.

- **Death Valley National Park:** Its inhospitable climate makes it the state's most unlikely tourist attraction. But the same conditions that thwarted settlers create some of the most dramatic landscapes you'll ever see. Mesmerizing rock formations, ever-changing dry lake beds, and often stifling heat provide the setting for relics of hardy 19th-century borax miners and (fool)hardy dwellers from the 1930s. See Chapter 16.
- **Torrey Pines State Reserve:** Poised on a majestic cliff overlooking the Pacific Ocean, this reserve is home to the rare torrey pine and numerous hiking trails. See Chapter 17.
- **Anza-Borrego Desert State Park:** The largest state park in the continental United States attracts the most visitors during the spring wildflower season, when a kaleidoscopic carpet blankets the desert floor. Others come year-round to hike the more than 100 miles of designated trails. See Chapter 17.

2 The Best Active Vacations

- **Surfing at Santa Cruz:** Up here they laugh at Southern California's reputation for surfing. The surfers of Santa Cruz claim that their town is the hottest spot in the Golden State, especially Steamer's Lane between the boardwalk and the lighthouse. See Chapter 6.
- **River Fishing on the Klamath in the Klamath National Forest:** In "Bigfoot Country," there's incredible fishing in one of the Golden State's most spectacular and unpopulated wildernesses. See Chapter 9.
- **White-Water Rafting on the Trinity, American, or Klamath River:** Our favorite is the Trinity River, flowing along Calif. 299 west from Weaverville. One of the prime territories for rafting and kayaking in California, it's been designated a Wild Scenic River. See Chapter 9.
- **Climbing Mount Shasta:** For experts who know how to handle an ice axe or crampon, guided expeditions reach the summit in 2 to 2¹/₂ days. Put yourself in the care of the experts at Shasta Mountain Guides, 1938 Hill Rd. (☎ 916/926-3117) at Mount Shasta. They'll even give you a crash course in rock climbing. See Chapter 9.
- **Skiing at One of Lake Tahoe's Resorts—Alpine Meadows, Squaw Valley, Heavenly, or Kirkland:** Narrow chutes, sheer faces, and towering cliffs attract the downhill skier. Squaw Valley and Alpine Meadows lie on Calif. 89 between Tahoe City and Truckee; Kirkland is reached along Calif. 89 south from South Lake Tahoe, and Heavenly is on U.S. 50 in South Lake Tahoe. See Chapter 9.
- **Rock Climbing in Yosemite:** Experts rate Yosemite as one of the finest climbing areas in the world—with vertical granite walls surrounding two-thirds of the valley. It's especially noteworthy at El Capitan and Half Dome. You'll have to enroll in the Yosemite Mountaineering School, however. After scaling the heights, you learn why the ancient Ahwahneechee people called Yosemite "the world's sacred belly, where nature's wonders spew forth." See Chapter 10.
- **Mountain Biking at Mammoth Mountain:** In summer, Mammoth becomes a veritable mountain-biking playground, with such challenging and thrilling trails as the Kamikaze Downhill. See Chapter 10.
- **Sea Kayaking Along the Monterey Coastline:** It's too cold and rocky for swimming, but it's ideal for exploring in a kayak. Take your business to the experts at Monterey Bay Kayaks, 693 Del Monte Ave., Monterey (☎ 408/373-KELP), who know the best takeoff points. See Chapter 12.

- **Exploring the Waters off Catalina Island:** This mecca for boaters is Southern California's answer to Capri and other jewels of the Mediterranean. The island's beaches and clear, cool coves are great for snorkeling and sunbathing. The surrounding sea is filled with marlin, porpoise, and phosphorescent flying fish. See Chapter 15.
- **Year-Round Action at Arrowhead and Big Bear Lakes,** nestled together in the San Bernardino Mountains: Within 2 hours of Los Angeles—yet with altitudes reaching over 10,000 feet—this resort area is popular year-round for skiing (or mountain biking along bare trails), fishing, waterskiing, sailboat and pontoon rentals, horseback riding, and outdoor ice skating. See Chapter 15.
- **Golfing the Desert Resorts—and More:** In addition to more than 80 lush golf courses, the desert playground in and around Palm Springs offers horseback riding, tennis, bicycle and roller-skate rentals, the giant Oasis Waterpark, hot-air ballooning, and guided tours of the surrounding desert canyons in your choice of vehicles: a modern Jeep or an authentic covered wagon pulled by a team of mules. See Chapter 16.
- **Big-Game Fishing at Point Loma:** Deep-sea boats operate out of most every marina in the state, but the most serious sea-hunters head straight for San Diego, where the open-ocean fishing is among the finest on the Pacific coast. H&M Landing (☎ 619/222-1144) offers excursions to the Point Loma Kelp Beds, where tuna, barracuda, and halibut regularly bite. See Chapter 17.
- **Scuba Diving & Snorkeling in the San Diego–La Jolla Underwater Park:** You can look at (but don't touch) a myriad of sealife—garibaldi, abalone, octopus, and more—in this unusual underwater park, which includes the shimmering La Jolla Cove and surroundings. You'll want a wetsuit in winter. See Chapter 17.
- **Cycling down Palomar Mountain:** The excitement takes over as gravity kicks in and you coast from the top of Palomar Mountain to its base. This 5,000-foot drop takes place over 16 miles. It's the thrill of a lifetime. See Chapter 17.

3 The Best Beaches

- **San Francisco's Ocean Beach:** At the end of Golden Gate Park, on the westernmost side of the city, Ocean Beach is gorgeous, but recommended for strolling and sunning only. Just offshore, the jagged Seal Rocks are inhabited by colonies of sea lions, among other creatures. See Chapter 5.
- **Stinson Beach:** Mount Tamalpais sweeps down to the sea at a point 6 treacherous miles north of Muir Beach on Calif. 1. Chilly waters and the threat of *Jaws* don't keep away thousands of sun worshippers and surfers. See Chapter 6.
- **Drake's Beach:** A massive stretch of white sand at Point Reyes National Seashore, west of Inverness. Winds and choppy seas make it rough for swimmers, but sun worshippers can have their Marin County tan for the day. If the rangers say it's all right, beach driftwood can make a romantic campfire in the early evening. See Chapter 8.
- **Manchester State Beach:** Take Calif. 1 8 miles north of Point Arena for a breezy introduction to the beaches of the far north. There are 5 miles of sand for beachcombing and surf fishing and huge driftwood logs along the beach. See Chapter 8.
- **Sand Dollar Beach:** The best Big Sur beach lies beyond Pacific Valley—ideal for swimming and surfing, with a panoramic view of Cone Peak, one of the coast's highest mountains. See Chapter 12.

- **Santa Barbara's Cabrillo Beach:** This wide swath of clean white sand hosts beach umbrellas, sandcastle builders, and spirited volleyball games. A grassy, parklike median keeps the happy beachgoers insulated from busy Cabrillo Boulevard. On Sunday, local artists display their wares beneath the elegant palm trees. See Chapter 13.
- **Malibu's Legendary Beaches:** Zuma and Surfrider beaches are the stretches of sand that were the inspiration for the 1960s surf music that embodies the Southern California beach experience. Surfrider, just up from Malibu Pier, is home to L.A.'s best waves. Zuma is loaded with amenities, including snack bars, rest rooms, and jungle gyms. In addition to some of the state's best sunbathing, you can walk in front of the Malibu Colony, a star-studded enclave of multi-million-dollar homes set in this seductively curving stretch of coast. See Chapter 14.
- **Hermosa Beach:** This is one of L.A.'s top beaches for family outings. It's also popular with the volleyball set. It offers wide sands, a paved boardwalk ("The Strand") that's great for strolling and biking, and loads of amenities—including plenty of parking. See Chapter 14.
- **La Jolla's Beaches:** *La Jolla* means "the jewel," and the beaches of La Jolla's cliff-lined coast truly are gems. Each has a distinct personality: Surfers love Windansea's waves; Torrey Pines and La Jolla Shores are popular for swimming and sunbathing; and Black's Beach is San Diego's unofficial (and illegal) nude beach. See Chapter 17.
- **Coronado Beach:** On the west side of Coronado extending to the Hotel del Coronado, this beautiful beach is uncrowded and great for watching the sunset. Marilyn Monroe romped in the surf here during the filming of *Some Like It Hot.* See Chapter 17.

4 The Best Walks

- **Golden Gate Park:** Strolling this magnificent park lets you escape the bustle of San Francisco and takes you through an array of attractions, beginning with the 1878 Conservatory of Flowers, but also including museums and a Japanese Tea Garden, and even a 430-foot-high man-made island, Strawberry Hill. End your walk by renting a rowboat and taking it for a spin. See Chapter 5.
- **Point Reyes National Seashore:** In Marin County, west of Inverness and a quarter mile north of Drake's Beach, Point Reyes Lighthouse, 6 miles to the west, will be your final goal. The scenery is among the most beautiful and enticing in the Golden State—especially the hike to Chimney Rock (follow the signs on your way to the lighthouse). See Chapter 8.
- **Mendocino Headlands State Park:** Between Mendocino and the Pacific is one of the most scenic nature trails in the north. From December to March the California gray whales pass by on their migration from the Arctic Ocean and Bering Sea to Baja California. Sunset vistas are worth the detour. See Chapter 8.
- **Yosemite National Park:** Relatively short and easy hikes will take you to Yosemite Falls, the highest waterfall in North America and the fifth highest in the world (upper falls at 1,430 feet), or to Bridalveil Falls, a ragged 620-foot cascade that can be wind-tossed as much as 20 feet from side to side. However, a more strenuous hike is a third option, the 3¹/₂-mile Yosemite Falls Trail, which rises to a height of 2,700 feet for one of the most panoramic vistas in the West. See Chapter 10.
- **The Beachfront Trails at Big Sur:** Take towering cliffs, rock-strewn beaches, and a backdrop of redwood forests and you have one of the most dramatic stretches

for coastline hiking in the world. Begin your adventure about 8 miles south of Point Lobos. See Chapter 12.

- **Cabrillo Peak in Morro Bay State Park:** This park offers a terrific day hike that culminates in a fantastic 360° view of surrounding hills and the distant ocean. There are hiking trails, but the best way to reach the top is by bushwacking straight up the gentle slope. See Chapter 13.

- **Beverly Hills' "Golden Triangle":** Defined by Wilshire Boulevard, Crescent Drive, and Santa Monica Boulevard, this is a window-shopper's fantasyland of tony shops with picture-perfect displays and sky-high price tags. It even boasts a cluster of shops built to resemble an Italian plaza, with its own faux-cobblestone "streets." If Rodeo Drive tariffs are out of your reach, don't worry; there are plenty of down-to-earth shops and eateries, plus an elegant Moorish-Mediterranean City Hall that's worth a look. See Chapter 14.

- **The L.A. Conservancy's Guided Walking Tours of Downtown Los Angeles:** The Conservancy conducts a dozen fascinating, information-packed tours of historic downtown L.A., seed of today's sprawling metropolis. The most popular is "Broadway Theaters," a loving look at movie palaces. Other intriguing ones include "Marble Masterpieces," "Art Deco," "Mecca for Merchants," and tours of the landmark Biltmore Hotel and City Hall. See Chapter 14.

- **Griffith Park:** This wooded enclave linking Hollywood with the San Fernando Valley has something for everyone. Be on the lookout for golf carts crossing near the picturesque Wilson and Harding golf courses, and for horseback riders from the nearby Equestrian Center. The L.A. Zoo and the Autry Museum lie at the northeast corner near I-5; the hills are loaded with hiking trails and picnic areas, and kids love the merry-go-round and pony rides. See Chapter 14.

- **From Crystal Pier (in Pacific Beach) South to the Jetty, & then North Along the Bayside to the Catamaran Hotel:** During the first part of this walk, you'll share the sidewalk with joggers, cyclists, and in-line skaters, and surfers will be testing their skill on the waves to your right. After you cross over to the Mission Bay side of Mission Boulevard, you'll experience the more subdued side of things: quiet water lapping onto white sand beaches, and the local residents tending their gardens. It's a lovely way to spend the day in San Diego. See Chapter 17.

- **From the San Diego Convention Center to Harbor Island:** This delightful stroll takes you around the waterfront of San Diego Bay. Along the way you'll pass Seaport Village, Tuna Bay, the cruise-ship terminal, the Embarcadero, and the Maritime Museum. The foot and cycle path offers a great view of Coronado and the ships plying the harbor. See Chapter 17.

5 The Best Skiing

- **Squaw Valley:** Located at Lake Tahoe, this is the most sophisticated and most Euro-chic resort in the area. It's as close as the Golden State gets to an alpine Swiss village. The Olympics pushed it into world-class status. Chair lifts send you to the heavens, as you scale five peaks. It boasts the most challenging and varied ski runs in the Sierra. See Chapter 9.

- **Alpine Meadows:** In a side canyon of the Truckee River, at an elevation of 6,835 feet, is the other "most famous" of Lake Tahoe's ski resorts. Alpine Meadows is not glitzy like Squaw Valley. It's a resort for skiers of all skills—from advanced to neophyte. Its season runs all the way from Thanksgiving until the Fourth of July. See Chapter 9.

- **Heavenly:** Heavenly (the "Valley" has been dropped from its name) is the third big ski challenger at Lake Tahoe (half of it lies in California, the other half in

Nevada). Its proximity to the casinos has made it even more popular. The slopes aren't Sun Valley or Aspen, but the après-ski life ("Look, there's Bill Cosby!") is just as good. Most of the slopes are intermediate. It boasts the Sierra's first-ever téléphérique. A day-care center for toddlers makes it family friendly, although prices might frighten most families. See Chapter 9.

- **Northstar Ski Resort:** Near Truckee, it's a family favorite, with nine lifts and an 1,800-foot vertical. It's been called "amusement park style" skiing—not too challenging and safe for most ages (residents call it "Flatstar"). Tracked Nordic skiing is offered in winter. Mount Pluto, at an elevation of 8,618 feet, is serviced by a gondola and some high-speed "detachables." See Chapter 9.
- **Kirkwood Meadows:** Kirkwood Meadows is on the way to becoming an "alpine village." One local cheerleader from the chamber of commerce predicts it will grow into "one of the best ski areas in the Golden State," though it's never going to be Aspen. At 7,800 feet, Kirkwood has the highest elevation in the Tahoe region and therefore "the driest and best snow"—or so they tout. Some fine Nordic ski facilities are found in the area, but you should go here more for relaxation than for any great ski challenge. See Chapter 9.
- **Mammoth Mountain Ski Area:** This mountain in the lower Sierra Nevada is as imposing as its name suggests. The town below offers a multitude of accommodations and markets, but little personality—Mammoth exists solely for the joy of the sport. The upper mountain is challenging and often severe (double-black-diamond runs), while the lower mountain has excellent novice and intermediate runs, along with a fine ski school. See Chapter 10.
- **Snow Summit Ski Resort:** This Big Bear resort is a favorite of Southlanders. Close enough for a day excursion yet alpine enough for some truly challenging skiing, Snow Summit offers amenities that include snack bars and restaurants at the base *and* summit of the mountain, breathtaking views of the pine-fringed lake below, and snow-making expertise that can double the length of the season. Wisely, ticket sales are limited to prevent crowding and to preserve snow conditions. Hey, you can even ski free on your birthday! See Chapter 15.

6 The Best Golf Courses

- **Silverado Country Club & Resort** (Napa): This 1,200-acre country club boasts not one but two championship 18-hole golf courses designed by Robert Trent Jones, Jr. They're among America's best. The weather is mild year-round, and the course is challenging but not daunting. It's a real R&R spot. See Chapter 7.
- **Pebble Beach Golf Course:** Situated along the famous 17-Mile Drive is the site of 10 national championships and the winter telecast of the celebrity-laden AT&T Pebble Beach National Pro-Am. The nearby raging Pacific and a scenic backdrop of the Del Monte Forest justify astronomical greens fees. See Chapter 12.
- **Spyglass Hill** (Pebble Beach): Five holes border the ocean, and the rest extend deep within Del Monte Forest. The holes here have been called "long and unforgiving" by golf magazines. Its slope rating of 143 makes it one of the toughest courses in California. See Chapter 12.
- **Poppy Hills** (Pebble Beach): Another course designed by Robert Trent Jones, Jr., *Golf Digest* has called it "one of the world's top 20 courses." Also used for AT&T festivities, it cuts right through the pines of Del Monte Forest. One golf pro said the course is "long and tough on short hitters." It's maintained in a state-of-the-art condition and, unlike some of its competitors, is rarely over-crowded. See Chapter 12.

- **The Links at Spanish Bay:** Perched along the 17-Mile Drive, the Links were designed by Robert Trent Jones, Jr., with a little help from Tom Watson and former USGA president Frank Tatum. Their aim was to simulate the experience of playing golf on true Scottish links. Its fescue grasses and natural fairways lead to rolls and unexpected bounces for your ball. Holes 14 to 18, taking you to the sea and back again through high dunes, call for some trick shot-making, but make the whole experience worthwhile. See Chapter 12.
- **Industry Hills Golf Course, Eisenhower Course** (Los Angeles): Designed by William Francis Bell in 1979, this course consistently ranks among *Golf Digest's* top 25 public courses. Often home to the U.S. Open qualifying rounds, the Eisenhower course has extra-large, undulating greens and the challenge of thick kikuyu roughs. See Chapter 14.
- **Westin Mission Hills Resort, Pete Dye Course** (Rancho Mirage): Since 1987, when course architect Pete Dye sculpted this links-style, par-70 challenger, players have wrangled with the pot bunkers, hidden pin placements, and carries over water that are his classic trademarks. Rolling fairways and railroad ties also characterize Dye's 6,706-yard classic. The course takes full scenic advantage of the lavender hills all around. See Chapter 16.
- **PGA West TPC Stadium Course** (La Quinta): The par-3 17th has a picturesque island green where Lee Trevino made Skins Game history with a spectacular hole-in-one. The rest of Pete Dye's 7,261-yard design is flat with huge bunkers, lots of water, and severe mounding throughout. The PGA West is part of the La Quinta Resort and Golf Club, which received *Golf* magazine's 1994 Gold Medal Award for the total golf resort experience. Now open for semiprivate play is the Mountain Course at La Quinta, another Dye design appearing regularly on U.S. top 100 lists. It's set dramatically against the rocky mountains, which thrust into fairways to create tricky doglegs. Small Bermuda greens are well guarded by boulders and deep bunkers. See Chapter 16.
- **Torrey Pines Golf Course** (La Jolla): Two gorgeous 18-hole championship courses overlook the ocean and provide players with plenty of challenge. In February the Buick Invitational Tournament is held here; the rest of the year these popular municipal courses are open to everybody. See Chapter 17.
- **Coronado Municipal Golf Course** (San Diego): This 18-hole, par-72 municipal course overlooking Glorietta Bay is located to the left of the Coronado Bay Bridge. It's the first thing you see when you arrive in Coronado—a fabulous welcome for duffers. See Chapter 17.

7 The Best Offbeat Travel Experiences

- **Hot-Air Ballooning over Napa Valley:** It's all the rage. Hotels throughout the valley arrange excursions. Flights are best right after sunrise, when the air is calm and cool. You'll fly away in the style of *Around the World in 80 Days,* and sometimes there's a catered champagne brunch at the end of the adventure. See Chapter 7.
- **Taking a Mud Bath at Indian Springs in Calistoga:** In this town's famous volcanic-ash mud—mixed with mineral water—you can get buck naked and covered in gooey mud. At a dozen or so places you can immerse yourself in the mud bath, followed by a mineral-water shower and a whirlpool bath, then a steam bath. It's perhaps the most relaxing experience in California. See Chapter 7.
- **Discovering "The Lost Coast":** The terrain was so rugged that the state of California couldn't extend Calif. 1 along the Pacific between Rockport and Eureka.

Today this isolated region remains pristine, with redwood trees perched precariously on cliffs some 200 feet above the rock-strewn coastline. The 75-mile drive is entered from U.S. 101 at Garberville, or, better yet, from a paved road from Humboldt Redwoods State Park, 3 miles north of Weott. See Chapter 8.

- **Panning for Gold in the Gold Country:** In the southern Gold Country, you can dig into living history and pan for gold. Several companies, including Gold Prospecting Expeditions (☎ 800/596-0009 or 209/984-4653) in Jamestown, offer dredging lessons and gold-panning tours. You'll quickly learn that this is backbreaking labor, although an adventure. And who knows? You might get lucky and launch a new Gold Rush. See Chapter 11.

- **Taking a Gastronomic Road Trip Between Bakersfield & the Gold Country:** Calif. 99 passes through fertile agricultural land and a series of small towns, each with a distinct ethnic heritage. Basque sheep farmers and bakers, Dutch dairies, Swedish and Armenian enclaves near Fresno, Portuguese and Italians near Modesto, and a French sausage maker in Lodi—they all represent the delicious diversity of California's central region. See Chapter 11.

- **Riding the Amtrak Rails Along the Southern California Coast:** Relive the golden age of train travel and see the natural beauty of California, avoiding the crowded highways at the same time. Spanish-style Union Station, a marble-floored Streamline Moderne masterpiece, is the Los Angeles hub. Trains run between L.A. and the romantic mission towns of San Juan Capistrano, San Diego, Santa Barbara, and San Luis Obispo. The scenery includes lush valleys, windswept coastline, and the occasional urban stretch. Call Amtrak (☎ 800/USA-RAIL) for information.

- **Discovering Downtown L.A.'s Public Art:** The wealth of public art on display in downtown Los Angeles is one of the city's best-kept secrets. Some works make political or social commentary (the black experience as represented by the life of former slave Biddy Mason in a multimedia exhibit between Broadway and Spring streets just south of 3rd Street, or Judd Fine's evolutionary chronicle *Spine* installed outside the Central Library). Others are abstract and open to a variety of interpretations. Pershing Square, a formerly untended eyesore bounded by 5th, 6th, Olive, and Hill streets, has been reincarnated as a modern sculpture garden. See Chapter 14.

- **Exploring Forest Lawn Memorial Park:** America's most famous cemetery is a wacky 300-acre park with more stars in the ground than Hollywood's Walk of Fame. In addition to Hollywood's most dearly departed, the cemetery contains 1,000 full-scale reproductions of Renaissance statuary, the enormous Great Mausoleum with its oversize stained-glass reproduction of *The Last Supper,* and the Church of the Recessional, where Ronald Reagan married his first wife, Jane Wyman. See Chapter 14.

- **Strolling Venice Beach:** All of humanity—for better and worse—is represented on a boardwalk framed by broad sands, swaying palms, and the sparkling blue Pacific. The day's carnival might include well-tanned body builders, outrageous street performers, scantily clad beach bunnies (bimbos *and* himbos), roving gangs of teens, psychedelic-era hippies, and much more. Experiment with style at the cheap sunglass stalls, grab an exotic dog at Jody Maroni's Sausage Kingdom, and make your way to the Santa Monica Pier to check out the historic photo gallery and carousel. See Chapter 14.

- **Skydiving over Southern California:** Enjoy a bird's-eye view of the Southland. Local schools offer instruction at all levels (including tandem jumps for first-timers). At the California City Skydive Center (☎ 800/2-JUMP-HI), in the Mojave

Desert, you can soar through the same skies as the space shuttle, which lands at nearby Edwards Air Force Base. Hemet and Perris are home to world-renowned schools, Skydiving Adventures at Hemet-Ryan Airport (☎ 800/526-9682) and the Perris Valley Skydiving School (☎ 800/832-8818), as is Skylark Airport at Lake Elsinore, where you'll find Jim Wallace Skydiving (☎ 800/795-DIVE).

- **Going to the Movies, San Diego Style:** Imagine sitting on the deck of the world's oldest merchant ship, watching a film projected on the "screen-sail"; floating on a raft in a huge indoor pool while a movie is shown on the wall; watching a silent movie accompanied by the San Diego Symphony; or sitting on the beach watching a movie that's projected on a floating barge. Only in San Diego! See Chapter 17.
- **Experiencing a San Diego Christmas:** Although visions of sugar plums don't dance in most people's heads when they think about San Diego, the area does offer a variety of unusual Christmas traditions. These include Christmas on the Prado in Balboa Park; the Coronado Christmas Celebration and Parade, where Santa arrives by ferry; and the Mission Bay Boat Parade of Lights and the San Diego Harbor Parade of Lights, where decorated boats of all sizes and types are the focus of attention. And it wouldn't be Christmas without the annual reading of Dr. Seuss's *The Grinch That Stole Christmas* at Loews Coronado Bay Resort. See Chapters 2 and 17.

8 The Best of Small-Town California

- **St. Helena:** A small town in the heart of the Napa Valley, St. Helena is known for its Main Street, which is lined with Victorian storefronts featuring intriguing wares. In a horse and buggy, Robert Louis Stevenson and his new bride, the cantankerous Fanny, made their way down this street. Go here for the old-timey, tranquil mood and the wonderful food. See Chapter 7.
- **Mendocino:** An artist's colony with a New England flavor, Mendocino serves as the backdrop for *Murder, She Wrote.* Perched on the clifftops above the Pacific Ocean, it's filled with small art galleries, general stores, weathered wooden houses, and elbow-to-elbow tourists. See Chapter 8.
- **Arcata:** If you're losing your faith in America, a few days spent at this Northern California coastal town will surely restore your patriotism. One of the best small towns in America, Arcata has it all: its own redwood forest and bird marsh, a charming town square, great family-owned restaurants, and even its own minor-league baseball team, which draws the whole town together for an afternoon of pure camaraderie. See Chapter 8.
- **Nevada City:** The whole town is a national historic landmark and the best place to understand Gold Rush fever. Settled in 1849, it offers fine dining and shopping and a stock of multigabled Victorian frame houses of the Old West. Relics of the cannibalistic Donner Party are on display at the 1861 Firehouse No. 1. See Chapter 12.
- **Pacific Grove:** Here you can escape from the crowds in Monterey, 2 miles to the west. Pacific Grove is known for its tranquil waterfront location and quiet, un-spoiled air. Thousands of Monarch butterflies flock here between October and March to make their winter home in Washington Park. See Chapter 12.
- **Cambria:** Near Hearst Castle, Cambria benefits from a constant stream of visitors, who bring the right amount of sophistication to this picturesque coastal town. Moonstone Beach holds a string of seaside lodges, while the village itself is filled

with charming B&Bs, artists' studios and galleries, and friendly shops. Don't miss Linn's Bakery and Restaurant, whose fresh olallieberry pies and other regional treats are well known throughout the Central Coast. See Chapter 13.

- **Ojai:** When Hollywood needed a Shangri-La for the movie *Lost Horizon*, they drove 1¹/₂ miles north to the idyllic Ojai Valley, an unspoiled hideaway of eucalyptus groves and small ranches warmly nestled among soft, green hills. Ojai is the amiable village at the valley's heart. It's a mecca for artists, free spirits, and weary city folk in need of a restful weekend in the country. See Chapter 13.
- **Ventura:** This charming mission town is filled with colorful Victorians. It's also home to a pleasantly eclectic old Main Street lined with thrift and antique shops, used record stores, friendly diners, and even old-time saloons operating beneath broken-down second-story hotels. Don't miss the historic mission on its landscaped plaza, and the Deco-era Greek Revival San Buenaventura City Hall looming over the town, bedecked with smiling stone faces of the founding Franciscan friars. See Chapter 13.
- **Julian:** This old mining town in the Cuyamaca Mountains near San Diego is well known today for its wildflower fields, the fall apple harvest, and tasty flavored breads from Dudley's Bakery. There's plenty of pioneer history here too, including a local history museum, an 1888 schoolhouse, and mining demonstrations. A smattering of antiques shops, plenty of barbecue, and an old-fashioned soda fountain operating since 1886 round out the experience. See Chapter 17.
- **Temecula:** This charming town, located in Riverside County 60 miles north of San Diego, is best known for its wineries and the excellent vintages they produce, as well as the annual hot-air balloon festival at harvest time. Since the wineries here are smaller than their counterparts in Northern California, and are mostly family-owned and -operated, you're more likely to be able to meet and talk with the vintners here. See Chapter 17.

9 The Best Family Vacation Experiences

- **San Francisco:** Ride the cable cars that "climb halfway to the stars" and visit the Exploratorium, the California Academy of Sciences (which includes the Steinhart Aquarium), the zoo, the ships at the maritime museum, Golden Gate Park, and much more. The City by the Bay is filled with unexpected pleasures for all members of the family and all ages. See Chapter 5.
- **Marine World Africa USA:** One of Northern California's most popular attractions is located on Marine World Parkway at Vallejo, an hour's drive northeast of San Francisco. This 160-acre wildlife theme park features animals of the air, land, and sea—some show-stopping performers. Killer whales, elephants, dolphins, sea lions—they're all in the act and you get a close-up look. See Chapter 6.
- **San Jose:** There's the Children's Discovery Museum, the Tech Museum of Innovation, and especially the architecturally bizarre Winchester Mystery House and Paramount's Great America. See Chapter 6.
- **Lake Tahoe:** California's Disneyland of outdoor adventure, Lake Tahoe has piles of family-fun things to do. Skiing, snowboarding, hiking, tobogganing, swimming, fishing, boating, waterskiing, mountain biking—the list is nearly endless. Even the casinos cater to kids while mom and pop play the slots. See Chapter 9.
- **Yosemite National Park:** Camping or staying in a cabin in Yosemite is a premier family attraction in California. Sites are scattered over 17 different campgrounds, and the rugged beauty of the Sierra Nevada surrounds you. During the day, the

family calendar is packed with hiking, bicycling, white-water trips, and even mountaineering to rugged, snowy peaks. See Chapter 10.

- **Monterey:** It's been called "Disneyland-by-the-Sea" because of all its tourist activities, including those on Cannery Row and Fisherman's Wharf. Check out the
state-of-the-art aquarium and have breakfast at the Bagel Bakery at 201 Lighthouse
Blvd. (the best family bargain in town). See Chapter 12.

- **Big Bear Lake:** Families flock year-round to this lake in the San Bernardino
Mountains, and not just for the skiing. Horseback riding, miniature golf, water
sports, and the Alpine Slide (kind of a snowless bobsled) are fun alternatives,
and you can see and learn about native wildlife at the Moonridge Animal
Park. The newly expanded village has a movie theater, arcade, and dozens of cutesy
bear-themed businesses. Most of the local lodging consists of clusters of woodsy
cabins that are perfect for families. See Chapter 15.

- **Disneyland:** The "Happiest Place on Earth" is family entertainment at its best.
Whether you're wowed by Disney animation come alive, thrilled by the roller-
coaster rides, or interested in the history and hidden secrets of this pop-culture
icon, you won't walk away disappointed. Stay at the nearby Disneyland Hotel
(connected directly to the park by monorail), a wild attraction unto itself, which
offers appealing packages including multiday access to the park. There's also a
terrific extra bonus: On most days, guests of the hotel get to enter the park early
and enjoy the major rides with no lines. Call ahead for the day's schedule. See
Chapter 15.

- **San Diego Zoo, Wild Animal Park, and Sea World:** San Diego boasts three of
the world's best animal attractions. At the Zoo, animals live in creatively designed
habitats such as Tiger River and Hippo Beach. At the Wild Animal Park, 3,000
animals roam freely over 2,200 acres. And Sea World, with its ever-changing animal shows and exhibits, is an aquatic wonderland. See Chapter 17.

10 The Best Architectural Landmarks

- **The Civic Center** (San Francisco): The creation of designers John Bakewell, Jr.,
and Arthur Brown, Jr., it is perhaps the most beautiful Beaux Arts complex in
America. See Chapter 5.

- **The Painted Ladies** (San Francisco): The so-called "Painted Ladies" are the city's
famous, ornately decorated Victorian homes. Check out the brilliant beauties
around Alamo Square. Most of the 14,000 extant structures date from the second
half of the 19th century. See Chapter 5.

- **Winchester Mystery House** (San Jose): The heiress to the Winchester rifle fortune, Sarah Winchester, created one of the major "Believe It or Not?" curiosities
of California, a 160-room Victorian mansion. It's been called the "world's strangest
monument to a woman's fear." When a fortune teller told her she wouldn't die
if she'd continue to build onto her house, her mansion underwent construction
day and night from 1884 to 1922. She did die eventually and the hammers were
silenced. See Chapter 6.

- **The Carson House** (Eureka): A splendidly ornate Victorian—one of the state's
most photographed and flamboyant Queen Anne–style structures. It was built in
1885 by the Newsom brothers for William Carson, the local timber baron. Today it's the headquarters of a men's club. See Chapter 8.

- **Mission San Carlos Borromeo del Rio Carmelo** (Carmel): The second mission
founded in California in 1770 by Father Junípero Serra (who is buried here) is

perhaps the most beautiful. Its stone church and tower dome have been authentically restored, and a peaceful garden of California poppies adjoins the church. Sights include an early kitchen and the founding father's spartan sleeping quarters. See Chapter 12.

- **The Control Tower and Theme Building at Los Angeles International Airport:** The spacey *Jetsons*-style "Theme Building," which has always loomed over LAX, unmistakably signaling your arrival, has been joined by a brand-new silhouette. The main control tower, designed by local architect Kate Diamond to evoke a stylized palm tree, is tailored to present Southern California in its best light. Only authorized personnel are allowed to make the ascent, but you can still enjoy the view from the Theme Building's observation lounge. See Chapter 14.
- **Los Angeles's Central Library:** The city rallied to save the downtown library when an arson fire nearly destroyed it in 1986; the triumphant result has returned much of its original splendor. Working in the early 1920s, architect Bertram G. Goodhue employed the Egyptian motifs and materials popularized by the recent discovery of King Tut's tomb, combined with the more modern use of concrete block. See Chapter 14.
- **Tail o' the Pup** (Los Angeles): At first glance, you might not think twice about this hot dog–shaped bit of kitsch on West Hollywood's San Vicente Boulevard, just across from the Beverly Center. But locals adored this closet-sized wiener dispensary so much that when it was threatened by the developer's bulldozer, they spoke out en masse to save it. One of the last remaining examples of 1950s representational architecture, the "little dog that could" also serves up a great Baseball Special. See Chapter 14.
- **The Gamble House** (Pasadena): The Smithsonian Institution calls this Pasadena landmark, built in 1908, "one of the most important houses in the United States." Architects Charles and Henry Greene created a masterpiece of the Japanese-influenced Arts and Crafts movement. Tours are conducted of the spectacular interior, designed by the Greenes down to the last piece of teak furniture and co-ordinating Tiffany lamp, and executed with impeccable craftsmanship. After you're done, stroll the immediate neighborhood to view several more Greene and Greene creations. See Chapter 15.
- **Balboa Park** (San Diego): These Spanish/Mayan-style buildings were originally built as temporary structures for the Panama-California Exposition between 1915 and 1916. Although many have been rebuilt over the years, a few of the original buildings still remain, and are worth seeking out. See Chapter 17.
- **Hotel Del Coronado** (Coronado): The "Hotel Del" stands in all its ornate Victorian red-tiled glory on some of the loveliest beach in Southern California. Built in 1888, it's one of the largest remaining wooden structures in the world. Even if you're not staying, stop by to take a detailed tour of the splendidly restored interiors, elegant grounds, and fascinating minimuseum of the hotel's spirited history. On your way to Coronado, you can't miss the Coronado Bay Bridge, an architectural landmark in its own right. Crossing the bridge by car or bus is an undeniable thrill because you can see Mexico, the San Diego skyline, Coronado, the naval station, and San Diego Bay. See Chapter 17.

11 The Best Museums

- **The Exploratorium** (San Francisco): The hands-on, interactive Exploratorium boasts 650 exhibits that help to show how things work. You use all your senses and stretch them to a new dimension. Every exhibit is designed to be useful. See Chapter 5.

- **The Oakland Museum:** This one might be dubbed the "Museum of California." The colorful people and history of the Golden State, and its sometimes overpowering art and culture, are here. Everything from the region's first inhabitants to today's urban violence is depicted. See Chapter 6.

- **California State Railroad Museum** (Sacramento): Old Sacramento's biggest attraction, this 100,000-square-foot museum was once the terminus of the Transcontinental and Sacramento Valley railways. The largest museum of its type in the United States, it displays 21 locomotives and railroad cars, among other attractions. One sleeping car simulates travel, with all the swaying and flashing lights of lonely towns passed in the night. See Chapter 11.

- **Petersen Automotive Museum** (Los Angeles): This museum is a natural for Los Angeles, a city whose personality is so entwined with the popularity of the car. Impeccably restored vintage autos are displayed in life-size dioramas accurate to the last period detail (including an authentic 1930s-era service station). Upstairs galleries house movie-star and motion-picture vehicles, car-related artwork, and visiting exhibits. See Chapter 14.

- **J. Paul Getty Museum** (Malibu): This exact replica of a villa buried by Vesuvius in A.D. 79 is the perfect setting for a world-renowned collection of Greek and Roman antiquities. Fueled by a bottomless endowment from billionaire oil magnate J. Paul Getty, the foundation has built an awesome collection that also includes European paintings and furnishings. There's a surprisingly eclectic parade of visiting exhibits, as well as a splendid Pacific view from the Roman pool garden. See Chapter 14.

- **Autry Museum of Western Heritage** (Los Angeles): This is a treat for both young and old. Relive California's historic cowboy past, and see how the period has been depicted by Hollywood through the years, from Disney cartoon re-creations to founder Gene Autry's "singing cowboy" films to popular 1960s TV series. Highlights include a life-size wooly mammoth and a glimmering vault of ornate frontier firearms. See Chapter 14.

- **Norton Simon Museum of Art** (Pasadena): This Pasadena museum is seen by millions each January 1 as a picturesque backdrop for the Rose Parade. What TV viewers miss, however, are the treasures inside, carefully collected by wealthy art lover Norton Simon and his wife, actress Jennifer Jones. The collection, spanning 2,000 years, includes Asian art and works of the Renaissance masters, but the museum's strength is its modern collection. Fine impressionist (Cézanne, Renoir, Van Gogh) and later (Kadinsky, Picasso) works are well complemented by the 19th- and 20th-century sculpture gardens, home to works by Rodin and others. See Chapter 15.

- **Museum of Contemporary Art** (San Diego): MCA is actually one museum with two locations: one in La Jolla, the other downtown. The museum is known internationally for its permanent collection, focusing primarily on work produced since 1950. See Chapter 17.

- **The Museums of Balboa Park** (San Diego): Located in a relaxed, verdant setting, the museums here offer unique cultural experiences. Highlights include the Aerospace Historical Center, Museum of Man, Museum of Photographic Arts, Model Railroad Museum, Natural History Museum, and the Lily Pond and Botanical Building. Check in at the Hospitality Center for a map and "Passport to Balboa Park," a low-cost pass to a combination of the museums. See Chapter 17.

12 The Best Views

- **Coit Tower** (San Francisco): The round 1933 tower atop Telegraph Hill opens onto a panoramic 360° view of the City by the Bay. In the distance the Marin Headlands unfold. In a city known for its views and vantage points, Coit Tower is the scenic show-stopper. See Chapter 5.
- **The Summit of Mount Tamalpais:** Twenty miles north of San Francisco, "Mount Tam" gives you a 100-mile panoramic sweep in all directions, from the foothills of the Sierras to the western horizon. The sunset there equals any Hemingway ever wrote about. See Chapter 6.
- **Mount Shasta as Seen from Black Butte:** The view of venerable Mount Shasta is best from Black Butte, which sits next to the 14,000-foot-plus behemoth itself. The 6,325-foot dome of Black Butte is reached after a 3-hour hike to the top. The majesty of the site turned fabled naturalist John Muir's "blood to wine." See Chapter 9.
- **Glacier Point in Yosemite National Park:** A sweeping 180° panorama of the High Sierras unfolds from 3,200 feet above the valley. Glacier Point looks out over Nevada and Vernal falls, the Merced River, and the snow-covered Sierra peaks of Yosemite's backcountry. See Chapter 10.
- **San Joaquin Valley:** This fertile valley is part of California's geographic and economic center. Roadside stops along I-5 offer panoramic views of 11 million rich acres of grapes, figs, almonds, carrots, asparagus, corn, and more. See Chapter 11.
- **The Coastline at Garrapata State Park:** You'll see 4 miles of the California coastline from Garrapata State Park, a 2,879-acre preserve in the Big Sur area. Rock-strewn beaches, towering cliffs, and redwood forests combine to form what may be the world's most dramatic coastal panorama. See Chapter 12.
- **Santa Barbara Mission:** Gazing seaward from the church's majestic steps, you can take in a panoramic view of Santa Barbara's delightful Spanish-style red-tile roofs, plus the California coast and azure Pacific in all their splendor. It's a postcard-worthy vista throughout the day, from the pastel shades of dawn to the midday shimmer of the sea to the fiery brilliance of sunset. See Chapter 13.
- **Griffith Observatory and Planetarium** (Los Angeles): For an outlook on urban Los Angeles without compare, head to this spot in the Hollywood Hills. Great ornate bronze doors lead into this 1935 Classic Moderne edifice (immortalized in *Rebel Without a Cause*). The view over the city from the hilltop balconies can, on a clear day, stretch to the Pacific. The lights of Hollywood below sparkle seductively at night, and the observatory's telescope can illuminate the myriad moons of Jupiter for you. See Chapter 14.
- **Rim of the World Highway** (Lake Arrowhead): This aptly named road winds toward Lake Arrowhead along a mountain ridge above San Bernardino. The view of the vast, flat valley floor beyond the evergreen fringe is breathtaking. At this altitude (about 5,500 feet), where the air is crisp and clean, it's easy to imagine you're floating above the earth. See Chapter 15.
- **The Colorado Desert:** If you think the desert is barren and ugly, you'll quickly change your mind. From the sweeping panorama atop Mt. San Jacinto (accessible by the Palm Springs Aerial Tramway) to the vast, other-worldly wind-turbine fields scattered throughout the valley, the visual splendor of this area mirrors the spirituality felt here by Native Americans and 20th-century spa-goers alike. From sunrise to sunset, natural light and shadow perform magic, transforming the shapes and colors of the arid hills. See Chapter 16.

- **Cabrillo National Monument** (near San Diego): From this vantage point, on the tip of Point Loma, you're treated to a spectacular vista of the ocean, San Diego Bay, Los Coronados Islands, and the mountains that ring the city to the east. Simply spectacular. See Chapter 17.
- **Mount Soledad** (San Diego): For a 360° view of La Jolla, Del Mar, downtown San Diego, inland San Diego, the Pacific Ocean, the mountains, and—on a clear day—even Mexico, Mount Soledad can't be beat. And it can't be missed, either: This La Jolla landmark is topped by a large white cross. See Chapter 17.

13 The Best Luxury Hotels

- **Auberge du Soleil** (Rutherford; ☎ 707/963-1211): The "Inn of the Sun," a Relais & Châteaux member in a 33-acre olive grove, stands in vineyards in the Napa Valley. This French country-style inn is the Wine Country's best resort. Each of the spacious villas is named after a region of France. It's very private, discreet, and romantic. See Chapter 7.
- **Meadowood Resort** (St. Helena; ☎ 707/963-3646): A retreat of towering charm and style, this 256-acre wine-country estate was inspired by New England's grand turn-of-the-century cottages. With its plethora of sports facilities and stress-relieving treatments, it attracts such clients as megabuck novelist Danielle Steel. See Chapter 7.
- **The Estate by the Elderberries** (Oakhurst; ☎ 209/683-6860): Close to Yosemite, the Château Sureau and Erna's Elderberry House, established in 1984, evoke the best of Europe. Exquisite furnishings, individually decorated rooms, and a cuisine worthy of the stars make for a memorable lodging and dining experience on the doorway to the wilderness. See Chapter 10.
- **Stonepine** (Carmel Valley; ☎ 408/659-2245): A mile-long driveway leads to this exquisite château on a private 330-acre estate that was built by a San Francisco banking family in the 1920s. Polo fields and stables evoke an era that seems straight out of *The Great Gatsby*. You'll be suitably pampered. See Chapter 12.
- **Ventana Inn** (Big Sur; ☎ 408/667-2331): A luxurious wilderness resort on 243 mountainous oceanfront acres, it's chic, tranquil, and hip. This pioneer sylvan retreat at Big Sur is a magnet for celebrities. Accommodations in one- and two-story buildings—each "worthy of the wild"—blend in with the dramatic Big Sur coastline. The cuisine is first-rate. See Chapter 12.
- **The Four Seasons Biltmore** (Santa Barbara; ☎ 805/969-2261): Opened in 1927 (and extensively refurbished in 1988), the Biltmore has palm-studded formal gardens and a prime beachfront location along "America's Riviera." Meander through the elegant Spanish/Moorish arcades and walkways, all accented by exquisite Mexican tile, then play croquet on manicured lawns or relax at the Coral Casino Beach and Cabana Club. The rooms, too, are the epitome of refined luxury, and the service couldn't be more friendly and accommodating. See Chapter 13.
- **Hotel Bel-Air** (Los Angeles; ☎ 310/472-1211): Nestled in the foothills above UCLA, this is the choice of visiting European royalty, world leaders, and top celebrities. The graceful hotel was built in the 1920s, its grounds landscaped like a fairy-tale kingdom: Stone footbridges pass over koi-filled streams, flowering trees surround a swan-filled pond, and flagstone paths lead to richly traditional rooms. See Chapter 14.
- **The Inn on Mt. Ada** (Santa Catalina Island; ☎ 310/510-2030): With only six guest rooms, this former mansion of the wealthy Wrigley family is one of the most exclusive B&B experiences you'll ever have. The hilltop inn's hefty rates include

all your meals (and thoughtful snacks laid out each afternoon), plus the use of a golf cart to putter around this auto-eschewing island paradise. You'll feel like an honored guest at a friend's Mediterranean villa. See Chapter 15.

- **Ritz-Carlton Laguna Niguel** (Dana Point; ☎ 714/240-2000): This jewel in the Ritz-Carlton chain is well known for its warmth, charm, picture-perfect setting, and impeccable service. On dramatic cliffs overlooking 2 miles of prime beach, the Ritz is furnished in an easy yet elegant nautical/seashore color scheme, accented by well-chosen antiques and fine art. See Chapter 15.

- **La Quinta Resort and Club** (La Quinta; ☎ 619/564-4111): This luxury resort, set in a grove of palms at the base of the rocky Santa Rosa Mountains, is surrounded by some of the desert's best golf courses. Single-story Spanish-style cottages are surrounded by a gardenlike setting and 24 "private" swimming pools. The tranquil lounge/library in the unaltered original hacienda hearkens back to the early days of the resort, when Clark Gable, Greta Garbo, Frank Capra, and other luminaries regularly escaped to the seclusion of La Quinta's casitas. See Chapter 16.

- **Loews Coronado Bay Resort** (Coronado; ☎ 619/424-4000): This lovely hideaway occupies a secluded 15-acre peninsula, 30 minutes from the airport and 4¹/₂ miles from downtown Coronado. Each room is very well appointed with elegant furnishings and large marble bathrooms. See Chapter 17.

- **Hyatt Regency San Diego** (☎ 619/232-1234): This impressive monolith enjoys a waterfront location and features a contemporary three-story lobby of green marble and Italian limestone. Views from the rooms are spectacular. See Chapter 17.

14 The Best Moderately Priced Hotels

- **Savoy Hotel** (San Francisco; ☎ 415/441-2700): This hotel is not only well appointed, affordable, and centrally located, but also has one of the city's better mid-range restaurants adjoining the lobby. See Chapter 5.

- **Burgundy House Country Inn** (Yountville; ☎ 707/944-0889): This retreat in California's Wine Country evokes a small country inn in France. Built in the early 1890s, it was once a brandy distillery, but now offers cozy, old-fashioned guest rooms, with lots of delightful touches such as bouquets of fresh flowers. See Chapter 7.

- **St. Orres** (Gualala; ☎ 707/884-3303): Designed in a Russian style—complete with two Kremlinesque onion-domed towers—the St. Orres offers secluded accommodations constructed from century-old timbers salvaged from a nearby mill. One of the most eye-catching inns on California's north coast. See Chapter 8.

- **Albion River Inn** (Albion; ☎ 707/937-1919): Easily one of the best rooms-with-a-view on the California coast, the Albion River Inn is dripping with romance. Perched on a cliff overlooking the rugged shoreline, most of the luxuriously appointed rooms have a Jacuzzi tub-for-two elevated to window level. Add champagne and you're guaranteed to have a night you won't soon forget. See Chapter 8.

- **Coloma Country Inn** (Coloma; ☎ 916/622-6919): Deep in the heart of California's northern Gold Country, this 1852 farmhouse stands on 5 acres of land. The rooms are decorated with stenciling and furnished with antiques, and old-fashioned country quilts cover the beds. Fresh flowers from the surrounding gardens brighten the house. See Chapter 11.

- **The Jabberwock Bed & Breakfast** (Monterey; ☎ 408/372-4777): This place, only 4 blocks from Cannery Row, was once a convent. Set in its own gardens with waterfalls, it was named after an episode in Lewis Carroll's *Through the Looking Glass*. Each room is individually decorated, one with a fireplace. See Chapter 12.

- **Bath Street Inn** (Santa Barbara; ☎ 805/682-9680): This is one of the most immaculate, sweetest B&Bs in California. The inn makes special efforts to coddle guests and also has a wonderfully peaceful back deck shaded by an enormous wisteria. See Chapter 13.
- **Hollywood Roosevelt** (Los Angeles; ☎ 213/466-7000): This hotel, overlooking the Walk of Fame, is a legendary survivor from Hollywood's golden age. Centrally located for sightseeing, it offers terrific city views, one of the city's most elegant lobbies, and evening entertainment at the popular art deco Cinegrill. The first Academy Awards ceremony was held here in 1929, and legends claim that the hotel is haunted by the ghosts of Marilyn Monroe and Montgomery Clift. See Chapter 14.
- **Casa Malibu** (Malibu; ☎ 310/456-2219): This beachfront motel will fool you from the front. Its cheesy 1970s entrance, right on the noisy Pacific Coast Highway, belies the quiet restful charm found within. Situated around the courtyard garden are 21 rooms, many with private decks above the Malibu sands. Rooftops and balconies are festooned with bougainvillea vines, creating an effect reminiscent of a Mexican seaside village. There's easy beach access, and one elegant suite that was Lana Turner's favorite. See Chapter 14.
- **Sommerset Suites Hotel** (San Diego; ☎ 619/692-5200): This terrific bargain is also a good choice for those who find traditional hotels too impersonal. The staff is friendly and helpful, and in the late afternoon they serve complimentary snacks, soda, beer, and wine in the cozy guest lounge. See Chapter 17.
- **Ocean Park Inn** (San Diego; ☎ 619/483-5858): This three-story standout, located right on Pacific Beach's lively beach path, is visually appealing both inside and out. Behind the hotel's modern Spanish-Mediterranean facade is a sharply designed marble lobby that gives way to the less splendid, but completely comfortable, guest rooms. See Chapter 17.

15 The Best Alternative Accommodations

- **An Elegant Victorian Mansion** (Eureka; ☎ 707/444-3144): Yes, that's the name of the inn. Guests relive the golden age of Victoria in an authentic way here—right down to the music and entertainment. At this 1888 house the butler greets you in morning dress. Stay in the Lily Langtry Room, named after the actress and king's mistress who boarded here when she performed locally. See Chapter 8.
- **Camping at Yosemite's Tuolumne Meadows:** It's especially memorable in late spring when it's carpeted with wildflowers. At an elevation of 8,600 feet, this is the largest alpine meadow in the High Sierras and a gateway to the "High Country." A large campground is operated here by park authorities, with a full-scale naturalist program. See Chapter 10.
- ***Delta King* Riverboat** (Sacramento; ☎ 916/444-5464): This paddlewheeler is the only major floating hotel in California (with the exception of the *Queen Mary* at Long Beach). In the 1930s it carried passengers between San Francisco and California's capital, but now it's permanently moored here, its former cabins turned into bedrooms and its old staterooms serving hungry diners. See Chapter 11.
- **Oceanfront Camping at Big Sur:** Kirk Creek Campground, about 3 miles north of Pacific Valley, offers camping with dramatic ocean views and access to the beach. But there are dozens more. Take your pick. See Chapter 12.

- **Olallieberry Inn** (Cambria; ☎ 805/927-3222): Nestled in the charming town of Cambria, this 1873 Greek Revival house, furnished in a romantic floral-and-lace Victorian style, is a perfect base for exploring Hearst Castle. The gracious innkeepers have your comfort and convenience at heart, providing everything from directions to Moonstone Beach to restaurant recommendations—and a scrumptious breakfast in the morning, of course. See Chapter 13.
- **Madonna Inn** (San Luis Obispo; ☎ 805/543-3000): You can't miss this Pepto Bismol–colored San Luis Obispo landmark when you're driving down U.S. 101. Every room of this family-run Bavarian-style château is unique, reflecting a love of old-world motifs, uncommon building materials, and the color pink. Try the rock-lined "Caveman" room, the frilly "Victorian" room, the atmospheric "Waterfall" room, or another of the 109 different theme rooms. This is a design genre all its own—it's an experience not to be missed! See Chapter 13.
- **The Venice Beach House Historic Inn** (Venice; ☎ 310/823-1966): This delightful B&B, in a sprawling 1911 bungalow just 2 blocks from the beach and boardwalk, is a great alternative to the standard cookie-cutter L.A. hotel. The nine guest rooms are all furnished with antiques and period artwork. The wood-paneled living room, bright and airy alcove, cozy patio, and lush garden are captivating. The nearby Venice Pier offers bicycle and roller-skate rentals—perfect for exploring this offbeat neighborhood. See Chapter 14.
- **Two Bunch Palms** (Desert Hot Springs; ☎ 619/329-8791): This spiritual sanctuary in Desert Hot Springs has been drawing weary city-dwellers with its healing mineral springs since Chicago mobster Al Capone built this hideaway in the 1930s. Two Bunch Palms later became a playground for the movie community, but today it's a friendly and informal haven offering full spa services, quiet bungalows nestled among the palms, and trademark pools of steaming mineral water. See Chapter 16.
- **Crystal Pier Hotel** (San Diego; ☎ 619/483-6983): Occupying a historic private pier that extends into the Pacific Ocean, this property affords guests the unusual experience of actually sleeping *over* the ocean. Ideal for beach-loving families. See Chapter 17.

16 The Best Places to Get Away from It All

- **The Mount Shasta Area:** The region around Mount Shasta is a remote swath of Northern California. "Lonely as God and white as a winter moon," wrote Joaquin Miller in 1873, and it's still true at this 14,000-foot-plus dormant volcano, which Native Americans called "the resting place of the Great Spirit." Here, in the region at the top of California, you can wander away from everything and everybody. Go in late spring when the wildflowers first burst into bloom and the trout are jumping. See Chapter 9.
- **Sequoia & Kings Canyon National Parks:** They have only a fraction of Yosemite's crowds and they're stunningly beautiful. This is a land of grandiose scenery separated by Kings Canyon, the deepest chasm in the continental United States. Virgin forests carpet the parks. Use them for hiking or wilderness camping almost unequaled in America. Autumn is our favorite time to visit. Almost everyone disappears, and you get to experience crisp days in fall colors and long, lingering Indian summers. See Chapter 10.
- **The Ventana Wilderness** (Big Sur): The U.S. Forest Service maintains 167,323 scenic acres straddling the Santa Lucia mountains. Cascading streams, waterfalls,

deep pools, and thermal springs take you back to Eden. Bring your Adam or Eve so you won't get lonely in the midst of all this nature. See Chapter 12.

- **The San Ysidro Ranch** (Montecito; ☎ 805/969-5046): This ultra-private guest ranch opened in 1893, and has since been the hideaway of writers (Somerset Maugham, John Steinbeck), film stars (Katherine Hepburn, David Niven), and Jackie and Jack Kennedy, who honeymooned here. Each isolated cottage has a wood-burning fireplace and welcomes pets. The ranch has riding stables, tennis and bocce ball courts, fitness facilities, and the acclaimed Stonehouse Restaurant. See Chapter 13.

- **Channel Islands National Park:** Just off the coast of Ventura is a world removed from the bustle of Southern California. The islands are a wild and storm-blown region of sharp cliffs, curving grasslands, and rocky coves punctuated by the barking of elephant seals and sea lions. Camping among the archipelago's many endemic plant species and fascinating array of animals (including the endangered brown pelican and indigenous fox) is a splendid way to steep yourself in the beauty of this untamed preserve. See Chapter 13.

- **The Huntington Library, Art Collections, and Botanical Gardens** (near Pasadena): This daytime Pasadena-area getaway is many treats in one. The former estate of railroad baron Henry Huntington is a spectacular botanical garden whose highlights include Japanese and Zen gardens, an oft-filmed statuary lawn, a camellia garden, and tranquil lily ponds. The Italianate main house is a gallery of European paintings, and scholars flock to study at the Huntington Library, one of the world's finest collections of rare manuscripts and first editions (including a Gutenberg bible). A superb bookstore and delightful tearoom round out this peaceful retreat. See Chapter 15.

- **The Pine Hills Area of Julian:** A half dozen bed-and-breakfast inns are located in this wonderfully quiet small town, where birdsong is the loudest sound you'll hear. See Chapter 17.

17 The Best Restaurants for California Cuisine

- **Silks** (San Francisco; ☎ 415/885-0999): It's been hailed as one of the top restaurants in America. This pocket of posh is a virtual valentine to the cuisine of the Pacific Rim. From the seared lobster and scallops to the signature grilled yakitori quail with sweet-potato purée, the dishes are not only beautiful to behold but also a joy to the palate. See Chapter 5.

- **Chez Panisse** (Berkeley; ☎ 510/548-5525): This is the culinary domain of Alice Waters, often called "the queen of California cuisine." Her food captivates the senses and the imagination. Although originally inspired by the Mediterranean, her kitchen has found its own style. Even Bill Clinton deserted the Big Mac for some Chez Panisse delights, such as grilled fish wrapped in fig leaves with red-wine sauce and Seckel pears poached in red wine with burnt caramel. See Chapter 6.

- **Terra** (St. Helena; ☎ 707/963-8931): One of the Napa Valley's premier dining rooms is the creation of Lissa Doumani and her Japanese husband, Hiro Sone. On every gastronome's tour of the Wine Country, it's a celebration of the region's bounty—sublime, flavorful, well crafted. The wine list is a tribute to the Golden State, emphasizing sometimes almost unknown selections from the small estates. See Chapter 7.

- **John Ash & Co.** (Santa Rosa; ☎ 707/527-7687): A "restaurant for all seasons," this southwestern-inspired dining room overlooks a vineyard. Its innovative creator, John Ash, has been called "the Daniel Boone of pioneering in wine-country cooking." The lush, bountiful richness of Sonoma County—from its succulent lamb to its vine-ripened fruits—is richly flavored and attractively presented at this premier choice for dining in the area. See Chapter 7.

- **Erna's Elderberry House** (Oakhurst; ☎ 209/683-6800): It's like a beacon shining across the culinary wasteland of the region around Yosemite. A six-course menu—changed nightly—is presented, an almost perfect blend of continental and Californian. The food is bountiful, and is as fully satisfying as is the elegant European ambience. Fresh, fresh, fresh—and no natural flavor is cooked beyond recognition. Ingredients are deftly and skillfully handled to bring out their natural taste. See Chapter 10.
- **Ian's** (Cambria; ☎ 805/927-8649): The menu changes daily and reflects chef Mark Sahaydak's take on the local bounty. His individual artistry is apparent in dishes like porcini mushroom ravioli with spicy Italian sausage, and sautéed scallops in a crème fraîche and chardonnay sauce flavored with sun-dried tomatoes. Ian's wine list reflects the very best of local and regional vineyards. See Chapter 13.
- **The Ranch House** (Ojai; ☎ 805/646-2360): This restaurant has been placing its emphasis on using the freshest vegetables, fruits, and herbs since it opened its doors in 1965, long before it became a national craze. If you stroll through the restaurant's lush herb garden before your meal, you might later recognize the freshly snipped sprigs that will aromatically transform your simple meat, fish, or game dish into a work of art. See Chapter 13.
- **Four Oaks** (Los Angeles; ☎ 310/470-2265): California cuisine with a French accent is served beneath trees festooned with twinkling lights at this canyon hideaway. The country-cottage ambience and chef Peter Roelant's superlative blend of fresh ingredients with luxurious continental flourishes make the Four Oaks a Frommer's favorite luxury. Appetizers like lavender-smoked salmon with crisp potatoes and horseradish crème fraîche complement mouth-watering dishes like roast chicken with sage, Oregon forest mushrooms, artichoke hearts, and port-balsamic sauce. See Chapter 14.
- **Spago** (West Hollywood; ☎ 310/652-4025): Everybody's heard of the dining dynasty launched by wunderchef Wolfgang Puck. The original is still the best, serving up gourmet pizzas from the wood-burning oven in a Hollywood "A-list" atmosphere. The menu also contains innovative pasta dishes like shrimp and lobster tortellini with crispy carrots and ginger-lobster curry, plus meat and game dishes with fruit and herb accents. They're supposed to move from their hard-to-find location into Beverly Hills in early 1997, so be sure to ask whether they've moved yet when you call to reserve. See Chapter 14.
- **George's at the Cove** (La Jolla; ☎ 619/454-4244): This popular restaurant gets raves for its seafood dishes, creative pastas, ocean view, and great sunsets in summer. If you dine here, be sure to try the smoked-chicken soup. See Chapter 17.

18 The Best Culinary Experiences

- **Dungeness Crab at San Francisco's Fisherman's Wharf:** Crabs, which are best consumed as soon as possible after being cooked, emerge right from boiling pots onto your plate. You crack the shells and pick the delectable meat out. Gastronomes treasure even the edible organs (crab butter) inside the carapace. See Chapter 5.
- **Steaks at Harris'** (San Francisco; ☎ 415/673-1888): This is the great steak restaurant of San Francisco, a tradition since the founding of the Old West. Owner

Ann Lee Harris, who grew up on a cattle ranch and married the owner of the largest feedlot in California, knows her steaks. They hang in a glass-windowed aging room, cut thick New York style or else as T-bones. See Chapter 5.

- **A Decadent Meal in the Wine Country:** Have yours at the fabled Mustards Grill (Yountville; ☎ 707/944-2424); it's been called "the quintessential Napa Valley wine restaurant." It's noisy and fun as you sample the fare, many platters straight from a wood-burning oven. Try the grilled Sonoma rabbit, or calf's liver with caramelized onions. Make sure to finish with the Jack Daniels chocolate cake. See Chapter 7.

- **Fresh Pacific Salmon:** Plump, firm, with a brightly colored flesh, salmon is best when consumed along the northern coast, especially in a restaurant at sunset overlooking the water. Memories are made of this. Although many species are available, the best known is the Chinook or king salmon. The leanest and most delicately flavored salmon appears in the late spring. The fish is caught in the Pacific just prior to its migration upstream to spawn. This salmon is in prime condition, as it has been feeding for years on rich marine bounty. See Chapter 8.

- **Roadside Strawberries and Peaches in the Central Valley:** You can sail through the Golden State's rich agricultural heartland and fill your car or your mouth with some of the finest fruit (vegetables, too) grown in America. The peaches rival those of Georgia, and there are more than 150 varieties of nectarines grown in the valley. When you see baskets of strawberries, tipped so that their luscious scarlet fruit is spilling out, you'll slam on the brakes. See Chapter 11.

- **The Pastry Shops of Solvang:** It's easy to dismiss Solvang as a tacky tourist trap, but, if truth be told, the town's bakeries are among California's very best. Many Santa Barbarans regularly make the 40-minute drive to this inland hamlet just to buy dessert. See Chapter 13.

- **A Sunset Horseback Ride Through Griffith Park to a Mexican Feast:** This culinary/equine excursion departs Friday evenings from Beachwood Stables in the Hollywood Hills just before dusk, winding up in Burbank at the modest but tasty—especially coming off the trail!—Viva Restaurant. Tie up your steed outside and saunter in for a steaming plate of enchiladas accompanied by an ice-cold cerveza, just like the real *vaqueros* (cowboys). For information, call the Sunset Ranch (☎ 213/464-9612).

- **Grand Central Market** (Los Angeles; ☎ 213/624-2378): Fresh produce stands, exotic spice and condiment vendors, butchers and fishmongers, and prepared-food counters create a noisy, fragrant, vaguely comforting atmosphere in this L.A. mainstay. The gem of this airy, cavernous complex is the fresh juice bar at the southwest corner. A market fixture for many years, it dispenses dozens of fresh varieties from an elaborate system of wall spigots (just like an old-fashioned soda fountain), deftly blending unlikely but heavenly combinations. See Chapter 14.

- **Sunday Champagne Brunch Aboard the *Queen Mary*** (Long Beach; ☎ 310/435-3511 or 310/432-6964): This elegant ocean liner was the world's largest, finest vessel when she was built in 1934, and the grandeur of those Atlantic crossing days remains. A sumptuous buffet-style feast, accompanied by harp soloist and ice sculpture, is presented in the richly wood-furnished first-class dining room. Walk off your overindulgence on the spectacular teak decks and through the art deco interiors. See Chapter 15.

- **A Date with the Coachella Valley:** Some 95% of the world's dates are farmed here in the desert. While the groves of date palms make evocative scenery, it's their savory fruit that draws visitors to the National Date Festival in Indio each February. Amid the Arabian Nights parade and dusty camel races, you can feast on an exotic array of plump Medjool, amber Deglet Noor, caramel-like Halawy, and buttery Empress. The rest of the year date farms and markets throughout the valley sell dates from the season's harvest, as well as date milkshakes, sticky date coconut rolls, and more. See Chapter 16 and the "Calendar of Events" in Chapter 2.

- **San Diego County Farmers' Markets:** The bountiful harvest of San Diego County is sold on various days at moveable markets throughout the area. Finds are fresh local fruits, vegetables, and flowers, as well as specialty items such as raw apple cider (in the fall), macadamia nuts, and rhubarb pies. See Chapter 17.

19 The Best Destinations for Serious Shoppers

- **San Francisco:** It has been called "a boutique town on the Bay." It's filled with hundreds of small and smart specialty shops, selling unusual clothes, books, antiques, jewelry, and gifts, much of it from the Pacific Rim. Of all the great stores in San Francisco, our favorite remains Gump's, on Post Street, between Grant Avenue and Kearny Street. Founded by German immigrants in 1865, the landmark store is known worldwide for its "treasures of Asia," including jade and pearls—plus the largest selection of fine crystal and china in the United States. See Chapter 5.
- **Mendocino/Fort Bragg:** Mendocino is tailor-made for art gallery hopping, antiquing, and wine-tasting. And there's even better shopping just a short drive up the coast at Fort Bragg, especially along the 300 block of North Franklin Street, which is lined with antiques stores. See Chapter 8.
- **Carmel:** Some 600 buildings in this serene little town are devoted to shops and boutiques. They sell virtually everything—fashions, housewares, art, imported goods, baskets, you name it. Seek out Carmel Plaza, a multilevel complex of boutiques and craft shops, and especially the Barnyard, with its authentic early California barns, now converted into 60-plus shops, boutiques, and restaurants. See Chapter 12.
- **Santa Monica:** The entire city is a shopper's paradise. In addition to the movie theater–laden Third Street Promenade and the more traditional multilevel Santa Monica Place, you can browse the shops—some funky, some down to earth—and trendy cafés of Main Street and the upscale stores of quaint Montana Avenue, or lose yourself in the expansive Fred Segal complex where, in addition to a string of unusual boutiques, you'll find a fantastic ladies' milliner. See Chapter 14.
- **West 3rd Street,** between La Cienega Boulevard and Fairfax Avenue, in Los Angeles: The Beverly Center? Bypass that unsightly behemoth and instead stroll in its shadow along West 3rd Street. You'll enjoy an eclectic mix of new and vintage clothing boutiques, intimate cafes, and specialty shops, interspersed with 1940s-era storefronts housing drapery-makers, leather workers, stationery printers, and other craftspeople. The cluttered blocks around Orlando and Sweetzer avenues hold such treasures as the Chado Tea Room, the Traveler's Bookcase and Cook's Library specialty bookstores, Janice McCarty clothing designs, and Polkadots & Moonbeams boutique. See Chapter 14.
- **South Coast Plaza** (The Orange Coast): This is the suburban shopping mall taken to its grandest extreme. With more "anchor stores" than several malls put together (including Nordstrom and Saks Fifth Avenue), South Coast Plaza is also home to a branch of Tiffany & Co., a Chanel boutique, a Versace salon, and a host of unusually highbrow shops. If your budget is in a more reasonable range, never fear—

all the familiar stores are here, next to some unique Southern California specialties and a mind-boggling selection of restaurants. See Chapter 15.

- **Horton Plaza:** The Disneyland of shopping malls, this place is right in the heart
of San Diego and covers 6¹/₂ city blocks. More than 140 specialty shops, a seven-
screen cinema, three department stores, and a variety of restaurants and short-
order eateries sprawl over myriad levels. See Chapter 17.

20 The Best of the Performing Arts

- **San Francisco Opera:** This world-class company performs at the War Memorial
Opera House, which is modeled after the Opéra Garnier in Paris. The opera season opens in September with a gala and runs through December. This was the first
municipal opera in the United States, and its brilliant members have been
acclaimed by critics throughout the world. See Chapter 5.
- **American Conservatory Theater** (San Francisco): The ACT is one of the nation's
leading regional theaters, dating from 1967. It has been called the American
equivalent of the British National Theatre, the Berliner Ensemble, and the
Comédie Française in Paris. Both classical and experimental works are brilliantly
performed. See Chapter 5.
- **Monterey Jazz Festival:** When the third weekend of September rolls around, the
Monterey Fairgrounds hosts this fabled classic, drawing jazz fans from around the
world. The 3-day festival (which is usually sold out about a month in advance) is
known for presenting the sweetest jazz west of the Mississippi. It even draws fans
from that city of jazz, New Orleans. See Chapter 12 and "Calendar of Events" in
Chapter 2.
- **Carmel Bach Festival:** For more than 50 years Carmel has hosted an annual
3-week celebration honoring Johann Sebastian Bach and his contemporaries. It
culminates in a candlelit concert in the chapel of the Carmel Mission. It starts
in mid-July, and tickets must be ordered way in advance. See Chapter 12 and
"Calendar of Events" in Chapter 2.
- **The Hollywood Bowl:** This iconic outdoor amphitheater is the summer home of
the Los Angeles Philharmonic, a stage for visiting virtuosos—including the occasional pop star—and the setting for several splendid fireworks displays throughout the summer. It's customary to have a gourmet picnic before the performance,
either at your seat or on the grounds; at evening's end, the aisles are littered with
empty wine bottles. Those lucky enough to obtain a box seat can set their own
private table. See Chapter 14.
- **The Viper Room:** Head to this West Hollywood closet for a glimpse of L.A.'s hippest scene. Owner Johnny Depp took this small but historic club space on the
famous Sunset Strip and gave it an atmospheric art deco vibe. He hangs out
here regularly with all his trend-setting friends; visiting celebrities and musicians
can be found mingling and listening to live bands every night of the week. After
midnight or so, don't be surprised if big-name recording artists take the stage
for an impromptu jam. See Chapter 14.
- **The Groundling Theater** (Hollywood): Many Groundlings alumni have hit the
big time, graduating to *Saturday Night Live,* TV sitcoms, and motion pictures. The
ensemble is best known for split-second improvisation and offbeat, irreverent
original skits, all performed in their small, intimate theater on Melrose Avenue.
You're bound to bust a gut here. See Chapter 14.
- **Festival of the Arts & Pageant of the Masters in Laguna Beach:** These events
draw enormous crowds to the Orange County coast every July and August.

Begun in 1932 by a handful of area painters, the festival has grown to show-case hundreds of artists. In the evening, crowds marvel at the Pageant of the Masters' *tableaux vivants,* where costumed townsfolk pose convincingly inside a giant frame and depict famous works of art, accompanied by music and narration. See Chapter 15.

- **Old Globe Theatre:** This Tony Award–winning theater, fashioned after Shakes-peare's original stage, produced the revival of *Damn Yankees* and has billed such notable performers as John Goodman, Marsha Mason, Cliff Robertson, Jon Voight, and Christopher Walken. See Chapter 17.
- **La Jolla Playhouse:** Winner of the 1993 Tony Award for Outstanding American Regional Theater, the LJ Playhouse stages six productions each year in its 500-seat Mandell Weiss Theater and 400-seat Mandell Weiss Forum on the campus of UCSD. This is where the Tony Award–winning production of *Tommy* was launched. See Chapter 17.

2 Planning a Trip to California

In the pages that follow, we've compiled everything you need to know to handle the practical details of planning your trip in advance—airlines, how to make camping reservations, a calendar of events, driving laws, and more.

1 Visitor Information & Money

VISITOR INFORMATION

For information on the state as a whole, contact the **California Office of Tourism,** 801 K St., Suite 1600, Sacramento, CA 95812 (☎ **800/862-2543**), and ask for their free information packet. In addition, almost every city and town in the state has a dedicated tourist bureau or chamber of commerce that will be happy to send you information on its particular parcel. These are listed under the appropriate headings in the geographically organized chapters that follow.

Foreign travelers should also see Chapter 4, "For Foreign Visitors," for entry requirements and other pertinent information.

INFORMATION ON CALIFORNIA'S PARKS To find out more about California's national parks, contact the **Western Region Information Center,** National Park Service, Fort Mason, Building 201, San Francisco, CA 94123 (☎ **415/556-0560**).

For general state park information, contact the **California Department of Parks and Recreation,** P.O. Box 942896, Sacramento, CA 94296-0001 (☎ **916/653-6995**). Some 10,000 campsites are on the department's reservation system, and can be booked up to 8 weeks in advance by calling **Mistix** (☎ **800/444-7275**). In the past it has been practically impossible to get through to this line, and campers have complained long and loud. The Parks Department has finally heard their pleas, and in June 1995 some improvements were implemented, including additional operators. Hours for making reservations have been extended; you can now call Monday to Saturday from 8am to 8pm and on Sunday from 8am to 5pm (Pacific time). Plans are in the works for taking reservations by fax, and the Parks Department is also planning to post parks information, includinga reservations form that can be mailed or faxed, on the Internet.

For information on fishing and hunting licenses, contact the **California Department of Fish and Game,** License and Revenue Branch, 3211 S St., Sacramento, CA 95816 (☎ **916/227-2244** for license information, or 916/227-2266 for 24-hour information).

MONEY

The ubiquitous Bank of America accepts Plus, Star, and Interlink cards, while First Interstate Bank is on-line with the Cirrus system. Both banks have dozens of branches all around California. For the location of the nearest **Cirrus** ATM, dial 800/424-7787, and for the **Plus** system, 800/843-7587. You can also locate Plus ATMs on the web at **http://www.visa.com,** and Cirrus ATMs at **http://www.mastercard.com.** Most ATMs will make cash advances against MasterCard and Visa. American Express cardholders can write a personal check, guaranteed against the card, for up to $1,000 in cash at an American Express office (see "Fast Facts" in the city chapters for locations).

Major credit cards are accepted at establishments throughout the state. U.S. dollar traveler's checks are also widely accepted for goods and services, and can be exchanged for cash at banks and most check-issuing offices. Foreign travelers should also see Chapter 4, "For Foreign Visitors," for monetary descriptions and currency-exchange information.

2 When to Go

California's climate is so varied that it's impossible to generalize about the state as a whole.

San Francisco's temperate marine climate means relatively mild weather year round. In summer temperatures rarely top 70°F (pack sweaters, even in August) and the city's famous fog rolls in most mornings and evenings. In winter the mercury seldom falls below freezing and snow is almost unheard of. Because of San Francisco's fog, summer rarely sees more than a few hot days in a row. Head a few miles inland, though, and it's likely to be clear and hot.

The Central Coast shares San Francisco's climate, though it gets warmer as you get farther south. Seasonal changes are less pronounced south of San Luis Obispo, where temperatures remain relatively stable year round. The northern coast is rainier and foggier; winters tend to be mild but wet.

Summers are refreshingly cool around Lake Tahoe and in the Shasta Cascades—a perfect climate for hiking, camping, and other outdoor activities and a popular escape for residents of California's sweltering deserts and valleys who are looking to beat the heat. Skiers flock to this area for terrific snowfall from late November to early April.

Southern California is usually much warmer than the Bay Area, and it gets significantly more sun. This is the place to hit the beach. Even in winter, daytime thermometer readings regularly reach into the 60s and higher. Summers can be stifling inland, but Southern California's coastal communities are always comfortable. Don't pack an umbrella—when it rains, Southern Californians go outside to look at the novelty. It's possible to sunbathe throughout the year, but only die-hard enthusiasts and wet-suited surfers venture into the ocean in winter. The water is warmest in summer and fall, but even then the Pacific is too chilly for many.

The Southern California desert is sizzling hot in summer; temperatures regularly top 100°F. Winter is the time to visit the desert resorts (and remember, it gets surprisingly cold at night in the desert).

San Francisco's Average Temperatures (°F)

	Jan	Feb	Mar	Apr	May	June	July	Aug	Sept	Oct	Nov	Dec
Avg. High	56	59	60	61	63	64	64	65	69	68	63	57
Avg. Low	46	48	49	49	51	53	53	54	56	55	52	47

Los Angeles's Average Temperatures (°F)

	Jan	Feb	Mar	Apr	May	June	July	Aug	Sept	Oct	Nov	Dec
Avg. High	65	66	67	69	72	75	81	81	81	77	73	69
Avg. Low	46	48	49	52	54	57	60	60	59	55	51	49

CALIFORNIA CALENDAR OF EVENTS

January

- ✪ **Tournament of Roses,** Pasadena. This spectacular parade down Colorado Boulevard features lavish floats, music, and extraordinary equestrian entries, followed by the Rose Bowl Game. Call 818/449-4100 for details or just stay home and watch it on TV (you'll have a better view). January 1.

- **AT&T Pebble Beach National Pro-Am,** Pebble Beach. A PGA-sponsored tour where pros are teamed with celebrities to compete on three world-famous golf courses. Call 408/649-1533. Lasts a week; dates vary.

- **Gold Discovery Celebration,** Coloma. A celebration of the fateful day that rocketed California to riches, with gold-panning demonstrations, musical entertainment, Gold Rush skits, and historic house tours. Call 916/622-6198. January 24.

- ✪ **Chinese New Year Festival and Parade.** The largest Chinese New Year Festival in the United States is San Francisco's, which includes a Golden Dragon parade with lion-dancing, marching bands, street fair, flower sale, and festive food. Call 415/982-3000 for exact date and schedule.

    L.A.'s celebration is colorful as well, with dragon dancers parading through the streets of downtown's Chinatown. Chinese opera and other events are scheduled. Contact the L.A. Chinese Chamber of Commerce at 213/617-0396 for this year's schedule.

February

- **National Date Festival and Riverside County Fair,** Indio. Coachella Valley dates and produce are featured at this annual desert festival, which also includes an Arabian Nights Pageant and camel and ostrich races. Call 619/863-8247 for details. February 14-23.

- ✪ **Fresno County Blossom Trail.** A 67-mile driving tour featuring the fruit and nut orchards in full bloom. Call 209/233-0836 for details. Late February to late March.

March

- **Russian River Wine Road Barrel Tasting,** Healdsburg. The vintners showcase wines still in the barrel, about-to-be-released vintages, and also some old gems from their cellars. Tastings are free and food is available to enhance the wines. Each year by February 1, a list of participants is released with the featured wines. Send a SASE to RRWR, P.O. Box 46, Healdsburg, CA 95448, or call 707/433-6782. First weekend in March.

- **Ocean Beach Kite Festival,** San Diego. Kite building, decorating, and flying are all demonstrated and contested. Phone 619/224-0189 for details. Early March.

- **Snowfest,** Truckee. A 10-day winter carnival with parades, ski challenges, polar-bear swim, children's carnival, and fireworks. Call 916/583-7625. Often early to mid-March, but dates vary.
- **Return of the Swallows,** San Juan Capistrano. An annual event with a parade, dances, and special programs. Call 714/248-2048 for details. Mid-March.
- **American Indian Festival and Market,** Los Angeles. A showcase and festival of Native American arts and culture at the L.A. Natural History Museum. The fun includes traditional dances, storytelling, and a display of arts and crafts as well as a chance to sample ethnic foods. Museum admission includes festival tickets. For further details, call 213/744-3314. Late March.
- **Redwood Coast Dixieland Jazz Festival,** Eureka. Three days of jazz featuring 12 of the best Dixieland groups, including a variety of jam sessions. Call 707/445-3378. Last weekend in March.

April

- ✪ **San Francisco International Film Festival.** One of America's oldest film festivals, featuring more than 100 films and videos from more than 30 countries. Tickets are relatively inexpensive, and screenings are very accessible to the general public for two weeks early in the month. Call 415/931-FILM for details.
- **Red Bluff Roundup Rodeo,** Red Bluff. A 2-day rodeo with saddle-bronc riding, steer wrestling, bareback riding, brahma-bull riding, team roping, and calf roping. For more information, call the Red Bluff Chamber of Commerce at 916/527-6220. Usually the second or third weekend in April.
- **Toyota Grand Prix,** Long Beach. An exciting weekend of Indy-class auto racing and entertainment in and around downtown Long Beach, drawing world-class drivers from the United States and Europe. Contact the Grand Prix Association at 800/752-9524 or 310/436-9953. Mid-April.
- ✪ **Renaissance Pleasure Faire,** San Bernardino. One of America's largest Renaissance festivals, this annual happening, set in Glen Ellen Regional Park in L.A.'s relatively remote countryside, is a re-created Elizabethan marketplace with costumed performers and living-history displays. For ticket information, phone 800/523-2473. Weekends from mid-April to June.
- **La Jolla Easter Hat Parade.** Prizes are awarded in several different categories. Call 619/454-2600 for more information. Easter Sunday.
- **Fisherman's Festival,** Bodega Bay. Fishing vessels, decorated with ribbons and banners, sail out for a Blessing of the Fleet, while landlubbers enjoy music, lamb, an oyster barbecue, an arts and crafts fair, and a boat parade. Late April, but dates vary.
- **Asparagus Festival,** Stockton. The spring harvest festival is celebrated with food and a variety of entertainment. Call 209/943-1987. Late April.
- ✪ **Ramona Pageant,** Hemet. A unique outdoor pageant that portrays the lives of the Southern California Mission Indians. The play was adapted from Helen Hunt Jackson's 1884 novel *Ramona.* Call 909/658-3111 for details. Late April to early May.
- **Del Mar National Horse Show.** Horse and rider teams compete in national championships. Held at the Del Mar Fairgrounds. Call 619/792-4288 or 619/755-1161 for more information. Late April to early May.

May

- ✪ **Cinco de Mayo.** A week-long celebration of one of Mexico's most jubilant holidays takes place throughout the city of Los Angeles. The fiesta's Carnival-like atmosphere is created by large crowds, live folkloric music, dancing, food, and historical reenactments. The main festivities are held downtown in El Pueblo de Los Angeles State Historic Park, with other events around the city. For information and schedule, call 213/628-1274.

There's also a Cinco de Mayo celebration in San Diego, featuring folkloric music, dance, food, and historical reenactments. Held in Old Town. Call 619/296-3161 or 619/220-5422 for more details.

- **Avenue of the Giants Marathon.** A scenic marathon along redwood-lined Avenue of the Giants and Humboldt Redwoods State Park, starting about 40 miles south of Eureka. Call 707/443-1226. Dates vary.
- **Redondo Beach Wine Festival.** The largest outdoor wine-tasting event in Southern California. For exact dates and this year's locations, contact the Redondo Beach Chamber of Commerce at 310/376-6912. Early May.
- **Luther Burbank Rose Parade and Festival,** Santa Rosa. Marching bands, floats, food, and roses everywhere honor horticulturalist Luther Burbank. Call 707/542-ROSE. Mid-May.
- **Venice Art Walk,** Venice Beach. An annual weekend event which gives visitors a chance to take docent-guided tours, visit five artist's studios, or take a Sunday self-guided art walk through private studios and homes of more than 50 emerging and well-known artists. Phone 310/392-8630, ext. 342. Mid-May.
- ✪ **Calaveras County Fair and Jumping Frog Jubilee,** Angels Camp. The event inspired by Mark Twain's story "The Celebrated Jumping Frog of Calaveras County." Entrants from all over the world arrive with their frog participants. There's also a children's parade, livestock competition, rodeo, carnival, and fireworks. Call 209/736-2561 for information. Third weekend in May.
- **Russian River Wine Festival,** Healdsburg. Five hours of superb tasting of wines, Sonoma County food specialties, and signature dishes from local chefs. Music and crafts too, all on the Healdsburg Plaza. Call 707/433-6782. Usually the third Saturday in May.
- **Bay to Breakers Foot Race,** Golden Gate Park, San Francisco. One of the city's most popular annual events, it's really more fun than run. Thousands of entrants show up dressed in their best Halloween-style costumes for the approximately $7^1/_2$-mile run across the park. Call 415/777-7770. Third Sunday in May.
- ✪ **Carnival,** San Francisco. The Mission District's largest annual event is a week-long series of festivities that culminates in a parade on Mission Street. More than a half-million spectators line the route, and the samba musicians and dancers continue to play on 14th Street, near Harrison, at the end of the march. Call the Mission Economic and Cultural Association at 415/826-1401 for details. Memorial Day weekend.
- **Great Monterey Bay Squid Festival.** The squid in all its glory is the focus of the celebration here, which maintains that "a day without squid is a day in hell." Squid-cleaning and squid-cooking demonstrations are followed by a taste of the squid, which—as shown here—can be used in virtually everything but ice cream. Festival fare includes arts and crafts, educational exhibits, and the usual entertainment. For details, contact the festival at 408/649-6547. Memorial Day weekend.
- **Cross-County Kinetic Sculpture Race,** Arcata. Wild and crazy human-powered amphibious vehicles race for 3 days from Arcata to Ferndale across mud, sand, roadway, and water. Call 707/725-3851. Memorial Day.

June
- **Pony Express Celebration and Re-Ride,** Folsom. Horses and riders follow the same route that the Pony Express took, starting in Missouri and ending with a

major celebration in Folsom, about 20 miles east of Sacramento. Much of the route parallels U.S. 50 in El Dorado County. Call 916/621-5885 or 916/985-2707. Dates vary.

- **Music in the Mountains,** Nevada City. A 3-week classical music festival. For information, call MIM at 916/265-6124. Dates vary.
- **Playboy Jazz Festival,** Los Angeles. Bill Cosby is the traditional master of ceremonies, presiding over top artists at the Hollywood Bowl. Call 310/246-4000. Mid-June.
- **Lesbian and Gay Freedom Day Parade.** It's celebrated all over the state, but San Francisco's party draws up to half a million participants. The parade's start and finish has been moved around in recent years to accommodate road construction, but traditionally it begins and ends at Civic Center Plaza, where hundreds of food, art, and information booths are set up around several sound stages. Call 415/ 864-3733 for information. Usually the third or last weekend of June.
- **Mariachi USA Festival,** Los Angeles. A 2-day family-oriented celebration of Mexican culture and tradition at the Hollywood Bowl, where festival-goers pack their picnic baskets and enjoy music, ballet, folklorico, and related performances by special guests. Call 213/848-7717. Late June.
- **Hot Air Balloon Classic,** Windsor. Hundreds of brilliant silken balloons float silently across the sky above, while gawkers enjoy a food and crafts fair. Call 707/ 838-7285. Usually the last weekend in June.
- **Rough and Ready Secession Celebration and Chili Cookoff,** Rough and Ready. This event celebrates the town's secession from the Union in 1850 in protest against a mining tax. It soon rejoined on the Fourth of July. Food, entertainment, and more. Call 916/432-4186 or 916/273-4328. Usually the fourth Saturday in June.
- **Pony Express Celebration and Re-Ride,** Folsom. Horses and riders follow the same route that the Pony Express took, starting in Missouri and ending with a major celebration in Folsom, about 20 miles east of Sacramento. Much of the route parallels U.S. 50 in El Dorado County. Call 916/621-5885 or 916/985-2707. Dates vary.
- **Music in the Mountains,** Nevada City. A 3-week classical music festival. For information, call MIM at 916/265-6124. Dates vary.

July

- **Independence Day,** statewide. It's celebrated all over the state, of course, but it's terrific in Pasadena, which offers Southern California's most spectacular display of fireworks following an evening of live entertainment at the Rose Bowl. Phone 818/ 577-3100 for further information. July 4.
- ✪ **Festival of Arts and Pageant of the Masters,** Laguna Beach. A fantastic performance-art production in which live actors re-create famous old masters paintings. Call 800/487-FEST or 714/497-6582; ticket prices range from $15 to $40. Early July through late August.
- **Carmel Bach Festival.** A 3-week festival honoring Johann Sebastian Bach and his contemporaries. It culminates in a candlelit concert in the chapel of the Carmel Mission. Call 408/624-1521. Dates vary.
- **Mammoth Lakes Jazz Jubilee.** A 3-day festival featuring 15 bands on 10 different stages, plus food, drink, and dancing—all under the pine trees and stars. Call 619/934-2478. Dates vary.
- **Shakespeare at the Beach,** Lake Tahoe. A bewitching experience of the Bard at Sand Harbor on the shore beneath the stars. Call 702/832-1606. Three weeks in late July and early August.

- **Gilroy Garlic Festival.** A gourmet food fair with more than 85 booths serving gar-licky food from almost every ethnic background, plus close to 100 arts, crafts, and entertainment booths. Call 408/842-1625. Last full weekend in July.

- **International Surf Festival,** Los Angeles. Four beachside cities—Hermosa Beach, Manhattan Beach, Redondo Beach, and Torrance—collaborate in the oldest international surf festival in California. Competitions include surfing, boogie boarding, sand-castle building, and other beach-related categories. Contact the International Surf Festival Committee at 310/376-6911 for information. End of July.

August

- **Sonoma County Showcase and Wine Auction,** at the Sonoma County Wine and Visitors Center and at different wineries. Four days of wine tastings and celebra-tions plus a wine auction. Call 707/586-3795. Usually the first weekend in August.

- **Old Spanish Days Fiesta,** Santa Barbara. The city's biggest annual event, this 5-day festival features a grand parade with horse-drawn carriages, two Spanish marketplaces, a carnival, a rodeo, and dancers. Call 805/962-8101. Early August.

- **Nisei Week Japanese Festival,** Little Tokyo, Los Angeles. This week-long celebra-tion of Japanese culture and heritage is held in the Japanese American Cultural and Community Center Plaza. Festivities include parades, food, music, arts, and crafts. Call 213/687-7193. Mid-August.

- **California State Fair,** at the California Exposition grounds, Sacramento. A gala celebration, with livestock, carnival food, exhibits, entertainment on 10 diff-erent stages, plus thoroughbred racing and a 1-mile monorail for panoramic views over the scope of it all. Call 916/263-3000. Late August to early September.

September

- **Sausalito Art Festival.** A juried exhibit of more than 180 artists, it's accompanied by music provided by Bay Area jazz, rock, and blues performers and international cuisine enhanced by wines from some 50 different Napa and Sonoma producers. Parking is impossible; take the Red & White Fleet (☎ 415/546-2628) ferry from Fisherman's Wharf to the festival site. Call 415/332-3555 for information. Labor Day weekend.

- **San Diego Street Scene.** The historic Gaslamp Quarter is transformed into an urban food and music festival. Call 619/557-8487 for more information. Early September.

- ✪ **Monterey Jazz Festival.** Top names in traditional and modern jazz perform at one of the oldest annual jazz festivals in the world. Call 408/373-3366 for schedule and ticket information. Mid-September.

- **San Francisco Blues Festival,** on the grounds of Fort Mason. The largest outdoor blues music event on the West Coast. Local and national musicians perform back-to-back during 2 marathon days. Call 415/826-6837. Usually in mid-September.

- **Los Angeles County Fair,** at the Los Angeles County Fair and Exposition Cen-ter, in Pomona. Horse racing, arts, agricultural displays, celebrity entertainment, and carnival rides are among the attractions of the largest county fair in the world. Call 909/623-3111 for information. Late September.

- **Cabrillo Festival,** San Diego. A week-long fair commemorating the exploration of the West Coast by Juan Rodríguez Cabrillo in 1542. A reenactment of the event takes place at the Cabrillo National Monument. Call 619/557-5450 for more information. Late September.

- **Watts Towers Day of the Drum Festival,** Los Angeles. Performances from Afro-Cuban folkloricos to East Indian tabla players. Phone 213/847-4646. Late September.
- **Catalina Island Jazz Trax Festival.** Great contemporary jazz artists travel to the island to play in the legendary Casino Ballroom. The festival is over two consecutive 3-day weekends. Call 800/866-TRAX or 619/458-9586 for more information. Late September or early October.
- **Tuolumne County Wild West Film Festival and Rodeo,** Sonora. A gathering of western film stars and rodeo legends, plus arts and crafts, entertainment, a rodeo, and an awards dinner. Call 209/533-4420. Last weekend in September.

October
- **Gold-Panning Championships and Historic Demonstration Day,** Coloma. Gold-panning contests, food, crafts, music, and tours. Living history demonstrations of spinning, weaving, cooking, and doll-making. Call 916/622-6198. Dates vary.
- **Sonoma County Harvest Fair,** at the Sonoma County Fairgrounds. A 3-day celebration of the harvest with exhibitions, art shows, and annual judging of the local wines. Call 707/545-4203. Dates vary.
- **Annual Bob Hope Celebrity Golf Tournament,** Riverside. Bob Hope is the honorary chairman of this annual event. For ticket and other information, contact the Riverside Convention and Visitors Bureau at 909/222-4700. Dates vary.
- **Western Regional Final Championship Rodeo,** at the Lakeside Rodeo Grounds, Calif. 67 and Mapleview Avenue, Lakeside. Top cowboys from 11 western states compete in seven rodeo events including calf roping, barrel racing, bull riding, team roping, and steer wrestling. Call 619/561-6070 for more information. Mid-October.
- **Whale Festival,** Long Beach. Join in building a life-size whale from sand, and enjoy a family sand-sculpture contest, food, crafts, children's activities, entertainment, booths on sea life and issues, and a watermelon feast. Call 310/548-7562. Late October.
- **Pumpkin and Art Festival,** Half Moon Bay. Features hundreds of artisans' booths, pumpkin carvings, music, and a contest for the largest pumpkin. Colorful in the extreme. Call 415/726-9652. Usually late October, but dates vary.
- **Halloween,** San Francisco. The City by the Bay celebrates with a fantastical parade organized at Market and Castro streets, and a mixed gay-straight crowd revels in costumes of extraordinary imagination. October 31.

November
- **Doo Dah Parade,** Pasadena. An outrageous spoof of the Rose Parade, featuring participants such as the Briefcase Brigade and a kazoo band. Call 818/449-3689. The Sunday before Thanksgiving.
- **Hollywood Christmas Parade.** This spectacular star-studded parade marches through the heart of Hollywood. For information, phone 213/469-2337. The first or second Sunday after Thanksgiving.
- **San Diego Dixieland Jazz Festival.** More than 30 bands perform foot-stomping jazz at the Town & Country Hotel. Call 619/297-5277 for more information. Late November.

December
For a special "Only in California" holiday season, see box below.
- **Truckers Christmas Light Convoy,** Eureka. Big rigs decorated and festooned with lights compete for cash prizes in this lumber town. Call 707/442-5744 for dates and time.

Christmas in San Diego

Christmas in San Diego offers a number of unique activities:

• **Christmas on the Prado,** Balboa Park. Celebrated since 1977 as a weekend of evening events, held the first Friday and Saturday in December. Includes carol sing-a-long and food booths. Free admission to all museums. Call 619/239-0512. First weekend.

• **Coronado Christmas Celebration and Parade.** Santa's arrival by ferry is followed by a parade along Orange Avenue. Call 619/437-8788 or 435-8895. First Friday.

• **Mission Bay Boat Parade of Lights,** from Quivira Basin in Mission Bay. Concludes with the lighting of a 320-foot tower of Christmas lights at Sea World. Saturday in mid-December. Call 619/276-8200.

• **San Diego Harbor Parade of Lights,** from Shelter Island to Harbor Island to Seaport Village. Decorated boats of all sizes and types participate, and spectators line the shore and cheer for their favorites. Held since 1971. On Sunday in mid-December; check the local newspaper for the exact day and time.

—Elizabeth Hansen

---

3 Getting There

BY PLANE

All major U.S. carriers serve the San Francisco, Sacramento, San Jose, Los Angeles, and San Diego airports. Domestic airlines flying in and out of these cities include **Alaska Airlines** (☎ 800/426-0333), **American Airlines** (☎ 800/433-7300), **Delta Air Lines** (☎ 800/221-1212), **Northwest Airlines** (☎ 800/225-2525), **Southwest Airlines** (☎ 800/435-9792), **TWA** (☎ 800/221-2000), **United Airlines** (☎ 800/241-6522), and **USAir** (☎ 800/428-4322). Foreign travelers should also see "Getting to the U.S." in Chapter 4 for a list of airlines offering overseas flights into California.

The lowest round-trip fares to the West Coast from New York fluctuate between about $400 and $500; from Chicago they range from $300 to $400. The lowest round-trip fare between Los Angeles and San Francisco is about $198. Sometimes it's even lower.

You might be able to get a great deal on airfare by calling a consolidator, such as **Travac,** 989 Ave. of the Americas, New York, NY 10018 (☎ **800/TRAV-800** or 212/563-3303), or **Unitravel,** 1177 N. Warson Rd. (P.O. Box 12485), St. Louis, MO 63132 (☎ **800/325-2222** or 314/569-0900).

BY CAR

Here are some handy driving times if you're on one of those "see the U.S.A." car trips. From Phoenix, it's about 6 hours (okay, 7 if you drive the speed limit) to Los Angeles on I-10. Las Vegas is 265 miles northeast of Los Angeles (about a 4- or 5-hour drive).

San Francisco is 227 miles southwest of Reno, Nevada, and 577 miles northwest of Las Vegas. It's a long day's drive 640 miles south from Portland, Oregon, on I-5.

Of course, if you have time on your hands, the ultimate nostalgic road trip into California is along Route 66, "America's Main Street," which runs from the shores of Lake Michigan and winds through eight states before ending at the L.A. coast.

Before you set out on a big car trip, you might want to join the **American Automobile Association (AAA)** (☎ **800/222-4357**), which has hundreds of offices nationwide. Members receive excellent maps (they'll even help you plan an exact itinerary) and emergency road service.

BY TRAIN

Amtrak (☎ **800/USA-RAIL**) connects California with about 500 American cities. Trains bound for both Northern and Southern California leave daily from New York and pass through Chicago and Denver. The journey takes about 3 1/2 days, and seats fill up quickly. As of this writing, the lowest round-trip fare was $266 from New York and $240 from Chicago. These heavily restricted tickets are good for 45 days and allow up to three stops along the way.

The *Sunset Limited* is Amtrak's regularly scheduled transcontinental service, originating in Florida and making 52 stops along the way as it passes through Alabama, Mississippi, Louisiana, Texas, New Mexico, and Arizona before arriving in Los Angeles. The train, which runs three times weekly, features reclining seats, a sightseeing car with large windows, and a full-service dining car. Round-trip coach fares begin at $286; sleeping accommodations are available for an extra charge.

Ask about special family plans, tours, and other money-saving promotions the rail carrier may be offering. Call for a brochure outlining routes and prices for the entire system.

BY BUS

Greyhound/Trailways (☎ **800/231-2222**) can get you here from anywhere cheaply, if not in great comfort. Round-trip fares vary depending on your point of origin, but few, if any, ever exceed $200.

4 Getting Around

BY CAR

California's freeway signs frequently indicate direction by naming a town rather than a point on the compass. If you've never heard of Canoga Park you might be in trouble—unless you have a map. The best state road guide is the comprehensive Thomas Bros. **California Road Atlas,** a 300+-page book of maps with schematics of towns and cities statewide. It costs $20 but is a good investment if you plan to do a lot of exploring. Smaller, accordion-style maps are handy for the state as a whole or for individual cities and regions. These foldout maps usually cost $2 to $3 and are available at gas stations, pharmacies, supermarkets, and tourist-oriented shops everywhere.

For **road conditions,** call 916/445-7623 in Northern California, 213/628-7623 in Southern California.

If you're heading into the Sierras or Shasta-Cascades for a winter ski trip, top up on antifreeze and carry snow chains for your tires (chains are mandatory in certain areas). Here are a few sample distances between key California cities:

Los Angeles

96 miles SE of Santa Barbara
103 miles W of Palm Springs

continues

Los Angeles, *cont.*
120 miles NW of San Diego
332 miles SE of Monterey
379 miles SE of San Francisco
383 miles S of Sacramento
659 miles SE of Eureka

San Francisco
87 miles SW of Sacramento
115 miles NW of Monterey
278 miles SE of Eureka
321 miles NW of Santa Barbara
379 miles NW of Los Angeles
548 miles NW of San Diego

Sacramento
87 miles NE of San Francisco
185 miles NE of Monterey
304 miles SE of Eureka
383 miles N of Los Angeles
391 miles NE of Santa Barbara
484 miles NW of Palm Springs

RENTALS   California is one of the cheapest places in America to rent a car. The best-known firms, with locations throughout the state and at most major airports, include **Alamo** (☎ 800/327-9633), **Avis** (☎ 800/331-1212), **Budget** (☎ 800/527-0700), **Dollar** (☎ 800/421-6868), **Hertz** (☎ 800/654-3131), **National** (☎ 800/328-4567), and **Thrifty** (☎ 800/367-2277).

Most rental firms pad their profits by selling a Loss/Damage Waiver (LDW), which usually costs an extra $9 per day. Before agreeing to this, however, check with your insurance carrier and credit- and charge-card companies. Many people don't realize that they are already covered by either one or both.

For renters, the minimum age is usually 19 to 25.

Finally, think about splurging on a convertible. Few things in life can match the feeling of flying along the California coast with the sun smiling on your shoulders and the wind whipping through your hair.

DRIVING RULES   California law requires both drivers and passengers to wear seat belts. Children under 4 years or 40 pounds must be secured in an approved child safety seat. Motorcyclists must wear a helmet. Auto insurance is mandatory; the car's registration and proof of insurance must be carried in the car.

You can turn right at a red light, unless otherwise indicated—but be sure to come to a stop first. Pedestrians *always* have the right-of-way.

BY PLANE

In addition to the major carriers listed above in "Getting There," several smaller airlines provide service within the state, including **America West** (☎ 800/235-9292), **American Eagle** (☎ 800/433-7300), **Skywest** (☎ 800/453-9417), **Shuttle by United** (☎ 800/241-6522), **Southwest** (☎ 800/435-9792) and **USAir Express** (☎ 800/428-4322).

BY TRAIN

Amtrak (☎ **800/USA-RAIL**) runs trains up and down the California coast, connecting Los Angeles with San Francisco and all points in between. A one-way ticket can often be had for as little as $50. The coastal journey, aboard Amtrak's *Coast Starlight,* is a fantastically beautiful trip that runs from Seattle to Oakland; crosses Salinas, the artichoke capital of the world; climbs San Luis Obispo's bucolic hills; drops into Santa Barbara; then runs down the Malibu coast into Los Angeles. You can then continue on to San Diego. It's a popular journey—make reservations well in advance.

FAST FACTS: California

AAA If you're a member of the American Automobile Association and your car breaks down, call 800/AAA-HELP for 24-hour emergency roadside service.

American Express To report lost or stolen traveler's checks, call 800/221-7282. Local office locations are listed in the appropriate chapters throughout this book.

Car Rentals See "Getting Around," earlier in this chapter.

Climate See "When to Go," earlier in this chapter.

Driving Rules See "Getting Around," earlier in this chapter.

Earthquakes In the rare event of an earthquake, you should know about a few simple precautions that every California schoolchild is taught: If you're in a tall building, don't run outside; instead, move away from windows and toward the building's center. Crouch under a desk or table, or stand against a wall or under a doorway. If you're in bed, get under the bed or stand in a doorway, or crouch under a sturdy piece of furniture. When exiting the building, use stairwells, *not* elevators.

If you're in your car, pull over to the side of the road and stop, but wait until you're away from bridges or overpasses, and telephone or power poles and lines. Stay in your car.

If you're out walking, stay outside and away from trees, power lines, and the sides of buildings. If you're in an area with tall buildings, stand in a doorway.

Emergencies To reach the police, ambulance service, or fire department, dial **911** from any telephone. No coins are needed at pay phones.

Information See "Visitor Information & Money," earlier in this chapter.

Liquor Laws Liquor and grocery stores, as well as some drugstores, can legally sell packaged alcoholic beverages between 6am and 2am. Most restaurants, nightclubs, and bars are licensed to serve alcoholic beverages during the same hours. The legal age for the purchase and consumption of alcoholic beverages is 21; proof of age is strictly enforced.

Maps Local maps can usually be obtained free from area tourist offices. State and regional maps are sold at gas stations, in drugstores, and in tourist-oriented shops all around the state; the Thomas Bros. maps are the best. And included with this book is a full-color foldout sheet map that is useful for navigating the entire state.

Pets Many chain hotels and motels accept dogs (though some require a deposit or impose size restrictions). Some good bets, with their toll-free reservation numbers, include Best Western (☎ 800/528-1234), Comfort Inns (☎ 800/228-5150), Holiday Inns (☎ 800/HOLIDAY), La Quinta Inns (☎ 800/531-5900), Red Lion

Inns (☎ 800/547-8010), and Motel 6 (no nationwide number). But remember that managers of individual establishments are free to set or change their pet policy, so it's vital that you contact the hotel itself to confirm your dog's reservation instead of relying solely on these central reservation numbers.

It's not a good idea to bring your dog to any of California's national parks—for your pet's own protection. It's just not safe for dogs to wander in these areas, where they might have dangerous encounters with wildlife.

The *California Dog Lover's Companion* (Foghorn Press) is a huge and incredibly useful resource, with lodging recommendations plus ratings of hundreds of parks and beaches, plus details on where Fido is allowed to romp off-leash. You'll learn that San Francisco is an unusually dog-friendly destination, and that dogs are welcome at Pismo Beach and on the sands at Carmel. *On the Road Again with Man's Best Friend* (Macmillan) is another great reference tool, with detailed reviews of accommodations where dogs are welcome.

Taxes   California's state sales tax is 7.75%. Some municipalities impose an additional percentage, so tax varies throughout the state. Hotel taxes are almost always higher than tariffs levied on goods and services.

Time   California and the entire West Coast are in the Pacific time zone, 3 hours earlier than the East Coast.

Tourist Offices   See "Visitor Information & Money," earlier in this chapter, as well as specific city chapters later in this guide.

For Foreign Visitors 3

This chapter will provide some specifics about getting to the United States as economically and effortlessly as possible, plus some helpful information about how things are done in California—from sending mail to making a local or long-distance telephone call.

1 Preparing for Your Trip

ENTRY REQUIREMENTS

DOCUMENT REGULATIONS   Canadian nationals need only proof of Canadian residence to visit the United States. Citizens of the United Kingdom and Japan need only a current passport. Citizens of other countries, including Australia and New Zealand, usually need two documents: a valid passport with an expiration date at least 6 months later than the scheduled end of their visit to the United States and a tourist visa, available at no charge from a U.S. embassy or consulate.

To get a tourist or business visa to enter the United States, contact the nearest American embassy or consulate in your country; if there is none, you'll have to apply in person in a country where there is a U.S. embassy or consulate. Present your passport, a passport-size photo of yourself, and a completed application, which is available through the embassy or consulate. You may be asked to provide information about how you plan to finance your trip or show a letter of invitation from a friend with whom you plan to stay. Those applying for a business visa may be asked to show evidence that they will not receive a salary in the United States. Be sure to check the length of stay on your visa; usually it's 6 months. If you want to stay longer, you may file for an extension with the Immigration and Naturalization Service once you're in the country. If permission to stay is granted, a new visa is not required unless you leave the United States and want to reenter.

MEDICAL REQUIREMENTS   No inoculations are needed to enter the United States unless you're coming from, or have stopped over in, areas known to be suffering from epidemics, particularly cholera or yellow fever.

If you have a disease requiring treatment with medications containing narcotics or drugs requiring a syringe, carry a valid signed prescription from your physician to allay any suspicions that you're smuggling drugs. The brands you're accustomed to buying in your country may not be available here, so your prescription should be in generic form.

CUSTOMS REQUIREMENTS   Every adult visitor may bring in, free of duty: 1 liter of wine or hard liquor; 200 cigarettes or 100 cigars (but no cigars from Cuba) or 3 pounds of smoking tobacco; and $100 worth of gifts. These exemptions are offered to travelers who spend at least 72 hours in the United States and who have not claimed them within the preceding 6 months. It is altogether forbidden to bring foodstuffs (particularly cheese, fruit, cooked meats, and canned goods) and plants (vegetables, seeds, tropical plants, and so on) into the country. Foreign tourists may bring in or take out up to $10,000 in U.S. or foreign currency with no formalities; larger sums must be declared to Customs on entering or leaving.

INSURANCE

Unlike most other countries, the United States does not have a national health-care system. Because the cost of medical care is extremely high, we strongly advise all travelers to secure health insurance coverage before setting out on their trip.

You may want to take out a comprehensive travel policy that covers (for a relatively low premium) sickness or injury costs (medical, surgical, and hospital); loss or theft of your baggage; trip-cancellation costs; guarantee of bail in case you're arrested; and/or costs of accident, repatriation, or death. Such packages (for example, "Europe Assistance" in Europe) are sold by automobile clubs at attractive rates, as well as by insurance companies and travel agencies and at some airports.

MONEY

The U.S. monetary system has a decimal base: One American **dollar ($1)** = 100 **cents** (100¢). Dollar bills commonly come in $1 (a "buck"), $5, $10, $20, $50, and $100 denominations (the last two are not welcome when paying for small purchases and are usually not accepted in taxis or at subway ticket booths). There are six coin denominations: 1¢ (one cent or a "penny"), 5¢ (five cents or a "nickel"), 10¢ (ten cents or a "dime"), 25¢ (twenty-five cents or a "quarter"), 50¢ (fifty cents or a "half dollar"), and the $1 pieces (which are relatively uncommon).

American Express, Thomas Cook, and Barclay's Bank traveler's checks in U.S. dollars are accepted at most hotels, motels, restaurants, and large stores. Sometimes picture identification is required.

Credit and charge cards are the method of payment most widely used: Visa (BarclayCard in Britain), MasterCard (EuroCard in Europe, Access in Britain, Diamond in Japan), American Express, Discover, Diners Club, enRoute, JCB, and Carte Blanche, in descending order of acceptance. You can save yourself trouble by using "plastic" rather than cash or traveler's checks in 95% of all hotels, motels, restaurants, and retail stores. A credit or charge card can also serve as a deposit for renting a car, as proof of identity, or as a "cash card," enabling you to draw money from automatic-teller machines (ATMs) that accept them.

You can telegraph money, or have it telegraphed to you very quickly using the **Western Union** system (☎ **800/325-6000**).

SAFETY

While tourist areas are generally safe, crime is on the increase everywhere, and U.S. urban areas tend to be less safe than those in Europe or Japan. Visitors should always stay alert. This is particularly true of large U.S. cities. It's wise to ask the city's or area's tourist office if you're in doubt about which neighborhoods are safe.

DRIVING Recently more and more crime has involved cars and drivers. If you drive off a highway into a doubtful neighborhood, leave the area as quickly as possible. If you have an accident, even on the highway, stay in your car with the doors locked until you assess the situation or until the police arrive. If you're bumped from behind on the street or are involved in a minor accident with no injuries and the situation appears to be suspicious, motion to the other driver to follow you to a police station or a well-lit public area. Never get out of your car in such situations.

If you see someone on the road who indicates a need for help, *don't* stop. Note the location, drive on to a well-lighted area, and call the police at 911.

Park in well-lighted, well-traveled areas if possible. Always keep your car doors locked, whether attended or unattended. Never leave any packages or valuables in sight. If someone attempts to rob you or steal your car, *don't* try to resist the thief/carjacker—report the incident to the police department immediately.

2 Getting to the U.S.

A number of U.S. airlines offer service from Europe to the United States. If they don't have direct flights from Europe to California, they can book you straight through on a connecting flight. You can make reservations by calling the following numbers in the U.K.: American (☎ 0181/572-5555), Continental (☎ 04412/9377-6464), Delta (☎ 0800/414-767), and United (☎ 0181/990-9900).

And of course many international carriers serve LAX and/or San Francisco International Airport. Helpful numbers to know include **Virgin Atlantic** (☎ 0293/747-747 in the U.K.), **British Airways** (☎ 0345/222-111 in the U.K.), and **Aer Lingus** (☎ 01/844-4747 in Dublin or 061/415-556 in Shannon). **Qantas** (☎ 008/177-767 in Australia) has flights from Sydney to Los Angeles and San Francisco; you can also take United from Australia to the West Coast. **Air New Zealand** (☎ 0800/737-000 in Auckland or 3/379-5200 in Christchurch) also offers service to LAX. Canadian readers might book flights on **Air Canada** (☎ 800/268-7240 or 800/361-8620 in Canada), which offers direct service from Toronto, Montréal, Calgary, and Vancouver to San Francisco, Sacramento, Los Angeles, and San Diego.

The visitor arriving by air, no matter what the port of entry, should cultivate patience and resignation before setting foot on U.S. soil. Getting through Immigration control may take as long as 2 hours on some days, especially summer weekends, so have your guidebook or something else to read handy. Add the time it takes to clear Customs and you'll see that you should make a very generous allowance for delay in planning connections between international and domestic flights—figure on 2 to 3 hours at least.

For the traveler arriving by car or by rail from Canada, the border-crossing formalities have been streamlined to the vanishing point. And if you're traveling by air from Canada, Bermuda, and some places in the Caribbean, you can sometimes go through Customs and Immigration at the point of departure, which is much quicker.

3 Getting Around the U.S.

For information on Getting Around by car, see "Getting Around" in Chapter 3.

BY PLANE On their trans-Atlantic or trans-Pacific flights, some large U.S. airlines offer special discount tickets for any of their U.S. destinations (American Airlines' Visit USA program and Delta's Discover America program, for example). The tickets or coupons are not on sale in the United States and must be purchased before you leave your point of departure. This system is the best, easiest, and fastest way to see the United States at low cost. You should obtain information well in advance from your travel agent or the office of the airline concerned, since the conditions attached to these discount tickets can be changed without advance notice.

BY TRAIN   International visitors can also buy a **USA Railpass,** good for 15 or 30 days of unlimited travel on Amtrak, the national passenger rail corporation. The pass is available through many foreign travel agents. Prices in 1996 for a 15-day pass were $245 off-peak (August 21 to June 16), $355 peak; a 30-day pass cost $350 off-peak, $440 peak. (With a foreign passport, you can also buy passes at some Amtrak offices in the United States including locations in San Francisco, Los Angeles, Chicago, New York, Miami, Boston, and Washington, D.C.) Reservations are generally required and should be made for each part of your trip as early as possible.

Visitors should also be aware of the limitations of long-distance train travel in the United States. With a few notable exceptions, service is rarely up to European standards: Delays are common, routes are limited and often infrequently served, and fares are rarely significantly lower than discount airfares. Thus, cross-country train travel should be approached with caution.

BY BUS   The cheapest way to travel the United States is by bus. Greyhound/Trailways, the sole nationwide bus line, offers an **Ameripass** for unlimited travel for 7 days at $179, 15 days at $289, 30 days at $399, and 60 days at $599. Bus travel in the United States can be both slow and uncomfortable, so this option is not for everyone. In addition, bus stations are often located in undesirable neighborhoods.

FAST FACTS: For the Foreign Traveler

Automobile Organizations   Auto clubs will supply maps, suggested routes, guidebooks, accident and bail-bond insurance, and emergency road service. The major auto club in the United States, with 955 offices nationwide, is the American Automobile Association (AAA). Members of some foreign auto clubs have reciprocal arrangements with the AAA and enjoy its services at no charge. If you belong to an auto club, inquire about AAA reciprocity before you leave. The AAA can provide you with an International Driving Permit validating your foreign license, although drivers with valid licenses from most home countries don't really need this permit. You may be able to join the AAA even if you're not a member of a reciprocal club. To inquire, call 619/233-1000. In addition, some automobile-rental agencies now provide these services; inquire about their availability when you rent your car.

Business Hours   Offices are usually open Monday to Friday from 9am to 5pm. Banks are open Monday to Friday from 9am to 3pm or later and sometimes on Saturday morning. Shops, especially those in shopping complexes, tend to stay open late: until about 9pm Monday to Friday and until 6pm on Saturday and Sunday.

Climate   See "When to Go" in Chapter 2.

Currency Exchange   The "foreign-exchange bureaus" so common in Europe are rare in the United States. They're at major international airports, and there are a few in most major cities, but they're nonexistent in medium-size cities and small towns. Try to avoid having to change foreign money, or traveler's checks denominated in other than U.S. dollars, at small-town banks, or even at branches in a big city; in fact, leave any currency other than U.S. dollars at home (except the cash you need for the taxi or bus ride home when you return to your own country); otherwise, your own currency may prove more nuisance to you than it's worth.

Drinking Laws   The legal age to purchase and drink alcohol is 21.

Electric Current   The United States uses 110–120 volts, 60 cycles, compared to 220–240 volts, 50 cycles, as in most of Europe. Besides a 100-volt transformer, small appliances of non-American manufacture, such as hair dryers or shavers, will require an adapter plug with two flat, parallel pins. The easiest solution to the power struggle is to purchase dual-voltage appliances that operate on both 110 and 220 volts and then all that's required is a U.S. adapter plug.

Embassies/Consulates   All embassies are located in Washington, D.C. Listed here are the West Coast consulates of the major English-speaking countries. The Australian Consulate is located at Century Plaza Towers, 19th Floor, 2049 Century Park East, Los Angeles, CA 90067 (☎ 310/229-4800). The Canadian Consulate is at 550 S. Hope St., 9th Floor, Los Angeles, CA 90071 (☎ 213/346-2700). The Irish Consulate is located at 655 Montgomery St., Suite 930, San Francisco, CA 94111 (☎ 415/392-4214). The New Zealand Consulate is at 12400 Wilshire Blvd., Los Angeles, CA 90025 (☎ 310/207-1605). Contact the U.K. Consulate at 11766 Wilshire Blvd., Suite 400, Los Angeles, CA 90025 (☎ 310/477-3322).

Emergencies   Call **911** for fire, police, and ambulance. If you encounter such traveler's problems as sickness, accident, or lost or stolen baggage, call Traveler's Aid, an organization that specializes in helping distressed travelers. (Check local telephone directories for the location nearest you.) U.S. hospitals have emergency rooms, with a special entrance where you will be admitted for quick attention.

Gasoline (Petrol)   One U.S. gallon equals 3.75 liters, while 1.2 U.S. gallons equals 1 Imperial gallon. A gallon of unleaded gas (short for gasoline), which most rental cars require, costs about $1.30 if you fill your own tank (it's called "self-serve"); about 10¢ more if the station attendant does it (called "full-service").

Holidays   On the following national legal holidays, banks, government offices, post offices, and many stores, restaurants, and museums are closed: January 1 (New Year's Day), third Monday in January (Martin Luther King, Jr., Day), third Monday in February (Presidents' Day), last Monday in May (Memorial Day), July 4 (Independence Day), first Monday in September (Labor Day), second Monday in October (Columbus Day), November 11 (Veterans Day / Armistice Day), last Thursday in November (Thanksgiving Day), and December 25 (Christmas Day). The Tuesday following the first Monday in November is Election Day and is a legal holiday in presidential election years (next in 2000).

Legal Aid   If you are stopped for a minor infraction (for example, of the highway code, such as speeding), never attempt to pay the fine directly to a police officer; you may be arrested on the much more serious charge of attempted bribery. Pay fines by mail, or directly into the hands of the clerk of the court. If you're accused of a more serious offense, it's best to say and do nothing before consulting a lawyer. Under U.S. law, an arrested person is allowed one telephone call to a party of his or her choice. Call your embassy or consulate.

Mail   Mailboxes are blue with a blue-and-white logo, and carry the inscription *U.S. Mail.* Within the United States, it costs 20¢ to mail a standard-size postcard and 32¢ to send an oversize postcard (larger than 4¼ by 6 inches, or 10.8cm by 15.4cm). Letters that weigh up to 1 ounce (that's about five 8- by 11-inch, or 20.5cm by 28.2cm, pages) cost 32¢, plus 23¢ for each additional ounce. A postcard to Mexico costs 30¢; a half-ounce letter, 35¢. A postcard to Canada costs 30¢; a 1-ounce letter, 40¢. A postcard to Europe, Australia, New Zealand, the Far East, South America, and elsewhere costs 40¢, while a letter is 60¢ for each half-ounce.

Taxes   In the United States there is no VAT (value-added tax) or other indirect tax at a national level. There is a $10 Customs tax, payable on entry to the United States, and a $6 departure tax. Sales tax is levied on goods and services by state and local governments, however, and varies by state, county, and city. It is not included in the price tags you'll see on merchandise and is not refundable.

Telephone & Fax   Pay phones can be found on street corners, as well as in bars, restaurants, public buildings, and stores, and at service stations. Some accept 20¢; most are 25¢. If the telephone accepts 20¢, you may also use a quarter (25¢) but you won't receive change.

In the past few years many American companies have installed "voice-mail" systems, so be prepared to deal with a machine instead of a receptionist if you're calling a business number.

For long-distance or international calls, it's most economical to charge the call to a telephone charge card or a credit card—or you can use a lot of change. The pay phone will instruct you how much to deposit and when to deposit it into the slot at the top of the telephone box.

For long-distance calls in the United States, dial 1 followed by the area code and number you want. For direct overseas calls, first dial 011, followed by the country code (Australia, 61; Republic of Ireland, 353; New Zealand, 64; United Kingdom, 44; and so on), and then by the city code (for example, 171 or 181 for London, 21 for Birmingham, 1 for Dublin) and the number of the person you wish to call.

Before calling from a hotel room, always ask the hotel phone operator if there are any telephone surcharges. There almost always are, and they're often as much as 75¢ or $1, even for a local call. These charges are best avoided by using a public phone, calling collect, or using a telephone charge card.

For reversed-charge or collect calls and for person-to-person calls, dial 0 (zero, not the letter "O") followed by the area code and number you want; an operator will then come on the line, and you should specify that you are calling collect, or person-to-person, or both. If your operator-assisted call is international, immediately ask to speak with an overseas operator.

For local directory assistance ("Information"), dial 411; for long-distance information dial 1, then the appropriate area code and 555-1212.

Time   California is on Pacific time, which is 3 hours earlier than on the U.S. East Coast. For instance, when it's noon in San Diego, it's 3pm in New York and Miami; 2pm in Chicago, in the central part of the country; and 1pm in Denver, Colorado, in the midwestern part of the country. California, like most of the rest of the United States, observes daylight saving time during the summer; in late spring, clocks are moved ahead 1 hour and then are turned back again in the fall. This results in lovely long summer evenings, when the sun sets as late as 8:30 or 9pm.

Tipping   Some rules of thumb: bartenders, 10% to 15%; bellhops, at least 50¢ per bag, or $2 to $3 for a lot of luggage; cab drivers, 10% of the fare; cafeterias and fast-food restaurants, no tip; chambermaids, $1 per day; checkroom attendants, $1 per garment; theater ushers, no tip; gas-station attendants, no tip; hairdressers and barbers, 15% to 20%; waiters and waitresses, 15% to 20% of the check; valet parking attendants, $1.

On the Road: Seeing California by Car

4

The cult of the car was born in California. We've assumed that you'll be driving as you explore, and there's no better way to see this spectacular state. Perhaps the most famous scenic drive in the United States follows Calif. 1 as it twists and turns, hugging the Pacific coast.

The great thing about driving, of course, is that you can go as you please, stopping to explore offbeat sights and little-known destinations. Here are three great drives that will get you started.

1 Ghost Towns of the Gold Country

by Lisa Stone-Norman

The scene of California's original get-rich-quick scheme is hundreds of miles from the fistfuls of money made today in Hollywood and Silicon Valley. The crannies of the Sierra foothills hide the real hardscrabble genesis of the Golden State, where a few gutsy pioneers accidentally shoveled pure gold in 1848.

In a brief decade, nearly 400,000 people stampeded to California to try to pan their piece of the Gold Rush. Long before the rush petered out, a small but lucky percentage of the famed forty-niners and others extracted millions of dollars in precious metal from the Mother Lode; most everybody else eventually went home—or stayed put—empty-handed.

Long before the gold was gone, however, the boomtowns of the Sierra became famous for the colorful characters who dug, drank, gambled, and lusted through their quest to eke precious gold out of its 200-million-year-old hiding place in the stony earth. Criminal Charles "Black Bart" Bolton shot up the towns and stole gold dust from a fledgling bank called Wells Fargo. Budding journalist Mark Twain wrote about it—but no one really knows if Twain ever wore a pair of the popular canvas pants cunningly riveted by young merchant Levi Strauss.

Today the legacy of the famous and forgotten fortune seekers lives on in a chain of more than 100 ghost towns and abandoned mines that dot Calif. 49. Driving from Coloma to Columbia, you'll discover picturesque villages that are doing a better business now than in the old days, thanks to painstakingly restored boardwalks stocked with antiques and collectibles. You'll also enjoy quiet ghost towns, sparsely populated or empty testaments to how—not so long ago— a new generation of Californians scratched their way to a living.

Start: Coloma (32 miles east of downtown Sacramento—halfway between Sacramento and South Lake Tahoe).

Finish: Columbia (55 miles south of Sacramento, 39 miles east of Stockton, and 120 miles east of the San Francisco Bay Area).

Time: This 1-day tour is perfect for visitors to Sacramento and South Lake Tahoe who are interested in seeing the heart of the Gold Country. The area also is accessible to visitors to the San Francisco Bay Area who want a look at rural California and aren't afraid of a little driving. History buffs interested in staying overnight and exploring the twisting 120-mile stretch between Downieville and Mariposa won't be disappointed.

Begin your tour in **Coloma,** where gold was first discovered in 1848. The pretty ghost town overlooks the south fork of the American River. Getting there from U.S. 50 is easy: Turn north at the stoplight in Placerville, where signs advertise Calif. 49; look for a vintage, brick-red Southern Pacific Railroad caboose as a landmark.

The crowded, corrugated tin roofs that line the start of the 8-mile drive from Placerville to Coloma testify to a mining past. Closer to Coloma the homes give way to windmills, cattle-grazing lands, and fruit orchards—the tools miners' descendants use to make a living nowadays.

Upon approaching Coloma, follow the signs to the Marshall Monument, or Calif. 153 (California's shortest highway at three-tenths of a mile). At its end you'll find the:

1. **James Marshall Monument and Gravesite.** On a knoll beyond the parking lot stands the huge, bronze statue of James Wilson Marshall. It doubles as his gravestone and points to the spot where he discovered gold on January 24, 1848, while building a sawmill. As the story goes, the New Jersey carpenter managed to keep the news to himself for only a few minutes before he shouted to work crews. Although word of his find spread as far away as Mexico and China, Marshall never ended up making a dime from his discovery. He ended his days as a carpenter and blacksmith in nearby Kelsey, unrecognized for his contribution.

The view from the monument is beautiful, especially in spring when the green hills sprout wildflowers. Nearby picnic tables are scattered beneath huge oak trees. The site and its public rest rooms are kept tidy by a resident park ranger. The state requests a $5 parking fee, which visitors may pay here or at the next stop.

Upon leaving the park, cross Calif. 49 and enter Coloma. Turn left onto Main Street and drive through the ghost town until on the left appears the:

2. **Marshall Gold Discovery State Historic Park.** A quick tour of this museum will bring you up to speed on Gold Country lingo, from "placer" gold, which erodes from quartz, to how miners "coyoted," or dug the metal out of the earth. You can learn how to pan for gold at the river and pick up an old-town walking tour map. The museum (☎ 916/622-1116) is open daily from 10am to 5pm. (For park information, call 916/622-3470.)

Coloma was quickly mined out, but its boom brought 10,000 people to the settlement and lasted long enough for residents to build a schoolhouse, a gunsmithy, a general store, and a tiny, tin-roofed post office. The miners also planted oak and mimosa trees that shade the street during hot summers. A few stores open to sell light fare and jewelry from March to early fall; traditionally, a beer garden opens next to the restored Weller House, the last remaining evidence of the 13 guest houses the town boasted at its peak.

Farther up Main Street is a huge replica of the mill Marshall was building when he made his discovery. The largest building in town, the mill is powered by electricity during the summer months. Across the street are two restored stone

Ghost Towns of the Gold Country

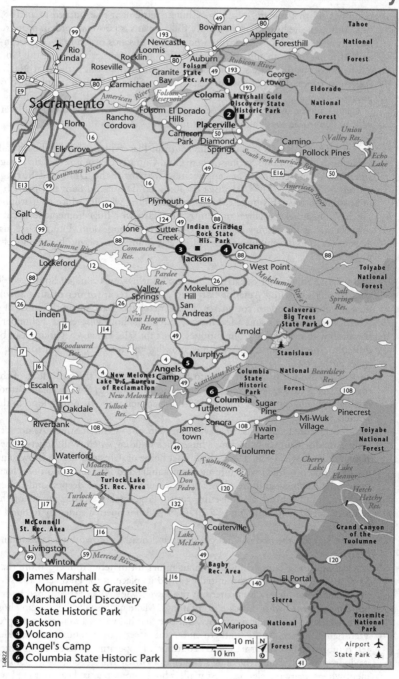

Legend:
1. James Marshall Monument & Gravesite
2. Marshall Gold Discovery State Historic Park
3. Jackson
4. Volcano
5. Angel's Camp
6. Columbia State Historic Park

0 | 10 mi
0 | 10 km

N

Airport ✈
State Park ✦

I-0822

buildings, all that remains of a large Chinese settlement that burned in an 1883
fire. Although the history of these early Californians is poorly recorded, proof remains that the Midas touch favored no race. Thousands of Chinese-, Mexican-,
and African-American miners worked their way to prosperity during the Gold
Rush, boosting the state's multicultural flavor at the same time that Native
American tribes, displaced and diseased by the influx of foreign people, died or
moved on.

Leave Coloma by taking Main Street back to Calif. 49. Travel through Placerville and continue south along the twisting road.

☕ **TAKE A BREAK**   A few miles south of Placerville is the tiny boardwalk
community of Diamond Springs, where Gold Country charm is served up alongside such urban comforts as cappuccino. Watch for the **Diamond Springs
Hotel,** 545 Main St. (☎ 916/621-1730; open daily from 8am to 9pm). It's
impossible to miss this huge red barn of a building with its white wraparound
porches. The hotel specializes in country breakfasts with huge homemade biscuits
as authentic as the twangy music piped in to the dining room. Lunches are just
as generous, and the children's menu offers everything from peanut butter and jelly
to Jell-O.

About 12 miles after departing Diamond Springs on Calif. 49 South, you'll
pass through bustling Amador City and Sutter Creek, former mining towns
now devoted to modern commerce. Local merchants have made the most of a
refurbished boardwalk and a few historic buildings; both villages are a shopper's
paradise, with everything from antiques to art for sale. However, parking can be
difficult, especially during the summer months, and travelers may opt to drive 5
miles farther to:

3. **Jackson.** Turn left off Calif. 49 onto Jackson Gate Road, the back door of the
town. After 3 or 4 miles you'll pass the dramatic white St. Sava Serbian Orthodox Church and cemetery. Built in 1894, the church is the first of its kind in the
United States.

A few hundred yards past St. Sava's, turn left onto Church Street. At no. 225
is the **Amador County Museum,** a huge brick building where Will Rogers filmed
Boys Will Be Boys in 1920. Today the former home of Armstead Calvin Brown and
his 11 children is filled with mining memorabilia and information on two local
mines, the Kennedy and the Argonaut, that were among the deepest and richest
in the nation. Behind the museum, tour a large-scale working model of the
Kennedy for $1. The museum (☎ 209/223-6386) is open Wednesday to Sunday
from 10am to 4pm.

Turn right at the end of Church Street and head for downtown Jackson and
Main Street.

Although the Kennedy and Argonaut mines ultimately produced more than
$140 million in gold, Jackson initially earned its place in the gold rush as a sup-
ply center. That history is apparent in the town's wide Main Street, lined by tall
buildings adorned with intricate iron railings. Make no mistake: This is no ghost
town—Jackson is a modern minicity, but one that has worked to preserve its pre-
Victorian influence. At the southern end of the street is the famous **National Hotel,** rumored to be California's oldest continuously operating hotel since it opened
its doors in 1862. Today the hotel's **Louisiana House Bar,** a cool, dark establishment where weary travelers can rest while a honky-tonk pianist beats out ragtime,
does plenty of business.

Take a good look at the **Wells Fargo Club and Charcoal Broiler,** located diagonally across the street from the hotel. This two-story brick structure with its wooden balcony and awning is an original 1851 Wells Fargo building.

Upon leaving Jackson, follow the signs back to Calif. 49 South. Once back on the highway, begin looking immediately for Calif. 88 east. Turn left onto Calif. 88 and travel 12 miles to:

4. Volcano. Unrestored and beautiful, this is one of the most authentic ghost towns in the central Sierra. The town got its name in 1848, after miners mistook the origin of the enormous craggy boulders that lie in the center of the village. The dark rock and blind window frames of a few backless, ivy-covered buildings give the town's main throughfare a haunted look. Sprinkled between boarded up buildings, about a hundred residents do business in the same sagging wooden storefronts that a population of 8,000 frequented nearly 150 years ago.

The overwhelming thing you'll notice about Volcano is the silence of its streets. But the now-quiet tiny burg has a rich history: Not only was this boomtown once home to 17 hotels, courts of quick justice, and the state's first lending library, but Volcano gold supported the Union during the Civil War. Residents even smuggled a huge cannon to the front line in a hearse (it was never used). The story goes that had the enthusiastic blues fired it, **"Old Abe"** would have exploded, it was so overcharged. The cannon sits in the town center today, under a rusting weathervane.

Looming over the small buildings is the stately **St. George Hotel** (☎ 209/296-4458), a three-story, balconied building that testifies to the $90 million in gold mined in and around the town. Its ivy-covered brick and shuttered windows will remind you of colonial New England. The 20-room hotel still operates Wednesday to Sunday and serves meals and libations in its full bar and restaurant.

Take Calif. 88 back to Calif. 49 and drive south 16 miles. Along the way, take note of the brick remains of **Butte Store.** The storefront is all that remains of Butte City, a camp that sprang up—and almost as quickly died—in the shadow of **Mokelumne Hill.** You'll want to stop at:

5. **Angel's Camp,** the site of "The Jumping Frog of Calaveras County," the Mark Twain story that made both him and the town famous overnight. It's a tale of frontier espionage—a champion frog croaks after being poisoned with buckshot by the competition. The town's Jumping Frog Jubilee is an annual celebration in the third week of May. Now you'll understand the recurring theme of amphibians painted on the boardwalk, which has flourished since 1860.

☕ **TAKE A BREAK**   Stop for a late lunch at **Piaggi's Restaurant and the Frog Pond Creamery,** 1262 S. Main St., where the settings and prices are modest but no one has ever left the premises hungry. The homemade chili is great—order it with onions and cheese—as are the enormous hamburgers. (*Beware:* The regular patty weighs more than a pound and is easily twice the size of the large onion kaiser roll it comes on.)

Continue 7 miles down Calif. 49 to:

6. Columbia State Historic Park, an antique metropolis that has more standing relics of early mining days than almost any ghost town in the Gold Country. Allow at least 2 hours to explore it. Columbia is very popular, however, so expect crowds in summer.

In Columbia's heyday its 15,000 residents built 150 gambling houses, one of the first public schools in California, 17 dry-goods stores, and a full-fledged Chinatown. Today cars are banned from its dusty streets, giving the shady town an authentic and uncommercial feel. Merchants still do business behind some storefronts, as horse, stagecoach, and pedestrian traffic wanders by.

Start your tour at the beautiful, two-story **Fallon Hotel and Theater** (☎ 209/ 532-1470). Like many buildings in Columbia, the hotel was built with bricks in 1857 to withstand the fires that regularly swept the town. The state has spent more than $1 million to restore the hotel and its antique furnishings, many of which are original to the Fallon. Its 14 rooms and full-service restaurant offer every convenience. Seasonal performances go on in the Fallon's quaint theater, courtesy of drama students from the University of the Pacific. The company rehearses down the street at Eagle Cotage (its traditional spelling), a former upscale boardinghouse for luckier miners.

Between the two buildings is the tiny office of the *Columbia Gazette,* the local paper that's still published once a year. The basement is home to a free museum on the history of California newspapers.

Up the road, on Main Street, is the **Wells Fargo Express** building. Constructed in 1858, the structure is notable for its lacework iron railing and, inside, a scale that gold-rush bankers used to weigh more than 1.4 million ounces of gold. The scale is fabled to be so precise that it can weigh a pencil signature on a piece of paper.

If you wait long enough in front of Wells Fargo, the **Columbia Stage** will pull up. The town's stables operate the stage and a livery year round for visitors interested in a horse or pony tour of the town and cemetery. Call 209/532-0663 for information and reservations.

Nearby is an open-air example of how residents mined an estimated $90 million in gold in and around the town before 1870. An intricate system of miniature sawmills and tunnels delivers water to the area, where you can try your hand at panning for gold today. The large boulders and nearby grassy park make it perfect for children.

Kids will also get a kick out of the schoolhouse, built in 1861, which has been restored with desks and slates. Farther down Main Street is the **Columbia Museum** and another beautiful old guesthouse, the **City Hotel** (☎ 209/532-1479), built in 1856. Behind the iron grillwork and French doors on the second floor are two of the hotel's 10 luxurious Victorian rooms.

⚫ **WINDING DOWN**   Pull up a stool at the **Douglass Saloon** (open daily from 10am to 5pm) on Columbia's Main Street. Inside the swinging doors of the classic western bar you can sample homemade sarsparilla and wild cherry, drinks the saloon has been serving since 1857. The storefront's large shuttered windows open onto a dusty main street, so put up your boots, relax awhile, and watch the stagecoach go by.

2 The Missions of the Central Coast

by Stephanie Avnet

For those who grew up along California's coast between the Bay Area and the Mexican border, grammar-school field trips to the beautifully restored old Spanish missions scattered throughout the region were a matter of course. For restless school kids, though, the day's greatest excitement was leaving the classroom temporarily behind. Many had more enthusiasm for scratching initials into the metallic back of a school bus seat than for learning about Franciscan friars who ventured north from Mexico more than 200 years ago.

Nearly everyone can remember similar school-age experiences. However, maybe your boredom wasn't just a result of your pint-sized attention span. Maybe if those long-gone school trips were as interesting as this driving tour, we all would have lifted our heads from behind those school bus seats.

Today, take an extraordinary opportunity to step back in time—not just to relive what might be your own history, but California's as well—by seeking out the six historic missions along the central coast. What's more, the drive will give you a panoramic view of modern California. From surf-pounded coastlines to rich agricultural valleys, from upscale college towns to working-class farm communities and even sparsely populated ranchland, you'll see that the missions act as the chain linking everything together.

In fact, the 21 missions *were* originally laid out as links in a chain by the Spanish friars, led by Father Junípero Serra, who were the state's earliest European settlers. Serra, born on Mallorca in 1713, was a Franciscan friar whose life work began when he was sent to the New World as administrator of the church's missions in Baja (lower) California. Shortly after arriving, he was charged with founding missions at the ports of San Diego and Monterey in the little-explored Alta (upper) California, a Spanish territory populated with "heathen" natives and threatened by Russian imperialism.

He was constantly thwarted by insufficient supplies, resistant natives, and Spanish bureaucratic red tape, yet Serra ultimately went on to found a total of nine thriving missions before his death in 1784. Recognized by many in both religious and secular circles for the role he played in spreading the Christian faith and establishing the strong Spanish legacy in California, Fr. Junípero Serra was a candidate for sainthood and was beatified by the Vatican in 1988.

Serra and his band of Spanish pilgrims spaced their colonial missions at roughly 1-day intervals (on horseback, that is!) along El Camino Real (the royal road) that stretched up through California from Mexico. Present-day U.S. 101 runs true to this historic road along most of its blacktopped path. At several of the missions along this tour you'll be able to walk along portions of the original road used by the Spanish to supply and oversee these colony outposts.

Start: Santa Barbara (95 miles northwest of downtown Los Angeles).
Finish: San Juan Bautista (92 miles south of San Francisco and 35 miles east of the Monterey Peninsula).
Time: Two days are recommended for seeing all six missions along this 270-mile drive. San Luis Obispo, Paso Robles, or Morro Bay is recommended for the overnight stop after seeing Mission San Luis Obispo.

Begin your tour in **Santa Barbara,** whose picturesque coastal location is complemented by the prevailing Spanish-Moorish architectural style, largely influenced by the city's imposing mission. From U.S. 101, exit at Mission Street and follow the beige-and-brown Historic Landmark signs, which are extremely well placed and helpful all along the drive, to the first stop on our tour. While cruising along Mission Street, notice the variety of architectural styles and eras. Just before the mission itself is **Plaza Junipero,** a small neighborhood of elegant Craftsman bungalows; two short stone replicas of a traditional mission *campanario* (bell tower) mark the gateway to the community. Just beyond Plaza Junipero is:

1. Santa Barbara Mission Virgen y Martir. Founded in 1786 and still inhabited by Franciscan friars, it's known as the "Queen of the Missions." The design of its imposing church, differing from the standard mission simplicity, incorporates many Moorish and classical elements. Santa Barbara's residents embraced the church's distinctive look as the town grew during the 1920s and 1930s, incorporating red roof tiles, thick stucco walls, arches, and outdoor arcades into the design of the town's new buildings.

Pause at the top of the church's majestic stairs for a moment to behold the panorama of city and sea. Its interior is well lit thanks to a row of high windows along each side. Notice the extreme depth of the outer walls, and the single trompe l'oeil window to the left of the altar.

Although the grounds directly in front of the mission have been paved over for parking, the beauty of the rustic Moorish fountain, built in 1808, hasn't been spoiled. In its shallow waters you'll see fish, lily pads, and previous visitors' coins tossed in for good luck. Nearby is the remarkably well preserved *lavanderia* (laundry basin), fed through a whimsical bear's head carved in stone.

As with most of the missions, it's worthwhile to tour the museum and gift shop established in the restored padres' quarters. A highlight of this museum is the collection of historical photographs of the buildings and surrounding area, some dating from the 1850s, featuring brown-robed friars tending the old orchards and gardens. The gift shop, meanwhile, has an extensive selection of crucifixes, religious statuary, and pottery crafted by local artisans.

Don't miss the cemetery outside the church, its yard populated with centuries of headstones, vaults, and mausoleums. Shaded by a majestic Australian fig tree, it's still in use to this day. While you're in the cemetery, be sure to take a minute to study the church's exterior. Over the door are three sets of skull and crossbones. Upon careful examination, you'll see that only one is carved in stone—two sets are *real* bones embedded in the plaster.

Mission Santa Barbara is open to the public daily from 9am to 5pm. Admission is $3 per person; allow 30 to 45 minutes to see all of its sights. For further information, call 805/682-4713.

Upon leaving the mission, return to U.S. 101 via Mission Street, or take palm tree–lined State Street west through the heart of Old Town Santa Barbara, past its attractive cafés, bookstores, and vintage clothing shops.

☕ **TAKE A BREAK**   If you're ready for a treat, stop by **Andersen's Danish Bakery and Restaurant**, at 1106 State St. near Figueroa Street (☎ 805/962-5085). Reservations recommended on weekends. Danish Ms. Andersen greets you herself (when she's not baking) and offers substantial (and cheap!) portions of New York steak, chicken or crab salad, and array of other edibles (including an honest-to-goodness smörgåsbord). And both the indoor and alfresco tables offer great people-watching along State Street.

Leaving Santa Barbara, drive north on U.S. 101, which turns sharply inland just past Gaviota, as the scenery changes from dramatic coastline to warm agricultural valleys. The cars sharing the roadway with you might change, too; many drivers in this area, inspired by the scenery, relive the heyday of motor touring with vintage autos.

At Buellton, take Calif. 246 west into the **Lompoc Valley.** This region produces half of all the flower seeds sold in the world. If you plan your trip for late spring or early summer, you'll be rewarded with a dazzling rainbow, as over 200 varieties blossom into a colorful patchwork across the countryside.

After traveling 15 miles on Calif. 246, past ornate gateways to distant ranches and roadside produce stands (do stop and sample the wares), you'll reach:

Missions of the Central Coast

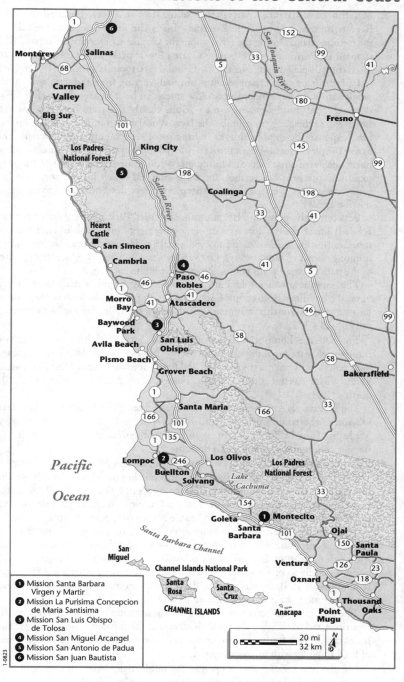

1. Mission Santa Barbara Virgen y Martir
2. Mission La Purisima Concepcion de Maria Santisima
3. Mission San Luis Obispo de Tolosa
4. Mission San Miguel Arcangel
5. Mission San Antonio de Padua
6. Mission San Juan Bautista

2. **Mission La Purísima Concepción de María Santísima,** founded in 1787. Reconstructed in its still-rural setting, this is the most extensively rebuilt of the mission chain. During the Depression, the Civilian Conservation Corps (CCC) restored La Purísima, which is now a state historic park. Inside the museum, an interesting display documents the CCC and the restoration process.

La Purísima's open arrangement is unusual, varying from the standard "quadrangle" around a large inner yard. Allow at least an hour to tour the grounds. The reconstructed buildings and work stations clearly illustrate how the Spanish Empire used the clergy to colonize the New World with minimal military support (and expense) by establishing fully functional settlements for converting the native peoples. The mission's intricate water-supply system, with its many elaborately decorated aqueducts and fountains, is still relatively intact. Be sure to stop to admire the pens of livestock and farm animals, which include some mighty impressive steers. Reportedly, the sheep are direct descendants of the original mission herds.

Between early spring and late autumn, costumed Park Service volunteers reenact daily life at the mission. You can enjoy the sights and smells of craft demonstrations (tortilla making, soap and candle making, leatherworking, blacksmithing, spinning, weaving, and pottery). On Sunday the volunteers conduct nature walks of the park's diverse plant communities and wildlife habitats.

The grounds at Mission La Purísima are open to the public daily from 7am to 6pm; the buildings close at 5pm. Admission is $5 per car; allow 60 to 90 minutes for your visit. For further information, including a schedule of living-history events, call 805/733-3713.

To leave the Lompoc Valley, follow Calif. 1 north. This route takes you through softly rolling hills past Vandenberg Air Force Base, which helps drive the local economy. Turn off at Calif. 135 and follow it toward Santa Maria for 1 mile. Exit at Clark Avenue and turn right. Follow Clark 2 miles to rejoin U.S. 101 north.

You'll certainly know when you've have entered the city limits of **San Luis Obispo**—who could miss the Pepto-Bismol–pink neon sign of the flamboyant **Madonna Inn**? Exit at Broad Street and follow the signs to the center of this attractive college town, where you'll find the:

3. **Mission San Luís Obispo de Tolosa,** founded in 1772. Father Junípero Serra chose this valley for the site of his fifth mission based on tales told to him of friendly natives and bountiful food (including grizzly bears—yum!). Here, the traditional red-tile roof was first used atop a California mission, after the original thatched tule roofs repeatedly fell to hostile Native Americans' burning arrows.

Today the site illustrates how a city growing up around historic structures can expertly incorporate new development without compromising historical value. Although the church has seen some disastrous restorations—the most offensive being the addition of wood siding and a New England–style steeple in 1880 (since removed)—in 1961 the city preserved the creek area fronting the mission, creating what is now the pedestrian **Mission Plaza.**

The former padres' quarters are an excellent museum chronicling both Native American and missionary life through all eras of the mission's use. Domestic and social artifacts are featured in the collection. The gift shop carries a fine selection of fired clay tiles with mission designs.

Mission San Luís Obispo is open to the public daily from 9am: to 5pm May to September, and to 4pm October to April. Admission is $1 per person; allow

30 to 45 minutes to tour the mission and its grounds. For further information, call 805/543-6850.

☕ **TAKE A BREAK**   Local art hangs on the walls and fresh, healthy cuisine is prepared using local ingredients at **Cafe Big Sky,** 1121 Broad St. (☎ 805/ 545-5401). Most everything on the menu, like shrimp tacos, herb-infused roasted chicken, and lighter meals such as white bean and yellowtail tuna salad and a charcoal-broiled eggplant sandwich, is inventive and tasty. The folk-artsy fervor of San Luis really shines here.

About 25 miles north of San Luis Obispo on U.S. 101 is the town of **Paso Robles,** so named for the region's plentiful oak trees. Almond orchards are also abundant, coloring the countryside pink and white during early spring. The valley's rich soils host many vineyards and award-winning wineries; most offer tours and tastings. Their wines and other local edibles are readily available and make great souvenirs and gifts. Eight miles north of Paso Robles is:

4. **Mission San Miguel Arcangel,** founded in 1824. This mission, still run by the Franciscan order and inhabited by brown-robed friars, is less spoiled by restoration than many of its counterparts. Its modest exterior hides one of this tour's treats: The church interior is one of the most elaborate and best preserved of the entire chain. Painted and decorated by area Native Americans under the supervision of Spanish designer Estevan Munras, the walls and woodwork glow with luminous colors untouched since their original application. Behind the altar, and its statue of San Miguel (St. Michael), is splendid tilework featuring a radiant Eye of God.

Mission San Miguel is open to the public daily from 9:30 am to 4:30pm; the church remains open until 5pm. Admission is $1 per family; allow 30 minutes to see the sights. For further information, call 805/467-3256.

Fourteen miles north of San Miguel, turn off U.S. 101 onto County Hwy. G18 and follow it northwest for 30 minutes, past Jolon, to:

5. **Mission San Antonio de Padua,** founded 1771. The tranquil land upon which the mission sits was once part of the William Randolph Hearst ranch; it now belongs to Fort Hunter-Liggett, a U.S. military training base. **The Hacienda,** adjacent to the mission, is often mistaken for Mission San Antonio itself. Originally Hearst's secondary ranch house, designed by Julia Morgan to complement the opulent Hearst Castle, this mission-revival building now functions as an officers' club and VIP housing for Hunter-Liggett. If you visit on a weekday between 11am and 1pm, you can visit the Hacienda—the club welcomes civilians for lunch.

More than any other mission in the chain, San Antonio feels as though time has stood still. The countryside remains much as it was when the padres chose this setting among the oaks. The colonnade outside the original padres' quarters still shows brick exposed by cattle constantly rubbing themselves against the scratchy surface.

Restorative interest in the mission group began in the early 1900s, after painters and photographers were drawn to the picturesque decay of sites like San Antonio. Subsequent displays of their works stimulated tourist interest, followed by philanthropic campaigns to preserve the missions.

Be aware that much of the quadrangle is in use by today's Franciscans and is thus off-limits to visitors. You may not be aware when you see the friars at work; they usually cast aside their traditional robes for a more practical daily wardrobe of jeans and T-shirts. The rest of the mission, including its first-rate museum, is open to the public Monday to Saturday from 9:30am to 4:30pm and on Sunday from 11am to 5pm. Admission is $1 per person; allow an hour to see the mission and its grounds. For further information, call 408/385-4478.

To rejoin U.S. 101 after your visit, follow County Hwy. G14 north for 25 minutes to the intersection at King City. About 60 miles north on U.S. 101 is **San Juan Bautista,** your final destination on this tour.

San Juan Bautista is a charming mission town that works hard to honor its pioneer heritage by retaining the flavor of a 19th-century village. The mission complex is perched in a picturesque farming valley, surrounded by the restored buildings of the original city plaza. From U.S. 101, take Calif. 156 east (south) to the center of town and:

6. **Mission San Juan Bautista,** founded 1797. Here you'll see the largest church in the mission chain and the only one in unbroken service since its founding. Like Mission San Luís Obispo, it once sported an incongruous wooden steeple but was mercifully decapitated by a storm in 1915. Inside, the church's three-aisle plan and large, theatrical altar inspired many Native Americans to convert, thus creating one of the largest congregations in all of California. The small museum contains many musical instruments and transcriptions, evidence of the mission's musical focus— it once boasted a formidable Native American boys' choir.

East of the church, perched at the edge of an abrupt drop created by the movement of the San Andreas Fault, is a marker pointing out the path of the old El Camino Real. Accompanying the marker are seismographic measuring equipment and an earthquake science exhibit.

There's much to see on the restored city plaza in addition to the mission. One Saturday morning I witnessed wedding preparations at the church *and* a group of costumed historians reenacting a Spanish-American War battle on the center lawn. Be sure to visit the **San Juan Bautista State Historic Park.** The park is comprised of not only the old Plaza Hotel with its classic frontier barroom and furnished rooms, but also the Plaza Hall, its adjoining stables and blacksmith shop, and the Castro House, where the Breen family lived after traveling here with the ill-fated Donner Party in 1846. A local artist specializing in nostalgic portraiture still operates a studio on the Plaza Hotel's upper floor, accessible from the outside balcony.

Allow $1^1/_2$ to 2 hours to see the entire plaza. Mission San Juan Bautista is open to the public daily from 9:30am to 5pm from May to October; it closes at 4:30pm the rest of the year. Admission is $2 per person. For further information, call 408/ 623-4528. San Juan Bautista State Historic Park is open daily from 10am to 4:30pm. Admission to the park buildings is $2 per person (this charge is separate from your entrance fee to the mission). For further information (including events schedules), call 408/623-4881.

☕ **WINDING DOWN**   End your tour with a visit to the **Jardines de San Juan,** 115 3rd St. (☎ 408/623-4466), where authentic Mexican food is served outdoors under graceful mulberry trees. Local performers (often a splendid guitar/ mandolin duo) will entertain you as you enjoy enormous platters, all accompanied by coarse corn tortilla chips and two excellent homemade salsas. The restaurant is open Sunday to Thursday from 11:30am to 9pm and on Friday and Saturday from 11:30am to 10pm. If you're not in the mood for Mexican food, more eateries and several fun antiques shops line 3rd Street, the "Main Street" of San Juan Bautista.

3 Historic Route 66

by Stephanie Avnet

Route 66—immortalized in film, song, literature, memory, in the popular imagination. But is anything really left of this great snaking highway, a dependable, comforting spirit John Steinbeck called "the Mother Road"? What of the path to adventure traveled by Tod and Buz in their trademark red Corvette on the namesake 1960s TV series? Well, it's still there, if you're willing to look for it.

Until the final triumph of the multilane superslab in the early 1960s, Route 66 was the *only* route west, from the windy Chicago shores of Lake Michigan to L.A.'s golden Pacific beaches, if you were traveling by car. "America's Main Street" rambled through eight states; today in each one there are enthusiastic organizations dedicated to preserving its remnants. California is fortunate to have a lengthy stretch of the original highway, many miles of which still proudly wear the designation "California State Highway 66."

Picturesque relics of a bygone era—single-story motels, friendly two-pump gas stations—exist beside their modern neighbors, inviting nostalgia for a slower, simpler time. So pop some Glenn Miller or Doris Day into the tape deck, eschew the fast pace of the present day, and prepare to transport yourself back to a time when the vacation began the moment you backed out of the driveway.

Start: Downtown San Bernardino (11 miles north of Riverside; 53 miles west of Palm Springs).
Finish: South Pasadena (6 miles northeast of downtown Los Angeles).
Time: Allow several hours to meander along this 59-mile stretch of the old route. As Route 66 emerged from the Mojave Desert and wriggled through the Cajon Pass, hot and weary travelers strained for a glimpse of:

1. **San Bernardino,** the next friendly watering hole and a signpost that Los Angeles was now within range. Located in the northeast "elbow" where Interstate 10 meets Interstate 215, downtown San Bernardino is easily reached from Los Angeles, San Diego, the desert communities, and other points north and east. During the early 1900s this land was fragrant with orange groves; the former Mormon settlement quickly prospered, earning the region a lasting sobriquet, "the Inland Empire."

    The year 1928 saw the grand opening of an elegant movie palace, the **California Theater,** at 562 W. 4th St., only 1 block from famous Route 66. From I-215, exit on 5th Street east. Turn right at F Street, then make a left on 4th Street, where you can pull over to view the theater. Lovingly restored and still popular for nostalgic live entertainment and the rich tones of its original Wurlitzer pipe organ, the California was a frequent site of Hollywood "sneak previews." Here humorist Will Rogers made his last public appearance, in 1935. (Following his death, the highway was renamed the "Will Rogers Memorial Highway" in his honor, but it remains popularly known as Route 66.) Notice the intricate relief of the theater's stone facade, and peek into the lobby to see the red velvet draperies, rich carpeting, and gold bannistered double staircase leading up to the balcony.

    From the theater, turn left on E Street to 5th Street, then turn left (west) and continue over the freeway. Although the first stretch is a little drab, have faith—after about a mile you'll enter the community of:

2. **Rialto.** Where 5th Street becomes Foothill Boulevard, you'll need to be on the lookout for Meriden Avenue, site of the fanciful **Wigwam Motel.** Built in the 1950s (along with an identical twin motor court in Holbrook, Arizona), these

Historic Route 66

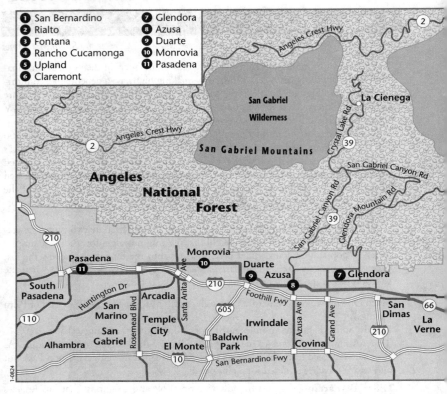

1. San Bernardino
2. Rialto
3. Fontana
4. Rancho Cucamonga
5. Upland
6. Claremont
7. Glendora
8. Azusa
9. Duarte
10. Monrovia
11. Pasadena

stucco teepees lured many a road-weary traveler in for the night with their whimsy. Their catchy slogan, "Sleep in a wigwam, get more for your wampum," has been supplanted today by the more to-the-point "Do it in a teepee." But as with many of the motor courts we'll pass on this drive, you need only picture a few large, shiny Buicks, T-bird convertibles, and "woodie" station wagons pulling in for the night and your imagination will begin to sense the welcoming charm of days gone by.

Continuing west on Foothill Boulevard, look out for the **Golden Embers** restaurant. After that, you'll pass into the town of:

3. **Fontana,** whose name in Italian means "fountain city." There isn't too much worth stopping for along this stretch, but definitely slow down to have a look at the **motor-court hotels** lining both sides of the road. They're of various vintages, all built to cater to the once-vigorous stream of travelers passing through. Although today they're dingy, the melody of their names once again conjures up those glory days: **Ken-Tuck-U-Inn, Rose Motel, Moana, Dragon, Sand & Sage, Sunset, 40 Winks, Redwing.**

At 15395 Foothill Blvd. is **Bono's Italian Deli,** here since 1936. Recently closed, it faces an uncertain future, for this stretch of highway is relatively desolate.

Soon you'll pass the I-15 junction and be driving through:

4. **Rancho Cucamonga,** whose fertile soil still yields a reliable harvest. You might see impromptu **produce stands** springing up by the side of the road; stop and pick up a fresh snack. If you're blessed with clear weather, gaze north at the gentle slope

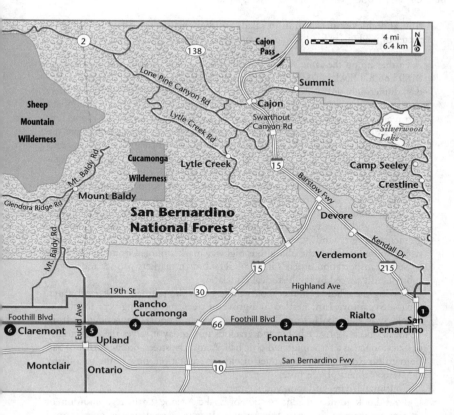

of the **San Gabriel Mountains** and you'll understand how Foothill Boulevard got its name. The construction codes in this community are among the most stringent in California, designed to respect the region's heritage and restrict runaway development. All new buildings are Spanish-Mediterranean in style and amply landscaped.

Rancho Cucamonga has earnestly preserved two historic wineries. First you'll pass the **Virginia Dare Winery,** at the northwest corner of Haven Avenue, whose structures now house part of a large business park / shopping mall, but retain the flourish of the original (1830s) winery logo.

At Archibald Avenue, look near the northwest corner for the lonely remnants of a **1920s-era gas station.** Empty now, those service bays have seen many a Ford, Studebaker, or Packard in need of a helping hand. The **New Kansan Motel** (on the northeast corner of Hellman) must have seemed welcoming to Dust Bowl refugees.

Next you'll see the **Thomas Vineyards,** at the northeast corner of Vineyard Avenue, established in 1839. Legend holds that the first owner mysteriously disappeared, leaving hidden treasure still undiscovered on the property. The winery's preserved structures now hold two eateries (including the Roadhouse Cafe, below), a country crafts store, and a bookstore housed in the former brandy still.

☕ TAKE A BREAK   If all this driving has made you hungry, the **Roadhouse Cafe** (☎ 909/941-8793; open for lunch and dinner daily) offers hearty steaks, ribs, fish, and chicken in addition to salads and lighter lunches. Share one of their batter-dipped, deep-fried whole onions, served with a zesty dipping sauce.

Farther up on the same side of Foothill Boulevard is the **Magic Lamp Inn,** at 8189 Foothill Blvd. (☎ 909/981-8659; open for lunch and dinner Tuesday to Friday, dinner only on Saturday and Sunday). Built in 1957, the Magic Lamp offers excellent continental cuisine (nothing *nouvelle* about Route 66!) in a setting that's part manor house and part "Aladdin" theme park. Dark, stately dining rooms lurk behind a funky banquette cocktail lounge punctuated by a psychedelic fountain/fire pit and a panoramic view. The genie bottle theme is everywhere, from the restaurant's dinnerware to the plush carpeting, which would be right at home in a Las Vegas casino. Lovers of kitsch and hearty retro fare shouldn't pass this one up.

Even if you don't stop to eat, be sure to stop in the shopping mall behind the Thomas Winery to tour the **Route 66 Territory Museum and Visitor's Bureau,** a minimuseum and gift shop. Stop in and look at the exhibits of old gas pumps, road signs, and other relics. You'll marvel at the array of books, maps, glasswear, garments, jewelry, and other souvenirs. Many items bear the original black-on-white Route 66 shield, the ubiquitous highway marker purged from the old route by state transportation officials in 1984. The brown markers you see today were subsequently placed by the historical associations.

Leaving the Thomas Winery, pass underneath the railroad tracks and watch for the **Sycamore Inn,** nestled in a grove of trees and looking very much like an old-style stagecoach stop. This reddish-brown wooden house, dating from 1848, has been a private home and gracious inn; today it serves the community of Cucamonga as a restaurant and civic hall. Across the street, on the corner of San Bernardino Road, there's a wonderful old service station, now home to a flashy car-stereo/cellular-phone store.

Continue driving and soon you'll enter:

5. Upland. Look north at the intersection of Euclid Avenue for the regal **monument to pioneer women.** Just past San Antonio Avenue, keep your eyes open toward the right for a great old **Winchell's Donuts** sign set back from the street. The junk-food theme continues nicely when you reach Benson Avenue, where a classic 1950s-style **McDonald's** stands on the southeast corner, its golden arches flanking a low, white walk-up counter with outdoor stools. The fast-food chain has its roots in this region: Richard and Maurice McDonald opened their first burger joint in San Bernardino in 1939. The successful brothers expanded their business, opening locations throughout Southern California, until entrepeneur Ray Kroc purchased the chain in 1955 and franchised McDonald's nationwide.

Pretty soon you'll be in the community of:

6. Claremont, known these days for the highly respected group of **Claremont Colleges.** You'll pass several of them along this eucalyptus-lined boulevard. In days gone by, drivers would cruise along this route for mile upon mile, through orchards and open fields, the scenery punctuated only by ambling livestock or a rustic wood fence. You'll pass through **La Verne,** home of **La Paloma** Mexican café, a fixture on the route for many years.

When you approach the start of I-210, keep to the left, passing under the on-ramp and into **San Dimas,** a ranchlike community where you must pay attention to the *horse crossing* street signs. At the corner of Cataract Avenue, a covered wagon announces the **Pinnacle Peak** restaurant, guarded by a giant steer atop the roof. In a block or two, the street name changes to Alosta Avenue and you'll be in:

7. Glendora, named in 1887 by founder George Whitcomb for his wife, Ledora. Look for the **Golden Spur** on the right-hand side. It began 70 years ago as a ride-up hamburger stand for the equestrian crowd; unfortunately, the restaurant has been remodeled in boring stucco, leaving only the original sign, with its neon cowboy boot, as a reminder of its colorful past. On the northeast corner of Grand Avenue stands the "world famous" **Derby East** restaurant. It's not affiliated with the legendary Hollywood watering hole, but was clearly built in the 1940s to capitalize on both its famous namesake and the nearby Santa Anita Racetrack. Past the Derby is the **Palm Tropics,** one of the best-maintained old motels along the route.

Soon you'll enter:

8. Azusa, where Alosta Avenue will curve to rejoin Foothill Boulevard at the **Foothill Drive-In Theater,** Southern California's last single-screen drive-in. As you cruise by, think of the days when our cars were an extension of our living rooms (with the great snacks mom wouldn't allow at home), and the outdoor theaters were filled every summer evening by dusk.

Continuing to the intersection with Cerritos Avenue, notice the **skeleton of one of the earliest McDonald's,** standing sadly abandoned. Soon you'll also pass the elegant 1932 Azusa City Hall and Auditorium, whose vintage lamposts and Moorish fountain enhance a charming courtyard.

You'll know when you've entered **Irwindale**—it smells just like the industrial area it is. Very soon you'll cross over the wide but nearly dry **San Gabriel River;** glance left from the bridge to see cars streaming along the Interstate that supplanted Route 66. Now you're in:

9. Duarte, and briefly on Huntington Drive, lit by graceful and ornate **double streetlamps** on the center median. This stretch also has many fabulous old motor courts; see if you can spot the **Capri, Ohio, Evergreen, Ranch Inn,** and the **Filly.** Farther along, look for the **"Route 66" gas station** (at the corner of Mt. Olive), and yet another example of the "wagon wheel / Wild West" theme restaurants, **The Rails.** Its super-tall dining sign will let you know when you're getting close.

Just inside the:

10. Monrovia city limits, turn right on Mountain Avenue to catch up with the 1930s alignment of Route 66. Make a left turn on Foothill Boulevard; you'll pass some splendid Craftsman bungalows and other historic homes.

Look for Magnolia Avenue and the outrageous **Aztec Hotel** on the northwest corner. Opened in 1925, the Aztec was a local showplace, awing guests with its overscale, dark Native American–themed lobby, garish Mayan murals, and exotic Brass Elephant bar. An arcade of shops once held the city's most prominent barbershop, beauty salon, and pharmacy. Little has changed about the interior, and a glance behind the front desk will reveal the original cord-and-plug telephone switchboard still in use. If you care to wet your whistle, stop into the bar before continuing on.

Nearby, at the southeast corner of Mayflower, a life-size plastic cow—a splendid example of this auto-age phenomenon—marks **Bob's Dairy.** If you've been observant, you'll have seen many drive-thru dairies along our route (mostly Alta-Dena brand). Bob's has all the typical features, including the refrigerated island display case still bearing a vintage "Driftwood Dairy Products" price sign.

Continue west into the tree-lined residential streets of **Arcadia,** home to the **Santa Anita Racetrack** and the **Los Angeles Arboretum,** the picturesque former estate of "Lucky" Baldwin, whose Queen Anne cottage has been the setting for many movies and TV shows.

Continue straight on Foothill Boulevard to Rosemead Boulevard; turn left and then right on Colorado Boulevard. This is your last chance to spot remaining motels like the **Hi-Way Host, Astro** (fabulous *Jetsons*-style architecture), **Siesta Inn, Swiss Lodge,** and **Saga Motor Hotel.** Colorado Boulevard leads into:

11. **Pasadena,** a charming city with many elegant historic buildings and a restored Old Town. If you're thinking about taking home some music reminiscent of your Route 66 experience, stop into **Canterbury Records** (☎ 818/792-7184; open daily), at the corner of Hudson Avenue. It has L.A.'s finest selection of big-band and pop vocalists on CD and cassette; perhaps you'll choose one of the many renditions of Bobby Troup's homage, "(Get Your Kicks on) Route 66."

Continue along Colorado Boulevard and turn left at Fair Oaks Avenue, keeping your eyes peeled as you pass the intersection with Green Street to see the rear view of the landmark **Castle Green Hotel.** Drive over the Pasadena Freeway (I-110) south on-ramp, which would take you onto L.A.'s historic first freeway, the **Arroyo Seco** (opened in 1940), to downtown Los Angeles. But continue instead along Fair Oaks Avenue to Mission Street and the **Fair Oaks Pharmacy** (☎ 818/799-1414; open daily), a fixture on the northwest corner since 1915. If you share my belief that there's no finer end to a grand adventure than ice cream, stop for an authentic ice-cream soda, sparkling phosphate, "Route 66" sundae, or old-fashioned malt (complete with the frosty mixing can), all served by today's fresh-faced "soda jerks" from behind the marble counter. They also serve soup, sandwiches, and other snacks. The Fair Oaks is still a dispensing pharmacy, and offers a variety of charming gifts, including an abundance of "Route 66"–themed items.

☕ **WINDING DOWN**   From this point on, the path of Route 66 changed many times over the years as Los Angeles grew. It ran through downtown L.A. via either Mission Street/Figueroa or Huntington/Broadway, caught up with Sunset Boulevard for a stretch, and ended up cruising toward the beach on Santa Monica Boulevard. Most remnants have been obscured by the city's zealous development; of the few remaining in Santa Monica, most fell victim to the disastrous 1994 earthquake. But the *complete* Route 66 experience includes the final stretch into the city, and that breathtaking first view of the ocean. So if you decide to explore further, look for the **Dolores Restaurant** at 11407 Santa Monica Blvd., the last of what was once a prominent chain of L.A.-area drive-ins. Near the ocean, notice the 1922 **Claude Short Dodge** dealership at 1201 Santa Monica Blvd., and the **Crocodile Cafe** at the corner of Ocean, which operated until recently as the Belle-Vue Restaurant, marking the unofficial "end of the line."

For more information, contact the **California Historic Route 66 Association** (☎ 714/289-8666) or the **U.S. Route 66 Association,** P.O. Drawer 5323, Oxnard, CA 93031. There's also a quarterly *Route 66 Magazine,* P.O. Box 66, Laughlin NV 89028-0066.

San Francisco 5

by Erika Lenkert and Matthew R. Poole

Consistently rated one the top tourist destinations in the world, San Francisco is awash with multiple dimensions. Its famous, thrilling streets go up and they go down; its multifarious citizens—and their adopted cultures, architectures, and cuisines—glean from San Antonio to Singapore; and its politics range from hyper-liberalism to an ever-encroaching wave of conservatism. Even something as mundane as fog takes on a new dimension as it creeps from the ocean and slowly envelopes San Francisco in a resplendent blanket of mist.

The result is a wee bit o' heaven for everyone. In a city so multi-faceted, so enamored with itself, it's truly hard not to find what you're looking for. Feel the cool blast of salt air as you stroll across the Golden Gate. Stuff yourself on Chinatown dim sum. Browse the Haight for incense and crystals. Walk along the beach, pierce your nose, see a play, rent a Harley . . . the list is endless. It's all happening in San Francisco, and everyone's invited.

1 Orientation

ARRIVING
BY PLANE

Two major airports serve the Bay Area: San Francisco International and Oakland International. All the major national rental-car companies have offices at these two locations.

SAN FRANCISCO INTERNATIONAL AIRPORT   Dubbed "SFO," San Francisco's major airport (☎ 415/761-0800) is 14 miles south of downtown directly on U.S. 101.

If you rent a car, it will take you about 40 minutes to reach downtown during rush hour; otherwise it's 20 to 25 minutes. A cab to downtown will cost $25 to $30, plus tip.

The **SFO Airporter** bus (☎ 415/495-8404) picks up passengers in front of the baggage claim area every 15 to 30 minutes from 6:20am to midnight daily and stops at several downtown hotels— the Grand Hyatt, San Francisco Hilton, San Francisco Marriott, Westin St. Francis, Parc Fifty Five, Hyatt Regency, and Sheraton Palace. No reservations are needed. It costs $9 one-way, $15 round-trip ($5 each way for children 2 to 16 accompanied by an adult).

Other private shuttle companies offer door-to-door airport service, in which you share a van with other passengers. The **SuperShuttle**

(☎ **415/558-8500**) charges $11 to downtown; a second passenger pays only $8 each way, and the entire van can be rented for $38 for up to seven passengers. The **Yellow Airport Shuttle** (☎ **415/282-7433**) charges $10 per person. Each shuttle stops every 20 minutes or so and picks up passengers from the marked areas outside the terminals' upper level. Reservations are required only for the return trip to the airport and should be made 1 day prior to departure. These shuttles usually get you to downtown San Francisco in 45 to 60 minutes, but demand that they pick you up 2 hours before your flight, 3 hours during holidays.

The San Mateo County Transit system, **SamTrans** (☎ **800/660-4287** in Northern California, or 415/508-6200) runs two buses between the airport and the Transbay Terminal at 1st and Mission streets. Bus no. 7B costs $1 and takes about 55 minutes; bus no. 7F costs $2 and takes only 35 minutes, but permits only one carry-on bag. Both buses run daily, every half hour from about 6am to 7pm, then hourly until about midnight.

OAKLAND INTERNATIONAL AIRPORT   Located about 5 miles south of downtown Oakland, at the Hegenberger Road exit of Calif. 17 (U.S. 880), Oakland International Airport (☎ **510/577-4000**) is used primarily by passengers with East Bay destinations. Some San Franciscans, however, prefer this less crowded airport when flying during busy periods.

Taxis from here to the center of San Francisco are expensive, costing approximately $45, plus tip; trip time is about an hour.

If you make advance reservations, the **AM/PM Airporter** (☎ **510/547-2155**) will take you from the Oakland Airport to your San Francisco hotel at any time of day. Allow about 50 to 60 minutes. The price depends on the number of passengers sharing the van, but is usually $35 to $45 or less per person; get a quote when you call. There are also shuttle services waiting for passengers at the airport. These are privately owned and vary in price, but usually cost less than $20 per person.

The cheapest way downtown is via **Bay Area Rapid Transit (BART)** (☎ **415/992-2278**), the high-speed rail system linking San Francisco with the East Bay. The **AirBART shuttle bus** (☎ **510/562-8428**) runs about every 15 minutes from Terminals 1 and 2 and will take you to BART for $2. BART fares vary depending on your destination; the trip to downtown San Francisco costs $2.15 and takes 20 minutes once onboard. AirBART operates Monday to Saturday from 6am to midnight and on Sunday from 8am to midnight.

BY CAR

If you're driving in from the north, U.S. 101 crosses the Golden Gate Bridge at the northernmost tip of the peninsula and runs directly through the city.

Approaching from the east, Interstate 80 crosses the San Francisco–Oakland Bay Bridge and terminates in the city's South of Market district.

Both I-280 and U.S. 101 come up the peninsula from the south and drop into the city via several downtown off-ramps.

BY TRAIN

Passengers on **Amtrak** (☎ **800/USA-RAIL**) arrive at the Emeryville depot just north of the East Bay side of the Bay Bridge. Free shuttles connect the depot with San Francisco's Ferry Building and CalTrain Station; they depart at 40-minute intervals and the trip takes about 45 minutes.

Since none of the major car-rental companies has an office at the train station, you'll have to pick up your car from downtown Oakland or San Francisco. **Hertz** (☎ **800/654-3131**) will reimburse your cab fare up to $5 from the train station to its Oakland office at 1001 Broadway, 2 miles away.

By Bus

Greyhound/Trailways (☎ 800/231-2222) buses arrive and depart from the Transbay Terminal at 1st and Mission streets.

VISITOR INFORMATION

The **San Francisco Visitor Information Center,** on the lower level of Hallidie Plaza, 900 Market St., at Powell Street (☎ 415/391-2000), provides information in several languages. It's open Monday to Friday from 9am to 5:30pm, on Saturday from 9am to 3pm, and on Sunday from 10am to 2pm.

There's an **events hotline** (☎ 415/391-2001) with a recorded message about current cultural, theater, music, sports, and other special events.

The **Visitors Information Center of the Redwood Empire Association,** 2801 Leavenworth St., San Francisco, CA 94103 (☎ 415/543-8334), publishes an annual *Redwood Empire Visitors' Guide* ($3 by mail, free in person) that covers the city, Marin County, and areas farther north. Open Monday to Friday from 9am to 5pm.

CITY LAYOUT

San Francisco occupies the tip of a 32-mile-long peninsula between San Francisco Bay and the Pacific Ocean. Its land area measures about 46 square miles. Twin Peaks, in the geographic center of the city, is more than 900 feet high.

San Francisco is easy to negotiate. The city's downtown streets are arranged in a grid, except for Market Street and Columbus Avenue, which cut across the grid at right angles to each other. Hills appear to distort this pattern, however, and can seem disorienting. But as you learn your way around, these same hills will become your landmarks and reference points.

MAIN ARTERIES & STREETS   Market Street, with the tall office buildings of the Financial District at its northeast end, is the city's main thoroughfare. One block beyond lies the Embarcadero and the bay.

The Embarcadero curves north along San Francisco Bay, terminating at Fisherman's Wharf. Aquatic Park and the Fort Mason complex are located farther west around the bay, occupying the northernmost point of the peninsula.

From the eastern perimeter of Fort Mason, **Van Ness Avenue** runs due south, back to Market Street.

The areas listed above form a rough triangle, with Market Street as its southeastern, the waterfront as its northern, and Van Ness Avenue as its western boundary. Within this triangle lie most of the city's main tourist sights.

STREET MAPS   San Francisco Visitor Information Center gives away a decent but limited map; if you intend to stick to the typical tourist areas, it will serve you well. The maps printed in the free tourist weeklies *Bay City Guide* and *Key* are also good for average visitors. These magazines can be found at most hotels, attractions, and in the San Francisco Visitor Information Center.

The Neighborhoods in Brief

Union Square   Union Square is the commercial hub of the city. Most major hotels and department stores are crammed into the area surrounding the actual square (named for a series of violent pro-Union mass demonstrations staged here on the eve of the Civil War), and there are a plethora of upscale boutiques, restaurants, and galleries tucked between the larger buildings.

Nob Hill   Bounded by Bush, Larkin, Pacific, and Stockton streets, Nob Hill is one of the genteel, old-money districts in the city, still occupied by the major power brokers and the social institutions they frequent. Here in the 1870s the Big Four built

San Francisco at a Glance

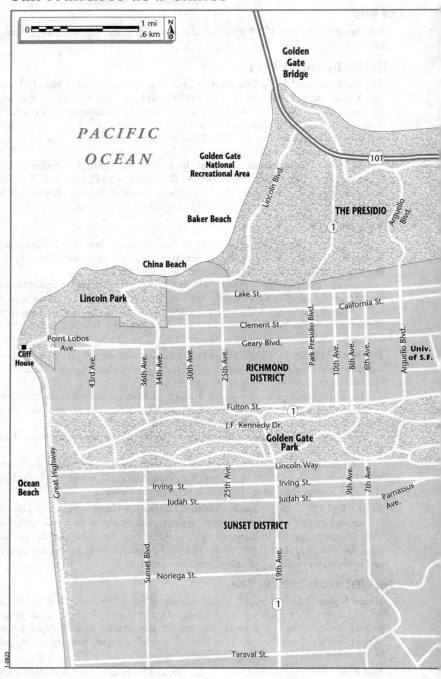

PACIFIC OCEAN

Golden Gate Bridge

101

Golden Gate National Recreational Area

Lincoln Blvd.

THE PRESIDIO

Arguello Blvd.

Baker Beach

1

China Beach

Lincoln Park

Lake St.

California St.

Clement St.

Point Lobos Ave.

Cliff House

Geary Blvd.

Park Presidio Blvd.

10th Ave.

8th Ave.

6th Ave.

Arguello Blvd.

Univ. of S.F.

43rd Ave.

36th Ave.

34th Ave.

30th Ave.

25th Ave.

RICHMOND DISTRICT

Fulton St.

1

J.F. Kennedy Dr.

Golden Gate Park

Lincoln Way

Ocean Beach

Great Highway

25th Ave.

Irving St.

Irving St.

9th Ave.

7th Ave.

Judah St.

Judah St.

Parnassus Ave.

SUNSET DISTRICT

Sunset Blvd.

19th Ave.

Noriega St.

1

Taraval St.

1-0825

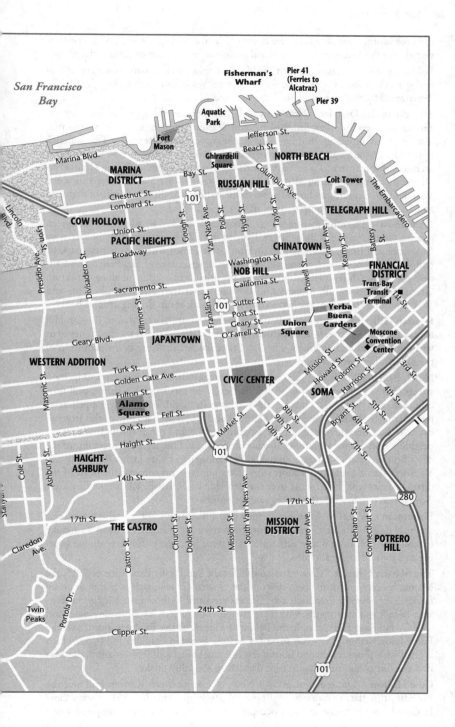

San Francisco Bay

Fisherman's Wharf

Pier 41 (Ferries to Alcatraz)

Pier 39

Aquatic Park

Fort Mason

Jefferson St.

Beach St.

Ghirardelli Square

NORTH BEACH

Marina Blvd.

MARINA DISTRICT

Bay St.

Columbus Ave.

Coit Tower

RUSSIAN HILL

Chestnut St.

Lombard St.

101

COW HOLLOW

Union St.

PACIFIC HEIGHTS

Broadway

Washington St.

NOB HILL

California St.

Sacramento St.

Sutter St.

Post St.

Geary St.

O'Farrell St.

TELEGRAPH HILL

The Embarcadero

Gough St.

Van Ness Ave.

Polk St.

Hyde St.

Taylor St.

CHINATOWN

Grant Ave.

Kearny St.

Powell St.

Battery St.

FINANCIAL DISTRICT

Trans-Bay Transit Terminal

1st St.

Presidio Ave.

Divisadero St.

Fillmore St.

Franklin St.

101

Union Square

Yerba Buena Gardens

Moscone Convention Center

Geary Blvd.

JAPANTOWN

WESTERN ADDITION

Turk St.

Golden Gate Ave.

Fulton St.

Alamo Square

Fell St.

CIVIC CENTER

SOMA

Masonic St.

Mission St.

Howard St.

Folsom St.

Harrison St.

3rd St.

Oak St.

Haight St.

Market St.

8th St.

9th St.

10th St.

Bryant St.

4th St.

5th St.

6th St.

7th St.

280

HAIGHT-ASHBURY

101

14th St.

Cole St.

Ashbury St.

17th St.

17th St.

Deharo St.

Connecticut St.

POTRERO HILL

Claredon Ave.

THE CASTRO

Castro St.

Church St.

Dolores St.

Mission St.

South Van Ness Ave.

MISSION DISTRICT

Potrero Ave.

Twin Peaks

Portola Dr.

24th St.

Clipper St.

101

Lincoln Blvd.

their mansions, most of which were destroyed by the earthquake in 1906 or else converted, like the Fairmont and the Flood mansions, into hotels or private clubs.

SoMa South of Market (dubbed "SoMa") is predominantly warehouses and industrial spaces sprinkled with eclectic shops, galleries, restaurants, and clubs. It's officially demarcated by the Embarcadero, U.S. 101, and Market Street.

The Financial District Northeast of Union Square, this area bordered by the Embarcadero and Market, 3rd, Kearny, and Washington streets is the city's business district and stomping ground for many major corporations. Its pointy Transamerica Pyramid, at Montgomery and Clay streets, is one of the district's most conspicuous architectural features. To its east stands the sprawling Embarcadero Center, an 8½-acre complex housing offices, shops, and restaurants. Farther east still is the World Trade Center, standing adjacent to the old Ferry Building. Ferries to Sausalito and Larkspur still leave from this point.

Chinatown The official entrance to Chinatown is marked by a large red-and-green gate on Grant Avenue at Bush Street. Beyond lies a 24-block labyrinth, bordered by Broadway and Bush, Kearny, and Stockton streets, filled with restaurants, markets, temples, and shops—and of course, a substantial percentage of San Francisco's Chinese residents. Chinatown is a great place for urban exploration all along Stockton, Grant, and Portsmouth Square, and the alleys that lead off them like Ross and Waverly. This area is jam-packed so don't even think about driving around here.

Russian Hill Extending from Pacific to Bay and from Polk to Mason, Russian Hill is marked by steep streets, lush gardens, and high-rises occupied by the moneyed as well as by the more bohemian. The San Francisco Art Institute is at the bottom of the hill at Chestnut and Jones.

North Beach The Italian quarter, which stretches from Montgomery and Jackson streets to Bay Street, is one of the best plac es in the city to grab a coffee, pull up a cafe chair, and do some serious people-watching. Its nightlife is equally happening—restaurants, bars, and clubs along Columbus and Grant avenues bring folks from all over the Bay Area here to fight for a parking place and romp through the festive neighborhood. Down Columbus toward the Financial District are the remains of the city's Beat Generation landmarks, including Ferlinghetti's City Lights Bookstore and Vesuvio's Bar. Broadway—a short strip of sex joints—cuts through the heart of the district. Telegraph Hill looms over the east side of North Beach, topped by Coit Tower, one of San Francisco's best vantage points.

Fisherman's Wharf North Beach runs into Fisherman's Wharf, which was once the busy heart of the city's great harbor and waterfront industries. Today it's a tacky tourist area with little if any authentic waterfront life, except for recreational boating and some friendly sea lions.

The Marina District Created on landfill for the Pan Pacific Exposition of 1915, the Marina boasts some of the best views of the Golden Gate, as well as plenty of grassy fields alongside San Francisco Bay. Streets are lined with elegant Mediterranean-style homes and apartments, which are inhabited by the city's well-to-do singles and wealthy families. Here, too, is the Palace of Fine Arts, the Exploratorium, and the Fort Mason Center. The main street is Chestnut between Franklin and Lyon, which is lined with shops, cafes, and boutiques. Because of its landfill foundation, the Marina was one of the city's hardest-hit districts in the 1989 quake.

Cow Hollow Located west of Van Ness Avenue, between Russian Hill and the Presidio, this flat, grazable area supported 30 dairy farms in 1861. Today Cow Hollow is largely residential and occupied by the city's young and yuppie. Its two primary commercial thoroughfares are Lombard Street, known for its many relatively inexpensive motels; and Union Street, a flourishing shopping sector filled with restaurants, pubs, cafes, and shops.

Japantown   Bounded by Octavia, Fillmore, and California streets and Geary Boulevard, Japantown shelters only about 4% of the city's Japanese-American population, but it's still a cultural experience to explore these few square blocks and the shops and restaurants within them.

The Civic Center   Although millions of dollars have been expended on brick sidewalks, ornate lampposts, and elaborate street plantings, the southwestern section of Market Street remains downright dilapidated. The Civic Center, at the "bottom" of Market Street, is an exception. This large complex of buildings includes the domed City Hall, the Opera House, Davies Symphony Hall, and the city's main library. The landscaped plaza connecting the buildings is the staging area for San Francisco's frequent demonstrations for or against just about everything.

Haight-Ashbury   Part trendy, part nostalgic, part funky, "The Haight," as it's most commonly known, was the soul of the psychedelic and free-loving 1960s and the center of the counterculture movement. Today the neighborhood straddling upper Haight Street on the eastern border of Golden Gate Park is more gentrified, but the commercial area still harbors all walks of life. Aging hippies mingle with grungy, begging street kids outside Ben & Jerry's Ice Cream (where they may still be talking about Jerry Garcia), nondescript marijuana dealers whisper "buds" as shoppers pass, and most people walking down the street have a glow-in-the-dark hair color. But you don't need to be a freak or wearing tie-dye to enjoy the Haight: The food, shops, and bars cover all tastes. From Haight, walk south on Cole Street to a more peaceful and quaint neighborhood.

The Castro   One of the liveliest streets in town, Castro is practically synonymous with San Francisco's gay community, even though technically it's only a street in the Noe Valley district. Located at the very end of Market Street, between 17th and 18th streets, Castro supports dozens of shops, restaurants, and bars catering to the gay community. Open-minded straight people are welcome, too.

The Mission District   The Mexican and Latin American populations, along with their cuisine, traditions, and art, make the Mission District a vibrant area to visit. Because some parts of the neighborhood are poor and sprinkled with the homeless, gangs, and drug addicts, many tourists duck into Mission Dolores, cruise by a few of the 200 amazing murals, and head back downtown. But there's plenty more to see. There's a substantial community of lesbians around Valencia Street, several alternative arts organizations, and most recently the ultimate in young hipster nightlife. New bars, clubs, and restaurants are popping up on Mission between 18th and 24th streets and on Valencia at 16th Street. Don't be afraid to visit this area, but do use caution at night.

2 Getting Around

BY PUBLIC TRANSPORTATION

The **San Francisco Municipal Railway,** better known as **Muni** (☎ **415/673-6864**), operates the city's cable cars, buses, and Metro streetcars. For detailed route information, phone Muni, check the map in the Yellow Pages, or purchase a route map ($2) at the San Francisco Visitor Information Center (see "Orientation," above) or another store.

The **fare** on buses and Metro streetcars is $1 for adults (payable in change or bills) and 35¢ for children 5 to 17 and seniors 65 and over. Cable cars cost $2, $1 for seniors from 6 to 7am and from 9pm to midnight (they're packed primarily with tourists). Exact change is required on all vehicles except cable cars.

"Passports," allowing unlimited rides on buses, Metro streetcars, and cable cars, cost $6 for 1 day, $10 for 3 days, and $15 for 7 consecutive days. The passport also grants admission discounts at 24 of the city's major attractions, including the Museum of Modern Art, the Exploratorium, and the museums in Golden Gate Park. They're available at the Visitor Information Center (see "Orientation," above) and the TIX booth at Union Square.

BY CABLE CAR   There are three lines operating daily from 6:30am to 12:30am. The most scenic—and exciting—is the Powell-Hyde line, which follows a zig-zag route from the corner of Powell and Market streets, over both Nob and Russian hills, to a turntable at Victorian Square in front of Aquatic Park. The Powell-Mason line starts at the same intersection and climbs over Nob Hill and down to Bay Street, just 3 blocks from Fisherman's Wharf. The California Street line begins at the foot of Market Street and runs straight through Chinatown and over Nob Hill to Van Ness Avenue. All riders must exit at the last stop and wait in line for the return trip.

BY BUS   Buses service the city, Marin County, and the East Bay. Some are powered by overhead electric cables; others use conventional gas engines. All are numbered and display their destinations on the front. Stops are designated by signs, curb markings, and yellow bands on adjacent utility poles. Many buses travel along Market Street or pass near Union Square and run daily from about 6am to midnight, after which there is infrequent all-night "Owl" service. If you can help it, for safety purposes avoid taking buses late at night.

Popular tourist routes are nos. 5, 7, and 71, all of which run to Golden Gate Park; nos. 41 and 45, which travel along Union Street; and no. 30, which runs between Union Square and Ghirardelli Square.

BY METRO STREETCAR   Five of Muni's six Metro streetcar lines, designated J, K, L, M, and N, run underground downtown where they stop at the BART stops along Market Street—Embarcadero, Montgomery, Powell, and the Civic Center—and in the outer neighborhoods. The J line goes to Mission Dolores; the K, L, and M lines to Castro Street; and the N line parallels Golden Gate Park. Metros run about every 15 minutes (more frequently during rush hours), operating Monday to Friday from 5am to 12:30am, on Saturday from 6am to 12:20am, and on Sunday from 8am to 12:20am.

The most recent streetcar addition is not a newcomer at all, but San Francisco's beloved rejuvenated 1930s cars. The beautiful green-and-cream colored F-Market line runs from downtown Market Street to the Castro and back.

BY BART   BART, an acronym for **Bay Area Rapid Transit** (☎ **415/992-2278**), is a high-speed rail network connecting San Francisco with the East Bay—Oakland, Richmond, Concord, and Fremont, as well as southern Daly City. Four stations are located along Market Street (see "By Metro Streetcar," above). Fares range from 90¢ to $3.55, depending on how far you go. Tickets are dispensed from machines in the stations. Children 4 and under ride free. Trains run every 15 to 20 minutes, Monday to Friday from 4am to midnight, on Saturday from 6am to midnight, and on Sunday from 8am to midnight. A line to the airport is scheduled to open in 1997.

BY CAR

You don't need a car to explore downtown San Francisco and in central areas—in fact, it can be your worst nightmare. But for exploring outside the city, driving is the way to go.

You may turn right at a red light (unless otherwise indicated), after making a complete stop and yielding to traffic and pedestrians. Cable cars always have the right-of-way, as do pedestrians at intersections and crosswalks. San Francisco's many one-way streets can create confusion, but most road maps of the city indicate which way traffic flows.

RENTAL CARS   Among the national car-rental companies operating in San Francisco are **Alamo** (☎ 800/327-9633), **Avis** (☎ 800/331-1212), **Budget** (☎ 800/527-0700), **Dollar** (☎ 800/800-4000), **Hertz** (☎ 800/654-3131), **National** (☎ 800/227-7368), and **Thrifty** (☎ 800/367-2277).

In addition to the big chains, there are dozens of regional rental places in San Francisco, many of which offer lower rates. These include **A-One Rent-A-Car,** 434 O'Farrell St. (☎ 415/771-3977), and **Bay Area Rentals,** 229 7th St. (☎ 415/621-8989).

PARKING   Street parking is extremely limited in the city and is particularly tough in Chinatown, around Nob Hill, by Fisherman's Wharf, in North Beach, and on Telegraph Hill. If there are no meters, note the signs and curb colors indicating parking regulations. *Red* means no stopping or parking; *blue* is reserved for disabled drivers with a California-issued disabled plate; *white* means there's a 5-minute limit; *green* indicates a 10-minute limit; and *yellow* and *yellow-black* curbs are for commercial vehicles only. Don't park at a bus stop or in front of a fire hydrant; watch out, too, for street-cleaning signs. If you violate the law, you might be "booted" (immobilized) or towed away, and that can cost you as much as $100. To get your car back, you must obtain a release from the nearest district police department, then go to the towing company to pick up the vehicle.

Take special care when parking on a hill. Apply the hand brake, put the car in gear, and turn your wheels—toward the curb when facing downhill, away from the curb when facing uphill. Curbing your wheels will not only prevent a possible "runaway" but will also keep you from getting a ticket—an expensive fine that's aggressively enforced.

Parking garages charge between $1 and $5 per hour (less by the day). In Chinatown, the cheapest place to park is the **Portsmouth Square Garage** at 733 Kearny St. (join the line to the entrance between Clay and Washington streets). At the Civic Center, try the **Civic Center Plaza Garage** between Polk and Larkin streets, and downtown, head for the **Sutter-Stockton Garage** at 330 Sutter St. At Fisherman's Wharf/Ghirardelli Square, try the garage on Beach between Hyde and Columbus, which charges $3.75 an hour to a $10 maximum; or the **Ghirardelli Square Garage** at 900 North Point, which offers 90 minutes of free parking with restaurant validation (60 minutes with retail validation), otherwise $1.50 per half hour, to $12 maximum for 12 hours.

BY TAXI

If you're downtown during rush hours or leaving from a major hotel, you can easily hail a cab. Otherwise, call one of the following companies to arrange a ride: **Veteran's Cab** (☎ 415/552-1300), **Desoto Cab Co.** (☎ 415/673-1414), **Luxor Cabs** (☎ 415/282-4141), **Yellow Cab** (☎ 415/626-2345), **City** (☎ 415/468-7200), and **Pacific** (☎ 415/986-7220). Rates are approximately $2 for the first mile and $1.80 for each mile thereafter.

BY FERRY

The **Golden Gate Ferry Service** (☎ **415/923-2000**) operates between the San Francisco Ferry Building, at the foot of Market Street, and downtown Sausalito (30 minutes) and Larkspur (45 minutes).

Daily service to Sausalito is frequent except on New Year's Day, Thanksgiving Day, and Christmas Day; phone for schedules. The ride takes half an hour and costs $4.25 for adults, $3.20 for kids 6 to 12, and $2.10 for seniors and the disabled.

The Larkspur ferry is primarily a weekday commuter service, with limited service on weekends. The 13-mile trip takes about 45 minutes and costs $2.50 for adults, $1.90 for kids 6 to 12, and $1.25 for seniors and the disabled; on weekends, prices rise to $4.25, $3.20, and $2.10, respectively.

The **Blue and Gold Fleet,** Pier 39, Fisherman's Wharf (☎ **415/705-5444** or 510/522-3300), operates daily from the Ferry Building and Pier 39 to Oakland, Alameda, and Vallejo. Fares to Oakland are $3.75 for adults, $1.50 for children, and $2.50 for seniors; to Vallejo, $7.50, $4, and $6, respectively. This service will also take you to Marine World Africa USA on a package trip that includes boat, bus shuttle, and admission; call for prices.

The **Red & White Fleet,** Piers 41 and 43$^1/_2$ (☎ **800/229-2784** or 415/546-2700), operates from Pier 43$^1/_2$ to Sausalito and Tiburon. Ferries also operate to Angel Island and Vallejo daily in summer and weekends only in winter. On weekdays ferries operate from Tiburon to the Ferry Building. Round-trip fares are $9 for adults, $8 for children 12 to 18, and $4.50 for children 5 to 11. Sausalito/Tiburon fares are $11 for adults and seniors, $5.50 for children.

Note: At press time the Blue and Gold Fleet had just purchased the Red & White Fleet and schedule changes were yet to be determined. Call either number for updated schedules and fare changes.

FAST FACTS: San Francisco

American Express   American Express has offices at 295 California St., at Battery Street (☎ 415/536-2686); and at 455 Market St., at 1st Street (☎ 415/536-2600) in the Financial District. Both are open Monday to Friday from 9am to 5pm and on Saturday from 9am to 2pm. To report lost or stolen traveler's checks, call 800/221-7282.

Baby-sitters   Try Temporary Tot Tending (☎ 415/355-7377, or 415/871-5790 after 6pm), which employs licensed teachers, and charges by the hour for children from 3 weeks to 12 years of age. It's open Monday to Friday from 6am to 7pm (weekend service is available only during convention times).

Camera Repair   Brooks Cameras, 125 Kearny St., between Post and Sutter (☎ 415/362-4708), stocks cameras and accessories and offers authorized repair service and 1-hour photo finishing.

Convention Center   The Moscone Convention Center, 774 Howard St. (☎ 415/974-4000), is between 3rd and 4th streets.

Dentist   In an emergency, see your hotel concierge or contact the San Francisco Dental Society (☎ 415/421-1435) for 24-hour referral to a specialist.

Doctor   Saint Francis Memorial Hospital, 900 Hyde St., between Bush and Pine streets on Nob Hill (☎ 415/353-6566), operates a physician-referral service.

Emergencies   Dial **911** for police, ambulance, or the fire department. Emergency **hotlines** include the Poison Control Center (☎ 800/523-2222) and Rape Crisis (☎ 415/647-7273).

Hospitals   Saint Francis Memorial Hospital, 900 Hyde St., between Bush and Pine streets on Nob Hill (☎ 415/353-6000), provides urgent-care service 24 hours.

Information   See "Visitor Information" under "Orientation," earlier in this chapter.

Liquor Laws   Liquor and grocery stores, as well as some drugstores, sell alcohol between 6am and 2am, as do bars and restaurants. The legal age for purchase and consumption is 21; proof of age is required.

Newspapers/Magazines   The city's two main dailies are the rather mediocre *San Francisco Chronicle* and the *San Francisco Examiner*. Get the combined Sunday edition for the "Datebook" of the week's events. The free weekly *San Francisco Bay Guardian* is indispensable for nightlife information; it's widely distributed on street corners and at city cafés and restaurants. *Key* and *San Francisco Guide* are also useful and are found in hotels and outlets in major tourist areas.

Pharmacies   There are Walgreens pharmacies all over town, including one on Divisadero Street at Lombard (☎ 415/931-6415) that's open 24 hours.

Police   Dial 911 in an emergency. For other matters, call 415/553-0123.

Post Office   The office closest to Union Square is inside Macy's department store, 121 Stockton St. (☎ 415/956-3570).

Safety   We don't recommend walking alone late at night in the Tenderloin, between Union Square and the Civic Center; the Mission District, around 16th and Mission streets; the Fillmore area, around lower Haight Street; and the SoMa area south of Market Street.

Taxes   An 8.5% sales tax is added at the register for all goods and services purchased in San Francisco. The city hotel tax is 12%. There is no airport tax.

Transit Information   For 24-hour information, call 415/673-6864.

Useful Telephone Numbers   These include: American Express Global Assist (for cardholders only; ☎ 800/554-2639), highway conditions (☎ 415/557-3755), KFOG Entertainment Line (☎ 415/777-1045), KMEL's Movie Phone Line (☎ 415/777-FILM), and the Grateful Dead Hotline (☎ 415/457-6388).

Weather   Call 415/936-1212 to find out when the next fog bank is rolling in.

3 Accommodations

San Francisco is an outstanding hotel town, especially considering its relatively small size. We can't cover them all in this guide, so if you'd like a larger selection, check out *Frommer's San Francisco,* which has dozens of other options.

Most of the hotels listed below are within easy walking distance of Union Square and are accessible via cable car. Union Square is near the city's major shops, the Financial District, and all transportation. Prices listed below do not include state and city taxes, which total 12%. Other hidden extras include parking and hefty surcharges for telephone use.

The hotels below are classified by area and by price as follows: **Very Expensive,** more than $175 per night for a double room; **Expensive,** $130 to $175 per night; **Moderate,** $80 to $130 per night; and **Inexpensive,** less than $80 per night. These categories reflect the price of an average double room during the high season, which runs approximately from April-September (in reality, rates don't vary much because the city is so popular year-round). But remember: These are "rack" or published rates, which are the highest charged. You can almost always get a better deal if you actively inquire about packages and special rates. Always ask about weekend discounts, corporate rates, and family plans, for example.

Bed and Breakfast International, P.O. Box 282910, San Francisco, CA 94128 (☎ **800/872-4500** or 415/696-1690; fax 415/696-1699), or on the World Wide Web at **http://www.bbintl.com,** offers a selection of B&Bs ranging from $60 to $150 per night. There's a 2-night minimum. Accommodations range from simple rooms in private homes to luxurious, full-service carriage houses, houseboats, and Victorian homes.

Almost all hotels offer no-smoking rooms; inquire when you make a reservation if it's important to you.

UNION SQUARE
VERY EXPENSIVE

The Clift Hotel. 495 Geary St. (at Taylor St., 2 blocks west of Union Sq.), San Francisco, CA 94102. ☎ **800/437-8243** in the U.S., or 415/775-4700. Fax 415/441-4621. 326 rms, 31 suites. A/C MINIBAR TV TEL. $255–$400 double; from $405 suite. Continental breakfast $12.50 extra. AE, CB, DC, MC, V. Parking $23. Cable car: Powell-Hyde or Powell-Mason line (2 blocks east). Bus: 2, 3, 4, 30, 38, or 45.

At the Clift, located in the city's Theater District, 2 blocks from Union Square, the staff excels at pampering its guests and even manages to be cordial to the droves of tourists who wander slackjawed through the palatial lobby. The decor of the guest rooms leans toward old-fashioned, with high ceilings, elaborate moldings and woodwork, Georgian reproductions, and marble bathrooms with everything from hair dryers to plush terry-cloth robes. Thoughtful extras include padded hangers, individual climate controls, two-line telephones, and a scale in your dressing room. The Clift's "Young Travelers Program" provides traveling families with toys and games, diapers, bottles, children's books, and other amenities. The hotel also accepts—and pampers—pets.

Dining/Entertainment: The French Room, open for breakfast, lunch, and dinner, specializes in seasonally appropriate California-French cuisine. The hotel's dramatic Redwood Room, which opened in 1933 and remains one of San Francisco's most opulent piano bars, has beautiful 22-foot-tall fluted redwood columns and is also famous for its Gustav Klimt murals. The lobby lounge serves cocktails daily and a traditional English tea Monday to Saturday.

Services: Concierge, room service (24 hours), twice-daily maid service, overnight laundry and shoe polishing, 1-hour pressing, evening turndown, complimentary in-room fax and computers.

Facilities: 24-hour business center, extensive fitness facility, gift shop.

✪ **Hotel Monaco.** 501 Geary St. (at Taylor St.), San Francisco, CA 94102. ☎ **800/214-4220** or 415/292-0100. Fax 415/292-0111. 177 rms, 24 suites. A/C MINIBAR TV TEL. From $170 double; from $295 suite. Call for discounted rates. AE, DC, DISC, JCB, MC, V. Parking $20. Bus: 2, 3, 4, 27, or 38.

This remodeled 1910 Beaux Arts building debuted in June 1995 and is the new diva of Union Square luxury hotels. For $24 million, the Kimpton Group did this place right—from the cozy main lobby with a two-story French inglenook fireplace to the guest rooms with canopy beds, Chinese-inspired armoires, bamboo writing desks, bold stripes, and vibrant colors. Everything is brand-spanking new, in the best of taste, and as playful as it is serious. The decor, combined with the breathtaking neighboring restaurant, make this our favorite luxury hotel in the city. The only downside—which can be considered major—are that the rooms are just too darn small, and some views are less than desirable.

Dining/Entertainment: The hotel's restaurant, the Grand Cafe, is the best hotel dining room downtown. It's grand, in the true sense of the word, with sky-high ceilings, elaborate 1920s to 1930s style, and an amazing collection of local art. The kitchen got off to a shaky start, but is steadily improving.

Services: Concierge, computer, complimentary wine hour nightly, overnight shoeshine, valet/laundry, two-line phones, secretarial services.

Facilities: Health club with steam, sauna, and massage; meeting and banquet facilities.

✪ **Prescott Hotel.** 545 Post St. (between Mason and Taylor sts.), San Francisco, CA 94102. ☎ **800/283-7322** or 415/563-0303. Fax 415/563-6831. 167 rms, 35 suites. A/C MINIBAR TV TEL. $175 standard double; $235 concierge level double (including breakfast and evening cocktail reception); from $265 suite. AE, CB, DC, MC, V. Parking $21. Cable car: Powell-Hyde or Powell-Mason line (1 block east). Bus: 2, 3, 4, 30, 38, or 45.

The Prescott has always been one of our favorite hotels in San Francisco. The staff treats you like royalty, the rooms are beautiful and immaculate, the location—1 block from Union Square—is perfect, and room service is provided by Postrio, one of the best restaurants in the city (see "Dining," later in this chapter). Dark tones of green, plum, and burgundy blend well with the cherrywood furnishings in each of the soundproofed rooms; the view, alas, isn't so pleasant.

Dining/Entertainment: The hotel provides preferred seating at Postrio Restaurant. Be sure to make reservations when you book your room.

Services: Concierge, room service (from the Postrio), twice-daily maid service, nightly turndown, same-day valet/laundry service, overnight shoeshine, complimentary morning coffee and tea, evening wine and hors d'oeuvres in the living room, limousine service weekday mornings to the Financial District.

Facilities: Access to off-premises health club, including swimming pool, free weights, and sauna.

Westin St. Francis. 335 Powell St. (between Geary and Post sts.), San Francisco, CA 94102. ☎ **800/228-3000** or 415/397-7000. Fax 415/774-0124. 1,192 rms, 83 suites. A/C MINIBAR TV TEL. Main building, $195–$325 double; from $225 suite. Tower, $265–$305 double; from $375 suite. Additional person $30 extra. Continental breakfast $12.50 extra. AE, DC, DISC, JCB, MC, V. Parking $24. Cable car: Powell-Hyde or Powell-Mason line (direct stop). Bus: 2, 3, 4, 30, 45, or 76.

At the turn of the century Charles T. Crocker and a few of his wealthy buddies decided that San Francisco needed a world-class hotel, and up went the St. Francis. Since then, hoards of VIPs have hung their hats and hosiery here, including Emperor Hirohito, Elizabeth II, Mother Teresa, King Juan Carlos of Spain, the shah of Iran, and all the U.S. presidents since Taft. The 32-story Tower was added in 1972, doubling the capacity and adding the requisite banquet and conference centers (as well Club Oz, the hotel's rooftop dance club). The older rooms of the main building vary in size and have more old-world charm than the newer Tower rooms, but the Tower is remarkable for its great views of the city once you rise above the 18th floor. Though it's too massive to offer the personal service you get at the smaller deluxe hotels on Nob Hill, few other hotels in San Francisco can match the majestic aura of the St. Francis.

Dining/Entertainment: Club Oz, a popular dance club with a hefty cover on weekend nights, is open nightly. The lobby-level Dewey's sports bar offers a do-it-yourself luncheon buffet, and burgers and pizzas at night. The Dutch Kitchen, also on the lower level, offers a basic breakfast menu. The Compass Rose is open daily for lunch and afternoon tea (3 to 5pm), with live music, dancing, champagne, cocktails, and caviar tasting in the evening.

Services: Room service (24 hours), voice-mail, baby-sitting referral, Westin Kids Club (great for families), laundry.

Facilities: Fitness center, business center, tour and car rental desks, barber/beauty salon, gift shop.

EXPENSIVE

✪ **Hotel Triton.** 342 Grant Ave. (at Bush St.), San Francisco, CA 94108. ☎ **800/433-6611** or 415/394-0500. Fax 415/394-0555. 140 rms, 7 suites. A/C MINIBAR TV TEL. $119–179 double; $199–279 suite. Continental breakfast $7.75 extra. AE, DC, DISC, MC, V. Parking $20. Cable car: Powell-Hyde or Powell-Mason line (2 blocks west).

Hotelier magnate Bill Kimpton requisitioned a cadre of local artists and designers to "do their thing" to his latest acquisition, the Hotel Triton. The result was San Francisco's first three-star hotel to finally break the boring barrier. Described as vogue, chic, retro-futuristic, and even neo-baroque, the Triton begs attention, from the Dalí-esque lobby to the sumptuous designer suites à la Jerry Garcia, Wyland (the ocean artist), and Joe Boxer.

A mild caveat: Don't expect perfection; many of the rooms could use a little touching up here and there (stained curtains, chipped furniture), and service isn't as snappy as it could be.

Dining/Entertainment: The Café de la Presse, a European-style newsstand and outdoor cafe, serves breakfast, lunch, and dinner. In the hotel lobby, complimentary coffee is served each morning and wine each evening.

Services: Room service, same-day laundry.

Facilities: Business center, exercise room.

Hotel Vintage Court. 650 Bush St. (between Powell and Stockton sts.), San Francisco, CA 94108. ☎ **800/654-1100** or 415/392-4666. Fax 415/433-4065. 106 rms, 1 suite. A/C MINIBAR TV TEL. $119–$159 double; $275 penthouse suite. AE, CB, DC, DISC, MC, V. Parking $16. Cable car: Powell-Hyde or Powell-Mason line (direct stop). Bus: 2, 3, 4, 30, 45, or 76.

Consistent personal service has prompted a loyal clientele at this European-style hotel located 2 blocks north of Union Square. Accented with dark wood, deep green, and rose, the lobby is welcoming enough to actually spend a little time in, especially when the nightly complimentary California wines are being poured. Each tidy room, renovated in 1995, mimics a wine country excursion with its floral bedspreads, matching drapes, and trellised carpeting.

Dining/Entertainment: Serving traditional French fare, Masa's is one of the top restaurants in San Francisco (see "Dining," later in this chapter). Breakfast is available in the dining room.

Services: Free morning transportation to the Financial District, tour desk, car-rental service.

Facilities: Access to off-premises health club.

Sir Francis Drake. 450 Powell St. (at Sutter St.), San Francisco, CA 94102. ☎ **800/227-5480** or 415/392-7755. Fax 415/677-9341. 412 rms, 5 suites. A/C MINIBAR TV TEL. $149–$199 double; $185–$600 suite. AE, CB, DC, DISC, MC, V. Parking $23. Cable car: Powell-Hyde or Powell-Mason line (direct stop). Bus: 2, 3, 4, 45, or 76.

It took a change of ownership and a multi-million-dollar restoration to save the Sir Francis Drake from becoming a Starbucks, but now this stately old queen is once again housing guests in grand fashion. Granted, this vunerable septuagenarian is still showing signs of age, but the price of imperfection is certainly reflected in the room rate: a good $100 less per night than its Nob Hill cousins. The new Sir Francis Drake is a hotel for people who are willing to trade a chipped bathroom tile or oddly matched furniture for the opportunity to vacation in pseudo-grand fashion: The

Beefeater doorman will handle your bags as you enter the elegant, captivating lobby; later, you can sip cocktails at the super-chic Starlight Lounge, and dine at Scala's Bistro, one of the hottest new restaurants in the city. Here, you'll live like the King or Queen of Union Square—but without the giant credit card bills.

Dining/Entertainment: The Scala Bistro, at the lobby level, serves excellent Italian cuisine in a stylish setting. (see "Dining," later in this chapter). The Cafe Expresso, a small Parisian-style corner café, does an equally commendable job serving coffees, pastries, and sandwiches daily. The Starlight Room on the 21st floor offers cocktails, entertainment, and dancing nightly with a panoramic view of the city.

Services: Concierge, room service, business services, valet.

Facilities: Exercise room, extensive meeting facilities.

✪ **White Swan Inn.** 845 Bush St. (between Taylor and Mason sts.), San Francisco, CA 94108. ☎ **415/775-1755.** Fax 415/775-5717. 23 rms, 3 suites. MINIBAR TV TEL. $145–$160 double; $195 romance suite; $250 two-room suite. Additional person $15 extra. Rates include full breakfast. AE, MC, V. Parking $19. Cable car: California Street line (1 block north). Bus: 1, 2, 3, 4, 27, or 45.

If the 50-plus teddy bears in the lobby don't cure homesickness, complimentary homemade cookies, tea, and coffee will. The romantically homey rooms are warm and cozy—the perfect place to snuggle up with a good book. They're also quite big, with hardwood entryways, rich, dark-wood furniture, and working fireplaces. The decor is English elegance at its best, if not to excess, with floral prints almost everywhere. Wine and hors d'oeuvres are served every evening. Its location—2½ blocks from Union Square—makes this 1900s building a charming and serene choice with service and style to satisfy the most discriminating traveler.

Dining/Entertainment: Breakfast is served in a room just off a tiny garden. Also served are afternoon tea, hors d'oeuvres, sherry, wine, and home-baked pastries. No smoking.

Services: Concierge, laundry, evening turndown, morning newspaper, overnight shoeshine.

Facilities: Access to an off-premises health club.

MODERATE

Andrews Hotel. 624 Post St. (between Jones and Taylor sts.), San Francisco, CA 94109. ☎ **800/926-3739** or 415/563-6877. Fax 415/928-6919. 43 rms, 5 suites. MINIBAR TV TEL. $86–$109 double; $119 petite suite. Rates include continental breakfast and evening wine. AE, DC, MC, V. Parking $15. Cable car: Powell-Hyde or Powell-Mason line (3 blocks east). Bus: 2, 3, 4, 30, 38, or 45.

Two blocks west of Union Square, the Andrews was formerly a Turkish bath before its conversion in 1981. As is fitting with Euro-style hotels, the rooms are small but well maintained and comfortable; white lace curtains and fresh flowers add a light touch. The bathrooms in general tend to be tiny and some have showers only; but for the price and location—a few blocks from Union Square—the Andrews is a safe bet for an enjoyable stay in the city. An added bonus is the adjoining Fino Bar & Ristorante, which offers complimentary wine to its hotel guests in the evening.

Beresford Arms. 701 Post St. (at Jones St.), San Francisco, CA 94109. ☎ **800/533-6533** or 415/673-2600. Fax 415/474-0449. 92 rms, 52 suites. MINIBAR TV TEL. $99 double; $115 Jacuzzi suite; $150 parlor suite. Additional person $10 extra; children 11 and under stay free in parents' room. Senior-citizen discount available. Rates include continental breakfast. AE, CB, DC, DISC, MC, V. Parking $15. Cable car: Powell-Hyde line (3 blocks east). Bus: 2, 3, 4, 27, or 38.

Every time we visit the Beresford Arms, its lobby always seems filled with happy, chatty Europeans. Maybe it's the Jacuzzi whirlpool bathtubs and bidets that keep them smiling, or the "Manager's Social Hour" with free wine and snacks. The price is fair, too, especially for a large, reasonably attractive (though a bit old-fashioned) suite with a choice of wet bar or fully equipped kitchen—a key for families. Modest business services are available, as is valet or self-parking.

✪ **Commodore International.** 825 Sutter St. (at Jones St.), San Francisco, CA 94109. ☎ **800/338-6848** or 415/923-6800. Fax 415/923-6804. 113 rms. TV TEL. $69–$89 double or twin. AE, DC, MC, V. Parking $12. Bus: 2, 3, 4, 27, or 76.

Before its present owners revamped the aging Commodore from top to bottom, it was pretty bad. But San Francisco hotelier Chip Conley let his hip-hop decor designers do their magic and it's now one groovy hotel. Stealing the show is the Red Room, a Big Apple–style bar and lounge that reflects no other spectrum but ruby red (you gotta see this one). Appealing to the masses, Chip left the first four floors as standard no-frills—though quite clean and comfortable—rooms, while converting the top two floors in neo-deco overtones (well worth the extra $10 per night). Adjoining the hotel is the Titanic Café, a cute little diner serving buckwheat griddlecakes and dragon fire salads.

Ⓢ **Hotel Bedford.** 761 Post St. (between Leavenworth and Jones sts.), San Francisco, CA 94109. ☎ **800/227-5642** or 415/673-6040. Fax 415/563-6739. 137 rms, 7 suites. MINIBAR TV TEL. $109–$129 double; from $175 suite. Continental breakfast $8.50 extra. AE, CB, DC, JCB, MC, V. Parking $18. Cable car: Powell-Hyde or Powell-Mason line (4 blocks east). Bus: 2, 3, 4, or 27.

For the price and location, 3 blocks from Union Square, the Bedford offers a darn good deal. You won't be paying for lavish furniture, but you'll find large, clean, sunny rooms, not to mention an incredibly enthusiastic staff. Each accommodation is furnished with a king- or queen-size bed or two double beds, a VCR, writing desk, and armchair. Many rooms have priceless views of the city.

The hotel's Wedgewood Lounge is a mahogany bar opposite the registration desk. The Canvas Café, an enormous eatery (open daily for beakfast),is located behind the lobby. Room service is available only for breakfast, but there's valet parking, complimentary wine in the lobby each evening, a video library, and free morning limousine service to the Financial District.

✪ **Hotel Diva.** 440 Geary St. (between Mason and Taylor sts.), San Francisco, CA 94102. ☎ **800/553-1900** or 415/885-0200. Fax 415/346-6613. 98 rms, 12 suites. A/C TV TEL. $119 double; $139 junior suite; $300 villa suite. Rates include continental breakfast. AE, DC, DISC, JCB, MC, V. Parking $17. Bus: 38 or 38L.

Appropriately named, the Diva is the prima donna of San Francisco's modern hotels and one of our favorites. A showbiz darling when it opened in 1985, the Diva won "Best Hotel Design" from *Interiors* magazine for its sleek, ultramodern interiors. A stunning profusion of curvaceous glass, marble, and steel mark the Euro-tech lobby, while the rooms—each spotless and neat—are softened with utterly fashionable "Italian Modern" furnishings. Nary a beat is missed with the toys and services either: VCRs (with a discreet video vending machine), Nintendo, pay-per-view, valet parking, room service, complimentary room-delivered breakfast, and on-site fitness and business centers complete the package. Insider Tip: Reserve one of the rooms ending in "09," which come with extra-large bathrooms with vanity mirrors and makeup tables.

Kensington Park Hotel. 450 Post St. (between Powell and Mason sts.), San Francisco, CA 94102. ☎ **800/553-1900** or 415/788-6400. Fax 415/399-9484. 82 rms, 2 suites. TV TEL. $115 double; $350 suite. Additional person $10 extra. 50% discount for post-midnight check-in. Rates include continental breakfast. AE, CB, DC, MC, V. Parking $16. Cable car: Powell-Hyde or Powell-Mason line (2 blocks east).

A cheery, eager-to-please staff, tasteful accommodations, and extra efforts prove that the Kensington really cares about its guests. The rooms are reminiscent of Olde England, with traditional ornate mahogany furnishings, beautiful damask fabrics, and enormous armoires. The bathrooms may be small, but they're sweetly appointed in brass and marble. Complimentary coffee and croissants are available on each floor every morning from 7 to 10am; complimentary tea, sherry, and cookies every afternoon; and a complimentary piano-accompanied wine hour on Thursday. Guests have access to an off-premises health club. In addition, there's a concierge, room service, same-day laundry, a morning newspaper, and a complimentary morning limo to the Financial District; fax and secretarial services are available.

The Raphael. 386 Geary St. (at Mason St.), San Francisco, CA 94102. ☎ **800/821-5343** or 415/986-2000. Fax 415/397-2447. 150 rms, 2 suites. A/C TV TEL. $109–$139 double; $160–$225 suite. Additional person $10 extra. Corporate and weekend discounts available. Continental breakfast $8.30 extra. AE, CB, DC, DISC, MC, V. Parking $16. Cable car: Powell-Hyde or Powell-Mason line (2 blocks east). Bus: 2, 3, 4, 30, 38, or 45.

From the old-style lobby and stained glass–capped elevators to the mishmash of furniture in each room, this place has the feeling it's been around forever. The staff is amazingly friendly and helpful, and the price for the location (just a block from Union Square) can't be beat. Unfortunately, the most exciting spaces are the fabulously funky hallways. The rooms are less artistic but do offer an eclectic collection of period reproductions, plenty of space, two phones, makeup mirrors, and hair dryers. Extra touches include a rose on arrival and complimentary coffee in the lobby. You'll also get 24-hour room service, twice-daily maid service, laundry/valet, and nightly turndown.

Savoy Hotel. 580 Geary St. (between Taylor and Jones sts.), San Francisco, CA 94102. ☎ **800/227-4223** or 415/441-2700. Fax 415/441-2700. 70 rms, 13 suites. MINIBAR TV TEL. $115–$125 double; from $155 suite. Ask about package, government, senior, and corporate rates. Rates include continental breakfast. AE, CB, DC, DISC, MC, V. Parking $16. Bus: 2, 3, 4, 27, or 38.

Both travelers and *Travel & Leisure* magazine agree that the Savoy is an excellent—and affordable—small hotel a few blocks off Union Square. The medium-size rooms are cozy French provincial, with 18th-century period furnishings, featherbeds, and goose-down pillows—plus modern such conveniences such as remote-control color TVs and hair dryers. Other perks include: triple sheets, turndown service, full-length mirrors, and two-line telephones. Guests also enjoy concierge service and overnight shoeshine free of charge. In addition to continental breakfast, rates include complimentary late-afternoon sherry and tea served in the Brasserie Savoy, a seafood restaurant that brings even the locals downtown for dinner (see "Dining," later in this chapter).

Warwick Regis. 490 Geary St. (between Mason and Taylor sts.), San Francisco, CA 94102. ☎ **800/827-3447** or 415/928-7900. Fax 415/441-8788. 40 rms, 40 suites. A/C MINIBAR TV TEL. $120–$155 double; from $150 suite. AE, DC, DISC, MC, V. Parking $18. Cable car: Powell-Hyde or Powell-Mason line. Bus: 2, 3, 4, 27, or 38.

Louis XVI may have been a rotten monarch, but he certainly had taste. Fashioned in the style of pre-Revolutionary France (circa 18th century), the Warwick is awash with pristine French and English antiques, Italian marble, chandeliers, four-poster beds, hand-carved headboards, and the like. The result is an expensive-looking hotel that, for all its pleasantries and perks, is surprisingly affordable when compared to its Union Square contemporaries. Honeymooners should splurge on the Fireplace Rooms with canopy beds—oo la la! Amenities include 24-hour room and concierge service, twice-daily maid service, complimentary shoeshine and newspaper, and valet parking. Adjoining the lobby is the fashionable La Scene Café, the perfect place to start your day with a latte and end it with a nightcap.

INEXPENSIVE

Brady Acres. 649 Jones St. (between Geary and Post sts.), San Francisco, CA 94102. ☎ **800/ 627-2396** or 415/929-8033. Fax 415/441-8033. 25 rms. MINIBAR TV TEL. $60–$85 double. MC, V. Oct–Apr, weekly rentals only; call for daily availability. Parking garage nearby. Bus: 2, 3, 4, 27, or 38.

Inside this small, four-story brick building is a penny-pincher's dream come true. Enter through a black-and-gold door and you'll find everything you need to keep home-away-from-home costs to a minimum; the small but very clean rooms have a microwave oven, small refrigerator, toaster, and coffee maker; hair dryer and alarm clock; direct-dial phone with free local calls; an answering machine; color TV, and VCR. The baths are newly renovated, and a coin-operated washer and dryer are located in the basement, along with free laundry soap and irons. Keep in mind that during the high season you can only rent by the week.

Golden Gate Hotel. 775 Bush St. (between Powell and Mason sts.), San Francisco, CA 94108. ☎ **800/835-1118** or 415/392-3702. Fax 415/392-6202. 23 rms, 14 with bath. TV. $65–$69 double without bath, $95–$109 double with bath. Rates include continental breakfast. AE, CB, DC, MC, V. Parking $12. Cable car: Powell-Hyde or Powell-Mason line (1 block east). Bus: 2, 3, 4, 30, 38, or 45.

Among San Francisco's small hotels occupying historic turn-of-the-century buildings are some real gems, and the Golden Gate Hotel is one of them. It's 2 blocks north of Union Square and 2 blocks down (literally) from the crest of Nob Hill, with cable car stops at the corner for easy access to Fisherman's Wharf and Chinatown (the city's theaters and best restaurants are also within walking distance). But the best thing about the Golden Gate Hotel is that this is a family-run establishment: John and Renate Kenaston are hospitable innkeepers who take obvious pleasure in making their guests comfortable. Each individually decorated room has handsome furnishings (plenty of wicker) from the early 1900s, quilted bedspreads, and fresh flowers. Request a room with clawfoot tub if you enjoy a good, hot soak. Most, but not all rooms have phones. Complimentary afternoon tea is served daily from 4 to 7pm.

Grant Plaza Hotel. 465 Grant Ave. (at the corner of Pine St.), San Francisco, CA 94108. ☎ **800/472-6899** or 415/434-3883. Fax 415/434-3886. 72 rms. TV TEL. $42–$65 double. MC, V. Parking $9.50. Cable car: Powell-Hyde or Powell-Mason line (2 blocks west).

You won't find any free little bottles of shampoo here (there's little more than a soap dispenser in the small showers and bathrooms), but you will find cheap accommodations and basic—and we mean basic—rooms right in the middle of the Union Square/Chinatown action. The pattern-crazy lobby isn't easy on the eye, but it's mostly a thoroughfare anyway, so who could care? Many of the small rooms in this six-story building overlook Chinatown's main street. The corner rooms on the higher floors are both larger and brighter. Note that no visitors are permitted in the rooms after 11pm, and no breakfast is served.

NOB HILL
VERY EXPENSIVE

Fairmont Hotel and Tower. 950 Mason St. (at California St.), San Francisco, CA 94108. ☎ **800/527-4727** or 415/772-5000. Fax 415/772-5013. 538 rms, 62 suites. A/C MINIBAR TV TEL. Main building, $199–$299 double; from $620 suite. Tower, $239–$300 double; from $500 suite. Additional person $30 extra. Continental breakfast $9.95 extra. AE, CB, DC, DISC, MC, V. Parking $25. Cable car: California Street line (direct stop).

The granddaddy of Nob Hill's elite cadre of ritzy hotels, the Fairmont wins top honors for the most awe-inspiring lobby in San Francisco. Even if you're not staying at the Fairmont, it's worth a side trip to gape at its massive, marble Corinthian columns, vaulted ceilings, velvet chairs, gilded mirrors, and spectacular wraparound staircase. Unfortunately, such ostentation doesn't carry over to the guest rooms, which are surprisingly ordinary aside from the spectacular views from those on the top floors. The rooms do, however, sport goose-down pillows, electric shoe buffers, bath scales, large walk-in closets, and multiline phones with private voice-mail.

Dining/Entertainment: Masons serves contemporary California cuisine, with live music Tuesday to Sunday. The Bella Voce Ristorante features Italian-American cuisine served by staff who occasionally pause for an aria or Broadway selection. The Crown offers deli lunches, dinner buffets, and Sunday brunches accompanied by a panoramic view of the Bay Area. The Tonga Restaurant and Hurricane Bar offer Chinese and Polynesian specialties in a tropical ambience, as well as dancing and a generous happy hour. Afternoon tea is served daily in the hotel's lobby.

Services: Concierge (24 hours), room service (24 hours), twice-daily maid service, evening turndown, laundry/valet, complimentary shoeshine, baby-sitting, doctor on-call, complimentary morning limousine to the Financial District.

Facilities: Health club, business center, barbershop, beauty salon, pharmacy, shopping arcade.

Huntington Hotel. 1075 California St. (between Mason and Taylor sts.), San Francisco, CA 94108. ☎ **800/227-4683,** or 800/652-1539 in California, or 415/474-5400. Fax 415/474-6227. 110 rms, 30 suites. MINIBAR TV TEL. $190–$240 double; $290–$790 suite. Special packages available. Continental breakfast $9.95 extra. AE, CB, DC, MC, V. Parking $19.50. Cable car: California Street line (direct stop). Bus: 1.

One of the kings of Nob Hill, the stately Huntington Hotel has long been a favorite retreat for Hollywood stars and political VIPs who desire privacy and security. Family-owned since 1924—an extreme rarity among large hotels—the Huntington eschews pomp and circumstance; absolute privacy and unobtrusive service are its mainstay. Though the lobby, decorated in a grand 19th-century style, is rather petite, the guest rooms are quite large and feature Brunschwig and Fils fabrics and bed coverings, French-style furnishings, and views of the city.

Dining/Entertainment: The Big Four restaurant offers expensive seasonal continental cuisine in one of the city's most handsome dining rooms. Live piano music plays nightly in the lounge.

Services: Concierge, room service, complimentary limousine to the Financial District and Union Square, overnight shoeshine, laundry, evening turndown, complimentary morning newspaper, complimentary formal tea or sherry service upon arrival.

Facilities: Access to off-premises health club and spa.

Mark Hopkins Inter-Continental. 1 Nob Hill (at California and Mason sts.), San Francisco, CA 94108. ☎ **800/327-0200** or 415/392-3434. Fax 415/421-3302. 390 rms, 28 suites. A/C MINIBAR TV TEL. $180–$230 double; from $375 suite. Continental breakfast $9.50 extra. AE, CB, DC, MC, V. Parking $23. Cable car: California Street line (direct stop). Bus: 1.

Built in 1926 on the spot where railroad millionaire Mark Hopkins's turreted mansion once stood, the 19-story Mark Hopkins caters mostly to convention-bound corporate executives who can write off the high rates. Each neoclassical room comes with all the fancy amenities you'd expect from a world-class hotel, including custom furniture, plush fabrics, sumptuous baths, and extraordinary views of the city. (*Tip:* The even-numbered rooms on the higher floor overlook the Golden Gate Bridge.) A minor caveat with the hotel is that it has only three guest elevators, making a trip to your room during busy periods akin to pouring molasses.

Dining/Entertainment: The plush and decidedly formal Nob Hill Restaurant offers international cuisine with a California flair nightly as well as a continental buffet breakfast each morning. Off the lobby, the Nob Hill Terrace serves lunch, afternoon tea, cocktails, and dinner daily. The world-renowned Top of the Mark lounge offers cocktails daily from 4pm to 1:30am, Sunday brunch from 10am to 2pm, and dancing to live music Wednesday to Saturday nights.

Services: Concierge, room service (24 hours), evening turndown, overnight shoeshine, laundry, limousine, valet parking, multilingual guest relations.

Facilities: Business center, health club, Executive Club floor, car-rental desk.

✪ **Ritz-Carlton San Francisco.** 600 Stockton St. (between Pine and California sts.), San Francisco, CA 94108. ☎ **800/241-3333** or 415/296-7465. Fax 415/296-0288. 292 rms, 44 suites. A/C MINIBAR TV TEL. $275 double; $395 club-level double; from $575 suite. Weekend discounts and packages available. Continental breakfast $14.50 extra; breakfast buffet $18.50 extra; Sunday brunch $42 extra. AE, CB, DC, DISC, MC, V. Parking $27. Cable car: Powell-Hyde or Powell-Mason line (direct stop).

Ranked among the top hotels in the world by readers of *Condé Nast Traveler,* the Ritz-Carlton has been the benchmark of San Francisco's luxury hotels since it opened in 1991; without queston, it's the top hotel in the city. A Nob Hill landmark, this former Metropolitan Insurance headquarters was completely gutted and refitted with fine furnishings, fabrics, and artworks, including a pair of Louis XVI French blue marble-covered urns with gilt mounts, and 19th-century Waterford candelabras. The rooms offer every possible service and amenity, including in-room safes and Italian-marble bathrooms with double sinks, telephones, name-brand toiletries, and plush terry bathrobes. The more expensive rooms take advantage of the hotel's location—the south slope of Nob Hill—and have good views of the city. Club rooms, located on the eighth and ninth floors, have a dedicated concierge, separate elevator-key access, and complimentary meals throughout the day.

Dining/Entertainment: The Ritz Carlton Dining Room, voted among the nation's top restaurants by several magazines, serves dinner Monday to Saturday (see "Dining," later in this chapter). The Terrace Restaurant, less formal than the Dining Room, offers Mediterranean cuisine and outdoor dining in the courtyard. The lobby lounge serves afternoon tea and cocktails and sushi daily with low-key live entertainment from 3pm to 1am. For a real splurge, Sunday brunch in the courtyard is easily one of the best in town.

Services: Concierge, room service (24 hours), same-day valet, child care, complimentary morning newspaper and shoeshine.

Facilities: Business center, an outstanding fitness center with pool, gift boutique, car-rental desk, VCR and video library.

EXPENSIVE

Nob Hill Lambourne. 725 Pine St. (between Powell and Stockton sts.), San Francisco, CA 94108. ☎ **800/274-8466** or 415/433-2287. 9 rms, 11 suites. A/C MINIBAR TV TEL. $155 double; $175–$250 suite. Rates include continental breakfast and wine hour. AE, CB, DC, DISC, MC, V. Valet parking $20, self-parking $15. Cable car: California Street line (1 block north).

One of San Francisco's top "business-boutique" hotels, the Nob Hill Lambourne bills itself as an urban spa, offering on-site massages, facials, body scrubs, aromatherapy, waxing, manicures, pedicures, and yoga lessons to ease corporate-level stress. Even without this "hook," the Lambourne deserves a top-of-the-class rating. Sporting one of San Francisco's most stylish interiors, the hotel flaunts the comfort and quality of its contemporary French design. Top-quality hand-sewn mattresses and goose-down comforters are complemented by a host of in-room accouterments that include fax machines, VCRs, stereos, kitchenettes, and coffeemakers. The bathrooms contain oversize tubs and hair dryers, as well as an "honor bar" of pamperings like geranium and orange bath oil, herbal lip balm, and jasmine moisturizer. On Friday and Saturday all guests are invited to enjoy complimentary wine and hors d'oeuvres and a 15-minute neck and shoulder massage.

Services: Evening turndown, business services.

Facilities: Spa treatment room.

SOMA
VERY EXPENSIVE

ANA Hotel San Francisco. 50 3rd St. (between Market and Mission sts.), San Francisco, CA 94103. ☎ **800/262-4683** or 415/974-6400. Fax 415/495-6152. 641 rms, 26 suites. A/C MINIBAR TV TEL. $220–$250 double; from $380 suite. Continental breakfast $8.75 extra. AE, DC, DISC, JCB, MC, V. Parking $23. Muni Metro: All Market Street trams. Bus: All Market Street routes.

The hotel's large number of rooms and fine location—just 1 block south of Market Street and 1 block from the Moscone Convention Center—makes the ANA attractive to both groups and business travelers. The guestrooms have floor-to-ceiling windows and are well outfitted with three telephones (with voice-mail and dataport for computer modem connection). Corner suites look across the Bay Bridge to 3COM Park (formerly Candlestick Park), and Executive Level rooms include continental breakfast and evening hors d'oeuvres.

Dining/Entertainment: The Café Fifty-Three serves three meals daily, plus a special Sunday brunch and offers garden-terrace seating. The adjacent lobby bar serves cocktails, wine, beer, and appetizers.

Services: Concierge, room service, twice-daily maid service, laundry/valet.

Facilities: Fitness center, business center, complimentary use of nearby tennis club, gift shop.

Sheraton Palace Hotel. 2 New Montgomery St. (at Market St.), San Francisco, CA 94105. ☎ **800/325-3535** or 415/392-8600. Fax 415/543-0671. 517 rms, 33 suites. A/C MINIBAR TV TEL. $295–$355 double; from $650 suite. Additional person $25 extra; children 17 and under sharing existing bedding stay free in parents' room. Weekend rates and packages available. Continental breakfast $13.50 extra; deluxe continental $15.75 extra. AE, DC, DISC, JCB, MC, V. Parking $20. Muni Metro: All Market Street trams. Bus: All Market Street routes.

The original 1875 Palace was one of the world's largest and most luxurious hotels—and every time you walk through the doors, you'll be reminded how incredibly majestic "old" luxury really is. The hotel was rebuilt after the 1906 quake and renovated in 1989, but the most spectacular attribute here is still the old regal lobby and the Garden Court, a San Francisco landmark that has been restored to its original 1909 grandeur. The court is flanked by a double row of massive Italian-marble, Ionic columns and is topped by 10 huge chandeliers. The real heart-stopper, however, is the 80,000-pane stained-glass ceiling. Regrettably, the rooms have a standardized, chain-hotel appearance. The fourth-floor health club features a skylight-covered lap pool, whirlpool, sauna, and exercise room.

Dining/Entertainment: The Garden Court serves American cuisine, afternoon tea Monday to Saturday, and drinks Monday to Saturday nights. Maxfields's Restaurant, a traditional San Francisco grill, has turn-of-the-century charm and is open daily for lunch and dinner. Kyo-ya is an authentic Japanese restaurant with a separate street entrance. The Pied Piper Bar is named after the $2.5-million Maxfield Parrish mural that dominates the room.

Services: Concierge, room service (24 hours), evening turndown, laundry/valet.

Facilities: Business service center, health club, lobby-level shops.

EXPENSIVE

Hotel Milano. 55 5th St. (between Market and Mission sts.), San Francisco, CA 94103.
☎ **800/398-7555** in the U.S., or 415/543-8555. Fax 415/543-5843. 108 rms. A/C MINIBAR
TV TEL. $129–$189 double. Additional person $19 extra. Continental breakfast $6 extra.
AE, MC, V, AE, DC, JCB, MC, V. Parking $19. Bus: All Market Street routes.

Contemporary Italian design, simple and elegantly streamlined rooms, and its central location make the Hotel Milano a popular choice for tourists and businesspeople
alike. The guest rooms feature everything a business executive could want—from
fax/computer-modem hookups to a Nintendo game system. Other features include
in-room safes and soundproof windows. Some have spa tubs, bidets, double lavato-
ries, and televisions with VCRs.

Dining/Entertainment: At press time, Michel Richard's Bistro M had just closed
its doors. It has yet to be decided what kind of eatery will take its place.

Services: Concierge, room service, laundry/valet.

Facilities: Fitness center and spa with steam and sauna, business center.

THE FINANCIAL DISTRICT

Galleria Park Hotel. 191 Sutter St. (at Kearny St.), San Francisco, CA 94104. ☎ **800/
792-9639** or 415/781-3060. Fax 415/433-4409. 162 rms, 15 suites. A/C MINIBAR TV TEL.
$159–$179 double; from $245 suite. Continental breakfast $7.95 extra. AE, CB, DC, DISC, MC,
V. Parking $14. Muni Metro: All Market Steet trams. Bus: All Market Street routes.

From its impressive black-marble facade and stylized lobby—complete with fireplace
and crystal skylight—to its beautifully appointed rooms and suites, the Galleria Park
has been totally restored in the art nouveau style of its original 1911 construction.
A good, upscale business-class hotel, the Galleria Park offers all the expected neces-
sities and some unusual extras, such as a rooftop jogging track.

Dining/Entertainment: Perry's Downtown serves American fare and has a bar.
The adjacent lounge features a pianist nightly. The Brasserie Chambord serves an
inspired country cuisine. Both restaurants are open daily for breakfast, lunch, and
dinner.

Services: Concierge, room service.

Facilities: Rooftop running track and park, fitness room.

NORTH BEACH / FISHERMAN'S WHARF
EXPENSIVE

Tuscan Inn. 425 North Point St. (at Mason St.), San Francisco, CA 94133. ☎ **800/648-4626**
or 415/561-1100. Fax 415/561-1199. 209 rms, 12 suites. A/C MINIBAR TV TEL. $165–$188
double; $208–$228 suite. Rates include evening fireside wine reception. AE, DC, DISC, MC, V.
Parking $13. Cable car: Powell-Mason line. Bus: 15, 32, or 42.

Like an island of respectability in a sea of touristy schlock, the Tuscan exudes a level
of style and comfort far beyond its neighboring competitors. Splurge on valet parking—it's cheaper than the wharf's outrageously priced garages—then saunter your
way toward the plush lobby warmed by a grand fireplace. Even the rooms, each
equipped with writing desks, armchairs, and handsome burgundy floral-print bedspreads, are a cut above. The only caveat is the lack of scenic views—a small price
to pay for a good hotel in a great location.

Dining/Entertainment: The adjoining Café Pescatore, open for breakfast, lunch,
and dinner, serves standard Italian fare in a airy, semi-alfresco setting.

Services: Concierge, valet parking, room service, laundry service, voice-mail.

MODERATE

✪ **Hotel Bohème.** 444 Columbus St. (between Vallejo and Green sts.), San Francisco 94133.
☎ **415/433-9111.** Fax 415/362-6292. 15 rms. TV TEL. $115 double. AE, DISC, DC, MC, V.

> ### 🙂 Family-Friendly Hotels
>
> **Westin St. Francis** *(see p. 75)*   Kids like the St. Francis because everyone 11 and under is given a Kids Club hat on arrival and special sports bottles (with complimentary refills in the hotel's restaurants). Their siblings ages 3 to 7 are given dinosaur soaps, sponges, and coloring books. Parents get some extra help, too, in seeing that their kids are supervised.
>
> **The Clift Hotel** *(see p. 74)*   The hotel's Young Travelers Program offers amenities from bottles and diapers to toys, games, coloring books, information about family-oriented attractions, special treats from room service, and small-size terrycloth robes—all designed to make kids feel as pampered as their parents.
>
> **Stanyan Park Hotel** *(see p. 89)*   A great moderately priced choice for families, the Stanyan Park is ideally located across from Golden Gate Park—for those times when your kids need to let off steam. Each of the one- and two-bedroom suites has a full kitchen, and can sleep up to six comfortably. Free tea and cookies are served each afternoon.

Parking $20 at nearby public garage. Cable car: Powell-Mason line. Bus: 12, 15, 30, 41, 45, or 83.

Although located on the busiest strip in North Beach, this recently renovated hotel's style and demeanor are more reminiscent of a prestigious home in upscale Nob Hill. The rooms are small but hopelessly romantic, with gauze-draped canopies and walls artistically accented with lavender, sage green, black, and pumpkin. It's a few steps to some of the greatest cafes, restaurants, bars, and shops in the city, and Chinatown and Union Square are within walking distance.

Washington Square Inn. 1660 Stockton St. (between Filbert and Union sts.), San Francisco, CA 94133. ☎ **800/388-0220** or 415/981-4220. Fax 415/397-7242. 16 rms, 11 with bath. TEL. $85–$95 double without bath, $95–$165 double with bath, $180 double with bath and park view. Rates include continental breakfast. AE, DC, DISC, JCB, MC, V. Parking $17. Bus: 15, 30, 39, or 45.

Reminiscent of a traditional English inn right down to the cucumber sandwiches served during afternoon tea, this small, comely bed-and-breakfast is ideal for those who prefer a quieter, more subdued environment than the commotion of downtown San Francisco. It's located across from Washington Square in the North Beach district and within walking distance of Fisherman's Wharf and Chinatown. Each room is decorated in English floral fabrics with quality European furnishings and plenty of fresh flowers. Five of the rooms share baths. A continental breakfast is included in the rates, as are afternoon tea, wine, and hors d'oeuvres.

INEXPENSIVE

San Remo. 2237 Mason St. (at Chestnut St.) San Francisco, CA 94133. ☎ **800/352-REMO** or 415/776-8688. Fax 415/776-2811. 59 rms, none with bath; 1 suite. $55–$65 double; $85 suite. AE, DC, MC, V. Parking $8. Cable car: Powell-Mason line. Bus: 15, 22, or 30.

Located in a quiet North Beach neighborhood and within walking distance of Fisherman's Wharf, the San Remo's rooms are small and bathrooms shared, but all is forgiven when it comes time to pay the bill. The rooms are decorated in a cozy country style with brass and iron beds, oak, maple, or pine armoires, and wicker furnishings; most have ceiling fans. The shared bathrooms—each one immaculately clean—feature clawfoot tubs and brass pull-chain toilets with oak tanks and brass fixtures.

COW HOLLOW / PACIFIC HEIGHTS
VERY EXPENSIVE

✪ Sherman House. 2160 Green St. (between Webster and Fillmore sts.), San Francisco, CA 94123. ☎ **800/424-5777** or 415/563-3600. Fax 415/563-1882. 8 rms, 6 suites. TV TEL. $200–$400 double; from $600 suite. Continental breakfast $14 extra. AE, CB, DC, MC, V. Parking $16. Cable car: Powell-Hyde line. Bus: 22, 41, or 45.

Built in 1876 by philanthropist/music publisher Leander Sherman, this magnificent Pacific Heights Victorian doubled as his home and playhouse for such guest stars as Enrico Caruso, Lillian Russell, and Victor Herbert. Today the Sherman House sets the standard in San Francisco for privacy, personal service, and sumptuous furnishings. All rooms are individually decorated with authentic antiques in French Second Empire, Biedermeier, or English Jacobean styles and contain queen-size canopy featherbeds along with ultra-rich tapestry fabrics and down comforters; all except one have fireplaces. The rooms also feature both TVs and stereos, and black granite bathrooms complete with bathrobes and whirlpool baths.

Dining/Entertainment: The dining room has a very fine reputation, but because of a zoning dispute it's now open only to guests, which may affect its standards.

Services: Concierge, room service, butler (who will discreetly unpack luggage), massage, personalized shopping, private chauffeuring.

Facilities: Business center.

EXPENSIVE

Jackson Court. 2198 Jackson St. (at Buchanan St.), San Francisco, CA 94115. ☎ **415/929-7670.** 10 rms. TV TEL. $122–$170 double. Rates include continental breakfast. AE, MC, V. Parking on street only. Bus: 12, 22, or 24.

If you crave a blissfully quiet vacation while swathed in elegant surroundings, this is the place. Each room is individually furnished with superior-quality antique furnishings; two have wood-burning fireplaces (de rigueur in the winter). The Blue Room, for example, features a brass-and-porcelain bed, Renaissance-style sofa, and inviting window seat, while the Garden Suite has handcrafted wood paneling and a large picture window looking out at the private garden patio. After breakfast, spend the day browsing the shops along nearby Union and Fillmore streets, then return in time for afternoon tea.

Union Street Inn. 2229 Union St. (between Fillmore and Steiner sts.), San Francisco, CA 94123. ☎ **415/346-0424.** Fax 415/922-8046. 5 rms, 1 carriage house. TV TEL. $125–$175 double; $225 carriage house. Rates include breakfast, hors d'oeuvres, and evening beverages. AE, MC, V. Parking $10. Bus: 22, 41, 45, or 47.

One of the most delightful B&Bs in California, this two-story Edwardian may front perpetually busy (and trendy) Union Street, but it's quiet as a church on the inside. All the individually decorated rooms are comfortably furnished with canopied or brass beds with down comforters, fresh flowers, bay windows (beg for one with a view of the garden), and private baths (some with Jacuzzi tubs). Breakfast is served either in the parlor, in your room, or on an outdoor terrace overlooking a lovely English garden. The ultimate honeymoon retreat is the private carriage house behind the inn, but any room at this warm, friendly inn is guaranteed to please.

MODERATE

Bed & Breakfast Inn. 4 Charlton Court (off Union St., between Buchanan and Laguna sts.), San Francisco, CA 94123. ☎ **415/921-9784.** 11 rms, 7 with bath; 2 suites. $70–$90 double without bath; $115–$140 double with bath; $190–$275 suite. Rates include continental breakfast. No credit cards. Parking $10 a day at nearby garage. Bus: 41 or 45.

San Francisco's first bed-and-breakfast is composed of a trio of Victorian houses—all gussied up in English country style—hidden in a cul-de-sac just off Union Street. While it doesn't have quite the casual ambience of neighboring Union Street Inn, the Bed & Breakfast Inn is loaded with charm. Each room is uniquely decorated with family antiques, original art, and a profusion of fresh flowers. Breakfast (freshly baked croissants, orange juice, and coffee, tea, or cocoa) is either brought to your room on a tray with flowers and a morning newspaper, or served in a sunny Victorian breakfast room with antique china.

JAPANTOWN & ENVIRONS
EXPENSIVE

○ **The Archbishop's Mansion.** 1000 Fulton St. (at Steiner St.), San Francisco, CA 94117. ☎ **800/543-5820** or 415/563-7872. 15 rms. TV TEL. $129–$385 double. Rates include continental breakfast. AE, MC, V. Free parking. Bus: 19, 31, or 38.

One thing is for certain: The archbishop who built this 1904 belle époque beauty was no Puritan. Drippingly romantic, the Archbishop's Mansion is one of the most opulent and fabulously adorned B&Bs you could possibly hope to stay in. The Don Giovanni Suite—larger than most San Francisco houses—comes with a huge, angel-encrusted four-poster bed imported from a French castle, a palatial fireplace, elaborately embroidered linens, and a seven-head shower that you'll never want to leave. Slightly closer to earth is the Carmen Suite, which has a deadly romantic combination of clawfoot bathtub fronting a toasty, wood-burning fireplace. In the morning breakfast is delivered to the guest rooms, and in the evening complimentary wine is served in the elegant parlor. Services include laundry/valet, concierge, limousine service, and complimentary morning newspaper.

○ **Hotel Majestic.** 1500 Sutter St. (between Octavia and Gough sts.), San Francisco, CA 94109. ☎ **800/869-8966** or 415/441-1100. Fax 415/673-7331. 51 rms, 9 suites. TV TEL. $125–$160 double; from $250 suite. Continental breakfast $8.50 extra. AE, DC, MC, V. Parking $14. Bus: 2, 3, or 4.

Built in 1902, the Majestic meets every professional need while retaining the ambience of a luxurious old-world hotel. The rooms are furnished with French and English antiques, the centerpiece of each being a large four-poster canopy bed. You'll also find custom-made, mirrored armoires and antique reproductions. Conveniences include a full-size, well-lit desk and clock-radio; extra bathroom amenities include bathrobes. Some rooms also have fireplaces.

Dining/Entertainment: The Café Majestic and Bar serves California and continental cuisine in a romantic setting and continues to intrigue a local clientele. Cocktails are offered in the adjacent bar complete with French mahogany bar.

Services: Concierge, room service, laundry/valet, complimentary newspaper, and afternoon sherry.

MODERATE

○ **Queen Anne Hotel.** 1590 Sutter St. (between Gough and Octavia sts.), San Francisco, CA 94109. ☎ **800/227-3970** or 415/441-2828. Fax 415/775-5212. 45 rms, 4 suites. TV TEL. $99–$150 double; $175 suite. Additional person $10 extra. Rates include continental breakfast. AE, DC, MC, V. Parking $12. Bus: 2, 3, or 4.

This majestic four-story 1890 Victorian was restored to its original integrity in 1981 and renovated in 1995. Walk under rich, red drapery to the immaculate and lavish "grand salon" lobby complete with English oak paneling and period antiques. The rooms follow suit with antique armoires, marble-top dressers, and other Victorian pieces. Some have corner turret bay windows that look out on tree-lined streets, as well as separate parlor areas and wet bars; others have cozy reading nooks and fire-places. All guest rooms have a telephone in the bathroom, a computer hookup, and a refrigerator. Services include a concierge, room service, morning newspaper, and complimentary afternoon tea and sherry. There's also access to an off-premises health club with a lap pool.

CIVIC CENTER
EXPENSIVE

✪ The Inn at the Opera. 333 Fulton St. (at Franklin St.), San Francisco, CA 94102. ☎ **800/ 325-2708** or 415/863-8400. Fax 415/861-0821. 30 rms, 18 suites. MINIBAR TV TEL. $140– $190 double; from $200 suite. Additional person $15 extra. Rates include European buffet break-fast. AE, MC, V. Parking $19. Bus: 5, 21, 47, or 49.

Judging from its mild-mannered facade and offbeat location behind the Opera House, few would ever guess that the Inn at the Opera is one of San Francisco's— if not California's—finest small hotels. But don't take my word for it—Luciano Pavarotti, Plácido Domingo, Mikhail Baryshnikov, and dozens of other stars of the stage throw their slumber parties here regularly, requisitioning the Act IV Restaurant (the inn's luxurious dining room and lounge) along with a floor or two of rooms. Queen-size beds with huge stuffed pillows are standard in each pastel-hued guest room, along with elegant furnishings, wet bars, microwave ovens, refrigerators, and bouquets of fresh flowers. The baths include hair dryers, scales, terrycloth robes, and French milled soaps. The larger rooms and suites are especially recommended for those who need elbow room; typical of small hotels, the least expensive "standard" rooms are short on space.

    Dining/Entertainment: The Act IV Restaurant, the hotel's fine dining room, pro-vides an intimate setting for dinner, while the adjacent lounge with its leather chairs, glowing fire, and soft piano music is a favorite city meeting place (see "Dining," later in this chapter).

    Services: Concierge, room service (24 hours), laundry/valet, evening turndown, complimentary light pressing and overnight shoeshine, staff physician, complimen-tary limousine service to the Financial District, morning newspaper.

    Facilities: Business center.

MODERATE

Abigail Hotel. 246 McAllister St. (between Hyde and Larkin sts.), San Francisco, CA 94102. ☎ **800/243-6510** or 415/861-9728. Fax 415/861-5848. 59 rms, 1 suite. TV TEL. $84 double; $129 suite. Additional person $10 extra. Rates include continental breakfast. AE, CB, DC, MC, V. Parking $12. Muni Metro: All Market St. trams. Bus: All Market St. routes.

The Abigail doesn't get much press, but it's one of the better medium-priced hotels in the city. It was built in 1925 to house celebrities performing at the world-renowned Fox Theater, but what the Abigail lacks in luxury is more than made up in charm. The rooms, while on the small side, are clean, cute, and comfortably furnished with cozy antiques and down comforters. Morning coffee, pastries, and complimentary newspapers greet you in the beautiful faux-marble lobby, while lunch and dinner are served downstairs in the "organic" restaurant, the Millennium. Access to a nearby health club, as well as laundry and massage services, are available upon request.

Phoenix Inn. 601 Eddy St. (at Larkin St.), San Francisco, CA 94109. ☎ **800/248-9466** or 415/776-1380. Fax 415/885-3109. 42 rms, 2 suites. TV TEL. $99–$109 double; $139–$150 suite. Rates include continental breakfast. AE, DC, MC, V. Free parking. Bus: 19, 31, or 38.

Situated on the fringes of San Francisco's less-then-pleasant Tenderloin district, this retro 1950s-style hotel has been described as the hippest hotel in town, a gathering place for visiting rock musicians, writers, and filmmakers who crave a dose of Southern California—hence the palm trees and pastel colors here. The focal point is a small, heated outdoor pool adorned with a neo-paisley mural by artist Francis Forlenza and ensconced in a modern-sculpture garden.

The rooms, while far from plush, are comfortably equipped with bamboo furnishings, potted plants, and original local art. In addition to the usual amenities, the inn's own closed-circuit channel shows films exclusively made in or about San Francisco. Services include an on-site massage therapist, concierge, laundry/valet, room service, and—whahoo!—free parking. Adjoining the hotel is Miss Pearl's Jam House restaurant/club, featuring spicy island cuisine and the reggae sounds to go with it.

HAIGHT-ASHBURY

Stanyan Park Hotel. 750 Stanyan St. (at Waller St.), San Francisco, CA 94117. ☎ **415/751-1000.** Fax 415/668-5454. 30 rms, 6 suites. TV TEL. $85–$105 double; from $135 suite. Additional person $20 extra. Rates include continental breakfast. AE, CB, DC, DISC, MC, V. Parking $5. Muni Metro: N line. Bus: 7, 33, 71, or 73.

This charming, three-story establishment is decorated with antique furnishings, Victorian wallpaper, and pastel quilts, curtains, and carpets. The tub/shower baths come complete with massaging shower head, shampoos, and fancy soaps. There are one- and two-bedroom suites. Each has a full kitchen, and formal dining and living rooms, and can sleep up to six comfortably; they're ideal for families. Complimentary tea and cookies are served each afternoon.

4 Dining

San Francisco's dining is some of the best in the world. Since our space is limited, we had to make tough choices. For a greater selection of reviews, see *Frommer's San Francisco.*

The restaurants below are divided by area and by price (for an average dinner), as follows: **Expensive,** more than $45 per person; **Moderate,** $25 to $45 per person; **Inexpensive,** $25 or under per person. If you want a table at a top restaurant, make your reservation weeks ahead.

UNION SQUARE / NOB HILL
EXPENSIVE

✪ **Charles Nob Hill.** 1250 Jones St. (at Clay St.). ☎ **415/771-5400.** Reservations recommended. Main courses $16–$26. AE, DC, MC, V. Daily 5:30–10pm. Cable car: California or Powell-Hyde line. Bus: 1, 12, 27, or 83. FRENCH.

We never knew beef could actually melt in your mouth until Aqua owner Charles Condy bought the historic restaurant "Le Club" and introduced us to the culinary magic of Aqua's executive chef Michael Mina (it really did melt!). The menu lists "classically inspired light French fare," which is served in two divided dining rooms with velvet banquettes, fresh floral arrangements, and the loud buzz of the older socialite crowd. Definitely start with the scallop and black truffle pot pie, and for the main course you might choose the poêle (melt-in-your-mouth) of beef tenderloin with wild mushroom and potato torte, balsamic-glazed onions, and foie gras, or a delicate seared red snapper with chive and preserved-lemon jus, artichoke, and chanterelle ragoût. No matter what, don't drive here unless you valet it—you may spend more than an hour looking for parking.

✪ **Fleur de Lys.** 777 Sutter St. (at Jones St.). ☎ **415/673-7779.** Reservations required. Main courses $27–$34; five-course tasting menu $65; four-course vegetarian menu $55. AE, CB, DC, MC, V. Mon–Thurs 6–10pm, Fri–Sat 5:30–10:30pm. Bus: 2, 3, 4, 27, or 38. FRENCH.

Imagine a large version of Jeannie's (as in *I Dream of Jeannie*) live-in bottle: dark, cozy, with 700 yards of floor-to-ceiling hand-painted fabric enclosing the room. Throw in dimly lit French candelabras, an enormous floral centerpiece, and about 20 tables filled with well-dressed diners (wear a dinner jacket!). Welcome to one of the most renowned dining rooms in San Francisco. Fleur de Lys does everything seriously—and with chef Hubert Keller (who was President Clinton's first guest chef at the White House) in the kitchen, it's impossible to go wrong. You can order à la carte, from the five-course tasting menu, or from the four-course vegetarian menu. Start with the blue potato chips with cauliflower purée and caviar or the crispy sweetbreads. Main courses might include herb-crusted salmon with mushrooms and spinach-noodle pie or lamb loin with black truffles. Combined with a selection of 300 French and California wines and sumptuous desserts and it's an overall dining fantasy.

✪**Masa's.** In the Hotel Vintage Court, 648 Bush St. (at Stockton St.). ☎ **415/989-7154.** Reservations required (accepted up to 21 days in advance). Main courses $30–$38.50; fixed-price dinner $68–$75. AE, CB, DC, DISC, MC, V. Tues–Sat 6–9:30pm. Closed first week in Jan and fourth week in July. Cable car: Powell-Mason or Powell-Hyde line. Bus: 2, 3, 4, 30, or 45. FRENCH.

Chef Julian Serrano's brilliant cuisine matched with a flawless wine list and exemplary (even unpretentious) service have solidified Masa's reputation as one of the country's great French outposts. Either fixed price or à la carte, dinner is a memorable expense-be-damned experience from start to finish. If you wish, you can simply leave the decisions up to the kitchen. Serrano's passion for using only the highest-quality ingredients accounts for the restaurant's four-star ranking—and four-figure prices. A typical dinner may begin with the Sonoma foie gras in a madeira-truffle sauce, or poached lobster with potatoes, fried leek, and a truffle vinaigrette. Main dishes may include medallions of New Zealand fallow deer with Zinfandel sauce and caramelized green apples, or the Atlantic black bass with a saffron sauce. The desserts, as you'd imagine, are heavenly.

✪**Postrio.** 545 Post St. (between Mason and Taylor sts.). ☎ **415/776-7825.** Reservations required. Main courses $6–$15 at breakfast, $14–$15 at lunch, $20–$26 at dinner. AE, CB, DC, DISC, MC, V. Mon–Fri 7–10am, 11:30am–2pm, and 5:30–10:30pm; Sat–Sun 9am–2pm. (Bar, daily 11:30am–2am.) Cable car: Powell-Mason or Powell-Hyde line. Bus: 2, 3, 4, or 38. AMERICAN.

Ever since chefs Anne and David Gingrass left the kitchen here to start their own enterprise, rumors have been flying that San Francisco's top restaurant isn't what it used to be. If its owners are crying, however, they're crying all the way to the bank, because it's a rare night when the kitchen doesn't perform to a full house. Eating, however, is only half the reason one comes to Postrio. After squeezing through the perpetually swinging bar—which, in its own right, dishes out excellent tapas and pizzas from a wood-burning oven in the corner—guests are forced to make a grand entrance down the antebellum staircase to the cavernous dining room below (it's everyone's 15 seconds of fame, so make sure your fly is zipped).

The menu, prepared by brothers Mitchell and Steven Rosenthal, combines Italian, Asian, French, and California styles with mixed results. When we last visited, the sautéed salmon was a bit overcooked, but the accompanying plum glaze, wasabi mashed potatoes, and miso vinaigrette were outstanding. Despite the prime-time rush, service was friendly and infallible, as was the presentation.

✪**Ritz-Carlton Dining Room.** In the Ritz-Carlton San Francisco, 600 Stockton St. (at California St.). ☎ **415/296-7465.** Reservations recommended. Fixed-price menu $45–$59.

AE, DC, DISC, MC, V. Mon–Sat 6am–10pm. Cable car: Powell-Hyde or Powell-Mason line (direct stop). CALIFORNIA/FRENCH.

Never a hotel to do anything second best, the Ritz-Carlton hotel is renowned for pampering its guests as if they were royalty—and the Dining Room is no exception. On our last visit, no less then five tuxedoed wait staff were surreptitiously attending to our needs (no half-empty water glasses in *this* joint) as we fussed over the wine list and debated the proper pronunciation of "*tatin*." The setting, as you would imagine, is quite regal and sumptuous: The crystal chandeliers, rich brocade, elegant table settings, cushy high-backed chairs, and live harp music reek of formality. Unfortunately, celebrity Chef Gary Danko—winner of the 1995 James Beard Award, the Academy Award of the food world—is no longer with the Ritz. His replacement, Chef Sylvain Portay, now runs the kitchen with similar aplomb, but the loss in noticeable—dishes such as the roast Maine lobster and striped bass filet were quite good, but certainly not of the four-star caliber that Danko's fans are accustomed to. A few dishes, however, were outstanding, particularly the crayfish bisque (one of the best dishes we have ever tasted) and the risotto with butternut squash and roasted squab. Dessert, alas, was also deigned for mere mortals, though the warm port-poached pear in vanilla sauce was superb.

The menu, which changes monthly, offers a choice of three-, four-, or five-course dinners ranging from $45 to $59, the latter of which includes wine pairing per course by Master Sommelier Emmanuel Kemiji for an additional $37. The Dining Room also features the country's only "rolling" cheese cart, laden with at least two dozen individually ripened cheeses.

MODERATE

✪ **Brasserie Savoy.** In the Savoy Hotel, 580 Geary St. (at Jones St.). ☎ **415/474-8686.** Reservations recommended. Main courses $11–$17. AE, DC, DISC, JCB, MC, V. Daily 6:30–11am and 5:30–10pm. Bus: 2, 3, 4, 27, or 38. CALIFORNIA/FRENCH.

The atmosphere here is French bistro, with a bright, busy dining room, black-and-white marble floors, and tables with beige and black leather, and woven chairs. The food is consistent, affordable, and delicious. Choices may include beef tenderloin with port sauce and green peppercorn butter, or duck breast with mille feuille of potato and mushrooms served with a date purée and coffee sauce. On the lighter side, the crayfish risotto with red and green peppers, scallions, celery, and chive-lemongrass butter is a perfect dish. Among the appetizers, the napoleon of braised rabbit with red onions, mushrooms, kalamata olives, and anise tuiles is a preferred choice, if it's offered, or any one of several freshly made salads. To finish, try the innovative crème brûlée.

✪ **Rumpus.** 1 Tillman Place (off Grant Ave., between Sutter and Post sts.). ☎ **415/421-2300.** Reservations recommended. Main courses $12–$17. AE, DC, MC, V. Mon–Thurs 11:30am–2:30pm and 5:30–10pm, Fri–Sat 11:30am–2:30pm and 5:30–11pm, Sun 5:30–10pm. CALIFORNIA.

Tucked into a small cul-de-sac off Grant Avenue, Rumpus is a fantastic new restaurant serving well-prepared California fare at reasonable prices. The perfect place for a business lunch, shopping break, or dinner with friends, Rumpus is architecturally playful, colorful, and buzzing with conversation. Like most restaurants in town, ahi tuna tartare is on the starters list. It is, however, wonderfully fresh, savory, and spiced with wasabi caviar. The pan-roasted chicken's crispy and flavorful crust is almost as delightful as the perfectly cooked chicken and mashed potatoes beneath it; and the quality cut of New York steak comes with a sweet-potato mash. If nothing else, make sure to stop in here for one of the best desserts we've ever had: the puddinglike chocolate-brioche cake.

◑ Scala's Bistro. In the Sir Francis Drake Hotel, 432 Powell St. (at Sutter St.). ☎ **415/ 395-8555.** Reservations recommended. Lunch/dinner main courses $8–$17; breakfast $6–$9. AE, CB, DC, DISC, MC, V. Daily 6:30am–midnight. Cable car: Powell-Hyde line. Bus: 2, 3, 4, 30, 45, or 76. FRENCH/ITALIAN.

Firmly entrenched at the base of the refurbished Sir Francis Drake Hotel, this latest venture by husband-and-wife team Giovanni (the host) and Donna (the chef) Scala is one of the best new restaurants in the city. The Parisian-bistro/old-world atmosphere blends just the right balance of elegance and informality, which means it's perfectly okay to have some fun here (and apparently most people do).

Drawing from her success at the Bistro Don Giovanni in Napa, Donna has put together a fantastic array of Italian and French dishes that are priced surprisingly low. Start with the earth and surf calamari appetizer (better than anything we've sampled along the Mediterranean) or the grilled portabello mushrooms. Generous portions of the moist, rich duck-leg confit will satisfy hungry appetites, but if you can only order one thing, make it Scala's signature dish: the seared salmon. Finish with the creamy Bostini cream pie, a dreamy combo of vanilla custard and orange-chiffon cake with a warm chocolate glaze.

THE FINANCIAL DISTRICT
EXPENSIVE

◐ Aqua. 252 California St. (between Battery and Front sts.). ☎ **415/956-9662.** Reservations recommended. Main courses $26–$32; six-course tasting menu $65; vegetarian tasting menu $45. AE, DC, MC, V. Mon–Fri 11:30am–2pm and 5:30–10:30, Sat 5:30–10:30pm. Bus: All Market St. routes. SEAFOOD.

Without question, Aqua is San Francisco's finest seafood restaurant. Chef Michael Mina dazzles his customers with a bewildering juxtaposition of earth and sea. The salmon, for example, is first glazed in ginger, then spiced with sweet orange marmalade that contrasts perfectly with the sour reduction sauce of braised red cabbage. Mina's passion for exotic mushrooms pervades most dishes, for taste as well as for show (Mina is, to a fault, amazingly adept at the art of presentation). His desserts are equally impressive, particularly the spiced pumpkin brioche with cream cheese ice cream, and the chocolate tasting plate—a feast for the eyes as well as the palate.

◐ Silks. In the Mandarin Oriental Hotel, 222 Sansome St. (between Pine and California sts.). ☎ **415/885-0999.** Reservations recommended. Fixed-price menu $32 for two courses, $39 for three courses, $47 for four courses. AE, DC, MC, V. Mon–Fri 7am–2pm and 6–9:30pm, Sat–Sun 6–9:30pm. Bus: 2, 38, or 42. CALIFORNIA/ASIAN.

Though the atmosphere is rather somber, Silks is still regarded as one of the better dining rooms in the city. Changing quarterly, the menu melds California and Asian ingredients and styles together, and is offered in two-, three-, or four-course meals. Main courses may include coriander-crusted tuna with soba noodles, Asian-marinated lamb loin and spicy satay, and the signature grilled yakitori quail with sweet-potato purée, star anise, and foie gras wontons. Follow with such desserts as banana cake with slices of caramelized bananas and two kinds of ice cream.

MODERATE
Splendido. 4 Embarcadero Center (at Clay and Drum sts.). ☎ **415/986-3222.** Reservations accepted. Main courses $14–$23. AE, DC, DISC, MC, V. Mon–Fri 11:30am–2:30pm and 5:30–10pm, Sat–Sun 5:30–10pm. Bus: 15, 45, or 76. MEDITERRANEAN/AMERICAN.

Warm olivewood, flickering candles, rustic stone walls, hand-painted tiles, and hand-hewn beams create the illusion of an old Mediterranean getaway in the middle of metropolitan Embarcadero Four. When the weather is pleasant you can eat under a canopy on the outdoor patio, or choose the seating in front of the open kitchen. But it's not the decor alone that procures kudos from *Gourmet* and other culinary magazines. The food is beautifully presented, lovingly prepared, and consistently delicious—from the starters, which might include fish soup, or crispy crab cakes to the main courses of grilled swordfish served on a bed of sweet white corn and braised leeks. Save some room for dessert—some say that the tiramisù with chocolate pine-nut bark is the best in town.

○ **Tadich Grill.** 240 California St. (between Battery and Front sts.). ☎ **415/391-1849.** Reservations not accepted. Main courses $12–$19. MC, V. Mon–Fri 11am–9:30pm, Sat 11:30am–9:30pm. Muni Metro: All Market Street trams. Bus: All Market Street routes. SEAFOOD.

This famous, venerated California institution arrived with the Gold Rush in 1849 and claims to be the very first to broil seafood over mesquite charcoal, back in the early 1920s. For a light meal you might try one of the delicious seafood salads, such as shrimp or prawn Louis. Hot dishes include baked avocado with shrimp diablo, baked casserole of stuffed turbot with crab and shrimp à la Newburg, and charcoal-broiled petrale sole with butter sauce, a local favorite. Almost everyone gets a side order of big, tasty french fries.

CHINATOWN

○ **House of Nanking.** 919 Kearny St. (at Columbus Ave.). ☎ **415/421-1429.** Reservations not accepted. Main courses $4.95–$7.95. No credit cards. Mon–Fri 11am–10pm, Sat noon–10pm, Sun 4–10pm. Bus: 9, 12, 15, or 30. CHINESE.

To the unknowing passerby, the shoebox-sized House of Nanking has "greasy dive" written all over it. To its legion of fans, however, the wait—sometimes up to an hour—is worth what's coming on the plate. Located on the edge of Chinatown just off Columbus Avenue, this inconspicuous little diner is one of San Francisco's worst-kept secrets. When the line is reasonable, we drop by for a plate of pot stickers (still the best we've ever tasted) and chef/owner Peter Fang's signature shrimp-and-green-onion pancake served with peanut sauce. Seating is tight, so prepare to be bumped around a bit, and don't expect good service—it's all part of the Nanking experience.

NORTH BEACH & FISHERMAN'S WHARF
EXPENSIVE

A. Sabella's. Fisherman's Wharf, 2766 Taylor St. (at Jefferson St.), 3rd Floor. ☎ **415/771-6775.** Reservations accepted. Main courses $9–$41. Daily 11am–3:30pm and 5–10:30pm. AE, DC, MC, V. Cable car: Powell-Mason line. ITALIAN/SEAFOOD.

The Sabella family has been serving seafood in San Francisco since the turn of the century and has operated A. Sabella's restaurant on the wharf continuously since 1920. Catering heavily to the tourist trade, the menu doesn't take any chances—traditional steak, seafood, and pasta dishes line the menu. Where A. Sabella's really shines, however, is in the shellfish department—the 1,180-gallon saltwater tank allows for fresh crab, abalone, and lobster year round, which means that no restaurant in the city can touch A. Sabella's when it comes to feasting on fresh Dungeness crab out of season. A nice touch is the live piano music played nightly in the large, formal dining room overlooking the wharf.

MODERATE

Bix. 56 Gold St. (between Sansome and Montgomery sts.). ☎ **415/433-6300.** Reservations recommended. Main courses $5–$12 at lunch, $11–$25 at dinner. AE, CB, DC, DISC, MC, V. Mon–Thurs 11:30am–11pm, Fri–Sat 11:30am–midnight, Sun 5–10pm. Bus: 15, 30, 41, or 45. CALIFORNIA.

Bix is better known for its martinis than for its menu. Curving Honduran mahogany, massive silver columns, and deco-style lighting set the stage for dancing to live music, though most locals settle for chatting with the friendly bartenders and noshing on appetizers. While the ultra-stylish setting tends to overshadow the food, Bix actually serves some pretty good grub. The lobster linguine with fresh prawns and mussels in a sun-dried tomato broth is the undisputed favorite, followed by the grilled filet mignon with mushrooms and chicken hash à la Bix.

✪ **Moose's.** 1652 Stockton St. (between Filbert and Union sts.) ☎ **415/989-7800.** Reservations recommended. Main courses $8.50–$25. AE, CB, DC, MC, V. Mon–Thurs 11:30am–11pm, Fri–Sat 11:30am–midnight, Sun 10:30am–11pm. Bus: 15, 30, 41, or 45. CALIFORNIA.

This is where Nob Hill socialites and local politicians come to dine and be seen. But Moose's isn't just an image. In fact, the dining room itself is rather sparse and unintimate, but the food—well, that's a different story. Everything that comes out of Moose's kitchen is way above par. The appetizers are innovative, fresh, and well balanced (try Mediterranean fish soup with rouille and croûtons cooked in the wood-fired oven), and the main courses (especially the meats) are perfectly prepared. The menu changes every few months and might include a grilled veal chop with potato galette and a variety of pasta, chicken, and fish dishes. A new chef had just come on board at press time; cross your fingers that he maintains the quality expected from Moose's.

INEXPENSIVE

Mario's Bohemian Cigar Store. 566 Columbus Ave. ☎ **415/362-0536.** Sandwiches $5–$6. No credit cards. Daily 10am–11pm. Closed Dec 24–Jan 1. Bus: 15, 30, 41, or 45. ITALIAN.

The century-old bar—small, well worn, and perpetually busy—is best known for its focaccia sandwiches, including meatball and eggplant. Wash it all down with an excellent cappuccino or a house Campari as you watch the tourists stroll by. And no, they don't sell cigars.

❺ **Pasta Pomodoro.** 655 Union St. (at Columbus Ave.). ☎ **415/399-0300.** Main courses $4–$6.50. No credit cards. Mon–Fri 11am–11pm, Sat noon–midnight, Sun noon–11pm. ITALIAN.

There's usually a 20-minute wait for a table, but after you're seated you'll be surprised at how promptly you're served. Every dish is fresh and sizable, and best of all, they're a third of what you'd pay elsewhere. Winners include the spaghetti frutti di mare, with calamari, mussels, scallops, tomato, garlic, and wine; or cavatappi pollo with roast chicken, sun-dried tomatoes, cream, mushrooms, and parmesan. Avoid the cappellini Pomodoro or ask for extra sauce—it tends to be dry.

Their second location, 2027 Chestnut St., at Fillmore St. (☎ 415/474-3400), is equally good, but cramped and noisy. The latest additon to the burgeoning Pasta Pomodoro empire is in the Castro at 2304 Market St., at 16th St. (☎ 415/558-8123).

COW HOLLOW / PACIFIC HEIGHTS / THE MARINA DISTRICT
EXPENSIVE

✪ **Harris'.** 2100 Van Ness Ave. (at Pacific Ave.). ☎ **415/673-1888.** Reservations recommended. Main courses $18–$30. AE, CB, DC, DISC, JCB, MC, V. Mon–Fri 6–11pm, Sat–Sun 5–11pm. Bus: 38 or 45. AMERICAN.

Proprietor Ann Lee Harris knows steaks; she grew up on a cattle ranch and married the owner of the largest feedlot in California. In 1976 the couple opened the Harris Ranch Restaurant on Interstate 5 in central California, where they built a rock-solid reputation up and down the coast. The steaks, which can be seen hanging in a glass-windowed aging room, are cut thick—either New York style or T-bone—and are served with a baked potato and seasonal vegetables. Harris' also offers roast duckling, lamb chops, fresh fish, lobster, and venison, buffalo, and other types of game. Those who like sweetbreads rave about the restaurant's sautéed brains in brown butter.

✪ **La Folie.** 2316 Polk St. (between Green and Union sts.). ☎ **415/776-5577.** Reservations recommended. Main courses $22–$28; five-course tasting menu $45. AE, DC, JCB, MC, V. Mon–Sat 5:30–10:30pm. Bus: 19, 41, 45, 47, 49, or 76. FRENCH.

The minute you walk through the door you'll know why this is many locals' favorite restaurant. The country-French decor is tasteful but not too serious, with whimsical chandeliers and a cloudy sky painted overhead. The staff is friendly, knowledgeable, and very accommodating; the food is outstanding. Unlike many renowned chefs, La Folie's Roland Passot is in the kitchen nightly—and it shows. Each of his California-influenced French creations is both an architectural and a culinary masterpiece. Best of all, they're served in a relaxed and comfortable environment. Start with an appetizer such as the roast quail and foie gras with salad. Main courses are not petite as in many French restaurants, and all are accompanied by flavorful and well-balanced sauces. Try the rôti of quail and squab stuffed with wild mushrooms and wrapped in crispy potato strings or the roast venison with vegetables, quince, and huckleberry sauce. Finish off with any of the delectable desserts.

MODERATE

The Elite Café. 2049 Fillmore St. (between Pine and California sts.). ☎ **415/346-8668.** Reservations not accepted. Main courses $11–$22. AE, DC, DISC, MC, V. Mon–Sat 5–11pm, Sun 10am–3pm and 5–10pm. Bus: 41 or 45. CAJUN/CREOLE.

This place is always bustling with Pacific Heights' beautiful people who come for fresh oysters, blackened filet mignon with Cajun butter, redfish with crab and Créole cream sauce, or any of the other well-spiced Cajun dishes. The high-backed booths provide more intimate dining than the crowded tables and bar. Brunch is good too, when Benedict, sardou, and many more egg dishes are offered along with bagels and lox.

✪ **Greens Restaurant, Fort Mason.** Building A, Fort Mason Center (enter Fort Mason opposite the Safeway at Buchanan and Marina sts.). ☎ **415/771-6222.** Reservations recommended 2 weeks in advance. Main courses $10–$13; fixed-priced dinner $38; brunch $7–$10. DISC, MC, V. Mon–Sat 8am–9pm, Sun 9am–2pm. (Bakery, Tues–Sat 9:30am–4:30pm, Sun 10am–3pm.) Bus: 28 or 30. VEGETARIAN.

Executive chef Annie Somerville (author of *Fields of Greens*) uses local organic produce to cook with the seasons in this old warehouse with enormous windows overlooking the bridge and the bay. A weeknight dinner might feature such appetizers as tomato, white-bean, and sorrel soup, or grilled asparagus with lemon, Parmesan cheese, and watercress. Main courses might include spring vegetable risotto with asparagus, peas, shiitake and crimini mushrooms, and Parmesan cheese; or Sri Lankan curry made of new potatoes, cauliflower, carrots, peppers, and snap peas stewed with tomatoes, coconut milk, ginger, and Sri Lankan spices. A five-course dinner is served on Saturday. An extensive wine list is available. The adjacent bakery sells homemade breads, sandwiches, soups, salads, and pastries to take home.

✪ **Pane e Vino.** 3011 Steiner St. (at Union St.). ☎ **415/346-2111.** Reservations recommended. Main courses $7.50–$18. AE, MC, V. Mon–Sat 11:30am–2:30pm and 5–10pm, Sun 5–10pm. Bus: 41 or 45. ITALIAN.

Pane e Vino is one of San Francisco's top—and most authentic—Italian restaurants. The food is consistently excellent (be careful not to fill up on the outstanding breads served upon seating), the prices reasonable, and the mostly Italian-accented staff always smooth and efficient under pressure (you'll see). The two small dining rooms, separated by an open kitchen emitting heavenly aromas, offer only limited seating, so expect a wait even if you have reservations. The fare includes a hugely popular chilled artichoke stuffed with bread and tomatoes, the antipasti of mixed grilled vegetables, which always spurs a fork fight, and a broad selection of pastas. Other specialties are grilled fish and meat dishes. The top dessert picks are any of the Italian ice creams, the crème caramel, and (but of course) the creamy tiramisù.

⭐ **PlumpJack Café.** 3127 Fillmore St. (between Filbert and Greenwich sts.). ☎ **415/ 563-4755.** Reservations recommended. Main courses $14–$20. AE, MC, V. Mon–Fri 11:30am– 2pm and 5:30–10:30pm, Sat 5:30–10:30pm. Bus: 41 or 45. CALIFORNIA/MEDITERRANEAN.

Wildly popular among San Francisco's style-setters, this small Cow Hollow restaurant is the "in" place to dine. This is partly due to the fact that it's run by one of the Getty clan (as in J. Paul), but mostly because chef Maria Helm's food is just plain good and the whimsical decor is a veritable work of art. Though the menu changes weekly, you might find on the menu roasted portobello mushroom with vegetable stuffing, reggiano, and cippolini onions; pasta; or roast local halibut with grilled asparagus and blood-orange chervil vinaigrette. Top it off with an apricot soufflé or the chocolate Kahlúa torte. The extensive California wine list is sold at next to retail, with many wines available by the glass.

INEXPENSIVE

Swan Oyster Depot. 1517 Polk St. (between California and Sacramento sts.). ☎ **415/ 673-1101.** Reservations not accepted. Seafood cocktails $5–$8; clams and oysters on the half shell $6–$7.50 per half dozen. No credit cards. Mon–Sat 8am–5:30pm. Bus: 27. SEAFOOD.

Almost 85 years old and looking even older, this tiny hole-in-the-wall with the city's friendliest servers is little more than a narrow fish market that decided to slap down some stools. There are only 20 or so seats jammed shoulder-to-shoulder along a long, marble bar. Most patrons come for a quick cup of chowder or a plate of half-shelled oysters that arrive chilling on crushed ice. The menu is limited to fresh crab, shrimp, oyster, and clam cocktails, Maine lobster, and Boston-style clam chowder. Fish is only available raw or smoked and to go. Beer and wine are available.

⭐ **Zinzino.** 2355 Chestnut St. (at Divisadero St.). ☎ **415/346-6623.** Reservations accepted only for parties of six or more. Main courses $7.50–$9.50 at lunch, $4–$9 at brunch. MC, V. Tues–Fri 5:30–10pm, Sat–Sun 10am–4pm and 5:30–10pm. Bus: 22 or 30. ITALIAN.

Zinzino may look like a tiny trattoria from the outside, but you could fit a small nuclear sub in the space from the sun-drenched facade to the shaded back patio of this former launderette. Italian movie posters, magazines, and furnishings evoke memories of past vacations, but we rarely recall the food in Italy being this good (and certainly not this cheap). Start off with the crispy calamari (second only to Scala's earth and turf) or the roasted jumbo prawns wrapped in crisp pancetta and bathed in a tangy basalmic reduction sauce. The perfect light lunch for two is a half eggplant, half a house-spiced Italian sausage pizza (a mere $4.50 per person), savored with the requisite glass of chianti at the marble-top wine bar. The huge focaccia sandwiches are also a big hit with the handful of locals who are privy to this San Francisco sleeper.

CIVIC CENTER
EXPENSIVE

Act IV. In the Inn at the Opera, 333 Fulton St. (at Frankin St.). ☎ **415/553-8100.** Reservations recommended. Main courses $5–$12 at lunch, $19–$28 at dinner; breakfast $5–$10. AE, MC, V. Mon–Thurs 7–10am, 11:30am–2pm, and 5:30–10pm; Fri–Sat to 10:30pm. Bus: 5. CALIFORNIA.

This small, intimate haven with its dark-wood furnishings, Belgian tapestries, and elegant table settings is a popular venue for après-opera noshing. Large portions of fresh, well-prepared meats and vegetables dominate each dish, such as the wonderful rack of lamb in a superb reduction sauce flavored with roasted garlic, carrots, turnips, and a potato gratin. The grilled Virginia striped bass with a tangy citrus vinaigrette and lemon aïoli is another good choice. Perhaps the main reason people come here, though, is to listen to the live entertainment and for the chance encounter with the steady stream of celebrities who frequent the hotel.

✪ **Stars.** 150 Redwood Alley (between McAllister and Golden Gate off Van Ness Ave.). ☎ **415/861-7827.** Reservations required. Main courses $23–$28. AE, MC, V. Mon–Fri 11:30am–2pm and 6–9:30pm, Sat–Sun 6–9:30pm. Bus: 19, 31, or 38. CALIFORNIA.

San Francisco's celebrity hot spot nonpareil, Stars is the brainchild of superstar chef Jeremiah Tower. Swathed in glimmering hardwoods, brass, and mirrors, this large, loud, and vibrant restaurant features the longest bar in the city, which does little to guarantee you'll find a free stool when the place is hopping. Critics complain that the quality of the food is slipping while prices are heading in the opposite direction, but it obviously doesn't deter local celebrities like Robin Williams and Mayor Willie Brown from making regular appearances.

Though the menu changes daily, among the half-dozen main courses you might find a braised veal ragoût with egg noodles, cipollini onions, and wild mushrooms; or sea scallops with braised Belgian endive, lobster-cream sauce, and tarragon. The desserts are extraordinary, from the signature chocolate soufflé pastry to the banana-nut torte.

MODERATE

✪ **Hayes Street Grill.** 320 Hayes St. (near Franklin St.). ☎ **415/863-5545.** Reservations recommended. Main courses $13.50–$18.25. AE, DC, MC, V. Mon–Fri 11:30am–2pm and 5–8:30pm, Sat 6–10:30pm, Sun 5–8:30pm. Bus: 19, 31, or 38. SEAFOOD.

This small, no-nonsense seafood restaurant has built a solid reputation among San Francisco's picky epicureans for its impeccably fresh fish. Choices ranging from Hawaiian swordfish to Puget Sound salmon—cooked to perfection, naturally—are matched with your sauce of choice (Szechuan peanut, tomato salsa, herb shallot butter, etc.), and a side of their signature french fries. Fancier seafood specials are available too, such as bay scallops with chanterelle and shiitake mushrooms, as well as an impressive selection of dirt-fresh salads and local grilled meats. Finish with the outstanding crème brûlée.

✪ **Zuni Café.** 1658 Market St. (at Franklin St.). ☎ **415/552-2522.** Reservations recommended. Main courses $16–$22.50. AE, MC, V. Tues–Sat 7:30am–midnight, Sun 7:30am–11pm. Muni Metro: All Market St. trams. Bus: 6, 7, 71, or 75. MEDITERRANEAN.

Even factoring in the snotty service, the Zuni Café is still one of our favorite places in the city to have lunch. Its expanse of windows and prime Market Street location guarantee good people-watching. For the full effect, sit at the bustling, copper-top bar and peruse the foot-long oyster menu (half a dozen or so varieties on hand at all times); you can also sit in the stylish, exposed-brick dining room or on the outdoor patio. Though changing, the menu always includes meat and fish, either grilled or braised in the kitchen's brick oven.

SOMA
EXPENSIVE

✪ **Boulevard.** 1 Mission St. (at Embarcadero and Steuart Sts.). ☎ **415/543-6084.** Reservations recommended. Main courses $17.75–$22. AE, DC, MC, V. Mon–Fri 11:30am–2pm and 5:30–10:30pm, Sat–Sun 5:30–10:30pm. Bus: 15, 30, 32, 42, or 45. AMERICAN.

Art nouveau interior-vaulted brick ceilings, floral-design banquettes, and fluid, tulip-shaped lamps set a dramatic scene for equally impressive dishes. Start with the delicate, soft egg ravioli with spinach, ricotta, and shaved white truffles; then embark on such wonderful concoctions as wood oven–roasted sea bass on a bed of sun-dried tomato and roasted-garlic mashed potatoes. Vegetarian items, such as roasted Portobello mushrooms layered with mashed sweet potatoes, are also offered. Three levels of formality—bar, open kitchen, and main dining room—keep things from getting too snobby.

✪ **Hawthorn Lane.** 22 Hawthorn Lane (at Howard St., between 2nd and 3rd sts.). ☎ **415/777-9779.** Reservations recommended. Jackets for men appropriate but not required. Main courses $9.50–$13 at lunch, $19.50–$24 at dinner. CB, DC, DISC , JCB, MC, V. Mon–Thurs 11:30am–2pm and 5:30–10pm, Fri 11:30am–2pm, Sun 5:30–10pm. BART: Montgomery station. Muni Metro: F, J, K, L, M, or N. Bus: 12, 30, 45, or 76. CALIFORNIA.

Anne and David Gingrass left Postrio to head the kitchen at Hawthorn Lane, where their seasonal menus reflect the Asian and European influences that made them famous under Wolfgang Puck. The bar area is comfortable and inviting, with both cocktail tables and bar seating. The dining room isn't too fancy or pretentious, but is well lit and decorated with bright artwork. But where the Gingrasses' expertise really shines is in the food. The bread alone is worth writing home about. Each dish arrives beautifully presented with whimsical accents. If it's on the menu, don't pass up the black cod appetizer served with a miso glaze and spinach rolls. The light, flaky seafood tempura with a vegetable salad is another show-stopper, as is the main course of quail glazed with maple and perched on the most delightful potato gratin. The desserts are as good to look at as they are to eat.

MODERATE

✪ **Bizou.** 598 4th St. (at Brannan St.). ☎ **415/543-2222.** Reservations recommended. Main courses $10.50–$17.50. AE, MC, V. Mon–Thurs 11:30am–2:30pm and 5:30–10pm, Fri 11:30am–2:30pm and 5:30–10:30pm, Sat 5:30–10:30pm. Bus: 15, 30, 32, 42, or 45. FRENCH/ITALIAN.

Bizou's friendly and professional service staff, fresh and creative fare, and sizable portions keep locals coming back again and again. The menu's starters include pizzas, grilled calamari with a citrus salsa and salsa verde, and batter-fried green beans with dipping sauce. The main courses may include sautéed sea bass with olive couscous, fennel, bay leaf, and dried orange peel; or grilled veal tenderloin with sautéed spinach, and garlic mashed potatoes bathing in a buttery mustard sauce. Our only complaint is that literally every dish is so rich and powerfully flavored (including the salads) that it's a bit of a sensory overload.

✪ **Fringale Restaurant.** 570 4th St. (between Brannan and Bryant sts.). ☎ **415/543-0573.** Reservations recommended at least a week in advance. Main courses $9–$18; lunch $4–$12. AE, MC, V. Mon–Fri 11:30am–2:30pm and 5:30–10:30pm, Sat 5:30–10:30pm. Bus: 30 or 45. FRENCH.

One of San Francisco's top restaurants, Fringale—colloquial French for "sudden urge to eat"—has enjoyed a week-long waiting list since the day chef/co-owner Gerald Hirigoyen first opened this small SoMa bistro. Sponged, eggshell-blue walls and other muted sand and earth tones provide a serene dining environment, which is all but shattered when the 15-table room inevitably fills with Hirigoyen's fans. For starters, try his potato and goat cheese galette with black olives. Among the dozen or so main courses you might find a filet of tuna basquais, pork tenderloin confit with onion and apple marmalade, or macaroni gratin with mushrooms. The desserts are worth savoring too, particularly the hazelnut and roasted almond mousse cake or the signature crème brûlée with vanilla bean.

✪ **Lulu.** 816 Folsom St. (at 4th St.). ☎ **415/495-5775.** Reservations recommended. Main courses $7–$13 at lunch, $9–$17 at dinner. AE, MC, V. Mon–Fri 7am–midnight, Sat 9am–midnight, Sun 9am–11pm. Bus: 15, 30, 32, 42, or 45. CONTINENTAL.

It's the energy of this enormous, converted warehouse dining room, the pizzas sliding in and out of the wood-fired oven, and the chefs communicating via headsets that make dining here not just a meal but a beloved event. The main room seats 170, but even as you sit amid a sea of stylish diners, the room somehow feels warm and convivial.

Don't pass up the roasted mussels piled high on an iron skillet; the chopped salad with lemon, anchovies, and tomatoes; the pork loin with fennel, garlic, and olive oil; and any of the other wonderful dishes. Everything is served "family style" and is meant to be shared. Save room for dessert—opt for the gooey chocolate cake that oozes with chocolate to be scooped up with the side of melting ice cream.

INEXPENSIVE

Hamburger Mary's. 1582 Folsom St. (at 12th St.). ☎ **415/626-5767.** Reservations recommended. Main courses $6–$9; breakfast $5–$9. AE, DC, DISC, MC, V. Mon–Thurs 11am–1am, Fri 11:30am–2am, Sat 10am–2am, Sun 10am–1am. Bus: 9, 12, 42, or 47. AMERICAN.

San Francisco's most alternative burger joint attracts all kinds—from the late-night SoMa dance club crowd to gays, lesbians, and bikers. The restaurant's kitsch decor includes thrift-shop floral wallpaper, family photos, garage-sale prints, stained glass, religious drawings, and Oriental screens. You'll get to know the bar well—it's where you'll stand with the tattooed masses while you wait for a table. Don't despair—they mix a good drink, and people-watching is what you're here for anyway. Sandwiches, salads, and vegetarian dishes provide an alternative to the famous greasy burgers.

HAIGHT-ASHBURY

✪ **Cha Cha Cha.** 1801 Haight St. (at Schrader St.). ☎ **415/386-5758.** Reservations not accepted. Tapas $4–$7; main courses $9–$13. No credit cards. Sun–Thurs 11:30am–4pm and 5–11pm, Fri–Sat 11:30am–4pm and 5–11:30pm. Muni Metro: N line. Bus: 6, 7, 66, 71, or 73. CARIBBEAN.

Cha Cha Cha is not a meal, it's an experience. Put your name on the mile-long list, crowd into the minuscule bar, and drink sangría while you wait. When you finally do get seated (it usually takes at least an hour), you'll dine in a loud (and we mean *loud*) dining room with Santería altars, banana trees, and plastic, tropical tablecloths. Order from the tapas menu and share the dishes family style (there are main courses, too). The fried calamari, fried new potatoes, Cajun shrimp, and mussels in saffron broth are all bursting with flavor and are accompanied by rich, luscious sauces—but whatever you choose, you can't go wrong. This is the kind of place where you take friends in a partying mood, let your hair down, and make an evening of it. If you want all the flavor without the festivities, come during lunch.

S **Zona Rosa.** 1797 Haight St. (at Shrader St.). ☎ **415/668-7717.** Burritos $3.50–$5. No credit cards. Daily 11am–10:30pm. Muni Metro: N line. Bus: 6, 7, 66, 71, or 73. MEXICAN.

This is a great place to stop and get a cheap (and healthy) bite. The most popular items here are the burritos, which are made to order and include your choice of beans (refried, whole pinto, or black), meats, or vegetarian ingredients. You can sit on a stool at the window and watch all the Haight Street freaks strolling by, relax at one of five colorful interior tables, or take it to go and head to Golden Gate Park (it's just 2 blocks away). Zona Rosa is one of the best burrito places around.

THE RICHMOND DISTRICT
EXPENSIVE

✪ **Alain Rondelli.** 126 Clement St. (between 2nd and 3rd aves.). ☎ **415/387-0408.** Reservations necessary Fri–Sat. Main courses $16–$19; tasting menu from $45. MC, V. Tues–Sun 5:30–10:30pm. Bus: 2 or 38. FRENCH.

French chef Alain Rondelli does more than simply serve exquisite—and innovative—French food; he dishes up a gastronomic experience you're likely to dream about for years to come. You may order à la carte, but you'd be better off ordering from the 6-, 9-, 12-, or 20-course tasting menus (for the entire table only). To complete the experience, wine can be ordered by the half glass. The grandest conjuration of all is that after such a didactic and tantalizing feast, you'll feel light as a feather, entirely satiated but not overly full, and you'll float out the front door onto Clement street as relaxed as if you just had a massage. If you're debating between dining here and at La Folie, bear in mind that Rondelli's portions are smaller and the atmosphere is far more formal.

Fountain Court. 354 Clement St. ☎ **415/668-1100.** Reservations accepted. Most main courses $6.50–$10.50. AE, DC, MC, V. Daily 11am–3pm and 5–10pm. SHANGHAI.

The decor is nothing special here, but the food sure is. We went with a crowd and ordered about a half-dozen dishes. Each was better than the last. Start with the pot stickers, which will arrive at your table in a bamboo steamer. A dining companion declared the garlic prawns were better than sex—we don't know if we'd go that far, but they were pretty darn good. Specials are offered nightly. When we where there, the special dishes were garlic crab (superb) and soft-shell turtle (less successful). We loved the spicy orange and sautéed eel. You can't go wrong here.

✪ Hong Kong Flower Lounge. 5322 Geary Blvd. (between 17th and 18th aves.). ☎ **415/668-8998.** Most main dishes $6–$11; dim sum dishes $1.20–$3.20. Mon–Fri 11am–2:30pm and 5–9:30pm, Sat–Sun 10am–2:30pm and 5–9:30pm. Bus: 1, 2, or 38. CHINESE/DIM SUM.

You know you're at a good Chinese restaurant when most people waiting for a table are Chinese. And if you come for dim sum, be prepared to stand in line because you won't be the only one who's heard that this is the best in town—us included, since the Hong Kong Flower Lounge has been one of our very favorite restaurants for years now. It's not the pink-and-green decor or the live fish swimming in the tank, or even the beautiful marble bathrooms—it's simply that every little dish that comes our way is so darn good. Don't pass up tarot cake, salt-fried shrimp, shark-fin soup, and shrimp or beef crêpes.

✪ Kabuto Sushi. 5116 Geary Blvd. (at 15th Ave.). ☎ **415/752-5652.** Sushi $3–$8 apiece; main courses $12–$20. AE, MC, V. Tues–Sat 5:30–11pm. Bus: 2, 28, or 38. JAPANESE.

Chopsticking fish-and-rice delicacies is one of the most joyous and adventurous ways to dine, and Kabuto is one of the best (and most expensive) places to do it. Chef Sachio Kojima, who presides over the small, ever-crowded sushi bar, constructs each dish with smooth, lightning-fast movements known only to master chefs. If you're big on wasabi, ask for the stronger stuff Kojima serves on request.

THE MISSION DISTRICT
MODERATE

Val 21. 995 Valencia St. (at 21st St.). ☎ **415/821-6622.** Reservations recommended. Main courses $11–$16. MC, V. Mon–Fri 5:30–10pm, Sat–Sun 10am–2pm and 5:30–10pm. Muni Metro: J line to 16th St. Station. CALIFORNIA.

The hip, eclectic decor, perpetually friendly service, and hefty portions of multi-ethnic fare have made Val 21 one of the Mission District's most popular restaurants. The menu changes frequently, although you might find such dishes as artichoke empanada, southwestern blackened chicken, or grilled salmon in a red-curry sauce (plenty of vegetarian plates, too). Sometimes the menu gets a little too creative, sending mixed messages to your mouth, but the overall dining experience makes it worth the trip. Weekends they also serve brunch.

Woodward's Garden. 1700 Mission St. (at Duboce Ave.). ☎ **415/621-7122.** Reservations required. Main courses $14–$17. Dinner seatings Wed–Sun at 6, 6:30, 8, and 8:30pm. MC, V. Bus: 14, 26, or 49. AMERICAN.

If you find yourself parking along a dank industrial street where no decent restaurant would dare to set up shop, you're in the right place. Woodward's Garden, named after a turn-of-the-century amusement center in the same location, is the kind of gem many San Franciscans don't even know about. And good thing—there are only nine tables in the entire place. Its simple decor and intimate—okay, tiny—environment make for sincerely romantic dining. And with so few tables, both the kitchen (formerly of Postrio and Greens) and the service staff are attentive enough to make you feel that they opened their doors just for you. Don't traipse down here without reservations—or a car, for that matter.

5 The Top Attractions

✪ **Alcatraz Island.** Pier 41, near Fisherman's Wharf. ☎ **415/705-1045.** Admission (including ferry trip and audio tour) $10 adults, $8.25 seniors 62 and older, $4.75 children 5–11. Advance purchase advised. Summer, daily 9:15am–4:15pm; winter, daily 9:30am–2:45pm. Ferries depart twice an hour, at 15 and 45 minutes after the hour (arrive at least 20 minutes before sailing time).

Visible from Fisherman's Wharf, Alcatraz Island (known as "The Rock") has seen a checkered history. It was discovered in 1775 by Juan Manuel Ayala, who named it after the many pelicans that nested on the island. From the 1850s to 1933, when the army vacated the island, it served as a military post protecting the bay shoreline. In 1934 the buildings of the military outpost were converted into a maximum-security federal prison. Given the sheer cliffs, treacherous tides and currents, and frigid temperatures of the waters, it was believed to be totally escape-proof. Among the infamous gangsters who were penned in cell blocks A through D were Al Capone, "Machine Gun" Kelly, and Alvin Karpis. Inmate Robert Stroud became famous as the Birdman of Alcatraz because he was an expert in ornithological diseases.

It cost a fortune to keep inmates imprisoned here because all supplies, including water, had to be shipped in. In 1963, after an apparent escape in which no bodies were recovered, the government closed the prison, and in 1972 it became part of the Golden Gate National Recreation Area. The wildlife that was driven away during the military and prison years has begun to return—the black-crested night heron and other sea birds are nesting here again—and a new trail has been built that passes through the island's nature areas. Tours, including an audio tour of the prison block and a slide show, are given by the park's rangers, who entertain their guests with interesting anecdotes.

It's a popular excursion and space is limited, so purchase tickets as far in advance as possible. The tour is operated by **Red & White Fleet** (☎ **800/229-2784** in California, or 415/546-2700) and can be charged to a credit card (AE, MC, V; $2 per ticket service charge on phone orders). Tickets may also be purchased in advance from the Red & White Fleet ticket office on Pier 41.

Wear comfortable shoes and take a heavy sweater or windbreaker because the island is cold even when the sun's out. The National Park Service also notes that there are a lot of steps to climb on the tour.

For those who want to get a closer look at Alcatraz without going ashore, two boat-tour operators offer short circumnavigations of the island (see "Organized Tours," later in this chapter).

✪ **The Cable Cars.** ☎ **415/673-6864.** Fare $2 ($1 seniors 6–7am and 9pm–midnight).

Designated official historic landmarks by the National Park Service in 1964, the city's beloved cable cars clank across the hills like mobile museum pieces. Each weighs

Major San Francisco Attractions

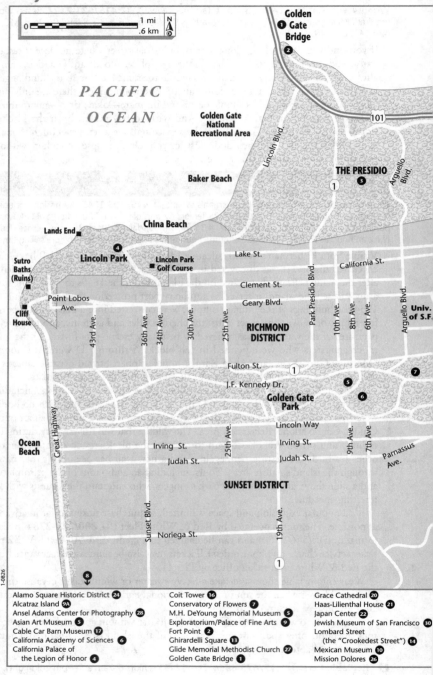

PACIFIC OCEAN

Golden Gate Bridge ❶
❷
Golden Gate National Recreational Area

THE PRESIDIO ❸

Baker Beach

Lincoln Blvd.

101

Arguello Blvd.

Lands End
China Beach

Lincoln Park ❹
Lincoln Park Golf Course

Sutro Baths (Ruins)

Cliff House
Point Lobos Ave.

Lake St.
California St.
Clement St.
Geary Blvd.

Park Presidio Blvd.
10th Ave.
8th Ave.
6th Ave.
Arguello Blvd.
Univ. of S.F.

43rd Ave.
36th Ave.
34th Ave.
30th Ave.
25th Ave.

RICHMOND DISTRICT

Fulton St. ❶
J.F. Kennedy Dr.
❺
Golden Gate Park ❻
❼

Lincoln Way

Ocean Beach

Great Highway

Irving St.
25th Ave.
Irving St.
Judah St.
Judah St.
9th Ave.
7th Ave.
Parnassus Ave.

SUNSET DISTRICT

Sunset Blvd.
19th Ave.

Noriega St.

❶

❽

1-0826

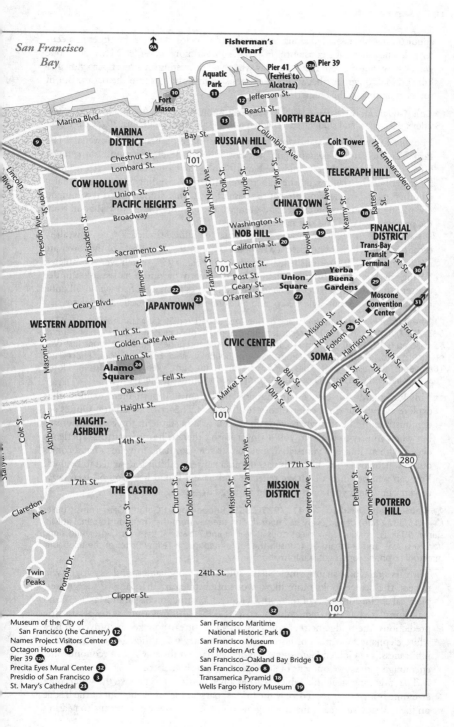

San Francisco Bay

Fisherman's Wharf

9A

Aquatic Park

10 Fort Mason

Pier 41 (Ferries to Alcatraz) **11**

12A Pier 39

12 Jefferson St.

Beach St.

Marina Blvd.

13

NORTH BEACH

MARINA DISTRICT

Bay St.

RUSSIAN HILL

Columbus Ave.

Coit Tower

9

Chestnut St.

Lombard St.

101

14

16

TELEGRAPH HILL

The Embarcadero

COW HOLLOW

Lincoln Blvd.

Union St.

15

Grant Ave.

Kearny St.

Battery St.

Lyon Ave.

PACIFIC HEIGHTS

Broadway

Van Ness Ave.

Polk St.

Hyde St.

Taylor St.

CHINATOWN

17

18

Presidio Ave.

Divisadero St.

Fillmore St.

Gough St.

21

Washington St.

NOB HILL

California St.

Powell St.

19

FINANCIAL DISTRICT

Trans-Bay Transit Terminal

20

Sacramento St.

Franklin St.

101

Sutter St.

1st St.

30

Post St.

Union Square

Yerba Buena Gardens

29

Geary Blvd.

Geary St.

O'Farrell St.

27

Moscone Convention Center

31

22

23

JAPANTOWN

WESTERN ADDITION

Masonic St.

Turk St.

Golden Gate Ave.

CIVIC CENTER

Mission St.

Howard St.

Folsom St.

Harrison St.

28

3rd St.

4th St.

Fulton St.

SOMA

Bryant St.

5th St.

6th St.

Alamo Square **24**

Fell St.

Oak St.

Market St.

8th St.

9th St.

10th St.

7th St.

280

Haight St.

Cole St.

Ashbury St.

HAIGHT-ASHBURY

14th St.

26

South Van Ness Ave.

17th St.

Stanyan St.

25

17th St.

THE CASTRO

Church St.

Dolores St.

Mission St.

MISSION DISTRICT

Potrero Ave.

Deharo St.

Connecticut St.

POTRERO HILL

Claredon Ave.

Castro St.

Twin Peaks

Portola Dr.

24th St.

Clipper St.

32

101

Museum of the City of
San Francisco (the Cannery) **12**
Names Project Visitors Center **25**
Octagon House **15**
Pier 39 **12A**
Precita Eyes Mural Center **32**
Presidio of San Francisco **3**
St. Mary's Cathedral **23**

San Francisco Maritime
National Historic Park **11**
San Francisco Museum
of Modern Art **29**
San Francisco–Oakland Bay Bridge **31**
San Francisco Zoo **8**
Transamerica Pyramid **18**
Wells Fargo History Museum **19**

about 6 tons and is hauled along by a steel cable, enclosed under the street in a center rail. They move at a constant $9^1/2$ m.p.h.—never more, never less. This may strike you as slow, but it doesn't feel that way when you're cresting an almost perpendicular hill and look down at what seems like a bobsled dive straight into the ocean. But in spite of the thrills, they're perfectly safe.

✪ **Coit Tower.** Atop Telegraph Hill. ☎ **415/362-0808.** Admission (to the top of the tower) $3 adults, $2 seniors and students, $1 children 6–12. Daily 10am–6pm. Bus: 39 ("Coit").

In a city known for its panoramic views and vantage points, Coit Tower is "The Peak." Located atop Telegraph Hill, just east of North Beach, the round, stone tower offers 360° views of the city and the bay. If you're there on a clear day, it's wonderful to get here by walking up the Filbert Steps (thereby avoiding a traffic nightmare) and then taking in the panorama at the base of the tower. (In fact, we'd recommend not paying the admission charge and going to the top; the view is just as good from the parking area and you can see the murals for free.)

Completed in 1933, the tower is the legacy of Lillie Hitchcock Coit, a wealthy eccentric who left San Francisco a $125,000 bequest. Inside the base of the tower are the impressive WPA murals titled *Life in California, 1934,* which were completed during the New Deal by more than 25 artists, many of whom had studied under master muralist Diego Rivera. The individual frescoes form a unified whole, all done in traditional Mexican-style fresco, and all done with the same scale and palette.

✪ **The Exploratorium.** In the Palace of Fine Arts, 3601 Lyon St. (at Marina Blvd.). ☎ **415/563-7337,** or 415/561-0360 for recorded information. Admission $9 adults, $7 senior citizens, $5 children 6–17, $2.50 children 3–5, free for children 2 and under, free for everyone first Wed of each month. Memorial Day–Labor Day and holidays, Wed 10am–9:30pm, Thurs–Tues 10am–6pm; the rest of year, Tues and Thurs–Sun 10am–5pm, Wed 10am–9:30pm. Closed Thanksgiving and Christmas Day. Bus: 30 from Stockton St. to the Marina stop.

This fun, hands-on science fair contains more than 650 permanent exhibits that explore everything from color theory to Einstein's Theory of Relativity. Optics are demonstrated in booths where you can see a bust of a statue in three dimensions—but when you try to touch it, you discover it isn't there! The same surreal experience occurs with an image of yourself: When you stretch your hand forward, a hand comes out to touch you—but the hands pass in midair. Every exhibit is designed to be used. You can whisper into a concave reflector and have a friend hear you 60 feet away, or you can design your own animated abstract art—using sound.

✪ **Golden Gate Bridge.** ☎ **415/921-5858.** Bridge-bound Golden Gate Transit buses (☎ 415/332-6600) depart every half hour during the day from the Transbay Terminal at Mission and 1st sts., making convenient stops at Market and 7th sts., at the Civic Center, and along Van Ness Ave. and Lombard St. (consult the route map in the Yellow Pages of the telephone directory or phone for schedule information).

With its gracefully swung single span, spidery bracing cables, and sky-high twin towers, the bridge looks more like a work of abstract art than one of the greatest practical engineering feats of the 20th Century. Construction began in May 1937 and was completed at the then-colossal cost of $35 million. Contrary to pessimistic predictions, the bridge neither collapsed in a gale or earthquake nor proved to be a white elephant. A symbol of hope when the country was afflicted with widespread joblessness, the Golden Gate single-handedly changed the Bay Area's economic life, encouraging the development of areas north of San Francisco.

The mile-long steel link, which reaches a height of 746 feet above the water, is an awesome bridge to cross. To view the bridge, park in the lot at the foot of the bridge on the city side and make the crossing by foot. Back in your car, continue to Marin's

Vista Point, at the bridge's northern end. Look back and you'll be rewarded with one of the most famous cityscape views in the world.

Millions of pedestrians walk across the bridge each year. You can walk out onto the span from either end. Note that it's usually windy and cold, and the bridge vibrates. Still, walking even a short way is one of the best ways to experience the immense scale of the structure.

Museum of Modern Art. 151 3rd St. (2 blocks south of Market St., across from Yerba Buena Gardens). ☎ **415/357-4000.** Admission $7 adults, $3.50 seniors and students 14–18, free for children 13 and under, free for everyone the first Tues of each month. Tues–Wed and Fri–Sun 11am–6pm, Thurs 11am–9pm. Docent tours offered daily. Closed holidays. Muni Metro: J, K, L, or M to Montgomery Station. Bus: 15, 30, or 45.

Swiss architect Mario Botta, in association with Hellmuth, Obata & Kassabaum, designed this $62 million building, which doubled the musuem's space when it opened South of Market in 1995. MOMA's collection consists of more than 15,000 works, including close to 5,000 paintings and sculptures by such artists as Henri Matisse, Jackson Pollock, and Willem de Kooning (although all are not on display simultaneously). Other artists represented include Diego Rivera, Georgia O'Keeffe, Paul Klee, the Fauvists, and exceptional holdings of Richard Diebenkorn. MOMA was also one of the first museums to recognize photography as a major art form; its extensive collection includes over 9,000 photographs by such notables as Ansel Adams, Alfred Steiglitz, Edward Weston, and Henri Cartier-Bresson.

Docent-led tours are offered daily. Times are posted at the museum's admission desk. Phone for current details of upcoming special events.

The Caffè Museo, located on the right of the museum entrance, sets a new precedent for museum food with flavorful and fresh soups, sandwiches, and salads that are as respectable as those served in many local restaurants.

Don't miss the Museum Store, which carries a wonderful array of architectural gifts, books, and trinkets. It's one of the best stores in town.

GOLDEN GATE PARK

This landmark urban green space is a narrow strip—3 miles long and 1½ miles wide—stretching from the Pacific coast inland. Enter the park at Kezar Drive, an extension of Fell Street, or take Bus 16AX, BX, 6, 7, 66, or 71. For information, head first to the McClaren Lodge and Park Headquarters (open Monday to Friday).

There are several special gardens in the park—notably the rhododendron dell, the rose garden, and at the western edge of the park, a springtime array of thousands of tulips and daffodils around a Dutch windmill.

Proceeding from east to west, you'll come first to the **Conservatory of Flowers.** Built for the 1894 Midwinter Exposition, this striking glass structure was modeled on the famous greenhouse at Kew Gardens in London. It contains a rotating display of plants and shrubs at all times of the year. The orchids in particular are a highlight.

The **Japanese Tea Garden** is a quiet haven of cherry trees, shrubs, and bonsai, crisscrossed by winding paths and high-backed bridges crossing over pools of water. Focal points and places for contemplation include the massive bronze Buddha that was cast in Japan in 1790 and donated by the Gump family, the Shinto wooden pagoda, and the Wishing Bridge (its reflection in the water looks as if it completes a circle).

Some 6,000 plant species grow in the **Srybing Arboretum and Botanical Gardens,** among them some very ancient plants in a special "primitive garden" and a grove of California redwoods.

Strawberry Hill, a 430-foot-high artificial island, lies at the center of **Stow Lake.** A path encircles it leading from the rustic bridge around to the Chinese Pavilion. The boathouse on the lake rents pedalboats, rowboats, and other craft.

In addition, the park contains numerous recreational facilities: tennis courts; baseball, soccer, and polo fields; a golf course; riding stables; fly-casting pools; and boat rentals at the Strawberry Hill boathouse. See Section 9, "Outdoor Activities & Spectator Sports," later in this chapter, for details on each facility.

The park is also home to the following:

M. H. De Young Memorial Museum. In Golden Gate Park near 10th Ave. and Fulton St. ☎ **415/750-3600,** or 415/863-3330 for recorded information. Admission (including the Asian Art Museum and California Palace of the Legion of Honor) $6 adults, $4 seniors 65 and over, $3 youths 12–17, free for children 11 and under (fees may be higher for special exhibitions); reduced admission for everyone the first Wed of each month. Wed–Sun 10am–4:45pm (to 8:45pm the first Wed of the month). Bus: 44.

Best known for its American art from colonial times to the 20th century, this museum displays paintings, sculpture, furniture, and decorative arts by such diverse talents as Paul Revere, Winslow Homer, John Singer Sargent, and Georgia O'Keeffe. Note in particular the American landscapes, as well as the trompe-l'oeil and still-life works from the turn of the century. There's also an important textile collection, with primary emphasis on rugs from Central Asia and the Near East. Other collections on view include ancient art from Egypt, Greece, and Rome; decorative art from Africa, Oceania, and the Americas; and British art by Gainsborough, Reynolds, Lawrence, Raeburn, and others. Special temporary exhibits are staged. Docent tours are offered daily; call for times.

The museum's Café de Young is exceptional. In summer visitors can dine in the garden, among bronze statuary. The cafe is open Wednesday to Sunday from 10am to 4pm.

Asian Art Museum. In Golden Gate Park near 10th Ave. and Fulton St. ☎ **415/668-8921,** or 415/752-2635 for the hearing impaired. Admission (including the M. H. de Young Memorial Museum and California Palace of the Legion of Honor) $6 adults, $4 seniors 65 and over, $3 youth 12–17, free for children 11 and under (fees may be higher for special exhibitions); reduced admission for everyone the first Wed (all day) and first Sat (10am–noon) of each month. Wed–Sun 10am–4:45pm. Bus: 44.

Adjacent to the M. H. de Young Museum and the Japanese Tea Garden, this museum can only display about 1,800 pieces from its vast collection of 12,000 at any given time. About half the works exhibited are in the ground-floor Chinese and Korean galleries, including sculpture, paintings, bronzes, ceramics, jades, and decorative objects. There's also a wide range of exhibits from Pakistan, India, Tibet, Japan, and Southeast Asia, including the world's oldest-known dated Chinese Buddha. The museum's daily guided tours are recommended; call for times.

California Academy of Sciences. On the Music Concourse of Golden Gate Park. ☎ **415/221-5100,** or 415/750-7145 for recorded information. Admission: Aquarium and museum, $7 adults, $4 students 12–17 and seniors 65 and over, $1.50 children 6–11, free for children 5 and under, free for everyone the first Wed of every month; planetarium shows, $2.50 adults, $1.25 children 17 and under and seniors 65 and over. Sunday before Labor Day to July 3, daily 10am–5pm; July 4–Saturday Day, daily 10am–7pm; first Wed of every month 10am–9pm. Muni Metro: N line ("Judah") to Golden Gate Park. Bus: 5 ("Fulton"), 44 ("O'Shaughnessy"), or 71 ("Haight-Noreiga").

This group of three related museums—the Steinhart Aquarium, the Morrison Planetarium, and the Natural History Museum—is clustered around the Music Concourse. The **Steinhart Aquarium** houses some 14,000 specimens, including

Golden Gate Park

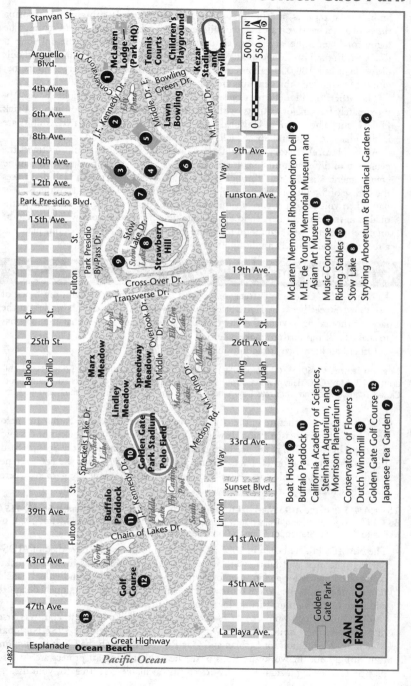

Stanyan St.

Arguello Blvd.

4th Ave.

6th Ave.

8th Ave.

10th Ave.

12th Ave.

Park Presidio Blvd.

15th Ave.

25th St.

Balboa

Cabrillo

39th Ave.

43rd Ave.

47th Ave.

Esplanade

Ocean Beach

Pacific Ocean

Conservatory Dr.

McLaren Lodge — (Park HQ)

Tennis Courts

Children's Playground

Kezar Stadium and Pavilion

J.F. Kennedy Dr.

Lily Pond

Middle Dr. E.

Bowling Green Dr.

Lawn Bowling

M.L. King Dr.

9th Ave.

Funston Ave.

Lincoln Way

Park Presidio By-Pass Dr.

St.

Stow Lake Dr.

Strawberry Hill

Cross-Over Dr.

Transverse Dr.

19th Ave.

Lloyd Lake

Marx Meadow

Speedway Meadow

Overlook Dr.

Middle Dr.

Elk Glen Lake

Mallard Lake

Metson Dr.

M.L. King Dr.

St.

St.

26th Ave.

Irving

Judah

Lindley Meadow

Golden Gate Park Stadium Polo Field

Spreckels Lake Dr.

Spreckels Lake

Metson Lake

Medson Rd.

33rd Ave.

Sunset Blvd.

Buffalo Paddock

J.F. Kennedy Dr.

Middle

Fly Casting Pool

South Lake

Lincoln

41st Ave

Fulton

Chain of Lakes Dr.

North Lake

45th Ave.

Golf Course

La Playa Ave.

Great Highway

SAN FRANCISCO

Golden Gate Park

- McLaren Memorial Rhododendron Dell ❷
- M.H. de Young Memorial Museum and Asian Art Museum ❸
- Music Concourse ❹
- Riding Stables ❿
- Stow Lake ❽
- Strybing Arboretum & Botanical Gardens ❻
- Boat House ❾
- Buffalo Paddock ⓫
- California Academy of Sciences, Steinhart Aquarium, and Morrison Planetarium ❺
- Conservatory of Flowers ❶
- Dutch Windmill ⓭
- Golden Gate Golf Course ⓬
- Japanese Tea Garden ❼

N

500 m
550 y

0

1-0827

107

amphibians, reptiles, marine mammals, and penguins. It contains a California tidepool and a hands-on area where children can touch starfish and sea urchins. The living coral reef is the largest display of its kind in the country and the only one in the West. In the Fish Roundabout, visitors are surrounded by fast-swimming schools of fish kept in a 100,000-gallon tank. Seals and dolphins are fed every 2 hours, beginning at 10:30am; the penguins are fed at 11:30am and 4pm.

The **Morrison Planetarium** presents sky shows as well as laser-light shows. Approximately four major exhibits, with titles such as "Star Death: The Birth of Black Holes" and "The Universe Unveiled," are presented each year. Related exhibits are in the adjacent Earth and Space Hall. Call for show schedules and information.

At the **Natural History Museum,** the Wattis Hall of Human Cultures traces the evolution of different human cultures and shows how they adapted to their natural environment. Visitors walk through an exhibit in McBean-Peterson Hall that traces the course of 3.5 billion years of evolution from the earliest life forms to the present day. Then you can experience a simulation of two of San Francisco's biggest earthquakes in the Hohfeld Earth and Space Hall, determine what your weight would be on other planets, see a real moon rock, and learn about the rotation of our planet at a replica of Foucault's Pendulum.

6 Exploring the City

Known as the "crookedest street in the world," the whimsically winding block of **Lombard Street** between Hyde Street and Leavenworth Street puts smiles on the faces of thousands of visitors each year. The elevation is so steep that the road has to snake back and forth to make a descent possible.

Other San Francisco attractions include the following:

Mission Dolores. 16th St. (at Dolores St.). ☎ **415/621-8203.** Admission $2 adults, $1 children 5–12. May–Oct, daily 9am–4:30pm; Nov–Apr, daily 9am–4pm; Good Fri 10am–noon. Closed Thanksgiving and Christmas Day. Muni Metro: J line to the corner of Church and 16th sts. Bus: 22.

This is the oldest structure in the city, built on order of Franciscan Father Junípero Serra by Father Francisco Palou. It was constructed of 36,000 sun-baked bricks and dedicated in June 1776 at the northern terminus of El Camino Real, the Spanish road from Mexico to California. It's a moving place to visit to observe the cool, serene buildings with their thick adobe walls and most of all, the cemetery-gardens where the early settlers are buried.

The NAMES Project AIDS Memorial Quilt Visitors Center. 2362-A Market St. ☎ **415/863-1966.** Free admission. Daily noon–10pm, Thurs–Tues noon–7pm. Muni Metro: J, K, L, or M line to Castro St. Station; or F line to Church and Market sts.

The NAMES Project began in 1987 as a memorial to those who have died of AIDS. Sewing machines and fabric were acquired, and the public was invited to make coffin-sized panels for a giant memorial quilt. More than 28,000 individual panels now commemorate the lives of those who have died. Each has been uniquely designed and sewn by the victims' friends, lovers, and family members.

The Quilt, which would cover 11 football fields if laid out end to end, was first displayed on the Capitol Mall in Washington, D.C., during the 1987 National March on Washington for Lesbian and Gay Rights. Although the Quilt is often on tour throughout the world, portions of the heart-wrenching art project are on display here. A sewing machine and fabrics are also available here, free, for your use.

The San Francisco Experience. At Fisherman's Wharf, on the waterfront at Embarcadero and Beach St. ☎ **415/388-6032.** Admission $7 adults, $6 seniors 55 and over, $4 children 5–16.

Jan–Mar, shows daily every half hour 10am–8:30pm; the rest of the year, shows daily every half hour 10am–9:30pm. Call for details; the show was planning to relocate in 1996.

Two centuries of San Francisco history are condensed into about 30 minutes in this multimedia show that lets you see, hear, and experience events from the city's past. From the city's founding to the Gold Rush, the Great Earthquake, and the Summer of Love, the life and times of San Francisco are conveyed in a light and informative manner on a 70- by 35-foot screen. In addition, some unique city features and events are simulated in 3-D, including a San Francisco "fog" that really rolls in.

ARCHITECTURAL HIGHLIGHTS

The Alamo Square Historic District contains many of the city's 14,000 Victorian **"Painted Ladies,"** homes that have been restored and ornately painted by residents. The small area—bordered by Divisadero Street on the west, Golden Gate Avenue on the north, Webster Street on the east, and Fell Street on the south, about 10 blocks west of the Civic Center—has one of the city's largest concentrations of these. One of the most famous views of San Francisco, which you'll see on postcards and posters all around the city, depicts sharp-edged Financial District skyscrapers behind a row of Victorians. This view can be seen from Alamo Square at Fulton and Steiner streets.

Built in 1881 to a design by Brown and Bakewell, **City Hall** and the **Civic Center** are part of a City Beautiful complex done in the beaux arts style. The dome rises to a height of 308 feet on the exterior and is ornamented with occuli and topped by a lantern. The interior rotunda soars 112 feet and is finished in oak, marble, and limestone with a monumental marble staircase leading to the second floor.

The **Flood Mansion,** 1000 California St., at Mason, was built in 1885–86 for James Clair Flood who, thanks to the Comstock Lode, rose from a bartender to one of the city's wealthiest men. The house cost $1.5 million (the fence alone carried a price tag of $30,000!). It was designed by Augustus Laver and modified by Willis Polk after the earthquake to accommodate the Pacific Union Club.

The **Haas-Lilienthal House,** 2007 Franklin St., at Washington (☎ 415/441-3004), is one of the city's most flamboyant Queen Anne–style Victorians. The 1886 structure features all the architectural frills of the period, including dormer windows, flying cupolas, ornate trim, and wistful turrets. The house is maintained by the Foundation for San Francisco's Architectural Heritage, which offers tours 2 days a week for $5 for adults, $3 for seniors and children 6 to 12; it's open on Wednesday from noon to 3:15pm and on Sunday from 11am to 4:15pm.

The **Garden Court,** in the Sheraton Palace Hotel, 2 New Montgomery St. (☎ 415/392-8600), is an enclosed courtyard covered by a lofty iridescent glass roof that's supported by 16 Doric marble columns. Rebuilt in 1909 after the Great Earthquake and meticulously restored, it's worth seeing.

The **Octagon House,** 2645 Gough St., at Union Street (☎ 415/441-7512), is an eight-sided, cupola-topped house dating from 1861. Its architectural features are extraordinary, especially the circular staircase and ceiling medallion. Inside, you'll find furniture, silverware, and American pewter from the Colonial and Federal periods. There are also some historic documents, including signatures of 54 of the 56 signers of the Declaration of Independence. Even if you're not able to visit during open hours, this strange structure is worth a look. It's open on the second Sunday and second and fourth Thursday of each month from noon to 3pm; closed January and holidays.

The **Palace of Fine Arts,** on Baker between Jefferson and Bay streets, is the only building to survive from the Pan Pacific Exhibition of 1915. Constructed by Bernard Maybeck, it was rebuilt in concrete using molds taken from the original in the 1950s.

The **Transamerica Pyramid,** 600 Montgomery St., is the tallest structure in San Francisco's skyline—48 stories tall and capped by a 212-foot spire. It was completed in 1972.

Although the **San Francisco–Oakland Bay Bridge** (☎ **510/464-1148** for information) is visually less appealing than the Golden Gate Bridge (see "The Top Attractions," earlier in this chapter), in many ways it's more spectacular. Opened in 1936, before the Golden Gate, it's 8¹/₄ miles long, one of the world's longest steel bridges. It's not a single bridge at all, but actually a dovetailed series of spans joined in midbay—at Yerba Buena Island—by one of the world's largest (in diameter) tunnels. To the west of Yerba Buena, the bridge is really two separate suspension bridges, joined at a central anchorage. East of the island is a 1,400-foot cantilever span, followed by a succession of truss bridges.

Yerba Buena Center/Gardens, between Mission and Howard streets, at 3rd Street, opened in 1993 adjacent to the Moscone Convention Center. It's the city's version of New York's Lincoln Center. The center consists of two buildings, a 755-seat theater designed by James Stewart Polshek, and the Arts Forum, which was conceived by Fumihiko Maki and which features three galleries and a space for dance. The complex also includes a 5-acre garden featuring several artworks, the most dramatic being a mixed-media memorial to Martin Luther King, Jr., created by sculptor Houston Conwill, poet Estella Majoza, and architect Joseph de Pace. It features 12 glass panels, each inscribed with quotations from King, sheltered behind a 50-foot-high waterfall.

CHURCHES

Glide Memorial United Methodist Church. 330 Ellis St. ☎ **415/771-6300.** Services held Sun at 9 and 11am. Muni Metro: Powell. Bus: 37.

There would be nothing special about this plain Tenderloin-area church if it weren't for its exhilarating pastor, Cecil Williams. Williams's enthusiastic and uplifting preaching and singing with the homeless and poor people of the neighborhood has attracted nationwide fame. Go for an uplifting experience.

Grace Cathedral. California St. (between Taylor and Jones sts.). ☎ **415/776-6611.** Free admission. Cable car: California line.

The initial design was begun in 1928–29 by architect Lewis P. Hobart on the site of the Crocker mansion, but it wasn't completed until 1964. Although it looks as if it's made of stone, in fact it's constructed of reinforced concrete that was beaten to achieve a stonelike effect. Among the more interesting features of the building are its stained-glass windows, particularly those by the French Loire studios depicting such modern figures as Thurgood Marshall, Robert Frost, and Albert Einstein; the replicas of Ghiberti's bronze "Doors of Paradise" at the east end; the series of religious frescoes completed in the 1940s by Polish artist John de Rosen; and the 44-bell carillon.

MUSEUMS

Ansel Adams Center for Photography. 250 4th St. ☎ **415/495-7000.** Admission $4 adults, $3 students, $2 seniors and children 12–17. Tues–Sun 11am–5pm (to 8pm the first Thurs of each month). Muni Metro: Powell. Bus: 9X, 30, or 45.

This popular SOMA museum features five separate galleries for changing exhibitions of contemporary and historical photography. One area is dedicated solely to displaying the works and exploring the legacy of Ansel Adams.

Cable Car Barn Museum. Washington and Mason sts. ☎ **415/474-1887.** Free admission. Apr–Oct, daily 10am–6pm; Nov–Mar, daily 10am–5pm. Cable car: Both Powell St. lines stop at the museum.

If you've ever wondered how cable cars work, this nifty museum will explain (and demonstrate!) it all to you. Yes, this is a museum, but the Cable car Barn is no stuffed shirt. It's the living powerhouse, repair shop, and storage place of the cable-car system and is in full operation. The exposed machinery, which pulls the cables under San Francisco's streets, looks like a Rube Goldberg invention. Watch the massive groaning and vibrating winches as they thread the cable that hauls the cars through a huge figure-8 and back into the system via slack-absorbing tension wheels. You can go through the room where you can see the cables operating underground. There's also a shop where you can buy a variety of cable-car gifts.

✪ **California Palace of the Legion of Honor.** In Lincoln Park at 4th Ave. and Clement St. ☎ **415/750-3600,** or 415/863-3330 for recorded information. Admission (including the Asian Art Museum and M. H. de Young Memorial Museum) $6 adults, $4 seniors 65 and over, $3 youths 12–17, free for children 11 and under (fees may be higher for special exhibitions), free for everyone the second Wed of each month. Tues–Sun 10am–4:45pm (10am–8:45pm the first Sat of the month). Bus: 18 or 38.

Designed as a memorial to California's World War I casualties, this neoclassical structure is an exact replica of the Legion of Honor Palace in Paris, right down to the inscription HONNEUR ET PATRIE above the portal. Reopened after a 2-year, $29-million renovation and seismic upgrading project that was stalled by the discovery of almost 300 turn-of-the-century coffins, the museum's collection contains paintings, sculpture, and decorative arts from Europe, as well as international tapestries, prints, and drawings. The chronological display of more than 800 years of European art includes a fine collection of Rodin sculpture.

The Jewish Museum San Francisco. 121 Steuart St. (between Mission and Howard sts.). ☎ **415/543-8880.** Admission $3 adults, $1.50 students and seniors, free for everyone the first Mon of each month. Mon–Wed noon–6pm, Thurs noon–8pm, Sun 11am–6pm.

This museum hosts a variety of shows that concentrate on immigration, assimilation, and identity of the Jewish community in the United States and around the world. They are illustrated by paintings, sculpture, photographs, and installation art. The museum is moving in 1998 to the nearby Yerba Buena Gardens area.

Mexican Museum. Building D, Fort Mason, Marina Blvd. (at Laguna St.). ☎ **415/441-0404.** Admission $3 adults, $2 children 11 and over, free for children 10 and under and for everyone the first Wed of the month. Wed–Sun noon–5pm. Bus: 76 to 28.

This gallery, which will be relocating to the Yerba Buena Center area in 1998, maintains a collection of art covering pre-Hispanic, colonial, folk, Mexican fine art, and Chicano/Mexican-American art. A recent show featured religious works by New Mexican women.

San Francisco Maritime National Historical Park and Museum. At the foot of Polk St. (near Fisherman's Wharf). ☎ **415/556-3002.** Admission: Museum, free; ships, $2 adults, $1 children 11–17, free for children 10 and under and for seniors 63 and over. Museum, daily 10am–5pm. Ships, May 16–Sept 15, daily 10am–6pm; Sept 16–May 15, daily 9:30am–5pm. Closed New Year's Day, Thanksgiving, and Christmas Day. Cable car: Hyde Street line to the last stop. Bus: 19, 30, 32, 42, or 47.

Shaped like an art deco ship and located near Fisherman's Wharf, the National Maritime Museum is filled with sailing, whaling, and fishing lore. Exhibits include intricate model craft, scrimshaw, and a collection of shipwreck photographs and historic marine scenes, including an 1851 snapshot of hundreds of abandoned ships, deserted en masse by crews dashing off to participate in the Gold Rush. The museum's walls are lined with finely carved, painted wooden figureheads from old windjammers.

Two blocks east, at Aquatic Park's Hyde Street Pier, are several historic ships that are open to the public. The *Balclutha,* one of the last surviving square-riggers, was built in Glasgow, Scotland, in 1886 and was used to carry grain from California around Cape Horn at a near-record speed of 300 miles a day; it rounded the treacherous cape 17 times in its career. Visitors are invited to spin the wheel, squint at the compass, and imagine they're weathering a mighty storm. Kids can climb into the bunking quarters, visit the "slop chest" (galley to you, matey), and read the sea chanties (clean ones only) that decorate the walls.

The 1890 *Eureka* still carries a cargo of nostalgia for San Franciscans. It was the last of 50 paddle-wheeled ferries that regularly plied the bay; it made its final trip in 1957. Restored to its original splendor, the side-wheeler is loaded with deck cargo, including antique cars and trucks.

The black-hulled, three-masted *C. A. Thayer,* built in 1895, was used in the lumber trade carrying logs from the Pacific Northwest to the carpentry shops of California.

Other historic ships docked here include the tiny two-masted *Alma,* one of the last scow schooners to bring hay to the horses of San Francisco; the *Hercules,* a huge 1907 oceangoing steam tug; and several others.

At the pier's small-boat shop, visitors can follow the restoration progress of historic boats from the museum's collection. It's behind the maritime bookstore on your right as you approach the ships.

Wells Fargo History Museum. 420 Montgomery St. (at California St.). ☎ **415/396-2619.** Free admission. Mon–Fri 9am–5pm. Closed bank holidays. Muni Metro: Montgomery St. Bus: Any to Market St.

Wells Fargo, one of California's largest banks, was founded on the frontier, and this museum displays hundreds of frontier relics. In the center of the main room stands a Concord stagecoach, which opened the West as surely as the Winchester rifle and the iron horse locomotive. On the mezzanine you can take an imaginary ride in a replica stagecoach or send a telegraph message in code using a telegraph key and the codebooks, just the way the Wells Fargo agents did more than a century ago.

Yerba Center of the Arts Galleries. 701 Mission St. ☎ **415/978-2700.** Admission $4 adults, $2 seniors and students, free for everyone Thurs 11am–3pm. Tues–Sun 11am–6pm. Muni Metro: Powell or Montgomery. Bus: 9X, 30, or 45.

Cutting-edge computer art and multimedia shows are on view in the high-tech galleries. The initial exhibition, "The Art of *Star Wars,*" which featured the special effects created by George Lucas for the film, was a prime example.

EXPLORING SAN FRANCISCO'S NEIGHBORHOODS

THE CASTRO   Castro Street around Market and 18th streets is the center of the city's gay community, anchored by the bookstore, **A Different Light,** and the many stores, restaurants, bars, and other institutions that cater to the community. Among the landmarks are **Harvey Milk Plaza,** the **NAMES Project,** and the **Castro Theater,** a 1920s movie palace. (See Section 7, "Organized Tours," later in this chapter, for details on a walking tour of the area.)

CHINATOWN   California Street to Broadway and Kearny to Stockton streets are the boundaries of today's Chinatown. San Francisco is home to the second-largest community of Chinese in the United States (about 33% of the city's population is Chinese), but the majority of them don't live or work in these 24 blocks, although they do return to shop and dine here on weekends.

The **gateway** at Grant and Bush marks the entry to Chinatown. Walk up Grant, which has become the tourist face of Chinatown, to California Street and Old St. Mary's. The square alongside it contains Bufano's monumental **statue of Sun Yat-sen,** founder of the Chinese Republic, who had an office in the Montgomery Block and worked toward the overthrow of the emperor from here.

What a Long, Strange Trip It's Been

San Francisco's rock bands were a key element of the counterculture scene that blossomed in the city in the mid-1960s; their free-form improvisation was one of the primary expressions of the hippies' "do your own thing" principle. Until 1995 you could still experience something of that scene by attending a concert by the Grateful Dead, the quintessential psychedelic rock band. Amid all the tie-dye shirts and blissful smiles remained a set of musical values that dated back to the days of Ken Kesey and his Merry Pranksters: a no-holds-barred reliance on spontaneous improvisation, even at the expense of clarity.

San Francisco was deeply saddened in August 1995 by the death of the band's leader, Jerry Garcia, one of the city's cultural icons. Jerry played in a number of Bay Area bands before founding the Dead in 1965; they were soon headlining in counterculture strongholds like Bill Graham's Fillmore Theater in San Francisco. From June 1966 through the end of 1967 the Dead lived communally at 710 Ashbury St. in the Haight and played numerous free concerts there. As 1967's "Summer of Love" brought the flower children into full bloom, the Dead set the tone for one enormous citywide house party, liberally seasoned with ample doses of marijuana and acid.

The Grateful Dead played together for nearly 30 years. Over that span, they have released numerous LPs; *American Beauty, Workingman's Dead,* and *Europe '72,* all on Warner Brothers, are some of their better records. If you ever caught one of their concerts, you got a small glimpse of Haight-Ashbury in 1967. For now, Haight Street windows are full of memorials to Jerry Garcia, and you'll find Dead memorabilia readily available in small shops throughout the neighborhood if you'd like to take home a reminder of the band that meant so much to San Francisco.

—*Ian Wilker*

The **Chinese Historical Society of America,** at 650 Commercial St. (☎ **415/ 391-1188**), has a small but interesting collection relating to the Chinese in San Francisco.

The heart of Chinatown is at **Portsmouth Square,** where the Chinese practice tai chi in the morning. This square was the center of early San Francisco and the spot where the American flag was first raised on July 9, 1846. From the square, Washington Street leads up to Waverly Place, where you can discover three temples.

A block north of Grant, Stockton Street is the main shopping drag of the community; it's lined with grocers, fishmongers, tea sellers, herbalists, noodle parlors, and restaurants. Here, too, is the **Kon Chow Temple** at no. 855, above the Chinatown Post Office.

Explore at your leisure, or see Section 7, "Organized Tours," later in this chapter, if you'd like to join a walking tour.

FISHERMAN'S WHARF & THE NORTHERN WATERFRONT   Few cities in America are as adept at wholesaling their historical sites as San Francisco, which has converted Fisherman's Wharf into one of the most popular tourist destinations in the world. Unless you come really early in the morning, you won't find any traces of the traditional waterfront life that once existed here—the only fishing going on around here now is for tourist dollars.

Originally called Meigg's Wharf, this bustling strip of waterfront got its present moniker from generations of fishers who used to base their boats here. Today the bay has become so polluted with toxins that bright-yellow placards warn against eating fish from these waters. A small fleet of fewer than 30 boats still operates from here, but basically Fisherman's Wharf has been converted into one long shopping mall stretching from Ghirardelli Square at the west end to Pier 39 at the east. Some people love it, others can't get far enough away from it, but most agree that Fisherman's Wharf, for better or for worse, has to be seen at least once in your life.

Ghirardelli Square, at 900 North Point, between Polk and Larkin streets (☎ 415/775-5500), dates from 1864 when it served as a factory making Civil War uniforms, but it's best known as the former chocolate-and-spice factory of Domingo Ghirardelli. The factory has been converted into a 10-level mall containing 50-plus stores and 20 dining establishments. Scheduled street performers play regularly in the West Plaza. The stores generally stay open until 8 or 9pm in the summer and 6 or 7pm in the winter.

The Cannery, at 2801 Leavenworth St. (☎ 415/771-3112), was built in 1894 as a fruit-canning plant and converted in the 1960s into a mall containing 50-plus shops and several restaurants and galleries, including **Jacks Cannery Bar** (☎ 415/931-6400), which features 83 beers on tap. Vendors' stalls and sidewalk cafes are set up in the courtyard amid a grove of century-old olive trees, and on summer weekends street performers are out in force entertaining tourists. The **Museum of the City of San Francisco** (☎ 415/928-0289), which traces the city's development with displays and artifacts, is on the third floor. The museum is free and is open Wednesday to Sunday from 10am to 4pm.

Pier 39, on the waterfront at Embarcadero and Beach Street (☎ 415/981-8030), is a 4^1/$_2$-acre waterfront complex a few blocks east of Fisherman's Wharf. Ostensibly a re-creation of a turn-of-the-century street scene, it features walkways of aged and weathered wood salvaged from demolished piers. But don't expect a slice of old-time maritime life. This is the busiest mall of the group, with more than 100 stores. In addition, there are some 20 or so restaurants and snack outlets, some with good views of the bay. Two marinas accommodating 350 boats flank the pier and house the Blue and Gold bay sightseeing fleet.

In recent years some 600 California **sea lions** have taken up residence on the adjacent floating docks. They sun themselves and honk and bellow playfully. The latest major addition to Fisherman's Wharf is **Underwater World,** a $38-million, 707,000-gallon marine attraction filled with sharks, stingrays, and more, all witnessed via a moving footpath that transports visitors through clear acrylic tunnels.

The shops are open daily from 10:30am to 8:30pm. Cable car: Powell-Mason line to Bay Street.

THE MISSION DISTRICT   Once inhabited almost entirely by Irish immigrants, the Mission District is now the center of the city's Latino community, an oblong area stretching roughly from 14th to 30th streets between Potrero Avenue in the east and Dolores on the west. Many of the city's finest Victorians still stand in the outer areas, though many seem strangely out of place in the mostly lower-income neighborhoods. The heart of the community lies along 24th Street between Van Ness and Potrero avenues, where dozens of excellent ethnic restaurants, bakeries, bars, and specialty stores attract people from all over the city. Walking through the Mission District at night isn't a good idea, but it's usually quite safe during the day and highly recommended.

For an even better insight into the community, go to the **Precita Eyes Mural Arts Center,** 348 Precita Ave., at Folsom Street (☎ 415/285-2287), and take one of the hour-long tours conducted on Saturday, which cost $4 for adults, $3 for seniors, $1 for under-18s. You'll see 70 murals in an 8-block walk. Every year they also hold a Mural Awareness Week (usually the second week in May) when tours are given daily. Other signs of cultural life include a number of progressive theaters—Eureka, Theater Rhinoceros, and Theater Artaud, to name only a few.

At 16th and Dolores is the **Mission San Francisco de Assisi** (better known as Mission Dolores), the city's oldest surviving building (see the separate listing above) and the district's namesake.

NOB HILL   When the cable car was invented in 1873, this hill became the city's most exclusive residential area. The Big Four and the Comstock Bonanza kings built their mansions here, but the structures were all destroyed by the 1906 earthquake and fire. Only the Flood mansion, which serves today as the Pacific Union Club, and the Fairmont (which was under construction when the earthquake struck) were spared. Today the area is home to some of the city's most upscale hotels and also **Grace Cathedral,** which stands on the Crocker mansion site. Stroll around and enjoy the views, and perhaps pay a visit to Huntington Park.

NORTH BEACH   In the late 1800s an enormous influx of Italian immigrants into North Beach firmly established this aromatic area as San Francisco's "Little Italy." Today dozens of Italian restaurants and coffeehouses continue to flourish in what's still the center of the city's Italian community. Walk down Columbus Avenue any given morning and you're bound to be bombarded with the wonderful aromas of roasting coffee and savory pasta sauces. Though there are some interesting shops and bookstores in the area, it's the dozens of eclectic little cafes, delis, bakeries, and coffee shops that give North Beach its Italo-bohemian character.

For a proper perspective of North Beach, sign up for a guided **Javawalk** with coffee-nut Elaine Sosa (see "Organized Tours," later in this chapter).

PARKS, GARDENS & ZOOS

In addition to Golden Gate Park (see Section 5, "The Top Attractions," earlier in this chapter), the Golden Gate National Recreation Area, and the Presidio (see Section 8, later in this chapter), San Francisco boasts more than 2,000 additional acres of parkland, most of which is perfect for picnicking.

Lincoln Park, at Clement Street and 34th Avenue, a personal favorite of ours, occupies 270 acres on the northwestern side of the city and contains the California Palace of the Legion of Honor (see "Museums," above) and a scenic 18-hole municipal golf course. But the most dramatic feature of the park is the 200-foot cliffs that overlook the Golden Gate Bridge and San Francisco Bay. Take bus no. 38 from Union Square to 33rd and Geary streets, then transfer to bus no. 18 into the park.

✪ **San Francisco Zoo and Children's Zoo.** Sloat Blvd. and 45th Ave. ☎ **415/753-7080.** Admission: Main zoo, $7 adults, $3.50 seniors and youths 12–15, $1.50 children 3–11, free for children 2 and under if accompanied by an adult; Children's Zoo, $1 per person, free for children under 3. Main zoo, daily 10am–5pm; Children's Zoo, daily 11am–4pm. Muni Metro: L line from downtown Market St. to the end of the line.

Located between the Pacific Ocean and Lake Merced, in the southwest corner of the city, the San Francisco Zoo is among America's highest-rated animal parks. Begun in 1889 with a grizzly bear named Monarch donated by the *San Francisco Examiner,* the zoo now sprawls over 65 acres and is growing. It attracts up to a million visitors each year. Most of the 1,000-plus inhabitants are contained in landscaped enclosures guarded by concealed moats. The innovative Primate Discovery Center is particularly noteworthy for its many rare and endangered species. Expansive outdoor atriums, sprawling meadows, and a midnight world for exotic nocturnal primates house such species as the owl-faced macaque, ruffed-tailed lemur, black-and-white colobus monkeys, patas monkeys, and emperor tamarins, pint-size primates distinguished by their long, majestic mustaches.

Other highlights include Koala Crossing, which is linked to the new Australian WalkAbout exhibit that opened in 1995, housing kangaroos, emus, and walleroos; Gorilla World, one of the world's largest exhibits of these gentle giants; and Penguin Island, home to a large breeding colony of Magellanic penguins. The new Feline Conservation Center is a wooded sanctuary and breeding facility for the zoo's endangered snow leopards, Persian leopards, and other jungle cats. Musk Ox Meadow is a 2^1/$_2$-acre habitat for a herd of rare white-fronted musk oxen brought from Alaska. The Otter River exhibit features waterfalls, logs, and boulders for the North American otters to climb on. And the Lion House is home to rare Sumatran and Siberian tigers; Prince Charles, a rare white Bengal tiger; and the African lions (you can watch them being fed at 2pm Tuesday to Sunday).

At the Children's Zoo, adjacent to the main park, the barnyard is alive with strokable domestic animals such as sheep, goats, ponies, and a llama. Also of interest is the Insect Zoo, which showcases a multitude of insect species, including the hissing cockroach walking sticks.

A free, informal walking tour of the zoo is available on weekends at 11am. The Zebra Zephyr train tour takes visitors on a 20-minute "safari" daily (in winter, only on weekends). The tour is $2.50 for adults, $1.50 for children 15 and under and for seniors.

7 Organized Tours

ORIENTATION TOURS

Gray Line, Transbay Terminal, 1st and Mission streets (☎ **800/826-0202** or 415/558-9400), offers several daily itineraries with free transfers from centrally located hotels to departure points. Reservations are required for most tours.

THE 49-MILE SCENIC DRIVE

The self-guided, 49-mile drive is one easy way to orient yourself and to grasp the beauty of San Francisco and its extraordinary location. Beginning in the city, it follows a rough circle around the bay and passes virtually all the best-known sights, from Chinatown to the Golden Gate Bridge, Ocean Beach, Seal Rocks, Golden Gate Park, and Twin Peaks. Originally designed for the benefit of visitors to San Francisco's 1939–40 Golden Gate International Exposition, the route is marked with blue-and-white seagull signs. Although it makes an excellent half-day tour, this mini-excursion can easily take longer if you decide, for example, to stop to walk across the Golden Gate Bridge or to have tea in Golden Gate Park's Japanese Tea Garden.

The **San Francisco Visitor Information Center,** at Powell and Market streets (see "Tourist Information" in "Orientation," earlier in this chapter), distributes free route maps. Since a few of the Scenic Drive marker signs are missing, the map will come in handy. Try to avoid the downtown area during the weekday rush hours from 7 to 9am and 4 to 6pm.

BOAT TOURS

One of the best ways to look at San Francisco is from a boat bobbing on the bay. There are several cruises to choose from, many of which start from Fisherman's Wharf. There are two major companies.

The **Red & White Fleet,** at Pier 41, Fisherman's Wharf (☎ **800/229-2784** in California, or 415/546-2700), is the city's largest boat-tour operator, offering more than half a dozen itineraries on the bay. The fleet's primary ships are two-toned,

Seeing The City by Seaplane

For those of you seeking a little thrill and adventure during your vacation, consider booking a flight with **San Francisco Seaplane Tours,** the Bay Area's only seaplane tour company. For more than 50 years this locally owned outfit has provided its customers an opportunity to see the city from a bird's-eye view, flying directly over San Francicso at an altitude of about 1500 feet. Sights along the 30-and 45-minute guided excursions include the Golden Gate and Bay bridges, Alcatraz, the Pacific coastline, Tiburon, and Sausalito. Half the fun, however, is taking off and landing on the water (which is surprisingly smooth).

Trips depart from, Pier 39 and Sausalito, with prices ranging from $74 to $89 per adult for the 30-minute Golden Gate Tour. For $104 per person you can take the horribly romantic Champagne Sunset Flight, which includes a bottle of bub-bly and a cozy backseat for two. Family discounts and children's rates are available, and cameras are welcome (on calm days, the pilot will even roll the window down). For more information or reservations, call **415/332-4843.**

double- and triple-deckers, capable of holding 150 to 500 passengers. You can't miss the observation tower ticket booths, at Pier $43^1/_2$, located next to the Franciscan Restaurant.

The Golden Gate Bay Cruise is a 45-minute cruise by the Golden Gate Bridge, Angel Island, and Alcatraz Island. Tours cost $16 for adults, $12 for juniors 12 to 18 and for seniors 62 and older, and $8 for children 5 to 11. Tour prices include audio narration in six languages: English, French, German, Japanese, Mandarin, and Spanish. They depart from Pier 41 and Pier $43^1/_2$ several times daily. The Blue and Gold Fleet acquired this company in 1996 so details may vary. Call for departure schedules.

The **Blue and Gold Fleet,** at Pier 39, Fisherman's Wharf (☎ **415/705-5444**), tours the bay year round in a sleek, 400-passenger sightseeing boat, complete with food and beverage facilities. The fully narrated, $1^1/_4$-hour cruise passes beneath the Golden Gate and Bay bridges, and comes within yards of Alcatraz Island. Frequent daily departures from Pier 39's West Marina begin at 10am in summer and at 11am in winter. Tickets cost $16 for adults, $8 for juniors 5 to 17 and for seniors 62 and over; children 4 and under sail free.

SPECIAL-INTEREST TOURS

MOVING PARTY   Three Babes and a Bus (☎ 415/552-2582) is perhaps the world's hippest scheduled tour operator. This unique company runs regular night-club trips for out-of-towners and locals who want to experience the city's night scene. The Babes' ever-changing $3^1/_2$-hour itinerary waltzes into four different clubs per night, cutting in front of every line with priority entry. The party continues en route, when the Babes entertain. Their bus departs from locations throughout the city. Phone for complete information and reservations. The tour costs $30, including club entrances, and runs on Friday and Saturday nights only, from 9:30pm to 1:30am.

EXPLORING THE CASTRO   Cruisin' the Castro (☎ 415/550-8110) will give you a totally new insight into the gay community's contribution to the political maturity, growth, and beauty of San Francisco. Tours are personally conducted by Ms. Trevor Hailey, who was involved in the development of the Castro in the 1970s and knew Harvey Milk, the first openly gay politician elected to office in the United States.

Tours are conducted Tuesday to Saturday from 10am to 1:30pm, and begin at Harvey Milk Plaza, atop the Castro Street Muni station. The cost includes lunch at the Lutie Pietia. Reservations are required. Prices are $30 for adults, $25 for seniors 62 and older and for children 16 and under.

A HIPPIE TOUR   The Grateful Dead's crash pad, Janis Joplin's house, and other monuments to the "Summer of Love"—Rachel Heller will take you to the city's hippie haunts. Tours begin at 9:30am on Tuesday and Saturday and cost $15 per person. For reservations call **Haight-Ashbury Walking Tours** (☎ **415/221-8442**).

NORTH BEACH CAFE SOIREE   **Javawalk** is a 2-hour walking tour by self-described "coffeehouse lizard" Elaine Sosa. Aside from visiting cafes, Javawalk also serves up a good share of historical and architectural trivia. Sosa keeps the tour interactive and fun, and it's obvious that she knows a multitude of tales and trivia about the history of coffee and its North Beach roots. Tours are Tuesday to Saturday at 10am. The price is $20 per person, $10 for kids 12 and under. For information and reservations call 415/673-9255.

AN INSIDER'S TOUR OF CHINATOWN   Founded by author, TV personality, cooking instructor, and restaurant critic Shirley Fong-Torres, **Wok Wiz Chinatown Walking Tours** (☎ **415/355-9657**) takes you into nooks and crannies not usually seen by tourists. Each of her guides is intimately acquainted with all of Chinatown's backways, alleys, and small businesses. You'll learn about dim sum (a "delight of the heart") and the Chinese tea ceremony; meet a Chinese herbalist; stop at a pastry shop to observe rice noodles being made; watch artist Y. K. Lau do his delicate brush painting; learn about jook, a traditional Chinese breakfast; stop in at a fortune-cookie factory; and visit a Chinese produce market and learn to identify the vegetables used in Chinese cuisine.

Tours are conducted daily from 10am to 1:30pm and include a Chinese lunch. The tour begins in the lobby of the Chinatown Holiday Inn at 750 Kearny St. (between Washington and Clay streets). Groups are generally limited to 12, and reservations are essential. Prices (including lunch) are $35 for adults, $33 for seniors 60 and older, and $25 for children 11 and under.

Shirley Fong-Torres also operates a gastronomical tour that starts with a Chinese breakfast in a noodle house, moves to a wok shop, and then makes further stops at a vegetarian restaurant, a rice-noodle factory, and a supermarket before taking a break for a dim sum luncheon. It's offered every Saturday for $50, including lunch.

8 Golden Gate National Recreation Area & the Presidio

GOLDEN GATE NATIONAL RECREATION AREA

No urban shoreline is as stunning as San Francisco's. The Golden Gate National Recreation Area, wrapping around the northern and western edge of the city and run by the National Park Service, lets visitors fully enjoy it. Along this shoreline are several landmarks. From its edge visitors have views of the bay and the ocean. MUNI provides transportation to most sites, including Aquatic Park, the Cliff House, and Ocean Beach. For more information, contact the National Park Service at 415/556-0560. For additional information, see Section 9, "Outdoor Activities & Spectator Sports," later in this chapter.

Here's a brief rundown of the major features of the recreation area, starting at the northern section and moving westward around the coastline:

Aquatic Park, adjacent to the Hyde Street Pier, is a small swimming beach, although it's not that appealing and the water's ridiculously cold.

Fort Mason Center occupies an area from Bay Street to the shoreline and consists of several buildings and piers that were used during World War II. Today they're occupied by a variety of museums, theaters, and cultural, educational, and community organizations, as well as by Greens vegetarian restaurant, which affords views of the Golden Gate Bridge. For information about Fort Mason events, call 415/441-5705. Park headquarters is also at Fort Mason.

Farther west along the bay, **Marina Green,** at the northern end of Fillmore, is a favorite spot for kite-flying or watching the sailboats on the bay and the birds gliding above. Next stop along the bay is the St. Francis Yacht Club. From here begins the 3¹/₂-mile paved **Golden Gate Promenade,** a favorite biking and hiking path, which sweeps along Crissy Field, leading ultimately to Fort Point under the Golden Gate Bridge. This promenade defines the outer limits of the **Presidio** (see below).

Fort Point (☎ **415/556-1373**), a National Historic Site sitting directly under the Golden Gate Bridge, was built in 1853 to protect the narrow entrance to the harbor. You might recognize it from Alfred Hitchcock's *Vertigo;* the master of suspense filmed some of the most important scenes here. During the Civil War the brick Fort Point was manned by 140 men and 90 pieces of artillery to prevent a Confederate takeover of California. Rangers in Civil War regalia lead regular tours and sometimes fire the old cannons. Call 415/556-1693 for schedules and information.

Lincoln Boulevard sweeps around the western edge of the bay to two of the most popular beaches in San Francisco. **Baker Beach,** a small and beautiful strand just outside the Golden Gate where the waves roll ashore, is a fine spot for sunbathing, walking, or fishing—it's packed on sunny days. Because of the cold water and the roaring currents that pour out of the bay twice a day, swimming is not advised here for any but the most confident. (You'll also see some nude sunbathers here.)

Here you can pick up the **Coastal Trail,** which leads through the Presidio (see below). A short distance from Baker, **China Beach** is a small cove where swimming is permitted. Changing rooms, showers, a sundeck, and rest rooms are available.

A little farther along the coast appears **Lands End,** looking out to **Pyramid Rock.** Both a lower and an upper trail provide hiking opportunities amid windswept cypress and pine on the cliffs above the Pacific.

Still farther along the coast lies **Point Lobos,** the **Sutro Baths,** and the **Cliff House.** The latter has been serving refreshments to visitors since 1863. Here you can view the **Seal Rocks,** home to a colony of sea lions and many marine birds. There's an **information center** here (open daily 10am to 4:30pm; ☎ **415/556-8642**) and the kids will enjoy the **Musée Mécanique,** an authentic old-fashioned arcade with 150 coin-operated amusements. Only traces of the Sutro Baths remain today northeast of the Cliff House. This swimming facility was a major summer attraction that could accommodate 24,000 people, but it burned down in 1966. A little farther inland at the western end of California Street is **Lincoln Park,** which contains a golf course and the Palace of the Legion of Honor.

From the Cliff House, the Esplanade continues south along the 4-mile-long **Ocean Beach,** which is not suitable for swimming. At the southern end of Ocean Beach is another area of the park around **Fort Funston** where there's an easy loop trail across the cliffs (call the ranger station at 415/239-2366). Here, too, you can watch the hang gliders taking advantage of the high cliffs and strong winds.

Farther south along Interstate 280, **Sweeney Ridge,** which can only be reached by car, affords sweeping views of the coastline from the many trails that crisscross this

Golden Gate National Recreation Area & the Presidio

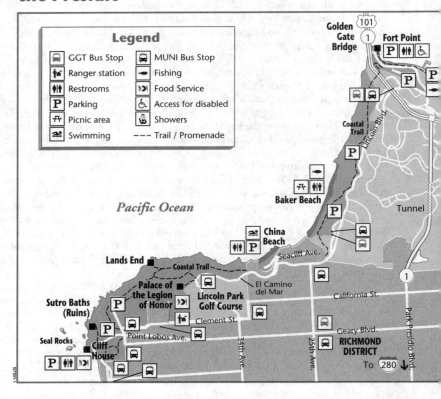

1,000 acres of land. It was from here that the expedition led by Don Gaspar de Portola first saw San Francisco Bay in 1769. It's in Pacifica and can be reached via Sneath Lane off Califorina 35 (Skyline Boulevard) in San Bruno.

THE PRESIDIO

In 1989 the Department of Defense announced what many had long thought impossible: The U.S. Army, which had held the Presidio as a military base since before the Civil War, was pulling out and leaving the most prized piece of real estate in San Francisco to the National Park Service as an example of post–Cold War retrofitting. Now an urban national park, it combines historical, architectural, and natural aspects.

The 1,480-acre area incorporates a variety of terrain—coastal scrub, dunes, and prairie grasslands that shelter many rare plants and more than 150 species of birds, some of which nest here. There are also more than 350 historic buildings to see, a scenic golf course to play, a national cemetery to visit, and a variety of terrains and natural habitats to explore. The National Park Service offers a number of walking and biking tours around the Presidio; reservations are required.

Walkers and joggers will enjoy the forests of the Presidio. It was once a bleak field of wind-blasted rock, sand, and grass, but in a strangely humanitarian gesture, 60,000 trees were planted in the 1880s to make the place more livable for the troops. Today, on the 2-mile **Ecology Loop Trail,** walkers can see more than 30 different

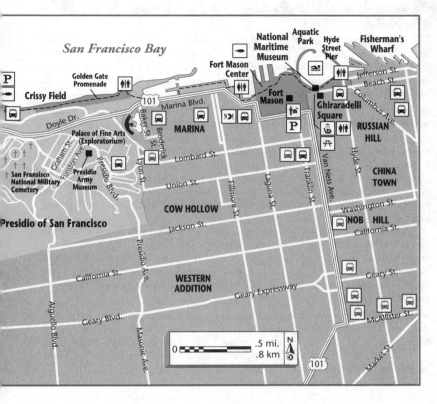

species of those trees, including redwood, spruce, cypress, and acacias. Hikers can follow the 2½-mile **Coastal Trail** from Fort Point along this part of the coastline all the way to Land's End. It follows the bluff top from Baker Beach to the southern base of the Golden Gate Bridge.

Anyone interested in the military history of the Presidio must stop at the **Presidio Army Museum,** loaded with military arcana from 200 years of base history. The museum, at the corner of Lincoln Boulevard and Funston Avenue, tells its story in dioramas, exhibitions, and photographs. It's open Wednesday to Sunday from 10am to 4pm.

Crissy Field is a former airfield that in recent years has become known as one of the see-and-be-seen proving grounds of California's windsurfing culture. Between March and October hundreds come to try their hand. The Crissy beach provides easy water access and plenty of room to rig up; it's not recommended for the inexperienced. This is also a popular place for joggers en route from the Marina District to Fort Point and back. At the west end of Crissy Field is a pier that can be used for fishing and crabbing.

For schedules, maps, and general information about ongoing developments at the Presidio, the best source is the **Golden Gate National Recreation Area Headquarters** at Fort Mason, Building 102, San Francisco, CA 94123 (☎ **415/556-2236**). On the west side of Montgomery Street on the main parade ground, it's open daily from 10am to 5pm. Bus: 28, 76, or 82X.

9 Outdoor Activities & Spectator Sports

OUTDOOR ACTIVITIES

The prime places to enjoy all kinds of recreational activities in San Francisco have already been described earlier in this chapter. See Section 5, "The Top Attractions," for a complete description of Golden Gate Park; and Section 8 for complete details on Golden Gate National Recreation Area and the Presidio, which comprise most of the city's shoreline.

BEACHES There are only two beaches in San Francisco that are safe for swimming: **Aquatic Park,** which is adjacent to the Hyde Park Pier and not very memorable; and **China Beach,** a small cove on the western edge of the South Bay (changing rooms, showers, a sundeck, and rest rooms are available).

Baker Beach, a small, beautiful strand just outside the Golden Gate, isn't the best place for swimming because of the strong currents, but it's popular for sunbathing (nude in certain sections), walking, picnicking, and fishing. It's wonderful to sit here on a sunny day and take in the view of the bridge. You'll climb down a very long flight of stairs from the street to reach the beach.

Ocean Beach, at the end of Golden Gate Park, on the westernmost side of the city, is San Francisco's largest beach (4 miles long). Just offshore, at the northern end of the beach in front of Cliff House, are the jagged Seal Rocks, which are inhabited by various shore birds and a large colony of barking sea lions. Bring binoculars. Ocean Beach is for strolling or sunning, but don't swim here—the tides are tricky, and each year bathers and surfers drown in the rough waters.

BICYCLING Two city-designated bike routes are maintained by the Recreation and Parks Department. One winds for $7^1/_2$ miles through Golden Gate Park to Lake Merced; the other traverses the city, starting in the south, and follows a route over the Golden Gate Bridge. A bike map is available from the San Francisco Visitor Information Center and from bicycle shops all around town.

A massive new seawall, constructed to buffer Ocean Beach from storm-driven waves, doubles as a public walk and bikeway along 5 waterfront blocks of the Great Highway between Noriega and Santiago streets. It's an easy ride from Cliff House or Golden Gate Park.

Park Cyclery, 1749 Waller St. (☎ **415/752-8383**), is one of two shops in the Haight Street/ Stanyan Street area that rent bikes. Next to Golden Gate Park, the cyclery rents mountain bikes exclusively, along with helmets, locks, and accessories. The charge is $5 per hour, $25 per day, and it's open Thursday to Tuesday from 10am to 6pm.

There's also great biking in the Presidio. From there you can venture across the Golden Gate Bridge and into the Marin hills.

BOATING At the **Golden Gate Park Boat House,** at Stow Lake (☎ **415/752-0347**), you can rent a rowboat or pedalboat by the hour and steer over to Strawberry Hill, a large, round island in the middle of the lake, for lunch. There's usually a line on weekends. It's open June to September, daily from 9am to 4pm; the rest of the year, Tuesday to Sunday from 9am to 4pm.

CITY STAIR-CLIMBING You don't need a Stairmaster in San Francisco. The **Filbert Street Steps,** 377 of them running between Sansome Street and Telegraph Hill, scale the eastern face of Telegraph Hill, from Sansome and Filbert past charming 19th-century cottages and lush gardens. Napier Lane, a narrow wooden plank walkway, leads to Montgomery Street. Turn right and follow the path to the end of the cul-de-sac where another stairway continues to Telegraph's panoramic summit.

The **Lyon Street Steps,** between Green Street and Broadway, comprise another historic stairway street, containing four steep sets of stairs totaling 288 steps. Begin at Green Street and climb all the way up, past manicured hedges and flower gardens, to an iron gate that opens into the Presidio. A block east, on Baker Street, another set of 369 steps descends to Green Street.

FISHING   **New Easy Rider Sport Fishing,** 225 University Ave. in Berkeley (☎ **415/285-2000**), makes daily salmon runs from Fisherman's Wharf from June to October. Fishing equipment is available; the cost of $49 per person includes bait. Reservations are required. Departures are daily at 6am, returning at 2pm; in summer there's a second daily departure at 3pm, returning at dusk.

If you'd like to stay on land, there's a pier at the west end of Crissy Field in the Presidio that can be used for fishing and crabbing.

GOLF   The **Golden Gate Park Course,** 47th Avenue and Fulton Street (☎ **415/751-8987**), is a nine-hole course over 1,357 yards and is par 27. All holes are par 3, tightly set, and well trapped with small greens. Greens fees are very reasonable: $10 per person Monday to Friday, $13 on Saturday and Sunday. The course is open daily from 9am to dusk.

The **Lincoln Park Golf Course,** 34th Avenue and Clement Street (☎ **415/221-9911**), San Francisco's prettiest municipal course, has terrific views and fairways lined with Monterey cypress trees. Its 18 holes encompass 5,081 yards, for a par 68. Greens fees are $23 per person Monday to Friday, $27 on Saturday and Sunday. The course is open daily from 9am to dusk.

RUNNING   The **Bay to Breakers Foot Race** is an annual 7.5km run from downtown to Ocean Beach. Around 80,000 entrants gather—many dressed in wacky, innovative, and sometimes X-rated costumes—for what's considered one of San Francisco's favored trademark events. It's sponsored by the *San Francisco Examiner* and is held the third Sunday of May. Call 415/777-7770 for details.

The **San Francisco Marathon** is held annually in the middle of July. For further information, contact USA Track & Field at 415/391-2123.

SKATING   Although people skate in Golden Gate Park all week long, Sunday is best, when John F. Kennedy Drive, between Kezar Drive and Transverse Road, is closed to automobiles. A smooth "skate pad" is located on your right, just past the Conservatory.

Skates on Haight, 1818 Haight St. (☎ **415/752-8376**), is the best place to rent either in-line or conventional skates, and is located only 1 block from the park. Protective wrist guards and knee pads are included free. The cost is $7 per hour for in-line skates, $6 per hour for "conventionals." Major credit/charge card and ID deposit are required. The shop is open Monday and Wednesday to Friday from 11:30am to 6:30pm, and on Saturday and Sunday from 10am to 6pm.

TENNIS   More than 100 courts maintained by the San Francisco Recreation and Parks Department (☎ **415/753-7001**) are available free, on a first-come, first-served basis. The exceptions are the 21 courts in Golden Gate Park; a $4 to $6 fee is charged for their use, and courts must be reserved in advance for weekend play. Call the number above on Wednesday from 7 to 9pm, or on Thursday and Friday from 9am to 5pm.

WINDSURFING   **Crissy Field** in the Presidio is a mecca for experienced windsurfers. There's easy access to the water and plenty of room to rig up. It's best between March and October.

Work It Out

While San Francisco has plenty to offer in the way of outdoor exercise and activities, there are also plenty of indoor places to relieve stress, work up a sweat, or treat your body to a little TLC.

The **San Francisco Bay Club,** at 150 Greenwich St., at Battery Street (☎ **415/433-2200**), is one of the most exclusive and extensive gym-cum-spas in the Bay Area. Celebrities such as Tom Cruise, Cindy Crawford, and Hugh Grant have flexed a few muscles here when on location, and regular members include the city's old and new elite. The club takes up almost a full block and offers three floors teeming with health equipment, including two pools (one's heated); tennis, squash, racquetball and basketball courts; aerobics and yoga; free weights, cardiovascular, and Nautilus equipment; a sundeck; sauna, steam, and whirlpool; and a cafe. Although walk-in guests are not permitted, sign up for any of the luxurious spa treatments and you're extended full work-out privileges for the day. Services include massage, facials, manicures, and pedicures.

A more spiritual workout can be found at **The Mindful Body,** a center for movement, body, and personal inner work. It's located at 2876 California St., between Broderick and Divisadero (☎ **415/931-2639** for class schedules). After an intense yoga or stretch class, guided meditation, or massage, you'll be a new person.

Adventurers can hone their skills at the **Mission Cliffs Rock Climbing Center,** 2295 Harrison St., at 19th Street (☎ **415/550-0515**). For $12 (plus $6 if you need rental equipment) you can climb 14,000 feet of terrain and 2,000 square feet of boulders. Lessons, which cost extra and include kid and outdoor programs, can be arranged. Once you're worn out, relax in the sauna.

If getting your heart rate up seems like a chore, take a less painful approach at the **Metronome** (☎ **415/252-9000**), which offers ballroom, swing, Latin, nightclub, and salsa dance classes for individuals and groups. Call for information on class times, package deals, and weekend dance parties.

SPECTATOR SPORTS

BASEBALL   The **San Francisco Giants** and star leftfielder Barry Bonds play at 3COM Park (formerly Candlestick Park), at Giants Drive and Gilman Avenue (☎ **415/467-8000**), from April to early October. The stadium is off U.S. 101, about 8 miles south of downtown. Tickets are usually available up until game time, but seats can be very far from the action. Tickets may be obtained at 3COM Park, by phone from the number above, or through BASS Ticketmaster (☎ 510/762-2277). Special express bus service is available from Market Street on game days; call Muni (☎ 415/673-6864) for pickup points and schedule information. Bring a coat, as this 60,000-seat stadium is known for chilly winds.

The **Oakland A's** play at the Oakland Coliseum Complex, at the Hegenberger Road exit off I-880 (☎ **510/430-8020**). The stadium holds close to 50,000 spectators and is serviced by BART's Coliseum station. Tickets are available from the Coliseum Box Office or by phone through BASS Ticketmaster (☎ 510/762-2277).

BASKETBALL   Perennially in search of a center, the **Golden State Warriors** play at the Oakland Coliseum Complex, at the Hegenberger Road exit off I-880, in Oakland (☎ **510/638-6300**). The season runs from November to April, and most games are played at 7:30pm. Tickets are available at the arena, and by phone through BASS Ticketmaster (☎ 510/762-2277).

FOOTBALL   The **San Francisco 49ers** play at 3COM Park, Giants Drive and Gilman Avenue (☎ **415/468-2249**), off U.S. 101, about 8 miles south of downtown. Games are played on Sunday from August to December; kickoff is usually at 1pm. Tickets sell out early in the season, but are available at higher prices through ticket agents beforehand and from scalpers at the gate. Ask your hotel concierge or visit City Box Office, 141 Kearny St. (☎ 415/392-4400). Special express bus service is available from Market Street on game days; call Muni (☎ 415/673-6864) for pickup points and schedule information.

Newly returned to the Bay Area in 1995, the **Oakland Raiders** play in the Oakland Coliseum (see "Basketball," above, for location and ticket information). Eccentric owner Al Davis is widely regarded as the George Steinbrenner of football.

The **University of California Golden Bears,** 61 Harmon Gym, University of California, Berkeley (☎ **800/GO-BEARS** or 510/642-5150), play their home games in Memorial Stadium, on the university campus. Tickets are usually available at game time. Phone for schedules and information.

HORSE RACING   Thoroughbred races are held at **Golden Gate Fields,** Gilman Street, off I-80 in Albany (☎ **510/559-7300**), from January to March and from April to the end of June. The park is on the seashore, 10 miles northeast of San Francisco. Call for admission prices and post times.

The nearest autumn racing is at **Bay Meadows,** 2600 S. Delaware St., off U.S. 101, in San Mateo (☎ **415/574-7223**), about 20 miles south of downtown San Francisco. The course hosts races 4 or 5 days each week from September to January. Call for admission and post times.

10 Shopping

Like its population, San Francisco's shopping is both worldly and intimate. Every persuasion, style, era, and fetish is represented here, not in a big, tacky shopping mall, but rather in hundreds of quaint and dramatically different boutiques scattered throughout the city.

The sales tax in San Francisco is 8.5%.

MAJOR SHOPPING AREAS

Union Square & Environs   San Francisco's most congested and popular shopping mecca is centered around Union Square and enclosed by Bush, Taylor, Market, and Montgomery streets. Most of the big department stores and many high-end specialty shops are in this area. Be sure to venture to Grant Avenue, Post and Sutter streets, and Maiden Lane.

Chinatown   Chinatown is the antithesis of Union Square, as the shops along Grant Avenue sell an eclectic variety of cheap goods, T-shirts, knockoffs, and other tourist-oriented trinkets. Most stores in Chinatown are open daily from 10am to 10pm.

Union Street   The Cow Hollow section of this trendy street, between Van Ness Avenue and Steiner Street, is the place for antiques, handcrafts, hip fashions, and deluxe glassware.

Haight Street   The 6 blocks of upper Haight Street, between Central Avenue and Stanyan Street, are still the best place to shop for inexpensive, funky styles; antique and vintage clothing; Grateful Dead memorabilia; and kitsch. Along this street there's a healthy mix of boutiques, secondhand shops, and inexpensive restaurants.

Fillmore Street   Some of the best shopping in town is packed into 5 blocks of Fillmore Street in Pacific Heights. From Jackson to Sutter streets, Fillmore is the perfect place to grab a bite and peruse the high-priced boutiques, craft shops, and incredible houseware stores.

Fisherman's Wharf & Environs   The nonstop strip of waterfront malls that runs along Jefferson Street includes hundreds of shops, restaurants, and attractions. Ghirardelli Square, Pier 39, the Cannery, the Anchorage, and the San Francisco shopping center are the major complexes.

SHOPPING A TO Z
ART

The *San Francisco Gallery Guide,* a comprehensive, bimonthly publication listing the city's current shows, is available free by mail. Send a self-addressed stamped envelope to San Francisco Bay Area Gallery Guide, 1369 Fulton St., San Francisco, CA 94117 (☎ 415/921-1600), or pick one up at the San Francisco Visitor Information Center (see "Orientation," earlier in this chapter). Most of the city's major art galleries are clustered downtown in the Union Square area, especially in the 400 and 500 blocks of Bush and Sutter.

BOOKS

✪ **Charlotte's Web.** 2278 Union St. (between Steiner and Fillmore sts.). ☎ **415/441-4700.**

A children's bookstore, Charlotte's Web is notable for its particularly knowledgeable owner, who sells everything from cloth books for babies to histories and poetry for young adults.

✪ **City Lights Bookstore.** 261 Columbus Ave. (at Broadway). ☎ **415/362-8193.**

Owned by Lawrence Ferlinghetti, the renowned Beat poet, this excellent three-level bookshop prides itself on a comprehensive collection of fiction, art, poetry, and political paperbacks, as well as more mainstream books.

A Clean Well-Lighted Place. 601 Van Ness Ave. ☎ **415/441-6670.**

Voted best bookstore by the *San Francisco Bay Guardian,* this store has good new fiction and nonfiction sections as well as music, mystery, and cooking sections.

McDonald's Bookshop. 48 Turk St. ☎ **415/673-2235.**

San Francisco's biggest used-book shop claims to stock more than a million volumes, including out-of-print, esoteric, and hard-to-find books in all categories and languages.

Rand-McNally Map and Travel. 595 Market St. ☎ **415/777-3131.**

Hands down the best travel bookstore in the city, this corner shop features maps, atlases, and travel guides to all destinations, as well as educational games, toys, and globes.

Thomas Bros. Maps & Books. 550 Jackson St. (at Columbus Ave.). ☎ **800/969-3072** or 415/981-7520.

Thomas Bros. sells street, topographic, and hiking maps depicting San Francisco, California, and the world. A selection of travel-related books is also sold.

FACTORY OUTLETS

There are many factory-outlet stores in San Francisco, selling overstocked and discontinued fashions at very good prices. Many are located south of Market Street, in the city's warehouse district.

Esprit Outlet Store. 499 Illinois St. (at 16th St.). ☎ **415/957-2550.**

All the Esprit collections and Susie Tompkins merchandise are available here at 30% or more off regular prices. In addition to clothes, the store sells accessories, shoes, and other assorted items. Open Monday to Friday from 10am to 8pm, on Saturday from 10am to 7pm, and on Sunday from 11am to 5pm.

New West. 426 Brannan St. (between 3rd and 4th sts.). ☎ **415/882-4929.**

This SoMa boutique offers top designer fashions—from shoes to suits—at rock-bottom prices. There are no cheap knockoffs here, just good men's and women's clothes and accessories. New West also has its own stylish clothing line. Open Monday to Saturday from 10am to 5pm and on Sunday from noon to 5pm.

The North Face. 1325 Howard St. (between 9th and 10th sts.). ☎ **415/626-6444.**

Well known for its sporting, camping, and hiking equipment, this off-price outlet carries a good selection of high-quality skiwear, boots, sweaters, and goods such as tents, packs, and sleeping bags.

FASHION
Children's Fashions
Minis by Profili. 2042 Union St. (between Webster and Buchanan sts.). ☎ **415/567-9537.**

Christina Profili, a San Franciscan clothing maker who used to design for The Gap, owns this children's clothing store that features her line of pint-sized pants, shirts, and dresses.

Men's Fashions
Citizen Clothing. 536 Castro St. (between 18th and 19th sts.). ☎ **415/558-9429.**

Stylish (but not faddish) pants, tops, and accessories.

MAC. 5 Claude Lane (off Sutter St. between Grant Ave. and Kearny St.). ☎ **415/837-0615.**

The more classic than corporate man shops here for imported tailored suits in new and intriguing fabrics. Their women's store is located at 1543 Grant Ave. (☎ 415/837-1604).

Women's Fashions
Métier. 50 Maiden Lane (at Grant Ave. and Kearny St.). ☎ **415/989-5395.**

Classic and sophisticated creations for women include European ready-to-wear lines and designer fashions.

Solo Fashion. 1599 Haight St. (at Clayton St.). ☎ **415/621-0342.**

While you're strolling upper Haight, stop in here for a good selection of upbeat, contemporary, English-style street wear, along with a collection of dresses designed exclusively for this shop.

FOOD
Joseph Schmidt Confections. 3489 16th St. (at Sanchez St.). ☎ **415/861-8682.**

Chocolate takes the shape of exquisite sculptural masterpieces—such as long-stemmed tulips and heart-shaped boxes—that are so beautiful you'll be hesitant to bite the head off your adorable chocolate panda bear. But once you do, you'll know why this is the most popular chocolatier in town. The prices are also remarkably reasonable.

Pure T. 2238 Polk St. (between Vallejo and Green sts.). ☎ **415/441-7878.**

If you're asked to bring dessert to a dinner party or are simply aching for a treat, it would be a sin to miss out on what we consider the best ice cream shop in the city.

The freshly made, all-natural ice creams here redefine "gourmet." They're light and delicate to the taste and flavored with—you guessed it—pure tea. Treat your tongue to scoop of black currant or Thai tea and you'll be hooked.

GIFTS

Exploratorium Store. In the Palace of Fine Arts, 3601 Lyon St. ☎ **415/561-0390.**

The best museum gift shop in the city is this fanciful store inside a hands-on science museum. Gifts include Space Age Super Balls, high-bouncing rubber balls that never seem to slow down; chime earrings and magnets; and other gizmos and gadgets.

Off Your Dot. 2241 Market St. (between Sanchez and Noe sts.). ☎ **415/252-5642.**

Wonderfully attractive and artistic handmade gifts cover almost every inch of this Castro-district store. There's everything from wall art to candles, picture frames, lamps, and glasswork here and most of it is locally made—and prices are the best in town.

Quantity Postcards. 1441 Grant St. (at Green St.). ☎ **415/986-8866.**

You'll find the perfect postcard for literally everyone you know here (there are hundreds of thousands), as well as some depictions of old San Francisco, movie stars, and Day-Glo™ posters featuring concert-poster artist Frank Kozik.

HOUSEWARES

Fillamento. 2185 Fillmore St. (at Sacramento St.). ☎ **415/931-2224.**

Fillamento's three floors are always packed with shoppers searching for the most classic, artistic, and refined housewares. Whether you're looking to set a good table or revamp your bedroom, you'll find it all here.

Gump's. 135 Post St. (between Kearny St. and Grant Ave.). ☎ **415/982-1616.**

Founded almost a century ago, San Francisco's favored house-and-home store offers gifts and treasures ranging from Asian antiquities to contemporary art glass and exquisite jade and pearl jewelry. Many items are made specifically for the store. Gump's also has one of the most revered window displays each holiday season.

The Wok Shop. 718 Grant Ave. (at Clay St.). ☎ **415/989-3797.**

This shop has every conceivable implement for Chinese cooking, including woks, circular chopping blocks, bamboo steamers—you name it—plus handmade linens from China and more.

Zinc Details. 1905 Fillmore St. (between Bush and Pine sts.). ☎ **415/776-2100.**

One of our favorite stores in the city, Zinc Details offers an amazing collection of locally handcrafted glass vases, pendant lights, ceramics, and furniture. Each piece is a true work of art created specifically for the store (except vintage items).

JEWELRY

Old & New Estates. 2181A Union St. (at Fillmore St.). ☎ **415/346-7525.**

Buy yourself a bauble, treat yourself to a trinket at this shop featuring top-of-the-line antique jewelry: pendants, diamond rings, necklaces, bracelets, and natural pearls.

Pearl Empire. 127 Geary St. (between Stockton St. and Grant Ave.). ☎ **415/362-0606.**

The Pearl Empire has been importing jewelry directly from Asia since 1957. It specializes in unusual pearls and jade, and offers restringing on the premises.

MARKETS/PRODUCE

Farmers Market. Embarcadero, in front of the Ferry Building. ☎ **510/528-6987.**

Every Saturday from May to November, Northern California fruit, vegetable, bread, and dairy vendors join local restaurateurs in selling fresh delicious edibles. There's no better way to enjoy a bright San Francisco morning than strolling this gourmet street market and snacking your way through breakfast. You can also pick up locally made vinegars and oils—they make wonderful gifts.

VINTAGE CLOTHING

Ⓢ **Aardvark's.** 1501 Haight St. (at Ashbury St.). ☎ **415/621-3141.**

One of San Francisco's largest secondhand-clothing dealers, Aardvark's has seemingly endless racks of shirts, pants, dresses, skirts, and hats from the last 30 years.

Buffalo Exchange. 1555 Haight St. (between Clayton and Ashbury sts.). ☎ **415/431-7733.**

On upper Haight, this store is crammed with antique and new fashions from the 1960s, 1970s, and 1990s—including everything from suits and dresses to neckties, hats, handbags, and jewelry. A second shop is located at 1800 Polk St., at Washington Street (☎ 415/346-5741).

La Rosa. 1711 Haight St. (at Cole). ☎ **415/668-3744.**

High-quality, dry-cleaned secondhand formal suits and dresses are this shop's specialty, but you'll also find sport coats, slacks, and shoes.

WINES

Wine Club San Francisco. 953 Harrison St. (between 5th and 6th sts.). ☎ **415/512-9086.**

The Wine Club is a discount warehouse that offers bargain prices on over 1,200 domestic and foreign wines. Bottles cost $4 to $1,100, and they only mark up wholesale prices 6% to 12%.

11 San Francisco After Dark

To find out what's hot, check the *San Francisco Bay Guardian* and the *San Francisco Weekly,* available free at bars and restaurants, and from street-corner boxes. *Key,* a free tourist monthly available in hotels and at attractions, is also useful. Also check the Sunday edition of the *Chronicle,* which contains a **"Datebook"** section.

THE PERFORMING ARTS

Tix Bay Area, on Stockton Street, between Post and Geary (☎ 415/433-7827), sells half-price tickets to theater, dance, and music performances on the day of the show only; tickets for Sunday and Monday events are sold on Saturday. It also sells advance, full-price tickets for most performances. The service charge is $1 to $3, and only cash or traveler's checks are accepted for half-price tickets. Tix is open Tuesday to Thursday from 11am to 6pm and on Friday and Saturday from 11am to 7pm.

Tickets to most theater and dance events can also be obtained through **City Box Office,** 153 Kearny St., Suite 402 (☎ 415/392-4400), and **BASS Ticketmaster** (☎ 510/762-2277). You can also try Wherehouse stores throughout the city; the most convenient is at 30 Powell St.

From mid-June to August, one of the best free programs is the **Stern Grove Midsummer Music Festival,** 44 Page St., Suite 604D, San Francisco, CA 94102 (☎ 415/252-6252), held every Sunday during the summer at 2pm in Stern Grove Park. It opens traditionally with the San Francisco Symphony Orchestra; other performances include ballet, jazz, and theater. Stern Grove is located near 19th Avenue and Sloat Boulevard; arrive early for a good view, and bring a picnic.

CLASSICAL MUSIC

In addition to the San Francisco Symphony (see below), there are a couple of other minor companies. Acclaimed by the *New York Times* as "the country's leading early-music orchestra," the **Philharmonia Baroque Orchestra,** 57 Post St., Suite 705 (☎ **415/391-5252**), usually performs at the Herbst Theatre from September to April. Tickets are $20 to $30. And the **San Francisco Contemporary Music Players,** 44 Page St., Suite 604a (☎ **415/252-6235,** or 415/978-ARTS for the box office), features modern chamber works by international artists. Tickets are $14 for adults, $10 for seniors 65 and older, and $6 for students.

San Francisco Symphony. Performing in Louise M. Davies Hall, 201 Van Ness Ave. (at Grove St.). ☎ **415/864-6000.** Tickets $10–$68.

Founded in 1911, the internationally respected San Francisco Symphony is now under the baton of Michael Tilson Thomas. The season runs from September to May. Summer symphony activities include a Composer Festival and a Summer Pops series.

OPERA

In addition to the renowned San Francisco Opera (see below), the **Pocket Opera,** 333 Kearny St., Suite 703 (☎ **415/989-1855**), performs on weekends from mid-February to mid-June. This comic company stages performances in English of well- and not-so-well-known operas accompanied by a chamber orchestra. The staging is intimate and informal, lacking lavish costumes and sets. Tickets run $18 to $25.

✪ **San Francisco Opera.** War Memorial Opera House, 301 Van Ness Ave. near Grove St. ☎ **415/864-3330.** Tickets $25–$135; $8 standing room sold after 10:30am on the day of performance.

The San Francisco Opera was the first municipal opera in the United States, and is one of the city's cultural icons. It features celebrated stars, along with promising newcomers, in traditional and avant-garde productions, all with English supertitles. The season starts in September and runs 14 weeks, with performances nightly (except Monday) and matinees on Sunday. Performances in January and February 1997 will be staged elsewhere while the Opera House is being retrofitted. The fall of 1997 will be the 75th anniversary season, which will be held in the newly restored Opera House.

THEATER

The theater district is concentrated in a few blocks west of Union Square.

The city has a wide variety of offerings, many more than we have space to cover here—check the publications mentioned above to see what's currently in production. One good bet is **The Magic Theatre,** Building D, Fort Mason Center, Marina Boulevard at Buchanan Street (☎ **415/441-8822**), a highly acclaimed company that presents the works of new playwrights and has nurtured such luminaries as Sam Shepard and Jon Robin Baitz. The season usually runs from September to July with performances Wednesday to Sunday. Tickets cost $14 to $23; $12 for students, children, and seniors. There's also **Theatre Rhinoceros,** 2926 16th St. (☎ **415/861-5079**), which was America's first (and still the foremost) theater ensemble devoted solely to works addressing gay and lesbian issues.

○ **American Conservatory Theater (ACT).** Performing at the Geary Theater, 415 Geary St. (at Mason St.). ☎ **415/749-2228.** Tickets $14–$47.50.

The troupe is so venerated that ACT has been compared to the British National Theatre, the Berliner Ensemble, and the Comédie Française. The season runs from October to May and features both classical and experimental works. The theater sustained severe damage in the 1989 earthquake and only recently reopened after undergoing renovation and seismic stabilization.

Lorraine Hansberry Theatre. 620 Sutter St. (at Mason St.). ☎ **415/474-8800.**

San Francisco's top African-American theater group performs in a 300-seat theater in the Sheehan Hotel. Special adaptations from literature are performed along with contemporary dramas, classics, and world premières.

DANCE

In addition to local companies, top traveling troupes such as the Joffrey Ballet and American Ballet Theatre make regular appearances here. The primary modern dance spaces include the **Theatre Artaud,** 450 Florida St., at 17th Street (☎ 415/621-7797); the **Cowell Theater,** at Fort Mason Center (☎ 415/441-3400); **Dancer's Group/Footwork,** 3221 22nd St., at Mission Street (☎ 415/824-5044); and the **New Performance Gallery,** 3153 17th St., at Shotwell (☎ 415/863-9834). Check the local papers for schedules or contact the theater box offices directly.

○ **San Francisco Ballet.** ☎ **415/861-5600** for tickets and performance location, or 415/865-2000. Tickets $10–$75.

Winner of high international praise, the San Francisco Ballet is the oldest permanent ballet company in the United States. Under the artistic direction of Helgi Tomasson, the company performs an eclectic repertoire of full-length neoclassical and contemporary ballets. The season opens with performances of *The Nutcracker* in December and continues through May at the War Memorial Opera House, Van Ness Avenue and Grove Street.

The Opera House closed in January 1996 for 18 months for seismic renovations. Meantime, the ballet will perform in alternative theaters.

MAJOR CONCERT & PERFORMANCE HALLS

There are a number of other venues, of course; we've only listed the few that provide particularly memorable settings for visiting performers. Check the publications listed above to find out who's playing during your visit in venues throughout the city.

Center for the Arts. Yerba Buena Gardens, at the corner of 3rd and Howard sts. ☎ **415/978-2787.**

This brand-new center features cutting-edge dance, music, and theater in the 755-seat proscenium-stage theater; dance and other events in the multiuse Forum; and theater, dance, and other performances outside on the Esplanade Stage.

The Great American Music Hall. 859 O'Farrell St. (between Polk and Larkin sts.). ☎ **415/885-0750.**

This historic venue boasts an ornate interior—with carved plaster cupids on the ceiling and a wraparound balcony supported by huge marble pillars. You'll be seated at a table to hear whatever pop, rock, blues, jazz, country, or bluegrass performer is booked.

Herbst Theatre. 401 Van Ness Ave. at McAllister St. ☎ **415/621-6600,** or 415/392-4400 for the box office.

This is the top hall for local and visiting musicians and artists. The 928-seat auditorium was the site of the 1945 signing of the United Nations Charter. Its walls are hung with eight paintings commissioned for the 1915 Panama Pacific International Exposition, created by renowned muralist Frank Brangwyn.

THE CLUB & MUSIC SCENE

The hippest dance places are South of Market Street (SoMa), in former warehouses, whereas the most popular music and cafe culture is still centered in North Beach.

CABARET & COMEDY

Bay Area Theatresports. At the Bayfront Theater, in the Fort Mason Center, Building B, 3rd Floor. ☎ **415/824-8220.** Tickets $8.

This is an improvisational tournament in which four-actor teams compete against each other, taking on improvisational challenges from the audience. Monday only.

Beach Blanket Babylon. At Club Fugazi, 678 Green St. between Columbus Ave. and Powell St. ☎ **415/421-4222.** Tickets $18–$45.

A San Francisco tradition, *Beach Blanket Babylon* is a comedic musical send-up, best known for its outrageous costumes and oversize headdresses. It's been playing almost 22 years now and still almost every performance sells out. Persons under 21 are welcome at Sunday matinees at 3pm when no alcohol is served; photo ID is required for evening performances. It's wise to write for tickets at least 3 weeks in advance, or obtain them through TIX.

Cobb's Comedy Club. In the Cannery at Fisherman's Wharf, 2801 Leavenworth St. ☎ **415/928-4320.** Cover $5 Mon, $8–$15 Tues–Sun—plus a two-drink minimum.

Cobb's features national headliners. There's comedy every night, including a 13-comedian All-Pro Monday showcase (a 3-hour marathon). The club is open to those 18 and over, and to those 16 and 17 if they're accompanied by an adult.

Finocchio's. 506 Broadway (at Kearny St.). ☎ **415/982-9388.** Cover $12–15.

For more than 50 years this family-run cabaret club has showcased the city's best female impersonators in a funny, kitschy show. Three different revues are presented nightly (usually Thursday to Saturday at 8:30, 10, and 11:30pm), and a single cover is good for the entire evening. There's no minimum, and drinks begin at $2.75. Parking is available next door at the Flying Dutchman.

Punchline. 444 Battery St., plaza level (between Washington and Clay sts.). ☎ **415/397-4337,** or 415/397-7573 for recorded information. Cover $6–$15 Mon–Sat, $5 Sun—plus a two-drink minimum.

This is the largest comedy club in the city. Three-person shows with top national and local talent are featured Tuesday to Saturday. Showcase night is Sunday, when 15 to 20 rising stars take the mike. There's an all-star showcase or a special event on Monday nights. Buy tickets in advance if you don't want to wait in line.

ROCK & BLUES CLUBS

The Fillmore. 1805 Geary Blvd. (at Fillmore St.). ☎ **415/346-6000.** Cover varies with the performer.

Reopened after years of neglect, the Fillmore, made famous by promoter Bill Graham in the 1960s, is once again attracting big names. Check the local listings magazines, or call the theater for information on upcoming events.

The Saloon. 1232 Grant Ave. at Green St. ☎ **415/989-7666.** Cover $3–$6 Fri–Sat.

An authentic Gold Rush survivor, this North Beach dive is the oldest extant bar in the city, popular with both bikers and daytime pinstripers. There's live blues several nights a week.

Slim's. 333 11th St. (at Folsom St.). ☎ **415/522-0333.** Cover $10–$20.

New Orleans–style Slim's is co-owned by Boz Scaggs, who sometimes takes the stage under the name "Presidio Slim." This glitzy restaurant/bar seats 300, serves California cuisine, and specializes in excellent American music—home-grown rock, jazz, blues, and alternative music—almost nightly.

JAZZ & LATIN CLUBS

Cesar's Latin Palace. 3140 Mission St. ☎ **415/648-6611.** Cover $5–$8.

Live Latin bands perform to a very mixed crowd—ethnically, economically, and generationally. Plenty of dancing and drinking.

❍ Jazz at Pearl's. 256 Columbus Ave. (at Broadway). ☎ **415/291-8255.** No cover (but there's a two-drink minimum).

One of the best venues for jazz in the city, where ribs and chicken go with the sounds. The live jams last until 2am nightly.

Mason Street Wine Bar. 342 Mason St. (at Geary St.). ☎ **415/391-3454.** No cover, except for special performances.

This contemporary bar offers live jazz nightly. Small cabaret tables with black club chairs face a small stage. More than 100 different wines are served from the half-moon-shaped bar; glasses begin at $4.

330 Ritch. 330 Ritch (between 3rd and 4th sts. off Townsend St.). ☎ **415/541-9574.**

If you can find the place, you must be cool. It's located on a 2-block-long alley in SoMa and even locals have a hard time remembering how to get there. But once you do, expect happy hour cocktails (specials on a few select mixed drinks and draft brews), pool tables, and a hip young crowd at play. Weekends, the place really livens up with disco or salsa themes.

Masons and the New Orleans Room. In the Fairmont Hotel, 950 Mason St. (at California St.). ☎ **415/772-5259.** Cover varies.

Cabaret reigns at Masons and the adjoining New Orleans Room features jazz. Call for information on featured entertainers.

DANCE CLUBS

The club scene is always changing. Most of the venues below are promoted as different clubs on various nights of the week, each with its own look, sound, and style. Discount passes and club announcements are often available at hip clothing stores and other shops along upper Haight Street.

Three Babes and a Bus (☎ 415/552-2582) runs regular nightclub trips on Friday and Saturday nights to the city's busiest clubs.

Club DV8. 540 Howard St. ☎ **415/777-1419,** or 415/957-1730 for recorded information. Cover $5 Thurs and Sun, $10 Fri–Sat; usually free before 10pm.

This SoMa club has been attracting the black-garb crowd longer than any other establishment. Two DJs spin music on separate dance floors. The decor mixes trompe l'oeil, pop art, candelabra, mirrors, and some extraordinary Dalí-esque props.

Club 1015. 1015 Folsom St. (at 6th St.). ☎ **415/431-1200.** Cover $10–$15.

Three levels and three dance floors have made this a stylish stop along the nightclub circuit. Weekends are best, when the club is a carnival of hip people. Currently, Dakota (☎ 415/431-1200) is held on Friday from 10pm to 6am and features four different sounds—1970s, progressive house, funk, and rare groove. Saturday is gay night (☎ 415/431-BOYS). For other nights, call ahead.

Paradise Lounge. 1501 Folsom St. (at 11th St.). ☎ **415/861-6906.** Cover $3–$15.

Labyrinthine Paradise features three dance floors simultaneously vibrating to different beats. Smaller auxiliary spaces include a pool room with half a dozen tables. Poetry readings are also given.

Sound Factory. 525 Harrison (at 1st St.). ☎ **415/543-1300.** No cover before 10pm, $10 after 10pm.

Columnist Herb Caen, who dubbed this the "mother of all discos," would never be found shaking it all night at this disco theme park. The maze of rooms and nonstop barrage of house, funk, lounge vibes, and club classics attract swarms of young urbanites looking to rave it up until sometimes as late as 6am. Management tries to eliminate the riffraff by enforcing a dress code (no sneakers, hooded sweatshirts, or sports caps).

THE BAR & CAFE SCENE

Below is a good cross section of the best the city has to offer.

Albion. 3139 16th St. (between Valencia and Guerrero sts.). ☎ **415/552-8558.**

Artistic types and various SoMa hipsters cocktail here. Live music is played on Sunday between 5 and 8 and ranges from ragtime and blues to jazz and swing.

Edinburgh Castle. 950 Geary St. (between Polk and Larkin sts.). ☎ **415/885-4074.**

Opened in 1958, this legendary Scottish pub is known for unusual British ales on tap and the best selection of single-malt scotches in the city. It's decorated with Royal Air Force mementos, steel helmets, and an authentic Ballantine caber, used in the annual Scottish games. Avoid Saturday nights unless you like bagpipes. Fish and chips are always available.

Gordon-Biersch Brewery. On the Embarcadero, 2 Harrison St. ☎ **415/243-8246.**

This large brew-restaurant serves decent food and tasty brews to a lively yuppie crowd. There are several beers to choose from, ranging from light to dark.

✪ Harry Denton's. 161 Steuart St. between Mission and Howard. ☎ **415/882-1333.** No cover Sun–Tues, $3 Wed, $5 Thurs, $10 Fri–Sat.

Early evening it's filled with working "suits" and secretaries on the prowl. But when the stately restaurant with mahogany bar, red velvet furnishings, and chandeliers clears away the dining utensils and turns up the music, a glitzy crowd pulls up to valet with their boogie shoes on. The front lounge features R&B or jazz performers while there's disco and pop dancing in the back room.

Johnny Love's. 1500 Broadway. ☎ **415/931-6053.**

This is the city's quintessential singles bar. There's a small dance floor and live music several nights a week; when it's jumping, this joint is a real scene. Love's serves decent food too, but your money's best spent on drinks.

Julie's Supper Club. 1123 Folsom (at 7th St.). ☎ **415/861-0707.** Cover $5 Fri–Sat unless a full meal is ordered.

Crowded and lively, Julie's offers an array of appetizers and live music on Friday and Saturday nights to a mixed crowd of twenty- and thirty-somethings.

Perry's. 1944 Union St. (at Laguna St.). ☎ **415/922-9022.**

An attractive bar for the thirty-something singles crowd, with mahogany paneling and a pressed-tin ceiling. There's a dining room, too.

✪ **The Redwood Room.** In the Clift Hotel, 495 Geary St. at Taylor St. ☎ **415/775-4700.**

This magnificent art deco–style room, completely done in redwood paneling, features a fabulous martini menu and a pianist who specializes in tunes from the 1930s and 1940s.

20 Tank Brewery. 316 11th St. (at Folsom St.). ☎ **415/255-9455.**

This huge, upscale bar is known for good ale, plus pizzas, sandwiches, chilis, and assorted appetizers. Live jazz is performed 2 nights a week. Other nights you can amuse yourself with darts, shuffleboard, and dice. Check 'em out on the Web: **http:// www.20tank.com.**

POOL HALLS

Chalkers Billiards Club. 101 Spear St. (at Mission St.). ☎ **415/512-0450.**

Poolhall meets men's smoking club at this enormous classy billiards joint. Food and drinks are delivered to the 31 cherrywood tables that you can rent by the hour. Happy hour on weekdays from 5 to 7pm offers more beer for your buck.

The Great Entertainer. 975 Bryant St. (at 8th St.). ☎ **415/861-8833.**

This is another glorified pool hall, with 42 pool tables, plus shuffleboard, darts, table tennis, and a video arcade. Drinks, pizza, and other dishes accompany the games.

NORTH BEACH BARS & CAFES

San Francisco in general, and North Beach in particular, is loaded with Italian-style cafés where patrons are encouraged to linger.

Caffè Greco. 423 Columbus Ave. between Green and Vallejo sts. ☎ **415/397-6261.**

The Caffè Greco opened in the late 1980s and has quickly become one of the best places to linger. Sophisticated and relaxed, it serves beer, wine, a good selection of coffees, focaccia sandwiches, and desserts.

Caffè Trieste. 601 Vallejo St. at Grant Ave. ☎ **415/392-6739.**

Opera is always on the jukebox at this classic Italian coffeehouse, and on Saturday afternoon it's live when the family performs arias to the assembled crowd.

Savoy Tivoli. 1434 Grant Ave. between Green and Union sts. ☎ **415/362-7023.**

Euro- and wanna-be Euro-trash crowd the few pool tables and indoor and patio seating to smoke cigarettes and look cool at this popular trendy bar.

Specs' Adler Museum Cafe. 12 Saroyan Place off Columbus Ave. ☎ **415/421-4112.**

Specs' is one of the liveliest and most likable pubs in North Beach. Maritime flags hang from the ceiling, while the exposed brick walls are lined with posters, photos, and various oddities.

Vesuvio. 255 Columbus Ave. at Broadway. ☎ **415/362-3370.**

This is one of North Beach's best beatnik-style hangouts. Popular with neighborhood writers, artists, songsters, and wanna-bes, Vesuvio also gets its share of longshoremen, cab drivers, and businesspeople. In addition to well-priced drinks, Vesuvio has good coffee/espresso.

COCKTAILS WITH A VIEW

The Carnelian Room. In the Bank of America Building, 555 California St. (between Kearny and Montgomery sts.). ☎ **415/433-7500.**

This 52nd-floor room offers panoramic views of the city. In addition to cocktails, sunset dinners are served nightly, for about $45 per person. Jackets and ties are required for men. The restaurant has one of the most extensive wine lists in the city— 1,275 selections, to be exact.

✪ **The Crown Room.** In the Fairmont Hotel, 950 Mason St. 24th floor. ☎ **415/772-5131.**

Of all the bars listed here, the Crown Room, reached by an external glass elevator, is definitely the plushest. The panoramic view from the top will encourage you to linger. In addition to drinks, dinner buffets are served for $31.

Harry Denton's Starlight Room. In the Sir Francis Drake Hotel, 450 Powell St. at Union Square 21st floor. ☎ **415/395-8595.** Cover $5–$10.

Tourists and locals sip cocktails at sunset and boogie down to live swing and big-band tunes after dark in this classic 1930s San Francisco room with red-velvet banquettes, chandeliers, and fabulous views. Jackets recommended for men.

✪ **Top of the Mark.** In the Mark Hopkins Hotel, California and Mason sts. ☎ **415/392-3434.**

One of the most famous cocktail lounges in the world opened here in 1939 and was renovated in 1996. During World War II countless Pacific-bound servicemen toasted their good-bye to the States here. The glass-walled room features an unparalleled view. Sunday brunch is served from 10am to 2pm, costing about $28.

GAY BARS & CLUBS

As with straight establishments, gay bars and clubs target varied clienteles. The major lesbian community is in Oakland, though there are a few hangouts in the city. In San Francisco, gay life is centered in the Castro, with establishments also in SoMa, along Polk Street, and in the Mission District. Check the gay paper the *Bay Area Reporter* or the *San Francisco Bay Guardian* for more information about what's currently hot.

Alta Plaza. 2301 Fillmore St. (at Clay St.). ☎ **415/922-1444.**

Pacific Heights' wealthy gays flock to this classy Fillmore establishment with both bar and restaurant. It's especially festive on Friday and Saturday during happy hour.

Badlands. 4121 18th St. at Casto St. ☎ **415/626-9320.**

This popular cruise bar is decorated with license plates from all over the country. Neon throws a stream of multicolored light on the patrons, many of whom are clad in tight Levis.

Castro Station. 456 Castro St.between 17th and 18th sts. ☎ **415/626-7220.**

A well-known gay hangout, this bar is popular with the leather and Levis crowd, and trendy boys from around the country show up here looking for action.

The Cinch Saloon. 1723 Polk St. (near Washington St.). ☎ **415/776-4162.**

Among the popular attributes of this cruisy neighborhood bar are the outdoor patio, Sunday barbecue or buffet, and progressive music and videos. 49er fans also gather here for televised games. The bar attracts a mixed crowd of gays, lesbians (now that there are almost no exclusively lesbian bars left in San Francisco), and gay-friendly straight folk.

Detour. 2348 Market St. (near Castro St.). ☎ **415/861-6053.**

Right in the heart of gay San Francisco, this bar attracts a young crowd of guys, with its low lighting and throbbing house music. Chain-link fences seem to hold in the action, while a live DJ spins a web of popular hits. Special events, including the Saturday go-go dancers, keep this place jumping.

The End Up. 401 6th St. (at Harrison St.). ☎ **415/543-7700.** Cover varies.

It's a different nightclub every night of the week, but regardless of who's throwing the party, the place is always jumping with the DJ's blasting tunes. There are two pool tables, a flaming fireplace, an outdoor patio, and a mob of gyrating souls on the dance floor. Some nights are straight, so call for gay nights.

Metro. 3600 16th St. (at Market St.). ☎ **415/703-9750.**

With modern art on the walls, the Metro provides the gay community with high-energy dance music and the best view of the Castro district from its large balcony. The bar seems to attract people of all ages who enjoy the friendly bartenders and the highly charged, cruisy atmosphere. There's also a Chinese restaurant on the premises.

The Mint. 1942 Market St. (at Laguna St.). ☎ **415/626-4726.**

Come out of the closet—and the shower—and into the Mint, where every night you can sing show tunes at this gay and lesbian karaoke bar. Along with song, you'll encounter a mixed 20- to 40something crowd who like to combine cocktails with do-it-yourself cabaret.

Nightshift. 469 Castro St. (between 17th and 18th sts.). ☎ **415/626-4876.**

Deep in the heart of the Castro district, young men and their pursuers show up here, enjoying the low lighting, the sexually charged atmosphere, and even the occasional exhibition of a local artist's work. The age group ranges from the early 20s to the 50s, and it's a convivial place with sometimes exciting shows. For would-be Jeff Strykers, "The Battle of the Bulge" (an underwear contest) takes place on the second Sunday of the month.

Rawhide II. 280 7th St. (at Folsom St.). ☎ **415/621-1197.**

Gay or straight, this is one of the city's top country-western dance bars, patronized by both sexes. Free dance lessons are offered Monday to Thursday from 7:30 to 9:30pm.

The Stud. 399 9th St. (at Harrison St.). ☎ **415/863-6623.**

The Stud has been around for 30 years, is one of the most successful gay establishments in town, and is mellow enough for straights as well as gays. The music here is a balanced mix of old and new, retro-disco for guys on Wednesday and women's nights on Thursday and Saturday.

6

Side Trips from San Francisco

by Erika Lenkert and Matthew R. Poole

Without question, the Bay City is captivating. But don't let it ensnare you to the point of ignoring its environs, which contain a multitude of natural spectacles like Mount Tamalpais and Muir Woods; scenic communities like Tiburon and Sausalito; and cities like gritty Oakland and its youth-oriented next-door neighbor, Berkeley. A little farther north stretch the valleys of Napa, Sonoma, and Alexander, the finest wine region in the nation. And to the south lies the digital wonderland of Silicon Valley and surf-city Santa Cruz.

1 Oakland

10 miles E of San Francisco

Although it's less than a dozen miles from San Francisco, the city of Oakland is worlds apart from its sister city across the bay. Originally little more than a cluster of ranches and farms, Oakland exploded in size and stature practically overnight as the last mile of transcontinental railroad track was laid down in 1869. Major shipping ports soon followed, and to this day Oakland has retained its hold as one of the busiest industrial ports on the West Coast.

The price for all this economic success, however, is Oakland's lowbrow reputation as a predominantly working-class city, forever in the shadow of San Francisco's Euro-chic spotlight. Even the city's NFL football team, the Oakland Raiders, has a proud and long-standing reputation for being mean, tough, and dirty (a cherished antithesis to their mortal enemy, the golden-boy 49ers). But with all its shortcomings and bad press, Oakland still has a few pleasant surprises up its sleeve for the handful of tourists who venture this way. Rent a sailboat on Lake Merritt, stroll along the waterfront, explore the fantastic Oakland Museum—all great reasons to hop across the bay and spend a fog-free day exploring one of California's largest and most ethnically diverse cities.

ESSENTIALS

GETTING THERE   You can take Bay Area Rapid Transit (BART) from San Francisco to Oakland. Your fare will range from 80¢ to $3, depending on your station of origin; children 4 and under ride free. Exit at the 12th Street station for downtown Oakland.

If you're driving from San Francisco, take I-80 across the San Francisco–Oakland Bay Bridge. Exit at Grand Avenue south for the Lake Merritt area.

CITY LAYOUT   Downtown Oakland is bordered by Grand Avenue on the north, I-980 on the west, the Inner Harbor on the south, and Lake Merritt on the east. Between these landmarks are three BART stations (12th Street, 19th Street, and Lake Merritt), City Hall, the Oakland Museum, Jack London Square, and several other sights.

WHAT TO SEE & DO

Lake Merritt is the city's primary tourist attraction. Three miles in circumference, the tidal lagoon was bridged and dammed in the 1860s and is now a wildlife refuge that's home to flocks of migrating ducks, herons, and geese. At the **Sailboat House,** in Lakeside Park along the north shore (☎ **510/444-3807**), you can rent sailboats, rowboats, pedalboats, and canoes for $6 to $12 per hour.

If you'd like to catch a big-league baseball game, the **Oakland A's** play at the Oakland Coliseum, at the Hegenberger Road exit from I-880 (☎ **510/430-8020**). Tickets are available from the Coliseum Box Office or by phone through BASS Ticketmaster (☎ 510/762-2277). The **Oakland Raiders** also play at the Coliseum (☎ **800/949-2626** for ticket information). The stadium holds close to 50,000 spectators and is serviced by BART's Coliseum station.

For a recorded update on Oakland's arts and entertainment happenings, phone **510/835-2787.**

Children's Fairyland. In Lakeside Park, Grand Ave. and Bellevue Dr. ☎ **510/452-2259.** Admission $3 adults, $2.50 children 12 and under. Summer, Mon–Fri 10am–4:30pm, Sat–Sun 10am–5:30pm; spring and fall, Wed–Sun 10am–4:30pm; winter, Fri–Sun and holidays 10am–4:30pm. BART: 19th St. station; then walk north along Broadway and turn right on Grand Ave. to the park. From I-580 south, exit at Grand Ave.; Children's Fairyland is at the far end of the park, on your left at Bellevue Ave.

Located on the north shore of Lake Merritt, this is one of the most imaginative children's parks in the United States, enough so that it inspired Walt Disney to construct Disneyland. Kids can peer into old Geppetto's workshop, watch the Mad Hatter eternally pouring tea for Alice, see Noah's Ark overloaded with animal passengers, and view Beatrix Potter's village of storybook characters. Fairy tales also come alive during puppet-show performances at 11am, 2pm, and 4pm.

✪ **Oakland Museum of California.** 1000 Oak St. (at 10th St.). ☎ **510/238-3401.** Admission $5 adults, $3 students and seniors, free for children 6 and under, free for everyone Sun 4–7pm. Wed–Sat 10am–5pm, Sun noon–7pm. Closed New Year's Day, July 4, Thanksgiving, and Christmas Day. BART: Lake Merritt station (1 block south of the museum). From I-880 north, take the Oak St. exit; the museum is 5 blocks east at Oak and 10th sts. Alternatively, take I-580 to I-980 and exit at the Jackson St. ramp.

The Oakland Museum includes just about everything you'd want to know about the state, its people, history, culture, geology, art, environment, and ecology. It's actually three museums in one, exhibiting works by California artists from Bierstadt to Diebenkorn; artifacts from California's history, from Pomo Native American basketry to Country Joe McDonald's guitar; and re-creations of California habitats from the coast to the White Mountains.

There are 45-minute guided tours leaving the gallery information desks on request. There's a fine cafe, a gallery (☎ 510/834-2296) selling works by California artists, and a book and gift shop.

Jack London Square. Broadway and Embarcadero. BART: 12th St. station; then walk south along Broadway (about half a mile) or take bus no. 51a to the foot of Broadway. Take I-880 to Broadway, turn south, and go to the end.

The Bay Area

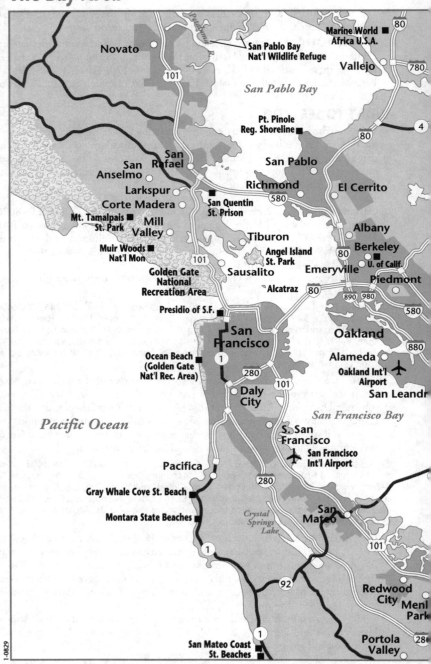

Novato

San Pablo Bay
Nat'l Wildlife Refuge

Marine World
Africa U.S.A.

Vallejo

80

780

San Pablo Bay

Pt. Pinole
Reg. Shoreline

80

4

San
Rafael

San
Anselmo

Larkspur

Corte Madera

Mt. Tamalpais
St. Park

San Pablo

Richmond

El Cerrito

San Quentin
St. Prison

580

Mill
Valley

Muir Woods
Nat'l Mon

Tiburon

Angel Island
St. Park

Albany

Berkeley

U. of Calif.

Emeryville

Piedmont

101

Golden Gate
National
Recreation Area

Sausalito

Alcatraz

80

980
890

580

Presidio of S.F.

San
Francisco

Oakland

880

Ocean Beach
(Golden Gate
Nat'l Rec. Area)

1

280

101

Alameda

Oakland Int'l
Airport

San Leandr

Daly
City

San Francisco Bay

Pacific Ocean

S. San
Francisco

San Francisco
Int'l Airport

Pacifica

280

Gray Whale Cove St. Beach

Montara State Beaches

Crystal
Springs
Lake

San
Mateo

101

1

92

Redwood
City

Menl
Park

San Mateo Coast
St. Beaches

1

Portola
Valley

28

1-0829

140

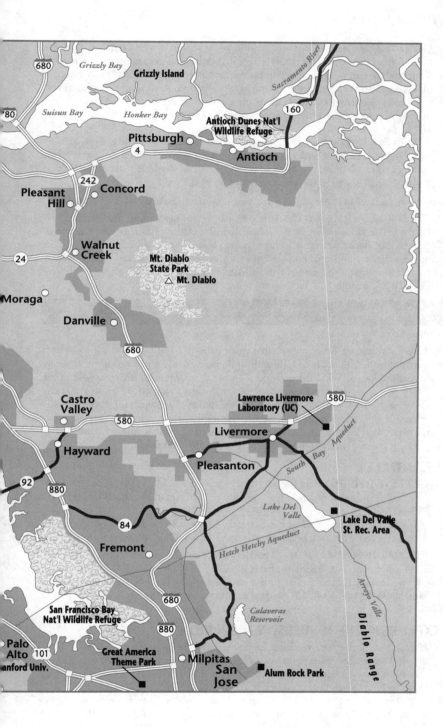

Grizzly Bay

Grizzly Island

680

Suisun Bay

Honker Bay

Sacramento River

80

Antioch Dunes Nat'l
Wildlife Refuge

160

Pittsburgh

4

Antioch

242

Concord

Pleasant
Hill

Walnut
Creek

24

Mt. Diablo
State Park
△ Mt. Diablo

Moraga

Danville

680

Castro
Valley

Lawrence Livermore
Laboratory (UC)

580

580

Livermore

Hayward

Pleasanton

South Bay Aqueduct

92

880

Lake Del
Valle

Lake Del Valle
St. Rec. Area

84

Hetch Hetchy Aqueduct

Fremont

Arroyo Valle

680

San Francisco Bay
Nat'l Wildlife Refuge

Calaveras
Reservoir

Diablo Range

880

Palo
Alto
anford Univ.

101

Great America
Theme Park

Milpitas

San
Jose

Alum Rock Park

141

Oakland's only patent tourist area, this low-key version of San Francisco's Fisherman's Wharf shamelessly plays up the fact that Jack London spent most of his youth along this waterfront. The square fronts the harbor, housing a tourist-tacky complex of boutiques and eateries that are about as far away from the "call of the wild" as you can get. In the center of the square is the small, reconstructed, rustic Yukon cabin in which London lived while prospecting in the Klondike during the Gold Rush of 1897.

At 56 Jack London Sq., at the foot of Webster Street, you'll find a more authentic memorial, the **First and Last Chance Saloon,** where London did some of his writing and much of his drinking. The corner table he used has remained exactly as it was 75 or so years ago (except for his photos on the wall).

Alice Arts Center. 1428 Alice St. (4 blocks from downtown Oakland). ☎ **510/238-7221.**

The $14-million Alice Arts Center houses six performing groups: the Oakland Ballet, the Oakland Ensemble Theater, the CitiCentre Dance Theatre (a jazz, Caribbean, and African dance ensemble), Dimensions Dance Theater (the Bay Area's oldest modern dance company), Four Seasons Concerts, and the Oakland Youth Orchestra. Dimensions also performs in downtown's spectacular Paramount Theatre (☎ 510/893-2300).

2 Berkeley

10 miles NE of San Francisco

Berkeley would be little more than a quaint sleepy town east of the big city if it weren't for the University of California at Berkeley, world renowned for its first-rate education, its 15 Nobel Prize winners—more than any other university—and the 1960s protests that led to the most infamous student riots in U.S. history. Today there's still hippie idealism in the air, but the radicals have aged, the 1960s are only present in tie-dye and paraphernalia shops, and the students are altogether less angstridden. Still, it's a charming town teeming with all types of people, a beautiful campus, vast parks, great shopping, and some incredible restaurants.

ESSENTIALS

GETTING THERE   The Berkeley BART station is 2 blocks from the university. The fare from San Francisco is under $3. For information, call **BART** at **510/793-2278.**

If you're driving from San Francisco, take I-80 east to the University exit. Count on walking some distance because you won't find a parking spot near the university.

VISITOR INFORMATION   The **Berkeley Convention and Visitors Bureau,** 1834 University Ave., 1st Floor, Berkeley, CA 94703 (☎ **510/549-7040**), can answer your questions and even find accommodations for you. Phone the **Visitor Hotline** (☎ 510/549-8710) for general information on events and happenings in Berkeley.

EXPLORING THE UNIVERSITY & ENVIRONS

Hanging out is the preferred Berkeley pastime and the best place to do it is on **Telegraph Avenue,** the street that leads to the campus's southern entrance. Most of the action lies between Bancroft Way and Ashby Avenue where coffeehouses, restaurants, shops, great book and record stores, and craft booths swarm with life.

Pretend you're local: Plant yourself at a cafe, sip a latte, and ponder something intellectual while you survey the town's unique residents bustling by. Bibliophiles must stop at **Cody's Books,** 2454 Telegraph Ave. (☎ **510/845-7852**), to peruse its

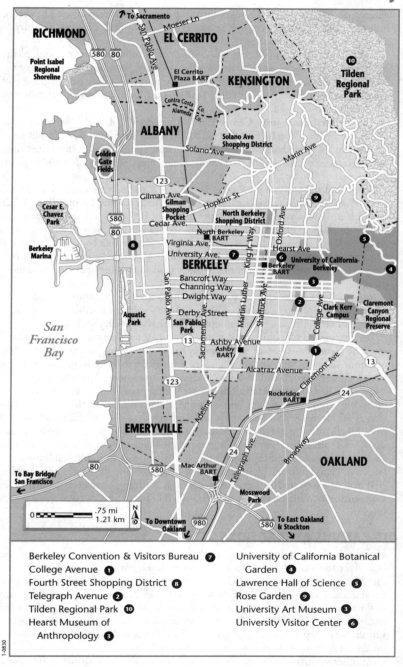

Berkeley

RICHMOND

EL CERRITO

To Sacramento

Moeser Ln

580 80

Point Isabel
Regional
Shoreline

El Cerrito
Plaza BART

KENSINGTON

10
Tilden
Regional
Park

ALBANY

Contra Costa Co.
Alameda Co.

Solano Ave
Shopping District

Golden
Gate
Fields

Solano Ave

Marin Ave

123

Gilman Ave.

Hopkins St

9

Cesar E.
Chavez
Park

Gilman
Shopping
Pocket

Cedar Ave.

North Berkeley
Shopping District

North Berkeley
BART

Oxford Ave.

580

80

Virginia Ave.

Hearst Ave

5

Berkeley
Marina

University Ave.

7

BERKELEY

King Jr. Way

University of California-
Berkeley

6

4

Berkeley
BART

Bancroft Way
Channing Way
Dwight Way

Martin Luther

Shattuck Ave.

3

San
Francisco
Bay

Aquatic
Park

Derby Street

2

Clark Kerr
Campus

Claremont
Canyon
Regional
Preserve

San Pablo Ave.

San Pablo
Park

College Ave.

13

Sacramento St.

Ashby Avenue
Ashby
BART

1

123

Alcatraz Avenue

13

Adeline St.

Rockridge
BART

Claremont Ave.

24

EMERYVILLE

Telegraph Ave.

Broadway

OAKLAND

80

580

24

Mac Arthur
BART

To Bay Bridge/
San Francisco

0   .75 mi
1.21 km

N

Mosswood
Park

To Downtown
Oakland

980

580

To East Oakland
& Stockton

1-0830

Berkeley Convention & Visitors Bureau 7
College Avenue 1
Fourth Street Shopping District 8
Telegraph Avenue 2
Tilden Regional Park 10
Hearst Museum of
    Anthropology 3

University of California Botanical
    Garden 4
Lawrence Hall of Science 5
Rose Garden 9
University Art Museum 3
University Visitor Center 6

143

gargantuan selection of titles, independent press books, and magazines. The avenue is also packed with street vendors selling everything from T-shirts and jewelry to *I Ching* and tarot-card readings.

UC Berkeley itself is worth a stroll as well. It's a beautiful old campus with plenty of woodsy paths, architecturally noteworthy buildings, and of course many of the 31,000 students scurrying to and from classes. Among the architectural highlights of the campus are a number of buildings by Bernard Maybeck, Bakewell and Brown, and John Galen Howard.

The **Visitor Information Center** at 101 University Hall, 2200 University Ave., at Oxford Street (☎ **510/642-5215**), has regularly scheduled free campus tours on Monday, Wednesday, and Friday at 10am and 1pm (no tours are offered from mid-December to mid-January). The office also supplies self-guided walking-tour brochures.

You'll find the university's southern entrance at the northern end of Telegraph Avenue, at Bancroft Way. Walk through the main entrance into **Sproul Plaza.** When school is in session you'll encounter the gamut of Berkeley's inhabitants here: the colorful homeless, rambling political zealots, chanting Hare Krishnas, and ambitious students. You'll also find the Student Union, complete with a bookstore, cafes, and an information desk on the second floor where you can pick up a free map of Berkeley, as well as the local student newspaper (also found in dispensers throughout campus).

You might be lucky enough to stumble upon some impromptu musicians or a heated—and sometimes absurd—debate. There's always something going on, so stretch out on the grass for a few minutes and take in Berkeley's vibes.

For viewing more traditional art forms, there are some noteworthy museums here, too. The **Hearst Museum of Anthropology** is open Wednesday and Friday to Sunday from 10am to 5pm, and on Thursday from 10am to 9pm. Admission is $2 for adults, $1 for seniors, and 50¢ for children 15 and under; Thursday it's free for everyone. The **Lawrence Hall of Science,** offering hands-on science exploration, is open daily from 10am to 5pm, and is a wonderful place to watch the sunset. Admission is $6 for adults, $4 for seniors and children 7 to 18, and $2 for children 3 to 6. Finally, the **University Art Museum** is open Wednesday and Friday to Sunday from 11am to 5pm, and on Thursday from 11am to 9pm. Admission is $6 for adults, $4 for seniors and children 12 to 17. This museum includes a substantial collection of Hans Hofmann paintings, a sculpture garden, and the Pacific Film Archive.

If you're interested in notable off-campus buildings, contact the **Berkeley Convention & Visitors Bureau** at 510/549-7040 for an architectural walking-tour brochure.

OFF-CAMPUS ATTRACTIONS

Unbeknownst to many travelers, Berkeley has some of the most extensive and beautiful parks around. If you want to wear out the kids or if you enjoy hiking, swimming, or just getting a breath of California air and sniffing a few roses, jump in your car and make your way to **Tilden Park** (☎ **510/843-2137**), where you'll find plenty of flora and fauna, hiking trails, an old steam train and merry-go-round, a farm and nature area for kids, and a chilly arbor-encircled lake. Call for further information. On the way, stop at the colorful terraced **Rose Garden,** located in north Berkeley on Euclid Avenue between Bay View and Eunice Street.

Another worthy nature excursion is the **University of California Botanical Garden,** in Strawberry Canyon on Centennial Drive (☎ **510/642-3343**), which features a vast collection of herbage ranging from cacti to redwoods.

The cozy downstairs restaurant strewn with blossoming floral bouquets is an appropriately warm environment to indulge in the fixed-price four-course gourmet dinner, which is served Tuesday to Thursday. On Friday and Saturday it's four courses plus an apéritif, and Monday is bargain night with a three-course dinner for $35. The menu, which changes daily, is posted outside the restaurant each Saturday for the following week. Meals are complemented by an excellent wine list.

MODERATE

O Chamé. 1830 4th St. (near Hearst). ☎ **510/841-8783.** Reservations necessary Fri–Sat. Main courses $7–$16.50. AE, DC, MC, V. Mon–Thurs 11:30am–3pm and 5:30–9pm, Fri 11:30am–3pm and 5:30–9:30pm, Sat 5:30–9:30pm. JAPANESE.

Spare and plain in its decor, with ochre-colored walls marked with etched patterns, this spot has a meditative air to complement the traditional and experimental Japanese-inspired cuisine. The menu, which changes daily, offers meal-in-a bowl dishes (from $7 to $11) that allow a choice of soba or udon noodles in a clear soup with a variety of toppings (from shrimp and wakame seaweed to beef with burdock root and carrot); appetizers and salads, which include a flavorsome melding of grilled shiitake mushrooms and sweet peppers and Portobello mushrooms, watercress, and green onion pancakes; a sashimi of the day; and specials which always include a delicious roasted salmon.

Rivoli. 1539 Solano Ave. ☎ **510/526-2542.** Reservations recommended. Main courses $10.25–$15. MC, V. Mon–Thurs 5:30–9:30pm, Fri 5:30–10pm, Sat 5–10pm, Sun 5–9pm. CALIFORNIA.

This small restaurant is one of the favored dinner destinations in the East Bay. It's not the well-appointed atmosphere, floral art, or small garden with magnolias that keeps the locals coming back (though the atmosphere is good). It's the food. If it's available, start with the Portobello mushroom fritters with lemon aïoli and shaved Parmesan or the ahi tuna tartare with ginger vinaigrette. Next try the braised pork chili verde with tomatillos, cilantro, chipotle, sour cream, red-onion salsa, and corn sticks; the grilled top sirloin with marsala jus, gorgonzola gnocchi, and sautéed baby spinach; or the chicken breast with currants and red wine topped off with a saffron-brioche stuffing. For a finish, opt for the blood-orange granita or the bitter-sweet-chocolate and walnut tart with butterscotch sauce and espresso cream. Bon appétit.

INEXPENSIVE

Bette's Oceanview Diner. 1807A 4th St. ☎ **510/644-3230.** Breakfast $5–7.50. No credit cards. Mon–Thurs 6:30am–2:30pm, Fri–Sun 6:30am–4pm. AMERICAN.

Situated in the middle of Berkeley's blooming chi-chi shopping area, Bette's may look like an old-style diner, but one glance at the menu and you'll know they've risen to match their surroundings. Sure, there are pancakes, eggs, and all the breakfast basics on the menu, but Bette's leaves out the grease and substitutes advanced culinary style. Savor any of the fresh housemade morning buns or scones and surge on with a delightful mound of an omelet filled with fresh ingredients such as roasted red bell pepper with herb-cream cheese. Other specialties include soufflé pancakes (banana rum, apple brandy, fresh berry, and chocolate swirl), and grate-to-order potato pancakes.

Blue Nile. 2525 Telegraph Ave. ☎ **510/540-6777.** Reservations needed Fri–Sat. Main courses $6.50–$7.50. MC, V. Mon–Sat 11:30am–10pm, Sun 5–10pm. ETHIOPIAN.

Step through the beaded curtains into the Blue Nile and the African paintings and music will summon your appetite to other parts of the world. But the journey doesn't end there—be prepared to savor such flavorful specialties as doro wat (a spiced stew of beef, lamb, or chicken, served with a fluffy crêpe injera) or gomen wat (mustard greens sautéed in cream) with no utensils other than your fingers. Sure, you could convince the service staff to drum up a fork or two, but don't bother. After all, when in Africa. . . . No appetizers are served, but meals come with a small salad.

Cafe Intermezzo. 2422 Telegraph Ave. ☎ **510/849-4592.** Most items $3.25–$5.65. No credit cards. Daily 10:30am–10:30pm. SOUPS/SANDWICHES.

Pay no heed to the line out the door; counter people whip up orders with such fervor that you'll be happily munching in 5 to 10 minutes on what we consider the best and most enormous salads in the Bay Area. The dressings aren't any fancier than Italian or poppy seed, but the salads are literally a trough of fresh greens with kidney and garbonzo beans, sprouts, avocado, egg, and cucumber. One salad is a meal for two, and comes with thick fresh slices of bread, and slabs of butter. Soups and sandwiches here are also delicious and one of the best deals around.

The Cambodiana's. 2156 University Ave. (between Shattuck and Oxford). ☎ **510/843-4630.** Reservations recommended, especially Fri–Sat. Main courses $7.50–$13; fixed-price dinner $11. AE, DC, JCB, MC, V. Mon–Fri 11:30am–3pm and 5–10pm, Sat–Sun 5–10pm. CAMBODIAN.

For those who relish the spicy cuisine of Cambodia, this is quite a find. The decor is as colorful as the fare—brilliant blue, yellow, and green walls with Breuer-style chairs. Especially tasty are the curry (chicken, beef, etc.) or naga dishes with a sauce of tamarind, turmeric, lemongrass, shrimp paste, coconut-milk galinga, shallots, lemon leaf, sugar, and green chili. This sauce may also smother salmon, prawns, chicken, or steak. Another tempting dish is the chicken chaktomuk, prepared with pineapple, red peppers, and zucchini in soy-and-oyster sauce. There's also an excellent-value three-course fixed-price dinner.

BERKELEY AFTER DARK

Blake's, 2367 Telegraph Ave. (☎ **510/848-0886**), was recently voted the town's best bar by the student newspaper. Three floors provide a variety of entertainment ranging from a pool table to dancing. There's an unspectacular but cheap full-service restaurant and bar. The draws here are the music, affordable prices, and down-home atmosphere, not the food.

The **Triple Rock Brewery and Alehouse,** 1920 Shattuck Ave., at Hearst (☎ **510/843-2739**), is a top-notch Berkeley favorite for a fresh brew—it pipes its ale directly

The Sage of Aquarius

Are you curious about the direction your life is taking? Need a little assistance in making those important decisions? Consider spending an afternoon in Berkeley having an astrological consultation by **Aquarius Astrological Services,** who are so renowned for their accuracy that even licensed psychologists have been known to drop in for a little astrological assistance. The AAS is run by a former world traveler who has solid academic credentials and an impressive 30-year background in astrology and Eastern religions. You can write for an appointment if you know when you're going to be in the area, or you can have them send you a 25-page report for your birth horoscope. Send your request to Aquarius Astrological Services, P.O. Box 894, Berkeley, CA 94701-0894, or call them at **510/549-3345.**

from the glass-enclosed brewery to the bar where sandwiches and chilis are also served. Play a game of shuffleboard, or on a sunny afternoon head to the rooftop deck.

3 Sausalito

5 miles N of San Francisco

Just off the northern end of the Golden Gate Bridge is the eclectic little town of Sausalito, a slightly bohemian, nonchalant, and studiedly quaint adjunct to San Francisco. With approximately 7,500 residents, Sausalito feels rather like St. Tropez on the French Riviera—minus the starlets and the social rat race. It has its quota of paper millionaires, but they rub their permanently suntanned shoulders with a good number of hard-up artists, struggling authors, shipyard workers, and fishers. Next to the swank restaurants, plush bars, and antiques shops and galleries, you'll see hamburger joints, beer parlors, and secondhand bookstores.

Above all, Sausalito has scenery and sunshine, for once you cross the Golden Gate Bridge you're out of the San Francisco fog patch and under blue California sky (hopefully).

ESSENTIALS

Ferries of the **Red & White Fleet** (☎ **800/229-2784** in California, or 415/ 546-2700) leave from Pier 43¹/₂ (Fisherman's Wharf) in San Francisco and charge $11 round-trip, $5.50 for kids 5 to 11. Boats run on a seasonal schedule; phone for departure information.

If you're driving from U.S. 101 north, take the first right after the Golden Gate Bridge (Alexander exit). Alexander becomes Bridgeway in Sausalito.

EXPLORING THE TOWN

Sausalito's main touring strip is Bridgeway, which runs along the water, but those in the know make a quick detour to Caledonia Street, which runs parallel to, and 1 block inland from, Bridgeway. Caledonia Street is less congested than Broadway, and there's a far better selection of cafes and shops.

Bay Model Visitors Center. 2100 Bridgeway. ☎ **415/332-3871.** Free admission. Summer, Tues–Fri 9am–4pm, Sat–Sun 10am–6pm; winter, Tues–Sat 9am–4pm.

The U.S. Army Corps of Engineers uses this high-tech 1¹/₂-acre model of San Francisco's bay and delta to resolve problems and observe what impact any changes in water flow will have. The scale model reproduces the rise and fall of tides, the flows and currents of water, and the mixing of fresh and salt water, and indicates trends in sediment movement. There's a 10-minute film that explains it all and a tour, but the most interesting time to visit is when it's actually being used, so call ahead.

SHOPPING

The town is a mecca for shoppers seeking handmade, original, and offbeat clothes and footwear as well as arts and crafts. The best offbeat shops are found in the alleys, malls, and second-floor boutiques reached by steep, narrow staircases on and off Bridgeway. Additional shops are on Caledonia Street a block inland. Here are a few highlights:

Village Fair, 777 Bridgeway, containing 30 stores, is Sausalito's closest approximation to a mall. One store, **Quest Gallery** (☎ **415/332-6832**), features fine ceramics, contemporary glass, hand-painted silks, woven clothing, and jewelry, all by Californian artists, many of whom sell exclusively through this store. The **Burlwood Gallery,** 721 Bridgeway (☎ **415/332-6550**), sells redwood furniture plus fine jewelry, metal sculptures, hand-blown glass, Oriental rugs, and other interesting gifts. The **Pegasus Leather Company,** 28 Princess St., off Bridgeway (☎ 415/332-5624), stocks ultra-soft, richly colored leathers. They will custom-make clothing and accessories for no extra charge. The **Sausalito Country Store,** 789 Bridgeway (☎ 415/332-7890), sells handmade country-style items—ceramic, stuffed, and painted-wood animals, aprons, baskets, embossed quilt prints, and lithographs—made by local artists and artisans. The **Stoneflower Gallery,** 795 Bridgeway (☎ 415/332-2995), specializes in wood, ceramics, and unusual handcrafted creations with a somewhat ethnic flair.

WHERE TO STAY

Casa Madrona. 801 Bridgeway, Sausalito, CA 94965. ☎ **800/567-9524** or 415/332-0502. Fax 415/332-2537. 36 rms and suites. MINIBAR TEL. $105–$245 double; $435 Madrona Villa suite. Rates include breakfast. Additional person $10 extra. Two-night minimum stay on weekends. AE, MC, V. Parking $5.

Sooner or later most visitors to Sausalito look up and wonder at the ornate mansion on the hill. It's part of Casa Madrona, a hideaway-by-the-bay built in 1885 by a wealthy lumber baron. The epitome of luxury in its day, the mansion had slipped into decay when it was saved by Henri Deschamps and converted into a hotel and restaurant. Successive renovations and extensions have added a rambling New England–style building to the hillside below the main house.

Now a certified historic landmark, the hotel offers rooms, suites, and cottages. The 16 newest units are each uniquely decorated by different local designers. The "1,000 Cranes" is Asian in theme, with lots of ash and lacquer. "Artist's Loft" is reminiscent of a rustic Parisian artist's studio, complete with easel, brushes, and paint. Rooms in the mansion are also decorated in a variety of styles; some have Jacuzzis, while others have fireplaces. The newest rooms are located on the water with panoramic views of the San Francisco skyline and bay.

The **Casa Madrona Restaurant** (☎ 415/331-5888) serves contemporary American cuisine. It's open for lunch Monday to Friday, for dinner nightly, and for Sunday brunch from 10am to 2:30pm. A meal will cost $25 to $35 without wine.

✪ **Inn Above The Tide.** 30 El Portal (Next to the Sausalito Ferry Landing), Sausalito, CA 94965. ☎ **800/893-8433** or 415/332-9535. Fax 415/332-6714. 28 rooms, 2 suites. AC TV TEL. $185–$400 double. Rates include continental breakfast. AE, MC, V.

Perched directly over the bay atop well-grounded pilings, this former luxury apartment complex underwent a $4 million dollar transformation into one of Sausalito's— if not the Bay Area's—finest accommodations. It's the view that clinches it: Every room comes with an unparalleled panorama of the San Francisco Bay, including a postcard-quality vista of the city glimmering in the distance. Should you manage to tear yourself away from your private deck (we were tempted to drag our mattress outside), within the sumptuously appointed room you'll find a romantic little fireplace, a vast sunken tub with Jacuzzi jets, remote-control air-conditioning, and wondrously comfortable queen- or king-size beds. Soothing shades of pale green and blue highlight the decor, which blends in well with the bayscape outside. Be sure to request that your breakfast and newspaper be delivered to your deck, then cancel your early appointments: on sunny mornings, nobody checks out early.

WHERE TO DINE

Feng Nian Chinese Restaurant. 2650 Bridgeway. ☎ **415/331-5300.** Reservations accepted. Main courses $6.50–$14; lunch specials $4–$5.50. AE, DISC, MC, V. Mon and Wed–Thurs 11:30am–9:30pm, Fri–Sat 11:30am–10pm, Sun 12:30–9:30pm. CHINESE.

A pretty restaurant serving fine-quality Chinese food, Feng Nian has such a wide selection of appetizers that a combination of several would make a delicious meal in
itself. The crispy roast duck is a personal favorite, but if you'd like an assortment, try
the flaming combination (enough for two) that includes egg roll, fried prawns,
paper-wrapped chicken, barbecued ribs, fried chicken, and teriyaki. There are nine
soups, including a truly exceptional, rich crabmeat/shark's-fin soup with shredded
crab-leg meat. The restaurant offers more than 90 main dishes, including a number
of main courses for vegetarians.

Guernica. 2009 Bridgeway.☎ **415/332-1512.** Reservations recommended. Main courses
$10–$18. AE, MC, V. Daily 5–10pm. FRENCH/BASQUE.

Established in 1976, Guernica is one of those funky old kind of restaurants that you'd
probably pass up for something chicer and more modern down the street if you didn't
know better. You don't know about Guernica's legendary paella valenciana? Well now
you do, so be sure to call ahead and order it in advance, and bring a partner because
it's served for two but will feed three.

Horizons. 558 Bridgeway. ☎ **415/331-3232.** Reservations accepted Mon–Fri only. Main
courses $9–$15; salads and sandwiches $6–$8. AE, MC, V. Mon–Fri 11am–11pm, Sat–Sun
10am–11pm. SEAFOOD/AMERICAN.

Eventually every San Franciscan ends up at Horizons to meet a friend for Sunday
Bloody Marys. It's not much to look at from the outside, but it gets better as you
head past the funky dark-wood interior toward the waterside terrace. On warm days
it's worth the wait for alfresco seating if only to watch dreamy sailboats glide past San
Francisco's distant skyline. The food here can't touch the view, but it's well portioned
and satisfying enough. Seafood dishes are the main items, including steamed clams
and mussels, freshly shucked oysters, and a variety of seafood pastas. In fine Marin
tradition, Horizons has a herb tea and espresso bar, and is a totally non-smoking
restaurant.

WHERE TO STOCK UP FOR A PICNIC—AND WHERE TO ENJOY IT

Even Sausalito's naysayers have to admit that it's hard not to enjoy eating your way
down Bridgeway on a warm, sunny day. If the crowds are too much or the prices too
steep at the bayside restaurants, grab a bite to go for an impromptu picnic in the park
fronting the marina.

You can get anything from a snack to a meal at **The Stuffed Croissant, Etc.,**
43 Caledonia St. (☎ **415/332-7103**). There are all sorts of gourmet croissants, including those filled with almond-chicken salad or Italian pizza, as well as bagels,
soups, and stews. Hot, cheap meals such as chicken curry with rice are also popular.
For dessert there's carrot cake, pecan bars, fudge and peanut brownies, and more.
Open daily.

The classic old **Venice Gourmet Delicatessen,** 625 Bridgeway (☎ **415/
332-3544**), has all the makings for a superb picnic: wines, cheese, fruits, stuffed vine
leaves, mushroom-and-artichoke salad, quiche, delicious sandwiches (made to order
on sourdough bread), olives, and fresh-baked pastries. Open daily from 9am to 6pm.

Small, clean, cute, and cheap, the **Café Soleil,** 37 Caledonia St. (☎ **415/
331-9355**), whips up some good soups, salads, and sandwiches along with killer
smoothies. Order to-go at the counter, then take your goods a block over to the marina for a dockside lunch. Open daily from 7am to 6:30pm.

As the name says, the specialty at the tiny, narrow **Hamburgers,** 737 Bridgeway.
(☎ **415/332-9471**), is juicy flame-broiled hamburgers—arguably Marin County's
best. Look for the rotating grill in the window off Bridgeway, then stand in line and

salivate with the rest (chicken burgers are a slightly healthier option). Order a side of fries, grab a bunch of napkins, then head over to the park across the street. Open daily from 11am to 5pm.

Caledonia Kitchen, 400 Caledonia St. (☎ **415/331-0220**), is the sort of place you wish were just around the corner from your house—a beautiful little cafe serving a huge assortment of fresh salads, soups, chili, sandwiches, and inexpensive entrees like herbed roast chicken or vegetarian lasagne for only $4.95. Continental-style breakfast items and good coffee and espresso drinks are also on the menu. Open daily from 8am to 8pm.

4 Tiburon & Angel Island

8 miles N of San Francisco

A federal and state wildlife refuge, Angel Island is the largest of the San Francisco Bay's three islets (the others are Alcatraz and Yerba Buena). The island has been, at various times, a prison, a quarantine station for immigrants, a missile base, and even a favorite site for duels. Nowadays, though, most of the people who visit here are content with picnicking on the large green lawn that fronts the docking area; loaded with the appropriate recreational supplies, they claim a barbecue, plop their fannies down on the lush green grass, and wile away an afternoon free of phones, television, and traffic. Hiking, mountain biking, and guided tram tours are also popular options. During the warmer months you can go **camping** at a limited number of sites (reservations are required; ☎ **800/444-7275**).

The same ferry from San Francisco to Angel Island will also take you to Tiburon, situated on a peninsula of the same name that looks like a cross between a fishing village and a Hollywood western set—imagine San Francisco reduced to toy dimensions. This seacoast town rambles over a series of green hills and ends up at a spindly, multicolored pier on the waterfront, like a Fisherman's Wharf in miniature. But in reality it's an extremely plush patch of yacht-club suburbia, as you'll see by both the marine craft and the homes of their owners.

Tiburon's Main Street is lined with ramshackle, color-splashed old frame houses that shelter boutiques, souvenir stores, antiques shops, and art galleries. Other roads are narrow, winding, and hilly, and lead up to dramatically situated homes. The view of San Francisco's skyline and the islands in the bay is reason enough to pay the price to live here. The main pastime is to stroll along the waterfront, pop into the stores, and wind up at a restaurant for lunch or dinner. Stop in and enjoy a taste of the Wine Country at **Windsor Vineyards,** 72 Main St. (☎ **800/214-9463** or 415/435-3113), in their Victorian tasting room, which dates from 1888. Some 35 choices are available for tasting daily from 10am to 6pm.

ESSENTIALS

Ferries of the **Red & White Fleet** (☎ **800/229-2784** in California, or 415/546-2628 or 415/546-2700) leave San Francisco from Pier 43¹/₂ (Fisherman's Wharf) and travel to both Tiburon and Angel Island. Boats run on a seasonal schedule; phone for departure information. The round-trip fare is $11 to Tiburon, $9 to Angel Island; half price for kids 5 to 11. (*Note:* The Red & White Fleet is slated to be consolidated into the Blue and Gold Fleet by 1997, but will probably keep the same schedule and fares.)

Alternatively, you can drive to Tiburon, a trip of 40 minutes from San Francisco. Take U.S. 101 to the Tiburon/Belvedere exit and then follow Tiburon Boulevard all the way into downtown. Once you're there you can board the **Angel Island Ferry** (☎ **415/435-2131** or 415/388-6770) for the 15-minute hop to the island. The round-trip costs $5 for adults, $3 for children 5 to 11, and $1 for bikes. Catch the ferry from the dock at Tiburon Boulevard and Main Street.

WHERE TO DINE

✪ **Guaymas.** 5 Main St. ☎ **415/435-6300.** Reservations accepted. Main courses $12–$18. AE, CB, DC, MC, V. Mon–Fri 11:30am–9:30pm, Sat 11:30am–10:30pm, Sun 10:30am–9:30pm. Ferry: Walk about 10 paces from the landing. From U.S. 101, exit at Tiburon/Calif. 131, follow Tiburon Blvd. 5 miles, and turn right onto Main St.; the restaurant is situated directly behind the bakery. MEXICAN.

Guaymas offers authentic Mexican regional cuisine and a spectacular panoramic view of San Francisco and the bay. In good weather the two outdoor patios are almost always packed with diners soaking in the sun and scene. Inside, beige walls are hung with colorful Mexican artwork, illuminated by modern track lighting. Should you be feeling chilled, to the rear of the dining room is a beehive-shaped adobe fireplace.

Guaymas is named after a fishing village on Mexico's Sea of Cortez, and both the town and the restaurant are famous for their camarones (giant shrimp). The restaurant also features ceviche, handmade tamales, and charcoal-grilled beef, seafood, and fowl. Save room for dessert—especially the outrageously scrumptious fritter with "drunken" bananas and ice cream. In addition to a good selection of California wines, Guaymas offers an exceptional variety of tequilas, Mexican beers, and mineral waters flavored with flowers, grains, and fruits.

Sam's Anchor Café. 27 Main St. ☎ **415/435-4527.** Reservations accepted. Main courses $8–$16. AE, MC, V. Mon–Thurs 11am–10pm, Fri 11am–10:30pm, Sat 10am–10:30pm, Sun 9:30am–10pm. Ferry: Walk from the landing. From U.S. 101, exit at Tiburon/Calif. 131; follow Tiburon Blvd. 4 miles and turn right onto Main St. SEAFOOD.

Summer Sundays are liveliest in Tiburon, when weekend boaters tie up to the docks at waterside restaurants like Sam's—the kind of place where you and your cronies can take off your shoes and have a fun, relaxed time eating burgers and drinking margaritas outside on the pier. The fare is pretty typical—sandwiches, salads, and seafood such as deep-fried oysters—but its quality and selection are inconsequential: Beers, burgers, and a designated driver are all you really need.

Sweden House Bakery-Café. 35 Main St. ☎ **415/435-9767.** Reservations not accepted. Omelets $6.50–$7; sandwiches $6–$8. MC, V. Mon–Fri 8am–6pm, Sat–Sun 8am–7pm. Ferry: Walk from the landing. From U.S. 101, exit at Tiburon/Belvedere; follow Tiburon Blvd. 5 miles and turn right onto Main St. SWEDISH/AMERICAN.

This small, cozy cafe with gingham-covered walls adorned with copperware and kitchen utensils is a local favorite. On sunny mornings there's no better seat in the Bay Area than on the bakery's terrace, where you can nurse an espresso and pastry while gazing out over the bay. Full breakfasts are served too, all accompanied by toasted Swedish limpa bread; skip the eggs-and-bacon routine and go with the tasty Swedish pancakes—lingonberry, blueberry, and apple. At lunch there's typical American fare plus traditional open-face sandwiches, including avocado and bacon or asparagus tips rolled in Danish ham. Beer and wine are available.

5 Muir Woods & Mount Tamalpais

15 miles N of San Francisco

by Andrew Rice

When he's not on the road for *Outside, Islands,* and a number of
other magazines, travel writer and environmental reporter Andrew
Rice lives and writes in San Francisco. He has recently authored
Outside Magazine's Adventure Guide to Northern California
(Macmillan Travel), and is currently at work on a companion
volume to *Southern California* and *Baja.*

Muir Woods is one of the best-preserved wilderness regions that lie in the shadow
of a major U.S. metropolitan area. Leave San Francisco, cross the Golden Gate
Bridge, and within 20 minutes you can experience the old-growth coastal redwoods
of Northern California much as they were prior to the influx of European settlers in
the 19th century.

While the rest of Marin County's redwood forests were being devoured to feed the
building spree that was San Francisco around the turn of the century, the trees of
Muir Woods, in a remote ravine on the flanks of Mount Tamalpais, escaped destruction while loggers went for easier pickings. By 1905, however, lumber companies had
designs on the 200-foot-tall, 800-year-old giants. They were thwarted when farsighted
congressman, philanthropist, and conservationist William Kent purchased the grove
for $45,000. But only 2 years later the trees faced a different threat: The local water
agency sought to condemn the land and build a dam on Redwood Creek that would
have inundated the forest. Kent appealed to President Theodore Roosevelt and in
1908 secured the national monument status that the woods enjoy today. It was on
Kent's request that the park was named after John Muir.

Muir Woods is a small park, only 553 acres tucked in a V-shaped canyon, but the
national monument is completely encircled by enormous **Mount Tamalpais State
Park,** lending it a wildness beyond its size.

The monument is 17 miles north of San Francisco, with well-marked signs leading from U.S. 101. From U.S. 101 you can enter the park from either Calif. 1 or the
Panoramic Highway. The national monument visitor center and the state park both
sell good hiking maps for a small fee. Muir Woods is open every day from 8am to
sunset. Admission is free. For more information, contact **Muir Woods National
Monument,** Mill Valley, CA 94941 (☎ **415/338-2595**).

There is no picnicking, camping, or accommodations in Muir Woods. The nearest
campground is a first-come, first-served 13-site walk-in camp at Pan Toll Station of
the heavily wooded **Alice Eastwood Group Camp** in Mount Tamalpais State Park.
Reservations are required; call 800/444-7275.

HIKING   Most visitors know the easy, paved loop trail that leaves from the visitor center and circles along the banks of Redwood Creek into the heart of the
monument's **Bohemian and Cathedral Groves.** Hikers seeking more solitude should
consider the longer trails, such as the **Fern Creek Loop,** 4 miles of spectacular canyon and redwood views; or the more strenuous **Dipsea Loop,** an 8-mile mix of shady
creekside, high ridges, and ocean views. On busy weekends, when the 200-space visitor center parking area can be a real headache, consider avoiding the traffic jam by
choosing the **Hassle Free Loop,** which begins on the Panoramic Highway in Mount
Tamalpais State Park and descends into the redwood grove and fern canyon via the
Panoramic Trail, Ocean View Trail, and Fern Canyon Trail—a total of about

5 miles. It's also a short but steep hike from this parking area to the top of **Mount Tamalpais,** one of the best views in the Bay Area.

6 Marine World Africa USA

30 miles NE of San Francisco, 10 miles S of Napa

Marine World Africa USA, on Marine World Parkway in Vallejo (☎ **707/ 643-6722**), is a kind of Disney–meets–Wild Kingdom theme park, offering aquatic and other trained-animal performances.

GETTING THERE   The **Blue and Gold Fleet** (☎ 415/705-5555) operates high-speed ferries from Pier 41 at Fisherman's Wharf. The scenic cruise, passing Alcatraz and the Golden Gate Bridge, takes 80 minutes, plus a brief bus ride. The round-trip, including park admission, is $39 for adults, $32 for seniors 62 and over and students 13 to 18, and $23.50 for kids 4 to 12. Service is limited; call for departure times.

By car from San Francisco, take I-80 north to Calif. 37 and follow the signs to the park; it's less than an hour's drive.

SEEING THE PARK   A variety of events are scheduled continuously throughout the day. There's a Killer Whale and Dolphin Show (the front seven rows of seats are saved for guests who want a thorough drenching). Shark Experience, a moving walkway through a clear acrylic tunnel, brings visitors through a 300,000-gallon tropical shark-filled tank.

Cross a bridge over a waterfall, past the flamingos, and you enter "Africa USA." Here you'll find the Elephant Encounter, where visitors can meet the park's 11 Asian and African elephants. In addition to shows, elephant rides costing $3 per person are offered. At Tiger Island you can see trainers and Bengal tigers playing and swimming together. An informative show about the park's exotic and endangered animals is performed in the Wildlife Theater.

The Bird Show is one of the park's best and proves that the birds' peanut-sized brains are capable of more than we think! There's also an enclosed Butterfly World, a Small Animal Petting Kraal (with llamas), and Gentle Jungle, a playground that combines education, fun, and adventure. Here, inside the Prairie Crawl, children can crawl through burrows in the prairie dog village and pop up into Plexiglas domes so they can see the world from these animals' point of view.

Finally there's a 55-acre lake that's the stage for a Waterski and Boat Show April to October.

Admission is $25.95 for adults, $21.95 for seniors 60 and over, $17.95 for kids 4 to 12, and free for children 3 and under. Credit/charge cards are accepted. The park is open from Memorial Day to Labor Day, daily from 9:30am to 6pm; the rest of the year, Wednesday to Sunday from 9:30am to 5pm.

7 San Jose & Environs

San Jose: 45 miles SE of San Francisco

THE HEART OF SILICON VALLEY: SAN JOSE

Some may mourn the San Jose of yesterday, a sleepy small town of orchards, crops, and cattle, but those days are long gone. Founded in 1717 and previously dwelling in the shadows of San Francisco, San Jose is now Northern California's largest city. With surveys that declare it one of the safest and sunniest cities in the country and rank it the fifth most popular place to live in America, San Jose is a force to be reckoned with. Today the prosperity of Silicon Valley has transformed what was once an agricultural backwater into a thriving city of restaurants, shops, a state-of-the-art light-rail system, a sports arena (Go Sharks!), and a reputable art scene.

ESSENTIALS

GETTING THERE   BART (☎ 510/793-2278) travels from San Francisco to Fremont in 1¼ hours; you can take a bus from there. **Cal train** (☎ 415/291-5651) operates frequently from San Francisco and takes about an hour and 25 minutes.

VISITOR INFORMATION   Contact the **San Jose Convention & Visitors Bureau**, 333 W. San Carlos St., Suite 1000, San Jose, CA 95110 (☎ 408/295-9600).

GETTING AROUND   Light Rail (☎ 408/321-2300) is best for getting around. A ticket is good for 2 hours and stops include Paramount's Great America, the Convention Center, and downtown museums. Or you can use the historic **trolleys,** which operate in a loop around downtown (summer only). Tickets can be purchased at Light Rail stations.

MUSEUMS WORTH SEEKING OUT

Downtown San Jose has several museums worth mentioning. The **Tech Museum of Innovation,** 145 W. San Carlos St., between Market Street and Almaden Boulevard (☎ 408/279-7150), is a small museum that allows visitors to grapple with modern technology. For example, visitors can use CAD (computer-aided design) to create a bicycle and then test it in a wind tunnel, or learn about DNA (how do they develop bigger and better vegetables?) by experimenting with genetic models. Admission is $6 for adults, $4 for children 6 to 18 and seniors; open Tuesday to Sunday from 10am to 5pm.

The **San Jose Museum of Art,** 110 S. Market St. (☎ 408/294-2787), is collaborating with New York's Whitney Museum for shows that trace the development of 20th-century American art. The series will include works by Franz Kline, Louis Nevelson, Andy Warhol, and many others. Look for renovations in the Historic Wing, which is reopening in 1997. Admission is $6 for adults, $3 for children 6 to 17 and seniors. Open Tuesday to Sunday 10am to 5pm (to 8pm on Thursday).

The **Children's Discovery Museum,** 180 Woz Way (☎ 408/298-5437), offers more than 150 interactive exhibits for kids, as well as shows and workshops that explore science, the humanities, the arts, and technology. "ArtWorks Too!" is an art center offering a different art project for kids to work on each month, while "Bubbalogna," an exhibit that explores the whimsical and scientifically intriguing world of bubbles, also draws rave reviews. Smaller kids enjoy dressing up in costumes and playing on the fire truck. Admission is $6 for adults, $5 for seniors, and $4 for children 2 to 18. Open Tuesday to Saturday from 10am to 5pm and on Sunday from noon to 5pm.

The **San Jose Historical Museum,** 1600 Senter Rd. (☎ 408/287-2290), occupies 25 acres in Kelley Park and features 26 original and replica buildings that have been restored to represent life in 1880s San Jose. The usual cast of characters is here—the doctor, the printer, the postmaster—with an occasional local surprise, such as the 1888 Chinese temple and the original Stevens fruit barn. Admission is $4 for adults, $3 for seniors, and $2 for children 4 to 17. Open Monday to Friday from 10am to 4:15pm and on Saturday and Sunday from noon to 4:15pm.

The **Rosicrucian Egyptian Museum & Planetarium,** 1342 Naglee Ave. (☎ 408/947-3636), is associated with a religious order that traces its origins back to the ancient Egyptians, who strongly believed in an afterlife and reincarnation. On display are human and animal mummies, funerary boats, and canopic jars, as well as jewelry, pottery, and bronze tools. There's also a replica of an Egyptian nobleman's tomb. Admission is $6.75 for adults, $4 for seniors, and $3.50 for children 7 to 15. It's open daily from 9am to 5pm. Call for show times at the planetarium, which is only open on weekdays and costs $4 for adults and $3 for children.

THEME PARK THRILLS

Paramount's Great America, Great America Parkway (off U.S. 101), Santa Clara (☎ 408/988-1776), provides 100 acres of family entertainment. A pretty cool place to lose your lunch, the park includes such favorites as the Top Gun suspended jet coaster, the Days of Thunder auto-racing simulator, a 3-acre Nickelodeon Center for children, and the new "Drop Zone," the world's tallest free-fall ride. Be sure to check for concerts and special events. Admission is $27.95 for adults, $18.95 for seniors, and $13.95 for children 3 to 6. It's open March through October 22 on Saturday and Sunday from 10am to 9pm (hours are extended on Labor Day weekend). To get there from San Francisco, take U.S. 101 south for about 45 miles to the Great America Parkway exit.

WHERE TO STAY

Fairmont. 170 S. Market St., San Jose, CA 95113. ☎ **408/998-1900.** Fax 408/287-1648. 541 rms and suites. A/C MINIBAR TV TEL. $179–$219 double; $219–$400 suite. AE, DC, DISC, JCB, MC, V.

Ideally situated near the Convention Center and the Center of Performing Arts, this hotel is in a landmark building. A popular spot to have afternoon tea or cocktails, the lobby attracts many who are just passing through. From the lobby to the rooms, which offer many modern features, the emphasis is on comfort. Amenities include 24-hour room service, concierge, laundry/valet, and a rooftop pool on the fourth floor surrounded by tropical foliage. Three restaurants are available, including Les Saisons for fine French/continental cuisine, a Chinese restaurant, and a coffee shop that's nicely accented with a massive marble soda fountain.

Hotel de Anza. 233 W. Santa Clara St., San Jose, CA 95113. ☎ **800/843-3700** or 408/286-1000. Fax 408/286-0500. 100 rms and suites. A/C MINIBAR TV TEL. $155–$170 double; $295 suite. Special weekend rates available. AE, DC, MC, V.

Located downtown in a landmark art deco building, this hotel is small enough to provide personal service. The room decor may reflect a 1930s style in the furnishings, but the amenities are state of the art. There are three telephones in each room, including one with a data line and fax port (computers and fax machines are supplied on request), plus voice-mail service. Additional amenities include a VCR and complimentary tapes. Bathrobes, a hair dryer, a makeup mirror, a TV, and a telephone are also available in each bathroom. There's room service, laundry/valet, complimentary shoeshine, nightly turndown, and a health club with Nautilus machines. There's a club lounge as well as La Pastaia restaurant, which serves fine Italian cuisine.

WHERE TO DINE

Emile's. 545 S. 2nd St. ☎ **408/289-1960.** Reservations recommended. Main courses $16.50–$28. AE, MC, V. Tues–Sat 6–10pm. CONTEMPORARY EUROPEAN.

Chef/proprietor Emile Mooser uses local ingredients to produce a tasty, contemporary cuisine. To start, try the scallops and spinach wrapped in filo on citrus emulsion, or Mooser's interesting variation on French onion soup, made with gorgonzola and gruyère cheese. Follow with a roasted, peppered pork tenderloin, served on roasted Granny Smith apples that bring out the flavor perfectly. Mirrors and recessed lighting, and large, bold floral arrangements create an elegant atmosphere. For dessert, select the chocolate mousse flavored with dark rum and served with raspberry coulis.

Paolo's. 333 W. San Carlos St. ☎ **408/294-2558.** Reservations recommended. Main courses $7–$20. AE, MC, V. Mon–Fri 11am–2:30pm and 5:30–10pm, Sat 5:30–10pm. NORTHERN ITALIAN.

Paolo's occupies the ground floor of a high-rise office building. The restaurant attracts a business crowd at lunchtime and a rather cultured crowd in the evening. The cuisine is refined northern Italian, with innovative flourishes. Among the appetizers, for instance, the beef carpaccio is served with a piquant vegetable sauce. The main dishes might include sea scallops roasted with whole garlic, cherry tomatoes, and thyme, or a classic roasted quail with white raisins, grappa, and natural juices. Desserts also stretch beyond the typical Italian favorites to include a chocolate torte with orange-caramel sauce, or lemon-curd tart with toasted coconut and pistachio nuts. An extensive wine list features over 600 selections.

SAN JOSE AFTER DARK

Characteristically lively San Jose brings them in from all over once the sun goes down. Originally a red-light district, this South Bay city is now a haven for hip-hop fans, and boasts quite an alternative scene. Happening nightclubs include the new **Cactus Club,** 417 S. 1st St. (☎ **408/491-9300**), offering live rock. **Agenda,** at 3399 S. 1st St. (☎ **408/287-3991**), is a trilevel restaurant, bar, and blues club with a SoHo feel, while **The Usual,** at 400 S. 1st St. (☎ **408/535-0330**) is an eclectic music and dance club. Those who want more—and then some—should pay a visit to **San Jose Live,** at 150 S. 1st St. (☎ **408/294-5483**). The "Señor Frog's" of California, this popular nightspot has two dance floors, a sports bar, "dueling" pianists, comedians, big-screen "boob-tubes," arcades, pool tables, and too much else to mention, much like its famous sibling club.

OFF THE BEATEN TRACK: SARATOGA

Walk down Saratoga's Main Street and you're bound to get the feeling that the real world has yet to infiltrate this sprawl of expensive shops, restaurants, and homes that's not unlike a miniature Carmel. In addition to marveling at the seeming isolation of the town, be sure to check out the many small wineries in the area such as **The Mountain Winery** (☎ 408/741-5183) and **Mariani Winery & Saratoga Vineyards** (☎ 408/741-2930).

WHERE TO STAY IN SARATOGA

The Inn at Saratoga. 20645 4th St., Saratoga, CA 95070. ☎ **800/338-5020** or 408/867-5020. Fax 408/741-0981. 45 rms, 4 suites. A/C MINIBAR TV TEL. $150 double; $225–$255 double with whirlpool bath; from $400 suite. Rates include continental breakfast. AE, DC, MC, V.

This small hotel overlooking Saratoga Creek and Wildwood Park provides a tranquil atmosphere. The rooms are spacious enough to contain sitting alcoves, with floor-to-ceiling windows that take advantage of the bucolic views. All are pleasantly decorated in a contemporary style with floral bedcovers; the suites have pencil four-posters and some offer whirlpool baths. Modern amenities include VCRs and computer-capable communications jacks. A continental breakfast that has all the trimmings, including scrumptious house-made pastries, is available in the lobby or out on the attractive patio. Extra perks include complimentary newspaper, nightly turndown, and laundry/valet service.

The Winchester Mystery House

Begun in 1884, the Winchester Mystery House, at 525 S. Winchester Blvd., San Jose (☎ **408/247-2101**), is a monument to one woman's paranoia. It's the legacy of Sarah L. Winchester, widow of the son of the famous rifle magnate. After the deaths of her husband and baby daughter, Mrs. Winchester consulted a seer, who proclaimed that the family had been targeted by the evil spirits of those killed with Winchester repeaters, and that the spirits would only be appeased by perpetual construction on the Winchester mansion. Convinced that she'd live as long as the building continued, the widow used much of her $20 million inheritance to finance the construction, which went on 24 hours a day, 7 days a week, 365 days a year, for 38 years. (Ricki Lake would have loved to have had her as a guest, we're sure.)

As you can probably guess, this is no ordinary home. With 160 rooms, it sprawls across half a dozen acres. And it's full of disturbing features: a staircase leading nowhere; a Tiffany window with a spider-web design; doors that open onto blank walls. There are 13 bathrooms, 13 windows and doors in the old sewing room, 13 palms lining the main driveway, 13 hooks in the seance room, and chandeliers with 13 lights. Such schemes were designed to confound the spirits that seemed to plague the heiress.

Touring the house and grounds costs $12.95 for adults, $9.95 for seniors, and $6.95 for children 6 to 12. Tours leave about every 15 minutes. The house is open daily from 9am to 8pm.

WHERE TO DINE IN SARATOGA

✪ **Le Mouton Noir**. 14560 Big Basin Way, Saratoga. ☎ **408/867-7017**. Reservations required. Main courses $17.50–$26. AE, DC, MC, V. Mon–Fri 6–9pm, Sat 11:30am–2pm and 5:30–9pm, Sun 5–9pm. INTERNATIONAL.

The extraordinary food at Le Mouton Noir can satisfy a variety of tastes. Lovers of Asian food will enjoy the grilled swordfish with lemongrass, ginger, garlic, and soy with clear rice noodles, while fans of classic European fare will love the red wine–marinated tenderloin of beef with truffle mashed potatoes. Culinary top billing, however, goes to the tender venison from New Zealand or the duck in sweet orange glaze. Among the extravagant desserts, choose the Tía María or the pots de crème, and top it off with a fine dessert wine. The decor is elegant and countrified—a little too much so for us—but Martha Stewart would be proud. Try not to be too hungry when you arrive, as the portions are slightly meager, in typical California cuisine fashion.

EN ROUTE TO SANTA CRUZ: GILROY & SAN JUAN BAUTISTA

A short drive down U.S. 101 from San Jose, **Gilroy** is famous for its garlic festival, which is held in July. Recently it has become known for its outlet shopping, too. For information, contact the **Gilroy Visitor's Bureau** (☎ 408/842-6436).

A little farther down, U.S. 101 brings you to **San Juan Bautista,** a historic town with a definite Spanish-Mexican flavor. **Mission San Juan Bautista** (open daily from 9:30am to 4:30pm) is a serene outpost that looks out over meadowlands, and you can imagine how isolated it must have been when it was built in 1797. The interior walls are decorated with frescoes, while the reredos has six hand-carved painted wooden statues, including a life-size polychrome figure of San Juan Bautista. More than 4,000 Native Americans are buried in the cemetery beside the church.

A grassy plaza spreads in front of the mission; around it stand a nunnery (built in 1815), the Castro House, the Plaza Hotel (1858), and stables, which together constitute the **San Juan Bautista Historic Park** (☎ 408/623-4881). Admission is $2 for adults, $1 for children, and it's open Wednesday to Sunday from 10am to 4:30pm.

The Castro House was the home of the Mexican administrator, José María Castro. In 1848 it was purchased by the Breen family, members of the Donner party who had survived 111 days stranded in the snow-bound Sierra Nevada in 1846.

The Plaza Hotel was a major stop on the stagecoach route in the mid-1800s when 10 or so stages passed through here daily. Once the railroad bypassed the town in 1876 it became a quiet backwater, which is why it has survived intact. The town's main street is lined with antique stores that are worth browsing and several Mexican restaurants. The big event here is the Annual Flea Market and Antique Show held in August. For additional information, contact the **San Juan Bautista Chamber of Commerce** (☎ 408/623-2454).

8 Santa Cruz

77 miles SE of San Francisco

For a small bayside city, Santa Cruz has a lot to offer. The main show, of course, is the Beach Boardwalk, the West Coast's only seaside amusement park, which attracts millions of visitors each year. But past the arcades and cotton candy is a surprisingly diverse and energetic city that has a little of something for everyone. Shopping, hiking, mountain biking, sailing, fishing, kayaking, surfing, wine tasting, golfing, whale watching—the list of things to do here is almost endless, making Santa Cruz one of the premier family destinations on the California coast.

ESSENTIALS

For information, contact the **Santa Cruz County Conference and Visitors Council,** 701 Front St., Santa Cruz, CA 95060 (☎ 800/833-3494, or 408/425-1234). It's open Monday to Saturday from 9am to 5pm and on Sunday from 10am to 4pm.

Special events include the **Santa Cruz Hot & Cool Jazz Festival** (☎ 408/662-1912) in July, **Shakespeare Santa Cruz** (☎ 408/459-2121) in July and August, and the **Cabrillo Music Festival** (☎ 408/426-6966) in August.

WHAT TO SEE & DO: SURF, SUN & OTHER FUN

One of the top amusement parks in the nation, the privately owned **Santa Cruz Beach Boardwalk** (☎ 408/426-7433) draws more than three million visitors a year to its 27 rides and multitudes of arcades, shops, and restaurants. The park has two national landmarks—a 1924 wooden Giant Dipper rollercoaster and a 1911 carousel complete with hand-carved wooden horses and a 342-pipe band organ. It's open daily in the summer, from Memorial Weekend to Labor Day, and on weekends and holidays throughout the spring and fall, from 11am on. Admission to the boardwalk is free, but an all-day "unlimited rides" pass will set you back about $18. Call for more information.

Here, too, at 400 Beach St. is **Neptune's Kingdom** (☎ 408/426-7433), an enormous indoor family recreation center where the main feature is a two-story miniature golf course. Also on Beach Street is the **Municipal Wharf** (☎ 408/429-3628) and pier, lined with shops and restaurants—a beachfront strip that's serenaded by the sea lions below. (This is where you can pick up your UC Santa Cruz Banana Slugs

T-shirt, just like the one John Travolta sported in *Pulp Fiction.*) You can also crab and fish from here. Open daily from 7am to 9am. **Stagnaro's** (☎ **408/427-2334**) operates fishing and whale-watching trips from the pier from November to April.

Farther down on West Cliff Drive you'll come to a favorite surfing spot, **Steamers Lane,** where you can watch the surfers coasting onto the beach. If you want to find out more about this local sport that's been practiced here for 100 years, then go to the memorial lighthouse, which contains the **Santa Cruz Surfing Museum** (☎ **408/429-3429**), open in summer Wednesday through Monday from noon to 5pm, and in winter Thursday to Monday from noon to 4pm.

Continue along West Cliff and you'll eventually reach **Natural Bridges State Beach,** 2531 W. Cliff Dr. (☎ **408/423-4609**), a large sandy beach with nearby tidepools and hiking trails. It's also home to a large colony of Monarch butterflies that roost and mate in the nearby eucalyptus grove.

Other Santa Cruz beaches worth noting are: **Bonny Doon,** at Bonny Doon Road and Calif. 1, an uncrowded sandy beach and a major surfing spot accessible by a steep walkway; **Pleasure Point Beach,** East Cliff Drive at Pleasure Point Drive; and **Twin Lakes State Beach,** which is ideal for sunning and also provides access to Schwann Lagoon, a bird sanctuary.

In addition to many cultural and sporting events, the UC Santa Cruz also has the **Long Marine Laboratory and Aquarium,** 100 Shaffer Rd. (☎ **408/459-4308**), where you can observe the activities of marine scientists and the species kept in tidepool touch-tanks and aquariums. Open Tuesday to Sunday from 1 to 4pm.

The **Santa Cruz Harbor,** 135 5th Ave. (☎ **408/475-6161**), is the place to head for boat rentals, open-boat fishing (cod, shark, and salmon), and whale-watching trips. Operators include **Santa Cruz Sportfishing, Inc.,** Santa Cruz Yacht Harbor (P.O. Box 3176), Santa Cruz, CA 95063 (☎ **408/426-4690**); and **Shamrock Charters,** 2210 E. Cliff Dr., Santa Cruz, CA 95062 (☎ **408/476-2648**).

There's a great bike route along the 2-mile cliff walk. Bikes—mountain, kids, tandem, hybrid—are available by the hour, day, or week from the **Bicycle Rental and Tour Center,** 415 Pacific Ave., at Front Street (☎ **408/426-8687**), open daily from 10am to 6pm. Figure on paying $25 a day, which includes helmet, lock, and pack.

There are several public golf courses, the best being the **Pasatiempo Golf Club,** at 18 Clubhouse Rd. (☎ **408/459-9155**), rated among the top 100 courses in the United States.

Hikers, bikers, and birders in need of some direction can call **The Tour Center** (☎ **408/426-8687**), where experienced local guides specialize in hiking, biking, and birding, as well as water-sport tours.

Sea kayaking, another fun beach activity, is also available. Outfitters include **The Kayak Connection,** 413 Lake Ave., Suite 4 (☎ **408/479-1121**), and **Vision Quest Kayaking,** at Building 2 on the Wharf (☎ **408/425-8445**), which has kayak, sail, and waterbike rentals available.

Surfing equipment can be rented at the **Cowell's Beach n Bikini Surf Shop,** 109 Beach St. (☎ **408/427-2355**), and also from the **Club Ed Surf School,** on Cowell Beach in front of the Dream Inn (☎ **408/459-9283**). You could also soar above the bay on a parasailing trip courtesy of **Pacific Parasail,** 58 Municipal Wharf (☎ **408/423-3545**). All the outfitters above also offer lessons.

IN NEARBY CAPITOLA

South along the coast lies the small attractive community of Capitola, at the mouth of the Soquel Creek, a spawning ground for steelhead and salmon. You can fish without a license from the **Capitola Wharf,** 1400 Wharf Rd. (☎ **408/462-2208**), or you can rent a fishing boat from **Capitola Boat and Bait** (☎ **408/462-2208**).

Capitola Beach fronts the Esplanade. Surf fishing and clamming are popular pastimes at Capitola's **New Brighton State Beach,** 1500 State Park Dr. (☎ **408/ 475-4850**), where camping is also allowed.

Other Capitola pastimes? Antiquing! Explore the many stores along Soquel Drive between 41st and Capitola avenues.

Still farther south around the bay is Aptos, home to the 10,000-acre **Forest of Nisene Marks State Park** (☎ **408/724-1266**), which has hiking trails that wind through redwoods and past abandoned mining camps. It was also the epicenter of the 1989 earthquake.

About 25 miles north of Santa Cruz the **Año Nuevo State Reserve,** New Years Creek Road, off Calif. 1 in Pescadero (☎ **800/444-7275**), offers guided walks into the northern elephant seal rookery from December to March. The walks take 2¹/₂ hours and cover 3 miles. Reservations are necessary. Self-guided walks are possible with a permit in summer.

In the redwood-forested mountains behind Santa Cruz are quite a few wineries, although visitors may not be familiar with the labels because the product is small and consumed locally. Most are clustered around Boulder Creek and Felton or around Capitola. All offer tours by appointment; some feature regular tastings, including the **Bargetto Winery,** 3535 N. Main, Soquel (☎ **408/475-2258**), which has a courtyard wine-tasting area overlooking the creek. For additional information, contact **Santa Cruz Mountains Winegrowers Association** (☎ **408/479-WINE**).

WHERE TO STAY

Casa Blanca Inn. 101 Main St. (at Beach St.), Santa Cruz, CA 95060. ☎ **408/423-1570.** Fax 408/423-0235. 34 rms. TV TEL. High season (May–Sept), $95–$300 double. Low season (Aug–Apr), $58–$195 double. AE, CB, DC, MC, V.

Across from the wharf in a heavily trafficked area, this motel along the waterfront was once the Mediterranean-style Cerf Mansion, dating from 1918. Other motel-style accommodations have grown up around the main building. Originally the home of a Federal judge, it offers individually decorated bedrooms, some with brass beds and velvet draperies. Some units contain fireplaces and terraces, and all are equipped with microwaves and coffeemakers. Most of the rooms have views of the water. There's a restaurant on the premises (see "Where to Dine," below) that serves good seafood in a romantic ocean-view setting.

Darling House. 314 W. Cliff Dr., Santa Cruz, CA 95060. ☎ **408/458-1958.** 8 rms, 2 with bath. $95 double without bath, $225 double with bath. AE, DISC, MC, V.

This lovely Spanish-style house, designed in 1910 by William Weeks, architect of Santa Cruz's Coconut Grove, has a panoramic view of the Pacific Ocean and is situated in a quiet residential area within walking distance of the boardwalk and lighthouse. The gardens are fragrant with citrus and orchids, and contain some stately palms, too. From the tiled front veranda, guests enter an elegant interior, the focal point of which is the dining room handcrafted from tiger oak. Throughout, the house boasts fine architectural features such as beveled glass, antiques, and handsome fireplaces. Each of the eight rooms is individually decorated, and though all have sinks, only two come with private bath. The Pacific Ocean Room, decorated like a sea captain's quarters, features a fireplace, a telescope, and one of the finest ocean views in Santa Cruz. A backyard hot tub is available for guests. Breakfast includes oven-fresh breads and pastries, fruit, and homemade granola made with walnuts from the Darlings' own farm.

IN NEARBY CAPITOLA

The Inn at Depot Hill. 250 Monterey Ave. (near Park Ave.), Capitola, CA 95010. ☎ **800/ 57-B-AND-B** or 408/462-3376. Fax 408/462-3697. 8 rms, 4 suites. A/C TV TEL. $165–$250 double. Rates include breakfast, afternoon tea or wine and hors d'oeuvres, and after-dinner dessert. AE, MC, V.

Located a few blocks from the bayfront, this converted railroad station has been beautifully designed and decorated with great attention to detail and to every aspect of comfort, thanks to innkeeper Suzanne Lankes. All rooms have wood-burning fireplaces, VCRs and stereos, telephones with fax/modem capability, bathrobes, hair dryers, two-person showers, and full baths. Thoughtful touches include dimmer light switches; fine fabrics; linens; closet lights, makeup remover, and lint remover in the bathrooms; nightlights that function as flashlights; and needlepointed DO NOT DISTURB signs. Each room is decorated in the style of a particular country, such as the terra-cotta–walled Portofino Room, patterned after an Italian villa right down to the frescoes and stone cherub. Regular guests usually pick a different room with each visit.

The evening wine and hors d'oeuvres and the breakfast are of similar prime quality, and they can be enjoyed either in your room or out in the garden courtyard on wrought-iron tables shaded by market umbrellas.

WHERE TO DINE

Cafe Bittersweet. 2332 Mission St. (near King St.) ☎ **408/423-9999.** Reservations recommended. Main courses $10–$16. MC, V. Tues–Thurs and Sun 5:30–9pm, Fri–Sat 5:30–10pm. MEDITERRANEAN.

In an unlikely small strip development, this light, airy restaurant—occupying a single room with white walls and terra-cotta–tile floors—has developed a reputation for fine cuisine since it opened in 1992. The menu features only five main dishes, which ensures quality. Start with the grilled shrimp over greens with garlic, sage, and white beans, or one of the fresh salads. Follow with the richly flavored veal medallions with a brandied wild-mushroom sauce. We also enjoyed the inventive mushroom moussaka, which layers eggplant and potatoes with a mixture of exotic mushrooms; the whole thing is topped with béchamel and kassari asiago and Parmesan cheeses.

Casablanca Restaurant. 101 Main St. (at Beach St.). ☎ **408/426-9063.** Reservations recommended. Main courses $14–$20. AE, DC, MC, V. Sun–Thurs 5–9pm, Fri–Sat 5–10pm, Sun 9:30am–2pm. CONTINENTAL.

The candlelit dining room at the Casa Blanca Inn was obviously built for romance, right down to the stellar views of the shimmering bay. For a stimulating start, try the Sicilian red clam chowder, or the fire-roasted Anaheim chili stuffed with herbed chèvre and served with tomatillo salsa. Among the 10 or so main courses, we'd recommend any of the fresh seafood dishes, perhaps the red snapper sautéed with capers, scallions, and lemon-butter sauce. The award-winning book-length wine list is excellent.

O'Mei. 2316 Mission St. ☎ **408/425-8458.** Reservations suggested Fri–Sat. Main courses $7–$11. AE, MC, V. Mon–Thurs 11:30am–2pm and 5–9:30pm, Fri 11:30am–2pm and 5–10pm, Sat 5–10pm. SZECHUAN.

O'Mei's (pronounced Oh-*may*) mini-mall location may not be very inviting, but the fantastic food served here more than makes up for it. The menu features some unusual specialties such as apricot-almond chicken and wine-braised chicken livers, along with more familiar dishes such as chicken with cashews or Szechuan shrimp. Dinner starts with a dim sum–style tray of exotic offerings such as sesame-cilantro-eggplant salad or pan-roasted peppers with feta cheese. Recommended choices are the sliced rock cod in black-bean/sweet-pepper sauce and the black-date and sweet-potato chicken.

IN NEARBY CAPITOLA

Shadowbrook. 1750 Wharf Rd., Capitola. ☎ **408/475-1511.** Reservations accepted. Main courses $14–$25. AE, DC, MC, V. Mon–Thurs 5:30–9:30pm, Fri 5:30–10pm, Sat 4:30–11pm, Sun 10am–2:15pm and 4:30–9pm. AMERICAN/CONTINENTAL.

Shadowbrook, one of Capitola's most venerable and romantic restaurants, occupies a serene setting above the Soquel Creek. To reach the restaurant, diners have to either take the cable-driven "hillavator" down or walk the long, steep bank of steps beside a running waterfall. At the bottom is a log cabin built in the 1920s, which has been enlarged and now contains a series of dining rooms on different levels— the wood-paneled Wine Cellar, the airy Garden Room, the Fireplace Room, and the creekside Greenhouse.

The menu doesn't hold many surprises, featuring thick-cut prime rib and steaks, along with seafood such as scampi and grilled trout, plus pasta dishes including lasagne primavera. Prawn cocktails, deep-fried artichoke hearts, and baked brie are among the appetizers. Standout desserts are the mud pie and Bailey's cheesecake.

The Wine Country 7

by Erika Lenkert and Matthew R. Poole

California's Napa and Sonoma valleys are two of the most famous wine-growing regions in the world. The workaday valleys that are a way of life for thousands of vintners are also a worthy trip for any wine lover. Hundreds of wineries are nestled among the vines of this beautiful countryside—and most are open to visitors. Even if you can only visit California's celebrated Wine Country as a day trip from San Francisco, it's well worth the drive.

Conveniently, most of the large wineries—as well as most of the hotels, shops, and restaurants—are located along a single road, Calif. 29, which starts at the mouth of the Napa River, near the north end of San Francisco Bay, and continues north to Calistoga and the top of the growing region. Every Napa Valley town and winery listed here can be reached from this main thoroughfare. The Sonoma Valley towns and wineries are over the ridge, due west of Napa Valley, roughly along Calif. 12.

1 Napa Valley

Many of the California wines you've been enjoying with your meals in San Francisco hail from this warm, narrow valley about 90 minutes north of the city. Napa Valley's fame as the state's premier wine-growing region was established by its Cabernet Sauvignon, made from Cabernet grapes that, except for the white Chardonnay grape, are allocated more growing acres than any other.

Napa Valley is home to more than 250 wineries, as well as to an exceptional selection of fine restaurants and hostelries for every taste and budget. If you can, plan on spending more than a day here; it will take you a couple of days to tour even a small number of the valley's wineries. The valley is just 35 miles long, so any of the valley towns—Napa, Yountville, Rutherford, Oakville, St. Helena, Calistoga—make a good base, allowing you to wine, dine, shop, and sightsee without traveling very far. Don't pass up the valley if you only have a day to spare, though; even a few hours spent here will introduce you to this beautiful region and its bounty, and give you a taste of the wine-making process.

ESSENTIALS

GETTING THERE   From San Francisco, cross the Golden Gate Bridge and continue north on Calif. 101. Turn east on Calif. 37 (toward Vallejo), then north on Calif. 29, the main road through the

Wine Country (don't worry, there's plenty of signs showing the way). You really can't get lost—there's just one north-south road, on which most of the wineries, hotels, shops, and restaurants are located.

VISITOR INFORMATION   While you're in San Francisco, you can pick up free Wine Country maps and brochures from the **Wine Institute,** at 425 Market St., Suite 1000, San Francisco, CA 94105 (☎ 415/512-0151).

Once you're in the Napa Valley, stop at the **Napa Valley Conference and Visitors Bureau,** 1310 Town Center Mall (off 1st Street), Napa, CA 94559 (☎ 707/ 226-7455), for a variety of local information. All over Napa and Sonoma you can pick up a very informative free weekly publication called the *Wine Country Review.* It will give you the most up-to-date information on the area's wineries and related events.

If you need help organizing your Wine Country vacation, contact **Wine Country Referrals,** P.O. Box 543, Calistoga, CA 94515 (☎707/942-2186; fax 707/ 942-4681). It's a knowledgeable company that specializes in the area and offers extensive rental information on inns, hotels, motels, resorts, and vacation homes, as well as wineries, limousine tours, restaurants, spas, ballooning, gliders, and train rides.

WHEN TO GO   The best time to visit California's Wine Country is during the autumn harvest season, when the grapes have ripened and all the wineries are in full production—it's quite a show. Spring has its own rewards: The entire valley is blanketed in wildflowers. Summer? Say hello to hot weather and heavy traffic.

TOURING THE WINERIES

Most wineries offer tours daily from 10am to 5pm. The tours usually chart the process of wine-making from the grafting and harvesting of the vines to the pressing of the grapes and the blending and aging of the wines in oak casks. They vary in length, detail, and formality, depending on the winery. Most tours are free.

Our favorite wineries are listed below, organized geographically from south to north along Calif. 29, beginning in the village of Napa (visits to all are free unless otherwise indicated). You can't miss them—each winery bears a large sign to ensure that you won't. In addition to those listed here, be sure to stop at some of those you pass along the way. Some of our most memorable Wine Country experiences haven't been on tours or in formal tasting halls, but at the mom-and-pop wineries throughout the region. These are the places where you'll make discoveries, pick up bottles that are only sold from the proprietor's front room, and talk with the colorful people who made the wine they're selling you with their own hands. The big, commercially oriented wineries offering tours are not to be missed, for sure, but don't pass up the other, more personal side of the Wine Country experience either.

Trefethen Vineyards. 1160 Oak Knoll Ave., Napa. ☎ 707/255-7700. Daily 10am–4:30pm. Tours by appointment only. From Calif. 29, take Oak Knoll Avenue east.

A tour of this winery (available by appointment only) is well worth arranging. The main structure, built in 1886, is listed on the National Register of Historic Places. The bucolic brick courtyard is surrounded with oak and cork trees. Although it's one of the valley's oldest wineries, Trefethen didn't produce its first Chardonnay until 1973; since then the vineyard has won awards year after year. Tastings take place in their inviting wood-beamed, jazz-filled tasting room.

Newlan Vineyards. 5225 Solano Ave., Napa. ☎ 707/257-2399. Tours by appointment only. Tasting daily 10am–5pm.

This small, family-owned winery produces only about 10,000 cases a year. It was founded in 1967, when physicist Bruce Newlan planted 11 acres of cabernet

The Wine Country

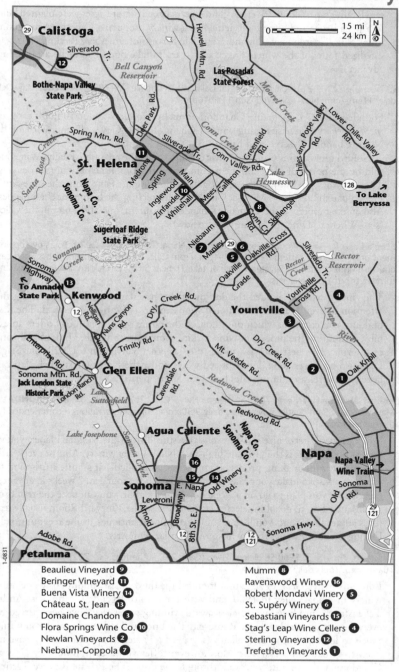

Beaulieu Vineyard **9**
Beringer Vineyard **11**
Buena Vista Winery **14**
Château St. Jean **13**
Domaine Chandon **3**
Flora Springs Wine Co. **10**
Newlan Vineyards **2**
Niebaum-Coppola **7**

Mumm **8**
Ravenswood Winery **16**
Robert Mondavi Winery **5**
St. Supéry Winery **6**
Sebastiani Vineyards **15**
Stag's Leap Wine Cellars **4**
Sterling Vineyards **12**
Trefethen Vineyards **1**

sauvignon grapes along dry creek. Three years later 16 more acres were planted, and in 5 years Bruce and his wife, Jonette, had a winery producing Cabernet Sauvignon, Pinot Noir, Chardonnay, Zinfandel, and late harvest Johannesberg Riesling. The personalized tours of the winery are excellent; try to take one (it must be arranged in advance).

✪ **Domaine Chandon.** California Dr. (at Calif. 29), Yountville. ☎ **707/944-2280.** May–Oct, daily 11am–6pm; Nov–Apr, Wed–Sun 11am–6pm.

Founded in 1973, Domaine Chandon annually produces about 500,000 cases of *méthode champenoise* sparkling wines—Chandon Brut Cuvée, Carneros Blanc de Noirs, Chandon Réserve, and Etoile.

Guided tours of this California-style champagne house are offered daily. Wines are sold by the bottle or glass and are accompanied by complimentary hors d'oeuvres. There's also a gift shop and a small gallery housing artifacts from the vineyard's French parent company, Moët et Chandon, chronicling the history of champagnes. Also on the property is the Domaine Chandon restaurant, one of the best in the valley (see "Where to Dine" in "Yountville," below).

Stag's Leap Wine Cellars. 5766 Silverado Trail, Napa. ☎ **707/944-2020.** Tours by appointment only. Sales and tasting daily 10am–4pm. From Calif. 29, take Yountville Cross Road east and turn right (south) on Silverado Trail; or take Trances Street or Oak Knoll Avenue east and turn left (north) to the cellars.

The vintner who has guided the destiny of this now-famous winery, garnering the attention of even France's most noted wine experts, is Warren Winiarski. The first building you come to, which once housed the entire operation, today offers an exhibit illustrating the process of wine-making from start to finish. Undoubtedly one of the vineyard's best-known wines is the Cabernet Sauvignon Cask 23, but Stag's Leap also produces good, lower-priced wines under the Hawk Crest label. You can taste current releases during sales hours for $3 per person.

Robert Mondavi Winery. 7801 St. Helena Hwy. (Calif. 29), Oakville. ☎ **800/MONDAVI.** May–Oct, daily 9am–5:30pm; Nov–Apr, daily 9:30am–4:30pm. Reservations recommended for the guided tour.

You'll probably recognize this mission-style spread from the Mondavi labels you've seen at home. This is the ultimate high-tech Napa Valley winery: Almost every variable in the wine-making process is computer controlled—it's quite intriguing to watch. It's wise to make your reservations for the guided tour 1 to 2 weeks in advance, especially if you plan to go on a weekend. After the tour, you can taste the results of all this attention to detail in selected current wines. The Vineyard Room usually features an art show, and you'll find some exceptional antiques in the reception hall. During the summer the winery hosts outdoor jazz concerts.

Beaulieu Vineyard. 1960 St. Helena Hwy. (Calif. 29), Rutherford. ☎ **707/963-2411.** Daily 10am–5pm. Tours daily 11am–4pm.

Bordeaux native Georges de Latour founded the third-oldest continuously operating winery in Napa Valley in 1900, and with the help of legendary oenologist André Tchelistcheff, produced world-class award-winning wines that have been served by every American president since Roosevelt. The brick and redwood tasting room isn't much to look at, but with Beaulieu's (say *bowl-you*) stellar reputation, they have no need to visually impress. They do, however, offer you a complimentary glass of Chardonnay the minute you walk through the door. The Private Reserve Tasting Room nearby offers tastes of reserve wines for a small fee. A free tour explains the wine-making process and the vineyard's history.

✪ **Flora Springs Wine Co..** 1978 W. Zinfandel Lane (just off Calif. 29), St. Helena. ☎ **707/ 963-5711.** Open by reservation only; call ahead or write.

While this handsome stone winery dates back to Napa Valley's early days, the Flora Springs label didn't appear until 1978. The label is well known for its barrel-fermented chardonnay, a Cabernet Sauvignon, and "Trilogy," a Bordeaux-style blend.

Flora Springs offers an excellent 1-hour "familiarization seminar," which can be tailored to suit all levels of wine enthusiast. Limited to groups of 10, the course is held Monday to Saturday by appointment only. The program begins in the vineyards, where you'll taste the grapes. While the grapes are being crushed, you taste the must (the just-pressed juice) and see how it ultimately becomes a beautiful, clear wine. Then you're taught how to evaluate wines: You'll blind-taste different ones and learn how wines change with age and how to distinguish between them. You'll also learn to pair wines with different foods. Who knows, it may just prove to be the most interesting and enjoyable—not to mention educational—time you spend in the Wine Country.

Beringer Vineyards. 2000 Main St. (just north of St. Helena's business district, on Calif. 29), St. Helena. ☎ **707/963-7115.** Tours daily 9:30am–5pm.

This remarkable Rhine House, with its hand-dug tunnels carved out of the mountainside, is the site of the original Beringer winery. Beringer Vineyards was founded in 1876 by brothers Jacob and Frederick; the family owned it until 1971, when it was purchased by the Swiss firm of Nestlé, Inc. It's the oldest continuously operating winery in Napa Valley. ("What about Prohibition?" you might ask; Beringer made "sacramental" wines during the dry years.)

The modern working winery on the opposite side of the road is not open to the public. Tasting of current vintages is conducted during sales hours in the Rhine House; reserve wines are available in the Founders' Room (upstairs in the Rhine House). A modest fee is charged per taste. Tours are conducted by very knowledgeable guides.

Sterling Vineyards. 1111 Dunaweal Lane (half a mile east of Calif. 29), Calistoga. ☎ **800/ 726-6136,** or 707/942-3344. Sales and tasting daily 10:30am–4:30pm. Visitor fee $6 per person.

This winery—an imposing one, owned by the Seagram Classics Wine Company and producing more than 200,000 cases per year—is probably more startling in appearance than any of its neighbors. Perched atop an island of rock, it looks more like a Greek or Italian monastery than a Napa winery. Yet reaching this isolated facility is relatively easy and fun—an aerial gondola, which offers panoramic views of the valley, provides a quick ride up the hill.

The very informative tour is self-directed. You'll go downstairs to fermentors, then down to the first aging cellar, and farther down still to the final aging cellar.

SETTLING INTO THE VALLEY: THE TOWN OF NAPA

Driving into Napa, you might wonder why you spent over an hour getting here only to find that the Wine Country is really just a long strip of industrial spaces, motels, and cheesy discount stores. But have no fear; the town of Napa serves mainly as the commercial center of the Wine Country and the gateway to Napa Valley—hence, the high-speed freeway that whips you right past it and on to the "tourist" towns of St. Helena and Calistoga.

WHAT TO SEE & DO BEYOND THE WINERIES

If you have plenty of time and a penchant for Victorian architecture, however, the **Napa Valley Conference and Visitors Bureau,** 1310 Napa Town Center Mall, off

1st St. (☎ **707/226-7459**), offers self-guided walking tours of the town's historic buildings, and there are a few other activities and attractions worth stopping for.

The Napa Valley Wine Train. McKinstry Street Depot, 1275 McKinstry St. (near 1st St. and Soscol Ave.). ☎ **800/427-4124** or 707/253-2111. Train fare, $30 for daytime rides, $22 for evening rides. Meal supplements, $22 for brunch, $25 for lunch, $39.50 for dinner $39.50. Departures Mon at 11:30am; Tues–Fri at 11:30am and 6pm; Sat–Sun and holidays 8:30am, noon, and 6pm. Reduced departure schedule Jan–Feb.

You don't have to worry about drinking and driving if you visit the Wine Country aboard the Wine Train, a rolling restaurant that makes a 3-hour, 36-mile journey through the vineyards of Napa, Yountville, Oakville, Rutherford, and St. Helena (*Tip:* Sit on the west side for the best views.). The vintage-style cars—finished with polished Honduran mahogany paneling and etched-glass partitions—evoke the opulent sophistication of the 1920s and 1930s. Gourmet meals are served by an attentive staff, complete with all the appropriate details—damask linen, bone china, silver flatware, and etched crystal. The menus are fixed, consisting of three or four courses, which might include poached Norwegian salmon court bouillon or Black Angus filet mignon served with a cabernet and roquefort sauce.

In addition to the dining rooms, the train pulls a Wine Tasting Car ($5 for four tastings), a Deli Car, and three 50-passenger lounges. *Fair Warning:* Photos are taken before you board; so if you want to capture the moment on film, be prepared.

Hitting the Links

South of downtown Napa, 1.3 miles east of Calif. 29 on Calif. 12, is **The Chardonnay Club (☎ 707/257-8950),** a challenging 36-hole land-links golf complex with first-class service. You pay just one fee, which makes you a member for the day. Privileges include the use of a golf cart, the practice range (including a bucket of balls), and services usually found only at a private club (the day that we played, a snack cart came by on the course with a full complement of sandwiches and soft drinks—and at the end of the round my clubs were cleaned). The course ambles through and around 325 acres of vineyards, hills, creeks, canyons, and rock ridges. There are three nines of similar challenge, all starting at the clubhouse so that you can play the 18 of your choice. Five sets of tees provide you with a course measuring from 5,300 yards to a healthy 7,100. Starting times can be reserved up to 2 weeks in advance.

Greens fees (including mandatory cart and practice balls) are $60 Monday to Thursday ($45 after 1pm), $80 Friday to Sunday ($55 after 1pm). The course is open daily year-round. Chardonnay Club services include the golf shop, locker rooms, and a restaurant and grill.

WHERE TO STAY

Expensive

✪ **Silverado Country Club & Resort.** 1600 Atlas Peak Rd., Napa, CA 94558. ☎ **800/532-0500** or 707/257-0200. Fax 707/257-2867. 281 studios, 28 suites. A/C MINIBAR TV TEL. $195 studio; $255 one-bedroom suite; $365–$470 two- or three-bedroom suite. Breakfast $8.50 extra. Golf and promotional packages available. AE, CB, DC, MC, V. Free parking. Drive north on Calif. 29 to Trancas St.; then turn east to Atlas Peak Rd.

If you long for the opulence of an East Coast country club, bring your racquet and golf clubs and fork over big dollars to play at the Silverado, a 1,200-acre resort in the Wine Country foothills. When stacked up against many of California's poshest resorts, this place comes off more like a suburban country club than a retreat for the rich and famous. The accommodations range from very large studios with a king-size bed, kitchenette, and a roomy, well-appointed bath, to one-, two-, or three-bedroom cottage suites, each with a wood-burning fireplace. All rooms are individually decorated with country home–style furnishings. The best accommodations, as you'd imagine, are the cottage suites—clustered in private, low-rise groupings, they all share tucked-away courtyards and peaceful walkways that provide a sense of privacy despite the resort's size.

Dining/Entertainment: The Royal Oak is the quintessential steak and seafood restaurant. Vintner's Court offers superb California and Pacific Rim cuisine with a view of the surrounding eucalyptus and well-tended flower beds. The Silverado Bar & Grill is a large indoor terrace/bar and outdoor deck that serves breakfast, lunch, and cocktails.

Services: Concierge, room service, laundry.

Facilities: The hotel's two golf courses were very cleverly designed by Robert Trent Jones, Jr. The **South Course** is 6,500 yards, with a dozen water crossings; the **North Course** is 6,700 yards, somewhat longer but a bit more forgiving. A staff of pros is on hand to provide pointers. The greens fee is $105 for 18 holes on either course, including a mandatory cart. There are also tennis courts and several swimming pools, as well as a tour desk. Non-smoking rooms are available.

Moderate

🅢 Cedar Gables Inn. 486 Coombs St. (at Oak St.), Napa, CA 94559. ☎ **800/309-7969** or 707/224-7969. Fax 707/224-4838. 6 rms. $109–$169 double ($10 less in winter). Rates include breakfast. AE, MC, V. From Calif. 29 north, exit onto 1st St. and follow the signs to downtown.

This is easily one of Napa's best buys, located in a quiet, tree-filled residential area. The Cedar Gables is an imposing 1892 Victorian mansion made inviting by the personal attention of innkeepers Margaret and Craig Snasdell. The rooms—all with private baths—are decorated with tapestries and antiques, and painted in rich, old-world colors. Some have fireplaces, four have whirlpool tubs, and all feature brass, wood, or iron queen-size beds. The inn's cozy sunken family room is home to a large-screen TV and roaring fireplace—the perfect place to cuddle up with your sweetie pie. Wine and cheese are served in the evening.

Château Hotel. 4195 Solano Ave., Napa, CA 94558. ☎ **800/253-6272** in California or 707/253-9300. Fax 707/253-0906. 115 rms, 6 suites. A/C TV TEL. Apr–Oct, $115 double; Nov–Mar, $100 double; from $155 suite. Rates include buffet breakfast. AE, CB, DC, MC, V. Free parking. From Calif. 29 north, turn left just past Trower Ave., at the entrance to the Napa Valley wine region.

The Château is a contemporary two-story motel complex that tries to evoke the aura of a French country inn, but it isn't fooling anybody—a motel's a motel. The rooms and bathrooms are spacious and have separate vanity/dressing areas; most have refrigerators. Ten rooms are especially designed for disabled guests, and non-smoking units are available. If you're used to a daily swim, the Château also has a heated pool and spa.

🅢 Tall Timbers Chalets. 1012 Darms Ln., Napa, CA 94558. ☎ **707/252-7810.** 8 cottages. A/C MINIBAR TV. $105 cottage for two Sun–Fri, $150 Sat. Additional person $10 extra. AE, MC, V. Free parking. From Calif. 29 north, turn left onto Darms Ln. 8 miles north of Napa.

This group of eight roomy whitewashed cottages surrounded by pines and eucalyptus is one of the best bargains in Napa Valley. All the cottages are decorated in a simple, homey fashion and are well furnished; amenities include refrigerators, toaster-ovens, and coffeemakers. It's really pleasant to find, on your arrival, a

---

Adventures Aloft: Hot-Air Ballooning

Fancy grape juice isn't the only thing the Wine Country has to offer. Believe it or not, Napa Valley is the most popular hot-air-balloon "flight corridor" in the *world*. Northern California's temperate weather allows for ballooning year round, and on summer weekends it's a rare day in the valley when you don't see at least one of the colorful airships floating above the vineyards.

Trips usually depart early in the morning when the air is cooler and the balloons have better lift. Flight paths vary with the direction and speed of the changing breezes, so "chase" crews on the ground must follow the balloon to its undetermined destination. Most flights last about an hour and end with a traditional champagne celebration and breakfast. Reservations are required, and should be made as far in advance as possible. Prices range from $165 to $195 per person for the basic package; wedding, wine tasting, picnic, and lodging packages are also available. For more information or reservations, call Napa's **Bonaventura Balloon Company** (☎ **800/FLY-NAPA,** or 707/944-2882), a highly reputable organization owned and operated by pilot Joyce Bowen, or **Adventures Aloft** (☎ **800/944-4408,** or 707/944-4408), Napa Valley's oldest hot-air-balloon company.

---

basket of fresh fruit in the breakfast nook, breakfast treats in the refrigerator, and a complimentary bottle of champagne. There are no phones in the cottages, but you'll have access to one in the main office. Each unit can sleep four (there's a bedroom plus a queen-size sofa bed in the living room); several have decks. No smoking is allowed in the cottages.

Inexpensive
Napa Valley Budget Inn. 3380 Solano Ave., Napa, CA 94558. ☎ **707/257-6111.** 58 rms. A/C TV TEL. $56–$79 double. AE, DC, DISC, MC, V. Free parking. From Calif. 29 north, turn left at the Redwood Rd. turnoff and go 1 block to Solano Ave.; then turn left and go half a block to the motel.

The best thing going for this no-frills inn is its excellent location—close to Calif. 29 and just across the street from convenient shopping. The rooms are simple, clean, and comfortable. There's a small heated pool on the premises.

WHERE TO DINE
Bistro Don Giovanni. 4110 St. Helena Hwy. (Calif. 29; just north of Salvador Ave.). ☎ **707/224-3300.** Reservations recommended Sat–Sun. Main courses $11–$15. AE, DC, MC, V. Daily 11am–10pm. NORTHERN ITALIAN.

Donna and Giovanni Scala—who also run the fantastic Scala's Bistro in San Francisco (see Chapter 6)—serve refined Italian fare prepared with top-quality ingredients and a California flair at this large, lively, Mediterranean-style restaurant. Terra-cotta tiles, an open kitchen, café-style chairs, and an enormous painting of the Italian flag set the scene. The menu features pastas, risottos, pizzas (baked in a wood-burning oven), and half a dozen other main courses such as braised lamb shank and Niman Schell bistro burgers. Less traditional appetizers include a grilled pear with a frisée-and-arugula salad with bleu cheese, caramelized walnuts, and bacon, while the matchstick zucchini sprinkled with parmesan cheese has become a signature dish. Pasta lovers should go for the farfalle with asparagus, porcini, wild mushrooms, pecorino cheese, and truffle oil; the seared filet of salmon with tomato, white wine, and chive sauce is another winner. Alfresco dining among the vineyards is available— and highly recommended on a warm, sunny day.

La Boucane. 1778 2nd St. (1 block east of Jefferson St.). ☎ **707/253-1177.** Reservations recommended. Main courses $14–$21. MC, V. Mon–Sat 5:30–10pm. FRENCH.

You'll be graciously welcomed into the domain of chef-owner Jacques Mokrani, who took this 1885 "Victorian lady" and refurbished it in a traditional French style with antiques and lots of chintz. The dinner-only menu is also classically French, featuring such dishes as duck à l'orange, sole meunière, and tournedos forestière. Try the poulet sauté Boucane, prepared with cognac, shallots, mushrooms, and sherry. To start, there are escargots and prawns provençal, and to finish, a traditional chocolate mousse and crème caramel. Granted, La Boucane isn't on the road to glory, but its tried-and-true French fare is better than most in the area.

The Red Hen Cantina. 5091 St. Helena Hwy. (Calif. 29). ☎ **707/255-8125.** Reservations recommended for large parties only. Main courses $8–$14. AE, DC, MC, V. Sun–Thurs 11am–9pm, Fri–Sat 11am–10pm. MEXICAN.

This popular taquería serving moderately priced food looks like a Swiss chalet that got lost somewhere south of the border. Seafood dishes supplement the traditional burritos, tacos, and pollo méxicano (chicken strips sautéed in white wine, onion, mushrooms, and tomatoes). What you get isn't bad, but it loses something in the translation this far north. Your best bet is to rest your weary bones at a patio table adorned with chips, salsa, and a cool margarita.

YOUNTVILLE

Founded by George Calvert Yount, the first white American to settle in the valley, Yountville lacks the small-town charm of neighboring St. Helena and Calistoga—for better or worse, the town lacks a rambunctious Main Street—but it does serve as a good base for exploring the valley and has a handful of excellent restaurants and inns.

WHAT TO SEE & DO BEYOND THE WINERIES

At the center of the village is **Vintage 1870** (☎ 707/944-2451), once a winery (from 1871 to 1955) and now a gallery with specialty shops selling antiques, wine accessories, country collectibles, and more; it's also home to three restaurants.

WHERE TO STAY

Expensive

Vintage Inn. 6541 Washington St., Yountville, CA 94599. ☎ **800/351-1133** or 707/944-1112. Fax 707/944-1617. 72 rms, 8 minisuites; 4 villas. A/C TV TEL. $150–$275 double; $240–$325 minisuite or villa. Rates include continental breakfast. Additional person $25 extra. AE, CB, DC, MC, V. Free parking. From Calif. 29 north, take the Yountville exit and turn left onto Washington St.

Built on an old 23-acre winery estate in the center of town, this sprawling, contemporary accommodation sits on land that once belonged to pioneer George C. Yount, who received it as a Spanish land grant. Famed designer Kipp Stewart, who also designed the sybaritic Ventana Inn at Big Sur, was responsible for creating this high-priced hideaway, which boasts four villas. You'll enter via a handsome reception lounge with a brick fireplace, lavender couches, and shuttered windows. The rooms are well equipped, with fireplaces, ceiling fans, oversize beds, coffeemakers, refrigerators, plush bathrobes, tubs with Jacuzzi jets, and a complimentary bottle of wine.

Dining: A California/continental champagne breakfast (cereals, yogurt, pastries, egg salad, and fruit) is served in the Vintage Club, as is afternoon tea.

Facilities: 60-foot swimming pool (heated year round), outdoor heated whirlpool, two tennis courts, bikes for rent; ballooning can be arranged. Non-smoking rooms are available.

Services: Concierge, limousine (to the wineries), laundry/valet, nightly turndown.

Moderate

❍ Burgundy House Country Inn. 6711 Washington St. (P.O. Box 3156), Yountville, CA 94599. ☎ **707/944-0889.** 5 rms. A/C. $125 double. Rates include breakfast. MC, V. Free parking. From Calif. 29 north, take the Yountville exit and turn left onto Washington St.

This small, distinctly French country inn—built in the early 1890s out of local fieldstone and river rock—successfully manages to retain its vintage charm. Originally a brandy distillery, it still features thick stone walls and hand-hewn post-and-lintel beams, a rustic decor enhanced today by antique country furnishings. Each of the five cozy guest rooms has comfortable beds with colorful quilted spreads and private baths; all are non-smoking rooms. Delightful touches include fresh flowers in each of the rooms and a complimentary decanter of local white wine. The full breakfast can be taken inside or outdoors in the inn's pretty garden.

Napa Valley Lodge. 2230 Madison St., Yountville, CA 94599. ☎ **800/368-2468** or 707/944-2468. Fax 707/944-9362. 55 rms and suites. $120–$210 double. MC, V. Rates include continental breakfast.

If you don't mind the corporate feel or a view of the highway beyond the swimming pool, the Napa Valley Lodge offers ultra-clean and spacious accommodations—including two-room suites—that are ideal for families. The rooms are better appointed than many in the area, and many have vaulted ceilings and fireplaces. All come with a king- or queen-size bed, wicker furnishings, coffeemakers, and either a private balcony or patio. The cheapest rooms are darker, motel style, and at ground level, but if you don't want to hang out there, you can always head to the swimming pool, garden spa, sauna, or fitness center. Extras include a concierge, complimentary extended continental breakfast buffet, VCR access, afternoon tea and cookies in the lobby, and Friday-evening wine tasting in the library.

WHERE TO DINE

Expensive

❍ Domaine Chandon. 1 California Dr. ☎ **707/944-2892.** Reservations required. Main courses $13–$17 at lunch, $24–$28 at dinner. AE, DC, MC, V. Summer, Mon–Tues 11:30am–2:30pm, Wed–Sun 11:30am–2:30pm and 6–9:30pm; winter, Wed–Sun 11:30am–2:30pm and 6–9:30pm. Closed the first 3 weeks of Jan. From Calif. 29 north, take the Yountville exit; the restaurant is on the west side of the highway. CALIFORNIA/FRENCH.

One of California's most celebrated restaurants is found at this French-owned champagne house, hidden in an idyllic locale off Calif. 29 beside a tree-shaded creek. The multilevel restaurant's large picture windows take full advantage of the vineyard views. At night, when candles illumine the fir-paneled room, it's quite romantic. On fairweather days you can dine alfresco.

Chef Philippe Jeanty, a native of Champagne, has presided over the well-trained staff here since 1977. He has a knack for original seasonings and a sound classic technique that reflects his background. The cuisine is full of flavor and carefully orchestrated to go with the Napa Valley wines offered. Main courses change daily, but might include caramelized scallops with mashed potatoes and a chardonnay-mushroom sauce, or chicken pot pie with fresh veggies and a creamy chardonnay sauce. At dinner, try the grilled Atlantic salmon wrapped in pancetta with a tangy onion sauce, or venison tournedos with a sweet-potato Napoléon, fava beans, and huckleberry-merlot sauce. Superb desserts include île flotante with caramel, almonds, and crème anglaise, or banana-coconut cream pie brûlée; other offerings suggest that desserts are not the chef's forte. The impeccable wine list includes some vintage dessert wines and cognacs.

⭐ **The French Laundry.** 6640 Washington St. (at Creek St.) ☎ **707/944-2380.** Reservations required. Prix-fixe menu $49—$57. AE, MC, V. Tues—Thurs 5:30–9:30pm, Fri–Sun noon–1:30pm and 5:30–9:30pm. AMERICAN/FRENCH.

If your restaurant has the chutzpah to post neither a sign nor an address, it had better be good. Fortunately, the French Laundry restaurant—housed in a converted fieldstone cottage that was once a French steam laundry—*is* that good. Though this Yountville institution has been around since 1978, it wasn't until renowned chef/owner Thomas Keller bought the restaurant a few years back that it caught the attention of epicureans worldwide.

Dinner is an all-night affair, a 2- to 3-hour event that, when it's finally over, you're ready to sit down and do all over again—truly, it's that wonderful. Technically, the prix-fixe menu offers a choice of four or five courses (including a vegetarian menu), but after a slew of cameo appearances from the kitchen, everyone starts to lose count. Signature dishes include Keller's "tongue in cheek" (a marinated and braised round of sliced lamb tongue and tender beef cheeks) and pan-seared sea bass with braised artichoke bottoms and slow-roasted tomatoes. Portions are small, but only because Keller wants his guests to taste as many different things as possible—nobody leaves hungry. The excellent service staff is well acquainted with the wide selection of regional wines; even so, the house charges a mere $5 corkage fee (undoubtedly set low to mollify local diners). On warm summer nights, of which the Wine Country has an abundance, consider requesting a table in the flower-filled garden.

Moderate

Mark Allen. 6795 Washington St. ☎ **707/944-0168.** Reservations accepted (recommended Sat–Sun). Main courses $12.95–$18.95. AE, MC, V. Daily 11:30am–3pm and 5–10pm. CALIFORNIA.

Pacific Rim–influenced California food has made its way up to the Wine Country at Mark Allen, a quaint, airy restaurant that opened in the summer of 1995 in the heart of Yountville. Following a Wine Country trend, chef/owner Mark Allen (who formerly presided at San Francisco's Inn at the Opera) styled his restaurant and café in a casually sophisticated fashion, with Mediterranean ceramic and tile floors and modern formal table settings. The food is equally as interesting, with such choices as tempura-battered prawns with a spicy bean-sprout salad in a soy-mustard vinaigrette starter, or main courses like grilled pork chops with butternut squash raviolis topped with maple/sun-dried-cherry sauce. Word around town is that Mark Allen is the new hot spot in Napa Valley.

✪ **Mustards Grill.** 7399 St. Helena Hwy. (1 mile north of Yountville on Calif. 29). ☎ **707/944-2424.** Reservations required. Main courses $11–$17. CB, DC, MC, V. Apr–Oct, daily 11:30am–10pm; Nov–Mar, daily 11:30am–9pm. CALIFORNIA.

Food critics writing about this place invariably call it "the quintessential Napa Valley wine restaurant." Opened in 1983 by a trio of innovators who also founded San Francisco's Fog City Diner (see Chapter 5), it just may be. A bronze of a bowler-hatted gentleman greets you at the door of the barnlike building. Inside, you'll find a bilevel, black-and-white tiled dining room with cathedral ceilings, a small bar, and a glass-enclosed outer dining area. The atmosphere is often boisterous and noisy. The blue-jeaned, white-shirted servers are friendly and knowledgeable.

Warm, crusty baguettes served with sweet butter are immediately brought to the table. Among the appetizers are such gems as home-smoked salmon with pasilla corncakes and crème fraîche, and garlicky goat cheese toasted on bread with arugula and sun-dried tomatoes. Seasonal main courses range from wood-burning-oven specialties like calf's liver with caramelized onions, bacon, and homemade chili sauce or smoked Long Island duck with 100-almond/onion sauce, to grilled items such as Sonoma rabbit with wild-mushroom cacciatore and filet mignon with merlot sauce. The Jack Daniels chocolate cake with chocolate sauce and the crumble-top banana cheesecake with caramel sauce are the top to-hell-with-the-calories dessert choices. Featured local wines range from $4 to $9 a glass. If you bring your own, the restaurant charges a $10 corkage fee.

We've known this place since it opened, and, quite frankly, it has its good and bad days, but we keep coming back. A sign of their commitment to both quality and style: If you order a burger (they make superb ones here), it comes with homemade catsup. Not bad.

Napa Valley Grille. 6795 Washington St. (on Calif. 29 at Madison St.). ☎ **707/944-8686.** Reservations recommended. Main courses $12–$22; lunch $7–$14. AE, DISC, MC, V. Mon–Thurs 11:30am–9:30pm, Fri–Sat 11:30am–10pm, Sun 10am–9:30pm. CALIFORNIA/MEDITERRANEAN.

Both upscale and casual at the same time, this big, bright, and airy dining room is as Californian as it gets. Smoky scents from the restaurant's wood-burning oven permeate the room; the oven's products include house-smoked barbecued baby back ribs and hickory-roasted game hen. Start with the smoked chicken spring rolls with watermelon-jicama slaw, and follow them with a pasta, such as black-pepper fettuccine or rigatoni with mixed vegetables, or the respectable paella. A large selection of salads, like warm cabbage with spicy beef, and sandwiches, such as fried oysters on a baguette, are available at lunch. Sunday brunch is popular here, particularly when patio seating is available.

Inexpensive

The Diner. 6476 Washington St. (between Mission and Oak sts.). ☎ **707/944-2626.** Reservations not accepted. Breakfast $4–$8; lunch $6–$10; dinner $8–$13.25. No credit cards. Tues–Sun 8am–3pm and 5:30–9pm. AMERICAN/MEXICAN.

This down-home diner, decorated in pink and featuring a functioning Irish Waterford wood stove and rotating art exhibits, is presided over by hearty empress Cassandra Mitchell, a fourth-generation San Franciscan who believes in giving people good food—and plenty of it. The menu is extensive, the portions huge, and the food satisfying. Breakfast offers such staples as oatmeal with walnuts and raisins, as well as French toast and standard egg dishes, but regulars tend to go for the local sausages, house potatoes, and cornmeal pancakes with house maple syrup. At lunch and dinner there's an assortment of Mexican and American dishes such as roast free-range chicken with fresh vegetables, giant burritos, big ol' burgers, and thick sandwiches made with house-roasted meats and house-baked bread.

OAKVILLE & RUTHERFORD
STOCKING UP FOR A NAPA VALLEY PICNIC

Driving farther north on the St. Helena Highway (Calif. 29) brings you to the Oakville Cross Road and the ✪ **Oakville Grocery Co.,** 7856 St. Helena Hwy., in Oakville (☎ **707/944-8802**), one of the finest gourmet food stores this side of New York's Dean & Deluca. Here you can put together the provisions for a memorable picnic or for a very special custom gift basket. You'll find the best breads, the choicest selection of cheeses in the northern Bay Area, pâtés, fresh foie gras (domestic and French, seasonally), smoked Norwegian salmon, smoked sturgeon and smoked pheasant (by special order), fresh caviar (Beluga, Sevruga, and Osetra), and an exceptional selection of California wines, of course. The grocery will prepare a picnic basket for you themselves with 24 hours' notice. Delivery service is available to some areas. It's open daily from 10am to 6pm.

WHERE TO STAY
Expensive

✪ Auberge du Soliel. 180 Rutherford Hill Rd., Rutherford, CA 94573. ☎ **707/963-1211.** Fax 707/963-8764. 50 rms and suites. A/C TV TEL MINIBAR. Weekdays $175–$750 double; weekends $250–$850 double from April to November. Rates are discounted Dec–Mar. AE, DC, DISC, MC, V. From Rutherford turn right on Calif. 128 and go three miles to the Silverado Trail; turn left and head north about 200 yards to Rutherford Hill Rd., then turn right.

Auberge du Soliel is the kind of place you'd imagine movie stars would frequent for a clandestine affair or a weekend retreat. It's set high above the Napa Valley in a 33-acre olive grove (as you stroll the terraced pathways to your private cottage, you may find a groundsworker gathering sun-ripened olives in baskets), and each accommodation is quiet, indulgent, and luxuriously romantic. The Mediterranean-style rooms are large enough to get lost in—and you might want to, once you discover all the amenities. The bathtub alone, an enormous hot tub complete with bath salts and a skylight overhead, will entice you to grab a glass of California red and settle in for a while. A wood-burning fireplace is surrounded by oversized, cushy furniture with bright, playfully pink pillows. Fresh flowers and original art, combined with terra-cotta floors and natural wood and leather furnishings, whisk you out of the Wine Country and into the Southwest, but once you step out onto the private balcony, you'll know you've left this planet and gone straight to heaven. Views of the valley are nothing less than spectacular, and each sun-washed deck is entirely exclusive. Auberge du Soleil, or "inn of the sun," also has a celestial swimming pool and work-out room with one of the grandest views around. All in all, it's one of the best places we've ever stayed.

Dining: See "Where to Dine," below.

Services: 24-hour room service; twice-daily maid service; laundry/valet; complimentary shoeshine.

Facilities: Outdoor pool with sun deck, massage rooms, 3 tennis courts, exercise room, beauty salon. Sculpture and nature trail with picnic areas that crisscross the property.

Rancho Caymus. 1140 Rutherford Rd. (P.O. Box 78), Rutherford, CA 94573. ☎ **800/845-1777,** or 707/963-1777. Fax 707/963-5387. 26 suites. A/C MINIBAR TV TEL. $125–$155 suite for two; from $235 Master Suite; $295 two-bedroom suite. Rates include continental breakfast. AE, DC, MC, V. From Calif. 29 north, turn right onto Rutherford Rd. / Calif. 128 East; the hotel is ahead on your left.

This Spanish-style hacienda inn was the creation of sculptor Mary Tilden Morton (of Morton Salt). Her family originally constructed this $4-million retreat, with two floors opening onto wisteria-covered balconies. Wantin each room in the hacienda to be a work of art, Morton hired the most skilled craftspeople of her day. She designed the adobe fireplaces herself, based on old designs, and wandered through Mexico and South America purchasing artifacts for the property.

The guest units are situated around a whimsical garden courtyard adorned with wrought-iron patio furniture and an enormous outdoor fireplace. The decor inside is on the funky side: mismatched overly varnished dark-wood furnishings, braided rugs—kind of like a visit to grandma's house. It's extremely cozy, however, and the accommodations are decent-sized split-level suites with queen-size beds. Other amenities include a wet bar, a sofa bed in the sitting area, and a small private patio. Twenty-two of the suites have wood-burning fireplaces and five have kitchenettes and whirlpool tubs. The rooms and public areas are full of character, with hand-carved black walnut furniture, stained-glass windows, and wall hangings woven by

Ecuadorian Otavalon Indians. Breakfast, which includes fresh fruit and breads and is included in the rates, is served in the inn's Mont St. John restaurant.

WHERE TO DINE

Auberge du Soleil. 180 Rutherford Hill Rd., Rutherford. ☎ **707/963-1211.** Reservations recommended. Main courses $25–$30; fixed-price dinner $60. AE, DISC, MC, V. Daily 7–11am, 11:30am–2:30pm, and 6–9:30pm. WINE COUNTRY CUISINE.

The Auberge du Soleil may be better known for its inn, but it was the restaurant that started all the fuss about this world-class resort. Frenchman Claude Rouas spent $1.5 million (an unheard-of amount for a Wine Country restaurant at the time) building the restaurant in 1981, and it became such an instant success that the inn soon followed.

Alfresco dining on the wisteria-canopied deck is taken to an entirely new level here, particularly on warm summer nights when diners are rewarded with a gorgeous view of Napa Valley fading with the sunset. Inside, a magnificent stucco fireplace, huge wood pillars, and fresh flowers combine to create a warm, rustic ambience. Chef Andrew Sutton characterizes his cuisine as "Wine Country," a reflection of the region's produce and international influences: Pacific Rim, southwestern, and Mediterranean styles predominate. Your potato-crusted Chilean sea bass, for example, may come with caraway-Savoy cabbage and truffled-beet relish. Signature dishes include roasted lobster sausage with fennel salad and mustard-seed vinaigrette, and grapevine-smoked salmon with walnut-wheat croutons and relish of roasted shallots and capers. The crisp-seared foie gras with black lentils and frisee salad is also quite good. Regardless of what you order, be sure to arrive before sunset and beg for terrace seating.

ST. HELENA

Located 17 miles north of Napa on Calif. 29, this former Seventh-Day Adventist village manages to maintain a pseudo–Old West feel while simultaneously catering to upscale shoppers with deep pockets—hence **Vanderbilt's,** purveyor of fine housewares, at 1429 Main St. It's a quiet, attractive little town hosting a slew of beautiful old homes and first-rate restaurants and accommodations. Assuming you can find a parking space, a stroll along Main Street is highly recommended.

WHAT TO SEE & DO BEYOND THE WINERIES

Literary buffs and other romantics will want to visit the **Silverado Museum,** at 1490 Library Lane (☎ 707/963-3757), which is devoted to the life and works of Robert Louis Stevenson, who honeymooned here in 1880 in an abandoned Silverado Mine bunk house. More than 8,000 museum items include original manuscripts, letters, photographs, and portraits, plus the desk he used in Samoa. It's open Tuesday to Sunday from noon to 4pm; admission is free.

BIKING THE VALLEY   The quieter northern end of the valley is an ideal place to rent a bicycle and ride the Silverado Trail. **St. Helena Cyclery,** at 1156 Main St.(☎ 707/963-7736), rents bikes for $7 per hour or $25 a day, including rear rack and picnic bag.

WHERE TO STAY

Very Expensive

◖Meadowood Resort. 900 Meadowood Lane, St. Helena, CA 94574. ☎ **707/963-3646.** Fax 707/963-3532. 85 rms and suites. A/C MINIBAR TV TEL. $320–$465 double; from $540 one-bedroom suite; from $830 two-bedroom suite; from $1,180 three-bedroom suite; from $1,520 four-bedroom suite. Two-night minimum stay. Ask about promotional offers and off-season rates. AE, DC, DISC, MC, V.

Named one of the top 10 resorts in the United States by *Condé Nast Traveler,* Meadowood is the Wine Country's version of a wealthy grownups' summer camp. The resort, tucked away on 250 acres of pristine mountainside amid a forest of madrone and oak trees, is quiet and exclusive enough to make you forget that busy wineries are 10 minutes away. Many accommodations are individual suites so far removed from the common areas that you have to drive to get to them (lazier folks can opt for more centrally located accommodations). Inside, the suites are decorated with American country classics, and are equipped with beamed ceilings, private patios, stone fireplaces, and wilderness views. Guests can spend their days using the nine-hole golf course, tennis courts, croquet lawns, swimming pools, and health spa, or hiking inn the surrounding areas. Those who actually want to leave here to do some wine tasting can check in with John Thoreen, the hotel wine tutor, whose sole purpose is to help guests better understand and enjoy Napa Valley's "liquid poetry." Each year the Napa Valley wine auction is held here in June.

Dining: See "Where to Dine," below, for our recommendation of the Restaurant at Meadowood.

Facilities: Golf, croquet, two outdoor pools with sundeck, massage rooms, 7 tennis courts, exercise room, hiking trails, and an executive conference center.

Expensive

Bartels Ranch and Country Inn. 1200 Conn Valley Rd., St. Helena, CA 94574. ☎ **707/ 963-4001.** Fax 707/963-5100. 4 rms. A/C TV TEL. $135–$315 double. AE, DC, DISC, JCB, MC, V. From downtown St. Helena, turn east on Pope St., cross Silverado Trail, and continue onto Howell Mountain Rd.; bear right onto Conn Valley Rd. and the inn is 2 miles ahead on the left.

This palatial ranch-style retreat, perched on 60 acres of rolling meadows studded with fig trees, cypress, and old oaks, is run by ebullient innkeeper Jamie Bartels, who designed the 7,000-square-foot stone ranch house and has decorated it with her own collection of butterflies and other mementos. The four individually decorated rooms provide every conceivable comfort—fireplaces, VCRs, balconies—plus conveniences like ironing boards, hair dryers, and private baths. The "champagne suite" has a heart-shaped Jacuzzi in the bathroom, while the Blue Valley room has a private deck and Jacuzzi. The house has a communal sundeck and pool, as well as a games room filled with books, a pool and Ping-Pong table, and a stereo. The bountiful breakfasts consist of fresh fruits, breads, and egg dishes; complimentary wine, fruit, and cheese are served each afternoon. Forever aiming to please, Jamie provides her guests with picnic supplies, lends them bicycles, and arranges massages or wine-country tours. A bocce ball court, croquet grounds, and access to horseback riding and tennis courts are other outdoor options.

Harvest Inn. 1 Main St., St. Helena, CA 94574. ☎ **800/950-8466** or 707/963-9463. 54 rms. A/C TV TEL. $185–$220 double. AE, DC, DISC, MC, V.

If you like your accommodations loaded with 20th-century luxuries yet reminiscent of an Olde English inn, you'll like the Harvest Inn. Ornate brick walkways—constructed with bricks harvested from turn-of-the-century San Francisco homes—cross the beautifully landscaped grounds to this Tudor-style inn. Each of the immaculate rooms—ranging from the Earl of Ecstasy to Camelot—are furnished in dark Tudor style with oak beds and dressers, black leather chairs, and antique furnishings; most have brick fireplaces, wet bars, and refrigerators. Facilities include a wine bar, heated swimming pools, and outdoor spas.

Hotel St. Helena. 1309 Main St., St. Helena, CA 94574. ☎ **707/963-4388.** 17 rms, 14 with bath; 1 suite. A/C TEL. $140 double without bath; $190 double with bath; $250 suite. Rates include continental breakfast. AE, DC, MC, V.

This downtown hotel occupies a historic 1881 building, the oldest wooden structure in St. Helena. The hotelkeepers celebrated the building's 100th birthday with a much-needed renovation and now it's more comfortable than ever. The hallways are cluttered with stuffed animals, wicker strollers, and other memorabilia. Most of the rooms have been similarly decorated, with brass beds, wall-to-wall burgundy carpeting, and oak or maple furnishings. There's a garden patio and wine bar, and TVs are available upon request. Smoking is discouraged.

The Inn at Southbridge. 1020 Main St., St. Helena, CA 94574. ☎ **800/520-6800** or 707/967-9400. Fax 707/967-9486. 21 rms. MINIBAR, TV, TEL. $175–$225 double. AE, DC, DISC, JCB, MC, V.

Eschewing the lace-and-latticework theme that plagues most Wine Country inns, the new Inn at Southbridge takes an unswervingly modern, pragmatic approach to accommodating its guests. Instead of stuffed teddy bears in the rooms you'll find terrycloth robes, fireplaces, bathroom skylights, down comforters, private balconies, and a host of other little luxuries. The decor is upscale Pottery Barn–trendy, for some a welcome departure from quaintly traditional hotel-style stuff; more functional touches include voice-mail and fax modems. On the premises is the brand-new restaurant Tomatina, which is owned and run by the owners of Tra Vigne, an Italian restaurant conveniently located next door, see "Where to Dine," below. There's a concierge and guests receive privileges at sibling resort Meadowood (for golf, tennis, croquet, spa, and fitness swimming).

Wine Country Inn. 1152 Lodi Ln., St. Helena, CA 94574. ☎ **707/963-7077.** Fax 707/963-9018. 24 rms. A/C TEL. $115–$248 double. Rates include breakfast. MC, V.

Just off the highway behind the Freemark Abbey Vineyard, this attractive wood-and-stone inn—complete with a French-style mansard roof and turret—overlooks a pastoral landscape of Napa Valley vineyards. The rooms are furnished with iron or brass beds and pine country furnishings; most have fireplaces and private terraces overlooking the valley, while others have private hot tubs. One of the inn's best features—besides the absence of televisions—is the outdoor pool, which is attractively set into the hillside.

Moderate

Ⓢ El Bonita Motel. 195 Main St. (at El Bonita Ave.), St. Helena, CA 94574. ☎ **800/541-3284**, or 707/963-3216. 26 rms. A/C MINIBAR TV TEL. $79–$120 double. AE, DC, MC, V.

This 1930s art deco motel was built a bit too close to Calif. 29 for comfort, but the 2^1/$_2$ acres of beautifully landscaped gardens behind the hotel (away from the road) help even the score. The rooms, while small, are spotlessly clean and decorated with new furnishings; all contain microwave ovens and coffeemakers, while some have kitchens or whirlpool baths. Families, attracted to the larger bungalows with kitchenettes, often consider El Bonita one of the best values in Napa Valley, especially considering that the motel comes with a heated outdoor pool, Jacuzzi, sauna, and a new massage facility.

WHERE TO DINE

Expensive

Restaurant at Meadowood. In the Meadowood Resort, 900 Meadowood Lane. ☎ **707/963-3646**. Reservations recommended. Fixed-price dinner $45 for meat or fish, $39 vegetarian. AE, DC, DISC, MC, V. Daily 6–10pm. AMERICAN/FRENCH.

One of Napa's more ambitious four-course dinners is served at Meadowood, a top-rated resort with a gazebo-style clubhouse dining room overlooking the golf course.

Chef Roy Breiman brought his southern French-influenced menu to the restaurant a few years back after leaving renowned Ernie's of San Francisco. He's obviously comfortable in his new kitchen because every course is well balanced and delicious. You might start dinner with a flavorful warm quail salad with smoky lentils and soy sauce, robust but not too heavy. Next try a crispy-skinned salmon trout served with exotic mushrooms and truffle oil—superb. And for a main course, sample the roast Moscovy duck flavored with cinnamon, star anise, and orange; it's not only impressive in presentation, but also skillfully prepared, with the fat well cooked off the skin. The delicious desserts include caramelized banana with currants and vanilla ice cream. The vegetarian four-course meals are just as tasty as the meat dinners, featuring, for example, couscous served with layered zucchini flavored with anise seeds, and crispy strudel with artichokes, onions, and wild mushrooms. Take a little stroll around the tranquil grounds afterward.

✪ **Terra.** 1345 Railroad Ave. (between Adams and Hunt sts.). ☎ **707/963-8931.** Reservations recommended. Main courses $14–$23. DC, MC, V. Sun–Thurs 6–9pm, Fri–Sat 6–10pm. CONTEMPORARY AMERICAN.

St. Helena's restaurant of choice, Terra is the creation of Lissa Doumani and her husband, Hiro Sone, a master chef who hails from Japan and once worked with Wolfgang Puck at Spago in L.A. Sone makes full use of the region's bounty; he seems to know how to coax every nuance of flavor from his fine local ingredients. The simple dining room is a perfect foil for Sone's extraordinary food. Among the appetizers, the terrine of foie gras with apple, walnut, and endive salad and the home-smoked salmon with cucumber-dill salad, caviar, and sour cream are the stars of the show. The main dishes successfully fuse different cooking styles: Try the grilled salmon with Thai red-curry sauce or the sake-marinated sea bass with shrimp dumplings in shiso broth. A recommended finale? The apple crostata with vanilla-bean ice cream and cinnamon/apple-cider sauce.

✪ **Tra Vigne Restaurant and Cantinetta.** 1050 Charter Oak Ave. (at Calif. 29). ☎ **707/963-4444** for the restaurant, 707/963-8888 for the Cantinetta. Reservations recommended. Main courses $12.50–$16 in the restaurant, $4–$8 in the Cantinetta. CB, DC, DISC, MC, V. Restaurant, daily 11:30am–9:30pm; Cantinetta, daily 11:30am–6pm. ITALIAN.

If you can only dine at one restaurant while visiting the Wine Country, make it Tra Vigne. Sure, there are a few fancier places in town, but there's no restaurant that measures up to the combined qualities of this restaurant's atmosphere, food, and prices. The enormous dining room, with 30-foot ceilings, a hand-carved bar, and ultramodern Italian light fixtures, packs 'em in every night. And whether diners are seated next to the immense curved windows that open onto a large veranda, on the veranda itself (heated during cold nights), or in the center of the bustling scene, they're usually thrilled just to have gotten a seat. Even though it's tempting, don't fill up on the wonderful bread served with housemade flavored olive oils (sold at the adjoining cantinetta); instead, save plenty of room for the robust California dishes cooked with Italian flair that have made this place everyone's favorite.

The menu features about seven or so pizzas, including a succulent version with caramelized onions, thyme, and gorgonzola. Other dishes of the day might include a grilled and cedar-planked tuna with herb salad and roasted tomato vinaigrette or a grilled Sonoma rabbit with teleme-layered potatoes, oven-dried tomatoes, and mustard-pan sauce, and a dozen or so antipasti. The pastas are equally tempting, including ceppo with sausage, spinach, potatoes, sun-dried tomatoes, and pecorino. And the delicious desserts might include warm apple tart with candied walnut crust, sweet gorgonzola, and caramel sauce.

The restaurant's adjoining café, called the Cantinetta, offers a small selection of sandwiches, pizzas, and lighter meals (I've never had a better focaccia in my life). They also pack picnics, and sell about 20 flavored olive oils infused with everything from roasted garlic to lavender, as well as other creative cooking ingredients.

Trilogy. 1234 Main St. (at Hunt Ave.). ☎ **707/963-5507.** Reservations required. Main courses $14.50–$20. DC, MC, V. Tues–Fri noon–2pm and 5–9pm, Sat 5–9pm. Closed 3 weeks in Dec. CALIFORNIA/FRENCH.

The creation of Diane Pariseau, this small, low-key restaurant is a favorite of Wine Country moguls, with a wine list that's probably second to none in the valley. Pariseau and her assistant do virtually everything themselves, turning out exceptionally fresh food prepared with a fine-honed technique. Though a standard à la carte menu is available, the real treat here is the $48 four-course prix-fixe menu, with each course accompanied by the appropriate glass of top-quality wine ("The best deal around," says Parisean). The menu changes daily, but such delectable cuisine as fresh corn crêpes or a wild-mushroom ragoût are typical of the offerings here. Other selections may include goat-cheese gnocchi with sun-dried tomato and roasted-garlic sauce, or pan-roasted monkfish wrapped in smoked bacon with braised cabbage (accompanied by a peppery 1993 Jade Mountain Syrah, of course).

Moderate

Brava Terrace. 3010 St. Helena Hwy. ☎ **707/963-9300.** Reservations recommended. Main courses $8–$15. AE, DC, DISC, MC, V. Thurs–Tues noon–9pm. CALIFORNIA/MEDITERRANEAN.

Fred Halpert earned acclaim as the head chef at the Portman Hotel in San Francisco, but in 1991 he struck out on his own, setting up shop in the Wine Country, where he became a hit almost at once. The main dining room has an open kitchen and a handsome stone fireplace; there's also a glass-enclosed dining area and a large terrace with umbrella-covered tables. Halpert is always searching for new taste sensations; fortunately, that experimentation is backed up by a thorough training in the flavors and zest of Provence and other culinary locales.

The food is both good and reasonably priced. You can order a simple sandwich of grilled portobello mushrooms with mozzarella, red onions, and rosemary aïoli, or go whole hog for such main courses as coq au vin or a grilled pork chop with barbecue sauce. There's always a fish, a pasta, and a risotto of the day. Be sure to try the spicy fries—a heartburn special—or the garlic "smashed" potatoes. If your stomach can handle this wild and robust mixture of flavors and food, finish your meal with the chocolate-chip crème brûlée. A dozen selections of wine by the glass are available. Beware: Service can be slow on weekends.

CALISTOGA

Sam Brannan, entrepreneur extraordinaire and California's first millionaire, made his first bundle of wealth by supplying miners during the Gold Rush. Flushed with success, he went on to take advantage of the natural geothermal springs at the north end of Napa Valley by building a hotel and spa here in 1859. Flubbing a speech comparing this natural California wonder to the Saratoga Springs resort on the East Coast, he serendipitously coined the term Calistoga, and it stuck.

This small, simple resort town still remains popular—and uncomplicated—today, particularly with city folk who come here to unwind. Calistoga's main street is still only about 6 blocks long, and no building is taller than two stories. It's a great place to relax and indulge in mineral waters, mud baths, Jacuzzis, massages—and, of course, wine.

FIND THE NEW YOU: TAKE A CALISTOGA MUD BATH

The one thing you should do while you're in Calistoga is what people have been doing here for the last 150 years: Take a mud bath. The natural baths are composed of local volcanic ash, imported peat, and naturally boiling mineral water, all mulled together to produce a thick mud that simmers at a temperature of about 104°F.

Once you overcome the hurdle of deciding how best to place your naked body into the mushy stone tub, the rest is pure relaxation—you soak with surprising buoyancy for about 10 to 12 minutes. A warm mineral-water shower, a mineral-water whirlpool bath, and a mineral-water steam room visit follow. Afterward, a relaxing blanket-wrap will cool your delighted body down slowly. All of this takes about 1¹/₂ hours and costs about $45; with a massage, add another half-hour and $20 (we recommend a full hour). The outcome is a rejuvenated, revitalized, squeaky-clean you. (*Note:* Mud baths aren't recommended for those who are pregnant or have high blood pressure.)

The spas also offer a variety of other treatments, such as hand and foot massages, herbal wraps, acupressure face-lifts, skin rubs, and herbal facials. Prices range from $35 to $125, and appointments are necessary for all services; call at least a week in advance.

Indulge yourself at any of these Calistoga spas: **Dr. Wilkinson's Hot Springs,** 1507 Lincoln Ave. (☎ 707/942-4102); the **Lincoln Avenue Spa,** 1339 Lincoln Ave. (☎ 707/942-5296); the **Golden Haven Hot Springs Spa,** 1713 Lake St. (☎ 707/942-6793); and the **Calistoga Spa Hot Springs,** 1006 Washington St. (☎ 707/942-6269).

WHAT TO SEE & DO BEYOND THE MUD BATHS & WINERIES

There's plenty to do in Calistoga even beyond the world-famous mud baths and wineries.

Calistoga Depot, at 1458 Lincoln Ave. (on the site of Calistoga's original 1868 railroad station), now houses a variety of shops, some of which are housed in six restored passenger cars dating from 1916 into the 1920s.

Old Faithful Geyser of California, at 1299 Tubbs Lane (☎ **707/942-6463**), is one of only three Old Faithful geysers in the world. It's been blowing off steam at regular intervals for as long as anyone can remember. The 350°F water spews out to a height of about 60 feet every 40 minutes or so, day and night (varying with natural influences such as barometric pressure, the moon, tides, and tectonic stresses). The performance lasts about 3 minutes. You'll learn a lot about the origins of geothermal steam on your visit. You can bring a picnic lunch with you and catch the show as many times as you wish. An exhibit hall, gift shop, and snack bar are open every day. Admission is $5 for adults, $4 for seniors, $2 for children 6 to 12, and free for children 5 and under. Open daily: in summer from 9am to 6pm, and in winter from 9am to 5pm. To get there, follow the signs from downtown Calistoga; it's between Calif. 29 and Calif. 128.

You won't see thousands of trees turned into stone, but you'll still find many interesting petrified specimens at the **Petrified Forest,** 4100 Petrified Forest Rd. (☎ **707/942-6667**). Volcanic ash blanketed this area after the eruption of Mount St. Helena three million years ago. As a result you'll find redwoods that have turned to rock through the slow infiltration of silicas and other minerals, as well as petrified seashells, clams, and marine life indicating that water covered this area even before the redwood forest. Admission is $3 for adults, $1 for children 4 to 11, and free for children 3 and under. Open daily: in summer from 10am to 5:30pm, and in winter from 10am to 4:30pm. To get there from Calif. 128, turn right onto Petrified Forest Road, just past Lincoln Avenue.

BICYCLING   Cycling enthusiasts can rent bikes from **Getaway Bikes,** 1117 Lincoln Ave. (☎ **800/499-BIKE** or 707/942-0332). Full-day tours ($89), which include lunch and a visit to three or four wineries, are available, as are downhill cruises ($39) for people who hate to pedal. On weekdays they'll even deliver bikes to you.

GLIDER RIDES   Calistoga offers a unique way of seeing its vineyard-filled valleys—from a glider. These quiet "birds" leave from the **Calistoga Gliderport,** 1546 Lincoln Ave. (☎ **707/942-5000**). The 20-minute rides are $79 for one, $110 for two (weight limits apply); 30-minute rides are also available.

WHERE TO STAY

Expensive

Brannan Cottage Inn. 109 Wapoo Ave. (at Lincoln Ave.), Calistoga, CA 94515. ☎ **707/942-4200.** 6 rms. A/C. $160 double. Rates include full breakfast. MC, V.

At the east end of town on a quiet side street stands this cute little 1860 cottage, complete with the requisite white picket fence. It's one of Sam Brannan's original resort cottages, as well as the only structure left remaining at its original location. Now listed on the National Register of Historic Places, the inn was massively restored through a community effort to salvage an important piece of Calistoga's heritage. The six spacious, cozy rooms are decorated with country-style antiques, down comforters, and white lace curtains. More important, each room also has an air-conditioner, ceiling fan, private bath, and its own entrance. There's a comfortable parlor with reproduction wingback chairs, and a pleasant brick terrace furnished with umbrella tables. A full buffet-style breakfast is served in the outdoor garden, weather permitting.

Mount View Hotel. 1457 Lincoln Ave. (in downtown Calistoga), Calistoga, CA 94515. ☎ **707/942-6877.** Fax 707/942-6904. 22 rms, 8 suites, 3 cottages. A/C TV TEL. $110–$140 double; $155–$200 suite; $200 cottage. Packages available. AE, MC, V.

Listed on the National Register of Historic Places, the Mount View Hotel offers 1920s- and 1930s-style "European Eclectic" rooms, three self-contained cottages, and eight suites named for the movie idols of those eras—all of which are non-smoking. The Carole Lombard Suite has peach-colored walls and light-green carpeting, while the Tom Mix Suite has a western theme (of course). The cottages have queen-size beds, wet bars, private decks, and hot tubs; all rooms have a private bath, air-conditioning, and television. A heated swimming pool, European spa, and Jacuzzi are on the premises, as is one of our favorite Napa Valley restaurants, Catahoula's (see "Where to Dine," below). Tennis courts, nature trails, and a nine-hole golf course are also nearby. Be forewarned: There's a 2-night minimum stay during high-season weekends.

Moderate

Dr. Wilkinson's Hot Springs. 1507 Lincoln Ave. (in downtown Calistoga), Calistoga, CA 94515. ☎ **707/942-4102.** 42 rms. A/C MINIBAR TV TEL. Summer, $79–$119 double. Winter, $59–$119 double. Weekly discounts and packages available. AE, MC, V.

This spa/resort was originally established by "Doc" Wilkinson, who arrived in Napa Valley just after World War II. The rooms range from Victorian-style accommodations with sundecks and garden patios to rather basic and functional motel-like rooms, similar to Janet Leigh's room in Psycho. All rooms have drip coffeemakers and refrigerators; some have kitchens. Non-smoking rooms are available. Facilities include three mineral-water pools (two outdoor and one indoor), a Jacuzzi, a steam room, mud baths, and a health club. Facials and all kinds of body treatments are available in the salon.

WHERE TO DINE

All Seasons Café. 1400 Lincoln Ave. (at Washington St.). ☎ **707/942-9111.** Reservations recommended Sat–Sun. Main courses $13–$19. MC, V. Thurs–Tues 11am–3pm and 5:30–10pm (brunch Sat–Sun 9am–noon). (Wine shop, Thurs–Tues 11am–8pm.) CALIFORNIA.

Wine Country devotees often wend their way to the All Seasons Café in downtown Calistoga because of its extensive wine list and knowledgeable staff. The trick here is to buy a bottle of wine from the café's wine shop, then bring it to your table: The cafe adds a corkage fee of $7.50 instead of tripling the price of the bottle (as is done at most restaurants). The menu is diverse, ranging from pizzas and pastas to such main courses as braised lamb shank "osso buco" in an orange, madeira, and tomato sauce. Anything with the house-smoked salmon or spiced sausages is also a safe bet. Chef John Coss saves his guests from any major faux pas by matching wines to his dishes on the menu, so you know what's just right for his grilled duck breast or duck confit pizza.

۞ Catahoula. 1457 Lincoln Ave. ☎ **707/942-2275.** Reservations recommended. Main courses $11–$20. MC, V. Mon and Wed–Thurs noon–2:30pm and 5:30–10pm, Fri noon–2:30pm and 5:30–10:30pm, Sat noon–3:30pm and 5:30–10:30pm, Sun noon–3:30pm and 5:30–10pm. AMERICAN/SOUTHERN.

Named after the official hound of the state of Louisiana, the Catahoula features that beloved dog everywhere—on the metal sculptures over the bar and in the photos in the restaurant and the saloon. The domain of chef Jan Birnbaum, formerly of New York's Quilted Giraffe and San Francisco's Campton Place, this restaurant is the current favorite in town. And with good reason: It's the only place in Calistoga where you can get a decent rooster gumbo, and you'd have to travel all over Louisiana to find another pan-fried jalapeño-pecan catfish like the one that's served here. Catahoula's funky and fun, and the food that comes out of the wood-burning oven—like the roast duck with chili-cilantro potatoes or the whole roasted fish with lemon broth, orzo, and escarole—is exciting. Start with the spicy gumbo ya ya with andouille sausage, and finish with what may be a first for many non-Southerners: buttermilk ice cream.

Smokehouse Café. 1458 Calistoga Ave. (in downtown Calistoga). ☎ **707/942-6060.** Main courses $5–$15. No credit cards. Daily 6am–10pm. REGIONAL AMERICAN.

Jack Hunter, the Smokehouse Café's ebullient meat-master, guarantees that you'll leave his restaurant well fed and completely satisfied. And he's right: Who would've guessed that the best spareribs and house-smoked meats in Northern California would come from this little kitchen in Calistoga? Here's the winning game plan: Start with the delta crayfish cakes (better than any wimpy crab cakes you'll find in San Francisco) and husk-roasted Cheyenne corn, then move on to the slow pig sandwich, a half slab of ribs, or housemade sausages—all of which take up to a week to prepare (not while you wait, luckily). The clincher, though, is the fluffy all-you-can-eat cornbread dipped in pure syrup, which comes with every full-plate dinner. Kids are especially catered to—a rarity in these parts—and patio dining is available during the summer for breakfast, lunch, and dinner.

Wappo Bar & Bistro. 1226B Washington St. (off Lincoln Ave.). ☎ **707/942-4712.** Main courses $8.50–$14.50. AE, DC, MC, V. Wed 11:30am–2:30pm, Thurs–Mon 11:30am–2:30pm and 6–9:30pm. INTERNATIONAL.

One of the best alfresco dining experiences in the Wine Country is under Wappo's honeysuckle and vine-covered arbor, but you'll also be comfortable inside this small bistro at one of the well-spaced, well-polished tables. The menu offers a wide range of choices: roast vegetables with polenta, rabbit pie with wild mushrooms and puff pastry, and chicken with morels served with a side of chive mashed potatoes, for example. The desserts of choice are the black-bottom coconut cream pie and the strawberry rhubarb pie.

2 Sonoma Valley

Sonoma is often thought of as the "other" Wine Country, forever in the shadow of Napa Valley. Truth is, even though there are far fewer wineries here (and far, far fewer tourists), its wines have actually won more awards than Napa's. Sonoma County, which stretches west to the coast, is more rural and less traveled than its neighbor to the east. Small family-owned wineries are its mainstay, just like back in the old days of wine making when everyone started with the expectation of going broke and loved every minute of it. Unlike the corporate-run tours at many Napa Valley wineries, tastings on the west side of the Mayacamas Mountains are usually free and low-key, and come with plenty of friendly banter between the winemakers and their guests.

ESSENTIALS

GETTING THERE   From San Francisco, cross the Golden Gate Bridge and stay on U.S. 101 north. Exit at Calif. 37 (toward Vallejo); after 10 miles, turn north onto Calif. 121. After another 10 miles, turn north onto Calif. 12 (Broadway), which will take you into the town of Napa. From there, take Calif. 121 south to Calif. 12. We know this all sounds confusing, but don't worry—the roads are well marked with signs.

VISITOR INFORMATION   Before you begin your explorations of the area, visit the **Sonoma Valley Visitors Bureau,** 453 1st St. East, Sonoma, CA 95476 (☎ **707/ 996-1090;** fax 707/996-9212). The office, located right on the Plaza in the town of Sonoma, offers free maps and brochures about local happenings. It's open daily: from 9am to 7pm in the summer and 9am to 5pm in the winter. An additional office has recently been added a few miles south of Sonoma at 25200 Arnold Dr. (Calif. 121; ☎ **707/996-1090**); it's open daily from 9am to 5pm.

The **Sonoma County Convention and Visitors Bureau,** 5000 Roberts Lake Rd., Suite A, Rohnert Park, CA 94928 (☎ **800/326-7666** or 707/586-8100; fax 707/ 586-8111), offers a free 48-page visitors guide with information about the whole county. They're also happy to provide lots of specialized information. Write as far in advance as possible. It's open daily from 9am to 5pm.

WHEN TO GO   As with Napa, he best time to visit Sonoma is during the autumn harvest season when the grapes have ripened and all the wineries are in full production—it's quite a show. Again, spring has its own rewards: the entire valley is blanketed in wildflowers. Summer? As we mentioned before—hot weather and heavy traffic.

TOURING THE WINERIES

Like its sister valley, Napa, Sonoma Valley produces some of the finest wines in the nation. What makes a trip to Sonoma so pleasant is the intimate quality of so many of its vineyards—most of the wineries here are still family owned. California's first winery, Buena Vista, was founded in Sonoma Valley in 1857, and it's still in operation today (see below). Today Sonoma is home to about 35 wineries and 13,000 acres of vineyards. Chardonnay is the variety for which Sonoma is most noted, representing almost a quarter of the valley's vine acreage.

The wineries here tend to be a little more spread out than they are in Napa, but they're still easy to find. The visitors bureaus listed above will provide you with maps to the valley's wineries. We've listed our favorite ones below; they, and the towns that follow, are listed roughly from south to north.

Ravenswood Winery. 18701 Gehricke Rd., Sonoma. ☎ **707/938-1960.** Fax 707/938-9459. Daily 10am–4:30pm. Reservations required for tours.

This small, traditional winery in the Sonoma Hills, built right into the hillside to keep it cool inside, crushed its first grapes in 1976 for its inaugural Zinfandel. The winery is best known for its reds, especially its big, bold Zinfandels, but it also produces a merlot, a Cabernet Sauvignon, and some whites. You'll be able to taste these as well as some younger blends, which are less expensive than the older vintages. Tours follow the wine-making process from grape to glass, and include the oak-barrel aging rooms. A "Barbecue in the Vineyards" is held each weekend from Memorial Day to the end of September (call for details).

Sebastiani Vineyards Winery. 389 4th St. East, Sonoma. ☎ **800/888-5532** or 707/ 938-5532. Daily 10am–5pm (last tour begins at 4pm).

Although Sebastiani doesn't occupy the most scenic setting or structures in Sonoma Valley, its place in the history and development of the region is unique, and it does offer an interesting and informative guided tour. The 25-minute tour, through aging stone cellars containing more than 300 carved casks, is well worth the time. You can see the winery's original turn-of-the-century crusher and press, as well as a large collection of oak-barrel carvings. If you don't want to take the tour, go straight to the tasting room, where you can sample an extensive selection of wines. A picnic area is adjacent to the cellars.

Buena Vista. 18000 Old Winery Rd., Sonoma. ☎ **707/938-1266.** Daily 10:30am–4:30pm.

Buena Vista, the patriarch of California wineries, is located slightly northeast of the town of Sonoma. It was founded in 1857 by Count Agoston Haraszthy, the Hungarian émigré who is called the father of the California wine industry. A close friend of Gen. Mariano Vallejo, the Mexican administrator who helped build Sonoma, Haraszthy returned from Europe in 1861 with 100,000 of the finest vine cuttings, which he made available to all wine growers. Although Buena Vista's wine-making now takes place in an ultramodern facility outside Sonoma, the winery still maintains a complimentary tasting room here, inside the restored 1862 Press House. There's also a self-guided tour that you can follow anytime during operating hours and a guided tour at 2pm daily.

Château St. Jean. 8555 Sonoma Hwy. (Calif. 12), Kenwood. ☎ **707/833-4134.** Self-guided tours, daily 10am–4:30pm. Tasting room, daily 10am–4:30pm.

This winery, founded in 1973, is at the foot of Sugarloaf Ridge, just north of Kenwood and east of Calif. 12. A private drive takes you to what was once a 250-acre country retreat, built in 1920. Château St. Jean is notable for its exceptionally beautiful buildings, well-landscaped grounds, and elegant tasting room. A well-manicured lawn is now a picnic area, complete with a fountain and benches.

There's a self-guided tour with detailed descriptions and photographs of the wine-making process. When you're done with it, be sure to walk up to the top of the tower for a view of the valley. Back in the tasting room, Château St. Jean offers several Chardonnays, a Cabernet Sauvignon, a Fumé Blanc, a Merlot, a Riesling, and a Gerwürtztraminer. Since 1984 the winery has been part of the Suntory family of premium wineries.

The toll-free, interactive Château St. Jean "wine line" (☎ 800/332-WINE) offers free recorded reports on the Sonoma Wine Country, including updated information on vineyard conditions and what's happening at the winery, interviews with winemakers and growers, and descriptions of currently available wines.

SETTLING INTO THE VALLEY: THE TOWN OF SONOMA

Sonoma owes much of its appeal to Mexican Gen. Mariano Guadalupe Vallejo, who fashioned this pleasant, slow-paced town after a typical Mexican village—right down to the central plaza, Sonoma's geographical and commercial center. The Plaza sits at the top of a T formed by Broadway (Calif. 12) and Napa Street. Most of the surrounding streets form a grid pattern around this axis, making Sonoma easy to negotiate. The Plaza's Bear Flag Monument marks the spot where the crude Bear Flag was raised in 1846, signaling the end of Mexican rule; the symbol was later adopted by the state of California. The 8-acre park at the center of the Plaza, with two ponds frequented by ducks and geese, is perfect for an afternoon siesta in the cool shade.

WHAT TO SEE & DO BEYOND THE WINERIES

The best way to see the town of Sonoma is to follow the **Sonoma Walking Tour,** available from the Sonoma Valley Visitors Bureau (see "Visitor Information" in "Essentials," above). Highlights include General Vallejo's 1852 Victorian-style home; the Sonoma Barracks, erected in 1836 to house Mexican army troops; and the Blue Wing Inn, an 1840 hostelry built to accommodate tourists and new settlers while they erected homes in Sonoma—John Frémont, Kit Carson, and Ulysses S. Grant were all guests.

The **Mission San Francisco Solano de Sonoma,** on Sonoma Plaza at the corner of 1st Street East and Spain Street (☎ 707/938-1519), was founded in 1823. It was the northernmost—as well as the last—mission built in California. It was also the only one established on the northern coast by the Mexican rulers, who wished to protect their territory against expansionist Russian fur traders. It's now part of Sonoma State Historic Park. Admission is $2 for adults, $1 for children 6 to 12, and free for children 5 and under. It's open daily from 10am to 5pm; closed New Year's Day, Thanksgiving, and Christmas Day.

The **Arts Guild of Sonoma,** 140 E. Napa St. (☎ 707/996-3115), showcases the work of local artists. Exhibits change frequently and include a wide variety of styles and media. Admission is free. Open Wednesday to Monday from 11am to 5pm.

SHOPPING   Most of the town's shops, which offer everything from food and wines to clothing and books, are located around the Plaza, including **The Mercato,** a small shopping center at 452 1st St. East that houses several good stores selling unusual wares.

BICYCLING   You can rent a bike or in-line skates at the **Goodtime Bicycle Company,** 18503 Calif. 12 (☎ 707/938-0453). They'll happily point you to easy bike trails. They also provide a picnic on request. Bikes cost $5 per hour or $25 a day. Bikes are also available from **Sonoma Valley Cyclery,** 20093 Broadway (☎ 707/935-3377), for $6 per hour or $20 a day. For additional biking information in Sonoma County, call the friendly folks at **Dave's Bikes Sport**, 353 College Ave., in Santa Rosa (☎ 707/528-3283).

WHERE TO STAY

Very Expensive

Sonoma Mission Inn & Spa. 18140 Calif. 12, Boyes Hot Springs, CA 94576. ☎ **800/862-4945** or 707/938-9000. Fax 707/938-4250. 170 rms, 3 suites. A/C MINIBAR TV TEL. Apr–Oct, $140–$295 Historic Inn room; $180–$365 Wine Country room; from $325 suite. Nov–Mar, $115–$260 Historic Inn room; $155–$350 Wine Country room; from $325 suite. AE, DC, MC, V. From central Sonoma, drive 3 miles north on Calif. 12.

More than 30 years ago the lifeblood of this historic resort—a natural mineral hot spring—ran dry, and it wasn't until 1991 that a new source of liquid inspiration was discovered 1,100 feet directly beneath the inn: 127°F natural artesian mineral water, piped directly into the world-class spa's two pools and whirlpools.

The Sonoma Mission Inn & Spa is a sprawling 1920s-era resort housed in a three-story pink Mediterranean-style structure—complete with mission towers—and set on 8 landscaped acres of well-groomed lawns, bougainvillea, pines, and eucalyptus. The mission theme reappears in the lobby, with its beamed ceiling and large fireplace—it's the sort of place where Clara Bow or Mary Pickford would have felt at home, though you're more likely to see Barabra Streisand or Harrison Ford strolling around in their aquatic skivvies.

The rooms—all well equipped and comfortable, but short on style—are furnished in a modern theme with framed watercolors, ceiling fans, and extra amenities like bathroom scales, hair dryers, and oversize bath towels. The larger Wine Country rooms are in a newer building and furnished with king-size beds, down comforters, desks, and refrigerators; some offer fireplaces, and many have balconies. The older Historic Inn Rooms are slightly smaller; most are furnished with queen-size beds. All rooms have VCRs and come with a complimentary bottle of wine.

Dining: The Grille, run by chef Toni Sakaguchi, is known for its low-calorie, low-sodium, and low-cholesterol California "spa" cuisine—rack of Sonoma lamb or grilled Petaluma chicken breast, for example—and its 200 varieties of Napa and Sonoma wines. The casual Cafe, serving an eclectic array of modestly priced dishes for lunch and dinner, is renowned for its bountiful all-American breakfasts.

Services: Concierge, room service, valet, laundry.

Facilities: Full spa facilities with full range of treatments and nutritional consultation; health club; tennis courts. The tariff for individual spa and salon services ranges from $35 to $199. The use of the spa's bathhouse, which includes a sauna, steam room, whirlpool, outdoor exercise pool, and gym with weight equipment, costs $10 weekdays, $20 weekends, but is complimentary with any spa service. Guests have use of the nearby 18-hole Sonoma Golf Club.

Moderate

El Dorado Hotel. 405 1st St. West (at W. Spain St.), Sonoma, CA 95476. ☎ **800/289-3031** or 707/996-3030. Fax 707/996-3148. 27 rms. A/C TV TEL. Summer, $105–$145 double. Winter, $85–$110 double. Rates include continental breakfast and a split of wine. AE, MC, V.

The El Dorado Hotel may look like a 19th-century Wild West relic from the outside, but you won't be sleeping on a rickety antique bed and bathing in a cramped clawfoot tub here—inside it's all 20th-century deluxe. Each modern, handsomely appointed guest room—designed by the same folks who put together the Auberge du Soleil in Rutherford (see "Napa Valley," earlier in this chapter)—has French windows and small terraces; some offer lovely views of the Plaza, while others overlook the hotel's private courtyard and heated pool. Each guest room has a canopy bed and a private bath with plush towels and hair dryers. All rooms (except those for the disabled) are on the second floor. The two rooms on the ground floor are off the private courtyard; each has its own partially enclosed patio. Services include a concierge, laundry, in-room massage, bicycle rental, and access to a nearby health club.

Breakfast, served either inside or out, includes coffee, fruits, and freshly baked breads and pastries. Within the hotel is Piatti, a popular restaurant serving regional Italian cuisine (see "Where to Dine," below).

✪ Sonoma Chalet. 18935 5th St. West (at the northwest end of town), Sonoma, CA 95476. **☎ 707/938-3129.** 3 rms, 3 cottages, 1 suite. Apr–Oct, $95–$140 double. Nov–Mar, $80–$130 double. Rates include continental breakfast. AE, MC, V.

This is one of the few accommodations in Sonoma that's truly secluded; it's on the outskirts of town, in a peaceful country setting overlooking a 200-acre ranch. The accommodations are in a Swiss-style farmhouse and several cottages, but they're by no means rustic—all were delightfully decorated by someone with an eye for color and a concern for comfort. They have clawfoot tubs, beds covered with country quilts, Oriental carpets, comfortable furnishings, and private decks; some have woodstoves. A breakfast of fruit, yogurt, pastries, and cereal is served either in the country kitchen or in your room (and the gaggles of ducks, chickens, and ornery geese that wander the grounds will be glad to help you finish off the crumbs).

Sonoma Hotel. 110 W. Spain St. (at 1st St. West), Sonoma, CA 94576. **☎ 800/468-6016** or 707/996-2996. Fax 707/996-7014. 17 rms, 5 with bath. Summer, $75–$85 double without bath, $115–$125 double with bath. Winter, Sun–Thurs, $65 double without bath, $95 double with bath; Fri–Sat, $75 double without bath, $115–$125 double with bath. Rates include continental breakfast. AE, MC, V. Free parking.

This cute little historic hotel on Sonoma's tree-lined Plaza still retains the same ambience that it did over a century ago when it first opened. With an emphasis on European-style elegance and comfort, each room is decorated in an early California style, with antique furnishings, fine woods, and floral-print curtains. Some of the rooms feature brass beds, and all are blissfully devoid of phones and TVs. Five of the third-floor rooms share immaculate baths (and significantly reduced rates), while rooms with private baths have deep clawfoot tubs with overhead showers. Perks include nightly turndown, continental breakfast, and a bottle of wine on arrival. The hotel also has a small restaurant and bar.

Inexpensive

Ⓢ El Pueblo Inn. 896 W. Napa St., Sonoma, CA 94576. **☎ 800/900-8844** or 707/996-3651. 38 rms. A/C TEL. May–Oct, $70–$80 double. Mar–Apr and Nov, $60–$70 double. Dec–Feb, $59 double (higher rates during holidays). AE, DISC, JCB, MC, V.

It ain't the Ritz, but this inn offers some of the best-priced accommodations around. It's located on Sonoma's main east-west street 8 blocks from the center of town. The rooms here are pleasant enough, with post-and-beam construction, exposed brick walls, light-wood furniture, and geometric prints. A drip coffee machine with packets of coffee in each room should be a comfort to early risers. An outdoor pool (heated on cold days) is a refreshing respite from the *Blazing Saddles*–type weather. If possible, reservations should be made at least a month in advance for the spring and summer months.

WHERE TO DINE

Moderate

Depot Hotel Restaurant and Garden. 241 1st St. West (3 blocks north of W. Spain St.). **☎ 707/938-2980.** Reservations recommended. Main courses $7–$16 at dinner. AE, DC, DISC, MC, V. Wed–Thurs 11:30am–2pm and 5–9pm, Fri 11:30am–2pm and 5–9:30pm, Sat 5–9:30pm, Sun 5–9pm. NORTHERN ITALIAN.

Where to Stock Up for a Gourmet Picnic, Sonoma Style

Sonoma has plenty of restaurants, but on a sunny day the Wine Country is really made for a picnic. Sonoma's Plaza Park is a perfect place to set up a gourmet spread; there are even picnic tables available. Below are Sonoma's top spots for stocking up for such an alfresco fete:

If you want to pick up some specialty fare on your way into town, stop at **Angelo's Wine Country Deli**, 23400 Arnold Dr. (☎ **707/938-3688**). Angelo's sells all types of smoked meats, special salsas, and homemade mustards. The deli is known for its half-dozen types of homemade beef jerky. It's open daily from 9am to 6pm.

The **Sonoma Cheese Factory**, on the Plaza at 2 Spain St. (☎ **707/996-1000**), offers an extraordinary variety of imported meats and cheeses; a few are set out for tasting every day. The factory also sells caviar, gourmet salads, pâté, and homemade Sonoma Jack cheese. Sandwiches are available, too. While you're there, you can watch a narrated slide show about cheesemaking. The factory is open weekdays from 8:30am to 5:30pm and weekends from 8:30am to 6pm.

At 315 2nd St. East, 1 block north of East Spain Street, is the **Vella Cheese Company** (☎ **800/848-0505** or 707/938-3232), established in 1931. The folks at Vella pride themselves on making cheese into an award-winning science, their most recent victory being "U.S. Cheese Championship 1995–96" for their Monterey Dry Jack. Other cheeses range from flavorful High Moisture Jack to a mild Daisy and a razor-sharp Raw Milk Cheddar. Among other cheeses for which Vella has become famous is Oregon Blue, made at Vella's southern Oregon factory—rich, buttery, and even spreadable, it's one of the few premier bleus produced in this country. Any of these fine handmade, all-natural cheeses can be shipped directly from the store. The Vella Cheese Company is open Monday to Saturday from 9am to 6pm and on Sunday from 10am to 5pm.

Of course, you're going to need something to wash down all this gourmet fare. Head to the **Wine Exchange,** at the Mercado, 452 1st St. East (☎ **707/938-1794**), which carries more than 600 domestic wines and has a full wine-tasting bar. The beer connoisseur who's feeling displaced in the Wine Country will be happy to find more than 280 beers from around the world here too, including a number of exceptional domestic beers. The Wine Exchange is open daily from 10am to 6pm, with wine and beer tastings daily.

Michael Ghilarducci has been the chef and owner here for the past 11 years, so you know he's either independently wealthy or an excellent cook. Fortunately, it's the latter. Located 1 block north of the Plaza in a handsome and historic 1870 stone building, the Depot Hotel offers pleasant outdoor dining in an Italian garden complete with a central reflection pool and cascading Roman fountain. The menu is unwaveringly Italian, filled with a plethora of classic dishes such as spaghetti bolognese and veal alla parmigiana. Start with the bounteous antipasto misto and end the feast with a dish of the chef's handmade Italian ice cream and fresh-fruit sorbets.

✪ **East Side Oyster Bar & Grill.** 133 E. Napa St. ☎ **707/939-1266.** Reservations recommended. Main courses $9–$15. AE, DC, MC, V. Mon–Sat 11:30am–2:30pm and 5:30–9:30pm, Sun noon–9:30pm. Closed Tues–Wed in winter. INTERNATIONAL.

This is one of Sonoma's most popular restaurants, opened by Charles Saunders, who gained fame and a following at the Sonoma Mission Inn & Spa in 1992. If possible, dine on the vine-entwined brick patio, which on cool nights is warmed by a fire. Saunders is blessed with an unerring sense of proportion and flavor; he knows how to keep both the visiting and local food lovers coming back for more. The emphasis is on seafood, although there will certainly be a local bird of the day— perhaps pheasant or chicken—as well as sandwiches. Our favorite dish is the drunken clam pasta: fresh linguine and Manila clams simmering in a broth of garlic, smoked chili peppers, Spanish chorizo, oregano, and a splash of golden tequila (it makes us hungry just thinking about it). Top it all off with the New Orleans–style praline meringue layered with chocolate ganache in a pool of bourbon-spiked crème anglaise—wow!

Piatti. In the El Dorado Hotel, 405 1st St. West (at W. Spain St.). ☎ **707/996-2351.** Reservations recommended. Main courses $7–$12. AE, MC, V. Mon–Thurs 11:30am–2:30pm and 5–10pm, Fri–Sat 11:30am–11pm, Sun 11:30am–10pm. ITALIAN.

This local favorite is known for serving reasonably priced food in a rustic Italian-style setting with delightful patio seating. The bright, sun-filled restaurant occupies the ground floor of the rejuvenated El Dorado Hotel, a 19th-century landmark. Tasty pizzas emerge from a wood-burning oven. There are also satisfying pastas, such as lasagne al pesto and spaghetti con agnello (with fresh mushrooms and lamb ragoût). Other dishes include a wonderful roast vegetable appetizer, rotisserie chicken with creamy mashed potatoes, and a good scaloppine pizzaiola. Granted, there are far fancier restaurants in the area, but not many that can fill you up at these prices.

Swiss Hotel. 18 W. Spain St. (at 1st St. West). ☎ **707/938-2884.** Reservations recommended. Main courses $8–$16. MC, V. Daily 11:30am–2:30pm and 5–9pm. (Bar, daily 11am–2am.) CONTINENTAL/NORTHERN ITALIAN.

The historic Swiss Hotel, located right in the town center, is a Sonoma landmark, complete with slanting floors and aged beamed ceilings. The long turn-of-the-century oak bar at the left of the entrance is adorned with black-and-white photos of pioneering Sonomans. The bright white dining room and rear dining patio are pleasant spots to enjoy pastas, sandwiches, and California-style pizzas (baked in a wood-burning oven) for lunch. Dinner might start with a warm winter salad of pears, walnuts, radicchio, and bleu cheese. Main courses run the gamut; we like the prawn linguine with a spicy tomato sauce, the filet mignon wrapped in a cheese crust, and the duck in an orange-honey sauce.

Inexpensive

Feed Store Café & Bakery. 529 1st St. West (at Napa St.). ☎ **707/938-2122.** Reservations accepted; recommended on Sun. Main courses $5–$9. MC, V. Daily 7am–4pm. CALIFORNIA.

This attractive, airy restaurant has a small fountain-cooled courtyard, a helpful staff, and first-rate, reasonably priced food served in bountiful portions. For breakfast, there are more varieties of eggs than you can imagine. For lunch, quesadillas, burgers, and the crowd-pleasing Jalisco club sandwich (a grilled chicken-breast Mexican burrito) are all good choices.

Under the same roof is the Bakery at the Feed Store, offering a great selection of baked goods, from small coffee cakes and muffins to New York cheesecake. The homemade breads are ideal for picnics.

La Casa. 121 E. Spain St. (at 1st St. East). ☎ **707/996-3406.** Reservations recommended on weekends and summer evenings. Main courses $6–$11. AE, CB, DC, DISC, MC, V. Daily 11:30am–10pm. MEXICAN.

This no-nonsense Mexican restaurant, on the Sonoma Plaza across from the mission, serves great enchiladas, fajitas, and chimichangas. To start, try the black-bean soup or the ceviche made of fresh snapper, marinated in lime juice with cilantro and salsa, and served on crispy tortillas. Follow that with tamales prepared with corn husks spread with corn masa, stuffed with chicken filling, and topped with a mild red chili sauce. Or, you might opt for the delicious suiza (deep-dish chicken enchiladas), or the fresh snapper Veracruz, if it's on the menu. Wine and beer are available.

GLEN ELLEN

This small Wine Country town about 7 miles north of Sonoma hasn't changed much since the days when Jack London settled on his Beauty Ranch, about a mile west. Today **Jack London State Park,** on London Ranch Road (☎ **707/938-5216**), is home to the House of Happy Walls, a museum built by Jack's wife, Charmian, to house and display a considerable collection of artifacts from the author's life. Jack London settled here in 1913 and began building his 26-room Wolf Mansion, which was destroyed by fire shortly before completion. The cottage that the Londons occupied is still there, though, along with the ruins of the mansion and the Londons' graves. Admission is $5 per car, $4 per car for seniors 62 and over. The park is open daily: in summer from 10am to 7pm and in winter from 10am to 5pm. The museum is open daily from 10am to 5pm.

HORSEBACK RIDING   This is ideal riding country. The **Sonoma Cattle Company & Napa Valley Trail Rides,** in Jack London State Park (☎ **707/996-8566**), offers guided tours on horseback. You'll ride on the same trails that London once followed, right past the writer's eucalyptus grove and wood-frame cottage on your way to the top of Mount Sonoma, where you'll have great views of the surrounding countryside. Rides are $40 for 2 hours and are available by appointment daily, weather permitting. For reservations, write P.O. Box 877, Glen Ellen, CA 95442.

WHERE TO STAY

✪ **Beltane Ranch.** 11775 Sonoma Hwy., Glen Ellen, CA 95442. ☎ **707/996-6501.** 4 rms. $120–$160 double. No credit cards (checks accepted).

On the slopes of the Mayacamas Mountains, surrounded by 1,600 acres of scenic rolling pastures, is one of our favorite Wine Country retreats—the Beltane Ranch, an honest-to-Betsy 1892 double-porched farmhouse. It's part of local legend, having once been owned by "Mammy" Pleasant, a former slave and abolitionist who, among other professions, was a madam and the mistress of English millionaire Thomas Bell. Mammy was suspected of his murder but was never convicted.

Beginning in the 1930s the Heins family used the ranch to raise turkeys, but when Rosemary Wood inherited it in 1981, she turned it into a B&B. The gardens are filled with irises and roses; a terrace surrounding the house looks out over the flowers and the fields beyond. Guests can use the comfortable parlor with the brick fireplace and woodstove. The rooms are comfortably furnished in a homey style and with the occasional family antique. Facilities include hiking trails and a tennis court.

Glenelly Inn. 5131 Warm Springs Rd., Glen Ellen, CA 95442. ☎ **707/996-6720.** 8 rms. $105–$140 double. Rates include breakfast and afternoon refreshments. MC, V. From Calif. 12, take Arnold Drive to Warm Springs Road.

Back in 1916 this was a wayside inn for train passengers. Today the inn evokes that gentler time with its wicker-furnished, country-style, antique-filled rooms. The "Valley of the Moon" room on the upper level has a woodstove, brass bed, and pine armoire. Others have pine four-posters or sleigh beds; most have clawfoot tubs. Down comforters, bathrobes, ceiling fans, and good reading lamps add to the comfort of the immaculate peach-and-white rooms. Best of all, the guest rooms are all only steps away from the trellised gardens and hot tub.

KENWOOD

At the north end of the valley is the tiny town of Kenwood, home to 10 or so wineries and several inns and restaurants.

WHERE TO STAY

✪ **Kenwood Inn & Spa.** 10400 Sonoma Hwy., Kenwood, CA 95452. ☎ **800/353-6966** or 707/833-1293. 12 rms. Apr–Oct, $195–$315 double (2-night minimum on weekends). Nov–Mar, $165–$275 double. Rates include breakfast and a bottle of wine. AE, MC, V.

Inspired by the villas of Tuscany, the Kenwood Inn & Spa's honey-colored Tuscan-style buildings, flower-filled flagstone courtyard, and provincial views of vineyard-covered hills are enough to make any northern Italian homesick. The sumptuous rooms—all equipped with fireplaces, balconies, feather beds, and down comforters—have been exquisitely decorated with imported tapestries and furnishings. Room 10, for example, is serenely fashioned in white and pale beige; torchères light the fireplace and Romanesque-style nooks shelter plants or books. A celebrated three-course breakfast is served poolside or in the Mediterranean-style kitchen. Available spa treatments include massage, aromatherapy, and sea-mineral body wraps, as well as fitness regimens and yoga. A minor caveat is the road noise, which even the Mediterranean music pumped into the courtyard fails to filter out.

WHERE TO DINE

✪ **Kenwood Restaurant & Bar.** 9900 Sonoma Hwy. ☎ **707/833-6326.** Reservations recommended. Main courses $12.50–$23.50. MC, V. Tues–Sun 11:30am–9pm. CALIFORNIA/CONTINENTAL.

This is what California Wine Country dining should be (but what it often, disappointingly, is not). From the terrace of the Kenwood you can enjoy a view of the vineyards as you dine at umbrella-covered tables. On nippy days you can retreat inside to the Sonoma-style roadhouse, with its shiny wood floors and pine ceiling. The decor—cushioned rattan chairs set at white cloth-covered tables—is discreetly simple, with a long oak bar on one side and a painted vine on the wall behind it.

The chef, Max Schacher, serves first-rate cuisine, complemented by a reasonably priced wine list. The menu is perfectly balanced between tradition and innovation, and the finely crafted cooking is marked by the heightened, distinctive flavors of California's Wine Country. Great starters are the Dungeness crab cake with herb mayonnaise; the super-fresh sashimi with ginger, soy, and wasabe; and the wonderful Caesar salad. Main-dish choices might include poached salmon in a creamy sorrel sauce or braised Sonoma rabbit with grilled polenta. But the Kenwood doesn't take itself too seriously: Sandwiches and burgers are also available.

SANTA ROSA

Santa Rosa is Sonoma's county seat. With a population of 120,000, it clearly suffers from suburban sprawl. Nevertheless, there are a few good reasons to stop here while you're in the Wine Country.

WHAT TO SEE & DO BEYOND THE WINERIES

The **Luther Burbank Home and Gardens,** at Santa Rosa and Sonoma avenues (☎ 707/524-5445), is reason enough to visit Santa Rosa on its own. Burbank was a famous horticulturist who lived here for 50 years and introduced more than 800 new varieties of plants to the world. You can tour the gardens for free. House tours are given from April to October for a $2 admission fee.

Across the street in Juilliard Park is a **museum dedicated to Robert Ripley,** 492 Sonoma Ave. (☎ **707/524 5233**), housed in a building made from a single California redwood. Ripley lived in Santa Rosa, where he compiled his "Believe It or Not" column of bizarre facts and discoveries he made on his many trips around the world.

The town has a lively cultural scene. It supports a symphony, a ballet company, and several theater companies as well as the **Luther Burbank Center for the Arts,** at 50 Mark West Springs Rd. (☎ **707/546-3600**).

SHOPPING   The best shopping can be found at **Railroad Square,** the landmark railroad depot that has been converted into a specialty shopping area between 3rd and 5th streets, just west of U.S. 101. The casually upscale complex includes a variety of specialty shops (most offering great bargains in spring and autumn), antiques outlets, a restaurant, and a chocolate factory. Most shops are open daily from 10am to 7:30pm.

GOLF   Local golfers rank the golf course at **Fountaingrove,** 1525 Fountaingrove Pkwy., in Santa Rosa (☎ **707/579-4653**), as one of the best—if not *the* best—in Sonoma County. This 18-hole, par-72 course sprawls over hilly terrain in the midst of the Sonoma Wine Country, with just a smattering of oak trees to interrupt the landscape. Technically this is a private course, but it opens its doors to nonmembers willing to pay the requisite fees. Greens fees, including the mandatory cart, are $50 Monday to Thursday, $65 on Friday, and $80 on Saturday and Sunday. Discount twilight rates are available after 1pm daily. Tee times can be reserved up to a week in advance.

WHERE TO STAY

Fountaingrove Inn. 101 Fountaingrove Pkwy., Santa Rosa, CA 95403. ☎ **800/222-6101** or 707/578-6101. 85 rms. A/C TV TEL. $125 double. Rates include buffet breakfast. AE, DC, MC, V. From U.S. 101 north, exit at Mendocino Ave. and turn right.

This contemporary complex of redwood, oak, and stone sits on the site of the old Fountaingrove Ranch. "Quaint" isn't a word that springs to mind here, but if all you're looking for is a comfortable, fully appointed place to relax after a long day of wine-tasting, the Fountaingrove Inn will do the trick. The functional rooms are done in oak and accented with brass and mirrors; amenities include dressing alcoves, double closets, and workspaces with modem jacks. Services range from room service and baby-sitting to laundry, valet, courtesy limo, in-room massage, bicycle rental, and complimentary newspaper delivery. The outdoor pool and Jacuzzi have a view of the ranch's historic round barn. The restaurant, Equus (designed around a horse theme), serves fine California cuisine and has a great wine list.

The Gables Bed & Breakfast. 4257 Petaluma Hill Rd., Santa Rosa, CA 95404. ☎ **707/ 585-7777.** 7 rms, 1 cottage. $110–$150 double; $190 cottage. Rates include full breakfast. AE, DISC, MC, V. From U.S. 101, exit at Rohnert Park Expressway, turn right, go 2¹/₂ miles to Petaluma Hill Rd., and turn left; from Calif. 12, turn right on Sonoma Ave., left on Santa Rosa Ave., and left again on Petaluma Hill Rd.

This landmark inn, a High Victorian Gothic Revival house with 15 gables crowning keyhole-shaped windows, is on a well-traveled road, but the surrounding 3¹/₂ acres of fields provides all the privacy you'll need. The spacious rooms—even the "smaller" ones are large—are furnished in Victorian style with brass or pencil four-poster beds, down comforters, and clawfoot tubs; some have marble fireplaces. The small, creekside William and Mary's Cottage in the backyard is a real charmer, complete with a woodstove, double whirlpool tub, loft bed, and a kitchenette. Breakfast is served on the back deck in nice weather.

Vintners Inn. 4350 Barnes Rd., Santa Rosa, CA 95403. ☎ **800/421-2584,** or 707/575-7350. Fax 707/575-1426. 44 rms. A/C TV TEL. $125–$155 double Sun–Thurs, $148–$195 double Fri–Sat. Rates include buffet breakfast. AE, DC, MC, V. From U.S. 101 north, exit at River Rd. and turn left on Barnes Rd.

This attractively designed modern hostelry, constructed in Mediterranean style around a brick courtyard and fountain, is set among 45 acres of vineyards. The exceptionally large, beam-ceilinged rooms are furnished with European pine and French provincial pieces; many have wood-burning fireplaces and all have patios or balconies with views of the vineyards or plaza. Cereals, breads, waffles, and fruit juice are served each morning in the cathedral-like dining room. Guests have access to a whirlpool and a trellis-covered sundeck, and some rooms are handicapped-accessible. But the best reason to stay here is that one of Sonoma's finest restaurants, John Ash & Co. (see "Where to Dine," below), is right next door.

WHERE TO DINE

✪ **John Ash & Co..** 4330 Barnes Rd. ☎ **707/527-7687.** Reservations recommended. Main courses $14.95–$22.95. AE, MC, V. Mon 5–9pm, Tues–Thurs 11:30am–2pm and 5–9pm, Fri–Sat 11:30am–2pm and 5–10pm, Sun 10:30am–2pm and 5–9pm. Cafe menu served Tues–Sun 11:30am–close. Hours change seasonally. From U.S. 101, exit west at River Rd. CALIFORNIA.

The bounty of California is celebrated at this southwestern-inspired restaurant that was launched by John Ash, culinary director of Fetzer Vineyards' Valley Oaks Food & Wine Center in Hopland. Ash, an innovative chef, is considered the "Daniel Boone" of Wine Country cooking. The dining rooms are light and airy with high vaulted ceilings, terra-cotta–tile floors, and large, local landscapes on the walls. There's also alfresco dining on the heated terrace with pleasant views of the surrounding vineyards.

Ash isn't around all the time anymore, but a talented chef, Jeffrey Madura, has followed in his footsteps. Whenever possible, he uses Sonoma-grown foods: luscious lamb and other meats, vegetables, and fruits. The dishes are attractively presented and richly flavored, as you'll discover when you cut into one of the pork chops, which are smoked and grilled with a caramelized apple-bacon compôte and port reduction sauce, or the grilled salmon with wild mushroom and oven-roasted tomato relish. A cafe menu, served all day, features such items as Dungeness crab cakes with serrano chili mayonnaise. To finish, we recommend the spectacular white-chocolate bread pudding with a pecan-bourbon sauce.

Lisa Hemenway's. 714 Village Court Mall (at Sonoma Ave. and Farmer's Lane). ☎ **707/ 526-5111.** Reservations recommended. Main courses $14–$20. AE, DC, MC, V. Mon–Sat 11:30am–2:30pm and 5:30–9:30pm, Sun 11:30am–2:30pm (brunch) and 5:30–9pm. Go east on Calif. 12, north on Farmer's Lane, then right on Sonoma Ave. CALIFORNIA/INTERNATIONAL.

In spite of her restaurant's unpromising location in a homely suburban mall, chef/owner Lisa Hemenway, an alumna of John Ash & Co. (see above), plays to a full house almost every night—so you know she must be doing something right. Her eclectic range of international cuisine means that just about anything may end up on the menu, from chicken-and-lemongrass hash in grilled cabbage leaves to duck breast roasted with chestnut-apple-marsala sauce. End the experience with Lisa's signature Hungarian torte. You can dine indoors on upholstered cane chairs or, preferably, outside on the sun-soaked patio. A spinoff, Lisa Hemenway's Tote Cuisine—a deli and tea room offering the makings for a celestial picnic—is just across the way.

3 Healdsburg & the Russian River Valley

Going north from Santa Rosa, instead of driving up U.S. 101, you may want to opt for a route that will take you through some beautiful countryside, much quieter than Napa and Sonoma valleys, planted with vineyards and fruit trees. At its heart is Healdsburg, an appealing small town situated on the Russian River and named after Harmon Heald, a native of Ohio who helped found the town in 1867. Its growth has since been fueled by the wine industry. Healdsburg is centered around a small plaza surrounded by restaurants, hotels, and stores.

ESSENTIALS

GETTING THERE   From U.S. 101, go west on River Road and turn right onto Wohler Road, which will carry you across the Russian River and onto Westside Road, where the Davis Bynum, Rochioli, and Hop Kiln vineyards are located. Westside Road eventually leads into West Dry Creek Road, which ends at the Ferrari Carano Vineyard. From Westside Road, you can turn right and take Lambert Bridge Road past the Dry Creek Vineyard and turn right on Dry Creek Road into Healdsburg.

To get directly to Healdsburg, however, simply take the Central Healdsburg exit off U.S. 101.

VISITOR INFORMATION   For information on the wineries in the area, contact or stop by the **Healdsburg Area Chamber of Commerce,** 217 Healdsburg Ave., Healdsburg, CA 95448 (☎ **707/433-6935**). The office is open Monday to Friday from 9:30am to 12:30pm and 1:30 to 4:30pm, and on Saturday and Sunday from 10am to 2pm, but winery maps are available around the clock on a rack outside the door.

Both the Russian River and Lake Sonoma offer great recreational opportunities; call the **Lake Sonoma Visitor Center** (☎ **707/433-9483**) for information on what's available. The **Parks and Recreation Department** (☎ **707/431-3301**) can direct you to public pools and tennis courts.

TOURING THE WINERIES

Kendall Jackson (☎ 707/433-7102) and **Windsor Vineyards** (☎ 707/433-2822) both have tasting rooms in town. Healdsburg is surrounded by about 60 more wineries, all within about a 30-minute drive. Our favorites closest to town are the award-winning **Alderbrook** (☎ 707/433-5987) on Westside Road, and **Foppiano** (☎ 707/433-7272), **Rodney Strong** (☎ 707/431-1533), and **Piper Sonoma** (☎ 707/433-8843) along the Old Redwood Highway. Farther out you'll find **Dry Creek** (☎ 707/433-7272), known for its Cabernet and Sauvignon Blanc; **Alexander Valley** (☎ 707/433-7209), known for its Chardonnay and Gewürztraminer grown at the south end of the valley and its Zinfandel grown at the north; **Chalk Hill** (☎ 707/838-4306), primarily known for its Chardonnay; and the eponymous **Russian River** (☎ 707/433-0490), famous for its Chardonnay, Pinot Noir, and sparkling wines.

WHAT TO SEE & DO BEYOND THE WINERIES

The **Healdsburg Museum,** 221 Matheson St. (☎ **707/431-3325**), has interesting local history exhibits and an outstanding photographic archive. Open Tuesday to Sunday from 11am to 4pm; admission is free.

BICYCLING   Bikes—including tandem cycles—can be rented from **Spoke Folk Cyclery,** at 249 Center St. in the downtown plaza (☎ **707/433-7171**), for $25 a day (they're closed on Tuesday). They also offer day-long Wine Country bike tours for $50, including Dry Creek Valley, Alexander Valley, and Russian River Valley.

CANOEING Canoes and kayaks can be put in on the Russian River at Memorial Beach at the south end of Healdsburg (this spot is great for swimming, too). For rentals or canoe trips, contact **W. C. "Bob" Trowbridge,** a small rental shop and general store located at 20 Healdsburg Ave. (☎ **800/640-1386,** or 707/433-7247). Prices for rentals range from $18 to $42 per day; multiday rentals are also available.

WHERE TO STAY

In addition to the Madrona Manor, below, there's also the dependable and inexpensive **Best Western Dry Creek Inn**, 198 Dry Creek Rd. (☎ **800/222-5784** or 707/433-0300).

Madrona Manor. 1001 Westside Rd., Healdsburg, CA 95448. ☎ **800/258-4003,** or 707/433-4231. Fax 707/433-0703. 18 rms, 3 suites. A/C TEL. $140–$205 double; from $240 suite. Rates include breakfast. AE, DC, MC, V. From U.S. 101, exit at Healdsburg Ave. and turn left onto Mill St., which runs into Westside Rd.

Ever since John and Carol Muir restored this Gothic-Victorian mansion and turned it into a family-friendly inn in 1982, the Madrona has been one of Northern California's most acclaimed addresses. The multigabled country inn and adjoining Carriage House, both dating from 1881, are ensconced on 8 beautiful (and blissfully quiet) acres on the outskirts of Healdsburg. The best rooms are on the mansion's second floor, each furnished with fine antiques such as an acorn-carved bed, a Georgian table and chair, and brass lamps. Another luxurious spread boasts a carved sun and inlay work on the matching bed and dresser, handsome fireplace tiles, a clawfoot tub, and a huge private balcony. The Carriage House has eight rooms that have been renovated and furnished with rosewood from Nepal. The most secluded accommodation is the Garden Cottage, a suite outfitted in rattan with private gardens and sheltered deck. All rooms have fireplaces; eight open onto large balconies. There's a well-decorated small parlor and other common rooms for guests to relax in. A trio of dining rooms is done in traditional Queen Anne style. The outdoor pool is set in the beautiful gardens.

Todd, John and Carol's son, trained at the celebrated Chez Panisse, and has brought considerable talent to the running of the Madrona Manor Restaurant. He's an innovator who makes much use of local produce, including vegetables grown in the kitchen garden. He smokes some of the meats and fish himself, and bakes bread better than the late James Beard. After tasting his Peking duck flavored with coconut and almonds, you'll be a loyal fan.

WHERE TO DINE

✪ Bistro Ralph. 109 Plaza St. ☎ **707/433-1380.** Reservations recommended. Main courses $13–$18. MC, V. Mon–Fri 11:30am–closing, Sat–Sun 5:30pm–closing (closing time depends on business). CALIFORNIA.

This culinary oasis is known for its down-home Northern California cooking. Bistro Ralph is the showcase of Ralph Tingle, the former executive chef of the late Fetzer Vineyards Sun Dial Grill in Mendocino, where he earned his well-deserved reputation. His new restaurant thrives on local foodstuffs, and Tingle's intelligent, imaginative cuisine focuses on bringing out their natural flavors, and does so exceedingly well, appropriately using wines in good measure to accent his dishes. The limited menu, which changes weekly, might offer a succulent braised rabbit stew with smoked-duck sausage and couscous, a grilled Bodega Bay salmon with stewed leeks and port-compound butter, or grilled flank steak marinated in rice vinegar, chiles, ginger, and brown sugar. The appetizers are also brimming with flavor. There's a wide selection of local wines, including about 15 varieties by the glass.

The Northern Coast

by Erika Lenkert and Matthew R. Poole

8

Heading north from San Francisco, you'll come upon a California that hardly resembles the southern half of the state. It's an entirely different landscape, in climate as well as flora and fauna. You can forget about California's fabled surfing-and-bikini scene this far north; instead, you'll find miles and miles of rugged coastline with broad beaches and tiny bays harboring dramatic rock formations—from chimney stacks to bridges and blowholes—carved by the ocean waves.

The best time to visit is in the spring or fall. In spring, the headlands are carpeted with wildflowers—golden poppy, iris, and sea foam—and in fall the sun shines clear and bright. Summers are typically cool and windy, with the ubiquitous fog burning off by the afternoon.

You may think you've already arrived in Alaska when you hit the beaches of Northern California. Take a dip in the sea and you'll soon agree with the locals: The Arctic waters along the north coast are best left to the seals when it comes to swimming. But that doesn't mean you can't enjoy the beaches, whether by strolling along the water or taking in the panoramic views of towering cliffs and seascapes. Unlike their southern counterparts, the beaches along the north coast are not likely to be crowded, even in summer.

As you head north toward Oregon, there's an amazing string of golden beaches, all clearly marked off Calif. 1 and easily accessible. Though there are lots of options, the following beaches are our favorites, going from south to north: Muir Beach (just off Calif. 1 and about 3 miles from Muir Woods); Duxbury Reef, known for its tidepools (at Bolinas, get on Mesa Road and turn left on Overlook Drive, then right on Elm Avenue, which will take you to the parking lot); Point Reyes National Seashore at Limantour Beach; Tomales Bay State Park, reached by Sir Francis Drake Boulevard right off Calif. 1 (go along Pierce Point Road until you come to the park); Fort Ross State Park, some 9¹/₂ miles north of the town of Jenner; Sea Ranch, off Calif. 1 south of Gualala; ✪ **Manchester State Beach,** some 9¹/₂ miles north of Point Arena; and Agate Beach in Patrick's Point State Park, which is known for its tidepools and is off U.S. 101, about 25 miles north of Eureka.

The most scenic way to reach Mendocino and points north is to drive from San Francisco along the coast via Calif. 1, one of the most beautiful drives in the world. The larger freeway, U.S. 101, runs

The Northern Coast

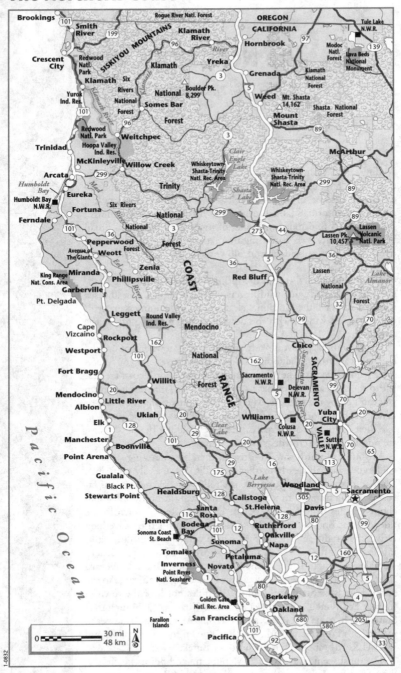

inland through Healdsburg and Cloverdale and is faster, but doesn't provide the spectacular views of coastal cliffs and windswept beaches you'll see on Calif. 1. If you decide to take the scenic route, turn toward the coast on Calif. 20 at Willits.

1 Point Reyes National Seashore

by Andrew Rice

Point Reyes is a 100-square-mile peninsula of dark forests, wind-sculpted dunes, endless beaches, and plunging sea cliffs. Aside from its beautiful scenery, it also boasts historical treasures that offer a window into California's coastal past, including lighthouses, turn-of-the-century dairies and ranches, the site of Sir Francis Drake's 1579 landing, plus a complete replica of a coastal Miwok Indian village.

The national seashore system was created to protect rural and undeveloped stretches of the coast from the pressures of soaring real estate values and increasing population, preserving both the natural features and unique culture of the coast. Nowhere is the success of the system more evident than at Point Reyes. Layers of human history coexist peacefully here with one of the world's most dramatic natural settings. Residents of the surrounding towns—**Inverness, Point Reyes Station,** and **Olema**—have steadfastly resisted runaway development. You won't find any strip malls or fast-food joints here—just a laid-back coastal town with cafes and country inns where gentle living prevails. The park, a 71,000-acre hammer-shaped peninsula jutting 10 miles into the Pacific and backed by Tomales Bay, is loaded with wildlife, ranging from tule elk, birds, and bobcats to gray whales, sea lions, and white sharks. During Audubon's annual Christmas bird count, Point Reyes, with as many as 350 different varieties, is regularly found to have the largest concentration of diverse bird species in the continental United States. The **Point Reyes Bird Observatory** (☎ **415/868-1221**), an ornithological research organization located in the park, is open to the public and offers tours and special programs.

Though the peninsula's people and wildlife live in harmony above the ground, the situation beneath the soil is much more volatile. The infamous San Andreas fault separates Point Reyes, the northernmost land mass on the Pacific Plate, from the rest of California, which rests on the North American Plate. Point Reyes is making its way toward Alaska at a rate of about 2 inches per year, but there have been times when it has moved much faster. In 1906 Point Reyes jumped north almost 20 feet in an instant, leveling San Francisco and jolting the rest of the state. The half-mile **Earthquake Trail,** near the Bear Valley Visitor Center, illustrates this geological drama with a loop through an area torn by the slipping fault. Shattered fences, rifts in the ground, and a barn knocked off its foundation by the quake illustrate how alive the earth is here. If that doesn't convince you, a seismograph in the visitor's center will.

The **Bear Valley Visitor Center** (☎ **415/663-1092**), just outside Olema, is the best place to begin your visit. In addition to the earthquake trail, here you'll find maps and information plus great natural history and cultural displays. Two features of the center are particularly fascinating. **Kule Loklo,** a restored coastal Miwok Indian village, often hosts displays of dancing, basketmaking, Native American cooking, and indigenous art; and the Park Service's **Morgan Horse Ranch** is the only working horse-breeding farm in the national park system. The best time to visit Kule Loklo is during July when it hosts an annual **Native American Celebration** and the whole village comes to life. Classes in Native American crafts and skills are offered intermittently throughout the year. Call 415/479-3281 for more information.

The weather at Point Reyes is very fickle. The point itself is the foggiest place on the West Coast. Generally the seasons here are reversed: Summer is cold and foggy, while winter is clear and, if not exactly warm, often at least tolerable. There are no hard-and-fast rules about the weather, though. Winter storms can rage for weeks and sometimes the summer fog stays away. The best plan is to take advantage of variations in local weather by being flexible with your itinerary: Save indoor sightseeing for rainy or foggy days, and hit the beach or go hiking when the sun comes out. In wooded areas keep an eye out for poison oak's waxy three-leaf clusters. Also be sure to check for ticks, as the Lyme disease–carrying black-legged tick is common here.

Though the park is heavily visited, crowds are only a problem at a few places and only during certain times. If you visit the lighthouse on a weekend or holiday during whale season, be prepared to wait for the shuttle at Drake's Beach and to have to deal with a lot of people. The trails leaving from Bear Valley tend to be more crowded on weekends than others. Try the Five Brooks or Palomarin Trailhead to avoid hordes of backcountry tourists.

Rangers lead special programs year round, from wildlife hikes and history lessons to habitat restoration. All are free. Call the Bear Valley Visitor Center for up-to-date schedules. Other groups, such as the Marin chapter of the **Sierra Club** (☎ 510/526-8969), the **Golden Gate Audubon Society** (☎ 510/843-2222), and **Oceanic Society Expeditions** (☎ 415/474-3385), run special excursions and outings to the park. During whale season the Oceanic Society takes naturalist-led whale-watching boats from the San Francisco Marina to Point Reyes every weekend that the weather permits. The all-day trip costs $48 for adults and $46 for kids and senior citizens; no children under 10 are allowed.

BEACHES   Beachgoers have their work cut out for them here. The **Great Beach** is one of California's longest. It's also one of the windiest, and home to large and dangerous waves. You can't swim here, but the beachcombing is some of the best in the world. Tidepoolers should go to **McClure's Beach** at the end of Pierce Point Road during low tide or hike out to **Chimney Rock.** Swimmers will want to stick to **Limantour Beach** or ✪ **Drake's Beach** in the protected lee of Point Reyes. Sir Francis Drake reputedly landed the *Pelican* (later rechristened the *Golden Hind*) on the sandy shore of Drake's Bay in June 1579, to replenish supplies and make repairs before sailing home to England. Drake's Beach is now home to the Kenneth C. Patrick Visitor Center, which has exhibits on the area's whale fossil beds, and Drake's Beach Cafe, the only food concession in the park, which is famous for its great oysters.

HIKING   There's a little of everything for hikers here. Some 32,000 acres of the park are crisscrossed by 70 miles of trails and are set aside as wilderness where no motor vehicles or bicycles are allowed. The **Bear Valley Trail** leads through wooded hillsides until it reaches the sea at **Arch Rock,** where Coast Creek splashes into the sea through a "sea tunnel;" the full hike from trailhead to Rock is about 8 miles round-trip. More relaxing is the 4$^{1}/_{2}$-mile **Estero Trail,** a favorite with birders, which meanders along the edge of Limantour Estero and Drake's Estero. *Estero* is the Spanish word for estuary and these brackish waters draw flocks of waterfowl and shorebirds as well as many raptors and smaller species. Near Wildcat Camp on the Coast Trail is **Alamere Falls,** which can also be reached via the Palomarin Trail or Five Brooks Trail in the south of the park. **Tomales Point Trail,** 11 miles round-trip, gives hikers a tour of the park's rugged shoreline and also passes through wilderness that's home to the park's herd of tule elk.

Point Reyes National Seashore & Bodega Bay

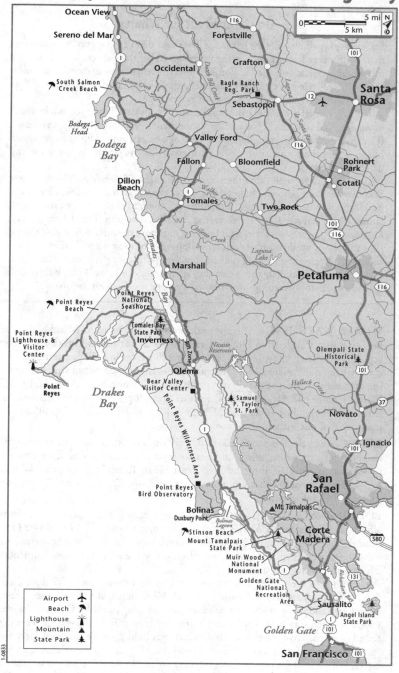

Ocean View
Sereno del Mar
Forestville
116
5 mi
5 km
N
101

Occidental
Grafton
Santa Rosa

South Salmon
Creek Beach
Salmon Creek
Dutch Bill Creek
Ragle Ranch
Reg. Park
Sebastopol
12

Bodega
Head
Valley Ford
116

Bodega
Bay
Fallon
Bloomfield
Rohnert
Park

Dillon
Beach
Tomales
Walker Creek
Two Rock
Cotati

Chileno Creek
Laguna
Lake
101
116

Marshall
Petaluma
116

Point Reyes
National
Seashore
Tomales Bay
State Park
Inverness
Point Reyes
Beach
Tomales Bay
Salt Zone
Nicasio
Reservoir
Olompali State
Historical
Park
101

Point Reyes
Lighthouse &
Visitor
Center
Olema
Bear Valley
Visitor Center
Samuel
P. Taylor
St. Park
Halleck Creek
Novato
37

Point
Reyes
Drakes
Bay
Point Reyes Wilderness Area
101
Ignacio

San
Rafael

Point Reyes
Bird Observatory
Bolinas
Duxbury Point
Bolinas
Lagoon
Stinson Beach
Mount Tamalpais
State Park
Mt. Tamalpais
Corte
Madera
580

Muir Woods
National
Monument
Golden Gate
National
Recreation
Area
1
131
Richardson Bay
Sausalito
Angel Island
State Park

Golden Gate
101
Airport
Beach
Lighthouse
Mountain
State Park

San Francisco
101

1-0833

203

On the Lookout for Whales

Each year gray whales (it's the barnacles that make them appear gray) migrate from their winter breeding grounds in the warm waters off the Baja coast to their summer feeding grounds off Alaska. You can observe them as they undertake this enormous 10,000-mile journey; the California coastline from Redwood National Park south to the Mexican border offers a perfect vantage.

In many coastal towns you can book a charter boat that will take you out in search of whales. And sometimes you can even spot them from land. During peak season (December to March), you might see dozens of whales from the Point Reyes Lighthouse, where there's a visitor center with great displays on whale migration (for details, see below).

If you're lucky, you'll catch the whales performing a few of their classic moves. You may see their powerful flukes rising out of the water in preparation for a dive. You'll certainly see their spouts, formed by the condensed moisture of their exhalation, which can rise 10 to 15 feet in the air and can be seen from 10 miles away. Occasionally you may see their heads popping out above the surface for a look around (in a maneuver whale watchers call "spyhopping"), or their whole bodies lurching right out of the water in what's called a "breach." Why they perform the last two is a mystery. Some speculate that when they spyhop they're actually checking coastal landmarks. As for breaching, who knows? Perhaps it's sheer jubilation.

WHALE WATCHING   During peak season (December to March), the Park Service runs a shuttle from Drake's Beach to the **Point Reyes Lighthouse,** where watchers have been known to see as many as 100 whales in a single afternoon. Even if the whales don't materialize, the lighthouse itself, a fabulous old structure teetering high above the sea at the tip of a promontory, is worth a visit. The **Lighthouse Visitor Center** (☎ 415/669-1534) features great displays on whale migration and maritime history. Two other spots, Chimney Rock and Tomales Point, offer just as many whales, but without the crowds.

BIKING   Bicycles are permitted in the park but not on the wilderness area trails, and plotting a course exclusively on the bike trails can be tricky. Check with the visitor center for specific information. **Trail Head Rentals** in Olema (☎ 415/663-1958) rents nice Fisher mountain bikes for about $24 a day and also is a good source of trail information.

LODGING & CAMPING   The only lodging within Point Reyes is the rustic but affordable ($9 per night) **AYH Hostel** on Limantour Road (☎ 415/663-8811). A beautiful old ranch complex 2 miles from Limantour beach that was converted into bunkhouse sleeping quarters, the hostel fills up early. Reservations are recommended. The maximum stay is 3 nights.

Camping in the park is limited to four hike-in camps. Two, **Wildcat Camp** (a 6½-mile hike) and **Coast Camp** (a 1.8-mile hike), sit just above the beach. They're often foggy and damp, so bring a good tent and sleeping bag. **Sky Camp** (a 1.7-mile hike) and **Glen Camp** (4.6 miles), set in the woods away from the sea, are more protected from the coastal elements. Individual sites hold up to eight people and have picnic tables and food lockers. Pit toilets and drinking water are available. Camping is free, but permits are required and stays are limited to 4 days. Sites can be reserved up to 2 months in advance by calling 415/663-1092 Monday to Friday from 9am to noon only. Dogs are not permitted on any trails or in the campgrounds.

WHERE TO STAY NEARBY

Blackthorne Inn. 266 Vallejo Ave. (off Sir Francis Drake Blvd., south of Inverness; P.O. Box 712), Inverness, CA 94937. ☎ **415/663-8621.** 5 rms, 3 with bath. $110 double without bath, $190 double with bath. Rates include buffet breakfast. MC, V.

This elaborate redwood home with its octagonal widow's walk, spiral staircase, turrets, and multiple decks looks more like a super-deluxe treehouse than a B&B. Our favorite—and the most expensive—unit is the Eagle's Nest, an octagonal room enclosed by glass and topped with a private sundeck with a catwalk leading to the private outhouse. The largest room is the Studio, virtually a suite with a private entrance and deck, while the smallest room is the Hideaway, which also has a private entrance and a sitting area facing the woods; both are furnished with wicker and decorated with floral fabrics and modern lithographs. The main sitting room in the house features a large stone fireplace, a skylight, and stained-glass windows and is surrounded by a huge deck. Guests have use of the hot tub on the top deck.

✪ **Manka's Inverness Lodge.** P.O. Box 1110, Inverness, CA 94937. ☎ **800/58-LODGE** or 415/669-1034. Fax 415/669-1598. 9 rms, 2 luxury cabins, 1 fishing cabin. $100–$165 double from $175 cabin. AE, MC, V.

This immediately lovable old hunting lodge is one of our favorite places to stay—and dine—on the coast. Every room resembles the sort of rustic old mountain cabin you read about in Jack London novels, and the restaurant has that perfect balance of countryfied charm and polished refinement. In addition to the standard rooms in the main lodge (which are anything but standard with their tree-limb bedsteads, billowy down comforters, and bucolic furnishings), there are two luxuriously appointed cabins adjacent to the inn, a quartet of smaller, less expensive rooms in the redwood annex, and a drippingly romantic 19th-century hunting cabin located down the road.

The lodge's reputation is built on its restaurant, which dominates the bottom floor. The specialty of the house is game and fish, including oysters from Tomales Bay. Prices range from $18 to $22. The limited menu might feature pheasant with a madeira jus, mashed potatoes and a wild huckleberry jam, black buck antelope chops with sweet-corn salsa, or everybody's favorite, pan-seared elk tenderloin. It's open for dinner Thursday to Monday, with a brunch on Sunday.

WHERE TO DINE

✪ **Station House Cafe.** 11180 Main St., Point Reyes Station. ☎ **415/663-1515.** Reservations recommended. Breakfast $4–$6.50; main courses $9–$16. DISC, MC, V. Sun–Thurs 8am–9pm, Fri–Sat 8am–10pm. AMERICAN.

A local favorite, the Station House Cafe is known for its good food and animated atmosphere, particularly when the live music fires up on weekends. For breakfast, we recommend a fritatta with asparagus, goat cheese, and olives, which always seems to taste better if you're sitting outside on the shaded garden patio. Luncheon specials might include two-cheese polenta served with sautéed fresh spinach and grilled garlic-buttered tomatoes. The menu changes every week, but always features locally grown beef and a good selection of fresh fish. Rounding out the menu are homemade chili, steamed clams, fresh soup made daily, and fish and chips. The cafe has an extensive list of fine California wines, plus local imported beers.

2 · Along the Sonoma Coast

TOMALES BAY

From Point Reyes Station, Calif. 1 travels north along the eastern edge of Tomales Bay. It's a pleasant drive, with worthwhile attractions along the route. Stop in at one of the oyster farms near the town of **Marshall** and pick out some choice samples from the tanks. The **Tomales Bay Oyster Company,** 15479 Calif. 1, Tomales (☎ 415/663-1242), for example, sells its wares by the dozen or in sacks of 100, in case you're on your honeymoon. It's open daily from 9am to 5pm. You can gather your own clams in the bay itself, or take part in the windsurfing, kayaking and hang gliding that are also available, especially at **Dillon Beach** at the mouth of the bay. Kayak trips, including 3-hour sunset outings, 3¹/₂-hour full-moon paddles, day trips, and longer excursions, are organized by **Tomales Bay Kayaking,** P.O. Box 833, Marshall, CA 94940-0833 (☎ 415/663-1743). Prices start at $45. Rentals begin at $16 for 2 hours for a single seater.

BODEGA BAY

Beyond the tip of the Point Reyes Peninsula the road curves around toward the coastal village of Bodega Bay, which supports a fishing fleet of 300 boats. As you drive north, Bodega Bay is a good place to stop for lunch or to stroll around town. There are several interesting shops and galleries, though the best show in town is at **Tides Wharf,** where the fishing boats come in to unload their daily catch, which is promptly gutted and packed in ice.

Bodega Head State Park is a great vantage point for whale watching during the annual migration season from January to April. At **Doran Beach** there's a large bird sanctuary (willets, curlews, godwits, and more), and the University of California Marine Biology Lab next door conducts guided tours on Friday afternoon.

The **Bodega Harbour Golf Links,** 21301 Heron Dr. (☎ 707/875-3538), enjoys a panoramic oceanside setting. It's an 18-hole Scottish-style course designed by Robert Trent Jones, Jr. A new warm-up center and practice facility has been added, which is free of charge to registered golfers. And you can go horseback riding through some spectacular local scenery by contacting **Chanslor Horse Stables** (☎ 707/875-2721).

One of the bay's major events is the **Fisherman's Festival,** in April. The local fishing boats, decorated with ribbons and banners, sail out for a Blessing of the Fleet, while landlubbers enjoy music, a lamb and oyster barbecue, and an arts and crafts fair. Another fun event is the **Bodega Bay Sandcastle Building Festival** at Doran Beach.

A few miles inland, the tiny town of Bodega, with a population of 100, is famous as the setting of Alfred Hitchcock's *The Birds;* fans will want to visit the Potter School House and St. Teresa's Church.

For more information, stop in at the **Bodega Bay Area Visitors Center,** 850 Calif. 1, Bodega Bay, CA 94923 (☎ 707/875-3422). It has lots of brochures about the town and the surrounding area, including maps of the Sonoma Coast State Beaches and the best local fishing spots.

WHERE TO STAY

✪ **Bodega Bay Lodge.** 103 Calif. 1, Bodega Bay, CA 94923. ☎ **800/368-2468** or 707/875-3525. 78 rms. $150–$190 Sun–Thurs, $175–$215 double Fri–Sat. 2-night minimum stay on weekends. AE, DC, DISC, MC, V.

This is easily the best hotel in Bodega Bay—every room at the Bodega Bay Lodge has a private balcony with sweeping views of the bay and bird-filled marshes. As if that weren't enough, they even throw in a fireplace, a stocked minibar, and plush furnishings and fabrics in handsome hues of cardinal and green. And as an added bonus, guests have complimentary access to a fitness center and sauna, as well as to a beautiful fieldstone spa and heated pool perched above the bay and surrounded by flower gardens.

The lodge's Duck Club Restaurant also enjoys a reputation as Bodega Bay's finest. Large picture windows take advantage of the bay view, a sublimely romantic setting for chef Jeff Reilly's Sonoma County cuisine. Entrees include farm-fresh asparagus strudel, roasted Petaluma duck, and fresh fish caught by the Bodega fleet. Breakfast and dinner are served daily.

Inn at the Tides. 800 Coast Hwy. (Calif. 1; P.O. Box 640), Bodega Bay, CA 94923. ☎ **800/ 541-7788** or 707/875-2751. Fax 707/875-3023. 86 rms. TV TEL. Summer, $125–$195 double Sun–Thurs, $145–$230 double Fri–Sat. Winter rates drop about 20%. Rates include continental breakfast. Golf packages available. AE, MC, V.

The larger (and, in our opinion, less appealing) of Bodega Bay's two upscale lodgings—the other is the Bodega Bay Lodge—the Inn at the Tides consists of a cluster of condolike wood complexes perched on the side of a gently sloping hill. The selling point here is the view, as each unit is staggered just enough to guarantee a view of the bay across the highway. While all the rooms are large and comfortably furnished, the decor suffers from a lack of inspiration; natural tones predominate in a "nouveau Californian" theme that may have worked in the 1970s but just looks out of date now. The amenities, though, are first-rate, such as the heated indoor/outdoor pool, Jacuzzi, and Finnish sauna.

The restaurant, the Bay View, is open for dinner Wednesday to Sunday. It offers sea views and has a romantic, somewhat formal ambience, though it suffers from a so-so reputation. The owners, to their credit, have recently poured a bundle of money into revitalizing it, including hiring an aspiring new chef, Clay Summers.

WHERE TO DINE

Tides Wharf Restaurant. 835 Calif 1. ☎ **707/875-3652.** Reservations recommended. Main courses $10–$24. AE, DC, MC, V. Daily 7:30am–9:30pm (last order). SEAFOOD.

It isn't as secluded or as intimate as you might have wanted (in summer, as many as 1,000 diners a day pass through here), but it evokes all the nostalgia of the 1950s, when it served as one of the settings for Hitchcock's *The Birds.* Don't expect the weather-beaten, board-and-batten luncheonette you saw in the movie: The place has been gentrified, enlarged, and redecorated many times since, although it retains the original bar used in the film. There are views over the water, and the tables are cramped but convivial. The bill of fare is what you might expect at a chowderhouse in Boston, with fish and chips, barbecued oysters, oysters Rockefeller, and all the seafood that the owners (who send their own fishing boat out into the Pacific every day) can dredge up from the cold blue waters offshore. Try the terrific open-face crab sandwich served with melted cheese on sourdough bread. Land-locked items such as prime rib and pasta are also available.

THE SONOMA COAST STATE BEACHES, JENNER & FORT ROSS STATE HISTORIC PARK

Along 13 winding miles of Calif. 1—from Bodega Bay to Goat Rock Beach in Jenner—stretch the ✪ **Sonoma Coast State Beaches.** These beaches are ideal for walking, tidepooling, abalone picking, fishing, and birdwatching for such species as blue heron, cormorant, osprey, brown and white pelicans, and more. Each beach is clearly marked from the road, and numerous pullouts are provided for parking. Even if you don't stop at any of the beaches, the drive alone is spectacular.

At **Jenner,** the Russian River empties into the ocean. Penny Island, in the river's estuary, is home to otters and many species of birds, while out on the ocean rocks there's a colony of harbor seals. Goat Rock Beach is a popular breeding ground for the seals; pupping season begins in March and lasts until June.

From Jenner, a 12-mile climb along some very dramatic coastline will bring you to **Fort Ross State Historic Park** (☎ 707/847-3286), a reconstruction of the fort that was established here in 1812 by the Russians as a base for seal and otter hunting (it was abandoned in 1842). At the visitor center you can view the silver samovars and elaborate table services that the Russians used. The fenced compound contains several buildings, including the first Russian Orthodox church ever built on the North American continent outside Alaska. The park also offers beach trails and picnic grounds on more than 1,000 acres. Admission is free, but parking is a hefty $5.

North from Fort Ross the road continues to **Salt Point State Park.** It's 3,500-acre expanse contains 30 campsites, 14 miles of hiking trails, dozens of tidepools, a pygmy forest, and old Pomo village sites. Your best bet is to pull off the highway at any place that catches your eye and start exploring on foot. At the north end of the park, branch off inland on Kruse Ranch Road to the 317-acre **Kruse Rhododendron Reserve** (☎ 707/847-3221), an aesthetic miracle in April and May. Some rhododendrons grow to a height of 18 feet under the redwood and fir canopy.

WHERE TO DINE

River's End. Calif. 1., Jenner. ☎ **707/865-2484.** Reservations recommended. Main courses $13–$33 at dinner. MC, V. Mon–Fri 11am–9:30pm, Sat–Sun 10am–9:30pm. INTERNATIONAL.

Outwardly unpretentious yet deceptively urbane, this small seaside restaurant offers an artfully rustic setting, with big windows overlooking the California coast, the sea, and whatever seals and sea lions happen to be cavorting offshore. The menu is wonderfully eclectic, the product of a German-born chef who whips up versions of Indonesian bahmi goreng, a selection of Indian curries, beef saté, beef Wellington, seafood, and steaks. A solarium holds the overflow from the main dining room, but it's only available for seating when the place gets crowded. After dinner, take the remainder of your wine to the outside deck and enjoy the sunset.

GUALALA & POINT ARENA

Back on Calif. 1 going north you'll pass through Sea Ranch, a series of condominium beach developments, until you reach Gualala (pronounced wah-*la*-la). To access the beaches along this stretch of coast you'll have to cross private property, and your entrance may therefore be restricted at any time. Still, there are about 10 or so public beaches that are ideal for walking.

The **Gualala River,** adjacent to the town of the same name, is suitable for canoeing, rafting, and kayaking since all powerboats and jet skis are forbidden. Along its banks you're likely to see osprey, heron, egrets, and ducks as well as steelhead, salmon, and river otters in the waters. Canoes, kayaks, and bicycles can be rented in Gualala for 2 hours, a half day, or a full day from **Adventure Rents,** behind the Gualala Hotel on Calif. 1 (☎ 707/884-4386). A bike for 2 hours costs $15, a canoe (which seats two to five people) costs $25 for a half day, and a double kayak for the whole day costs $60. **Gualala Kayak,** 39175 S. Calif. 1, next to the Chevron station (☎ 707/884-4705), specializes in river and sea kayaking. A single kayak costs $20 for 2 hours, $35 for a day, and a double kayak costs $65 for a day. Prices include everything from instruction to shuttle service.

Point Arena lies a few miles north of Gualala. Most folks stop here for the view at the **Point Arena Lighthouse** (☎ 707/882-2777), which was built in 1870 after 10 ships ran aground here on a single night during a storm. A $2.50 fee covers parking, entrance to the lighthouse museum, and a surprisingly interesting tour of the six-story, 145-step lighthouse. It's open daily from 11am to 3:30pm.

WHERE TO STAY

✪ Old Milano Hotel. 38300 Calif. 1, Gualala, CA 95445. ☎ **707/884-3256.** 6 rms, none with bath; 1 suite; 2 cottages. $85 double with garden view, $115 double with ocean view; $170 master suite; $140 cottage. Rates include breakfast. MC, V.

This romantic hotel lies just north of Gualala and has a spellbinding view of Castle Rock from the front porch and sloping lawn. The inn was built in 1905 on 3 acres and is listed in the National Register of Historic Places. It has enchanting flower and herb gardens and a superbly situated hot tub, from which you look directly out to the ocean. The rooms are all decorated differently, often with rare antiques. Upstairs, six rooms share two bathrooms, each with double showers. The most alluring units are the Vine Cottage, which has a sleeping alcove, reading loft, and woodstove; and an honest-to-Betsy train caboose, a romantically private space with woodstove and two upstairs brakeman's seats.

Dining/Entertainment: A full breakfast is served either in your room or in the parlor. Chef Madeleine Jordan offers pricey California cuisine—rack of Sonoma lamb, poached salmon, roasted Peking duck—served in an intimate dining room lit by candlelight and, on cool nights, by roaring fires in the stone fireplaces.

✪ St. Orres. 36601 Calif. 1 (P.O. Box 523), Gualala, CA 95445. ☎ **707/884-3303.** Fax 707/884-3903. 8 rms, none with bath; 12 cottages. $65 double rooms on side, $80 double with ocean view; $85–$270 cottage for two, depending on size. MC, V.

An extraordinary building designed in Russian style—complete with two onion-domed towers—St. Orres lies 1¹/₂ miles north of Gualala. The complex was built in 1972 with century-old timbers salvaged from a nearby mill. It offers secluded cottage-style accommodations on 42 acres, as well as eight rooms in the main building (these eight accommodations are handcrafted and share three bathrooms decorated in brilliant colors). Other accommodations are very private. Some have a full bath, wet bar, sitting area with Franklin stove, and French doors leading to a deck with a distant ocean view. Seven cottages lie beside St. Orres Creek and have exclusive use of a spa facility that includes a hot tub, sauna, and sundeck. The most luxurious is Pine Haven, with two bedrooms, two redwood decks, two baths, a tiled breakfast area, a beach stone fireplace, and wet bar.

Dining/Entertainment: The hotel is especially well known for its intimate restaurant (the St. Orres), a 17-seat charmer set below one of the main building's onion domes. Light filters through stained-glass windows onto strands of ivy that cascade down from the upper balcony. The only offering is a $30 three-course fixed-price meal that features game from the surrounding fields and forests. Dishes are inspired by Pacific Northwest cuisine, and include wild boar, pheasant, venison, quail, and rack of lamb. Reservations are essential. It's open daily for dinner only; closed weekdays the first 2 weeks of December. MasterCard and Visa are accepted for hotel guests only; otherwise, no credit cards.

NORTH FROM POINT ARENA

Driving north from Point Arena, you'll pass Elk (a cute place to stop for lunch), Manchester, Albion, and Little River on your way to Mendocino.

WHERE TO STAY

Greenwood Pier Inn. 5928 Calif. 1. (P.O. Box 336), Elk, CA 95432. ☎ **707/877-9997.** Fax 707/877-3439. 5 rms, 6 cottages and duplexes. $100–$225 double. Rates include continental breakfast. AE, MC, V.

The Greenwood Pier Inn, perched on the edge of a dramatic bluff, is an eclectic, New Age kind of place. It's the unique domain of Kendrick and Isabel Petty, who operate a complex combining a cafe, country store, garden shop, and accommodations. Kendrick is an artist and passionate gardener whose collages, tile, and marble work can be seen in the interiors of several of the buildings in the complex and also outside in the gardens. Of the accommodations, which are in various buildings in addition to the main inn, the Cliffhouse is the top choice, a seaside redwood cabin complete with a fireplace, a large deck, and an upper-level bathtub with ocean views. All the rooms have private decks, fireplaces, or woodstoves, and lie within 100 feet of the cliff edge; they have no TV or phone, but each has a private bath and access to a hot tub overlooking the ocean. A continental breakfast is delivered to your room; lunch and dinner are served daily in the cafe.

✪ **Harbor House.** 5600 S. Calif. 1 (P.O. Box 369), Elk, CA 95432. ☎ **707/877-3203.** 6 rms, 4 cottages. $200, 265 double; $175–$225 cottage for two. Rates discounted in Jan, Feb, and Mar. Additional person $50 extra. Rates include full breakfast and four-course dinner. No credit cards.

While the Greenwood Pier Inn is home to the New Age, the redwood-sided two-story Harbor House is very, very traditional. It was built in 1916 by the president of the Goodyear Redwood Lumber Co. as a hideaway for corporate executives and their wives. This is not a hotel, but an upmarket B&B offering 3 acres of gardens, access to a private beach, and views overlooking the Pacific. None of the units has a TV or phone, and that's how guests here like it. Five of the rooms in the main building have their own fireplaces, many are furnished with antiques originally purchased by the lumber executives, and all have private baths. The cottages tend to be small, but contain fireplaces and private decks.

The restaurant here always maintains two of its tables for nonguests, who should make reservations as far in advance as possible. Set dinners, which change nightly, cost $26 and feature both California and Pacific Northwest cuisine, making use of local herbs, freshly baked breads, and vegetables from the inn's own gardens.

Timber Cove Inn. 21780 Calif. 1, Jenner, CA 95450. ☎ **707/847-3231.** Fax 707/847-3704. 47 rms. $115–$150 double with pond view, $195–$230 double with ocean view, $295–$360 double with private hot tub, fireplace, and balcony. AE, MC, V.

Three miles north of Fort Ross, on a rocky promontory overlooking the ocean, this hotel was built with contemplation and meditation in mind. The massive redwood buildings are architecturally integrated with their surroundings. A stone-lined Japanese pond flanks the entrance path to the timbered lobby with its large walk-in fireplace. Adjacent is the dining room, which has sweeping views of the ocean. The rooms are built of redwood and decorated with large pieces of driftwood. Throughout the complex are arrangements of wild flowers and prints by Ansel Adams, many of them scenes of Timber Cove. About half the rooms have fireplaces, and a number have sunken tiled tubs with ocean views. The most expensive are 1,000-square-foot corner units with private hot tub, fireplace, and balcony.

WHERE TO DINE

Ledford House. 3000 N. Calif. 1, Albion. ☎ **707/937-0282.** Reservations recommended. Main courses $18–$21. AE, MC, V. Wed–Sun 5–9pm. CALIFORNIAN/FRENCH.

If James Beard were alive today, he'd feel right at home at this innovative but simply decorated restaurant standing on a bluff, with views of the Pacific and of the pounding surf. The kitchen offers self-styled "new American cuisine," experimenting with the rich bounty of the Golden State to fashion the produce into rich combinations and harmonious flavors. One part of the menu is reserved primarily for pastas and hearty stews suitable for this far northern setting, such as Antoine's cassoulet, a jumble of pork, lamb, garlic sausage, and duck confit slowly cooked with white beans. For a taste of California, try the salmon primavera with lemon-caper butter; or the red snapper braised with tomatoes, onions, garlic, and white wine. In the evening there's often live jazz emanating from the lounge.

3 Mendocino

Mendocino is, to our minds, *the* premier destination on California's north coast. Despite (or because of) its relative isolation, it emerged as one of Northern California's major centers for the arts in the 1950s. It's easy to see why artists were—and still are—attracted to this idyllic community, a cluster of New England–style sea captain's homes and small stores set on headlands overlooking the ocean. If fact, Mendocino is so picturesque that it has been the backdrop for dozens of movies, as well as the TV series *Murder, She Wrote.*

At the height of the logging boom Mendocino became an important and active port. Its population was about 3,500, and eight hotels were built, along with 17 saloons and more than a dozen bordellos. Today it has only about 1,000 residents, most of whom reside on the north end of town. On summer weekends the population seems more like 10,000 as droves of tourists drive up from the Bay Area. But despite the crowds, Mendocino still manages to retain its small-town charm.

ESSENTIALS

GETTING THERE   The fastest route from San Francisco is via U.S. 101 north to Cloverdale. From there, take Calif. 128 west to Calif. 1, then go north along the coast. It's about a 4-hour drive. (You could also take U.S. 101 all the way to Ukiah or Willits and cut over to the west from there.) The most scenic route from the Bay Area, if you have the time and your stomach doesn't mind the twists and turns, is to take Calif. 1 north along the coast the entire way; it's at least a 5- to 6-hour drive.

VISITOR INFORMATION   There's a small information office up the coast in Fort Bragg, stocked with lots of free brochures and maps available for purchase. Visit the **Fort Bragg / Mendocino Coast Chamber of Commerce,** 332 N. Main St. (P.O. Box 1141), Fort Bragg, CA 95437 (☎ **800/726-2780** or 707/961-6300).

EXPLORING THE TOWN

Stroll through town, enjoying the architecture, and browse through the dozens of galleries and shops. Our favorites include the **Highlight Gallery,** 45052 Main St. (☎ 707/937-3132), for its handmade furniture, pottery, and other craftwork; **Old Gold,** 6 Albion St. (☎ 707/937-5005), which carries a great selection of antique and contemporary jewelry and watches; and the **Gallery Bookshop,** at Main and Kasten streets (☎ 707/937-2665), which has a wonderful collection of new and used books, including children's books. Another popular stop is **Robert's Jams & Preserves,** at 440 Main St. (☎ 707/937-1037), which offers free tastings of their gourmet wares on little bread chips.

After exploring the town, walk out on the headlands that wrap around the town and constitute ✪ **Mendocino Headlands State Park.** (The visitor center for the park is in Ford House on Main Street.) Three miles of trails wind through the park, giving visitors panoramic views of sea arches and hidden grottoes. If you're here at the right time of year, the area will be blanketed with a carpet of wildflowers, and when we last stopped by in August 1995 you could pick fresh blackberries beside the trails. The headlands are home to many unique species of birds, including black oyster-catchers. Behind the Mendocino Presbyterian Church on Main Street is a trail leading to stairs that take you down to the beach, a small but picturesque stretch of sand where driftwood formations have washed ashore.

On the south side of town, **Big River Beach** is accessible from Calif. 1; it's good for picnicking, walking, and sunbathing.

In town, stop by the **Mendocino Art Center,** 45200 Little Lake Rd. (☎ 707/ 937-5818), the town's unofficial cultural headquarters. It's also known for its gardens, three galleries, and shops that display and sell local fine arts and crafts. Pick up a copy of the center's monthly magazine, *Arts and Entertainment,* which lists upcoming events throughout Mendocino. Admission is free; open daily from 10am to 5pm.

For a special treat, go to **Sweetwater Gardens,** 955 Ukiah St. (☎ **800/300-4140** or 707/937-4140), which offers group and private saunas and hot-tub soaks by the hour. Additional services include Swedish or deep-tissue massages. Reservations are recommended. Private tub prices are $8 per person per half hour, $11 per person per hour. Group tub prices are $7.50 per person with no time limit. Special discounts are available on Wednesday. Open Monday to Thursday from 2 to 10pm and Friday to Sunday from noon to 11pm.

ENJOYING THE OUTDOORS

Explore the Big River by renting a canoe, sea cycle, kayak, or outrigger from **Catch a Canoe & Bicycles Too** (☎ 707/937-0273), located on the grounds of the Stanford Inn by the Sea (see "Where to Stay," below). If you're lucky you'll see some osprey, blue herons, harbor seals, deer, and wood ducks. These same folks will also rent you a mountain bike (much better quality than your usual bike rental) so you can head up Calif. 1 and explore the nearby state parks on two wheels.

Horseback riding (both English and western) on the beach and into the redwoods is offered by **Ricochet Ridge Ranch,** 24201 N. Calif. 1, Fort Bragg (☎ 707/ 964-PONY).

Aside from Mendocino Headlands State Park, there are several other state parks near Mendocino; all are within an easy drive or bike ride and make for a good day's outing. Information on all the parks' features, including maps of each one, is found in a brochure called "Mendocino Coast State Parks," available from the visitor center in Fort Bragg. These areas include Manchester State Park, located where the San Andreas fault sweeps to the sea; Jug Handle State Reserve; and Van Damme State Park, with a sheltered, easily accessible beach.

Our favorite of these parks, located directly on Calif. 1 just north of Mendocino, is **Russian Gulch State Park** (☎ 707/937-5804). It's one of the region's most spectacular parks, where roaring waves crash against the cliffs that protect the park's California coastal redwoods. The most popular attraction is the Punch Bowl, a collapsed sea cave that forms a tunnel through which waves crash, creating throaty echoes. Inland there's a scenic paved biking path and visitors can also hike along miles of trails, including a gentle, well-marked 3-mile Waterfall Loop that winds past tall redwoods and damp green foliage to a 36-foot-high waterfall. Admission is $5. Thirty camping sites enjoy a beautiful setting and are available from April to mid-October ($14 per night). Phone 800/444-7275 for reservations.

Fort Bragg is just a short distance up the coast; deep-sea fishing charters are available from its harbor.

WHERE TO STAY
EXPENSIVE

✪ **Stanford Inn by the Sea.** N. Calif. 1 and Comptche Ukiah Rd. (P.O. Box 487), Mendocino, CA 95460. ☎ **800/331-8884** or 707/937-5615. Fax 707/937-0305. 23 rms, 10 suites. TV TEL. $175–$225 double; $200–$485 suite. Rates include buffet breakfast. AE, DC, MC, V.

Just south of town, this rustic but ever-so-sumptuous lodge occupies 11 acres of land abutting the Big River. The grounds are captivating, including tiers of elaborate gardens, a pond for duck and geese, and fenced pastures containing horses, curious llamas, and old gnarled apple trees.

The rooms, all with private baths, are luxuriously furnished in forest green and burgundy tones, and offer such special touches as thick terrycloth robes and heavenly down comforters. They're made even more appealing with fresh flowers and works by local artists. All have fireplaces or stoves, stereos and VCRs (there's an extensive library of tapes available from the front desk), and private decks from which you can look out onto the Pacific. Second honeymooners should inquire about the romantic River Cottage suite; families will want the big ol' renovated barn. Pets are welcome here, and receive the royal treatment.

Dining/Entertainment: A breakfast buffet is served every morning (you can take a tray back to your room) in the new breakfast room, and afternoon wine and hors d'oeuvres are offered as well.

Services: Concierge, laundry, in-room massage, courtesy car, baby-sitting.

Facilities: There's a gorgeous solarium-style indoor hot tub and pool surrounded by tropical plants, as well as a new exercise room. Mountain bikes and canoes are available on the property from Catch a Canoe and Bicycles Too (bike rentals are complimentary with your stay).

MODERATE

⑤ Joshua Grindle Inn. 44800 Little Lake Rd. (P.O. Box 647), Mendocino, CA 95460. ☎ **800/ GRINDLE** or 707/937-4143. 10 rms. July–Sept and Fri–Sat year round, $95–$175 double. Oct–June, $90–$155 double Sun–Thurs. Rates include full breakfast. AE, MC, V.

When it was built in 1879 this stately Victorian was one of the most substantial and impressive houses in Mendocino, owned by the town's wealthiest banker. It's covered with redwood siding and surrounded by a wraparound porch and large emerald lawns, and today it's proud of its heritage as the oldest B&B in Mendocino. From its prettily planted gardens there's a view across the village to the distant bay. There are five rooms in the main house, two in the cottage, and three in the watertower. All have well-lit, comfortably arranged sitting areas; some offer fireplaces. Each is individually decorated: the library, for example, has a New England feel with its four-poster pine bed, floor-to-ceiling bookcase, and 19th-century tiles around the fireplace depicting many of the Aesop's fables; the sunny and spacious master room has a wood-burning fireplace, granite whirlpool tub, and separate shower. Sherry is served in the parlor in front of the fireplace and breakfast is offered in the dining room.

✪ MacCallum House. 45020 Albion St. (P.O. Box 206), Mendocino, CA 95460. ☎ **800/ 609-0492** or 707/937-0289. 18 rms, 5 suites. $120–$190 double from $140 suite. Additional person $15 extra. MC, V. From U.S. 101, turn right onto Albion Street in downtown Mendocino.

A historic 1882 gingerbread Victorian mansion, MacCallum House is one of Mendocino's top hostelries. Originally owned by local matriarch Daisy MacCallum, the house still bears the imprint of this daughter of the town's richest lumber baron. It remained in the family until 1974, when it was turned into a bed-and-breakfast. Now owned by resident proprietors Melanie and Joe Redding, the home has been preserved with all of its original furnishings and contents—right down to Daisy's Christmas cards and books of pressed flowers. Boasting an occasional Tiffany lamp or authentic Persian carpet, each uniquely decorated guest room is exquisitely furnished with many original pieces—a Franklin stove, a handmade quilt, a cushioned rocking chair, or a child's cradle. More important, each has its own private bath. The luxurious barn suite, complete with a stone fireplace, can accommodate up to six adults.

The MacCallum House Restaurant (☎ 707/937-5763) has a sterling reputation. The menu changes seasonally, but a meal might start with broiled oysters bathed with garlic-basil butter and move on to a local salmon filet or pan-broiled tenderloin with shiitake mushrooms. It's open for dinner Friday to Tuesday from 4:30 to 9pm; closed January to mid-February.

Mendocino Hotel & Garden Suites. 45080 Main St., Mendocino, CA 95460. ☎ **800/ 548-0513** or 707/937-0511. Fax 707/937-0513. 51 rms, 37 with bath; 6 suites. TEL. $65–$80 double without bath, $80–$160 double with bath; $190–$225 suite. Additional person $20 extra. Rates slightly lower Dec–Mar and weekdays year round. AE, MC, V.

Right in the heart of town, this 1878 hotel evokes California's Gold Rush days. Beveled-glass doors open into a Victorian-style lobby and parlor where you might expect to see Mae West. The hotel's decor combines antiques and reproductions, like the oak reception desk from a demolished Kansas bank. Remington paintings (what else would do?), stained-glass lamps, and Persian carpets contribute to the Wild West aura. The guest rooms feature hand-painted French porcelain sinks with floral designs, quaint wallpaper, old-fashioned beds and armoires, and photographs and memorabilia of historic Mendocino. About half the rooms are located in four handsome small buildings behind the main house. Many of the deluxe rooms have fireplaces or wood-burning stoves, as well as more modern bathrooms and good views. The suites have an additional parlor, as well as a fireplace or balcony.

Breakfast and lunch are served in the Garden Room, while dinner is offered in the Victorian-style dining room. Room service is available daily from 8am to 9pm.

✪ **Rachel's Inn.** N. Calif. 1 (P. O. Box 134), Mendocino, CA 95460. ☎ **707/937-0088.** 9 rms. $96–$190 double Sun–Thurs, $110–$190 double Fri–Sat. Rates include breakfast. MC, V.

Two miles south of Mendocino, this B&B is set on an acre of land that abuts 82 acres of state park and is just a short walk from the beach. Two things make this inn special: One is Rachel herself, an attentive host who loves the Mendocino coast and who was responsible for organizing against the threat of offshore oil drilling in the 1980s. The second of the B&B's distinctive qualities is that, unlike most inns in town, it's *not* decorated in Laura Ashley style. Instead it has a refreshing contemporary style, with modern art for decoration, and an emphasis on comfort. From the house, guests can walk down to the cove, and there's also a trail from the house across the headlands. Rachel cooks a superb breakfast of huevos rancheros or something similar, plus fruit, baked goods, and cereals. The main house, built in the 1860s, contains four rooms, including the parlor suite, which has its own sitting room with piano and ocean view. The South Room is a state-of-the-art unit that's specially equipped for disabled guests, with an extra-large shower with seat into which you can wheel a wheelchair. All rooms have a private bath.

INEXPENSIVE

✪ **Mendocino Village Inn.** 44860 Main St. (P.O. Box 626), Mendocino, CA 95460. ☎ **800/ 882-7029** or 707/937-0246. 13 rms, 11 with bath; 1 suite. $75 double without bath, $90–$175 double with bath; $175 suite. Rates include full breakfast. No credit cards.

Although there's a street running between the Mendocino Village Inn and the ocean, it's certainly close to the water. A garden of flowers, plants, and frog ponds fronts the large blue-and-white guesthouse, which was built in 1882 by a local doctor and was later occupied by famed local artist Emmy Lou Packard.

Innkeepers Bill and Kathleen Erwin have decorated each room differently. The Queen Anne Room features a four-poster canopy bed, and the sentimental Maggie's Room is named for a child who etched her name in the window glass almost a century ago (you can still see it). Except for two attic rooms, all have private baths and four rooms have private outside entrances. Complimentary beverages are served in the evening.

IN NEARBY ALBION

✪ **Albion River Inn.** N. Calif. 1 (P.O. Box 100), Albion, CA 95410. ☎ **707/937-1919.** 14 rms, 6 Jacuzzi suites. TEL. $160–$190 double; $225–$250 Jacuzzi suite. Rates include full breakfast. AE, MC, V.

A quarter mile north of Albion, this modern establishment, perched on a bluff some 90 feet above the Pacific, overlooks the mouth of the Albion River. The rooms are all attractively decorated in a contemporary style with comfortable furnishings. You'll find wingbacks placed in front of the fireplace, down comforters on the king-size beds, well-lit desks, and earthenware lamps beside the bed. Additional amenities include a coffeemaker, bathrobes, and decks in all but two rooms. *Insider tip:* If you really want to impress your sweetie, reserve one of the rooms with a Jacuzzi, which have large picture windows that offer dazzling views of the coast.

Dining/Entertainment: The cuisine at the inn's restaurant changes daily but the view from the tables remains the same—stellar. Fresh local produce is used whenever possible with each dish. Entree favorites include grilled sea bass, ginger-barbecued salmon, and braised Sonoma rabbit. For dessert, the homemade ice cream is smooth and loaded with flavor. Soft piano entertainment adds to the romantic atmosphere on weekends.

IN NEARBY LITTLE RIVER

✪ **Glendeven.** 8221 N. Calif. 1, Little River, CA 95456. ☎ **800/822-4536** or 707/937-0083. Fax 707/937-6108. 10 rms, 1 cottage. Main house, $90–$105 double Mon–Thurs, $100–$105 double Fri–Sun and all of Aug. Annex, $140–$160 double Mon–Thurs, $125–$140 double Fri–Sun and all of Aug. Cottage, $220 Mon–Thurs, $240 Fri–Sun and all of Aug. Rates include continental breakfast. AE, MC, V.

Named one of the 12 best inns in America by *Country Inns* magazine, this 1867 farmhouse has been converted into an accommodation of exceptional styling and comfort by its designer/owners, Jan and Janet DeVries. The accommodations are spread across 2¹/₂ acres that encompass the main house, the Barn, and an addition known as Stevenscroft. Each room is individually decorated with a well-balanced mixture of antiques and contemporary pieces. We prefer two rooms in the farmhouse (misleadingly called suites, they're really just large rooms). The King's Suite includes an antique walnut bed, and the Eastlin Suite is furnished with a French rosewood bed. The five rooms in the modern annex are large and spacious, but perhaps with less charm. Guests are also housed in a fantastic converted Barn House Suite (the cottage), which can accommodate up to five (perfect for families or groups), and in the Stevenscroft, which has high peaks, a gabled roof, and a barnlike setting. Adjacent to the inn are the numerous fern-lined canyon trails of Van Damme State Park.

Heritage House. 5200 N. Calif. 1, Little River, CA 95456. ☎ **800/235-5885** or 707/ 937-5885. Fax 707/937-0318. 68 rms. Summer, $190–$350 double. Winter, rates drop about 15% in midweek. Rates include breakfast and dinner. Additional person $65 extra. MC, V. Closed Jan 2 to mid-Feb and from after Thanksgiving until Christmas.

This resort was used as the backdrop for the film *Same Time, Next Year.* Most of the rooms at this traditional country club–style property have views of the ocean and rugged coastline. Built in 1877 as a farmhouse and surrounded by 37 seafront acres, the main building's most infamous moment came when it served as a hideout for bandit "Baby Face" Nelson. Much of the inn as you see it dates from 1949, and has been renovated several times since. Only three guest rooms are located in the ivy-covered New England–style main building; the rest are in cottages. The accommodations are decorated with original antiques and locally made furnishings. There's no swimming pool either—just wooded walkways along the dramatic coastline.

The Heritage House dining room offers a $35 fixed-price dinner. The menu changes seasonally, but might include black mussel and saffron chowder and crisp, seared Cornish game hen. Men must wear jackets and reservations are essential.

WHERE TO DINE
EXPENSIVE

✪ **Cafe Beaujolais.** 961 Ukiah St. ☎ **707/937-5614.** Reservations recommended. Main courses $16–$20. No credit cards. Daily 5:45–9pm. AMERICAN/FRENCH.

This is one of Mendocino's—if not Northern California's—top dining choices, owned and managed since 1977 by California chef and entrepreneur Margaret Fox. The venerable French country–style tavern is set in a turn-of-the-century house; rose-colored carnival-glass chandeliers add a burnish to the oak floors and heavy oak tables adorned with flowers. On warm summer nights, request a table at the enclosed deck overlooking the "designer" gardens.

Though the Cafe Beaujolais started out as a breakfast and lunch place, it's strictly a dinner house now (yes, their famed weekend brunch has been discontinued). The menu usually lists about five main courses, such as Yucatecan-Thai crab cakes with spicy avocado salsa and achiote-roasted tomato sauce, or free-range chicken stuffed with eggplant, mushrooms, cheese, garlic, and fresh herbs from local organic farmers. Tuesday to Thursday the cafe offers a prix-fixe Country Menu, which includes an appetizer, an entree (usually a meat dish), and dessert for $20 to $25—a pretty good deal for Beaujolais-quality cuisine.

The 955 Ukiah Street Restaurant. 955 Ukiah St. ☎ **707/937-1955.** Reservations recommended. Main courses $11–$18. MC, V. Wed–Sun 6–10pm. Closed 1 week in June and from after Thanksgiving weekend to Christmas. CALIFORNIA/FRENCH.

Shortly after this building's construction in the 1960s, the region's most famous painter, Emmy Lou Packard, commandeered its premises as an art studio for the creation of a series of giant murals. Today it's a large but surprisingly cozy restaurant, accented with massive railway ties and vaulted ceilings. The tables on the mezzanine level can get a little cramped; if possible, request a window table overlooking the gardens. The cuisine is creative and reasonably priced, a worthy alternative to the perpetually booked Cafe Beaujolais next door. It's hard to recommend a particular main dish, although the phyllo-wrapped red snapper with pesto and lime has a zesty tang, and the crispy duck with ginger, apples, and a Calvados sauce would earn enthusiastic friends in Normandy.

MODERATE

Bay View Café. 45040 Main St. ☎ **707/937-4197.** Reservations not accepted. Dinner $6–$15. No credit cards. Tues–Wed 8am–3pm, Thurs–Mon 8am–9pm. AMERICAN.

This reasonably priced cafe is one of the most popular in town, and the only place around besides the Mendocino Hotel that serves breakfast ("And we're *way* better," says the owner). From the second-floor dining area of the café there's a sweeping view of the Pacific and faraway headlands; to reach it, climb a flight of stairs running up the outside of the town's antique water tower, then detour sideways. Surrounded by dozens of ferns suspended from the ceiling, you'll find a menu with southwestern selections (the marinated chicken breast is very popular), a good array of sandwiches (our favorite is the hot crabmeat with avocado slices), fish and chips, and the fresh catch of the day. Breakfast ranges from the basic bacon-and-eggs to eggs Florentine and honey-wheat pancakes.

The Mousse Cafe. 390 Kasten St. (at Albion St.). ☎ **707/937-4323.** Reservations required for dinner. Main courses $11–$16. No credit cards. Mon–Thurs 11:30am–9pm, Fri 11:30am–10:30pm, Sat 10am–10:30pm, Sun 10am–9pm. CONTINENTAL/CALIFORNIAN.

The setting is a turn-of-the-century clapboard house inspired by the architecture of New England, set in a pleasant garden. In 1995 the place was gutted and the interior was redone; the result is a brand-new, bright, streamlined appearance. The menu includes many local items, particularly organic herbs and vegetables (try the Caesar salad). We enjoyed roast chicken with garlic mashed potatoes, plus a swordfish special with fresh vegetables. The Blackout cake is a chocoholic's fantasy. The food is good and the service is friendly. Our only complaint is that the tables are a bit too close together, especially if it's crowded.

IN NEARBY LITTLE RIVER

Little River Restaurant. 7750 N. Calif. 1, Little River. ☎ **707/937-4945.** Reservations required. Main courses $16.50–$22. No credit cards. July 11–Oct 15, dinner seatings Fri–Tues at 6 and 8:30pm; the rest of the year, dinner seatings Fri–Mon at 6 and 8:30pm. PACIFIC/NORTHWESTERN.

Charming, small-scale, and personal, this restaurant occupies a complex that contains a general market and the hamlet's only post office, across the road from the much larger Little River Inn, with which this place is sometimes confused. The Little River Restaurant is the personal culinary statement of Jeri Barrett, who might be the only chef in the neighborhood who routinely quotes Elizabeth Barrett Browning. It enjoys a winning reputation for dishes like rack of lamb in a brandy-garlic sauce, tenderloin of pork with a ginger-flavored scallion sauce, and red snapper sautéed with lemon-dill butter and shallots. Beer and wine are served, but no hard liquor. Because there are only seven tables, making and keeping your reservations here is extremely important.

4 Fort Bragg

Mendocino County's commercial center—hence the site of most of the area's fast-food restaurants and supermarkets—Fort Bragg is far more down to earth than Mendocino. Inexpensive motels and cheap eats used to be its only attraction, but over the past few years gentrification has quickly spread throughout the town as the logging and fishing industries have continued to decline. With no room left to open new shops in Mendocino, many gallery, boutique, and restaurant owners have moved up the road. The result is a huge increase in Fort Bragg's tourist trade, particularly during the annual Whale Festival in March and during Paul Bunyan Days over Labor Day weekend.

To explore the town properly, make your first stop at the **Fort Bragg / Mendocino Coast Chamber of Commerce,** 332 N. Main St. (P.O. Box 1141), Fort Bragg, CA 95437 (☎ **800/726-2780** or 707/961-6300), and pick up a free walking map. The friendly staff will also answer any other questions about Mendocino, Fort Bragg, and the surrounding region.

SHOPPING & EXPLORING

The town doesn't boast as many well-coiffed stores and galleries as its dainty cousin to the south, but it does have some worthwhile shopping spots. Antiques shops line the 300 block of North Franklin Street, 1 block east of Main Street, while the **old train depot,** at 401 N. Main St. (☎ 707/964-6261), has been turned into a shopping center and historical museum with logging equipment and restored steam trains.

Fort Bragging Rights:
Cutting-Edge Theater Comes to the Mendocino Coast

Living proof that poor, maligned ol' Fort Bragg is on the road to respect is its up-start new theatrical company, the **Warehouse Repertory Theatre.** Determined to make Fort Bragg the Ashland of California, this cadre of highly talented profes-sional actors from around the country have finally answered the age-old Mendocino County question of "So, what is there to do around here at night?" From Shakespeare to Shepard, no play is too shocking or sultry for artistic director Meg Patterson and her crew, who have been bathed in nothing but kudos for the fresh, significant works they have brought to the north coast.

The Warehouse's season runs from late February to December, with performances Thursday to Saturday (and the occasional Monday) at 8pm, with Sunday matinees at 2pm. For information about current shows, future plays, or to reserve tickets (which range from $10 to $15), call the box office (☎ **707/961-2940**).

For the Shell of It, 344 N. Main St. (☎ 707/961-0461), stocks handmade jew-elry, baskets, and collectibles made of shells or designed around a nautical theme. **The Hot Pepper Jelly Company,** 330 N. Main St. (☎ 707/961-1422), is famous for the assortment of Mendocino food products that it offers—dozens of varieties of pep-per jelly, plus local mustards, syrups, and biscotti along with hand-painted porcelain bowls, unusual baskets, and more. The **Mendocino Chocolate Company,** 542 N. Main St. (☎ 707/964-8800), makes and sells homemade chocolates and truffles, which it ships all over the world. Painters, jewelers, sculptors, weavers, potters, and other local artists display their works at **Northcoast Artists,** 362 N. Main St. (☎ 707/964-8266). At **Windsong,** 324 N. Main St. (☎ 707/964-2050), you'll find a clutter of colorful kites, cards, candles, and other gifts.

Fort Bragg is the county's sportfishing center. Just south of town, **Noyo's Fish-ing Center,** 3245 North Harbor, Noyo (☎ **707/964-7609**), is a good place to buy or rent tackle, and the best source of information on local fishing boats. Lots of party boats leave from the town's harbor, as do whale-watching tours.

Lost Coast Adventures, North Coast Divers Supply, 19275 S. Harbor Dr. (☎ **800/961-1143,** or 707/961-1143), offers scuba diving, fishing, and whale-watching expeditions, as well as kayak tours of the coastline and coastal rivers.

Fort Bragg is also the home of the **Mendocino Coast Botanical Gardens,** 18220 N. Calif. 1 (☎ **707/964-4352**), about 8 miles north of Mendocino. This clifftop public garden, set among the pines along the rugged coast, nurtures rhodo-dendrons, fuchsias, azaleas, and a multitude of flowering shrubs. The area contains bridges, streams, canyons, dells, picnic areas, and trails for easy walking. Admission is $5 for adults, $4 for seniors 60 and over, $3 for children 13 to 17, $1 for children 6 to 12, and free for children 5 and under. (Children under 18 must be accompa-nied by an adult.) Open March to October, daily from 9am to 5pm; November to February, daily from 9am to 4pm.

From Fort Bragg, the **Skunk Train** (☎ **707/964-6371**) gives riders a fine tour of the area's redwoods. Locals have always said of the logging trains that "You can smell 'em before you can see 'em"—which explains the nickname. The trains, which can be boarded at the Fort Bragg Depot at the foot of Laurel Avenue in Fort Bragg (2 blocks from the Grey Whale Inn), travel 40 miles inland along the Redwood High-way (U.S. 101) to Willits. It's a scenic route through the redwood forest, crossing

31 bridges and trestles and cutting through two deep tunnels. The round-trip takes 6 to 7 hours, allowing plenty of time for lunch in Willits before you return on the afternoon train. Half-day trips are offered on weekends throughout the year, and daily from mid-June to early September (in summer call for reservations). The trains run year round but schedules vary so call for exact times. Tickets cost $26 round-trip, $21 one-way; children 5 to 11 board for half price.

Three miles north of Fort Bragg off Calif. 1 lies **Mackerricher State Park** (☎ 707/937-5804), a popular place for biking, hiking, and horseback riding. This enormous 1,700-acre park has 142 campsites and 8 miles of shoreline. For a true biking or hiking venture, travel the 8-mile-long "Haul Road," an old logging road that provides fine ocean vistas all the way to Ten Mile River. Harbor seals make their home at the park's Laguna Point Seal Watching Station, reached via an elevated wooden gangway (truly a pleasant walk).

WHERE TO STAY

Grey Whale Inn. 615 N. Main St., Fort Bragg, CA 95437. ☎ **800/382-7244** or 707/964-0640. Fax 707/964-4408. 11 rms, 5 suites. TEL. $100–$170 double; $180 suite. Rates include buffet breakfast. Discounted winter rates available midweek Nov–Mar. AE, DISC, JCB, MC, V.

A comfortable B&B 6 blocks from the beach and 2 blocks from the Skunk Train depot, this 1915 landmark was originally built as a hospital. The spacious and airy redwood building has become a well-run, relaxed inn, furnished partly with antiques and plenty of local art. Each guest room is unique: Two have ocean views, three have fireplaces, and one has a whirlpool tub; two have private decks and one offers a shower with wheelchair access. The buffet breakfast includes homemade bread or coffeecake and fresh fruit. No smoking.

Pudding Creek Inn. 700 N. Main St., Fort Bragg, CA 95437. ☎ **800/227-9529** or 707/964-9529. Fax 707/961-0282. 10 rms. $70–$130 double. Rates include breakfast. AE, DISC, MC, V.

The Pudding Creek Inn is actually two separate houses, built in 1884 by a Russian count. They're connected by an enclosed pebbled garden court filled with flowering plants, a stone fountain, and patio furnishings. Although some of the rooms are rather small, each is uniquely decorated, comfortable, and colorful, and has a private bath.

Despite its name, the Main House contains fewer rooms than the adjacent two-story annex. The Count's Room features a huge stone fireplace and a king-size brass bed. It's a beautiful room, but faces the noisy highway. The rooms in back are quieter; the best is called Interlude, and contains a king-size bed, oversize shower, and fireplace. The B&B's guest phone is located in the garden. There's a TV and recreation room, plus a parlor where afternoon tea, wine, and cheese are served. A full buffet breakfast is offered in an attractive room that contains tall bay windows, antique tables, and a fireplace.

WHERE TO DINE

North Coast Brewing Company. 444 N. Main St. ☎ **707/964-3400.** Reservations accepted for large parties only. Main courses $6–$17. DISC, MC, V. Summer, Tues–Sun 2–11pm. Winter, Tues–Fri 4–11pm, Sat 2–11pm. AMERICAN.

This homey brew pub is the most happening place in town, especially at happy hour when the bar and dark-wood tables are occupied by boisterous locals. The building that houses the pub is a dignified, century-old redwood structure, which in previous lives has functioned as a mortuary, an annex to the local Presbyterian church, an art studio, and administrative offices for the College of the Redwoods. Beer is brewed on the premises, in large copper vats that are displayed behind plate glass. A pale ale, a pilsner, a stout, and a fourth seasonal brew are always available. Standard brew-pub fare, such as burgers and barbecued chicken sandwiches, are supplemented by more substantial dishes, ranging from linguine with smoked mushrooms to a hefty pile of country-style Carolina barbecued pork. After lunch, browse the retail shop or take a free tour of the brewery.

The Restaurant. 418 Main St. ☎ **707/964-9800.** Reservations recommended. Lunch $6:50–$10; dinner $14–$20. MC, V. Mon–Tues 5–9pm, Thurs–Fri 11:30am–2pm and 5–9pm, Sat 5–9pm, Sun 9am–1pm and 5–9pm. PACIFIC NORTHWESTERN/CALIFORNIA.

This authentic local restaurant is housed in a Victorian building. The art on the walls is by a local artist, who also plays jazz bass and sometimes performs here on weekends. The menu features four fish and four meat dishes, including chicken marsala and grilled halibut with sweet-pepper relish. There are also a few vegetarian specialties, including grilled polenta with melted mozzarella and sautéed mushrooms topped with tomato-herb sauce and parmesan cheese. The tangy appetizers are likely to include corn fritters with fresh pineapples and chili sauce, and shrimp relleno with green-tomato sauce.

5 The Avenue of the Giants & Ferndale

From Fort Bragg, Calif. 1 continues north along the shoreline for about 30 miles before turning inland to Leggett and U.S. 101, known as the "Redwood Highway," which runs north to Garberville. Six miles beyond Garberville, the Avenue of the Giants begins around Phillipsville; it's an alternative route that roughly parallels U.S. 101, and there are about half a dozen interchanges between U.S. 101 and the Avenue of the Giants if you don't want to drive the whole thing. It's one of the most spectacular scenic routes in the west (California 254), cutting along the Eel River through the 51,000-acre Humboldt Redwoods State Park. The Avenue ends just south of Scotia; from here, it's only about 10 miles to the turnoff to Ferndale, about 5 miles west of U.S. 101.

For more information or a detailed map of the area, go to the **Humboldt Redwood State Park Visitor Center,** P.O. Box 276, Weott, CA 95571 (☎ **707/946-2263**), just north of Hidden Springs State Campground, 2 miles south of Weott. The **Chimney Tree,** Avenue of the Giants (P.O. Box 395), Garberville, CA 95542 (☎ **707/923-2265**), is another place to secure information about the area.

About 33 miles long, the Avenue of the Giants was left intact for sightseers when the freeway was built. The giants, of course, are the majestic coast redwoods (*Sequoia sempervirens*); more than 50,000 acres of them make up the most outstanding display in the redwood belt. Their rough-bark columns climb 100 feet or more without a branch and soar to a total height of more than 340 feet. They're immune to insects, and their bark is fire resistant, so they've survived for thousands of years. The oldest dated coast redwood is more than 2,200 years old.

The state park has three **campgrounds** with 248 campsites: Hidden Springs, half a mile south of Myers Flat; Burlington, 2 miles south of Weott, near park headquarters; and Albee Creek State Campground, 5 miles west of U.S. 101 on the Mattole Road north of Weott. You'll also come across picnic and swimming facilities, motels, resorts, restaurants, and numerous resting and parking areas.

Sadly, the route has several tacky attractions that attempt to turn the trees into some kind of freak show. Our suggestion is to skip these and appreciate the trees by taking advantage of the trails and the campgrounds off the beaten path. As you drive along, you'll see numerous parking areas with short loop trails leading into the forest. From south to north the first of these "attractions" is the **Chimney Tree** (☎ 707/923-2265), where J. R. R. Tolkien's Hobbit is rumored to reside. This living, hollow redwood is more than 1,500 years old. Nearby is a gift shop and a burger place. Then there's the **One-Log House,** a small apartmentlike house built inside a log. At Myers Flat, midway along the Avenue, you can also drive your car through a living redwood at the **Shrine Drive Thru Tree.**

A few miles north of Weott is **Founders Grove,** named in honor of those who established the Save the Redwoods League in 1918. Farther north, close to the end of the Avenue, stands the 950-year-old Immortal Tree, just north of Redcrest. Near Pepperwood at the end of the Avenue, the Drury Trail and the Percy French Trail are two good short hikes. The park itself is also good for mountain biking. Ask the rangers for details. For more information, contact **Humboldt Redwoods State Park,** P.O. Box 100, Weott, CA 95571 (☎ 707/946-2409).

WHERE TO STAY & DINE NEAR THE SOUTHERN ENTRANCE TO THE AVENUE OF THE GIANTS

Benbow Inn. 445 Lake Benbow Dr., Garberville, CA 95542. ☎ **800/355-3301** or 707/923-2124. Fax 707/923-2897. 55 rms, 1 cottage. A/C TEL. $120–$220 double; $295 cottage. AE, DISC, MC, V.

This national historic landmark overlooking the Eel River, off U.S. 101, was designed by Albert Farr in 1925; pretty Benbow Lake State Park is right out the front door. It's built in a mock-Tudor style, and guests enter through a grand hall with cherrywood wainscoting. The rooms in the main building have fireplaces, TVs, private entrances, and patios, and some have VCRs, too. A comfortable annex, with elegant woodwork, was added in the 1980s. Bicycles are available.

Complimentary afternoon tea and scones are served in the lobby at 3pm (there's mulled wine in winter), plus complimentary hors d'oeuvres in the lounge. The dramatic high-ceilinged dining room opens onto a spacious terrace and offers internationally inspired main courses ($12 to $20).

FERNDALE

Beyond the Avenue of the Giants and west of U.S. 101, the village of Ferndale has been declared a historic landmark because of its many Victorian homes and storefronts, including a smithy and a saddlery. About 5 miles inland from the coast and close to the redwood belt, Ferndale is one of the best-preserved Victorian hamlets in Northern California. In spite of its unbearably cute shops, it's nonetheless a vital part of the northern coastal tourist circuit. The small town has a number of artists in residence, and is also the home of one of the oddest California events, the **World Championship Great Arcata to Ferndale Cross-Country Kinetic Sculpture Race,** a bizarre 3-day event run every Memorial Day weekend. The race, which draws more than 10,000 spectators, is run over land and water in whimsically designed human-powered vehicles. Stop in at the museum at 780 Main St. if you want to see some recent race entries.

WHERE TO STAY

✪ **Gingerbread Mansion.** 400 Berding St. (P.O. Box 40), Ferndale, CA 95536. ☎ **800/952-4136** or 707/786-4000. Fax 707/786-4381. 5 rms, 5 suites. $140–$180 double; $150–$350 suite. Additional person $40 extra. Rates include continental breakfast and afternoon tea. AE, MC, V.

This peach-and-yellow structure with stained glass and other fine architectural details is one of Ferndale's most photographed Victorians; it was built in 1899 as the home of a local doctor and his family. Run by Ken and Sandie Torbert, it's beautifully furnished with antiques. Some of the large guest rooms have two old-fashioned clawfoot tubs for bubble baths for two, and others offer fireplaces. The latest addition is the attic-level Empire Suite, a lavish spare-no-expense blowout with Ionic columns, massage-jet shower, two fireplaces, and a king-size bed draped with Royal Sateen linens. Bathrobes and extra-large thick towels are provided. The beds are turned down for the night, and you'll find hand-dipped chocolates on the nightstand. The mansion has bicycles and umbrellas for guests to use. Smoking is only permitted on the verandas.

When you rise, there's morning coffee or tea outside your door, enough to sustain you until your breakfast of fruit, cheese, muffins, breads, cakes, and a baked egg dish. Afternoon tea with sandwiches, pastries, fresh fruit, and Devonshire cream is also served.

WHERE TO DINE

Curley's Grill. 460 Main St. ☎ **707/786-9696.** Reservation recommended. Main courses $9–$18. DISC, MC, V. Daily 11:30am–9pm (last order). CALIFORNIA GRILL.

Set in what looks like a clapboard Victorian farmhouse, across the street from Ferndale's Repertory Theater, this is a bright and lively restaurant that specializes exclusively in California-inspired grilled foods. Don't think for a moment that the menu is limited to steaks, however: Owner Curley Tait offers items that you may never have considered grillable, including polenta with a sausage-tomato sauce, a medley of Pacific seafish, and some of the freshest vegetables on the California coast. The interior decor is a vaguely art deco setting showcasing local artists' works, but the best seating is behind the kitchen in the secluded back patio. Curley's also offers a small but interesting selection of California wines.

6 Eureka & Environs

EUREKA

At first glance Eureka (pop. 27,000) doesn't look very appealing; fast-food restaurants, cheap motels, and shopping malls predominate on the main thoroughfare. But if you turn west off U.S. 101 anywhere between A and M streets, you'll discover Old Town Eureka along the waterfront, which is worth exploring. It has a large number of Victorian buildings, a museum, and some good-quality stores and restaurants.

The **Clarke Memorial Museum,** 240 E St. (☎ 707/443-1947), has a fine collection of Native American baskets and other historic artifacts. The other popular attraction is the extraordinary architectural gem, the **Carson House,** built in 1884–86 for lumber baron William Carson. A three-story conglomeration of ornamentation, it's designed in a melange of styles—Queen Anne, Italianate, Stick, and Eastlake. It took 100 men more than 2 years to build. Today it's a private club, so you can only marvel at the exterior of this 18-room mansion—said to be the most photographed Victorian home in America—from the sidewalk. Across the street stands the **"Pink Lady,"** designed for William Carson as a wedding present for his son. Both testify to the wealth that was once made in Eureka's lumber trade. As early as 1856 there were already seven sawmills producing two million board feet of lumber every month.

Humboldt Bay, where the town stands, was discovered by whites in 1850. In 1853 Fort Humboldt was established to protect the white settlements from local Native American tribes. Ulysses S. Grant was stationed here for 5 months until he resigned after serious disputes with his commanding officer about his drinking. The fort was abandoned in 1870. Today the fort offers a self-guided trail past a series of logging exhibits, plus a reconstructed surgeon's quarters and a restored fort hospital, used today as a museum housing Native American artifacts and military and pioneer paraphernalia. **Fort Humboldt State Historic Park** is at 3431 Fort Ave. (☎ **707/ 445-6567**). Admission is free; open daily from 9am to 5pm.

Humboldt Bay supplies a large portion of California's fish, and Eureka has a fishing fleet of about 200 boats. To get a better view (and perspective) of the bay and surrounding waters, you can board skipper Leroy Zerlang's *Madaket*—the oldest passenger-carrying vessel in operation in the United States, so they say—for a 75-minute **Humboldt Bay Harbor Cruise** (☎ 707/445-1910), departing daily from the foot of C Street in downtown Eureka.

More active water recreation includes fishing for halibut, king salmon, steelhead, and even shark, depending on the season. A license is required and can be secured for 1 day. For information, contact **Larry's Guide Service,** 3380 Utah St. (☎ **707/ 444-0250**). Fishing information can also be obtained from the **Eureka Fly Shop,** 505 H St. (☎ **707/444-2000**), and kayaks and sailboats can be rented from **Hum Boats,** located on F Street (☎ **707/443-5157**), which also provides tours and lessons.

Humboldt County is also suitable for biking, because it's relatively uncongested. Bikes can be rented from **Pro Sport Center,** 508 Myrtle Ave. (☎ **707/443-6328**).

Humboldt Bay is an important stopover point along the Pacific Flyway and is the winter home for thousands of migratory birds. South of town, the **Humboldt Bay National Wildlife Refuge,** 1020 Ranch Rd., Loleta, CA 95551 (☎ **707/733-5406**), provides an opportunity to see many of the 200 or so species that live in the marshes and willow groves—Pacific black brant, western sandpiper, northern harrier, great blue heron, and green-winged teal. The egret rookery on the bay, best viewed from Woodley Island Marina across the bay en route to Samoa, is spectacular. Peak viewing for most species of waterbirds and raptors is between September and March. The refuge's entrance is off U.S. 101 north at the Hookton Road exit; cross the overpass and turn right onto Ranch Road.

For information, contact the **Eureka/Humboldt County Convention and Visitors Bureau,** 1034 2nd St., Eureka, CA 95501 (☎ **800/346-3482** or 707/ 443-5097; fax 707/443-5115), or the **Eureka Chamber of Commerce,** 2112 Broadway, Eureka, CA 95501 (☎ **800/356-6381** or 707/442-3738).

WHERE TO STAY

✪ An Elegant Victorian Mansion Bed & Breakfast Experience. 14th and C sts., Eureka, CA 95501. ☎ **707/444-3144.** Fax 707/442-5594. 5 rms. $85–$165 double. Rates include breakfast. MC, V.

For anyone interested in social history and design, this is a special experience. Those who just want comfort, service, a true gourmet breakfast, and a lovely garden to enjoy, will also find this lodging ideal. The 1888 house is the labor of love of owners Doug and Lily Vieyra, who have combed the country for the wallpapers, fabrics, and designs that now provide the most authentic Victorian atmosphere we have ever encountered in the United States. The wallpapers are extraordinary, including brilliant blues, golds, jades, and reds in intricate patterns that feature peacocks and mythological figures. Doug has paid attention to every detail, from the butler who greets you in morning dress down to the silent movies and period music on the phonograph. The rooms are individually furnished. The Van Gogh Room contains the Belgian bedroom suite of Lily's mother. The Lily Langtry Room, named after the actress and king's mistress who stayed here when she performed locally, features a four-poster bed and Langtry memorabilia. Services include laundry and Swedish massage. Bikes and a sauna are available, and croquet is played on the manicured lawn, where ice-cream sodas and lemonade are served in the afternoon. No smoking is allowed.

☉ Hotel Carter. Carter House and Bell Cottage, 301 L St., Eureka, CA 95501. ☎ **800/ 404-1390** or 707/445-1390. Fax 707/444-8062. 29 rms, 2 suites. TV TEL. $65–$145 double; $95–$225 suite. AE, DC, MC, V. From U.S. 101 north, turn left onto L St. and go to 3rd.

At the north end of Eureka's Old Town is the original building that launched Carter's renowned hostelry empire: the Carter House. Copied from a famous 1884 San Francisco Victorian, it was constructed by Mark Carter as a family home in 1982. Soon afterward Mark and his wife, Christi Carter, began taking guests, and before long they built another 20-room hotel across the street. Later the pretty Victorian Bell Cottage was acquired. The 20 rooms in the large full-service hotel are furnished in modern style with pine four-posters. The suites have such luxury appointments as VCRs, fireplaces, and Jacuzzis with distant views of the waterfront from the Jacuzzi tubs. There are seven rooms in the original house, which is furnished with antiques, Oriental rugs, and modern artworks. The Bell Cottage's rooms are also individually decorated in fine style. On ground level is one of Eureka's finest restaurants (see "Where to Dine," below).

WHERE TO DINE

Ramone's Bakery & Cafe. 209 E St. ☎ **707/445-2923.** Main courses $4–$6. No credit cards. Cafe, Mon–Sat 7am–6pm, Sun 8am–5pm. BAKERY.

Ramone's combines a bakery on one side with a small cafe on the other. The baked items are extraordinary—try any one of the croissants, danish, or muffins and you won't be disappointed. Alas, the once-popular restaurant has closed down, but you can still find a few lunch specials to choose from among the breads and pastries. At any time of the day it's a great place to stop in for a light, inexpensive meal and cup of coffee. There's a second location at 2223 Harrison St. in Eureka, as well as two more in Arcata: 600 F St., and 747 13th St. at Wildberries Marketplace.

☉ Restaurant 301. In the Hotel Carter, 301 L St. ☎ **707/444-8062.** Reservations required in summer. Main courses $10–$18. AE, DC, DISC, MC, V. Daily 6–9pm. CALIFORNIA.

The large, light, and airy dining room adjacent to the hotel's lobby has tall windows looking out on the waterfront. It's one of the best restaurants in the area, with most of the herbs and many of the vegetables picked fresh from the hotel's organic gardens across the street. Predominantly Californian, the cuisine displays Asian accents—for example, in the tiger prawns with sesame, ginger, and soy, and the chicken with spicy peanut sauce. If you're an oyster lover, start with a few Humboldt Bay oysters roasted with barbecue sauce. The hotel's proprietor, Mark Carter, offers an excellent and extensive wine list, courtesy of his 301 Wine Shop in the hotel.

Samoa Cookhouse. Cookhouse Rd., Samoa. ☎ **707/442-1659.** Reservations accepted only for large groups. Main courses $10.95. AE, MC, V. Mon–Sat 6am–3:30pm and 5–10pm, Sun 6am–10pm. From U.S. 101, take Samoa Bridge to the end and turn left on Samoa Rd. then take the first left. AMERICAN.

When lumber was king, cookhouses like this one dating from 1885 were common and were the hub of the community. Here the millmen and longshoremen at the Hammond Lumber Company came to chow down three hot meals before, during, and after their 12-hour workday. The food is still hearty—though not particularly healthy—and served family style at long red-checkered cloth-covered tables; nobody leaves hungry. The price includes soup, salad, fresh-baked bread, the main course, and dessert (usually pie). The lunch and dinner menu still features a different dish each day—roast beef, fried chicken, or pork chops. Breakfast typically includes eggs, sausage, bacon, pancakes, and all the orange juice and coffee you can drink. Adjacent to the dining room is a small museum featuring memorabilia from the lumbering era.

ARCATA

From Eureka it's only 7 miles to Arcata, one of our favorite towns on the northern coast. Sort of a cross between Mayberry and Berkeley, it has an undeniable small-town flavor—right down to the bucolic town square—yet possesses that intellectual and environmentally conscious esprit de corps so characteristic of university towns (Arcata is the home of Humboldt State University).

There are loads of things to do here. On Wednesday, Friday, and Saturday evenings between June and July, Arcata's semi-pro baseball team, the **Humboldt Crabs,** take part in America's favorite pastime at Arcata Ballpark, at 9th and F streets. Also worth a stop are the **Humboldt State University Natural History Museum,** 1315 G St. (☎ 707/826-4479), which is open Tuesday to Saturday; **Tin Can Mailman,** 10th and H streets (☎ 702/822-1307), a wonderful used-book store with more than 130,000 titles; **Redwood Park,** at the east end of 11th Street, which has an outstanding playground for kids and miles of forested hiking trails; and the **Humboldt Brewing Company,** 10th and I streets (☎ 702/826-BREW), creators of the heavenly Red Nectar Ale (call for tour information).

The **Arcata Marsh and Wildlife Sanctuary,** at the foot of South I Street (☎ 707/ 826-2359), is another worthwhile excursion. The 154-acre sanctuary—which doubles as Arcata's integrated wetland wastewater-treatment plant—is a popular stopover for march wrens, egrets, and other waterfowl, including the rare Arctic loon. Each Saturday at 8:30am (rain or shine) the Audubon Society gives free 1-hour guided tours at the cul-de-sac at the foot of South I Street.

Heading east from Arcata, Calif. 299 leads to the **Trinity River** in the heart of **Six Rivers National Forest.** Willowcreek and Somes Bar are the prime recreational centers for the area. Here visitors can sign up for canoeing, rafting, and kayaking trips with such outfitters as **Aurora River Adventures,** P.O. 938, Willow Creek, CA 95573 (☎ 800/562-8475, or 916/629-3843), which offers some offbeat, educationally oriented adventures that are great for kids, as well as gnarly Class V trips for the more daring. Other outfitters include **Laughing Heart Adventures/Trinity Outdoor Center,** Willow Creek (☎ 916/629-3516); **Big Foot Rafting Company,** Willow Creek (☎ 800/722-2223, or 916/629-2263); and **Klamath River Outfitters,** 3 Sandy Bar Rd., Somes Bar (☎ 916/469-3349).

A few miles north of Willow Creek lies the Hoopa Indian Reservation. In the Hoopa Shopping Center, the **Hoopa Tribal Museum** (☎ 916/625-4110) archives the culture and history of the native people of Northern California—their ceremonial regalia, basketry, canoes, and tools. Open Monday to Friday from 8am to 5pm.

WHERE TO STAY

Hotel Arcata. 708 9th St., Arcata, CA 95521. ☎ **800/344-1221** or 707/826-0217. Fax 707/826-1737. 32 rms. TV TEL. $110–$150 double. Rates include continental breakfast. AE, DC, DISC, MC, V.

This is the town's most prominent hotel, and many guests are parents visiting their ungrateful offspring at Humboldt State University. Located at the northeast corner of the town plaza, its handsome turn-of-the-century brick facade belies a rather bland, modern interior; few of its original furnishings remain. The bedrooms have a rather characterless decor, but they're safe and comfortable lodgings nonetheless. On the premises, under different management, is a Japanese restaurant, Tomo.

✪ **The Lady Anne.** 902 14th St., Arcata, CA 95521. ☎ **707/822-2797.** 5 rooms. $90–$130 double. Rates include breakfast. MC, V.

Easily Arcata's finest lodging, this Queen Anne–style bed-and-breakfast is kept in top-notch condition by innkeepers Sharon Ferrett and Sam Pennisi, who also served a term as Arcata's mayor. The large, cozy guest rooms are individually decorated with period antiques, lace curtains, Oriental rugs, and English stained glass. For second honeymooners there's the Lady Sarah Angela Room with its four-poster bed and pleasant bay view. The Cinnamon Bear Room sleeps up to four on its king-size trundle beds, which makes it an obvious choice for parents with kids in tow. Breakfast is served in the grand dining room, warmed on winter mornings by a toasty fire. On summer afternoons the recreation of choice is to lounge on the veranda with a book or play a game of croquet on the front lawn. Several good dining options are only a few blocks away at Arcata Plaza.

WHERE TO DINE

Abruzzi/Plaza Grill. 791 8th St. (at H St.). ☎ **707/826-2345** (Abruzzi) or 707/826-0860 (Plaza Grill). Reservations recommended. Abruzzi, main courses $8–$18. Plaza Grill, platters and salads $5–$10. AE, DISC, MC, V. Plaza Grill, Sun–Mon 5–10, Tues–Fri 5–11pm. Abruzzi, Thurs–Fri 11:30–2pm and 5–10pm, Sat–Wed 5–10pm. ITALIAN/AMERICAN.

The best way to review your dining options in Arcata is to stroll to the downtown area's most distinctive minimall, the Jacoby Storehouse (a deftly converted mid-19th-century warehouse) and peer into both of these restaurants.

Abruzzi, on the street level, is the more formal and substantial of the two, and is generally acknowledged as the best restaurant in town. Menu items include chicken Frascati (with artichoke hearts, mushrooms, and marsala), pastas, veal dishes, and well-seasoned filet steaks.

On the building's third floor is the Plaza Grill. Despite efforts to make it more upscale, it can't seem to shake its image as a college-student burger joint. The menu, however, is more substantial than you'd think, with a choice of salads, sandwiches, fish platters, and burgers.

TRINIDAD & PATRICK'S POINT STATE PARK

Back on U.S. 101 north of Arcata, you'll come to Trinidad, a tiny coastal fishing village of some 400 people. One of the smallest incorporated cities in California, it occupies a peninsula 25 miles north of Eureka. If you're not into fishing, there's little to do in town expect poke around at the handful of shops, walk along the busy pier, and wish you owned a house here.

Five miles north of Trinidad takes you to the 640-acre **Patrick's Point State Park,** 4150 Patrick's Point Dr. (☎ 707/677-3570), which has one of the finest ocean access points in the north at sandy **Agate Beach.** It's suitable for driftwood picking, rockhounding, and camping on a sheltered bluff. The park contains a re-creation of a Sumeg village, which is actively used by the Yurok people and neighboring tribes. A self-guided tour takes you to replicas of family homes and sweat houses.

WHERE TO STAY

✪ **The Lost Whale Inn.** 3452 Patrick's Point Dr., Trinidad, CA 95570. ☎ **800/677-7859** or 707/677-3425. Fax 707/677-0284. 8 rms. Summer, $130–$160 double. Winter, $80–$130 double. Rates include country breakfast. AE, MC, V.

This modern version of a blue-and-gray Cape Cod–style house is set on 4 acres of seafront land studded with firs, alders, spruces, and redwoods. Its owners cater to children (there's a playground on the premises and mini-zoo up the street) and adults (there's also a Jacuzzi with a view of the sea), and claim (arguably) that it's the only hotel in the state of California with its own private beach. Afternoon tea and an artfully prepared and presented breakfast are included in the rates.

The inn's name derives from a civic drama that unfolded in Trinidad the year it was built: A whale was stranded on the rocks offshore. Although somewhat reticent, the owners will tell you the story if you ask. The decor is eclectic, with lots of statuary and paintings, and an outdoor deck facing the surf. Part of the grounds are devoted to a kitchen garden with fresh herbs and vegetables. The rooms are comfortable, and don't have phones or TVs, so you can escape from the rest of the world. Families should inquire about the furnished homes—including a wonderful farmhouse—that the innkeepers also rent out.

Trinidad Bay Bed & Breakfast. 560 Edwards St. (P.O. Box 849), Trinidad, CA 95570. ☎ **707/677-0840.** 2 rms, 2 suites. $125 double; $155 suite. Rates include breakfast. MC, V. Closed Dec–Jan.

Set 175 feet above the ocean, all rooms at this picturesque Cape Cod–style home have sweeping views of Trinidad Bay—on a clear day, you can see up to 65 miles of the rugged coastline. Your hosts are Paul and Carol Kirk, two seasoned innkeepers who have created what many visitors think is the most charming inn around. Rare for an older B&B, both the rooms and the suites have private bathrooms. The decor throughout is an eclectic mix of New England–style antiques and more recent reproductions. If it's available, opt for the Mauve Fireplace Suite, with its wraparound window, large wood-burning fireplace, king-size bed, and private entrance.

WHERE TO DINE

❂ **Larrupin Café.** 1658 Patrick's Point Dr. ☎ **707/677-0230.** Reservations required. Main courses $10–$20. No credit cards. Summer, Wed–Mon 5–9pm; winter, Thurs–Sun 5–9pm. AMERICAN.

On a quiet country road 2 miles north of Trinidad, this highly praised restaurant sports an eclectic blend of Indonesian and African artifacts mingled with paintings by Northern California artists and massive bouquets of flowers. The food is often barbecued over mesquite fires, and includes fish (halibut and ahi tuna, among others) that are basted with lemon-butter and served with a portion of mustard-flavored dill sauce. Other items include barbecued Cornish game hen served with an orange-and-brandy glaze. For appetizers, the barbecued oysters are perfectly delightful, especially in winter, when a fireplace casts a welcome warmth.

The Seascape Restaurant. Beside the Pier at the foot of Bay Street. ☎ **707/677-3762.** Reservations accepted. Full dinners $9–$20. MC, V. Daily 7am–9pm. CALIFORNIA.

Established in the 1940s, this is an unpretentious cross between a cafe and a diner, with three dining rooms, overworked but cheerful waitresses, and a nostalgic aura. Folks pop in for coffee or snacks from early morning till after sundown, but by far the biggest seller here is the Trinidad bay platter ($15.95). Heaped with halibut, scallops, shrimp, and accompanied by salad and rice pilaf, it's even more popular than the prawn brochette, which draws a close second.

ORICK

From Trinidad it's about another 15 miles to Orick. You can't miss it—just look for the dozens of burl stands alongside the road. Carved with chisels and chainsaws, these former redwood logs have been transformed into just about every creature you can imagine—perhaps a gift for your mother-in-law?

At the south end of Orick is the town's only saving grace, the sleek **Redwood National Park Information Center,** P.O. Box 7, Orick, CA 95555 (☎ 707/ 488-3461). If you plan to spend any amount of time exploring the park, stop here first and pick up a free map; the displays of fauna and wildlife aren't too bad, either. It's open daily from 9am to 5pm.

The first of the parks that make up Redwood National Park, **Prairie Creek,** is 6 miles north of Orick. About 14 miles farther on is the mouth of the **Klamath River,** famous for its salmon, trout, and steelhead. Tours aboard a jet boat take visitors upriver from the estuary to view bear, deer, elk, osprey hawks, otters, and more along the riverbanks. It's about $20 for a 30-mile trip. For information, contact **Klamath River Jet Boat Tours,** Klamath (☎ 800/887-JETS or 707/482-7775). From Klamath it's another 20 miles to Crescent City, gateway to the other parks that make up Redwood National Park.

7 Crescent City, Gateway to Redwood National Park

Crescent City itself has little to offer, but it makes a good base for exploring Redwood National Park and the Smith River, one of the great recreational rivers of the West. The **Battery Point Lighthouse,** at the foot of A Street (☎ 707/464-3089), which is accessible on foot only at low tide, houses a museum with exhibits on the coast's history. Tours of the lighthouse are offered April to September, Wednesday to Sunday from 10am to 4pm, weather permitting.

In addition to the national park, another draw is the **Smith River Recreation Area,** east of Jedediah Smith State Park and part of Six Rivers National Forest. The headquarters is at the Gasquet Ranger Station, 10600 U.S. 199, Gasquet, CA 95543 (☎ 707/457-3131), which is reached via U.S. 199 from Crescent City (19 miles, about a 30-minute drive). Maps of the forest can be obtained here, at the Supervisor's Office in Eureka, or at the Redwood National Park centers in Orick and Crescent City.

The 300,000-plus acres of wilderness offer camping at five modest-sized campgrounds (all with less than 50 sites), along the Smith River. Sixteen trails attract hikers from across the country. The easiest short trail is the **McClendon Ford,** which is 2 miles long and drops from 1,000 to 800 feet in elevation to the south fork of the river. Other activities include mountain biking, white-water rafting, kayaking, and fishing for salmon and trout.

For information, contact the **Crescent City–Del Norte County Chamber of Commerce,** 1001 Front St., Crescent City, CA 95531 (☎ 707/464-3174).

WHERE TO STAY

Crescent Beach Motel. 1455 Redwood Hwy. South (U.S. 101), Crescent City, CA 95531. ☎ **707/464-5436.** 28 rms. TV. Summer, $63–$68 double. Winter, $49–$52 double. AE, DISC, MC, V.

Near the highway, about 2 miles south of town, this single-story structure is the only local motel set directly on the beach. It has simple, old-fashioned bedrooms, without phone or cooking facilities, but with an undeniably rustic, outdoorsy appeal. Four of the units face the highway; try to get one of the others, which all have decks and doors opening directly onto the sands. There's no restaurant or bar on the premises, but one of the city's most popular restaurants, the Beachcomber (see "Where to Dine," below), is located next door.

Curly Redwood Lodge. 701 Redwood Hwy. South (U.S. 101), Crescent City, CA 95531. ☎ **707/464-2137.** 36 rms. TV TEL. Summer, $59–$64 double. Winter, $37–$39 double. AE, DC, MC, V.

This is a blast from the past, the kind of place where you might have stayed as a kid during one of those cross-country vacations in the family station wagon. It was built in 1959 on grasslands across from the town's harbor, and completely trimmed with lumber from a single ancient redwood. Although they're not full of the latest high-tech gadgets, the bedrooms are among the largest and best-soundproofed in town, and certainly the most evocative of a bygone, more innocent age. In winter about a third of the bedrooms (the ones upstairs) are locked and sealed. Overall, the aura is more akin to Oregon than to anything you might imagine in California.

WHERE TO DINE

Beachcomber. 1400 U.S. 101. ☎ **707/464-2205.** Reservations recommended. Main courses $6–$15. MC, V. Thurs–Tues 5–9pm. SEAFOOD.

The decor is as predictably nautical as its name implies: rough-cut planking, a scattering of artfully arranged driftwood, fishnets, and buoys dangling above a dimly lit space. The restaurant lies beside the beach, 2 miles south of Crescent City's center. Its fans cite it as one of the two best restaurants in town. The cuisine is a joy to fish lovers who prefer not to mask the flavor of their seafood with complicated sauces. Most of the dishes are grilled over madrone-wood barbecue pits, a technique perfected since this place was established in 1975. Pacific salmon, halibut, lincod, Pacific snapper, oysters, and steamer clams are house specialties, dishes for which visitors line up, especially on Friday and Saturday night.

Harbor View Grotto Restaurant & Lounge. 150 Starfish Way. ☎ **707/464-3815.** Reservations recommended. Main courses $6–$9 at lunch, $8–$35 at dinner. MC, V. Daily 11:30am–l0pm. SEAFOOD/STEAKS.

This is the best-established nonchain restaurant in town, specializing in fresh seafood at market prices since 1961. Completely renovated in December 1995, it has pleasant views of the ocean and harbor from both the dining room and the lounge. It's capped with a miniature lighthouse inspired by Crescent City's Battery Point Lighthouse, and staffed with the family of the original founders. The "light eaters" menu includes a cup of white chowder (made fresh daily), salad, a main course, and vegetables; heavy eaters can choose from three different cuts of prime rib. Menu items include fresh fish from local fishing fleets, such as Pacific snapper or salmon. Crab or shrimp Louis, as well as crabmeat and shrimp sandwiches, are perpetually popular.

8 Redwood National & State Parks

by Andrew Rice

When he was governor of California, Ronald Reagan once said that if you've seen one redwood, you've seen them all. He couldn't have been more wrong. Redwood National and State Parks are living proof. While he was right that one 367-foot-tall coast redwood (the world's tallest, located in the Tall Trees Grove) does in fact look pretty much like the next one, Reagan was guilty of not seeing the forest for the trees.

It's impossible to explain the feeling you get in the old-growth forests of Redwood National and State Parks without resorting to *Alice in Wonderland* comparisons. Like a tropical rain forest, the redwood forest is a multistoried affair, the tall trees being only the top layer. Everything is so big, misty, and primeval; flowering bushes cover the ground, 10-foot-tall ferns line the creeks, and the smells are rich and musty. It's so *Jurassic Park* that you can't help but half expect to turn the corner and see a dinosaur.

When Archibald Menzies first noted the botanical existence of the coast redwood in 1794, more than two million acres of redwood forest carpeted the north coast. By 1965 heavy logging had reduced that to 300,000 acres and it was obvious something had to be done if any redwoods were to survive. The state created several parks around individual groves in the 1920s, and in 1968 the federal government created Redwood National Park.

The 110,000-acre park offers a lesson in bioregionalism. When the park was first created to protect the biggest coast redwoods, the federal government allowed loggers to clear much of the surrounding area. Redwoods in the park began to suffer as the quality of the Redwood Creek drainage declined from upstream logging. In 1978 the government purchased the entire watershed, having learned that you can't preserve individual trees without preserving the ecosystem they depend on. In April 1994 the National Park Service and the California Department of Parks and Recreation signed an agreement to manage the four Redwood parks cooperatively.

JUST THE FACTS

Frankly, all those huge trees and ferns wouldn't have survived for 1,000 years if it didn't rain one heck of a lot. Count on rain (or at least a heavy drizzle) during your visit, then get ecstatic when the sun comes out—it can happen anytime. Spring, of course, is the best season for wildflowers. Summer is foggy (it's called "the June gloom," but often includes July). Fall is the warmest, sunniest (relatively!) time of all, and winter isn't bad, though it's cold and wet (try 60 inches of rain), and some park facilities are closed. A storm can provide the most introspective time to see the park, since you'll probably be alone. And after a storm passes through, sunny days often follow.

The north coast used to be one of those places where people left their keys in the ignition in case someone had to move their car. But no more. Lock your car and put valuables in the trunk or take them with you.

Admission to the national park is free, but to enter any of the three state parks (which contain the best redwood groves) you'll have to pay a $6 day-use fee. It's good at all three.

SEEING THE HIGHLIGHTS

A number of scenic drives cut through the parks. Steep, windy **Bald Hills Road** will take you back into the Redwood Creek watershed and up to the shoulder of 3,097-foot Schoolhouse Peak. Don't even think of driving a motor home up here or pulling a trailer.

The partially paved 8-mile **Coastal Drive** wanders among redwood groves and along the banks of the Klamath River. The southern section is okay for RVs, but don't go past Alder Camp Road going north or Flint Ridge heading south. Watch for the old World War II radar tracking station disguised as a barn and farmhouse to fool the Japanese.

SPORTS & ACTIVITIES

No one has ever lacked for things to do at Redwood National and State Parks. Everything from river kayaking to birdwatching is available here. In addition to the

Redwood National & State Parks

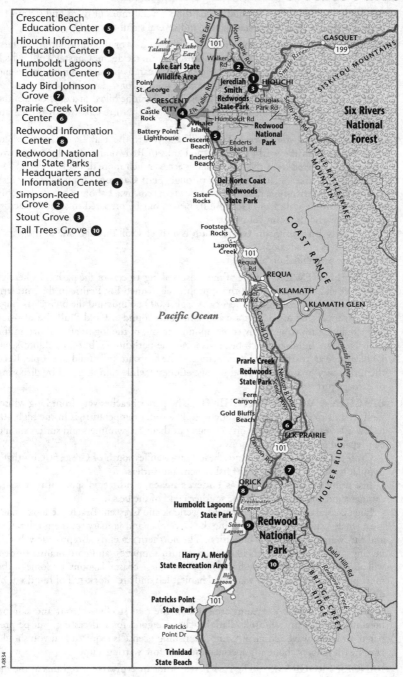

Pacific Ocean

1-0834

231

redwoods, the park includes miles of coastline, several miles of rivers and streams, a herd of elk, three California state parks, and several small towns.

HIKING   The park map and guide, available at any of the information centers, provides a good map of hiking trails. Backpackers can tackle the **Coastal Trail,** which runs the entire length of the park, as near the ocean as possible. There are several backcountry camps on the route making for a great 3- or 4-day trip.

More manageable segments of the Coastal Trail can be hiked in a day. One of the nicest runs is from Crescent Beach south into the Del Norte Coast Redwoods State Park.

The 8-mile **Redwood Creek Trail** will take you to the Tall Trees Grove, where the tallest trees in the world grow on the banks of Redwood Creek. In winter two bridges are removed from the trail, making access much more difficult.

Smaller day hikes include the walk through **Fern Canyon,** an unbelievably lush grotto of sword, five-finger, and maidenhair ferns cut by a babbling brook. It's only about a $1^1/_2$-mile walk from Gold Bluffs beach, but be prepared to scramble across the creek several times on your way.

The **Lady Bird Johnson Grove Loop** is a short stroll through one of the park's lushest groves of redwoods.

Pets are prohibited on all park trails.

WILDLIFE VIEWING   One of the most striking aspects of the park is its herd of Roosevelt elk, usually found in the appropriately named Elk Prairie in the southern end of the park. These gigantic deer can weigh 1,000 pounds and the bulls carry huge antlers from spring to fall. Elk are also sometimes found at Gold Bluffs Beach—it's an incredible rush to suddenly come upon them out of the fog or after a turn in the trail. Nearly a hundred black bears also call the park home, but are seldom seen. Unlike those at Yosemite and Yellowstone, these bears are still afraid of people. Keep them that way by observing food-storage etiquette while camping and by disposing of garbage properly.

BEACHES & WHALE WATCHING   The park's beaches vary from long white-sand strands to cobblestone pocket coves. The water temperature is in the high 40s to low 50s year round and it's often rough out there, so swimmers and surfers should be prepared for adverse conditions.

Crescent Beach is a long sandy beach just 2 miles south of Crescent City that's popular with beachcombers, surf fishermen, and surfers.

Just south of Crescent Beach is **Endert's Beach,** a protected spot with a hike-in campground and tide pools at the southern end of the beach.

High coastal overlooks (like Klamath overlook and Crescent Beach overlook) make great whale-watching outposts during the December and January southern migration and the March/April return migration. The northern sea cliffs also provide valuable nesting sites for marine birds like auklets, puffins, murres, and cormorants. Birders will also thrill at the park's freshwater lagoons. These coastal lagoons are some of the most pristine shorebird and waterfowl habitat left and are chock-full of hundreds of different species.

FISHING   The area's streams are some of the best steelhead trout and salmon breeding habitats in California. Park beaches are good for surf casting, but be prepared for heavy wave action. A California fishing license is required and you should check with rangers about any special closures before wetting a line.

RANGER PROGRAMS   The Park Service runs **interpretive programs** at the the Hiouchi, Crescent Beach, and Redwood information centers during the summer months, and year round at the park headquarters in Crescent City (☎ 707/ 464-6101). State rangers lead campfire programs and numerous other activities throughout the year. Call the **Parks Information** service for both the national and state parks (☎ 707/464-6101) to get current schedules and events.

CAMPING & LODGING

Five small campgrounds are located in the national park proper. Four are walk-in camps and are free, but to use them you must get a permit from the visitor center in advance. The fifth, a car-camping strip along the freeway at Freshwater Lagoon, requests an $8 donation.

Most car campsites are in the **Prairie Creek and Jedediah Smith State Parks,** which lie entirely inside the national park. Sites there are $14 per night and can be reserved by calling the state's infuriating Destinet reservation system (☎ 800/ 444-7275), which requires an additional $6.75 reservation fee. Be prepared to deal with a truly annoying computer before you call and know exactly what campground and, if possible, which site you'd like. (The state park service has promised improvements in this system, but we'll see.)

An interesting option is the **boat-in campground** at Stone Lagoon in Humboldt Lagoons State Park. Reachable only by canoe, kayak, or rowboat, it's on the bank of the lagoon and a short walk to the ocean beach.

Farther from the park attractions—but also farther from the crowds—are four **National Forest Campgrounds** in the mountains above the park. Sites are $8 per night and can be reserved by calling 800/280-2267—where an actual person can help you make decisions.

The **Redwood AYH Hostel,** at 14480 U.S. 101, near Klamath (☎ 707/ 482-8265), is the only lodging actually inside the park. This very inexpensive turn-of-the-century inn has kitchen facilities, three showers, and 30 beds in shared rooms. The staff leads nature walks and is well versed in local history.

A number of bed-and-breakfasts and funky roadside motels are available in the surrounding communities of Crescent City, Orick, and Klamath. The **Crescent City / Del Norte Chamber of Commerce** (☎ 800/343-8300) can steer you toward a proper match (and see the preceding two sections of this chapter for our favorite recommendations).

9

The Far North: The Shasta Cascades & Lake Tahoe

by Erika Lenkert and Matthew R. Poole

Dominated by the snowcapped Mt. Shasta—visible for 100 miles around—California's northern mountains are largely remote and uncrowded. This vast region, often called "The Far North," stretches from the valleys east of the coastal range all the way west to the gambling casinos at the border of Nevada. It begins at the olive orchards north of Sacramento and reaches northward to the Oregon border. A virtual outdoor playground for Californians, the area is so vast that the state of Ohio would fit comfortably within its borders.

This beautiful region offers myriad opportunities for hiking, climbing, skiing, white-water rafting, and cycling. The Far North is also filled with attractions, both man-made and natural, ranging from the Shasta Dam to Lava Beds National Monument, which has dozens of caves for you to explore. Lassen Volcanic National Park will give you a look at three sides of a volcano, and there's even a ski area here that's active in winter.

One of the most celebrated natural attractions in the Golden State is Lake Tahoe, lying 6,225 feet above sea level in the Sierra Nevada mountains. It straddles the border between Nevada and California, with gambling on the Nevada side. Although the lake has been marred by overdevelopment, especially along the southern and eastern shores, the western coastline still provides quiet havens for hiking and cycling, whereas the surrounding mountains offer some of the best skiing in the United States.

Tahoe's beaches are generally overcrowded in summer, but the water rarely gets above 68°F. When the crowds become too much, head for the wilderness that rings the lake. Its 15 downhill skiing resorts and 11 cross-country centers form the largest concentration of skiing facilities in America, and the place buzzes with activity—and skiers—from late November to early April, depending on snow conditions.

1 Lava Beds National Monument

by Andrew Rice

Lava Beds takes a while to grow on you. It's a seemingly desolate, windy place with high plateaus, cinder cones, and rolling hills covered with lava cinders, sagebrush, and tortured-looking junipers. Miles of land just like it cover most of this corner of California. So why, asks the first-time visitor, is this a national monument? The answer lies underground.

The earth here is like Swiss cheese, so porous in places that it actually makes a hollow sound. When lava pours from a shield volcano it doesn't cool all at once; the outer edges cool first and the core keeps flowing, forming underground tunnels like a giant pipeline system.

More than 330 lava-tube caves lace the earth at Lava Beds, caves that are open to the public to explore on their own or with park rangers. Where most caves lend themselves to a fear of getting lost with their huge chambers, multiple entrances, and bizarre topography, these are simple, relatively easy-to-follow tunnels with little room to go wrong. The feeling once inside is that this would be a great place for a game of hide and seek.

In the winter of 1872–73, a band of 155 Modoc Indians held off a siege by more than 500 well-armed U.S. cavalrymen for nearly 6 months using the lava flows as hideouts in a deadly game of cat and mouse. By May, weakened by starvation and exhausted, almost all the Modocs had been captured or killed. On June 1, 1873, their leader, "Captain Jack," surrendered with the last of his tribe. He and three other Modoc leaders were hanged. The surviving members of his band were banished to a reservation in Oklahoma.

JUST THE FACTS

Park elevations range from 4,000 to 5,700 feet, and this part of California can get cold any time of year. Summer is the best time to visit, with average temperatures in the 70°s Fahrenheit; winter temperatures plunge down to about 40°F in the day and as low as 20°F by night. Summer is also the best time to participate in ranger-led hikes, cave trips, and campfire programs. Check at the visitor center for schedules.

SEEING THE HIGHLIGHTS

There's very little of historical note remaining above ground here besides a white cross. It marks the spot where Gen. E. R. S. Canby was killed during "peace" meetings with the Modocs, an act that led to the final bloodbath. He was charged with returning the Modocs to a reservation in Oregon where they were to be housed with a rival tribe.

A hike to **Schonchin Butte** (three-quarters of a mile, one-way) will give you a good perspective on the wildly stark beauty of the monument and nearby Tule Lake Valley. Wildlife lovers should keep their eyes peeled for terrestrial animals like mule deer, coyote, marmots, and squirrels, while watching overhead for bald eagles and 24 species of hawks, as well as enormous flocks of ducks and geese headed to the Klamath Basin, one of the largest waterfowl wintering grounds in the Lower 48. Sometimes the sky goes dark with ducks and geese during the peak migrations.

CAVES & HIKES

The caves at **Lava Beds** are open to the public with very little restriction or hassle. All you need to see most of them is a good flashlight or headlamp, sturdy walking shoes, and a sense of adventure. Many of the caves are entered by ladders or stairs, others still by holes in the side of a hill. Once inside, walk far enough to round a corner and then shut off your light—a chilling experience, to say the least.

One-way **Cave Loop Road,** just southwest of the visitor center, is where you'll find many of the best cave hikes. About 15 lava tubes have been marked and made accessible. Two are ice caves, where the air temperature remains below freezing all year and ice crystals form on the walls. If exploring on your own gives you the creeps, check out **Mushpot Cave.** Almost adjacent to the visitor center, this cave has been outfitted with lights and a smooth walkway; you'll have plenty of company.

Hardened spelunkers will find enough remote and relatively unexplored caves in the monument, many requiring specialized climbing gear, to keep themselves busy.

Above ground, several trails crisscross the monument. The longest of these, the 8.2-mile (one-way) **Lyons Trail** spans the wildest part of the monument, where you're likely to see plenty of animals. The **Whitney Butte Trail,** 3.4 miles (one-way), leads from Merill Cave along the shoulder of 5,000-foot Whitney Butte to the edge of the Callahan Lava Flow and the monument boundary.

PICNICKING, CAMPING & ACCOMMODATIONS

The 40-unit **Indian Well Campground** near the visitor center has spaces for tents and small RVs year round, with water available only during the summer. The rest of the year you'll have to carry water from the nearby visitor center.

Two **picnic grounds,** Fleener Chimneys and Captain Jacks Stronghold, have tables but no water; open fires are prohibited.

There are no hotels or lodges in the monument, but numerous services are available in nearby Tulelake and Klamath Falls. For more information, call or write **Lava Beds National Monument,** P.O. Box 867, Tulelake, CA 96134 (☎ **916/ 667-2282**).

2 Mt. Shasta & the Cascades

In this section we'll take I-5 north through the Sacramento Valley and up into the Cascades. Chances are, your first glimpse of Mt. Shasta's majestic, snowcapped peak will be a memorable one. A dormant volcano with a base 17 miles in diameter, it stands in virtual isolation and can be seen from more than 100 miles away. When John Muir first saw Shasta from 50 miles away in 1874, he wrote: "[I] was alone and weary. Yet my blood turned to wine, and I have not been weary since." He went on to describe it as "the pole star of the landscape"—which indeed it is.

ESSENTIALS

GETTING THERE   From San Francisco, take I-80 to I-505 to I-5 to Redding. From the coast, pick up Calif. 299 east a few miles north of Arcata to Redding.

Redding Municipal Airport, 6751 Airport Rd. (☎ 916/224-4331), is serviced by United Express. Amtrak stops in Dunsmuir and Redding.

VISITOR INFORMATION   Regional information can be secured from the following: **Shasta Cascade Wonderland Association,** 14250 Holiday Rd., Redding, CA 96003 (☎ 800/326-6944 or 916/275-5555); the **Mt. Shasta Chamber of Commerce,** 300 Pine St., Mt. Shasta, CA 96067 (☎ 800/926-4865 or 916/ 926-4865); the **Redding Convention and Visitors Bureau,** 777 Auditorium Dr., Redding, CA 96001 (☎ 800/874-7562 or 916/225-4100); and the **Trinity County Chamber of Commerce,** 317 Main St. (P.O. Box 517), Weaverville, CA 96093 (☎ 800/487-4648 or 916/623-6101).

WILLIAM B. IDE ADOBE STATE HISTORIC PARK

En route to Mt. Shasta from the south, you may want to stop near Red Bluff at William B. Ide Adobe State Historic Park, 21659 Adobe Rd. (☎ **916/529-8599**), for a picnic along the Sacramento River. The 3-acre park commemorates William B. Ide, the first and only president of the Republic of California, proclaimed on June

14, 1846, by those who led the Bear Flag Rebellion against the Mexicans who were excluding Americans from California. The republic lasted only 3 weeks before the American victory in the Mexican-American War made California a state in the Union. The adobe home dates from 1852. Some historians say that it was not the home of Mr. Ide, but it does give visitors an idea of frontier life. In the summer the park is open daily from 8am to sunset; the house is open noon to 4pm; call ahead in winter. Parking is $3 per vehicle.

REDDING & SHASTA

The major town and gateway to the region is Redding, the hub of the panoramic Shasta-Cascade region, lying at the top of the Sacramento Valley. From here you can either turn westward into the wilderness-forest of Trinity and the Klamath Mountains, or north and east into the Cascades and Shasta Trinity National Forest.

In Redding, with its fast-food joints, gas stations, and cheap motels, summer heat generally ranges above nearly 100°F all summer. A city of some 60,000, Redding is the transportation hub of Northern California. It has little of interest to detain you, but is mainly used as a base for exploring the natural wonders nearby. Information is available from the **Redding Convention and Visitors Bureau,** 777 Auditorium Dr., Redding, CA 96001 (☎ **800/874-7562** or 916/225-4100), which is west of 1-5 on Calif. 299. It's open Monday to Friday from 8am to 5pm and on Saturday and Sunday from 9am to 5pm.

Horse lovers will want to know about the **Wild Horse Sanctuary,** which can be reached via either Calif. 36 from Red Bluff or Calif. 44 from Redding. The sanctuary was established by Jim Clapp, who saved 80 horses that were scheduled to be destroyed. The sanctuary is only 23 miles from Mt. Lassen, and visitors can view the horses and also take 2- and 3-day pack trips through the ruggedly beautiful foothills of Mt. Lassen. Two-day trips cost $235 per person. For information, call 916/474-5770.

Ahead and northeast, Mt. Shasta rises to a height of more than 14,000 feet. From Redding, I-5 cuts north over the Pit River Bridge, crossing Lake Shasta and leading eventually to the mount itself.

Before striking north, however, you may want to explore Lake Shasta and see Shasta Dam. Another option is to take a detour west of Redding to Weaverville, Whiskeytown-Shasta Trinity National Recreation Area, and Lake Trinity (see below).

About 3 miles west, stop at the old mining town of Shasta, which has been converted into **Shasta State Historic Park** (☎ **916/243-8194**). Shasta was founded on gold, and was the "Queen City" of the northern mines in the Klamath range. Its life, though, was short, and it expired in 1872 when the Central Pacific Railroad bypassed it in favor of Redding. Today the business district is a ghost town, complete with a restored general store and a Masonic hall. The 1861 courthouse has been converted into a museum where you can view the jail and a gallows out back, plus the remarkable collection of Californian art assembled by Mae Helen Bacon Boggs, including works by Maynard Dixon, Grace Hudson, and many others. Open Wednesday to Sunday from 10am to 5pm. Admission is $2 for adults, $1 for children 6 to 12, and free for children 5 and under.

Continue along Calif. 299 west to Calif. 3 north, which will take you to Weaverville and then to the west side of the lake and Trinity Center.

WHERE TO STAY

Redding also has a **Red Lion Motor Inn** (☎ 916/221-8700) and a **La Quinta Inn** (☎ 800/325-2525 or 916/221-8200), both fine motel choices.

Tiffany House Bed and Breakfast Inn. 1510 Barbara Rd., Redding, CA 96003. ☎ **916/ 244-3225.** 3 rms, 1 cottage. $75–$95 double; $125 cottage. Rates include breakfast. AE, DISC, MC, V.

Despite the fact that this two-story gray-and-white house wasn't built until 1939, everyone in town refers to it as a Victorian. A sweeping view of the Lassen Mountain Range is visible from the oversize deck, which seems to float above a garden in back. There's also a swimming pool. The bedrooms have crocheted bedspreads, one has a clawfoot tub in the bathroom, and all contain some kind of reproduction Tiffany lamp, as the inn's name would imply.

WHERE TO DINE

Jack's Grill. 1743 California St., Redding. ☎ **916/241-9705.** Reservations not accepted. Main courses $7.25–$18.25. AE, DISC, MC, V. Mon–Sat 4–11pm. STEAKHOUSE.

This is a local favorite, established in 1938 in a building originally constructed in 1835 as a secondhand-clothing store. The second floor served as a brothel in the late 1930s, and an entrepreneur named Jack Young set up the main floor as a steakhouse (his establishment serviced all of a body's needs, you might say). Today it's an earthy, well-established steakhouse. Waiting for a table over drinks in the bar is part of the fun. Good old-fashioned red meat is supplemented by a couple of seafood dishes such as deep-fried jumbo prawns and ocean scallops. Prices include salad, hot garlic bread, and baked or french-fried potatoes. It's a very fetching spot, with good honest tavern food and a jovial crowd. Be prepared for a long wait on weekends.

WEAVERVILLE

Weaverville was a gold-mining town in the 1850s, and part of the history of the place is captured at the **Jake Jackson Memorial Museum–Trinity County Historical Park,** 508 Main St. (☎ 916/623-5211). It displays the usual collection of memorabilia, from firearms to household items. It's interesting for what it tells about the residents of the town—Native Americans, miners, pioneers, and especially the Chinese. In the gold rush era, the town was half Chinese, with a Chinatown of about 2,500 residents. Admission is free. It's open May to October, daily from 10am to 5pm; in April and November, daily from noon to 4pm; closed December to March.

Across the parking lot you can view the oldest continuously used Taoist temple in California at the **Joss House State Historic Park** (☎ 916/623-5284). Although technically it's open Wednesday to Sunday from 10am to 5pm, hours tend to be irregular, so call ahead. Admission is $2 for adults, $1 for children 6 to 13, and free for children 5 and under.

WHERE TO DINE

Weaverville isn't exactly packed with exciting dining choices, so up here you take what you can get.

The Mustard Seed. 252 S. Main St. ☎ **916/623-2922.** All items under $6.95. No credit cards. Mon–Sat 7am–3pm, Sun 8am–3pm. AMERICAN/MEXICAN.

This century-old, yellow-fronted Victorian house stands in the town's historic core. At breakfast the favorite items are the Belgian waffles with crushed almonds and the omelets—the best in town. Lunch brings an array of tacos, burritos, quiches, and veggie dishes for the dedicated cauliflower and broccoli lovers in the area.

The Pacific Brewery. 401 S. Main St. ☎ **916/623-3000.** Main courses $8–$14. MC, V. Daily 6am–9pm. AMERICAN.

Redding/Mt. Shasta Area

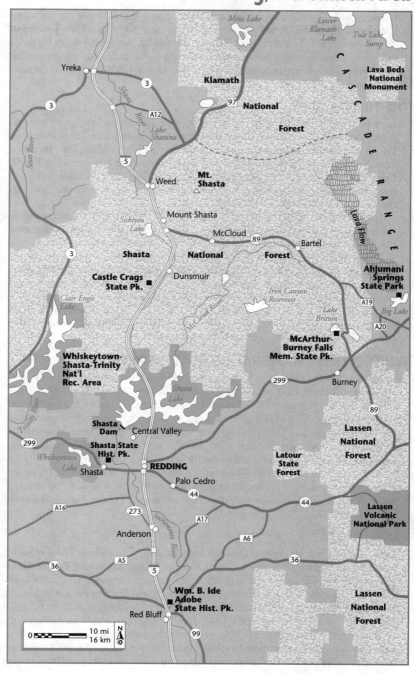

Honest, good food at reasonable prices is served here—that is, if you can get a pre-occupied staff member to pay you some attention. Start with the shrimp cocktail or the nachos, then follow with steak or pasta primavera, salmon steak, or breast of chicken in a mushroom-garlic-wine sauce. Mud pie is the traditional favorite conclusion. Several microbrews are available on tap. The decor is 100% Americana; the same can be said for the diners.

THE TRINITY ALPS

West of Weaverville stretch the Trinity Alps, with Thompson Peak rising to more than 9,000 feet. The second-largest wilderness area in the state lies between the Trinity and Salmon rivers and contains more than 55 lakes and streams. Its alpine scenery makes it popular with hikers and backpackers. You can access the **Pacific Crest Trail** west of Mt. Shasta at Parks Creek, South Fork Road, Whalen Road, and also from Castle Crags State Park. For trail and other information, contact the Forest Service in Weaverville at 916/623-2121.

The **Fifth Season,** 300 N. Mt. Shasta Blvd. (☎ **916/926-3606**), offers mountaineering and backpack rentals and will provide trail maps and other information concerning Shasta's outdoor activities.

Living Waters Recreation (☎ **916/926-5446**) offers half-day to 2-day rafting trips on the Upper Sacramento, Klamath, Trinity, and Salmon rivers. **Trinity River Rafting Company** on Calif. 299W in Big Flat (☎ **916/623-3223**) also operates white-water trips along the Trinity, Salmon, and Klamath rivers.

For additional outfitters and information, contact the **Trinity County Chamber of Commerce,** 317 Main St., Weaverville, CA 96093 (☎ **800/487-4648** or 916/623-6101).

WHISKEYTOWN NATIONAL RECREATION AREA

In adjacent Shasta County, the Whiskeytown National Recreation Area is on the eastern shore of Trinity Lake, a quiet and relatively uncrowded lake with 157 miles of shoreline. When this reservoir was created, it was officially named Clair Engle, after the politician who created it. But locals insist on calling it Trinity after the name of the river that used to rush through the region past the towns of Minersville, Stringtown, and an earlier Whiskeytown. All these were destroyed when the river was dammed. They now lie submerged under the lake's glassy surface.

Both Lake Trinity and the Whiskeytown National Recreation Area are in the Shasta Trinity National Forest, 2.1 million acres of wilderness with 1,269 miles of hiking trails. For information on trails, contact **Shasta Trinity National Forest** (☎ **916/246-5222**).

LAKE SHASTA

Now we'll continue heading north on I-5 from Redding. Travel about 12 miles north and take the Shasta Dam Boulevard exit to the **Shasta Dam and Power Plant** (☎ **916/275-4463**), which has an overflow spillway three times higher than Niagara Falls. The huge dam—3,460 feet long, 602 feet high, and 883 feet thick at its base—holds back the waters of the Sacramento, Pit, and McCloud rivers. A dramatic sight indeed, it's a vital component of the Central Valley water project. At the visitors center is a series of photographs and displays covering the dam's construction period. You can either walk or drive over the dam, but far more interesting are the free 45-minute tours given daily: on the hour from 9am to 5pm in the summer, and at 10am, noon, and 2pm from Labor Day to Memorial day. The guided tour takes you deep within the dam's many chilly corridors (not a good place for claustrophobes) and below the spillway. It's an entertaining way to beat the summer heat.

Lake Shasta has 370 miles of shoreline and attracts anglers (bass, trout, and king salmon), waterskiers, and other boating enthusiasts—two million, in fact, in summer. The best way to enjoy the lake is aboard a houseboat, which can be rented from several companies: **Antlers Resort & Marina,** P.O. Box 140, Antlers Rd., Lakehead, CA 96051 (☎ 800/238-3924); **Packers Bay Marina,** 16814 Packers Bay Rd., Lakehead, CA 96051 (☎ 800/331-3137); and **Lakeshore Marina,** 20479 Lakeshore Dr., Lakehead, CA 96051 (☎ 916/238-2303).

For information and additional houseboat rentals, contact the **Redding Convention and Visitors Bureau,** 777 Auditorium Dr., Redding, CA 96001 (☎ **800/874-7562** or 916/225-4100).

While you're here, you can visit **Lake Shasta Caverns** (☎ 916/238-2341). These caves contain 20-foot-high stalactite and stalagmite formations—60-foot-wide curtains of them in the great Cathedral Room. To see the caves, drive about 15 miles north of Redding on I-5 to the O'Brien/Shasta Caverns exit. A ferry will take you across the lake and a short bus ride will follow to the cave entrance for an hour-long tour. Admission is $12 for adults and $6 for children. The caverns are open daily year round, with tours every half hour in summer from 9am to 4pm, and every hour in winter from 9am to 3pm.

Farther north, off I-5 about 35 miles north of Redding, you'll reach **Castle Crags State Park** (☎ 916/235-2684), a 4,300-acre park with 64 campsites and 28 miles of hiking trails. Here granite crags that were formed 225 million years ago tower more than 6,500 feet above the Sacramento River. The park is filled with dogwood, oak, cedar, and pine as well as tiger lilies, azaleas, and orchids in summer. You can walk the 1-mile Indian Creek nature trail or take the easy 1 1/2-mile Root Creek Trail.

Back on I-5 the road curves around past the old railroad town of Dunsmuir and on into Mt. Shasta.

MT. SHASTA

A volcanic mountain with eight glaciers, ✪ **Mt. Shasta** is a towering peak of legend and lore. It stands alone, always snowcapped, unshadowed by other mountains, and can be seen from 125 miles away. Although dormant since 1786, that doesn't mean it could not erupt, and indeed there are hot sulfur springs bubbling at the summit. The springs saved John Muir on his third ascent of the mountain in 1875. Caught in a severe snowstorm, he and his partner took turns submersing themselves in the hot mud to survive.

Many New Agers are convinced that Mt. Shasta is the center of an incredible energy vortex. These young devotees flock to the foot of the mountain, perhaps hoping to connect with their inner selves. In 1987 the foothills of the mountain were host to the worldwide Harmonic Convergence, calling for a planetary union and a new phase of universal harmony. Yoga, massage, meditation, and metaphysics are all the rage here. These New Agers seem to coexist harmoniously with people who never get more metaphysical than listening to the lyrics in a Dolly Parton song.

Those who don't want to climb can drive up to about 8,000 feet. From Mt. Shasta City, drive 14 miles up the Everitt Memorial Highway to the end of the road near Panther Meadow. Along the way you'll be able to stop and see the Sacramento River Canyon, the Eddy Mountains to the west, and glimpses of Mt. Lassen to the south. At the **Everitt Vista Turnout,** you can take the short hike through the forests to a lava outcrop overlooking the McCloud area.

Continue on to **Bunny Flat,** a major access point for climbers in the summer and also for cross-country skiing and sledding in winter. The highway ends at the Old Ski Bowl Vista, providing panoramic views of Mt. Lassen, Castle Crags, and the Trinity Mountains.

While in Mt. Shasta, visit the **Fish Hatchery** at 3 N. Old State Rd. (☎ 916/926-2215), which was built in 1888. Here you can observe rainbow and brown trout being hatched to stock rivers and streams statewide—and indeed millions are produced here annually. You can feed them via coin-operated food dispensers, and on certain Tuesdays during the fall and winter observe the spawning process. Admission is free, and it's open daily from 8am to sunset. Adjacent to the hatchery is the **Sisson Museum,** which displays a smattering of local history exhibits. It's open daily from 10am to 5pm in summer, from noon to 4pm in winter, and admission is free.

MOUNTAIN CLIMBING   Mt. Shasta attracts thousands of hikers each year, from timid first-timers to serious mountaineers who search for the most difficult path up. The hike isn't technically difficult, but it's a demanding ascent that takes about 8 hours of continuous exertion, particularly when the snow softens up. (*Tip:* Start real early, while the snow is still firm.) Before setting out, hikers must secure a permit by signing in at the trailhead or at the **Mt. Shasta Ranger District Office,** which also gives out plenty of good advice for amateur climbers. The office is at 204 W. Alma St., off North Mount Shasta Boulevard in Mount Shasta (☎ 916/926-4511). Be sure to wear good hiking shoes, carry crampons and an ice ax, as well as a first-aid kit, a quart of water per person, and a flashlight in case it takes longer than anticipated. Sunblock is an absolute necessity.

All the requisite equipment can be rented at **The Fifth Season,** 300 N. Mt. Shasta Blvd. (☎ 916/926-3606). The weather can be extremely unpredictable, and every year hikers die on this volcano, usually from making stupid mistakes. Traditionally climbers make the ascent from the Sierra Lodge at Horse Camp, which can be reached from the town of Shasta via Alma Street and the Everitt Memorial Highway or from Bunny Flat.

For more information and also supervised trips, contact **Shasta Mountain Guides,** 1938 Hill Rd. (☎ 916/926-3117). This outfit offers a 2-day climb that follows the traditional John Muir route and costs $235. They also offer a glacier climb and rock climbing in Castle Crags State Park, plus cross-country and telemark skiing, too.

SKIING   In winter, visitors can ski at **Mt. Shasta Ski Park,** 104 Siskiyou Ave., Mt. Shasta, CA 96067 (☎ 916/926-8600), which has 22 runs with 80% snowmaking and three chair lifts; a fourth lift is in the works at press time. A day pass costs under $30. There's also a Nordic Ski center with 15^{1}/$_{2}$ miles of groomed trails. In summer you can ride the chair lifts to scenic views, mountain bike down the trails (an all-day pass is $9), or practice on the two-story climbing wall. Access to the chair lifts is 10 miles east on Mt. Shasta on its southern slopes via Calif. 89 from McCloud. For information, call 916/926-8600. The ski lodge's number is 916/926-8610.

WATER SPORTS   Although the source of the headwaters of the Sacramento River is found here, water does not gush down from the mountain. Instead, it's accumulated at the base. At Shasta's base lies **Lake Siskiyou,** a popular lake for boating, swimming, and fishing, and a great vantage point for photographs of Mt. Shasta and its reflection. Waterskiing is not allowed, but windsurfing is available, and boat rentals are offered at **Lake Siskiyou Camp Resort,** 4239 W. A. Barr Rd., Mt. Shasta (☎ 916/926-2618).

GOLF & TENNIS   Golfers should head for the 27-hole Robert Trent Jones, Jr., golf course at the **Lake Shastina Golf Resort,** 5925 Country Club Dr., Weed (☎ 916/938-3201), or the 18-hole course at the **Mt. Shasta Resort,** 1000 Siskiyou Lake Blvd., Mt. Shasta (☎ 916/926-3030). The resort also has tennis courts.

OTHER OUTDOOR ACTIVITIES   In and around Mt. Shasta you'll find a variety of suppliers and sports outfitters, including the Fifth Season (see "Mountain Climbing," above).

Mt. Shasta offers some excellent mountain biking. In the summer the **Mt. Shasta Ski Park** (☎ **916/926-8610**) rents everything you'll need for a complete day of mountain biking, including bikes and helmets. An all-day chair lift pass is only $9.

For fishing information, go to **Hart's Guide Service,** 965 Lassen Lane (☎ **916/ 926-2431**), or contact **Mt. Shasta Fly Fishing** (☎ **916/926-6648**).

For an offbeat trip, contact the **Rainbow Ridge Ranch** (☎ **916/926-5794**) and join one of their llama-trekking trips. Trips last from 3 to 5 days and cost from $400.

WHERE TO STAY

Best Western Tree House. I-5 and Lake St. (P.O. Box 236), Mt. Shasta, CA 96067. ☎ **800/ 545-7164** or 916/926-3101. Fax 916/926-3542. 95 rms. A/C TV TEL. $66–$149 double. AE, CB, DC, MC, V.

Just off the main highway, this motor inn offers rooms that are typically furnished with Scandinavian-style furnishings. Some accommodations have decks and refrigerators, which make them a family favorite. Facilities include a rustic dining room and lounge with a stone fireplace. There's also a huge indoor pool that's usually deserted, as well as an exercise room. Frankly, this is the best place to stay in the town of Mt. Shasta, far superior to its competitors, and it keeps its prices low. Downhill and cross-country skiing are possible within a 10-mile drive.

✪ **McCloud Guest House.** 606 W. Colombero Dr. (P.O. Box 1510), McCloud, CA 96057. ☎ **916/964-3160.** 5 rms. $80–$95 double. Rates include continental breakfast. MC, V.

A veranda wraps around this bungalow-style house with dormer windows that's set among oak and pine trees on the lower slopes of Mt. Shasta, off Calif. 89, west of McCloud. The house was built in 1907 as a residence for the president of the McCloud River Lumber Company. In 1984 innkeepers Bill and Patti Leigh and Dennis and Pat Abreu restored it to fine condition. Upstairs there's a large comfortable parlor for guests with a pool table. Off the parlor are the five individually decorated rooms with white iron beds. Three of the rooms have clawfoot tubs and two have a shower but no tub.

On the ground floor there's an atmospheric dining room with leaded and stained-glass interior decoration. The menu offers a fine selection of Italian chicken, veal, pasta, and seafood dishes.

Mt. Shasta Ranch B&B. 1008 W. A. Barr Rd., Mt. Shasta, CA 96067. ☎ **916/926-3870.** 9 rms, 4 with bath; 1 cottage. TV. $45–$60 double without bath, $85 double with bath; $95 cottage for three. Rates include continental breakfast. AE, MC, V. Take the Central Mt. Shasta exit off I-5 to W. A. Barr Road.

The Mt. Shasta Ranch was conceived and built in 1923 by one of the country's most famous horse trainers and racing tycoons, H. D. ("Curley") Brown, as the centerpiece of a private retreat and thoroughbred horse ranch. Despite the encroachment of nearby buildings, the main house and its annex are still available as a cozy B&B with touches of nostalgia and the occasional antique. Four bedrooms (those with private bath) are in the main house; the remaining five share two bathrooms in the carriage house. It's a 30-minute trek to the shores of nearby Lake Siskiyou, or you could stay here to enjoy the hot tub and Ping-Pong tables.

Railroad Park Resort. 100 Railroad Park Rd., Dunsmuir, CA 96025. ☎ **916/235-4440.** Fax 916/235-4470. 28 rms, 4 cabins. A/C TV TEL. $55–$80 double rooms. $73 double cabin. Additional person $5 extra. AE, DISC, MC, V. Take Railroad Park Exit off I-5, 1 mile south of Dunsmuir.

Lying a quarter of a mile from the Sacramento River, this is an offbeat accommodation that kids enjoy. It's located at the foot of Castle Crags and contains several facilities—a restaurant and lounge, a campground and RV park, and fishing ponds, as well as the caboose motel. The railroad cabooses have been converted into rooms, leaving their pipes, ladders, and lofts in place. They're furnished with modern brass beds, table and chairs, dressers, and TV. They're located around the fenced-in kidney-shaped pool and whirlpool. The restaurant and lounge are also in vintage railroad cars.

Stewart Mineral Springs Resort. 4617 Stewart Springs Rd., Weed, CA 96094. ☎ **800/ 322-9223** or 916/938-2222. 3 teepees (suitable for 1–4 people), 4 dorm rms (for 1–4 people), 6 motel rms (for 1 or 2 people), 5 cabins with kitchens (for 1–4 people), 1 large A-frame house (suitable for 10–15 people). $15 teepee for one ($5 for each additional person up to four); $30 dorm room for one ($10 for each additional person up to four); $37.50 motel double; $45 cabin with kitchen for two; $300 A-frame house for up to 15. MC, V. Closed Dec–Mar 1 or even later depending on snow.

Stewart Mineral Springs is one of the most unusual health spas in California, loaded with lore and legends while making few concessions to modernity. It lies above coldwater springs that Native Americans valued for their healing powers. Don't expect anything approaching a European spa or big-city luxury here. Established in 1875, the site is deliberately rustic, with as few intrusions from the urban world as possible (no phones or TVs). Designed in a somewhat haphazard compound of about a dozen buildings, 4 miles west of the town of Weed, it occupies a 37-acre site of sloping, forested land accented with ponds, gazebos, and decorative bridges, and riddled with hiking and nature trails and freshwater streams. There are no restaurants on site, and the spa facilities are often beside campers and RVs that hook up to facilities at a nearby campsite.

Activities revolve around hiking, nature watching, and taking the healing waters of the legendary springs. The bathhouse is the curative headquarters of the resort, and contains 13 private cubicles where water from the springs is heated and run into tubs for soaking. A staff member will describe the rituals involved in the immersion process: A 20-minute soak is followed with a visit to a nearby sauna and an immersion in the chilly waters of Parks Creek, just outside the bathhouse. Other feel-good options include massages ($30 per half-hour session), herbal body wraps ($65 for a 90-minute experience), and facials ($15).

If you opt for treatment and R&R here, you won't be alone. Despite its rusticity, young Hollywood has discovered the place, including many of the actors from *The Young and the Restless* and *Guiding Light*, San Francisco 49ers football players, and local newscasters.

Wagon Creek Inn. 1239 Woodland Park Dr., Mt. Shasta, CA 96067. ☎ **800/995-9260** or 916/926-0838. Fax 916/926-0855. 3 rms, 1 with bath. $65 double without bath; $75 double with bath. Rates include continental breakfast. MC, V. From I-5 take the Central Mt. Shasta exit to Old Stage Road and turn right onto Woodland Park Drive.

Loretta Lynn would feel at home in one of these country-style rooms inside this log cabin home located about 2¹/₂ miles from Mt. Shasta. The King Room has its own bath; the other two share. Guests can use the living room with fireplace, TV, and VCR. It's a homey, inexpensive place where pets and kids are welcome.

WHERE TO DINE

Lily's. 1013 Mt. Shasta Blvd., Mt. Shasta. ☎ **916/926-3372.** Reservations recommended. Main courses $9.50–$16. MC, V. Mon–Fri 7am–9pm, Sat–Sun 7am–9:30pm. AMERICAN.

Set in a white-clapboard turn-of-the-century house in a residential neighborhood south of the town center, this friendly little restaurant has a front porch, a picket fence, a back garden, and tables scattered randomly in both front and back. It's popular for breakfast, when chunky breads and omelets ($5 to $6) start the morning off right. Lunch and dinner dishes—polenta, enchiladas, scampi al Roma, kung pao shrimp—span the globe.

Michael's. 313 N. Mt. Shasta Blvd., Mt. Shasta. ☎ **916/926-5288.** Main courses $13–$17. AE, MC, V. Tues–Fri 11am–2:30pm and 5–9pm, Sat noon–9pm. ITALIAN/AMERICAN.

Since 1980 Michael and Lynn Kobseff have enjoyed a devoted following of Shasta locals at their small but venerable restaurant. It stands across from a Hallmark store, in the midst of the town's main commercial street. The menu offers a variety of worthy Italian dishes along with steaks. Among the pasta dishes, opt for the manicotti or the cannelloni alla romana, with veal, chicken, spinach, and cheese in a marinara sauce. Dinners include soup, salad, garlic bread, and coffee. Thursday, Friday, and Saturday are prime rib nights.

MCARTHUR-BURNEY FALLS MEMORIAL STATE PARK

On its way to Lassen Volcanic National Park (see below) from Mt. Shasta, Calif. 89 east loops back south to ✪ **McArthur-Burney Falls Memorial State Park** (☎ 916/335-2777). One of the spectacular features of this 768-acre park is a waterfall that cascades over a 129-foot cliff. Theodore Roosevelt once called the falls "the eighth wonder of the world." Giant springs lying a few hundred yards upstream feed the falls and keep them flowing, even during California's legendary dry spells.

The half-mile **Headwater Trail** will take you to a good vantage point above the falls. If you're lucky you can observe the black swifts that nest in the mossy crevices behind the cascade. Other birds to look for include barn and great horned owls, the belted kingfisher, the common flicker, and even the Oregon junco. The year-round park also has a mile-long nature trail, 128 campsites, picnicking grounds, and good fishing for bass, brown trout, rainbow trout, and brook trout. For camping reservations, call 800/444-7275.

From here, Lassen Volcanic National park lies about 40 miles south.

3 Lassen Volcanic National Park

by Andrew Rice

Lassen Volcanic National Park is a remarkable reminder that North America is still forming, and that the ground below is alive with the forces of creation and, sometimes, destruction. Lassen Peak is the southernmost peak in a chain of volcanoes (including Mount Saint Helens) that stretches all the way from British Columbia.

Though it's dormant, Lassen Peak is still very much alive. It last awakened in May 1914, beginning a cycle of eruptions that spit lava, steam, and ash until 1921. The eruptions climaxed in 1915 when Lassen blew its top, sending a mushroom cloud of ash 7 miles high that was seen from hundreds of miles away. The peak itself has been dormant for nearly a century now, but the area still boils with a ferocious intensity: Hot springs, fumaroles, and mud pots are all indicators that Lassen hasn't had its last word. Monitoring of geothermal features in the park shows that they're getting hotter, not cooler, and some scientists take this as a sign that the next big eruption in the Cascades is likely to happen here.

Until then, the park gives visitors an interesting chance to watch a landscape recover from the massive destruction brought on by an eruption. To the northeast of Lassen Peak is the aptly named Devastated Area, a huge swath of volcanic destruction steadily repopulating with conifer forests. Botanists have revised their earlier

The "Wild Man" of Lassen

The Lassen area was inhabited by four groups of Native Americans before the arrival of whites. The Atsugewi, Maidu, Yana, and Yahi all used portions of the park as their summer hunting grounds. The white man's diseases and encroachment into their territory quickly decimated their population. By the turn of the century they were thought to be gone from the wilds of the Lassen area. In 1911, however, a nearly naked Native American man was discovered by butchers at a slaughterhouse in Oroville. When they couldn't communicate with him, the sheriff locked the man in a cell.

News of the "Wild Man" found a receptive audience among anthropologists at the University of California at Berkeley, who quickly rescued the man. Ishi, as he came to be known, turned out to be the last of the Yahi tribe and lived at the university's Museum of Anthropology for 5 years before succumbing to tuberculosis. Ishi, through sharing his knowledge with anthropologist Alfred Kroeber and others, is responsible for much of what is known about Native American culture in California.

theories that forests must be preceded by herbacious growth after watching the Devastated Area immediately revegetate with a diverse mix of different conifer species.

The 106,000-acre park is a place of great beauty. The flora and fauna here are an interesting mix of species from the Cascade Range, which stretches north from Lassen, and species from the Sierra Nevada, which stretches south. The resulting blend accounts for an enormous diversity of plants; 715 distinct species have been identified in the park. Though it's snowbound in winter, Lassen is an important summer feeding ground for transient herds of mule deer and numerous black bears.

In addition to the volcano and all its geothermal features, Lassen Volcanic National Park includes miles of hiking trails, huge alpine lakes, large meadows, cinder cones, lush forests, cross-country skiing, and great camping. Only one major road, Calif. 89 (the Park Road), crosses the park in a 39-mile half circle with entrances and visitor centers at either end. Three-quarters of the park is designated wilderness.

JUST THE FACTS

Most visitors enter the park at the Southwest Entrance Station, drive through the park, and leave through the Northwest Entrance, or vice versa. Two other entrances lead to remote portions of the park. Warner Valley is reached from the south on the road from Chester. The Butte Lake entrance is reached by a cut-off road from Calif. 44 between Calif. 89 and Susanville.

Ranger stations are clustered near each entrance and provide the full spectrum of interpretive displays, ranger-led walks, informational leaflets, and emergency help. The largest visitor center is located just outside the Northwest Entrance Station before Manzanita Lake. The park information number for all requests is 916/595-4444, or write Lassen Volcanic National Park, P.O. Box 100, Mineral, CA 96063-0100.

Because of the dangers posed by the park's thermal features, rangers ask that you remain on trails at all times. Fires are allowed in campgrounds only; please make sure they're dead before leaving them. Mountain bikes are prohibited on all trails.

Lassen is one of the least-visited parks in the lower 48 states, so crowd control isn't as big a consideration here as in other places. Unless you're here on the Fourth of July or Labor Day weekend, you won't encounter anything that could rightly be called

Lassen Volcanic National Park

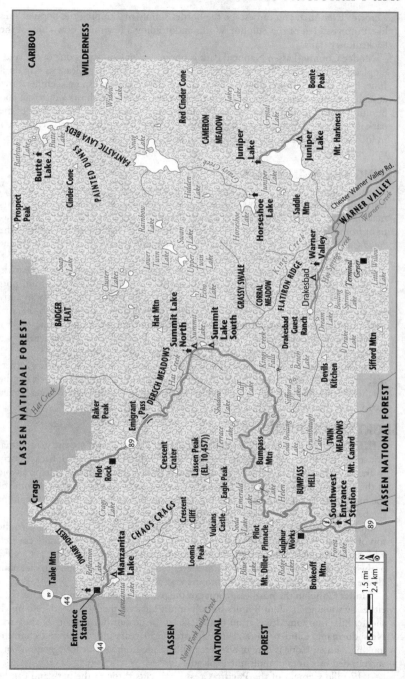

CARIBOU

WILDERNESS

Red Cinder Cone

Bonte
Peak

CAMERON
MEADOW

Widow
Lake

Lake
Lake

Crystal
Lake

Mt. Harkness

Juniper
Lake

Juniper
Lake

BADGER
FLAT

Bathtub
Lake

Butte
Lake

Butte
Lake

Cinder Cone

Prospect
Peak

PAINTED DUNES

FANTASTIC LAVA BEDS

Snag
Lake

Ghost Creek

Hidden
Lake

Rainbow
Lake

Swan
Lake

Upper
Twin
Lake

Lower
Twin
Lake

Cluster
Lakes

Soap
Lake

Horseshoe
Lake

Horseshoe
Lake

Juniper
Lake

Saddle
Mtn

Chester Warner Valley Rd.

WARNER VALLEY

Warner Creek

Kings Creek

Warner
Valley

Drakesbad

Hot Spring Creek

Boiling
Spring
Lake

Terminal
Geyser

Little Willow
Lake

Spring
Lake

Sifford Mtn

LASSEN NATIONAL FOREST

LASSEN NATIONAL FOREST

CORRAL
MEADOW

FLATIRON RIDGE

GRASSY SWALE

Echo
Lake

Summit
Lake

Summit Lake
North

Summit
Lake
South

Drakesbad
Guest
Ranch

Dream
Lake

Drake
Lake

Kings Creek
Falls

Bench
Lake

Sifford
Lakes

Devils
Kitchen

Crumbaugh
Lake

Cold Boiling
Lake

TWIN
MEADOWS

Mt. Canard

Hat Mtn

Hat Creek

DERSCH MEADOWS

Summit
Lake

Cliff
Lake

Shadow
Lake

Terrace
Lake

Bumpass
Mtn

Bumpass
Lake

BUMPASS
HELL

Southwest
Entrance
Station

LASSEN NATIONAL FOREST

LASSEN NATIONAL FOREST

Raker
Peak

Emigrant
Pass

89

Hot
Rock

Crescent
Crater

Crescent
Cliff

Lassen Peak
(EL. 10,457)

Eagle Peak

Emerald
Lake

Lake
Helen

CHAOS CRAGS

Vulcans
Castle

Pilot
Pinnacle

Soda
Lake

Crags

DWARF FOREST

Table Mtn

Manzanita
Lake

Reflection
Lake

Manzanita
Lake

Loomis
Peak

Cragg
Lake

Blue
Lake

Ridge
Lakes

Mt. Diller

Brokeoff
Mtn.

Forest
Lake

Sulphur
Works

i

89

44

89

44

Entrance
Station

LASSEN

NATIONAL

FOREST

North Fork Bailey Creek

Manzanita Creek

N

0   1.5 mi
     2.4 km

247

a crowd. Even then you can escape the hordes simply by skipping the popular sites like Bumpass Hell or the Sulphur Works and heading a few miles down any of the backcountry trails.

Modoc County (Lassen National Park is not in Lassen County) is one of the coldest places in California. Winter begins in late October and doesn't release its grip until June. Even in the summer you should plan for possible rain and snow. Temperatures at night can drop below freezing at any time. Winter, however, shows a different and beautiful side of Lassen that more people are starting to appreciate. Since most of the park is over a mile high and the highest point is 10,457 feet high, snow accumulates in incredible quantities. Don't be surprised to find snowbanks lining the Park Road into July.

SEEING THE HIGHLIGHTS

The highlight of Lassen is, of course, the volcano and all its offshoots: hot springs, fumaroles, mud pots, etc. You can see many of the most interesting sites in a day, making it possible to visit Lassen as a short detour from I-5 or U.S. 395 on the way to or from Oregon. Available at park visitors centers (see "Just the Facts," below), the *Road Guide to Lassen Park* is a great traveling companion that will explain a lot of the features you'll see as you traverse the park.

Bumpass Hell, a 1¹/₂-mile walk off the Park Road in the southern part of the park, is the largest single geothermal site in the park—16 acres of bubbling mud pots cloaked in a stench of rotten-egg-smelling sulfur. The name comes from an early Lassen traveler, Bumpass, who lost a leg after he took a shortcut through the area while hunting and plunged into a boiling pool. Don't make the same error.

Sulphur Works is another stinky, steamy example of Lassen's residual heat. Two miles from the southwest park exit, the ground roars with seething gases.

Boiling Springs Lake and **Devil's Kitchen** are two of the more remote geothermal sites; they're located in the Warner Valley section of the park, which can be reached by hiking from the main road or entering the park through Warner Valley Road from the small town of Chester.

SPORTS & ACTIVITIES

HIKING   Most Lassen visitors drive through in a day or two, see the geothermal hot spots, and move on. That leaves 150 miles of trails and expanses of backcountry to the few who take the time to get off-road. The "Lassen Trails" booklet available at the visitor centers (see "Just the Facts," below) gives good descriptions of some of the most popular hikes and backpacking destinations. Anyone spending the night in the backcountry must have a wilderness permit issued at the ranger stations.

Probably the most popular hike is the 2¹/₂-mile climb from the Park Road to the top of **Lassen Peak.** The trail may sound short, but it's steep and generally covered with snow until late summer. At 10,457 feet in elevation, though, you'll get a view of the surrounding wilderness that's worth every step. On clear days you can see south all the way to the Sierra and north into the Cascades.

Cinder Cone, in the northeast corner of the park, is another worthy hike, reached either by walking in about 8 miles from Summit Lake on the Park Road, or a much shorter hike (but long drive) from Butte Lake at the far northeast corner of the park. Now dormant, Cinder Cone is appoximately 250 years old. Black and charred-looking, Cinder Cone is bare of any sort of life (aside from very little vegetation) and surrounded by dunes of multihued volcanic ash.

A 17-mile segment of the **Pacific Crest Trail** cuts through the park and can be accessed via the Warner Valley Road or by a long hike from Hat Lake. The most interesting section of the trail for nonthrough hikers is the 5-mile segment south of Warner Valley leading to Boiling Springs Lake and Terminal Geyser.

CANOEING & KAYAKING   Paddlers can take canoes, rowboats, and kayaks on any of the park lakes except Reflection, Emerald, Helen, and Boiling Springs. Motors, including electric motors, are strictly prohibited on all park waters. Park lakes are full of trout and fishing is popular. You must have a current California fishing license.

CROSS-COUNTRY SKIING   The Park Road usually closes because of snow in November, and most years it doesn't open until June, so cross-country skiers have their run of the park. Marked trails of all skill levels leave from Manzanita Lake at the north end of the park and Lassen Chalet at the south. You can ski the 30-mile course of the road in a long day or an easy overnight. For safety reasons the park requires all skiers to register at the ranger stations before heading into the backcountry, whether for an overnight or just the day.

Park staff also lead snowshoe hikes into the park emphasizing ecology and winter survival.

CAMPING

Backcountry camping is allowed almost everywhere, and traffic is light. Ask about closed areas when you get your wilderness permit.

Car campers have their choice of seven park campgrounds, more than enough to handle the half-million visitors who come to Lassen every summer. So few people camp in Lassen that there's no reservation system except for the **Lost Creek Group Campground,** and stays are granted a generous 14-day limit. Fees are $45 per night per group. Sites do fill up on weekends, so your best bet is to get to the park early on Friday to secure a place to stay.

If the park is packed, there are 43 campgrounds in surrounding Lassen National Forest, so you'll find a site somewhere.

By far the most "civilized" campground in the park is at **Manzanita Lake,** where you can find hot showers, flush toilets, and a camper store. When Manzanita fills up, rangers open the **Crags Campground** overflow camp, about 5 miles away, which is much more basic. On the southern end of the park you'll find **Southwest Campground,** a walk-in camp directly adjacent to the Lassen Chalet parking lot.

ACCOMMODATIONS

Only one lodge operates inside Lassen Park: the **Drakesbad Guest Ranch.** Famous for its rustic cabins, lodge, and steaming hot-spring pool, Drakesbad is deluxe as only a place with no electricity or phones can be, with handmade quilts on every bed and kerosene lamps to read by. Full meal service is available and is very good. Rates begin at around $115 per guest, per night, double occupancy. Since the lodge is extremely popular and only open from June to September, reservations are taken as far as a year in advance. The spa is only for guests, but horseback-riding trips are available for day visitors as well as overnight guests. You can also arrange meals for a day visit. For prices and reservation information contact the **California Parks Co.,** 2150 N. Main St., Suite 5, Red Bluff, CA 96080 (☎ **916/529-3376,** or 916/529-1512 off-season).

▪JUST OUTSIDE THE PARK

Ⓢ **The Bidwell House.** 1 Main St. (P.O. Box 1790), Chester, CA 96020. ☎ **916/238-3338.** 14 rms, 12 with bath; 1 cottage with kitchenette. $60–$65 double without bath, $78–$115 double with bath; $153 cottage for two. Rates include full breakfast. MC, V.

In 1901 Gen. John Bidwell, a California senator who made three unsuccessful bids for the U.S. presidency, built a country retreat and summer home here for his beloved young wife, Annie. Although he died before ever living in the house, Annie eventually moved here and used it as a base for missionary work, converting scores of local Native Americans to Christianity. After her death, when Chester had developed into a prosperous logging hamlet, the building, with its farmhouse-style design and spacious veranda, was converted into the headquarters for a local ranch.

Today the house sits at the extreme eastern end of Chester, adjacent to a rolling meadow. The lake is visible across the road, and inside, Ian and Kim James maintain one of the most charming B&B inns in the region. Seven of the rooms have Jacuzzi tubs, and two offer wood-burning stoves. Breakfast is presented with fanfare and incorporates many gourmet touches, including home-baked breads and scrumptious omelets.

4 Lake Tahoe

Lake Tahoe has long been California's most popular recreational playground. In summer you can enjoy boating and water sports, plus in-line skating, bungee jumping, camping, ballooning, horseback riding, bicycling, parasailing—the list is endless. In winter Lake Tahoe becomes one of the nation's premier ski destinations with its 13 downhill resorts and 15 cross-country skiing centers. There's also sleigh riding, ice skating, snowmobiling, and—more increasingly—snowshoeing. Year-round activities include tennis, fishing, Vegas-style gambling, and big-name entertainment on the Nevada border.

And that's not the half of it, for there's also the lake.

It's disputable whether Lake Tahoe is the most beautiful lake in the world, but it's certainly near the top of the list. It's famous for its 99.997% pure water (a white dinner plate at a depth of 75 feet would be clearly visible from the surface!), and so immense that the water it contains—close to 40 trillion gallons—could cover the entire state of California with $14^1/_2$ inches of water. Its average depth is 989 feet, although it reaches 1,645 feet in places, making it the second-deepest lake in the United States (after Crater Lake, Oregon) and the eighth deepest in the world.

More important to the visitor, however, is this region's pristine beauty: the play of light during the day, which transforms the color of the lake from a dazzling emerald to blues and rich purples; the snowy mountaintops reflecting off the water; the fresh, crisp air; and the deep green of the trees carpeting the expanse of the valley. It's a sight that no one should miss—and one that nobody forgets.

ESSENTIALS

GETTING THERE   It's a 4-hour drive from San Francisco; take I-80 east to Sacramento, then U.S. 50 to the lake's south shore, or I-80 east to Calif. 89 south to reach the lake's north shore. From Los Angeles, it's a grueling 9-hour drive; take I-5 through the Central Valley to I-80 east at Sacramento, then U.S 50 east. If the weather's good and you can spare a few additional hours, it's really worth avoiding the Interstate for the scenic drive on U.S. 395 and U.S. 50, which lie along the corridor between the towering peaks of the eastern Sierras and the Inyo Mountain Range.

Reno/Tahoe International Airport, 40 miles northeast of Lake Tahoe (about a 50-minute drive), offers regularly scheduled service on 13 national airlines, including American (☎ 800/433-7300), Delta (☎ 800/221-1212), and United/United

Express (☎ 800/241-6522). If you make the big bucks, Trans World Express (☎ 800/221-2000) has direct flights daily from many cities—including Los Angeles and San Francisco—to **South Lake Tahoe Airport** (☎ 916/542-6180), just south of town.

Amtrak (☎ 800/USA-RAIL) services Truckee, 10 miles north of the lake; shuttle service is available to North Lake Tahoe from the station. Trains connect with the rest of the state through Sacramento.

VISITOR INFORMATION   Call the **Tahoe North Visitors & Convention Bureau** in Tahoe City (☎ **800/824-6348** or 916/583-3495), or stop by the **North Lake Tahoe Chamber of Commerce,** 245 N. Lake Blvd., Tahoe City (☎ **916/581-6900**); it's open Monday to Friday from 8:30am to 5pm and on Saturday and Sunday from 9am to 4pm.

In South Lake Tahoe, there's the **South Lake Tahoe Visitors Authority,** 1156 Ski Run Blvd. (☎ **800/288-2463** or 916/544-5050), and the **South Lake Tahoe Chamber of Commerce,** 3066 Lake Tahoe Blvd. (☎ **916/541-5255**), which is open Monday to Friday from 8:30am to 5pm and on Saturday from 9am to 4pm (it's closed on major holidays).

SKIING & OTHER WINTER ACTIVITIES

Tahoe offers California's best skiing, with 13 downhill ski resorts and 15 cross-country centers. The ski season usually lasts from November into May, but frequently extends into summer (in 1993 and 1995 there was skiing until July 4!). Lift tickets usually cost about $42 per day, $30 per half day, and $6 for children 12 and under. Five of the top areas—Alpine Meadows, Heavenly Resort, Kirkwood, Northstar-at-Tahoe, and Squaw Valley—offer an interchangeable Ski Lake Tahoe lift ticket.

If you've come to ski, contact both visitor offices (see above) for information about ski packages offered by almost every hotel and resort on the lake—you're likely to save a bundle. The following are some of Tahoe's most popular resorts.

✪ **Alpine Meadows.** P.O. Box 5279, Tahoe City, CA 96145. ☎ **800/441-4423** or 916/583-4232.

Six miles from Tahoe City, Alpine's high elevation (8,637 feet) gives it a long skiing season that lasts until Memorial Day. The mid-sized resort—ranked by readers of *Snow Country* magazine as their favorite resort in California—is mainly considered a mountain for intermediate and advanced skiers, with 40% groomed for intermediate skiers, 35% for advanced, and 25% for beginners. There are no on-site lodgings or additional sports facilities.

Diamond Peak. 1210 Ski Way, Incline Village, NV 89451. ☎ **702/832-1177** or 702/831-3249.

One of Tahoe's smaller—and less crowded and expensive—ski resorts, Diamond Peak plugs itself as the "premier family ski resort." It's primarily a mountain for intermediates (49%), with 33% of the mountain groomed for advanced and 18% for beginners. Kids love the new snowboard park. There's cross-country skiing too, and lodging in nearby Incline Village.

✪ **Heavenly Resort.** P.O. Box 2180, Stateline, NV 89449. ☎ **702/586-7000.**

Celebrating its 40th anniversary, this South Lake Tahoe legend is one of the area's largest ski resorts, with 4,800 acres of ski terrain and snowmaking on 66% of the trails. The vertical drop is 3,500 feet, the steepest in the region. The terrain is 45% intermediate, 35% advanced, and 20% beginner. There are 25 lifts, including a

Lake Tahoe & Environs

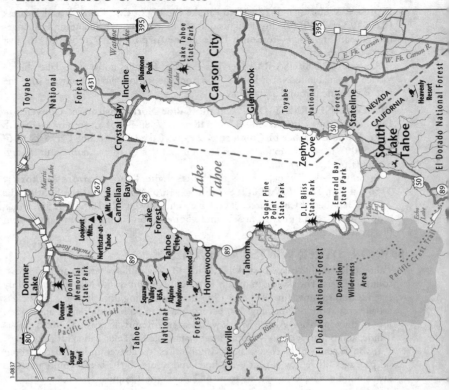

50-passenger aerial tram and three high-speed detachable quads. It straddles the state borders. Heavenly West on the California side has easier trails than Heavenly North, which is predominantly intermediate territory. It's less crowded, however, on the Nevada side.

✪ **Kirkwood.** Off Calif. 88 (P.O. Box 1), Kirkwood, CA 95646. ☎ **209/258-6000.**

Kirkwood's only drawback is that it's 30 miles (45 minutes) from South Lake Tahoe on Calif. 88; otherwise, this is one of the top ski areas in Tahoe, with one of the highest average snowfalls after Squaw Valley (Alpine Meadows is third) and excellent spring skiing often running into June. The 2,300 acres of skiable terrain is 50% intermediate, 35% advanced/expert, and 15% beginner. There are 11 lifts—including three triple chairs—accessing 65 trails.

✪ **Northstar-at-Tahoe.** P.O. Box 129, Truckee, CA 96160. ☎ **800/466-6784** or 916/ 562-1010.

More than 50% snowmaking coverage and a full-time kids' program make Northstar a top choice in Tahoe for families. It offers 2,000 acres of downhill skiing with 60 runs and 37 miles of cross-country trails, plus sleigh rides and snowmobiling. It has 12 lifts, including a six-passenger express gondola and four express quad chairs. Facilities include on-site lodging and five restaurants. It's only 45 minutes from the Reno-Tahoe airport.

Ski Homewood. 5145 Westlake Blvd. (P.O. Box 165), Homewood, CA 95718. ☎ **916/ 525-2992.**

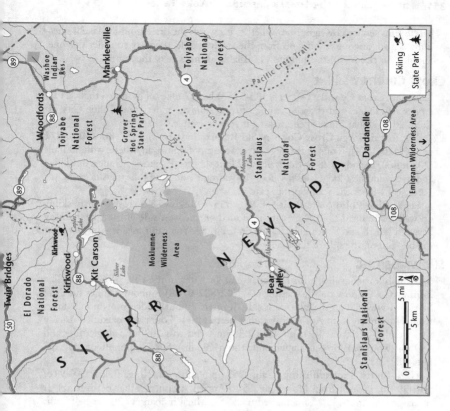

Homewood is one of our favorite small ski areas, a homey little resort with lean lift lines and gorgeous views of the lake. The ski area covers 1,260 acres and offers 57 trails and 10 lifts. It's a good family resort, with child care for 2- to 5 year-olds and a special ski and play program for kids 6 to 12. It's 6 miles south of Tahoe City and 19 miles north of South Lake Tahoe. *Hot Tip:* The best ski deal in Tahoe is the 2-for-1 special on Wild Wednesdays, which usually start in January: Buy one all-day adult lift ticket and receive one free.

✪ **Squaw Valley USA.** Squaw Valley, CA 96146. ☎ **800/545-4350** or 916/583-6985.

Site of the 1960 Olympic Winter Games, Squaw is almost every serious skier's favorite resort, simply because it offers the most challenging array of runs. Squaw's terrain is 25% for beginners, 45% intermediate, and 30% advanced/expert/insane. There are 33 chair lifts, including a 120-passenger cable car. It's famous for the chutes called the Palisades and the acrobatic skiing that they inspire. Skiing is spread across six mountains.

The **Squaw Creek Cross-Country Ski Center** at the Resort at Squaw Creek (☎ **916/583-6300**) has 400 acres for touring and 28 miles of groomed trails.

Sugar Bowl. P.O. Box 5, Norden, CA 95724. ☎ **916/426-3651.**

Though ranked by *Ski* magazine in 1994 as one of the top 30 resorts in the nation, Sugar Bowl's *best* attribute is its location: If you're driving to Tahoe from the Bay Area via Interstate 80, it's about an hour's drive closer than Squaw Valley. Known for its deep snowpack (does "powder skiing" mean anything to you?), the mid-sized resort has 58 runs serviced by eight lifts. Whether it's worth the drive from the lake is questionable, but anyone coming up from the valley should seriously consider this one. Should you choose to stay, lodging is available at the base of the resort.

CROSS-COUNTRY SKIING

Lakeview Cross Country (☎ 916/583-9353) has 37 miles of groomed trails, a full-service day lodge, and three warming huts. It's only 2 miles from Tahoe City off Calif. 28 at Dollar Point Shell, making it very accessible.

The **Royal Gorge Cross-Country Ski Resort,** Soda Springs (☎ 800/500-3871 or 916/426-3871), is one of the largest cross-country facilities anywhere, with 88 trails (203 miles), including 28 novice trails, and four ski lifts. Facilities include a day lodge and two wilderness lodges, a ski school, 10 warming huts, and four trailside cafés. It's 1 mile off I-80 at the Soda Springs exit.

Sugar Pine Point State Park (☎ 916/525-7982) also has cross-country skiing on well-maintained trails. The park is located on the west side of the lake, halfway between North and South Lake Tahoe on Calif. 89. You can't miss it—just look for the big sign on the side of the road.

SNOWMOBILING

Snowmobiles are available for rent at several locations in the Lake Tahoe area. The **Zephyr Cove Snowmobile Center** (☎ 702/882-0788) is about 4 miles north of Stateline, Nevada, on the lake's east side. It offers 2-hour guided snowmobile tours from November 26 to April 15 (weather permitting). Tours are scheduled usually thrice daily—at 10am, 12:15pm, and 2:30pm—and cost $69 for a single rider and $99 for two people on one snowmobile (limit 400 lb.). Special moonlight tours are also offered.

High Sierra Snowmobiling, Calif. 267 and Calif. 28, Kings Beach (☎ 916/546-9909), is open from November 15 to April 1 (again, weather permitting). It offers no trail tours, just a manicured track, for which it charges $30 per half hour. High Sierra is open daily from 9am to 4:30pm.

ICE SKATING

One of the world's most unusual ice rinks is 8,200 feet above sea level at **Squaw Valley's High Camp** (☎ 916/583-6985). The ice is accessible only by cable car—a scenic ride that's included with rink admission. Skating costs $17 for adults, $10 for children, including cable-car ride and skate rentals. After 4pm the prices drop to $9 for adults and $6 for children. The rink is open year round, daily from 10am to 9pm. Call first, as the rink closes a few days in the spring and fall for repairs.

SUMMER ACTIVITIES

BALLOONING   View the lake and the Sierras in a hot-air balloon suspended 10,000 to 12,000 feet in the air. **Lake Tahoe Balloons,** South Lake Tahoe (☎ 916/544-1221), offers 1- to 1¹/₂-hour flights followed by a champagne brunch at Café Roma at Caesars.

BIKING   There are miles of excellent paved bike paths around the lake. The 3.4-mile **Pope-Baldwin Bike Path** on the south shore runs parallel to Calif. 89 and through Camp Richardson and the Tallac Historic Site. In South Lake Tahoe another paved path runs from El Dorado Beach along the lake paralleling U.S. 50. Along the west shore there are 15 miles of paved pathways, extending from Tahoe City in three directions. On the northeast shore, Incline Village also has a 2¹/₂-mile trail from Gateway Park on Calif. 28.

You can rent bikes in Tahoe City at **Porter's Ski and Sport,** 501 N. Lake Blvd. (☎ 916/583-2314), and in Incline Village also at **Porter's,** 885 Tahoe Blvd. (☎ 702/831-3500). In South Lake Tahoe, go to **Anderson's Bike Rental** on the lake side of Calif. 89 at 13th Street (☎ 916/541-0500). Bike rentals usually cost $4 per hour, $11 for 4 hours, and $18 per day.

BOAT RENTALS   Several companies rent a variety of boats—canoes, powerboats, and pedalboats. Among them are the **Zephyr Cove Resort Marina** (☎ 702/588-3833), which rents all three; **Paradise Watercraft,** at Camp Richardson Resort (☎ 916/541-7272); **Tahoe Keys Boat Rentals,** at Tahoe Keys Marina (☎ 916/544-8888 or 916/541-8405), which only rents powerboats; and **North Tahoe Marina,** Calif. 28, 1 mile west of Calif. 267, Tahoe Vista (☎ 916/546-8248), which rents skis and tow lines along with 18- to 21-foot motorboats. Canoes and kayaks can be rented from **Tahoe Paddle & Oar** in Tahoe City (☎ 916/581-3029).

FISHING   Fishing in the crystalline clear waters of the lake presents a special challenge to anglers. Deep-water fishing for mackinaw trout is good year-round. Surface fishing for Kokanee salmon is best in May and June, whereas fishing for rainbow trout is ideal in the fall and winter months.

There are dozens of charter companies offering daily excursions on Lake Tahoe year round. **Mickey's Big Mack Charters,** Tahoe City (☎ **916/546-4444,** or 800/877-1462 after 6pm), is a well-respected outfit, led by experienced guide Mickey Daniels. All the fishing gear is provided, but you'll need a license, which can be purchased on the boat. Call for requirements and reservations. Mickey's boats depart from the Sierra Boat Co., in Carnelian Bay, about 5 miles north of Tahoe City. Five-hour trips cost $65 per person and depart daily year round, in the early morning and late afternoon; exact times vary according to season. Other fishing specialists include: **Blue Ribbon Fishing Charters,** South Lake Tahoe (☎ **916/541-8801**), and **Tahoe Sportfishing,** Ski Run Marina, 900 Ski Run Blvd., South Lake Tahoe (☎ **916/541-5448**).

GOLF   There are two Robert Trent Jones, Jr., championship courses in the area: the **Incline Village Championship Course,** 955 Fairway Blvd. (☎ 702/832-1144), and the **Squaw Creek Golf Course,** at the Resort at Squaw Creek (☎ 916/583-6300), which is the most expensive course ($115 on weekends) at Tahoe. Other challenging courses include the **Northstar Golf Course,** Basque Drive (☎ 916/562-2490), which has water hazards on 14 holes and was designed by Robert Muir Graves, and South Lake's **Edgewood Tahoe** (☎ 702/588-3566), site of the Isuzu Celebrity Gold Championship, with 18 holes and a driving range.

HIKING   The mountains surrounding Lake Tahoe are crisscrossed with hiking trails graded for all levels of experience. Before setting out, you may wish to contact the local visitors bureau for a map and more in-depth information on particular trails. Some of the most popular trails are:

Eagle Falls/Eagle Lake: One of the best trails for novice hikers, the Eagle Falls walk offers a cascading reward. The trail begins at Eagle Picnic Area, directly on Calif. 89 across from Emerald Bay.

Emerald Bay/Vikingsholm: From the parking area, 1½ miles above Tahoe's prettiest inlet, you can hike down to Vikingsholm, a 38-room replica of a medieval Scandinavian castle. The trail begins at the parking area on the north side of Emerald Bay, on Calif. 89.

Loch Levon Lakes: An easy but beautiful walk to three lakes, the Loch Levon Trail is perfect for hikers who wish to stay on the beaten path. To reach the trailhead, take

I-80 to the Big Bend exit and look for the sign PRIVATE ROAD PUBLIC TRAIL across from the Big Bend ranger station.

Shirley Lake: In Squaw Valley, near the tram line, this excellent hike has the advantage of a one-way adventure; you can take the tram up and hike down or vice versa. The trail begins at the end of Squaw Peak Road, next to the tram building.

HORSEBACK RIDING   Camp Richardson Corral, South Lake Tahoe (☎ 916/541-3113), offers a variety of trail rides and pack trips. A 2-hour trail ride is $35, whereas pack trips cost $150 per day, including packer, livestock, food, boat, and tackle. From December to March, sleigh rides are offered.

Northstar Stables, 2499 Northstar Dr. at Calif. 267 (☎ 916/562-1230), at the resort of the same name, offers a variety of trail rides, lessons, and pack trips. Special breakfast and dinner rides are also available. Children 6 and under are not allowed on trail rides. Northstar is on the north side of Lake Tahoe, between Kings Beach and Truckee. Prices range from $5 for pony rides to $23 for 1 1/2 hours, $50 for half-day rides, and $100 for a full day. Call for pack-trip information. Open year-round, daily from 9am to 5pm; when winter prohibits trail rides, sleigh rides are available.

Squaw Valley Stables, 1525 Squaw Valley Rd. (☎ 916/583-7433), offers trail rides and lessons for all ages and riding levels. Squaw Valley is about 5 miles north of Tahoe City. Prices range from $18 to $55 per person. Open mid-May to early September, daily from 8:30am to 4:30pm.

Sunset Ranch, U.S. 50, South Lake Tahoe (☎ 916/541-9001), is the only stable to allow unescorted riding. A quarter of a mile west of the Lake Tahoe Airport, Sunset Ranch offers rides to both children and adults along the open meadows that abut the Truckee River. Prices are $20 per hour, or $30 per hour for two people on a single horse. Open year-round, daily from 9am to 6pm.

INLINE SKATING   Although there are trails all around Lake Tahoe, the best ones for blading are the well-paved BICYCLE AND PEDESTRIANS ONLY paths that hug the Truckee River and Calif. 89, between Tahoe City and Squaw Valley. Rollerblades and other inline skates can be rented from the nearby **Squaw Valley Sport Shop,** Tahoe City (☎ 916/583-6278). The shop charges $5 per hour (a $10 minimum) or $15 a day (the price covers wrist guards and other protective gear). Squaw Valley is open Sunday to Thursday from 9am to 6pm and on Friday and Saturday from 9am to 7pm.

JET-SKIING   The **Lighthouse Watersports Center,** 950 N. Lake Blvd., Tahoe City (☎ 916/583-6000), rents jet skis, paddle boats, and canoes during the summer months. Reservations are recommended for jet-ski rentals. Jet skis cost $35 per half hour and $60 per hour; paddle boats and canoes go for $15 per half hour and $20 for 2 hours. The water-sports center is open June to September, daily from 9am to 6pm.

In South Lake Tahoe, the place to rent is **Lakeview Sports,** 3131 U.S. 50, across from the El Dorado Campground (☎ 916/544-0183 or 916/541-8405). They also rent mountain bikes, inline skates, and boats.

MOUNTAIN BIKING   At both **Northstar** (☎ 916/562-1010) and **Squaw Valley** (☎ 916/583-6985), you can ride the cable car with your bike and cycle the trails all the way down. Call for complete information.

PARASAILING   Lake Tahoe Parasailing, Tahoe City (☎ 916/583-7245), charges $40 to $50 (depending on your time aloft) and $70 for a tandem flight. Rides are offered from Memorial Day to Labor Day, daily from 8am to 3pm. Boats operate from the Tahoe Boat Co. Marina. Boat and Waverunner rentals are also available.

RIVER RAFTING   After 6 years of draught, the Truckee River—Lake Tahoe's only outlet—is now dumping plenty of water for a swift, but gentle, ride. Rafts seat anywhere from 2 to 14 people and cost about $25 for adults and $20 for kids (no kids under 5); the season runs from Memorial Day weekend to Labor Day. Rafting outfits include **Truckee River Raft Rental** (☎ 916/583-0123), **Fanny Bridge Rafts** (☎ 916/581-0123), and **Truckee River Rafting / Mountain Air Sports** (☎ 916/583-7238).

TENNIS   All the major resorts have tennis courts open to the public on a fee basis. Call the **Resort at Squaw Creek** (☎ 916/583-6300) and **Northstar** (☎ 916/562-0321) for information and reservations.

Budget-minded players looking for good local courts should visit **Tahoe Lake School,** Grove Street, Tahoe City, where two lighted courts are available free, on a first-come, first-served basis. **South Tahoe Intermediate School,** Lyons Avenue, off U.S. 50, has eight lighted courts. It charges a manageable $3 per hour.

WATERSKIING   North Tahoe Marina, Calif. 28, 1 mile west of Calif. 267, Tahoe Vista (☎ **916/546-8248**), rents skis and tow lines along with 18- to 21-foot motorboats. Other powerboat toys, including tubes, kneeboards, and wetsuits, are also available. Rates are $65 to $95 per hour. Open May to October 1, daily from 8am to 6pm.

WINDSURFING   Easy winds and relatively calm conditions make Lake Tahoe an ideal place to learn. At Carnelian Bay, **Lakeside Chalets,** 5240 N. Lake Blvd., Carnelian Bay (☎ **916/546-5857**), rents boards and offers lessons by appointment June to September. Windsurfers cost $20 per initial hour and $10 per hour thereafter ($50 to $60 a day).

LAKE CRUISES

The best way to experience the lake is to get out on it. **M.S. *Dixie II,*** at the Zephyr Cove Marina (☎ **702/588-3508**), a 570-passenger vessel with bars, a dance floor, and a full dining room, offers daily cruises year round, which may include breakfast, champagne brunch, and dinner. The Zephyr Cove Marina is on U.S. 50 in Nevada, 4 miles north of Stateline in South Lake Tahoe. Bay cruises cost $14 for adults and $5 for children 11 and under; breakfast and brunch cruises, $18 for adults and $9 for children 11 and under; dinner cruises, $26 to $36 for adults, $10 for children 11 and under. Call for schedules.

The *Tahoe Queen* (☎ **800/238-2463** or 916/541-3364), a 500-passenger stern-wheeler, operates year round, offering daily Emerald Bay cruises, sunset dinner-dance cruises, and shuttle service between the lake's north and south shores during the ski season. There are large outdoor and indoor viewing decks and a glass bottom for peering deep into the lake. The Emerald Bay Cruise costs $14 for adults and $5 for children 11 and under; the dinner cruise, $18 for adults and $9.50 for children 11 and under (dinner optional, menu selections from $15); round-trip North/South Shore Ski Shuttle, $18 for adults and $9 for children 11 and under. The *Tahoe Queen* departs from the Ski Run Marina, just west of Stateline. Call to confirm rates and schedules.

The North Shore version of the *Tahoe Queen* is the *Tahoe Gal* (☎ **800/218-2464** or 916/583-0141), a Mississippi River paddlewheeler that departs from the Lighthouse Marina in Tahoe City (behind Safeway). Cruises include Emerald Bay ($18 for adults, $8 for children), champagne breakfast ($15 for adults, $5 for children), sunset cocktail ($15 for adults, $5 for children), dinner ($35 for adults, $17 for children), and scenic shoreline ($15 for adults, $5 for children).

Woodwind **Sailing Cruises,** in the Zephyr Cove Resort, on U.S. 50, Zephyr Cove, Nevada (☎ **702/588-3000**), offers daily sailing trips aboard a 41-foot trihull craft that takes up to 30 passengers. The boat's glass bottom allows for good underwater viewing. Reservations are recommended. Trips cost $14 for adults, $7 for children 2 to 11, and free for children under 2. It leaves April to October, daily at 11:30am and 1, 2:30, and 4pm. There's also a sunset champagne cruise for $20 (adults only).

A DRIVE AROUND THE LAKE

Other than cruising over it, the next best way to contemplate the lake is to drive the 72 miles around it, though at times it can be completely clogged with traffic. Although the lake has never frozen over, the roads that surround it do; many are closed in winter, making this trip possible during the summer season only. If your car sports a tape player, consider buying *Drive Around the Lake,* a drive-along audio cassette that contains facts, tales and legends, places of interest, and just about everything else you could possibly want to know about the lake. It's available at numerous giftshops or at the South Lake Tahoe Chamber of Commerce (see "Visitor Information" in "Essentials," above).

We'll start at the California–Nevada border in South Lake Tahoe and loop around the western shore on Calif. 89 to Tahoe City and beyond. U.S. 50, which runs along the south shore, is an ugly strip of motels and overdevelopment that obliterates any view of the lake unless you're staying at one of these developments. Keep heading west and you're soon free of this ugly zone.

First stop is the **Tallac Historic Site,** a cluster of rustic mansions that were built 100 years ago and are currently being restored by the Forest Service. A little farther on you'll find the Forest Service's **Lake Tahoe Visitors Center,** located along Taylor Creek, which offers nature trails and also an opportunity to view Kokanee salmon making their way upstream to spawn.

From here Calif. 89 climbs northward. Soon you'll be peering down into beautiful **Emerald Bay,** a 3-mile-long inlet containing tiny Fanette Island, which has an old stone teahouse clearly situated at its peak. It was built by Ms. Lora Knight, who also built Vikingsholm (see below).

Across Calif. 89 from Emerald Bay, there's another parking area. From here it's a short but steep quarter-mile hike to a footbridge above Eagle Falls. Then it's about 1 mile to Eagle Lake. Register at the trailhead. **Emerald Bay State Park** (☎ **916/ 988-0205**) offers 100 camping sites on the south side of the bay.

It's not surprising that someone chose to build a mansion right here overlooking the bay—**Vikingsholm,** Emerald Bay, Calif. 89 (☎ **916/525-7277** or 916/ 525-7232). This 38-room mansion was built in 1929, a replica of a medieval Viking castle. It's so striking that a paved parking area on the highway had to be built for all the gawkers. Tree branches shaped like spears jut out from the gutters to ward off evil spirits. Inside, carved dragon heads decorate the ceiling beams. A layer of sod blankets the roof, which sprouts wildflowers in the spring. You can visit Vikingsholm by hiking down a steep 1¹⁄₂-mile trail (but remember, you have to come back up, too). The mansion is open for tours, every hour on the half hour, during summer only. Admission is $2 for adults, $1 for children 6 to 17, and free for kids 5 and under. It's open July to Labor Day, daily 10am to 4pm.

From here it's only about 2 miles to **D. H. Bliss State Park** (☎ **916/525-7277**), where you'll find one of the lake's best beaches. It gets very crowded in summer, so get there early before all the parking places are occupied. The park also contains 168 campsites and several trails, including one along the shoreline.

About 7 miles farther on, **Sugar Pine Point State Park** (☎ 916/525-7982) is the largest (2,000 acres) of the lake's parks and also the only one that has year-round camping. In summer there are several beaches in the park plus a nature trail; in winter there's cross-country skiing on well-maintained trails.

For a thrill, sign up with **Cal'Vada Aircraft, Inc.** (☎ 916/525-7143), and fly in their small planes, which take off and land on the lake. Trips range from 20 minutes to an hour long. There's usually a two-person minimum for each tour, and the cost is anywhere from $50 to $90 per person. Call for reservations. The seaplane base is in **Homewood,** on the west shore of the lake, 6 miles south of Tahoe City.

It's a clear drive through the small town of Homewood (site of the ski resort of the same name) to **Tahoe City,** which is smaller and much more appealing than South Lake Tahoe, although it, too, has its share of strip development.

At Tahoe City, Calif. 89 turns off to **Truckee** and to the Alpine Meadows and Squaw Valley ski resorts. **Squaw Valley** is only 5 miles out, and a ride on the Squaw Valley cable car (☎ 916/583-6985) rewards visitors with incredible vistas summer or winter from 2,000 feet above the valley floor. In addition to the views, visitors can enjoy ice skating, swimming, tennis, and bungee jumping at the High Camp Bath and Tennis Club. The cable car operates year round, daily from 8am to 4pm. A ticket costs $12 for adults, $9 for seniors 65 and older, $5 for children 4 to 12, and free for kids 3 and under. From Squaw Valley, it's another 5 or so miles to the railroad town of Truckee and **Donner State Park,** with its museum and monument to the Donner Party Expedition of 1846.

If you continue around the lake on Calif. 28, you'll reach Carnelian Bay, Tahoe Vista, and Kings Beach before crossing the state line into Nevada to Crystal Bay, Incline Village, the Ponderosa Ranch, and Sand Harbor Beach. **Kings Beach State Recreation Area** (☎ 916/546-7248) is 12 miles east of Tahoe City and in summer is jammed with sunbathers and swimmers. From Incline Village, a 4-mile side trip up the Mt. Rose Highway leads to an overlook of the entire Tahoe Basin.

Remember Hoss and Little Joe Cartwright? The **Ponderosa Ranch,** Calif. 28, Incline Village (☎ 702/831-0691), is a theme park inspired by the popular 1960s television show *Bonanza*. The original 1959 Cartwright Ranch House can be visited, along with a western township complete with blacksmith's shop and staged gun battles. There are also such activities as pony rides and a petting farm. The barbecue grill is almost always fired up, and breakfast hayrides—on tractor-pulled wagons—are offered for an extra $2. Admission is $9.50 for adults, $5.50 for children 5 to 11, and free for kids 4 and under. It's open mid-April to October only, daily from 9:30am to 5pm.

Also at Incline Village is **Sand Harbor,** one of the best beaches on the lake (though it can get incredibly crowded in summer).

South of Sand Harbor, if you wish, you can then turn inland to Spooner Lake and Carson City, capital of Nevada, or continue south along Calif. 28 to an outcropping called **Cave Rock,** where the highway passes through 25 yards of solid stone. Farther along is **Zephyr Cove,** from which the tour boats depart. You'll then return to Stateline and South Lake Tahoe, your original starting point.

WHERE TO STAY
SOUTH SHORE/SOUTH LAKE TAHOE
Very Expensive

✪ **Embassy Suites Resort Lake Tahoe.** 4130 Lake Tahoe Blvd., South Lake Tahoe, CA 96150. ☎ **800/988-9850** or 916/544-5400. Fax 916/544-4900. 400 suites. A/C MINIBAR TV TEL. $150–$240 suite for two. Additional person $20 extra. Packages available. Rates include continental breakfast. AE, DC, MC, V.

Stayin' Alive: The Saga of the Donner Party

The experience of the Donner Party is a grim testament to the perils that awaited those on the overland journey to the West. In 1846 the 89-member group, led by George and Jacob Donner, set out from Springfield, Illinois. They had read a book by Lansford Hastings that recommended turning off the regular California trail at Fort Bridger. This they did, but they were unable to make contact with Hastings and suffered a series of delays.

On October 23 they began the climb over the Sierras. Five days later they were stopped in their tracks, near Truckee Lake, by the first snowstorm of the winter. They camped and tried to protect themselves against the cold, but by mid-December it was clear that they needed to go for help. A party of 15 of the strongest, including five women and two Native American guides, set off with 6 days' rations to try to reach civilization. The journey turned into a harrowing nightmare.

Along the way, four of the party died; their flesh was stripped, cooked, and eaten by fellow members of the party. Two more men died and were eaten. The two Native Americans, who refused to eat human flesh, were shot and devoured. On January 10, 1847, after 32 days, the seven survivors staggered into a Native American village. A rescue party went back and recovered the survivors at the original site. They, too, had succumbed to cannibalism. Only 45 of the original 89 members of the Donner party survived.

Standing near the state line, this is the only real hotel on California's south shore, and it's in a class by itself, competing for the upscale gambling crowd and the convention business with Nevada's glittering casino hotels across the way. Family skiers fill up the place in winter. A Bavarian-style hotel of character, it rises nine floors, the roofline pierced with a double layer of dormers. The accommodations are nothing unusual for those who've stayed at Embassy Suites before: dark hardwood furniture, tasteful fabrics, well-chosen carpets, and such useful extras as microwaves.

Dining/Entertainment: Zackary's restaurant serves American and international dishes around the clock. Turtles sports bar opens onto an outdoor deck; it keeps its wood-fired pizza oven busy at night and turns into a disco later in the evening.

Facilities: Whirlpool, indoor pool, a basic gym.

Tahoe Seasons Resort. 3901 Saddle Rd. (off Ski Run Blvd.; P.O. Box 5656), South Lake Tahoe, CA 96157. ☎ **800/540-4874** or 916/541-6700. Fax 916/541-0653. 183 suites. A/C TV TEL. Winter/summer, $140–$210 suite for two. Spring/fall, $105–$160 suite for two. AE, MC, V.

Big, modern, and loaded with luxuries, the Tahoe Seasons lies in a relatively uncongested residential neighborhood at the base of the Heavenly Valley Ski Resort, 2 miles from Tahoe's casinos. Every unit here is a suite; all but 10 have gas fireplaces, and all have huge whirlpool spas, VCRs, refrigerators, microwaves, and coffeemakers. Skiing isn't the only activity around here: You can play a round of tennis on the roof, swim in the heated outdoor pool, or hop aboard the free casino shuttles. The ambience is rustic Californian, a style appreciated by the droves of second honeymooners who come here to lose their shirts, in more ways than one. An on-site restaurant and cocktail lounge provides, among other things, room service. Be sure to inquire about the seasonal "Romance" packages.

Expensive

Caesar's Tahoe. 55 U.S. 50 (P.O. Box 5800), Lake Tahoe, NV 89449. ☎ **800/648-3353** or 702/588-3515. 410 rms, 31 minisuites, 7 executive suites. A/C TV TEL. $110–$195 double; $375 minisuite; $650 executive suite. Additional person $10 extra. AE, DC, MC, V.

This 16-story hotel, built in the early 1980s, has all the glitter, the glitz, and the campy references to Roman mythology that Caesar's Palace in Las Vegas has had perfected for decades. It's a more intimate version of its Las Vegas counterpart, recently spruced up with a mere $16-million renovation. We consider its plasticized Roman theme one of the most fun establishments in Tahoe. Mythological figures even cavort across the elevators taking you up to your oversize room, where views of the lake stretch out beginning at a point across the highway.

The guest rooms are furnished with contemporary hardwood pieces and fully equipped with extra-large tubs (Roman style, of course) and two phones. King- or queen-size beds await you, often with padded scalloped headboards à la Mae West. The suites have unique themes, such as the Hollywood Suite, which comes complete with faux palm trees. Suites can only be guaranteed at check-in, presumably because high rollers are difficult to evict on schedule.

Dining/Entertainment: There are six in-house restaurants, the most popular being the Broiler Room. It's all here: grill, yogurt shop, buffets, an Asian dining room, and even an Italian restaurant by the pool. But Planet Hollywood is the venue that packs 'em in—everyone from tourists to the occasional visiting pop star.

Services: Concierge, room service (24 hours), laundry/valet, babysitting.

Facilities: A 24-hour casino plus showrooms with major entertainment; indoor lagoon-style swimming pool, tennis courts, fitness room with Universal machines plus massage therapists.

✪ Fantasy Inn. 3696 Lake Tahoe Blvd., South Lake Tahoe, CA 96150. ☎ **800/367-7736** or 916/541-6666. Fax 916/541-6798. 53 rms. A/C TV TEL. $115–$195 double Sun–Thurs; $155–$240 double Fri–Sat. Packages available. AE, DC, DISC, MC, V.

Even the "fantasy" industry is downsizing: At one time there were five Fantasy Inns around Lake Tahoe and Reno, but, alas, now there is only one hotel left in Tahoe that caters exclusively to the adults-only, all-romance market. Despite a theme that in less skilled hands would be tacky, leering, and lecherous, this place actually is outfitted in relatively good taste with goodly amounts of fun. Its erotic undercurrent isn't particularly discreet, thanks to sexually provocative art and a choice of porno flicks coming over the VCR whenever they're called for. Nonetheless, the place has provided love nests for hundreds of couples (including an occasional scattering of same-sex couples). It opened in 1993, and as such is one of the newest hotels in town.

Set on the California side, about 1 1/2 miles from the state line, it offers little in the way of outside diversions (presumably, you'll bring your own). There's no restaurant, no breakfast served, and no casino on-site.

The room decors mingle camp with a sense of fun and (usually) discreet tastefulness. All units have lots of mirrors (on both walls and ceilings), surround-sound stereo systems, twin shower heads for those communal showers, provocative art, and accoutrements designed for two. Theme suites (Antony & Cleopatra, Romeo & Juliet, Caesar's Indulgence, and the Sultan's Tent, for example) might have round beds or "waveless water beds." Our favorite of all, Graceland, has a bed shaped like a heart and enough Elvis memorabilia to give you something to talk about after your passions have been satiated.

Harrah's Casino Hotel. U.S. 50 (at Stateline; P.O. Box 8), Lake Tahoe, NV 89449. ☎ **800/ 427-7247** or 702/588-6611. Fax 702/586-6607. 540 rms, 40 junior suites and suites. TV TEL. $119–$180 double; $179–$280 junior suite; $486–$918 suite. AE, CB, DC, DISC, MC, V.

In hot competition with Caesar's for supremacy, this modern Vegas-style palace in an 18-story concrete-and-glass tower is deliberately glitzy and flashy. It stands astride the California–Nevada state line, and for legal reasons, of course, all the gambling facilities are on the Nevada side. Connected to Harvey's Casino Resort (see below) by a tunnel, it's a consistently high-rated hotel, an impressive achievement for such a sprawling complex.

The rooms are among the largest in Tahoe—each with two bathrooms and those thick fluffy white towels Sinatra was always demanding. Each accommodation has a bay window overlooking the lake or the Sierra mountain range. Key-card locks, soundproofing, and walk-in closets are additional room features. Recent additions include full no-smoking floors, as well as an enormous Family Fun Center designed to keep the kids perpetually busy while mom and dad work the slots.

Dining/Entertainment: There are seven restaurants, the most glamorous of which are on the upper floors. Big names in show biz headline at the casino's South Shore Room, which serves international dinners. The dinner-only Summit Restaurant on the 16th floor offers panoramic views of the lake and mountains, which are often better than the food. Other choices include a 24-hour coffee shop, an Italian café, an Asian eatery, and a split-level rooftop steakhouse. Buffets are also served on the rooftop. A sports bar is just one of many drinking meccas.

Services: Concierge, room service (24 hours), valet, overnight laundry, shoeshine, ski shuttle, baby-sitting.

Facilities: Casino, glass-enclosed swimming pool, health club, arcade, showroom, car-rental desk.

Harvey's Casino Resort, Lake Tahoe. U.S. 50 (at Stateline Ave.), Stateline, NV 89449. ☎ **800/HARVEYS** or 702/588-2411. Fax 702/588-6643. 704 rms, 36 suites. TV TEL. July–Labor Day, $115–$195 double. The rest of the year, $99–$180 double. Year-round, $179–$500 suite. Rates include continental breakfast. AE, CB, DC, DISC, MC, V.

Harvey's was born in Lake Tahoe in the 1940s, during the great expansion of Las Vegas, and it reflects a Vegas sensibility in its design. Originally the resort contained only a 12-story tower, which is referred to today as the Mountain Tower, but in 1986 the hotel's size was more than doubled with the addition of a 19-story Lake Tower. Today it's the largest hotel in Tahoe, boasting an 88,000-square-foot casino (Tahoe's largest), eight restaurants, and a cabaret with some of the most glittering, be-spangled entertainment in town. More than a hotel, Harvey's is, frankly, something like a city unto itself, and it's connected to its neighbor, Harrah's, by a tunnel. Try to get a room in the newer tower where every room has a view of both Lake Tahoe and the surrounding Sierra.

Dining/Entertainment: There are eight restaurants, often filled with convention revelers. Llewellyn's, on the 19th floor with panoramic views of the lake, is the premier restaurant, serving contemporary cuisine. There's also the Sage Room, a traditional western steakhouse (ribeye to venison), buffet restaurant, seafood grotto, pizzeria, a burger pitstop, and the very popular Mexican venue, El Vaquero. The Emerald Theater cabaret showroom features top artists and revues, and the adjacent Emerald Lounge has live entertainment nightly.

Services: Concierge, room service (24 hours), laundry/valet, shoeshine, ski shuttle.

Facilities: Casino, swimming pool, three tennis courts, arcade, health club and spa, car-rental desk, children's day camp and family fun center. The hotel also has its own wedding chapel, whose view of the lake has been the site of thousands of marriages.

Horizon Casino Resort. U.S. 50 (P.O. Box C), Lake Tahoe, NV 89449. ☎ **800/648-3322** or 702/588-6211. Fax 702/588-0349. 509 rooms, 30 suites. A/C TV TEL. Winter, $69–$119 double. Summer, $99–$149 double. Year round, from $325 suite. Additional person and lake-view rooms $10 extra; children 11 and under stay free in parents' room. AE, DC, MC, V.

This massive hotel stands next to the even larger and better known Harvey's, but it charges a lot less for basically the same facilities. Rising in a pair of towers (with 9 and 15 floors, respectively), the Horizon was radically renovated in 1994. Its original core, built in the 1960s, was the High Sierra Hotel, whose trademark Old West trappings were ripped out in favor of today's glitzy but bland modern style. The lobby is now a sea of white marble and mirrors, and the rooms, although less campy, are smoother and more tasteful (but less amusing for lovers of kitsch). The upper floors, naturally, open onto the best views of mountain and lake. The place is so big that if you've had too much to drink, you may never find your way to the room with your number on it.

Dining/Entertainment: The 24-hour coffee shop often attracts hard-core gamblers in the wee hours. There's also a buffet room and a run-of-the-mill steakhouse (many guests head over to the new Planet Hollywood across the way at Caesar's). The lounge features karaoke but turns up few promising Sinatras. Second-string performers, often from Los Angeles, perform in the cabaret room, which has a two-drink minimum. The casino is more upmarket than some of its patrons.

Services: Room service (24 hours), valet parking, a helpful staff who seem adjusted to their hotel's being a runner-up.

Facilities: Fitness center, outdoor swimming pool and hot tubs open to wind, ski-rental shop, arcade, wedding chapel.

Moderate

Best Western Station House Inn. 901 Park Ave., South Lake Tahoe, CA 96150. ☎ **800/822-5953** or 916/542-1101. Fax 916/542-1714. 96 rms, 2 suites, 2 chalets. A/C TV TEL. $98–$118 double; $125–$150 suite; $175–$200 chalet. AE, DC, MC, V.

Trimmed with redwood, the Best Western Station House Inn was built in the late 1970s, nestling amid pines 2 blocks off U.S. 50. It's one of the few hotels in town that has its own private "gated" beach on the lake, and it has an in-house restaurant, Lew MarNell's. It's not a particularly exciting hotel, but it's clean, competent, and eminently acceptable. The bedrooms are done in a modern style with oak furnishings. The staff is friendly but not particularly polished. There's a free shuttle to the casinos and most ski resorts.

Lakeland Village Beach & Ski Resort. 3535 Lake Tahoe Blvd. (P.O. Box 1356), South Lake Tahoe, CA 96150. ☎ **800/822-5969** or 916/544-1685. Fax 916/541-3539. 212 condo apts. A/C TV TEL. $75–$345 apt for two. AE, MC, V.

Between Ski Run Boulevard and Fairway Avenue off U.S. 50—that's a mile northeast of the casino district and a mile from Heavenly Valley—this condo complex is clustered on 19 lightly forested acres. In many ways it represents a real-estate dream gone sour. It was built in the 1970s as one of the region's most ambitious developments. Although about 60 of them were bought by full- or part-time residents, the rest couldn't be sold. The developers' solution involved transforming the complex into a hybrid half-residential apartment complex, half-holiday resort.

Don't expect any particular sense of community here—everything about the design seems focused on privacy and anonymity. The layout is a complicated labyrinth of buildings whose wood sides blend into the surrounding landscape. The only drawback is the proximity to the traffic headed into Lake Tahoe, although some units, placed out among the grounds, are quieter than those in the main lodge, which lies adjacent to the road. The only hotel services are daily maid service and continental breakfast served in the two-story lobby.

When you check in, be prepared for a baffling choice of layouts, as the resort's staff will present an array of floor plans that would confuse even the most jaded conventioneers. The units, ranging from studios to four-bedroom lakeside apartments, are streamlined California architecture, and many units have upstairs sleeping lofts. There are no restaurants on the premises, although complimentary shuttle buses carry gamblers to the nearby casinos, a grocery store is within walking distance, and all units have fully equipped kitchens. Perks include two outdoor pools, three saunas, tennis and volleyball courts, bicycle rentals, a health club, a large private beach opening directly onto the lake, and access to a boat dock.

NORTH SHORE/TAHOE CITY

Expensive

Chinquapin Resort. 3600 N. Lake Blvd. (P.O. Box 1923), Tahoe City, CA 96145. ☎ **916/583-6991.** Fax 916/583-0937. 172 town houses/condo apts. TV TEL. $162–$225 one-bedroom unit; $153–$209 two-bedroom unit; $209–$408 three-bedroom unit; $219–$472 four-bedroom unit. MC, V.

Built in the 1970s on 95 acres of land on the north shore of Lake Tahoe, this complex lies 3 miles east of Tahoe City and is convenient for easy access to the area's ski resorts, golf courses, restaurants, and shopping. It consists of a series of town houses and condos on forested lakefront land, including a mile of shoreline. The one- to four-bedroom units range in size from 950 to 2,800 square feet. The development offers some 20 different floor plans, and redwood trim and fireplaces are featured in every accommodation, some of which have their own saunas. All are fully furnished, containing a kitchen (with all the equipment), fireplace, washer, and dryer, and the rooms are attractively decorated. Some one-bedroom units are more expensive than two-bedrooms because of their lakefront location. At all times, about a third of the units are available to rent and the rest in use by their owners.

Facilities: Two sandy beaches, seven tennis courts, a swimming pool, a pier, saunas, a sand volleyball court, and all the jogging, walking, and hiking trails an aspiring Bill Clinton would ever need.

Hyatt Regency Lake Tahoe. Country Club at Lakeshore (P.O. Box 3239), Incline Village, NV 89451. ☎ **800/233-1234** or 702/832-1234. Fax 702/831-7508. 446 rooms, 22 suites, 24 cottages. A/C TV TEL. Winter, from $155 double, from $255 suite; summer, from $240 double, from $355 suite. AC, DC, DISC, MC, V.

If you like to gamble but hate those gauche, racy casinos that line the California–Nevada border, you might want to consider this Hyatt in Incline Village. Far, far classier and quieter than the casino/hotels you'll find along Stateline, the Hyatt is a resort hotel first and a casino second. Far more inviting than the baccarat tables is the resort's exquisite private beach, loaded with watertoys—catamaran cruises, jet skis, parasailing—available to guests.

While the hotel itself isn't exactly an architectural masterpiece inside or out, the adjoining lakeside cottages are a wee bit o' heaven for families—or honeymooners—who want beachfront access and large, comfortable rooms with unobstructed panoramas of the lake. A bonus for families is the popular Camp Hyatt, which lets kids 3 to 12 get a break from their parents for the day.

Dining/Entertainment: The Hyatt's Lone Eagle Grill offers fine American cuisine and lakefront dining in a rustic "lodge" atmosphere with large wooden beams and an enormous 20-foot fireplace. There's also the intimate Ciao Mein Trattoria, which mixes Asian and Italian styles, and the Sierra Café, which serves inexpensive burgers, soups, fajitas, buffets, and breakfasts. The small casino runs 24 hours, and includes an arcade and cabaret entertainment.

Services: Room service (24 hours), Camp Hyatt for kids, business services, valet.

Facilities: Outdoor heated pool and spa, health club, tennis courts, 55-foot catamaran, ski-rental shop.

✪ The Resort at Squaw Creek. 400 Squaw Creek Rd. (P.O. Box 3333), Olympic Valley, CA 96146. ☎ **800/327-3353** or 916/583-6300. Fax 916/581-6632. 196 rms, 201 suites. A/C MINIBAR TV TEL. $180–$250 double; $280–$395 suite. AE, CB, DC, DISC, MC, V. Valet parking $10, free self-parking.

The only deluxe resort on the California side of the lake, the $130-million Resort at Squaw Creek opened in 1990 amid controversy about its environmental impact. It's located in an inconspicuous corner of the valley at the base of Snow King Mountain, so you can't beat the resort's ski-in/ski-out access to Squaw Valley skiing. In fact, a chair lift lands just outside the door. Don't ski? Don't worry. There are lots of other sports facilities to keep active travelers happy.

The resort, 6 miles northwest of Tahoe City, encompasses two buildings connected by a shopping promenade, evocative of a luxurious Sierra lodge. One, of a harmonious design inspired by Frank Lloyd Wright, houses public areas, restaurants, and meeting areas. In jarring contrast, the other multistory building is made of black glass and steel, and contains the guest rooms, often filled with well-heeled skiers or business types on expense accounts. A waterfall cascades from the lobby to the pool area.

The accommodations are not particularly spacious but they're well equipped, containing ample closets, good lighting, ironing board, hair dryer, and a speakerphone telephone. (If only they had desks.) The suites, with spacious entertaining areas and additional TVs and telephones, come in a baffling array of sizes, each with a name the staff expects everyone to understand instantly (executive suites, panorama suites, vista suites, junior suites).

Dining/Entertainment: Glissandi, the resort's top restaurant, serves French-American cuisine in a window-wrapped dining room. Cascades is open for all-day buffet-style casual dining. The Ristorante Montagna has tables both indoors and out. The Sweet Potatoes Deli is open early for coffee, light bites, and picnic-style lunches. Bullwhackers Pub is a combination steakhouse and sports bar, with a pool table, regular live entertainment, and happy-hour specials.

Services: Concierge, room service, overnight laundry, supervised children's activities.

Facilities: 18-hole golf course, three heated swimming pools, three outdoor whirlpools, eight tennis courts, fitness center, shopping arcade, $18^1/_2$ miles of groomed cross-country skiing trails (marked for hiking and biking in summer), ice-skating rink (in winter only), equestrian center with riding stables.

✪ The Shore House. 7170 N. Lake Blvd, Tahoe Vista, CA 96148. ☎ **800/207-5160** or 916/546-7270. 9 rms. $125–$165 double. Rates include breakfast. MC, V.

If you're looking for a cozy, romantic bed-and-breakfast right on Lake Tahoe's shoreline, you'll be hard pressed to find a better one than the Shore House. Hosts Marty and Barb are an immediately likable pair who have made pampering an art form, whether they're personally cooking your breakfast—Marty's an ex-chef—or planning a foolproof itinerary for your day.

There are nine individually decorated rooms to choose from, each with its own entrance, fabulous rough-hewn log furniture (handmade in Idaho), private bathroom, mini-fridge, and blissfully comfortable featherbed. All guests have access to a private and pristine patch of lakeside beach and landscaped lawn that overlook the entire lake.

Boat owners can even make use of their six buoys and private dock. Planning on tying the knot? No problem: Marty's a minister of the Universal Life church, and Barb can provide the marriage license (talk about a full-service B&B). Sure, prices are a bit steep, but if you looking for a romantic weekend you won't soon forget, it's worth every penny.

Moderate

Meeks Bay Resort. P.O. Box 411, Tahoma, CA 96142 (summer); P.O. Box 70248, Reno, NV 89570 (winter). ☎ **916/525-7242** in summer, or 702/829-1997 in winter. 21 cabins. TEL. $75 cabin for two per night, $575–$2,800 per week. No credit cards. Closed Sept 25–June 11.

Lying 10 miles south of Tahoe City on Calif. 89, the Meeks Bay Resort is one of the oldest hostelries on the lake and something of a historical landmark. This wide, sweeping lakefront curve fronts the best fine-sand beach in Tahoe. Known centuries ago to the Washoe Indians, Meeks Bay was opened as a public campground in 1920. During the next 50 years the resort grew to include cabins and other improvements, and attracted many celebrities from Southern California. Acquired by the U.S. Forest Service in 1974, the property is now operated, under a special-use permit, from June 15 to September 15 only. Most rentals are on a weekly basis and consist of cabins both on the lake and on the adjacent hillside. Units vary in size, sleeping 2 to 12, and are modest without being austere. Each has a full kitchen, and some have fireplaces. Facilities include a beachfront cafe and canoe and kayak rentals.

On the grounds, the Kehlet Mansion is the resort's first-rate accommodation. Owned at one time by William Hewlett, cofounder of the Hewlett-Packard Corporation, and later the summer residence of billionaire Gordon Getty, this pretty little house, on a rock that juts out into the lake, is one of the best places to stay in all of Tahoe. The mansion has seven bedrooms, three bathrooms, a large kitchen and living room, and water on three sides. The entire house is rented by the week, sleeps a dozen, and costs just $2,800 for Wednesday-to-Wednesday bookings.

Sunnyside Lodge. 1850 W. Lake Blvd. (off Calif. 89; P.O. Box 5969), Tahoe City, CA 96145. ☎ **800/822-2754** or 916/583-7200. 23 rms. May 24–Oct 6, $145–$160 double. Apr 7–May 23 and Oct 7–Dec 12, $110–$125 double. Dec 13–Apr 6, $130–$145 double. Rates include continental breakfast. AE, MC, V.

Built as a private home in 1908, this hotel and restaurant stands 2 miles south of Tahoe City. It's one of the grand old lodges still left on the lake, and looks very much like a giant wooden cabin, with its typical Northern California architecture, complete with dormers, steep pitched roofs, and natural-wood siding. Stretching across the building, a large deck fronts a tiny marina. Directly on the lake, the place is rustic but fairly sophisticated, with about two dozen individually decorated bedrooms with homey bark-covered timber tables and chairs as well as both contemporary and antique-style prints. Lakefront rooms, the most desirable, go for $15 more than the others. Only four have no views at all (unless you find parked cars attractive). Five units have rock fireplaces and two have wet bars; 10 are no-smoking. Most of the lodge's ground floor is dominated by the popular Sunnyside Restaurant (see "Where to Dine," below).

Inexpensive

Lake of the Sky Motor Inn. 955 N. Lake Blvd. (P.O. Box 227), Tahoe City, CA 96145. ☎ **916/583-3305.** 23 rms. Apr 30–June 13, $50–$65 double. June 14–Sept 21, $74–$89 double. Sept 22–Apr 29, $50–$89 double. AE, CB, DC, DISC, MC, V.

Not much more than a 1960s-style A-frame motel in the heart of Tahoe City, the Lake of the Sky Motor Inn offers decent accommodations in a central location, only steps away from shops and restaurants. The place is popular with budget travelers and skiers, some of whom can be seen grabbing a very early morning cup of coffee and obviously itching to get out and tackle the wilderness. Accommodations throughout have almost no style, but the housekeeping is good and the comfort level in tiptop motor-inn tradition. There's a heated swimming pool as well as a barbecue area.

WHERE TO DINE
SOUTH SHORE/SOUTH LAKE TAHOE
Moderate

Cantina Los Tres Hombres. 765 Emerald Bay Rd. ☎ **916/544-1233.** Main courses $7–$13. AE, MC, V. Daily 11:30am–10:30pm. MEXICAN.

While this restaurant's cavernous tiki-bar interior can easily be mistaken to represent the South Seas, the food is unmistakably south-of-the-border. Los Tres Hombres' bar and adjacent dining area are two of the busiest rooms in South Lake Tahoe. The menu is well priced and extensive, although it sticks to the tried-and-true Californian-Mexican specialties such as tacos, burritos, and enchiladas. The chiles rellenos (cheese-stuffed peppers, battered and fried) get a thumbs-up, as does the crabmeat- and mushroom-stuffed enchilada. The dishes are unimaginative but the portions are mountainous. Service is brisk but not unfriendly, and some patrons may have had more than their share of tequila.

Nepheles. 1169 Ski Run Blvd. ☎ **916/544-8130.** Main courses $12–$18. AE, MC, V. Daily 5–10pm. CALIFORNIA.

En route to the Heavenly Ski Resort, this old home, complete with stained-glass windows, stops passing drivers, some of whom come in to sample the wares. Although the cuisine may range around the world for its inspiration, it's basically Californian, using market-fresh ingredients deftly handled by the kitchen. To give you a taste of the north woods, menu items nightly feature whatever game is in season—venison, elk, or wild boar.

The menu offers the usual steaks for the ol' boys, but more exciting dishes as well, including swordfish in pineapple and a garlic-cilantro salsa (how California can you get?), or perhaps duck in the classic orange sauce enlivened with a healthy dash of bourbon. If you demand ketchup here with your meal, it's likely to be a bottle from Indonesia. For dessert, consider their popular "decadence," served at the ultra-private hot tubs adjoining the restaurant.

Scusa! 1142 Ski Run Blvd. ☎ **916/542-0100.** Main courses $9–$15. MC, V. Daily 5–10pm. ITALIAN.

Also on the trail to the Heavenly Ski Resort, this cozy Italian eatery may have a decor that errs a little garishly on the neon side, but the food more than compensates. Dishes are interspersed with enough surprises to keep the locals happy. The place is civilized, basic but clean, and the staff is usually cheerful and knowledgeable unless they're rushed or having a bad hair day. Among the specialties are a smoked chicken and ravioli made with cheese ravioli, sun-dried tomatoes, capers, black olives, and sage butter, and a savory baked penne with smoked mozzarella, prosciutto, roasted garlic, and focaccia crust.

The Swiss House. 787 Emerald Bay Rd. ☎ **916/542-1717.** Main courses $10–$17. AE, MC, V. Daily 5–9pm. SWISS/CONTINENTAL.

The ambience of this South Lake Tahoe spot is genuine enough and warmly appreciated by diners, especially those arriving from the ski slopes in winter to find a fire blazing away. Despite its name, the place is not exactly into yodeling and cowbells, but the dishes are often alpine. The operation seems to run like Swiss clockwork, and, although we've had better Wiener schnitzels than this, the ones served here are perfectly adequate. There's also cheese fondue and raclette to take you back to the old country; it's warmly flavored but so filling you might not be able to finish. Other dishes include the inevitable steaks or something more refined like salmon en croute.

Inexpensive

Yellow Sub. U.S. 50 and 983 Tallac Ave. ☎ **916/541-8808.** Sandwiches $3–$6. No credit cards. Daily 10:30am–10pm. SANDWICHES.

When it comes to picnic supplies, there's stiff competition in South Lake Tahoe: three sandwich shops on this single block alone. Still, our favorite is Yellow Sub, with its 21 kinds of overstuffed subs, made in 6-inch and 12-inch varieties. The shop is hidden in a small shopping center across from the El Dorado Campground.

NORTH SHORE/TAHOE CITY

Expensive

✪ **Wolfdale's.** 640 N. Lake Blvd., Tahoe City. ☎ **916/583-5700.** Reservations recommended. Main courses $15–$20. MC, V. Wed–Mon 6–10pm (July–Aug open daily). CALIFORNIA/JAPANESE.

Although it's one of Tahoe's top restaurants, situated in an idyllic lakeside setting, Wolfdale's is visually modest. Behind a rather unassuming wood-shingle exterior is a simple, clean interior that combines country-style American furnishings with Japanese-style blond woods and screens.

Meals here might begin with tea-smoked duck with peanut noodles and mango chutney or sashimi with ginger and wasabi. The spinach salad tossed with smoked local trout, olives, and grated eggs is particularly memorable. The main courses are equally inventive and include grilled game hen with Thai dipping sauce or Alaskan halibut and sea scallops wrapped in Swiss chard with leek sauce. The chefs are capable and they know how to put a personal spin on regional ingredients. They also dare to be innovative and aren't afraid of blending the flavors and textures of East and West.

Moderate

Sunnyside Restaurant. In the Sunnyside Lodge, 1850 W. Lake Blvd., Tahoe City. ☎ **916/583-7200.** Main courses $13–$19. AE, MC, V. July–Sept, daily 10am–10pm (brunch Sun 9:30am–2pm). Oct–June, daily 5:30–9:30pm. SEAFOOD/AMERICAN.

Located about 2 miles south of Tahoe City on Calif. 89, the Sunnyside Restaurant, at the Sunnyside Lodge (see "Where to Stay," above) is worth a detour. In summer, when the sun is shining there's no more highly coveted table in Tahoe than one on Sunnyside's lakeside veranda. Guests can also dine in the lodge's more traditional dining room with its 1930s aura.

Nothing out of the ordinary here. At lunch the menu has fresh pastas, burgers, chicken, and fish sandwiches, together with a variety of soups and salads. Dinners are fancier, with such main courses as Australian lobster tail, oven-roasted shiitake pork tenderloin, and lamb chops (broiled and served with fresh mint). All dinners come with San Francisco–style sourdough bread, the chef's starch of the day, and a Caesar salad or cup of creamy chowder.

Tahoe House Restaurant and Bäckerei. 625 W. Lake Blvd., Tahoe City. ☎ **916/583-1377.** Main courses $9–$18. AE, DISC, MC, V. Bakery, daily 6am–10pm (deli lunch from 11am, dinner 5–10pm). SWISS/CALIFORNIA.

Serving Tahoe's skiers, boaters, and sunbathers for nearly two decades, Tahoe House is one of the oldest Swiss restaurants on the lake, located at the "Y" in Tahoe City. Though not a trendsetter, it's known locally as a reliable venue for good food at reasonable prices. Chef-owner Barbara Vogt's menu features some Swiss-German dishes such as Wiener schnitzel, Rahmschnitzel (veal with creamy mushroom sauce), grilled Bratwurst, and pork Cordon Bleu. Steaks and seafood also satisfy, as do several pastas. The full-service European-style bakery items and desserts are wonderful, as exemplified by home-baked tortes, truffles, and chocolates. Dishes are based on the seasonal availability of ingredients, and usually only the freshest and best are used. In keeping with the new trend in healthy cooking, Vogt has added a selection of lighter choices, including vegetarian dishes straight from the Vogts' farm.

Inexpensive

Bridgetender Tavern and Grill. 30 W. Lake Blvd. (at Fanny Bridge), Tahoe City. ☎ 916/583-3342. Burgers/salads/ribs $5–$7. No credit cards. Daily 11am–2am. PUB FARE.

Though it's located at Fanny Bridge, in one of the most popular tourist areas in North Lake, the Bridgetender is a locals' hangout through and through. Still, they're surprisingly tolerant of out-of-towners, who come for the cheap grub and huge selection of draft beers. The tavern is built around a trio of Ponderosa pines that meld in with the decor so well you hardly notice. Big, burly burgers, salads, pork ribs, and such round out the menu, and the daily beer specials—posted on the wall in Day-Glo colors—are definitely worth going over. During the summer months, dine outside among the pines.

✪ **Fire Sign Café.** 1785 W. Lake Blvd., Tahoe City. ☎ 916/583-0871. Breakfast/lunch $4–$9. MC, V. Daily 7:30am–2pm. AMERICAN.

Choosing a place to have breakfast in North Tahoe is a no-brainer: Since the late 1970s the Fire Sign Café has been the locals' choice for starting out their day, which explains the lines out the door on weekend mornings. Just about everything is made from scratch, such as the soft buttermilk biscuits and coffee cake that accompany the big ol' plates of bacon and eggs or blackberry-buckwheat pancakes. Even the salmon for the chef/owner Bob Young's legendary salmon omelet is smoked in-house. Lunch—burgers, salads, sandwiches, burritos, etc.—is also quite popular, particularly when the outdoor patio is open.

Izzy's Burger Spa. 100 W. Lake Blvd. (at Fanny Bridge), Tahoe City. ☎ 916/583-4111. Burgers $3.50–$6. No credit cards. Mon–Fri 11am–7pm, Sat–Sun 11am–8pm. BURGERS.

It's just a simple, wooden A-frame building containing a small short-order grill, but Izzy's Burger Spa flips an unusually hefty and tasty burger and an equally enticing grilled chicken breast sandwich. On a sunny day the best seats are at the picnic tables set out front. The restaurant is directly across from the Tahoe Yogurt Factory.

Tahoe Yogurt Factory. 125 W. Lake Blvd., Tahoe City. ☎ 916/581-5253. Coffee $1; espresso $1.30–$2.60; yogurt $1.50–$3.25; sandwiches $2–$4. No credit cards. Daily 6am–6pm (to 10pm in summer). YOGURT/SANDWICHES.

This small coffee shack, located at the "Y" in Tahoe City, is frequently mentioned as "the best little cafe in Tahoe"—perhaps an overstatement—but it does have its devotees. There's not much more to it than basic croissants, bagels, muffins, sandwiches, smoothies, and excellent java. Small tables are placed outdoors in the summer.

✪ **Za's.** 395 N. Lake Blvd. (across from the fire station), Tahoe City. ☎ 916/583-1812. Main courses $6–$10. MC, V. Daily 4:30–9:30pm. ITALIAN.

The sign used to say PIZZA'S until half of it fell off, which is just as well because there's a whole lot more to Za's than just pizza. One of the most popular restaurants in North Tahoe, this little gem serves great Italian food at bargain prices. Example: A hefty plate of smoked chicken fettuccine in a garlic-cream sauce with roasted bell peppers, fresh artichoke hearts, and mushrooms sells for under $10. Start with Pudge's Plate—a pleasing platter of fresh-roasted veggies doused in a balsamic vinaigrette—and a tumbler or two of chianti, then take a pick from the wide range of pastas, calzone, and pizzas. Za's is a bit hard to find (look behind Pete-n-Peter's Saloon), but *mama-mia,* is it worth the search!

TAHOE AFTER DARK

Tahoe is not known particularly for its nightlife, although there's always something going on in the showrooms of the major casino hotels located in Stateline, just east of South Lake Tahoe. Call **Harrah's** (☎ 916/588-6611), **Harvey's** (☎ 916/588-2411), **Caesar's** (☎ 916/588-3515), and the **Lake Tahoe Horizon** (☎ 916/588-6211) for current show schedules and prices. Most cocktail shows cost $12 to $40, and headliners are likely to include the likes of Jay Leno or perhaps Johnny Mathis.

There's usually live music nightly in **Bullwhackers Pub,** at the Resort at Squaw Creek (☎ 916/583-6300), 5 miles west of Tahoe City. The **Pierce Street Annex,** 850 N. Lake Blvd. (☎ 916/583-5800), behind the Safeway in Tahoe City, has pool tables, shuffleboard, and DJ dancing every night. It's one of the livelier places around.

The High Sierra: Yosemite, Mammoth Lakes & Sequoia & Kings Canyon

10

By Erika Lenkert and Matthew R. Poole

The national parks of California's Sierra are a mecca for travelers across the globe. The big attraction is Yosemite, of course, but the entire region is the stuff from which postcards are made.

It was in Yosemite that naturalist John Muir found "the most songful streams in the world . . . the noblest forests, the loftiest granite domes, the deepest ice sculptured canyons." Even today few visitors would disagree with Muir's early impressions as they explore this land of waterfalls, towering cliffs, wilderness, snow fields, alpine lakes, river beaches, and waterfalls. Yosemite Valley is riddled with dramatic waterfalls, sheer walls, and domes and peaks reaching toward the sky. The valley is the most central and accessible part of the park, stretching for some 20 miles, all the way from Wawona Tunnel in the west to Curry Village in the east. If you visit during spring or early fall, you'll encounter fewer problems with crowds.

Across the heart of the Sierra Nevada, in east-central California, sprawl Sequoia and Kings Canyon national parks, administered as one entity. Their peaks stretch across some 1,300 square miles, taking in the giant sequoias for which they're fabled. This a land of alpine lakes, granite peaks, and deep canyons. At 14,495 feet, Mount Whitney is the highest point in the lower 48 states.

Another big attraction in the area is Mammoth Lakes, one of the major playgrounds of California, where you can enjoy dozens of recreational activities in a setting of lakes, streams, waterfalls, and rugged meadows that bring the Austria countryside to mind. Acting as giant geological cleaners, glaciers in unrecorded times carved out much of this panoramic region, as did volcanic activity.

Because of the vast popularity of the parks and natural areas, facilities can be strained at peak visiting times. Always secure your reservations in advance if possible (and that definitely includes camping). You'll be glad you did.

1 Merced: Gateway to Yosemite

Merced is an ideal overnight stop en route to the park. It also has several sights worth visiting if you have the time.

Families enjoy **Applegate Park & Zoo,** at 25th and R streets, (☎ **209/385-6840**),which has a small zoo and picnic areas. Admission is nominal and it's open daily from 10am to 5pm.

For out-of-state visitors, however, what's compelling about Merced is its location at the center of the Central Valley (see Chapter 12). Also known as the San Joaquin Valley, this is one of California's most important agricultural regions. For example, you can explore the **Buchanan Hollow Nut Company,** 6510 Minturn Rd., LeGrand (☎ **209/389-4594**), a family-owned nut-processing and packaging plant where you can purchase some of the produce or ship gift boxes home.

You can acquire an agricultural history on Calif. 140 en route to Yosemite. The **Merced Agricultural Museum,** 4498 E. Calif. 140 (☎ **209/383-1912**), is a collection of assorted machinery that includes antique gas engines and horse-drawn buggies. Anyone who appreciates early technology will get a kick out of a visit. A donation is requested, and it's open Tuesday to Sunday from 10am to 4pm.

For a completely different experience, kids and flying enthusiasts will want to visit the **Castle Air Museum,** Santa Fe and Buhach roads, Atwater (☎ **209/723-2178**). On display outside at this former airbase are 42 historic aircraft, including the B-17, the workhorse of World War II, and the SR-71, which flies at three times the speed of sound. To reach the museum, take the Buhach exit off Calif. 99 to Santa Fe Drive and turn left. Admission is free, and it's open daily from 10am to 4pm.

ESSENTIALS

GETTING THERE   If you're driving from San Francisco, take I-580 east to I-5 south to Calif. 140 east. Merced Municipal Airport, 20 Macready Dr. (☎ 209/385-6873), is serviced by United Air Express. Amtrak, which operates along the Central Valley from Sacramento to Bakersfield, stops at Merced.

VISITOR INFORMATION   For information, contact the **Merced Conference and Visitors Bureau,** 690 W. 16th St., Merced, CA 95340 (☎ **800/446-5353** or 209/384-3333).

WHERE TO STAY

Best Western Pine Cone Inn. 1213 V St. (at West 13th St.), Merced, CA 95340. ☎ **800/528-1234** or 209/723-3711. Fax 209/722-8551. 94 rms. A/C TV TEL. $62 double, $72 double with refrigerator/microwave. Additional person $5 extra. AE, DC, MC, V.

Set about a mile north of Merced's center, relatively isolated from its neighbors, the two-story Pine Cone Inn was built in the 1960s and renovated in 1995. It's probably your best option in Merced. The bedrooms are cozy if bland, and painted in shades of hunter green. Rooms contain two phones and a coffeemaker. There's a run-of-the-mill restaurant on the premises, and a swimming pool. The inn's bar is open until 11pm.

Holiday Inn Express. 730 Motel Dr., Merced, CA 95340. ☎ **800/HOLIDAY** or 209/383-0333. Fax 209/383-0643. 65 rms. A/C TV TEL. $75 double. Rates include continental breakfast. 10% discounts for AAA or AARP members. AE, DC, MC, V.

Built in 1992, this is one of the newest hotels in Merced, and was designed in the blandly anonymous Holiday Inn format. Its three stories rise about a mile south of the town center. It's a good choice for families. The bedrooms are hardly inspired, but they're clean and comfortable, with modern amenities. It may be so hot outside you'll literally worship the hotel's outdoor pool and the air-conditioning in your room. Only continental breakfast is served here, but several fast-food joints lie within walking distance.

Ramada Inn. Calif. 99 and Childs Ave., Merced, CA 95340. ☎ **800/2-RAMADA** or 209/723-3121. Fax 209/723-0127. 112 rms. A/C TV TEL. $69 double Sun–Thurs, $79 double Fri–Sat. AE, MC, V.

New owners are working hard to make this more than merely a safe and relatively inexpensive stopover en route to Yosemite. The rather unremarkable building lies 3 miles south from the center of Merced, and though some of the decor may be motel-bland, new textiles have recently been added and a few larger rooms now have marble bathrooms. On the premises is a swimming pool, which comes as a blessed relief during the real summer scorchers. There's also a fairly basic restaurant that will fill you up, nothing else.

WHERE TO DINE

The Branding Iron. 640 W. 16th St. ☎ **209/722-1822.** Reservations accepted. Main courses $13–$20. AE, MC, V. Mon–Fri 11:30am–2pm and 5:30–9pm, Sat–Sun 5:30–9pm. STEAK/SEAFOOD.

This is by far the most animated, most popular, and most frenetic steak and seafood house in Merced. Set in the heart of town, behind its trademark green awnings, it has plank-sided walls accented with burned-in marks from branding irons. The portions are massive. Prime rib is the most consistently popular, although seafood, chicken, and lobster (the most expensive item) tie for close seconds. Soup, salad, potato, and vegetables all accompany the main course.

Ⓢ **Lenny's.** 1052 W. Main St. (at R St.). ☎ **209/722-0350.** Dinner platters $10–$16. AE, MC, V. Mon–Fri 7am–9:30pm, Sat 7am–10pm, Sun 9am–9pm. ITALIAN.

This is one of the two most visible restaurants in Merced, feeding a stream of newcomers who tend to return after they've explored Yosemite. The menu proudly offers old-world recipes handed down from the owner's family for several generations, with lots of all-American twists. Loaded with pastas and at least 15 other dishes, the lunchtime buffet is probably the region's best bargain ("awesome," pronounced one local). Dinners are more elaborate, usually featuring chicken, veal, pasta, and vegetarian dishes. All sauces, as well as all the sausages, are made on the premises in the style of long-ago Italy.

You won't lack for visual distraction here. Glass-fronted refrigerators, set end-to-end, display more than 150 kinds of beers, and one corner of the place is devoted to an espresso bar.

2 Yosemite National Park

by Andrew Rice

This area first became widely known to white men when a troop of U.S. soldiers in the Mariposa Battalion, sent to chase down a band of Native Americans, stumbled upon this natural wonder and were awestruck by its beauty. They regaled their friends with tales of its impossible geography when they got home, and Yosemite's popularity has been steadily increasing ever since.

It's a place of record-setting statistics: the highest waterfall in North America and three of the world's 10 tallest waterfalls (Upper Yosemite Falls, Ribbon Falls, and Sentinel Falls); the tallest and largest single granite monolith in the world (El Capitan); the most recognizable mountain (Half Dome); one of the world's largest trees (the Grizzly Giant in the Mariposa Grove); and literally thousands of rare plant and animal species.

What most sets the valley apart is its incredible geology. The Sierra Nevada were formed between 10 and 80 million years ago when a tremendous geological uplift pushed layers of granite lying under the ocean up into an incredible mountain range.

Cracks and rifts in the rock gave erosion a start at carving canyons and valleys. Then, during the last ice age, at least three glaciers flowed through the valley, sheering vertical faces of stone and hauling away the rubble. The last glacier retreated 10,000 to 15,000 years ago, but left its legacy in the incredible number and size of the waterfalls pouring into the valley from hanging side canyons. From the 4,000-foot-high valley floor, the 8,000-foot tops of El Capitan, Half Dome, and Glacier Point look like the top of the world, but they're small in comparison to the highest peaks in the park, some of which reach almost 14,000 feet. The 7-square-mile valley is really a huge bathtub drain for the combined runoff of hundreds of square miles of snow-covered peaks.

High country creeks flush with snowmelt catapult over the abyss left by the glaciers and form an outrageous variety of falls, from tiny ribbons that never reach the ground to the torrents of Nevada and Vernal falls. Combined with the shadows and lighting of the deep valley, the effect of all this falling water is mesmerizing. On a clear spring morning you'll see more rainbows than you can count and a base note of roaring water echoes through the entire valley.

All that vertical stone gets put to use by hundreds who flock to the park for some of the finest climbing anywhere. Sharp-eyed visitors will spot a lot of climbers hanging off the sheer faces of Yosemite's famous walls, such as El Capitan and Half Dome. Sometimes spending as long as 10 days slung from the rock, the world's best climbers are here to see and be seen proving their mettle. At the base of the big walls you'll find climbers of all abilities practicing moves and belaying techniques on smaller pitches.

The valley is also home to beautiful meadows and the Merced River. When the last glacier retreated, its debris dammed the Merced and formed a lake. Eventually sediment from the river filled the lake and created the rich and level valley floor we see today. Tiny Mirror Lake was created later by rockfall that dammed up Tenya Creek; the addition of a man-made dam in 1890 made it more of a lake than a pond. Rafters and inner tubers enjoy the slow-moving Merced during the heat of summer.

Deer and coyote frequent the valley, often causing vehicular mayhem as one heavy-footed tourist slams on brakes to whip out the Handi-cam while another rubber-necker, mesmerized by Bambi too, drives right into him. Metal crunches, tempers flare, and the deer daintily hops away, doubtlessly amused at the stupidity it just witnessed.

Bears, too, are at home in the valley. The name "Yosemite" derives from the Native American word *Yohamite,* "killer among us." Grizzlies are gone from the park now, but black bears are plentiful. Rather than posing pretty for the cameras in broad daylight, they make their presence known through late-night plundering of ice chests and food in the campgrounds.

Right in the middle of the valley's thickest urban cluster is the **Valley Visitor Center** (☎ **209/372-0299**), with exhibits that will teach you about glacial geology, history, and the park's flora and fauna. Check out the **Indian Cultural Museum** next door for insight into what life in the park was once like. Excellent exhibits highlight the Miwok and Paiute cultures that thrived here; the museum has a great collection of baskets and other artifacts. Behind the center is a re-creation of Ahwahneechee village, a Native American settlement like those that once existed here. The Museum Gallery houses a number of fine Ansel Adams prints as well as other artists' work.

You'll also find much history and memorabilia from the career of nature writer John Muir, one of the founders of the conservation movement. Muir's name is virtually synonymous with Yosemite (see box below).

Yosemite National Park

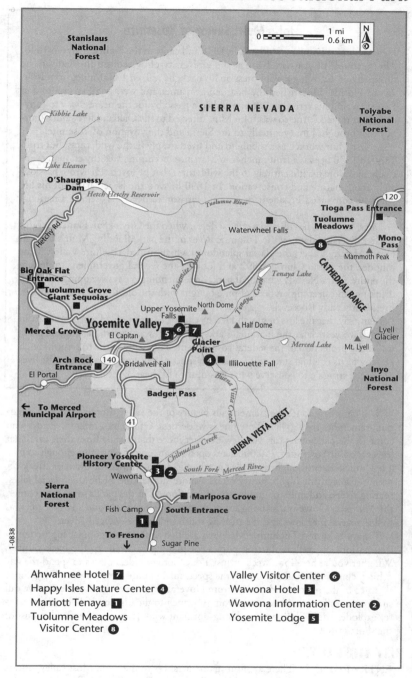

Stanislaus National Forest

SIERRA NEVADA

Tolyabe National Forest

Kibbie Lake

Lake Eleanor

O'Shaugnessy Dam

Hetch Hetchy Reservoir

Tuolumne River

120

Tioga Pass Entrance

Waterwheel Falls

Tuolumne Meadows

8

Mono Pass

Mammoth Peak

Big Oak Flat Entrance

Tuolumne Grove Giant Sequoias

Yosemite Creek

Tenaya Lake

Tenaya Creek

CATHEDRAL RANGE

Lyell Glacier

Merced Grove

Yosemite Valley

Upper Yosemite Falls

North Dome

Half Dome

El Capitan

5 6 7

Glacier Point

Merced Lake

Mt. Lyell

Arch Rock Entrance

140

Bridalveil Fall

4

Illilouette Fall

Inyo National Forest

El Portal

Badger Pass

Buena Vista Creek

← To Merced Municipal Airport

41

BUENA VISTA CREST

Chilnualna Creek

Pioneer Yosemite History Center

Wawona

3 2

South Fork Merced River

Sierra National Forest

Fish Camp

Mariposa Grove

South Entrance

1

To Fresno
↓

Sugar Pine

1-0838

Ahwahnee Hotel **7**

Happy Isles Nature Center **4**

Marriott Tenaya **1**

Tuolumne Meadows
   Visitor Center **8**

Valley Visitor Center **6**

Wawona Hotel **3**

Wawona Information Center **2**

Yosemite Lodge **5**

John Muir: Savior of Yosemite

He was born in Dunbar, Scotland, in 1838 and came to the United States in 1848. After a couple of years studying at the University of Wisconsin in Madison, he dropped out. Carrying a plant press on his back, he walked 1,000-miles from Indiana to Florida. Dissatisfied, he boarded a steamer and went via Panama to San Francisco. On his arrival in 1868, he asked a passerby for the nearest way to "anyplace that is wild." And so was John Muir directed to the Oakland ferry and a journey that brought him eventually to the Sierra and the salvation of Yosemite.

At first Muir worked as a shepherd and lived simply in the wilderness, but from 1880 to 1890 he was a fruit rancher in Martinez, becoming wealthy enough eventually to devote his life entirely to the wilderness that he loved. He wrote passionately about nature and conservation. In 1890 he won the largest battle of his life when he convinced President Benjamin Harrison to declare Yosemite a national park.

Later, however, he suffered a critical defeat when the City of San Francisco built a water diversion dam on the Tulomne River in the park, flooding Muir's beloved Hetch Hetchy Valley, the glacial splendor of which rivaled Yosemite Valley. Muir founded the Sierra Club in 1892 and lobbied the federal government to declare the entire Sierra Nevada a national park, once spending 3 days swapping tall tales, drinking, and sleeping on beds of pine boughs with the old Rough Rider himself, President Teddy Roosevelt.

Many say that the loss of Hetch Hetchy caused Muir to die of a broken heart in 1914. Two years later the National Parks legislation was passed, placing the parks under the protection of the federal government. Today the battle to return Hetch Hetchy to its original state still rages. The spirit of this great conservationist lives on, as the struggle to conserve what was dear to his heart continues.

While it's easy to let the tremendous beauty of the valley monopolize your attention, remember that 95% of Yosemite is wilderness. Of the four million visitors who come to the park each year, very few ever get more than a mile from their car. That leaves most of Yosemite's 750,000 acres open for anyone adventurous enough to hike a few miles. Even though the valley is a hands-down winner for dramatic freak-of-nature displays, the high country offers a more subtle kind of beauty: glacial lakes, roaring rivers, and miles of granite spires and domes. In the park's southwest corner, the Mariposa Grove is a striking forest of rare sequoias, the world's largest trees, as well as several meadows and the rushing south fork of the Merced River.

Tenaya Lake and Tuolumne Meadows are two of the most popular high-country destinations, as well as starting points for many great trails to the backcountry. Whether you're here for a week or just a day, both are ideal places to spend the day fishing, climbing, or hiking among the spectacular granite of the high country. Since this area of the park is under snow from November to June, the short season we call summer is really more like spring. From snowmelt to the first snowfall, the high country explodes with wildflowers and long-dormant wildlife trying to make the most of the short season.

JUST THE FACTS

ENTRY POINTS   There are four main entrances to the park. Most valley visitors enter through the **Arch Rock Entrance Station** on Calif. 140. The best entrance for the Mariposa Grove and Wawona is the **South Entrance** on Calif. 41 from Mariposa. If you're going to the high country you'll save a lot of time by coming in through the **Big Oak Flat Entrance,** which puts you straight onto Tioga Road without forcing you to deal with the congested valley. The **Tioga Pass Entrance** is only open in summer and is only really relevant if you're coming from the east side of the Sierra (in which case it's your only choice). A fifth, little-used entrance is the **Hetch Hetchy Entrance** in the euphonious Poopenaut Valley, on a dead-end road.

FEES   It's $5 per car per week to enter the park or $3 per person per week. Annual Yosemite Passes are a steal at only $15. Wilderness permits are free, but reserving them requires a $3 fee.

VISITOR CENTERS & INFORMATION   There's a central, 24-hour recorded information line for the park (☎ **209/372-0200**). All visitor-related service lines including hotels, and information can be accessed by Touch-Tone phone at **209/ 372-1000.**

By far the biggest visitor center is the **Valley Visitor Center** (☎ 209/372 0299). The **Wawona Ranger Station** (☎ 209/372-0564) and **Big Oak Flat Information Center** (☎ 209/372-0615) give general park information. For interesting biological and geological displays about the high sierra, as well as trail advice, the **Tuolumne Meadows Visitor Center** (☎ 209/372-0263) is great. All three can provide you with maps plus more newspapers, books, and photocopied leaflets than you'll ever read.

REGULATIONS   Rangers in the Yosemite Valley spend more time being cops than being rangers. They even have their own jail, so don't do anything here you wouldn't do in your hometown—this isn't the Wild West. Despite the pressure, park regulations are pretty simple. Wilderness permits are required for all overnight backpacking trips. Fishing licenses are required. Utilize proper food storage methods in bear country. Don't collect firewood around campgrounds. No off-road bicycle riding. Dogs are allowed in the park but must be leashed and are forbidden from trails. Don't feed the animals.

SEASONS   Winter is one of the nicest times to visit the valley. It isn't crowded, as it is during summer, and a dusting of snow provides a stark contrast to all that granite. To see the waterfalls at their best, come in spring when snowmelt is at its peak. Fall can be cool, but it's beautiful and much less crowded than summer.

The high country is under about 20 feet of snow from November to May, so unless you're snow camping, summer is pretty much the only season. Even in summer, thundershowers are an almost-daily occurrence and snow is not uncommon. Mosquitoes can be a plague during the peak of summer but get better after the first freeze.

RANGER PROGRAMS   Even though they're overworked just trying to keep the peace, Yosemite's wonderful rangers also take time to lead a number of educational and interpretive programs ranging from backcountry hikes to fireside talks to snowcountry survival clinics. Call the main park information number with specific requests for the season and park area you'll be visiting. Also a great service are the free painting, drawing, and photography classes offered spring through fall and on holiday weekends in winter at the Art Activity Center next to the Museum Gallery.

Avoiding the Crowds

Unfortunately, popularity isn't always the greatest thing for wild places. Over the last 20 years, tourist-magnet Yosemite Valley has set records for the worst crowding, noise, crime, and traffic in any California national park. More than 4.1 million visitors came in 1995.

The park covers more than 1,000 square miles, but most visitors flock to the floor of Yosemite Valley, a 1-mile-wide, 7-mile-long freak of glacial scouring that tore a deep and steep valley from the solid granite of the Sierra Nevada. It's still one of the most beautiful places on earth, but the Yosemite Valley becomes a total zoo anytime between Memorial Day and Labor Day. To make it worse, the National Park Service, which once called for eliminating auto traffic in the valley and reducing infrastructure inside the park, has done the opposite, continuing to allow kitschy concession signs, rinky-dink curio shops, an auto-repair garage, several hotels, a post office, a small hospital, and last but certainly not least, a jail, to turn Yosemite Valley into an urban mess, albeit a pretty one.

Cars line up bumper to bumper on almost any busy weekend. Until now, federal authorities did not show enough courage to implement one of several plans that would reduce traffic. But in 1995 Yosemite's new superintendent closed the entrances to the park 11 times between Memorial Day and mid-August when the number of visitors reached the park's quota; she turned away 10,000 vehicles. We'll see in future years whether or not she's successful in implementing measures to control crowds and preserve the quality of the visitor experience. In the meantime, to enjoy the reasons all those people flock to the valley without having to deal with the hordes themselves, my best advice is to try to come before Memorial Day or after Labor Day.

If you must go in summer, try to do your part to help out. It's not so much the numbers of people that are ruining the valley, but their insistence on driving from attraction to attraction within the valley. Once you're here, park your car and bike, hike, or ride the shuttle buses that go everywhere in the valley. Curry Village and Yosemite Lodge also both rent bikes in the summer (☎ 209/372-8367). It may take longer to get from point A to point B, but you're in one of the most gorgeous places on earth—so why hurry?

SEEING THE HIGHLIGHTS
THE VALLEY

First-time visitors are often completely dumbstruck as they enter the valley from the west. The first two things you'll see are the delicate and beautiful **Bridal Veil Falls** and the immense face of **El Capitan,** a beautiful and anything-but-delicate 3,593-foot-tall solid-granite rock. A short trail leads to the base of Bridal Veil, which at 620 feet tall is only a medium-sized fall by park standards, but one of the prettiest.

This is a perfect chance to get those knee-jerk tourist impulses under control early: Resist the temptation to rush around bagging sights like they're feathers for your cap. Instead, take your time and look around. One of the best things about the valley is that many of its most famous features are visible from all over. Instead of rushing to the base of every waterfall or famous rock face and a getting a crick in your neck from staring straight up, go to the visitor center and spend a half hour learning something about the features of the valley. Buy the excellent "Map and Guide to Yosemite Valley" for $2.50; it describes many excellent hikes and short nature walks. Then go take a look. Walking and biking are the best way to get around. To cover longer distances, the park shuttles run frequently and everywhere.

If you absolutely must see it all and want to have someone tell you what you're seeing, the **Valley Floor Tour** is a 2-hour narrated bus or open-air tram tour (depending on season) that provides an introduction to the valley's natural history, geology, and human culture for $15. Purchase tickets at valley hotels or call **209/372-1240** for advance reservations.

Three-quarters of a mile from the visitor center is the **Awahnee Hotel.** Unlike the rest of the hotel accommodations in the park (see "Where to Stay," below), the

Ahwahnee actually lives up to its surroundings. The native granite-and-timber lodge was built in 1927 and reflects an era when grand hotels were, well, grand. Fireplaces bigger than most Manhattan studio apartments warm the immense common rooms. Parlors and halls are filled with antique Native American rugs. Don't worry about what you're wearing unless you're going to dinner—this is Yosemite, after all.

The best single view in the valley is from **Sentinel Bridge** over the Merced River. At sunset, Half Dome's face functions as a projection screen for all the sinking sun's hues from yellow to pink to dark purple and the river reflects it all. Ansel Adams took one of his most famous photographs from this very spot.

VALLEY WALKS & HIKES   Yosemite Falls is within a short stroll of the visitor center. You can actually see it better elsewhere in the valley, but it's really impressive to stand at the base of all that falling water. The wind, noise, and blowing spray generated when millions of gallons catapult 2,425 feet through space onto the rocks below is sometimes so strong you can barely stand on the bridge below.

If you want more, the **Yosemite Falls Trail** zigzags 3¹/₂ miles from Sunnyside Campground to the top of Upper Yosemite Fall. This trail gives you an inkling of the weird, vertically oriented world climbers enter when they head up Yosemite's sheer walls. As you climb this narrow switchback trail, the valley floor drops away until people below look like ants, but the top doesn't appear any closer. It's a little unnerving at first. Plan on spending all day on this 7-mile round-trip because of the incredibly steep climb.

A mile-long trail leads from the Valley Stables (shuttle bus stop 17; no car parking) to **Mirror Lake.** The already-tiny lake is shrinking every year as it fills with silt, becoming a meadow, but the reflections of the valley walls and sky on its surface remain one of the park's most introspective sights.

Also accessible from the Valley Stables or nearby Happy Isles is the best valley hike of all—the **John Muir Trail** to Vernal and Nevada falls. It follows the Sierra crest 200 miles south to Mt. Whitney, but you only need go 1¹/₂ miles round-trip to get a great view of 317-foot Vernal Fall. Add another 1¹/₂ miles and 1,000 vertical feet for the climb to the top of Vernal Fall on the **Mist Trail,** where you'll get wet as you climb directly alongside the falls. On top of Vernal and before the base of Nevada Fall is a beautiful little valley and deep pool. For a truly outrageous view of the valley and one heck of a workout, continue on up the Mist Trail to the top of Nevada Fall. From 2,000 feet above Happy Isles where you began, it's a dizzying view straight down the face of the fall. To the east is an interesting profile perspective on Half Dome. Return either by the Mist Trail or the slightly easier John Muir Trail for a total 7-mile round-trip hike.

Half Dome may look insurmountable to anyone but an expert rock climber, but thousands every year take the popular cable route up the backside. It's almost 17 miles round-trip and a 4,900-foot elevation gain from Happy Isle on the John Muir Trail. Many do it in a day, starting at first light and rushing home to beat nightfall. A more relaxed strategy is to camp in the backpacking campground in Little Yosemite Valley just past Nevada Fall. From here the summit is an easy striking distance to the base of Half Dome. You must climb up a very steep granite face using steel cables installed by the park service. During summer boards are installed as crossbeams, but they're still far apart. Wear shoes with lots of traction and bring your own leather gloves for the cables (your hands will thank you). The view from the top is an unbeatable vista of the high country, Tenaya Canyon, Glacier Point, and the awe-inspiring abyss of the valley below. When you shuffle up to the overhanging lip for a look down the face, be extremely careful not to kick rocks or anything else onto the climbers below who are earning this view the hard way.

THE SOUTHWEST CORNER

This corner of the park is densely forested and gently sculpted in comparison to the stark granite that makes up so much of the park. Coming from the valley, Calif. 41 passes through a long tunnel. Just prior to the entrance is **Tunnel View,** site of another famous Ansel Adams photograph, and the best scenic outlook of the valley accessible by automobile. Virtually the whole valley is laid out below: Half Dome and Yosemite Falls straight ahead in the distance, Bridalveil to the right, and El Capitan to the left.

A few miles past the tunnel, Glacier Point Road turns off to the east. Closed in winter, this winding road leads to a picnic area at ✪ **Glacier Point,** site of another fabulous view of the valley, this time 3,000 feet below. Schedule at least an hour to drive here from the valley and an hour or two to absorb the view. This is a good place to study the glacial scouring of the valley below; the Glacier Point perspective makes it easy to picture the valley below filled with sheets of ice.

Some 30 miles south of the valley on Calif. 41 is the **Wawona Hotel** and the **Pioneer Yosemite History Center.** In 1879 the Wawona was the first lodge built in the state reserve that would later become the national park. Its Victorian architecture evokes a time when travelers spent several days in horse-drawn wagons to get to the park. What a welcome stop it must have been. The Pioneer center is a collection of early homesteading log buildings across the river from the Wawona.

One of the primary reasons Yosemite was first set aside as a park was the **Mariposa Grove** of sequoias. (Many good trails lead through the grove.) These huge trees have personalities that match their gargantuan size. Single limbs on the biggest tree in the grove, the Grizzly Giant, are 10 feet thick. The tree itself is 209 feet tall, 32 feet in diameter, and more than 2,700 years old. Totally out of proportion with the size of the trees are the tiny cones of the sequoia. Smaller than a baseball and tightly closed, the cones won't release their cargo of seeds until opened by fire.

THE HIGH COUNTRY

The high country of Yosemite has the most grandiose landscape in the entire Sierra Nevada. Dome after dome of beautifully crystalline granite reflects the sunlight above deep-green meadows and icy-cold rivers.

Tioga Pass is the gateway to the high country. At times it clings to the side of steep rock faces; in other places it weaves through canyon bottoms. Several good campgrounds make it a pleasing overnight alternative to fighting summertime crowds in the valley, though use is increasing here, too. Unlike the valley, a car is vital to getting around as the only public transportation is the once-a-day bus to Tuolumne Meadows. Leaving the valley at 8am, the bus will let you off anywhere along the way. The driver waits 2 hours at Tuolumne Meadows, which isn't much time to see anything, then heads back down to the valley, returning around 4pm. The one-way fare is $12, slightly less to intermediate destinations.

Tenaya Lake is a popular windsurfing, fishing, canoeing, sailing, and swimming spot. The water is very chilly. Many good hikes lead into the high country from here and the granite domes surrounding the lake are popular with climbers. Fishing here varies greatly from year to year.

Near the top of Tioga Pass is stunning **Tuolumne Meadows.** This enormous meadow covering several square miles is bordered by the Tuolumne River on one side and spectacular granite peaks on the other. The meadow is cut by many stream channels full of trout, and herds of mule deer are almost always present. The **Tuolumne Meadows Lodge** and store is a welcome counterpoint to the overdeveloped valley. In winter the canvas roofs are removed and the buildings fill with snow.

You can buy last-minute backpacking supplies here, and there's a basic burgers-and-fries cafe.

TUOLUMNE MEADOWS HIKES & WALKS   So many hikes lead from here into the backcountry that it's impossible to do them justice. A good day hike is the 5-mile climb to **Cathedral Lake**. This steep but shady trail passes an icy-cold spring and traverses several meadows.

On the far bank of the Tuolumne from the meadow a trail leads downriver, eventually passing through the grand canyon of the Tuolumne and exiting at Hetch Hetchy. Shorter hikes will take you downriver past rapids and cascades.

An interesting geological quirk is the **Soda Spring** on the far side of Tuolumne Meadow from the road. This bubbling spring gushes carbonated water from a hole in the ground. A small log cabin marks its site.

For a great selection of Yosemite high-country hikes and backpacking trips, consult some of the specialized guidebooks to the area. *Tuolumne Meadows*, a hiking guide by Jeffrey B. Shaffer and Thomas Winnett, and *Yosemite National Park* by Thomas Winnett and Jason Winnett, both published by Wilderness Press, are two of the best.

YOSEMITE SPORTS & ACTIVITIES

BIKING   Biking is the perfect way to see the valley. Eight miles of bike paths in addition to the valley roads make this an even better option. You can rent one-speeds at the Yosemite Lodge or Curry Village for $5 per hour or $16.25 per day. If you want a fancier bike you'll have to bring it from home. All trails in the park are closed to mountain bikes.

FISHING   The Merced River in the valley is catch and release only, and barbless hooks are required. High-country lakes and streams are literally leaping with trout. A California license is required and available in the park at the Yosemite Village Sportshop.

HORSEBACK RIDING   Three stables offer scenic day rides and multiday pack excursions in the park. **Yosemite Valley Stables** (☎ 209/372-8348) is open spring through fall. The other two—**Wawona** (☎ 209/375-6502), and **Tuolumne Stables** (☎ 209/372-8427)—only operate in summer. Day rides vary from $30 to $60, depending on length. Multiday backcountry trips cost roughly $100 per day and must be booked almost a year in advance. The park wranglers can also be hired to make resupply drops at any of the backcountry High Sierra camps if you want to arrange for a food drop while on an extended trip.

ROCK CLIMBING   Much of the most important technical advancement in rock climbing came out of the highly competitive Yosemite Valley climbing scene of the 1970s and 1980s. Though other places have taken some of the limelight, Yosemite is still one of the most desirable climbing destinations in the world.

The **Yosemite Mountaineering School** runs classes for beginners through advanced climbers (☎ **209/372-8444** in the valley, or 209/372-8435 at Tuolumne Meadows). Considered one of the best climbing schools in the world, it offers a basic lesson for $100 per person per day that will teach you basic body moves and rappelling, and will take you on a single pitch climb. Classes run from early spring to early October in the valley, less often in Tuolumne Meadows.

SKIING   Yes, there is an alpine ski area in Yosemite, but it isn't much of one. Opened in 1935, **Badger Pass** (☎ **209/372-8430**) is the oldest operating ski area in California. Four chairs and two T-bars cover a compact mountain of beginner and intermediate runs. At $28 per day for adults and $13 for children on weekends (about

20% cheaper midweek), it's a great place to learn how to ski or snowboard. If you're a good skier or boarder already, don't bother.

Yosemite is a better destination for cross-country skiers and snowshoers. Both the Badger Pass ski school and the mountaineering school run trips and lessons for all abilities, ranging from basic technique to trans-Sierra crossings. If you're on your own, Crane Flat is a good place to go, as is the groomed track up to Glacier Point, a 20-mile round-trip.

ICE SKATING   In winter the **Curry Village Ice Rink** is a lot of fun. It's outdoors and melts quickly when the weather warms up. Rates are $5 for adults, $4.50 for children. Skate rentals are available.

CAMPING

Campgrounds in Yosemite can be reserved up to 4 months in advance through **DESTINET** (☎ 800/436-7275). During the busy season all valley campsites sell out within hours of becoming available on the service.

VALLEY CAMPGROUNDS

The five car campgrounds in the valley are always full except in the dead of winter. All are located along the Merced River and cost $15 per night. All have drinking water, flush toilets, pay phones, fire pits, and a heavy ranger presence. Showers are available for a cost at Curry Village. Three campgrounds—**North Pines, Upper Pines,** and **Lower River**—allow small RVs (less than 35 feet long). **Upper River** is for tents only. If you're expecting a real nature experience, skip camping in the valley unless you like doing so with 4,000 strangers.

Sunnyside Campground is the only walk-in campground in the valley and fills up with climbers since it's only $3 per night. Hard-core climbers used to live here for months at a time, but the Park Service has cracked down on that. It still has a much more bohemian atmosphere than at any of the other campgrounds.

ELSEWHERE IN THE PARK

Outside the valley things start looking up for campers. Two campgrounds near the south entrance of the park, **Wawona** and **Bridalveil Creek,** offer a total of 210 sites with all the amenities. Wawona is open year-round on a first-come, first-served basis. Because it sits well above snowline at more than 7,000 feet, Bridalveil is open in summer only. Both cost $10 per night.

Crane Flat, Hodgdon Meadow, and Tamarack Flat are all in the western corner of the park near the Big Oak Flat Entrance.

Crane Flat is the nearest to the valley, about a half-hour drive, with 166 sites, water, flush toilets, and fire pits. Its rates are $12 per night, and it's open from May to October. **Hodgdon Meadow** is directly adjacent to the Big Oak Flat entrance at 4,800 feet elevation. It's open year-round and charges $12 per night. Facilities include flush toilets, running water, a ranger station, and pay phones. It's one of the least crowded low-elevation car campgrounds, but there's not a lot to do here.

Tamarack Flat is a waterless, 52-site campground with pit toilets, open June to October. It's a bargain at $6 per night.

High-country car campers can choose between Tuolumne Meadows, White Wolf, Yosemite Creek, or Porcupine Flat. All are above 8,000 feet and open in summer only.

✪ **Tuolumne Meadows** is the largest campground in the park, with more than 300 spaces, but it absorbs the crowd well and has all the amenities, including campfire programs and slide shows in the outdoor amphitheater. Half the sites are reserved in advance. The rest are set aside on a first-come, first-served basis. Rates are $12 per night.

White Wolf, west of Tuolumne Meadows, is the other full-service campground in the high country, with 87 sites available for $10 per night. It offers a drier climate than the meadow and doesn't fill up as quickly.

Two primitive camps, **Porcupine Flat** and **Yosemite Creek,** are the last to fill up in the park. Both have pit toilets and no running water, and charge $6 per night.

ACCOMMODATIONS
IN THE PARK

The grand **Ahwahnee Hotel** (☎ 209/252-4848) is one of the most romantic and beautiful hotels in California. With its ballroom, pool, tennis, gourmet dining, outstanding views, and high-digit price tag, it's a special-occasion sort of affair. Rooms are booked a year in advance. Try to reserve one of the cottages, which cost the same as rooms in the main hotel but are more spacious.

The next best thing (and much more moderately priced) is the **Wawona Hotel** (☎ 209/252-4848), near the south entrance. Now a National Historical Landmark, the Wawona is a romantic throwback to another century. That has its ups and downs. Private bathrooms were not a big hit yet in the 19th century and rooms were small to hold in heat. Still, the Wawona is a great place to play make-believe. It offers a restaurant, pool, stables, and a lounge.

Yosemite Lodge (☎ 209/252-4848) is the next step down in Yosemite Valley accommodations. It's actually a huge complex, not a lodge, with an array of accommodations ranging from luxurious suites with outdoor balconies and striking views of Yosemite Falls to one-room cabins with shared baths in a separate building. There's a pool. Two restaurants and a cafeteria serve mediocre meals. Rates are moderate.

Curry Village (☎ 209/252-4848) is the valley's low-rent district. This compound of almost 200 cabins and 400 tent cabins varies widely in quality. Some have private baths; others share campground-style bathrooms. Ironically, the oldest cabins are the nicest. Shoddy construction gives the others a slapped-together appearance, not to mention making them cold and drafty in winter. The tent cabins have wood floors and canvas walls; without real walls to stop noise, they lack any sort of privacy, but they're fun in that summer camp way. You'll have to sustain yourself with fast food from the Curry Village shopping center, as no cooking is allowed in the rooms. Rates are inexpensive to moderate.

An intriguing option bridging the gap between backpacking and staying in a hotel are Yosemite's five backcountry **High Sierra Camps.** These wilderness lodges are simple tent cabins and cafeteria tents located in some of the most beautiful, remote parts of the park. The five camps—Glen Aulin, May Lake, Sunrise, Merced Lake, and Vogelsang—make for good individual destinations. Or you can link several together, since they're arranged in a loose loop about a 10-mile hike from each other—a nice wilderness circuit. Overnight rates include a tent cabin, breakfast, dinner, bathrooms, and showers. High Sierra camp reservations are accepted beginning in December for the following summer and usually book solid by January. Contact **High Sierra Reservations,** Yosemite Park and Curry Co., 5410 E. Home Ave., Fresno, CA 93727 (☎ **209/454-2002**).

OUTSIDE THE PARK

✪ **The Estate by the Elderberries.** 48688 Victoria Lane (P.O. Box 577), Oakhurst, CA 93644. ☎ **209/683-6860** (Château du Sureau), or 209/683-6800 (Erna's Elderberry House restaurant). Fax 209/683-0800. 9 rms. A/C TEL. $310–$410 double. Rates include full breakfast. Additional person $65 extra. AE, MC, V.

If you're in search of the perfect marriage of luxurious lodging and decadent dining, the Château du Sureau and Erna's Elderberry House in Oakhurst, a 20-minute drive from the southern entrance to Yosemite along Calif. 41, give even Wine Country retreats a run for their money. The restaurant was established in 1984 and has been hailed as one of the best places to dine in the state. The château—"built to look old"—dates only from 1991 and is set back off the road on the crest of a hill. From the restaurant at the front of the property, a pathway leads through fragrant gardens past fountains to the house, which resembles a French château complete with turret and terra-cotta–tile roof.

The interior is exquisitely furnished with fine antiques, rugs, and fabrics. Each room is decorated differently, one with a large French canopy bed decked out in French toile, another with a mother-of-pearl inlay Victorian-style bed. All have king-size beds with the finest Italian linens, goose-down comforters, wood-burning fireplaces, wrought-iron balconies, and CD sound systems with a selection of discs. TVs are available on request. The bathrooms are finished with hand-painted French tiles, and some rooms have whirlpool tubs.

Dining/Entertainment: The restaurant offers impeccable food, ambience, and service without being stuffy. The six-course $58 prix-fixe menu changes daily. A smaller three-course menu is available for $45. You might find a salmon en croûte to start, followed by quail filled with sausage spoonbread and served with huckleberry sauce and six seasonal vegetables. After a salad, a dessert such as cranberry walnut cake with pumpkin ice cream would finish the repast.

Services: Room service (24 hours), twice-daily maid service, coffee and refreshments in the lobby.

Facilities: Outdoor pool and sundeck.

✪ **Tenaya Lodge.** 1122 Calif. 41, Fish Camp, CA 93623. ☎ **800/635-5807** or 209/683-6555. Fax 209/683-8684. 224 rms, 20 suites. A/C MINIBAR TV TEL. Winter, $89 double Sun–Thurs, $129 double Fri–Sat. Summer, $199 double Sun–Thurs, $219 double Fri–Sat. Add $20–$80 for suites. Buffet breakfast $10 per couple. Children stay free in parents' room. AE, DC, MC, V.

This three- and four-story resort opened in 1990 on a 35-acre tract of forested land loaded with hiking trails. It's the centerpiece of Fish Camp, a village whose only other attraction is a gas station and a general store. Inside, the decorative theme is a cross between an Adirondack hunting lodge and a southwestern pueblo. The lobby is dominated by a massive river-rock fireplace rising three stories. This is probably the best resort outside the southern entrance to Yosemite, with a likable staff well seasoned by the training methods of the Marriott chain. The rooms are ultramodern, with three phones and other amenities, including in-room safes.

Dining/Entertainment: Since there aren't lots of other options in town, the three restaurants draw huge crowds.

Services: Room service.

Facilities: Indoor and outdoor swimming pools, on-site massage specialists, health club, games room, sleigh and hay rides (depending on the season).

3 Mammoth Lakes

High in the Sierras, just southeast of Yosemite, Mammoth Lakes is surrounded by glacier-carved, pine-covered peaks that soar up from flower-filled meadows. It's an alpine region of sweeping beauty and one of Californians' favorite playgrounds for hiking, biking, horseback riding, skiing, and more. It's also home to one of the top-rated ski resorts in the world.

ESSENTIALS

GETTING THERE   It's a 6-hour drive from San Francisco via Calif. 120 over the Tioga Pass in Yosemite (closed in winter), 5 hours north of Los Angeles via Calif. 14 and U.S. 395, and 3 hours south of Reno, Nevada, via U.S. 395. In winter, Mammoth is accessible via U.S. 395 from the north or the south.

Sierra Mountain Airways (☎ 800/22-GO-FLY) and **Mountain Air Express** (☎ 800/788-4247) service Mammoth Lakes Airport on U.S. 395.

VISITOR INFORMATION   For information, contact the **Mammoth Lakes Visitors Bureau,** Calif. 203 (P.O. Box 48), Mammoth Lakes, CA 93546 (☎ **800/ 367-6572** or 619/934-2712).

ENJOYING THE OUTDOORS

Mammoth Lakes is at the heart of several wilderness areas and is cut through by the San Joaquin and Owens rivers. Mammoth Mountain overlooks the Ansel Adams Wilderness Area to the west and the John Muir Wilderness Area to the southeast, and beyond to the Inyo National Forest and the Sierra National Forest.

The ✪ **Mammoth Mountain Ski Area,** P.O. Box 24, Mammoth Lakes, CA 93546 (☎ **800/832-7320** or 619/934-2571), is the central focus for both summer and winter activities. Visitors can ride the lifts to see panoramic vistas; those who want an active vacation have a world of options.

DOWNHILL & CROSS-COUNTRY SKIING   In winter Mammoth Mountain has more than 3,500 skiable acres, a 3,100-foot vertical drop, 150 trails (22 with snowmaking), and 31 lifts, including two high-speed quads. The terrain is 30% beginner, 40% intermediate, and 30% advanced. It's known for power sun, ideal spring skiing conditions, and anywhere from 8 to 12 feet of snow.

The **June Mountain Ski Area** (☎ **619/648-7733**), 20 minutes north of Mammoth, is smaller and offers many summer activities. It has 500 skiable acres, a 2,590-foot vertical drop, 35 trails, and eight lifts, including two high-speed quads. The terrain is 35% beginner, 45% intermediate, and 20% advanced. It's at the center of a chain of lakes—Grant, Silver, Gull, and June—which can be viewed on a scenic driving loop around Calif. 158. It's especially beautiful in the fall when the aspens are ablaze with gold. Cross-country ski centers are at **Tamarack Lodge** (☎ 619/934-2442) and **Sierra Meadows Ski Touring Center** (☎ 619/934-6161). There's also snowmobiling, dog sledding, snowshoeing, and sleigh rides.

MOUNTAIN BIKING   In summer the mountain becomes one huge bike park and climbing playground. The **Bike Center** at the base of the mountain has rentals and accessories. The bike park is famous for its Kamikaze Downhill Trail, the obstacle arena where riders can test their balance and skill and the slalom course. There's also an area designed for kids. A pass granting unlimited access to the gondola and the trail system is $23 for adults, $12 for children 12 and under; to the trails only, it's $12 for adults, $6 for children. The park operates daily from 9am to 6pm, from about July 1 to September 29 and then weekends only to October 13. In town, mountain bikes can also be rented from the **Footloose Sports Center** at the corner of Canyon and Minaret (☎ 619/934-2400). The **NORBA National Mountain Bike Championships** are held here in the summer.

CLIMBING   Climbing and orienteering courses are offered by **Mammoth Mountain Adventure Connection** (☎ 619/934-0606).

TROUT FISHING   Mammoth Lakes Basin sits in a canyon a couple of miles west of town. Here are the lakes—Mary, Mamie, Horseshoe, George, and Twin—that have made the region known for trout fishing. Southeast of town, Crowley Lake is also famous for trout fishing, as are the San Joaquin and Owens rivers. In addition, there are plenty of other lakes in which to spin your reel. For fishing information and guides, contact **Rick's Sport Center,** at Calif. 203 and Center Street (☎ 619/934-3416); **The Trout Fitter,** in the Shell Mart Center, Main Street and Old Mammoth Road (☎ 619/924-3676); and **Kittredge Sports,** Main Street and Forest Trail (☎ 619/934-7566), which rents equipment, supplies guides, teaches fly-fishing, and offers backcountry trips and packages.

KAYAKING   Kayaks are available at Crowley Lake from **Caldera Kayaks** (☎ 619/935-4942) for $30 a day. This outfit also offers half- and full-day trips on Crowley and on Mono Lake and provides instruction, as well.

PACK TRIPS   The region is also an equestrian's paradise, and numerous outfitters offer pack trips. Among them are: **Red's Meadows Pack Station,** Red's Meadows, past Minaret Vista (☎ 800/292-7758 or 619/934-2345); **Mammoth Lakes Pack Outfit,** Lake Mary Road, past Twin Lakes (☎ 619/934-2434), which offers 1- to 6-day riding trips and semiannual horse drives, plus other wilderness workshops; and **McGee Creek Pack Station,** McGee Creek Road, Crowley Lake (☎ 619/935-4324).

HIKING   Trails abound in the Mammoth Lakes Basin area. They include the half-mile-long **Panorama Dome Trail,** which is just past the turnoff to Twin Lakes on Lake Mary Road, leading to the top of a plateau that provides a view of the Owens Valley and Lakes Basin. Another trail of interest is the 5-mile-long **Duck Lake Trail,** starting at the end of the Coldwater Creek parking lot with switchbacks across Duck Pass past several lakes to Duck Lake. The head of the **Inyo Craters Trail** is reached via gravel road, off the Mammoth Scenic Loop Road. This trail takes you to the edge of these craters and a sign that explains how they were created.

For additional trail information and maps, contact the **Mammoth Ranger Station** (☎ 619/924-5500). For equipment and maps, go to **Footloose Sports Center** at the corner of Canyon and Minaret (☎ 619/934-2400), which also rents inline skates and mountain bikes.

OTHER SUMMERTIME FUN   Golf can be enjoyed at **Snowcreek Golf Course,** Old Mammoth Rd. (☎ 619/934-6633). Adventurers will also want to go hot-air ballooning with the **High Sierra Ballooning Co.** (☎ 619/934-7188).

EXPLORING THE SURROUNDING AREA

Bodie, one of the most authentic ghost towns in the West, lies about an hour's drive north of Mammoth, past the Tioga Pass entrance to Yosemite. In 1870 more than 10,000 people lived in Bodie; today it's an eerie shell. En route to Bodie, you'll pass **Mono Lake,** near Lee Vining, which has startling tufa towers arising from its surface—limestone deposits formed by underground springs. It's a major bird-watching area—about 300 species nest or stop here during their migrations.

CAMPING

There are more than 700 campsites available in the area. These sites open on varying dates in June, depending on the weather. The largest campgrounds are at Convict Lake, Twin Lakes and Cold Water (both in the Mammoth Lakes Basin), and Red's Meadow. For additional information, call the **Mammoth Ranger Station** at **619/924-5500.**

The Mammoth Lakes Region

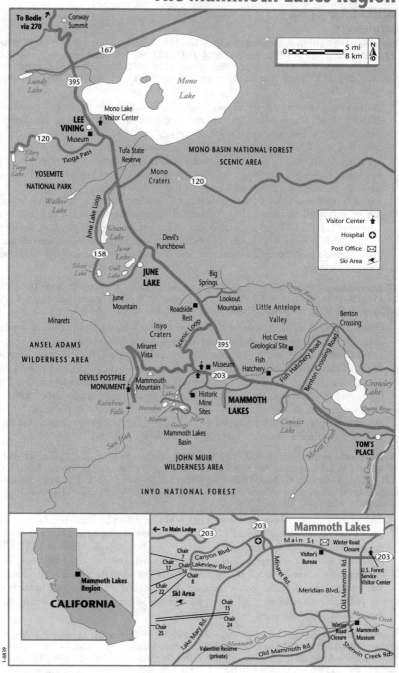

To Bodie via 270
Conway Summit
167
Lundy Lake
395
Mono Lake
Mono Lake Visitor Center
LEE VINING
Museum
120
Ellery Lake
Tioga Lake
Tioga Pass
YOSEMITE NATIONAL PARK
Walker Lake
Tufa State Reserve
MONO BASIN NATIONAL FOREST SCENIC AREA
Mono Craters
120
June Lake Loop
Grant Lake
Devil's Punchbowl
158
June Lake
Silver Lake
Gull Lake
JUNE LAKE
Minarets
June Mountain
ANSEL ADAMS WILDERNESS AREA
Inyo Craters
Roadside Rest
Scenic Loop
Big Springs
Lookout Mountain
Little Antelope Valley
Owens River
Benton Crossing
Minaret Vista
395
Hot Creek Geological Site
Benton Crossing Road
Fish Hatchery Road
DEVILS POSTPILE MONUMENT
Mammouth Mountain
Museum
203
Fish Hatchery
Crowley Lake
Rainbow Falls
Twin Lakes
Historic Mine Sites
MAMMOTH LAKES
Owens River
Horseshoe
Mamie
George
Mary
Convict Lake
TOM'S PLACE
San Joaqin
Mammoth Lakes Basin
JOHN MUIR WILDERNESS AREA
McGee Creek
Rock Creek
INYO NATIONAL FOREST

Visitor Center
Hospital
Post Office
Ski Area

0 5 mi
0 8 km
N

Mammoth Lakes Region
CALIFORNIA

Mammoth Lakes

← To Main Lodge 203
203
Main St Winter Road Closure
Chair 7
Canyon Blvd.
Chair 17 Chair 16
Lakeview Blvd
Chair 8
Chair 22
Ski Area
Chair 15
Chair 24
Chair 25
Lake Mary Rd.
Valentine Reserve (private)
Minaret Rd.
Visitor's Bureau
Meridian Blvd.
203
U.S. Forest Service Visitor Center
Old Mammoth Rd.
Mammoth Creek
Winter Road Closure
Mammoth Museum
Old Mammoth Rd
Sherwin Creek Rd.

1-0839

WHERE TO STAY
MODERATE

Mammoth Mountain Inn. Minaret Rd. (P.O. Box 353), Mammoth Lakes, CA 93546. ☎ **800/ 228-4947** or 619/934-2581. Fax 619/934-0701. 173 rms, 40 one-bedroom condo apts (suitable for up to four people). A/C TV TEL. Winter, $110–$210 double; from $225 condo apt. Summer, $99–$130 double; from $145 condo apt. Special ski and mountain biking packages available. AE, MC, V.

Conveniently located opposite the ski lodge, this modern accommodation started out in 1954 as only one building, but was enlarged a decade later into a newer, glossier complex. It was last remodeled in the early 1990s. With a certain rustic charm, it looks very much like a mountain resort with wood siding. The bedrooms are well equipped and pleasantly furnished, but not inspired. It appeals to families, offering supervised children's activities, free cribs, a playground, box lunches for picnics, a games room, and even picnic tables.

You'll have your pick of sports facilities, including bicycles, fishing or hiking guides, downhill or cross-country skiing, sleighing, horseback riding, and even haywagon rides. The hotel has a snack bar and offers barbecues, and room service is also available. The rather standard restaurant serves breakfast, lunch, and dinner. Extras include free airport transportation and occasional entertainment. A whirlpool spa is also on site.

✪ Sierra Lodge. 3540 Main St. (Calif. 203), Mammoth Lakes, CA 93546. ☎ **800/356-5711** or 619/934-8881. Fax 619/934-7231. TV TEL. Winter, $100–$130 double Sun–Thurs, $120– $150 double Fri–Sat. Summer, $75 double Sun–Thurs, $85 double Fri–Sat. MC, V.

Opened in 1991 in the heart of the resort near the ski shuttle, this two-story inn deliberately abandoned the tried-and-true rustic-woodsy theme used in the resort's other hotels in favor of a glossy, big-city decor of pop-modern prints, track lighting, streamlined detailing, and—as a concession to the mountains—rock-built fireplaces in the public areas. Breakfast is the only meal served, but many restaurants are nearby. The bedrooms, in synch with the public areas, are glossy and modern, proud of their divergence from the town's rustic tone. The rooms are spacious and furnished in typical contemporary styling, each equipped with a kitchenette. Facilities include an outdoor Jacuzzi and a fireside room for relaxing. No smoking.

Snow Goose Inn. 57 Forest Trail (P.O. Box 946), Mammoth Lakes, CA 93546. ☎ **800/ 874-7368** or 619/934-2660. Fax 619/934-5655. 15 rms, 2 suites. TV TEL. Winter, Sun–Thurs, $78 double, $148 suite; Fri–Sat, $98 double, $168 suite. Summer, $68 double; $98 suite. Rates include breakfast, evening wine, and appetizers. Doubles with kitchens $5–$10 extra. Special packages available. AE, MC, V.

This place is managed by owners who run it as if it were a bed-and-breakfast rather than a traditional hotel. Set half a block off the main street, near a number of restaurants, the Snow Goose was built in two separate two-story buildings in 1967. The bedrooms are comfortably and attractively furnished, and two offer kitchens. The two-bedroom suites can accommodate four in a two-story space with dinette, kitchen, and living room complete with a fireplace. Antiques add a graceful note to some of the public rooms, and the staff is helpful and will direct you to cross-country and downhill skiing possibilities 3 miles away.

Tamarack Lodge. Twin Lakes Rd. (off Lake Mary Rd.) P.O. Box 69, Mammoth Lakes, CA 93546. ☎ **800/237-6879** or 619/934-2442. 10 rms, 5 with bath; 25 cabins. TEL. Summer, $70 double without bath, $85–$105 double with bath; $85–$260 cabin. Winter, $80 double without bath, $95–$140 double with bath; $110–$300 cabin. Special packages available. DISC, MC, V.

Winter Driving in the Sierras

Winter driving in the Sierra Nevada range can be dangerous. While the most hazardous roads are often closed, others are negotiable by four-wheel-drives or with tire chains. Be prepared for sudden blizzards, and protect yourself by taking these important pretrip precautions:

- Check road conditions before setting out by calling **800/427-7623.**
- If you're driving a rental car, let the rental company know you're planning to drive in snow, and ask whether the antifreeze is prepared for cold climates.
- Make sure your heater and defroster work.
- Always carry chains. If there's a blizzard, the police will not allow vehicles without chains on certain highways. You'll have to pay about $40 to "chain up" at the side of the road.
- Recommended items include an ice scraper, a small shovel, sand or burlap for traction if you get stuck, warm blankets—and an extra car key (it's surprisingly common for motorists to lock their keys in the car while putting on tire chains).

The lodge and cabin accommodations at this rustic lakeside retreat are nothing fancy, but that's exactly what's kept guests coming here since the 1920s. Folks relax in front of a fire burning in the stone hearth in the sitting room or hang out in their rooms, which are intentionally rustic with knotty-pine walls and modern furnishings. The cabins, which can accommodate two to nine people, are dotted around the property and offer a variety of configurations, from studios with wood-burning stove and shower to two-bedroom/two-bath accommodations with fireplace. Each cabin has a fully equipped kitchen, but there's no daily maid service (fresh towels are provided at the front desk). In the main lodge there are rooms with private baths and with shared bath.

The lodge has a very popular cross-country ski center with more than 25 miles of trails and skating lanes, ski rentals, and a ski school. Boat and canoe rentals are also available. The dining room, overlooking Twin Lakes, offers Californian and continental fare.

Ⓢ White Horse Inn. 2180 Old Mammoth Rd. (P.O. Box 2326), Mammoth Lakes, CA 93456. ☎ **800/982-5657** or 619/924-3656. 5 rms. Winter, $75–$135 double. Summer, $90–$105 double. Rates include breakfast. DISC, MC, V.

Set about a mile southwest of the resort's center, this establishment occupies a gray-and-white gabled house built in the 1950s. Unlike its competitors, there's no flowery Laura Ashley decor here. Each accommodation is furnished eclectically and with wit, each with a distinct theme such as all Chinese antiques or a furniture ensemble from Austria and Mexico. A country breakfast is included as part of the price, and in nice weather you'll enjoy it on an outdoor deck. Wine and cheese are served near a billiard table during the early evening. There's a hot tub on the premises and a communal kitchen reserved for the use of guests.

WHERE TO DINE
MODERATE

✪ Anything Goes Café. 645 Old Mammoth Rd. ☎ **619/934-2424.** Reservations strongly recommended for dinner. Main courses $13–$18. MC, V. Tues 7am–3pm, Thurs–Mon 7am–3pm and 5:30–9:30pm. CALIFORNIA.

This cafe is about half a mile outside town, near the golf course, in an old "but not antique" building. Customers order lunch directly at the counter, which helps retain the low noontime prices. Overstuffed deli sandwiches, salads, and platters of California-inspired chicken and pastas are all the rage. Despite the informality of the lunch hour, it's obvious that the hardworking owners are directing the seasonings from their perch in the kitchens.

Dinners, on the other hand, are more formal, with table service, tablecloths, candlelight, and more attention to the nuances of the cuisine. The menu changes weekly, but the dinner menu will feature about six or so main courses. For example, you might find breast of chicken marinated in orange juice, ginger, shallots, garlic, and soy, then oven roasted until crispy; or lamb shanks braised with figs, pinot noir, and garlic, then finished with Dijon mustard. Special attention is paid to desserts here, with emphasis on pies (the peach and strawberry-apricot are especially good) and homemade sweets.

✪ **Nevados.** Main St. (at Minaret Rd.) ☎ **619/934-4466.** Reservations recommended. Main courses $14–$23; fixed-price meal $26. AE, DC, DISC, MC, V. Daily 6–9:30pm. EUROPEAN/ CALIFORNIA.

What is it that makes this restaurant a favorite with the locals? Well, owner/host Tim Dawson is on hand nightly to ensure that their every need is met; the innovative cuisine is fresh and homemade; and the moist and tasty bread is house-baked. The clincher, though, is the fixed-price meal which consists of a first course such as soft-shell crab, salad, or ahi tuna and California spring roll; a main course featuring the likes of linguine with wild mushrooms, snow peas, red bell peppers, and herbs; and desert (love that warm pear and almond tart). Throw in the casual-but-sweet ambience (white tablecloths, candles, and French country murals) and the extensive selection of wines, single-malt scotches, and single-batch bourbons, and it's no wonder this is the hangout for ski instructors and race coaches.

The Restaurant at Convict Lake. Convict Lake Rd. ☎ **619/934-3803.** Reservations recommended. Main courses $14–$28. AE, MC, V. Summer, daily 11am–3pm and 5:30–9:30pm; winter, daily 5:30–9:30pm. CONTINENTAL/FRENCH.

This noteworthy restaurant, which manages to be both elegant and rustic at the same time, is set 5 miles south of the sometimes congested heart of Mammoth Lake, and therefore provides a refreshing change of pace from in-town restaurants. It's in a woodsy-looking, plank-sided, oversized cabin, and stands adjacent to a lakefront marina. Tables are placed around a copper-hooded, free-standing fireplace and windows overlook a forest of aspen.

Try such classic dishes as duck breast with Grand Marnier and sun-dried-cherry sauce, garnished with candied-orange zest. In season, the venison, pan-seared with kalamata olives, toasted cumin, and oven-dried tomatoes and served with a fine herb glaze, is worth the trip here. To start, there's an unusual carpaccio of lamb with aged Monterey Jack cheese, Pommery mustard, and rosemary aïoli.

✪ **Skadi.** In the Sherwin Plaza III Shopping Mall, 587 Old Mammoth Rd. ☎ **619/934-3902.** Reservations recommended. Main courses $9.50–$20. AE, MC, V. Daily 5:30–10pm. ECLECTIC.

The minimall where this restaurant is located (a half-mile south of Mammoth Lake's center) may not be the home of the Viking goddess of skiing and hunting whose name this restaurant bears, but she wouldn't have cared once she saw the view—it encompasses most of the mountains for miles around. Everybody likes this place— it's perfect for an après-ski cocktail at the 14-seat bar, a snack from the substantial selection of appetizers and desserts, or a full-blown dinner on the town.

The decor here evokes a big-city postmodern aura that's a welcome change after all that local alpine rusticity. Main courses are self-proclaimed "Alpine cuisine" and include such dishes as smoked trout Napoleon or grilled venison with lingonberries and a game sauce. Finish the evening with crème brûlée or the frozen macadamia-nut parfait.

Whiskey Creek. 18 Main St. (at Minaret Rd.), Mammoth Lakes. ☎ **619/934-2555.** Reservations recommended. Main courses $9–$16. AE, DC, MC, V. Daily 5:30–10pm. AMERICAN.

If you favor the Charthouse upscale surf-and-turf chain in every town you visit, you've found your dining spot here. It's not exactly a culinary adventure, but the fare is hearty and the view is splendid. The building is designed with wraparound windows to encompass a sweeping view over the snow-clad mountains. Isolated on a corner lot about three-quarters of a mile from the town center, it combines a rustically elegant restaurant with a rock-and-roll club. You can dine and boogie in rapid order. Live music begins every night at 9pm and continues to at least 1am, and entrance is free unless there's a well-known band (and even then, the cover is no more than $5 per person).

Although this restaurant is known for its beef, there are some other fine dishes on the menu, including rack of lamb with a jalapeño-mint jelly and even meatloaf with a mild horseradish sauce. People lust after the smashed potatoes. For an appetizer, try the duck quesadilla with roasted peppers, Jack cheese, and tomatillo salsa. A microbrewery, the Mammoth Brewing Company (brewery tours as well), is a welcome addition to an already-bubbly atmosphere.

4 Devils Postpile National Monument

by Andrew Rice

Just a few miles outside the town of Mammoth Lakes, Devils Postpile National Monument is home to one of nature's most curious geological freak shows. Formed when molten lava cracked as it cooled, the 60-foot-high blue-gray basalt columns that form the postpile look more like some sort of enormous eerie pipe organ or a jumble of giant pencil leads than anything you'd expect to see made from stone. The three- to seven-sided columns formed underground and were exposed when glaciers scoured this valley in the last ice age some 10,000 years ago. Similar examples of columnar basalt are found in Ireland and Scotland.

Because of its high elevation (7,900 feet) and heavy snowfall, the monument is open only from summer until early fall. The weather in the summer is usually clear and warm, but afternoon thundershowers can soak the unprepared. Nights are still cold, so bring good tents and sleeping bags if you'll be camping. The Mammoth Lakes region is famous for its beautiful lakes—but unfortunately all that water also means lots of mosquitoes. Plan for them.

From late June until early September cars are prohibited in the monument between 7:30am and 5:30pm because of the small roads' inability to handle the traffic. Visitors must take a shuttle bus from the Mammoth Mountain Inn to and from locations in the monument. While it takes some planning, the resulting peace and quiet is well worth the trouble and makes you wonder why the Park Service hasn't implemented similar programs at Yosemite Valley and other traffic hot spots.

HIKING There's more to Devils Postpile than a bunch of rocks, no matter how impressive they might be. Located on the banks of the San Joaquin River in the heart of a landscape of granite peaks and crystalline mountain lakes, the 800-acre park is a gateway to a hiker's paradise. Short paths lead from here to the top of the postpile, and to Soda Springs, a spring of cold carbonated water.

A longer hike (about 1¹/₄ miles) from the separate Rainbow Falls trailhead will take you to spectacular **Rainbow Falls,** where the entire middle fork of the San Joaquin plunges 101 feet off a lava cliff. From the trail a stairway and short trail lead to the base of the falls and swimming holes below.

The **John Muir Trail,** which connects Yosemite National Park with Kings Canyon and Sequoia national parks, and the **Pacific Crest Trail** both run through here. Named after the famous conservationist and author who's largely credited with saving Yosemite and popularizing the Sierra Nevada as a place worth preserving, the 211-mile John Muir Trail traverses some of the most rugged and remote parts of the Sierra. There are two accesses to it in Devils Postpile, one via the ranger station, the other from Rainbow Falls Trailhead. From here you can hike as far as your feet will take you north or south.

Note that mountain bikes are not permitted on trails.

CAMPING   While most visitors stay in or around Mammoth Lakes, the monument does maintain a 21-site campground with piped water, flush toilets, fire pits, and picnic tables on a first-come, first-served basis. Rates are $8 per night. Bears are common in the park, so proper food storage measures must be taken. Leashed pets are permitted on trails and in camp. Call the National Park Service (☎ 619/934-2289) for details. There are several other U.S. Forest Service campgrounds nearby, including **Red's Meadow** and **Upper Soda Springs** (☎ 619/924-5500).

5 Visalia: Gateway to Sequoia & Kings Canyon

Visalia is the gateway to Sequoia and Kings Canyon national parks. It's on Calif. 198 east of Calif. 99, halfway between the coast and the Sierras and halfway between Los Angeles and Sacramento. The town is pleasant enough, with some very fine Victorian and Colonial Revival homes. Pick up a walking tour pamphlet at the convention and visitors bureau if you're interested in strolling (see "Essentials," below).

In stride with its surroundings, Vasalia has consciously preserved its natural wilderness in the form of 18 public parks, which cover almost 400 acres. Especially popular is the **Mooney Grove Park,** at 2700 S. Mooney Blvd., which is filled with the remainder of a great oak forest that once reigned here. There's also a lagoon with islands, a boathouse, and fish ponds. Another of the park's monuments to the past is the famous and moving statue *The End of the Trail* by James Earle Fraser. It depicts a battle-weary brave, head dropped to his chest, spear tip down, astride an exhausted pony. In 1968 the original was removed to the National Cowboy Hall of Fame in Oklahoma City and replaced by this copy cast in bronze.

Also in the park, the **Tulare County Museum,** at 2700 S. Mooney Blvd. (☎ 209/733-6616), displays some fine collections and several restored historic buildings, including the Visalia Jail and Witt's Blacksmith Shop where C. V. Witt designed his world-famous cattle brands. Admission is $2 for adults and $1 for children 12 and under. It's open Wednesday to Monday from 10am to 4pm.

At the **Central California Chinese Cultural Center,** 500 S. Akers (☎ 209/625-4545), a temple complex and museum, the Chinese in the valley gather to preserve their traditions and cultural heritage. At the center, visitors can view Chinese artifacts, archeological objects, and paintings inside, and contemplate the 8-foot bronze statue of Confucius in the courtyard. Admission is free and it's open year-round. Call in advance for visiting hours.

In nearby Hanford, **China Alley** is all that remains of a Chinese community that once numbered 600 in the late 19th century. Here you can see the Taoist Temple (1893) and the L. T. Sue Herb Company. Also in Hanford and worth visiting is the **Fox Theatre,** dating from the 1920s. It seats more than 1,000 and has an original Wurlitzer organ. **Courthouse Square** is a shopping complex; in the square an old 1930s carousel has been restored to its former brilliance.

ESSENTIALS

GETTING THERE   If you're driving from San Francisco, take I-580 east to I-5 south to Calif. 198 east. The **Visalia Municipal Airport,** 9500 Airport Dr. no. 1 (☎ **209/651-1131**), is served by United Express (☎ **800/748-8853** or 209/651-2202). **Amtrak (☎ 800/USA-RAIL)** stops at nearby Hanford, and there's a shuttle from there to Visalia.

VISITOR INFORMATION   For information, contact the **Visalia Convention and Visitors Bureau,** 815 W. Center St., Visalia, CA 93291 (☎ **800/524-0303** or 209/738-3435).

WHERE TO STAY

✪ **Ben Maddox House.** 601 N. Encina St., Visalia, CA 93291. ☎ **800/401-9800** or 209/739-0721. 4 rms. TV TEL. $60 double without bath, $75–$90 double with bath. Rates include breakfast. AE, MC, V.

Set in a residential street of Victorian homes, 4 blocks from the town's main street, the Ben Maddox House is an impressive sight with its triangular gable punctuated with a round window and two extremely tall palm trees looming over the front yard. The house, built in 1876, is constructed of redwood, and its rooms retain their original dark-oak trim and white-oak floors. The guest rooms are decorated with late 18th- and 19th-century furnishings and the two front rooms have French doors leading to two small porch sitting areas. A swimming pool and hot tub are open to guests in the back, and a full breakfast is served.

Radisson Hotel. 300 S. Court St., Visalia, CA 93291. ☎ **800/333-3333** or 209/636-1111. Fax 209/636-8224. 201 rms, 7 suites. A/C MINIBAR TV TEL. $100–$130 double; $225–$450 suite. Additional person $15 extra. AE, CB, DC, MC, V.

Lying 7 blocks from the town center, this eight-story chain hotel is the finest in Visalia. It's a family favorite, and is often visited by those en route to Sequoia and Kings Canyon national parks. Cribs are provided free—thankfully, as some of the attractively furnished rooms open onto balconies. This is certainly not the most glamorous Radisson in California, but it's serviceable in every way, and contains a whirlpool, wet bars in the suites, and even offers room service until 2am. Free airport transfers are arranged as well. There is exercise equipment, and the hotel also maintains a fleet of bikes. The restaurant serves breakfast, lunch, and dinner, with last seating at 10pm. You can also patronize the local bar, and entertainment is provided on Friday and Saturday nights. The hotel has a pool with poolside service.

❸ **The Spalding House.** 631 N. Encina St., Visalia, CA 93291. ☎ **209/739-7877.** Fax 209/625-0902. 3 suites. $85 suite for two. Rates include breakfast. MC, V.

This Colonial Revival house built in 1901 has been carefully restored by owners Wayne and Peggy Davidson. Handcrafted beveled-glass doors lead into the entry hall and the music room with its 1923 Steinway player grand piano. Readers will particularly enjoy the library, which is lined with more than 1,500 books. There's a TV in the living room and Oriental rugs and antiques are combined with classic reproductions throughout the house. All the rooms are suites with a sitting room, bedroom, and private bath, but no phone. It's totally non-smoking.

WHERE TO DINE

Michael's on Main. 123 W. Main St. ☎ **209/635-2686.** Reservations required. Main courses $15–$22. AE, DC, MC, V. Mon–Thurs 11am–3pm and 5–10pm, Fri 11am–3pm and 5–11pm, Sat 5–11pm. CALIFORNIA.

Join the debate in Visalia—many claim that Michael's on Main is better than the Vintage Press (see below). The main dishes at Michael's range from fresh seafood such as blackened ahi tuna to grilled items including pork tenderloin with port/wild-mushroom sauce or grilled filet of rabbit. In season, game is available. There are also several luscious pastas—a favorite is the rigatoni Bellini, tossed with wild mushrooms, sun-dried tomatoes, smoked duck, and quattro formaggi (four cheese) sauce.

✪ The Vintage Press. 216 N. Willis St. ☎ **209/733-3033.** Reservations recommended. Main courses $12–$25. AE, CB, DC, MC, V. Mon–Thurs 11:30am–2pm and 6–10:30pm, Fri–Sat to 11pm. AMERICAN/CONTINENTAL.

The local debate notwithstanding, this is the best restaurant within a surrounding 100-mile radius, a culinary stopover of widely acknowledged merit in the gastronomic wasteland between Los Angeles and San Francisco. Everything about it was designed to imitate a fin-de-siècle gin mill in gold-rush San Francisco, with a bar imported from that city manufactured by the Brunswick Company (of bowling-alley fame), lots of antiques bought at local auctions, and glittering panels of leaded glass and mirrors. The place is big enough (250 seats) to feed a boatload of gold-rush hopefuls, and has a bustling bar/lounge where live music by a piano player is presented Thursday to Saturday from 5:30 to 9pm.

The menu is supplemented by daily specials—a zesty rack of lamb roasted in a cabernet sauce with rosemary and pistachios, for example. The regular menu offers about a dozen meat and fish dishes, with steaks supplemented by such dishes as red snapper with lemon, almonds, and capers, or pork tenderloin with Dijon mustard, red chili, and honey. To start, we recommend a selection of farm-raised fresh oysters on the half shell or the wild mushrooms with cognac in puff pastry.

6 Sequoia & Kings Canyon National Parks

by Andrew Rice

It's only about 200 road miles between Yosemite and Sequoia and Kings Canyon national parks, but the two Sierra Nevada parks are worlds apart. Where the National Park Service has taken every opportunity to modernize, accessorize, and urbanize Yosemite, leading to a frenetic tourist scene much like the cities so many of us strive to escape, at Sequoia and Kings Canyon they've treated the wilderness beauty of the park with respect and care. Only one road loops through the park, the Generals Highway, and no road traverses the Sierra here. The park service doesn't recommend vehicles over 22 feet long use the steep and windy stretch between Potwisha Campground and the Giant Forest in Sequoia National Park. As a result the park is much less accessible by car than most, but spectacular for those willing to head out on foot.

The Sierra Nevada tilts upward as it runs south. **Mt. Whitney,** at 14,495, feet the highest point in the Lower 48 states, is just one of many high peaks in Sequoia and Kings Canyon. The Pacific Crest Trail reaches its highest point here too, crossing north to south through both parks. Besides the rocky, snow-covered peaks, Sequoia and Kings Canyon are also home to the largest groves of giant sequoias in the Sierra Nevada, as well as the headwaters of the Kern, Kaweah, and Kings rivers. A few small, high-country lakes are home to some of the only remaining pure-strain golden trout.

Sequoia & Kings Canyon National Parks

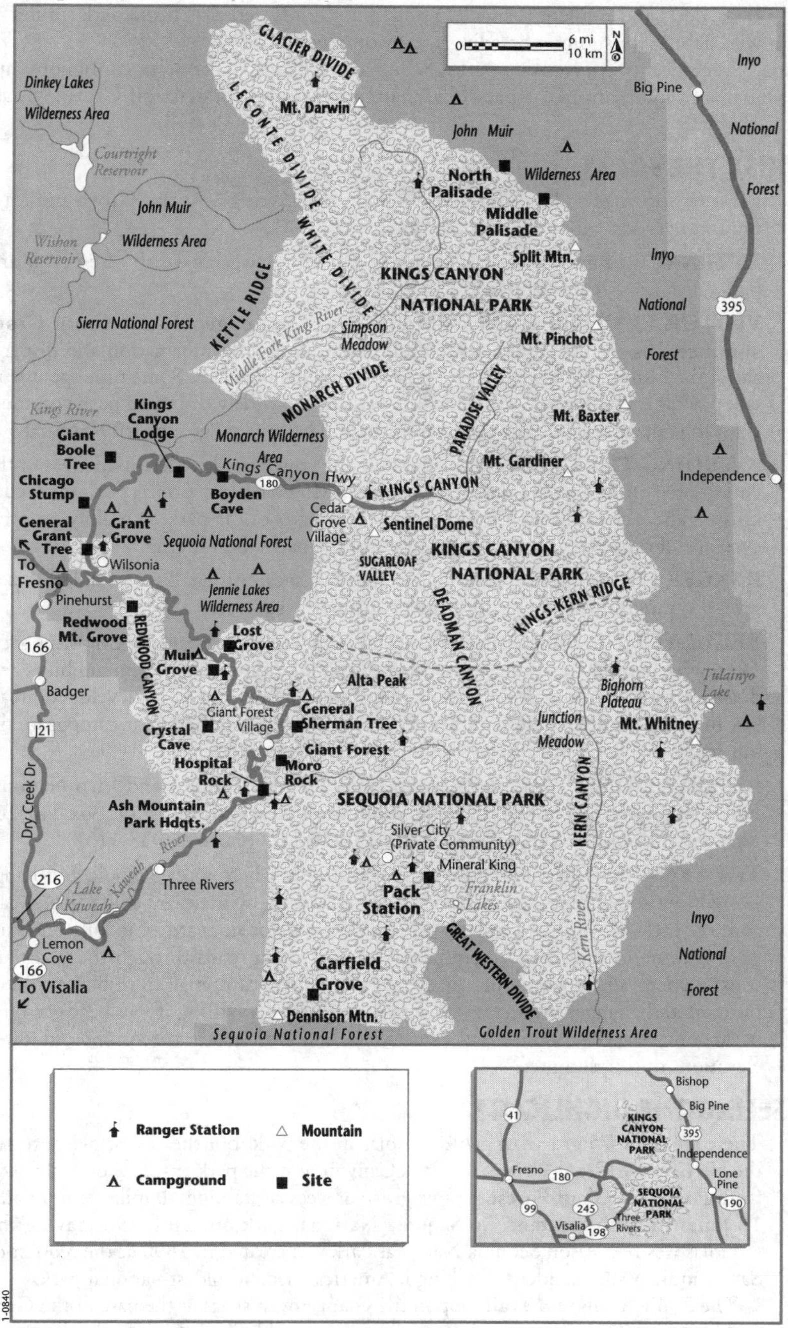

6 mi
10 km
0
N
GLACIER DIVIDE
LECONTE DIVIDE
WHITE DIVIDE
Mt. Darwin
John Muir
Wilderness Area
North Palisade
Middle Palisade
Split Mtn.
Big Pine
Inyo
National
Forest
Dinkey Lakes
Wilderness Area
Courtright Reservoir
John Muir
Wilderness Area
Wishon Reservoir
Sierra National Forest
KETTLE RIDGE
KINGS CANYON
NATIONAL PARK
Middle Fork Kings River
Simpson Meadow
MONARCH DIVIDE
Mt. Pinchot
395
PARADISE VALLEY
Mt. Baxter
Kings River
Kings Canyon Lodge
Giant Boole Tree
Monarch Wilderness Area
Kings Canyon Hwy
180
Mt. Gardiner
Independence
KINGS CANYON
Chicago Stump
Boyden Cave
Cedar Grove Village
Sentinel Dome
General Grant Tree
Grant Grove
Sequoia National Forest
KINGS CANYON
NATIONAL PARK
To Fresno
Wilsonia
SUGARLOAF VALLEY
Jennie Lakes Wilderness Area
Pinehurst
Redwood Mt. Grove
REDWOOD CANYON
DEADMAN CANYON
KINGS-KERN RIDGE
166
Lost Grove
Muir Grove
Badger
Alta Peak
Bighorn Plateau
Tulainyo Lake
General Sherman Tree
Giant Forest Village
Junction Meadow
Mt. Whitney
J21
Crystal Cave
Giant Forest
Hospital Rock
Moro Rock
Dry Creek Dr
Ash Mountain Park Hdqts.
SEQUOIA NATIONAL PARK
KERN CANYON
River
Silver City (Private Community)
Mineral King
216
Lake Kaweah
Kaweah
Three Rivers
Pack Station
Franklin Lakes
Lemon Cove
166
To Visalia
GREAT WESTERN DIVIDE
Kern River
Inyo
National
Forest
Garfield Grove
Dennison Mtn.
Sequoia National Forest
Golden Trout Wilderness Area
Ranger Station
Mountain
Campground
Site
Bishop
Big Pine
41
KINGS CANYON NATIONAL PARK
395
Independence
Fresno
180
Lone Pine
99
245
SEQUOIA NATIONAL PARK
190
Visalia
198
Three Rivers
1-0840

Bear, deer, and numerous smaller animals and birds depend on the park's miles of wild habitat for summer breeding and feeding grounds.

Technically two separate parks, Sequoia and Kings Canyon are contiguous and managed jointly from the park headquarters near Ash Mountain off Calif. 198 east of Visalia.

JUST THE FACTS

Most visitors make a loop through the parks by entering at Grant Grove and leaving through Ash Mountain, or vice versa.

ENTRANCE FEES   A $5-per-car fee is good for 1 week's worth of entry at any park entrance. An annual pass is $15.

VISITOR CENTERS & INFORMATION   The **Lodgepole** and **Grant Grove** visitor centers are the largest, with a full selection of park information and displays about the history, biology, and geology of this incredible place. Some time spent here will pay off by letting you decide which parts of the widely dispersed park you most want to concentrate on. For visitor information before you go, call **209/565-3134.**

AVOIDING THE CROWDS   To escape the crowds and see less-used areas of the park, enter on one of the dead-end roads to Mineral King, South Fork, or Cedar Grove. The lack of through traffic makes these parts of the park incredibly peaceful even at full capacity, and they're gateways to the parks' best hiking.

RANGER PROGRAMS   Park rangers lead hikes, campfire talks, and slideshows at several campgrounds and visitor centers during the summer.

REGULATIONS   Wilderness permits are required for all backpacking trips. You can reserve permits in advance by writing the park headquarters. Mountain bikes and dogs are forbidden on all park trails (dogs are only permitted in developed areas, but must be leashed). The Park Service allows firewood gathering at campgrounds, but removing wood from living or standing trees is forbidden.

RESERVATIONS   You can reserve permits for Mt. Whitney and Inyo National Forest by phone, fax, or mail through **Wilderness Reservations,** P.O. Box 430, Big Pine, CA 93513 (☎ **888/374-3773** or 619/938-1136; fax 619/938-1137).

THE SEASONS   In the middle to high altitudes, where most Sequoia and Kings Canyon visitors are headed, summer is short and the winters are cold. Spring can come as early as April and as late as June. Snow is not unheard of in July and August. Afternoon showers are common. Only the main roads through the parks are usually open during winter months when the climate can range from bitter cold to pleasant and changes minute by minute. Be ready for anything if you head into the backcountry on skis. Mosquitoes, poison oak, and rattlesnakes are common in lower elevations during summer.

SEEING THE HIGHLIGHTS

There are some 75 groves of giant sequoias in the park, but the easiest places to see the big trees are **Grant Grove,** in Kings Canyon near the park entrance on Calif. 180 from Fresno, or **Giant Forest,** a huge grove of trees containing 40 miles of footpaths 16 miles from the entrance to Sequoia National Park on Calif. 198. Saving the sequoias was the reason Sequoia National Park was created in 1890 at the request of San Joaquin Valley residents, making it America's second-oldest national park.

The 2-mile **Congress Trail** loop in the Giant Forest starts at the base of the **General Sherman Tree,** the largest living thing in the world. Single branches of this monster are more than 7 feet thick. Each year it grows enough wood to make a 60-foot-tall tree of normal dimensions. Other trees in the grove are nearly as large, and many of the peaceful-looking trees have also been saddled with strangely militaristic and political monikers like General Lee and Lincoln. Longer trails lead to remote reaches of the grove and nearby meadows.

Unlike the coast redwoods, which reproduce by sprouting or by seeds, giant sequoias only reproduce by seed. The tiny cones require fire to open, so decades can pass between generations. Adult sequoias don't die of old age and are protected from fire by thick bark. The huge trees have surprisingly shallow roots, and most die when they topple in high winds or heavy snows. These groves, like the ones in Yosemite, were first explored by conservationist and nature writer John Muir.

Besides the sequoia groves, Sequoia and Kings Canyon are home to the most pristine wilderness in the Sierra Nevada. At **Roads End** on the Kings Canyon Highway (open from May to November) you can stand by the banks of the Kings River and stare up at 5,000-foot-tall granite walls rising above the river, the deepest canyon in the United States.

Near Giant Forest Village, **Moro Rock** is a 6,725-foot-tall granite dome formed by exfoliation of layers of the rock. A quarter-mile trail scales the dome for a spectacular view of the adjacent Kaweah Canyon. The trail gains 300 feet in 400 yards, so be ready for a climb.

Boyden Cavern, on Calif. 180 in neighboring Sequoia National Forest, is a large cave where you can take a 45-minute tour to see stalactites and stalagmites. A fee is charged; call 209/736-2708 for details.

Crystal Cave is located 15 miles from the Calif. 198 park entrance and an additional 7 miles to cave parking. Here you can take a 50-minute tour of Crystal's beautiful marble interior. The tour costs $4 for adults and children 12 and older, $2 for children 6 to 11 and senior citizens, and free for kids 5 and under. Tickets are not sold at the cave and must be purchased at the Lodgepole or Foothills visitor center at least 1 1/2 hours in advance. Be sure to wear sturdy shoes and bring a jacket.

HIKING THE PARKS

Hiking and backpacking are what this park is really all about. Some 700 miles of trails connect canyons, lakes, and high alpine meadows and snow fields.

Some of the park's most impressive hikes start in the **Mineral King** section in the southern end of Sequoia. Beginning at 7,800 feet, trails lead onward and upward to destinations like Sawtooth Pass, Crystal Lake, and the old White Chief Trail to the now-defunct White Chief Mine. Once an unsuccessful silver-mining town in the 1870s, Mineral King was the center of a pitched battle in the late 1970s and early 1980s when developers sought to build a huge ski resort here. They were defeated when Congress added Mineral King to the park, and the wilderness remains unspoiled.

The **John Muir Trail,** which begins in Yosemite Valley, ends here just below Mount Whitney. For many miles it coincides with the **Pacific Crest Trail** as it skirts the highest peaks in the park. This is the most difficult part of the Pacific Crest, remaining above 10,000 feet most of the time and crossing 12,000-foot-tall passes.

Other hikers like to explore the end of the park from **Cedar Grove** and **Roads End.** The **Paradise Valley Trail** is a fairly easy day trip by park standards leading to beautiful Mist Falls. The **Copper Creek Trail** immediately rises into the high wilderness around Granite Pass at 10,673 feet, one of the most strenuous day hikes in the park.

If the altitude and steepness are too much for you at these trailheads, try some of the longer hikes in the **Giant Forest** or **Grant Grove.** These forests are woven with interlocking loops that allow you to take as short or as long a hike as you want. The 6-mile **Trail of the Sequoias** in Giant Forest will take you to the grove's far eastern end where some of the finest trees are. In Grant Grove, a fascinating side trip, is the 100-foot walk through the hollow trunk of the Fallen Monarch. The fallen tree has been used for shelter for more than 100 years and is tall enough inside that you can walk through without bending over.

Perhaps the most traversed trail to the park is the **Whitney Portal Trail.** It runs from east of the park near Lone Pine, through Inyo National Forest, to the summit of Mt. Whitney. Overnight and day-use permits are required. They're limited and available by writing to Wilderness Office, Sequoia and Kings Canyon National Parks, Three Rivers, CA 93271. Permits are required for all overnight trips to the back-country; call 209/565-3708 for information. Though it's a straightforward walk to the summit and it's possible to bag it in a very long day hike, you'd better be in really good shape before attempting it. Almost half the people who attempt Whitney, including those who camp partway up, don't reach the summit. Weather, altitude, and fatigue can all conspire to stop even the most prepared party.

The official park map and guide gives good road maps for the parks, but for serious hiking you'll want to check out *Sierra South: 100 Back-Country Trips* by Thomas Winnett and Jason Winnett (Wilderness Press). Another good guide is *Kings Canyon Country,* a hiking handbook by Ginny and Lew Clark. The Grant Grove, Lodgepole, Cedar Grove, and Foothills visitor centers all sell a complete selection of maps and guidebooks to the park.

OTHER OUTDOOR ACTIVITIES

FISHING   Trout fishing in the lower altitudes is fairly limited, mostly along the banks of the Kings and Kaweah rivers. A few high-country lakes are refuges for trout and are not stocked with hatchery fish. Before venturing into the high country, inquire at a ranger station about the area you'll be visiting to find out about closures or specific regulations. A California fishing license is required for everyone over 16 years old. Tackle and licenses are available at several park stores.

SKIING & SNOWSHOEING   Sequoia Ski Touring, near Giant Forest Village (☎ 209/565-3381), offers complete rentals and trail maps for 35 miles of Sequoia backcountry trails. In Kings Canyon, Sequoia Ski Touring in Grant Grove (☎ 209/335-2314) provides the same services and an even-wider selection of trails. People with their own equipment are welcome on all trails in the park at no cost. Trail maps are available at the visitor centers. On winter weekends park rangers lead introductory snowshoe hikes (snowshoes provided for $1) at both areas. The roads to Cedar Grove and Mineral King are closed in winter.

RAFTING & KAYAKING   Only recently have professional outfitters begun taking experienced rafters and kayakers down the Class IV and V Kaweah and Upper Kings rivers outside the parks. Contact Sequoia National Forest at 209/784-1550 for a current listing of companies running trips. This is only for the very adventurous.

CAMPING & ACCOMMODATIONS

There are 13 campgrounds in the park, offering the most convenient and economical accommodations here, although none have hookups. Only one accepts reservations: **Lodgepole Campground** on the Kaweah River in Sequoia (☎ 209/565-3134 for reservations). Others are first-come, first-served and often fill up on weekends. Three campgrounds—Azalea, Lodgepole, and Potwisha—are open year round. The rest are open from snowmelt to September. Call **800/365-2267** for camping formation. Even in summer campers should prepare for rain and cold temperatures. Bring a good tent and warm sleeping bags.

Two large campgrounds in Sequoia are **Dorst** and **Lodgepole.** Both are close to the Giant Forest. Lodgepole is within a short stroll of a restaurant, gas station, and a visitor center. With more than 200 sites each, they tend to be the noisiest campgrounds in Sequoia. Lodgepole is the most expensive in the park at $14 per site. Dorst is $12.

Smaller and more peaceful are **South Fork, Potwisha, Buckeye Flats, Atwell Mill,** and **Cold Springs.** South Fork, Atwell Mill, and Cold Springs have pit toilets and are $6 per night. The others, with flush toilets, running water, and public phones, charge $12.

Campers in the remote Cedar Grove area of Kings Canyon National Park near the Kings River gorge can choose from **Moraine, Sentinel, Sheep Creek,** and **Canyon View,** a group camp. All four have flush toilets and are convenient to some of the park's best hiking. The small **Cedar Grove Village** offers a restaurant, store, showers, and gas. Sites are $12.

Three campgrounds in the Grant Grove area will put you near the sequoias without the noise and crowds of Giant Forest Village. All three—**Sunset, Azalea,** and **Crystal Springs**—have flush toilets and phones. Azalea has an RV disposal site and ranger station. Showers are nearby. The charge is $12 per site.

Lodging in the parks ranges from rustic one-room cabins with no bath or heat to a luxury motel. None of the complexes is very big. All lodging in the park is operated by the park concessionaire, **Sequoia Guest Services,** P.O. Box 789, Three Rivers, CA 93271 (☎ **209/561-3314** for information and reservations).

The heaviest concentration of accommodations is in Giant Forest, where you'll find something in every price and taste range. Grant Grove offers a variety of cabins with private or shared baths. Cedar Grove is the site of an 18-room motel. Each room has its own bath and two queen-size beds.

11

The Gold Country & the Central Valley

By Erika Lenkert and Matthew R. Poole

On the morning of January 24, 1848, a carpenter named James Marshall was working on John Sutter's mill in Coloma when he made an exciting discovery: He stumbled on a gold nugget on the south fork of the American River. Despite Sutter's wishes to keep the find a secret, word leaked out, a word that would change the fate of California—and John Sutter—almost overnight: *Gold!*

The news spread like wildfire, and a frenzy seized the nation—the Gold Rush was on. Within 3 years the population of the state grew from a meager 15,000 to more than 265,000. Most of these newcomers were single men under the age of 40, and not far behind were the thousands of merchants, bankers, and women who made their fortunes catering to the miners.

Sacramento grew quickly as a supply town at the base of the surrounding goldfields. Although the Gold Country boom lasted less than a decade, as the gold supply was quickly exhausted and many towns shrank or disappeared, Sacramento continued to grow as the fertile Central Valley south of it exploited another source of wealth by becoming the vegetable and fruit garden of the nation.

A trip along Calif. 49 from the northern mines to the southern mines will give visitors a sense of what life might have been like on the rough mining frontier. (See Chapter 5 for a detailed driving tour.) The towns along this route seem frozen in time, with the main streets boasting raised wooden sidewalks, double-porched buildings, ornate saloons, and Victorian storefronts. Each town tells a similar story of sudden wealth and explosive growth, yet each has left behind a different imprint. Any fan of movie westerns will recognize the setting—hundreds, perhaps even thousands, of movies have been shot in these towns.

The broad Central Valley, 240 miles long and 50 miles wide, is California's bread basket, the source of much of its bounty that's shipped across the nation and overseas. Much of the history of California has revolved around the struggle for control of the water used to irrigate the valley (it receives less than 10 inches of rainfall per year) and to make this inland desert bloom. Despite the frequent scarcity of water, in the sprawling valley a breathtaking panorama of orange and pistachio groves, grape vines, and strawberry fields stretches uninterrupted for miles.

1 Sacramento

Sacramento, with a population of 370,000, is one of the state's fastest-growing cities. In addition to being the state capital, it's a thriving shipping and processing center for the fruit, vegetables, rice, wheat, and dairy goods that are produced in the fruitful Central Valley. It's a prosperous and politically charged city, with broad tree-shaded streets lined with some impressive Victorians and well-crafted bungalows. At its heart sits the Capitol building—Sacramento's main attraction—in a well-maintained park replete with flower gardens and curious squirrels. It's far from a tourist town, but it has its share of touristy activities. Visitors and locals alike enjoy spending the day walking through Old Sacramento or floating down the American River.

ESSENTIALS

GETTING THERE   If you're driving from San Francisco, Sacramento is located about 90 miles east on I-80. From Los Angeles, take I-5 through the Central Valley directly into Sacramento. From North Lake Tahoe, get on I-80 west, and from South Lake Tahoe take U.S. 50.

The **Sacramento Metropolitan Airport** (☎ 916/929-5411), 12 miles northwest of downtown Sacramento, is served by about a dozen airlines, including **American** (☎ 800/433-7300), **Continental** (☎ 800/525-0280 or 916/369-2700), **Delta** (☎ 800/221-1212 or 916/446-3464), **Northwest** (☎ 800/225-2525), and **United** (☎ 800/241-6522).

AAA Taxi and Shuttle Service (☎ 916/334-5555) will get you from the airport to downtown; they charge a flat rate of $15 to the capital, a bargain compared to the $30 a conventional taxi would cost.

Amtrak (☎ 800/USA-RAIL) trains serve Sacramento daily.

ORIENTATION   Suburbia sprawls around Sacramento, but its downtown area is relatively compact. Getting around the city is made easy by a gridlike pattern of streets that are designated by numbers or letters. The state Capitol, on 10th Street between N and L streets, is the key landmark. From the front of the Capitol, M Street—which is at this point called Capitol Mall—runs 10 straight blocks to Old Sacramento, one of the city's oldest sections.

VISITOR INFORMATION   The **Sacramento Convention and Visitors Bureau,** 1421 K St., Sacramento, CA 95814 (☎ **916/264-7777**; fax 916/264-7788), provides plenty of helpful information for tourists. Once in the city, visitors can also stop by the **Sacramento Visitor Center,** 1104 Front St. (☎ **916/264-7777,** or 916/442-7644 on weekends and holidays), in Old Sacramento; it's usually open daily from 9am to 5pm.

EXPLORING THE STATE CAPITOL & ENVIRONS

In town, you'll want to stroll around **Old Sacramento,** 4 square blocks at the foot of the downtown area that have become a major attraction. The blocks contain more than 100 restored buildings, including restaurants and shops. Although the area has cobblestone streets, wooden sidewalks, and Gold Rush–era architecture, the high concentration of T-shirt shops and other gimmicky stores has turned it into a sort of historical Disneyland. While you're there, be sure to stop at the new **Discovery Museum,** at 101 I St. (☎ **916/264-7057**), which houses dozens of hands-on exhibits and demonstrations on California's history, as well as plenty of fascinating scientific and technological gizmos and doodads. It's open Tuesday to Sunday from 10am to 5pm; admission is $3.50 for adults, $2 for kids 6 to 17.

California State Capitol. 10th St. (between N and L sts.). ☎ **916/324-0333.** Free admission. Daily 9am–4pm. Tours offered every hour on the hour. Closed New Year's Day, Thanksgiving, and Christmas Day.

Closely resembling a scale model of the U.S. Capitol in Washington, D.C., the domed California state Capitol, built in 1869 and massively renovated in 1976, is Sacramento's most distinctive landmark, and the stage of many important political dramas in California history: In 1969 armed members of the Black Panther party marched into the building to assert their right to carry guns; in 1980 then-governor Ronald Reagan announced his candidacy for president here; and in 1995 the building was beseiged by protesters attempting to prevent the passage of Proposition 187, a measure that imposed new restrictions on California's illegal immigrant population. Daily guided tours, offered every hour on the hour, provide insight into both the building's architecture and the workings of the government it houses. Visitors are led through seven historic, antique-filled offices into the Senate and Assembly chambers, where the government functions—or at least *tries* to—today.

✪ **California State Railroad Museum.** 125 I St. (at 2nd St.). ☎ **916/552-5252,** ext. 7245. Admission $5 adults, $2 children 6–12. Daily 10am–5pm.

Well worth visiting, this museum is one of the highlights of Old Sacramento. You won't miss much if you bypass the memorabilia displays and head straight for the museum's 21 shiny locomotives and rail cars, beautiful antiques that are true works of art. Afterward you can watch a film on the history of the western railroads that's actually quite good, and peruse related exhibits that tell the amazing story of the building of the transcontinental railroad. Before you leave, choose a souvenir from the new museum store's huge selection of railroad books, videos, and collector's items. This museum is not just for train buffs, and even the hordes of schoolchildren that typically mob this place shouldn't dissuade you from visiting.

April to September, on weekends and holidays, steam locomotive rides depart on the hour from 10am to 5pm from the Central Pacific Passenger Station at K and Front streets. Fares are $5 for adults, $2 for children 6 to 12.

Towe Ford Museum of Automotive History of California. 2200 Front St. ☎ **916/442-6802.** Admission $5 adults, $4.50 seniors, $2.50 youths 14–18, $1 children 5–13, free for children 4 and under. Daily 10am–6pm.

This is one of the world's largest collections of antique Fords. More than 180 cars represent nearly every Ford model manufactured between 1903 and 1953. Antique fire, mail, and commercial trucks are also on display.

✪ **Crocker Art Museum.** 216 O St. (at 3rd St.). ☎ **916/264-5423.** Admission $4.50 adults, $2 children 7–17, free for children 6 and under. Wed and Fri–Sun 10am–5pm, Thurs 10am–9pm. Closed major holidays.

This museum houses a truly outstanding collection of Californian art. Donated to the city of Sacramento by the widow of Judge E. B. Crocker over a century ago, the museum itself is an imposing Italianate building, with an ornate interior of carved and inlaid woods. The Crocker Mansion Wing, the museum's most recent addition, is modeled after the Crocker family home and contains works by Northern Californian artists from the 1960s to the present. The adjoining museum shop features unique art-related gifts.

Downtown Sacramento

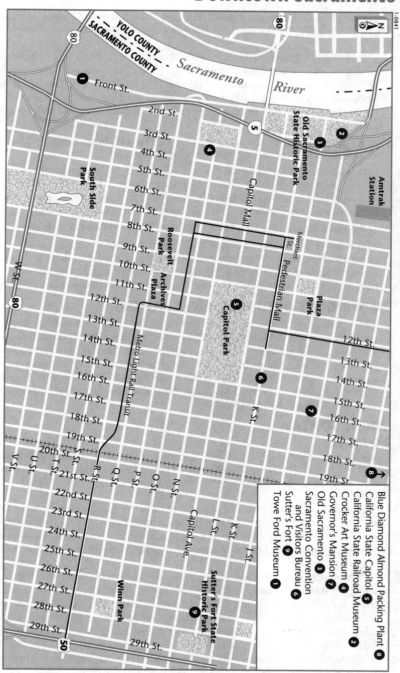

1-0841

N

YOLO COUNTY
SACRAMENTO COUNTY

Sacramento River

Front St.
2nd St.
3rd St.
4th St.
5th St.
6th St.
7th St.
8th St.
9th St.
10th St.
11th St.
12th St.
13th St.
14th St.
15th St.
16th St.
17th St.
18th St.
19th St.
20th St.
21st St.
22nd St.
23rd St.
24th St.
25th St.
26th St.
27th St.
28th St.
29th St.

W St.

South Side Park

Roosevelt Park

Archives Plaza

Old Sacramento State Historic Park

Capitol Mall

Merchant St.

Pedestrian Mall

Plaza Park

Amtrak Station

Capitol Park

Metro Light Rail Transit

K St.

V St.
U St.
T St.
R St.
Q St.
P St.
O St.
N St.

Capitol Ave.

L St.
K St.
J St.

Winn Park

Sutter's Fort State Historic Park

29th St.

Blue Diamond Almond Packing Plant **8**
California State Capitol **5**
California State Railroad Museum **4**
Crocker Art Museum **4**
Governor's Mansion **2**
Old Sacramento **3**
Sacramento Convention and Visitors Bureau **6**
Sutter's Fort **7**
Towe Ford Museum **1**

303

Governor's Mansion. 16th and H sts. ☎ **916/324-0539.** Admission $2 adults, $1 children 6–12, free for children 5 and under. Daily 10am–4pm. Hour-long guided tours offered on the hour.

The 15-room, Victorian-style Governor's Mansion was home to 13 of California's governors before 1967, when Ronald Reagan decided he needed to build even fancier digs. Now operated as a historical museum, the mansion is a turn-of-the-century landmark, complete with 14-foot ceilings, Italian marble fireplaces, Oriental rugs, ornate chandeliers, and French mirrors—all reflecting the tastes and styles of California's first families.

Sutter's Fort State Historic Park. 2701 L St. ☎ **916/445-4422.** Admission $2 adults, $1 children 6–12, free for children 5 and under. Daily 10am–5pm.

John Augustus Sutter established this outpost in 1839, and the park, restored to its 1846 appearance, tries to recapture the pioneering spirit of 19th-century California. The usual exhibits are on hand—a blacksmith's forge, a cooperage, a bakery, and a jail—on a self-guided audio tour. Historic demonstrations are staged daily.

Blue Diamond Almond Packing Plant. 1701 C St. ☎ **916/446-8439.** Free admission.

This is the world's largest almond-packaging plant, and one of the city's most offbeat attractions. Here you'll see how almonds are sorted, cracked, sliced, halved, and roasted, and you'll learn all about the nuts' long journey from tree to table. Guided tours have been discontinued, but the visitors center shows a 20-minute video of plant operations.

ENJOYING THE OUTDOORS: RIVER RAFTING

The American and Sacramento rivers lie nearby, and rafting is immensely popular, especially on warm weekends. Several Sacramento area outfitters rent rafts for 4 to 15 people, along with life jackets and paddles. Their shuttles drop you and your entourage upstream and meet you 3 to 4 hours later at a predetermined point downstream. Recommended outfitters include **River Rat,** 4053 Pennsylvania Ave., Fair Oaks (☎ 916/966-6777), and **American River Raft Rentals,** 11257 S. Bridge St., Rancho Cordova (☎ 916/635-6400).

WHERE TO STAY
EXPENSIVE

Hyatt Regency Sacramento. 1209 L St., Sacramento, CA 95814. ☎ **800/233-1234** or 916/443-1234. Fax 916/321-6699. 500 rms, 30 suites. A/C MINIBAR TV TEL. $165–$180 double; $200 club-level double; from $250 suite. AE, DC, DISC, MC, V. Valet parking $10; self-parking $6.

Sacramento's top hotel stands right in the heart of downtown, directly across from the California state Capitol and near the convention center. It's *the* high-status address for visiting politicos and is popular with conventioneers as well. Its facilities and services are unmatched in the city, leaving first-class independent travelers with little choice but to stay here.

While the rooms themselves are not spectacular, they conform to a very high standard. The best are the corner units with views facing the state Capitol. All rooms are equipped with full-length mirrors, hair dryers, and cable TVs with dozens of movies available on demand. The most expensive rooms are on the Regency Club floor, where you'll have a private concierge and a private lounge where complimentary breakfast, beverage services, and hors d'oeuvres are provided.

Dining/Entertainment: Dawson's, the hotel's top restaurant, serves lunch and dinner and is worth a visit even if you're not staying at the Hyatt. Ciao Yama serves Italian/Japanese cuisine.

Services: Concierge, room service, evening turndown, overnight laundry, lobby shoeshines.

Facilities: Swimming pool, Jacuzzi, exercise room, gift shop, car-rental desk.

MODERATE

Abigail's Bed-and-Breakfast. 2120 G St., Sacramento, CA 95816. ☎ **800/858-1568** or 916/441-5007. Fax 916/441-0621. 5 rms. A/C TV TEL. $100–$160 double. Rates include breakfast. AE, DISC, MC, V.

A boardinghouse for women during World War II, this 1912 Colonial Revival mansion has since been converted into a quaint and comfortable B&B with several pretty sitting areas, an outdoor spa in the rear garden, and two house cats, Sabrina and Abigail. The home's five rooms—all with private bath—are furnished with queen-size wood or brass beds and an assortment of antiques, including a chair or small settee. Anne's Room, the B&B's best, contains an enormous mahogany four-poster bed. Every room comes with terry robes and reproductions of antique radios. A telephone and TV are available upon request.

✪ **Amber House Bed-and-Breakfast.** 1315 22nd St., Sacramento, CA 95816. ☎ **800/755-6526** or 916/444-8085. Fax 916/552-6529. 9 rms. A/C TV TEL. $99–$219 double. Rates include breakfast. AE, CB, DC, DISC, MC, V.

Just 8 blocks from the Capitol, Amber House, a bucolic old home built in 1905 and currently owned and run by Michael and Jane Richards, offers individually decorated rooms named for famous artists and writers. The accommodations are located in two adjacent historic houses: the Poet's Refuge, a well-crafted 1905 home with five rooms, and the Artist's Retreat, a Mediterranean-style house built in 1913. The Renoir Room is the B&B's best, containing a canopied king-size bed and a Jacuzzi big enough for three. All rooms have hair dryers, VCRs, phones with computer jacks and voice-mail, and marble bathrooms—eight with whirlpool bathtubs for two.

Amber House effectively combines elegant surroundings with impeccable service. A beautiful living room and intimate library are available for guests' use. A full breakfast is served at the time and location you request—either in your room, in the large dining room, or outside on the veranda. Coffee and a newspaper are brought to your door early every morning. And additional perks include room, concierge, and laundry service, as well as free use of bicycles kept on the B&B's premises.

⑤ **Best Western Ponderosa Inn.** 1100 H St., Sacramento, CA 95814. ☎ **800/528-1234** or 916/441-1314. Fax 916/441-5961. 98 rms. A/C TV TEL. $75–$135 double. Rates include continental breakfast. AE, CB, DC, DISC, MC, V.

You'd never know from the plain motel-like exterior that this is one of the best values in Sacramento. The rooms here are as up-to-date as any offered by upscale hotels such as the Hilton and the Sheraton, and include well-coordinated furnishings, cable TV, a telephone with voice-mail, and valet and laundry service. There's also a swimming pool in the courtyard, and complimentary coffee and pastries are served each morning in the lobby.

✪ ***Delta King* Riverboat.** 1000 Front St., Old Sacramento, CA 95814. ☎ **800/825-5464** or 916/444-5464. 44 rms, 1 suite. A/C TV TEL. Sun–Thurs, $99 double; $400 captain's quarters suite. Fri–Sat, $139 double; $400 captain's quarters suite. Rates include continental breakfast. AE, DC, DISC, MC, V.

The *Delta King* carried passengers between San Francisco and Sacramento in the 1930s. Permanently moored in Sacramento since 1984, the riverboat underwent a $9-million restoration that enlarged all the staterooms and refurbished the popular restaurant, and is now a gimmicky but nonetheless charming hotel. Staying here can be quite a novelty, but the boat's cramped quarters can wear thin, especially if you're planning to spend a lot of time in your room. All rooms are nearly identical and have private baths and low ceilings. The captain's quarters, a particularly pricey suite, is a unique, mahogany-paneled stateroom, complete with an observation platform and private deck.

The *Delta King's* Pilothouse Restaurant is popular for local office parties. When the weather is nice there's dining on outside decks with views of Old Sacramento. The Paddlewheel Saloon, which overlooks the boat's 17-ton paddlewheel, features regular live entertainment.

○ **Sterling Hotel.** 1300 H St., Sacramento, CA 95814. ☎ **800/365-7660** or 916/448-1300. Fax 916/448-8066. 13 rms, 3 suites. A/C TV TEL. Sun–Thurs, $110–$145 double; $175 suite. Fri–Sat, $125–$175 double; $225 suite. Rates include continental breakfast. AE, DC, MC, V.

Set in the heart of Sacramento, 6 blocks from the Capitol, this inn occupies a white-fronted Victorian mansion originally built in the 1890s and heavily renovated in 1995. The Sterling has all the charm of a small, well-managed, sophisticated inn, with tasteful decor, a scattering of antiques—and a Jacuzzi in every room. It also has a carefully tended front lawn, covered in a well-maintained carpet of grass and attractive flower beds.

The Sterling's dining room, the Chanterelle, which serves well-prepared continental cuisine in a dignified setting furnished with antique reproductions, is known as one of Sacramento's better restaurants. Main courses range from $13 to $19, and advance reservations are recommended.

INEXPENSIVE

Sacramento Vagabond Inn. 909 3rd St., Sacramento, CA 95814. ☎ **800/522-1555** or 916/446-1481. Fax 916/448-0364. 107 rms. A/C TV TEL. $80 double. Rates include continental breakfast. Additional person $15 extra; children 16 and under stay free in parents' room. AE, CB, DC, DISC, MC, V.

A reliable choice within walking distance of the state Capitol, the Vagabond Inn has a heated swimming pool and a host of free features, including local phone calls, weekday newspapers, and continental breakfast. The bedrooms are clean and comfortable, but not exceptional. Stay here for the economy and the convenient location. There's an adjoining 24-hour coffee shop as well as a cocktail lounge.

WHERE TO DINE
EXPENSIVE

○ **Biba.** 2801 Capitol Ave. ☎ **916/455-2422.** Main courses $16–$20. AE, MC, V. Mon–Thurs 11:30am–2:30pm and 5:30–9:30pm, Fri 11:30am–2:30pm and 5:30–10:30pm, Sat 5:30–10:30pm. ITALIAN.

Locals flock to this sleek neo–art deco restaurant to sample the classical Italian cuisine of Bologna-born owner Biba Caggiano. Although the menu changes seasonally, you can expect to find about 10 or so pastas and 10 or so main courses. There might be a delicate pappardelle with a fresh seafood sauce, or a more pungent spaghetti alla siciliana, which combines eggplant, fresh tomatoes, capers, garlic, and anchovies. For a main course, the osso buco with madeira wine is excellent, but save room for the double-chocolate trifle made with dark and white chocolate, Grand Marnier–soaked pound cake, and raspberry purée.

MODERATE

Capitol Grill. 2730 N St. ☎ **916/736-0744.** Reservations recommended. Main courses $6.50–$19. AE, DC, DISC, MC, V. Mon 11am–10pm, Tues–Fri 11am–11pm, Sat 5–11pm, Sun 5–10pm. AMERICAN/SEAFOOD.

One of the liveliest restaurants in the city, the Capitol Grill is popular with Sacramento's see-and-be-seen crowd, a good-looking throng of 20- and 30-somethings without any Los Angeles–style attitude (they're looking for a date, not a producer). An excellent selection of well-prepared dishes includes sea scallops with grilled scallions and ginger-soy butter, and grilled lamb loin with French lentils, fried artichokes, and garlic sauce. We recommend the shrimp pot stickers or chicken quesadilla as starters.

⭐ **Harlow's.** 2714 J St. ☎ **916/441-4693.** Main courses $10–$17. AE, DC, MC, V. Mon–Thurs 11:30am–2pm and 6–9:30pm, Fri 11:30am–2pm and 6–10pm, Sat 6–10pm. ITALIAN/CALIFORNIA.

This comfortable, casual, and very popular spot has a 1930s air that might have pleased Jean Harlow herself. If you've got a hot date for the night, suggest meeting at the bar: It's Sacramento's most fashionable place to see and be seen. The pastas are superb here—ranging from the simple cannelloni in a rich meat sauce to the elaborate gnocchi in gorgonzola-cream sauce. The main dishes are equally well prepared, such as the scampi diavola, which has a piquant horseradish/mustard/cream sauce. Top it all off with the chocolate pâté.

Paragary's Bar and Oven. 1401 28th St. ☎ **916/452-3335.** Reservations recommended for parties of six or more. Main courses $10–$17. AE, DC, DISC, MC, V. Mon–Thurs 11:30am–11pm, Fri 11:30am–midnight, Sat 5pm–midnight, Sun 5–10pm. ITALIAN.

Occupying two distinct dining rooms just across the street from the Capitol Grill, Paragary's vies with its neighbor for "best moderately priced restaurant" status in Sacramento's downtown. The fireplace room is more formal than the brighter cafe, which is outfitted with bentwood chairs and white Formica tables. During good weather the best seats are on the sidewalk. The same menu is served no matter where you sit, with the best dishes coming from the kitchen's wood-burning pizza oven. Some of the more unusual gourmet pizza toppings are prosciutto, new potatoes, goat cheese, roasted garlic, artichokes, smoked salmon, and grilled eggplant.

The Rusty Duck. 500 Bercut Dr. ☎ **916/441-1191.** Reservations recommended. Main courses $13.95–$21.95. AE, DC, DISC, MC, V. Mon–Thurs 11am–10pm, Fri 11am–11pm, Sat 4:30–11pm, Sun 10am–10pm. Exit from I-5 at Richards Blvd. SEAFOOD/CALIFORNIA.

Set about 2 miles northwest of Sacramento's commercial core beside the American River, this building was inspired by a hunting lodge in Massachusetts. Rough-hewn cedar planks, river rocks, and concrete, all entwined with strands of ivy, create a kind of bucolic charm, despite the nearby roar of I-5's traffic.

At the Duck, politicos mingle with TV stars (Alan Alda dined here the night we did, though not with us) over one of the most diverse menus in the area. A perpetual favorite is salmon rolled in mustard seed and thyme, and served with citrus-flavored watercress sauce. Also popular is the charcoal-broiled swordfish with a brandy, white wine, oyster, and herb sauce accompanied with a dollop of red Cajun butter.

INEXPENSIVE

💲 **Aïoli.** 1800 L St. ☎ **916/447-9440.** Reservations recommended. Main courses $9–$18. AE, MC, V. Daily 10am–midnight. SPANISH.

Its fans, of whom there are many, call this the most authentic and charming Spanish restaurant in California, and they may be right. Set about 4 blocks south of the Capitol, on the street level of a high-rise apartment building, it's outfitted like a bistro you might find in Andalusia, with a large folkloric dining room and a back garden. Your fellow diners might include local media figures who are regulars here and friends of the cosmopolitan staff, some of whom were born of multilingual families in Algiers. Menu items include a saffron-laden paella (prepared only for two or more), a zarzuela of shellfish, gazpacho, chorizos a la plancha (grilled spicy sausages), and grilled shrimp basted with herbs and olive oil.

Fox & Goose Public House. 1001 R St. (at 10th St.). ☎ **916/443-8825.** Main courses $6–$10. Daily 7am–2pm. MC, V. BREAKFAST/AMERICAN-STYLE LUNCH.

The Fox is basically a giant beer hall that caters to the city's politicians, but we mention it here for its locally famous breakfasts, which include golden-brown waffles and a variety of omelets, including one that's stuffed with smoked salmon, cream cheese, and onions. They offer a pretty good lunch, too.

Tower Café. 1518 Broadway. ☎ **916/441-0222.** Main courses $7–$12. AE, MC, V. Mon–Thurs 7–11am, 11:30am–4pm, and 4:30–10pm; Fri 7–11am, 11:30am–4pm, and 4:30–11pm; Sat 4:30–11pm; Sun 8am–2pm and 4:30–10pm. Open later for dessert and drinks only.

The Tower Café gets its name from the building in which it's located: a grand old 1939 movie house with a tall art deco spire. The restaurant occupies the same space in which a small mom-and-pop music store once stood. This former resident, Tower Records, has since grown into America's second-largest record retailer. While it's unlikely that Tower Café will share the phenomenal success of its predecessor, it's not because of the food or surroundings. Both are good, and even with its perpetually sluggish service, this restaurant remains our favorite Sacramento lunch spot. On warm days it seems as if everyone in the city is lunching here (in fact, recent patrons have included the President and his staff), and crowd watching can be a real treat. Dishes reflect a variety of international flavors, from the Jamaican jerk chicken and African piri piri to the Thai pad Thai and Brazilian chicken salad.

2 The Gold Country

Cutting a swath for 350 miles along Calif. 49, the Gold Country stretches from Sierra City almost to the foothills of Yosemite. It still looks like a western movie set, with its mine sites, caverns, and Wild West saloons, along with ghost towns and architecture that would make Gene Autry or Roy Rogers feel right at home.

Drive along Calif. 49 and stop wherever your mood dictates. We've gone there before you to highlight some of the best places to explore. We found the drive best in April when most of the wildflowers burst into bloom. Motels, fast-food joints, and various convenience stores await you all along the route.

If you'd like to explore this area by following a structured driving tour, see "Ghost Towns of the Gold Country" in Chapter 4.

Placerville, east of Sacramento along U.S. 50, is in the approximate middle of the Gold Country. The northern Gold Country incorporates Placerville itself and other towns in the north, while the southern Gold Country along Calif. 49 includes such towns as Amador City, Sutter Creek, and Jackson.

THE NORTHERN GOLD COUNTRY: NEVADA CITY & GRASS VALLEY

Lying about 60 miles northeast of Sacramento, Nevada City and Grass Valley might be your best centers here. If you're driving from San Francisco, take I-80 to Calif. 49 and follow the signs. For information about the area, go to the **Grass Valley/Nevada County Chamber of Commerce,** 248 Mill St., Grass Valley, CA 95945 (☎ **916/273-4667**), or the **Nevada City Chamber of Commerce,** 132 Main St., Nevada City, CA 95959 (☎ **916/265-2692**).

These two towns were at the center of the hard-rock mining fields of Northern California. Grass Valley, in fact, was California's richest mining town, producing more than $400 million worth of gold in a century. Both are attractive to visit, although we'd rank Nevada City number one: Its wealth of Victorian homes and storefronts makes it one of the most appealing small towns in California; its entire downtown has been designated a National Historic Landmark. It has attracted a number of artists and writers in recent years and there are several fine bookstores on the main street, a good selection of restaurants, and some high-quality shops to browse through.

NEVADA CITY

Rumors of miners pulling a pound of gold a day out of Deer Creek brought hundreds of fortune-seekers to the area in 1849. Within a year it was a boisterous town of 10,000. Initially named Deer Creek Dry Diggins, it was renamed in 1850. In its heyday everyone who was anyone visited this rollicking western outpost with its busy red-light district. Mark Twain lectured here in 1866, telling the audience about his trips to the Sandwich Islands (Hawaii). Former President Herbert Hoover also lived and worked here as a gold miner.

Pick up a walking-tour map at the chamber of commerce, 132 Main St., and stroll the streets lined with impressive Victorian buildings, including the Firehouse, complete with bell tower and gingerbread decoration. The National Hotel (1854–56) is here, as is the Nevada Theatre (1865), one of the oldest theaters in the nation and still operating as such, today home to the Foothill Theatre Company. The Firehouse contains a museum that displays mementos from the Donner Party, a Maidu Indian basket collection, and an altar from a temple originally located in the Chinese section of Grass Valley. It's open in summer daily from 11am to 4pm; in winter it opens a half hour later and is closed Wednesday.

If you want to see the source of much of the city's wealth, visit **Malakoff Diggins State Historic Park,** 23579 N. Bloomfield Rd. (☎ **916/265-2740**), 26 miles northeast of Nevada City. In the 1870s North Bloomfield, then located in the middle of this park, had a population of 1,500. Some of the buildings have been reconstructed and refurnished to show what life was like then. The 3,000-acre park also offers several hiking trails, swimming at Blair Lake, and 30 campsites that can be reserved through Mystix by calling 800/444-7275. The museum is open daily in summer from 10am to 5pm, but in winter is only open on weekends from 10am to 4pm. To reach the park, take Calif. 49 toward Downieville for 11 miles. Turn right onto Tyler-Foote Crossing Road for 17 miles. The name will change to Curzon Grade and then to Backbone. When the road turns into gravel, turn right onto Derbec Road and into the park.

Another 6 miles up Calif. 49 from the Malakoff Diggins turnoff will bring you to Pleasant Valley Road, the exit that will take you (in about 7 miles) to a **covered bridge,** one of the most impressive in the country. Built in 1862, it's 225 feet long and was crossed by many a stagecoach.

GRASS VALLEY

In contrast to Nevada City's "tourist town" image, Grass Valley is the commercial/retail center of the region. The **Empire Mine State Historic Park,** 10791 E. Empire St., Grass Valley (☎ **916/273-8522**), is just outside town. This mine, which once had 367 miles of underground shafts, produced an estimated 5.8 million ounces of gold between 1850 and 1956 when it closed. Here you can look down the shaft of the mine, walk around the mine yard, and stroll through the gardens of the mine owner. From March to November, tours are given daily and a mining movie is shown. You can also enjoy picnicking, cycling, mountain biking, or hiking in the

784-acre park. It's open year-round. Admission to the museum is $2 for adults, $1 for children.

In town, visitors can pick up a walking-tour map at the chamber of commerce and explore the historic downtown area along Mill and Main streets. There are also a couple of museums that history buffs will want to visit: the **Grass Valley Museum,** in Mount Saint Mary's Convent and Chapel on South Church Street (☎ **916/ 272-4725**), and the **North Star Mining Museum** (☎ **916/273-4255**).

Grass Valley was, for a time, the **home of Lola Montez,** singer, dancer, and paramour of the rich and famous. A replica of the home that she bought and occupied in 1853 can be viewed at 248 Mill St. (☎ **916/273-4667**). It now houses the chamber of commerce, but it does contain some memorabilia of her 2-year stay. Down the street Lotta Crabtree, Montez's famous protegée, lived at 238 Mill St., now an apartment house. Also pop into the **Holbrooke Hotel** at 212 Main St. to see the signature of Mark Twain, who stayed here. The saloon has been in continuous use since 1852, and it's the place to meet the locals and have a tall cold one.

The surrounding region offers many recreational opportunities on its rivers and lakes and in the Tahoe National Forest. You can enjoy fishing, swimming, and boating at **Scotts Flat Lake** near Nevada City (east on Calif. 20), and at **Rollins Lake** on Calif. 174, between Grass Valley and Colfax. White-water rafting is available on several rivers. **Tributary Whitewater Tours,** 20480 Woodbury Dr., Grass Valley, CA 95949 (☎ **800/672-3846** or 916/346-6812), offers half-day to 3-day trips from March to October. In winter you can ski at Sugar Bowl Ski resort and Royal Gorge (only 45 minutes away), or at Squaw Valley, Alpine Meadows, and Northstar, a little more than an hour away over the Donner Pass (see Chapter 9). The region is also ideal for mountain biking. The chambers of commerce publish a trail guide, but there's nowhere to rent a bike in either Nevada City or Grass Valley—bring your own wheels. For regional hiking information, contact **Tahoe National Forest headquarters,** at Coyote Street and Calif. 49 in Nevada City (☎ **916/265-4531**).

From Nevada City, you have two choices about where to drive. You can take the 160-mile Yuba Donner Scenic Loop north along Calif. 49 through Downieville and Sierra City to Truckee before heading back to Nevada City via I-80 and Calif. 20. Or you can drive from Nevada City to Grass Valley in 15 minutes, and from there pick up Calif. 49—the Gold Country route—south to Auburn.

GOING UP TO DOWNIEVILLE: A GREAT SIDE TRIP

For a wonderful sidetrip from Nevada City or Grass Valley, visit the tiny mountain town of Downieville, located an hour's drive up Calif. 49 at the junction of the Yuba and Downie rivers. Back in the 1850s more than 5,000 prospectors worked the mines and streams around the town. Nowadays the population has dwindled to about 300, but the Gold Rush–era buildings and boardwalks still remain, looking pretty much the same as they did over a century ago.

As you stroll along the crooked Main Street, be sure to stop in at the **Downieville Museum**—housed in a funky old Chinese store—and the **Sierra County Courthouse** (☎ **916/289-3215**), which keeps some of the gold dug out of Ruby Mine on display. Inside the old stone Craycroft Building is the **Downieville Bakery** (☎ **916/ 289-0108**), a good place to load up on snacks for the trip back.

WHERE TO STAY
Nevada City
✪ **Deer Creek Inn Bed & Breakfast.** 116 Nevada St., Nevada City, CA 95959. ☎ **800/ 655-0363** or 916/265-0363. Fax 916/265-0980. 5 rms. A/C. $95–$140 double. Rates include breakfast. MC, V.

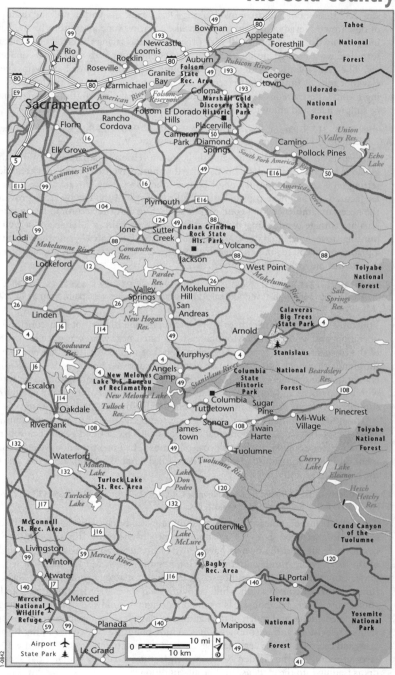

Tahoe National Forest

Eldorado National Forest

Union Valley Res.

Echo Lake

Toiyabe National Forest

Salt Springs Res.

Calaveras Big Trees State Park

Stanislaus

National Forest

Beardsleys Res.

Toiyabe National Forest

Cherry Lake

Lake Eleanor

Hetch Hetchy Res.

Grand Canyon of the Tuolumne

Yosemite National Park

Sierra National Forest

Bowman
Applegate
Foresthill
Rubicon River
Newcastle
Loomis
Rocklin
Auburn
Folsom State Rec. Area
Georgetown
Rio Linda
Roseville
Granite Bay
Coloma
Marshall Gold Discovery State Historic Park
Carmichael
American River
Folsom Reservoir
Sacramento
Rancho Cordova
Folsom
El Dorado Hills
Placerville
Camino
Pollock Pines
Florin
Cameron Park
Diamond Springs
South Fork American River
American River
Elk Grove
Consumnes River
Cosumnes River
Galt
Plymouth
Lodi
Ione
Sutter Creek
Indian Grinding Rock State His. Park
Volcano
Mokelumne River
Comanche Res.
Jackson
West Point
Lockeford
Pardee Res.
Mokelumne River
Valley Springs
Mokelumne Hill
San Andreas
Linden
New Hogan Res.
Arnold
Woodward Res.
Murphys
Angels Camp
New Melones Lake U.S. Bureau of Reclamation
New Melones Lake
Columbia State Historic Park
Stanislaus River
Escalon
Columbia
Tuttletown
Sugar Pine
Mi-Wuk Village
Pinecrest
Oakdale
Tullock Res.
Sonora
Jamestown
Twain Harte
Riverbank
Waterford
Tuolumne
Modesto Lake
Turlock Lake St. Rec. Area
Lake Don Pedro
Tuolumne River
Turlock Lake
McConnell St. Rec. Area
Couterville
Livingston
Winton
Merced River
Lake McLure
Atwater
Bagby Rec. Area
El Portal
Merced National Wildlife Refuge
Merced
Planada
Mariposa
Le Grand

Airport
State Park

0   10 mi
0   10 km

N

311

An 1887 three-floor Victorian overlooking Deer Creek and within walking distance of downtown Nevada City, this inn feels like a warm home away from home. The individually decorated rooms, all with private verandas facing the creek or town, are furnished with assorted antiques and four-poster or canopy beds with down comforters. The ceiling fans provide adequate cooling in summer; most bathrooms have clawfoot tubs. A full breakfast is served either out on the deck or in the formal dining room. Guests are invited to try a little panning of their own, fish, play croquet, or simply relax and enjoy the lawn and landscaped gardens along the creek.

Flume's End. 317 S. Pine St., Nevada City, CA 95959. ☎ **916/265-9665.** 6 rms, 1 cottage. A/C. $75 double; $135 cottage. Rates include breakfast. MC, V.

Innkeepers Steve and Terrianne and their golden retriever, Jamar, make warm and gracious hosts at this modern B&B, located a short drive from town in a creekside setting on 3 acres of tranquil woods. Some of the rooms have private decks, two offer Jacuzzis, and all have private baths. And the gurgle of the nearby creek provides the necessary ambience for a good night's sleep. Our favorite accommodation is the separate cottage overlooking the waterfalls, which contains a kitchenette, a wood-burning stove, a secluded deck, and two comfortable living areas—one that contains a piano and fireplace, and another that features a TV, a refrigerator, and a wet bar. A generous buffet breakfast is served.

National Hotel. 211 Broad St., Nevada City, CA 95959. ☎ **916/265-4551.** 43 rms, 30 with bath. A/C TV TEL. $68 double without bath, $113 doubles; 7 suites with bath, from $113 suite. AE, MC, V.

You can't miss this classic three-story Victorian, the oldest hotel in continuous operation west of the Rocky Mountains. It's located near what was once the center of the town's red-light district. The lobby is full of mementos from that era, hence the grandfather clock and early square piano. The suites are replete with Gold Rush–era antiques and large, cozy beds. Most rooms have private baths, and some come with canopy beds and romantic love seats. A definite bonus on typically sweltering summer days is the secluded swimming pool filled with cool mountain water.

The hotel's Victorian dining room, which serves traditional items such as prime rib, steaks, lobster tail, and homemade desserts, also has a Gold Rush atmosphere: The tables, for example, are lit with coal-oil lamps. The hotel provides live entertainment on Friday and Saturday nights. There's also a popular Sunday brunch, one of the best in the county.

✪ Red Castle Inn. 109 Prospect St., Nevada City, CA 95959. ☎ **916/265-5135.** 7 rms. $100–$150 double. Rates include breakfast. MC, V.

This hillside inn occupies a four-story Gothic Revival brick house built in 1860; it's situated in a secluded spot with a panoramic view of the town. It has an elegant but comfortable air, and the owners have a love of literature and music. The highlight of the week is the Sunday afternoon "Conversations with Mark Twain" in which guests can engage the great author (or at least a reasonable facsimile thereof—a costumed actor) in conversation while enjoying such specialties as lemon tarts and a choice cup of tea. The house has retained its original woodwork, plaster moldings, ceiling medallions, and much of the handmade glass. It lacks any modern intrusions such as televisions and telephones. Guests enjoy bountiful five-course buffet breakfasts, and can relax on the verandas that encircle the first two floors of the house. Our favorite rooms are the Garden Room, which features a canopy bed and has French doors leading into the gardens, and the air-conditioned three-room garret unit tucked under the eaves, furnished with sleigh beds and featuring Gothic arched windows.

Grass Valley

Holbrooke Hotel. 212 W. Main St., Grass Valley, CA 95945. ☎ **800/933-7077** or 916/ 273-1353. Fax 916/273-0434. 26 rms, 2 suites. A/C TV TEL. $55–$106 double; $95–$145 suite. AE, DC, DISC, MC, V.

This Victorian-era white clapboard building was a rollicking saloon during the Gold Rush days, and then evolved into a place for exhausted miners to "rack out." It's the oldest and most historic hotel in town. It has hosted a number of legendary figures since it opened its doors: Ulysses S. Grant, Benjamin Harrison, Grover Cleveland, and Gentleman Jim Corbett, among others. Nineteen of the rooms are in the main building. The remainder are in an adjacent annex, a house occupied long ago by the hotel's owner. The rooms have high ceilings; the front rooms are large and have access to the balconies. Each is decorated with an eclectic collection of Gold Rush– era furniture.

✪ **Murphy's Inn.** 318 Neal St., Grass Valley, CA. 95945. ☎ **916/273-6873.** 8 rms. A/C TV. $95–$140 double. Rates include breakfast. AE, MC, V.

This 1866 Colonial Revival house that was built for Edward Coleman, owner of the North Star mine, has been turned into a crackerjack B&B. Today it stands at the center of well-tended gardens complete with fountains, a fish pond, and a tall sequoia. Guests can relax in the gardens, on the porch, where trimmed ivy baskets hang decoratively, or in two very well furnished and comfortable living rooms with fireplaces. The bedrooms are equally alluring, all decorated in a chintzy Victorian style, but each with its own unique charm. Some have fireplaces, others offer private balconies, and two, the Maid's Quarters and the East Room, have a skylight. Two of the most spacious units, both with fireplaces and one with a full kitchen, are in the Donation Day House.

WHERE TO DINE

Nevada City

Friar Tucks. 111 N. Pine St. ☎ **916/265-9093.** Main courses $14–$20. AE, MC, V. Sun–Thurs 5–9:30pm, Fri–Sat 5–10pm. INTERNATIONAL.

A local favorite, this restaurant consists of a series of rustic, dimly lit rooms furnished with high-backed oak booths. The menu is eclectic, offering everything from cheese fondues and Swiss meatballs to teriyaki steak, Tuck's bouillabaisse, and duck with raspberry sauce, and the accompanying wine list is surprisingly impressive. With the flavor and ambience of a British pub, the bar is a popular local hangout, and has a guitar player who entertains nightly from 7pm.

🅢 **Gourmet to Go.** 110 York St. ☎ **916/265-5697.** Lunch items $4–$8. No credit cards. Mon–Fri 11am–3pm. DELI.

Little more than a small room with a counter and barely enough room for a cooler of soft drinks, the Gourmet to Go is just that: a seatless deli serving homemade gourmet offerings to go at low prices. Excellent sandwiches, salads, pastas, soups, espresso, desserts, and a handful of specials are wrapped for the road. Don't know where to go with your goods? Ask the deli staff, who will probably send you to nearby Pioneer Park for an impromptu picnic among the pines.

✪ **Potager.** 320 Broad St. ☎ **916/265-5697.** Main courses $13–$24. AE, MC, V. Tues–Thurs 6–9pm, Fri 6–9:30pm, Sat 5:30–9:30pm, Sun 5–9pm. INTERNATIONAL.

Formerly Peter Selaya's California Restaurant, Potager (pronounced Poh-ta-*zhay*) offers the most creative and cosmopolitan cuisine in town, served in an intimate woodside setting enhanced by private dining niches. Natural meats and organic produce are the mainstay here, such as the Bradley Ranch beef Wellington, beef wrapped in a puff pastry and topped with mushroom duxelle and cabernet/foie-gras sauce. Another recommended choice is the house-made wild-boar sausage, served with Potager's prize-winning chipotle-cherry sauce, grilled polenta, and fresh vegetables from the chef's own kitchen garden. Other handmade items include a superb ravioli and top-notch desserts.

Grass Valley

The Dining Room at the Holbrooke Hotel. 212 W. Main St. ☎ **916/273-1353.** Reservations recommended Fri–Sat night. Main courses $12–$19. AE, DC, DISC, MC, V. Mon–Sat 11:30am–2pm and 5:30–9pm, Sun 10am–2pm (brunch) and 5:30–9pm. AMERICAN.

This hotel dining room is the most formal place in town—an ironic twist, given its past life as a Gold Rush saloon and a flophouse for drunken miners. In its way it's the most authentic and nostalgic restaurant in a town filled with worthy hardworking competitors. Menu items include free-range chicken topped with proscuitto and gruyère cheese, roasted duck breast in a cranberry-honey sauce, and a changing assortment of dishes inspired by the whimsy of the chef, Andres Chavez. Should your arteries need further hardening, Saturday and Sunday are "prime rib" nights.

☉ The Old California. 341 E. Main St. ☎ **916/273-7341.** Main courses $5–$14. MC, V. Mon–Thurs 11:30am–2pm and 5–9:30pm, Fri 11:30am–2pm and 5–10pm, Sat 5–10pm. PRIME RIB/AMERICAN.

Located about half a mile east of the commercial center of town, this restaurant has a very loyal clientele who swear by its prime rib. It occupies a sprawling, turn-of-the-century building that once housed a bordello that thrived for a while beginning around 1901. Inside, you'll find lots of old-time memorabilia and photos of earlier and lustier eras. A platter of prime rib, with salad and vegetables, is a bargain at $8.95, although other choices include boneless breast of chicken, vegetarian pastas, prawns, calamari steak, and fish platters of the day, such as grilled filets of red snapper seasoned with herbs. The most expensive item on the menu, priced at $13.95, is a heaping platter with 16 ounces of prime rib cooked any way you like it.

☉ Pasta Luigi. 760 S. Auburn St. ☎ **916/477-0455.** Reservations recommended. Main courses $8–$13.50. AE, MC, V. Tues–Sun 5–9pm. ITALIAN.

This is the closest thing in town to a neighborhood Italian restaurant. It's a thoroughly charming, unpretentious spot, packed most nights with happy locals who couldn't care less about the less-than-trendy location. Menu items include a zesty cioppino, linguine zingarella (a "gypsy sautée" of Italian sausages, peppers, garlic, and onions), a classic veal scaloppine, and cappellini alla contadina, with diced chicken, fresh basil, olive oil, and tomatoes.

AUBURN, COLOMA & PLACERVILLE

From Grass Valley it's a short drive along Calif. 49 south to Auburn. If you're driving straight from San Francisco, take I-80 to U.S. 50 and follow the signs from there.

For information, contact the **Auburn Area Chamber of Commerce,** 601 Lincoln Way, Auburn (☎ 916/885-5616); **Placer County Tourism,** 13460-A Lincoln Way, Auburn (☎ 916/887-2111); or the **El Dorado County Chamber of Commerce,** 542 Main St., Placerville (☎ 916/621-5885).

In Auburn you might want to linger in the Old Town and browse the stores. Auburn also has the **Placer County Museum,** 101 Maple St. (☎ **916/889-6500**), a state-of-the-art exhibit on the history of Placer County, including a remarkable Native American collection, a restored sheriff's office, and mining displays. The museum is open Tuesday to Sunday from 10am to 4pm. Admission is free.

How to Pan for Gold

Find a gold pan—ideally a 12- to 15-inch steel pan. Place the pan over an oven burner, or better yet, in a camp fire. This will darken the pan, making it easier to see any flakes of placer gold. Find some gravel, sand, or dirt in a stream that looks promising or feels lucky. Almost fill the pan with dirt and then place it under water and keep it there while you break up the clumps of mud and clay and toss out any stones. Then grasp the pan with both hands. Holding it level, rotate it in swirling motions. This will cause the heavier gold to loosen and settle to the bottom of the pan. Drain off the dirty water and loose stuff. Keep doing this until gold and heavier minerals called "black sand" are left in the pan. Carefully inspect the black sand for nuggets or speck traces of gold. You just might be lucky.

You can dredge for gold from June 1 to October 15, but you'll need a dredging permit. Apply for one at Regional 2 Headquarters, **California Department of Fish & Game,** 1701 Nimbus Rd., Rancho Cordova, CA 95670 (☎ 916/355-0978). Or you can sign up for one of the many dredging lessons and gold-panning tours offered in the Gold Country towns. Try calling **Gold Prospecting Expeditions** (☎ **800/596-0009** or 209/984-4653).

Auburn is en route to the site of the original discovery that started it all: **Coloma,** where gold was discovered in 1848. About 70% of the quiet, appealing town lies in the **Marshall Gold Discovery State Historic Park** (☎ **916/622-3470**), which preserves the spot where James Wilson Marshall discovered gold along the banks of the south fork of the American River. Although Marshall and his partner, John Sutter, tried to keep the discovery secret, the word soon leaked out. Sam Brannan, who ran a general store at Fort Sutter, secured some gold samples himself, and then headed for San Francisco, where he ran through the streets shouting, "Gold! Gold! Gold! From the American River!" San Francisco was soon half emptied as men rushed off to seek their fortunes at the mines. A self-guided trail leads to the site of this momentous event.

Over the next 50 years, 125 million ounces of gold were taken from the Sierra foothills (worth $50 billion today), fueling the rapid development of California and the nation. But it didn't line the pockets of the man who discovered it. Marshall died in poverty and his grave site stands here on a hill; his statue is pointing to the spot where he made his discovery. It's a pleasant hike up to the top, from which you can survey the whole valley.

Other attractions in the park include the Gold Discovery Museum, which relates the story of the Gold Rush, and a number of Chinese stores, all that remains of the once-sizable local Chinese community. The park also has three picnic areas, four trails, recreational gold panning, and a number of buildings and exhibits relating the way of life that prevailed here in the 19th century. Admission is $5 per vehicle, and it's open daily (except major holidays) from 10am to 5pm.

Folks also come here for white-water thrills on the American River. The **White Water Connection,** Coloma (☎ **916/622-6446**), offers half-day to 3-day trips on the American, Klamath, Salmon, and Stanlislaus rivers.

Eight miles south of Coloma is **Placerville.** Although its main street has a string of historic Victorian buildings, don't come here expecting a cute mining town—it's a modern commercial center. But there's the **El Dorado County Historical Museum,** 100 Placerville Dr. (☎ **916/621-5865**), which features a large collection of Native American baskets, plus some remarkable examples of transportation that won the West. Admission is free and it's open Wednesday to Saturday from 10am to 4pm and on Sunday from noon to 4pm. The other attraction is **Hangtown's Gold Bug Park,** 2501 Bedford Ave. (☎ 916/642-5238), a 61-acre park where visitors can follow a self-guided tour through the gold mine. Admission is $2, and it's open daily in summer from 10am to 4pm (only on weekends in spring, fall, and winter).

East of Placerville, U.S. 50 leads out to the small towns of Camino and Pollock Pines. This hilly and forested area is worth visiting to explore **Apple Hill,** which has close to 30 apple and other fruit orchards, plus a number of small, family-operated wineries, including the **Boeger Winery,** 1709 Carson Rd., Placerville (☎ 916/622-8094), which has an atmospheric tasting room and produces Merlot and Zinfandel; **Lava Cap,** 2221 Fruitridge Rd., Placerville (☎ 916/621-0175), which produces a wide range of varietals; the **Madrona Vineyards,** High Hill Road, Camino (☎ 916/644-5948), which produces Chardonnay, Riesling, and Zinfandel; and **El Dorado,** 3551 Carson Rd., Camino (☎ 916/644-2854), which specializes in Chardonnay, Cabernet, and Merlot.

For a free map listing all of El Dorado County's wineries, call the **El Dorado Winery Association** (☎ 800/306-3956 or 916/446-6562).

WHERE TO STAY

Auburn

Auburn Inn. 1875 Auburn Ravine Rd., Auburn, CA 95603. ☎ **800/272-1444** or 916/885-1800. Fax 916/888-6424. 78 rms, 3 suites. A/C TV TEL. $60–$66 double; $100–$120 suite. Rates include buffet continental breakfast. AE, DC, DISC, MC, V. From I-80, take the Auburn Ravine Rd./Forest Hill exit.

Set on the town's eastern outskirts, near the highway leading to Reno, Nevada, this hotel is better maintained and equipped than some of its newer competitors. It has a two-story motel-style design and a vaguely Colonial Revival decor, and was completely remodeled in 1995 with all new furniture. There's also a swimming pool on the premises, and a Jacuzzi-style spa. Close attention is paid to security and locks, and there are rooms and facilities for the disabled. Lots of dining choices are nearby.

Coloma

✪ **Coloma Country Inn.** 345 High St., Coloma, CA 95613. ☎ **916/622-6919.** 5 rms, 3 with bath; 2 suites. $88–$99 double; $120–$170 suite. No credit cards.

In the middle of the state park, this restored 1852 country farmhouse situated on 5 landscaped acres is a very romantic place to stay. It's made even more inviting by the warmth of innkeepers Alan and Cindi Ehrgott. To add to the experience, Alan doubles as a veteran balloon pilot, and you can sign up for an hour-long flight, which takes off from a balloon field just a short walk away from the B&B when you book your room (the B&B/Balloon package is $215 per person). You can also make arrangements for white-water–rafting trips.

The rooms are very prettily decorated with stenciling and plenty of fresh flowers from the surrounding gardens, and are furnished with antiques and quilts. The two suites in a separate cottage, one of which has a full kitchen, are exceptionally appealing. Afternoon tea and lemonade are served in the garden gazebo, and guests have the use of bicycles and also of the comfortable parlor and the front porch. There's an old pond on the property where kids can feed the ducks. A breakfast of fresh fruit, fresh-baked goods, and juice and coffee is served in the formal dining room. If you're bringing children, advance notice is needed. Smoking is not permitted.

✪ **Vineyard House.** Cold Springs Rd., Coloma, CA 95613. ☎ **916/622-2217.** 7 rms, 2 with bath. $95 double without bath, $130 double with bath. AE, MC, V.

Adjacent to Marshall Gold Discovery Park off Calif. 49, this inn occupies a large Italianate house that was built between 1876 and 1878; it was once the social center of the area and the home of a state senator. It's on the site of an award-winning winery. Downstairs it features a large granite-walled wine cellar, which now makes a very agreeable saloon.

The rooms are all furnished differently, based on characters from the Gold Rush era. The Lola Montez Room, for example, is decorated in rich reds and Spanish lace and has a private bath with a clawfoot tub. The restaurant, which consists of five period-furnished rooms, serves traditional fare such as chicken and dumplings and prime rib. There's bluegrass and jazz entertainment on Friday and Saturday in the saloon.

Placerville

Chichester-McKee House. 800 Spring St., Placerville, CA 95667. ☎ **916/626-1882.** 3 rms, none with bath. A/C. $80–$90 double. AE, DC, MC, V. Turn off Calif. 49 at Coloma St., turn right on High St., then right again on Wood St. to the parking area behind the house.

A handsome Victorian featuring fretwork and stained glass, this home—the first in Placerville to have indoor plumbing—was built in 1892 for a lumber baron. Today it's furnished with the doll collection and other personal effects of innkeepers Bill and Doreen Thornhill, who are happy to give sightseeing advice. Each room contains a brass or iron bed, Oriental rugs, a crocheted bedspread or quilt, country-oak furnishings, a sink and toilet, and bathrobes for the shared bath down the hallway. Guests can relax in the parlor or the library. An elaborate breakfast of crêpes, quiches, eggs Benedict, and "Bill's Special Blend" coffee is served in the dining room.

WHERE TO DINE

Auburn

✪ **The Headquarter House.** 14500 Musso Rd. ☎ **916/878-1906.** Reservations recommended. Main courses $9–$20. AE, DC, MC, V. Daily 11am–9:30 or 10pm. Drive northeast from Auburn's center along I-80 and exit at the Bell exit. AMERICAN/INTERNATIONAL.

Three miles east of Auburn's center is one of the area's most popular and consistently reliable restaurants. Many of its windows overlook the eighth hole of a nine-hole golf course; it's the unofficial watering hole and celebration (or commiseration) site of anyone playing on the course. A pianist performs Thursday to Sunday from 6 to around 10pm. If you prefer to dine outside, there's a deck with a half-dozen individual gazebos, each suitable for up to six diners. Menu items include steaks, prime rib, and such seafood dishes as salmon from the nearby Middlefork River, served in a lobster/pink-peppercorn sauce. No smoking is allowed inside.

Placerville

$ **Lil' Mama D. Carlo's.** 482 Main St. ☎ **916/626-1612.** Reservations recommended. Main courses $8–$15. MC, V. Sun–Thurs 3–9pm, Fri–Sat 3–10pm. ITALIAN.

If you're in the mood for Italian food, there's a little *ristorante* on Placerville's Main Street that's been placating hungry locals for the past 17 years. Just about everything coming out of the kitchen at Lil' Mama D. Carlo's is made from scratch, such as their giant ravioli hand-stuffed with ricotta, Parmesan, and spinach, or their tangy lasagne with seasoned pork sausage and thick layers of fresh Parmesan and mozzarella cheese. All entrees come with a choice of salad or minestrone soup—made fresh daily—and garlic bread. The best part, however, is the price: Most pastas are under $10, and the entire selection of El Dorado County wines is under $15.

Smith Flat House. 2021 Smith Flat Rd. ☎ **916/621-0667.** Main courses $11–$16. AE, DC, MC, V. Mon 11:30am–2pm, Tues–Sat 11:30am–2pm and 5–9pm, Sun 5–9pm. (Saloon, Mon–Thurs 10:30am–midnight, Fri–Sat 10:30am–1:30am, Sun 3pm–midnight.) AMERICAN.

Set at the western end of Placerville's historic center, behind a balcony where desperado shootouts might have taken place, this is probably the first building you'll see as you drive east into town from Sacramento. If there's a standard local favorite in Placerville, it must be the Smith Flat House. Fabled as the final milepost on the Lake Tahoe Wagon Trail, this place has lived through many incarnations—it's been everything from a Pony Express depot drop-off to a dance hall with "wicked" show girls. Beginning in 1853 it fed whiskey and (probably unpalatable) food to miners and cattle farmers streaming in from the surrounding fields. Today it revels in nostalgia for the Old West. There's a saloon in the cellar with a circular mine shaft that's said to lead to the heart of the Mother Lode. Reasonably well-prepared meals are served in the street-level restaurant. The food is hearty and very American, and no one leaves here hungry. Mainly steaks, chicken, and grilled or deep-fried seafood or fish fill the limited dinner menu.

Zachary Jacques. 1821 Pleasant Valley Rd. ☎ **916/626-8045.** Reservations recommended. Main courses $14–$20. AE, MC, V. Wed–Sat 5:30–9:30pm, Sun 5–8:30pm. FRENCH.

Zachary Jacques is easily the best restaurant in town. The French cuisine, which changes with the seasons, is well prepared and carefully presented, with an emphasis on fresh vegetables and fish. Start with the champignons farcis en croûte—mushroom caps stuffed with spinach, Brie, sun-dried tomatoes, and basil, then baked in puff pastry. Specialties include rack of lamb Valréas, with Dijon mustard, rosemary, and garlic; and lapin ardèchoise, fresh rabbit sautéed with leeks and served with whole-grain mustard sauce. Wednesday diners have a bonus option: cassoulet maison, a classic country dish with white beans, duck, sausages, and lamb.

THE SOUTHERN GOLD COUNTRY

From Placerville, continue south along Calif. 49 via Plymouth and Drytown to reach three appealing mining towns—Amador City, Sutter Creek, and Jackson. If you're coming straight here from San Francisco, take I-80 to Calif. 4. You can either follow Calif. 4 all the way to Angels Camp to pick up Calif. 49 north, or you can turn off Calif. 4 to Calif. 99 north at Stockton and pick up Calif. 88 to Jackson.

For information, contact the **Amador County Chamber of Commerce,** 125 Peek St., Jackson (☎ 209/223-0350).

Before you reach these towns you may want to turn off Calif. 49 to explore the Shenandoah Valley around Plymouth. Take Shenandoah Road east to explore the **Amador County Wine Country,** which is known for its zinfandel and, more recently, for sauvignon blanc and chenin blanc. The wineries are small and family owned; any tour or tasting will most likely be given by the owner. There are several wineries on Shenandoah Road (Sonny Grace, Sobon Estate, and Vino Noceto), Bell Road (Karly and Story), and Steiner Road (with at least six). Bell and Steiner both branch off from Shenandoah.

Although **Amador City** sounds large and impressive, it's in fact tiny. Basically, it's a widening in the road with a few very browsable shops and the Imperial Hotel, which has one of the finest dining rooms in the area.

Sutter Creek is a small, attractive town with lots of 19th-century homes and worthwhile antiques stores.

Jackson, the county seat of Amador County, is livelier. Take time to stroll through the town, browsing in the stores and noting the Victorian buildings.

South of Jackson on Calif. 49 is one of the most evocative mining towns of the region—**Mokelumne Hill.** The town basically consists of one street overlooking a valley with a few old buildings, but somehow its sad, abandoned air has the mark of authenticity. It's not gussied up—it's just the unvarnished way it has remained for decades. At one time the hill was dotted with tents and wood and tarpaper shacks, and the town boasted a population of 15,000, including an old French quarter and a Chinatown. But now many of its former residents are merely memorialized in the town's Protestant, Jewish, and Catholic cemeteries.

WHERE TO STAY
Amador City

Imperial Hotel. Main St. (Calif. 49; P.O. Box 195), Amador City, CA 95601. ☎ **800/ 242-5594** or 209/267-9172. 6 rms. A/C. $80–$95 double. AE, MC, V.

Right on Calif. 49, this hotel occupies a brick Victorian that was built in 1879. The individually decorated rooms—all with private bath—are upstairs above the dining room and are furnished with brass, iron, or pine beds; two come with private balconies. Our favorite room is one containing hand-painted furnishings by local artist John Johannsen. Amenities include hair dryers and heated towel bars in all rooms, as well as newspaper delivery and in-room massage upon request. The restaurant, serving American/continental cuisine, has a sterling reputation, and hotel guests can take advantage of room service when it's open (see "Where to Dine," below).

Sutter Creek

✪ **The Foxes.** 77 Main St. (P.O. Box 159), Sutter Creek, CA 95685. ☎ **209/267-5882.** Fax 209/267-0712. 7 rms. A/C. $120–$165 double. Rates include breakfast. DISC, MC, V.

This clapboard house with a decorous front porch was built in 1857 and is the town's most elegant hostelry. The seven rooms are all uniquely decorated, each with a queen-size bed and down comforters. Three, including the Garden Room and the Fox Den, have wood-burning fireplaces. The Victorian Fox Den also has a little library of its own, and features a 9-foot-tall Renaissance Revival bed and a separate sitting room. Three of the rooms have TVs tucked in armoires, and all have private baths. Breakfast, cooked to order, can be served in your room or in the gazebo in the garden.

Gold Quartz Inn. 15 Bryson Dr., Sutter Creek, CA 95685. ☎ **800/752-8738** or 209/ 267-9155. Fax 209/267-9170. 24 rms. A/C TV TEL. $80–$150 double. AE, DISC, MC, V.

Just off Calif. 49 outside Sutter Creek, the Gold Quartz Inn is one of the town's premier B&Bs, a modern establishment designed in Queen Anne style. Its amenities and first-class bedrooms make it comparable to a deluxe small hotel. The rooms are decorated with antique reproductions and furnished with iron or brass beds, and all have private baths. Some units have their own porches, the only place in the hotel where smoking is allowed. Afternoon tea and a full breakfast are served daily in the dining rooms, and the adjacent parlor offers an array of sofas and a VCR with a movie library. Free laundry service is also available.

Jackson

Court Street Inn. 215 Court St., Jackson, CA 95642. ☎ **800/200-0416** or 209/223-0416. 8 rms. A/C. $95–$130 double. Rates include breakfast. AE, DISC, MC, V.

Two blocks from Main Street, this Victorian home—listed on the National Register of Historic Places—was built in 1870 and sports elegant details such as eyelash shutters, embossed ceilings, and a Carerra marble fireplace. Our favorite unit is the Muldoon Room, with its oak-manteled fireplace, handsome four-poster king-size bed, and Victorian cradle. Romantics should select the Peiser Room, which has a wicker canopy bed. All the rooms are very nicely decorated and some have fireplaces and whirlpool or clawfoot tubs. There's a porch where guests can relax on the swing, and a hot tub is also available for star-gazing. Complimentary evening refreshments are served. TVs are available on request. No smoking is allowed inside.

WHERE TO DINE
Amador City
Imperial Hotel. Main St. (Calif. 49). ☎ **209/267-9172.** Reservations recommended. Main courses $14–$21. AE, MC, V. Daily 5–9pm. AMERICAN/CONTINENTAL.

This restored 1879 hotel has been recommended already, but even if you aren't staying here, its restaurant is worth a detour. There are only about seven main dishes offered on the seasonal menu, but whatever you choose will be tasty and well prepared. To start, try the sun-dried tomato polenta, topped with prosciutto and Parmesan, and served with a roasted tomato sauce. To follow, you might select the local version of cioppino, a tomato-based fresh seafood stew accented with zinfandel. If you put your name on the waiting list for their New Year's celebration, you might get a seat by the year 2000—it's that popular.

Sutter Creek
Ron and Nancy's Palace. 76 Main St. ☎ **209/267-1355.** Reservations recommended on weekends. Main courses $9–$16. AE, DC, MC, V. Daily 11:30am–3pm and 5–9pm (last order). AMERICAN/CONTINENTAL.

Set in a rustic building originally built in 1884 as a stable, this place is not run by the former first couple, but is the palace of Ron and Nancy Gottheiner, experienced San Francisco restaurateurs. Many visitors come just for the two-fisted drinks served in the bar/lounge, where a battle for your attention will rage between the Elvis memorabilia favored by Nancy and the Oakland Raiders memorabilia prized by Ron. (The bar, incidentally, remains open through the afternoon, even when the restaurant area is closed.) In the three dining rooms, light from the windows is filtered through panels of stained glass.

Most dishes are enhanced with a dash of vermouth, marsala, or California wines. One of the most popular lunchtime dishes is a steak croissant sautéed in marsala and flavored with onions and herbs. Dinner items include linguines, prime rib, and a wildly popular pan-fried scampi with veal strips.

Jackson
Michael's. In the National Hotel, 2 Water St. ☎ **209/223-3448.** Reservations recommended. Main courses $11–$19. AE, MC, V. Fri–Sat 5:30–10pm, Sun 10:30am–2pm and 5:30–8:30pm. CALIFORNIA/AMERICAN.

The best and brightest aspect of the faded National Hotel is this restaurant down in the basement. Named after chef Michael Golsie, the restaurant offers well-prepared food that's traditional enough to appeal to assorted tastes. Entrees include veal with an Amador County zinfandel-raspberry sauce and shiitake mushrooms, and orange roughy with a light lemon-wine sauce. And there's always a vegetarian plate and a pasta of the evening.

Upstairs Restaurant. 164 Main St. ☎ **209/223-3342.** Reservations recommended. Main courses $12–$20. AE, MC, V. Tues–Fri 11:30am–2:30pm and 5:30–9pm, Sat–Sun 11:30am–3:30pm and 5:30–9pm. INTERNATIONAL.

The restaurant offers a limited, often-changing menu, but you might stumble on some true culinary gems—a red snapper cooked in strawberry-mint sauce, or duck julienned and served with a blackberry/ginger-port sauce, for example. Layne

McCollum, a graduate of California's Culinary Institute, is known as the town's finest and most sophisticated chef, with a reputation for imaginative and innovative cuisine. Crisp white linens, bowls of fresh flowers, and background music form a romantic backdrop to the restaurant's 12 tables.

CONTINUING SOUTH TOWARD JAMESTOWN

From Mokelumne Hill, Calif. 49 continues south, via San Andreas, 20 miles to **Angels Camp.** This is where Mark Twain heard the story that inspired his "The Celebrated Jumping Frog of Calaveras County." The frog jumping contest started in 1928 to mark the paving of the town's streets, and to this day the ribiting competition continues every third weekend in May. The record jump of 21 feet, 5³/₄ inches was achieved in 1986 by "Rosie the Ribiter," who beat the old world record by 4¹/₂ inches. Livestock exhibitions, pageants, cook-offs, arm-wrestling tournaments, carnival rides, and plenty of beer and wine keep the spectators entertained between jump-offs. For more information and entry forms ($3 per frog), call the **Jumping Frog Jubilee** headquarters at **209/736-2561.**

Angels Camp is built on hills that are honeycombed with mine tunnels. In the 1880s and 1890s five mines were located along Main Street—the Sultana, Angels, Lightner, Utica, and Stickle—and the town was bursting with the noise of the mills, as more than 200 stamps crushed the ore. Between 1886 and 1910 the five mines generated close to $20 million.

From Angels Camp, take a detour east along Calif. 4 to **Murphys,** a smaller and less commercial town than those along Calif. 49. Just off Calif. 4, a mile north of Murphys, are **Mercer Caverns** (☎ 209/728-2101), off Sheep Ranch Road. The caverns were discovered in 1885 by Walter Mercer and contain a variety of geological formations—stalactites, stalagmites, columns, curtains, flowstone, and more. Tours take 45 minutes; the caverns are open from Memorial Day to September, daily from 9am to 5pm; October to May, on Saturday and Sunday from 11am to 4pm. Admission is $5 for adults and $4.50 for children 10 and under.

Fifteen miles beyond Murphys on Calif. 4 is **Calaveras Big Trees State Park,** where you can see giant sequoias. Open daily; admission is $5 per car for day use.

From Murphys, get back onto Calif. 49, crossing the Stanlislaus River bridge over the Melones Reservoir to the most remarkable attraction in the area, **Columbia State Historic Park** (☎ 209/532-4301), which, though somewhat commercialized, is one of the best-maintained Gold Rush towns in the Mother Lode. The whole town has been preserved and functions as it did in the 1850s, with stagecoach rides, western-style Victorian hotels and saloons, a newspaper office, a working blacksmith's forge, and a Wells Fargo express office. The whole town comes to life in summer.

The county seat, **Sonora,** only a few miles south, is nestled in ravines and on hillsides. In Sonora you can visit the **Tuolumne County Museum and History Center,** 158 W. Bradford Ave. (☎ 209/532-1317), which is located in the 1857 county jail. Admission is free, and it's open daily year-round from 10am to 4pm.

About 4 miles down Calif. 49, **Jamestown** was the home of the Sierra Railroad Company. It's famous for its **Railtown 1897 State Historic Park** (☎ 209/984-3953), which features three original Sierra steam locomotives. These great machines were used in many a movie, including *High Noon* and *My Little Chickadee.* Rides are given on weekends from March to November. It's open daily year-round.

From Jamestown, Calif. 49 continues south across the huge Don Pedro Reservoir and through Coulterville and Bear Valley to **Mariposa,** on the fringes of Yosemite. It's another attractive hilly mining town with plenty of atmosphere.

WHERE TO STAY
Angels Camp
Cooper House Bed & Breakfast Inn. 1184 Church St. (P.O. Box 1388), Angels Camp, CA 95222. ☎ **800/225-3764,** ext. 326 or 209/736-2145. 3 suites. A/C. $90 suite for two. Rates include breakfast. AE, DISC, MC, V.

Once the home and office of a prominent community physician, Dr. George P. Cooper, the Cooper House is Angels Camp's only B&B, a small Arts and Crafts home mercifully positioned well away from the hustle and bustle of the town's Main Street. Owners/innkeepers Tom and Kathy Reese maintain three guest rooms, all with private bath. The Zinfandel Suite has its own private entrance and deck (alas, the bed is only a double), whereas the Chardonnay Suite has a king-size bed and an antique clawfoot bathtub. The third bedroom, the Cabernet Suite, is mid-sized, with a queen-size bed, an adjoining sun room, and a splendid garden view.

Murphys
○ **Dunbar House, 1880.** 271 Jones St. (P.O. Box 1375), Murphys, CA 95247. ☎ **800/ 692-6006** or 209/728-2897. 3 rms, 1 suite. A/C TV TEL. $115 double; $155 suite. Rates include breakfast. AE, MC, V.

This pretty Italianate home, built in 1880 for the bride of a local businessman, is one of the finest in the Gold Country. The inviting front porch, which overlooks the exquisite gardens, is decorated with wicker furniture and hanging baskets of ivy. Inside, the emphasis is on comfort and elegance. The rooms are furnished with quality antiques and equipped with every possible amenity you could wish for. The beds have lace-trimmed linens and down comforters, and each room has a wood-burning stove and personal refrigerator supplied with mineral water and a complimentary bottle of wine. Other unexpected extras include a TV/VCR (well hidden), makeup mirror, and hair dryer, plus his-and-hers reading lamps. The most expensive accommodation, the Cedar, is a two-room suite with a private sun porch, a whirlpool bath, and free champagne. Lemonade and cookies are offered in the afternoon, appetizers and wine in the early evening. Breakfast is served either in your room, the dining room, or the garden.

The Redbud Inn. 402 Main St., Murphys, CA 95247. ☎ **800/827-8533** or 209/728-8533. 10 rms, 2 suites. A/C. $90–$155 double; $225 suite. Rates include breakfast. AE, DISC, MC, V.

Despite its location in a small shopping development, this inn offers all the comforts of home in its individually decorated rooms. Each appeals to a different personality. The Carousel, for example, contains a four-poster bed, a woodstove, a spa tub, and a balcony, and is decorated with carousel horses. The Garden House is a two-bedroom/two-bath suite with a completely outfitted kitchen. And the most romantic of all is the Anniversary Suite, with a double-sided fireplace, enormous tiled spa tub, king-size bed, and private balcony. A full breakfast is served in the bay-windowed dining room, and wine and hors d'oeuvres in the parlor in the evening. Therapeutic massage is available by appointment.

Columbia
City Hotel. Main St. (P.O. Box 1870), Columbia State Park, CA 95310. ☎ **209/532-1479.** Fax 209/532-7027. 10 rms, none with bath. A/C. $75–$100 double. Rates include breakfast. AE, MC, V.

This pleasant hostelry has been operating since 1856, and offers guests access to a large parlor furnished with Victorian sofas, antiques, and Oriental rugs. The largest units are the two balcony rooms overlooking Main Street; the rooms off the parlor are also spacious. The hallway rooms are smaller but still nicely furnished with Renaissance Revival beds and antique pieces. Each room has a sink and toilet.

A large buffet breakfast is served in the dining room. The hotel has a full restaurant and also the What Cheer saloon, which boasts its original cherrywood bar.

Fallon Hotel. Washington St. (P.O. Box 1870), Columbia State Park, CA 95310. ☎ **209/ 532-1470.** 14 rms, none with bath. A/C. $55–$95 double. Rates include breakfast. AE, MC, V.

This hotel, which opened in 1857, has been restored and decorated to evoke the 1890s, when Columbia experienced a second boom. A classic two-story building with an upper balcony, the hotel has retained many of its original antiques and furniture. The largest rooms are the front balcony rooms. Each unit has a private sink and toilet, and showers are nearby down the hall. The rooms are furnished with high-backed Victorian beds, marble-top dressers, rockers, and similar oak pieces. A continental breakfast is served in the downstairs parlor.

Sonora

Ryan House. 153 S. Shepherd St., Sonora, CA 95370. ☎ **800/831-4897** or 209/533-3445. 3 rms, 1 suite. A/C. $90 double; $160 suite. Rates include breakfast. MC, V.

Built in 1855, this wood-frame farmhouse is complete with a resident dog and cat. In summer the small garden out front is a riot of color with roses, wisteria, iris, tulips, pansies, and azaleas. A full breakfast of French toast or sourdough waffles is served outdoors. The small parlor has a wood-burning stove, which guests gather around. The rooms are furnished with brass beds covered by handmade quilts, and other country furnishings; all have private baths and air-conditioning. The upstairs Garden View Suite has a private parlor with a gas-log stove of its own and a bathroom with a soaking tub for two.

✪ **Serenity.** 15305 Bear Cub Dr., Sonora, CA 95370. ☎ **800/426-1441** or 209/533-1441. 4 rms. A/C. $90–$130 double. Rates include breakfast. AE, MC, V. From Sonora take Business Calif. 108 east to Calif. 108 to Phoenix Lake Rd., turn left and proceed for 3 miles to Bear Cub Dr., and turn right.

This B&B, set on 6 acres outside town, affords an opportunity to enjoy the beauty, peace, and quiet of the area's deer-filled oak and pine forest. A modern wood house built in traditional style with a wraparound porch, it has all the comforts of home and then some. The beds are made with lace-trimmed linens, and each room has a sitting area and private bath. One unit has a four-poster; another, a white iron bed. If you're making a winter visit, reserve one of the upstairs rooms warmed by remote-control gas-log fireplace. Breakfast, served in the formal dining room, is a veritable feast.

Jamestown

The Jamestown Hotel. Main St. (P.O. Box 539), Jamestown, CA 95327. ☎ **209/984-3902.** Fax 209/984-4149. 7 rms, 1 suite. A/C. $70–$95 double; $125 suite. Rates include breakfast. AE, DISC, MC, V.

The most worked-over building in town, the Jamestown was originally built in 1858, and had burned down and been rebuilt twice before 1915. And there have been more recent improvements as well: To achieve the brick-fronted Victorian look it sports today, its current owners ripped out a lot of stucco and Spanish Revival paraphernalia before they were satisfied with its old-fashioned look.

Much of the interior is devoted to the restaurant, which is separately recommended (see "Where to Dine," below). The second floor, however, contains cozy bedrooms outfitted with antiques acquired along both coasts of North America. Each room is large, with lots of nostalgic charm, and each has a private bath containing a claw-foot tub.

National Hotel. 77 Main St. (P.O. Box 502), Jamestown, CA 95327. ☎ **800/894-3446** or 209/984-3446. Fax 209/984-5620. 11 rms, 5 with bath. A/C. $65 double without bath, $80 double with bath. Rates include continental breakfast. AE, MC, V.

Located in the center of town, this two-story classic western hotel has been operating since 1859, one of the 10 oldest continuously operating hotels in the state. The saloon has its original 19th-century redwood bar, and you can imagine what it must have been like when miners traded gold dust for drinks. The rooms above are now furnished with oak pieces and brass beds made up with quilts. Some rooms have private baths; others have access to a bath down the hall and guests in those rooms are provided with bathrobes for their convenience. The restaurant serves traditional American and continental food.

WHERE TO DINE

Jamestown

Jenny Lind Room. In the Jamestown Hotel, Main St. ☎ **800/205-4901** or 209/984-3902. Reservations recommended. Main courses $10–$17. AE, DISC, MC, V. Mon–Sat 11am–3pm and 5–9pm, Sun 10am–3pm (brunch) and 5–9pm. AMERICAN/INTERNATIONAL.

The Jenny Lind Room may not be the best restaurant in the Gold Country, but it's certainly the most authentic looking, a dark-wood affair with stuffed wingback chairs, a fireplace, and dozens of old photos. There are about 15 tables inside, plus another 13 on an outdoor deck, which is only open during clement weather. Menu items include escargots in mushroom caps cooked in garlic butter, and breast of chicken "Jerusalem," with artichokes, mushrooms, and lemon-scented cream sauce. There's also a Sunday champagne brunch served until 3pm, and live music on weekend nights.

✪ Michelangelo. 18228 Main St. ☎ **209/984-4830.** Reservations recommended. Main courses $11–$13. DISC, MC, V. Mon and Wed–Sat 5–10pm, Sun 4–9pm. ITALIAN.

Marble-top tables, bentwood chairs, and drop halogen lights over the tables set the modern Milan-style scene for the Italian cuisine, which ranges from pasta and pizza to more complex dishes such as veal with lemon and caper sauce or chicken saltimbocca. Our favorite pizza here is topped with fresh apple, chicken sausage, and roasted red peppers. Service is polite and professional. The **Smoke Café** across the street, a stylish Tex-Mex restaurant best known for its lively bar and wicked "After Burner" cocktail, is affiliated with the Michelangelo.

Sonora

✪ Good Heavens. 49 N. Washington St. ☎ **209/532-3663.** Main courses $5–$9. No credit cards. Tues–Sun 11am–2:30pm. AMERICAN.

This lunch-only cafe, with bentwood chairs and blue floral-patterned tablecloths, is known for offering only homemade items. The menu features a variety of unique sandwiches—cucumber and pesto cream, turkey and cranberry orange—plus an array of delicious soups, salads, and desserts. There are also serveral daily specials—everything from chile rellenos to crêpes and pastas—listed on the board outside. Each meal starts with fresh herb-and-cheese biscuits and a choice of freshly made jams, such as the decadent raspberry-chocolate or the tart orange marmalade. Don't leave without purchasing a jar or two of the jams, which are sold at the counter.

Hemingway's. 362 Stewart St. ☎ **209/532-4900.** Reservations accepted. Main courses $13–$15. AE, MC, V. Tues–Fri 11:30am–2pm and 5pm–closing, Sat–Sun 5pm–closing. INTERNATIONAL.

What's going to be on the menu at Hemingway's this season is anyone's guess. Last year it was a California/French theme, where dishes ranged from mahogany duckling with Grand Marnier glacé to lobster Newburgh. Then it was the "classic foods of Spain," such as paella a la valenciana, cordero al chilindrón (chicken with orange sauce), and an array of tapas, sopas, and ensaladas. The trick is to call ahead and see what's on the menu: If it sounds good, it probably *is* good. This place does a brisk business at night, especially on weekends, when the service staff—semiprofessional musicians moonlighting to make ends meet—take the occasional break to get behind the piano and bring a little extra atmosphere to your dinner.

3 The Central Valley & Sierra National Forest

The Central Valley (also known as the San Joaquin Valley) is about as far as you can get from California's glamorous movie-stars-in-stretch-limos image. This hot, flat strip of tract homes, fast-food joints, cheap motels, and minimalls stretches for some 225 miles, separating Los Angeles and San Francisco from the Sierra Nevada.

Between the coastal foothills and the western slopes of the Sierra Nevada mountain range, this 18,000-square-mile valley is central to the economy of the Golden State, in part because of its cultivated and irrigated fields, orchards, pastures, and vineyards.

The major traffic arteries through the valley are Calif. 99 and I-5. Calif. 99 links the agricultural communities while I-5 provides access routes to the roadside attractions in the valley. Rivers cutting through the valley offer recreation, fishing, boating, houseboating on the delta, and white-water rafting on the rapids. And the valley's spectacular landscapes provide unrivaled natural beauty; many visitors drive through in spring just to view the orchards in bloom.

Frankly, although each town in the Central Valley has some attractions, nearly all of them are minor. Consider the towns along the way merely places to grab a quick bite or find a bed for the night while you're pursuing your real interest in the area, which is adventure and communion with nature in one of the national forests.

The Central Valley towns and cities stand on the doorstep of some of America's greatest attractions, including Yosemite. See Chapter 10 for coverage of two Central Valley towns, Merced and Visalia, which are good gateways to Yosemite, and Sequoia and Kings Canyon, respectively.

Fresno, although not much in itself, is on the doorstep of the Sierra National Forest and nearby attractions like Roeding Park and the Millerton Lake State Recreation Area.

FRESNO

The running joke in California is that Fresno is the "gateway to Bakersfield." Although for most visitors Fresno is just a place to pass through en route to the state parks, it can be a good place to stop for food and lodging (see below).

Founded in 1874, in the geographic center of the state, Fresno lies in the heart of the Central Valley and has experienced incredible growth in recent years, and, like most growing cities, has been plagued by an increase in crime, drugs, and urban sprawl.

As the seat of Fresno County, however, the city handles more than $3 billion annually in agricultural production. It also contains the world's largest dried-fruit packing plant, Sun Maid, and Guild, one of the country's largest wineries.

Fresno has some good hotels and some surprisingly good restaurants (see below). However, be careful if you're looking for a bargain and plan to check into one of the cheap motels along the highway. Security may be questionable.

Once you're based in Fresno, you can explore the Sierra National Forest (the big one) or tackle more minor attractions such as Roeding Park and the Millerton Lake State Recreation Area, all of which are previewed below.

If you have any reason at all to be in Fresno, try to visit between late February and late March so you can drive the **Fresno County Blossom Trail.** This 67-mile tour is self-guided and takes in the beauty of California's agrarian bounty at its peak. The trail courses through fruit orchards in full bloom, and citrus groves with lovely orange blossoms and a heady natural perfume. The **Visitor's Bureau,** 808 M St. in Fresno (☎ **800/788-0836** or 209/233-0836), supplies full details, including a map.

ROEDING PARK

This park, at 890 W. Belmont Ave. (☎ **209/498-1551**), set 1½ miles southwest of Fresno's center (via Calif. 99), is the city's playground. It's not a wilderness retreat, but the oldest, largest, and best-known recreational park in the region. It occupies 157 acres of land dotted with flower beds and trees, and is definitely an urban park, with lots of visitors at all times of the day.

The park includes the Fresno Zoo, **Rotary Playland,** and Storyland. It's beautifully landscaped, with groves of trees, blue lakes, and flower gardens, along with eight championship tennis courts, two dance pavilions, horseshoe pits, slides, and playgrounds. Several areas, complete with tables, running water, and barbecue pits, have been set aside for picnics.

The **Fresno Zoo** (☎ **209/498-2671**) sprawls across 25 acres, and aims to provide a natural habitat for more than 700 birds, reptiles, and mammals. The zoo is home to the world's only computerized Reptile House, and has a new 2-acre enclosure for elephants, one of the few breeding centers for Asian elephants in North America. The zoo is open in summer, daily from 9am to 5pm; in winter, daily from 10am to 5pm. Admission is $4.50 for adults, $1 for children 4 to 14, and free for kids 3 and under.

Storyland (☎ **209/264-2235**) is tucked away in a corner of Roeding Park. It's a magical, Disney-like playground for children. You can follow the Crooked Mile, slide down Jack's Beanstalk, climb Owl's Tree, or have a drink at Mother Goose's Fountain. Children's plays, puppet shows, and other events round out the agenda. Storyland is open daily from 10am to 3pm May 3 to Labor Day, charging $1.75 admission for children over 3, and $2.75 for adults. Off-season it's open on Saturday, Sunday, and school holidays from 10am to 3pm; it's closed in December and January.

MILLERTON LAKE STATE RECREATION AREA

This 14,107-acre park, at 5290 Millerton Road, Friant, CA 93626 (☎ **209/822-2332**), lies 21 miles northeast of Fresno via Calif. 41. Set in the foothills of the Sierra Nevada, amid a landscape of rolling hills and scattered groves of oak trees, the lake was formed in 1941 when a dam was built to channel the sometimes destructive waters of the San Joaquin River, which had until then roared down from the High Sierras at seasonal intervals.

Measuring up to 7 miles in length (but usually less, depending on droughts in the nearby hills) the ribbon-shaped lake is accessed via Fresno or Madera. You can camp in the park for a charge of $12 to $15 a night. (Bring your own gear—no electricity or gas sources are available in the park.)

Entrance to the park costs $6 for a vehicle and $5 per boat or jet ski. Unless you're registered at one of the park's campsites (in which event you can stay overnight), the park's hours are from 7am to 10pm every day in summer, and 7am to 6pm daily in winter.

WHERE TO STAY

San Joaquin. 1309 W. Shaw Ave., Fresno, CA 93711. ☎ **800/775-1309** or 209/225-1309. Fax 209/225-6021. 68 suites. A/C TV TEL. $82–$89 junior suite; $129 one-bedroom suite with kitchen; $165 two-bedroom suite with kitchen; $195 three-bedroom suite with kitchen. Rates include breakfast. AE, DC, MC, V.

Set on the northern edge of Fresno, this hotel was conceived as an apartment complex in the 1970s. Around 1985 a lobby was added, the floor plans were adjusted, and the place was reconfigured as an all-suite hotel. Each suite is outfitted in a slightly different style, with light, contemporary colors and furniture. Room service is available from an independently managed restaurant down the street.

WHERE TO DINE

Nicola's. 3075 N. Maroa Ave. ☎ **209/224-1660.** Reservations recommended. Main courses $9.75–$33.95. AE, DC, MC, V. Mon–Thurs 11:30am–4pm and 5–10pm, Fri 11:30am–4pm and 5–11pm, Sat 5–11pm, Sun 4–10pm. ITALIAN/AMERICAN.

Restaurants come and go in Fresno, but Nicola's remains the enduring favorite of many a discriminating diner. It's also evidence that not everything in Fresno is fast food. Inside the well-upholstered, masculine setting where you can indulge in a stiff cocktail before dinner, you're likely to meet the town's district attorney and a judge or two. The place prides itself on its stuffed steak: a hearty slab of beef layered with ham and cheese, and drizzled with a white wine and mushroom au jus sauce (not exactly health food, but oh, so decadent). Other choices include veal scallopine, cioppino, capellini pescatore (angel-hair pasta with shellfish), and beefsteak with gorgonzola.

✪ **Veni, Vidi, Vici.** 1116 N. Fulton. ☎ **209/266-5510.** Reservations recommended. Main courses $16–$19. MC, V. Wed–Sun 5:30–10pm. Closed 2 weeks in early Jan. NORTHERN CALIFORNIA.

The most innovative and creative restaurant in Fresno occupies a prominent position about 6 miles south of the commercial center, in a funky neighborhood known as the Tower District. The place's rustic exterior strikes an interesting contrast to the polished and artful interior on the other side of the 15-foot doors, where the decor is accented with exposed brick walls, hanging mirrors, and chandeliers fashioned from twisted wire and metal leaves.

The menu changes with the inspiration of the chef, but might include roasted loin of pork with Chinese black-bean and citrus-flavored glaze, served with grilled Portobello mushrooms, sun-dried tomatoes, risotto, and red-pepper coulis; or a vegetarian moussaka with a ragoût of crimson lentils and fresh cucumber-yogurt sauce. This is the only restaurant in Fresno that makes its own ice cream (the flavor of the day when we arrived was Technicolor lime sorbet). Have a scoop or two with the restaurant's perennial dessert favorite: bittersweet chocolate cake.

SIERRA NATIONAL FOREST

Leaving Fresno's taco joints, used-car lots, and tract houses behind, an hour's drive east delivers you to the Sierra National Forest, a land of lakes and coniferous forests lying between Yosemite and Sequoia/Kings Canyon national parks. The entire eastern portion of the park is still unspoiled wilderness protected by the government, and development—some of it, unfortunately, beside the bigger lakes and reservoirs—is confined to the western side.

The 1.3-million-acre forest contains 528,000 acres of wilderness. The Sierra's five wilderness areas include Ansel Adams, Dinkey Lakes, John Muir, Kaiser, and Monarch (see below).

The forest offers plenty of opportunities for fishing, swimming, sailing, boating, camping, waterskiing, white-water rafting, kayaking, and horseback riding, all regulated by certain guidelines. Downhill and cross-country skiing, as well as hunting, are also available, depending on the season. Backpackers seeking to retreat to the wilderness will find solace here, as the park is traversed by some 1,100 miles of forest hiking trails.

In the lower elevations, summer temperatures can frequently reach 100°F, but in the higher elevations, more comfortable temperatures in the 70s and 80s are the norm.

After visiting the ranger station at Oakhurst (see below), take Calif. 41 to Calif. 49, the major road into the northern part of the national forest. This is more convenient for visitors approaching the park from Northern California. Calif. 168 via Clovis is the primary route from Fresno if you're headed for Shaver Lake. There's no approach road from the eastern Sierras, only from the west.

To learn about hiking, camping, or other activities, or to obtain the fire and wilderness permits needed for backcountry jaunts, visit one of the ranger stations in the park's western section. These include: **Mariposa Ranger District,** 43060 Calif. 41, Oakhurst (☎ 209/683-4665); **Minarets Ranger Station,** 57003 North Fork (☎ 209/877-2218); **Kings River District,** 34849 Maxon Road, Sanger, near the Pine Flat Reservoir (☎ 209/855-8321); and the **Pineridge Ranger Station,** 29688 Auberry Rd., Prather (☎ 209/855-5355).

Shaver Lake is one place where you can stock up on goods and supplies if you're going into the wilderness, but stores in Fresno carry much of the same stuff at lower prices. Cheaper supplies are also available in the town of Clovis outside Fresno (which you must pass through en route to the forest), especially at its **Peacock Market,** at Tollhouse Road (3rd Street) and Sunnyside Avenue (☎ 209/299-6627).

THE MAJOR WILDERNESS & RECREATION AREAS

First we'll preview the five major wildernesses, then we'll run down the other major scenic highlights of the forest system.

THE ANSEL ADAMS WILDERNESS   Divided between the Sierra and Inyo national forests, this wilderness area covers 228,500 acres. Elevations range from 3,500 to 13,157 feet. The frost-free period extends from mid-July through August, the best time for a visit to the park's upper altitudes.

Ansel Adams is dotted with scenic alpine vistas, including steep-walled gorges and barren granite peaks. There are several small glaciers in the north, and some fairly large lakes on the eastern slope of the precipitous Ritter Range. This vast wilderness has excellent stream and lake fishing, especially for rainbow, golden, and brook trout, and offers challenging mountain climbing in the Minarets Range. The wilderness is accessed by Tioga Pass Road in the north, U.S. 395 and Reds Meadow Road in the east, the Minarets Highway in the west, and Calif. 168 to High Sierra in the south.

DINKEY LAKES WILDERNESS   The 30,000-acre Dinkey Lakes area was created in 1984 and occupies the western slope of the Sierra Nevada, southeast of Huntington Lake and just northwest of Courtright Reservoir. Most of the wilderness, timbered, rolling terrain, is 8,000 feet above sea level, reaching its highest point (10,619 feet) at Three Sisters Peak. Sixteen lakes are clustered in the west-central region. You can reach the area on Kaiser Pass Road (north), Red/Coyote Jeep Road (west), Rock Creek Road (southwest), or Courtright Reservoir (southeast), generally from mid-June to late October.

JOHN MUIR WILDERNESS   Occupying 584,000 acres in the Sierra and Inyo national forests, the John Muir Wilderness—named after the turn-of-the-century naturalist—extends southeast from Mammoth Lakes along the crest of the Sierra Nevada for 30 miles before forking around the boundary of Kings Canyon National Park to Crown Valley and Mt. Whitney. Elevations range from 4,000 to 14,496 feet at Mt. Whitney, and many of the area's peaks surpass 12,000 feet.

Split by deep canyons, the wilderness is also a land of meadows (especially beautiful when wildflowers bloom), lakes, and streams. The South and Middle Forks of the San Joaquin River, the North Fork of Kings River, and many creeks draining into Owens Valley originate in the John Muir. Mountain hemlock, red and white fir, whitebark, and western pine dot the park's landscape. Temperatures vary wildly throughout any 24-hour period: Summer temperatures range from 25° to 85°F, and the only really frost-free period is between mid-July and August. The higher elevations are marked by barren expanses of granite splashed with many glacially carved lakes.

KAISER WILDERNESS   Immediately north of Huntington Lake and some 70 miles northeast of Fresno, Kaiser is a 22,700-acre forest tract commanding a view of the central Sierra Nevada. It was named after Kaiser Ridge, which divides the area into two different regions. Four trailheads provide easy access to the wilderness, but the northern half is much more open than the forested southern half; the primary point of entry is the Sample Meadow Campground. All other lakes are approached cross-country. Winter storms begin to blow in late October, and the grounds are generally snow-covered until early June.

MONARCH WILDERNESS   This area extends across 45,000 acres in the Sierra and Sequoia national forests. The Sierra National Forest portion of the region—about 21,000 acres—is very rugged and hard to traverse. Steep slopes climb from the Middle and Main Forks of Kings River, with elevations going from 2,400 to more than 10,000 feet. Rock outcroppings are found throughout Monarch, and most of the lower elevations are mainly chaparral covered with pine stands near the tops of the higher peaks.

HUNTINGTON LAKE RECREATION AREA   At 7,000 feet, this area is a 2-hour drive east of Fresno via Calif. 168. The lake is one of the reservoirs in the Big Creek Hydroelectric System, and has 14 miles of shoreline. It's a popular recreational area, offering camping, hiking, picnicking, sailing, swimming, windsurfing, fishing, and horseback riding. Or you can just appreciate the beauty. The main summer season stretches from Memorial Day to Labor Day. There are seven campgrounds and four picnic areas in the Huntington Lake Basin, plus numerous hiking and riding trails. For information, stop in at the **Easterwood Visitor Center** (☎ 209/ 893-6611), open May to September.

NEIDER GROVE OF GIANT SEQUOIAS   This 1,540-acre tract in the Sierra National Forest contains 101 mature giant sequoias in the center of the Sequoia range, south of Yosemite National Park. A visitor center stands near the Nelder Grove Campground, with historical relics and displays, including two restored log cabins. The Bull Buck Tree—at one time thought to be the largest in the world—has a height of 246 feet and a circumference at ground level of 99 feet. There's a mile-long, self-guided walk along the "Shadow of the Giants" National Recreational Trail in the southwest corner of the grove.

SPORTS & ACTIVITIES

FISHING   The many streams of the Sierra are home to rainbow, golden, brown, and brook trout. The best freshwater angling is in the Pineridge and Kings River ranger districts. Lower elevation reservoirs, such as Shaver Lake, Bass Lake, and Pine Flat reservoirs, are known for their black bass fishing.

Questions about fishing in the national forest can be directed to the **California Department of Fish and Game,** 1235 E. Shaw Ave., Fresno, CA 93710 (☎ **209/ 222-3761**).

SKIING   Lying 65 miles northeast of Fresno on Calif. 168, in the Sierra National Forest, the **Sierra Summit Ski Area** is known for its alpine skiing. It also offers marked trails for cross-country skiing and snowmobiling. Information about the district is available from the Pineridge Ranger Station, 29688 Auberry Rd., Prather (☎ 209/855-5355). The resort area has two triple- and three double-chair lifts, plus four surface lifts and 25 runs, the longest of which extends for 2¼ miles. There's a vertical drop-off of 1,600 feet. Other facilities include a lodge, snack bar, cafeteria, restaurant, and bar, all open daily from mid-November until mid-April. For a ski report, call 209/893-3311.

The ranger district has developed several marked cross-country trails along Calif. 168. They range from a 1-mile tour for beginners to a 6-mile trail for more advanced skiers.

WHITE-WATER RAFTING   The Upper Kings River, east of Pine Flat Reservoir, offers a 10-mile rafting run through Garnet Dike to Kirch Flat Campground. Rafting season is from late April to mid-July, with the highest waters in late May and early June. To get there, take Belmont Avenue east from Fresno (toward Pine Flat Reservoir) for about 63 miles.

Two commercial rafting companies that offer guided rafting trips on the Kings River are **Kings River Expeditions** (☎ 209/233-4881) and **Zephyr River Expeditions** (☎ 209/532-6249).

CAMPING   The Sierra National Forest seems like one vast campsite. Options range from unembellished, primitive wilderness camps to developed and often crowded campgrounds with snack bars, flush toilets, bathhouses, and RV hookups. For information and reservations, call the **National Forest Reservation Center** at **800/ 280-CAMP.**

The major campgrounds are the Shaver Lake area (first-come, first-served); the Huntington Lake area (which has six family campgrounds open from the end of June to Labor Day that must be reserved in advance); the Florence and Edison Lake area (first-come, first-served); the Dinkey Creek area (which has family and group camping by special permit); the Wishon and Courtright area (four campgrounds; first-come, first-served); the Pine Flat Reservoir (in the Sierra foothills, with two first-come/first served campgrounds available); and Upper Kings River, east of Pine Flat Reservoir (which has family campgrounds on a first-come, first-served basis).

The Monterey Peninsula & Big Sur Coast

12

By Erika Lenkert and Matthew R. Poole

Located about 120 miles south of San Francisco, the Monterey Peninsula and Big Sur coast comprise one of the world's most coveted shorelines. Skirted with cypress, rugged shores, and crescent-shaped bays, the indescribably beautiful marine backdrop has made this entire stretch of coastline a favorite seaside playground for travelers worldwide. Monterey reels in visitors with its Monterey Bay Aquarium and unparalleled outdoor activities; many consider it the golf and dive capital of the world. Pacific Grove is so peaceful and quaint that the butterflies choose it as their yearly mating ground. Pebble Beach attracts the world's golfing elite. Though packed with tourists who come for the beaches, shops, and restaurants, tiny Carmel-by-the-Sea somehow remains romantic and sweet. And Big Sur's dramatic and majestic coast, backed by pristine redwood forests and rolling hills, is one of the most breathtaking sites on earth.

Monterey and Pacific Grove occupy the northern half of the peninsula overlooking Monterey Bay, while Pebble Beach and Carmel-by-the-Sea look out over Carmel Bay and hug the peninsula's south coast. Between the north and south coasts, which are only about 5 miles apart, are at least eight golf courses, some of the state's most stunning homes and hotels, and 17-Mile Drive, among the most scenic coastal roads in the world. Inland lies Carmel Valley, with its elegant inns and resorts, golf courses, and guaranteed sunshine, even when the coast is socked in with fog.

Farther down the coast is Big Sur, a stunning 90-mile stretch of coast south of the Monterey Peninsula and west of the Santa Lucia Mountains.

1 Monterey

While its neighbors are romantic coastal hideaways, Monterey is the antithesis. A harbor-town-cum-tourist-trap, it's big enough that you have to drive from downtown to Cannery Row, and affected enough that chain hotels and restaurants have put the squeeze on boutique establishments. Plenty of history and heritage remains, but you'll have to weed though minimalls to find them. Its saving grace is the fantastic aquarium and beautiful Monterey Bay, where sea lions and otters still frolic in abundance.

You can save money by staying in an inexpensive motel in Monterey and easily driving into pricier Carmel-by-the-Sea to shop

The Monterey Peninsula

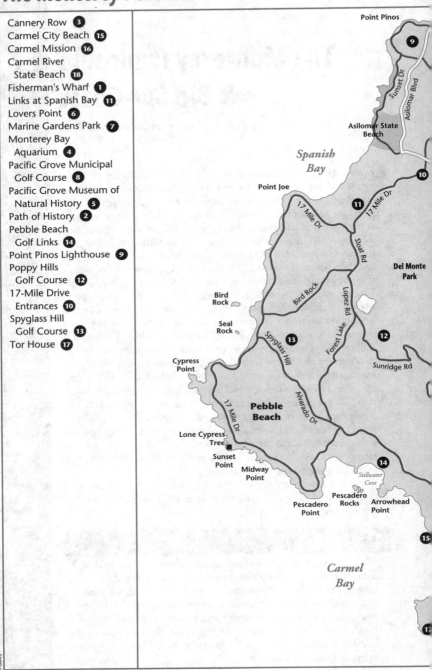

1-0843

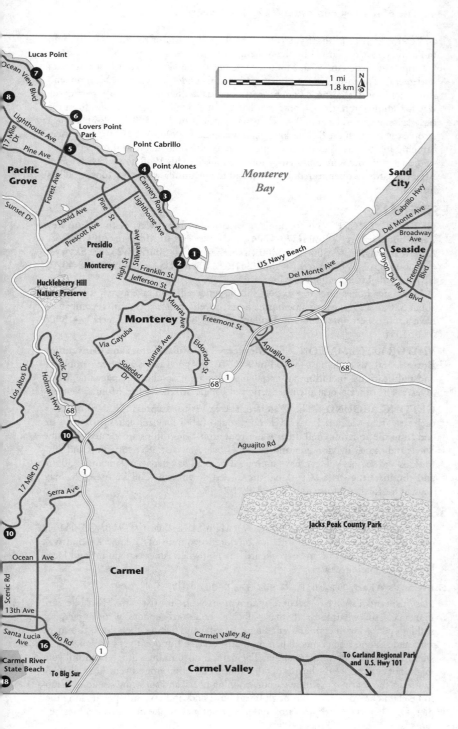

Lucas Point

7

8

Ocean View Blvd

6

Lighthouse Ave

117 Mile Dr

Lovers Point
Park

5

Pine Ave

Point Cabrillo

4 Point Alones

**Pacific
Grove**

Forest Ave

David Ave

Prescott Ave

Pine St

Sunset Dr

**Presidio
of
Monterey**

Cannery Row

3

Lighthouse Ave

Stillwell Ave

High St

**Huckleberry Hill
Nature Preserve**

1

Franklin St

2

Jefferson St

*Monterey
Bay*

**Sand
City**

Cabrillo Hwy

Del Monte Ave

Broadway
Ave

Seaside

US Navy Beach

Del Monte Ave

Canyon Del Rey

Fremont Blvd

1

Blvd

Monterey

Munras Ave

Freemont St

Via Gayuba

Munras Ave

Eldorado St

Aguajito Rd

68

Soledad
Dr

1

68

Scenic Dr

Los Altos Dr

Holman Hwy

68

10

1

Aguajito Rd

17 Mile Dr

Serra Ave

10

Jacks Peak County Park

Ocean Ave

Carmel

Scenic Rd

13th Ave

Santa Lucia
Ave

16

Rio Rd

1

Carmel Valley Rd

**To Garland Regional Park
and U.S. Hwy 101**

**Carmel River
State Beach**

18

To Big Sur

Carmel Valley

0 ____ 1 mi
1.8 km

N

and go to the beach. But if you can afford the full charm of the area, set up camp in Pacific Grove or Carmel-by-the-Sea and make Monterey a day trip.

Originally settled in 1770, Monterey was one of the West Coast's first European settlements. The town was the capital of California under the Spanish, Mexican, and American flags. California's state constitution was drafted here in 1849, paving the way for admission to the Union a year later. Many architectural buildings from the early colonial era still stand. A major whaling center in the 1800s, it also became a sardine center when the first packing plant was built in 1900. By 1913 the boats were bringing in 25 tons of sardines a night. Lives of the residents who thronged down to the 18 canneries were captured by John Steinbeck in his 1945 novel *Cannery Row*. After the sardines disappeared, the town and the peninsula went after tourist dollars instead.

ESSENTIALS

GETTING THERE   The region's most convenient runway, at the **Monterey Peninsula Airport** (☎ **408/373-1704**), is 3 miles east of Monterey on Calif. 68. **American Eagle** (☎ 800/433-7300), **Northwest** (☎ 800/225-2525), **Skywest** (☎ 800/453-9417), **United** (☎ 800/241 6522), and **USAir** (☎ 800/428-4322) have daily flights in and out of Monterey.

Many area hotels offer free airport shuttle service. If you take a taxi, it will cost about $20 to $25 to get to a peninsula hotel. Several national car-rental companies have airport locations, including **Dollar** (☎ 800/800-4000) and **Hertz** (☎ 800/654-3131).

VISITOR INFORMATION   The **Monterey Peninsula Visitors and Convention Bureau,** 380 Alvarado St. (☎ **408/649-1770**), has good maps and free pamphlets and publications, including an excellent visitors' guide and the magazine *Coast Weekly.* The office is near the intersection of Pacific Street and Del Monte Avenue.

GETTING AROUND   The **Waterfront Area Visitor Express (WAVE)** operates each year from Memorial Day weekend through Labor Day and takes passengers to and from the aquarium and other waterfront attractions. Stops are located at many hotels and motels in Monterey and Pacific Grove. At a cost of $1 for adults and 50¢ for kids and seniors you can have unlimited rides all day between 9am and 6:30pm and eliminate the stress of parking in crowded downtown. Call Monterey Salinas Transit for further information at **408/899-2555.**

SEEING THE SIGHTS

The **Steinbeck Center Foundation,** 371 Main St., Salinas (☎ **408/753-6411**), offers a self-guided tour or information on docent-led tours of "Steinbeck Country," which show visitors sites once frequented by renowned American author and local legend John Steinbeck.

Fisherman's Wharf. 99 Pacific St. ☎ **408/373-0600.**

Has "fisherman's wharf" become synonymous with "tourist trap?" Just like San Francisco's, this wharf is exactly that—albeit an honest-to-goodness wooden pier, it's still jam-packed with craft and gift shops, boating and fishing operations, fish markets, and seafood restaurants all baiting tourist dollars. But don't get us wrong—this wharf does have redeeming qualities. The natural surroundings are so beautiful you might not even notice the hoards of other tourists hovering around you. After all, who can resist the charm of a sunny harbor, bobbing boats, and surfacing sea lions? Grab some clam chowder in a sourdough bread bowl and find a seaside perch along the pier. Or when the wind picks up, find a bayfront seat at one of the seafood restaurants (see "Where to Dine," below).

If the seaside sights have got you itching to set sail, don't remain landlocked; boats depart regularly from Fisherman's Wharf and will lead you on a number of ocean adventures. See "Sports & Outdoor Activities," below, for details on some of the offerings.

Cannery Row. Monterey Bay (between David and Drake aves.). ☎ **408/649-6690.**

Once an industrious sardine-packing mecca immortalized by John Steinbeck as "a poem, a stink, a grating noise, a quality of light, a tone, a habit, a nostalgia, a dream," this area today is better described as a strip congested with wandering tourists, tacky gift shops, overpriced seafood restaurants, and an overall parking nightmare.

What changed it so dramatically? The silver sardines suddenly disappeared from Monterey's waters in 1948 as a result of overfishing, changing currents, and pollution. Fishermen left, canneries closed, and the Row fell into disrepair. But curious tourists continued to visit Steinbeck's fabled area, and where there are tourists, there are capitalists.

After visiting Cannery Row in the 1960s, Steinbeck wrote, "The beaches are clean where they once festered with fish guts and flies. The canneries which once put up a sickening stench are gone, their places filled with restaurants, antique shops, and the like. They fish for tourists now, not pilchards, and that species they are not likely to wipe out."

The Row is even more touristy today. The seaside strip's canneries and warehouses have been renovated and converted to restaurants, art galleries, hotels, factory outlets, and gift shops. Many of the larger buildings have become self-contained minimalls, stocked with a myriad of tacky tourist shops and eateries.

✪ **Monterey Bay Aquarium.** 886 Cannery Row. ☎ **800/756-3737,** 800/225-2277, or 408/648-4888. Admission $13.75 adults, $11.75 students and seniors 65 and over, $6 disabled visitors and children 3–12, free for children 2 and under. AE, MC, V. Daily 10am–6pm (opens at 9:30am summer and holidays).

The site of one of the world's most spectacular aquariums was not chosen at random. It sits on the border of one of the largest underwater canyons on earth (wider and deeper than even the Grand Canyon) and is surrounded by incredibly diverse local marine life.

Opened in 1984, the Monterey Bay Aquarium quickly gained fame as one of the best exhibit aquariums in the world, and it's one of the largest, too—home to more than 350,000 marine animals and plants. One of the living museum's main exhibits is a three-story, 335,000-gallon tank, with clear acrylic walls that give visitors an unmatched look at local sea life. A towering kelp forest, which rises from the floor of this oceanic zoo, gently waves with the water as hundreds of leopard sharks, sardines, anchovies, and other fish swim back and forth in an endless game of hide-and-seek.

In 1996 the outstanding Outer Bay exhibit opened, which features creatures that inhabit the open ocean. This tank—holding a million gallons of water—houses yellowfin tuna, large green sea turtles, barracuda, sharks, the very-cool giant ocean sunfish, and schools of bonito. The Outer Bay's jellyfish exhibit is guaranteed to amaze, and kids will love Flippers, Flukes, and Fun, a learning area for families.

Additional wet exhibits re-create other undersea habitats found in Monterey Bay. Everyone falls in love with the sea otters playing in their two-story exhibit. There are also coastal streams, tidal pools, a sand beach, and a petting pool, where you can touch living bat rays and handle sea stars. Visitors can also watch a live video link that regularly transmits from a deep-sea research submarine maneuvering thousands of feet below the surface of Monterey Bay.

You can avoid long lines at the gate by calling 800/756-3737 or 800/225-2277 and ordering tickets in advance.

FOLLOWING THE PATH OF HISTORY

About a dozen antique buildings are clustered around Fisherman's Wharf and the adjacent town. Collectively, they comprise the Path of History, and many are a part of the **Monterey State Historic Park,** 20 Custom House Plaza (☎ **408/649-7118**). A self-guided walking tour booklet is available that describes the route. You can pick up a copy at clearly marked points along the path, including the Cooper-Molera Adobe and Colton Hall (see below).

The path's best buildings are featured below; many don't have formal addresses, so they're listed according to the streets or street corners they fill. Path of History building hours vary from each other and change frequently, although in most cases they're open daily from 10am to 4pm in winter, and 10am to 5pm in summer. Call the Monterey State Historic Park for the latest information or go to the **State Park Visitor Center** at Stanton Center, 5 Custom House Plaza. A film on the history of Monterey is shown here free every 20 minutes, and guided walking tours of the Path leave from here daily at 10:15am, 12:30pm, and 2:30pm. The price is $2 for adults, $1.50 for youths 13 to 18, and $1 for children 6 to 12. Purchase of a $5 ticket guarantees admission over any 2-day period into each of the four buildings that charge admission fees. Otherwise, entrance to those four buildings costs $2 each.

Monterey Maritime Museum and History Center   This museum, at 5 Custom House Plaza (☎ **408/373-2469**), lets you view ship models and other collections that relate the area's seafaring history. Admission is $5 for adults, $3 for youths 13 to 18, $2 for children 6 to 12, and free for kids 5 and under. Open Tuesday to Sunday from 10am to 5pm (daily in July and August).

The Custom House   Dating from about 1827, this is the oldest government building in California, used by Mexican officials to inspect and tax ships trading on the California coast. It was here that Commodore John Sloat raised the stars and stripes to claim California for the United States.

California's First Theatre / Jack Swan's Tavern   In 1847 Jack Swan built a lodging house and tavern at Scott and Pacific streets. Three years later several U.S. soldiers decided to produce plays as a business venture. They used blankets as curtains, barrels and boards as benches, and turned a healthy profit on their very first night. Today the troupers of the **Gold Coast Theater Company** stage authentic 19th-century melodramas here. Call for reservations after 1pm Wednesday to Saturday at 408/375-4916. Tickets cost $8 for adults, $7 for children 13 to 19 and seniors 60 and over, and $5 for kids 12 and under. Show times are Wednesday to Saturday at 8pm in July and August, and on Friday and Saturday at 8pm the rest of the year.

Cooper-Molera Adobe   At the corner of Polk and Munras streets was the home of Capt. John Rogers Cooper, a successful merchant. It was built in the 1820s and 1830s, but was expanded and improved upon as he became wealthier. Today it's furnished with antiques that reveal much about his lifestyle.

Casa Soberanes   This colonial-era adobe house at 336 Pacific St., at Scott Street, was built during the 1840s. The home's cantilevered balcony and tile roof are of particular interest, as is the well-maintained interior, decorated with early New England furnishings and modern Mexican folk art.

Larkin House   Built in 1835, this balconied two-story adobe house at 510 Calle Principal, at Jefferson Street, was the home of Thomas Oliver Larkin, the U.S. consul to Mexico from 1843 to 1846. The house doubled as the consular office and is furnished with many fine antiques, including some original pieces. Next door is the house that was used by William Tecumseh Sherman; it now contains a museum depicting the roles of the two men in California history.

Stevenson House   Robert Louis Stevenson rented a second-floor room here during the autumn of 1879, and during his stay he wrote *The Old Pacific Capital,* an account of Monterey in the 1870s. Today the building has been restored and several rooms are devoted to Stevenson memorabilia.

Pacific House   Built in 1847, Pacific House, at 10 Custom House Plaza, was first used for military offices and supplies. Horses were corralled behind the building, which was also a popular spot for Sunday bull and bear fights. Pacific House later sheltered several small stores, and served successively as a public tavern, a courtroom, county clerk's office, newspaper office, law offices, a church, and a ballroom. The first floor now houses a museum of California history; the second floor has an extensive collection of Native American artifacts.

Colton Hall   This structure, at 522 Pacific St., was originally built as Monterey's town hall and public school. California's constitutional congress convened here in 1849. The Old Monterey Jail adjoins the property, its grim cell walls still marked with prisoners' scribblings.

Casa del Oro   Built by Thomas Oliver Larkin and used as a store by Joesph Bosta, this two-story adobe stands at the corner of Scott and Oliver streets. Today Casa del Oro is again a general store, which is operated by the volunteers of Historic Gardens of Monterey.

ENJOYING THE OUTDOORS

Cast your hook and your cares on a deep-sea-fishing expedition. Among the operators are **Chris' Fishing Trips,** 48 Fisherman's Wharf (☎ **408/375-5951**), which offers large party boats. Cod and salmon are the main catches, with separate boats leaving daily. Call for a complete price list and sailing schedule. Full-day excursions cost $27 to $40 per person.

Sam's Fishing Fleet, 84 Fisherman's Wharf (☎ **408/372-0577**), offers fishing excursions for cod, salmon, and whatever else is running, as well as seasonal whale-watching tours. Make reservations and bring lunch. Departures are at 7:30am Monday to Friday (salmon-fishing boats leave earlier) and at 6:30am on Saturday and Sunday. Check-in is 45 minutes prior to departure. Weekday prices are $27 for adults, $15 for children 11 and under; weekend and holidays cost $30 for adults, $19 for children. Equipment is $16 extra.

Kayaks can be rented from several outfitters for a spin around the bay. Contact **Monterey Bay Kayaks,** 693 Del Monte Ave. (☎ **800/649-5357** or 408/373-5357), on Del Monte Beach north of Fisherman's Wharf, which offers instruction, plus natural history tours that introduce visitors to the Monterey Bay National Marine Sanctuary. Prices start at $45 for the tours, $25 for rentals. To find out more, check them out on the Internet at **http://montereykayaks.com/tour.**

For bikes and in-line skates as well as kayak tours and rentals, contact **Adventures by the Sea,** at 299 Cannery Row (☎ **408/372-1807**). Bikes cost $6 per hour or $24 a day; kayaks are $25 per person; and skates are $12 for 2 hours, $24 for a day. Adventures also has other locations at 201 Alvarado Mall (☎ 408/648-7235) at the Doubletree Hotel and on the beach at Lovers Point in Pacific Grove.

Experienced scuba divers with their own equipment and one tank can contact **Twin Otters** (☎ **408/394-4235**), which specializes in scuba-diving trips along the reefs of Monterey and Carmel Bays.

A popular—and exhilarating—way to view Monterey Bay's spectacular scenery is via hot air balloon. Sunrise flights are offered daily, and sunset flights in fall and winter only. For information, contact **Balloons-by-the-Sea** (☎ **408/424-0111**).

North of Monterey at Marina State Beach, you can learn to hang-glide during a 3-hour course that includes five flights with **Western Hang Gliders,** Calif. 1 at Reservation Road, Marina (☎ **408/384-2622**). The cost is $89. More extensive packages and tandem lessons in Big Sur are available, too.

Need to keep the kids busy or feeling playful yourself? The **Dennis the Menace Playground** at Camino El Estero and Del Monte Avenue, near Lake Estero, is an old-fashioned playground created by Pacific Grove resident and famous cartoonist Hank Ketcham. It has bridges to cross, tunnels to climb through, and an authentic Southern Pacific Railroad engine teeming with wanna-be conductors. There's also a hot dog and burger stand, and a big lake where you can rent paddleboats or feed the ducks. The park is open daily from 10am to sunset.

WHERE TO STAY

It seems there are only three types of choices for accommodations in Monterey: lace-and-flowery B&Bs; large corporate-cum-beachy hotels; or run-of-the-mill motel digs. As well as how much you want to spend, consider which area you'd like to be in—beach, Cannery Row, wharf, secluded, central, etc.

EXPENSIVE

In addition to choices below, there are two chain hotels conveniently located near Fisherman's Wharf. The **Monterey Marriott,** 350 Calle Principal, at Del Monte Blvd. (☎ **800/228-9290** or 408/649-4234), offers some rooms with bay views and has a good rooftop restaurant serving California/Italian cuisine. It has an outdoor pool, health club, whirlpool, and saunas. There's also the **Doubletree Hotel at Fisherman's Wharf,** at 2 Portola Plaza (☎ **800/222-8733** or 408/649-4511). Both hotels are popular with business travelers and conventioneers.

○ **Hotel Pacific.** 300 Pacific St., Monterey, CA 93940. ☎ **800/232-4141** or 408/373-5700. Fax 408/373-6921. 105 suites. A/C TV TEL. $199–$249 suite for two. Rates include continental breakfast and afternoon tea. AE, DC, DISC, MC, V. Free parking.

If it's good enough for Martha Stewart, it's good enough for you. The day we arrived here we previewed the Grande Dame of Hospitality's room before she checked in. We were surprised that she chose a hotel that's not on the water, but once we saw the rooms, we understood why. Beyond the elegant Spanish/Mediterranean architecture of the common areas, each accommodation is situated in one of 16 buildings clustered around courtyards and gardens ingratiated with spas and fountains. The guest rooms are cozy southwestern/adobe-style junior suites with an overly fluffy soufflélike down comforter puffed atop a four-poster feather bed (for the full effect request a canopied one). Rustically stylish decor, terra-cotta–tiled floors, a fireplace surrounded by a cushy couch and seats, plus two TVs, three phones, gourmet coffee and tea—all make this a place where you'll want to kick your shoes off and stay awhile. Tiny closets are one of the few downsides. Laundry/valet service is available, and there's room service in the evenings. All this and it's close to the wharf (but not oceanfront) and across the street from the Monterey Conference Center.

Services/Facilities: Room service (evenings only), laundry/valet, 2 Jacuzzis.

Monterey Bay Inn. 242 Cannery Row, Monterey, CA 93940. ☎ **800/424-6242** or 408/ 373-6242. Fax 408/373-7603. 47 rms. MINIBAR TV TEL. $119–$329 double. Rates include continental breakfast delivered to your room. AE, CB, DC, DISC, MC, V. Free parking. From Calif. 1, take the Pacific Grove/Del Monte Ave. exit and follow the signs to Cannery Row; the hotel is near the aquarium.

We'd been under the impression that aside from its central location a short walk from the aquarium, there was no reason to stay on noisy, expensive Cannery Row. But when we stepped out onto our private patio at the Monterey Bay Inn and saw otters splashing around below us, our criticism melted into tranquil admiration. If you don't spend all your time on the balcony, you'll be pleased to discover that the spacious rooms escape appearing corporate and have light beachy decor and old Monterey photos on the walls. Most have king-size beds and convertible sofas, as well as dressing areas and combination baths stocked with terry cloth robes. Amenities include a refrigerator, VCR, and binoculars. Not surprisingly, ocean-view rooms cost substantially more than those that look onto a park, harbor, or Cannery Row. Parents with small children should take precautions with the sliding glass doors, which open to minimal balustrades.

Services: Room service (5 to 10pm).

Facilities: Sauna, fitness room, scuba facilities, beach and dive access, two hot tubs (one open 24 hours and the other boasts romantic bay views).

Monterey Plaza Hotel. 400 Cannery Row, Monterey, CA 93940. ☎ **800/631-1339**, 800/334-3999 in California, or 408/646-1700. Fax 408/646-5937. 285 rms, 7 suites. MINIBAR TV TEL. $160–$270 double; $405–$705 suite. Children 17 and under stay free in parents' room. Package plans available. AE, CB, DC, MC, V. Parking $10. From Calif. 1 take the Soledad Dr. exit and follow the signs to Cannery Row.

One of the most formal hotels in town, the Monterey Plaza encompasses three buildings, two on the water and one across the street, that are connected by a second-story "bridge." The public areas are elegantly decorated with imported marble, Brazilian teak, and attractive artwork. The stately bedrooms, which were renovated in 1996, are more upscale-corporate than most around town and have double or king-size beds, decor hinting at 17th-century Ming or 19th-century Biedermeier, and baths covered with Italian marble. Many units have balconies overlooking the water (sea otters included in the view). The least desirable rooms are across the street from the ocean. Extra bonuses include terrycloth robes, an exercise room, and an attentive and professional staff.

Dining/Entertainment: The Duck Club, the hotel's flagship dining room, has splendid views of the bay and serves an à la carte, primarily Italian menu prepared in an open Genovese exhibition kitchen. Schooners, with an outdoor terrace, is the new yacht-themed lounge/restaurant.

Services: Concierge, dry cleaning.

Facilities: Fitness room.

✪ **Old Monterey Inn.** 500 Martin St., Monterey, CA 93940. ☎ **800/350-2344** or 408/375-8284. Fax 408/375-6730. 9 rms, 1 cottage. $170–$240 double; $240 cottage. Rates include American breakfast. MC, V. Free parking. From Calif. 1, take the Soledad Dr. exit and turn right onto Pacific Ave., then left onto Martin St.

Ann and Gene Swett have done a masterful job of converting their comfortable family home into a three-story, half-timbered, vine-clad country inn. Away from the surf, on a 1-acre site off Pacific Avenue, it's a choice for romantics, with rose gardens, a bubbling brook, and brick and flagstone walkways shaded by a panoply of oaks creating an appropriate atmosphere for love. Each guest room enjoys peaceful garden views and cozy beds with goose-down comforters and pillows. Most rooms also have feather beds and wood-burning fireplaces, and two open onto private patios. Charmingly furnished and unique in character, they all owe a debt to Laura Ashley or Ralph Lauren. Special touches are evident throughout, including fresh fruit, flowers, and candies; sachets by the pillow; and books and magazines to read. The bathrooms come with hair dryers and complete toiletry packages. The cottage unit out back has antique wicker furniture, a fireplace, a sitting area, and an oversize bedroom with a king-size bed and a private patio.

Breakfast is also stellar, consisting of perhaps a soufflé or Belgian waffles. It's served either in your room, the dining room, or the rose garden. If you want to lunch on the beach, the Swetts will provide a picnic basket and towels. At 5pm guests are invited to have wine and hors d'oeuvres in front of a blazing fireplace.

Spindrift Inn. 652 Cannery Row, Monterey, CA 93940. ☎ **800/841-1879** or 408/646-8900. Fax 408/646-5342. 41 rms. MINIBAR TV TEL. $189–$229 double; $289–$349 double with ocean view. Rates include continental breakfast delivered to your room and afternoon tea. AE, DC, MC, V.

Down in the middle of honky-tonk Cannery Row, but right on a narrow stretch of beach, this four-story hotel is an island of continental style and grace in a sea of commercialism. It's elegant and well maintained, and the rooms are sweetly decorated with feather beds (a few with canopies), hardwood floors, wood-burning fireplaces, and either cushioned window seats or private balconies. The luxurious bathrooms are adorned with marble and brass fixtures. Extras include terrycloth robes and two telephones. The ocean views are definitely worth the extra cost. Services here include nightly turndown with a chocolate treat, daily newspaper, and room service from an Italian restaurant next door.

MODERATE

Munras Avenue and northern Fremont Avenue are lined with moderate and inexpensive family-style motels, some independently owned and some chains. They're not as central as the downtown options, but if transportation's not an issue, you can save a bundle by staying in one of these areas. If the selections below are full, try calling **Best Western** (☎ **800/528-1234**) for several other options. There's also the **Cypress Gardens Inn,** 1150 Munras Ave. (☎ **408/373-2761**), with a pool, hot tub, free movie channel, and continental breakfast; dogs are welcome.

The Arbor Inn. 1058 Munras Ave., Monterey, CA 93940. ☎ **408/372-3381.** Fax 408/372-4687. 54 rms. A/C TV TEL. $39–$69 double Mon–Thurs; $49–$129 double Fri–Sat. AE, DC, DISC, MC, V.

If life were a musical, you'd hear a Brady Bunch riff when you opened the door and peered into your guest room at this motel. The rooms are large and clean, and many have fireplaces, but the funky brown carpet, plaid couches, and 1970s color scheme aren't exactly *en vogue.* There's a hot tub on the property that looks a little worn, but it's tucked into a quiet spot away from the parking lot. A continental breakfast is served in a country-style dining room complete with fireplace. The rates are darn good here, considering that the motel is close to downtown and the waterfront. It changed hands recently, however, so expect some changes in 1997.

Fireside Lodge. 1131 10th St., Monterey, CA 93940. ☎ **408/373-4172.** Fax 408/655-5640. 24 rms. TV TEL. $69–$149 double. Rates include continental breakfast. AE, DC, DISC, MC, V.

Location is the primary draw to this hotel near Fisherman's Wharf and downtown. The room furnishings are relatively standard but attempt at coziness with wicker chairs set around the gas-heated brick fireplace. Amenities include an in-room tea/coffeemaker, a hot tub on the premises, and a continental breakfast served daily in the hotel's lobby.

✪ **The Jabberwock Bed & Breakfast.** 598 Laine St., Monterey, CA 93940. ☎ **408/372-4777.** Fax 408/655-2946. 7 rms, 3 with bath. $105 double without bath, $190 double with bath. Rates include full breakfast, afternoon appetizers, and bedtime cookies. MC, V.

One of the best B&Bs in the area, the Jabberwock (named after an episode in Lewis Carroll's *Through the Looking Glass*) is 4 short blocks back from Cannery Row. Although centrally located, the property is tranquil and its half-acre garden with waterfalls is a welcome respite from the downtown crowds. The seven rooms are all furnished differently, some more elegantly than others, but all with goose-down comforters and pillows. The Toves Room has a huge walnut Victorian bed; the Borogrove has a fireplace and a view of Monterey Bay; the Mimsey has a fine ocean view from its window seat, while the Wabe has an Austrian carved bed. A full breakfast is served in the dining room or in your own room. Evening hors d'oeuvres are also offered on the veranda, and a Vorpal Bear tucks each guest in with cookies and milk.

INEXPENSIVE

Pass up the charming B&Bs and waterfront rooms and opt for a motel to get the best rates in this town. Some reliable options are **Motel 6** (☎ 800/4-MOTEL6), **Super 8** (☎ 800/800-8000), or **Best Western** (☎ 800/528-1234).

Ⓢ **Cypress Tree Inn.** 2227 N. Fremont St., Monterey, CA 93940. ☎ **408/372-7586.** Fax 408/372-2940. 55 rms. TV TEL. $58–$92 double. MC, V.

Although it's not centrally located (2 miles from downtown), if you're on a budget and have transportation, you won't be sorry you saved your pennies if you stay here. The large rooms are spotless, and all but one has a combination tub-shower. Nine also have hot tubs. There's no shampoo, hair dryer, or in-room treats other than the taffy left by the maid, but the hostelry does have a hot tub, sauna, and guest coin-op laundry.

WHERE TO DINE

Cafe Fina. 47 Fisherman's Wharf. ☎ **408/372-5200.** Reservations recommended. Main courses $13–$17. AE, DC, MC, V. Mon–Fri 11:30–2:30pm and 5–10pm, Sat–Sun 11:30am–3pm and 5–10pm. Free parking at Heritage Harbor (at Scott and Pacific). ITALIAN/SEAFOOD.

While other pierside restaurants lure in tourists with little more than an outstanding view, the Cafe Fina's mesquite-grilled meats, well-prepared fresh fish, brick oven–baked pizzas, and an array of delicious salads and pastas give even locals a reason to head to the wharf. Combine the food with a million-dollar vista and a casual atmosphere, and Cafe Fina ranks hands down as the best choice on the pier.

✪ **Fresh Cream.** Heritage Harbor, 99 Pacific St. ☎ **408/375-9798.** Reservations recommended. Main courses $21–$30. AE, DC, MC, V. Fri 11:30am–2pm and 6–10pm, Sat–Thurs 6–10pm. FRENCH/CALIFORNIA.

Consistently rated one of the best places in California for fresh and innovative cuisine, Fresh Cream is a sure thing if you're looking for a memorable meal. The decor in the five dining rooms is elegantly understated to play up the emphasis on the food, though fresh flowers, oil lamps, and some tables with wharf views can't help but create ambience. But once the food comes out of the kitchen, you're liable to forget your surroundings entirely and become entranced by every well-presented and perfectly prepared plate. Start with the ravioli of lobster with lobster butter and black and gold caviar or the grilled prawns on whipped white beans with Castroville artichokes, pancetta bacon, and bouillabaisse. Venture on to a main dish such as the blackened ahi tuna sweetened with a pineapple-rum sauce; duck richly flavored with black-currant sauce; or veal loin with wild mushrooms and white-wine butter. Save room for a fluffy Grand Marnier soufflé or the sinful sac au chocolat.

✪ **Montrio.** 414 Calle Principal (at Franklin). ☎ **408/648-8880.** Reservations recommended. Main courses $14–$19. AE, DISC, MC, V. Mon–Thurs 11:30am–3pm and 5:30–10pm, Fri–Sat 11:30am–11pm, Sun 10am–10pm. AMERICAN BISTRO.

Big-city sophistication met old Monterey when Montrio hit the ground running here in March 1995. The enormous dining room is definitely the sharpest in town, mixing chic style with a playful canopied vineyard of modern light fixtures, clouds hanging from the ceiling, and the buzz of well-dressed diners. You can watch chefs scurry around in the open kitchen, but you're more likely to keep your eyes on the tasty dishes, such as the crispy Dungeness crab cakes with spicy rémoulade, hot goat-cheese salad with marinated veggies and toasted pumpkin seeds, a succulent grilled pork T-bone with apple, pear, and currant compôte, or an oven-roasted Portabello mushroom with polenta and ragoût of vegetables. Finish the evening with chocolate bread pudding with warm banana compôte and vanilla ice cream.

Whaling Station Inn. 763 Wave St. (between Prescott and Irving aves.). ☎ **408/373-3778.** Reservations recommended on weekends. Main courses $15–$30; fixed-price menu $27. AE, DC, DISC, MC, V. Daily 5–10pm. From Calif. 1, take the Soledad Dr. exit and follow the signs toward Cannery Row; turn left on Wave St. 1 block before Cannery Row. CONTINENTAL.

If you insist on eating on Cannery Row, come to this touristy, old-fashioned dining house known for its New York, porterhouse, and other steaks grilled over oak and mesquite. A 25-year tradition guarantees you an artichoke vinaigrette appetizer before your main course, which ranges from salad to pasta and the inevitable seafood dish. Famished folk will appreciate the fixed-price menu, which includes a salad or gnocchi, fresh fish or filet mignon with garlic mashed potatoes and garlic sauce, and dessert.

Wharfside Restaurant and Lounge. 60 Fisherman's Wharf. ☎ **408/375-3956.** Reservations recommended. Main courses $9–$18. AE, CB, DC, DISC, MC, V. Daily 11am–9:30pm. Closed the first 2 weeks of Dec. SEAFOOD.

A banner out front promises a "TASTE OF MONTEREY," which translates into a decent helping of fresh seafood served à la tourist trap. While the fare is okay, the real flavor is the Wharfside's casual upstairs nautically themed dining room where you'll get a great view from the end of Fisherman's Wharf. There's also downstairs and upper-deck outdoor seating where you can choose from seven different varieties of ravioli (made on the premises), such specialties as a Monterey bouillabaisse, or any of the house-made desserts. Daily specials usually include fresh seasonal fish, beef, and pasta. Clam chowder, sandwiches (including hot crab), and pizzas are on the regular menu.

2 Pacific Grove

Some compare 2.6-square-mile Pacific Grove—the locals call it "P.G."—to Carmel 20 years ago. Although tourists wind their way through here on oceanfront trails and dining excursions, the town remains quaint and peaceful—amazing considering that Monterey is a stone's throw away (a quarter of the Monterey Bay Aquarium is actually in Pacific Grove). While neighboring Monterey is comparatively congested and cosmopolitan, Pacific Grove is a community sprinkled with historic homes, blooming flowers, and the kind of tranquillity that inspires butterflies to flitter and frolic and deer to meander fearlessly across the road in search of another garden to graze.

ESSENTIALS

ORIENTATION   Lighthouse Avenue is the Grove's principal thoroughfare, running from Monterey to the lighthouse at the very point of the peninsula. Lighthouse Avenue is bisected by Forest Avenue, which runs from Calif. 1 (where it's called Holman Highway, or Calif. 68) to Lovers Point, a finger that sticks out into the bay in the middle of Pacific Grove.

VISITOR INFORMATION   Although the town is small, there is the **Pacific Grove Chamber of Commerce,** at the corner of Forest and Central avenues (☎ **408/373-3304**).

EXPLORING THE TOWN

Pacific Grove is a town to be strolled, so park the car, put on your walking shoes, and make an afternoon of it. Meander around George Washington Park and along the waterfront around the point. The **Point Pinos Lighthouse,** at the tip of the peninsula on Ocean View Boulevard (☎ **408/648-3116**), is the oldest working lighthouse on the West Coast. It dates from 1855 when Pacific Grove was little more than a pine forest. The museum and grounds are open free to visitors on Thursday, Saturday, and Sunday from 1 to 4pm.

Marine Gardens Park, a stretch of shoreline along Ocean View Boulevard on Monterey Bay and the Pacific, is renowned not only for its ocean views and colorful flowers, but also for its fascinating tidepool seaweed beds. Walk out to **Lovers Point** (named after Lovers of Jesus, not groping teenagers) and watch the sea otters playing in the kelp beds and cracking open an occasional abalone for lunch.

An excellent alternative, or complement, to the 17-Mile Drive (see Section 3, on Pebble Beach, later in this chapter) is the scenic drive or bike ride along Pacific Grove's **Ocean View Boulevard.** This coastal stretch starts near Monterey's Cannery Row and follows the Pacific around to the lighthouse point. There it turns into Sunset Drive, which runs along secluded **Asilomar State Beach.** Park on Sunset and explore the trails, dunes, and tidepools of this sandy stretch of shore. Look for purple shore crabs, green anemone, sea bats, starfish, and limpets, as well as all kinds of kelp and algae. The 11 buildings of the conference center established here by the YWCA in 1913 are historic landmarks that were designed by noted architect Julia Morgan. If you follow this route during winter months, a furious sea rages and crashes against the rocks.

To learn more about the marine and other natural life of the region, stop in at the **Pacific Grove Museum of Natural History,** 165 Forest Ave. (☎ **408/648-3116**). It has displays about the monarch butterflies and their migration, and also stuffed examples of the local birds and mammals. Admission is free and it's open Tuesday to Sunday from 10am to 5pm.

SEEING THE MONARCH BUTTERFLIES

Pacific Grove is widely known as "Butterfly Town, U.S.A."—a reference to the thousands of monarch butterflies that migrate here from November to February, traveling from as far away as Alaska. Many settle in the Monarch Grove sanctuary, a eucalyptus stand on Grove Acre Avenue off Lighthouse Avenue. George Washington Park, at Pine Avenue and Alder Street, is also famous for its "butterfly trees." To reach these sites, they may travel as far as 2,000 miles, covering 100 miles a day at an altitude of 10,000 feet.

Collectors beware: The town imposes strict fines for molesting butterflies.

A GOLFING ALTERNATIVE TO PEBBLE BEACH

Just as Ocean View Boulevard serves as an alternative to the 17-Mile Drive, the **Pacific Grove Municipal Golf Course,** 77 Asilomar Ave. (☎ **408/648-3177**), serves as a reasonably priced alternative to the high-priced courses at Pebble Beach (see below). The back nine holes of this 5,500-yard, par-70 course overlook the sea and offer the added challenge of coping with the winds. Views are panoramic, and the fairways and greens are better maintained than most semiprivate courses. There's a restaurant, pro shop, and driving range. Greens fees are $24 Monday to Thursday, and $28 Friday to Sunday; optional carts cost $23. Visa and MasterCard are accepted for greens fees, but not equipment rental.

FACTORY-OUTLET SHOPPING

The **American Tin Cannery Factory Outlet Center,** 125 Ocean View Blvd. (☎ 408/372-1442), is a warehouse of 45 factory-outlet shops. Labels represented here include Anne Klein, Joan & David, Bass Shoes, Carter's children's wear, Royal Doulton, Maidenform, London Fog, and Carole Little.

WHERE TO STAY

Hate making decisions? Call **Vacation Centers Reservations** at 408/466-6283 or **Resort II Me** at 800/449-1499; both will help you choose a hotel and make a reservation.

MODERATE

Centrella Inn. 612 Central Ave., Pacific Grove, CA 93950. ☎ **800/233-3372** or 408/372-3372. Fax 408/372-2036. 19 rms, 4 suites, 5 cottages. $95–$159 double; from $178 suite; from $195 cottage. Rates include buffet breakfast. MC, V.

A couple of blocks from the waterfront, and 2 blocks from Lovers Point Beach, the two-story Centrella is an old turreted Victorian that has been standing here since it was built as a boardinghouse in 1889. Today the rooms are decorated in a Victorian style, but they're somewhat plain—iron beds, plus side table, floor lamp, and armoire—although the bathrooms do have clawfoot tubs. In the back, connected to the house by brick walkways, are several private cottages and suites with living rooms with fireplaces, wet bars, TVs, and separate bedrooms and baths. Two have private decks; the others offer decks facing the rose garden and patio, which is set with umbrella tables and chairs. Cheese and hors d'oeuvres are served in the evening.

Gosby House. 643 Lighthouse Ave., Pacific Grove, CA 93950. ☎ **800/527-8828** or 408/375-1287. Fax 408/655-9621. 22 rms, 20 with bath. $85–$100 double without bath, $150 double with bath. Rates include full breakfast. From Calif. 1, take Calif. 68 to Pacific Grove, where it turns into Forest Ave.; continue on Forest to Lighthouse Ave., turn left, and go 3 blocks. AE, MC, V.

Originally a boardinghouse for Methodist ministers, this Victorian was established in 1887, 3 blocks from the bay. It's one of the oldest homes in the neighborhood, and it's still one of the most charming Victorians on the Monterey Peninsula. Each room is uniquely decorated, with floral-print wallpapers, lacy pillows, and antique furnishings. Twelve guest rooms have fireplaces, and all come with the inn's trademark teddy bears. The two Carriage House rooms merit special consideration. Each has a fireplace, deck, and extra large bathroom with spa tub.

The house has a separate dining room and parlor, where guests gather for breakfast and complimentary wine and snacks in the afternoon. Other amenities include complimentary newspaper, twice-daily maid service, and bicycles. Smoking is not allowed.

☉ Green Gables Inn. 104 5th St., Pacific Grove, CA 93950. ☎ **408/375-2095.** Fax 408/375-5437. 11 rms, 7 with bath; 1 suite. $100 double without bath; $160 double with bath; $160 suite. Rates include buffet breakfast. AE, MC, V. From Calif. 1, take the Pacific Grove exit (Calif. 68) and continue to the Pacific Ocean; turn right on Ocean View Blvd. and drive half a mile to 5th St.

A Queen Anne–style mansion, looking like an English country inn, this hotel dates from 1888 when a judge from Pasadena built it to shelter his mistress from the prying eyes of his hometown. Managed by hospitable innkeepers, this little gem may not be fancy, but it's comfortable. The rooms are divided between the main building and the carriage houses behind it. The less atmospheric carriage-house rooms are better for families. Most rooms have an ocean view and are individually decorated with dainty furnishings, including some antiques and an occasional four-poster bed. Carriage-house rooms enjoy private baths; most of those in the original home share two immaculate bathrooms. There's an antique carousel horse in the comfortable parlor, where complimentary wine, tea, and hors d'oeuvres are served each afternoon. Teddy bears populate every nook and cranny. No smoking.

Martine Inn. 255 Ocean View Blvd., Pacific Grove, CA 93950. ☎ **800/852-5588** or 408/373-3388. 20 rms. $135–$240 double. Rates include full breakfast. AE, DISC, MC, V.

One glance at the lavish Victorian interior and the incredible bay views and you'll know why this Mediterranean-style hotel is one of the best B&Bs in the area. Enjoy the vista via binoculars the management leaves out for guests or stroll the bayfront promenade. Always above par, the rooms have been recently redecorated but still maintain Victorian style. You'll pay more if you want a fireplace and ocean view. And be sure to request a room with a bathtub if it matters to you, some only have a shower. A full breakfast is served at lace-covered tables in the large front room; hors d'oeuvres are served in the evening. Guests also have access to two additional sitting quarters: a small room downstairs overlooking the ocean and a larger room with shelves of books. Amenities include newspaper delivery, free coffee and refreshments, Jacuzzi, and a billiards table.

Pacific Grove Inn. 581 Pine Ave., Pacific Grove, CA 93950, ☎ **800/732-2825** or 408/375-2825. 13 rms, 3 suites. TV TEL. $98–$138 double; $110–$170 suite. Rates include breakfast. AE, CB, DC, DISC, MC, V. From Calif. 1, take the Pacific Grove exit (Calif. 68) to the corner of Pine and Forest aves.

Located just 5 blocks from the beach, this stately renovated 1904 Queen Anne–style mansion is one of the town's architectural gems. Despite heavy Victorian embellishments, the elegant accommodations feel light, airy, and particularly spacious. They come with queen- or king-size beds and all have fireplaces. Afternoon tea is served in the parlor. No smoking.

✪ **Seven Gables Inn.** 555 Ocean View Blvd., Pacific Grove, CA. 93950. ☎ **408/372-4341.** 14 rms. $105–$225 double. Rates include breakfast and afternoon tea. 2-night minimum stay on weekends. MC, V.

On the coast road overlooking the sea, this sprawling compound of Victorian buildings was constructed in 1886 by the Chase family (as in Chase Manhattan Bank) and has been a B&B since 1982. It's named after the seven gables that cap the hotel. The inside is graced with a valuable collection of mostly European antiques. Everything here is opulent and gilded, including the rooms, which are scattered among the main house, cottages, and the guesthouse; all have ocean views. The accommodations are linked with verdant gardens filled with roses and marble sculpture. Rates include breakfast and afternoon tea accompanied by an array of pastries and homemade chocolates. If the hotel's booked, ask about the Grand View Inn, a comparable B&B next door that's run by the same owners.

INEXPENSIVE

✪ **The Wilkies Inn.** 1038 Lighthouse Ave., Pacific Grove, CA, 93950. ☎ **408/372-5960.** Fax 408/655-1681. 24 rms. $55–$95 double. Additional person $8 extra. 2-night minimum stay on weekends. AE, DISC, MC, V.

The decor here is basic motel style, but the owners did splurge on stylish bedspreads and special amenities for divers. All the squeaky-clean rooms come with coffeemakers and free movies and local calls. Some have microwaves or partial ocean views, two have a full kitchen, and you can have a refrigerator for a few extra dollars. Considering that this place consistently charges less than the other hotels in town, gets an A+ for service, and is located on a quiet tree-lined street in Pacific Grove (we watched a deer cross the street in midday), it's a great choice for the budget traveler.

WHERE TO DINE

EXPENSIVE

✪ **Fandango.** 223 17th St. ☎ **408/372-3456.** Reservations recommended. Main courses $11–$19; fixed-price dinner $20. AE, CB, DC, DISC, MC, V. Mon–Sat 11am–3:30pm and 5–9:30pm, Sun 10am–2:30pm (brunch) and 5–9:30pm. From Calif. 1, take the Pacific Grove exit (Calif. 68), turn left on Lighthouse Ave., and continue a block to 17th St. MEDITERRANEAN.

The term *fandango,* a Spanish dance, takes on new meaning here where it's your tongue instead of your feet that will rejoice. Provincial Mediterranean specialties from Spain to Greece to North Africa spice up the menu with such offerings as seafood paella with North African couscous (the recipe has been in the owner's family for almost 200 years), cassoulet maison, cannelloni niçoise, and a Greek-style lamb shank. Along with the fare, the atmosphere takes you straight to Europe in a fiesta of five up- and downstairs dining rooms cozied by roaring fires, wood tables, and antiqued walls. There's a very good international wine list, and a dessert menu that includes a Grand Marnier soufflé with fresh raspberry purée sauce and profiteroles. In winter ask to be seated in the fireplace dining room and in summer request the terrace room, but whenever you come, expect everything here to be lively and colorful, from the regional decor to the owner himself.

Joe Rombi's. 208 17th St. (at Lighthouse Ave.). ☎ **408/373-2416.** Reservations recommended. Main courses $12–$19. MC, V. Wed–Sun 5–10pm. ITALIAN.

Expect a fun night out at Joe Rombi's where enormous French antique posters line every portion of wall space, lighting is perfectly dimmed, and the food is very fresh (lasagnes and pastas are made that day by the owner himself). Joe will seat you at one of the 11 intimate tables and you'll immediately be served a basket of fresh housemade focaccia to munch while you peruse the limited menu of a handful of appetizers, soups, and salads, pizzas, pastas, and four main courses (some of which come with soup and salad). Go with the fish of the day—we had a halibut dish that any upscale San Francisco restaurant would be proud to present. The food here is good, but what really makes the place pop is the aura of Joe Rombi, who's always on hand to make sure that his customers' every need is fulfilled.

✪ **Melac's.** 663 Lighthouse Ave. ☎ **408/375-1743.** Reservations required. Main courses $19–$25; fixed-price dinners $28 and $45. AE, DC, MC, V. Tues–Fri 11:30am–2pm and 5:30–9:30pm, Sat 5:30–9:30pm. FRENCH.

Take an intimate dining room with brick walls, hand-painted French-country murals, and formally set tables, combine it with a husband-and-wife team (she's a graduate of Paris's Cordon Bleu, he's the friendly French host), and you've got Pacific Grove's favorite French restaurant. Elegant yet unpretentious, this is the place to romance amid a fireplace and a limited menu of finely prepared classic dishes—without the stuffiness often associated with French establishments. Expect such preparations as a delicious lobster ravioli appetizer with a tarragon-lobster sauce or gratin of baby leeks and chanterelles with reggiano Parmesan and Dijon mustard. Then choose from main courses of Atlantic salmon poached on a bed of dilled vegetables julienne and lemon-caper basmati rice pilaf and veal sweetbreads roasted between layers of puff pastry with minced wild mushrooms and cognac cream (each entree is served with dinner salad). If you want to go all out, opt for the "Petit" or "Grande Aventure," four- or six-course fixed-price dinners.

⚫ **The Old Bath House.** 620 Ocean View Blvd. ☎ **408/375-5195.** Reservations required. Main courses $14–$27.50. AE, DC, DISC, MC, V. Mon–Fri 5–10:30pm, Sat 4–11pm, Sun 3–10:30pm. CONTINENTAL.

A late 19th-century spot for beachside swimming pools, this restored Victorian restaurant with etched glass and leather furniture is perched on the edge of the earth overlooking Lovers Point. Though pricey and frequented by tourists, dinner here is a stately affair with undeniably knockout bay views and lovingly prepared cuisine, which makes it the perfect place for a romantic night out. You may find cream of lobster and wild-boar sausage on the starters menu. Although main courses vary, signature dishes include Dungeness crabs and duck merlot served with apples and a raspberry-merlot sauce. Complete your meal with hot pecan ice cream fritters.

MODERATE

The First Awakening. In the American Tin Cannery, 125 Ocean View Blvd. ☎ **408/372-1125.** Reservations not accepted. Breakfast $4–$7; lunch $5–$8. AE, DC, MC, V. Daily 7am–2:30pm. From Calif. 1, take the Pacific Grove exit (Calif. 68) and turn right onto Lighthouse Ave.; after a mile turn left onto Eardley Ave. and take it to the corner of Ocean View. AMERICAN.

What was once a dank canning factory is now a bright, huge, open restaurant, flooded with light from an entire wall of windows. Ceilings don't get much taller than these, and they're topped with an enormous skylight and hung with plants and industrial overhead fans.

Breakfast, the most important meal of the day here, includes 11 varieties of omelets; granola with nuts, fruit, and yogurt; walnut and wheat pancakes; and raisin French toast. At lunch there's a fine choice of salads and a foot-long list of sandwiches that encompasses everything from albacore to zucchini.

ⓢ The Fishwife at Asilomar Beach. 1996¹/₂ Sunset Dr. (at Asilomar Beach). ☎ **408/375-7107.** Reservations accepted. Main courses $8.25–$12.50. AE, DISC, MC, V. Mon and Wed–Sat 11am–10pm, Sun 10am–10pm. From Calif. 1, take the Pacific Grove exit (Calif. 68) and stay left until it becomes Sunset Dr.; the restaurant will be on your left about 1 mile ahead, as you approach Asilomar Beach. SEAFOOD.

This restaurant dates from the 1830s, when an enterprising sailor's wife started a small food market that became famous for its Boston clam chowder. Today locals still return for the savory soup as well as some of the finest seafood in Pacific Grove. Two bestsellers at dinner are calamari steak sautéed with shallots, garlic, tomatoes, and white wine; and prawns Belize, presented sizzling with red onions, tomatoes, fresh serrano chiles, jicama, lime juice, and cashews. There are also steak and pasta dishes on the menu, and all main courses come with fresh vegetables, bread, black beans, and rice or potatoes. Kids get their own color-in menu which has smaller portions for under $6.

Peppers Mexicali Cafe. 170 Forest Ave. ☎ **408/373-6892.** Reservations recommended. Main courses $5.50–$11. AE, DC, MC, V. Mon and Wed–Thurs 11:30am–10pm, Fri–Sat 11:30am–11pm, Sun 4–10pm. MEXICAN/LATIN AMERICAN.

Peppers is the kind of place where you can't help but feel at home. The dining room is casual and inviting, with wooden floors and tables, pepper art visible from every viewpoint, and a perpetual crowd of diners who come to suck up beers and savor spicy specialties such as well-balanced seafood tacos and fajitas or housesmade tamales and chile rellenos. Other fire-starters include the snapper Yucatán, which is cooked with chiles, citrus cilantro, and tomatoes, and grilled prawns with lime-cilantro dressing. Add a substantial selection of suds, an addicting compilation of chips and salsa, and a friendly service staff, and your taste buds are bound to bellow "Ole!"

3 Pebble Beach

Pebble Beach is a world in itself. Polo shirts, golf shoes, and big bankrolls are standard here, and if you need to ask how much accommodations and greens fees are, you definitely can't afford them. In this elite golfers paradise, endless grassy fairways are only interrupted by a few luxury resorts and cliffs where the ocean meets the land. It's also the site in winter of the **AT&T Pebble Beach National Pro-Am,** a celebrity tournament originally launched in 1937 by crooner Bing Crosby.

In 1980 tycoon Marvin Davis, czar of the real-estate partnership that owned the links, sold the 5,300-acre resort to Japanese developer Minoru Isutani for a whopping $840 million. Isutani outraged golfers worldwide when he turned around and tried to peddle 2,000 memberships in the proposed Pebble Beach National Golf Club, at $740,000 a membership.

Scandals, investigations, and even the recession in Japan caused Pebble Beach and its neighboring courses to hit bottom in 1992. Claims circulated that wealthy Japanese tourists were given preferential treatment over American golfers who showed up. In 1992 the Lone Cypress Company, with Japanese backing, acquired the Pebble Beach Resorts for $500 million (and considered it a bargain). In the last few years they've invested more than $24 million in the resort, and golfing magazines have cited notable improvements. Golfing critics now report that the links have never looked better, thanks in large part to the Jack Nicklaus design team who went to work to upgrade them.

THE 17-MILE DRIVE

The beautiful 17-Mile Drive demands a leisurely afternoon. Pack a picnic or make lunch reservations at Roy's in the Inn at Spanish Bay (see "Where to Stay & Dine," below), fork over $6 to enter the drive, and prepare to see some of the most exclusive coastal real estate in California.

The drive can be entered from any of three gates: Pacific Grove to the north, Carmel to the south, or Monterey to the east. The most convenient entrance from Calif. 1 is just off the main road at the Holman Highway exit. You may beat traffic by entering at the Carmel Gate and doing the tour backward.

Admission to the drive includes an informative map that lists 26 points of interest along the way. Aside from homes of the ultra-rich, highlights include Seal and Bird rocks, where you can see countless gulls, cormorants, and other offshore birds as well as seals and sea lions; and Cypress Point Lookout, which affords a 20-mile view all the way to the Big Sur lighthouse on a clear day. Also visible is the famous Lone Cypress tree, inspiration to so many artists and photographers, which you can admire from afar but to which you can no longer walk. The drive also traverses the Del Monte Forest, thick with tame blacktail deer, and often compared to some "billionaire's private game preserve."

One of the best ways to see 17-Mile Drive is by bike, but the ride toward Carmel is all downhill so unless you're in great shape, arrange for a ride back or simply do it by car.

GREAT GOLF COURSES

Locals tell us it's almost impossible to get a tee time unless you're staying at the resort. If you're one of the lucky few, you can choose from several famous courses along the 17-Mile Drive.

◐ PEBBLE BEACH GOLF LINKS   The most famous course is Pebble Beach Golf Links (☎ **800/654-9300** or 408/624-3811), at the Lodge at Pebble Beach (see "Where to Stay & Dine," below). It's home in winter to the AT&T Pebble Beach National Pro-Am, a celebrity-laden tournament watched on TV around the world. Jack Nicklaus has claimed: "If I could play only one course for the rest of my life, this would be it." He should know; he won both the 1961 U.S. Amateur and the 1972 U.S. Open here. Indeed, 10 national championships have been decided here. Herbert Warren Wind, dean of this century's golf writers, said, "There is no finer seaside golf course in creation"—and that includes the legendary Old Course at St. Andrews in Scotland. Built in 1919, this 18-hole course is 6,799 yards and par 72. It's precariously perched over a rugged ocean. Greens fees are a staggering $225 for resort guests—if they can get a slot (it's almost impossible for anyone else to play here).

◐ SPYGLASS HILL GOLF COURSE   Also frequented by celebrities is this course at Stevenson Drive and Spyglass Hill Road (☎ **800/654-9300** or 408/624-6611). Its slope rating of 143 means that it's one of the toughest courses in California. It's a justifiably famous links: 6,859 yards and par 72 with five oceanfront holes. The rest reach deep into the Del Monte Forest. Greens fees are $200, $175 for guests of the lodge or inn (see "Where to Stay & Dine," below). Reservations should be made a month in advance. There's an excellent Grill Room on the grounds.

◐ POPPY HILLS   This course, on the 17-Mile Drive (☎ **408/625-1513**), was named one of the world's top 20 courses by *Golf Digest*. It was designed by Robert Trent Jones, Jr., in 1986. Greens fees are $105, plus $30 cart rental. You can make reservations 30 days in advance.

◐ THE LINKS AT SPANISH BAY   This course, lying on the north end of 17-Mile Drive at the Pebble Beach Resort / Inn at Spanish Bay (☎ **408/624-3811**), is the most easily booked course. Serious golfers say it's the most challenging of the Pebble Beach links. Robert Trent Jones, Jr., Tom Watson, and Frank Tatum (former USGA president) designed the course to duplicate a Scottish links course. Greens fees are $150 for resort guests, $165 for nonguests. Required cart rental is an additional $20. Reservations can be made 60 days in advance.

DEL MONTE GOLF COURSE   At 1300 Sylvan Rd. (☎ **408/373-2436**) lies the oldest course west of the Mississippi, charging some of the most reasonable greens fees in the Pebble Beach area: $50 per player, plus a cart rental of $18. The course, often cited in magazines for its "grace and charm," is relatively short, only 6,339 yards. This seldom advertised course is actually part of the Pebble Beach complex.

WHERE TO STAY & DINE

✪ Inn at Spanish Bay. 2700 17-Mile Dr., Pebble Beach, CA 93953. ☎ **800/654-9300** or 408/647-7500. Fax 408/648-7899. 270 rms, 17 suites. MINIBAR TV TEL. $275–$350 double; from $575 suite. AE, CB, DC, MC, V. From Calif. 1 south, turn west onto Calif. 68 and south onto 17-Mile Dr.; the hotel is located on your right, just past the toll plaza.

Surrounded by the Links at Spanish Bay (see above), the Inn at Spanish Bay is a plush three- and four-story low-rise, lying 10 miles north of the Lodge at Pebble Beach and set on 236 manicured acres. Approximately half the rooms face the ocean and are more expensive than their counterparts that overlook the forest. Each accommodation contains about 600 square feet of floor space, a generous allowance, and has a private fireplace and either an outdoor deck or a patio. The baths are finished in Italian marble and the furnishings, all of which are custom made, include four-poster beds with down comforters.

Dining/Entertainment: Roy Yamaguchi, Hawaii's celebrity chef, opened Roy's, his only mainland outpost in April 1995. The menu features Euro-Asian cuisine and many of his signature dishes, plus some new ones inspired by California's regional ingredients. Roy has a way with sauces, and although he's probably not in the kitchen, his protégés whip up some great tiger prawn and salmon cakes with a sesame sauce, potstickers, and ravioli of shiitake, spinach, and ricotta. Main courses include grilled gingered chicken breast with soy glaze and sticky rice, grilled filet mignon with creamy wild-mushroom sauce, and wood-fired pizzas from the exhibition kitchen. Traps and the adjacent Lobby Lounge serve light meals; the Bay Club serves a gourmet Mediterranean menu. You can also have breakfast or lunch at the nearby Clubhouse Bar and Grill, overlooking the first fairway. A jazz band performs in the Lobby Lounge every day, but our favorite time is at dusk, when a bagpiper strolls the terrace with a skirling tribute to Scotland, with which Pebble Beach is "linked."

Services: Concierge, room service (24 hours), massages, evening turndown, overnight shoeshine, laundry/valet.

Facilities: World-class golf course, eight tennis courts (two lighted), a first-rate Ansel Adams Gallery, pro shops, award-winning fitness center, equestrian center, bicycles, heated swimming pool.

The Lodge at Pebble Beach. 17-Mile Dr., Pebble Beach, CA 93953. ☎ **800/654-9300** or 408/624-3811. Fax 408/649-8500. 161 rms, 12 suites. MINIBAR TV TEL. $330–$450 double; from $825 suite. 15% gratuity added. AE, CB, DC, MC, V. From Calif. 1 south, turn west on Calif. 68, south onto 17-Mile Dr., and follow the coastal road to the hotel.

For the combined cost of green fees and a room here, you could easily create a professional putting green in your own backyard—and still have some money left over. But if you're a dedicated hacker, you've got to play here at least once. Look on the bright side—at least you can expect ultra-plush, recently revamped rooms, which are equipped with every conceivable amenity, including refrigerators and wood-burning fireplaces. Most are in two-story cottage clusters, with anywhere from eight to a dozen units in each. Those opening onto the ocean carry the highest price tags.

Dining/Entertainment: The Cypress Room, which overlooks the 18th green and the bay, is a seafood grill. The Tap Room, patterned after an English pub and decorated with golfing memorabilia, offers everything from prime rib to thick-crust pizza. The Gallery, overlooking the first tee, is open only for breakfast and lunch. Club XIX, an opulent and pricey classical French dining room, offers extravagant dishes such as foie gras and truffles, and stuffed quail.

Services: Concierge, room service (24 hours), priority golf tee times, supervised children's facilities, barber, evening turndown, complimentary airport transportation, massage, laundry/valet.

Facilities: Outstanding golf course, 12 tennis courts, fitness room, horseback riding, beach, bicycles for rent, heated swimming pool, sauna, hiking trails, shopping arcade.

4 Carmel

If you visited the town officially known as Carmel-by-the-Sea dozens of years ago, you're likely to be of the school that criticizes its present-day overcommercialization. Carmel began as an artists' colony that attracted such luminaries as Robinson Jeffers, Sinclair Lewis, Robert Louis Stevenson, Ansel Adams, William Rose Benet, and Mary Austin. It was a nonconformist enclave where residents resisted assigning street numbers and lighting (they carried lanterns, which they considered more romantic).

Today Carmel may not be the bohemian artists' village seasoned travelers remember, but it's still an adorable (albeit touristy) town that knows how to celebrate its surroundings. Vibrant wildflower gardens flourish along each residential street, gnarled cypress trees reach up from white sandy beaches, and at the end of each day tourists magically disappear and the town for a split second seems undiscovered.

It's still intimate enough that there's no need for street numbers and establishments are a small collection of inns, restaurants, boutiques and a surprisingly high number of art galleries, all of whose locations are identified only by cross streets. It's not the town itself, but such hints as Saks Fifth Avenue, convertible roadsters cruising through town, intolerable traffic, and the price tags on B&Bs that remind us we're not in Kansas anymore, but rather a well-preserved upscale tourist haven.

ESSENTIALS

The **Carmel Business Association,** P.O. Box 4444, Carmel, CA 93921 (☎ **408/624-2522**), is above the Hog's Breath Inn on San Carlos between 5th and 6th streets. It distributes local maps, brochures, and publications. It's open June to August, Monday to Friday from 9am to 6pm, on Saturday from 11am to 6pm, and on Sunday from noon to 4pm; in winter, it closes on Sunday and is only open until 5pm on the other days. Pick up a copy of the *Carmel Gallery Guide* and a schedule of local events.

EXPLORING THE TOWN

A wonderful stretch of white sand backed by cypress trees, **Carmel Beach City Park** is a wee bit o' heaven on earth, though parking can be closer to that *other* hotter postmortem destination. There's plenty of room for families, surfers, and dogs with their owners (yes, pooches are allowed to run off-leash here). If the parking lot is full, there are some spaces on Ocean Avenue.

Farther south around the promontory, **Carmel River State Beach** is a less-crowded option with white sand and dunes, plus a bird sanctuary where brown pelicans, black oystercatchers, cormorants, gulls, curlews, godwits, and sanderlings make their home.

The ✪ **Mission San Carlos Borromeo del Rio Carmelo,** on Basilica Rio Road at Lasuen Drive, off Calif. 1 (☎ **408/624-3600**), is the burial ground of Father Junípero Serra and the second-oldest of the 21 Spanish missions he launched. Founded in 1771 on a scenic site overlooking the Carmel River, it remains one of the largest and most interesting of California's missions. The present stone church, with its gracefully curving walls and Moorish bell tower, was begun in 1793. Its walls are covered with a lime plaster made of burnt seashells. The old mission kitchen, the first library in California, the high altar, and the flower gardens are all worth visiting. More than 3,000 Native Americans are buried in the adjacent cemetery; their graves are decorated with seashells. A $2 donation is requested. The mission is open June to August, daily from 9:30am to 7:30pm; in other months, Monday to Saturday from 9:30am to 4:30pm and on Sunday from 10:30am to 4:30pm.

One of Carmel's prettiest homes and gardens is **Tor House,** 26304 Oceanview Ave. (☎ **408/624-1813,** or 408/624-1840 on Friday and Saturday only), built by California poet Robinson Jeffers. On Carmel Point, the house dates from 1918 and includes a 40-foot tower containing stones from around the world, which are embedded in the walls (there's even one from the Great Wall of China). Inside, an old porthole is reputed to have come from the ship on which Napoléon escaped from Elba in 1815. Admission is by guided tour only, and reservations are required. It's $5 for adults, $3.50 for college students, and $1.50 for high school students (no children under 12). Open on Friday and Saturday from 10am to 3pm.

SHOPPING

If shopping is more your bag, leave the car at the hotel or park and check out the town on foot. You'll be surprised at the amount of shops packed into this small town—over 500 boutiques offering unique fashions, baskets, housewares, and imported goods and a veritable cornucopia of art galleries. All the commercial action is packed along the small stretch of Ocean Avenue between Junipero and San Antonio avenues.

If you want to tour the galleries, pick up a copy of the *Carmel Gallery Guide* from the Carmel Business Association (see "Essentials," above).

Shoppers will enjoy **Carmel Plaza,** a multilevel complex of boutiques, craft stores, restaurants, and gourmet food outlets on Ocean Avenue at Junipero Street, or **The Barnyard,** on Calif. 1 at Carmel Valley Road (you'll have to take the car to this authentic early-Californian barn housing 60-plus shops and restaurants).

WHERE TO STAY

EXPENSIVE

Carriage House Inn. Junipero St., between 7th and 8th aves. (P.O. Box 1900), Carmel, CA 93921. ☎ **800/433-4732** or 408/625-2585. Fax 408/624-2967. 13 rms, 2 suites. MINIBAR TV TEL. $189–$250 double; $260 suite. Rates include continental breakfast. Additional person $15 extra. AE, CB, DC, DISC, MC, V. From Calif. 1, exit onto Ocean Ave. and turn left onto Junipero St.

If we had to choose between here and the neighboring Cobblestone Inn (see below), we'd pick this place hands-down. It's not that each room comes with a VCR (and free videos from the video library), wood-burning fireplaces, small refrigerators, and king-size beds with down comforters, or that most of the second-floor rooms have sunken tubs and vaulted beam ceilings and bottom-floor rooms have single whirlpool tubs. It's the luxurious atmosphere and superfluous pampering that comes with the cost of the room. Not only do guests receive breakfast delivered to their room, but there's also wine and hors d'oeuvres served in the afternoon and cappuccino in the evening. Plus, while almost all choices in the area are frill-and-lace, the Carriage House is a more mature, formal but cozy environment.

Cobblestone Inn. Junipero St. (between 7th and 8th aves., 1¹/₂ blocks from Ocean Ave.; P.O. Box 3185), Carmel, CA 93921. ☎ **800/841-5252** or 408/625-5222. Fax 408/625-0478. 21 rms, 3 suites. TV TEL. $145–$160 double; $175 suite. Rates include buffet breakfast. AE, MC, V.

The Cobblestone may not be Victorian like other properties owned by the Four Sisters Inns, but it's just as flowery, well kept, and cute, with hand-stenciled wall decorations, fireplaces, and a trademark abundance of teddy bears. The first floor is completely constructed of stones taken from the Carmel River (hence the name) and the rooms encircle a slate courtyard; some look out onto the brick patio where breakfast is sometimes served. The guest rooms vary in size; some can be small and none come with bathtubs, but the largest units include wet bars and sofas, and a separate bedroom. Guests have the use of a comfortable living room with large stone fireplace. No smoking is permitted.

Services include twice-daily maid service, morning newspaper, complimentary wine and hors d'oeuvres, and coffee and cookies. Bicycles are available to rent.

✪ **Highlands Inn.** Calif. 1 (P.O. Box 1700), Carmel, CA 93921. ☎ **800/538-9525** or 408/624-3801. Fax 408/626-1574. 42 rms, 100 spa suites. TV TEL. $295 double; $375–$425 spa suite. AE, DC, MC, V.

Four miles south of Carmel on a 12-acre bluff overlooking Point Lobos, this one- and two-story rustic yet luxurious establishment attracts the gamut; ranging from celebrities and honeymooners to business executives. There's plenty of character here: The old-style main lounge dates from 1916 and has panoramic coastal vistas and an assortment of comfortable furnishings to cuddle up on. The rooms are intimately distributed throughout a cluster of buildings terraced into the hillside. Since they were renovated in 1996, expect brand-new digs adorned with modern natural-wood furnishings and equipped with VCRs, coffeemakers, and hair dryers. Most have decks or balconies and wood-burning fireplaces. The suites have Jacuzzi tubs and completely equipped kitchens; the 42 rooms have showers but no tubs.

Dining/Entertainment: The two restaurants are well known for their fine cuisine. The Pacific's Edge Restaurant, which hosts an annual Masters of Food and Wine event, offers dramatic views and memorable cuisine. The California Market is more casual, and you can dine inside by the potbelly stove or on the alfresco redwood deck.

Services: Concierge, room service (limited), valet, newspaper delivery, in-room massage, twice-daily maid service, free shuttle.

Facilities: A well-landscaped kidney-shaped pool fringed by pine and cypress and reached via stairways cut into the hillside, rental bicycles, health club, sundeck.

✪ **La Playa.** Camino Real and 8th Ave. (P.O. Box 900), Carmel, CA 93921. ☎ **800/ 582-8900** or 408/624-6476. Fax 408/624-7966. 72 rms, 3 suites, 5 cottages. MINIBAR TV TEL. $120–$220 double; $215–$395 suite; $215–$495 cottage. AE, DC, MC, V.

Only 2 blocks from the beach and yet within walking distance of town, the four-story La Playa is a romantic Mediterranean-style villa built in 1904 with a Bermudan-pink facade. Norwegian artist Christopher Jorgensen ordered its construction for his bride, an heiress of the Ghirardelli chocolate dynasty. The guest rooms are arranged around a lawn and garden with a pool at the center. The stylish lobby, with a white marble fireplace, sets the elegant tone with its terra-cotta floors enhanced with Oriental rugs. The room furnishings are Spanish in style. Beds have carved headboards; windows are shielded with white shutters. The cottages have full kitchens, wet bars, garden patios, and wood-burning fireplaces.

Dining/Entertainment: The Terrace Grill, a riot of color, serves California cuisine and it's very relaxing in summer dining out on the alfresco terrace overlooking the gardens.

Services: Room service and nightly turndown (excluding cottages).

✪ **Mission Ranch.** 26270 Dolores St., Carmel, CA 93923. ☎ **800/538-8221** or 408/ 624-6436. Fax 408/626-4163. 29 rms, 2 cottages. TV TEL. $85–$225 double; $125 cottage. Rates include continental breakfast. AE, MC, V.

This venerable inn, constructed in the 1850s as a dairy farm, was purchased and restored by Clint Eastwood, Carmel's former celebrity-mayor, who wanted to preserve the vista of the nearby wetlands stretching out to the bay. With no condos in sight, the view today is inspiring.

Millions of dollars went into the historic property. There are several rooms scattered amid different structures, both old and new. As befits a ranch, even this one, the accommodations are decorated in a provincial style, with high-carved wooden beds dressed with handmade quilts. Homespun is the rule here. Some fixtures from the highly acclaimed Eastwood film *Unforgiven,* including a potbelly stove, are on display.

Rooms range from so-called regular (and less desirable) in the main barn to meadow-view units, each with a vista across the fields to the bay. All are equipped with whirlpool baths, fireplaces, and decks or patios. The Martin Family farmhouse contains six of the units, all arranged around a central parlor, while the Bunkhouse, the oldest structure on the property, contains separate living and dining areas, bedrooms, and a full kitchen.

Dining/Entertainment: Even if you're not staying here, call for a table at the Restaurant at Mission Ranch, where zest and flavor are put into essentially American cuisine. Refined touches in the food are evident, including the fresh tomatoes in the black-bean chili.

Facilities: Tennis courts, exercise room, pro shop.

MODERATE

Carmel is a great vacation spot for dogs, and the **Cypress Inn,** at Lincoln Street and 7th Avenue (☎ 408/624-3871), goes to great lengths to make you and your pooch feel at home. This lovely Mediterranean-style inn is owned by actress Doris Day.

Normandy Inn. Ocean Ave. (between Monte Verde and Casanova sts.; P.O. Box 1706), Carmel, CA 93921. ☎ **800/343-3825** in California, or 408/624-3825. Fax 408/624-4614. 41 rms, 4 suites, 3 cottages. TV TEL. $100–$150 double; $180–$200 suite; $250–$350 cottage. Rates include continental breakfast. Additional person $10 extra. AE, MC, V. From Calif. 1, exit onto Ocean Ave. and continue straight for 5 blocks past Junipero St.

This hotel's Tudor architecture is like something out of a storybook, especially with an array of colorful flowers brightening up the white walls. The guest rooms have French country decor and down comforters. Some are equipped with fireplaces and/or kitchenettes, and all come with coffeemakers. There's a small heated pool banked by a sweet flower garden, and a self-service laundry, and newspapers are delivered to your room daily.

But what really makes this hotel noteworthy is its location 3 blocks from the beach and its larger family-style units. The three cottages are an especially good deal and accommodate up to eight; each one has three bedrooms, two bathrooms, a fully equipped kitchen, a dining room, a living room with a fireplace, and a back porch. Be sure to reserve far in advance, especially in summer.

Sandpiper Inn at the Beach. 2408 Bay View Ave., Carmel, CA 93923. ☎ **800/633-6433** or 408/624-6433. Fax 408/624-5964. 16 rms. $115–$185 double; $115 cottage room. Rates include extended continental breakfast. AE, MC, V.

A garden of flowers welcomes visitors to this quiet, mid-scale Carmel standby that's been in business for more than 60 years. The inn's rooms, which are within both sight and sound of the surf, offer an array of well-kept accommodations. The highest priced are four-poster–bedded corner rooms with plenty of windows framing the ocean view. All are decorated with handsome country antiques and fresh flowers that are changed daily. Three have fireplaces.

☺ Village Inn. Ocean Ave. and Junipero St. (P.O. Box 5275), Carmel, CA 93921. ☎ **800/346-3864** in California, or 408/624-3864. Fax 408/626-6763. 34 rms, 2 suites. TV TEL. $69–$145 double; from $89 suite. Rates include continental breakfast. AE, MC, V. From Calif. 1, exit onto Ocean Ave. and continue straight to Junipero St.

Well run and centrally located, the Village Inn is nothing more than a motor lodge. The rooms, arranged around a courtyard/parking lot lined with potted geraniums, are outfitted with bland but functional decor. In addition to French country-style furniture, the guest rooms come equipped with refrigerators. Breakfast, accompanied by the morning newspaper, is served in the downstairs lounge.

WHERE TO DINE
EXPENSIVE

✪ Anton & Michel. At Court of the Fountain, Mission St. (between Ocean and 7th aves.). ☎ **408/624-2406.** Reservations recommended. Main courses $17.50–$22. AE, DC, MC, V. Daily 11:30am–3pm and 5:30–9:30pm. FRENCH/CONTINENTAL.

This elegant restaurant, just across from Carmel Plaza, serves traditional French cuisine in one of the most formal rooms in town. During the day it's best to dine fountainside on the patio or encased in the glass-wrapped terrace. The view is still charming in the evening when the courtyard is lit and the fountain's water sparkles with reflection. Decorated with French chandelier lamps and original oil paintings, the main dining room is a formal affair, though, as in most restaurants in town, patrons' attire does not need to match it. Appetizers include crab cakes with cilantro-pesto aïoli, or the delicate ravioli filled with goat cheese, sun-dried tomato, and shiitake mushroom mousse and served with a curry-cream sauce. French-inspired menu items include such entrees as a tender lamb Wellington in a pastry crust plus eclectic items such as a flavorful chicken breast Jerusalem, sautéed with olive oil, white wine, cream, mushrooms, and artichoke hearts.

Casanova. 5th Ave. (between San Carlos and Mission sts.). ☎ **408/625-0501.** Reservations recommended. Main courses $19–$33. MC, V. Mon–Fri 11:30am–3pm and 5–10:30pm, Sat–Sun 8am–3pm and 5–10:30pm. From Calif. 1, take the Ocean Ave. exit and turn right on Mission, then left onto 5th Ave. NORTHERN ITALIAN/SOUTHERN FRENCH.

Sure, Casanova serves up good food, but so do plenty of other places in town—at half the price. But the European ambience here *is* something special. The building, which once belonged to Charlie Chaplin's cook, is divided into two intimate Belgian chalet–like dining rooms perfect for leaning over a bottle of red and creating vacation memories. More festive folk step back to the Old World–style covered patio where it's bustling and crowded. Since all dinner entrees include antipasto and a choice of appetizers such as baked stuffed eggplant with rice, herbs, cheese, and tomatoes, $30 is actually not such a bad deal. The menu features typical Mediterranean cuisine: paella, homemade pastas, meats, and fish. Casanova also boasts an award-winning wine cellar featuring over 1,600 French, Californian, German, and Italian wines. A word of warning: They've recently acquired an adjoining building and will expand their seating capacity by 100. Since service can already be inattentive at times, we'll have to see if the kitchen and service staff rises to the occasion.

✪ Crème Carmel. San Carlos St. and 7th Ave. ☎ **408/624-0444.** Reservations recommended. Main courses $16.75–$21.75. AE, DC, MC, V. July–Aug, daily 5:30–9pm; Sept–June, Mon–Sat 5:30–9pm. CALIFORNIA/FRENCH.

The discreet location of Crème Carmel (tucked away in a courtyard) has not hurt its business any—it's still one of the most popular upscale dining spots in town for both tourists and locals. Art, fresh flowers, and a soaring tongue-and-groove ceiling provide a sweet setting for an evening robust with California-French flavor. The menu lists an array of decadently wonderful starters, such as prawn and goat-cheese tart with a jalapeño-and-shallot sauce, lobster with Maui onion pancakes and lobster sauce, or melt-in-your-mouth Sonoma foie gras. The main courses are equally special and might include Pacific salmon with roasted leeks and fresh basil sauce or beef tenderloin with a cabernet sauce, fresh horseradish, and potato cake.

MODERATE

✪ Flying Fish Grill. In Carmel Plaza, Mission St. (between Ocean and 7th aves.). ☎ **408/625-1962.** Reservations recommended. Main courses $14.50–$19.50. AE, DISC, MC, V. Daily 5–10pm. PACIFIC RIM/SEAFOOD.

We always feel more confident when a restaurant's kitchen is actually run by its owner—and a dinner experience here will confirm that chef/proprietor Kenny Fukumoto is in the house. Dark, romantic, and Asian-influenced, the dining room's atmosphere is intimate and unique with redwood booths (built by Kenny) and fish hanging (flying?) from the ceiling. The cuisine features fresh seafood with exquisite

Japanese accents. Start with some sushi, tempura, or any of the other exotic and tantalizing taste teasers. Then prepare your tongue for seriously sensational main courses. House favorites include a savory rare peppered ahi, which is blackened and served with mustard/sesame-soy vinaigrette and angel-hair pasta, and a pan-fried almond sea bass with whipped potatoes, Chinese cabbage, and rock shrimp stir-fry.

The Hog's Breath Inn. San Carlos St. (between 5th and 6th aves.). ☎ **408/625-1044.** Reservations not accepted. Main courses $9.50–$23. AE, DC, MC, V. Mon–Fri 11:30am–3pm and 5–10pm, Sat–Sun 11am–3pm and 5–10pm. From Calif. 1, take the Ocean Ave. exit and turn right onto San Carlos St. AMERICAN.

What's in a name? Well, if Clint Eastwood didn't own this place, we don't know what would inspire tourists to eat at a joint named after a pig's exhalation (how very Clint!). But clamor they do for one of the tree-trunk tables with plastic chairs along a brick patio. Tables in the wood-paneled dark-and-rustic dining room decorated with farm implements fill up too, though they're not as lively as outdoor seats. The fare here isn't remotely as legendary as the eatery's owner (whom you're not likely to see), but it's the perfect place to nosh on afternoon snacks (burgers, nachos, etc.) and throw back a few brews. The small dark bar with sports on the tube is the best place to pull up a stool and get loaded on a rainy day (or a sunny one for that matter).

Il Fornaio. Ocean Ave at Monte Verde. ☎ **408/622-5100,** or 408/622-5115 for the bakery. Reservations accepted. Main courses $8–$15. AE, DC, MC, V. Mon–Fri 7am–10:30pm, Sat–Sun 8am–11pm. ITALIAN.

We don't care if it is a chain—Il Fornaio is still one of our favorite restaurants because we know we're guaranteed a well-prepared mocha and thick chocolate-dipped biscotti at every outpost. There's also a great selection of salads (go with the simple house salad with shaved Parmesan, croutons, and a tangy light dressing), pastas, pizzas, and rotisserie chicken, duck, and rabbit fresh from the brick oven. The housemade breads and seeded breadsticks alone are enough of a reason to come through the door. We must admit that we were disappointed with tasty-but-measly $11 lasagne, so skip it and start with the seared swordfish antipasto with roast pepper and Dijon mustard; or decadent grilled polenta with sautéed wild mushrooms, provolone cheese, and Italian truffle oil. Move on to a gourmet pizza or a pasta such as the lobster filled with ricotta cheese, leeks, and a lemon-cream sauce or spaghetti with fresh shrimp, mussels, imported tuna, black olives, and garlic and tomato sauce. The large airy dining room and sunny terrace offer charming and diverse atmospheres. The Panetteria, a retail bakery, is the perfect place to pick up a gourmet picnic.

🟢 La Bohème. Dolores St. and 7th Ave. ☎ **408/624-7500.** Reservations not accepted. Fixedprice three-course dinner $19.75. MC, V. Daily 5:30–10pm. Closed 2 weeks before Christmas. From Calif. 1, exit onto Ocean Ave. and turn left onto Dolores St. FRENCH COUNTRY.

Like a set from Disney's "It's a Small World," La Bohème mimics a French street with cartoony asymmetrical shingled house facades and a painted blue sky overhead. Thankfully, the similarity stops with the decor and there are no dolls singing anywhere—in French or English. Dining here is utterly romantic French, served at cramped tables set with floral-print cloths in bright colors, hand-painted dinnerware, and vibrant floral bouquets. Dinner is a three-course, fixed-price feast, consisting of a large salad, a tureen of soup, and a main dish (perhaps breast of chicken with ginger-shallot sauce or filet mignon with cognac-cream sauce). Vegetarian specials are available nightly. Homemade desserts and fresh coffee are sold separately, and are usually worth the extra expense. Dress is casual. Curious on-line folks can learn more at **http://www.carmelnet.com/laboheme.**

INEXPENSIVE

🟢 **Caffè Napoli.** Ocean Ave. (between Dolores and Lincoln). ☎ **408/625-4033.** Reservations recommended. Main courses $8–$15. MC, V. Daily 11:30am–4pm and 5–10pm. ITALIAN.

The decor here is so quintessentially Italiana, with flags, gingham tablecloths, garlic, and baskets overhead, that we expected a flour-coated pot-bellied Padrino Napoli to emerge from the kitchen, embrace us wholeheartedly, and exclaim "Mange! Mange!" as he slapped down a bowl overflowing with sauce-drenched pasta. Of course there is no padrino here, and we received no welcoming hug, but we did indulge in the fine Italian fare that keeps locals coming back for more. If the wait is too long, the host will direct you around the corner to a sibling restaurant, Little Napoli, which serves the same food but in a slightly more upscale setting. The menu is straight Italian and includes seven salad choices, antipasti, pizza, and pasta.

🟢 **Little Swiss Cafe.** 6th Ave. (between Lincoln and Mission). ☎ **408/624-5007.** Reservations not accepted. Menu items $4.75–$7.50. No credit cards. Mon–Sat 7:30am–3pm, Sun 8am–2pm. CONTINENTAL.

Locals led us to this quirky little eatery designed to look like a Swiss cottage. Kids may love the old-fashioned, grandma-cute decor, but the grownups come for what they consider the best homemade blintzes and pancakes in town. Late risers rejoice— breakfast is served all day.

5 Carmel Valley

Inland from Carmel stretches Carmel Valley, where wealthy folks retreat beyond the reach of the coastal fog and mist. It's a scenic and perpetually sunny valley of rolling hills dotted with manicured golf courses and many a horse ranch.

Hike the trails in **Garland Regional Park,** 8 miles east of Carmel on Carmel Valley Road (dogs are welcome off-leash). The sun really bakes you out here, so bring lots of water. You could also sign up for a trail ride at the **Holman Ranch,** 60 Holman Rd. (☎ **408/659-2640**), 12 miles east of Calif. 1. **Golf** is offered at several resorts and courses in the valley, notably at Quail Lodge, 8000 Valley Green Dr. (☎ 408/624-2770), and Rancho Canada Golf Club, Carmel Valley Rd. (☎ 408/624-0111). While you're in the valley, taste the wines at the **Château Julien Winery,** 8940 Carmel Valley Rd. (☎ **408/624-2600**), which is open daily.

WHERE TO STAY

✪ **Quail Lodge Resort and Golf Club.** 8205 Valley Greens Dr., Carmel, CA 93923. ☎ **800/538-9516** or 408/624-1581. Fax 408/624-3726. 86 rms, 14 suites. TV TEL. Mar–Nov, $215–$275 double; $320–$590 suite. Dec–Feb, $180–$225 double; $255 suite. Additional person $25 extra. AE, CB, DC, MC, V. From Calif. 1 north, past the Carmel exits, after which the highway narrows to two lanes, turn left on Carmel Valley Rd. and continue 3 miles to Valley Greens Dr.

Quail Lodge—an executive golf haven—is one of the most highly regarded resort hotels in the country, lying in the foothills of the Santa Lucia Range and receiving five-star ratings for 20 years running. Its pastoral setting encompasses more than 850 acres of sparkling lakes, secluded woodlands, and rolling meadows. The guest rooms are in two-story balconied wings with terraces overlooking the pool or one of the 10 man-made lakes, or in cottages holding five accommodations each. Executive villas are the most expensive units.

Remodeled in 1996, the guest rooms are decorated in warm earth tones jazzed up with floral and striped patterns. Higher-priced accommodations, on the upper floors, have cathedral ceilings. Every room has a separate dressing area and an ample balcony;

some have fireplaces and wet bars. There's a coffeemaker in every room, supplied with freshly ground beans. Afternoon tea is served in the lobby from 3 to 5pm.

Dining/Entertainment: The renowned Covey Restaurant serves European fare in warmly elegant surroundings. Tables are covered with Belgian linens, set with Sienna china, adorned with fresh flowers, and topped with romantic gas lamps. The Caesar salad is exceptional. Main courses include Santa Barbara abalone and Muscovy duck with red currants and brandied cherries. Jackets are required for men, and reservations are essential.

Services: Concierge, room service, evening turndown, complimentary morning newspaper.

Facilities: 18-hole golf course designed by Robert Muir Graves, four tennis courts, two swimming pools, sauna, redwood hot tub, hiking and jogging trails, gift shops, nearby beauty salon.

Robles del Rio. 200 Punta del Monte, Carmel Valley, CA 93924. ☎ **800/833-0843** or 408/659-3705. 26 rms, 2 suites, 5 cottages. TV. $89–$145 double; from $200 suite; from $170 cottage. Rates include buffet breakfast. AE, MC, V.

Set among oak trees on a mountaintop, this rustic resort has beckoned many a luminary since its 1928 opening (Arthur Murray, Red Skelton, and Alistair Cook, for example). Whether the rooms are in the main lodge or in the cottages, the furnishings have a simple, rustic style with iron or wicker beds and either feature knotty-pine walls or a southern colonial look. The cottages have fireplaces, plus a kitchen or kitchenette. The restaurant opens onto panoramic views of the Carmel Valley.

Facilities: A well-landscaped pool, outdoor hot tub, tennis, horseback riding, hiking and jogging trails.

✪ Stonepine. 150 E. Carmel Valley Rd., Carmel Valley, CA 93924. ☎ **408/659-2245.** Fax 408/659-5160. 3 rms, 9 suites, 1 cottage. $225–$500 double; $225–$750 suite; $750 cottage. AE, MC, V.

Once through the electronically controlled gate, guests follow a mile-long winding driveway past the polo field and stables up to this hilltop château. The wisteria-clad mansion was built in the 1920s and was once part of the private estate of Henry Potter and Helen Crocker Russel of the San Francisco banking family, who raised thoroughbreds here. Framed by box hedges, the surrounding formal English gardens are laid out into separate rose, perennial, and fruit gardens.

The very comfortable accommodations in the château are each decorated and equipped differently. The most expensive boasts a fireplace and marble Roman bath with Jacuzzi, as well as his-and-hers bathrooms and dressing rooms, plus a sitting room. The Don Quixote Suite has French doors leading out to a garden patio, while the Venetian Suite contains a canopied bed and has a separate entrance. All are furnished with fine antiques and fabrics. The rooms in the Paddock House have access to a complete country kitchen and dining room. They all have Jacuzzi tubs, too. No children under 12 are allowed in the château accommodations, but they are welcome in the Paddock and the cottage.

Dining/Entertainment: A five-course dinner is served in the very formal dining room in the château—perhaps curry-mussel soup with cilantro, a salad, hazelnut-crusted salmon with tomato-ginger sauce, and a chocolate Grand Marnier cake.

Facilities: Beyond the gardens lie the Renaissance-inspired swimming pool, tennis court, and a soccer field. Other recreational facilities include the croquet lawn, archery range, and the Equestrian Center. The last offers four regimens in horsemanship, all available to guests.

WHERE TO DINE

Fish Ranch Restaurant. In the Crossoroads shopping center, 245 Crossroads Blvd. ☎ **408/625-1363.** Reservations recommended. Most main courses $12–$18. AE, MC, V. Daily 11:30am–4pm and 5–10pm. SEAFOOD.

Steven Spielberg, Clint Eastwood, Jason Priestly, and Brad Pitt are just a few of the celebrities who've been sighted recently at the hottest new restaurant in the Monterey Bay area. But stargazing isn't the only attraction here, for one of the best dining rooms around also has been known to serve stellar seafood. The atmosphere offers the kind of clever sophistication you'd expect from one of San Francisco's finer haunts. Look up at the ceiling—you'll notice the underwater fish-eye view, complete with a boat's bottom in a running stream and a passing rainbow trout overhead. The tables are dispersed both inside the warm, handsome dining room with whimsical light fixtures and a large fireplace and on the sunny patio overlooking the mountains.

The menu starts off with "Lures," or appetizers, such as Monterey Bay calamari served with wasabi tartar, or sautéed clams and mussels with leeks, tomatoes, and saffron–crème fraîche sauce. Main courses are arranged on a "Field and Stream" list and include ranch-made crab and ricotta ravioli in a tomato-and-basil nagé or cabernet-marinated lamb shank, minted rosemary sauce, and northern white beans. Don't worry if you're not fish-savvy—there are plenty of other options on the menu. *Take note:* The kitchen here is still having growing pains; and has on and off days. Come on a weekend night for live music.

⑤ Rio Grill. 101 Crossroads Blvd. ☎ **408/625-5436.** Reservations required. Main courses $10–$25. AE, DISC, MC, V. Daily 11:30am–11pm. From Calif. 1, take the Rio Rd. exit west for 1 block and turn right onto Crossroads Blvd. AMERICAN.

You won't mind waiting to be seated here—the lively lounge is one of the best in Carmel, attracting an interesting crowd. It's decorated with a cartoon mural of famous locals such as Clint Eastwood and the late Bing Crosby, as well as playful sculpture, cactus, and other vibrant art. The whimsical nature of the modern Santa Fe–style dining room belies the kitchen's serious preparations, which include home-made soups; a rich quesedilla with almonds, cheeses, and smoked-tomato salsa; barbecued baby back ribs from a wood-burning oven; and fresh fish from an open oak grill. The restaurant's good selection of wines includes some rare Californian vintages and covers a broad price range. As usual in this town, dress is casual.

6 The Big Sur Coast

Big Sur is more than a drive along one of the most dramatic coastlines on earth, or a peaceful evening amid a forest of towering California redwoods. It's a stretch of vast wilderness so ominously beautiful—especially when the fog glows in the moonlight—that it inspires all who walk its majestic paths.

Although there is an actual Big Sur Village approximately 25 miles south of Carmel, "Big Sur" refers to the entire 90-mile stretch of coastline between Carmel and San Simeon, blessed on one side by the majestic Santa Lucia Range and on the other by the rocky Pacific coastline. It's one of the most romantic and relaxing places on earth. There's little more to do than explore the mountains and beaches— or just perch yourself atop the cliffs and take in the California sea air.

ESSENTIALS

ORIENTATION Most of this stretch is state park, and Calif. 1 runs its entire length, hugging the ocean the whole way. Restaurants, hotels, and sights are easy to spot—most are situated directly on the highway—but without major towns as reference points, their addresses can be obscure. For the purposes of orientation, we'll use the River Inn as our mileage guide. Located 29 miles south of Monterey on Calif. 1, the inn is generally considered to mark the northern end of Big Sur.

VISITOR INFORMATION The **Monterey Peninsula Visitors and Convention Bureau,** 380 Alvarado St., Monterey (☎ **408/649-1770**), also has specialized information on places and events in Big Sur.

EXPLORING THE BIG SUR COAST

Big Sur offers visitors unspoiled tranquillity and unparalleled wild natural beauty— ideal for hiking, picnicking, camping, fishing, and beachcombing. The first settlers arrived here only a century ago, and the present highway making the area accessible was built in 1937. (Electricity only arrived in the 1950s, and it's still not available in the remote inland mountains.) Big Sur's mysterious, misty beauty has inspired several modern spiritual movements, the most famous being Esalen, the birthplace of the human potential movement. Even the tourist bureau bills the area as a place in which "to slow down . . . to meditate . . . to catch up with your soul." Take the board's advice and take your time—nothing better lies ahead.

The region affords a bounty of wilderness adventure opportunities. The inland **Ventana Wilderness,** which is maintained by the U.S. Forest Service, contains 167,323 acres straddling the Santa Lucia mountains and is characterized by steep-sided ridges separated by V-shaped valleys. The streams that cascade through the area are marked by waterfalls, deep pools, and thermal springs. The wilderness offers 237 miles of **hiking trails** that lead to 55 designated trail camps—a backpacker's paradise. One of the easiest trails to access is the **Pine Ridge Trail** at Big Sur station (☎ 408/667-2315).

From Carmel, the first stop along Calif. 1 is **Point Lobos State Reserve** (☎ 408/624-4909), 3 miles south of Carmel. Sea lions, harbor seals, sea otters, and thousands of seabirds reside in this 550-acre reserve. You can see whales in season, too. Trails follow the shoreline and lead to hidden coves. Note that parking is limited; on weekends especially, you need to arrive early to secure a place.

From here, cross the Soberanes Creek, passing ✪ **Garrapata State Park,** a 2,879-acre preserve with 4 miles of coastline. It's unmarked and undeveloped. To explore the trails, you'll need to park at one of the turnouts on Calif. 1 near Sobranes Point and hike in.

Ten miles south of Carmel, you'll arrive at North Abalone Cove. From here, Palo Colorado Road leads back into the wilderness to the first of the Forest Service camping areas at Bottchers Gap ($12 to camp, $5 to park overnight).

Continuing south, you'll cross two dramatic bridges at Rocky Creek and Bixby Creek, which will bring you to the **Point Sur Lighthouse,** at the 18$^{1}/_{2}$ mile marker. The **Bixby Bridge,** 13 miles south of Carmel, towers nearly 260 feet above Bixby Creek Canyon. It offers canyon and ocean views and several observation alcoves at regular intervals along the bridge. The lighthouse, which sits 361 feet above the surf on a volcanic rock promontory, was built in 1887–89, when only a horse trail provided access to this part of the world. Tours, which take 2 to 3 hours and involve a steep half-mile hike each way, are scheduled on most weekends. For information call 408/625-4419. Admission is $5 for adults, $3 for youths 13 to 17, $2 for children 5 to 12, and free for kids 4 and under.

About 3 miles south of the lighthouse is **Andrew Molera State Park** (☎ 408/667-2315), the largest state park on the Big Sur Coast (4,800 acres), but much less crowded than Pfeiffer Big Sur (see below). Miles of trails meander through meadows and along beaches and bluffs. Hikers and cyclists use the primitive trail camp about

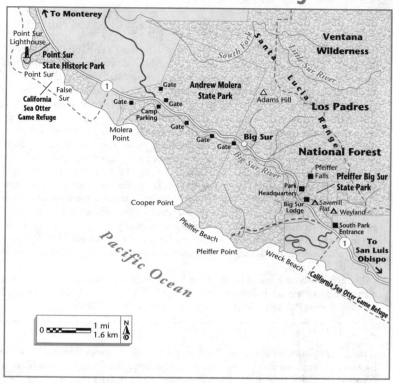

a third of a mile from the parking area. **Molera Big Sur Trail Rides** (☎ 408/625-5486) offers coastal trail rides for riders of all levels of experience. The 2½-mile-long beach, which is sheltered from the wind by a bluff, is accessible via a mile-long path flanked in spring by wildflowers. You can walk the entire length of the beach at low tide; otherwise take the bluff trail above the beach. The park also has campgrounds.

Back on Calif. 1, you'll soon reach the village of Big Sur, where commercial services are available.

About 26 miles south of Carmel you'll come on the **U.S. Forest Service Ranger Station,** where you can pick up maps and other information about the region. It's located in **Pfeiffer Big Sur State Park** (☎ 408/667-2315), an 810-acre park which offers 218 camping sites along the Big Sur River, picnicking, fishing, and hiking. It's a scenic park of redwoods, conifers, oaks, and open meadows. For this reason it gets very crowded. The Lodge in the park has cabins with fireplaces and other facilities (see "Camping," below). Sycamore Canyon Road (unmarked; it's the only paved road west of Calif. 1 between the Big Sur post office and the state park entrance) will take you 2 miles to sandy **Pfeiffer Beach,** which has an arch-shaped rock formation just offshore. It's open for day use only and is the only beach accessible by car. Admission to the park is $6, and it's open daily from dawn to dusk.

Back on Calif. 1, the road travels 11 miles past Sea Lion Cove to Julia Pfeiffer Burns State Park. High above the ocean is the famous Nepenthe restaurant, the retreat bought by Orson Welles for Rita Hayworth in 1944. A few miles farther south

Henry Miller at Big Sur

In 1944 author Henry Miller visited his friend, artist Jean Varda, on the Monterey Peninsula. After a 2-month stay, Varda drove Miller down the coast to Big Sur, where Miller fell in love with the remote region and decided to move there. Miller was by then already a legendary and controversial figure whose books, *Tropic of Capricorn* (1939) and *Tropic of Cancer* (1943), had been banned as indecent.

Rumors spread that he was a sex anarchist who was building a colony of followers in the remote region of Big Sur. The truth was that Miller had retreated here to cure his writer's block and to commune and heal in the presence of nature, away from the telephone and other distractions. Upon arriving in Big Sur he wrote, "Here I will find peace. Here I shall find the strength to do the work I was made to do."

And he did, in his house on Partington Ridge. He confided that every morning when he surveyed the view from his cabin door, "I blessed the trees, the birds, the dogs, the cats. I blessed the flowers, the pomegranates, the thorny cactus. I blessed men and women everywhere no matter on which side of the fence they happened to be."

Under the influence of the environment, he wrote *Big Sur* and *The Oranges of Hieronymus Bosch,* introducing the attractions of this remote region to the rest of the world.

Unfortunately, the rest of world came here to see it for themselves, and tourist intrusions and the rustic life became too hard for Miller to endure. In 1961 he moved south to Pacific Palisades, where he lived until his death in 1980.

is the **Coast Gallery,** the premier local art gallery, which shows lithographs of works by Henry Miller, whose fans will also want to stop at the **Henry Miller Memorial Library,** on Calif. 1, 30 miles south of Carmel and a quarter mile south of the **Nepenthe Restaurant** (☎ 408/667-2574). The library displays and sells books and artwork by Miller and houses a permanent collection of first editions. It also serves as a community art center, hosting concerts, poetry readings, and art exhibitions. The rear gallery room is a video-viewing space where films about Henry Miller can be seen. There's a sculpture garden, plus tables on the adjacent lawn where visitors can rest and enjoy the surroundings. Admission is free, and it's open Tuesday to Sunday from 11am to 5pm.

Julia Pfeiffer Burns State Park (☎ 408/667-2315) encompasses some of Big Sur's most spectacular coastline. To get a closer look, take the trail from the parking area at McWay Canyon, which leads under the highway to a bluff overlooking an 80-foot-high waterfall dropping directly into the ocean. It's less crowded here than at Pfeiffer Big Sur, and there are miles of trails to explore in the 3,580-acre park. Scuba divers can apply for permits to explore the 1,680-acre underwater reserve.

From here, the road skirts the Ventana Wilderness, passing Anderson and Marble Peaks and the **Esalen Institute,** before crossing the Big Creek Bridge to Lucia and several campgrounds farther south. **Kirk Creek Campground,** about 3 miles north of Pacific Valley, offers camping with ocean views and beach access. Beyond Pacific Valley, the **Sand Dollar Beach** picnic area is a good place to stop and enjoy the coastal view and take a stroll. A half-mile trail leads down to the sheltered beach, from which there's a fine view of Cone Peak, one of the coast's highest mountains. Two miles south of Sand Dollar is **Jade Cove,** a popular spot for rock hounds. From here, it's about another 27 miles past the Piedras Blancas Light Station to San Simeon (see Chapter 13).

WHERE TO STAY

Few area accommodations offer the kind of pampering luxury you'd expect in a fine urban hotel; even direct-dial phones and TVs (often considered philistine in these parts) are rare. Big Sur hotels are especially busy in summer, when advance reservations are required.

Big Sur Lodge. In Pfeiffer–Big Sur State Park, Calif. 1 (P.O. Box 190), Big Sur, CA 93920. ☎ **800/424-4787** or 408/667-3100. Fax 408/667-3110. 61 cabins. $79–$139 cabin for two; $99–$159 cabin with kitchen or fireplace; $109–$179 cabin with kitchen and fireplace. Rates include park entrance fees. MC, V. From Carmel, take Calif. 1 south 26 miles.

A family-friendly place to stay, Big Sur Lodge, sheltered by towering redwoods, sycamores, and broad-leafed maples, is situated in the state park. The rustic accommodations are motel-style cabins, and are all quite large, with high peaked cedar- and redwood-beamed ceilings. They're clean and heated, and have private baths and reserved parking spaces. Some have fireplaces and/or kitchenettes (bring your own cooking utensils, though). All offer porches or decks with views of the redwoods or the Santa Lucia Range. Cabins 34 to 50 will put you in Siberia.

An advantage to staying here is that you're entitled to free use of all the facilities of the park, including hiking, barbecue pits, and picnic areas. In addition, the lodge has its own large, outdoor heated swimming pool, gift shop, grocery stores, and laundry facilities. The lodge dining room is open for breakfast and dinner (and lunch in the summer). Evening menus, only slightly better than summer-camp food, feature fresh seafood, steaks, and pasta dishes. Reservations are recommended and should be made far in advance during summer months.

Deetjen's Big Sur Inn. Calif. 1, Big Sur, CA 93920. ☎ **408/667-2377.** 20 rms, 15 with bath. Sun–Thurs, from $70 double without bath, from $100 double with bath. Fri–Sat, from $85 double without bath, from $115 double with bath. MC, V.

In the 1930s before Calif. 1 was built, this homestead was an overnight stopping place on the coastal wagon road. It was begun by Norwegian homesteader Helmuth Deetjen who over the years built several accommodations constructed out of hand-hewn logs and lumber. The rooms are simple, rustic, and short on creature comforts, but they're set in a redwood canyon and make for a peaceful retreat. Single-wall construction means that the rooms are far from soundproof, so children under 12 are allowed only if families reserve both rooms of a two-room building. There's no insulation, so prepare to crank up the fire or wood-burning stove.

The restaurant consists of four intimate rooms lit by candlelight; they're made even more inviting by classical music playing in the background. The cuisine runs to classic American/continental favorites—steaks, lamb chops, grilled fish, and some vegetarian dishes.

✪ Post Ranch Inn. Calif. 1 (P.O. Box 219), Big Sur, CA 93920. ☎ **800/527-2200** or 408/667-2200. Fax 408/667-2824. 30 rms, 1 suite. TEL. $285–$545 double; $375 suite. Rates include breakfast. AE, MC, V.

Okay, so the attitude here can be a little stuffy. But that, in conjunction with some of the most amazing accommodations on earth, adds to the exclusivity of the ultra-elite Post Ranch Inn. Perched on 98 acres of pristine seaside ridges 1,200 feet above the Pacific, this resort opened in 1992 and was instantly declared one of the world's finest retreats. What's the big deal? The Post Ranch doesn't attempt to beat its stunning natural surroundings, but rather to join them. The wood-and-glass guest cottages are built around existing trees; some are elevated on stilts to avoid damaging native redwood root structures; and the ultra-private Ocean and Coast cottages are so close to the edge of the earth, you get the impression that you've joined the clouds (imagine that from your private spa tub). Other cottages are equally impressive in design and face the woodlands. Each room contains a fireplace, terrace, massage table, cassette and CD player, and wet bar filled with complimentary goodies. The bathrooms, fashioned out of slate and granite, feature spa tubs. There's also a small workout room and two heated outdoor pools and sundecks on the premises.

Dining/Entertainment: The Sierra Mar restaurant is open only to guests for continental breakfasts and to the public nightly for dinner (when there's a four-course fixed-price meal for $55). It, too, has floor-to-ceiling views of the ocean. The most acclaimed dish on the menu is the breast of duck with foie gras, quince, and walnuts.

Services: Room service, complimentary newspaper. An activities director substitutes for a concierge. Among the services available are massage, yoga, spa services, guided hikes, tarot reading, aromatherapy, and facials.

✪ **Ventana Inn.** Calif. 1, Big Sur, CA 93920. ☎ **800/628-6500** or 408/667-2331. Fax 408/667-2419. 56 rms, 4 suites. A/C MINIBAR TV TEL. $195–$440 double; from $525 suite. Rates include continental breakfast and afternoon wine and cheese. AE, CB, DC, DISC, MC, V.

Luxuriously rustic and utterly romantic, the Ventana Inn has been a highly popular wilderness outpost for over 20 years. Located on 243 mountainous oceanfront acres, the Ventana has an elegance that's atypical of the region and has continually attracted famous guests since its opening in 1975—Barbra Streisand, Goldie Hawn, and Francis Ford Coppola have all retreated here.

The accommodations, in one- and two-story buildings, are worthy of the wild, blending in with the magical Big Sur countryside. The guest rooms, somewhat old-fashioned, are located in 12 contemporary natural-wood buildings with slanted roofs that fit well into the landscape. The elegantly rustic and comfortable interiors have white stucco and cedar walls, wicker furnishings, and firm beds covered with hand-made quilted patchwork spreads. Each accommodation has a separate dressing room, VCR, refrigerator, and private terrace or balcony overlooking the ocean or forest. Most rooms offer wood-burning fireplaces, and some have hot tubs and high cathedral ceilings. A complete fitness center has recently been added. *Families take heed:* Children are permitted, but not exactly embraced.

Dining/Entertainment: The Ventana Restaurant is a worthwhile splurge; its food is absolutely first-rate, although service is often slow. The airy cedar interior has two large stone fireplaces, redwood tables, and cane and bentwood chairs, and is filled with ferns, potted plants, and fruit baskets. The large outdoor patio offers views over a dramatic expanse of ocean and 50 miles of Big Sur coast.

Services: Concierge, massage, newspaper delivery, twice-daily maid service, free coffee.

Facilities: Two 90-foot heated outdoor swimming pools, bathhouse, Japanese hot bath, sauna, fitness room, gift store, art gallery.

CAMPING

Big Sur Campground and Cabins. Calif. 1, 26 miles south of Carmel (half a mile south of the River Inn). ☎ **408/667-2322.** 81 tent sites, 40 with electricity and water hookup; 17 cabins, all with shower. $24 tent site for two; $24 RV hookup, plus $3 extra for electricity and water; $72–$144 cabin for two. Rates include entrance for your car. MC, V.

Each campsite here has its own wood-burning fire pit, picnic table, and freshwater faucet within 25 feet of the pitching area. Facilities include bathhouses with hot showers, laundry facilities, a river for swimming, a playground area, a volleyball/basketball court, and a grocery store. Open year-round.

Fernwood. Calif. 1, 31 miles south of Carmel (2 miles south of the River Inn). ☎ **408/ 667-2422.** 86 sites, 39 with electricity. $24 site for two without electricity, $27 site for two with electricity; $27 RV hookup. Additional person $3 extra. Car entrance $5 extra. MC, V.

Each site at this campground on 23 woodland acres has running water and a fire pit. About half overlook the river. The restaurant on the premises is open daily from 11:30am to 10pm and serves burgers, ribs, and other summer camp fare. An adjacent bar/cocktail lounge features live music on the weekends, and a grocery store sells wood, ice, beer, and other essentials.

Ventana Campground. Calif. 1, 28 miles south of Carmel (4¹/₄ miles south of the River Inn). ☎ **408/667-2688.** 75 sites. $24 site for two. Additional person $5 extra; $5 charge for a dog. Rates include entrance fee for your car. No credit cards.

The campsites on 40 acres of a redwood canyon here are spaced well apart for privacy. Each has a picnic table and fire ring, although there's no electricity and no RV hookups. Three bathhouses with hot showers (25¢ fee) are conveniently located. The closest coastal access is at Pfeiffer Beach, 3 miles away. The entrance to Ventana Campground is adjacent to the entrance to the resort of the same name (see above). To reserve a space, send 1 night's deposit, the dates you'd like to stay, and a stamped, self-addressed envelope at least 2 weeks in advance.

WHERE TO DINE

Fine dining can be enjoyed at the Ventana Inn anytime, and also at the Post Ranch for dinner (see "Where to Stay," above).

Glen Oaks Restaurant. Calif. 1, 26 miles south of Carmel. ☎ **408/667-2264.** Reservations recommended for dinner. Main courses $10–$16. MC, V. Daily 6–9pm. INTERNATIONAL.

Not much changes in this neck of the woods, but Glen Oaks is this year's exception. The down-home restaurant got a new owner and a new chef, and was redecorated in 1996. The atmosphere still complements the surroundings with beamed ceilings, a wood-burning copper-chimneyed fireplace, and plenty of plants and local art. Dinner specials change daily, but you can always count on a basket of homemade bread (baked daily) and some version of the house-smoked trout and salmon. Dinner features such main dishes as grilled marinated chicken. Desserts are prepared daily on the premises, and a small selection of Californian wines is available.

Nepenthe. Calif. 1, 30 miles south of Carmel (5 miles south of the River Inn). ☎ **408/ 667-2345.** Reservations accepted only for parties of five or more. Main courses $9–$25. AE, MC, V. Daily 11:30am–10pm. AMERICAN.

We scoff at a $10 burger and a $4 draft beer even when we're in the finest of San Francisco restaurants. But we'd cough up the cash all over again for an encore lunch on the terrace at Nepenthe. Think of it as a nominal admission to dine at heights only angels usually enjoy. Sitting 808 feet above sea level along the cliffs overlooking the ocean, Nepenthe's atmosphere is naturally celestial—especially when fog lingers above the water below.

Thankfully, the restaurant was intentionally constructed of redwood and adobe to unite it with the landscape and earth it stands on. The result? An unobtrusive wooden dining room (big wood-burning fireplace, redwood ceilings, and all) and large windows that frame the unearthly view. The fare, though good, will not send you to gastronomic heaven, but if the sun is shining and you're sipping a chardonnay, who cares? Lunch is basic: burgers, sandwiches, and salads. Dinner main courses include steak, broiled chicken, and fresh fish prepared any number of ways.

7   Pinnacles National Monument

by Andrew Rice

Once a little-known outpost of the national monument system, Pinnacles National Monument has become one of the most popular weekend climbing destinations in central California over the past decade. The mild winter climate and plentiful routes make this a perfect off-season training ground for climbers. It's also a popular haven for campers, hikers, and nature lovers. One of the most unique chaparral ecosystems in the world supports a large community of plant and animal life here, including one of California's largest breeding population of raptors.

The Pinnacles themselves—hundreds of towering crags, spires, and hoodoos—are seemingly out of place in the voluptuously rolling hills of the coast range. And they *are,* in fact, out of place, part of the eroded remains of a volcano formed 23 million years ago 195 miles south in the middle of the Mojave Desert. It was carried here by the movement of the San Andreas Fault, which runs just east of the park. (The other half of the volcano remains in the Mojave.) Because of this distinctive geology, Pinnacles was set aside as a national monument on January 16, 1908, though it wasn't developed for visitor use until the 1930s and 1940s.

You could spend days here without getting bored, but it's possible to cover the most interesting features in a weekend. With a single hike you can go from the lush oak woodland around the Bear Gulch Visitor Center to the dry and desolate crags of the high peaks, then back down through a half-mile-long cave complete with underground waterfalls.

JUST THE FACTS

ACCESS POINTS   Two entrances lead to the park. The **West Entrance** from Soledad and U.S. 101 is a dry, dusty, winding single-lane road (not suitable for trailers) with the best drive-up view of the park. It doesn't connect with the east side. The alternative route is via the **East Entrance.** Unless you're coming from nearby, take the longer drive on Calif. 25 to enter through the east. Because most of the peaks of the Pinnacles face east, and the watershed drains east, most of the interesting hikes and geologic features are on this side. No road crosses the park.

VISITOR CENTER   The first place you should go upon entering the park from the east is the **Bear Gulch Visitor Center** (☎ **408/389-4485**). This small center is rich with exhibits about the park's history, wildlife, and geology, and also has a great selection of nature handbooks and climbing guides for the Pinnacles. Climbers should check with rangers about closures and other information before heading out: Many routes are closed during hawk and falcon nesting season, and rangers like to know how many climbers are in the park.

Adjacent to the visitor center, the Bear Gulch picnic ground is a great place to fuel up before setting out on a hike or, if you're not planning on leaving your car, one of the best places to gaze up at dramatic spires of the high peaks (the ultimate spot is from the west side).

REGULATIONS & WARNINGS   Beware of poison oak, particularly in Bear Gulch. Rattlesnakes are common throughout the park but rarely seen. Bikes and dogs are prohibited on all trails, and no back country camping is allowed anywhere in the park.

Hiking through this variety of landscapes demands versatility. Come prepared with a good pair of hiking shoes, snacks, lots of water, and a flashlight.

Daytime temperatures often exceed 100°F in summer, so the best times of year to visit are spring, when the wildflowers are blooming, followed by fall. Crowds are common during spring weekends.

HIKING/SEEING THE HIGHLIGHTS

To see most of the park in a single, moderately strenuous morning, take the **Condor Gulch Trail** from the visitor center. As you climb quickly out of the parking area, the Pinnacles' wind-sculpted spires seem to grow taller. In less than 2 miles you're among them, and Condor Gulch intersects with the **High Peaks Trail.** The view from the top spans miles: the Salinas Valley to your west, the Pinnacles below, and miles of coast range to the east. After traversing the high peaks (including stretches of footholds carved in steep rock faces) for about a mile, the trail drops back toward the visitor center via a valley filled with eerie-looking hoodoos.

In another 1¹/₂ miles, you'll reach the reservoir marking the top of **Bear Gulch Cave.** You'll need your flashlight and might get wet, but this .6-mile-long talus cave is a thrill. From the end of the cave you're just a short walk through the most popular climbing area of the park away from the visitor center. It's also possible to hike just Bear Gulch and the cave, then return via the **Moses Spring Trail.** It's about 2 miles round-trip, but you'll miss the view from the top.

If you're coming from the west entrance, the **Juniper Canyon Trail** is a short (1.2 miles), but very steep, blast to the top of the high peaks. You'll definitely earn the view. Otherwise, try the short **Balconies Trail** to the monument's other talus cave, **Balconies Cave.** Flashlights are required here, too.

CAMPING

The national monument **campground** on the west side (☎ **408/389-4485**) is just an open field with a few pit toilets and picnic tables. To top things off, it's not open on spring weekends, prime visiting season. Rates are $10 per night.

The campground on the east side, privately run **Pinnacles Campground, Inc.** (☎ **408/389-4462;** $6 per person) is just outside the park off Calif. 25, 32 miles south of Hollister, with lots of privacy and space between sites, showers, a store, and a pool. It's close enough so you can hike into the park from the campground, though it will add a few miles to your outing. Though private campgrounds often are overdeveloped, the management here saw the benefits of leaving the surroundings natural. Park rangers hold campfire programs here on weekends. Dogs are not recommended.

13 The Central Coast

by Erika Lenkert and Matthew R. Poole

California's Central Coast—a spectacular amalgam of beaches, lakes, and mountains—is the state's most diverse region. The narrow strip of coast that runs for more than 100 miles from San Simeon to Ventura spans several climate zones and is home to an eclectic mix of students, middle-class workers, retirees, farmers, computer techies, and fishermen. The ride along Calif. 1, which follows the ocean cliffs, is almost always packed with rental cars, recreational vehicles, and bicyclists. Traffic may give your brakes a workout, but it also allows you to take longer looks at one of the most spectacular vistas in the world.

Whether you're driving from Los Angeles or San Francisco, Calif. 1 is the most scenic and leisurely route (U.S. 101 gets you there faster, but is less picturesque). Most bicyclists peddle from north to south, the direction of the prevailing winds. Those in automobiles may prefer to drive south to north, so they can get a better look at the coastline as it unfolds toward the west. No matter which direction you drive, break out the ol' camera—you're about to experience unparalleled beauty, California style.

1 San Simeon: Hearst Castle

Few places on earth compare to Hearst Castle. This 165-room estate of publishing magnate William Randolph Hearst, situated high above the coastal village of San Simeon atop a hill he called La Cuesta Encantada ("the Enchanted Hill"), is an ego trip par excellence. One of the last great estates of America's Gilded Age, it's an astounding, completely over-the-top monument to wealth—and to the power that money brings.

Hearst Castle is a sprawling compound of structures, constructed over 28 years in a Mediterranean Revival architectural style, set in undeniably magical surroundings. The focal point of the estate is the you-have-to-see-it-to-believe-it **Casa Grande,** a 100-plus-room mansion brimming with priceless art and antiques. Hearst acquired the majority of his vast European collection via New York auction houses, where he bought entire rooms (including walls, ceilings, and floors) and shipped them here. The result is an old-world castle done in a priceless mix-and-match style. You'll see fantastic 400-year-old Spanish and Italian ceilings, enormous 500-year-old fireplace mantels, 16th-century Florentine bedsteads, Renaissance paintings, Flemish tapestries, and innumerable other treasures.

Three opulent "west houses" also contain magnificent works of art. A lavish private movie theater was used to screen first-run films twice nightly—once for employees, and again for the guests and host. And then there are the swimming pools: The Roman-inspired indoor pool has intricate mosaic work, Carrara marble replicas of Greek gods and goddesses, and alabaster globe lamps that create the illusion of moonlight. The breathtaking outdoor Greco-Roman Neptune pool, flanked by marble colonnades that frame the distant sea, is one of the mansion's most memorable features.

In 1957, in exchange for a massive tax write-off, the Hearst Corporation donated the estate to the State of California (while retaining ownership of approximately 80,000 acres); the California Department of Parks and Recreation now administers it as a State Historic Monument.

TOURING THE ESTATE

Hearst Castle can be visited only by guided tour. Four distinct daytime tours are offered on a daily basis, each lasting almost 2 hours. Evening tours are also available most Friday and Saturday evenings during the spring and fall months. Wear comfortable shoes—you'll be walking about 1 1/2 miles, which includes between 150 and 350 steps to climb or descend. (Wheelchair tours are available by calling 805/927-2020 at least 10 days in advance.)

Tour 1, recommended for the first-time visitor, includes part of the gardens, a guesthouse, and the ground floor of the main house—including the movie theater, where you'll see Hearst's home movies.

Tour 2, takes in the upper part of the main house, including Hearst's private suite and study, the library, guest rooms, the kitchen, and the pools.

Tour 3, visits the north wing of Casa Grande, with its 10 guest suites and sitting rooms, pools, and gardens; it deals with construction changes over a 20-year period.

Tour 4, offered April to October only, doesn't go inside La Casa Grande itself; it focuses on the grounds and gardens and includes the wine cellar and two floors of the largest guesthouse.

Tour 5, the evening tour, is available during the spring and fall and is led by docents in period dress. This tour highlights Casa Grande, the pools and gardens, the largest guest cottage, and a 1930s newsreel shown in the theater.

Tours are conducted daily, beginning at 8:20am, except New Year's Day, Thanksgiving, and Christmas Day. Two to six tours leave every hour, depending on the season. Allow 2 hours between starting times if you plan on taking more than one tour. Reservations are recommended and can be made up to 8 weeks in advance. Tickets can be purchased by telephone through **Destinet** (☎ **800/444-4445**). Daytime tours cost $14 for adults, $8 for children 6 to 12. The evening tour costs $25 for adults, $13 for children 6 to 12.

Hearst Castle is located directly on Calif. 1, about 42 miles north of San Luis Obispo and 94 miles south of Monterey. From San Francisco or Monterey, take U.S. 101 south to Paso Robles, then Calif. 46 west to Calif. 1, and Calif. 1 north to the castle. From Los Angeles, take U.S. 101 north to San Luis Obispo, then Calif. 1 north to the castle. Park in the visitor center parking lot; a tour bus will take you the 5 miles up the hill to the estate.

NEARBY TOWNS: CAMBRIA & SAN SIMEON

After driving for close to an hour without passing anything but lush green hills and nature at its most glorious, it's a remarkably quaint surprise to roll into the adorable coastal mini-towns of Cambria and nearby San Simeon. Cambria, in particular, is so charming that the town itself is reason enough to make the drive. With little more than two streets' worth of shops, restaurants, and a handful of B&Bs, Cambria is the perfect place to escape the everyday, enjoy the endless expanses of pristine coastal terrain, and meander through little shops selling local artwork.

Gray whales pass through the area from late December to early February, and for the past few years hundreds of elephant seals have made the shore along Moonstone Beach Drive their year-round playground—much to the delight of locals and nature enthusiasts. Don't approach the seals, but rather watch them from the bluffs. They're wild animals and will bite if molested. The beaches and coves are a wonderful place for humans to frolic as well—stone collectors will be especially enamored by the natural bounty of jade and moonstones mingled with the sand.

WHERE TO STAY

Best Western Cavalier Inn. 9415 Hearst Dr. (Calif. 1), San Simeon, CA 93452. ☎ **800/ 826-8168** or 805/927-4688. 90 rms. TV TEL. $64–$149 double. AE, DISC, MC, V.

"Oceanfront" and "budget" are generally a contradiction, but this family-friendly hotel offers the best of both. Aside from the basics, the rooms are all outfitted with VCRs (video rentals are available next door), refrigerators, computer jacks, hair dryers, and cable TV with HBO; some even have fireplaces. Other bonuses include two outdoor heated pools, an exercise room, two restaurants, a launderette, a shopping center, and a video arcade.

Blue Dolphin Inn. 6470 Moonstone Beach Dr., Cambria, CA 93428. ☎ **805/927-3300.** 18 rms. TV. $75–$225 double. Rates include continental breakfast. AE, MC, V.

Voted in 1996 one of the best moderately priced California accommodations by *Los Angeles Times* readers, the Blue Dolphin offers high-quality rooms along the Cambria coastline. Designed in English country style, the guest rooms brim with frilly opulence and include gas fireplaces, refrigerators, hair dryers, and VCRs. Rooms 111, 112, and 113 have good ocean views from their private patios.

California Seacoast Lodge. 9215 Hearst Dr., San Simeon, CA 93452. ☎ **805/927-3878.** Fax 805/927-1781. 54 rms; 3 suites. June–Sept 15, $85–$95 double; from $185 suite. Sept 16– May, $50–$60 double; from $185 suite. Additional person $5 extra. Rates include continental breakfast. AE, MC, V.

You'll find clean, newly renovated accommodations at this hotel located 3 miles from the entrance to Hearst Castle. There are an array of options here; you can go budget with a basic room, kick in a few extra bucks for one of the most expensive doubles (which comes with king-size bed and fireplace), or splurge on a minisuite that's stocked with a fireplace, Jacuzzi, canopied bed, and French furnishings. There's also a glass-enclosed pool on the premises.

✪ Olallieberry Inn. 2476 Main St., Cambria, CA 93428. ☎ **888/927-3222** or 805/ 927-3222. Fax 805/927-0202. 8 rms, 1 suite. $85–$140 double; $165 cottage suite. Rates include a full breakfast and evening wine and hors d'oeuvres. MC, V.

The minute we walked into this 1873 Greek Revival house located on Cambria's main street, we knew this was our kind of place. The grounds were perfectly manicured but whimsically blooming with flora, the air smelled of baked brie and homemade bread (we'd come during the afternoon wine hour), and guests lounged on

The Central Coast

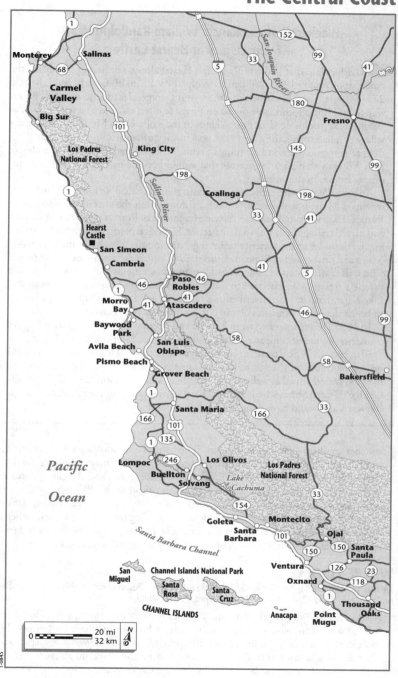

Weekends at the Ranch: William Randolph Hearst & the Legacy of Hearst Castle

The lavish palace that William Randolph Hearst always referred to simply as "the ranch" took root in 1919. William Randolph ("W.R." to his friends) had inherited 275,000 acres from his father, mining baron George Hearst, and was well on his way to building a formidable media empire. He often escaped to a spot known as "Camp Hill" on his newly acquired lands in the Santa Lucia Mountains above the village of San Simeon, the site of boyhood family outings. Complaining that "I get tired of going up there and camping in tents," Hearst hired Paris-trained architect Julia Morgan to design the retreat that would become one of the most famous private homes in the world.

An art collector with indiscriminate taste and inexhaustible funds, Hearst overwhelmed Morgan with interiors and furnishings from the ancestral collections of Europe. Each week, railroad cars carrying fragments of Roman temples, lavish doors and carved ceilings from Italian monasteries, Flemish tapestries, hastily rolled paintings by the old masters, ancient Persian rugs, and antique French furniture arrived—5 tons at a time—in San Simeon. *Citizen Kane,* which depicts a Hearst-like mogul with a similarly excessive estate called Xanadu, has a memorable scene of hoarded priceless treasures warehoused in dusty piles, stretching as far as the eye can see. Like Kane, Hearst, once described as a man with an "edifice complex," purchased so much that only a fraction of what he bought was ever installed in the estate.

In 1925 Hearst separated from his wife and began to spend time in Los Angeles overseeing his movie company, Cosmopolitan Pictures. His principal starlet, Marion Davies, became W.R.'s constant companion and hostess at Hearst Castle; this would be her main role for the rest of his life. The ranch soon became a playground for the Hollywood crowd as well as dignitaries like Winston Churchill and playwright George Bernard Shaw, who is said to have wryly remarked of the estate that "this is the way God would have done it if He had the money."

couches cradling a plate of delectables. The owners have a passion for cooking and gardening (the herb garden was recently featured in *Sunset* magazine), but the decor doesn't fall by the wayside: Victorian floral-and-lace reigns, and the guest rooms are lovingly and individually appointed; each has its private bath, although not all are en suite (some are across or down the hall). Follow the deck off the dining area to the backyard and you'll find rooms in a newer building overlooking a creek—they're remarkably charming and have a fireplace and private deck. The full breakfast—accompanied by olallieberry jam, of course—is guaranteed to impress.

WHERE TO DINE

✪ **Ian's.** 2150 Center St., Cambria. ☎ **805/927-8649.** Reservations highly recommended. Main courses $8–$22. AE, MC, V. Daily 5–9pm. CALIFORNIA.

Ask locals where they'd prefer to dine and they're likely to mention Ian's. Chef Mark Sahaydak's menu, which changes daily, reflects his take on the local bounty. His individual artistry is apparent in dishes like porcini-mushroom ravioli with spicy Italian sausage, and sautéed scallops in a crème fraîche and chardonnay sauce flavored with sun-dried tomatoes. Ian's wine list reflects the very best of local and regional vineyards.

Despite its opulence, Hearst promoted "the ranch" as a casual weekend home. He regularly laid the massive refectory table in the dining room with paper napkins and bottled ketchup and pickles to invoke a rustic camplike atmosphere. Folklore has it that the only formal dinner held here was in honor of President Calvin Coolidge. In Hearst's beautiful library, his priceless collection of ancient Greek pottery—one of the greatest collections of its kind in the world—is arranged casually among the rare volumes, like knickknacks.

The Hollywood crowd would take Hearst's private railway car from Los Angeles to San Luis Obispo, where a fleet of limousines waited to transport them to San Simeon. Those who didn't come by train were treated to a flight on Hearst's private plane from the Burbank airport (MGM head Irving Thalberg and his wife, Norma Shearer, preferred this mode of transportation). Hearst, an avid aviator, had a sizable landing strip built; Charles Lindbergh used it when he flew up for a visit in the summer of 1928.

Oh, if the walls could talk. Atop one of the castle's looming towers are the hexagonal Celestial Suites. One was a favorite of Clark Gable and Carole Lombard, who would be startled out of their romantic slumber by the clamor of 18 carillon bells directly overhead. David Niven, a frequent guest, was one of the unknown number who defied teetotaler Hearst's edict against liquor in private rooms; Niven was called upon more than once to explain the several "empties" under the bed (which Cardinal Richelieu once owned and slept in) in his customary suite.

W.R. and Marion Davies hosted frequent costume parties at the ranch, which were as intricately planned as a movie production. The most legendary, the Circus Party, was held to celebrate W.R.'s 75th birthday on April 29, 1938. Much of Hollywood attended to honor the tycoon, including grand dame Bette Davis—dressed as a bearded lady.

—Stephanie Avnet

Robin's. 4095 Burton Dr., Cambria. ☎ **805/927-5007.** Reservations recommended. Main courses $9–$14. MC, V. Mon–Sat 11am–9pm, Sun 5–9:30pm. ECLECTIC.

It's surprising to find such a culinarily adventuresome restaurant in a small town, but after hearing everyone rave about the salmon bisque appetizer; porcini raviolis with roasted-pepper/cream sauce, fresh spinach, basil, and parmesan; and other flavorful combinations such as Thai prawns in green curry with basmati brown rice, fruit chutney, and chapati, it became clear that both residents and visitors here have discerning palates. Robin's is a restaurant with something for everyone, from exotic dishes from Mexico, Thailand, India, and beyond to more straightforward preparations like a tasty salad or juicy steak and an array of vegetarian dishes. Don't miss dessert—try the espresso-soaked cake with mascarpone mousse and shaved chocolate or vanilla custard bread pudding. Temp your taste buds on-line at **http://www. Cambria-online.com.**

The Sow's Ear Cafe. 2248 Main St., Cambria. ☎ **805/927-4865.** Reservations recommended. Main courses $13–$18; early-bird specials $10.25–$12.25. AE, DISC, MC, V. Daily 5–8 or 9:30pm, depending on business. AMERICAN COUNTRY.

Although the name may be anything but romantic, the dining room definitely is. It's a casually elegant spot, lit just enough to catch the warmth of its rustic wooden surroundings—the perfect place to lean over a bottle of California red, fresh-baked bread, and a hearty plate of beer-spiced shrimp, chicken and dumplings, or baby pork ribs and whisper travel fantasies with a companion. Early dinner specials might consist of honey-lime-barbecued chicken, a fresh catch, and a vegetarian dish.

2 Morro Bay

Don't get the wrong impression when you first enter Morro Bay via U.S. 101. It may look like an industrial motel town accented with one remarkable rock protruding from the shoreline, but aside from its gigantic, absurdly placed oceanfront electrical plant and motel strip, it's just a sleepy seaside town northwest of San Luis Obispo.

Morro Bay is separated from the ocean by a long peninsula of sand dunes, which can reach up to 85 feet high. It's best known for dramatic **Morro Rock,** an enormous egg-shaped monolith that juts out of the water just offshore. Part of a chain of long-extinct volcanoes, the huge domed rock is a winter and fall sanctuary for thousands of migrating birds, including cormorants, pelicans, sandpipers, and the rare peregrine falcon. It's wonderful to watch them from the beach or from a window table of a bay-view restaurant.

Stop here for lunch, a little shopping (it's far more upscale here than in nearby Pismo Beach), and a walk around amazing Morro Rock. Some visitors make Morro Bay their base while visiting the area, but families seem to prefer to retreat to Pismo Beach where there's another great stretch of sandy shoreline.

ESSENTIALS

The **Morro Bay Chamber of Commerce,** 895 Napa St., Suite A1, Morro Bay, CA 93442 (☎ **800/231-0592** or 805/772-4467), offers armfuls of area information. It's open Monday to Friday from 8am to 5pm and on Saturday from 10am to 3pm.

EXPLORING THE AREA

Most visitors come to Morro Bay to ogle **Morro Rock,** the much-photographed Central Coast icon known as the "Gibraltar of the Pacific." It's definitely worth a gander (actually you couldn't miss it if you wanted to) and a few snapshots, but there's more to do in the area beyond this *morro,* or mini-volcanic peak.

BEACHES   Popular **Atascadero State Beach,** just north of Morro Rock, has gentle waves and lovely views. Rest rooms, showers, and dressing rooms are available. Just north of Atascadero is **Morro Strand State Beach,** a long, sandy stretch with normally gentle surf. Rest rooms and picnic tables are available here. Morro Strand has its own campgrounds; for information, call 805/772-2560, or reserve a spot through MISTIX (☎ 800/444-7275).

STATE PARKS   Cabrillo Peak, a morro located in the lovely ✪ **Morro Bay State Park** (☎ **805/772-7434**), makes for a terrific day hike, and offers fantastic 360° views from its summit. There's a faint zigzagging trail, but the best way to reach the top is by bushwhacking straight up the gentle slope—a hike that takes about 2 hours round-trip. To reach the trailhead, take Calif. 1 south and turn left at the Morro Bay State Park / Montana de Oro State Park exit. Follow South Bay Boulevard for three-quarters of a mile, then take the left fork another half a mile to the Cabrillo Peak dirt parking lot, located on your left.

Montana de Oro State Park ("Mountain of Gold") is fondly known as "petite Big Sur" because of its stony cliffs and rugged terrain. There's great swimming at Spooner's Cove and lots of easy hiking trails here, including a number that lead to spectacular coastal vistas or hidden forest streams. The Hazard Reef Trail will take you up on the Morro Bay Sandspit dunes. The park's campground is in the trees, across from the beach. For information, call the park rangers at 805/528-0513 or 805/772-7434, or reserve a spot through MISTIX (☎ 800/444-7275).

IN TOWN   In addition to soaking up the local color at the Embarcadero, visit the **Morro Bay Aquarium** (☎ 805/772-7647), which takes in injured and abandoned sea otters and seals and nurses them back to health, eventually releasing the recovered animals back to the sea. Open daily from 9am to 6pm in summer, to 5pm in winter.

WHERE TO STAY
Baywood Bed & Breakfast Inn. 1370 2nd St., Baywood Park, CA 93042. ☎ **805/ 528-8888.** 5 rms, 10 suites. TV TEL. $80–$110 double; $110–$150 suite. Additional person $15 extra. Rates include breakfast. MC, V.

Rarely will you find such affordable accommodations with so many extras as those offered at the Baywood. Each room at the two-story bayfront inn, located in Baywood Park just south of Morro Bay, is decorated in a distinct theme, so guests can cuddle in a floral and light-wood country cottage, stretch out in a stately 19th-century English affair, or saddle down in a southwestern suite. Every room has a private entrance, gas fireplace, microwave, coffeemaker, and refrigerator stocked with complimentary sodas and snacks; all but a few have ocean views. Breakfast is brought to your room, which tops off an already-romantic and pleasurable experience, or you can dine at the hotel's new Waterside Cafe, which serves breakfast, lunch, dinner, and Sunday brunch.

The Inn at Morro Bay. 60 State Park Rd., Morro Bay, CA 93442. ☎ **800/321-9566** or 805/ 772-5651. Fax 805/772-4779. 96 rms. TV TEL. $95–$265 double (highest rates on weekends). AE, MC, V.

One of the most upscale hotels on the San Luis coast is strategically sandwiched along the shoreline between monumental Morro Bay and an 18-hole golf course. Two-story Cape Cod–style buildings house guests and have contemporary interiors tempered by blond-wood cabinetry, polished brass fittings and beds, and reproduction 19th-century European furnishings. The best rooms enjoy unobstructed views of Morro Rock; those in back face the swimming pool and gardens.

WHERE TO DINE
Hoppe's at 901. 901 Embarcadero. ☎ **805/772-9012.** Reservations recommended. Main courses $12–$22. AE, DISC, MC, V. Mon and Wed–Thurs 5–9pm, Fri–Sun 11am–2pm and 5–9pm. CALIFORNIA.

Ask locals where to go for a special meal in Morro Bay and they're likely to send you to Hoppe's. Not only do diners get a stellar view of Morro Rock, but also an opportunity to savor chef/owner Wilhelm Hoppe's seasonally inspired cuisine. Favorites include the lobster ravioli appetizer with red curry in a peanut sauce or such entrees as smoked sea scallop lasagne with proscuitto and sun-dried tomatoes or roasted duck breast with tamarind, ginger, and mango.

3 San Luis Obispo

Because the actual town of San Luis Obispo is not visible from U.S. 101, even many Californians don't know that it's more than a McDonald's-and-gasoline stopover on the way to Southern California. But its secret location is exactly what keeps "San Luis" the quaint little Central Coast jewel that it is.

San Luis Obispo is neatly tucked into the mountains about halfway between San Francisco and Los Angeles and is surrounded by green pristine mountain ranges and

filled with college kids and friendly locals. The atmosphere is small-town casual—
the perfect place to meander and ponder a simpler, more carefree existence.

The town grew up around an 18th-century mission, and its dozens of historical
landmarks, quaint Victorian homes, shops, and restaurants are its primary attractions.
Today it's still quaint, almost undiscovered, and best ventured on foot. It also makes
a good base for an extensive exploration of the region as a whole. To the west of town,
a short drive away, are some of the state's prettiest swimming beaches; turning east,
you enter the Central Coast's wine country, home to dozens of respectable wineries.

ESSENTIALS

GETTING THERE   U.S. 101, one of the state's primary north-south roadways,
runs right through San Luis Obispo; it's the fastest land route here from anywhere.
If you're driving down along the coast, Calif. 1 is the way to go for its natural beauty
and oceanfront cliffs. If you're entering the city from the east, take Calif. 46 or 41.

VISITOR INFORMATION   The **San Luis Obispo Visitors Center,** 1039 Chorro
St., Suite E, San Luis Obispo, CA 93401 (☎ **805/781-2777;** fax 805/543-1255),
is located downtown, between Monterey and Higuera streets. This helpful office is
one of the best-run visitors bureaus we've ever come across. Drop in to ask questions
and to pick up maps, a calendar of events, or specialized information on local sights.
Ask for a "Path of History" map, which details many of the sights listed below. The
visitors bureau can also make reservations and issue tickets for Hearst Castle at San
Simeon. The center is open Tuesday to Friday from 8am to 5pm, and Saturday to
Monday from 10am to 5pm.

ORIENTATION   San Luis Obispo is about 10 miles inland, at the junction of
Calif. 1 and U.S. 101. The downtown is laid out in a grid, roughly centered around
the historic mission and its Mission Plaza (see below). Most of the main tourist sights
are around the mission, within the small triangle created by U.S. 101 and Santa Rosa
and Marsh streets.

EXPLORING THE TOWN

Definitely make a pit stop at the perpetually pink **Madonna Inn,** 100 Madonna Rd.
(off U.S. 101; ☎ **805/543-3300**), if for no other reason than to use its unique public restrooms (the men's has a waterfall urinal; the women's is a barrage of crimson and pink). Every over-the-top inch of this place is an exercise in excess, from
the dining room, complete with pink leather booths, pink table linens, and colored
sugar that's—you guessed it—piquantly pink, to the rock-walled, cave-like guest
rooms.

The Ah Louis Store. 800 Palm St. (at Chorro St.). ☎ **805/543-4332.** Usually Mon–Sat
2–5:30pm, but hours vary.

This establishment, practically unchanged since its opening in 1874, is still in the
hands of the original Cantonese family owners. Entrepreneurial Mr. Ah Louis was
lured to California by gold fever in 1856; emerging from the mines empty-handed,
he soon began a lucrative career as a labor contractor, hiring and organizing Chinese
crews that would build the railroad; later he opened this store. Ah Louis also founded
one of the country's first brickyards, built county roads, ran a vegetable and flower-
seed business, bred racehorses, and oversaw eight farms.

Today you can chat with Ah Louis's heir, Howard, while you browse through the
clutter of Asian merchandise. Ask for a free brochure detailing the family's history.
Hours are somewhat irregular, though, since Howard often just closes up and goes
fishing.

❂ **Farmer's Market.** Higuera St. (between Osos and Nipomo sts.). Thurs 6:30–9pm.

If you're lucky enough to be in town on a Thursday, there's no better activity than taking an evening stroll down Higuera Street, when the state's largest weekly street fair fills four downtown city blocks. You'll find much more here than fresh-picked produce—there's an ever-changing array of street entertainment, open-pit barbecues, food stands, and market stalls selling fresh flowers, cider, and other seasonal goodies. Surrounding stores stay open until 9pm.

Mission San Luis Obispo de Tolosa. 782 Monterey St. ☎ **805/543-6850.** Free admission ($1 donation requested). Summer, daily 9am–5pm (sometimes later); winter, daily 9am–4pm.

Founded by Father Junípero Serra in 1772, California's fifth mission was built with adobe bricks by Native American Chumash people. The mission remains one of the prettiest and most interesting structures in the Franciscan chain. For further details on the mission, see "The Missions of the Central Coast" driving tour in Chapter 5.

Mission Plaza, a pretty garden with brick paths and park benches fronting a meandering creek, still functions as San Luis Obispo's town square. It's the focal point for local festivities and activities, from live concerts to poetry readings and dance and theater productions. Check at the visitors center (see "Essentials," above) to find out what's on when you're in town.

At Mission Plaza you'll also find the **San Luis Obispo Art Center** (☎ 805/543-8562), whose three galleries display and sell an array of California-made art. Admission is free.

San Luis Obispo Children's Museum. 1010 Nipomo St. ☎ **805/544-KIDS.** Admission $3 adults and children 2 and older, free for kids under 2. July–Aug, Thurs–Tues 10am–5pm; Sept–June, Mon and Sat 10am–5pm, Thurs–Fri 1–5pm, Sun noon–5pm.

This terrific children's museum features a playhouse of interesting manipulatives for toddlers, an authentic reproduction of a Native American Chumash cave dwelling, a music room, a computer corner, a pint-sized bank and post office, and more. Special events like mask making, sing-alongs, and stage makeup classes are scheduled regularly; call for a current schedule.

San Luis Obispo County Historical Museum. 696 Monterey St. ☎ **805/543-0638.** Free admission. Wed–Sun 10am–4pm.

This little museum, run by the San Luis Obispo County Historical Society in a Carnegie library, houses an extensive research library and historical photograph collection. The permanent exhibit includes artifacts from Native American Chumash and early European settlers.

SHOPPING

Don't expect New York's Fifth Avenue here, but rather a few charming boutiques (among many uninteresting ones) scattered throughout town. The best place to exercise your credit/charge cards is on the downtown streets surrounding the mission, specifically the 5 blocks of **Higuera Street** from Nipomo to Osos streets, as well as a short stretch of **Monterey Street** between Chorro and Osos streets.

On Higuera Street, check out **Hands Gallery,** 777 Higuera St. (☎ 805/543-1921), which has a playful bright collection of local and internationally created art. Trinkets range from glass candies to vases, jewelry, and ceramics and can be viewed or bought Monday to Wednesday from 10am to 6pm, Thursday from 10am to 9pm, Friday and Saturday from 10am to 8pm, and Sunday from 11am to 5pm.

You might also want to check out **The Creamery,** 570 Higuera St., at Nipomo Street (☎ **805/541-0106**), which functioned as one of the state's most important milk-producing centers for more than 40 years. Restored, remodeled, and opened as a shopping and restaurant mall, the complex is centered around the creamery's old cooling tower. Antique freezer doors, overhead workhouse lights, and milk-can lamps pointedly remind visitors of the structure's original function.

Central Coast wineries are producing some excellent vintages, some of which are available for tasting at the **Central Coast Wine Room,** 10 Old Creamery Rd., Harmony (☎ **805/927-7337**). If you don't mind wading through the mediocre ones, you'll find some excellent selections from Paso Robles and the Edna Valley that compete favorably with those of Napa Valley. The tasting room is open daily from 11am to 5pm; tastings are $1.

WHERE TO STAY

In addition to what's listed below, there's a pristine branch of **Holiday Inn Express** (☎ 800/465-4329 or 805/544-8600); the **Best Western Olive Tree** (☎ 800/528-1234 or 805/544-2800), offering good-value apartment-style accommodations; and a great budget choice, reliable **Motel 6** (☎ 800/4-MOTEL 6, or 805/541-6992).

Ⓢ Adobe Inn. 1473 Monterey St., San Luis Obispo, CA 93401. ☎ **800/676-1588** or 805/549-0321. Fax 805/549-0383. 15 rms, 8 with kitchenette but no stove. TV TEL. $45–$95 double. Additional person $6 extra. Rates include breakfast. Seasonal discounts available. AE, DISC, MC, V.

Okay, it's not *actually* adobe, or even remotely close for that matter, but Michael and Ann Dinshaw have taken this old motor inn and given it a creatively homey atmosphere at unbeatable prices. Each spotless accommodation is named after a cactus, has a corresponding hand-painted sign on its door, and is individually decorated in southwestern style with quirky additions such as playfully painted cupboards or a windowside reading nook. Breakfast is served in a clean dining area that unfortunately faces the street, but coffee snobs will delight in a cup of locally roasted coffee. Plants adorn the inn's exterior and there's a mini-cactus garden and fountain beyond the parking lot. Michael or Ann is usually on-site and go out of their way to make guests happy and offer a slew of packages that explore the surrounding areas and attractions. This is a great bargain, all in all.

Apple Farm Inn. 2015 Monterey St., San Luis Obispo, CA 93401. ☎ **800/255-2040** or 805/544-2040. Fax 805/546-9495. 69 rms. A/C TV TEL. $95–$200 double. AE, DISC, MC, V.

Ultra-popular, the Apple Farm Inn is a peaceful getaway in a Disney plantation kind of way. Every square inch of the immaculate Victorian-style farmhouse is cheek-pinchingly cute with floral wallpaper, fresh flowers, and sugar-sweet colorful touches. No two rooms are alike, though all have a gas fireplace, large well-equipped bathroom, pine antiques, lavish country decor, and either a canopy, four-poster, or brass bed.

Some bedrooms open onto cozy turreted sitting areas with romantic window seats; others have bay windows and a view of San Luis Creek, where a working mill spins its huge wheel to power an apple press. An outdoor heated swimming pool and Jacuzzi are open year-round. Service here is outstanding and includes nightly turndown and a morning wake-up knock, delivered with complimentary coffee or tea and a newspaper. Other features include complimentary cribs and train and airport shuttle service. Cider is always on hand in the lobby.

⑤ Lamp Lighter Inn. 1604 Monterey St. (at Grove St.), San Luis Obispo, CA 93401. ☎ **800/ 547-7787** or 805/547-7777. Fax 805/547-7787. 29 rms, 11 suites. A/C TV TEL. $45–$80 double; from $69 suite. Rates include continental breakfast. AE, DISC, MC, V.

Even if you're not looking for a bargain, you'll be pleasantly surprised with the value of your dollar at this motel. The rooms boast traditional motel style and colors but look brand new, are squeaky clean, and have firm mattresses. Other bonuses are coffeemakers, refrigerators (except in three rooms), and a heated pool and whirlpool. Breakfast is served in the lobby by an amazingly enthusiastic staff.

◐ Madonna Inn. 100 Madonna Rd. (off U.S. 101), San Luis Obispo, CA 93405. ☎ **800/ 543-9666** or 805/543-3000. Fax 805/543-1800. 109 rms, 25 suites. TV TEL. $87–$180 double; from $145 suite. MC, V.

This one you've got to see for yourself. The creative imaginations of owners Alex and Phyllis Madonna gave birth to the wildest—and most superfluously garish—fantasy world this side of Graceland. The only decor consistency throughout the hotel is its color scheme, which is perpetual pink. Beyond that, it's a free-for-all. Every nook and cranny has been built to delight—even the men's room has a rock-waterfall urinal and clam-shell sinks. Each room offers a different thematic fantasy far beyond a creative paint job. One room features a trapezoidal bed—it's 5 feet long on one side and 6 feet long on the other. "Rock" rooms with zebra- or tiger-patterned bedspreads and stonelike showers and fireplaces conjure up thoughts of a Flintstones' Playboy palace. There are also blue rooms, red rooms, over-the-top Spanish, Italian, Irish, Alps, Currier and Ives, Native American, Swiss, and hunting rooms. The coffee shop, dining room, and two cocktail lounges are also outlandishly ornate. Even if you don't stay here, stop by and check it out.

WHERE TO DINE

Buona Tavola. 1037 Monterey St. ☎ **805/545-8000.** Reservations recommended. Main courses $8.25–$17. DC, DISC, MC, V. Mon–Thurs 11:30am–2:30pm and 5:30–9:30pm, Fri 11:30am–2:30pm and 5:30–10pm, Sat 5:30–10pm, Sun 5:30–9:30pm. NORTHERN ITALIAN.

While most eateries in town are burger-and-sandwich casual, Buona Tavola offers well-prepared Italian food in a more upscale environment. It's still the kind of place where you can stroll in wearing jeans, but the dining room with checkerboard floors and original artwork is warmer and more intimate than other spots in town. There's also backyard-terrace seating where you can enjoy your meal surrounded by magnolia, ficus, and grapevines. The menu boasts a number of salads on the antipasti list. Favorite pastas include agnolotti de scampi allo zafferand, which is homemade, filled with scampi, and served in a cream-saffron sauce. The spaghettini scoglio d'oro comes with lobster, sea scallops, clams, mussels, shrimp, and diced tomatoes in a saffron sauce. Others opt for the pollo scamiciato alla Vinaggia—a grilled boneless chicken marinated with garlic and herbs and served with a rosemary-mustard sauce. Don't worry—once you get through trying to pronounce your desired dish, the rest of the evening should be both relaxing and satisfying.

Cafe Big Sky. 1121 Broad St. ☎ **805/545-5401.** Main courses $6–$8 at lunch, $6–$11 at dinner; salads and sandwiches $5–$6; breakfast $4–$6. MC, V. Mon–Sat 7am–10pm, Sun 8am–4pm. AMERICAN.

The folk-artsy fervor of San Luis really shines at this southwestern mirage where local art, a blue star-studded ceiling, and a dragon canoe hanging in midair surround diners who come for fresh, healthy food. Most everything on the menu, like shrimp tacos and herb-infused roasted chicken, is created with local ingredients. Lighter meals, such as black-bean vegetarian chili, charcoal-broiled eggplant sandwich, and white bean and yellowtail tuna salad are equally inventive and tasty. The excellent breakfasts include buttermilk pancakes, a jambalaya omelet, turkey hash, and black-bean huevos rancheros.

SLO Brewing Company. 1119 Garden St. ☎ **805/543-1843.** Reservations accepted. Main courses $6–$9. AE, MC, V. Mon–Wed 11:30am–10:30pm, Thurs–Sat 11:30am–12:30am, Sun noon–5pm. AMERICAN.

This brew pub's homemade beer has created such a buzz that it's now not only locally downed but also nationally distributed. Three distinct variations—Pale Ale, Amber Ale, and Porter—are brewed from all-natural ingredients and wash down the menu's burgers and fried-food fare perfectly. Join the festive collegiate crowd at night, stop by for lunch, or check the place out on the Web at **http://www.slobrew.com.**

🅢 **Thai Classic.** 1101 Higuera St. (at Osos). ☎ **805/541-2025.** Reservations recommended on weekends. Most dishes $6–11. DISC, MC, V. Sun–Thurs 11am–10pm, Fri–Sat 11am–11pm. THAI.

It's not much to look at, that's for sure, but stare past the cheesy white booths and plain walls and focus on what's coming out of the kitchen, and you won't be sorry you came. There's an extensive vegetarian selection and trademark Thai appetizers such as satay with peanut and cucumber sauces, pahd Thai, and spring rolls. Locals favor the pineapple fried rice with shrimp, chicken, and cashews as well as the curry plates, all of which should be eaten family style. Lunch specials on weekdays are a real bargain at $3 to $4 for soup, salad, spring roll, fried wonton, steamed rice, and one of 21 main courses.

4 Pismo Beach

Just outside San Luis Obispo, Pismo's 23-mile-stretch of prime California beach makes flip-flops the shoes of choice, and most clothing shops feature the latest in surf fashion. It's all about beach life here, so bring your board, a good book, or if nothing else, your bathing suit.

If building sand castles or tanning isn't your idea of a tantalizing time, explore isolated dunes, cliff-sheltered tide pools, and old pirate coves. Bring your dog (Fido's welcome here) and play an endless game of fetch or go fishing—it's permitted from Pismo Beach Pier, which also offers arcade entertainment, bowling, and billiards. Pismo is also the only beach in the area that allows all-terrain vehicles on the dunes.

Unfortunately, the town itself consists of little more than tourist shops and surf-and-turf restaurants. San Luis Obispo is a far more charming place to stay in this area, but if you want a few days on a beautiful beach at half the price of an oceanfront room in Santa Barbara, Pismo is a perfect choice.

ESSENTIALS

The **Pismo Beach Chamber of Commerce and Visitors Bureau,** 581 Dolliver St., Pismo Beach, CA 93449 (☎ **800/443-7778** in California, or 805/773-4382), offers free brochures and information on local attractions, lodging, and dining. The office is open Monday to Friday from 9:30am to 5pm, on Saturday from 10am to 4pm, and on Sunday from noon to 4pm. You can peruse their information on the Internet at **http://webmill.com/pismo.**

WHAT TO SEE & DO
SEEING THE BUTTERFLIES

From late November to February, tens of thousands of migrating monarch butterflies take up residence in the area's eucalyptus and Monterey pine tree groves. The colorful butterflies form dense clusters on the trees, each hanging with its wings over the one below it, providing warmth and shelter for the entire group. During the monarchs' stay, naturalists at **Pismo State Beach** conduct 45-minute narrative walks every Saturday and Sunday at 11am and 2pm (call 805/772-2694 for tour information). The majority of the "butterfly trees" are located on Calif. 1, between Pismo Beach and Grover Beach, to the south.

BEACHES

Beaches in Pismo are exceptionally wide, making them some of the best in the state for sunning and playing. The beach north of Grand Avenue is popular with families, and well suited to jogging and strolling. North of Wadsworth Street, the coast becomes dramatically rugged as it rambles northward to Shell Beach and Pirates Cove. Some areas of the beach are open to all-terrain vehicles and automobiles.

OUTDOOR ACTIVITIES

CLAMMING Pismo Beach was one of the most famous places in America for clamming, so much so that the clam population was depleted almost to extinction. Government intervention has saved the clams, and you're now permitted to pick them up in limited numbers directly from the sand. Clams must measure at least $4^{1}/_{2}$ inches in diameter, and catches are limited to 10. You'll need to dig down about a foot to find them. Clam forks can be rented at **Pismo Bob's True Value Hardware**, 930 Price St. (☎ **805/773-6245**), for $5 per day.

FISHING No license is required to drop a line from Pismo Pier. Catches here are largely bottom fish like red snapper and ling cod. There's a bait-and-tackle shop on the pier.

HIKING You can trek along the **Guadalupe-Nipomo Dunes** year-round. This 18-mile strip of coastline 20 minutes south of Pismo has the highest beach dunes in the West. It's a great place for hiking and observing native plants and birds, including the California brown pelican, one of 200 species that migrate here each year.

HORSEBACK RIDING **Livery Stables,** 1207 Silver Spur Place (☎ **805/489-8100**), in Oceano (about 5 minutes south of Pismo Beach), is one of the very few places in the state that rents horses for riding on the beach. These are not guided rides; you rent the horses for $15 per hour and go at your own pace.

WHERE TO STAY

The Clamdigger. 150 Hinds Ave., Pismo Beach, CA 93449. ☎ **805/773-2342.** 10 studio cabins, 4 motel suites, 1 one-bedroom cottage. TV. $50–$75 cabin; $60–$90 suite; from $110 cottage. 7th night free if staying 6. AE, DISC, DC, MC, V.

Who cares about blow dryers, VCRs, and plush new furnishings? This adorable cluster of cabins just south of the pier offers a true old-style California beach vacation. Little more than a one-room shack on the beach (okay, it does have a bathroom), each cabin welcomes you with a stained-glass ship on the door, a queen-size bed, cable TV, a kitchenette with gas stove, a coffeemaker (bring your own ground beans), and basic furniture. The cottage has a queen-size bed and a hide-a-bed, a private deck, and sleeps up to four. The motel suites sleep up to six. The place has some history, too— Valentino stayed here when he filmed on location in the 1920s.

SeaVenture Resort. 100 Ocean View Ave., Pismo Beach, CA 93449. ☎ **800/662-5545** or 805/773-4994. Fax 805/773-0924. 50 rms. MINIBAR TV TEL. $99–$249 double. Rates include continental breakfast. Take U.S. 101 to the Price St. exit and turn west onto Ocean View (at the beach). AE, DC, DISC, MC, V.

If luxury accommodations overlooking the beach and an outdoor spa on your private deck sound like heaven to you, you don't have to die to get there, just stay at SeaVenture, a brand-new resort providing the most luxurious accommodations in Pismo. Most units here look directly onto the beach. Once in your room, you need only to drag your tired traveling feet through the thick forest-green carpeting, past the white country furnishings, and turn on your gas fireplace to begin what promises to be a relaxing stay. Then either opt for renting a movie from the video library, scheduling a massage, or simply bathing your weary bones in your own outdoor hydrotherapy spa tub. With the beach right outside your door, there's not much more you could ask for—although there *is*, in fact, more provided: a wet bar, refrigerator, coffeemaker, continental breakfast delivered to your room, and a pool and restaurant on the premises. Most rooms have ocean views and many have a private balcony overlooking the beach. Other bonuses include room service from 4 to 10pm, massage, and laundry.

Surf Motel. 250 Main St., Pismo Beach, CA 39449. ☎ **800/472-7873** or 805/773-2070. 33 rms. TV TEL. $65–$85 double (lower on off-season weekends). Rates include continental breakfast. MC, V.

Strategically located just half a block from the beach, the Surf Motel is a good bet if you want basic, clean accommodations. All rooms have refrigerators; some have fully stocked kitchenettes. The indoor swimming pool is open year-round. Unless you prefer modern and new motel amenities, however, you'll get more of Pismo's true flavor at the rustic oceanfront cottages of the Clamdigger.

WHERE TO DINE

PierSide Seafood. In the Boardwalk Plaza Mall, 175 Pomeroy St. ☎ **805/773-4411.** Reservations recommended on weekends. Main courses $9–$20. Summer, daily 10am–11pm; winter, daily 11am–9pm. AE, DISC, MC, V. AMERICAN.

If the food here is simply decent and the menu offers the same fare as everyone else in town (surf and turf), why bother dining here? Well, first of all, this two-story restaurant is practically on top of Pismo Pier, which provides it an unparalleled dining view. Second, the decor is fun: Mermaids and surfboards hang overhead and an array of trinkets and an ocean mural keep the eye wandering and interested throughout the meal. Finally, on a sunny day there's no better place to kick back than at one of the outdoor umbrella-topped tables. The place is *tourist maximus*, but few places here aren't.

Rosa's Italian Restaurant. 491 Price St. ☎ **805/773-0551.** Reservations recommended on weekends. Main courses $8–$15. AE, DISC, MC, V. Mon–Fri 11:30am–2pm and 4–9:30pm, Sat–Sun 4–10pm. ITALIAN.

Look beyond the boring decor and you'll find that Rosa's is the finest Italian-American restaurant in town. It ain't Italy, but fresh bread is made on the premises, as are the ravioli, canneloni, and other pastas. Veal parmesan, chicken cacciatore, and the fresh seafood dishes are dependably tasty. There are a few tables on a small heated patio, and though there's no ocean view, it'll be a welcome change from the overly abundant local surf-and-turf fare.

Splash Cafe. 197 Pomeroy St. (near Pismo Pier). ☎ **805/773-4653.** Most items $2.50–$5.75. No credit cards. Daily 10am–8pm. AMERICAN.

This beachy burger stand, with a short menu and just a few tables, gets high marks for its excellent clam chowder, served in a sourdough bread bowl. Fish and chips, burgers, hot dogs, and sandwiches are also available.

5 En Route to Santa Barbara: The Santa Ynez Valley

The compact and beautiful Santa Ynez Valley (surrounded by mountains of the same name) is located between San Luis Obispo and Santa Barbara. The valley is home to five small towns: Buellton, Santa Ynez, Los Olivos, Ballard, and Solvang, the region's top tourist draw.

SOLVANG

Founded in 1911 by Danish-Americans originally intent on preserving their heritage, the old-country town of Solvang ("sunny valley" in Danish) has prostituted its Scandanavian heritage into a popular and tacky tourist trap. The "quaint" village now looks as if Disney did Denmark, with white-and-blue fringed buildings housing hokey import shops and numerous pancake and pastry restaurants. Solvang's immense popularity has cost the town its charm. A trip here wouldn't ordinarily be worth going out of your way for, except that Solvang's bakeries are still among California's very best. Accordingly, it's worth a detour for lunch.

From U.S. 101 south, turn east (left) onto Calif. 246 at Buellton; it's a well-marked 20-minute drive along an extremely scenic two-lane road. From Santa Barbara, take U.S. 101 north to Calif. 154, a truly breathtaking 45-minute drive over San Marcos Pass.

Old Mission Santa Ines. 1760 Mission Dr., Solvang. ☎ **805/688-4815.** Free admission, but $3 donation requested. Summer, Mon–Sat 9am–7pm, Sun 1:30–7pm; winter, Mon–Sat 9am–4:30pm, Sun 1:30–4:30pm. From downtown Solvang, take Calif. 246 1 mile east to Mission Dr.

Founded in 1804, this perfectly restored mission is by far the oldest structure in town. The main building contains early Native American artifacts and relics once belonging to the missionaries. Like many other missions, Santa Ines still maintains an active congregation. The church, chapel, museum, and surrounding grounds are open to the public.

A BALD EAGLE HABITAT

On Calif. 154 between Solvang and Santa Barbara, the ✪ **Cachuma Lake Recreation Area** surrounds Cachuma Lake, which is both the primary town reservoir for Santa Barbara and a particularly beautiful habitat for the American bald eagle. In the winter months dozens of bald eagles migrate here from as far north as Alaska, where food is plentiful for them and human development is minimal. Over the last few years some have chosen to remain at Cachuma to raise their young. Perching on treetops and branches overlooking the water, the eagles hunt for trout and waterfowl. Other migratory birds also come in large numbers, including loons, white pelicans, and Canadian geese.

You can simply drive into the recreation area and go birding on your own, or you can board the *Osprey* (☎ **805/568-2460**), a 48-foot boat with viewing platforms at both bow and stern. Two-hour Eagle Cruises are offered November to February, Wednesday to Sunday at 10am; additional tours are offered on Friday and Saturday at 2pm. Wildlife Cruises, from which you can view deer, bobcats, and mountain lions, are offered March to October on Friday at 3pm, on Saturday at 10am and 3pm, and on Sunday at 10am. All cruises cost $10 for adults, $5 for children 11 and under; reservations are recommended. Contact the **Santa Barbara County Parks Department,** Star Route, Santa Barbara, CA 93105 (☎ **805/688-4658**).

WHERE TO STAY

There's no real reason to stay here, since there are so many great places to stay just to the north and south, but if you've just got to wake up here to eat more pastries, try Solvang's comfortable **Royal Scandinavian Inn** (☎ 800/624-5572 or 805/688-8000) or the good-value **Motel 6** (☎ 800/4-MOTEL6 or 805/688-7797), just west of Solvang in Buellton.

6 Santa Barbara

Between the Santa Ynez Mountains and the Pacific, charming, spoiled Santa Barbara is coddled by wooded mountains, caressed by baby breakers, and sheltered from tempestuous seas by rocky offshore islands. And it's just far enough from Los Angeles to make the big city seem at once remote and accessible. There are few employment opportunities and real estate is expensive here, so demographics have favored college students and rich retirees, thought of by the locals as the "almost wed and almost dead."

Downtown Santa Barbara is distinctive for its Spanish-Mediterranean architecture; all the structures sport matching red-tile roofs. But it wasn't always this way. Santa Barbara had a thriving Native American Chumash population for hundreds, if not thousands, of years. The European era began in the late 18th century, around a Presidio (fort) that's been reconstructed in its original spot. The earliest architectural hodgepodge was destroyed in 1925 by a powerful earthquake that leveled the business district. Out of the rubble rose the Spanish-Mediterranean town of today, a stylish planned community that continues to rigidly enforce its strict building codes.

ESSENTIALS

GETTING THERE   U.S. 101 runs right through Santa Barbara; it's the fastest and most direct route from north or south (2 hours from Los Angeles, 6 hours from San Francisco).

The **Santa Barbara Municipal Airport** (☎ 805/967-7111) is located in Goleta, about 10 minutes north of downtown Santa Barbara. Airlines serving Santa Barbara include **American Eagle** (☎ 800/433-7300), **Skywest/Delta** (☎ 800/453-9417), **United** (☎ 800/241-6522), and **USAir Express** (☎ 800/428-4322). **Yellow Cab** (☎ 805/965-5111) and other metered taxis line up outside the terminal; the fare is about $20 to downtown.

Amtrak (☎ 800/USA-RAIL) offers daily service to Santa Barbara. Trains arrive and depart from the **Santa Barbara Rail Station,** 209 State St. (☎ 805/963-1015). Fares can be as low as $20 from Los Angeles.

VISITOR INFORMATION   The **Santa Barbara Visitor Information Center,** 1 Santa Barbara St., Santa Barbara, CA 93101 (☎ **805/965-3021,** or 800/927-4688 to order a free destination guide), is on the ocean, at the corner of Cabrillo Street. The staff distribute maps, literature, an events calendar, and excellent advice. Be sure to ask for their handy guide to places of interest and public parking. The office is open Monday to Saturday from 9am to 4pm and on Sunday from 10am to 4pm; it closes 1 hour earlier in winter and 1 hour later in July and August. A second **Visitor Information Center,** open Monday to Friday from 9am to 5pm, is located at 504 State St., in the heart of downtown. Be sure to pick up a free copy of *Things to See and Do* at one of the offices.

Also make sure you pick up a copy of *The Independent,* an excellent free weekly paper with a comprehensive listing of events. It's available in shops and from sidewalk racks around town.

Downtown Santa Barbara

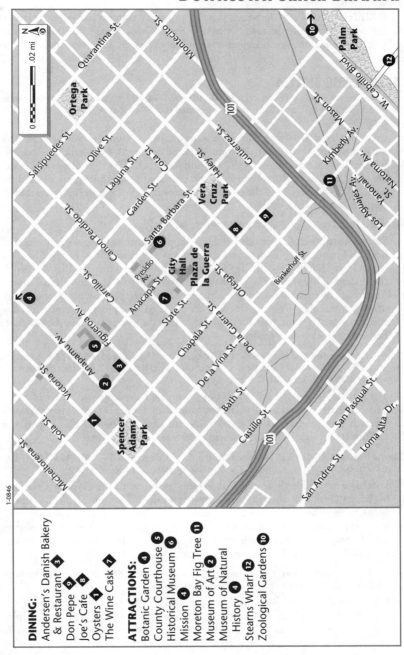

DINING:

Andersen's Danish Bakery
& Restaurant **3**
Don Pepe **9**
Joe's Cafe **8**
Oysters **1**
The Wine Cask **7**

ATTRACTIONS:

Botanic Garden **4**
County Courthouse **5**
Historical Museum **6**
Mission **4**
Moreton Bay Fig Tree **11**
Museum of Art **2**
Museum of Natural
History **4**
Stearns Wharf **12**
Zoological Gardens **10**

1-0846

385

ORIENTATION   State Street, the city's primary commercial thoroughfare, is the geographic center of town. It ends at Stearns Wharf and Cabrillo Street; the latter runs along the ocean and separates the city's beaches from touristy hotels and restaurants.

SEEING THE SIGHTS

County Courthouse. 1100 Anacapa St. ☎ **805/962-6464.** Free admission. Mon–Fri 8am–5pm, Sat–Sun and holidays 10am–5pm. Free guided tours Mon–Sat at 2pm, plus Wed and Fri at 10:30am.

Even murderers are afforded exquisite surroundings in stunning Santa Barbara, for the courthouse is the most flamboyant example of Spanish-Mediterranean architecture in the entire city. Built in 1929 to mimic a much older style, the ornate building is Santa Barbara's literal and figurative centerpiece. There are great views of the ocean, the mountains, and the city's terra-cotta–tile roofs from the observation deck atop the clock tower.

Moreton Bay Fig Tree. Chapala and Montecito sts.

Santa Barbara's best-known tree has a branch spread that would cover half a football field, and its roots run under more than an acre of ground. It is, hands down, the largest of its kind in the world. It's so broad, in fact, that an estimated 10,000 people could stand in its shade. Planted in 1877, it's a native of Moreton Bay in eastern Australia. The tree is related to both the fig and the rubber tree, but produces neither figs nor rubber. Once in danger of being leveled for a proposed gas station, and later threatened by excavation for nearby U.S. 101, the revered tree now shelters Santa Barbara's homeless community.

Santa Barbara Botanic Garden. 1212 Mission Canyon Rd. ☎ **805/682-4726.** Admission $3 adults, $2 children 13–19 and seniors 65 and over, $1 children 5–12, free for children 4 and under. Mon–Fri 9am–5pm, Sat–Sun 9am–6pm.

The gardens, about 1¹/₂ miles north of the mission, encompass 65 acres of native trees, shrubs, cacti, and wildflowers, and more than 5 miles of trails. They're at their aromatic peak just after spring showers. Docent tours are offered daily at 2pm, with additional tours on Thursday, Saturday, and Sunday at 10:30am.

Santa Barbara Historical Museum. 136 E. De La Guerra St. ☎ **805/966-1601.** Free admission, but donations requested. Tues–Sat 10am–5pm, Sun noon–5pm.

Local-lore exhibits include late 19th-century paintings of the California missions by Edwin Deakin; a 16th-century carved Spanish coffer from Majorca, home of Junípero Serra; and objects from the Chinese community that once flourished here, including a magnificent carved shrine from the turn of the century. A knowledgeable docent leads an interesting free tour every Wednesday, Saturday, and Sunday at 1:30pm.

✪ Santa Barbara Mission. Laguna and Los Olivos sts. ☎ **805/682-4713** or 805/682-4151. Admission $3 adults, free for children 15 and under. Daily 9am–5pm.

Established in 1786 by Father Junípero Serra and built by the Chumash Indians, this is a very rare example in physical form of the blending of Indian and Hispanic spirituality. Called the "Queen of the Missions" for its twin bell towers and graceful beauty, this hilltop mission overlooks the town and the Channel Islands beyond. Brochures are available in six languages, and docent-guided tours can be arranged in advance ($1 extra per person). See "The Missions of the Central Coast" driving tour in Chapter 4 for further details.

Santa Barbara Museum of Art. 1130 State St. ☎ **805/963-4364.** Admission $4 adults, $3 seniors 65 and over, $1.50 children 6–16, free for children 5 and under, free for everyone Thurs and the first Sun of each month. Tues–Wed and Fri–Sat 11am–5pm, Thurs 11am–9pm, Sun noon–5pm.

A trip here feels like an exclusive visit to the private galleries of a wealthy art collector. Works by Monet and other mid-quality oils by Dalí, Picasso, Matisse, Chagall, and Rousseau are displayed on a rotating basis in rooms that, for the most part, are ample, airy, and well lit. Quantitatively, the museum's strengths lie in early 20th-century western American paintings and 19th- and 20th-century Asian art. Qualitatively, the best are the antiquities and Chinese ceramics collections. Many pieces are often on loan to other museums, but good temporary exhibits show a high degree of reciprocity. Some awkward arrangements don't always make sense, and lighting could be improved on the placards. For the most part, though, SBMA is a jewel of a museum. Free docent-led tours are given Tuesday to Sunday at 1pm. Focus tours are held on Wednesday and Saturday at noon. A new wing to be completed in 1997 is slated to include more galleries, a larger gift shop, and a cafe.

Santa Barbara Museum of Natural History. 2559 Puesta del Sol Rd. (2 blocks uphill from the mission). ☎ **805/682-4711.** Admission $5 adults, $4 seniors and teens, $3 children. Mon–Sat 9am–5pm, Sun and holidays 10am–5pm.

This museum focuses on the study and interpretation of Pacific Coast natural history, which includes mammals, birds, marine life, plants, and insects and displays ranging from fossil ferns to the complete skeleton of a blue whale. Native American history is emphasized in exhibits including basketry, textiles, and a full-size replica of a Chumash canoe. An adjacent planetarium projects sky shows every Saturday and Sunday.

Santa Barbara Zoological Gardens. 500 Ninos Dr. ☎ **805/962-5339,** or 805/962-6310 for a recording. Admission $5 adults, $3 seniors and children 2–12, free for children under 2. Daily 10am–5pm (last admission is 1 hour before closing). Closed Thanksgiving and Christmas Day.

When you're driving around the bend on Cabrillo Beach Boulevard, look up—you might spot the head of a giraffe poking up through the palms. This is a thoroughly charming, pint-sized place, where all 700 animals can be seen in about 30 minutes. Most of the animals live in natural, open settings. The zoo has a children's Discovery Area, a miniature train ride, and a small carousel. The picnic areas (complete with barbecue pits) are underutilized and especially recommendable.

Stearns Wharf. At the end of State St.

In addition to a small collection of second-rate shops, attractions, and restaurants, the city's 1872-vintage pier offers terrific inland views and good drop-line fishing. The Dolphin Fountain at the foot of the wharf was created by local artist Bud Bottoms for the city's 1982 bicentennial.

BEACHES

Santa Barbara has an array of beaches perfect for stretching out on a towel, playing volleyball (a very popular sport around here), or frolicking seaside. **Hendry's Beach,** at the end of Cliff Drive, is popular with families, boogie-boarders who come to ride the excellent beach breaks, and sunset strollers. ✪ **Cabrillo Beach** is a wide swath of clean white sand that hosts beach umbrellas, sand-castle builders, and spirited volleyball games. A grassy, parklike median keeps the noise of busy Cabrillo Boulevard away. On Sunday local artists set up shop beneath the palms.

Note: A tragic oil spill off the coast of Santa Barbara in 1969 left surfers and sea critters dodging gobs of floating tar for the next 20 years. Although the area has finally cleared up, the staining brown substance still finds its way onto clothes and skin from time to time even if you don't go in the water (that's why the Four Seasons Biltmore hotel includes "Tar Off" in its baskets of toiletry goodies).

OUTDOOR ACTIVITIES

BICYCLING   A relatively flat, palm-lined 2-mile coastal pathway runs along the beach and is perfect for biking. More adventurous riders can peddle through town, up to the mission, or to Montecito, the next town over. The best mountain-bike trail begins at the end of Tunnel Road and climbs up along a paved fire road before turning into a dirt trail to the mountaintop.

Beach Rentals, 22 State St. (☎ **805/966-6733**), rents well-maintained one-speeds. They also have tandem bikes and surrey cycles that can hold as many as four adults and two children. Rates vary depending on equipment. Bring your driver's license or passport to expedite your rental. They're open daily from 8am to dusk.

GOLF   At the **Santa Barbara Golf Club,** 3500 McCaw Ave., at Las Positas Road (☎ **805/687-7087**), there's a great 6,009-yard, 18-hole course and driving range. Unlike many municipal courses, the Santa Barbara Golf Course is well maintained and was designed to present a moderate challenge for the average golfer. Greens fees are $24 Monday to Friday and $28 on weekends ($17 for seniors). Optional carts rent for $20 for 18 holes, $10 for 9 holes.

The 18-hole, 7,000-yard **Sandpiper** course, at 7925 Hollister Ave. (☎ **805/ 968-1541**), a scenic oceanside course, has a pro shop and driving range, plus a coffee shop. Greens fees are $60 Monday to Friday and $80 on Saturday and Sunday. Carts cost $24.

HIKING   The hills and mountains surrounding Santa Barbara have excellent hiking trails. One of our favorites begins at the end of Tunnel Road. Take Mission Canyon Road past the mission, turn right onto Foothill Road, and take the first left onto Mission Canyon Drive. Bear left onto Tunnel Road and park at the end (where all the other cars are). You can buy a trail map at the Santa Barbara Visitor Information Center (see "Essentials," above).

HORSEBACK RIDING   Several area stables rent horses, including the **Circle Bar B Ranch,** 1800 Refugio Rd. (☎ 805/968-3901), and **Rancho Oso,** Paradise Road, off Calif. 154 (☎ 805/964-8985).

POWERBOATING & SAILING   The **Sailing Center of Santa Barbara,** at the Santa Barbara Breakwater (☎ **800/350-9090** or 805/962-2826), rents sailboats from 13 to 50 feet, as well as powerboats and jet skis. Both crewed and bare-boat charters are available by the day or hour. Sailing instruction for all levels of experience is also available.

SKATING   The paved beach path that runs along Santa Barbara's waterfront is perfect for skating. **Beach Rentals,** 22 State St. (☎ **805/966-6733**), located nearby, rents both in-line and conventional roller skates. The $5-per-hour fee includes wrist and knee pads.

SPORTFISHING, DIVE CRUISES & WHALE WATCHING   **Sea Landing,** at the foot of Bath Street and Cabrillo Boulevard (☎ **805/963-3564**), makes regular sportfishing runs from specialized boats. It also offers a wide variety of other fishing and diving cruises. Food and drink are served on board, and rental rods and tackle are available. Rates vary according to excursion; call for reservations.

Whale-watching cruises are offered from February to April, when California gray whales make their migratory journey from Baja California, Mexico, to Alaska. Tours are $24 for adults and $14 for children; sightings of large marine mammals are guaranteed.

SHOPPING

State Street from the beach to Victoria Street is the city's main thoroughfare and has the largest concentration of shops. Many specialize in T-shirts and postcards, but there are a number of boutiques as well. If you get tired of strolling, hop on one of the electric shuttle buses (25¢) that run up and down State Street at regular intervals.

Also check out **Brinkerhoff Avenue** (off Cota Street, between Chapala and De La Vina streets), Santa Barbara's "antique alley." Most shops here are open Tuesday to Sunday from 11am to 5pm. **El Paseo,** at 814 State St., is a picturesque shopping arcade reminiscent of an old Spanish street. Built around an 1827 adobe home, the mall is lined with charming shops and art galleries.

WHERE TO STAY

Before you even begin calling around for reservations, keep in mind that Santa Barbara's accommodations are expensive—especially in summer. Then decide whether you'd like to stay beachside (even more expensive) or downtown. The town is small, but not small enough to happily stroll between the two areas.

Hot Spots Accommodations, 36 State St., Santa Barbara, CA 93101 (☎ **805/ 564-1637**), a one-stop shop for hotel and B&B rooms, keeps an updated list of what's available in all price categories. There's no charge for their services. Significantly discounted rates are often available at the last minute, when hotels need to fill their rooms.

Another option is **Accommodations Reservations Service** (☎ **800/292-2222**), a company that books rooms along California's coast from Oxnard to Monterey. The service is free and has information on all price ranges.

VERY EXPENSIVE

✪ **Four Seasons Biltmore.** 1260 Channel Dr. (at the end of Olive Mill Rd.), Santa Barbara, CA 93108. ☎ **800/332-3442** or 805/969-2261. Fax 805/969-4682. 234 rms, 24 suites. A/C MINIBAR TV TEL. $199–$475 double; from $650 suite. Additional person $30 extra. Special midweek and package rates available. AE, DC, MC, V.

The tattoo-and-lace taste of the now divorced couple Heather Locklear (*Melrose Place*) and Tommy Lee (Motley Crew) may have raised a few eyebrows in their day, but they regained our faith by getting married at the beach club next door from here (and later indulging in the hotel's infamously decadent Sunday brunch). But they weren't the first to celebrate in the area—other Hollywood highbrows such as Greta Garbo, Errol Flynn, and Bing Crosby also knew that the Biltmore is one of the most beautiful hotels in the country. Although it debuted in 1927, when Four Seasons acquired the property in 1987 they brought its beauty to its full potential with a $20-million renovation.

Today the hotel still captivates guests with Spanish Revival architecture, hand-painted Mexican tiles, and 19 acres of incredibly landscaped oceanfront gardens, but its aura is much lighter, warmer, and even *greener* with flora and fauna almost everywhere you look. Frankly, its beauty is beyond description, especially in the common areas such as the Patio restaurant, which has an oceanfront view, indoor and outdoor seating, and a retractable atrium roof. The guest rooms are appropriately less elaborate but come complete with the most comfortable beds, fluffy towels and robes, and the kind of bath soaps you can't help but pack in your luggage when you depart. They also come with striking views of the mountains or the ocean, and some have Spanish balconies and/or fireplaces, or private patios; all come with VCRs. If you've got the bucks, you can't do better than this.

Dining/Entertainment: This is resort dining at its finest. The elegant La Marina offers surprisingly innovative specialties. The Patio is more casual, serving three meals daily and Santa Barbara's best Sunday brunch. La Sala is a comfortable lounge serving afternoon tea and evening cocktails; there's live jazz on Wednesday and Friday nights.

Services: Concierge, room service (24 hours), overnight shoeshine, laundry service, twice-daily maid service including nightly turndown, in-room movies.

Facilities: Two outdoor heated pools, three lighted tennis courts, two health clubs, putting green, shuffleboard and croquet courts, beachfront cabanas, sundeck, complimentary bicycle use, special children's programs, beauty salon, gift shop.

✪ **San Ysidro Ranch.** 900 San Ysidro Lane (off U.S. 101), Montecito, CA 93108. ☎ **800/ 368-6788** or 805/969-5046. Fax 805/565-1995. 43 cottages, 15 suites. MINIBAR TV TEL. $240– $475 cottage for two; from $575 suite. AE, MC, V.

Imagine a summer camp for the wealthy: quaint winding trails overgrown with wildflowers and trees, peaceful rolling hills beyond, and 540 acres of lush countryside all around. San Ysidro Ranch is just that—a rustically indulgent retreat for those who are lucky enough to be able to afford it. This is the kind of place where the noisiest time of day is when the sun comes up and birds begin to celebrate their surroundings; a strenuous afternoon consists of leaning up from a poolside lounge chair to accept a bowl of complimentary berries from an accommodating pool hand.

Upon arrival, guests are escorted to their freestanding "cottages" (with their last name posted in rustic block letters next to the door), which were renovated in 1996 and are impeccably outfitted in country luxury, with a wood-burning stove or fireplace, outdoor terrace, goosedown comforter and Frette linens, VCR, and dozens of other amenities that'll pamper every aspect of your being. Each individually decorated accommodation feels more like a rich uncle's country home than a resort and boasts such intimate touches as books and magazines, fresh flowers, and a stereo with CDs.

The property also has tennis courts, a fitness center and exercise course, spa treatments, and a renowned restaurant. For 100 years, folks (such as Vivien Leigh and Laurence Olivier, who were married here) have come here to replenish themselves, and for good reason: One night here, and you'll feel like you've vacationed a week— but you won't be ready to leave, by any means.

EXPENSIVE

Montecito Inn. 1295 Coast Village Rd., Santa Barbara, CA 93108. ☎ **800/843-2017** or 805/ 969-7854. Fax 805/969-0623. 50 rms, 10 suites. $150–$195 double; from $205 suite. Rates include continental breakfast. 2-night minimum stay on weekends. AE, DISC, MC, V. From U.S. 101, take the Olive Mill Road exit and turn west on Olive Mill Road to Coast Village.

This Mediterranean-style inn isn't at 95% capacity year-round just because Charlie Chaplin built it in 1928 to serve as Hollywood elite's romantic retreat. It's in demand because it's professional and charming. The guest rooms are not as impressive as some of the common areas adorned with Chaplin memorabilia, but are well appointed with French provincial–style furnishings, floral prints, and hand-painted tiles in the small bathrooms; some have VCRs and refrigerators. The new luxury suites are eye-poppingly lavish, with large living rooms and bedrooms and Italian marble bathrooms bigger than many hotel rooms we've seen; Jacuzzi tubs and fireplaces put them over the top. The only drawback is the lack of views. Out back are a small heated pool, spa, and sauna. Athletic folks will enjoy the free touring bikes and exercise room.

The Upham. 1404 De La Vina St. (at Sola St.), Santa Barbara, CA 93101. ☎ **800/727-0876** or 805/962-0058. Fax 805/963-2825. 50 rms, 4 suites. TV TEL. $125–$190 double; from $255 suite. Rates include continental breakfast. AE, CB, DC, DISC, MC, V.

This upscale B&B located right in the heart of town celebrated its 125th anniversary in 1996. What's kept it so popular for so long? It could be the great service—it keeps businesspeople happy. Or maybe the European atmosphere, which makes foreigners feel right at home. Or per chance it's the accommodations themselves—they have private entrances and are distinctively outfitted with some truly impressive antiques and brass or four-poster beds; many even have private porches and fireplaces. Our only complaint: Our room was desperate for a paint job. Combined with the complimentary continental breakfast and evening wine and cheese served in the lobby and garden (with a feisty cat that hangs out at the gazebo), the Upham is a charming alternative to other downtown hotels. Louie's at the Upham, a cozy restaurant, is open for lunch and dinner.

MODERATE

In addition to those listed below, other highly recommendable, moderately priced accommodations are to be had at the **Best Western Encina Lodge and Suites** (☎ 800/526-2282 or 805/682-7277) and **Tropicana Inn and Suites** (☎ 800/468-1988 or 805/966-2219).

✪ **Bath Street Inn.** 1720 Bath St. (north of Valerio St.), Santa Barbara, CA 93101. ☎ **800/341-BATH**, 800/549-BATH in California, or 805/682-9680. 12 rms. TV TEL. $95–$175 double. Rates include breakfast. Midweek rates up to 25% off. AE, MC, V.

This is one of the cutest, most meticulously cared for B&Bs we've ever seen. The minute we walked in, a gracious innkeeper guided us to the redwood patio for a glimpse of an amazing wisteria canopy in bloom (lucky guests can have breakfast beneath the blooms). We were then treated to fresh-baked cookies, which are served with tea and wine each afternoon. After our snack, we wandered from room to room, astonished by the exquisite details of each nook and cranny throughout the three-story Victorian (two unique features include a semicircular "eyelid" balcony and a hipped roof). Each adorable (and immaculate) room is intimately and individually decorated with antiques, colorful wallpaper, and fresh flowers—and it has a private bath. Some include a Jacuzzi and/or a VCR. The common areas are equally attractive and include a third-floor reading nook with a VCR (there's a video library downstairs). No smoking is allowed in the house.

INEXPENSIVE

All the best buys fill up fast in the summer months, so be sure to reserve your room well in advance—even if you're just planning to stay at the nice, reliable **Motel 6** (☎ 800/4-MOTEL6 or 805/564-1392) near the beach, or the good-value **Sandpiper Lodge** (☎ 805/687-5326) just a little farther away.

Casa del Mar. 18 Bath St., Santa Barbara, CA 93101. ☎ **800/433-3097** or 805/963-4418. Fax 805/966-4240. 14 rms, 7 suites. TV TEL. $79–$154 double; from $114 suite. Rates include continental breakfast and wine-and-cheese social. Additional person $10 extra; $10 extra per pet. Midweek discounts available. AE, DISC, DC, MC, V. From northbound U.S. 101, exit at Cabrillo, turn left onto Cabrillo and head toward the beach; Bath is second street on right after the wharf. From southbound U.S. 101, take the Castillo exit, turn right on Castillo, left on Cabrillo, and left on Bath.

Very similar to the Franciscan Inn (see below) and just a half block away (even closer to the beach), Casa del Mar is another good-value motel with one- and two-room suites. The decor is old Spanish Mediterranean with a mish-mash of furnishings. Many rooms have kitchenettes, fridges, and stoves. The Jacuzzi here stays open half an hour later than the Francisan's.

⊙ **Franciscan Inn.** 109 Bath St. (at Mason St.), Santa Barbara, CA 93101. ☎ **805/963-8845.** Fax 805/564-3295. 53 rms, 25 suites. TV TEL. $65–$99 double; from $85 suite. Rates include continental breakfast. Additional person $8 extra. AE, CB, DC, MC, V.

One of the best bargains beachside can be found 1 block from the shore at the Franciscan Inn. The exterior is motel-like. Inside, the rooms are a quirky combination of country pine furnishings and floral and plaid prints. In some cases the decor just doesn't work, but the immaculate recently renovated rooms and the price more than make up for it. Several rooms have fully equipped kitchenettes and/or balconies, and most bathrooms come with tub. All rooms have coffeemakers, computer jacks, and VCRs; hair dryers are available upon request. The suites come complete with a living room, a separate kitchen, and sleeping quarters for up to four adults; one has a fireplace. Breakfast, afternoon appetizers, and a complimentary newspaper are included in the price, as is the use of the heated outdoor pool, Jacuzzi, and coin-operated laundry. Reservations should be made well in advance, especially for May to September.

Orange Tree Inn. 1920 State St., Santa Barbara, CA 93101. ☎ **800/LEM-ORNG** or 805/ 569-1521. 44 rms, 2 suites. A/C TV TEL. $65–$150 double; from $90 suite. AE, DISC, MC, V.

We'd personally prefer to stay by the beach, but if you want cheap downtown accommodations, you're safe with the Orange Tree. Don't get too excited, though—it's a motel, after all. Still, the rooms are newly renovated and have new carpets, bedspreads, and TVs. Most have a balcony or patio, and some have bathtubs. Guests also get free local calls and use of the pool.

WHERE TO DINE
EXPENSIVE

Citronelle. At the Santa Barbara Inn, 901 Cabrillo Blvd. ☎ **805/966-2285.** Reservations accepted. Main courses $22–$24. AE, DISC, MC, V. Daily noon–9pm. CALIFORNIA/FRENCH.

Chef Felicien Cueff heads the kitchen at Michel Richard's (of L.A.'s ultra-popular Citrus) upscale but casual restaurant. The dining room is remarkably airy and lined with windows that allow panoramic views of the ocean and promenade across the street. The atmosphere is peaceful and the room pleasantly quiet, except for the buzz of nearby diners and, on some evenings, live guitar music. Request a windowside table, order a bottle from the fine selection of wines, and dine à la carte or from the four- or five-course tasting menu. Each dish is delicately prepared, and meats and fish are always cooked to perfection. Most plates come with an exotic sauce that can, on occasion, overpower the subtle flavor of the courses themselves, but a few dishes we've sampled here are as fine as they come. If the roasted Chilean sea bass with lime sauce and mashed potatoes is on the menu, don't pass it up. Finish the meal with a dessert we've fantasized about ever since I cleaned the last crumb of it from my plate: creme brulee layered with caramelized phyllo dough.

Oysters. In Victoria Court, 9 W. Victoria St. (at State St.). ☎ **805/962-9888.** Reservations recommended on weekends. Main courses $9–$16. AE, DC, DISC, MC, V. Tues–Thurs 11:30am–2:30pm and 5–9pm, Fri–Sat 11:30am–2:30pm and 5–10pm, Sun 5–9pm. CALIFORNIA.

Whether you're in the intimate and formal dining room or basking on the sunny patio, you're sure to enjoy a well-prepared feast here. Most popular are the sautéed oysters with bacon, scallops, spinach, mushrooms, and hollandaise; the fresh fish of the day (a few choices and a selection of preparations); and capellini with shrimp, artichoke, tomato, sweet peppers, and basil. For dessert, even the richest chocolate-mousse cake should be passed up for the restaurant's home-churned ice cream.

○ Pan e Vino. 1482 E. Valley Rd., Montecito. ☎ **805/969-9274.** Reservations required. Pastas $8–$10; meat and fish dishes $11–$18. AE, MC, V. Mon–Sat 11:30am–9:30pm, Sun 5:30–9:30pm. ITALIAN.

The perfect Italian trattoria, Pan e Vino offers food as authentic as you'd find in Rome. The simplest dish, spaghetti topped with basil-tomato sauce, is so delicious it's hard to understand why diners would want to occupy their taste buds with more complicated concoctions. But this kitchen is capable of almost anything. A whole-artichoke appetizer, steamed, chilled, and filled with breading and marinated tomatoes, is absolutely fantastic. Pasta puttenesca, with tomatoes, anchovies, black olives, and capers, is always tops. Pan e Vino gets high marks for its terrific food, attentive service, and casual atmosphere. Although many diners prefer to eat outside on the intimate patio, some of the best tables are in the charming, cluttered dining room.

○ Wine Cask. In El Paseo Center, 813 Anacapa. ☎ **805/966-9463.** Reservations recommended. Main courses $8–$12 at lunch, $17–$23.50 at dinner. AE, DC, MC, V. Mon–Thurs 10am–9pm, Fri–Sat 10am–10pm, Sun 10am–9pm. ITALIAN.

Take a 15-year-old wine shop, a large dining room with a big stone fireplace, a few large abstract paintings, and hand-stenciled gold-leaf 1920s historic-landmark ceiling, and outstanding Italian fare. Mix them with an attractive staff and clientele, and you've got the Wine Cask—the most popular upscale dining spot in Santa Barbara. Whether you go for the dining room (request fireside for romance) or patio dining (yes, there are heat lamps), you'll be treated to such heavenly creations as lamb sirloin with twice-baked au gratin potatoes, green beans, baby carrots, port wine, and a roasted-garlic demi-glaze. Other options include potato and proscuitto-wrapped local halibut with sautéed spinach and shiitake mushrooms, cioppino sauce, and rouille; or grilled marinated chicken breast in a red-wine reduction with prosciutto, wild mushrooms, fresh rosemary, and sage. The wine list reads like a novel, with over 1,000 wines (ranging from $14 to $1,400) and has deservedly received the *Wine Spectator* award for excellence. There's also a happy hour at the beautiful maple bar from 4 to 6pm daily. This place is so in-the-know they sell cigars, too.

MODERATE

Brophy Bros. Clam Bar & Restaurant. Yacht Basin and Marina (at Harbor Way). ☎ **805/966-4418.** Reservations not accepted. Main courses $9–$16. AE, MC, V. Sun–Thurs 11am–10pm, Fri–Sat 11am–11pm. SEAFOOD.

First-class seafood combined with an unbeatable view of the marina makes dining here a favorite for both tourists and locals. Dress is casual, service is excellent, portions are huge, and everything on the menu is good. Favorites include New England clam chowder, cioppino (California fish stew), and any one of an assortment of seafood salads. The scampi is consistently good, as is all the fresh fish. A nice assortment of beers and wines is available. *But be forewarned:* The wait at this small place can be up to 2 hours on a weekend night.

Joe's Cafe. 536 State St. (at Cota St.). ☎ **805/966-4638.** Reservations recommended. Main courses $9–$17. AE, DISC, MC, V. Mon–Thurs 11am–11:30pm, Fri–Sat 11am–12:30am, Sun noon–9pm. AMERICAN.

Joe's may not be the hottest gourmet eatery in town, but it's been around so long (since 1928), it seems coming here is a generationally passed habit with locals and college students alike. The feel is hunting-lodge-cum-picnic and offers fare you'd expect from an old-school establishment: plenty of red meat dishes (five different steak options), southern fried chicken, and a shrimp dish and garden burger thrown in for good measure. Meals come with a barrage of side dishes. Weekends, the full bar turns out plenty of strong cocktails and late-night dinners to partying students.

📍 **Montecito Cafe.** 1295 Coast Village Rd. (off Olive Mill Rd.). ☎ **805/969-3392.** Reservations recommended. Main courses $7–$13. AE, MC, V. Daily 11:30am–2:30pm and 5:30–10pm. CALIFORNIA NOUVEAU.

Overlooking Montecito's shopping street, the light and airy Montecito Cafe provides diners a high-quality California culinary experience at an affordable price (some say it's the best value in town). Menu items include broiled oysters with lemon cream and goat cheese; a walnut-filled pork chop with lemon-herb sauce; and penne pasta with scallops, shrimp, and mussels in a saffron broth. The petit dining room itself is pleasantly simple, with well-set tables, a wall of windows, plants, a small fountain, and original art—it's the perfect place to impress a date.

Your Place. 22A N. Milpas St. (at Mason St.). ☎ **805/966-5151.** Reservations recommended. Main courses $7–$13. AE, DC, MC, V. Tues–Thurs and Sun 11am–10pm, Fri–Sat 11am–11pm. THAI.

There are an unusually large number of Thai restaurants in Santa Barbara, but when locals argue about which one is best, Your Place invariably ranks high on the list. Traditional dishes are prepared with the freshest ingredients and represent a wide cross section of Thai cuisine. It's best to begin with tom kah kai, a hot-and-sour chicken soup with coconut milk and mushrooms, ladled out of a hotpot tableside—enough for two or more. Siamese duckling, a top main dish, is prepared with sautéed vegetables, mushrooms, and ginger sauce. Like other dishes, it can be made mild, medium, hot, or very hot.

INEXPENSIVE

Andersen's Danish Bakery and Restaurant. 1106 State St. (near Figueroa St.). ☎ **805/ 962-5085.** Reservations recommended on weekends. Breakfast $4–$8; lunch $5–$8. No credit cards. Wed–Mon 8am–8pm. DANISH.

Remember how ice-cream parlors used to look? Well, pink and frilly does not describe this bakery's sweets, but old-style, family-restaurant decor does. Grandma will feel at home here and kids won't have a problem finding something they like on the menu (especially when it comes to dessert). Authentically Danish, Ms. Andersen greets you herself (when she's not baking) and offers substantial (and cheap!) portions of New York steak, chicken or crab salad, and an array of other edibles (including an honest-to-goodness smörgåsbord). Seating provides great State Street people-watching from both in- and outdoor tables.

La Super-Rica Taquería. 622 N. Milpas St. (between Cota and Ortega sts.). ☎ **805/ 963-4940.** Reservations not accepted. Main courses $3–$6. No credit cards. Sun–Thurs 11am–9:30pm, Fri–Sat 11am–10pm. MEXICAN.

Following celebrity chef Julia Child's lead, aficionados have deemed this place the state's best Mexican eatery. Excellent soft tacos are the restaurant's real forte. Unfortunately, portions can be quite small—you have to order two or three items in order to satisfy an average hunger. There's nothing grand about La Super-Rica except the food; you might want to get your order to go and take it to the beach.

Vintage: Central Coast

Have a penchant for a Pinot Noir? Craving a Sauvignon Blanc? Central California's dewy green hillsides and sun-kissed valleys have the perfect climate for grape growing. Though this budding wine country can't boast hundreds of wineries or as many awards as its Northern California neighbor, it's definitely coming into its own. And even if you don't know the difference between Ernest & Julio Gallo and Dom Perignon, this region is a wonderful place to spend a relaxing day.

Central California has two distinct wine regions. The Paso Robles Wine Country area is close to Cambria and San Luis Obispo. There are over 25 wineries here, with more than 100 vineyards. Among them is **Arciero Winery,** 6 miles east of U.S. 101 on Calif. 46 (☎ 805/239-2562), which is open Monday to Friday from 10am to 5pm, and in summer also on Saturday and Sunday from 10am to 6pm. **Bonny Doon** is at Sycamore Farms, 3 miles west of U.S. 101 on Calif. 46 (☎ 805/239-5614). It's open daily from 10:30am to 5:30pm. And **Wild Horse,** located at 1437 Wild Horse Winery Court in Templeton (☎ 805/434-2541), is open daily from 11am to 5pm except most major holidays.

For information on wine events, wineries, accommodations, and a winery map, write or call the **Paso Robles Vintners and Growers Association,** P.O. Box 324, Paso Robles, CA 93447 (☎ 805/239-VINE). Also contact the **San Luis Obispo County Visitors & Conference Bureau,** 1041 Chorro St., Suite E, San Luis Obispo, CA 93401 (☎ 800/634-1414 or 805/541-8000), for a free "Bounty of the County" food and wine tour map.

The Santa Ynez Mountains combined with coastal fog and ocean breezes make Santa Barbara County another prime grape-growing spot. There are more than 10,000 acres of vineyards here and dozens of wineries. The drive over the hills hovering above Santa Barbara alone make it worth the trip. But once you hit the wine country, you'll find some well-respected wineries amid the gorgeous Central California mountain range.

You'll be best off picking up a wine country touring map, which offers information on locations, hours of operation, and picnic and touring facilities. It's free at many hotels and shops around Santa Barbara, including the Wine Cask (see "Where to Dine" in the Santa Barbara section of this chapter). You can also order it by mail from the **Santa Barbara County Vintners Association,** P.O. Box 1558, Santa Ynez, CA 93460 (☎ 800/218-0881 or 805/688-0881).

A few recommended stops include the **Fess Parker Winery,** located at 6200 Foxen Canyon Rd., Los Olivos (☎ 805/688-1545), which is open daily from 10am to 4pm; the **Gainey Vineyard,** at 3950 E. Calif. 246, Santa Ynez (☎ 805/688-0558); **Firestone Vineyard,** at 5017 Zaca Station Rd., Los Olivos (☎ 805/688-3940), which is open daily from 10am to 4pm; and **Sunstone Vineyards & Winery,** at 125 N. Refugio Rd., Santa Ynez (☎ 800/313-WINE or 805/688-WINE), which is open daily from 10am to 4pm.

SANTA BARBARA AFTER DARK

To find out what's going on while you're in town, check the free weekly *The Independent,* or call the following venues direct: the **Center Stage Theater,** upstairs at the Paseo Nuevo Shopping Center, Chapala and De La Guerra streets (☎ 805/963-0408); the **Lobero Theater,** 33 E. Canon Perdido St. (☎ 805/963-0761); the

Arlington Theater, 1317 State St. (☎ 805/963-4408); and the **Earl Warren Showgrounds,** at Las Positas Road and U.S. 101 (☎ 805/687-0766).

Backstage. 18 E. Ortega. ☎ **805/730-7383.** Cover none–$7.

Santa Barbara's most cutting-edge alternative nightclub enjoys a Los Angeles–style warehouse setting and a mixed gay/straight crowd. Under high ceilings are two bars, a pool table, an indoor fountain, and one of the largest dance floors in town. Regular theme nights are interspersed with occasional live local bands.

Madhouse. 434 State St. ☎ **805/962-5516.** No cover.

Young singles pack into this warehouse-cum-cocktail lounge that's eclectically decorated with Oriental rugs and interesting trinkets hanging overhead. Order a drink from one of the attractive young bartenders or forge your way to the back room—a heated covered patio that's jazzed up with colorful hanging lamps—where there's another bar and a little extra elbow room.

Mel's. In the Paseo Nuevo Mall, 6 W. De La Guerra St. ☎ **805/963-2211.** No cover.

The compact bar of this old drinking dive in the heart of downtown attracts a good cross section of regulars.

The Wildcat Lounge. 15 W. Ortega. ☎ **805/962-7970.** No cover.

On a side street off State Street downtown, this small bar with retro funky decor, a CD jukebox, and a pool table keeps young local singles coming back for more.

7 The Ojai Valley

by Stephanie Avnet

In a crescent-shaped valley between Santa Barbara and Ventura, surrounded by mountain peaks, lies Ojai (pronounced "*O*-high"). It's a magical place, selected by Frank Capra as Shangri-La, the legendary utopia of his 1936 classic *Lost Horizon.* The spectacularly tranquil setting has made Ojai a mecca for artists and a particularly large population of New Age spiritualists, both drawn by the area's mystical beauty.

Life is low-key in the peaceful Ojai Valley. Perhaps the most excitement in town is during the first week of June, when the **Ojai Music Festival** draws world-reknowned contemporary jazz artists to perform in the Libbey Bowl amphitheater.

You're bound to hear folks wax poetic about something called the "pink moment." It's a phenomenon first noticed by the earliest Native American valley dwellers, when the brilliant sunset over the nearby Pacific is reflected onto the mountainside creating an eerie and beautiful pink glow.

ESSENTIALS

GETTING THERE The 45-minute drive south from Santa Barbara to Ojai is along two-lane Calif. 150, a beautiful road that's as curvaceous as it is stunning. From Los Angeles, take U.S. 101 north to Calif. 33, which winds through eucalyptus groves to meet Calif. 150—the trip takes about 90 minutes.

VISITOR INFORMATION The **Ojai Valley Chamber of Commerce,** 338 E. Ojai Ave., Ojai, CA 93023 (☎ 805/646-8126), distributes free area maps, brochures, and a *Visitor's Guide to the Ojai Valley,* which lists galleries and current events. Open Monday to Friday from 9:30am to 4:30pm and on Saturday and Sunday from 10am to 4pm.

ORIENTATION   Calif. 150 is called Ojai Avenue in the town center and is the village's primary thoroughfare.

EXPLORING TOWN & VALLEY

Small Ojai is home to more than 35 artists working in a variety of media; most have home studios and are represented in one of several galleries in town. The best for jewelry and smaller pieces is **HumanArts,** 310 E. Ojai Ave. (☎ 805/646-1525). They also have a home accessories annex, **HumanArts Home,** 246 E. Ojai Ave. (☎ 805/646-8245). Artisans band together each October for an organized **Artists' Studio Tour** (October 11 and 12 in 1997; for information call 805/646-8126). It's fun to drive from studio to studio at your own pace, meeting various artists and perhaps purchasing some of their work. Ojai's most famous resident is world-reknowned **Beatrice Wood,** who celebrated her 103rd birthday in 1996 while overseeing a traveling exhibition of her whimsical sculpture and luminous pottery.

Strolling the Spanish arcade shops downtown and the surrounding area will yield a treasure trove, including open-air **Bart's Books,** Matilija St. at Canada St. (☎ 805/646-3755), an Ojai fixture for many years; **Local Hero Books/Cafe,** 254 E. Ojai Ave. (☎ 805/646-3165), carries a large selection of New Age and philosophical titles and hosts readings and musical performances. In a town peppered with ladies' boutiques, designer **Barbara Bowman**'s two eponymous shops, at 125 and 133 E. Ojai Ave. (☎ 805/646-2670), stand out in a crowd.

Residents of the Ojai Valley *love* their equine companions—miles of bridle paths are painstakingly maintained, and HORSE CROSSING signs are everywhere. If you'd like to explore the equestrian way, call the **Ojai Valley Inn's Ranch & Stables** (☎ 805/646-5511, ext. 456).

Ojai has long been a haven for several esoteric sects of metaphysical and philosophical beliefs. The **Krotona Institute and School of Theosophy,** Calif. 33 and Calif. 150 at Hermosa Road (☎ 805/646-2653), has been in the valley since moving from Hollywood in 1926, and visitors are welcome at their library and bookstore.

In the **Lake Casitas Recreation Area** (☎ 805/649-2233 for visitor information) the incredibly beautiful Lake Casitas boasts nearly 32 miles of shoreline, and was the site of the 1984 Olympic canoeing and rowing events. You can rent rowboats and small powerboats year-round from the boathouse (☎ 805/649-2043), or enjoy picnicking and camping by the lakeside. Because the lake serves as a domestic water supply, swimming is not allowed. From Calif. 150, turn left onto Santa Ana Road, then follow the signs to the recreation area.

When Ronald Coleman saw Shangri-La in *Lost Horizon,* he was really admiring the Ojai Valley. To visit the breathtakingly beautiful spot where Coleman stood for his view of **Shangri-La,** drive east on Ojai Avenue, up the hill, and stop at the stone bench near the top; the view is spectacular.

✪ **Wheeler Hot Springs Spa & Restaurant.** 16825 Maricopa Hwy. (Calif. 33), 7 miles north of downtown. ☎ **800/9-WHEELER** or 805/646-8131. Fax 805/646-9787. Spa package for two (hot tub, massage, and dinner) $139–$165. Full-day, weekend brunch, and other combinations available, as well as spa services à la carte. AE, MC, V.

Nestled in a canyon and shaded by rustling palms, Wheeler is the place to purge all your inner demons. You'll be so relaxed after their pampering treatments that the walk across the gravel driveway to their world-class restaurant will be all you can manage. We recommend that you enjoy their famed mineral baths *à deux* in private redwood-lined and skylighted chambers each containing hot bubbling and cold plunge wooden tubs—after dunking back and forth, it's time for a soothing massage.

You can also come up just to dine on contemporary European cuisine prepared with a light touch, while listening to live jazz entertainment on the weekends.

WHERE TO STAY

Ojai Manor Hotel Bed & Breakfast. 210 E. Matilija, Ojai, CA 93023. ☎ **805/646-0961.** 6 rms, none with bath. $90–$100 double. Rates include breakfast and evening wine and spirits. MC, V.

Conveniently located 1 block off Ojai Avenue, this comfortable clapboard B&B was built as a schoolhouse in 1874 and is Ojai's oldest building. A cozy parlor and inviting wraparound porch help make up for the lack of private baths, and a cottage on the grounds houses a friendly beauty and massage salon. A typical guest room is simply furnished with throw rugs on the wooden floors and wrought-iron beds. Children over 12 are welcomed.

Ojai Rancho Motel. 615 W. Ojai Ave. (at Country Club Dr.), Ojai, CA 93023. ☎ **800/ 362-1434** or 805/646-1434. 12 rms. A/C TV TEL. $80–$135 double. AE, DISC, MC, V.

This classic ranch-style motel has been well kept up and presents an attractively rustic alternative to the pricey country club around the corner, but don't expect the same gracious service from their cranky front office. The rooms all come with microwave, refrigerator, and coffeemaker, and there's a heated outdoor pool, sauna, and Jacuzzi; two have a fireplace. The rooms in back look out on ranchland and tend to be quieter than the front rooms near the street.

Ojai Valley Inn. Country Club Dr. (off Calif. 33), Ojai, CA 93023. ☎ **800/422-OJAI** or 805/ 646-5511. Fax 805/646-7969. 207 rms, 15 suites. A/C MINIBAR TV TEL. $195–$260 double; from $345 suite. Packages available. AE, DC, MC, V.

In 1923 famous Hollywood architect Wallace Neff designed the clubhouse that's now the focal point of this quintessentially Californian colonial Spanish-style resort. The inn has carefully kept a sprawling ranch ambience while providing gracious, elegant service and amenities, along with a beautifully oak-studded Senior PGA Tour golf course. Many of the unusually spacious accommodations have fireplaces; most have sofas, writing desks, and secluded terraces or balconies that open onto expansive views of the valley and the magnificent Sierra Madre. Added comforts include coffeemakers, plush terry robes, and hair dryers. The inn is worth a splurge, and at press time they were even offering a midweek, AAA-member rate of $99.

Dining/Entertainment: There's the first-rate Vista Dining Room—a beautiful choice for a pleasant culinary adventure at breakfast, lunch, and dinner; it also puts out a terrific Sunday brunch spread. There's also a terrace grill overlooking the golf course and two lounges.

Services: Concierge, room service (24 hours), nightly turndown.

Facilities: Golf on the championship 18-hole, 6,258-yard course costs $95 for guests; greens fees include the use of a cart. There are eight hard-surface tennis courts (four lit for night play); charges are $12 per hour. "Camp Ojai" offers special children's programs including a supervised play area and activities during peak holiday periods. Two outdoor heated pools (including a 60-foot lap pool); state-of-the-art fitness center with exercise room, Jacuzzi, sauna, steam room; jogging trails; complimentary bicycles; horseback riding.

WHERE TO DINE
EXPENSIVE

L'Auberge. 314 El Paseo (at Rincon St.). ☎ **805/646-2288.** Reservations recommended. Main courses $15–$20. AE, MC, V. Mon–Fri 5:30–9pm, Sat–Sun 11am–2:30pm and 5:30–9pm. FRENCH/BELGIAN.

Possibly the most romantic of all the romantic restaurants in the Ojai Valley, L'Auberge is located in a 1910 mansion with a fireplace, chandeliers, and a charming terrace with an excellent view of Ojai's famous sunset "pink moment." The dinner menu is traditional, featuring scampi, frogs' legs, poached sole, tournedos of beef, sweetbreads, and duckling à l'orange. The weekend brunch menu offers a selection of crêpes. Service is expert and friendly, and this elegant house is an easy walk from downtown.

✪ **The Ranch House.** S. Lomita Ave. ☎ **805/646-2360.** Reservations recommended. Main courses $19–$24. AE, CB, DC, DISC, MC, V. Wed–Sat 6–8:30pm, Sun 11am–7:30pm (lunch served Apr–Sept, Wed–Sat; call for hours). CALIFORNIA

This restaurant has been placing emphasis on the freshest vegetables, fruits, and herbs in its cuisine since opening its doors in 1965, long before this practice became a national craze. Freshly snipped sprigs from the restaurant's lush herb garden will aromatically transform your simple meat, fish, or game dish into a work of art. From an appetizer of cognac-laced liver pâté served with their own chewy rye bread to leave-room-for desserts like fresh raspberries with sweet Chambord cream, the ingredients always shine through. And you'll dine in a magical setting, for the Ranch House offers alfresco dining year-round on the wooden porch facing the scenic valley, as well as in the romantic garden amid twinkling lights and stone fountains.

MODERATE

Lanna Thai. 849 E. Ojai Ave. ☎ **805/646-6771.** Reservations recommended on weekends. Main courses $8–$17. MC, V. Mon–Sat 11:30am–2:30pm and 4:30–9:30pm. THAI.

Chiedo Latawan Lopez, a transplant from northern Thailand, runs this cheerful, casual restaurant with a garden-style decor. His dishes contain little sugar and no MSG, but otherwise they're Thai traditionals. Fresh salmon poached in a spicy-and-sour broth, the house specialty, is terrific. Also worth trying is pla goong salad—grilled shrimp on spikes with julienned vegetables, lemongrass, mint, cilantro, and hot chiles. A children's menu is available.

Roger Keller's Restaurant. 331 E. Ojai Ave. ☎ **805/646-7266.** Reservations recommended on weekends. Main courses $8–$22. AE, MC, V. Daily 11:30am–10pm. AMERICAN/CONTINENTAL.

Installed in a former storefront in the center of downtown, Roger Keller's has a casual ambience with exposed brick walls, bare wooden tables, and works by local artists. The food is rich in both American and European bistro tradition. Linguine tossed with pesto and sun-dried tomatoes, topped with rock shrimp and bay scallops, is fantastic. Or try the filet mignon encrusted in cracked peppercorns and flamed with brandy. The small but well-selected wine list includes several good buys, and live piano music enhances the mood each Friday and Saturday evening.

INEXPENSIVE

Boccali's. 3277 Ojai–Santa Paula Rd. ☎ **805/646-6116.** Reservations not accepted. Pizza $9–$16; pasta $6–$9. No credit cards. Mon–Tues 4–9pm, Wed–Sun noon–9pm. ITALIAN.

This small, wood-frame restaurant, set among citrus groves, is a pastoral pleasure spot where patrons eat outside at picnic tables under umbrellas and twisted oak trees, or inside at tables covered with red-and-white-checked oilcloths. Pizza is the main dish served here, topped in California style with the likes of crab, garlic, shrimp, and chicken. Fresh lemonade, squeezed from fruit plucked from local trees, is the usual drink of choice, though both Miller and Michelob are available on tap.

Tottenham Court. In the Downtown Shopping Arcade, 242 E. Ojai Ave. ☎ **805/646-2339.** Reservations recommended for afternoon tea on weekends. Main courses $5–$10. AE, MC, V. Daily 9:30am–5:30pm. ENGLISH TEAROOM.

Besides being purveyors of a variety of British imports, Tottenham Court is a delightful change of pace for breakfast or lunch, offering a menu of quiches, salads, sandwiches, and pastries in addition to a traditional afternoon English tea service. They have a selection of English beers, and the store itself sells food items, gifts, and housewares imported from the U.K.

8 En Route to Los Angeles: Ventura

by Stephanie Avnet

Nestled between gently rolling foothills and the sparkling blue Pacific Ocean, Ventura may not have the cultural and gastronomic appeal of Los Angeles or even nearby Santa Barbara, but it does boast a picturesque setting and clean sea breezes typical of California coastal towns. Southland antique hounds know about Ventura's quirky collectible shops, and time-pressed vacationers zip up to charming bed-and-breakfast inns just an hour from Los Angeles. Ventura is also the headquarters and main point of embarkation for Channel Islands National Park (see below).

Most travelers don't bother exiting U.S. 101 for a closer look. But think about stopping to while away a couple of hours around lunchtime; sleepy Ventura's charm might even convince you to spend a night.

ESSENTIALS

GETTING THERE If you're traveling northbound on U.S. 101, exit at California Street; southbound, take the Main Street exit. If you're coming west on Calif. 33 from Ojai, there's also a convenient Main Street exit. By the way, don't let the directions throw you off; because of the curve of the coastline the ocean isn't always to the west, but is often southward.

VISITOR INFORMATION For a visitor's guide and genial answers to any questions you might have, stop in at the **Ventura Visitors & Convention Bureau,** 89-C S. California St., Ventura, CA 93001 (☎ **805/648-2075**). Open 8:30am to 5pm from Monday to Friday, 9am to 4pm Saturday, and 10am to 4pm on Sunday.

EXPLORING THE TOWN

Much of Ventura's recent development has taken place inland and to the south, so many folks overlook the charming seaside **Main Street,** the town's historic center, which grew outward from the Spanish Mission of San Buenaventura (see below). The best section for strolling is between the mission (to the north) and Fir Street (to the south).

Although Ventura stretches south to one of California's most picturesque little harbors (the jumping-off point for the Channel Islands; see below), the town has its own simple **pier** at the end of California Street. Exceptionally well maintained and favored by area fishermen, the wooden pier is charming and old-fashioned. It's fun to walk out over the water and gaze back at Ventura nestled against the hills.

Mission San Buenaventura. 225 E. Main St. ☎ **805/643-4318.** Free admission, but donations appreciated. Mon–Sat 10am–5pm, Sun 10am–4pm.

Founded in 1782 (current buildings date from 1815) and still in use for daily services, this whitewash and red-tile church lent its style to the contemporary civic buildings across the street. Step back into time by touring the mission's inside garden, where you can examine the antique water pump and olive press once essential to daily life here. Good for a quick history fix, the mission is small and near the rest of Ventura's action. Pick up a self-guided tour brochure in the adjacent gift shop for the modest donation of $1 per adult, 50¢ per child.

San Buenaventura City Hall. 501 Poli St. ☎ **805/658-4726.** Guided tours, $4 adults, $3 seniors, free for children 16 and under. Guided tours given May–Sept, Sat 11am–1pm.

This majestic neoclassical building was built in 1912 to serve as the Ventura County Courthouse. It sits on the hillside, regally overlooking old downtown and the ocean. To either side on Poli Street are some of Ventura's best preserved and most ornate late 19th- and early 20th-century houses. Full of architectural detail (like the carved heads of Franciscan friars adorning the facade) inside and out, City Hall can be fully explored by 1-hour escorted tours.

Ventura County Museum of History & Art. 100 E. Main St., Ventura. ☎ **805/653-0323.** Admission $3 adults, free for children 16 and under. Tues–Sun 10am–5pm.

This museum is worth visiting for its rich Native American Room, filled with Chumash treasures, and its Pioneer Room, which contains a collection of artifacts from the Mexican-American War (1846–48). The art gallery features revolving exhibits of local painters and photographers, and the museum has an enormous archive (20,000 and counting) of photos depicting Ventura County from its origin to the present.

WHERE TO STAY

Bella Maggiore Inn. 67 S. California St. (half a block south of Main St.), Ventura, CA 93001. ☎ **800/523-8479** or 805/652-0277. 24 rms and suites. TV TEL. $75–$150 double; $100–$130 suite. Rates include full breakfast and afternoon refreshments and appetizers. Additional adult $10 extra; additional child 11 and under $5 extra. AE, DISC, MC, V.

The Bella Maggiore is an intimate Italian-style inn whose simply furnished rooms (some with fireplaces, balconies, or bay window seats) overlook a romantic courtyard or roof garden. Complimentary breakfast is served each morning around the patio fountain, an intimate spot known to nonguests as Nona's Courtyard Cafe. A kind of European elegance pervades all but the reasonable rates here, and be sure to ask about midweek specials.

La Mer European Bed & Breakfast. 411 Poli St. (west of City Hall), Ventura, CA 93001. ☎ **805/643-3600.** 5 rms. $105–$155 double. Rates include full breakfast and complimentary wine in room. MC, V.

Perfect for a romantic getaway, La Mer is an 1890 Cape Cod–style home with a spectacular view of the ocean from the parlor and two of the five guest rooms, four with private entrances and each of which is furnished in a different international style. Whether you choose the "Madame Pompadour" French chamber with wood-burning stove, the "Vienna Woods" Austrian hideaway with a sunken bathtub, or one of three other rooms, you'll love this cozy little cottage. They offer generous midweek packages for couples that can include gourmet candlelit dinners, cruises to Anacapa Island, country carriage rides, therapeutic massages . . . or all of the above! Note that children are not accepted.

WHERE TO DINE

Rosarito Beach Cafe. 692 E. Main St. (at Fir St.). ☎ **805/653-7343.** Main courses $10–$19. AE, DISC, MC, V. Tues–Thurs 11:30am–2pm and 5:30–9pm, Fri–Sat 11:30am–2pm and 5–10pm, Sun 5:30–9pm. MEXICAN.

The 3-year-old Rosarito Beach Cafe really packs them into this 1938 Aztec Revival Moderne building and its welcoming outdoor patio. Diners in-the-know bring their palates for superb Baja-style cuisine whose tangy elements are borrowed from the Caribbean, delicious handmade tortillas, and a culinary sophistication rare in modest Ventura.

The Sportsman. 53 California St. (half a block south of Main St.). ☎ **805/643-2851.** Main courses $4–$14. AE, MC, V. Mon–Fri 11am–10pm, Sat 9am–2pm and 5–10pm, Sun 4–10pm. AMERICAN.

You might walk right by the inconspicuous facade of Ventura's oldest (since 1950) restaurant. Like the intriguingly "retro" lettering on the awning, the interior hasn't changed a lick since then: plush leather booths, brass lamps, wood-paneled bar, and a giant trophy swordfish on the back wall. The Sportsman looks "fancy" but is quite affordable (especially at breakfast and lunch), and serves up fine hearty breakfasts, burgers, steaks, and other grilled items. Or you can wet your whistle with $2.50 well drinks from the bar.

Yolie's Fresh Mex Grill. 26 S. Garden St. (at Main St., west of the mission). ☎ **805/652-0338.** Main courses $5–$13. AE, DISC, MC, V. Mon–Thurs and Sun 11am–9pm, Fri–Sat 11am–10pm. MEXICAN.

This colorful cantina's funny moniker is a nickname of the proprieter, Yolanda, and the place is better than its nondescript business-park exterior would lead you to believe. Yolie offers an impressive fresh salsa bar (authentic and delicious) as well as an admirable beer, margarita, and tequila menu. The patio and dining room are festooned with rainbow serapes and sombreros, and the kitchen quickly sends out traditional combination plates, as well as lighter and/or vegetarian adaptations. Yolie's all-day hours make it a good road-trip rest stop.

9 Channel Islands National Park

by Andrew Rice

There's nothing like a visit to the Channel Islands for discovering the sense of awe the explorers must have felt nearly 400 years ago. It's miraculous what 25 miles of ocean can do, for compared to the mainland, this is a wild and empty land. Whether you approach the islands by sea or air, you'll be bowled over by how untrammeled they remain, despite being next-door neighbors to Southern California's teaming masses.

Channel Islands National Park encompasses the five northernmost islands of the eight-island chain: Santa Barbara, Anacapa, Santa Cruz, Santa Rosa, and San Miguel. Tiny Santa Barbara Island sits very much by itself, about 46 miles off the Southern California coast. The other four are clustered in a 40-mile-long chain that begins with tiny Anacapa; it continues with Santa Cruz, then Santa Rosa, and ends with wild and windy San Miguel. The park also protects the ocean 1 mile offshore from each island, thereby prohibiting oil drilling, shipping, and other industrial uses.

The islands are the meeting point of two distinct marine ecosystems: The cold waters of Northern California and the warmer currents of Southern California swirl together here, creating an awesome array of marine life. On land, the relative isolation from mainland influences has allowed distinct species, like the island fox and the night lizard, to develop and survive here. The islands are also the most important seabird nesting area in California, and home to the biggest seal and sea lion breeding colony in the United States.

GETTING THERE Each of the five islands is relatively distinct and difficult to reach. Odds are you're only going to visit one island on a given trip, so it's a good idea to study your options before going.

Visit the **Channel Islands National Park Headquarters and Visitor Center,** 1901 Spinnaker Dr., Ventura, CA 93001 (☎ **805/658-5700**), to get aquatinted with the various programs and individual personalities of the islands through maps and displays. Rangers run interpretive programs both on the islands and at the center year-round. **Island Packers,** next door to the visitor center at 1867 Spinnaker Dr. (☎ **805/642-7688** for recorded information or 805/642-1393 for reservations), is the park's concessionaire for boat transportation to and from the islands; they're another great source of information.

There are no park fees, but getting to the islands is expensive—anywhere from $25 to $120 per person—since you must go by boat or fly out. Island Packers will take you on a range of regularly scheduled boat excursions, from 3½-hour nonlanding tours of the islands ($21 per person) to full-day tours of individual islands led by naturalists ($37 to $49 per person). Private yachts and commercial dive and tour boats from all over Southern California also visit the park on a regular basis.

Island Packers also arranges small-group tours by sea kayak to all five Channel Islands. Half- and whole-day excursions allow you to enjoy the rugged coastline, sea lions, and teeming tidepools of Anacapa, Santa Barbara, or Santa Rosa Island. Bring a picnic lunch. Fares range from $21 to $65 for adults, $14 to $45 for kids 12 and under. Two-day adventures to secluded and unspoiled San Miguel Island can also be arranged, with meals and berth accomodations included, for $215 to $235.

If you want to get to Santa Rosa in a hurry, **Channel Islands Aviation,** 305 Durley Ave., Camarillo, CA 93010 (☎ **805/987-1678**), will fly you there in one of their small, fixed-wing aircraft. If you just want a quick overflight and maybe a picnic stop with a quick hike, **Heli-Tours, Inc.,** at the Santa Barbara Airport (☎ **805/964-0684**), offers 3- to 4-hour flights to Santa Cruz Island.

THE WEATHER   The weather in the islands is unpredictable year-round: 30-m.p.h. winds can blow for days, or sometimes a fog bank will settle in and smother the islands for weeks at a time. Winter rains can turn island trails into mud baths. In general, plan on wind, lots of sun (bring sunscreen), cool nights, and the possibility of hot days. Water temperatures are in the 50s and 60s year-round. If you're camping, bring a good tent—if you don't know the difference between a good and a bad tent, the island wind will gladly demonstrate it for you.

CAMPING   Camping is permitted on all the park-owned islands, but is limited to 30 people per island per night. Camping is also allowed on Santa Cruz, through special arrangement with the private owners. Fires and pets are prohibited on all the islands. You must bring everything you'll need—there are no supplies on any of the islands. To reserve free camping permits for any of the islands, schedule your transportation, then call the visitor center (see "Getting There," above) no more than 90 days in advance (no more than 30 days in advance for San Miguel).

EXPLORING THE ISLANDS

SANTA BARBARA   As you come upon Santa Barbara Island after a typical 3-hour crossing, you'll think that someone took a single medium-sized grassy hill, ringed it with cliffs, and plunked it down in the middle of the ocean. When you drop anchor, you'll realize that your initial perception is basically on target. Landwise, there's just not a lot here. But the upside is that, of all the islands, Santa Barbara gives you the best sense of what it's like to be stranded on a desert isle. Being on Santa Barbara, far enough out to sea so that the mainland is almost invisible, gives you an idea of just how immense the Pacific really is.

Other than the landing cove, there's no access to the water's edge. The snorkeling in the chilly cove is great. You can hike the entire 640-acre island in a few hours; then it's time to stare out to sea. You won't be let down. The cliffs and rocks are home to elephant seals, sea lions, and swarms of seabirds such as you'll never see on the mainland. There's also a small campground, pit toilets, and a tiny museum chronicling island history. Visitors are welcome to camp for as long as they like between April and November, but unless you're a hermit, a weekend should do. Island Packers only schedules boats to Santa Barbara in summer and fall (see "Getting There," above).

ANACAPA Most people who visit the park come to Anacapa. It's only 11 sea miles from Ventura, an easy half-day trip. At only 1.1 square miles, Anacapa—actually three small islets divided by narrow stretches of ocean—is only marginally larger than Santa Barbara and, consequently, not a place for those who need a lot of space to roam around. Only East Anacapa is open to visitors, as the other two islets are important brown-pelican breeding areas. Several trails on the island will take you to beautiful overlooks of clear-watered coves and wild ocean. Arch Rock, a natural land bridge, is visible from the landing cove, where you'll clamber up 154 stairs to the island's flat top.

Camping is allowed on East Anacapa year-round, but don't bring more than you can carry the half mile from the landing cove. Bring earplugs and steer clear of the foghorn, which can leave permanent hearing damage. Most of the waters around the island, including the landing cove, are protected as a National Marine Preserve, where divers can look but not take anything. Pack a good wet suit, mask, fins and snorkel; you can dive right off the landing cove dock.

SANTA CRUZ By far the biggest of the islands—nearly 100 square miles—Santa Cruz is also the most diverse. It has huge canyons, year-round streams, beaches, cliffs, now-defunct early cattle ranches, Native American Chumash village sites, and seemingly endless displays of flora and fauna.

The island is still privately owned: the western nine-tenths by the Nature Conservancy, and the east end by the Gherini family. Access is allowed through agreements with the Park Service. Most visitors come to Scorpion Ranch and Smuggler's Ranch on the Gherinis' 6,000 acres (slated for future purchase by the Park Service). Unfortunately, the east end of the island has been badly overgrazed by feral sheep; much of the most beautiful land is on the Nature Conservancy property, which includes Santa Cruz's lush central valley and the islands' highest peaks. It's more difficult, but not impossible, to get access to the Conservancy land; Island Packers runs occasional trips to Prisoner's Harbor. At one point it was possible to arrange stays at Christy Ranch on the windswept west end of the island and visits to the Main Ranch in the central valley, but at press time flooding had closed most of the roads on the Conservancy property and access was restricted. Contact the Nature Conservancy (☎ 805/962-9111) for up-to-date information.

Valdez Cave (also known as Painted Cave) is a huge half-mile-long sea cave that you can enter only via dinghy or kayak at the island's northwest end. Contact Island Packers for the most current information on this as well as the entire, continually changing Santa Cruz access situation.

Island Packers runs day trips as well as overnights to Santa Cruz. Camping is allowed ($25 per night, including the boat ride from Ventura), or you can stay in the old ranch house at either Scorpion or Smuggler's Ranch; contact Horizons West at 800/430-2544 for rates and availability.

SANTA ROSA Windy Santa Rosa was California's only singly owned, private island until it was purchased by the Park Service for $30 million in the 1980s from the Vail and Vickers ranching company. As part of the purchase agreement, the Vails are allowed to ranch the island until 2011. Close to 6,500 cattle still call the 54,000-acre island home. You can camp in the old ranch compound on the island's northeast end, where you might be lucky enough to see the Vail and Vickers cowboys working the herd, just as they have for more than 100 years.

Santa Rosa is also home to a large concentration of endangered plant species, 34 of which occur only on the islands. And like Santa Cruz, Santa Rosa is home to the diminutive island fox, a tiny cousin of the red fox that has become nearly fearless as it has evolved in the predator-free island environment—they'll walk right through your camp if you let them. Santa Rosa also has great beaches, a benefit somewhat outweighed by the nearly constant winds.

SAN MIGUEL People often argue about what's the wildest place left in the lower 48 states. They bat around names like Montana, Colorado, and Idaho. Curiously, no one ever thinks to consider San Miguel. They should, for this 10,500-acre island is a wild, wild place. The wind blows constantly, and the island can be shrouded in fog for days at a time. Human presence is definitely not the status quo here.

Visitors land at Cuyler Harbor, a half-moon–shaped cove on the island's east end. Arriving here is like arriving on earth the day it was made: perfect water, perfect sand, outrageously blue water. Seals bask on the offshore rocks. The island's two most interesting features are the Caliche Forest, a sort of petrified forest left when the wind exposed sandstone casts of a forest that once stood on the island; and Point Bennett, the breeding ground of six separate species of seals and sea lions. During the winter, thousands carpet the beach; their barking is deafening.

The waters around San Miguel are the richest and most dangerous of all the islands. The island is exposed to wave action from all sides. Many ships have sunk here. A 3-foot-tall stone cross marks the burial place of Juan Rodríguez Cabrillo, the Spanish explorer credited with discovering the Channel Islands in 1542.

Island Packers' schedule to San Miguel is sporadic in summer and almost nonexistent in winter, so call ahead. Primitive camping is allowed near the ranger's residence, but no potable water is available and fires are prohibited.

THE EXTRA MILE: EXPLORING THE WATERS OFF THE CHANNEL ISLANDS A good portion of Channel Islands National Park is underwater. Scuba divers come here from all over the globe for the chance to explore stunning kelp forests, shipwrecks, and underwater caves, all with the best visibility in California. Everything from sea snails and urchins to orcas and great white sharks call these waters home. **Truth Aquatics** in Santa Barbara (☎ **805/962-1127**) is the best provider of single-day and multiday dive trips to all the islands. Boats from Ventura, San Pedro, and other Southern California ports also make regular visits.

14 Los Angeles

By Stephanie Avnet

Los Angeles is not a humble city. Like a celebrity who chooses a front table at Spago, L.A. is a star that just loves to be noticed.

And noticed it is. The movies, TV, and music that it issues forth are seen, heard, and felt throughout the world. The city is America's—and often the world's—popular tastemaker, its cultural barometer. When it comes to what's hot and what's not, Angelenos can confidently say that they heard—or started—the buzz here first.

L.A. is a cosmopolitan city in the true sense of the word—it's a cornucopia of lifestyles and cultures and a sometimes uneasy mix of races that's at once both thrilling and uncomfortable. It's not an easy place to master. The sprawling city has no cultural center, and its layout is difficult to grasp. Despite all appearances, however, L.A. is a very welcoming place. Often criticised for having few historical or cultural attributes, Los Angeles is anxious to prove its critics wrong, and any resident will gladly tell of the hidden corners and secret treasures that make living here a nonstop adventure.

The best way to approach this colossal, Technicolor city is with a critical conscience and tongue firmly in cheek. Recognize its influence and humor its self-importance. Keep in mind your media-made preconceptions, then discover L.A. for what it is: glitzy, grimy, glittery, powerful—the world capital of pop culture—and a city resplendent in the sunny climate and Mediterranean topography that have drawn admirers here for centuries. Put on your shades, take the top down, and get ready to roll—this is Hollywood.

1 Orientation

ARRIVING

BY PLANE

LOS ANGELES INTERNATIONAL AIRPORT (LAX)   Most visitors to the area fly into Los Angeles International Airport, better known as LAX (☎ **310/646-5252**). Situated oceanside just off I-405, between Santa Monica and Manhattan Beach, LAX is a convenient place to land; it's minutes away from all the city's beach communities, and about a half-hour drive from the Westside, Hollywood, or downtown.

Transportation from LAX   You'll probably be renting a car from LAX; you'll need one (see "Getting Around," later in this chapter). All the major car-rental firms provide shuttles from the terminals to

Area Code Change Notice

Please note that, effective June 14, 1997, the phone company plans to split the 818 area code. The eastern portion, including Burbank, Glendale and Pasadena, will change to the new area code **626.** You will be able to dial 818 until January 17, 1998, after which you will have to use 626.

their off-site branches. To reach Santa Monica and other northern beach communities, exit the airport, take Sepulveda Boulevard north, then follow the signs to Calif. 1 (Pacific Coast Highway, or PCH) north. To reach the southern beach communities, take Sepulveda Boulevard south, then follow the signs to Calif. 1 (PCH) south. To reach Beverly Hills or Hollywood, exit the airport via Century Boulevard, then take I-405 north to Santa Monica Boulevard east. To reach downtown, exit the airport via Century Boulevard, then take I-405 north to I-10 east. To reach Pasadena, exit the airport, turn right onto Sepulveda Boulevard south, then take I-105 east to I-110 north.

Many city hotels provide free shuttles for their guests; ask about transportation when you make reservations. You can also catch a **taxi** from your terminal. Taxis line up outside each terminal and rides are metered. Expect to pay about $30 to Hollywood and downtown, $25 to Beverly Hills, $20 to Santa Monica, and $45 to Pasadena, including a $2.50 service charge for rides originating at LAX.

The **Super Shuttle** (☎ 310/782-6600) offers regularly scheduled minivans from LAX to any location in the city. When traveling to the airport for your trip home, reserve your shuttle at least a day in advance. The city's MTA buses also go between LAX and many parts of the city; phone **MTA Airport Information** (☎ 800/ 252-7433 or 213/626-4455) for schedules and fares.

OTHER AREA AIRPORTS   One of the area's smaller airports might be more convenient for you, landing you closer to your destination and allowing you to avoid the traffic and bustle of LAX. **Burbank-Glendale-Pasadena Airport** (☎ 818/840-8840) is the best place to land if you're locating in Hollywood or the Valleys. This small airport has especially good links to Las Vegas and other southwestern cities. **Long Beach Municipal Airport** (☎ 310/421-8293), south of LAX, is the best place to land if you're visiting Long Beach or northern Orange County, and want to avoid L.A. entirely. The **Orange County/John Wayne International Airport** in Anaheim (☎ 714/252-5200) is closest to Disneyland, Knott's Berry Farm, and other Anaheim area attractions.

BY CAR

If you're driving in **from the north,** you have two choices: the quick route, along I-5 through the middle of the state; or the scenic route along the coast.

Heading south along I-5, you'll pass a small town called Grapevine. This marks the start of a mountain pass known as the Grapevine. Once you've reached the southern end of the mountain pass, you'll be in the San Fernando Valley, and you've arrived in Los Angeles County. To reach the beach communities and L.A.'s Westside, take I-405 south; to get to Hollywood, take Calif. 170 south to U.S. 101 south (this route is called the Hollywood Freeway the entire way); I-5 will take you through downtown and into Orange County.

If you're taking the scenic coastal route in from the north, take U.S. 101 to I-405 or I-5, or stay on U.S. 101, following the instructions as listed above to your final destination.

The Los Angeles Area at a Glance

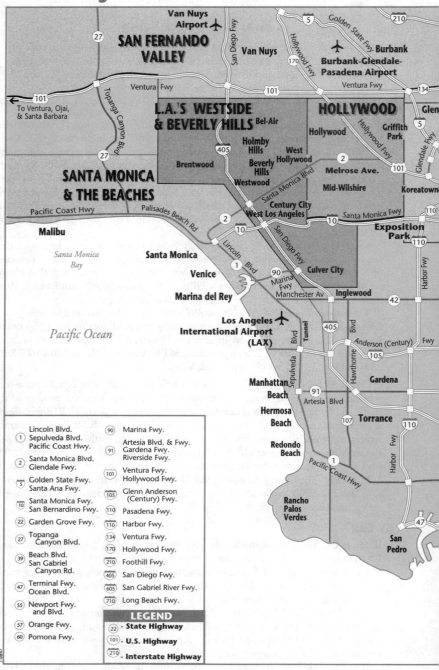

Legend and map labels:

SAN FERNANDO VALLEY
- Van Nuys Airport
- Van Nuys
- Burbank
- Burbank-Glendale-Pasadena Airport
- Golden State Fwy
- Ventura Fwy
- To Ventura, Ojai, & Santa Barbara

L.A.'S WESTSIDE & BEVERLY HILLS
- Bel-Air
- Holmby Hills
- Brentwood
- Beverly Hills
- West Hollywood
- Westwood
- Century City
- West Los Angeles
- Santa Monica Blvd

HOLLYWOOD
- Hollywood
- Griffith Park
- Glen
- Melrose Ave.
- Mid-Wilshire
- Koreatown

SANTA MONICA & THE BEACHES
- Malibu
- Santa Monica Bay
- Pacific Coast Hwy
- Palisades Beach Rd
- Santa Monica
- Venice
- Marina del Rey
- Pacific Ocean
- Los Angeles International Airport (LAX)
- Manhattan Beach
- Hermosa Beach
- Redondo Beach
- Rancho Palos Verdes
- San Pedro

- Culver City
- Inglewood
- Exposition Park
- Manchester Av
- Gardena
- Torrance
- Artesia Blvd
- Pacific Coast Hwy

Legend (route index)

- ① Lincoln Blvd. Sepulveda Blvd. Pacific Coast Hwy.
- ② Santa Monica Blvd. Glendale Fwy.
- 5 Golden State Fwy. Santa Ana Fwy.
- 10 Santa Monica Fwy. San Bernardino Fwy.
- 22 Garden Grove Fwy.
- 27 Topanga Canyon Blvd.
- 39 Beach Blvd. San Gabriel Canyon Rd.
- 47 Terminal Fwy. Ocean Blvd.
- 55 Newport Fwy. and Blvd.
- 57 Orange Fwy.
- 60 Pomona Fwy.
- 90 Marina Fwy.
- 91 Artesia Blvd. & Fwy. Gardena Fwy. Riverside Fwy.
- 101 Ventura Fwy. Hollywood Fwy.
- 105 Glenn Anderson (Century) Fwy.
- 110 Pasadena Fwy.
- 110 Harbor Fwy.
- 134 Ventura Fwy.
- 170 Hollywood Fwy.
- 210 Foothill Fwy.
- 405 San Diego Fwy.
- 605 San Gabriel River Fwy.
- 710 Long Beach Fwy.

LEGEND
- 22 - State Highway
- 101 - U.S. Highway
- 210 - Interstate Highway

1-0847

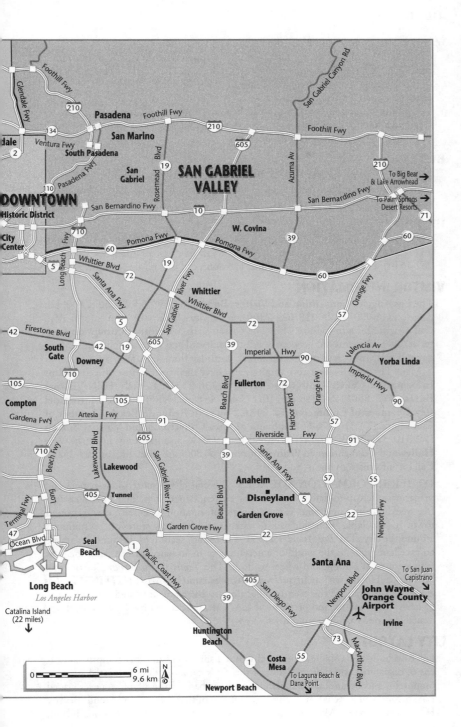

If you're approaching **from the east,** you'll be driving in on I-10. For Orange County, take Calif. 57 south. I-10 continues through downtown and terminates at the beach. If you're heading to Hollywood, take U.S. 101 north; if you're heading to the Westside, take I-405 north. To get to the beaches, take Calif. 1 (PCH) north or south, depending on your destination.

If you're coming in **from the south,** head north on I-5. At the southern end of Orange County, I-405 splits off to the west; take this road to the Westside and beach communities. Stay on I-5 to reach downtown.

BY TRAIN

Passengers arriving via **Amtrak** (☎ **800/USA-RAIL**) will disembark at Union Station, on downtown's northern edge. From the station, travelers can take one of the many taxis that line up outside the station.

BY BUS

The main Los Angeles bus station for arriving **Greyhound/Trailways** (☎ **800/ 231-2222**) buses is downtown at 1716 E. 7th St., east of Alameda (☎ 213/ 262-1514). For additional area terminal locations, call the toll-free number.

VISITOR INFORMATION

The **Los Angeles Convention and Visitors Bureau,** 633 W. 5th St., Suite 600, Los Angeles, CA 90071 (☎ **213/624-7300**), is the city's main source for information. Call or write for a free visitor's kit. The bureau staffs a **Visitors Information Center** at 685 S. Figueroa St., between Wilshire Boulevard and 7th Street; it's open Monday to Friday from 8am to 5:30pm and on Saturday from 8:30am to 5pm.

Many Los Angeles–area communities also have their own tourist offices: **Visitor Information Center Hollywood** (☎ 213/236-2331); **Beverly Hills Visitors Bureau** (☎ 800/345-2210 or 310/271-8174; fax 310/858-8032); **Marina del Rey Chamber of Commerce** (☎ 213/821-0555); **Redondo Beach Chamber of Commerce** (☎ 310/376-6911); **Santa Monica Convention and Visitors Bureau** (☎ 310/393-7593; Internet Website: http://www.ci.santa-monica.ca.us); **West Hollywood Convention & Visitors Bureau** (☎ 800/368-6020 or 310/289-2525). Call for information, hours, and locations.

OTHER INFORMATION SOURCES   Several city-oriented newspapers and magazines offer up-to-date information on current happenings. The *L.A. Weekly,* a free weekly listings magazine, is packed with information on current events around town. It's available from sidewalk newsracks and in many stores and restaurants around the city. The *Los Angeles Times* "Calendar" section of the Sunday paper is an excellent guide to the world of entertainment in and around L.A., and includes listings of what's doing and where to do it. The *Times* also maintains an Internet "Guide to Tinseltown" at **http://www.latimes.com/HOME/ENT/TINSEL.** *Los Angeles* magazine and the even trendier upstart *Buzz* are city-based monthlies full of news, information, and previews of L.A.'s art, music, and food scenes. Both are available at newsstands around town.

CITY LAYOUT

Los Angeles is not a single compact city, but a sprawling suburbia comprising dozens of disparate communities. Most of the city's communities are located between mountains and ocean, on the flatlands of a huge basin. Even if you've never visited L.A. before, you'll recognize the names of many of these areas: Hollywood, Beverly Hills, Santa Monica, Malibu. Ocean breezes push the city's infamous smog inland, toward dozens of less well-known residential communities, and through mountain passes into the suburban sprawl of the San Fernando and San Gabriel valleys.

Downtown Los Angeles—which isn't where most tourists will stay—is in the center of the basin, about 12 miles east of the Pacific Ocean. Most visitors will spend the bulk of their time either on the coast or on the city's Westside (see "The Neighborhoods in Brief," below, for complete details on all the city's sectors).

MAIN ARTERIES & STREETS

L.A.'s extensive freeway system connects the city's patchwork of communities; they work well together to get you where you need to be, although rush-hour traffic can sometimes be bumper-to-bumper. You might only drive on a couple of L.A's freeways, but here's an overview of the entire system:

U.S. 101, called the "Ventura Freeway" in the San Fernando Valley and the "Hollywood Freeway" in the city, runs across L.A. in a roughly northwest-southeast direction, from the San Fernando Valley to the center of downtown.

Calif. 134 continues as the Ventura Freeway after U.S. 101 turns into the city and becomes the Hollywood Freeway. The Calif. 134 branch of the Ventura Freeway continues directly east, through the valley towns of Burbank and Glendale, to **I-210** (the "Foothill Freeway"), which will take you through Pasadena and out toward the eastern edge of Los Angeles County.

I-5, otherwise known as the "Golden State Freeway" north of I-10 and the "Santa Ana Freeway" south of I-10, bisects downtown on its way from San Francisco to San Diego.

I-10, labeled the "Santa Monica Freeway" west of I-5 and the "San Bernardino Freeway" east of I-5, is the city's major east-west freeway, connecting the San Gabriel Valley to downtown and Santa Monica.

I-405, also known as the "San Diego Freeway," runs north-south through L.A's Westside, connecting the San Fernando Valley with LAX and the southern beach areas.

I-105, Los Angeles's newest freeway—called the "Century Freeway"—extends from LAX east to I-605.

I-110, commonly known as the "Harbor Freeway," starts in Pasadena as **Calif. 110** (the "Pasadena Freeway"); it turns into the Interstate in downtown Los Angeles and runs directly south, where it dead-ends in San Pedro. The section that's now the Pasadena Freeway is Los Angeles's historic first freeway, known as the Arroyo Seco when it opened in 1940.

I-710, also called the "Long Beach Freeway," runs in a north-south direction through East Los Angeles and dead-ends at Long Beach.

I-605, the "San Gabriel River Freeway," runs roughly parallel to I-710 farther east, through the cities of Hawthorne and Lynwood and into the San Gabriel Valley.

Calif. 1—called "Highway 1", the "Pacific Coast Highway," or simply "PCH"— is really a highway (more like a surface thruway) rather than a freeway. It skirts the ocean, linking all of L.A.'s beach communities, from Malibu to the Orange Coast.

The freeways are complemented by a complex web of surface streets. The major east-west thoroughfares connecting downtown to the beaches (listed from north to south) are Sunset Boulevard, Santa Monica Boulevard, Wilshire Boulevard, and Olympic, Pico, and Venice boulevards. The section of Sunset Boulevard that runs between Crescent Heights Boulevard and Doheny Drive is the famed Sunset Strip.

STREET MAPS

Because Los Angeles is so spread out, a good map of the area is essential. Foldout maps are available at gas stations, hotels, bookshops, and tourist-oriented shops around the city. If you're going to be in Los Angeles for a week or more, or plan on doing some extensive touring, you might want to invest in the all-inclusive *Thomas Guide,* a comprehensive book of city maps that depicts every single road in the city. The ring-bound edition is sold in most area bookstores and costs about $16. There's also an overview of the L.A. area included on th enclosed four-color sheet map.

THE NEIGHBORHOODS IN BRIEF

Los Angeles is a very confusing city, with fluid neighborhood lines and equally elastic labels. We've found that the best way to grasp the city is to break it into five regions—Santa Monica and the Beaches, Westside L.A. and Beverly Hills, Hollywood, Downtown, and the San Fernando Valley—each of which encompasses a more-or-less distinctive patchwork of city neighborhoods and independently incorporated communities.

SANTA MONICA & THE BEACHES

These are our favorite L.A. communities. The 60-mile beachfront stretching southward from Malibu to the Palos Verdes Peninsula has milder weather and less smog than the inland communities, and traffic is nominally lighter—except on summer weekends, of course. The towns along the coast each have their own mood and charm. We've listed them below from north to south:

Malibu, at the northern border of Los Angeles County, is 25 miles from downtown. Its particularly wide beaches, sparsely populated hills, and relative remoteness from the inner city make it extremely popular with rich recluses. With plenty of green space and dramatic rocky outcroppings, Malibu's rural beauty is unsurpassed in L.A.

Pretty **Santa Monica,** Los Angeles's premier beach community, is known for its long ocean pier, artsy atmosphere, and somewhat wacky residents. It's also noted for its particularly acute homeless problem. The 3rd Street Promenade, a pedestrians-only thoroughfare lined with great shops and restaurants, is one of the country's most successful revitalization projects.

Venice, a planned community in the spirit of its Italian forebear, was constructed with a series of narrow canals connected by quaint one-lane bridges. The area has been infested with grime and crime, but gentrification is in full swing. Some of L.A.'s most innovative and interesting architecture lines funky Main Street. Without question, Venice is best known for its Ocean Front Walk, a nonstop circus of skaters, sellers, and posers of all ages, colors, and sizes.

Marina del Rey, just south of Venice, is a somewhat quieter, more upscale community best known for its small-craft harbor, one of the largest of its kind in the world.

Manhattan, Hermosa, and **Redondo beaches,** as well as neighboring **Rancho Palos Verdes,** are relatively sleepy residential neighborhoods with modest homes, mild weather, and easy parking. These communities have excellent beaches for volleyballers, surfers, and sunworshippers, but there's not much else about these South Bay suburbs for visitors to get very excited about—when it comes to good restaurants or cultural activities, pickings are quite slim indeed.

L.A.'S WESTSIDE & BEVERLY HILLS

The Westside, an imprecise, misshapen L sandwiched between Hollywood and the city's coastal communities, includes some of the L.A.'s most prestigious neighborhoods, all with names you're sure to recognize:

Beverly Hills is roughly bounded by Olympic Boulevard on the south, Robertson Boulevard on the east, and Westwood and Century City on the west; it extends into the hills to the north. Politically distinct from the rest of Los Angeles, this famous enclave is best known for its palm tree–lined streets of palatial homes and high-priced shops (does Rodeo Drive ring a bell?), but it's the healthy mix of the filthy rich, tourists, and wannabes that creates a unique—and sometimes bizarre—atmosphere.

West Hollywood is a key-shaped community (go ahead, look at your map) whose epicenter is the intersection of Santa Monica and La Cienega boulevards. It's bounded on the west by Doheny Drive and on the south roughly by Melrose Avenue; the tip of the key extends east for several blocks north and south of Santa Monica Boulevard as far as La Brea Avenue, but it's primarily located to the west of Fairfax Avenue. Nestled between Beverly Hills and Hollywood, this politically independent town can feel either tony or tawdry, depending on which end of it you're in. In addition to being home to the city's best restaurants, shops, and art galleries, West Hollywood is the center of L.A.'s gay community.

Bel Air and **Holmby Hills,** located in the hills north of Westwood and west of the Beverly Hills city limits, comprise a wealthy residential area and feature prominently on most maps to the stars' homes.

Brentwood, the world-famous backdrop for the O.J. Simpson melodrama, is really just a tiny, quiet, relatively upscale neighborhood with the typical L.A. mixture of homes, restaurants, and strip malls. It lies west of I-405 and north of Santa Monica and West Los Angeles.

Westwood, an urban village that the University of California, Los Angeles (UCLA) calls home, is bounded by I-405, Santa Monica Boulevard, Sunset Boulevard, and Beverly Hills. The village, which used to be a hot destination for a night on the town, lost much of its appeal because of overcrowding, rudeness, and even street violence. There's still a high concentration of movie theaters, but we're all waiting for Westwood to regain the charm it once had.

Century City is a compact, busy, rather bland high-rise area sandwiched between West Los Angeles and Beverly Hills. Once the back lot of 20th Century Fox studios, Century City is home to the Shubert Theatre and the outdoor Century City Marketplace. Its three main thoroughfares are Century Park East, Avenue of the Stars, and Century Park West; it's bounded on the north by Santa Monica Boulevard and on the south by Pico Boulevard.

West Los Angeles is a label that basically applies to everything that isn't one of the other Westside neighborhoods. It's generally the area south of Santa Monica Boulevard, north of Venice Boulevard, east of the communities of Santa Monica and Venice, and west and south of Century City.

HOLLYWOOD

Yes, they still come. Young aspirants are attracted to this town like moths fluttering in the glare of neon lights. But Hollywood is now much more a state of mind than a glamour center. Many of the neighborhood's former movie studios have moved to less expensive, more spacious venues. Hollywood Boulevard is now one of the city's seediest strips. The area is now just a less-than-admirable part of the whole of Los Angeles, but the legend of the neighborhood as the movie capital of the world endures, and it's still home to several important attractions, such as the Walk of Fame and Mann's Chinese Theatre.

For our purposes, the label "Hollywood" extends beyond seedy Hollywood itself—centered around Hollywood and Sunset boulevards—to surrounding neighborhoods. It generally encompasses everything between Western Avenue to the east and Fairfax, Avenue to the west and from the Hollywood Hills (with its dazzling homes and million-dollar views) south.

Melrose Avenue, a scruffy but fun neighborhood, is the city's funkiest shopping district.

The stretch of Wilshire Boulevard that runs through the southern part of Holly-wood is known as the **Mid-Wilshire District,** or Miracle Mile. It's lined with contemporary apartment houses and office buildings; the stretch just east of Fairfax Avenue, now known as **Museum Row,** is home to almost a dozen museums, including the Los Angeles County Museum of Art, the La Brea Tar Pits, and that brand-new shrine to L.A. car culture, the Petersen Automotive Museum.

Griffith Park, up Western Avenue in the northernmost reaches of Hollywood, is one of the country's largest urban parks, and home to the Los Angeles Zoo and the famous Griffith Observatory.

DOWNTOWN

Roughly bounded by the U.S. 101, I-110, I-10, and I-5 freeways, L.A.'s downtown is home to a tight cluster of high-rise offices, the El Pueblo de Los Angeles Historic District, and the neighborhoods of Koreatown, Chinatown, and Little Tokyo. For our purposes, the residential neighborhoods of Silverlake and Los Feliz, Exposition Park (home to Los Angeles Memorial Coliseum, the L.A. Sports Arena, and several downtown museums), and East and South-Central L.A., the city's famous barrios, all fall under the downtown umbrella.

The construction of skyscrapers—facilitated by earthquake-proof technology—transformed downtown Los Angeles into the business center of the city. Despite the relatively recent construction of numerous cultural centers—including the Music Center and the Museum of Contemporary Art—and a few smart restaurants, down-town is not the hub it would be in most cities; the Westside, Hollywood, and the beach communities are all more popular.

THE SAN FERNANDO VALLEY

The San Fernando Valley, known locally as "The Valley," was nationally popular-ized in the 1980s by the notorious mall-loving "Valley Girl" stereotype. Snuggled between the Santa Monica and the San Gabriel mountain ranges, most of the Val-ley is residential and commercial, and off the beaten tourist track. But there are some attractions bound to draw you over the hill: **Universal City,** located west of Griffith Park between U.S. 101 and Calif. 134, is home to Universal Studios and CityWalk, a vast shopping and entertainment complex. And you may make a trip to **Burbank,** just north of Universal City, to see one of your favorite TV shows being filmed at the NBC or Warner Bros. studios. There are also many good restaurants and shops along Ventura Boulevard in and around **Studio City.**

Glendale is a largely residential community sandwiched between the San Fernando Valley and downtown L.A. You'll find the city's best sightseeing cemetery, Forest Lawn, there.

2 Getting Around

BY CAR

Despite its hassles, driving is the way to get around L.A. The golden rule is this: Always allow more time to get to your destination than you reasonably think it will take, especially during morning and evening rush hours.

RENTALS Los Angeles is one of the cheapest places in America to rent a car. Among the national firms operating in L.A. are: **Alamo** (☎ 800/327-9633), **Avis** (☎ 800/331-1212), **Budget** (☎ 800/527-0700), **Dollar** (☎ 800/800-4000), **Hertz** (☎ 800/654-3131), **National** (☎ 800/328-4567), and **Thrifty** (☎ 800/367-2277).

PARKING   Parking in L.A. is usually ample, but in some sections—most notably downtown and in Santa Monica, West Hollywood, and Hollywood—finding a space can be fraught with frustration. In most places, though, you'll be able to find metered street parking—carry plenty of quarters. When you can't, expect to valet or garage your car for somewhere between $4 and $10. Many restaurants and night-clubs, and even some shopping centers, offer valet parking; they usually charge about $3 to $5. Most of the hotels listed in this book offer off-street parking; it's often complimentary, but can cost as much as $20 per day in high-density areas.

DRIVING TIPS   On surface roads, you may turn right at a red light (unless otherwise indicated) after making a complete stop and yielding to traffic and pedestrians. Pedestrians always have the right-of-way at intersections and crosswalks.

Many Southern California freeways have designated car-pool lanes, also known as High-Occupancy-Vehicle (HOV) lanes. Some require two passengers, others three. The minimum fine for an HOV violation is $246. Most on-ramps are metered to control the traffic flow; carpools are exempt and pass in their own lane.

When it comes to radio traffic reporter jargon, the names of L.A.'s freeways (as opposed to their numbers) are usually used. A "SigAlert" is the term used for an unplanned freeway crisis (a serious accident) that will affect the movement of traffic for 30 minutes or more. When you hear "a big rig is blocking the number one lane," you can determine the lane by counting out from the center divider.

BY PUBLIC TRANSPORTATION

We've heard rumors about visitors to Los Angeles who have toured the city entirely by public transportation, but they can't be more than that—rumors. It's hard to believe that visitors can comprehensively tour this Auto Land without a car of their own. Still, if you're in the city for only a short time, are on a very tight budget, or don't expect to be moving around a lot, public transport might be for you. The city's trains and buses are operated by the **Los Angeles County Metropolitan Transit Authority (MTA),** 425 S. Main St., Los Angeles, CA 90013 (☎ **213/ 626-4455**).

FAST FACTS: Los Angeles

American Express   In addition to those at 327 N. Beverly Dr., Beverly Hills (☎ 310/274-8277), and at 901 W. 7th St., downtown (☎ 213/627-4800), offices are located throughout the city. To report lost or stolen cards, call 800/ 528-4800. To report lost or stolen traveler's checks, call 800/221-7282.

Baby-sitters   If you're staying at one of the larger hotels, the concierge can usually recommend a reliable baby-sitter. If not, contact the Baby-Sitters Guild in Glendale (☎ 818/552-2229) or Sitters Unlimited (☎ 800/328-1191).

Dentists   To find an area dentist, call the national Dental Referral Service (☎ 800/422-8338).

Doctors   Contact the Uni-Health Information and Referral Hotline (☎ 800/ 922-0000) for a free, confidential physician referral.

Emergencies   For police, fire, highway patrol, or in case of life-threatening medical emergencies, dial **911.**

Liquor Laws   Liquor and grocery stores can sell packaged alcoholic beverages between 6am and 2am. Most restaurants, nightclubs, and bars are licensed to serve alcoholic beverages during the same hours. The legal age for purchase and consumption is 21; proof of age is required.

Newspapers/Magazines The *Los Angeles Times* is a plump high-quality daily with strong local and national coverage and meager international offerings. Its Sunday "Calendar" section is an excellent and interesting guide to the world of entertainment in and around L.A. The free weekly events magazine *L.A. Weekly* is packed with news of events and a calendar of happenings around town; it's available from sidewalk newsracks and in many stores and restaurants around the city. *Los Angeles* magazine and *Buzz* are hip monthlies with good listings and entertainment news.

Police See "Emergencies," above. For nonemergency police matters, phone 213/485-2121 or 213/550-4951 in Beverly Hills.

Post Office Call 213/586-1467 to find the one closest to you.

Taxes The combined Los Angeles County and California state sales taxes amount to 8.25%; hotel taxes range from 12% to 17%, depending on the municipality you're in.

Taxis You can order a taxi in advance from Checker Cab (☎ 213/221-2355), L.A. Taxi (☎ 213/627-7000), or United Independent Taxi (☎ 213/483-7604).

Time For the correct time, call 853-1212 (good for all local area codes).

Weather Call Los Angeles Weather Information (☎ 213/554-1212) for the daily forecast. For beach conditions, call the Zuma Beach Lifeguard recorded information (☎ 310/457-9701).

3 Accommodations

by Jim Moore

Jim Moore was an assistant editor at Macmillan
Travel before he abandoned the concrete canyons
of New York City for sunny Southern California.

In sprawling Los Angeles, location is everything. Choosing the right neighborhood as a base can make or break your vacation; if you plan to while away a few days at the beach but base yourself downtown, for example, you're going to lose a lot of valuable relaxation time on the freeway. For business travelers, choosing a location is easy: Pick a hotel near your work—don't commute if you don't have to. For vacationers, though, the decision about where to stay is a more difficult one. Take into consideration where you'll be wanting to spend your time before you commit yourself to a base. But wherever you stay, count on doing a good deal of driving—no hotel in Los Angeles is convenient to everything.

In general, downtown hotels are business oriented; they're sometimes popular with groups, but are largely ignored by independent tourists. The top hotels here are very good, but cheaper ones can be downright nasty. If you're on a budget, locate elsewhere.

There are fewer hotels in Hollywood than the visitor would expect. The accommodations here, usually moderately priced, are generally well maintained but otherwise unspectacular. Hollywood is very centrally located between downtown and Beverly Hills, and it's within easy reach of Santa Monica. It's a great base if you're planning to do a lot of touring.

Most visitors stay on the city's Westside, a short drive from the beach and close to most of L.A.'s most colorful sights. The city's most elegant—and expensive—accommodations are in Beverly Hills and Bel Air; a few of the hotels in this neighborhood have become visitor attractions themselves. You'll find the city's best hotel values in West Hollywood, an exciting and convenient place to base yourself.

The relatively smogless coastal areas are understandably popular with visitors. Trendy Santa Monica and its neighbors are home to lots of hotels; book ahead, because they fill up quickly in the summer, when everyone wants to be by the water. Santa Monica also enjoys convenient freeway access to the popular tourist sights inland. Malibu and the South Bay communities (Manhattan, Hermosa, and Redondo beaches) are more out of the way, and hence quieter.

Families might want to head to the San Fernando Valley to be near Universal Studios, or straight to Anaheim or Buena Park for easy access to Disneyland and Knott's Berry Farm (see Chapter 11, "Easy Excursions from Los Angeles," for places to stay in the Anaheim area).

The hotels listed below are categorized first by area, then by price: Rates given are the rack (walk-in) rates for a standard room for two with private bath (unless otherwise noted); you can often do better. Ask about weekend packages and discounts, corporate rates, family plans, and any other special rates that might be available. The prices given do not include state and city hotel taxes, which run from 12% to a whopping 17%, depending on which community you're in. Be aware that most hotels make additional charges for parking (with in-and-out privileges, except where noted) and levy heavy surcharges for telephone use.

Several hotel reservations services offer one-stop shopping; they'll tell you what's available at many of L.A.'s hotels and book you into the one of your choice, all at no additional charge. These services are particularly helpful for last-minute reservations, when rooms are often scarce—or discounted. Here are two companies that serve the L.A. area: **Central Reservation Service,** 505 Maitland Ave., Suite 100, Altamonte Springs, FL 32701 (☎ **800/548-3311** or 417/339-4116; fax 407/339-4736); and the **Hotel Reservations Network,** 8140 Walnut Hill Lane, Suite 203, Dallas, TX 75231 (☎ **800/96-HOTEL** or 214/361-7311; fax 214/361-7299).

SANTA MONICA & THE BEACHES
VERY EXPENSIVE

Loews Santa Monica Beach Hotel. 1700 Ocean Ave. (south of Colorado Blvd.), Santa Monica, CA 90401. ☎ **800/223-0888** or 310/458-6700. Fax 310/458-6761. 349 rms, 22 suites. A/C TV TEL. $225–$315 double; from $450 suite. AE, CB, DC, EU, MC, V. Valet parking $15, self-parking $13.

If it weren't for Shutters, this would be the finest hotel in Santa Monica. Loews isn't exactly beachfront; it's on a hill less than a block away, but the unobstructed ocean views are fabulous. But realize that you're paying for location: The drone of the ice makers is audible in the hallways, and the plumbing is noisy at times—blemishes that you wouldn't expect from a hotel of this caliber. But it's still a great hotel. A dramatic, multistory glass and green-steel atrium lobby gives way to ample cookie-cutter rooms that are outfitted with the latest luxury amenities. This popular hotel doesn't need my recommendation to stir business; it has become something of a darling for industry functions, and it's booked to capacity in the summer months.

Dining/Entertainment: There are two restaurants and poolside snack service. There's live jazz in the lounge most nights.

Services: Concierge, room service (24 hours), overnight shoeshine, nightly turndown, baby-sitting, valet parking.

Facilities: VCRs on request, outdoor heated pool, Jacuzzi, fitness center with cardio machines, summer children's program, business center, bike and roller-skate rental.

○ **Shutters on the Beach.** 1 Pico Blvd. (at the beach), Santa Monica, CA 90405. ☎ **800/334-9000** or 310/458-0030. Fax 310/458-4589. 186 rms, 12 suites. TV TEL. $290–$475 double; from $675 suite. AE, DC, DISC, EU, MC, V. Parking $16.

Light and luxurious Shutters enjoys one of the city's most prized locations: directly on the beach (this is the only fine hotel to enjoy such a distinction in L.A.), a block from Santa Monica Pier. The guest rooms fall into two categories: cottagelike beachfront rooms and those housed in a taller tower. Although the beach-cottage rooms are plainly more desirable, when it comes to rates the hotel doesn't distinguish between them. The views and sounds of the ocean are the most outstanding qualities of the rooms, some of which have fireplaces and Jacuzzis; all have floor-to-ceiling windows that open. Showers come with waterproof radios, toy duckies, and biodegradable bath supplies. Despite this welcome whimsy, there's a relaxed and elegant atmosphere throughout the contemporary art–filled hotel—sort of like staying at the opulent Cape Cod estate of a very well-off friend (except for the quirky parade of humanity along the boardwalk out front). The small swimming pool on an elevated deck and the sunny lobby lounge overlooking the sand are two great places for spotting the celebrities who swear by Shutters as an alternative to smoggy Hollywood.

Dining/Entertainment: One Pico, the hotel's premier restaurant, is very well regarded. The best meals at the more casual Pedals are prepared on the wood-burning grill. The overdesigned Handle Bar offers good happy-hour specials.

Services: Concierge, room service (24 hours), overnight laundry, evening turn-down, in-room massage, valet parking.

Facilities: VCRs, outdoor heated pool, exercise room with cardio machines, Jacuzzi, sauna, sundeck, beach equipment rental, bicycle rental.

EXPENSIVE

In addition to the Hotel Oceana, another Santa Monica option in this price category is the recently renovated, reliable **Radisson Huntley Hotel** at 1111 2nd St., north of Wilshire Boulevard (☎ **800/333-3333** or 310/394-5454).

Hotel Oceana. 849 Ocean Ave., Santa Monica, CA 90403. ☎ **800/777-0758** or 310/393-0486. 63 suites. TV TEL. $170–$325 suite. AE, DC, DISC, MC, V. Rates include breakfast. Parking $10.

If you stayed in the former Oceana Suites Hotel, you won't even recognize the newly renovated and renamed Hotel Oceana. Excellently located in a residential neighborhood right on Ocean Avenue, this all-suite hotel is great for families. Upon walking into the newly built lobby, you'll know you've arrived at the beach; light and airy and capped by an enormous skylight, the lobby is completely covered with Jean Cocteau–inspired floor-to-ceiling murals. With the bright Matisse-inspired colors and cushy IKEA-ish furniture, the completely renovated suites appear to have been decorated by the set designer from *Friends*. Some suites have ocean views; VIP suites feature air-conditioning and two-person Jacuzzi tubs. In-room lunch and dinner service is provided by Wolfgang Puck's Cafe, but since all suites come with fully equipped kitchens, cooking for yourself is another option.

MODERATE

In addition to the hotels recommended below, another moderately priced option is **Courtyard by Marriott,** 13480 Maxella Ave., Marina del Rey (☎ **800/628-0908** or 310/822-8555), a resortlike hotel conveniently located only a few blocks from the marina and the Villa Marina Center.

✪ **Barnaby's Hotel.** 3501 Sepulveda Blvd. (at Rosecrans Blvd.), Manhattan Beach, CA 90266. ☎ **800/552-5285** or 310/545-8466. 123 rms. A/C. $144–$169 double. Rates include breakfast. AE, DC, DISC, EU, MC, V. Valet parking $4.

The most unusual hotel on the coast, Barnaby's sounds like a guesthouse, operates like a bed-and-breakfast, and feels like a quaint old hotel. The pink stuccoed facade and trademark green awnings give way to European-style guest rooms; each is decorated with antique headboards, lace curtains, hardcover books, and 19th-century prints. Some rooms feature balconies, chandeliers, and attractive but nonfunctioning fireplaces. The best rooms are in back and overlook the courtyard, where weddings and other functions are held. Romantic Barnaby's is an excellent place for couples and celebrants. Full English breakfasts are served buffet style. The hotel offers complimentary airport service as well as a glass-enclosed heated pool and Jacuzzi, and a sundeck.

✪ Casa Malibu. 22752 Pacific Coast Hwy. (about a quarter mile south of Malibu Pier), Malibu, CA 90265. ☎ **800/831-0858** or 310/456-2219. Fax 310/456-5418. 19 rms, 2 suites. TV TEL. $99–$135 double with garden view, $150 double with ocean view, $169 beachfront double; from $169 suite. Room with kitchen $10 extra. AE, EU, MC, V. Free parking.

I'm hesitant to crow too loudly about Casa Malibu—one of my favorite L.A. hotels—for fear that it'll be even harder to get a room here. The modest two-story motel wraps around a palm-studded inner courtyard with well-tended flowerbeds and cuppa d'oro vines climbing the facade. Just past the garden is the blue Pacific and a large swath of private Malibu beach for the exclusive use of hotel guests. The rooms are surprisingly contemporary and cheerful, with top-quality mattresses, bathrobes, coffeemaker, and refrigerator; some rooms come with a fireplace and/or air-conditioning. The king-size-bedded oceanfront rooms have balconies directly over the sand, making them some of the city's most coveted accommodations—they're a great place to watch the pelicans dive for fish in the late afternoon. If you've got a room without a view, you can only see the ocean from the communal balcony; but since the sound of the waves will put you soundly to sleep in any of the rooms, that criticism seems like complaining that the caviar is too cold.

Hotel Shangri-La. 1301 Ocean Ave., Santa Monica, CA 90401. ☎ **800/345-STAY** or 310/394-2791. Fax 310/451-3351. 8 studios, 47 suites. A/C TV TEL. $115 studio; from $155 suite. Rates include continental breakfast. AE, DC, DISC, EU, MC, V. Free parking.

Perched right on Ocean Avenue overlooking the Pacific and just 2 blocks from the Third Street Promenade, the Shangri-La has a great location. The small lobby opens to a large plant-filled courtyard (suprisingly lacking a pool) bordered on the north and west by the hotel. The rooms are accessed motel style, from outside balconies overlooking the courtyard. The rooms themselves are spacious, and almost all offer ocean views. The overall art deco feel of the hotel carries through into the rooms—the lamps and mirrors, even the faucets and doorknobs evoke the early part of the century. The large Formica-covered furniture, however, evokes the Starship Enterprise more than the Golden Age of Hollywood. There's a small ocean-view exercise room.

Marina del Rey Hotel. 13534 Bali Way (west of Lincoln Blvd.), Marina del Rey, CA 90292. ☎ **800/882-4000,** 800/862-7462 in California, or 310/301-1000. Fax 310/301-8167. 154 rms, 6 suites. A/C TV TEL. $140–$205 double; from $350 suite. Packages available. AE, CB, DC, EU, MC, V. Free parking.

This hotel, on a pier jutting into the harbor, is bounded on three sides by the world's largest man-made marina. The guest rooms are surprisingly well decorated, with fine contemporary furnishings and a few nautical nods. Most rooms have balconies or patios, as well as harbor views. The entrance and lobby were under renovation when I visited, but should be completed when you arrive. The Waterfront Bar & G overlooking the marina, serves California-style cuisine all day. Services and facilities include a concierge, room service, complimentary airport limousine, an outdoor heated waterside pool, sundeck, nearby tennis and golf, putting green, and car-rental service.

Marina International. 4200 Admiralty Way (west of Lincoln Blvd.), Marina del Rey, CA 90292. ☎ **800/529-2525** or 310/301-2000. Fax 310/301-6687. 110 rms, 25 bungalows. A/C TV TEL. $125–$300 double; from $150 bungalow. AE, CB, DC, EU, MC, V. Free parking.

This hotel's lovely rooms are bright, contemporary, and very, very private. Most rooms are decorated in a casual California style, with soft pastels and textured fabrics; all have balconies or patios. The bungalows are plush and absolutely huge—some are even split-level duplexes—with sitting areas and sofa beds. The Crystal Fountain serves continental fare indoors or out, and the hotel offers concierge, room service, and complimentary airport shuttle. There's an outdoor heated pool, whirlpool, sundeck, nearby golf and tennis, a business center, and a tour desk.

INEXPENSIVE

❍ **Venice Beach House Historic Inn.** 15 30th Ave. (off Pacific Ave.), Venice, CA 90291. ☎ **310/823-1966.** Fax 310/823-1842. 4 rms, none with bath; 5 suites. TV TEL. $85–$95 double; $130–$165 suite. Rates include continental breakfast. AE, EU, MC, V. Free parking.

This former family home, built in 1911, is now a fine bed-and-breakfast on one of Venice's unique sidewalk streets (a service alley provides access to rear garages). The interiors of this Victorian, with its hardwood floors, bay windows, lattice porch, and large Oriental rugs, will make you forget the hustle and bustle of the beach that's just steps away. Each of the nine guest units is different, outfitted with white rattan or antique wood furnishings; some are punctuated with country prints, others with shelves packed with worn hardcover books. One particularly romantic room has an ocean view and a fireplace. The four double rooms share baths. Continental breakfast—cereal, breads, juice, and coffee—is served in the comfortable downstairs sitting room; afternoon tea or cool lemonade is served with fresh-baked cookies every day. The inn can prepare picnic baskets for day excursions. *Beware:* The inn can get noisy, and despite its relative homeyness, it's not for everyone. Smoking is not permitted.

ACCOMMODATIONS NEAR LAX

If you have an early-morning flight and you need an airport hotel, here are two good, moderately priced choices: **Gateway Hotel–Los Angeles Airport,** 6101 W. Century Blvd., near Sepulveda Blvd. (☎ **800/325-3535** or 310/642-1111), a comfortable, California-style hotel that literally overlooks the runway; and the **Los Angeles Airport Marriott,** Century Boulevard at Airport Boulevard (☎ **800/228-9290** or 310/ 641-5700), a reliable choice for travelers on the fly. If you're looking for an inexpensive option, try the **Travelodge at LAX,** 5547 W. Century Blvd. (☎ **800/ 421-3939** or 310/649-4000), a otherwise standard member of the reliable chain with a surprisingly beautiful tropical garden surrounding the pool area.

L.A.'S WESTSIDE & BEVERLY HILLS
VERY EXPENSIVE

❍ **The Argyle.** 8358 Sunset Blvd., West Hollywood, CA 90069. ☎ **800/225-2637** or 213/ 654-7100. Fax 213/654-9287. 19 rms, 48 suites. TV TEL. $225 double; from $325 suite. AE, CB, DC, EU, MC, V.

Completed in 1929, this landmark 15-story hotel is one of the most pristine art deco buildings in the city; it was designed in the Streamline Moderne style, with a gunmetal-gray facade, rounded corners, and an intricate stepped pediment that's reminiscent of classical designs. It's also terrifically located, at the base of the Hollywood Hills between Beverly Hills and Hollywood. Formerly the St. James Club (and before that, Sunset Tower), the hotel has been home to Jean Harlow, Errol Flynn, and John Wayne (who once kept a cow on his balcony so he could have fresh milk every day). More recently it made an appearance in *The Player.* Purchased in 1995 by the Lancaster Group (which owns the Jefferson in Washington and the Tremont in Chicago), the Argyle is undergoing interior renovation and an exterior face-lift that was just completed. The rooms are on the small side, but they're lovely, with deco reproductions and specially commissioned handcrafted Italian furnishings, such as unique gondolalike beds. Corner rooms have marvelous rounded windows and spectacular city views. Though the hotel appears straight out of the 1920s, modern conveniences haven't been overlooked—all rooms come equipped with VCRs, CD players, fax machines, and space-age phones with display screens that do everything from tell the temperature to control the room's lighting.

Dining/Entertainment: Book a table at Fenix when you reserve your room. Ken Frank, one of the area's most respected restaurateurs, sold his celebrated French restaurant La Toque in order to cook here; it's one of the neighborhood's most prominent dining rooms.

Services: Concierge, room service (24 hours), laundry service, secretarial services.

Facilities: Heated outdoor pool, small exercise room with free weights and cardio machines, sundeck, car-rental desk.

✪ **Beverly Hills Hotel & Bungalows.** 9641 Sunset Blvd. (at Rodeo Dr.), Beverly Hills, CA 90210. ☎ **800/283-8885** or 310/276-2251. Fax 310/281-2905. 194 rms, 21 bungalows and garden suites. A/C TV TEL. $300–$350 double; from $300 bungalow; from $595 suite. AE, DC, EU, MC, V. Parking $15.

After a 4¹/₂-year, $100-million restoration, the Pink Palace is back. The famous stucco facade, impeccably landscaped grounds, and grand lobby have been restored to their former over-the-top glory, and then some: Despite declarations that the custom pink color has been painstakingly re-created, most everyone will tell you—myself included—that the hotel should now be known as the "Salmon Palace." Despite this controversy, the reborn hotel is glorious again. This is the kind of place where legends are made, and many were: This was center stage for deal—and star—making in Hollywood's golden days. Howard Hughes long maintained quite a complex here (he even kept a separate room for his personal food-taster). Dean Martin and Frank Sinatra once got into a big fistfight with other guests at the bar. In 1969 John Lennon and Yoko Ono checked into the most secluded bungalow under assumed names, only to station so many armed guards around their cozy hideaway that they might as well have put up a neon sign announcing their arrival. Inside observers claim that many of the Beverly Hills Hotel's Old Hollywood faithfuls defected to the nearby Peninsula, and have yet to return following the hotel's 1995 reopening, but plenty of current stars and industry hotshots can be found lazing around the pool Katherine Hepburn once dove into fully clothed.

The hotel was reconfigured to compete in today's luxury market. There are fewer rooms, each more spacious and loaded with modern amenities. Gone are the sorry plumbing and tiny bathrooms of yesteryear; today's larger ones are outfitted with double Grecian marble sinks, TVs, and telephones for sinkside deal making. The best original touches have been retained as well, like a butler at your service with the touch of a button. The bungalows are more luxurious than ever—and who knows who you'll have as a neighbor?

Dining/Entertainment: The iconic Polo Lounge is back, with the original atmosphere and traditional comfort fare, like Dutch apple pancakes or its signature guacamole; the veteran maître d' is back too, greeting the agents and stars here to close mega-bucks movie deals. The adjacent Polo Grill takes up the nouvelle torch, specializing in California cuisine. The famous Fountain Coffee Shop is back. The Tea Lounge is another new addition.

Services: Concierge, room service (24 hours), dry cleaning, laundry service, nightly turndown, airport limo service, massage, valet parking.

Facilities: VCRs (video rentals delivered to the rooms), large outdoor heated pool, fitness room with cardio machines, Jacuzzi, sundeck, car-rental desk, beauty salon, boutiques.

✪ **Hotel Bel-Air.** 701 Stone Canyon Rd. (north of Sunset Blvd.), Bel Air, CA 90077. ☎ **800/ 648-4097** or 310/472-1211. Fax 310/476-5890. 52 rms, 40 suites. $315–$435 double; from $495 suite. AE, DC, MC, V. Parking $12.50.

The Hotel Bel-Air is your address if you want to impress. This Mission-style hotel is truly one of the finest—and most beautiful—hotels in Southern California. It regularly wins praise for its attentive service and luxurious rooms. The grounds—11 acres of private park—are strikingly magical, lush with ancient trees, fragrant flowers, and a swan-dotted pond. The welcoming, richly traditional public rooms are filled with fine antiques. The guest villas, decorated in Mediterranean style with compulsive attention to detail, dot the property. The rooms and garden suites are equally stunning; all have two phones, a VCR, and a CD player. Some units have wood-burning fireplaces. The hotel is a natural for honeymooners and other celebrants, but families might be put off by the Bel-Air's relative formality, which is geared more to the jet-setting socialites and professionals who sojourn here.

Dining/Entertainment: It's worth having dinner at the Restaurant. Even if you don't stay here, you might consider brunch or lunch on the hotel's outdoor, woodsy terrace, or stop in for drinks at the cozy bar.

Services: Concierge, room service (24 hours), evening turndown, valet parking, welcome tea upon arrival.

Facilities: VCRs, large outdoor heated pool, health club (with treadmills, Stair-Masters, Lifecycles), sundeck, nature trails.

Hotel Nikko. 465 S. La Cienega Blvd., Los Angeles, CA 90048. ☎ **800/645-5687** or 310/ 247-0400. Fax 310/247-0315. 300 rms and suites. A/C TV TEL. $295–$395 double; from $600 suite. AE, DC, DISC, JCB, MC, V. Valet parking $16.50; free self-parking.

Finally—a hotel designed for business travelers whose primary goal isn't mimicking every other business hotel. The Nikko refers to its interior decoration as Pacific Rim (Organic Pacific Rim for the suites, which use all organic textiles), but well thought-out seems just as appropriate. Thanks to amenities such as in-room fax machines, three two-line phones, and large counter/desk space, the rooms function equally well as sleeping quarters and workspaces. And after a long day at work, the huge Japanese soaking tubs that come in all the bathrooms are perfect for unwinding. Registration is done at sit-down desks. In the guest rooms, shoji screens replace curtains, allowing light to filter through or block it out entirely.

Dining/Entertainment: Blending French and American dishes with Asian influences, Pangaea was named "L.A's Best New Restaurant of 1994" by *Esquire* magazine. On Sunday, Pangaea offers a 14-piece big-band brunch. The Nikko also has a cocktail lounge with nightly entertainment.

Services: Concierge, room service (24 hours), evening turndown, same-day dry cleaning and laundry.

Facilities: Heated pool, exercise room, sauna, business center, massage.

✪ Regent Beverly Wilshire. 9500 Wilshire Blvd. (east of Santa Monica Blvd.), Beverly Hills, CA 90210. ☎ **800/421-4354** or 310/275-5200. Fax 310/274-2851. 300 rms, 144 suites. A/C TV TEL. $255–$405 double; from $425 suite. AE, CB, DC, DISC, EU, MC, V. Parking $15.

If the Beverly Hills Hotel is where new money exhibits itself, then this is the place for seasoned sophisticates. But that doesn't mean that it hasn't seen its share of color: Actor Warren Beatty earned his playboy reputation while living here, and parts of *Pretty Woman* were filmed in one of the palatial suites. You just can't beat the location, close to Rodeo Drive shops and an easy cruise down Wilshire to just about anywhere else. Nobody lingers in the spacious, ornate lobby; tell your friends to meet you in the more private lounge. The rooms are refined, with a mix of period furniture, three phones, three TVs, and special double-glazed windows that ensure absolute quiet. Wilshire Wing rooms are unusually huge, but those on the Beverly side are prettier, and include balconies overlooking the pool. The bathrooms have an extra-deep soaking tub and a glass-enclosed shower that's large enough for two (or more). There's steward service on every floor and butlers can be called from a bedside bell.

Dining/Entertainment: The elegant dining room here—one of the hottest of the moment—is the only place on the Westside offering fine dining and live dance music. The Lounge, a European-style salon, serves a terrific tea from 3 to 5pm, light menus, and cocktails; at night it's packed with media moguls and beautiful hangers-on.

Services: Concierge, room service (24 hours), overnight shoeshine, nightly turndown, express checkout, valet parking.

Facilities: Small outdoor heated pool, large health club with cardio and weight machines and free weights, hot tubs, sundeck, massage, business center, shops.

Westwood Marquis Hotel & Gardens. 930 Hilgard Ave., Los Angeles, CA 90024-3033. ☎ **800/421-2317** or 310/208-8765. Fax 310/824-0355. 257 suites. A/C TV TEL. From $235 suite; from $325 penthouse suite. AE, DC, DISC, JCB, MC, V.

This terrific all-suite hotel near UCLA, which attracts behind-the-scenes industry types, offers accommodations that are straightforward without being boring. Hidden behind a severe concrete exterior, each stylish room is unique and loaded with amenities. The 15-story hotel underwent a major renovation in 1995; each suite was outfitted with multiline speakerphones and fresh textiles. South-facing suites have the best city and ocean views. Beware: The hotel can be noisy during graduation and other large school events.

Dining/Entertainment: The Garden Terrace serves breakfast, lunch, and Sunday champagne brunch; dinner is served in the Dynasty Room. There are cocktails and afternoon tea in the lounge, and cocktails and casual fare at the outdoor cafe.

Services: Concierge, room service (24 hours), dry cleaning, laundry service, nightly turndown, valet parking.

Facilities: Two outdoor heated pools, Jacuzzi, small fitness center, sundeck, flower shop, gift shop.

EXPENSIVE

Beverly Prescott Hotel. 1224 S. Beverwil Dr. (north of Pico Blvd.; P.O. Box 3065), Beverly Hills, CA 90212. ☎ **800/421-3212** or 310/277-2800. Fax 310/203-9537. 128 rms, 12 suites. A/C TV TEL. $190–$275 double; from $250 suite. AE, DC, DISC, EU, MC, V. Parking $15.

This hotel opened its doors in 1993, after a multimillion-dollar renovation that rendered the former Beverly Hillcrest unrecognizable. Managed by the Kimpton Group, owners of about a dozen top-quality boutique hotels in San Francisco, the Prescott is knowledgeably run and joyfully decorated; its comfortable, colorful, funky furnishings were carefully chosen by a confidently quirky designer. Thus it was in perfect character for the hoteliers to commission the late legendary rock musician and neckwear designer Jerry Garcia to remodel one of the suites. The resulting Garcia Suite is surprisingly sedate, designed with fish themes, subtly psychedelic fabrics, a top-of-the-line sound system, and an eclectic art collection that includes a dozen pieces by Captain Trips himself. Each room has an oversize TV screen, cordless phones, and a private balcony with good city views.

Dining/Entertainment: The former Sylvie is, at least for now, the Chez. Operated by the same folks who run Chez Melange and a handful of other local restaurants, it serves up robustly flavored fusion cuisine in a bright, Caribbean-influenced interior.

Services: Concierge, room service (24 hours), overnight laundry/shoeshine, free morning newspaper, nightly turndown, massage and manicure services, complimentary shuttle service to nearby business centers and shopping.

Facilities: Large outdoor heated pool, fitness room with cardio machines, sundeck, business center.

Century Plaza Hotel & Tower. 2025 Ave. of the Stars (south of Santa Monica Blvd.), Century City, CA 90067. ☎ **800/228-3000** or 310/277-2000. Fax 310/551-3355. 996 rms, 76 suites. A/C TV TEL. $150–$220 double; from $250 suite. AE, CB, DC, EU, MC, V. Valet parking $19.50, self-parking $10.

Located on a former Twentieth Century Fox backlot, this Westin-managed property sits on 10 of L.A.'s most centrally located acres. It's so close to film and TV's Century City nerve center that it has become the de facto home-away-from-home for countless rank-and-file industry execs and creative types. Because it's so huge (the main building has 19 floors; the tower has 30), the hotel is also a natural for conventions and meetings; there's always something going on here. All this makes it the antithesis of warm and cozy, but the rooms are large, the freeways nearby, and your anonymity is assured. Rooms in the Tower building were renovated in 1995 and are considerably nicer—and pricier—than those in the main building. They feature large sitting areas, two sinks, and a separate tub and shower stall—some rooms in the main building have only a shower (no tub). Tower suites are head and shoulders above Hotel ones.

Dining/Entertainment: The hotel has two restaurants and two lounges, but dine in only if you have to.

Services: Concierge, room service (24 hours), same-day laundry service, evening turndown, complimentary car service to/from Beverly Hills, valet parking.

Facilities: Two large outdoor heated pools, Jacuzzi, sundeck, two exercise rooms, business center, conference rooms, car-rental desk, airline desk, ticket agency, tour desk.

✪ Chateau Marmont. 8221 Sunset Blvd. (between La Cienega and Crescent Heights blvds.), West Hollywood, CA 90046. ☎ **800/242-8328** or 213/656-1010. Fax 213/655-5311. 63 rms, 53 suites, 4 bungalows. A/C TV TEL. $190 double; from $240 suite; from $550 bungalow. AE, CB, DC, EU, MC, V. Valet parking $12.50.

The Norman-style Chateau Marmont, perched in a curve of the Sunset Strip, is a landmark from 1920s-era Hollywood; step inside and you expect to find John Barrymore or Errol Flynn holding inebriated court in the baronial living room. Greta Garbo regularly checked in as "Harriet Brown," and Howard Hughes maintained a suite here for a while; Jim Morrison was only one of many to call this home in later years. This historical monument built its reputation on exclusivity and privacy, a posture that was shattered when John Belushi overdosed in Bungalow No. 2. Chateau Marmont is popular because it's close to the Hollywood action, and a luxurious world away at the same time. The standard rooms have views of the city and the Hollywood Hills; some have kitchenettes. Their faux English and Formica furnishings aren't too rustic—just enough that you'll enjoy their kitsch. The suites are large, and most come with cloth-canopied balconies. The poolside Cape Cod bungalows—large, secluded, cozy, with full kitchens—are some of the most coveted in town.

Services: Concierge, room service (24 hours), laundry service, nightly turndown.

Facilities: Large outdoor heated pool, small fitness room, sundeck.

⑤ **Le Montrose Suite Hotel.** 900 Hammond St., West Hollywood, CA 90069. ☎ **800/776-0666** or 310/855-1115. Fax 310/657-9192. 125 suites. $160–$475 suite. AE, CB, DC, EU, MC, V. Parking $13.

Nestled on a quiet residential street just 2 blocks from the bustling Strip, this all-suite hotel features large one-bedroom apartments that feel more like upscale condos than standard hotel rooms. Each has a large bedroom, kitchen, and bathroom, as well as a sizable sunken living room complete with gas fireplace, fax machine, and Nintendo games. You have to go up to the roof for anything resembling a view, but once you're up there, you can swim in the pool or play on the lighted tennis court. For location, quality, and price, this is one of L.A.'s best values, and is already popular among music industry clientele; let's hope that when this place catches on, prices will stay reasonable and reservations won't be hard to come by.

Dining/Entertainment: The Library Restaurant serves continental meals all day. Light bites are served poolside.

Services: Concierge, room service (7am to 10:45pm), nightly turndown, voice-mail, currency exchange.

Facilities: VCRs, video library, outdoor heated pool, small exercise room, Jacuzzi, sauna, sundeck, one lighted tennis court, complimentary bicycles.

Le Parc Hotel. 733 N. West Knoll Dr., West Hollywood, CA 90069. ☎ **800/5-SUITES** or 310/855-8888. Fax 310/659-7812. 154 suites. A/C TV TEL. $185–$265 suite. AE, DC, EU, MC, V. Parking $12.

Situated on a quiet residential street, Le Parc is a high-quality all-suite hotel with a pleasantly mixed clientele. Designers stay here because it's a few minutes' walk to the Pacific Design Center; patients and medical consultants check in because it's close to Cedars-Sinai; and tourists enjoy being near the Farmer's Market and Museum Row. The nicely furnished, apartmentlike units each have a kitchenette, dining area, living room with fireplace, and balcony. There's a swimming pool, a basketball hoop, and a tennis court (recently resurfaced and lit for night play) on the roof. What this hotel lacks in cachet it more than makes up for in value. Although your L.A. friends may not have heard of this place, thanks to an overall renovation in 1996 they'll be impressed when you invite them up for drinks. Cafe Le Parc is open from 6:30am to midnight and features a fully licensed bar.

MODERATE

Two good, moderately priced options near UCLA are the comfortable **Doubletree Hotel Los Angeles/Westwood,** 10740 Wilshire Blvd., at Selby Avenue (☎ **800/472-8556** or 310/475-8711); and the **Century Wilshire Hotel,** 10776 Wilshire Blvd., between Malcolm and Selby avenues (☎ **800/421-7223** outside California, or 310/474-4506), with large, somewhat worn units that nevertheless offer great value in an expensive neighborhood.

If you're traveling with a group or as a family, be sure to consider the suite hotels listed under "Expensive" above; they can become quite a deal when you realize that you can accommodate four (or more) in a suite.

Beverly Hills Inn. 125 S. Spalding Dr., Beverly Hills, CA 90212. ☎ **800/463-4466** or 310/278-0303. Fax 310/278-1728. 45 rms, 4 suites. A/C TV TEL. $125–$175 double; from $175 suite. Rates include breakfast. AE, DC, EU, MC, V. Free parking.

Once the nondescript Beverly Crest Hotel—so dull that you could pass it a hundred times without ever noticing it—this property underwent an enormous yearlong renovation and reopened in 1995; it's now a terrific place to stay. The inn is well located, within walking distance of both Rodeo Drive and Century City. The rooms, thoughtfully designed in a slightly Asian style, tend to be on the small side, but you get what you pay for here; prices go up for the larger rooms. The best overlook the pool and courtyard; those on the other side can keep an eye on their cars in the parking lot. Every room has a refrigerator. There's a sauna and exercise room, and a small bar aptly named the Garden Hideaway. At press time, a new bar and restaurant were scheduled to open shortly.

⑤ **Carlyle Inn.** 1119 S. Robertson Blvd. (south of Wilshire Blvd.), Los Angeles, CA 90035. ☎ **800/322-7595** or 310/275-4445. Fax 310/859-0496. 24 rms, 8 suites. A/C TV TEL. $120–$130 double; $190 suite. Rates include full breakfast. AE, DC, DISC, EU, MC, V. Parking $8.

Hidden on an uneventful stretch of Robertson Boulevard just south of Beverly Hills, this four-story inn is one of the best-priced finds in L.A. The hotel's exceedingly clever design has transformed an ordinary square lot in a high-density district into an delightfully airy hostelry. Despite its small size and unlikely location, architects have managed to create a multistory interior courtyard, which almost every room faces. Well-planned, contemporary interiors are fitted with recessed lighting, deco wall lamps, pine furnishings, and well-framed classical architectural monoprints. Amenities include coffeemakers and VCRs. The hotel's primary drawback is that it lacks views; curtains must remain drawn at all times to maintain any sense of privacy. The suites are only slightly larger than standard rooms.

Hyatt on Sunset. 8401 Sunset Blvd. (2 blocks east of La Cienega Blvd.), West Hollywood, CA 90069. ☎ **800/233-1234** or 213/656-1234. Fax 213/650-7024. 234 rms, 28 suits. A/C TV TEL. $140–$160 double; $350–$550 suite. Special weekend rates available. AE, CB, DC, DISC, EU, MC, V. Parking $10.

This aging 13-story chain hotel is favored by newly signed rock bands and other industry types for its Sunset Strip location: close to Tower Records, the Whisky A-Go-Go, the Roxy, and House of Blues. Except for its art deco lobby, there's nothing exceptional here; plans are in the works, however, for an overall renovation. The rectangular rooms are spacious; some have private balconies, and those on high floors enjoy skyline views. There's a heated rooftop swimming pool, a business center, and room service from 6am to midnight. A restaurant and a sports bar/deli serves sandwiches and pastas.

INEXPENSIVE

In addition to the hotels listed below, the **Los Angeles West Travelodge,** 10740 Santa Monica Blvd., at Overland Avenue (☎ **310/474-4576**), is a terrific option, offering pleasant, modern, recently renovated rooms and friendly service.

⑤ **Hotel Del Capri.** 10587 Wilshire Blvd. (at Westholme Ave.), Los Angeles, CA 90024. ☎ **800/444-6835** or 310/474-3511. Fax 310/470-9999. 36 rms, 45 suites. A/C TV TEL. $85–$105 double; from $110 suite. Rates include continental breakfast. AE, CB, DC, EU, MC, V. Free parking.

The Del Capri is one of the best values in trendy Westwood. This well-located and fairly priced hotel is popular with tourists, business travelers, and parents visiting their UCLA offspring. There are two parts to the property: a four-story building on the boulevard, and a quieter two-story motel that surrounds a kidney-shaped swimming pool. Though the rooms are beginning to show wear and tear, all are of good

🌐 Family-Friendly Hotels

The highest concentration of family-friendly accommodations—those that make families with kids their primary concern—are found close to Disneyland (see Chapter 16). That doesn't mean that families aren't welcome in L.A. hotels; in fact, a few welcome kids with open arms.

Loews Santa Monica Beach Hotel *(see p. 417)*   Offering comprehensive children's programs throughout the summer, and more like a resort than any other L.A. hotel, Loews boasts an unbeatable location—it's right by the beach and the boardwalk. What more could make the kids happy? They also offer baby-sitting services, so you can enjoy a kid-free evening on the town.

Hotel Oceana *(see p. 418)*   This is a spacious all-suite hotel overlooking the beach at Santa Monica. Kids will love the brightly colored walls and cushy furniture, and all suites come with Nintendo video games.

Century Plaza Hotel & Tower *(see p.424)*   The Century Plaza offers spacious, family-sized rooms and lots of facilities. Because it's a veritable city unto itself, older kids love to explore this labyrinthine hotel.

Sheraton Universal Hotel *(see p. 431)*   This Sheraton enjoys a terrifically kid-friendly location, adjacent to Universal Studios and the enormously fun CityWalk mall. Baby-sitting services are available to give mom and dad a break, and there's a large games room on the premises.

Le Parc Hotel *(see p.425)* and **Le Montrose Suite Hotel** *(see p. 425)*   These fairly comparable all-suite hotels are centrally located in West Hollywood. Multiple rooms means privacy for parents, and kitchenettes can cut down on restaurant and room-service bills.

quality and have electrically adjustable beds—a decidedly novel touch. The more expensive rooms are slightly larger and have whirlpool baths and an extra phone in the bathroom. Most of the suites have kitchenettes. The hotel provides free shuttle service to nearby shopping and attractions in Westwood, Beverly Hills, and Century City.

Park Sunset Hotel. 8462 Sunset Blvd., West Hollywood, CA 90069. ☎ **800/821-3660** or 213/654-6470. Fax 213/654-5918. 62 rms, 20 suites. A/C TV TEL. $75–$80 double; $150 suite. AE, CB, DC, DISC, EU, MC, V. Parking $5.

You'd think that the Park Sunset's location—right on the Strip—would make this one of the noisiest places to sleep in L.A. But all the guest rooms are in the back of the modest three-story hotel, away from the cars and cacophony. The rooms are well kept and surprisingly well decorated, though the carpets are a bit worn and the bathroom color schemes are a tad dated. Some rooms have balconies and/or kitchens, and corner rooms have panoramic city views. There's a small heated pool in a lush courtyard, and a continental restaurant on the lobby level.

Ⓢ Ramada Limited Hotel. 1052 Tiverton Ave. (near Glendon Ave.), Los Angeles, CA 90024. ☎ **800/631-0100** or 310/208-6677. Fax 310/824-3732. 27 rms, 9 suites. A/C TV TEL. $66–$76 double; from $75 suite. AE, CB, DC, DISC, EU, MC, V. Free parking.

This isn't a fancy place by any stretch of the imagination, but the rooms are comfortable and have recently been updated—they're in better condition than those in many hotels that cost more. Some have stoves, refrigerators, and stainless-steel countertops; others have microwave ovens. The bathrooms have marble vanities. Facilities include an exercise room, a lounge, and an activities desk.

San Vicente Inn. 837 N. San Vicente Blvd., West Hollywood, CA 90069. ☎ **310/854-6915.** 20 rms, suites, and cottages. TV TEL. $79–$179 double. Rates include continental breakfast. AE, CB, DC, EU, MC, V. Free parking.

West Hollywood's only gay-owned and -operated bed-and-breakfast is a thoroughly charming place, with rooms that are individually and cozily decorated. Some rooms have kitchens, but you won't really need one; lots of restaurants (and shops and bars) are just steps away. Guests have use of the garden patio, swimming pool, spa bath, and clothing-optional redwood sundeck.

HOLLYWOOD
MODERATE

Holiday Inn Hollywood. 1755 N. Highland Ave. (between Franklin and Hollywood blvds.), Hollywood, CA 90028. ☎ **800/465-4329** or 213/462-7181. Fax 213/466-9072. 448 rms, 22 suites. A/C TV TEL. $150 double; from $170 suite. AE, DC, DISC, EU, MC, V. Parking $6.50.

This 23-story hotel in the heart of Hollywood offers perfectly acceptable rooms that are both pleasant and comfortable—as long as you don't mind being on a busy thoroughfare and sharing the pavement with bikers, wannabe rockers, and the other colorful characters that make up the neighborhood melange. A major guest room renovation was completed in 1995, so the hotel's standard furnishings are now stain-free. The suites, which include small kitchenettes, are particularly good buys. There's a swimming pool, a sundeck, and a revolving rooftop restaurant.

⑤ **Hollywood Roosevelt.** 7000 Hollywood Blvd., Hollywood, CA 90028. ☎ **800/252-7466** or 213/466-7000. 311 rms, 19 suites. $109–$129 double; from $200 suite. AE, CB, DC, DISC, EU, MC, V. Valet parking $9.50.

This 12-story movie-city landmark is located on a slightly seedy, very touristy part of Hollywood Boulevard, across from Mann's Chinese Theatre and just down the street from the Walk of Fame. The Roosevelt was one of the city's grandest hotels when it opened its doors in 1927, and was home to the first Academy Awards ceremony. But like the starlets who once filled the lobby, its beauty faded; until a relatively recent nip-and-tuck, it seemed well on its way to Forest Lawn. The exquisitely restored two-story lobby features a Hollywood mini-museum. The rooms, however, are typical of chain hotels, far less appealing—in both size and decor—than the public areas; but a few are charmed with their original 1920s-style bathrooms. The suites are named after stars who stayed in them during the glory days; some have grand verandas, while others are rumored to be haunted by the ghosts of Marilyn Monroe and Montgomery Clift. High floors have unbeatable skyline views. David Hockney decorated the famous Olympic-size pool. The Cinegrill supper club draws locals with a zany cabaret show and guest chanteuses from Eartha Kitt to Cybill Shepherd.

INEXPENSIVE

Hollywood Celebrity Hotel. 1775 Orchid Ave. (north of Hollywood Blvd.), Hollywood, CA 90028. ☎ **800/222-7017,** 800/222-7090 in California, or 213/850-6464. Fax 213/850-7667. 32 rms, 6 suites. A/C TV TEL. $60–$70 double; from $75 suite. Rates include continental breakfast. AE, CB, DC, DISC, EU, MC, V. Free parking.

This small but centrally located hotel is one of the best budget buys in Hollywood. Located just half a block behind Mann's Chinese Theatre, it offers spacious, comfortable, art deco–style units. Breakfast is delivered to your door along with the newspaper every morning. Small pets are allowed, but a $50 deposit is required.

DOWNTOWN
VERY EXPENSIVE

Regal Biltmore. 506 S. Grand Ave. (between 5th and 6th sts.), Los Angeles, CA 90071. ☎ **800/245-8673** or 213/624-1011. Fax 213/612-1545. 640 rms, 43 suites. A/C TV TEL. $225–$235 double; from $350 suite. AE, CB, DC, DISC, EU, MC, V. Parking $20.

Built in 1923, the historic—and opulent—Biltmore is considered the grand dame of L.A. hotels. During the 1930s and 1940s the Academy Awards were held in the spectacular Crystal Ballroom—the first sketch of the Oscar statuette was scrawled on a linen napkin here—and the hotel was the top choice for presidents and the elite. You've seen the Biltmore in many movies, including *The Fabulous Baker Boys, Beverly Hills Cop,* and Barbra Streisand's *A Star Is Born;* the Crystal Ballroom appeared upside down in *The Poseidon Adventure.*

The 11-story hotel sparkles with Italian marble and traditional French-reproduction furnishings, but the hotel's overall elegance has been compromised by an ugly office tower that was added in the mid-1980s. Still, the sense of refinement and graciousness endures, with a vaulted, hand-painted lobby ceiling, attentively decorated—though small—rooms with marble baths, and some enchanting old-world suites with lofty living rooms and nonworking fireplaces.

Dining/Entertainment: Bernard's features high-quality continental cuisine. Smeraldi's serves homemade pastas and lighter California fare. Afternoon tea and evening cocktails are served in the lobby's stately Rendezvous Court. Libations are also available in the Grand Avenue Sports Bar.

Services: Concierge, room service (24 hours), dry cleaning, laundry service, newspaper delivery, nightly turndown, express checkout, valet parking.

Facilities: Beautiful, original 1923 tile- and brass-inlaid swimming pool, state-of-the-art health club, Jacuzzi, sauna, well-staffed business center.

Wyndham Checkers Hotel Los Angeles. 535 S. Grand Ave., Los Angeles, CA 90071. ☎ **800/996-3426** or 213/624-0000. Fax 213/626-9906. 173 rms, 15 suites. A/C TEL TV. $240 double; from $400 suite. AE, DC, DISC, EU, MC, V. Parking $18.

The atmosphere at the Wyndham Checkers, a boutique version of the Biltmore across the street, is as removed from "Hollywood" as a top L.A. hotel can get. Built in 1927, the hotel is protected by the City Cultural Heritage Commission as a Historic Cultural Monument. It has the feel of a grand old home, with cozy (and freshly upgraded) public areas such as a wood-paneled library. The top-of-the-line accommodations are outfitted with oversize beds and coffeemakers.

Dining/Entertainment: Checkers Restaurant is one of downtown's finest dining rooms (see the review in Chapter 6).

Services: Concierge, room service (24 hours), dry cleaning, laundry service, nightly turndown, express checkout, valet parking.

Facilities: Rooftop spa, heated lap pool, Jacuzzi, sundeck.

EXPENSIVE

In addition to the hotels listed below, downtown is home to local branches of the luxury chains, all of which are particularly suitable for business travelers, including the ultra-contemporary **Hotel Inter-Continental Los Angeles,** 251 S. Olive St. (☎ **213/617-3300**), the best-managed property in the neighborhood; the functional but sterile **Hyatt Regency Los Angeles,** 711 S. Hope St., at 7th Street (☎ **800/ 233-1234** or 213/683-1234), whose most outstanding features are absolutely enormous windows that offer great views of downtown from every room; and the spacious, warm **Sheraton Grande,** 333 S. Figueroa St., between 3rd and 4th streets (☎ **800/325-3535** or 213/617-1133), attractively decorated and located right in the heart of the downtown hustle.

New Otani Hotel & Garden. 120 S. Los Angeles St. (at 1st St.), Los Angeles, CA 90012. ☎ **800/421-8795,** 800/273-2294 in California, or 213/629-1200. Fax 213/622-0980. 434 rms, 20 suites. A/C TV TEL. $160–$250 double; from $550 Japanese-style suite. Cultural packages available. AE, CB, DC, EU, MC, V. Parking $11.

Most of the plush rooms in this anonymous 21-story concrete tower are Western style and comparable to other top downtown hotels in quality (and price). The best reason to stay here is to experience the New Otani's unique Japanese-style suites, outfitted with futons on tatami floors, Ofuro baths, and sliding rice-paper shoji screens. Hotel guests have exclusive use of the half-acre rooftop classical tea garden. The 1- and 2-night Japanese Experience cultural packages include suite accommodations, sake and Japanese appetizers served at check-in by a kimono-clad waitress, dinner in any of the hotel's restaurants, shiatsu massages, and a live bonsai tree to take home with you.

Dining/Entertainment: There are two Japanese restaurants, one California-style dining room, and a coffee shop (fresh-baked breads and pastries are a specialty). The beautiful Garden Grill, a Tokyo-style teriyaki grill, features rare Japanese Kobe beef (which is beer-fed and massaged daily!). Chefs prepare seafood and prime steaks.

Services: Concierge, room service (6am–11pm), same-day laundry service, nightly turndown, airport limousine service, valet parking.

Facilities: Japanese-style health club (with saunas, baths, and shiatsu massages). Golf and tennis are available at a nearby country club. Car-rental desk, arcade with more than 30 shops.

Westin Bonaventure. 404 S. Figueroa St. (between 4th and 5th sts.), Los Angeles, CA 90071. ☎ **800/228-3000** or 213/624-1000. Fax 213/612-4800. 1,368 rms, 155 suites. A/C TV TEL. $175–$215 double; from $190 suite. AE, CB, DC, EU, MC, V. Parking $18.50.

The 35-story Bonaventure is the hotel that locals most love to hate. It's certainly architecturally unique: The hotel's five gleaming glass silos—like giant mirrored rolls of paper towels—constitute one of downtown's most distinctive landmarks. This is an enormous convention hotel, designed on the scale of a mini-city. The six-story skylit lobby houses splashing fountains, gardens, trees, even a large lake. There's a tangle of concrete ramps and 12 glass-enclosed, high-speed elevators that appear to rise from the reflecting pools. The guest rooms begin on the 10th floor; each has a wall of windows offering good views, but they're smaller than similarly priced rooms in the neighborhood. One of the towers is a completely remodeled all-suite facility where rooms come with an additional parlor room and half-bath.

Dining/Entertainment: The rooftop Top of Five features panoramic views along with adequate, but not distinctive, continental cuisine. Ask for an exterior table—they're the only ones with the view. The views from the Bona Vista cocktail lounge are worth the price of a drink. There's nightly entertainment—jazz combos, cocktail-hour dancing—at the Sidewalk Cafe, a California bistro, and the adjacent Lobby Court.

Services: Concierge, room service (24 hours), nightly turndown, express checkout, valet parking, Executive Club level with upgraded facilities and services.

Facilities: Large outdoor pool, sundeck, business center (open Monday through Friday), conference rooms, car-rental desk, five levels of shops and boutiques.

INEXPENSIVE

Kawada Hotel. 200 S. Hill St. (at 2nd St.), Los Angeles, CA 90012. ☎ **800/752-9232** or 213/621-4455. Fax 213/687-4455. 115 rms, 1 suite. A/C TV TEL. $79–$119 double; $145 suite. AE, DC, DISC, EU, MC, V. Parking $6.60.

This pretty, well-kept, and efficiently managed hotel is a pleasant oasis in the otherwise gritty heart of downtown, conveniently located to the Civic Center, the Museum of Contemporary Art, and Union Station. Behind the clean three-story, redbrick exterior are over a hundred pristine rooms, all with handy kitchenettes and simple furnishings. The rooms aren't large, but they're extremely functional, each outfitted with a VCR (movies are available free of charge) and two phones. Nonsmoking rooms are available. The hotel's lobby-level restaurant features an eclectic international menu all day.

THE SAN FERNANDO VALLEY

In addition to the hotels listed below, another comfortable option close to Universal Studios is the **Radisson Valley Center,** 15433 Ventura Blvd. (at the junction of I-405 and U.S. 101), Sherman Oaks (☎ **818/981-5400**).

VERY EXPENSIVE

Sheraton Universal. 333 Universal Terrace Pkwy., Universal City, 91608. ☎ **800/325-3535** or 818/980-1212. Fax 818/985-4980. 417 rms, 25 suites. A/C TEL TV. $225 double; from $300 suite. AE, CB, DC, DISC, EU, MC, V. Valet parking $14, self-parking $10.

This 21-story concrete rectangle, situated on the grounds of Universal Studios, is a good-quality, mixed-use hotel catering to tourists, businesspeople, and industry folks visiting the studios' production offices. A major 1994 renovation updated every room with contemporary fabrics and floor-to-ceiling windows that actually open; each is equipped with Nintendo games. The hotel is very close to the Hollywood Bowl, and you can practically roll out of bed and into the theme park.

MODERATE

Beverly Garland Holiday Inn. 4222 Vineland Ave., North Hollywood, CA 91602. ☎ **800/BEVERLY** or 818/980-8000. Fax 818/766-5230. 258 rms, 12 suites. A/C TV TEL. $139–$149 double; from $189 suite. AE, DISC, DC, MC, V. Free parking.

Don't get confused by the name—this hotel is named for its owner, the actress Beverly Garland (of *My Three Sons* fame), not Beverly Hills. Grassy areas and greenery abound at this North Hollywood Holiday Inn, a virtual oasis in the concrete jungle that is most of L.A. The Southern California Mission-style buildings that make up the hotel are a bit dated, but if you grew up with *Brady Bunch* reruns, this only adds to the charm—it looks like something Mike Brady would have designed. Southwestern-themed fabrics complement the natural-pine furnishings in the recently renovated guest rooms; unfortunately, the painted cinderblock walls give off something of a college dorm feel. And if you don't smoke, make sure to ask for a nonsmoking room (the smoking rooms smell musty). There are a pool, sauna, and two tennis courts, and all rooms feature balconies. The Paradise Restaurant serves Polynesian-influenced cuisine throughout the day. A complimentary shuttle to Universal is available.

Sportsmen's Lodge. 12825 Ventura Blvd. (west of Coldwater Canyon), Studio City, CA 91604. ☎ **800/821-8511** or 818/769-4700. Fax 213/877-3898. 178 rms, 13 suites. A/C TV TEL. $92–$138 double; from $180 suite. AE, DC, DISC, EU, MC, V. Free parking.

It's been a long time since this part of Studio City was wilderness enough to justify the lodge's name. This sprawling motel has been enlarged and upgraded since those days, the most recent improvements, sprucing up the worn room furnishings, made within the last 3 years. Walking around the ponds and waterfalls out back, you come upon the surprise luxury of a heated, Olympic-size swimming pool surrounded by a fleet of chaise longues. It's hard to imagine that busy Ventura Boulevard is just across the parking lot. The guest rooms are large and comfortable but not luxurious; many have balconies, and refrigerators are available. The poolside suites (called executive studios) are the largest and best located of the accommodations here. There's a well-equipped exercise room and a variety of shops and service desks, and both golf and bowling are nearby. Complimentary afternoon tea is served in the lobby at 4pm. Caribou, the latest incarnation of the hotel's stunning glass-enclosed dining room, serves meat and game dishes in a hunting-lodge setting (but hopefully not any of the pretty swans frolicking out back!).

Universal City Hilton & Towers. 555 Universal Terrace Pkwy., Universal City, CA 91608. ☎ **800/HILTONS** or 818/506-2500. Fax 818/509-2031. 446 rms, 26 suites. A/C TV TEL. $125–$165 double; from $175 suite. AE, DC, DISC, EU, MC, V. Valet parking $13.

Though this 24-story hotel sits right outside the Universal Studios theme park, there's more of a conservative-business-traveler feel than the raucous family-with-young-children feel you might expect here. The large lobby is built almost entirely of glass, giving it an openness that doesn't feel hollow or empty. The rooms are tastefully decorated in light earth tones with English-style furniture. The Cafe Sierra serves California cuisine and is open for breakfast, lunch, dinner, and Sunday brunch. Services include concierge, 24-hour room service, dry cleaning and laundry, and express checkout. On the premises are a heated pool, a Jacuzzi, and a privately run health club available for guest use at no extra charge.

4 Dining

Any way you look at it—food, decor, service—Los Angeles is one of the world's great dining cities. When it comes to culinary innovation and architectural design, L.A.'s restaurants are tops, plus recent economic and social trends have led to a whole new crop of places serving bone-china cuisine at blue-plate prices. Our limited space forced us to make tough choices; for a greater selection of reviews, see *Frommer's Los Angeles.*

The restaurants below are categorized first by geographic area, then by price. Keep in mind that many of the restaurants listed as "Expensive" are moderately priced at lunch. Reservations are recommended almost everywhere, particularly on weekends and during peak lunch (noon to 1:30pm) and dinner (7 to 8:30pm) times.

SANTA MONICA & THE BEACHES
EXPENSIVE

✪ **Michael's.** 1147 3rd St. (west of Wilshire Blvd.), Santa Monica. ☎ **310/451-0843.** Reservations required. Main courses $15–$25. AE, CB, DC, DISC, MC, V. Tues–Fri noon–3pm and 6–10:30pm, Sat 6–10:30pm. CALIFORNIA.

If Wolfgang Puck is the father of contemporary California cuisine, then Michael McCarty is the grandfather. Born in New York and schooled in France, McCarty opened this self-consciously modern American restaurant in 1979, when he was only 25 years old. Those were exciting times: The walls were irreverently hung with works by David Hockney, Cy Twombly, and Jasper Johns; staff uniforms were designed by Ralph Lauren; and the unusually casual dining room had the added novelty of a dining patio and rock garden. Several top L.A. restaurants have since caught up with Michael's—most notably Puck's Spago, Joachim Splichal's Patina, and Michel

Richard's Citrus—but this fetching Santa Monica eatery remains one of the city's best. A recent price rollback has made dishes like Michael's simple grilled pork tenderloin with cream sauce and apples, and duck with Grand Marnier and oranges, even more appetizing. Spaghetti tossed in a creamy chardonnay sauce with large sea scallops, roasted sweet peppers, baby asparagus, and American golden caviar is just one example of the delicious, complex pastas here. Don't miss Michael's famous goat-cheese salad, served warm with walnuts and vinaigrette.

✪ **Valentino.** 3115 Pico Blvd. (west of Bundy Dr.), Santa Monica. ☎ **310/829-4313.** Reservations required. Pasta $12–$16; meat and fish dishes $18–$25. AE, CB, DC, DISC, MC, V. Mon–Thurs 5:30–10:30pm, Fri 11:30am–2:30pm and 5:30–11pm, Sat 5:30–11pm. ITALIAN.

All of Los Angeles ached for charming owner Piero Selvaggio when he lost 20,000 bottles of wine in the 1994 earthquake. But elegant Valentino never lost its position as *Wine Spectator* magazine's top wine cellar, and *New York Times* food critic Ruth Reichl calls this the best Italian restaurant in America. The creations of Selvaggio and his brilliant young chef, Angelo Auriana, make dinners here lengthy multicourse affairs (often involving several bottles of wine). You might begin with a crisp Pinot Grigio paired with caviar-filled cannoli; or crespelle, thin little pancakes with fresh porcini mushrooms and a rich melt of fontina cheese. Handmade pastas tossed with tender baby squid or sweet tiny clams are typical of first courses, though it really depends on what came to market the morning you visit. A rich Barolo is the perfect accompaniment to rosemary-infused roasted rabbit; the fantastically fragrant risotto with white truffles is one of the most magnificent dishes we've ever had. Jackets are all but required in the elegant dining room. What more can we say—go!

MODERATE

✪ **Abiquiu.** 1413 5th St. (between Broadway and Santa Monica Blvd.), Santa Monica. ☎ **310/395-8611.** Reservations required. Main courses $13–$18. AE, MC, V. Mon–Thurs 11:30am–2:30pm and 6–10pm, Fri 11:30am–2:30pm and 6–10:30pm, Sat 6–10:30pm, Sun 11:30am–2pm (brunch) and 6–10:30pm. CONTEMPORARY SOUTHWESTERN.

If you needed just one more morsel of proof that Los Angeles remains on the culinary edge, this is it. Chef/owner John Sedlar, one of the city's most gifted young chefs, named Abiquiu (pronounced "Ab-*i*-kyoo") after his northern New Mexico hometown. The dramatic, postmodern restaurant is Sedlar's vehicle for showing off his own brand of southwestern food, which relies heavily on yellow corn and green chiles. The specialty here is tamales, Mexican favorites that are traditionally made of meat and cornmeal and steamed in a corn husk—but this is no traditional restaurant. Of the dozens of gourmet varieties served here, none is better than the salmon mousse–filled corn-husk tamale, or the crab-and-lobster tamale steamed in a lobster shell. The menu includes "fusion" creations like an unbelievably fantastic lobster sushi roll with creamy green-chile sauce. Sedlar had his share of controversy when Catholics picketed his restaurant for serving dessert tamales on Madonna (not the pop star) plates. The chef just ordered more of this personally designed tableware, but has promised to quit stenciling shock messages like "D.O.A." on the plates' rims. Upstairs there's a dedicated tamale and tequila bar, for light bites and strong margaritas. Abiquiu is underpriced and busy; go early and arrive hungry.

Alice's. 23000 Pacific Coast Hwy. (at the Malibu Pier), Malibu. ☎ **310/456-6646.** Reservations recommended. Main courses $9–$18; lunch $7–$15. MC, V. Mon–Fri 11:30am–10pm, Sat–Sun 11am–11pm. CALIFORNIA.

Alice's has a long history as a Malibu fixture, situated on the Pacific Coast Highway on the pier above the beach. The dining room is glassed in on three sides and faces the ocean; rear tables sit on a raised platform so that everyone has a million-dollar view. It's a light and airy place, with a casual menu to match. Admittedly, most people are here for the one-of-a-kind atmosphere, but the food is a lot better than it needs to be. Seared yellowtail tuna is served simply, on a bed of spinach, with lemon and tarragon butter. Grilled chicken breast is marinated in garlic and soy and served with tomato-cilantro relish. Pastas and pizzas are also available, and there's a full bar.

Aunt Kizzy's Back Porch. In the Villa Marina Shopping Center, 4325 Glencove Ave., Marina del Rey. ☎ **310/578-1005.** Reservations not accepted. Main courses $8–$13. AE. Mon–Thurs 11am–11pm, Fri–Sat 11am–midnight, Sun 11am–3pm (brunch) and 4–11pm. SOUTHERN.

This is a real southern restaurant, owned by genuine southerners from Texas and Oklahoma. Kizzy's chicken Créole, jambalaya, and smothered pork chops are just about as good as it gets in this city. Almost everything comes with vegetables, red beans and rice, and corn muffins. Fresh-squeezed lemonade is served by the mason jar. These are huge meals that, as corny as it sounds, are as delicious as they are filling. Sunday brunches are all-you-can-eat affairs, served buffet style. The biggest problem with Aunt Kizzy's is its location, hidden in a shopping center that has too few parking spaces to accommodate its customers. Look for the restaurant to the right of Vons supermarket.

Camelions. 246 26th St. (south of San Vicente Blvd.), Santa Monica. ☎ **310/395-0746.** Reservations required. Main courses $14–$22; lunch $10–$13. AE, CB, DC, MC, V. Tues–Sun 11:30am–2:30pm and 6–9:30pm. CALIFORNIA/FRENCH.

Either indoors or out, dining here is one of Los Angeles's most romantic dining experiences. Camelions' three 1920s stucco cottages, each with beamed ceiling and a crackling fireplace, are built around an ivy-trellised brick patio. Contrary to its Provençal setting, the tasty French-inspired cuisine is plenty California trendy. Red lentil crêpes arrive garnished with smoked salmon and arugula salad, and roasted duck breast is sliced thin and fanned out over a plate of walnut-merlot sauce, accompanied by a risotto-and-berry timbale. There are traditional French dishes like sautéed rabbit stewed in a clay pot with sweet garlic. A large selection of sandwiches and salads (like spinach with warm new potatoes, bacon, and mustard vinaigrette) are available at lunch.

Inn of the Seventh Ray. 128 Old Topanga Canyon Rd. (on Calif. 27), Topanga Canyon. ☎ **310/455-1311.** Reservations required. Main courses $16–$25. MC, V. Mon–Fri 11:30am–3pm and 6–10pm, Sat 10:30am–3pm and 6–10pm, Sun 9:30am–3pm and 6–10pm. CALIFORNIA HEALTH FOOD.

Topanga Canyon has long been the home of leftover hippies and L.A.'s New Agers; it's a mountainous, sparsely populated area that's undeniably beautiful, even spiritual. This restaurant, a former church, is in the middle of the aura. People come here less for the food than for a romantic dining experience far from the bright lights of the city. About half the seating is outdoors, at tables overlooking a creek and endless tangles of untamed vines and shrubs. Inside, the dining room is rustic, with a sloped roof and a glass wall offering mountain views.

The inn was opened about 25 years ago by Ralph and Lucille Yaney, who preach some kind of mumbo-jumbo about the energy of food, and list menu items in order of their "esoteric vibrational value." Everything is prepared from scratch, and foods are organic and chemical- and preservative-free. The fish are caught in deep water far offshore and served the same day. They even sell unpasteurized wines. Ten main dishes are available daily, and all are served with hors d'oeuvres, soup or salad, and vegetables. The lightest dish, called Five Secret Rays, consists of lightly steamed vegetables served with lemon-tahini and caraway-cheese sauces; the densest dish—vibrationally speaking—is a 10-ounce New York steak cut from naturally fed beef.

INEXPENSIVE

Benny's Bar-B-Q. 4077 Lincoln Blvd. (south of Washington Blvd.), Marina del Rey. ☎ **310/ 821-6939.** Sandwiches $4–$6; dinner specials $7–$10. AE, MC, V. Mon–Sat 11am–10pm, Sun 2–10pm. BARBECUE.

It's mostly take-out at this cook-shack dive, but there are a few tables, where the city's luckiest diners gorge themselves on Los Angeles's best barbecued pork and beef ribs and hot-link sausages. Like almost everything on the menu, the barbecued chicken is bathed in a tangy hot sauce and served with baked beans and a choice of cole slaw, potato salad, fries, or corn on the cob. Beef, ham, and pork sandwiches are also available. To reach Benny's, find Lincoln Boulevard, then follow the heavy aroma.

Jody Maroni's Sausage Kingdom. 2011 Ocean Front Walk (north of Venice Blvd.), Venice. ☎ **310/306-1995.** Sandwiches $4–$6. No credit cards. Daily 10am–5:30pm. SANDWICHES/ SAUSAGES.

Your cardiologist might not approve, but Jody Maroni's all-natural, preservative-free "haut dogs" are some of the best weiners served anywhere. The grungy walk-up (or Rollerblade-up) counter looks fairly foreboding—you wouldn't know there was gourmet fare behind that aging hot dog–stand facade. At least 14 different grilled sausage sandwiches are served here. Bypass the traditional hot Italian and try the Toulouse garlic, Bombay curried lamb, all-chicken apple, or orange-garlic-cumin. Each is served on a freshly baked onion roll and smothered with onions and peppers. Burgers, hot dogs, BLTs, and rotisserie chicken are also served, but why bother?

Other locations include Santa Monica's Third Street Promenade, the Valley's Universal CityWalk (☎ 818/622-JODY), and inside LAX's Terminal 5, where you can pick up some last-minute vacuum-packed sausages for home.

☻ Kay 'n Dave's Cantina. 262 26th St. (south of San Vicente Blvd.), Santa Monica. ☎ **310/ 260-1355.** Reservations not taken. Main courses $5–$12. AE, MC, V. Mon–Thurs 7:30am– 9:30pm, Fri 7:30am–10pm, Sat 8am–10pm, Sun 8am–9:30pm. HEALTHY MEXICAN.

A beach community favorite for "really big portions of really good food at really low prices," Kay 'n Dave's cooks with no lard and has a vegetarian-friendly menu with plenty of meat items, too. Come early (and be prepared to wait) for breakfast, as local devotees line up for five kinds of fluffy pancakes, zesty omelets, or one of the best breakfast burritos in town. Grilled tuna Veracruz, spinach and chicken enchiladas in tomatillo salsa, seafood fajitas tostada, vegetable-filled corn tamales, and other Mexican specialties really are served in huge portions, making this mostly locals mini-chain a great choice to energize for (or reenergize after) an action-packed day of beach sightseeing. Bring the family—there's a kids' menu and crayons on every table.

Kay 'n Dave's also has cantinas in Malibu at 18763 Pacific Coast Hwy. (☎ 310/ 456-8800) and in Pacific Palisades at 15246 Sunset Blvd. (☎ 310/459-8118). The Malibu location opens later in the mornings.

L.A.'S WESTSIDE & BEVERLY HILLS
EXPENSIVE

☻ Four Oaks. 2181 N. Beverly Glen Blvd., Los Angeles. ☎ **310/470-2265.** Reservations required. Main courses $22–$29. AE, MC, V. Tues–Sat 11:30am–9:30pm and 6–10pm, Sun 10:30am–2pm and 6–10pm. CALIFORNIA.

Just looking at the menu here makes us swoon. The country-cottage ambience and chef Peter Roelant's superlative blend of fresh ingredients with luxurious continental flourishes make a meal at the Four Oaks one of our favorite luxuries. Dinner is served beneath trees festooned with twinkling lights. Appetizers like lavender-smoked salmon with crisp potatoes and horseredish crème fraîche complement mouthwatering dishes like roasted chicken with sage, Oregon forest mushrooms, artichoke hearts, and port-balsamic sauce. If you're looking for someplace special, head to this canyon hideaway—you won't be disappointed.

Lawry's The Prime Rib. 100 N. La Cienega Blvd. (north of Wilshire Blvd.), Beverly Hills. ☎ 310/652-2827. Reservations required. Main courses $19–$29. AE, CB, DC, DISC, MC, V. Mon–Fri 5–11pm, Sat 4:30–11pm, Sun 4–10pm. PRIME RIB/SEAFOOD.

Most Americans know Lawry's only as a brand of seasoned salt; the seasoning was invented here, conceived to flavor this restaurant's meats. Opened in 1938 by Lawrence Frank, Lawry's remains a serious family enterprise. Going to Lawry's is an old-world event; the main menu offerings are four cuts of prime rib that vary in size from two fingers to an entire hand. Every standing rib roast is dry-aged for 2 to 3 weeks, sprinkled with Lawry's famous seasoning, then roasted on a bed of rock salt. A carver wheels the cooked beef tableside, then slices it properly, rare to well done. The result is incredibly tender and juicy prime rib, some of the nation's very best. All dinners come with very mushy mashed potatoes, creamy whipped horseradish, Yorkshire pudding, and the Original Spinning Bowl Salad (while mixed greens, hard-boiled eggs, and chopped beets are spinning on a bed of crushed ice, they're drenched with dressing poured straight from the Lawry's bottle). Lawry's moved across the street from its original location a few years ago, but retained its throwback-to-the-30s clubroom atmosphere, complete with Persian-carpeted oak floors, high-backed chairs, and original European oils. Couples should opt for a table in either the Vintage or Oval Room (the latter seats larger parties as well).

Maple Drive. 345 N. Maple Dr. (at Alden Dr.), Beverly Hills. ☎ 310/274-9800. Reservations recommended. Main courses $17–$29; lunch $10–$18. AE, MC, V. Mon–Thurs 11:30am–2:30pm and 6–10pm, Fri 11:30am–2:30pm and 6–11pm, Sat 6–11pm. AMERICAN.

Owned by Liza Minelli, Dudley Moore, and producer/director Tony Bill, Maple Drive is one of the best traditional American restaurants in, well, America. Chef Leonard Schwartz cooks great meatloaf, terrific chili, and out-of-this-world veal chops (which regulars ask for Milanese style—lightly breaded and served with a squeeze of lemon). The restaurant attracts the biggest celebrities—Barbra, Elton, Arnold, and others who have enjoyed fame for so long they often seem tired of the attention; they enter through a second, more discrete, door and sit in relatively secluded booths in back of the multilevel dining room. That's a bonus for us nobodies; on warm nights, the best seats are out on the patio. Maple Drive is a classy place with great food, high prices, and live dinnertime jazz. Even if Clint isn't at the next table, it's worth lingering for the extraordinary desserts.

The same celebrity team also runs one of the beach's trendiest restaurants, **72 Market Street,** 72 Market St., just west of Pacific Avenue, Venice (☎ 310/392-8720), where Franco-American staples draw loyal crowds, along with the requisite meatloaf and chili.

○ Matsuhisa. 129 N. La Cienega Blvd. (north of Wilshire Blvd.), Beverly Hills. ☎ 310/659-9639. Reservations required. Main courses $14–$22; sushi $20–$30. AE, DC, MC, V. Mon–Fri 11:45am–2:45pm and 5:45–10:15pm, Sat–Sun 5:45–10:15pm. JAPANESE/PERUVIAN.

Japanese chef/owner Nobuyuki Matsuhisa arrived in Los Angeles via Peru and opened what may be the most creative restaurant in the entire city. A true master of fish cookery, Matsuhisa creates fantastic, unusual dishes by combining Japanese flavors with South American spices and salsas. Broiled sea bass with black truffles, sautéed squid with garlic and soy, and Dungeness crab tossed with chiles and cream are good examples of the masterfully prepared delicacies that are available in addition to thickly sliced nigiri and creative sushi rolls. Matsuhisa is also known for having some of the most hard-to-get tables in town. Both tight and bright, the restaurant's small, crowded main dining room suffers from bad lighting and precious lack of privacy. There's lots of action behind the sushi bar, and a frenetic service staff keeps the restaurant humming at a fiery pace. Stars are commonplace, though many are just walking through on their way to a private room. Matsuhisa is fantastically popular with hard-core foodies, who continually return for the savory surprises that come with every bite. Reserve early, unless you're happy starting your meal at 6 or 10pm.

✪ **Spago.** 1114 Horn Ave. (at Sunset Blvd.), West Hollywood. ☎ **310/652-4025.** Reservations required. Main courses $18–$28. DC, DISC, MC, V. Daily 6–11:30pm. CALIFORNIA.

Wolfgang Puck is more than a great chef: He's also a masterful businessman and publicist who has made Spago one of the best-known restaurants in America. Despite all the hoopla—and more than 15 years of service—Spago remains one of L.A.'s top-rated eateries. German-born Puck originally won fame serving imaginative "gourmet" pizzas. These individually sized thin-crust pies are baked in a wood-burning oven, topped with goodies like duck sausage, shiitake mushrooms, leeks, and artichokes, and other combinations once considered to be on the culinary edge. Of meat dishes, roast Sonoma lamb with braised shallots and grilled chicken with garlic and parsley are two perennial favorites. The celebrated (and far from secret) off-menu meal is Jewish pizza, a crispy pie topped with smoked salmon, crème fraîche, dill, red onion, and dollops of caviar. The restaurant has plans to move from its quirky, hard-to-find location into Beverly Hills early in 1997, so be sure to call ahead.

For perhaps the quintessential L.A. dining experience, be sure to try at least one of Puck's L.A. restaurants. In addition to Spago, he also has two terrific restaurants near the beach. **Chinois on Main,** 2709 Main St., Santa Monica (☎ **310/ 392-9025**), serves terrifically quirky East-meets-West Franco-Chinese cuisine. At **Granita,** in the Malibu Colony Mall, 23725 W. Malibu Rd., Malibu (☎ **310/ 456-0488**), Puck applies his signature California style to seafood—very successfully, of course.

MODERATE

Bombay Cafe. 12113 Santa Monica Blvd. (at Bundy Dr.). ☎ **310/820-2070.** Reservations not accepted. Main courses $9–$15. MC, V. Tues–Thurs 11:30am–10pm, Fri–Sat 11:30am–11pm, Sun 11:30am–4pm. INDIAN.

Indian is the cuisine of the moment in L.A., and nowhere is it done better than at the Bombay Cafe. The unlikely McRestaurant interior and storefront location (on the second floor of a nondescript mini-mall) belie excellent curries and kurmas that are typical of South Indian street food. Once seated, immediately order sev puri for the table; these crispy little chips topped with chopped potatoes, onions, cilantro, and chutneys are the perfect accompaniment to what's sure to be an extended menu-reading session. Also recommended are the burrito-like "frankies," juicy little bread rolls stuffed with lamb, chicken, or cauliflower. The best dishes come from the 800°F tandoor, and include spicy yogurt-marinated swordfish, lamb, and chicken. The food is served authentically spicy, unless you specify otherwise. The restaurant is phenomenally popular, and gets its share of celebrities: Meg Ryan and Dennis Quaid hired the Bombay Cafe to cater an affair at their Montana ranch. Only beer and wine are served.

Cava. In the Beverly Plaza Hotel, 8384 W. 3rd St. (at Orlando Ave.). ☎ **213/658-8898.** Reservations recommended on weekends. Main courses $8–$17; breakfast $3–$9; lunch $4–$14. AE, CB, DC, DISC, MC, V. Daily 6:30am–midnight. SPANISH.

Trendy types in the mood for some fun are attracted to Cava's great mambo atmosphere; the tapas bar is made festive with flamboyant colors and loud, lively flamenco really is live on weekends. The dining room is less raucous, with velvet drapes and tassels adorning the walls and comfortable booths. The cuisine is Spanish livened up with Caribbean touches (Cava is the invention of the team responsible for Cha Cha Cha in Silverlake), an influence reflected in dishes like black-bean tamales with tomatillo salsa and golden caviar; thick, dark tortilla soup; jerk chicken with sweet yams; and pan-seared shrimp in spicy peppercorn sauce. Spanish paella is stewed up three ways—with seafood, chicken and sausage, or all-vegetable—and is featured in Monday's all-you-can-eat "Paella Festival." If you have room for dessert, try the ruby-colored pears poached in port, the rice pudding, or the flan.

Kate Mantilini. 9101 Wilshire Blvd. (at Doheny Dr.), Beverly Hills. ☎ **310/278-3699.** Reservations suggested. Main courses $7–$16. AE, MC, V. Mon–Thurs 7:30am–1am, Fri 7:30am–3am, Sat noon–3am, Sun 10am–midnight. AMERICAN.

It's rare to find a restaurant that feels comfortably familiar yet trendy and cutting edge and is also one of L.A.'s few late-night eateries. Kate Mantilini fits the bill perfectly. One of the first to bring meatloaf back into fashion, Kate's offers a huge menu of upscale truckstop favorites like "white" chili (made with chicken, white beans, and Jack cheese), grilled steaks and fish, a few token pastas, and just about anything you could crave. At 2am nothing quite beats a steaming bowl of lentil-vegetable soup and some garlic-cheese toast—unless your taste runs to fresh oysters and a dry martini—Kate has it all. The huge mural of the Hagler-Hearns boxing match that dominates the stark, open interior provides the only clue to the namesake's identity—Mantilini was an early female boxing promoter, circa 1947.

۞ Locanda Veneta. 8638 W. 3rd St. (between San Vicente and Robertson blvds.). ☎ **310/274-1893.** Reservations required. Main courses $10–$22. AE, DC, DISC, MC, V. Mon–Thurs 11:30am–2:30pm and 5:30–10:30pm, Fri 11:30am–2:30pm and 5:30–11pm, Sat 5:30–11pm. ITALIAN/VENETIAN.

Locanda Veneta's citywide renown belies its tiny size and unpretentious setting. Its location, across from the unsightly monolith that is Cedars-Sinai Hospital, is a far cry from Venice's Grand Canal. And the single, loud, tightly packed dining room can sometimes feel like Piazza San Marco at the height of tourist season. But the sensible prices reflect the restaurant's efficient decor. While the dining room is decidedly unfancy, the kitchen is dead serious, making this restaurant a kind of temple for knowledgeable foodies, who flock here to sample the latest creations of chef Massimo Ormani, a gifted artist and culinary technician who's building a national reputation. The soups are excellent, seafood dishes extraordinary, and pastas as good as they can get. Signature dishes include pasta-and-bean soup, veal chops, lobster ravioli, shrimp risotto, and perfectly grilled vegetables. Insiders order linguine with rock shrimp, baby asparagus, and tomatoes—an uncharacteristically light off-menu meal.

Replay Country Store Cafe. 8607 Melrose Ave. (between San Vicente and La Cienega blvds.), West Hollywood. ☎ **310/657-6404.** Reservations suggested on weekends. Main courses $6–$13. AE, DISC, MC, V. Daily 10am–10pm. ITALIAN/CONTINENTAL.

The two things to remember at Replay are (1) don't buy the clothes, and (2) always order the soup. Most of the café's tables are on the wraparound wood porch of the overpriced boutique it's attached to. This faux country general store on trendy Melrose Avenue near the Pacific Design Center won't fool anyone into plunking down $150 for denim overalls, but the restaurant is one of West Hollywood's hidden treasures. Everything on the casual, vaguely Italian menu is outstanding, from gourmet pizzas to pasta with delicately puréed tomato-basil sauce; from the warm chicken salad's surprise combination of bleu cheese, walnuts and mandarin orange wedges to exquisite pastries for dessert. Each day a different soup, always a simple purée allowing the fresh ingredients to shine through, is ladled into wide bowls at your table from heavy copper saucepans.

INEXPENSIVE

✪ **The Apple Pan.** 10801 Pico Blvd. (east of Westwood Blvd.). ☎ **310/475-3585.** Main courses $6–$7. No credit cards. Tues–Thurs and Sun 11am–midnight, Fri–Sat 11am–1am. SAND-WICHES/AMERICAN.

There are no tables, just a U-shaped counter, at this classic American burger shack and L.A. landmark. Open since 1947, the Apple Pan is a diner that looks—and acts—the part. It's famous for juicy burgers, bullet-speed service, and its authentic frills-free atmosphere. The hickory burger is best, though the tuna sandwich also has its huge share of fans. Ham, egg salad, and swiss cheese sandwiches round out the menu. Definitely order fries and, if you're in the mood, the home-baked apple pie, too.

Dive! In the Century City Marketplace, 10250 Santa Monica Blvd. ☎ **310/788-3483.** Reservations accepted only for parties of 10 or more. Main courses $6–$15. AE, DC, MC, V. Sun–Thurs 11:30am–10pm, Fri–Sat 11:30am–11pm. SANDWICHES/AMERICAN.

"Prepare to dive!" the public address system cries without warning. Red lights flash, the room darkens, water bubbles through "portholes," video monitors go black . . . and a waitress casually delivers another Coke to an adjacent table. Owned by Steven Spielberg and Jeffrey Katzenberg, two-thirds of the new mega-company Dreamworks SKG, Dive! is the first of what the investors hope to be a series of submarine-themed restaurants. The restaurant-cum-theme-park's insulated underwater ambience is the ultimate in dining entertainment. Except for the fries and the thin-cut onion rings, however, the same cannot be said of the food, which is decent at best and bad at worst. The menu is mainly submarine sandwiches (get it?), along with salads and some wood-roasted dishes like salmon served with assorted dipping sauces, such as homemade ketchup and cheddar cheese sauce. Stick with the subs. The restaurant is perpetually packed; waiting patrons get a beeper that won't work outside, so they have to wait at the expensive bar, where there's a voyeuristic periscope exposing the goings-on down on Santa Monica Boulevard. At the requisite gift shop, you can purchase a souvenir menu sprinkled with puns and quotations. It costs $5, but it lights up.

✪ **Skewer.** 8939 Santa Monica Blvd. (between Robertson and San Vicente blvds.), West Hollywood. ☎ **310/271-0555.** Main courses $7–$9; salads and pitas $4–$7. AE, MC, V. Daily 11am–midnight. MIDDLE EASTERN.

Santa Monica Boulevard is the heart of West Hollywood's commercial strip, and Skewer's sidewalk tables are a great place to see all kinds of neighborhood activity. Inside is a New York–like narrow space with changing artwork adorning the bare brick walls. From the zesty marinated carrot sticks you get the moment you're seated, to sweet, sticky squares of baklava for dessert, this Mediterranean grill is sure to please. The cuisine features baskets of warm pita bread for scooping up traditional salads like baba ghanoush (grilled eggplant with tahini and lemon) and tabbouleh (cracked wheat, parsley, and tomatoes). Try marinated chicken and lamb off the grill, or dolmades (rice and meat-stuffed grape leaves) seared with a tangy tomato glaze.

The Source. 8301 W. Sunset Blvd. (between La Cienega Blvd. and Fairfax Ave.), West Hollywood. ☎ **213/656-6388.** Main courses $5–$11. AE, CB, DC, MC, V. Mon–Fri 8am–midnight, Sat–Sun 9am–midnight. CALIFORNIA HEALTH FOOD.

This is where Woody Allen met Diane Keaton for a typical L.A. lunch in *Annie Hall*—part of his New York–centric statement about health-crazy Los Angeles. The restaurant is painted with giant colorful sunflowers and daisies that sprout up against a green background; from the street it looks just like the 1960s throwback that it is. Today Jerry Seinfeld eats here along with other health-conscious Angelenos who enjoy the ultra-casual dining room and patio. Once strictly vegetarian, the Source's menu now integrates mainstream healthful cuisine like veggie-filled omelets and turkey burgers with favorites from their hippie days—brown-rice pancakes, "Mother's" eggplant, cheese and walnut loaf, and Magic Mushrooms (a hallucination-free source specialty). Devotees order the veggie burger en casserole and stick around for the date-nut cheesecake; drinks include yogurt shakes, beer, and wine.

HOLLYWOOD
EXPENSIVE

Campanile. 624 S. La Brea Ave. (north of Wilshire Blvd.). ☎ **213/938-1447.** Reservations required. Main courses $18–$28. AE, MC, V. Mon–Thurs 7:30am–2:30pm and 6–10pm, Fri 7:30am–2:30pm and 5:30–11pm, Sat 8am–1:30pm and 5:30–11pm, Sun 8am–1:30pm. CALIFORNIA/MEDITERRANEAN.

Built as Charlie Chaplin's private offices in 1928, this lovely building has a multi-level layout, with flower-bedecked interior balconies, a bubbling fountain, and a skylight through which diners can see the campanile (bell tower). Crisply contemporary, the dining rooms are successful amalgams of vintage and modern, making this one of the most attractive spaces in Los Angeles. The kitchen, headed by Spago alumnus chef/owner Mark Peel, gets a giant leg up from baker (and wife) Nancy Silverton, who runs the now-legendary La Brea Bakery next door. Meals here might begin with fried zucchini flowers drizzled with melted mozzarella or lamb carpaccio surrounded by artichoke leaves—a dish that arrives looking like one of van Gogh's sunflowers. Chef Peel is particularly known for his grills and roasts; try the grilled prime rib smeared with black-olive tapenade or papardelle with braised rabbit, roasted tomato, and collard greens. And don't skip dessert here—the restaurant's many enthusiastic sweets fans have turned Nancy Silverton's dessert book into a bestseller.

♦ Patina. 5955 Melrose Ave. (west of Cahuenga Blvd.). ☎ **213/467-1108.** Reservations required. Main courses $18–$26. AE, DC, DISC, MC, V. Sun–Mon 6–9:30pm, Tues–Thurs 11:30am–2pm and 6–9:30pm, Fri 11:30am–2pm and 6–10:30pm, Sat 6–10:30pm. CALIFORNIA/FRENCH.

Joachim Splichal, arguably L.A.'s very best chef, is also a genius at choosing and training top chefs to cook in his kitchens while he jets around the world. Patina routinely wins the highest praise from demanding gourmands, who are happy to empty their bank accounts for unbeatable meals that almost never miss their intended mark. The dining room is straightforwardly attractive, low key, well lit, and professional, without the slightest hint of stuffiness. The menu is equally disarming: "Mallard Duck with Portobello Mushrooms" gives little hint of the brilliant colors and flavors that appear on the plate. The seasonal menu features partridge, pheasant, venison, and other game in winter and spotlights exotic local vegetables in warmer months. Seafood is always available; if Maine lobster cannelloni or asparagus-wrapped John Dory is on the menu, order it. Patina is justifiably famous for its mashed potatoes and potato-truffle chips; be sure to include one (or both) with your meal.

MODERATE

Bar Bistro at Citrus. 6703 Melrose Ave. (west of Highland Ave.). ☎ **213/857-0034.** Reservations recommended. Main courses $12–$16. AE, MC, V. Mon–Thurs noon–2:30pm and 6–10pm, Fri noon–2:30pm and 6–10:30pm, Sat 6–10:30pm. CALIFORNIA FRENCH.

The recent partition of the dining room at Michel Richard's venerable Citrus to make way for this upstart was the most conspicuous illustration of how top restaurateurs are dealing with the changing economic climate. Here the menu selections resemble those at Citrus proper, but the prices are kept low with less expensive meats and without the use of time-consuming stock reductions. Thankfully, Richard's exquisite dessert selections each day are the same for both. While a meal here is indeed a bargain, it can be frustrating to gaze across at Citrus's mesmerizingly atmospheric dining room.

Chianti Cucina. 7383 Melrose Ave. (between Fairfax and La Brea aves.). ☎ **213/653-8333.** Reservations recommended. Main courses $12–$20. AE, CB, DC, MC, V. Chianti Cucina, Mon–Thurs and Sun 11:30am–11:30pm, Fri–Sat 11:30am–midnight; Ristorante Chianti, Sun–Thurs 5:30–10:30pm, Fri–Sat 5:30–11pm. TUSCAN.

Innocent passersby, and locals in search of a secret hideaway, go to the dimly lit, crimson-colored Ristorante Chianti, where waiters whip out flashlights so customers can read the menu. Cognoscenti, on the other hand, bypass this 60-year-old standby and head straight for Chianti Cucina, the bright, bustling eat-in "kitchen" of the more formal restaurant next door. Chianti Cucina features excellent meals at fair prices. The menu, which changes frequently, is always interesting and often exceptional. Hot and cold appetizers range from fresh handmade mozzarella and prosciutto to lamb carpaccio with asparagus and marinated grilled eggplant filled with goat cheese, arugula, and sun-dried tomatoes. As for main dishes, the homemade pasta is both superior and deliciously inventive. Try the black tortellini filled with fresh salmon, or the giant ravioli filled with spinach and ricotta.

Dar Maghreb. 7651 Sunset Blvd. (between Fairfax and La Brea aves.). ☎ **213/876-7651.** Reservations recommended. Fixed-price dinner $29. AE, CB, DC, MC, V. Tues–Fri 6–11pm, Sat 6:30–11pm, Sun 5:30–10:30pm. MOROCCAN.

If you're a lone diner in search of a quick bite, this isn't the place for you. Dinner at Dar Maghreb is an entertaining dining experience that increases exponentially the larger your party and the longer you linger. Enter an exotic Arab world of genie waitresses who wash your hands with lemon water and belly dancers who shimmy around an exquisite fountain in the center of a Koranic patio. You'll feel like a guest in an ornately tiled palace as you dine at traditional tables on either low sofas or goatskin cushions.

Nothing is available à la carte here. The fixed-price meal is a multicourse feast, starting with bread and traditional Moroccan salads, followed by b'stilla, an appetizer of shredded chicken, eggs, almonds, and spices wrapped in a flaky pastry shell and topped with powdered sugar and cinnamon. The main courses, your choice of lamb, quail, chicken, and more, are each sublimely seasoned and delectable. Perhaps it's the exotic atmosphere that makes everyone eat more than they expected, but you'll be thankful that desert is a simple fruit and nut basket, accompanied by warm spice tea poured dramatically into traditional glasses. All is eaten with your hands, a slithery sensual experience that grows on you as the night progresses.

Georgia. 7250 Melrose Ave. (at Alta Vista Ave.). ☎ **213/933-8420.** Reservations recommended. Main courses $14–$20. AE, MC, V. Mon–Sat 6:30–11pm, Sun 5:30–10pm. SOUTHERN.

Soul food and power ties come together at this calorie-unconscious ode to southern cooking in the heart of Melrose's funky shopping district. Owned by a group of investors that includes Denzel Washington and Eddie Murphy, the restaurant is popular with Hollywood's African-American crowd and others who can afford L.A.'s highest-priced pork chops, fried chicken, and grits. It's great for people-watching. The antebellum-style dining room is built to resemble a fine southern house, complete with mahogany floors, Spanish moss, and wrought-iron gates; a bourbon bar continues the theme. The smoked baby back ribs are particularly good and, like many other dishes, are smothered in onion gravy or rémoulade, and sided with corn pudding, grits, string beans, or an excellent creamy garlic cole slaw. Other recommendations include turtle soup, grilled gulf shrimp, and a Créole-style catfish that's more delicately fried than it would traditionally be.

Musso & Frank Grill. 6667 Hollywood Blvd. (at Cahuenga Blvd.). ☎ **213/467-7788.** Reservations recommended. Main courses $13–$22. AE, CB, DC, MC, V. Tues–Sat 11am–11pm. AMERICAN/CONTINENTAL.

A survey of Hollywood eateries that leaves out Musso & Frank is like a study of Las Vegas showrooms that fails to mention Wayne Newton. It's not that this is the best restaurant in town, nor is it the most famous, but as L.A's oldest eatery (since 1919), Musso & Frank is the paragon of Old Hollywood grill rooms, an almost kitschy glimpse into a meat-and-potatoes world that has remained the same for generations. This is where Faulkner and Hemingway drank during their screenwriting days, where Orson Welles used to hold court. The restaurant is still known for its bone-dry martinis and perfectly seasoned Bloody Marys. The setting is what you'd expect: oak-beamed ceilings, red-leather booths and banquettes, mahogany room dividers (complete with coathooks), chandeliers with tiny shades. The extensive menu is a veritable survey of American/continental cookery. Hearty dinners include veal scaloppine marsala, roast spring lamb with mint jelly, and broiled lobster. Grilled meats are the restaurant's specialties, as is the Thursday-only chicken pot pie. Regulars also flock in for Musso's trademark "flannel cakes," crêpe-thin pancakes flipped to order.

INEXPENSIVE

○ **Authentic Cafe.** 7605 Beverly Blvd. (at Curson Ave.). ☎ **213/939-4626.** Reservations not accepted. Main courses $8–$13; lunch $8–$13. AE, MC, V. Mon–Thurs 11:30am–10pm, Fri 11:30am–11pm, Sat 10am–11pm, Sun 10am–10pm. SOUTHWESTERN.

True to its name, this excellent restaurant serves authentic southwestern food in a casual atmosphere, a winning combination that has made it an L.A. favorite. The trendy dining room is known for hip people-watching, large portions, and good food; they (thankfully) recently expanded the dining room, easing what used to be an unbearable wait for tables. You'll sometimes find an Asian flair to chef Roger Hayot's southwestern-style meals. Look for brie, papaya, and chili quesadillas; other worthwhile dishes are the chicken casserole with a cornbread crust, fresh corn and red peppers in chile-cream sauce, and meatloaf with caramelized onions.

○ **El Cholo.** 1121 S. Western Ave. (south of Olympic Blvd.). ☎ **213/734-2773.** Reservations recommended. Main courses $7–$13. AE, DC, MC, V. Mon–Thurs 11am–10pm, Fri–Sat 11am–11pm, Sun 11am–9pm. MEXICAN.

There's *authentic* Mexican and then there's *traditional* Mexican—El Cholo is comfort food of the latter variety, south-of-the-border cuisine traditionally craved by Angelenos. They've been serving it up in this pink adobe hacienda since 1927, even though the once-outlying Mid-Wilshire neighborhood around them has turned into Koreatown. El Cholo's expertly blended margaritas, invitingly messy nachos, and classic combination dinners don't break new culinary ground, but the kitchen has perfected these standards over 70 years. El Cholo is the best of the bunch, and we wish they bottled their rich, dark-red enchilada sauce! Other specialties include seasonally available green-corn tamales and creative sizzling vegetarian fajitas that go *way* beyond just eliminating the meat. The atmosphere is festive, as people from all parts of town dine happily in the many rambling rooms that comprise the restaurant. There's valet parking as well as a free self-park lot directly across the street.

Pink's Hot Dogs. 709 N. La Brea Ave. (at Melrose Ave.) ☎ **213/931-4223.** Reservations not accepted. Hot dogs $2.10. Sun–Thurs 9:30am–2am, Fri–Sat 9:30am–3am. HOT DOGS.

Pink's isn't your usual guidebook recommendation, but then again, this crusty corner stand isn't your usual doggery either. The heartburn-inducing chili dogs are so decadent that otherwise-upstanding, health-conscious Angelenos crave them. Bruce Willis reportedly proposed to Demi Moore at the 58-year-old shack that grew around the late Paul Pink's 10¢ weiner cart. Pray the bulldozers stay away from this little nugget of a place.

Roscoe's House of Chicken 'n' Waffles. 1514 N. Gower St. (at Sunset Blvd.). ☎ **213/466-7453.** Reservations not accepted. Main courses $4–$11. No credit cards. Sun–Thurs 9am–midnight, Fri–Sat 9am–4am. AMERICAN.

It sounds like a bad joke: Only chicken and waffle dishes are served here, a rubric that also encompasses eggs and chicken livers. Its close proximity to CBS Television City has turned this simple restaurant into a kind of de facto commissary for the network. A chicken-and-cheese omelet isn't everyone's ideal way to begin the day, but it's de rigueur at Roscoe's. At lunch, few calorie-unconscious diners can resist the chicken smothered in gravy and onions—a house specialty that's served with waffles or grits and biscuits. Large chicken-salad bowls and chicken sandwiches also provide plenty of cluck for the buck. Homemade cornbread, sweet-potato pie, homemade potato salad, and corn on the cob are available as side orders, and wine and beer are sold.

Roscoe's can also be found at 4907 W. Washington Blvd., at La Brea Ave. (☎ 213/936-3730), and 5006 W. Pico Blvd. (☎ 213/934-4405).

✪ **Sofi Estiatorion.** 8030³/₄ W. 3rd St. (between Fairfax and Crescent Heights). ☎ **213/651-0346.** Reservations suggested. Main courses $7–$14. AE, DC, MC, V. Mon–Thurs noon–2:30pm and 5:30–10:30pm, Fri–Sat noon–2:30pm and 5:30–11pm, Sun 5:30–10:30pm. GREEK.

Look for the Aegean-blue awning over the narrow passageway leading from the street to this hidden Athenian treasure. Be sure to ask for a table on the romantic patio amid twinkling lights, and immediately order a plate of their thick, satisfying tzatziki (yogurt-cucumber-garlic spread) and a basket of warm pitas for dipping. Other specialties (recipes courtesy of Sofi's old-world grandmother) include herbed rack of lamb with rice, fried calamari salad, saganaki (kasseri cheese flamed with ouzo), and other hearty taverna favorites. Located near the Farmer's Market in a popular part of town, Sofi's odd, off-street setting has made it an insiders' secret.

DOWNTOWN
EXPENSIVE

Pacific Dining Car. 1310 W. 6th St. (at Witmer St.). ☎ **213/483-6000.** Reservations recommended. Main courses $20–$42; lunch $14–$29; breakfast $11–$20. AE, MC, V. Daily 24 hours (breakfast 11pm–11am). STEAKS.

It's 4am and you're in the mood for a well-marbled, patiently aged New York steak. Well, even in these health-conscious times there are still enough nocturnal carnivores in Los Angeles to justify not one, but two all-night Pacific Dining Car steakhouses. The flagship location, just a few short blocks from the epicenter of downtown, is dark and clubby, a vestige of an age when diners guiltlessly indulged in fist-sized medallions of beef. The mesquite-charred steaks are terrific indeed, a cut above the restaurant's other hearty offerings, like lamb and chicken. There's a good wine selection. A separate breakfast menu features egg dishes, salads, and mini-steaks.

A second restaurant is located in Santa Monica, at 2700 Wilshire Blvd., a block east of 26th Street (☎ 310/453-4000).

🙂 Family-Friendly Restaurants

Musso & Frank Grill *(see p. 442)* Prices notwithstanding, Hollywood's oldest restaurant is a simple family place that offers something for everyone. Located directly on the Walk of Fame, the restaurant is in the heart of touristland. Kids are pleased by the extensive menu that offers something for everyone. For adults, the restaurant offers unmistakable quality. And who else will serve you peas and cubed carrots—with absolutely no irony—just like mom used to?

Pink's Hot Dogs *(see p. 443)* On the other end of the scale, Pink's is an institution in its own right that has been serving politically incorrect franks for what seems like forever. Everyone loves Pink's chili dogs, but you may never get the orange stains out of your kid's clothes.

Dive! *(see p. 439)* This place was created by Steven Spielberg and Jeffrey Katzenberg with kids specifically in mind. It's a fun place, with surroundings designed to take your mind off the food.

Jerry's Famous Deli *(see p. 446)* Jerry's in Studio City is frequented mostly by industry types who populate this Valley community; their kids often sport baseball caps or production T-shirts from mom's or dad's latest project. It has the most extensive deli menu in town and a casual, coffee-shop atmosphere, so families flock to Jerry's for lunch, early dinner, and (crowded) weekend breakfast.

MODERATE

Cafe Pinot. In the L.A. Public Library, 700 W. 5th St. (between Grand and Flower sts.). ☎ 213/239-6500. Reservations recommended. Main courses $13–$22. AE, MC, V. Mon 11:15am–2:30pm and 5–9pm, Tues–Sat 11:15am–2:30pm and 5–9:30pm. CALIFORNIA/FRENCH.

Chef Joachim Splichal is quickly becoming the most dominant force on the L.A. restaurant scene. Modeled after Patina, his top-ranked restaurant, Cafe Pinot is designed to be less formal in atmosphere and lighter on the palate—and the pocketbook. Opened in 1995 in the gardens of the L.A. Public Library, Cafe Pinot's tables are mostly on the patio, shaded by umbrellas and the well-landscaped library courtyard. The restaurant's location makes it a natural for downtown business folk; at night there's free shuttle transportation to the Music Center. Splichal has installed a giant rotisserie in the kitchen, and the best meals come from it. The moist, tender mustard-crusted roast chicken is your best bet—unless it's Friday night when you can order the roast suckling pig with its crackling skin. Other recommendable dishes include duck leg confit, grilled calf's liver, and seared peppered tuna.

Cha Cha Cha. 656 N. Virgil Ave. (at Melrose Ave.), Silver Lake. ☎ 213/664-7723. Reservations recommended. Main courses $8–$15. AE, DC, DISC, MC, V. Sun–Thurs 8am–10:30pm, Fri–Sat 8am–11:30pm. CARIBBEAN.

Cha Cha Cha serves the West Coast's best Caribbean food in a fun and funky space on the seedy fringe of downtown. The restaurant is a festival of flavors and colors that are both upbeat and offbeat. It's impossible to feel down when you're part of this eclectic hodgepodge of pulsating Caribbean music, wild decor, and kaleidoscopic clutter; still, the intimate dining rooms cater to lively romantics, not obnoxious frat boys. Claustrophobes should choose seats in the airy covered courtyard. The very spicy black-pepper jumbo shrimp gets top marks, as does the paella, a generous mixture of chicken, sausage, and seafood blended with saffron rice. Other

Jamaican-, Haitian-, Cuban-, and Puerto Rican–inspired recommendations include jerk pork and mambo gumbo, a zesty soup of okra, shredded chicken, and spices. Hardcore Caribbeanites might visit for breakfast, when the fare ranges from plantain, yucca, onion, and herb omelets to scrambled eggs with fresh tomatillos served on hot grilled tortillas.

✪ **La Serenata de Garibaldi.** 1842 E. 1st St. (between Boyle and State sts.), Boyle Heights. ☎ **213/265-2887.** Reservations recommended. Main courses $9–$18; lunch $6–$11. AE, MC, V. Tues–Sun 11am–10pm. MEXICAN.

Once a humble neighborhood hangout indistinguishable from the many tiny and thriving Latino businesses on this Boyle Heights street, La Serenata grew to prominence as word of its superior cuisine spread to business lunchers in nearby downtown. Soon affluent patrons came from far and wide—menu prices are decidedly more Westside than East L.A.—including O.J.'s legal "dream team," who lunched here often during his trial. Seafood is the focus of the hardworking kitchen. Trademark dishes include shrimp in cilantro sauce and Mexican sea bass filets in a tangy chipotle sauce, plus a rich, simmered-all-day mole sauce served on giant shrimp or chicken. This brand of authentic Mexican cuisine, done so expertly, has made La Serenata a consistent draw despite its dodgy surroundings—if you'll enjoy the earthy ethnic neighborhood (across the street from Mariachi Plaza, where colorfully attired ensembles wait, instruments in hand, for an evening's work). The restaurant has a secure rear parking lot, and the food is worth the drive.

A smaller-scale sister restaurant called **La Serenata Gourmet** recently opened near the Westside Pavilion at 10924 W. Pico Blvd., Los Angeles (☎ **310/441-9667**).

INEXPENSIVE

The Original Pantry Cafe. 877 S. Figueroa St. (at 9th St.). ☎ **213/972-9279.** Main courses $6–$11. No credit cards. Daily 24 hours. AMERICAN.

An L.A. institution if there ever was one, this place has been serving huge portions of comfort food around the clock for more than 60 years. In fact they don't even have a key to the front door. Owned by L.A. Mayor Richard Riordan, the Pantry is especially popular with politicos, who come here for weekday lunches, and conference-goers en route to the nearby L.A. Convention Center. The well-worn restaurant is also a welcoming beacon to late-night clubbers, when downtown becomes a virtual ghost town. A bowl of celery stalks, carrot sticks, and whole radishes greets you at your Formica table, and creamy cole slaw and sourdough bread come free with every meal. Famous for quantity rather than quality, the Pantry serves huge T-bone steaks, densely packed meatloaf, macaroni and cheese, and other American favorites. A typical breakfast (served all day) might consist of a huge stack of hotcakes, a big slab of sweet cured ham, homefries, and coffee.

THE SAN FERNANDO VALLEY

Other conveniently located Valley restaurants include a dark, tasty Mexican dive called **Casa Vega,** 13371 Ventura Blvd. (at Fulton Ave.), Sherman Oaks (☎ 818/788-4868); **Iroha Sushi,** 12953 Ventura Blvd. (west of Coldwater Canyon), Studio City (☎ 818/990-9559), a tiny Japanese cottage hidden behind an ethnic art gallery; **Miceli's,** 3655 Cahuenga Blvd. (east of Lankershim), Universal City (☎ 818/508-1221), a cavernous, stained-glass-windowed Italian restaurant whose service staff sings showtunes or opera favorites in between serving lasagne and chianti; and **Talesai,** 11744 Ventura Blvd. (between Colfax and Laurel Canyon), Studio City (☎ 818/753-1001), whose minimalist decor and crisp white tablecloths complement a sophisticated and innovative Thai cuisine.

Du-par's Coffee Shop. 12036 Ventura Blvd. (1 block east of Laurel Canyon), Studio City. ☎ **818/766-4437.** Reservations not accepted. All items under $10. AE, MC, V. Sun–Thurs 6am–1am, Fri–Sat 6am–4am. AMERICAN/DINER.

It's been called a "culinary wax museum," the last of a dying breed, the kind of coffee shop Donna Reed took the family to for blue-plate specials. This isn't a trendy new theme place, it's the real deal—and that motherly waitress who calls everyone under 60 "hon" might've had this job for 20 or 30 years! It's popular among old-timers who made it part of their daily routine decades ago, show-business denizens who eschew the industry watering holes, a new generation who appreciates a tasty, cheap meal—well, everyone, really. It's common knowledge that Du-par's makes the best buttermilk pancakes in town, though some prefer the eggy, perfect French toast (extra-crispy around the edges, please). Mouth-watering pies (blueberry cream cheese, coconut cream, etc.) line the front display case, and can be had for a song.

There's another Du-par's in Los Angeles at the Farmer's Market, 6333 W. 3rd St. (☎ 213/933-8446), but it doesn't stay open as late.

Jerry's Famous Deli. 12655 Ventura Ave. (at Coldwater Canyon Blvd.), Studio City. ☎ **818/980-4245.** Reservations not accepted. Main courses $9–$14; breakfast $2–$11; sandwiches and salads $4–$12. AE, MC, V. Daily 24 hours. DELI.

Just east of Coldwater Canyon Avenue, here's a simple yet sizable deli where all the Valley's hipsters go to relieve their late-night munchies. This place probably has one of the largest menus in America—a tome that spans cultures and continents, from Central America to China to New York. From salads to sandwiches to steak and seafood platters, everything, including breakfast, is served all day. Jerry's is consistently good at lox and eggs, pastrami sandwiches, potato pancakes, and all the deli staples. It's also an integral part of L.A.'s cultural landscape, and a favorite of the show-business types who populate the adjacent foothill neighborhoods. It also has a full bar.

Pinot Bistro. 12969 Ventura Ave. (west of Coldwater Canyon Ave.), Studio City. ☎ **818/990-0500.** Reservations required. Main courses $16–$22; lunch $7–$13. AE, DC, DISC, MC, V. Mon–Thurs 11:30am–2:30pm and 6–10pm, Fri 11:30am–2:30pm and 6–10:30pm, Sat 5:30–10:30pm, Sun 5:30–9:30pm. CALIFORNIA/FRENCH.

When the Valley crowd doesn't want to make the drive to Patina, they pack into Pinot Bistro, one of restaurateur Joachim Splichal's other hugely successful restaurants. The Valley's only great bistro is designed with dark woods, etched glass, and cream-colored walls that scream "trendy French" almost as loudly as the rich, straightforward cooking. The menu is a symphony of California and continental elements that includes a beautiful warm potato tart with smoked whitefish, and baby lobster tails with creamy polenta—both studies in culinary perfection. The most popular dish here is chef Octavio Becerra's Frenchified Tuscan bean soup, infused with oven-dried tomatoes and roasted garlic and served over crusty ciabatta bread. The generously portioned main dishes continue the gourmet theme: baby lobster risotto, braised oxtail with parsley gnocchi, and puff pastry stuffed with bay scallops, Manila clams, and roast duck. The service is good, attentive and unobtrusive. Many regulars prefer Pinot Bistro at lunch, when a less expensive menu is served to a more easygoing crowd.

5 The Top Attractions

SANTA MONICA & THE BEACHES

✪ **J. Paul Getty Museum.** 17985 Pacific Coast Hwy. (Calif. 1), Malibu. ☎ **310/458-2003.** Free admission. Tues–Sun 10am–5pm (last entrance at 4:30pm).

When it opened in 1974, the Getty Museum was mocked as a filthy-rich upstart with a spotty art collection. It didn't help that the museum was pompously designed after a Roman villa buried at Pompeii. With about $60 million a year to spend, the Getty has repeatedly made headlines by paying record prices for some of the art world's trophies. But far from snatching up everything, the museum is buying intelligently and selectively—perhaps realizing its detractors' worst fears— methodically transforming what was once a rich man's pastime into a connoisseur's delight.

The most notable piece in the rich antiquities collection is *The Victorious Athlete,* a 4th-century B.C. Greek sculpture known as the Getty Bronze; it's believed to have been crafted by Lysippus, court sculptor to Alexander the Great. But the most compelling antiquity is the *Kouros,* a Greek sculpture of a nude youth. It's now widely believed to be fake, but, after years of scientific testing and scholarly debate, the legitimacy of the statue has yet to be resolved. In a classic example of turning lemons into lemonade, rather than shirking from the controversial spotlight, the museum has turned the debate into the focal point of their exhibit, displaying all the evidence both for and against the statue's authenticity.

Construction of the new Getty Center in Brentwood will be completed by the end of 1997, and the Malibu villa will close for 3 years of renovation. Some pieces will be displayed at the new center, which will have extensive research facilities in addition to public galleries. The Malibu Getty is a quintessential L.A. experience, however—try to visit while you still can.

Important: Parking is free, but you must phone for a parking reservation 7 to 10 days in advance. If you can't get a reservation, your best bet is to park in the lot of any restaurant on the Pacific Coast Highway (Calif. 1) and phone a cab (see "Getting Around," above). Walk-in visitors are not permitted.

Venice Ocean Front Walk. On the beach, between Venice Blvd. and Rose Ave.

Venice is one of the world's most engaging bohemias. It's not an exaggeration to say that no visit to L.A. would be complete without a stroll along the famous beach path, an almost surreal assemblage of every L.A. stereotype—and then some. Among stalls and stands selling cheap sunglasses, Mexican blankets, and "herbal ecstasy" pills swirls a carnival of humanity that includes bikini-clad roller skaters, tattooed bikers, muscle-bound pretty boys, panhandling vets, beautiful wannabes, and plenty of tourists and gawkers. On any given day you're bound to come across all kinds of performers: white-faced mimes, breakdancers, buskers, chainsaw jugglers, talking parrots, an occasional apocalyptic evangelist. Last time we were there, a man stood behind a table and railed against the evils of circumcision. "It's too late for us, guys, but we can save the next generation." But a chubby guy singing "Kokomo"—out of tune but with all his heart—cheered us up.

L.A.'S WESTSIDE & BEVERLY HILLS

Rancho La Brea Tar Pits/George C. Page Museum. 5801 Wilshire Blvd. (east of Fairfax Ave.), Los Angeles. ☎ **213/936-2230** or 213/857-6311. Admission $6 adults, $3.50 seniors 62 and older and students with ID, $2 children 5–12, free for kids 4 and under, free for everyone the second Tues of every month. Museum, Tues–Sun 10am–5pm; Paleontology Laboratory, Wed–Sun 10am–5pm; Tar Pits, Sat–Sun 10am–5pm.

An odorous, murky swamp of congealed oil continuously oozes to the earth's surface in the middle of Los Angeles. No, it's not a low-budget horror-movie set: It's the La Brea Tar Pits, an awesome, primal pool right on Museum Mile, where hot tar has been bubbling from the earth for over 40,000 years. The glistening pools, which look like murky water, have enticed thirsty animals throughout history. Thousands of mammals, birds, amphibians, and insects—many of which are now extinct—mistakenly crawled into the sticky sludge and stayed forever. In 1906 scientists began a systematic removal and classification of entombed specimens, including ground sloths, giant vultures, mastodons, camels, bears, lizards, even prehistoric relatives of today's beloved superrats. The best finds are on display in the adjacent George C. Page Museum of La Brea Discoveries, where an excellent 15-minute film documenting the recoveries is also shown. Archeological work is ongoing; you can watch as scientists clean, identify, and catalog new finds in the Paleontology Laboratory.

The Tar Pits themselves are only open on weekends; guided tours are given on Saturday and Sunday at 1pm. Swimming is prohibited.

HOLLYWOOD

Hollywood Sign. At the top of Beachwood Dr., Hollywood.

These 50-foot-high white sheet-metal letters have come to symbolize both the movie industry and the city itself. Erected in 1923 as an advertisement for a fledgling real estate development, the full text originally read HOLLYWOODLAND. The recent installation of motion detectors around the sign just made this graffiti tagger's coup a target even more worth boasting about. A thorny hiking trail leads to it from Durand Drive near Beachwood Drive, but the best view is from down below, at the corner of Sunset Boulevard and Bronson Avenue.

Hollywood Walk of Fame. Hollywood Blvd., between Gower St. and La Brea Ave; and Vine St., between Yucca St. and Sunset Blvd. ☎ **213/469-8311.**

More than 2,500 celebrities are honored along the world's most famous sidewalk. Each bronze medallion, set into the center of a granite star, pays homage to a famous television, film, radio, theater, or recording personality. Although about a third of them are just about as obscure as Andromeda—their fame simply hasn't withstood the test of time—millions of visitors are thrilled by the sight of famous names like James Dean (at 1719 Vine St.), John Lennon (at 1750 Vine St.), Marlon Brando (at 1765 Vine St.), Rudolph Valentino (at 6164 Hollywood Blvd.), Greta Garbo (6901 Hollywood Blvd.), Louis Armstrong (7000 Hollywood Blvd.), and Barbra Streisand (6925 Hollywood Blvd).

The sight of bikers, metalheads, druggies, hookers, and hordes of disoriented tourists all treading on memorials to Hollywood's greats makes for quite a bizarre tribute indeed. But the Hollywood Chamber of Commerce has been doing a terrific job sprucing up the pedestrian experience with filmstrip crosswalks, swaying palms, and more. And at least one weekend a month a privately organized group of fans calling themselves Star Polishers busy themselves scrubbing tarnished medallions.

Recent subway digging under the boulevard has caused the street to sink several inches. When John Forsythe's star cracked, authorities removed many others to prevent further damage. In the next few years, up to 250 stars, including those of Marilyn Monroe (6744 Hollywood Blvd.) and Elvis Presley (6777 Hollywood Blvd.) will be temporarily removed as the subway project expands.

The legendary sidewalk is continually adding new names. The public is invited to attend dedication ceremonies; the honoree is usually in attendance. Contact the **Hollywood Chamber of Commerce,** 6255 Sunset Blvd., Suite 911, Hollywood, CA 90028 (☎ **213/469-8311**), for information on who's being honored this week.

Mann's Chinese Theatre. 6925 Hollywood Blvd. (3 blocks west of Highland Ave.). ☎ **213/464-8111** or 213/461-3331. Movie tickets $7.50. Call for show times.

Stargazing in L.A.: Top Spots About Town for Sighting Celebrities

Celebrities pop up everywhere in L.A. If you spend enough time here, you'll surely bump into a few of them. If you're only in the city for a short time, however, it's best to go on the offensive.

Restaurants are your surest bet. Matsuhisa, The Ivy, and Maple Drive can almost guarantee sightings any night of the week. If you're not up to committing yourself to dining at one of these pricey hot spots, walk in confidently at 9pm and tell the maître d' that you just want to take a look at the dining room. The trendiest clubs and bars—Whisky, Viper Room, Tatou, and Roxbury—are second best for star sighting, but cover charges can be astronomical and the velvet ropes oppressive. And it's not always Mick and Rod and Madonna; a recent night on the town only turned up Yanni, Ralph Macchio, and Dr. Ruth.

Often, the best places to see members of the A-list aren't as obvious as a back-alley stage door or the front room of Spago. Shops along Sunset Boulevard, like Tower Records and the Virgin Megastore, are often star-heavy. Book Soup, that browser's paradise across the street from Tower, is usually good for a star or two. You'll often find them casually browsing the international newsstand (if they're not there to sign their latest tell-all autobiography). You might even pop into Sunset Strip Tattoo, where Cher, Charlie Sheen, Lenny Kravitz, and members of Guns 'N' Roses all got inked. A midafternoon stroll along Melrose Avenue might also produce a familiar face; check out Drake's Gift and Novelty Shop, Retail Slut, and Billy Martin's.

Keep your eyes peeled for celebrities—everyone does in L.A.—and you'll more than likely be rewarded. And don't feel bad if you only see Bob Denver. What greater sighting than Gilligan himself?

This is one of the world's great movie palaces, and one of Hollywood's finest landmarks. The Chinese Theatre was opened in 1927 by entertainment impresario Sid Grauman, a brilliant promoter who's credited with originating the idea of the paparazzi-packed movie "première." Outrageously conceived, with both authentic and simulated Chinese embellishments, gaudy Grauman's theater was designed to impress. Original Chinese heaven doves top the facade, and two of the theater's exterior columns once propped up a Ming Dynasty temple.

Visitors flock to the theater by the millions for its world-famous entry court, where stars like Elizabeth Taylor, Paul Newman, Ginger Rogers, Humphrey Bogart, Frank Sinatra, Marilyn Monroe, and about 160 others set their signatures and hand- and footprints in concrete. It's not always hands and feet, though: Betty Grable made an impression with her shapely leg, Gene Autry with the hoofprints of his horse, Champion, and Jimmy Durante and Bob Hope used their trademark noses.

Farmer's Market. 6333 W. 3rd St. (near Fairfax Ave.). ☎ **213/933-9211.** Mon–Sat 9am–6:30pm, Sun 10am–5pm.

The original market was little more than a field clustered with stands set up by farmers during the Depression so they could sell directly to city dwellers. It slowly grew into permanent buildings recognizable by the trademark shingled 10-story clocktower, and has evolved into a sprawling food marketplace with a carnival atmosphere, a kind of "turf" version of San Francisco's surfy Fisherman's Wharf. About 100 restaurants, shops, and grocers cater to a mix of workers from the adjacent CBS Television City complex, locals, and tourists, who are brought here by the busload.

Hollywood Area Attractions

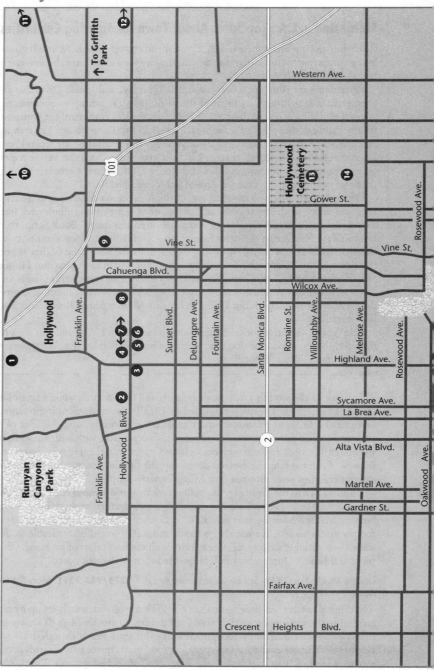

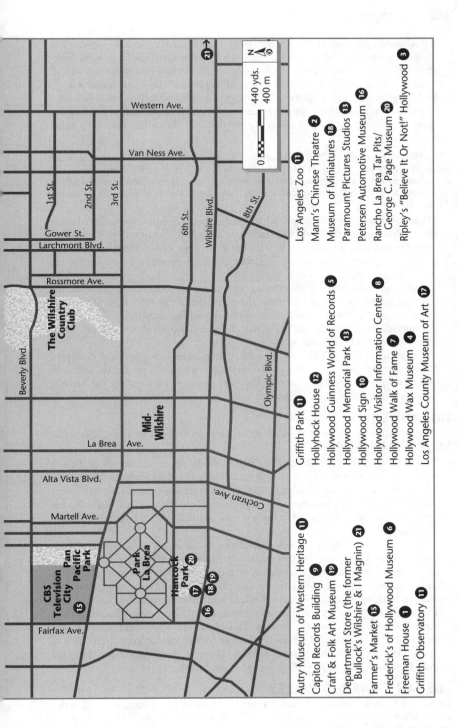

Western Ave.

Van Ness Ave.

1st St.
2nd St.
3rd St.

6th St.

Wilshire Blvd.

8th St.

Gower St.
Larchmont Blvd.

Rossmore Ave.

The Wilshire Country Club

Beverly Blvd.

Mid-Wilshire

Olympic Blvd.

La Brea   Ave.

Alta Vista Blvd.

Martell Ave.

Cochran Ave.

CBS Television City **15**

Pan Pacific Park

Park La Brea

Hancock Park **20**

17 **18** **19**

16

Fairfax Ave.

N

440 yds.
400 m
0

Los Angeles Zoo **11**

Mann's Chinese Theatre **2**

Museum of Miniatures **18**

Paramount Pictures Studios **13**

Petersen Automotive Museum **16**

Rancho La Brea Tar Pits/
George C. Page Museum **20**

Ripley's "Believe It Or Not!" Hollywood **3**

Griffith Park **11**

Hollyhock House **12**

Hollywood Guinness World of Records **5**

Hollywood Memorial Park **13**

Hollywood Sign **10**

Hollywood Visitor Information Center **8**

Hollywood Walk of Fame **7**

Hollywood Wax Museum **4**

Los Angeles County Museum of Art **17**

Autry Museum of Western Heritage **11**

Capitol Records Building **9**

Craft & Folk Art Museum **19**

Department Store (the former
Bullock's Wilshire & I Magnin) **21**

Farmer's Market **15**

Frederick's of Hollywood Museum **6**

Freeman House **1**

Griffith Observatory **11**

21

Retailers sell greeting cards, kitchen implements, candles, and souvenirs; but everyone comes here for the food stands, which offer oysters, Cajun gumbo, fresh-squeezed orange juice, roast beef sandwiches, fresh-pressed peanut butter, and all kinds of international fast foods. You can still buy produce here—no longer a farm-fresh bargain, but a better selection than the grocery stores offer. Don't miss Kokomo, a "gourmet" outdoor coffee shop that has become power breakfast spot for show-biz types. Red turkey hash and sweet-potato fries are the dishes that keep them coming back.

✪ **Griffith Observatory.** 2800 E. Observatory Rd. (in Griffith Park, at the end of Vermont Ave.). ☎ **213/664-1191,** or 213/663-8171 for the Sky Report, a recorded message on current planet positions and celestial events. Free admission; planetarium show tickets $4 adults, $3 seniors, $2 children. June–Aug, daily 12:30–10pm; Sept–May, Tues–Fri 2–10pm, Sat–Sun 12:30–10pm.

Made world famous in the film *Rebel Without a Cause,* Griffith Observatory's bronze domes have been Hollywood Hills landmarks since 1935. Most visitors never actually go inside; they come to this spot on the south slope of Mt. Hollywood for unparalleled city views. On warm nights, with the lights twinkling below, this is one of the most romantic places in L.A.

The main dome houses a planetarium, where narrated projection shows reveal the stars and planets that are hidden from the naked eye by the city's lights and smog. Mock excursions into space search for extraterrestrial life, or examine the causes of earthquakes, moonquakes, and starquakes. Presentations last about an hour. Show times vary, so call for information.

The adjacent Hall of Science holds exhibits on galaxies, meteorites, and other cosmic objects, including a telescope trained on the sun; a Foucault pendulum; and earth and moon globes 6 feet in diameter. On clear nights you can gaze at the heavens through the powerful 12-inch telescope.

DOWNTOWN

El Pueblo de Los Angeles Historic District. Enter on Alameda St. across from Union Station. ☎ **213/628-1274.**

This Los Angeles Historic District was built in the 1930s, on the site where the city was founded, as an alternative to the wholesale razing of a particularly unsightly slum. The result is a contrived nostalgic fantasy of the city's beginnings, a kitschy theme park portraying Latino culture in a Disneyesque fashion. Nevertheless, El Pueblo has proven wildly successful, as L.A.'s Latinos have adopted it as an important cultural monument.

El Pueblo is not entirely without authenticity. Some of L.A.'s oldest extant buildings are located here, and the area really does exude the ambience of Old Mexico. At its core is a Mexican-style marketplace on old Olvera Street. The carnival of sights and sounds is heightened by mariachis, colorful piñatas, and more than occasional folkloric dancing. Olvera Street, the district's primary pedestrian thoroughfare, and adjacent Main Street are home to about two dozen 19th-century buildings; one houses an authentic Mexican restaurant, La Golondrina. Stop in at the visitor center, 622 N. Main St. (☎ 213/628-1274); open Monday to Saturday from 10am to 3pm). Don't miss the Avila Adobe, at E-10 Olvera St. (open Monday to Saturday from 10am to 5pm); built in 1818, it's the oldest building in the city.

THE SAN FERNANDO VALLEY

Universal Studios. Hollywood Fwy. (Lankershim Blvd. exit), Universal City. ☎ **818/508-9600.** Admission $34 adults, $28 seniors 65 and older and children 3–11, free for kids 2 and under. Parking $5. Summer, daily 7am–11pm; the rest of the year, daily 9am–7pm.

Believing that filmmaking itself was a bona fide attraction, Universal Studios began offering tours to the public in 1964. The concept worked. Today Universal is more than just one of the largest movie studios in the world—it's one of the biggest amusement parks.

The main attraction continues to be the Studio Tour, a 1-hour guided tram ride around the company's 420 acres. En route you pass stars' dressing rooms and production offices before visiting famous backlot sets that include an eerily familiar Old West town, a clean New York City street, and the famous town square from the *Back to the Future* films. Along the way the tram encounters several staged "disasters," which we won't divulge here lest we ruin the surprise.

Other attractions are more typical of high-tech theme park fare, but all have a film-oriented slant. On Back to the Future—The Ride, you're seated in a mock time-traveling DeLorean and thrust into a fantastic multimedia rollercoasting extravaganza—it's far and away Universal's best ride. The Backdraft ride surrounds visitors with brilliant balls of very real fire spewing from imitation ruptured fuel lines. Kids love it. Like the movie that inspired it, the E.T. Adventure appeals to the heart; you ride simulated bicycles on an extraordinary special-effects adventure through principal parts of the film. A "Waterworld" live-action stunt show is thrilling to watch (and probably more successful than the film that inspired it), while the latest special effects showcase, Jurassic Park—The Ride, is short in duration but long on dinosaur illusions and computer magic lifted from the Universal blockbuster.

Universal Studios is really a fun place. But just as in any theme park, lines can be long; the wait for a 5-minute ride can sometimes last more than an hour. In summer the stifling Valley heat can dog you all day. To avoid the crowds, skip weekends, school vacations, and Japanese holidays.

6 TV Tapings

Being part of the audience for the taping of a television show might be the quintessential L.A. experience. This is a great way to see Hollywood at work, to find out how your favorite sitcom or talk show is made, and to catch a glimpse of your favorite TV personalities. But you might end up with tickets to a show that may never make an appearance in *TV Guide* rather than for one of your favorites, like *Mad About You* or *Friends*. Tickets to top shows are in greater demand than others, and getting your hands on them usually takes advance planning—and possibly some time waiting in line.

Request tickets as far in advance as possible. Several episodes may be shot on a single day, so you may be required to remain in the theater for up to 4 hours. If you phone at the last moment, you may luck onto tickets for your top choice. More likely, however, you'll be given a list of shows that are currently filming and you won't recognize many of the titles—studios are always taping pilots, few of which end up on the air. But you never know who may be starring in them—look at all the famous faces that have launched new sitcoms in the past couple of years. Tickets are always free, usually limited to two per person, and are distributed on a first-come, first-served basis. Many shows don't admit children under the age of 10; in some cases no one under the age of 18 is admitted.

Audiences Unlimited (☎ **818/506-0043** or 818/506-0067 for the ticket information hotline) distributes tickets for the top sitcoms, including *Murphy Brown,* *Seinfeld,* and *Frasier.* **Television Tickets** (☎ **213/467-4697**) distributes tickets for the most popular talk and game shows. Their services are free, and you can reserve by phone. Or you can get tickets directly from the networks:

ABC, 4151 Prospect Ave., Hollywood, CA 90027 (☎ **310/557-7777**). Taped messages on the hotline let you know what's currently going on. Order tickets for a taping either by writing 3 weeks in advance or by showing up the day of the taping.

CBS, 7800 Beverly Blvd., Los Angeles, CA 90036 (☎ **213/852-2345** or 213/852-2458 for the ticket information hotline). Call to see what's being filmed while you're in town. Tickets for tapings are distributed on a first-come, first-served basis; you can write in advance to reserve them or pick them up directly at the studio up to an hour before taping.

NBC, 3000 W. Alameda Ave., Burbank, CA 91523 (☎ **818/840-4444** or 818/840-3537). Call to see what's on while you're in L.A. Tickets for NBC tapings, including *The Tonight Show with Jay Leno,* can be obtained in two ways: Pick them up at the NBC ticket counter on the day of the show you want to see (they're distributed on a first-come, first-served basis at the ticket counter off California Avenue); or at least 3 weeks before your visit, send a self-addressed, stamped envelope with your ticket request to the address above.

7 Exploring the City

ARCHITECTURAL HIGHLIGHTS

Los Angeles is a veritable Disneyland of architecture. The city is home to an amalgam of distinctive styles, from art deco to Spanish revival to coffee-shop kitsch to suburban ranch to postmodern—and much more.

Cutting-edge, over-the-top styles that would be out of place in other cities, from the oversize hot dog that is Tail o' the Pup to the mansions lining the streets of Beverly Hills, are perfectly at home in movie city. The world's top architects, from Frank Lloyd Wright to Frank Gehry, have flocked to L.A., reveling in the artistic freedom they have here. Los Angeles has taken some hard criticism for not being a "serious" architectural center, but in terms of innovation and personal style, the city couldn't get higher marks.

Although much of it is gone, you'll still find some prime examples of the roadside art that defined L.A. in earlier days. The Famous Brown Derby is no more, but, along with Tail o' the Pup, you may come across a giant stack of 45 r.p.m. records, an oversize doughnut or two, and some new structures carrying on the tradition.

SANTA MONICA & THE BEACHES

When you're strolling the historic canals and streets of Venice, be sure to check out **Chiat/Day/Mojo Headquarters** at 340 Main St. What would otherwise be an unspectacular contemporary office building is made fantastic by a three-story pair of binoculars that frames the entrance to this advertising agency. The sculpture is modeled after a design created by Claes Oldenburg and Coosje van Bruggen.

When you're flying in or out of LAX, be sure to stop for a moment to admire the **Control Tower and Theme Building.** The spacey *Jetsons*-style "Theme Building," which has always loomed over LAX, has been joined by a brand-new silhouette. The main control tower, designed by local architect Kate Diamond to evoke a stylized palm tree, is tailored to present Southern California in its best light. You can go inside to enjoy the view from the Theme Building's observation lounge.

L.A.'S WESTSIDE & BEVERLY HILLS

In addition to the Argyle and Beverly Hills Hotels (see "Accommodations," earlier in this chapter), be sure to wind your way through the streets of Beverly Hills off Sunset Boulevard. Modern architecture lovers should check out the **Pacific Design**

Center at 8687 Melrose Ave. (see "Shopping," later in this chapter). Designed by Argentinean Cesar Pelli, the bold architecture and overwhelming scale of the Pacific Design Center aroused plenty of controversy when it was erected in 1975. Sheathed in gently curving cobalt-blue glass, the seven-story building, housing over 750,000 square feet of wholesale interior design showrooms, is known to locals as "the blue whale." Nearby on San Vicente Boulevard—on a totally different scale—is the iconic ❂ Tail o' the Pup. This is roadside art—and the wiener—at its best.

HOLLYWOOD

In addition to the Griffith Observatory and Mann's Chinese Theatre (see "The Top Attractions," earlier in this chapter), and the Hollywood Roosevelt Hotel (see "Accommodations," earlier in this chapter), don't miss the Capitol Records Building. This 12-story tower just north of the legendary intersection of Hollywood and Vine is one of the city's most recognizable buildings. Often, but incorrectly, rumored to have been made to resemble a stack of 45s on a turntable (it kinda does, really), this circular tower is nevertheless unmistakable. Nat "King" Cole, songwriter Johnny Mercer, and other 1950s Capitol artists populate a giant exterior mural.

Built between 1917 and 1920, Hollyhock House was the first Frank Lloyd Wright residence to be constructed in Los Angeles. The centerpiece of art-filled Barnsdall Park, the house, at 4800 Hollywood Blvd. (☎ 213/485-4581), is now owned by the city and operates as a small gallery and house museum, although it's undergoing extensive repairs for structural damamge from the 1994 earthquake.

Formerly Bullock's, then I. Magnin, the department store on Wilshire Boulevard at Vermont Avenue is a classy art deco gem featuring a stylish interior with mottled marble wall panels, cubist wall reliefs, and luxurious wood veneers. The main entrance faces the parking lot in the rear; the streetside facade was meant to be admired while flying past.

DOWNTOWN

Built in 1928, the 27-story City Hall, at 200 N. Spring St., remained the tallest building in the city for over 30 years. The structure's distinctive ziggurat roof was featured in the film *War of the Worlds,* but is probably best known as the headquarters of the *Daily Planet* in the *Superman* TV series. On a clear day the top-floor observation deck (open Monday to Friday from 10am to 4pm) offers views to Mount Wilson, 15 miles away.

On West 5th Street, between Flower Street and Grand Avenue, is one of L.A.'s early architectural achievements, the carefully restored ❂ Central Library (the majestic main entrance is actually on Flower Street). Working in the 1920s, architect Bertram G. Goodhue played on the Egyptian motifs and materials popularized by the discovery of King Tut's tomb, combining them with modern concrete block to great effect.

The 1893 Bradbury Building, at South Broadway and 3rd Street, is Los Angeles's oldest commercial building, and one of the city's most revered architectural landmarks. You've got to go inside to appreciate it. The glass-topped atrium is often used as a movie and TV set; you've seen it in *Chinatown* and *Blade Runner.*

Union Station, at Macy and Alameda streets, is one of the finest examples of California Mission–style architecture, built with the opulence and attention to detail that characterize 1930s W.P.A. projects. The cathedral-size, richly paneled ticket lobby and waiting area of this fantastic cream-colored structure stand sadly empty most of the time, but the MTA does use Union Station for Blue Line commuter trains.

The **Watts Towers,** at 1765 E. 107th St. (☎ **213/847-4646**), are more than a bit off the beaten track, but they warrant a visit. The fantastically colorful, 99-foot-tall concrete-and-steel sculptures are ornamented with mosaics of bottles, sea shells, cups, plates, generic pottery, and ceramic tiles. They were completed in 1954 by folk artist Simon Rodia, an immigrant Italian tile setter who worked on them for 33 years. Call for a tour schedule.

THE SAN FERNANDO VALLEY

At first glance the **Walt Disney Corporate Office,** at 500 S. Buena Vista St. (at Alameda Avenue) in Burbank, is just another neoclassical building. But wait a minute: Those aren't Ionic columns holding up the building's pediment . . . they're the Seven Dwarfs—giant-size, of course.

CHURCHES
SANTA MONICA & THE BEACHES

Wayfarers Chapel. 5755 Palos Verdes Dr. South, Rancho Palos Verdes. ☎ **310/377-1650.** Free admission. Daily 9am–5pm. Phone in advance to arrange a free escorted tour.

Constructed on a broad cliff with a steep face, the Wayfarers Chapel enjoys a fantastic spot overlooking the lashing waves of the Pacific. Designed by Frank Lloyd Wright, Jr., son of the more celebrated architect, the church is constructed of glass, redwood, and native stone. Known locally as the "glass church," Wayfarers is a memorial to Emanuel Swedenborg, an 18th-century Swedish philosopher who claimed to have visions of spirits and heavenly hosts.

L.A.'S WESTSIDE & BEVERLY HILLS

Church of the Good Shepherd. 505 N. Bedford Dr., Beverly Hills.

Built in 1924, this is Beverly Hills's oldest house of worship, and it has seen its share of joy and sorrow. In 1950 Elizabeth Taylor and her first husband, Nicky Hilton, were married here, and the funerals of Alfred Hitchcock, Gary Cooper, and Jimmy Durante were all held here.

MISSIONS

Two of the 21 missions built by Franciscan missionaries in the late 18th century along the California coast from San Diego to Sonoma are in the Los Angeles area. The valleys in which they're nestled in eventually took their names. In addition to the one listed below, see Mission San Gabriel under "Pasadena & Environs" in Chapter 16.

Mission San Fernando. 15151 San Fernando Mission Blvd., Mission Hills. ☎ **818/361-0186.** Admission $4 adults, $3 seniors and children 12 and under. Daily 9am–5pm. From I-5, exit at San Fernando Mission Blvd. east and drive 5 blocks to the mission.

Established in 1797, Mission San Fernando once controlled more than 1.5 million acres, employed 1,500 Native Americans, and boasted over 22,000 head of cattle and extensive orchards. The mission complex was destroyed several times, but was always faithfully rebuilt with low buildings surrounding grassy courtyards. The aging church was replaced in the 1940s, and again in the 1970s after a particularly destructive earthquake. The Convento, a 250-foot-long colonnaded structure dating from 1810, is the compound's oldest remaining part. Some of the mission's rooms, including the old library and the private salon of the first bishop of California, have been restored to their late 18th-century appearance. A half-dozen padres and many hundreds of Shoshone Indians are buried in the adjacent cemetery.

MUSEUMS & GALLERIES
SANTA MONICA & THE BEACHES

Museum of Flying. Santa Monica Airport, 2772 Donald Douglas Loop North, Santa Monica. ☎ **310/392-8822.** Admission $7 adults, $5 seniors, $3 children. Wed–Sun 10am–5pm.

Once headquarters of the McDonald Douglas corporation, the Santa Monica Airport is the birthplace of the DC-3 and other pioneers of commercial aviation. The museum celebrates this bit of local history with 24 authentic aircraft displays and some interactive exhibits. In addition to antique Spitfires and Sopwith Camels, there's a new kid-oriented learning area, where "hands-on" exhibits detail airplane parts, pilot procedures, and the properties of air and aircraft design. The shop is full of scale models of World War II birds; the coffee-table book *The Best of the Past* beautifully illustrates 50 years of aviation history.

L.A.'S WESTSIDE & BEVERLY HILLS

Museum of Tolerance. 9786 W. Pico Blvd. (at Roxbury Dr.). ☎ **310/553-8403.** Admission $8 adults, $6 seniors, $5 students, $3 children 3–12, free for children 2 and under. Advance purchase recommended. Mon–Thurs 10am–5pm, Fri 10am–3pm (to 1pm Nov–Mar), Sun 11am–5pm. Closed many Jewish and secular holidays; call for schedule.

The Museum of Tolerance is designed to expose prejudices and teach racial and cultural tolerance. It's located in the Simon Wiesenthal Center, an institute founded by the legendary Nazi-hunter. While the Holocaust figures prominently here, this is not just a Jewish museum—it's an academy that broadly campaigns for a live-and-let-live world. Tolerance is an abstract idea that's hard to display, so most of this $50-million museum's exhibits are high tech and conceptual in nature. Fast-paced interactive displays are designed to touch the heart as well as the mind, and engage both serious investigators and the MTV crowd. One of two major museums in America that deal with the Holocaust, the Museum of Tolerance is considered by some to be inferior to its Washington, D.C., counterpart, and visitors can be frustrated by the museum's policy of insisting that you follow a prescribed 2½-hour route through the exhibits.

Museum of Television and Radio. 465 N. Beverly Dr. (at Santa Monica Blvd.), Beverly Hills. ☎ **310/786-1000.** Admission $6 adults, $4 students and seniors, $3 kids 12 and under. Wed and Fri–Sun noon–5pm, Thurs noon–9pm. Closed New Year's Day, July 4, Thanksgiving, and Christmas.

Want to see the Beatles on *The Ed Sullivan Show* (1964) or Edward R. Murrow's examination of Joseph McCarthy (1954), watch Arnold Palmer win the 1958 Masters Tournament, relive childhood's *Winky Dink and You,* or listen to radio excerpts like FDR's first "Fireside Chat" (1933) and Orson Welles's famous *War of the Worlds* UFO hoax (1938)? All these, plus a gazillion episodes of *The Twilight Zone, I Love Lucy,* and other beloved series, can be viewed within the starkly white walls of architect Richard Meier's neutral, contemporary museum building. Like the ritzy Beverly Hills shopping district that surrounds it, the museum is more flash than substance. Once you gawk at the celebrity and industry-honcho names adorning every hall, room, and miscellaneous area, it becomes quickly apparent that "library" would be a more fitting name for this collection, since the main attractions are requested via sophisticated computer "catalogs" and viewed in private consoles. Although no one sets out to spend a vacation watching TV, it can be tempting once you start browsing the archives. The West Coast branch of the 20-year-old New York facility succeeds in treating our favorite pastime as a legitimate art form, with the respect history will prove it deserves.

For a preview, the museum's Internet Website is at **http://www.mtr.org/ camsm.htm.**

UCLA at the Armand Hammer Museum of Art and Cultural Center. 10899 Wilshire Blvd. (at Westwood Blvd.). ☎ **310/443-7000.** Admission $4.50 adults, $3 students and seniors 55 and over, $1 kids 17 and under, free for everyone Thurs 6–9pm. Tues–Wed and Fri–Sat 11am–7pm, Thurs 11am–9pm, Sun 11am–5pm.

Created in 1990 by the former chairman and CEO of Occidental Petroleum, the Armand Hammer Museum has had a hard time winning the respect of critics and the public alike. Barbs are usually aimed at both the museum's relatively flat collection and its patron's tremendous ego. Ensconced in a two-story Carrara marble building attached to the oil company's offices, the Hammer is better known for its high-profile and often provocative visiting exhibits, such as the opulent pre-Revolution treasures of Russian ruler Catherine the Great, or an exhibition entitled "Sexual Politics" assembed around avant-garde artist Judy Chicago's controversial 1970's feminist creation *The Dinner Party*. In conjunction with UCLA's Wight Gallery, a feisty gallery with a reputation for championing contemporary political and experimental art, the Hammer continues to present often daring and usually popular special exhibits, and it is most definitely worth calling ahead to find out what will be there during your visit to L.A.

The permanent collection (Armand Hammer's personal collection, which had been promised to the L.A. County Museum but was withdrawn in 1990 amid great controversy and criticism) consists mostly of traditional Western European and Anglo-American art. It contains noteworthy paintings by Toulouse-Lautrec, Degas, and van Gogh. Several canvases warrant special notice: John Singer Sargent's dramatic *Dr. Pozzi at Home* (1881) feels as though the doctor were an actor about to go on stage; it's a sophisticated masterpiece of salon painting. Rembrandt's *Juno* (1662), painted as a loving tribute to the artist's mistress, is one of the museum's most important pieces, and one of the finest Dutch paintings in any American collection.

HOLLYWOOD

✪ **Los Angeles County Museum of Art.** 5905 Wilshire Blvd. ☎ **213/857-6111,** or 213/857-6000 for a recording. Admission $6 adults, $4 students and seniors 62 and over, $1 children 6–17, free for kids 5 and under; regular exhibitions free for everyone the second Wed of every month. Tues–Thurs 10am–5pm, Fri 10am–9pm, Sat–Sun 11am–6pm.

This is one of the finest art museums in the United States. The huge complex was designed by three very different architects over a span of 30 years. The architectural fusion can be migraine inducing, but this city landmark is well worth delving into. If you fear getting lost forever, head straight for the Japanese Pavilion, which holds the museum's highest concentration of great art. Its exterior walls are made of Kalwall, a translucent material that, like shoji screens, permits the entry of soft natural light. Inside is a collection of Japanese Edo paintings that's rivaled only by the holdings of the emperor of Japan.

The Anderson Building, the museum's contemporary wing, is home to 20th-century painting and sculpture. Here you'll find works by Matisse, Magritte, and a good number of Dada artists.

The Ahmanson Building houses the rest of museum's permanent collections. Here you'll find everything from 2,000-year-old pre-Columbian Mexican ceramics to a unique glass collection spanning the centuries to 19th-century portraiture. The museum also has one of the nation's largest holdings of costumes and textiles, and an important Indian and Southeast Asian art collection.

The Hammer Building is primarily used for major special loan exhibitions. Free guided tours covering the museum's highlights depart on a regular basis from here. The museum has an Internet Website at **http://www.lacma.org.**

Craft & Folk Art Museum. 5800 Wilshire Blvd. (at Curson Ave.). ☎ **213/937-5544.** Admission $4 adults, $2.50 seniors students, free for children 11 and under. Tues–Sat 11am–5pm.

In 1965 a small restaurant and gallery called the Egg and the Eye began serving up eclectic arts and crafts exhibitions along with modest meals. The restaurant no longer exists, but the gallery has grown into one of the city's largest, opening in a prominent Museum Mile building in 1995. "Craft and folk art" is quite a large rubric that encompasses everything from clothing, tools, religious artifacts, and other everyday objects to wood carvings, papier-mâché, weaving, and metalwork.

The museum displays folk objects from around the world, but its strongest collection is masks from India, America, Mexico, Japan, and China. Special exhibitions planned for 1997 include a retrospective of California woodworker Sam Maloof (whose custom-made chairs grace many a celebrity home) and a collection examining parallels between Italy's rich textile heritage and traditional bread shapes and textures. The museum is well known for its annual International Festival of Masks, a colorful and ethnic celebration held each October in Hancock Park, across the street.

Museum of Miniatures. 5900 Wilshire Blvd. ☎ **213/937-MINI.** Admission $7.50 adults, $6.50 seniors, $5 students, $3 children. Tues–Sat 10am–5pm, Sun 11am–5pm.

With almost 200 exhibits, the Museum of Miniatures is the world's largest repository of diminutive mansions, pint-size automobiles, and intricately decorated mini-rooms. Completely unbeknownst to most Angelenos, miniatures-making is a thriving and popular art; in fact, almost everything here has been created within the last 15 years. And we're not talking mere dollhouses here (though it has those, too). The Museum of Miniatures has perfect one-twelfth-scale minis of an antebellum mansion, a Benedictine abbey, and an entire Victorian village. It even has an intricately detailed mini re-creation of Judge Lance Ito's famous courtroom, complete with prosecutors and the defense "dream team." Miniature 18-karat-gold train cars full of rubies, sapphires, and emeralds are pulled by an engine encrusted with almost 200 diamonds. Bring your life-size wallet, for the wonderful museum gift shop has lilliputian tea sets, very small clocks, and tiny Louis XV "chair" brooches.

○ Petersen Automotive Museum. 6060 Wilshire Blvd. (at Fairfax Ave.). ☎ **213/930-2277.** Admission $7 adults, $5 seniors and students, $3 children 5–12, free for kids 4 and under. Tues–Sun 10am–6pm.

When the Petersen opened in 1994, many locals were surprised that it had taken this long for the City of Freeways to salute its most important shaper. Indeed, this museum says more about the city than probably any other one in L.A. Named for Robert Petersen, the publisher responsible for *Hot Rod* and *Motor Trend* magazines, the four-story museum displays over 200 cars and motorcycles, from the historic to the futuristic. Cars on the first floor are depicted chronologically, in period settings. Other floors are devoted to frequently changing shows of race cars, early motorcycles, and famous movie vehicles. Recent exhibits have included the Flintstones' fiberglass and cotton movie car; a customized dune buggy, with seats made from surfboards, created for the Elvis Presley movie *Easy Come, Easy Go;* and a three-wheeled scooter that folds into a Samsonite briefcase, created in competition by a Mazda engineer. You can check it out on the Internet at **http://www.lam.mus.ca.us/petersen.**

The Frederick's of Hollywood Museum. 6608 Hollywood Blvd. ☎ **213/466-8506.** Free admission. Mon–Sat 10am–6pm, Sun noon–5pm.

Stargazing, Part II: The Less-Than-Lively Set

Almost everybody who visits L.A. hopes to see a celebrity—they are, after all, our most common export item. Celebrities usually don't cooperate, failing to gather in readily viewable herds. They occasionally tread predictable paths, frequenting certain watering holes, but on the whole, celeb-spotting is a chancy proposition.

There's a much much better alternative. An absolutely guaranteed method of being within 6 feet of your favorite star: Cemeteries. Cemeteries are *the* place for star (or at least headstone) gazing: The star is always available, and you're going to get a lot more up close and personal than you probably would to anyone who's actually alive. And L.A.'s a big place, with a lot of cemeteries—and there are a lotta stars in them thar hills. What follows is a guide to the most fruitful cemeteries, listed in order (more or less) of their friendliness to stargazers:

Weathered Victorian and deco memorials add to the decaying charm of **Hollywood Memorial Park,** 6000 Santa Monica Blvd., Hollywood (☎ **213/469-1181**). Fittingly, there's a terrific view of the HOLLYWOOD sign over the graves, as many of the founders of the community rest here. You'll see their names on the nearby street signs: the Gowers, the Wilcoxes, the Coles. The most notable tenant is Rudolph Valentino, who rests in an interior crypt. And there's silent director William Desmond Taylor (under his real name, William Deane Tanner), whose 1922 murder was an enormous scandal, ruining the careers of silent stars Mary Miles Minter and Mabel Normand, who were considered guilty by association. (Sidney Kirkpatrick's excellent *A Cast of Killers* delves into this decades-old mystery in great detail, even solving the crime at last.) Outside are Tyrone Power, Jr.; Douglas Fairbanks, Sr.; *Sheik* co-star Agnes Ayers; Cecil B. DeMille (facing Paramount, his old studio); Alfalfa from *The Little Rascals* (contrary to what you might think, the dog on his grave is not Petey); Hearst mistress Marion Davies; Charlie Chaplin's mother, Hannah, and son, Charlie, Jr.; John Huston; and a headstone for Jayne Mansfield (she's really buried in Pennsylvania with her family). In other mausoleums are the Talmadge sisters and "Bugsy" Siegel.

Catholic **Holy Cross Cemetery,** 6001 Centinela Ave., Baldwin Hills, hands out maps to the stars' graves. Religion makes for strange gravefellows: In one area, within feet of each other, lie Bing Crosby, Bela Lugosi (buried in his Dracula cape), and Sharon Tate; not far away are Rita Hayworth and Jimmy Durante. Also here are Tin Man Jack Haley and Scarecrow Ray Bolger, Mary Astor, John Ford, Spike Jones, gossip queen Louella Parsons, Mack Sennett, Elizabeth Taylor's first husband Conrad "Nicky" Hilton, and Rosalind Russell, as well as Gloria Morgan Vanderbilt.

The front office at **Hillside Memorial Park,** 6001 Centinela Ave., Baldwin Hills, can provide a guide to this Jewish cemetery, which has an L.A. landmark: the behemoth tomb of Al Jolson, another humble star. His rotunda, complete with bronze reproduction of Jolson in his Mammy pose and cascading fountain, is visible from I-405. Also on hand are Georgie Jessel, Jack Benny, Eddie Cantor, Vic Morrow, comic Dick Shawn, and *Fugitive* David Janssen.

You just know developers get stomach aches looking at **Westwood Memorial Park,** 1218 Glendon Ave., Westwood (☎ **310/474-1579;** the staff can direct you around), smack-dab in the middle of some of L.A.'s priciest real estate. But it's not going anywhere. Especially when you consider its most famous resident: Marilyn

Monroe. It's also got Truman Capote, John Cassavetes, Armand Hammer, Donna Reed, Edith Massey (John Waters's Egg Lady), Natalie Wood, *Playboy* playmate Dorothy Stratten (who was murdered by her husband; remember *Star 80*?), Darryl Zanuck, and Will and Ariel Durant, the husband and wife historian/writer team (most notably, the 11-volume *Story of Civilization*), who died within days of each other after a nearly 70-year romance.

Forest Lawn Glendale, 1712 S. Glendale Ave. (☎ 213/254-3131), likes to pretend it has no celebrities. The most prominent of L.A. cemeteries, it's also the most humorless, which is pretty silly when you realize they've done their darndest to turn their graveyard into an amusement park. What else would you call their regular "dramatic" (read: cheesy) unveilings (complete with music and narration) of such works of "art" as a reproduction of da Vinci's *Last Supper* in stained glass? The place is full of Bad Art, all part of the continuing vision of founder Hubert Eaton, bane of cemetery buffs everywhere. Eaton thought cemeteries—excuse me, *memorial parks*—should be happy places, uninterrupted by nasty thoughts of, ick, death. So he banished all those gloomy upright tombstones and monuments in favor of flat, pleasant, character-free, flush-to-the-ground slabs. Voilà! A rolling, parklike vista, easy on the eyes and easy to mow.

Contrary to what you've heard, Walt Disney was *not* frozen and placed under Cinderella's castle at Disneyland. He was cremated, and resides in a little garden to the left of the Freedom Mausoleum. Turn around and just behind you are Errol Flynn (in the Garden of Everlasting Peace) and Spencer Tracy (to right of the George Washington statue). In the Freedom Mausoleum are Alan Ladd, Clara Bow, Nat King Cole, Chico Marx, Gummo Marx, Larry Fine (of *The Three Stooges*), and Gracie Allen—finally joined by George Burns. In a columbarium near the Mystery of Life is Humphrey Bogart. Keep moving to your left and you should find Mary Pickford. Unfortunately, some of the best celebs—such as Clark Gable and Carole Lombard, W.C. Fields, and Jean Harlow—are in the Great Mausoleum, which you often can't get into unless you're visiting a relative.

You'd think a place that encourages people just to visit for fun would understand what the real attraction is. But no—Forest Lawn Glendale won't tell you where any of their illustrious guests are, so don't even bother asking. And this place is immense—and, frankly, dull in comparison to the previous cemeteries, unless you appreciate the kitsch value of the Forest Lawn approach to art.

Forest Lawn Hollywood Hills, 6300 Forest Lawn Dr. (☎ 800/204-3131), is slightly less anal than the Glendale branch, but the same basic attitude prevails. On the right lawn, beside the wall near the statue of George Washington, is Buster Keaton. Marty Feldman is in front of the next garden, over on the left. From Buster's grave, go up several flights of stairs to the last wall on the right—there's Stan Laurel. In the Courts of Remembrance are Lucille Ball, Charles Laughton, Freddie Prinze, George Raft, Forrest Tucker, and the not-quite-gaudy-enough tomb of Liberace. Outside, in a vault on the Ascension Road side, is Andy Gibb. Bette Davis's sarcophagus is in front of the wall, to the left of the entrance to the Courts. Also on the grounds are Ozzie Nelson, Ricky Nelson, Sammy Davis, Jr., Ernie Kovacs, Jack Webb, and John Travolta's mother, Helen.

—Mary Susan Herczog

God bless Frederick Mellinger, inventor of the push-up bra (originally known as the "Rising Star"). Frederick's of Hollywood opened this world-famous purple-and-pink art deco panty shop in 1947, and dutifully installed a small exhibition saluting all the stars of stage, screen, and television who glamorized lingerie. The collection now includes Madonna's pointy-breasted corset, a pair of Tony Curtis's skivvies, and a Cher-autographed underwire bra (size 32B). Some exhibits were lost during the 1992 L.A. riots, when looters ransacked the exhibit. Mercifully, the bra worn by Milton Berle on his 1950s TV show was saved.

○ **Autry Museum of Western Heritage.** 4700 Western Heritage Way, in Griffith Park. ☎ **213/667-2000.** Admission $7 adults, $5 seniors 60 and over and students 13–18, $3 children 2–12, free for kids under 2. Tues–Sun 10am–5pm.

If you're under the age of 45 you might not be familiar with Gene Autry, a Texas-born actor who starred in 82 westerns and became known as the "Singing Cowboy." Opened in 1988, Autry's museum is one of L.A.'s best. The enormous collection of art and artifacts of the European conquest of the West is remarkably comprehensive and intelligently displayed. Evocative exhibits illustrate the everyday lives of early pioneers, not only with antique firearms, tools, saddles, and the like, but with many hands-on exhibits that successfully stir the imagination and the heart. There's footage from Buffalo Bill's Wild West Show, movie clips from the silent days, contemporary films, the works of Wild West artists, and plenty of memorabilia from Autry's own film and television projects. The "Hall of Merchandising" displays Roy Rogers bedspreads, Hopalong Cassidy radios, and other items from the collective consciousness—and material collections—of baby boomers. You can have a look on the Internet at **http://www.questorsys.com/autry-museum.**

DOWNTOWN

California Museum of Science and Industry. 700 State Dr., Exposition Park. ☎ **213/744-7400,** or 213/744-2014 for the IMAX theater. Admission: Museum, free; IMAX theater, $6 adults, $4.75 youths 18–21, $4 seniors and children. Multishow discounts available. Daily 10am–5pm.

Celebrating Los Angeles's long-standing romance with the aerospace industry, this museum is best known for its collection of airplanes and other flying objects, including a Boeing DC3 and a DC8, and several rockets and satellites. Other industrial science exhibits include a working winery and a behind-the-scenes look at a functioning McDonald's restaurant. Exhibits on robotics and fiber optics thrill kids, as does the hatchery, where almost 200 chicks are born daily. Temporary exhibits are well planned and thoughtfully executed. The museum's IMAX theater shows up to three different films daily, from about 10am to 9pm. Most of the films are truly awesome exposés of events on earth and in space.

Japanese American National Museum. 369 E. 1st St. (at Central Ave.). ☎ **213/625-0414.** Admission $4 adults, $3 seniors and children 6–17, $2 students. Tues–Thurs and Sat–Sun 10am–5pm, Fri 11am–8pm.

Located in a beautifully restored historic building in Little Tokyo, the Japanese American National Museum is a private nonprofit institute created to document and celebrate the history of the Japanese in America. The museum's fantastic permanent exhibition chronicles Japanese life in America, while temporary exhibits highlight distinctive aspects of Japanese-American culture.

Los Angeles Children's Museum. 310 N. Main St. (at Los Angeles St.). ☎ **213/687-8800.** Admission $5; free for kids under 2. Summer, Tues–Fri 11:30am–5pm, Sat–Sun 10am–5pm; the rest of the year, Sat–Sun 10am–5pm.

This thoroughly enchanting museum is a place where children learn by doing. Everyday experiences are demystified by interesting interactive exhibits displayed in a playlike atmosphere. In the Art Studio, kids are encouraged to make finger puppets from a variety of media, and shiny rockets out of Mylar. Turn the corner and you're in the unrealistically clean and safe City Street, where kids can sit on a policeman's motorcycle or pretend to drive a bus or a firetruck. Kids (and adults) can see their shadows freeze in the Shadow Box, and play with giant foam-filled, Velcro-edged building blocks in Sticky City. Because this is Hollywood, the museum wouldn't be complete without its own recording and TV studios, where kids can become "stars."

Museum of Contemporary Art. 250 S. Grand Ave. and 152 N. Central Ave. ☎ **213/ 621-2766.** Admission $6 adults, $4 seniors and students, free for children 11 and under. Tues– Wed and Fri–Sun 11am–5pm, Thurs 11am–8pm.

This is Los Angeles's only institution exclusively devoted to art from 1940 to the present. Displaying works in a variety of media, it's particularly strong in works by Cy Twombly, Jasper Johns, and Mark Rothko, and shows are often superb. For many experts, MOCA's collections are too spotty to be considered world-class, and the conservative museum board blushes when offered controversial shows (they passed on a Whitney exhibit that included photographs by Robert Mapplethorpe). Nevertheless, we've seen some excellent exhibitions here.

MOCA is one museum housed in two buildings that are close to one another but not within walking distance. The Grand Avenue main building is a contemporary red sandstone structure by renowned Japanese architect Arata Isozaki. The museum restaurant, Patinette (☎ 213/626-1178), located here, is the casual dining creation of celebrity chef Joachim Splichal (see Patina in "Dining," earlier in this chapter). The museum's second space, on Central Avenue in Little Tokyo, was the "temporary" Contemporary while the Grand structure was being built, and now houses a superior permanent collection in a fittingly neutral warehouse-type space. An added feature here is a detailed timeline corresponding to the progression of works. Unless there's a visiting exhibit of great interest at the main museum, we recommend that you start at the Temporary—it's also easier to park down here!

Natural History Museum of Los Angeles County. 900 Exposition Blvd., Exposition Park. ☎ **213/744-3466.** Admission $6 adults; $3.50 children 12–17, seniors, and students with ID; $2 children 5–12; free for kids 4 and under; free for everyone the first Tues of every month. Tues– Sun 10am–5pm. Free docent-led tours offered daily at 1pm. Closed New Year's Day, Thanksgiving, and Christmas.

The "Fighting Dinosaurs"—they're not a high-school football team but the trademark symbol of this massive museum, *Tyrannasaurus rex* and triceratops skeletons poised in a stance so realistic that every kid feels inspired to imitate their *Jurassic Park* bellows. Opened in 1913 in a beautiful columned and domed Spanish Renaissance building, the museum is a 35-hall warehouse of the Earth's history, chronicling the planet and its inhabitants from 600 million years ago to the present day. There's a mind-numbing number of exhibits of prehistoric fossils, bird and marine life, rocks and minerals, and North American mammals. The best permanent displays include the world's rarest shark, a walk-through vault of priceless gems, and an Insect Zoo. The museum has an Internet Website at **http://www.lam.mus.ca.us/facmnh.**

PIERS

Slightly raffish and somewhat shabby, **Santa Monica Pier,** on Ocean Avenue at the end of Colorado Boulevard, is everything an old wharf is supposed to be. Built in 1909 as a passenger and cargo ship pier, the wooden wharf is now home to seafood

Downtown Area Attractions

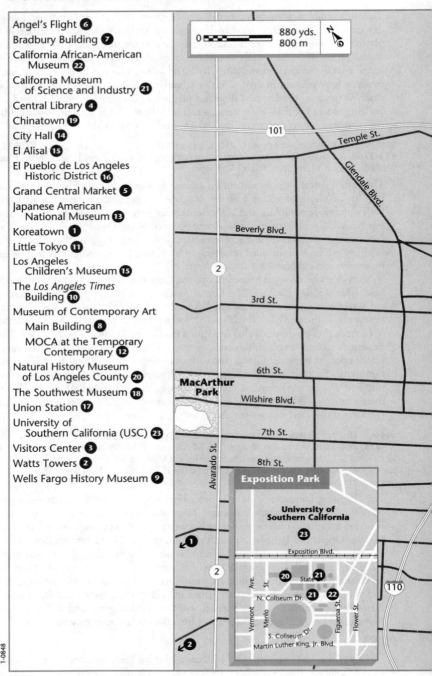

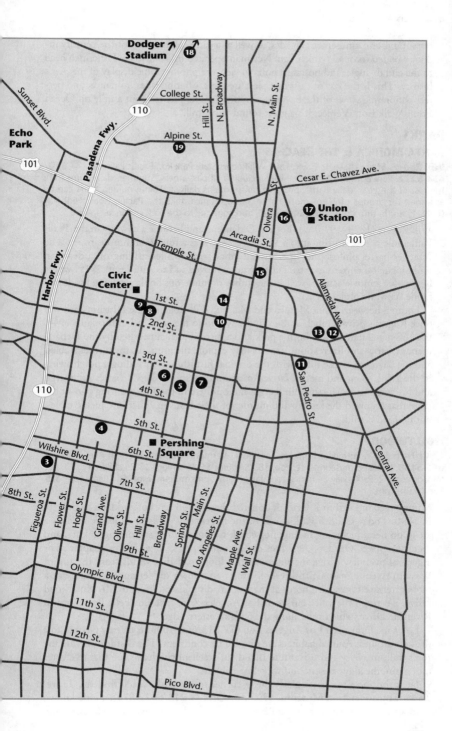

Dodger
Stadium

18

College St.

110

Echo
Park

101

Alpine St.

19

Cesar E. Chavez Ave.

17 Union
Station

16

101

Temple St.

Arcadia St.

Civic
Center

15

1st St.

14

9 8

2nd St.

10

3rd St.

13 12

6

4th St.

5 7

11

110

5th St.

4

Wilshire Blvd.

6th St.

Pershing
Square

3

7th St.

8th St.

Sunset Blvd.

Pasadena Fwy.

Harbor Fwy.

Hill St.

N. Broadway

N. Main St.

Olvera St.

Alameda Ave.

San Pedro St.

Central Ave.

Figueroa St.

Flower St.

Hope St.

Grand Ave.

Olive St.

Hill St.

Broadway

Spring St.

Main St.

Los Angeles St.

Maple Ave.

Wall St.

9th St.

Olympic Blvd.

11th St.

12th St.

Pico Blvd.

restaurants and amusement arcades, as well as a gaily colored turn-of-the-century indoor wooden carousel (which Paul Newman operated in *The Sting*). Fishermen head
to the end to angle, and nostalgia buffs to view the photographic display of the pier's
history. This is the last of the great pleasure piers, offering rides, romance, and perfect panoramic views of the bay and mountains. The pier is about a mile up Ocean
Front Walk from Venice; it's a great round-trip stroll.

PARKS
SANTA MONICA & THE BEACHES
Will Rogers State Historic Park. 1501 Will Rogers State Park Rd., Pacific Palisades. ☎ **310/
454-8212.** Park entrance $5 per vehicle, including all passengers. Summer, daily 8am–7pm;
the rest of the year, daily 8am–5pm. The house opens daily at 10am; guided tours can be
arranged for groups of 10 or more. From Santa Monica, take the Pacific Coast Highway
(Calif. 1) north, turn right onto Sunset Blvd., and continue to the park entrance.

Will Rogers (1879–1935) was born in Oklahoma and became a cowboy in the Texas
Panhandle before drifting into a Wild West show as a folksy, humorous roper. The
"cracker-barrel philosopher" performed lariat tricks while carrying on a deadpan
monologue on current events. The showman moved to Los Angeles in 1919, where
he become a movie actor as well as the author of numerous books detailing his down-
home "cowboy philosophy."

Located between Santa Monica and Malibu, Will Rogers State Historic Park was
once Rogers's private ranch and grounds. Willed to the state of California in 1944,
the 168-acre estate is now both a park and a historic site, supervised by the Department of Parks and Recreation. Visitors may explore the grounds, the former stables,
and the 31-room house filled with the original furnishings, including a porch swing
in the living room and many Native American rugs and baskets. Charles Lindbergh
and his wife, Anne Morrow Lindbergh, hid out here in the 1930s during part of the
craze that followed the kidnap and murder of their first son. There are picnic tables,
but no food is sold.

HOLLYWOOD
✪ **Griffith Park.** Entrances from Los Feliz Blvd., Vermont Ave., and Western Ave. ☎ **213/
665-5188.** Park and museum, free; zoo, $8.25 adults, $5.25 seniors, $3.25 children 2–12, free
for kids under 2. Park, daily 24 hours; zoo, daily 10am–5pm; museum Mon–Fri 10am–4pm, Sat–
Sun 10am–5pm.

Mining tycoon Griffith J. Griffith donated these 4,000 acres of parkland to the city
in 1896. Today Griffith Park is one of the largest city parks in America. There's a
lot to do here, including hiking, horseback riding, golfing, swimming, biking, and
picnicking (see "Outdoor Activities & Spectator Sports," later in this chapter). For
a general overview, drive the mountainous loop road that winds from the top of
Western Avenue, past Griffith Observatory, and down to Vermont Avenue. For a
more extensive foray, turn north at the loop road's midsection, onto Mt. Hollywood
Drive. To reach the golf courses or Los Angeles Zoo, take Los Feliz Boulevard to
Riverside Drive, which runs along the park's western edge.

L.A.'s medium-sized **Los Angeles Zoo** (☎ 213/666-4090) is an easy place to tote
the kids around. Animal habitats are divided by continent. The best features are the
zoo's walk-in aviary and Adventure Island, an excellent children's zoo that re-creates
mountain, meadow, desert, and shoreline habitats.

Near the zoo, in a particularly dusty corner of the park, you'll find the **Travel
Town Transportation Museum,** 5200 Zoo Dr. (☎ 213/662-5874), a little-known
outdoor museum with a small collection of vintage locomotives and old airplanes.
Kids love it.

TOURIST TRAPS

You've heard of all of the following attractions, of course, but you should know exactly what you're in for before you part with your dollars.

Hollywood Guinness World of Records. 6746 Hollywood Blvd., Hollywood. ☎ **213/ 463-6433.** Admission $7.95 adults, $6.50 seniors, $4.95 children 6–11. Sun–Thurs 10am– midnight, Fri–Sat 10am–2am.

Scale models, photographs, and push-button displays of the world's fattest man, biggest plant, smallest woman, fastest animal, and other superlatives don't make for a superlative experience.

The Hollywood Wax Museum. 6767 Hollywood Blvd., Hollywood. ☎ **213/462-8860.** Admission $9 adults, $7.50 seniors, $7 children 6–12, free for kids 5 and under. Sun–Thurs 10am–midnight, Fri–Sat 10am–2am.

Cast in the Madame Tussaud mold, the Hollywood Wax Museum features dozens of lifelike figures of famous movie stars and events. The "museum" is not great, but it can be good for a cheeky laugh or two. A "Chamber of Horrors" exhibit includes the coffin used in *The Raven*, as well as a diorama from the Vincent Price classic *The House of Wax*. The "Movie Awards Theatre" exhibit is a short film highlighting Academy Award presentations from the last four decades.

Ripley's "Believe It Or Not!" Hollywood. 6780 Hollywood Blvd. ☎ **213/466-6335.** Admission $8.95 adults, $7.95 seniors, $5.95 children 5–11.

Believe it or not, this amazing and silly "museum" is still open. A bizarre collection of wax figures, photos, and models depicts unnatural oddities from Robert Leroy Ripley's infamous arsenal. Our favorites include the skeleton of a two-headed baby, a statue of Marilyn Monroe sculpted with shredded money, and a portrait of John Wayne made from laundry lint.

8 Organized Tours

STUDIO TOURS
HOLLYWOOD

Paramount Pictures. 5555 Melrose Ave. ☎ **213/956-1777.** Tours $15 per person. Mon– Fri 9am–2pm.

Paramount's 2-hour walking tour around its Hollywood headquarters is both a historical ode to filmmaking and a real-life look at a working studio. Tours depart hourly; the itinerary varies, depending on what productions are in progress. Visits might include a walk through the sound stages of TV shows like *Entertainment Tonight, Frasier,* and *Wings.* Cameras, recording equipment, and children under 10 are not allowed.

THE SAN FERNANDO VALLEY

NBC Studios. 3000 W. Alameda Ave., Burbank. ☎ **818/840-3537.** Tours $6 adults, $5.50 seniors, $3.75 children 6–12. Mon–Fri 9am–3pm.

According to a security guard, John Wayne and Redd Foxx once got into a fight here after Wayne refused to ride in the same limousine as Foxx, who called the movie star a "redneck." Well, your NBC tour will probably be a bit more docile than that. The guided 1-hour tour includes a behind-the-scenes look at *The Tonight Show with Jay Leno* set, wardrobe, makeup, and set-building departments, and several sound studios. The tour includes some cool video demonstrations of high-tech special effects.

✪ Warner Brothers Studios. Olive Ave. (at Hollywood Way), Burbank. ☎ **818/972-TOUR.** Admission $29 per person. Mon–Fri 9am–4pm, Sat (summer only) 10am–2pm.

Warner Brothers offers the most comprehensive—and the least theme park–like—of the studio tours. The tour takes visitors on a 2-hour informational drive-and-walk jaunt around the studio's faux streets. After a brief introductory film, you'll pile into glorified golf carts and cruise past parking spaces marked *Clint Eastwood, Michael Douglas,* and *Sharon Stone,* then walk through active film and television sets. Whether it's an orchestra scoring a film or a TV program being taped or edited, you'll get a glimpse of how it's done. Stops may include the wardrobe department or the mills where sets are made. Whenever possible, guests visit working sets to watch actors filming actual productions. Reservations are required; children under 10 are not admitted.

SIGHTSEEING TOURS

Oskar J's Tours (☎ 818/501-2217) operates regularly scheduled panoramic motorcoach tours of the city. Buses (or plush minivans) pick up passengers from major hotels for morning or afternoon tours of Sunset Strip, the movie studios, Farmer's Market, Hollywood, homes of the stars, and other attractions. Tours vary in length from 2 to 5 hours and cost $25 to $50. Call for details and to make reservations.

Next Stage Tour Company offers a unique **Insomniacs' Tour of L.A.** (☎ 213/939-2688), a 3am tour of the predawn city that usually includes trips to the *Los Angeles Times;* the flower, produce, and fish markets; and the top of a skyscraper to watch the sun rise over the city. The fact-filled tour lasts about 6½ hours and includes breakfast. Tours depart twice monthly and cost $47 per person. Phone for information and reservations.

Grave Line Tours (☎ 213/469-4149) is a terrific journey through Hollywood's darker side. You're picked up in a renovated hearse and taken to the murder sites and final residences of the stars. You'll see the Hollywood Boulevard hotel where female impersonator–actor Divine died, the liquor store where John Belushi threw a temper tantrum shortly before his overdose, and the telephone pole that Montgomery Clift crashed his car into. Tours are $40 per person and last about 2½ hours. They depart at 9:30am daily from the corner of Orchid Street and Hollywood Boulevard, by Mann's Chinese Theatre. Reservations are required.

The **✪ L.A. Conservancy** (☎ 213/623-2489) conducts a dozen fascinating, information-packed walking tours of historic downtown L.A., seed of today's sprawling metropolis. The most popular is "Broadway Theaters," a loving look at movie palaces. Other intriguing ones include "Marble Masterpieces," "Art Deco," "Mecca for Merchants," "Terra-Cotta," and tours of the landmark Biltmore Hotel and City Hall. They're usually held on Saturday mornings, and cost $5. Call Monday to Friday between 9am and 5pm for exact schedule and information.

Heli USA Helicopter Adventures, 6033 W. Century Blvd. Suite 950, Los Angeles (☎ 800/443-5487), cruises the Paramount, Universal, Burbank, and Disney studios; hovers over the mega-estates of the stars in Beverly Hills and Bel Air; then winds up over Hollywood's Mann's Chinese Theatre, Sunset Strip, and the Hollywood sign. The cost of this helicopter "flightseeing" tour, including lunch or dinner, ranges from $99 to $149, depending on the itinerary.

9 Beaches

Los Angeles County's 72-mile coastline sports over 30 miles of beaches, most of which are operated by the **Department of Beaches & Harbors,** 13837 Fiji Way,

Marina del Rey (☎ **310/305-9503**). County-run beaches usually charge for parking ($4 to $8). Alcohol, bonfires, and pets are prohibited, so you'll have to leave Fido at home. For recorded surf conditions (and coastal weather forecast) call 310/457-9701. The following are the county's best beaches, listed from north to south:

EL PESCADOR, LA PIEDRA & EL MATADOR BEACHES   These relatively rugged and isolated beaches front a 2-mile stretch of the Pacific Coast Highway (Calif. 1) between Broad Beach and Decker Canyon roads, about 10 minutes' driving from the Malibu Pier. Picturesque coves with unusual rock formations, they're perfect for sunbathing and picnicking, but swim with caution as there are no lifeguards or other facilities. These beaches can be difficult to find, marked only by small signs on the highway. Visitors are limited by the small number of parking spots atop the bluffs. Descend to the beach via stairs that cling to the cliffs.

✪ ZUMA BEACH COUNTY PARK   Jam-packed on warm weekends, L.A. County's largest beach park is located off the Pacific Coast Highway (Calif. 1) a mile past Kanan Dume Road. While it can't claim to be the most lovely beach in the Southland, Zuma has the most comprehensive facilities: plenty of rest rooms, lifeguards, playgrounds, volleyball courts, and snack bars. The southern stretch, toward Point Dume, is Westward Beach, separated from the noisy highway by sandstone cliffs. A trail leads over the point's headlands to Pirate's Cove, once a popular nude beach.

PARADISE COVE   This private beach in the 28000 block of the Pacific Coast Highway (Calif. 1) charges $15 to park and $5 per person if you walk in. Changing rooms and showers are included in the price. The beach is often full by noon on weekends.

✪ MALIBU LAGOON STATE BEACH   Not just a pretty white-sand beach, but an estuary and wetlands area as well, Malibu Lagoon is the historic home of the Chumash Indians. The entrance is on the Pacific Coast Highway (Calif. 1) south of Cross Creek Road, and there's a small admission charge. Marine life and shorebirds teem where the creek empties into the sea, and the waves are always mild. The historic Adamson House is here, a showplace of Malibu tile now operating as a museum.

✪ SURFRIDER BEACH   Without a doubt, L.A.'s best waves roll ashore here. One of the city's most popular surfing spots, this beach is located between the Malibu Pier and the lagoon. In surf lingo, few "locals only" wave wars are ever fought here—surfing is not as territorial here as it can be in other areas, where out-of-towners can be made to feel unwelcome. Surrounded by all of Malibu's hustle and bustle, don't come to Surfrider for peace and quiet.

TOPANGA STATE BEACH   Noise from the highway prevents solitude at this short, narrow strip of sand located where Topanga Canyon Boulevard emerges from the mountains. Why go? Ask the surfers who wait in line to catch Topanga's excellent breaks. There are rest rooms and lifeguard services, but little else.

WILL ROGERS STATE BEACH   Three miles along the Pacific Coast Highway (Calif. 1) between Sunset Boulevard and the Santa Monica border are named for the American humorist whose ranch-turned-state historic park (see "Parks" in "Exploring the City," earlier in this chapter) is nestled above the palisades that provide the striking backdrop for this popular beach. A pay parking lot extends the entire length of Will Rogers, and facilities include rest rooms, lifeguards, and a snack hut in season. While the surfing is only so-so, the waves are friendly for swimmers of all ages.

Beaches & Coastal Attractions

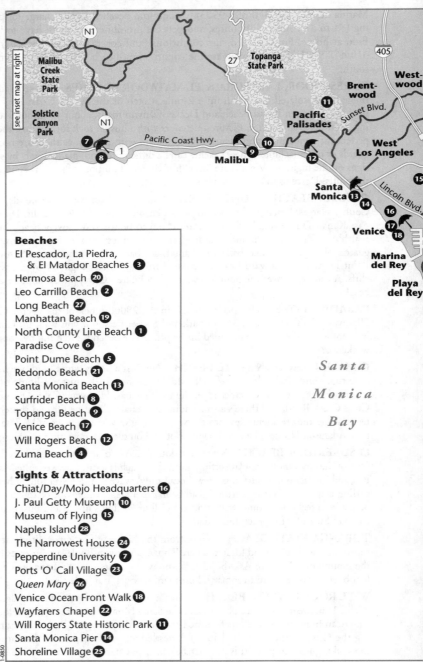

Beaches

El Pescador, La Piedra,
   & El Matador Beaches **3**
Hermosa Beach **20**
Leo Carrillo Beach **2**
Long Beach **27**
Manhattan Beach **19**
North County Line Beach **1**
Paradise Cove **6**
Point Dume Beach **5**
Redondo Beach **21**
Santa Monica Beach **13**
Surfrider Beach **8**
Topanga Beach **9**
Venice Beach **17**
Will Rogers Beach **12**
Zuma Beach **4**

Sights & Attractions

Chiat/Day/Mojo Headquarters **16**
J. Paul Getty Museum **10**
Museum of Flying **15**
Naples Island **28**
The Narrowest House **24**
Pepperdine University **7**
Ports 'O' Call Village **23**
Queen Mary **26**
Venice Ocean Front Walk **18**
Wayfarers Chapel **22**
Will Rogers State Historic Park **11**
Santa Monica Pier **14**
Shoreline Village **25**

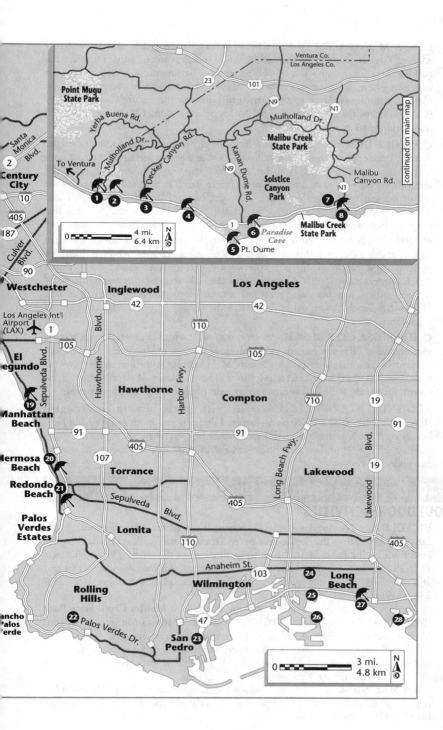

continued on main map

Ventura Co.
Los Angeles Co.

**Point Mugu
State Park**

Yerba Buena Rd.

Mulholland Dr.

To Ventura

Mulholland Dr.

Decker Canyon Rd.

N9

N1

**Malibu Creek
State Park**

Malibu
Canyon Rd.

**Solstice
Canyon
Park**

N9

Kanan Dume Rd.

N1

**Malibu Creek
State Park**

① ②
③
④
⑤ Pt. Dume
⑥ *Paradise Cove*
⑦ ⑧

0   4 mi.
6.4 km

N

23

101

Santa
Monica Blvd.

②

**Century
City**

10

405

187

Culver
Blvd.

90

Westchester   **Inglewood**   **Los Angeles**

42   42

Los Angeles Int'l
Airport
(LAX) ①

105

**El
Segundo**

Sepulveda Blvd.

⑲
**Manhattan
Beach**

91

**Hermosa
Beach** ⑳

**Redondo
Beach** ㉑

**Palos
Verdes
Estates**

107

405

Torrance

Hawthorne Blvd.

Hawthorne Fwy.

Harbor Fwy.

110

105

Compton

710

19

91   91

Lakewood

19

Lakewood Blvd.

405

Sepulveda
Blvd.

Lomita

405

110

Long Beach Fwy.

Anaheim St.

103

Wilmington

⑳④
**Long
Beach**

㉕

㉗

**Rolling
Hills**

㉒ Palos Verdes Dr.

47

㉖

㉘

**San
Pedro** ㉓

Rancho
Palos
Verde

0   3 mi.
4.8 km

N

SANTA MONICA STATE BEACH   The beaches on either side of the Santa Monica Pier are popular for their white sands and easy accessibility. There are big parking lots, eateries, and lots of well-maintained bathrooms. A paved beach path runs along here, allowing you to walk, bike, or skate to Venice and points south. Colorado Boulevard leads to the pier; turn north on the Pacific Coast Highway (Calif. 1) below the coastline's striking bluffs, or south along Ocean Avenue; you'll find parking lots in both directions.

✪ **VENICE BEACH**   Moving south from the city of Santa Monica, the paved pedestrian Promenade becomes Ocean Front Walk, and gets progressively wierder until it reaches an apex at Washington Boulevard and the Venice fishing pier. Although there are people who swim and sunbathe, Venice Beach's character is defined by the sea of humanity that gathers here, plus the bevy of boardwalk vendors and old-fashioned "walk-streets" a block away (see "The Top Attractions," earlier in this chapter). Park on the sidestreets or in the plentiful lots west of Pacific Avenue.

MANHATTAN STATE BEACH   The Beach Boys used to hang out (and surf, of course) at this wide, friendly beach backed by beautiful ocean-view homes. Plenty of parking on 36 blocks of sidestreets (between Rosecrans Avenue and the Hermosa Beach border) draw weekend crowds from the L.A. area. Manhattan has some of the best surfing around, along with rest rooms, lifeguards, and volleyball courts. Manhattan Beach Boulevard leads west to the fishing pier and adjacent seafood restaurants.

✪ **HERMOSA CITY BEACH**   A very, very wide white-sand beach with tons to recommend it, Hermosa extends to either side of the pier and includes "The Strand," a pedestrian lane that runs its entire length. Main access is at the foot of Pier Avenue, which itself is lined with interesting shops. There's plenty of street parking, rest rooms, lifeguards, volleyball courts, fishing pier, playgrounds, and good surfing.

REDONDO STATE BEACH   Popular with surfers, bicyclists, and joggers, Redondo's white sand and ice plant–carpeted dunes is just south of tiny King Harbor, along "The Esplanade" (South Esplanade Drive). Get there via the Pacific Coast Highway (Calif. 1) or Torrance Boulevard Facilities include rest rooms, lifeguards, and volleyball courts.

10 Outdoor Activities & Spectator Sports

OUTDOOR ACTIVITIES

BICYCLING   Los Angeles is great for biking. If you're into distance peddling, you can do no better than the flat 22-mile paved **Ocean Front Walk** that runs along the sand from Pacific Palisades in the north to Torrance in the south. The path attracts all levels of riders, so it gets pretty busy on weekends. For information on this and other city bike routes, phone the Metropolitan Transportation Authority (☎ 213/244-6539).

The best place to mountain bike is along the trails of **Malibu Creek State Park** (☎ 800/533-7275 or 818/880-0350), in the Santa Monica Mountains between Malibu and the San Fernando Valley. Fifteen miles of trails rise to a maximum of 3,000 feet and are appropriate for intermediate to advanced bikers. Pick up a trail map at the park entrance, 4 miles south of U.S. 101 off Las Virgenes Road, just north of Mulholland Highway. Park admission is $5 per car.

Sea Mist Rental, 1619 Ocean Front Walk, Santa Monica (☎ 310/395-7076), rents 10-speed cruisers for $5 per hour and $14 a day; 15-speed mountain bikes rent for $6 per hour and $20 a day.

FISHING   **Marina del Rey Sports Fishing,** 13759 Fiji Way (☎ **310/822-3625**), known locally as "Captain Frenchy's," has four deep-sea boats departing daily on half- and full-day ocean fishing trips. Of course, it depends on what's running when you're out, but bass, barracuda, halibut, and yellowtail tuna are the most common catches on these party boats. Excursions cost $20 to $25, including bait and tackle. Phone for reservations.

No permit is required to cast from shore or to drop a line from a pier. Local anglers will hate us for giving away their secret spot, but the best saltwater fishing spot in all of L.A. is at the foot of Torrance Boulevard in Redondo Beach. Centuries of tides and currents have created a deep underwater canyon here that's known among local fisherman as a glory hole.

GOLF   The greater Los Angeles area has more than 100 golf courses, which vary in quality from abysmal to superb. **American Golf Corp.,** 1633 26th St., Santa Monica (☎ **800/468-7952** or 310/829-4653; fax 310/829-4990), guarantees reserved tee times at more than 16 top area courses. The company can also arrange lessons and provide information on local tournaments.

It's best to book tee times at the following courses in advance.

Of the city's seven 18-hole and five 9-hole courses, you can't get more central than the **Rancho Park Golf Course,** 10460 W. Pico Blvd. (☎ **310/838-7373**), located smack-dab in the middle of L.A.'s Westside. The par-71 course has lots of tall trees, but not enough to blot out the towering Century City buildings next door. Greens fees are $17 Monday to Friday, and $22 on weekends. Rancho also has a 9-hole, par-3 course; fees are $5 weekdays, $6 on weekends (☎ **310/838-7561**).

The **Industry Hills Golf Club,** 1 Industry Hills Pkwy., City of Industry (☎ **818/810-4455**), has two 18-hole courses designed by William Bell. Together they encompass eight lakes, 160 bunkers, and long fairways. The Eisenhower Course, which consistently ranks among *Golf Digest*'s top 25 public courses, has extra-large, undulating greens and the challenge of thick kikuyu rough. An adjacent driving range is lit for night use. Greens fees are $45 weekdays and $60 on weekends, including cart.

HIKING   The Santa Monica Mountains, a small range that runs only 50 miles from Griffith Park to Point Mugu, on the coast north of Malibu, makes Los Angeles a great place for hiking. The mountains peak at 3,111 feet and are part of the **Santa Monica Mountains National Recreation Area,** a contiguous conglomeration of 350 public parks and 65,000 acres. Many animals make their homes in this area, including deer, coyote, rabbit, skunk, rattlesnake, fox, hawk, and quail. The hills are also home to almost 1,000 drought-resistant plant species, including live oak and coastal sage.

Hiking is best after spring rains, when the hills are green, flowers are in bloom, and the air is clear. Summers can be very hot; hikers should always carry fresh water. Beware of poison oak, a hearty shrub that's common on the West Coast. Usually found among oak trees, poison oak has leaves in groups of three, with waxed surfaces and prominent veins. If you come into contact with this itch-producing plant, bathe yourself in calamine lotion, or the ocean.

Santa Ynez Canyon, in Pacific Palisades, is a long and difficult climb that rises steadily for about 3 miles. At the top, hikers are rewarded with fantastic views over the Pacific. Also at the top is Trippet Ranch, a public facility providing water, rest rooms, and picnic tables. From Santa Monica, take the Pacific Coast Highway (Calif. 1) north. Turn right onto Sunset Boulevard, then left onto Palisades Drive. Continue for 2¹/₂ miles, turn left onto Verenda de la Montura, and park at the cul-de-sac at the end of the street, where you'll find the trailhead.

Temescal Canyon, in Pacific Palisades, is far easier than the Santa Ynez Trail and, predictably, far more popular with locals. It's one of the quickest routes into the wilderness. Hikes here are anywhere from 1 to 5 miles. From Santa Monica, take the Pacific Coast Highway (Calif. 1) north; turn right onto Temescal Canyon Road and follow it to the end. Sign in with the gatekeeper, who can also answer your questions.

Will Rogers State Historic Park, Pacific Palisades, is also a terrific place for hiking. An intermediate-level hike from the park's entrance ends at Inspiration Point, a plateau from which you can see a good portion of L.A.'s Westside. See "Parks" in "Exploring the City," earlier in this chapter, for complete information.

HORSEBACK RIDING   The **Los Angeles Equestrian Center,** 480 Riverside Dr., Burbank (☎ 818/840-9066), rents horses by the hour for western or English riding through Griffith Park's hills. There's a 200-pound weight limit, and children under 12 are not permitted to ride. Horse rental costs $13 per hour, and there's a 2-hour rental maximum. The stables are open Monday to Friday from 8am to 7pm and on Saturday and Sunday from 8am to 4pm.

Sunrise Downs Equestrian Center, 11900 Big Tujunga Canyon Rd., Tujunga (☎ 818/353-9410), offers 2-, 3-, and 4-hour guided day or evening horseback tours through the San Gabriel Mountains and the scenic San Fernando Valley. They charge $25 per hour per person, and there's a two-person minimum.

JET SKIING   **Nature Tours,** 1759 9th St., Suite 201, Santa Monica (☎ 310/452-7508), offers Personal Watercraft (PWC) rentals and lessons, teaching all levels of riders how to get the most out of jet skis and the more popular, sit-down style WaveRunners. Riders of all levels learn in the harbor's calm water then venture into open Santa Monica Bay. Rates range from $62 to $80 an hour for different size crafts—the larger ones even have a small ice-chest built in under the seat!

SCUBA DIVING   The best scuba diving and snorkeling in Los Angeles is off Catalina Island (see Chapter 16), and off Leo Carillo State Beach, near the Ventura County line. **Dive and Surf,** 504 N. Broadway, Redondo Beach (☎ 310/372-8423), arranges trips for all diving levels.

SKATING   The 22-mile-long **Ocean Front Walk** that runs from Pacific Palisades to Torrance is one of the premier skating spots in the country. Inline skating is especially popular, but conventionals are often seen here, too. Roller skating is allowed just about everywhere bicycling is, but be aware that cyclists have the right-of-way. **Spokes 'n Stuff,** 4175 Admiralty Way, Marina del Rey (☎ 310/306-3332), is just one of many places to rent wheels near the Venice portion of Ocean Front Walk. Skates cost $5 per hour; kneepads and wrist guards come with every rental.

SURFING   Shops near all top surfing beaches in the L.A. area rent boards, including **Zuma Jay Surfboards,** 22775 Pacific Coast Hwy., Malibu (☎ 310/456-8044). You'll find the shop about a quarter mile south of the Malibu Pier. Rentals are $20 per day, plus $8 to $10 for wetsuits in winter.

TENNIS   You'll find mostly hard-surface courts in California. If your hotel doesn't have a court, and can't suggest any courts nearby, try the well-maintained, well-lit **Griffith Park Tennis Courts,** on Commonwealth Road just east of Vermont Avenue. Or call the City of Los Angeles Department of Recreation and Parks (☎ 213/485-5555) to make a reservation at a municipal court near you.

SPECTATOR SPORTS

BASEBALL   Los Angeles has two major-league baseball teams. The **Los Angeles Dodgers** (☎ 213/224-1500) play at Dodger Stadium, 1000 Elysian Park, near

Sunset Boulevard. If you're lucky, you just may get to see Hideo Nomo, the Dodgers' Japanese sensation, pitch before a hometown crowd (Hideo is actually the second Japanese player to play in the Big Leagues, but the first to reach star status). If you go to a game, don't be surprised by the apparent apathy of the crowd; traffic is so bad getting to and from Dodger Stadium that the fans usually arrive late, around the second or third inning, and leave early—the stands empty out during the seventh inning. Dodgers' fans are an odd bunch.

The Disney-owned **California Angels** (☎ 714/634-2000) play at Anaheim Stadium, at 2000 S. State College Blvd. (near Katella Avenue) in Anaheim. More often than not, games are populated by displaced fans there to see the visiting team rather than diehard Angels' supporters. If you go to cheer on your hometown Yankees, Orioles, White Sox, or Twins, you'll probably be right at home in the crowd.

Since 1995's baseball strike, tickets to ball games have been very easy to get, though the best seats still go to season ticket holders.

BASKETBALL   Los Angeles has two National Basketball Association franchises: the **L.A. Lakers** (☎ 310/419-3100), who play at the Great Western Forum, 3900 W. Manchester Blvd. (at Prairie Avenue) in Inglewood; and the **L.A. Clippers** (☎ 213/745-0400), who hold court in the L.A. Sports Arena, 3939 S. Figueroa St., near downtown. Good seats to Lakers games are all but impossible to acquire, though tickets in the nosebleed section are often available. They're practically giving away tickets to Clippers games—except when they're playing the Lakers, of course.

FOOTBALL   Football fans are out of luck in L.A. these days. The two former Los Angeles–area NFL teams both left town in 1995: the Raiders went back to Oakland and the Rams ran for St. Louis.

HORSE RACING   The scenic **Hollywood Park Racetrack,** 1050 S. Prairie Ave., in Inglewood (☎ 310/419-1500), with its lakes and flowers, features thoroughbred racing from early April to July as well as in November and December. The $1-million Hollywood Gold Cup is run here. Well-placed monitors project views of the back stretch as well as stop-action replays of photo finishes. Citation, the track restaurant named after the Triple Crown–winning thoroughbred, features an eclectic menu that includes chicken, beef, pork, and ostrich dishes—but no horse meat, of course. Races are usually held Wednesday to Sunday. Post times are 1pm in summer (at 7pm on Friday) and 12:30pm in the fall. General admission is $6, $25 to the clubhouse.

One of the most beautiful tracks in the country, **Santa Anita Racetrack,** 285 W. Huntington Dr., Arcadia (☎ 818/574-7223), offers thoroughbred racing from October to mid-November and December to late April. The track was featured in the Marx Brothers' film *A Day at the Races* and in the 1954 version of *A Star Is Born.* On weekdays during racing season the public is invited to watch morning workouts from 7:30 to 9:30am. Post time is 12:30 or 1pm. Admission is $4.

ICE HOCKEY   The NHL's **L.A. Kings** (☎ 310/673-6003) play at the Great Western Forum at 3900 W. Manchester Blvd. (at Prairie Avenue) in Inglewood. The Disney-owned **Mighty Ducks** play at Arrowhead Pond, Anaheim (☎ 714/704-2500).

11 Shopping

Whether you take home souvenirs with traditional Southern California images, fine goods available only here, books on topics of local interest, or some quirky thing about which you can always say "I picked that up on my trip to L.A.," we guarantee you'll enjoy the diversity of the city's shopping scene as much as the residents do. Here's a rundown of the primary shopping areas, along with descriptions of a few of the best stores.

The **sales tax** in Los Angeles is 8.25%, but savvy shoppers know to have larger items shipped directly home and save the tax.

SANTA MONICA & THE BEACHES
3RD STREET PROMENADE
(FROM BROADWAY TO THE WILSHIRE BLVD., SANTA MONICA)

Packed with chain stores and boutiques as well as dozens of restaurants and a large movie theater, Santa Monica's pedestrians-only section of 3rd Street is one of the most popular shopping areas in the city. The Promenade bustles on into the evening with a seemingly endless assortment of street performers, and an endless parade of souls. Stores stay open late (often till 1 or 2am on the weekends) for the movie-going crowds. There's plenty of metered parking in structures on the adjacent streets, so bring lots of quarters!

Hennessey & Ingalls. 1254 3rd Street Promenade. ☎ **310/458-9074.**

This bookstore is devoted to art and architecture, from magnificent coffee-table photography books to graphic arts titles and obscure biographies of artists and art movements.

Mayhem. 1411 3rd Street Promenade. ☎ **310/451-7600.**

This shop sells autographed guitars and other music memorabilia from U2, Nirvana, Springsteen, Bon Jovi, Pearl Jam, and other rockers to collectors, including the owners of the Hard Rock cafes.

Midnight Special Bookstore. 1318 3rd Street Promenade. ☎ **310/393-2923.**

This medium-size general bookshop is known for its good small-press selection and regular poetry readings.

Na Na. 1228 3rd Street Promenade. ☎ **310/394-9690.**

This is what punk looks like in the 1990s: clunky shoes, knit hats, narrow-striped shirts, and baggy streetwear.

Puzzle Zoo. 1413 3rd Street Promenade. ☎ **310/393-9201.**

Puzzles have proved so popular here that the Zoo recently expanded to better accommodate a selection chosen "Best in L.A." by *Los Angeles* magazine. You'll find the double-sided World's Most Difficult Puzzle, the Puzzle in a Bottle, and collector's serial-numbered Ravensburger series, among others.

Pyramid Music. 1340 3rd Street Promenade. ☎ **310/393-5877.**

Seemingly endless bins of used compact discs and cassette tapes line the walls of this long, narrow shop on the Promenade. LPs, posters, cards, buttons, and accessories are also available.

MAIN STREET IN SANTA MONICA & VENICE
(BETWEEN PICO BLVD. & ROSE AVE.)

Another good strip for strolling, Main Street boasts a healthy combination of mall standards like The Gap as well as upscale, left-of-center individual boutiques. You'll also find plenty of casually hip cafes and restaurants. The primary strip connecting Santa Monica and Venice, Main Street has a relaxed, beach-community vibe that sets it apart from similar strips. The stores here straddle the fashion fence between upscale trendy and beach-bum edgy.

The Bey's Garden. 2919 Main St. (between Ashland and Pier sts.). ☎ **310/399-5420.**

This fragrant, esoteric shop sells aromatic oils, candles, herbal body treatments, and exotic soaps.

C.P. Shades. 2925 Main St., Santa Monica. ☎ **310/392-0949.**

Fans of C.P. Shades, a San Francisco ladies' clothier whose line is carried by many department stores and boutiques, will love this boutique devoted solely to their loose, casual cotton and linen separates. Their trademark monochromatic neutrals are meticulously arranged in an airy, well-lit store. There's also a C.P. Shades in Old Pasadena.

Horizons West. 2011 Main St.(south of Pico Blvd.), Santa Monica. ☎ **310/392-1122.**

Brand-name surfboards, wet suits, leashes, magazines, waxes, lotions, and everything else you need to catch the perfect wave are found here. Stop in and say "hi" to Randy, and pick up a free tide table.

Just in Case. 2718 Main St., Santa Monica. ☎ **310/399-3096.**

Featuring "cruelty-free" handbags, backpacks, luggage, agendas, wallets, and other items, this shop carries goods made of fabric and innovative materials like recycled rubber instead of animal skins.

Pepper's Eyeware. 2904 Main St. (between Ashland and Pier sts.). ☎ **310/392-0633.**

Lenscrafters they're not, but if you're looking for some truly sophisticated, finely crafted eyeware, this friendly shop is for you. Ask for frames by cutting-edge L.A. designers Bada and Koh Sakai.

Z Gallerie. 2728 Main St. (near Hill St.), Santa Monica. ☎ **310/392-5879.**

This California-based chain offers a good selection of framed and unframed poster art, Crate and Barrel–style furnishings, stylish kitchenware, and unusual gift items.

BERGAMOT STATION (2525 MICHIGAN AVE., SANTA MONICA)

Once a station for the Red Car trolley line, the industrial space of Bergamot Station (☎ **310/829-5854**) is now home to about two dozen art galleries, a café, a bookstore, and offices. Most of the galleries are closed Monday; the train yard is located at the terminus of Michigan Avenue west of Cloverfield Boulevard. Exhibits change often and vary widely, ranging from a Julius Shulman black-and-white photo retrospective of L.A.'s Case Study Houses, to a provocative exhibit of Vietnam War propoganda posters from the U.S. and Vietnam, to whimsical furniture constructed entirely of corrugated cardboard. A sampling of offerings includes:

The **Gallery of Functional Art** (☎ **310/829-6990**) features tables, chairs, beds, sofas, lighting, screens, dressers, bathroom fixtures, and other functional art pieces. Smaller items such as jewelry, watches, flatware, candlesticks, ceramics, and glass are also shown. All work is one of a kind or limited edition.

The **Rosamund Felson Gallery** (☎ **310/828-8488**) is well known for showcasing L.A.–based contemporary artists. This is a good place to get a taste of current trends.

Track 16 Gallery (☎ **310/264-4678**) has exhibitions that range from pop art to avant-garde inventiveness. *Always* see what's going on here.

L.A.'s WESTSIDE & BEVERLY HILLS
WEST 3RD STREET (BETWEEN FAIRFAX AVE. & ROBERTSON BLVD.)

You can shop till you drop on this newly trendy strip, anchored on the east end by the Farmer's Market. Many of Melrose Avenue's shops have relocated here, alongside some terrific up-and-comers, several cafes, and the much-lauded restaurant Locanda Veneta. "Fun" is more the catchword here than "funky," and the shops (including the vintage clothing stores) tend a bit more to the refined than do those along Melrose; you'd never find upscale bookshops dedicated to travel tomes and cookbooks in that neck of the woods—but you will here.

✪ **Chado Tea Room.** 8422 W. 3rd St. ☎ **213/655-4681.**

A temple for tea lovers, Chado is designed with a nod to Paris's reknowned Mariage Frères tea purveyor. One wall is lined with nooks whose recognizable brown tins are filled with over 250 different varieties of tea from around the world. Among the choices are 15 kinds of Darjeeling, Indian teas blended with rose petals, and ceremonial Chinese and Japanese blends. They also serve tea meals here, featuring delightful sandwiches and individual pots of any loose tea in the store.

The Cook's Library. 8373 W. 3rd St. ☎ **213/655-3141.**

There's a specialty bookshop for everyone in L.A.; this is where the city's top chefs find both classic and deliciously offbeat cookbooks and other food-oriented tomes. Browsing is welcomed, even encouraged, with tea, tasty treats, and rocking chairs.

Farmer's Market. 6333 W. 3rd St. (at Fairfax Ave.), Los Angeles. ☎ **213/933-9211.**

The city's most famous food carnival is also one of Hollywood's top attractions. Started during the Depression, the outdoor plaza has grown to include spice and candle shops, a friendly outdoor diner, and dozens of stands selling fresh and prepared foods for consumption on or off the premises. Closed evenings.

GOAT Cadeaux. 306 S. Edinburgh (at 3rd St. east of Crescent Heights). ☎ **213/651-3133.**

Cadeaux means "gifts" in French, and this is the kind of shop where you can always find just the right last-minute present. From unusual candles to antique bookends to carved wooden boxes to art deco picture frames, GOAT carries a intriguing variety.

Polkadots & Moonbeams. 8367 and 8381 W. 3rd St. ☎ **213/651-1746.**

This is actually two stores several doors apart, one carrying (slightly overpriced) hip young fashions for women, and a vintage store with clothing, accessories, and fabrics from the 1920s to the 1960s, all in remarkable condition.

Traveler's Bookcase. 8375 W. 3rd St. ☎ **213/655-0575.**

This store, one of the best travel bookshops in the West, stocks a huge selection of guidebooks and travel literature, as well as maps and travel accessories. A quarterly newsletter chronicles the travel adventures of the genial owners, who know firsthand the most helpful items to carry. Look for regular readings by well-known travel writers.

SUNSET STRIP
(BETWEEN LA CIENEGA BLVD. & DOHENY DR., WEST HOLLYWOOD)

The monster-size billboards advertising the latest rock god make it clear that this is rock 'n' roll territory. The "Strip" is lined with trendy restaurants, industry-oriented hotels, and dozens of shops offering outrageous fashions and chunky stage accessories. One anomaly is Sunset Plaza, an upscale cluster of Georgian-style shops resembling Beverly Hills at its snootiest.

Billy Martin's. 8605 Sunset Blvd., West Hollywood. ☎ **310/289-5000.**

Founded by the legendary Yankee manager in 1978, this chic men's western shop—complete with fireplace and leather sofa—stocks hand-forged silver and gold belt buckles, Lucchese and Liberty boots, and stable staples like flannel shirts.

✪ **Book Soup.** 8800 Sunset Blvd., West Hollywood. ☎ **310/657-1072.**

This has long been one of L.A.'s most celebrated bookshops, selling both mainstream and small-press books and hosting regular book signings and author nights. Book Soup, a great browsing shop, has a large selection of show-biz books and an extensive outdoor news and magazine stand on one side. The owners recently annexed an adjacent cafe space so they can better cater to hungry intellectuals. The resulting Book Soup Bistro has an appealing bar, a charming outdoor patio, and an extensive menu that includes alphabet soup.

North Beach Leather. 8500 Sunset Blvd., West Hollywood. ☎ **310/652-3224.**

This San Francisco–based shop has up-to-the-minute fashions from casual to elegant—particularly leather and suede jackets and dresses—at high Sunset Strip prices.

Sunset Strip Tattoo. 8418 W. Sunset Blvd., West Hollywood. ☎ **213/650-6530.**

Cher, Charlie Sheen, Lenny Kravitz, and members of the rock band Guns 'N' Roses all got inked at this celeb-magnet parlor, which has been a Sunset Strip fixture for 30 years.

Tower Records. 8811 W. Sunset Blvd., Hollywood. ☎ **310/657-7300.**

Tower insists that it has L.A.'s largest selection of compact discs—over 125,000 titles—despite the Virgin Megastore's contrary claim. Even if Virgin has more, Tower's collection tends to be more interesting and browser friendly. And the enormous shop's blues, jazz, and classical selections are definitely greater than the competition's. Open 365 days a year.

Virgin Megastore. 8000 Sunset Blvd., Hollywood. ☎ **213/650-8666.**

Some 100 CD "listening posts" and an in-store "radio station" make this megastore a music lover's paradise. Virgin claims to stock 150,000 titles, including an extensive collection of hard-to-find artists.

LA BREA AVENUE (NORTH OF WILSHIRE BLVD.)

This is L.A.'s artsiest shopping strip. Anchored by the giant American Rag, Cie. alterna-complex, La Brea is home to lots of great urban antiques stores dealing in deco, arts and crafts, 1950s modern, and the like (there's even a great antique-hardware store). You'll also find vintage clothiers, furniture galleries, and other warehouse-size stores, as well as some of the city's hippest restaurants, such as Campanile.

Dishes a la Carte. 5650 W. 3rd St. (at LaBrea Ave.), Los Angeles. ☎ **213/938-6223.**

Modeled after New York's *Fish's Eddie,* this little ceramics shop carries factory seconds and obsolete patterns of well- and little-known brands alike. You'll find Fiesta-ware next to locally hand-painted pieces and durable restaurant dishes.

✪ **Drea Kadilak.** 463 S. LaBrea Ave. (at 6th St.), Los Angeles. ☎ **213/931-2051.**

The art of millinery often seems to have gone the way of white afternoon gloves for ladies, but inventive Drea Kadilak charms you with her tiny hat shop. Designing in straw, cotton duck, wool felt, and a number of more unusual fabrics, she does her own blocking, will cheerfully take measurements for custom ladies' headware, is reasonably priced, and gives away signature hatboxes with your purchase.

Liz's Antique Hardware. 453 S. LaBrea Ave., Los Angeles. ☎ **213/939-4403.**

Stuffed to the rafters with hardware and fixtures of the last 100 years, Liz's thoughtfully keeps a cannister of wet-wipes at the register—believe us, you'll need one after sifting through bags and crates of doorknobs, latches, finials, and any other home hardware you can imagine needing. Perfect sets of Bakelite drawer pulls and antique ceramic bathroom fixtures are some of the more intriguing items. Be prepared to browse for hours, whether you're redecorating or not!

Mortise & Tenon. 444 S. LaBrea Ave., Los Angeles. ☎ **213/937-7654.**

For wood furniture with timeless appeal, Angelenos have been flocking to Mortise & Tenon's large, fun showroom. Farm-style tables, vaguely Gothic armoires, and faux-Craftsman chairs are complemented by simply styled and affordable accessories, including some refreshingly original CD-storage cabinets.

RODEO DRIVE & BEVERLY HILLS' GOLDEN TRIANGLE (SANTA MONICA BLVD., WILSHIRE BLVD. & CRESCENT DR.)

Everyone knows about **Rodeo Drive,** the city's most famous shopping street. Couture shops from high fashion's Old Guard are located along these three hallowed blocks, along with plenty of newer high-end labels. And there are two examples of the Beverly Hills version of mini-malls, albeit more insular and attractive—the **Rodeo Collection,** 421 N. Rodeo Dr., and **Two Rodeo,** at Wilshire Boulevard.

The 16-square-block area surrounding Rodeo Drive is known as the "Golden Triangle." Shops off Rodeo are generally not as name-conscious as those on the strip (you might actually be able to buy something!), but they're nevertheless plenty upscale. **Little Santa Monica Boulevard** has a particularly colorful line of specialty stores, and **Brighton Way** is as young and hip as relatively staid Beverly Hills gets.

The big names to look for here are **Giorgio Beverly Hills,** 327 N. Rodeo Dr. (☎ 800/GIORGIO or 310/274-0200); **Gucci,** 347 N. Rodeo Dr. (☎ 310/ 278-3451); **Hermès,** 343 N. Rodeo Dr. (☎ 310/278-6440); **Louis Vuitton,** 307 N. Rodeo Dr. (☎ 310/859-0457); **Polo/Ralph Lauren,** 444 N. Rodeo Dr. (☎ 310/281-7200); and **Tiffany & Co.,** 210 N. Rodeo Dr. (☎ 310/273-8880).

Barney's New York. 9570 Wilshire Blvd., Beverly Hills. ☎ **310/276-4400.**

The celebrated New York clothier opened this Beverly Hills satellite shop in 1994, and L.A. is already looking better. Saxophonist and former *The Tonight Show with Jay Leno* bandleader Branford Marsalis gets his Gaultiers here. Barney Greengrass, New York's "sturgeon king," has opened a restaurant on the top floor.

Neiman Marcus. 9700 Wilshire Blvd., Beverly Hills. ☎ **310/550-5900.**

Dallas has come to L.A., bringing distinctive men's and women's fashions, world-famous furs, precious jewels, unique gifts, and legendary personal service, which have made this one of the area's most successful department stores (despite its "Needless Mark-up" reputation).

PaceWildenstein. 9540 Wilshire Blvd., Beverly Hills. ☎ **310/205-5522.**

A stark, modern space ideal for showcasing the oversize contemporary pieces that draw art-minded members of L.A.'s entertainment elite like Steve Martin and David Geffen.

The Wine Merchant. 9701 Santa Monica Blvd. (at Roxbury), Beverly Hills. ☎ **310/278-7322.**

"The Wine Merchant to the Stars" is more like it. Linger while looking for the right bottle and you may run into a famous local.

BEVERLY BOULEVARD (FROM ROBERTSON BLVD. TO LABREA AVE.)

Every Picture Tells a Story. 7525 Beverly Blvd. (between Fairfax and LaBrea aves.), Los Angeles. ☎ **213/932-6070.**

This gallery, devoted to the art of children's literature, displays antique children's books as well as the works of over 100 illustrators, including lithos of *Curious George, Eloise,* and *Charlotte's Web.* Whether you're indulging your inner child or introducing your kids to their first "art gallery," you'll also enjoy the story readings and interactive workshops. Call to find out what's upcoming on the schedule.

Mysterious Bookshop. 8763 Beverly Blvd., West Hollywood. ☎ **310/659-2959.**

Over 20,000 used, rare, and out-of-print titles make this the area's best mystery, espionage, detective, and thriller bookshop. Author appearances and other special events are regularly hosted.

The Opera Shop. 8384 Beverly Blvd. (3 blocks east of La Cienega Blvd.), Los Angeles. ☎ **213/658-5811.**

If you can name more than three tenors, this pleasantly cluttered little gift shop is for you. Everything imaginable is available with an opera theme: musical motif jewelry, stationery, T-shirts, opera glasses (of course!), and tapes, videos, and CDs of your favorite productions.

Re-Mix. 7605^1/$_2$ Beverly Blvd. (between Fairfax and LaBrea aves.), Los Angeles. ☎ **213/936-6210.**

If you complain that they just don't make 'em like they used to . . . well, they do at Re-Mix. Selling only vintage (1940s to 1970s) but brand-new (as in unworn) shoes for men and women, it's more like a shoestore museum featuring wingtips, Hush Puppies, Joan Crawford pumps, and 1970s platforms. A rackful of unworn vintage socks all display their original tags and stickers, and the prices are downright reasonable. Celebrity hipsters and hep cats from Madonna to Roseanne are often spotted here.

✪ Second Time Around Watch Co. 8840 Beverly Blvd. (west of Robertson Blvd.), Los Angeles. ☎ **310/271-6615.**

The city's best selection of pre-1960s collectible timepieces includes dozens of classic Tiffanys, Cartiers, Piagets, and Rolexes. You might even find an 1850s Patek Philippe pocket watch.

HOLLYWOOD
MELROSE AVENUE (BETWEEN FAIRFAX & LA BREA AVES.)

It's showing some wear—some stretches have become downright ugly—but this is still one of the most exciting shopping streets in the country for cutting-edge fashions—and some eye-popping people-watching to boot. There are scores of shops selling the latest in clothes, gifts, jewelry, and accessories. Melrose is a playful stroll, dotted with plenty of hip restaurants and funky shops that are sure to shock. Where else could you find green patent-leather cowboy boots, a working 19th-century pocket watch, an inflatable girlfriend, and glow-in-the-dark condoms in the same shopping spree?

Aardvark's Odd Ark. 7579 Melrose Ave. ☎ **213/655-6769.**

This large storefront near the Venice Beach Walk is crammed with racks of antique and used clothes from the 1960s, 1970s, and 1980s. They stock vintage everything, from suits and dresses to neckties, hats, handbags, and jewelry. And they manage to anticipate some of the hottest new street fashions. There's another Aardvark's at 1516 Pacific Ave., Venice (☎ 310/392-2996).

Betsey Johnson Boutique. 7311 Melrose Ave., Los Angeles. ☎ **213/931-4490.**

The New York–based designer has brought her brand of fashion—trendy, cutesy, body-conscious womenswear in colorful prints and faddish fabrics—to L.A. Also in Santa Monica at 2929 Main St. (☎ 310/452-7911).

Where to Find Hollywood's Hand-Me-Downs

Admit it: Like everyone else, you've dreamed of being a glamorous movie or TV star. Well, you shouldn't expect to be "discovered" during your L.A. vacation, but you can live out your fantasy by dressing the part. Costumes from famous movies, TV show wardrobes, castoffs from celebrity closets—they're easier to find (and more affordable to own) than you might think.

A good place to start is **Star Wares,** 2817 Main St., Santa Monica (☎ **310/ 399-0224**). This deceptively small shop regularly has leftovers from Cher's closet, as well as celebrity-worn apparel from the likes of Joan Rivers, Tim Curry, and Kathleen Turner. They also stock movie production wardrobes and genuine collector's items. If the $5,000 *Star Trek* uniform or *Planet of the Apes* military regalia you covet is out of your price range, don't worry: You can still pick up one of Johnny Depp's *Benny and Joon* outfits, dresses from the closets of Lucille Ball and Greer Garson, or E.T.'s bathrobe, all of which are surprisingly affordable. Many pieces have accompanying photos or movie stills, so you'll know exactly who donned your piece before you. Open daily from noon to 6pm.

That isn't the case, however, at **The Place & Co.,** 8820 S. Sepulveda Blvd., Westchester (☎ **310/645-1539**), where the anonymity of their well-heeled clientele (sellers and buyers) is strictly honored. Here you'll find men's and women's haute couture—always the latest fashions and gently worn—at a fraction of the Rodeo Drive prices. All the designers are here—Ungaro, Bill Blass, Krizia, Donna Karan. You may even have seen that Armani suit or Sonia Rykiel gown you find in the racks on an Academy Awards attendee last year! Open Monday to Saturday from 10am to 6pm.

For sheer volume, you can't beat **It's A Wrap,** 3315 W. Magnolia Blvd., Burbank (☎ **818/567-7366**). Every item here is marked with its place of origin, and the list is staggering: *Melrose Place, Seinfeld, Baywatch, All My Children, Forrest Gump, The Brady Bunch Movie,* and so on. Many of these wardrobes (which include shoes

---

Boy London. 7519 Melrose Ave., Los Angeles. ☎ **213/655-0302.**

Once on the cutting edge of London's King's Road, Boy has toned down a bit, now selling shirts and other clothes emblazoned with its own logo. It's still cool, though.

Brian Jeffrey's Design Greenhouse. 7556 Melrose Ave., Los Angeles. ☎ **213/651-2539.**

This is one of the most beautiful stores on Melrose. Brian Jeffrey's is a professional decorator's dream store for interior plants, baskets and containers, candleholders, and wind chimes. It has floating lotus flowers, pressed eucalyptus, and candles galore. A festival for the senses, the shop is cluttered with terrific visuals, sweet smells, and the sounds of music.

Condomania. 7306 Melrose Ave., Los Angeles. ☎ **213/933-7865.**

A vast selection of condoms, lubricants, and kits creatively encourage safe sex.

L.A. Eyeworks. 7407 Melrose Ave., Los Angeles. ☎ **213/653-8255.**

This hometown designer has become world famous for its innovative styles and celebrity ad campaign. The shop on Melrose is the original storefront location. There are other locations throughout the L.A. metropolitan area.

and accessories) aren't outstanding but for their Hollywood origins: Jerry Seinfeld's trademark polo shirts, for instance, are standard mall-issue. Some collectible pieces, like Sylvester Stallone's *Rocky* stars-and-stripes boxers, are framed and on display. Open Monday to Saturday from 11am to 6pm and on Sunday from 11am to 4pm.

When you're done at It's A Wrap, stop in across the street at **Junk For Joy,** 3314 W. Magnolia Blvd., Burbank (☎ **818/569-4903**). A Hollywood wardrobe coordinator or two will probably be hunting through this wacky little store right beside you. The emphasis here is on funky items more suitable as costumes than everyday wear (the store is mobbed each year around Halloween). At press time they were loaded with 1970s polyester shirts and tacky slacks, but you never know what you'll find when you get there. Open Tuesday to Friday from 10am to 6pm and on Saturday from 11am to 6pm.

The grand dame of all wardrobe and costume outlets is **Western Costume,** 11041 Vanowen St., North Hollywood (☎ **818/760-0900**). In business since 1912, it still designs and executes entire wardrobes for major motion pictures; when filming is finished, the garments are added to their staggering rental inventory. This place is perhaps best known for outfitting Vivien Leigh in *Gone with the Wind.* Several of Scarlett O'Hara's memorable gowns were even available for rent until they were recently auctioned off at a charity event. Western maintains an "outlet store" on the premises, where damaged garments are sold at rock-bottom (nothing over $15) prices. If you're willing to do some rescue work, there are definitely some hidden treasures here. Open for rentals Monday to Friday from 8am to 5:30pm, and for sales Tuesday to Friday from 10am to 5pm.

Finally, don't miss **Golyester,** 136 S. LaBrea Ave. (☎ **213/931-1339**). This shop is almost a museum of finely preserved (but reasonably priced) vintage clothing and fabrics. The staff will gladly flip through stacks of *Vogue* magazines from the 1930s, '40s, and '50s with you, pointing out the star-studded original advertisements for various outfits in their stock. Open Monday to Saturday from 11am to 6pm.

Maya. 7452 Melrose Ave., Los Angeles. ☎ **213/655-2708.**

This rather plain-looking store houses a huge—and fascinating—variety of silver and turquoise rings and earrings from South America, Nepal, Bali, and central Asia. The shop's walls are cluttered with Asian and South American ceremonial and ornamental masks.

Retail Slut. 7308 Melrose Ave., Los Angeles. ☎ **213/934-1339.**

You'll find new clothing and accessories for men and women at this famous rock 'n' roll shop. The unique designs are for a select crowd (the name says it all), so don't expect to find anything for your next PTA meeting here.

Wasteland. 7428 Melrose Ave., Los Angeles. ☎ **213/653-3028.**

An enormous steel-sculpted facade fronts this L.A. branch of the Berkeley/Haight-Ashbury hipster hangout that sells vintage and contemporary clothes for men and women. There's a lot of leathers, denim, and some classic vintage—but mostly funky 1970s garb. This ultra-trendy store is a packed with the flamboyantly colorful polyester halters and bell-bottoms from the decade some of us would rather forget.

Farther West on Melrose

Name That Toon. 8483 Melrose Ave., Los Angeles. ☎ **213/653-5633.**

Several L.A. galleries sell clay, computer, and cel animation art, but none has a better selection than this well-stocked shop, which specializes in original production cels from Disney, Warner Brothers, Hanna-Barbera, Dr. Seuss, and Walter Lantz. Original Ren and Stimpy and Simpsons art is also available. Phone for information on artists' receptions, lecturers, and other special events.

Maxfield. 8825 Melrose Ave., West Hollywood. ☎ **310/274-8800.**

Some of L.A.'s best-quality avant-garde designs include men's and women's fashions by Yamamoto, Comme des Garçons, Dolce Gabbana, Jill Sander, and the like. Furniture and home accessories are also sold, and the store's provocative window display ranges from sharp political statements to a Jerry Garcia tribute.

HOLLYWOOD BOULEVARD (BETWEEN GOWER ST. & LA BREA AVE.)

One of Los Angeles's most famous streets is, for the most part, a sleazy strip. But along the Walk of Fame, between the T-shirt shops and greasy pizza parlors, you'll find some excellent poster shops, souvenir stores, and Hollywood memorabilia dealers that are worth getting out of your car for—especially if there's a chance of getting your hands on that long-sought-after Ethel Merman autograph or *200 Motels* poster.

Book City Collectibles. 6631 Hollywood Blvd., Hollywood. ☎ **213/466-0120.**

More than 70,000 color prints of past and present stars are available, along with a good selection of autographs from the likes of Lucille Ball ($175), Anthony Hopkins ($35), and Grace Kelly ($750).

Frederick's of Hollywood. 6606 Hollywood Blvd., Hollywood. ☎ **213/466-8506.**

Behind the garish pink-and-purple facade lies one of the most famous panty shops in the world. Everything from Spandex suits to bikini bras and sophisticated nighties is here. Even if you're not buying, stop in and pick up one of their famous catalogs.

Hollywood Book and Poster Company. 6349 Hollywood Blvd., Hollywood. ☎ **213/465-8764.**

Owner Eric Caidin's excellent collection of movie posters (from about $15 each) is particularly strong in horror and exploitation flicks. Photocopies of about 5,000 movie and television scripts are also sold for $10 to $15 each, and the store also carries music posters and photos.

The Last Moving Picture Show. 6307 Hollywood Blvd. (near Vine St.), Hollywood. ☎ **213/467-0838.**

Movie-related merchandise of all kinds is sold here, including stills from 1950s movies and authentic production notes from a variety of films.

DOWNTOWN

Since the late, lamented *grande dame* department store Bullock's closed in 1993 (its deco masterpiece salons were rescued to house the Southwestern Law School's library), downtown has become even less of a shopping destination than ever. Savvy Angelenos still go for bargains in the garment and fabric districts, florists and bargain hunters arrive at the vast Flower Mart before dawn for the city's best selection of fresh blooms, and families of all ethnicities stroll the Grand Central Market. Although many of the once-splendid streets are lined with cut-rate luggage and cheap electronics storefronts, shopping downtown can be a rewarding if gritty experience for the adventuresome.

Cooper Building. 860 S. Los Angeles St., downtown. ☎ **213/622-1139.**

The centerpiece of downtown's Garment District, the Cooper Building and surrounding blocks are full of shops selling name-brand clothes for men, women, and children at significantly discounted prices.

Golf Exchange. 830 S. Olive St. (between 8th and 9th sts.), downtown. ☎ **213/622-0403.**

L.A.'s golf megastore fills 10 rooms with clubs and accessories: An entire room is devoted to golf shoes, another to bags, another to used clubs, and so on. There's also an indoor driving range so you can try before you buy.

✪ **Grand Central Market.** 317 S. Broadway (between 3rd and 4th sts.), downtown. ☎ **213/624-2378.**

Opened in 1917, this bustling market has watched the face of downtown L.A. change while changing little itself. Today it serves Latino families, enterprising restaurateurs, and home cooks in search of unusual ingredients and bargain-priced fruits and vegetables. On weekends you'll be greeted by a lively mariachi band at the Hill Street entrance, near our favorite market feature—the fruit juice counter, which dispenses 20 fresh varieties from wall spigots and blends up the tastiest, healthiest "shakes" in town. Farther into the market you'll find produce sellers and prepared-food counters, plus spice vendors who seem sraight out of a Turkish alley, and a grain and bean seller who'll scoop out dozens of exotic rices and dried legumes.

La Plata Cigars. 1026 S. Grand Ave. (between 11th St. and Olympic Blvd.). ☎ **213/747-8561.**

Los Angeles's only cigar factory, family-run La Plata has been hand-rolling stogies since 1947. The public is welcome to visit the downtown factory and watch how Cuban artisans create these premium prizes. Afterward enter the shop's huge humidor to choose from thousands of fresh cigars in all sizes—for about half what the fancy places charge. Open Monday to Friday from 7am to 4:30pm.

Phoenix Bakery. 969 N. Broadway (Chinatown), downtown. ☎ **213/628-4642.**

The freshest, flakiest, sweetest almond cookies are baked right here in the heart of Chinatown. They come in three sizes and cost only pennies each. The bakery is also remarkable for its endless selection of special-occasion cake decorations—whatever theme you desire, from *Pocahontas* to *Sesame Street* to *Star Trek,* they have the plastic figures and accessories to make it memorable.

THE SAN FERNANDO VALLEY
STUDIO CITY (VENTURA BLVD. BETWEEN LAUREL CANYON & FULTON AVE.)

Long beloved by Valley residents, Studio City is conveniently located freeway- and canyon-close to Hollywood and the Westside. Ventura Boulevard has a distinct personality in each of the several Valley communities it passes through, but Studio City is where you'll find small boutiques and antiques stores, quirky little businesses (many dating from the 1940s and 1950s), and less conjested branches of popular chains like The Gap, Pier One Imports, and Blockbuster.

The Cranberry House (Studio City Antique Mall). 12318 Ventura Blvd. (2 blocks east of Whitsett), Studio City. ☎ **818/506-8945.**

Under a berry-colored awning, several storefront windows hint at the treasures within this antiques and collectibles store featuring over 100 different sellers. Be sure to haggle—even front-desk staff are often authorized by the individual dealers to strike a bargain.

Samuel French Book Store. 11963 Ventura Blvd., Studio City. ☎ **818/762-0535.**

This is L.A.'s biggest theater and movie bookstore. Plays, screenplays, and film books are all sold here, as well as scripts for Broadway and Hollywood blockbusters. Also in Hollywood at 7623 Sunset Blvd., between Fairfax and LaBrea avenues (☎ 213/ 876-0570).

Studio City Camera Exchange. 12174 Ventura Blvd. (1 block west of Laurel Canyon), Studio City. ☎ **818/762-4749.**

There's comfort in the 1940s architecture of this corner photography store—like an old friend, Studio City Camera is there if you need supplies, film, processing, batteries, frames, albums, used cameras (some quite collectible), or just to talk shop with fellow shutterbugs behind the counter.

UNIVERSAL CITYWALK (UNIVERSAL CENTER DR., UNIVERSAL CITY)

Technically an outdoor mall rather than a shopping area, Universal CityWalk (☎ 818/622-4455) gets mention here because it's so utterly unique. A pedestrian promenade next door to Universal Studios, CityWalk is dominated by brightly colored, outrageously surreal oversize storefronts. The heavily touristed faux street is home to an inordinate number of restaurants, including B.B. King's Blues Club, the newest Hard Rock Cafe, and a branch of the Hollywood Athletic Club featuring a restaurant and pool hall. This is consumer culture gone haywire—an egotistical eyesore not worth a special visit.

ELSEWHERE IN THE VALLEY

Arte de Mexico. 5356 Riverton Ave., North Hollywood. ☎ **818/769-5090.**

Seven warehouses full of carved furniture and wrought iron once sold only to moviemakers and restaurants is now open to the public. One of the most fascinating places in North Hollywood.

Piccolo Pete's Art Deco. 13814 Ventura Blvd., Sherman Oaks. ☎ **818/907-9060.**

A lovely shop selling art nouveau, deco, and moderne furnishings and art, including clocks, lighting fixtures, pottery, and dinnerware. A recent museum exhibition on art deco wasn't as nice as the perfect specimens in Piccolo Pete's, but expect their prices to reflect that perfection.

STORES WORTH SEEKING OUT ELSEWHERE IN THE CITY

California Map and Travel Center. 3211 Pico Blvd., Santa Monica. ☎ **310/829-6277.**

As the name says, this store carries a good selection of domestic and international maps and travel accessories, including guides for hiking, biking, and touring. Globes and atlases are also sold. Visit their Website at **http://www.mapper.com.**

Nordstrom. In the Westside Pavilion, 10830 W. Pico Blvd., West Los Angeles. ☎ **310/ 470-6155.**

Emphasis on customer service has won this Seattle-based chain a loyal following. Equally devoted to women's and men's fashions, the store has one of the best shoe selections in the city, and there are thousands of suits in stock.

✪ **Rhino Records.** 1720 Westwood Blvd., Westwood. ☎ **310/474-3786.**

This is L.A.'s premier alternative shop, specializing in new artists and independent-label releases. In addition to new releases, there's a terrific used selection; this is where record industry types come to trade in the records they don't want for the records they do, so you'll be able to find never-played promotional copies of brand-new releases at half the retail price. You'll also find the definitive collection of records on the Rhino label here.

Trashy Lingerie. 402 N. La Cienega Blvd., Hollywood. ☎ **310/652-4543.**

This shop will tailor-fit their house-designed clothes—everything from patent-leather bondage wear to elegant bridal underthings—for you. There's a $2 "membership" fee to enter the store, but, even for browsers, it's worth it.

12 Los Angeles After Dark

The *L.A. Weekly,* a free weekly paper available at sidewalk stands, shops, and restaurants, is the best place to find out what's going on about town, especially for club happenings. The "Calendar" section of the Sunday *Los Angeles Times* is also a good place to find out what's going on after dark.

For weekly updates on music, art, dance, theater, special events, and festivals, call the **Cultural Affairs Hotline** (☎ **213/688-ARTS**), a 24-hour directory listing a wide variety of events, most of which are free.

Ticketmaster (☎ 213/480-3232) and **Telecharge** (☎ 800/447-7400) are the major charge-by-phone ticket agencies in the city, selling tickets to concerts, sporting events, plays, and special events.

THE PERFORMING ARTS
CLASSICAL MUSIC & OPERA

Beyond the pop realms, music in Los Angeles generally falls short of that found in other cities. For the most part, Angelenos rely on visiting orchestras and companies to fulfill their classical music appetites; scan the papers to find out who's playing and dancing while you're in the city.

The **Los Angeles Philharmonic** (☎ 213/850-2000) isn't just the city's top symphony; it's the only major classical music company in Los Angeles. Finnish-born music director Esa-Pekka Salonen concentrates on contemporary compositions; despite complaints from traditionalists, he does an excellent job attracting younger audiences. Tickets can be hard to come by when celebrity players like Itzak Perlman, Issac Stern, Emanuel Ax, and Yo-Yo Ma are in town. In addition to regular performances at the **Music Center's Dorothy Chandler Pavilion,** 135 N. Grand Ave., downtown, the Philharmonic also plays a popular summer season at the Hollywood Bowl (see "Concerts Under the Stars," below).

Slowly but surely, the **L.A. Opera** (☎ 213/972-8001) is gaining both respect and popularity with inventive stagings of classic operas, usually with guest divas. The Opera also calls the Music Center home.

The 120-voice **Los Angeles Master Chorale** (☎ 213/626-0624) sings a varied repertoire that includes classical and pops compositions. Concerts are usually held at the Music Center from October to June.

CONCERTS UNDER THE STARS

✪ **Hollywood Bowl.** 2301 N. Highland Ave. (at Odin St.), Hollywood. ☎ **213/850-2000.**

Built in the early 1920s, the Hollywood Bowl is an elegant Greek-style natural outdoor amphitheater cradled in a small mountain canyon. This is the summer home of the Los Angeles Philharmonic Orchestra; internationally known conductors and soloists often sit in on Tuesday and Thursday nights. Friday and Saturday concerts often feature orchestral swing or pops concerts. The summer season also includes a jazz series; past performers have included Natalie Cole, Mel Torme, Dionne

Warwick, and Chick Corea. Other events, from Tom Petty concerts to an annual Mariachi Festival, are often on the season's schedule.

For many concertgoers, a visit to the Bowl is an excuse for an accompanied picnic under the stars. Gourmet picnics at the Bowl—complete with a bottle or two of wine—are one of L.A.'s grandest traditions. You can prepare your own, or order a picnic basket with a choice of hot and cold dishes and a selection of wines and desserts from the theater's catering department. A la carte baskets run $16.95 to $25.95 per person; appetizers and drinks are extra. Call **213/851-3588** the day before you go.

THEATER
Major Theaters & Companies

The Ahmanson Theater and Mark Taper Forum, the city's top two playhouses, are both part of the all-purpose **Music Center,** 135 N. Grand Ave., downtown. The **Ahmanson Theater** (☎ 213/972-7401) reopened in 1995, after a $71-million renovation that improved acoustics and seating. This theater is active year round, either with shows produced by the in-house Center Theater Group, or with traveling Broadway productions. In-house shows are usually revivals of major Broadway plays, starring famous film and TV actors; we saw *Dangerous Liasions* with Lynn Redgrave and Frank Langella, and *The Little Shop Around the Corner* with Pam Dawber and Christopher Reeve a few years ago. Traveling shows are usually West Coast premières of plays such as Neil Simon's *Broadway Bound* or Andrew Lloyd Webber's *Phantom of the Opera;* the renovated theater debuted with *Miss Saigon.* The Ahmanson is so huge that you'll want seats in the front third or half of the theater.

The **Mark Taper Forum** (☎ 213/972-0700) is a more intimate, circular theater staging contemporary works by international and local playwrights. Kenneth Branagh's Renaissance Theatre Company staged its only American productions of *King Lear* and *A Midsummer Night's Dream* at the Mark Taper, to give you an idea of the quality of the shows here. Productions are usually excellent, run with plenty of spirit and no shortage of controversy.

Ticket prices vary depending on the performance. Discounted tickets are usually available on the day of performance for students and seniors.

Big-time traveling troupes and Broadway-bound musicals that don't go to the Ahmanson head instead for the **Shubert Theater,** in the ABC Entertainment Center, 2020 Ave. of the Stars, Century City (☎ 800/233-3123). This plush playhouse presents major musicals on the scale of *Cats, Sunset Boulevard,* and *Les Misérables.*

Top-quality Broadway-caliber productions are also staged at the **UCLA James A. Doolittle Theater,** 1615 N. Vine St., Hollywood (☎ 213/462-6666 or 213/972-0700).

For the current schedule at any of the above theaters, check the listings in *Los Angeles* magazine or the "Calendar" section of the Sunday *Los Angeles Times,* or call the box offices directly at the numbers listed above.

Smaller Playhouses

Like New York's Off Broadway or London's fringe, Los Angeles's small-scale theaters often outdo the slick, high-budget shows. Because this is Tinseltown, movie and TV stars sometimes headline, but more often than not the talent is up-and-coming. Who knows—the unknown on stage today might be the next David Schwimmer tomorrow.

The **Colony Studio Theater,** 1944 Riverside Dr., Silver Lake (☎ 213/665-3011), has an excellent resident company that has played in this air-conditioned,

99-seat, converted silent-movie house for over 20 years. Recent productions include the musical *Candide* and the classic American comedy *The Front Page*.

The **Actors Circle Theater,** 7313 Santa Monica Blvd., West Hollywood (☎ 213/882-8043), is a 47-seater that's as acclaimed as it is tiny. Look for original contemporary works throughout the year.

The **Los Angeles Theater,** 615 S. Broadway (☎ 213/629-2939), is worth a trip no matter what's on. Built in 1931 by cinema architect S. Charles Lee, this grand movie palace was designed in the ornate baroque style of 18th-century France. Live theater began to be staged here in 1995.

In addition to those listed above, there are about 100 other stages of varying quality throughout the city. Tickets for most plays usually cost $10 to $30. Check newspaper listings for current offerings.

THE CLUB & MUSIC SCENE

By Steve Hochman and Heidi Siegmund Cuda

In addition to covering the pop music scene for the *Los Angeles Times*, Steve Hochman has written for such publications as *Rolling Stone, Spin*, and *Melody Maker*, as well as the on-line HotWired outlet to the adventure travel magazine *Escape*. Heidi Siegmund Cuda is the night club columnist and a feature writer for the *Los Angeles Times*, a contributing writer to *Entertainment Weekly*, and a pop music critic for *Pulse!* magazine. With Ice T, she co-authored *The Ice Opinion* (St. Martin's Press), a first-person narrative detailing the rapper's view of America, politics, and urban culture.

The L.A. club and music scene is truly something-for-everybody territory, from blues fanatics to leather freaks. *But be forewarned:* You're not in Kansas anymore. Or for that matter, San Francisco. Friendlier cities greet out-of-towners with arms extended and advice at hand. Travel to the City by the Bay, and a waiter might tip you off to the best restaurant or the hottest dance club for that moment in time. Sit in a Los Angeles café, however, and be grateful if you're acknowledged. It's nothing personal—it's more a matter of Social Darwinism. This is a town where only the strongest—and the most resourceful—survive, and too many folks are angling to get out of the cattle line, past the velvet rope, and into clubland's hot zones.

The competition is compounded by L.A.'s short attention span. What might have been the hip ticket last week could be belly up by the time you find the door. That said, don't lose all hope. A smart visitor has ammo: This guide, along with a current *L.A. Weekly* (which can be found for free at numerous around-town outlets on Thursday), offers a plethora of dance and music club information for the adventurous at heart.

Note: Unless otherwise noted, to enter the clubs listed below you must be at least 21—with ID to prove it.

LIVE MUSIC

It's a good bet that someone of interest will be in town during any one stay. The best way to see what's on is by checking the *L.A. Weekly*, available just about everywhere.

Mid-size Concerts

B.B. King's Blues Club. CityWalk, Universal City. ☎ 818/622-5464.

B.B. King's is a bit more "real" than the House of Blues. Its three-floor seating area, resembling an old southern club, is tastefully decorated, the music stays closer to authentic blues, and the ribs are terrific. It also offers a fine, though overpriced, Sunday gospel brunch.

Hollywood Palladium. 6215 Sunset Blvd., Hollywood. ☎ **213/962-7600.**

The big-band leaders who called this home in the 1940s might be horrified to see the chandeliers shaken by alternative rock's top names, and the dance floor turned into a swarming mosh pit. But for the last decade the 3,000- or 4,000-capacity hall has been a key venue for rockers on the way to bigger things, with the likes of Hole, Sonic Youth, and the Red Hot Chili Peppers headlining. Some unruly crowds have brought neighborhood concerns, but tight security—and we mean tight, with everything from lipstick to pens to gum being confiscated in thorough entry searches—has kept the hall open.

House of Blues. 8430 Sunset Blvd., West Hollywood. ☎ **213/650-0247.**

Depite its Disneyland-ish decor, this club—co-owned by some really strange bedfellows, including Hard Rock founder Issac Tigrett, Jim Belushi, Dan Ackroyd, Aerosmith, and Harvard University—does earnestly honor its namesake music with informative displays and a wealth of colorful folk art. Still, it's permeated with industry types more interested in being seen than hearing the music. Even so, there's enough top-notch music here to keep many who routinely bad-mouth the place coming back, and the food in the upstairs restaurant can be superb (reservations are a must). The Sunday gospel brunch, though a bit overpriced, is a rousing diversion.

John Anson Ford Theatre. 2580 Cahuenga Blvd. West. ☎ **213/464-2826.**

Once, during a late-1980s Ramones concert at this lovely alfresco facility, the punk sounds carried across U.S. 101 and into the ears of people who were trying to hear the L.A. Symphony play Beethoven at the Hollywood Bowl. They were not amused, and rock was virtually banned from the Ford for some time. But lately it's been back, and a night with a rising star under the stars (Alanis Morissette played there on her way to superstardom) can be wonderful. Parking, though, is nightmarish—prepare for a long walk uphill.

Mayan Theatre. 1038 S. Hill St. ☎ **213/746-4287.**

This is perhaps the strangest, yet coolest concert venue in town, with elaborate decor in the mode of a Mayan temple (or something). Another fine relic of L.A.'s glorious past, it's relatively new as a pop music house, holding about 1,000 for such performers as PJ Harvey, Ani DiFranco, and—before they got mega-huge—Bush. It's in a part of downtown L.A. where most people usually never go, but there's plenty of parking, and the interior makes it seem like another dimension.

The Palace. 1735 N. Vine St., Hollywood. ☎ **213/461-3504.**

A classic vaudeville house, this 1,200-capacity theater, just across Vine from the famed Capitol Records tower, has been the site of numerous significant alternative rock shows in the 1990s, including key appearances by Nirvana and Smashing Pumpkins. But its dominance has been challenged of late by several other venues of similar size.

✪ Wiltern Theatre. 3790 Wilshire Blvd. ☎ **213/380-5005.**

Saved from the wrecking ball in the mid-1980s, this WPA-era art deco showcase is perhaps the most beautiful theater in town. You could have an entertaining evening just sitting and staring at the ornate ceiling—but usually you don't have to. Countless national and international acts have played here, from Jerry Garcia to Joan Osborne, with such nonpop music events as Penn & Teller and top ballet troupes complementing the schedule.

Club Shows

Alligator Lounge. 3321 Pico Blvd., Santa Monica. ☎ **213/453-8477.**

An unassuming dive with a neighborhood feel, the Alligator has become one of the top sites for emerging roots and alternative music in recent years, and has been home to weekly New Music Mondays hosted by avant-garde guitarist Nels Cline with challenging music that crosses rock, jazz, and classical forms performed by Cline and his band, as well as guests drawn from the cream of category-busting musicians.

Al's Bar. 305 S. Hewitt St., downtown. ☎ **213/625-9703.** Cover varies.

Al's is the last of a dying breed of downtown hellholes that regularly attracts fun underground music. If you can brave the neighborhood, which is sketchy at best, a good time can almost always be had here.

Bar Deluxe. 1710 N. Las Palmas Ave., Hollywood. ☎ **213/469-1991.** Generally no cover.

This is the club to go to when you're looking for a hassle-free, no-lines affair. This dimly lit, black-and-red, voodoo-meets-hoodoo haven specializes in surf, blues, and rockabilly bands and is as comfortable as an old pair of Doc Martens.

Billboard Live. 9039 Sunset Blvd., West Hollywood. ☎ **310/786-1712.** Cover varies.

With a gala opening in August 1996 that closed down the Sunset Strip for the first time in history—so thousands of revelers could help Tony Bennett celebrate the birth of this three-tier, $5¹/₂ million club—this club promises to breath some life into the legendary Strip. Located on the former site of the seminal rock 'n' roll club Gazzari's, Billboard Live's ambitions loom large. Among its state-of-the-art distinctions: two gigantic exterior "Jumbotrons," which reveal the onstage performances to passersby and, during the day, feature continuous music programming; a unique "industrial plush" interior design (think corrugated metal draped in velvet); a "Tequila Library," where card-carrying members can order any tequila concoction under el sol; and numerous monthly performances selected from *Billboard*'s "Heatseekers" charts, so you can be the first to see the Next Big Thing. Ultimately, the 400-capacity club, the first of a dozen Billboard Live venues scheduled to be built over the next four years, is an excellent live music showcase.

Coconut Teaszer. 8117 Sunset Blvd. West Hollywood. ☎ **213/654-4773.**

In some ways this is a carry-over of the 1980s pre–alternative rock ethos, with hard-rockin' dudes mostly trying to impress record company talent scouts. It's a good place for local acts that you've never heard of, and most likely will never hear of again. But who knows—the night you're there may be the night a future superstar is discovered.

Doug Weston's Troubadour. 9081 Santa Monica Blvd., West Hollywood. ☎ **310/276-6168.** All ages, Cover varies.

The Troubadour has worked long and hard to shed its creepy 1980s Spandex-'n'-big-hair image, and it has emerged vibrant and vigorous once again. Turning 40 in 1997, the club counts the Byrds and the Eagles among the bands that virtually formed here, and even in the metal years saw Motley Crue and others rise to the big time. Today the Troub can be counted on for excellent sound, and a wide array of up-and-coming break-out bands and already-made-its. A fine, fine venue. All ages.

Dragonfly. 6510 Santa Monica Blvd., Hollywood. ☎ **213/466-6111.** Cover varies.

Not one to miss a trend, Dragonfly went from being a dance club scene that offered live music to becoming a live music scene that offers dancing. Currently the hip venue in the heart of Hollywood is attacking its band bookings with a vengeance. From "surprise" shows by top-notch local acts such as Rage Against the Machine and Porno for Pyros to surprising national acts—Run-D.M.C. at an alternative music club!—Dragonfly is soaring. Guests should also enjoy its cool outdoor patio and pillow room.

FM Station Live. 11700 Victory Blvd., North Hollywood. ☎ **818/769-2220.** Cover varies.

This is Hessian heaven, NoHo style. The last of the headbanger havens, FM Station keeps metal alive by booking tribute bands nearly 5 nights a week. Acts to look for are the Atomic Punks (a Van Halen cover band) and Sticky Fingers (you guessed it, a Rolling Stones tribute act). But no matter who's on stage, at FM Station it's always good time rock 'n' roll.

Jabberjaw. 3711 W. Pico Blvd., Los Angeles. ☎ **213/732-3463.** Cover varies.

This sweaty, arty coffeehouse is only fun if you like the national indie rock scene and a lot of java (no alcohol is served so all ages are welcome). When temperatures begin to soar, so does the discomfort factor, but guests are granted a reprieve on the club's outdoor patio. Nevertheless, this club is so tied in to the indie scene, a regular can cancel his subscription to *Flipside*.

Jack's Sugar Shack. 1707 Vine St., Hollywood. ☎ **213/466-7005.**

Jack doesn't mess around. The *Gilligan's Island* meets *The Love Boat* decor combined with a select booking policy makes this nightclub a tasty treat. Less interested in trends than in quality music, Jack's books national and local blues, country and western, and alternative music, and is the current host to Ronnie Mack's Barndance, a free Tuesday-night affair of alternative country music.

Lava Lounge. 1533 La Brea Ave., Hollywood. ☎ **213/876-6612.** Cover varies.

Described by its lovely owner, a former set decorator, as a "Vegas in hell" motif, the interior of this small bar and performance space located in a très-ugly strip mall is very inventive. Think tiki-tacky coupled with big-city chic. Live music includes jazz and surfabilly, and live regulars include Quentin Tarantino.

LunaPark. 665 N. Robertson Blvd., West Hollywood. ☎ **310/652-0611.** Cover none–$10.

Proprietor Jean-Pierre Boccarra has turned this bilevel retaurant/performance space into one of the most unpredictable yet reliable venues in the area—not just for music, which ranges from up-and-coming sensations (Ani DiFranco played her first L.A. show here) to global music stars (Cape Verde's "barefoot diva" Cesaria Evora), but for performance art, cabaret, and comedy, too.

McCabe's. 3101 Pico Blvd., Santa Monica. ☎ **213/828-4497.**

Since the early 1970s the back room of this earthy guitar shop has been the leading folk club in L.A., and possibly west of the Mississippi. Bonnie Raitt, Jackson Browne, and Linda Ronstadt are among those who played here early in their careers, and top-flight folk, country, and even rock musicians still return regularly to perform in an unbeatable, low-key, almost living room–esque setting.

The Opium Den. 1605¹/₂ Ivar St., Hollywood. ☎ **213/466-7800.** Cover varies.

Brent Bolthouse, an über-promoter on the Hollywood nightlife circuit, opened his first club on the site of the old Gaslight so his friends would have a comfortable, quality venue to perform in. With pals who appear in nearly every issue of *People,* this works in everyone's favor. Live alternative music is scheduled seven nights a week, with late-night dance parties occurring on Thursday, Friday, and Saturday. Stand-out performances include the Geraldine Fibbers, Rickie Lee Jones, Spain, and X.

Pan at the Faultline. 4216 Melrose Ave., Silver Lake. ☎ **213/662-LOVE** or 213/660-0889. Cover varies.

The precursor to Spaceland, Pan moved over to its current location, a gay leather bar, and voilà!—a star was born. Combining the fetish underground with local and national underground bands makes for interesting bedfellows. Add a decent sound system and a dash of style—this is not only one good-looking leather venue but interested parties can purchase all the fetish acoutrements on Visa and Amex at the club boutique—and you've got one of the coolest underground scenes in L.A. Pan is held bimonthly—usually the second and fourth Thursday—and plus all day on some Saturdays. Call for information.

The Roxy. 9009 Sunset Blvd. West Hollywood. ☎ **213/276-2222.**

Veteran record producer/executive Lou Adler opened this Sunset Strip club in the mid-1970s with concerts by Neil Young and a lengthy run of the pre-movie *Rocky Horror Show.* Since then it has remained among the top showcase venues in Hollywood—though it lost its unchallenged preeminence among cozy clubs to increased competition from the revitalized Troubadour and such new entries as the House of Blues.

Spaceland at Dreams. 1717 Silver Lake Blvd., Silver Lake. ☎ **213/413-4442.** Cover varies.

In less than a year promoter Mitchell Frank took over a spacious, dowdy bar on the eastern edge of Hollywood and turned it into one of the most happening nightspots in Los Angeles. With his eclectic bookings (everyone from the Foo Fighters and the Beasties to hometown faves Extra Fancy), Frank built a scene from scratch; Spaceland now rivals such Hollywood fixtures as the Whisky and Roxy as a place to see and be seen.

Union. 8210 Sunset Blvd., West Hollywood. ☎ **213/654-1001.** Cover: none Thurs–Tues., $5 Wed.

Otherwise known as the club that books avant-garde acid jazz artiste Toledo every Monday night, the Union is a comfortable bilevel venue with an outdoor patio and a piano bar, and averages 5 nights of live music weekly. Guests will hear acid jazz, straight jazz, and blues. On Wednesday promoter Brent Bolthouse takes over with "Soap," an inspired cocktail lounge atmosphere. But if you want something to remember L.A. by, see Toledo on Monday. A true original.

✪ **Viper Room.** 8852 Sunset Blvd., West Hollywood. ☎ **310/358-1880.** Cover varies.

This place is so delightfully hot that you might get singed on the way out. It's definitely a club to witness firsthand before exiting town—despite what you might have heard: Yes, Johnny Depp owns it (with partner Sal Jenco), and yes, River Phoenix overdosed here, and the combo either attracts or repulses clubgoers. But, hands down, the Viper Room has the most varied and exciting live music bookings in town. From Johnny Cash to Iggy Pop, the small, bilevel venue doesn't disappoint. The expensive sound system is a delight to true music fans, and there's enough stars on hand nightly to keep gazers excited.

The Whisky. 8901 Sunset Blvd., West Hollywood. ☎ **310/535-0579.** All ages, cover varies.

If you don't go to any other club in L.A., you must a go-go to the Whisky. The bilevel venue personifies L.A. rock 'n' roll, from Jim Morrison to X to Guns 'N' Roses. Every trend has passed through this club, and it continues to be the most vital venue of its kind. Recently an in-house booker was hired to bring more local music to the club, which already offers one of the best local showcases in town: Bianca's Hole on Monday nights, an always-free night of mostly L.A. bands.

DANCE CLUBS & BARS

To give outsiders an idea of the lightning speed with which dance clubs come and go in this town, the Roxbury doesn't even register on the map this year. It's still there, but folks aren't lining up like they used to, so we can't recommend it this time out. But no worries: There are plenty of sonic offerings to take its place, but best to move quickly and precisely. Take great pains to follow the recommended nights closely— you'll be glad you did.

Bossa Nova. Thursdays at the Pink, 2810 Main St., Santa Monica. ☎ **310/392-1077.** Cover $10.

DJs and label execs Jason Bentley and Bruno Guez bring their eclectic music tastes to this happening nightclub each week and guests DJs (including Tricky) round out the mood, which includes electronic, acid jazz, and more interesting musical treats than you can shake a stick at. An aural pleasure for all music fans.

Cherry. Fridays at the Love Lounge, 657 N. Robertson Blvd., West Hollywood. ☎ **310/659-0472.** Cover $10.

Deejay Mike Messex's Friday-night gig finds him digging deep into the 1980s for loads of glam rock, New Wave, and disco, keeping the dance floor packed all evening. Promoter Bryan Rabin knows how to keep the energy level high, with selective live performances—often with a homoerotic edge—as well as theme nights. A celebration of *Showgirls* was a must-see.

The Derby. 4500 Los Feliz Blvd., Los Feliz. ☎ **213/663-8979.** Cover $5.

This East Hollywood swing club is one Class A joint. The luscious club, located at a former Brown Derby site, was restored to its original luster and detailed with a heavy 1940s edge. This would explain the inordinate number of guests who come decked out in garb from that era to swing the night away to such musical acts as Big Bad Voodoo Daddy and the Royal Crown Revue (whose popularity soared after weekly bookings at the club).

El Floridita. 1253 N. Vine St., Hollywood. ☎ **213/871-8612.** Cover varies.

This Cuban restaurant-cum-salsa joint is hot, hot, hot. Despite its modest strip-lot locale, the tiny club attracts the likes of Jennifer Lopez, Sandra Bullock, Jimmy Smits, and Jack Nicholson, and the hippest nights continue to be Monday and Thursday, when Johnny Polanco and his swinging New York–flavored salsa band get the dance floor jumpin'.

The Garage. 4519 Santa Monica Blvd., Silver Lake. ☎ **213/683-3447.** Cover varies.

Another key Silver Lake club, this one sprang up from the underground and remains firmly planted therein. With a wide variety of weekly dance club promotions, this sparkling erstwhile garage attracts a comfortable gay/straight clientele with such events as Sucker, a Sunday beer bust hosted by drag diva Miss Vaginal Creme Davis; Hai

Karate, a dazzling Friday-night funky fest; and Ultra Saturdays, with hot Hollywood DJ Victor Rodriguez spinning deep house and soul.

The Gate. 643 N. La Cienega Blvd., West Hollywood. ☎ **310/289-8808.** Cover varies.

This is one despicable club, but folks seem to migrate here anyway. Perhaps the demise of Beverly Hills's Tatou encouraged the migration. Most famous for its repeated mentions in Faye Resnick's ode to Nicole Brown Simpson, the Gate attracts chemically altered, surgically enhanced Eurotrash bimbos and himbos, who enjoy its elaborate decor and gargoyles a-plenty. Dancing is scheduled Wednesday to Saturday—and don't wear shorts if you want to get in.

Saturday Night Fever. Saturdays at the Diamond Club, 7070 Hollywood Blvd., Hollywood. ☎ **213/848-9300** for location. Cover $10.

For nearly 5 years now this weekly disco party has been the biggest Saturday-night dance bash in Hollywood. Although it has moved numerous times since its inception, it continues to outgrow each venue, and the last consistent spot was at the Roxbury. Fever's currently going off at the Diamond Club, but owner Brent Bolthouse indicated at press time that he plans to move it yet again. Wherever it lands, it's sure to be the bomb: With popular L.A. DJ Mike Messex behind the main console, the temperature's always sizzling.

7969. 7969 Santa Monica Blvd., West Hollywood. ☎ **213/654-0280.** Cover varies.

Here's a fetish club that can't miss: Saturday features Sin-A-Matic, L.A.'s long-running, popular S&M industrial dance club, complete with whipping room. Monday and Friday offer a drag party. 7969's most popular night to date is Thursday's Grand Ville, a sexy dance club with a midnight striptease—emphasis on "tease." Also quite popular, among the ladies, that is, is Michelle's XXX Revue, a Tuesday-night lesbian hangout with an enormous number of topless women.

Soul Mama. Fridays at Checca, 7323 Santa Monica Blvd., Hollywood. ☎ **213/850-7471.** Cover $15.

L.A. used to be chock-full of decent hip-hop clubs, but in the past few years they've dropped like flies. Until things straighten up, Soul Mama—with its ample supply of hip-hop, funk, and old-school soul—will have to suffice.

COCKTAIL LOUNGES

Four Seasons Hotel Los Angeles. 300 S. Doheny Dr. (at Burton Way), Los Angeles. ☎ **310/273-2222.** No cover.

The sprawling lobby bar of this slightly pretentious but always eventful hotel serves as both celebrity magnet and unofficial parlour for monied regulars who virtually live in the high-rise. Decorated in the same comfortable but unremarkable neutral tones as the rest of the hotel, the bar is actually comprised of several sitting rooms and an outdoor patio, through which waft the sounds of the house pianist tinkling the ivories. The bartenders here have seen it all—no request is too outrageous, from a platter of oysters courtesy of the hotel's restaurant to a bowl of water for a canine companion (dogs served on patio only). The current cigar trend has found a home here: You may select from the bar's expansive humidor, but stay away if the smoke will offend you (or your dry cleaner).

Good Luck Bar. 1514 Hillhurst Ave. (between Hollywood and Sunset blvds.), Los Angeles. ☎ **213/666-3524.** No cover.

Until they installed a flashing sign—which simply reads "LUCK"—only locals and hipsters knew about this Kung Fu–themed room in the Los Feliz/Silverlake area. The dark red windowless interior boasts Oriental ceiling tiles, fringed Chinese paper lanterns, sweet-but-deadly drinks like the "Yee Mee Loo" (translated as "blue drink"), and a jukebox with selections from Thelonius Monk to Cher's "Half Breed." The spacious sitting room, furnished with mismatched sofas, armchairs, and banquettes, provide a great atmosphere for conversation or romance. Arrive early to avoid the throngs of L.A. scenesters.

Lounge 217. 217 Broadway (between Second and Third streets), Santa Monica. ☎ **310/281-6692.** Cover varies.

A lounge in the true sense of the word, these plush Art Deco surroundings just scream "martini"—and the bartenders stand ready to shake or stir up your favorite. Comfortable seating lends itself well to intimate socializing, or enjoying Monday's classical guitarist; Thursday night brings a torch singer and cigar bar. Come early on the weekends, when Lounge 217 hosts a more raucous late-night crowd.

Windows On Hollywood. in the Holiday Inn, 1755 N. Highland Ave., Hollywood. ☎ **213/462-7181.** No cover.

There's nothing like a revolving bar/restaurant to enjoy a panoramic view of the city; this one is 23 floors above the heart of Hollywood. While it scores low on the hipness scale, we're glad trendy bar-hoppers have taken their scene elsewhere, freeing up the prime window tables for you and me. The slowly revolving outer circle will show you downtown's skyline, the lights of Hollywood, and the hills to the north; the non-circulating center offers entertainment and dancing. If you're lucky, there'll be some young Sinatra wannabe providing a schmalty soundtrack for your cocktail hour.

COMEDY & CABARET

Except for the Cinegrill, which is in its own league, each of the following venues claims—and justly so—to have launched the careers of the comics who are now household names. The funniest up-and-comers are playing all the clubs (except for the Groundlings, which is an improvisation group), so you're probably best off choosing a club for its location. In addition to the venues listed below, see what's on at **Luna Park** (see "The Club & Music Scene" above) and **The Ice House** (see "Pasadena After Dark" in chapter 15).

The Cinegrill. In the Hollywood Roosevelt Hotel, 7000 Hollywood Blvd., Hollywood. ☎ **213/466-7000.**

There's something going on every night of the week here at one of L.A.'s most historic hotels. Some of the country's best cabaret singers pop up here regularly. The Cinegrill draws locals with a zany cabaret show and guest chanteuses from Eartha Kitt to Cybill Shepherd.

Comedy Store. 8433 Sunset Blvd., West Hollywood. ☎ **213/656-6225.**

You can't go wrong here: New comics develop their material, and established ones work out the kinks from theirs, at owner Mitzi Shore's (Pauly's mom) landmark venue.

The Best of the Comedy Store Room, which seats 400, features professional stand-ups continuously on Friday and Saturday nights. Several comedians are always featured, each doing about a 15-minute stint. The talent here is always first-rate, and includes comics who regularly appear on *The Tonight Show* and other shows.

or so comedians back-to-back nightly.
Sunday night is amateur night: Anyone with enough guts can take the stage for
3 minutes, so who knows what you'll get?

The Belly Room alternates between comedy stage and piano bar, with Wednesday night reserved for the "Gay and Lesbian Comedy Show."

○ Groundling Theater. 7307 Melrose Ave., Los Angeles. ☎ **213/934-9700.**

L.A.'s answer to Chicago's Second City has been around for over 20 years, yet
remains the most innovative and funniest group in town. Their collection of skits
changes every year or so, but they take new improvisational twists every night, and
the satire is often savage. In the current production, O.J. meets the Menendez brothers, and Universal CityWalk takes a hilarious beating. The Groundlings were the
springboard to fame for Pee-Wee Herman, Elvira, and former *Saturday Night Live*
stars Jon Lovitz, Phil Hartman, and Julia "It's Pat" Sweeney. Trust me—you haven't
laughed this hard in ages. Phone for show times and reservations.

Igby's Comedy Cabaret. 11637 W. Pico Blvd., West Los Angeles. ☎ **310/477-3553.**

Igby's is the best spot for comedy on the Westside. There's not a bad seat in the place.
The comics are well "stacked," so the night usually becomes racier the later it gets.
You can order from a full dinner menu during the show, as long as you don't mind
eating right under the comedian's nose.

The Improvisation. 8162 Melrose Ave., West Hollywood. ☎ **213/651-2583.**

A showcase for top stand-ups since 1975, the Improv offers something different
each night. The club's own television show, A&E's *Evening at the Improv,* is now
filmed at the Santa Monica location. Although there used to be a fairly active music schedule, the Improv is now mostly doing what it does best—showcasing
comedy. Owner Bud Freedman's buddies—like Jay Leno, Billy Crystal, and Robin
Williams—hone their skills here more often than you'd expect. But even if the
comedians on the bill the night you go are all unknowns, they won't be for long.
Shows are at 8pm on Thursday and Sunday, at 8:30 and 10:30pm on Friday and
Saturday.

THE OTHER BAR SCENE: L.A.'S TOP COFFEEHOUSES
by Steve Hochman

What cocaine was to disco, coffee is to grunge—not just the drug of choice, but the
fuel of the culture. Actually, it's just the latest application of the sacred bean to boho
lifestyle (imagine Maynard G. Krebs without access to a coffeehouse). Today, though,
coffee has gone beyond cliche and into ubiquitousness, with funky little coffeehouses
practically on every corner—in addition, of course, to the Starbucks that are overrunning the city.

L.A.'s romance with '90s coffee culture is hardly unique; every major urban city
in America is similarly enthralled. But a few of L.A.'s coffeehouses are distinctly
Angeleno in their funky characters, which basically range from seedy funky to arty
funky. They're definitely worth checking out if you're craving a half-caf cap non-fat
with a twist—and maybe some music or poetry to go with it.

The Abbey. 692 N. Robertson Blvd., West Hollywood. ☎ **310/289-8410.**

This coffeehouse in the heart of West Hollywood is really a cafe, offering full meals.
But it's also perhaps the best casual hangout in the heavily gay neighborhood, with

desserts galore. Lingering over an iced mocha on the patio with a few friends makes for a perfect evening time-waster.

Bourgeois Pig. 5931 Franklin Ave., Hollywood. ☎**213/962-6366.**

With a bit more of a bar atmosphere than the usual coffeehouse, this veteran, on a hot business strip at the Hollywood/Los Feliz border, is a youth and show-biz drone favorite. An added draw is the terrific newsstand next door.

Highland Grounds. 742 N. Highland Ave., Hollywood. ☎**213/466-1507.**

Pre-dating the coffeehouse explosion, this comfortable, relatively unpretentious place set the L.A. standard with a vast assortment of food and drink—not just coffee—and often first-rate live music, ranging from nationally known locals, such Victoria Williams, to open-mike Wednesdays for all-comers. The ample patio is often used for readings and record release parties.

Onyx/Sequel. 1804 N. Vermont Ave., Los Angeles. No phone.

These two cozy, adjacent rooms in the Los Feliz district offer generally friendly service, as well as a decent line-up of soup, sandwiches, and desserts to go with the beverages. Owner John has long supported local performers and visual artists, giving a home to spoken word and music nights that have drawn such luminaries as Ann Magnuson and Beck. But if you're looking for something fancy, go elsewhere. *Caveat:* The art on the walls generally tends toward the scary tortured-soul variety, which doesn't always sit well after a double espresso.

Equator. 22 Mills Place, Pasadena. ☎**818/564-8656.**

Airy and comfy, this brick room on a busy alleyway in the heart of resurgent Old Town Pasadena has withstood the challenge of a Starbucks that moved in a block away. The menu—with smoothies, soup, and desserts in addition to a wide variety of coffee drinks—and the friendly service keep people coming back. Even the post-Haring art on the walls gives a distinctive character, which has been used for scenes in such films and TV shows as "Beverly Hills, 90210" to *A Very Brady Sequel.*

(For complete coverage of Pasadena, see Chapter 15, "Side Trips from Los Angeles.")

LATE-NIGHT BITES

L.A. is no 24-hour town. Surprisingly, the city has only about a dozen bonafide restaurants that are open after hours; even fewer serve all night.

If you want a serious meal after 2am, head for one of the following places, all of which are open 24 hours: **Pacific Dining Car,** 1310 W. 6th St., at Witmer Street, downtown (☎ 213/483-6000), is the place for a well-marbled, patiently aged New York steak any time of day or night. For Westsiders, there's a Santa Monica location at 2700 Wilshire Blvd., a block east of 26th Street (☎ 310/453-4000). **The Original Pantry Cafe,** 877 S. Figueroa St., at 9th Street downtown (☎ 213/972-9279), has been serving huge portions of comfort food around the clock for more than 60 years; in fact, they don't even have a key to the front door. **Jerry's Famous Deli,** 12655 Ventura Blvd., at Coldwater Canyon Avenue, Studio City (☎ 818/980-4245), is where Valley hipsters go to relieve their late-night munchies.

Kate Mantilini, 9101 Wilshire Blvd., at Doheny Drive, Beverly Hills (☎ 310/278-3699), serves up stylish fare until 1am most weeknights, and to 3am on weekends. **Du-par's Coffee Shop,** 12036 Ventura Blvd., a block east of Laurel Canyon, Studio City (☎ 818/766-4437), only serves its blue-plate specials till 1am on weeknights; however, come the weekend, they're slingin' hash until 4am.

In addition to the restaurants mentioned above (see "Dining," earlier in this chapter, for details on each), another late-night option is **Canter's Fairfax Restaurant, Delicatessen & Bakery,** 419 N. Fairfax Ave. (☎ **213/651-2030**), a Jewish deli that's been a hit with late-nighters since it opened more than 65 years ago. If you show up after the clubs close, you're sure to spot a bleary-eyed celebrity or two alongside the rest of the after-hours crowd, chowing down on a giant pastrami sandwich, matzoh-ball soup, potato pancakes, or another deli favorite. Try a potato knish with a side of brown gravy—trust me, you'll love it.

Side Trips from Los Angeles

by Stephanie Avnet

The area within a 100-mile radius of Los Angeles is one of the most diverse regions in the world: There are arid deserts, rugged mountains, industrial cities, historic towns, alpine lakes, rolling hillsides, and sophisticated seaside resorts. You'll also find an offshore island that's been transformed into the ultimate city-dweller's hideaway, not to mention the Happiest Place on Earth.

1 Pasadena & Environs

11 miles NE of Los Angeles

Pasadena is part of the greater Los Angeles area, but this community is so far removed from the rest of the city, both physically and in spirit, that we think of it as a side trip.

Founded by midwesterners fleeing the cold winter of 1873, by the turn of the 20th century Pasadena had grown into a warm resort destination nestled among the orange groves. The tear-down epidemic that swept Los Angeles mercifully passed over Pasadena, allowing the city a refreshing old-time feel. Historic homes along tree-lined streets coexist with a revitalized downtown respectful of its old brick and stone commercial buildings.

Angelenos flock here to shop and dine, enjoying the opportunity to stroll a compact, manageable downtown area. Best known to the world as the site of the Tournament of Roses Parade each New Year's Day, Pasadena is also home to the California Institute of Technology. Caltech's scientists are the first to report earthquake activity worldwide. In addition, the school boasts 22 Nobel Prize winners among its alumni, and the Caltech-operated Jet Propulsion Laboratory is the birthplace of America's space program. Pasadena offers a richly diverse arts and entertainment scene, and is a favorite location for feature films and TV.

ESSENTIALS

GETTING THERE   If you're flying to L.A. and are planning to make Pasadena or another San Fernando or San Gabriel Valley town your base, see if you can land at the quiet, convenient **Burbank-Glendale-Pasadena Airport,** 2627 N. Hollywood Way, Burbank (☎ **818/840-8840**). See Section 1 in Chapter 14 for more airport and airline information.

California's first freeway, the 6-mile Arroyo Seco Parkway, opened in 1940, linking downtown Los Angeles and Pasadena. It later

Pasadena

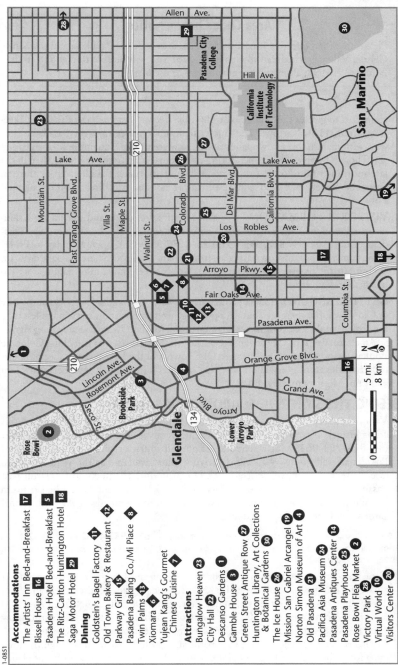

Accommodations
The Artists' Inn Bed-and-Breakfast **17**
Bissell House **16**
Pasadena Hotel Bed-and-Breakfast **5**
The Ritz-Carlton Huntington Hotel **18**
Saga Motor Hotel **29**

Dining
Goldstein's Bagel Factory **11**
Old Town Bakery & Restaurant **12**
Parkway Grill **15**
Pasadena Baking Co./Mi Piace **13**
Twin Palms **8**
Xiomara **6**
Yujean Kang's Gourmet
Chinese Cuisine **7**

Attractions
Bungalow Heaven **23**
City Hall **22**
Descanso Gardens **1**
Gamble House **3**
Green Street Antique Row **27**
Huntington Library, Art Collections
& Botanical Gardens **30**
The Ice House **26**
Mission San Gabriel Arcangel **19**
Norton Simon Museum of Art **4**
Old Pasadena **21**
Pacifica Asia Museum **24**
Pasadena Antiques Center **14**
Pasadena Playhouse **25**
Rose Bowl Flea Market **2**
Victory Park **28**
Virtual World **10**
Visitors Center **20**

1-0851

Area Code Change Notice

Please note that, effective June 14, 1997, the area code for Pasadena and the San Gabriel Valley is scheduled to change to **626**. You will be able to dial 818 until January 17, 1998, after which you will have to use 626.

---

connected to greater L.A.'s planned 1,500-mile freeway system as the **Pasadena Freeway (Calif. 110).** Narrower and curvier than modern freeways, the Pasadena Freeway, with its lush, overgrown landscaping, now seems like a quaint relic of an earlier era. Though bumper-to-bumper during rush hours, it's refreshingly traffic-free in the late morning and a lot of fun to drive. If you approach Pasadena from the San Fernando Valley, take the Calif. 134 Freeway east and exit directly onto Colorado Boulevard.

VISITOR INFORMATION   For a free destination guide and information, contact the **Pasadena Convention and Visitors Bureau,** 171 S. Los Robles Ave., Pasadena, CA 91101 (☎ 818/795-9311; fax 818/795-9656), open Monday to Friday from 8am to 5pm and on Saturday from 10am to 4pm. There's also a city-run Website **(http://www.ci.pasadena.ca.us),** which offers tourist information as well as business and government listings.

GETTING AROUND   Street parking can be scarce around the few blocks at the core of Old Town, but there are abundant public garages with friendly rates (often less than the change you'd feed your meter anyway). Look for the *Old Pasadena parking* signs.

An alternative is to take advantage of the free **Arts Buses** that run along Colorado Boulevard and Green Street through Old Town and the Lake Avenue shopping district. Shuttles come every 20 minutes (12 minutes during lunchtime) between 11am and 8pm Monday to Saturday.

SEEING THE SIGHTS IN & AROUND PASADENA

Various tours spotlighting architecture or neighborhoods are lots of fun, given this area's history of wealthy estates and ardent preservation. Call **Pasadena Heritage** (☎ 818/793-0617) for a schedule of guided tours, or pick up "Ten Tours of Pasadena," self-guided walking or driving maps available at the visitors bureau (see "Essentials," above). For a quick but profound architectural fix, stroll past Pasadena's grandiose and baroque **City Hall,** 100 N. Garfield Ave., 2 blocks north of Colorado; closer inspection will reveal its classical colonnaded courtyard, formal gardens, and spectacular tiled dome.

Descanso Gardens. 1418 Descanso Dr., La Cañada. ☎ 818/952-4402 or 818/952-4401. Admission $5 adults, $3 students and seniors 62 and over, $1 children 5–12, free for kids 4 and under. Daily 9am–4:30pm.

Camellias—evergreen flowering shrubs from China and Japan—were the passion of amateur gardener E. Manchester Boddy, who began planting them here in 1941. Today his Descanso Gardens contains more than 100,000 camellias in over 600 varieties, blooming under a 30-acre canopy of California oak trees. The shrubs now share the limelight with a 5-acre Rose Garden, home to hundreds of varieties.

This is really a magical place, with paths and streams that wind through the towering forest, bordering a lake and bird sanctuary. Each season features different plants: daffodils, azaleas, tulips, and lilacs in the spring; chrysanthemums in the fall; and so on. Monthly art exhibits are held in the garden's hospitality house.

There's also a beautifully landscaped Japanese-style teahouse which serves tea and cookies on Saturday and Sunday from 11am to 4pm. Free docent-guided walking tours are offered every Sunday at 1pm; guided tram tours, which cost $1.50, run Tuesday to Friday at 1, 2, and 3pm, and on Saturday and Sunday at 11am and 1, 2, and 3pm. Picnicking is allowed in specified areas.

○ **Gamble House.** 4 Westmoreland Place, Pasadena. ☎ **818/793-3334.** Admission $5 adults, $4 seniors, $3 students, free for children 11 and under. House tours, Thurs–Sun noon–3pm; bookshop, Tues–Sat 10am–4:30pm, Sun 11:30am–4:30pm. Closed holidays.

The huge two-story Gamble House, built in 1908 as a California vacation home for the wealthy family of Procter and Gamble fame, is a sublime example of Arts and Crafts architecture. Designed by the famous Pasadena-based Greene and Greene architectural team, the interior abounds with handcraftsmanship, including intricately carved teak cornices, custom-designed furnishings, elaborate carpets, and a fantastic Tiffany glass door. No detail was overlooked. Every oak wedge, downspout, air vent, and switchplate contributes to the unified design. Admission is by 1-hour guided tour only, which departs every 15 minutes. No reservations are necessary.

If you can't fit the tour into your schedule, but have a love of Craftsman design, visit the well-stocked bookstore and gift shop located in the former garage (you can also see the exterior and grounds of the house this way).

○ **Huntington Library, Art Collections, and Botanical Gardens.** 1151 Oxford Rd., San Marino. ☎ **818/405-2141.** Admission $7.50 adults, $6 seniors 65 and over, $4 students and children 12 and older. Tues–Fri noon–4:30pm, Sat–Sun 10:30am–4:30pm. Closed major holidays.

The Huntington Library is the jewel in Pasadena's crown. The 207-acre hilltop estate was once home to industrialist and railroad magnate Henry E. Huntington (1850–1927), who bought books on the same massive scale that he acquired businesses. The continually expanding collection includes dozens of Shakespeare's original works, Benjamin Franklin's handwritten autobiography, a Gutenberg Bible from the 1450s, and the earliest known manuscript of Chaucer's *Canterbury Tales.* Although some rarer works are only available to visiting scholars, the library has a regularly changing (and always excellent) exhibit showcasing different items in the collection.

If you prefer canvas to parchment, Huntington also put together a terrific 18th-century British and French art collection. His most celebrated paintings are Gainsborough's *The Blue Boy,* and *Pinkie,* a companion piece by Sir Thomas Lawrence depicting the youthful aunt of Elizabeth Barrett Browning. These and other works are displayed in the stately Italianate mansion on the crest of this hillside estate, so you can also get a glimpse of its splendid furnishings.

But it's the botanical gardens that draw most locals to the Huntington. The Japanese Garden is complete with traditional open-air Japanese house, koi-filled stream, and serene Zen garden; the cactus garden is exotic, the jungle garden intriguing, the lily ponds soothing—and there are plentiful benches scattered about encouraging you to sit and enjoy.

Because the Huntington surprises many with its size and the wealth of activities to choose from, first-timers might want to start by attending one of the regularly scheduled 12-minute introductory slide shows; or take the more in-depth 1-hour garden tour, given each day at 1pm.

We also recommend that you tailor your visit to include the popular English high tea served Tuesday to Sunday from 1:30 to 3:30pm. The charming tearoom overlooks the Rose Garden (home to 1,000 varieties displayed in chronological order of their breeding), and since the finger sandwiches and desserts are served buffet style, it's a genteel bargain (even for hearty appetites) at $11 per person. Phone 818/683-8131 for reservations.

Mission San Gabriel Arcangel. 537 W. Mission Dr., San Gabriel. ☎ **818/457-3035.** Admission $3 adults, $1 children 6–12 years, free for kids 5 and under. June–Sept, daily 10am–5:30pm; Oct–May, daily 9am–4:30pm. Closed holidays.

Founded in 1771, Mission San Gabriel Arcangel still retains its original facade, notable for its high oblong windows and large capped buttresses that are said to have been influenced by the cathedral in Cordova, Spain. The mission's self-contained compound encompasses an aqueduct, a cemetery, a tannery, and a working winery. In the church stands a copper font with the dubious distinction of being the first one used to baptize a Native Californian. The most notable contents of the mission's museum are Native American paintings depicting the Stations of the Cross, painted on sailcloth, with colors made from crushed desert flower petals. The mission is about 15 minutes south of Pasadena.

✪ Norton Simon Museum of Art. 411 Colorado Blvd., Pasadena. ☎ **818/449-6840.** Admission $4 adults, $2 students and seniors, free for children 11 and under. Museum, Thurs–Sun noon–6pm; bookshop, Thurs–Sun noon–5:30pm.

Named for a food-packing king and financier who reorganized the failing Pasadena Museum of Modern Art, the Norton Simon Museum has become one of California's most important museums. Comprehensive collections of masterpieces by Degas, Picasso, Rembrandt, and Goya are augmented by sculptures by Henry Moore and Auguste Rodin, including *The Burghers of Calais,* which greets you at the gates. The "Blue Four" collection of works by Kandinsky, Jawlensky, Klee, and Feininger is particularly impressive, as is a superb collection of Southeast Asian sculpture. *Still Life with Lemons, Oranges, and a Rose* (1633), an oil by Francisco de Zurbarán, is one of the museum's most important holdings. One of the most popular pieces is Mexican artist Diego Rivera's *The Flower Vendor / Girl with Lilies.*

Pacific Asia Museum. 46 N. Los Robles Ave., Pasadena. ☎ **818/449-2742.** Admission $3, free for children 11 and under, free for everyone on the third Sat of each month. Wed–Sun 10am–5pm.

The most striking aspect of this museum is the building itself. Designed in the 1920s in Chinese Imperial Palace style, it's rivaled in flamboyance only by Mann's Chinese Theatre in Hollywood (see Chapter 15). Rotating exhibits of Asian art span the centuries, from 100 B.C. to the current day. This manageably sized museum is usually worth a peek.

Virtual World. In the One Colorado Mall, 35 Hugus Alley (Colorado and Fair Oaks blvds.), Pasadena. ☎ **818/577-9896.** Admission $7 Mon–Fri before 5pm, $8 after 5pm; $9 Sat–Sun. Mon–Fri 10am–9pm, Sat–Sun 10am–8pm.

This is the ultimate "easy side trip" from Los Angeles. Several different adventures are offered at the world's first virtual-reality play center, including a run through the mining tunnels of Mars in the year 2053 and a jousting tournament on the fictitious desert planet Solaris VII. Many of the virtual worlds are set up like intergalactic war games, where you don heavy helmets and try to "neutralize" your friends. After the VR adventure, you can review your game from various angles on videotape.

SHOPPING

Pretty, compact Pasadena lends itself perfectly to many travelers' Number 1 pastime: shopping. The city's recent renovation efforts have focused unabashedly on creating an alternative to L.A.'s behemoth shopping malls, so Pasadena's streets are a true pleasure to stroll. As a general rule, stores are open 7 days a week from about 10am, and, while some close at the standard 5 or 6 o'clock, many stay open till 8 or 9pm to accommodate the before- and after-dinner/movie crowd.

OLD PASADENA   The focus of consumerism is along Colorado Boulevard between Pasadena Avenue and Arroyo Parkway, where you'll see the ongoing regentrification of a once-dingy downtown. It's known as **Old Pasadena,** and some old-time residents hate it as much as the scores of visitors love it. In our opinion it's one of the best parts about the L.A. area, but we hope they retain more of the mom-and-pop businesses currently being pushed out by the likes of Banana Republic, Urban Outfitters, Crate & Barrel, J. Crew, Victoria's Secret, Barnes & Noble, and Armani Exchange. As you move eastward, however, the mix does begin to include more eclectic shops and galleries comingling with dusty, pre-yuppie relics.

   Penny Lane, 12 W. Colorado Blvd. (☎ **818/564-0161**), a new and used CD store, also has a great selection of music magazines and kitschy postcards. The selection is less picked-over here than at many record stores in Hollywood. Around the corner at **Rebecca's Dream,** 16 S. Fair Oaks Ave. (☎ **818/796-1200**), men and women can both find vintage clothing treasures in this small and meticulously organized (by color scheme) store. Be sure to look up; vintage hats adorn the walls. Around the corner is the **Del Mano** gallery of contemporary crafts, 33 E. Colorado Blvd. (☎ **818/793-6648**), and it's a whole lot of fun to see the creations—some whimsical, some exquisite—of American artists working with glass, wood, ceramics, or jewelry.

   Even if you don't stop in, have a look at **Crown City Loan & Jewelry,** on the corner of Colorado and Raymond, a pawn shop that survived regentrification as musty as ever! Its haphazard window display (wooden elephant carvings, assorted wristwatches, an old accordion) thumbs its nose at the order all around. Farther down is **Tournament Souvenirs,** 88 E. Colorado Blvd. (☎ **808/395-7066**), which is exactly as it sounds: Rose Parade and Rose Bowl clothing, hats, pennants, glassware, and sports sippers for anyone visiting during the 51 *other* weeks of the year. Around the corner is a duo of related stores, **Distant Lands Bookstore and Outfitters,** 54 and 62 S. Raymond Ave. (☎ **818/449-3220**). The bookstore has a terrific selection of maps, guides, and travel-related literature, while the recently opened outfitters two doors away offers everything from luggage and pith helmets to space-saving and convenient travel accessories.

TAKING A BREAK   Serious shopping requires occasional periods of rest and refreshment, and there's no place better than one of Pasadena's many, many coffee cafes. In addition to the ubiquitous **Starbucks,** 117 W. Colorado Blvd. (☎818/577-4622), there's sleek, spacious **Espresso Cabaret,** 17 E. Colorado Blvd. (☎ **818/584-6505**), and the outdoor patio at **Micah's,** 88 N. Fair Oaks at Holly (☎ 818/795-9733). But our favorite is **Chatz of Pasadena,** 53 E. Union St. (☎ 818/584-9110), tucked away 1 block north of busy Colorado Boulevard. It's cozy and friendly, the kind of place that runs out of the best muffins early but never takes down old flyers from the cluttered bulletin board on the wall by the door.

OTHER SHOPPING VENUES   In addition to Old Town Pasadena, there are numerous good hunting grounds in the surrounding area. For example, antique hounds might want to head to the **Green Street Antique Row,** 985 to 1005 E. Green St., east of Lake Avenue, or the **Pasadena Antique Center,** on South Fair Oaks Boulevard south of Del Mar. Each has a rich concentration of collectibles dealers and can captivate browsers for hours.

You never know what you'll find at the **Rose Bowl Flea Market,** at the Rose Bowl, 991 Rosemont Ave., Pasadena (☎ **818/577-3100**). Built in 1922, the horseshoe-shaped Rose Bowl is one of the world's most famous stadiums, home to UCLA's football Bruins, the annual Rose Bowl Game, and an occasional Super Bowl. California's largest monthly swap meet, on the second Sunday of every month from 9am to 3pm, is a favorite of Los Angeles antique hounds (who know to arrive as early as 6:30am for the best finds). Antique furnishings, clothing, jewelry, and other collectibles are assembled in the parking area to the left of the entrance, while the rest of the flea market surrounds the exterior of the Bowl. Here, look for everything from used surf-boards and car stereos to one-of-a-kind lawn statuary and bargain athletic shoes. Admission is $5.

Book lovers will want to prowl through the rare and out-of-print treasures at **The Browser's Bookshop,** 659 E. Colorado Blvd., at El Molino (☎ **818/585-8308**), or its dusty neighbor **House of Fiction,** 663 E. Colorado Blvd. (☎ **818/449-9861**). For a world-class selection of big band, swing, pop vocalist, soundtracks, and other non–rock 'n' roll CDs, don't miss **Canterbury Records,** 805 E. Colorado Blvd., at Hudson (☎ **818/792-7184**).

Anglophiles will delight in the **Rose Tree Cottage,** 824 E. California Blvd., just west of Lake Avenue (☎ **818/793-3337**), and its charming array of all things British. This cluster of historic Tudor cottages surrounded by traditional English gardens holds three gift shops and a tearoom, where a superb $19.50 high tea is served thrice daily among the knickknacks (and supervised by the resident cat, Miss Moffett). In addition to imported teas, linens, and silver trinkets, the Rose Tree Cottage sells homemade English delicacies like steak-and-kidney pies, hot cross buns, and shortbread. It is also the local representative of the British Tourist Authority and offers a comprehensive array of travel publications.

WHERE TO STAY

In the listings below, parking is free unless otherwise noted.

EXPENSIVE

✪ **Ritz-Carlton Huntington Hotel.** 1401 S. Oak Knoll Ave. (west of Elliott), Pasadena, CA 91109. ☎ **800/241-3333** or 818/568-3900. Fax 818/568-3700. 355 rms, 22 suites, 6 cottages. A/C MINIBAR TV TEL. $145–$240 double; from $350 suite. AE, DC, MC, V. Parking $12.

Built in 1906 and still one of America's grandest hotels, the Spanish-Mediterranean Huntington gained popularity early on among celebrated writers, entertainers, political and business leaders, even royalty. Set on 23 meticulously landscaped acres, it seems a world apart from downtown Los Angeles, though it's only about 20 minutes away. Closed for 6 years after a particularly destructive earthquake, the hotel reopened in 1991 as a full replica of itself under the Ritz-Carlton banner. Each oversize guest room is dressed in conservatively elegant Ritz-Carlton style, with marble baths, thick carpets, terry robes, and the like. Behind the hotel is a bucolic Japanese garden that's great for strolling.

Dining/Entertainment: Locals of senior-citizen status love to celebrate in the Georgian Room, where continental meals are prepared by a classically trained French chef. The less formal Grill serves traditional fare in a comfortable clublike setting. The Cafe serves all day, either indoors or out; it's best on Sunday, for champagne brunch. High tea is served daily in the Lobby Lounge.

Services: Concierge, room service (24 hours), nightly turndown, baby-sitting.

Facilities: Olympic-size heated outdoor pool, small exercise room, outdoor Jacuzzi, sundeck, three lighted tennis courts, car-rental desk, mountain bike rental, pro shop, full-service spa/salon, shopping promenade.

MODERATE

The Artists' Inn Bed-and-Breakfast. 1038 Magnolia St., South Pasadena, CA 91030. ☎ and fax **818/799-5668.** 5 rms. A/C. $100–$120 double. Rates include full breakfast. Additional person $20 extra. AE, MC, V.

This Victorian-style inn, an unpretentious yellow-shingled home pleasantly furnished with wicker throughout, was built in 1895 as a farmhouse. Each of the five rooms is thematically decorated to reflect the style of a particular artist or period, including Impressionist, Fauve, and Van Gogh. The English Room, fitted with good-quality antique furnishings and cheerful rose-patterned wallpaper, is the best room in the house; it's also the only one with a king-size bed. The Italian Suite has a queen-size bed and an adjoining sun room with twin beds, a perfect choice for families. The inn is on a quiet residential street 5 minutes from the heart of downtown.

Bissell House. 201 Orange Grove Ave. (at Columbia St.), South Pasadena, CA 91030. ☎ **818/441-3535.** 4 rms. A/C. $100–$150 double. Rates include full breakfast on weekends, expanded continental breakfast weekdays, plus afternoon snacks and all-day beverages. AE, MC, V.

Hidden behind tall hedges that carefully isolate it from busy Orange Grove Avenue, this 1887 gingerbread Victorian is furnished with antiques and offers a delightful taste of life on what was once Pasadena's "Millionaire's Row." All rooms have private bath with both shower and tub (one an antique clawfoot, one a private whirlpool). There's a swimming pool and Jacuzzi on the beautifully landscaped grounds, and a downstairs library offers telephone and fax machine for guests' use.

INEXPENSIVE

Pasadena Hotel Bed & Breakfast. 76 N. Fair Oaks Ave. (between Union and Holly sts.), Pasadena, CA 91103. ☎ **800/653-8886** or 818/568-8172. Fax 818/793-6409. 10 rms, 1 with half-bath. A/C TV TEL. $65–$165 double. Rates include continental breakfast. AE, MC, V. Parking $5.

This old-style hostelry is definitely not for everyone. In true turn-of-the-century rooming-house style, the guest rooms all have washbasins but all but one must share hallway bathrooms (three full, two half). Part of the attraction here is the well-restored National Historic Register building, and part is the hotel's flawless location: It's the only accommodation *literally* in the heart of Old Pasadena. The guest quarters are small but comfortable, and all are second-story exterior rooms. The central sitting room/lounge is elegant and welcoming, and there's a lively coffeehouse in the courtyard behind the hotel where you can enjoy your breakfast and complimentary afternoon teas. Shuttle buses to the Rose Bowl depart 1 block away during major events.

Saga Motor Hotel. 1633 E. Colorado Blvd. (between Allen and Sierra Bonita aves.), Pasadena, CA 91106. ☎ **818/795-0431.** 69 rms, 1 suite. A/C TV TEL. $62–$69 double; $75 suite. Rates include continental breakfast. AE, CB, DC, MC, V.

This motel is a 1950s relic of old Route 66, a little bland by modern standards but with far more character than most others in its price range. The rooms are small, clean, and simply furnished with just the basics. The best rooms are in the front building surrounding the gated swimming pool, which is shielded from the street and inviting in warm weather. The grounds are attractive and surprisingly well kept, if you don't count the Astroturf "lawn" around the pool. The motel is about a mile from the Huntington Library and within 10 minutes of both the Rose Bowl and Old Pasadena.

WHERE TO DINE

During the past decade or so, Pasadena has grown into one of the premier dining destinations for Angelenos in the know. Superstar chefs have fled the super-competitive Westside restaurant scene to shine in this friendly suburb. As a result, there are many excellent and affordable eateries, plus a profusion of coffeehouses and casual bakery/cafes. Remember, this isn't really out-of-town, and no one thinks twice about hopping the freeway for dinner and a movie.

EXPENSIVE

Parkway Grill. 510 S. Arroyo Pkwy. (at California Blvd.), Pasadena. ☎ **818/795-1001.** Reservations recommended. Main courses $8–$23. AE, CB, DC, MC, V. Mon–Thurs 11:30am–2:30pm and 5:30–11pm, Fri 11:30am–2:30pm and 5pm–midnight, Sat 5pm–midnight, Sun 10am–2pm and 5–11pm. CALIFORNIA ECLECTIC.

This quintessentially Southern California restaurant has been one of the L.A. area's top-rated spots since it opened in 1985, quickly gaining a reputation for avant-garde flavor combinations and gourmet pizzas to rival Spago's. Although some critics find many of chef Hugo Molina's dishes too fussy, others thrill to appetizer innovations like lobster-stuffed cocoa crêpes or Dungeness crab cakes with ginger cream and two salsas. The stars of the menu are meat and game from the iron mesquite grill, followed by richly sweet (and substantial) desserts. The interior is vibrantly colored and architecturally, well, eclectic, for the building once knew life as a transmission shop! Located where the old Arroyo Seco Parkway glides into an ordinary city street, the Parkway Grill is within a couple of minutes' drive from Old Pasadena and thoughtfully offers free valet parking.

✪ Xiomara. 69 N. Raymond Ave. (1 block north of Colorado Blvd.), Pasadena. ☎ **818/796-2520.** Reservations recommended. Main courses $18–$23; fixed-price menu $25. AE, MC, V. Mon–Fri 11:30am–2:30pm and 5:30–10:30pm, Sat 5:30–10:30pm, Sun 5–10:30pm. COUNTRY FRENCH.

By any other name, Xiomara (pronounced "*See*-o-ma-ra") would still be one of the top restaurants in Los Angeles, despite the fact that it has never made Zagat's "top rated" list. Chef Patrick Healy's best dishes are rustic country concoctions like sausage-laden cassoulet, and veal shanks braised so long the meat practically falls off the bone. Chicken is simmered for an eternity in a sealed cast-iron pot with artichokes and carrots. The nightly fixed-price meal, a three-course menu determined by the chef's mood and the fresh ingredients at hand, is a remarkably good value. A long list of obscure country wines complements the menu. The dining room, a sleek black bistro setting, is as pleasing as the food, fitted with comfortable armchairs and presided over by the enthusiastic Xiomara herself. An oyster and clam bar features oyster shooters, ceviche, and a large selection of raw oysters and clams on the half shell.

MODERATE

❸ Twin Palms. 101 W. Green St. (at Delacey Ave.), Pasadena. ☎ **818/577-2567.** Reservations recommended on weekends. Main courses $9–$17. AE, CB, DC, MC, V. Mon–Thurs 11:30am–midnight, Fri–Sat 11:30am–1:30am, Sun 10:30am–midnight. MEDITERRANEAN/FRENCH.

Twin Palms is able to seat nearly 400 at spacious tables (no postage-stamp two-seaters here!) shaded by the fronds of 100-year-old palm trees. It's also busy, having become a hit with recession-weary Angelenos who come here for some of the best-value meals in the entire L.A. area. The quasi-outdoor and tented space creates a festival atmosphere, augmented by two lively bars and a bandstand with entertainment every night except Monday. Or come on Sunday until 1:30pm for the "Gospel Brunch," during which Twin Palms also offers alternative entertainment for children. Co-owner/chef Michael Roberts is as well known for his celebrity backers (including Kevin Costner) as he is for the French "comfort food" he created as a backlash against pricey haute cuisine. Everyone talks about the salt cod mashed potato brandade, a delicious appetizer that's big enough to serve four—for only $5. The best main courses come off the crackling rotisserie and outdoor grill; they include juicy, roasted sage-infused pork and honey-glazed coriander-scented duck. Sautéed dishes and salads are not as successful. A number of exciting wines are priced well, under $20.

Yujean Kang's Gourmet Chinese Cuisine. 67 N. Raymond Ave. (between Walnut St. and Colorado Blvd.), Pasadena. ☎ **818/585-0855.** Reservations recommended. Main courses $14–$21. AE, MC, V. Daily 11:30am–2:30pm and 5–10pm. CHINESE CONTEMPORARY.

Many Chinese restaurants put the word "gourmet" in their name, but few really mean—or deserve—it. Not so at Yujean Kang's, where Chinese cuisine is taken to an entirely new level. A master of "fusion" cuisine, the eponymous chef/owner snatches bits of techniques and flavors from both China and the West, comingling them in an entirely fresh way. Can you resist such provocative dishes as "Ants on Tree" (beef sauteed with glass noodles in chili and black sesame seeds) or lobster with caviar and fava beans, or Chilean sea bass in passionfruit sauce? Kang is a wine aficionado and has assembled a magnificent cellar of California, French, and particularly German wines. Try pairing a German Spätlese with tea-smoked duck salad. The red-wrapped dining room is less subtle than the food, but just as elegant.

INEXPENSIVE

Goldstein's Bagel Bakery. 86 W. Colorado Blvd. (at Delacey Ave.), Old Pasadena. ☎ **818/79-BAGEL.** Most items under $3. AE, MC, V. Sun–Thurs 6am–9pm, Fri–Sat 6am–10:30pm. BAKERY/DELI.

Join the locals who storm Goldstein's each morning for freshly baked (in the authentic New York style, they'll assure you) bagels—the reliable plain and onion are as good as exotic honey oat raisin or banana nut. In addition to six flavored cream cheeses, you can choose a bagel sandwich prepared with your choice of every deli ingredient under the sun. Centrally located in the heart of Old Pasadena, this is a good choice for snacks and light meals without interrupting the rhythm of your day.

Old Town Bakery & Restaurant. 166 W. Colorado Blvd. (at Pasadena Ave.), Pasadena. ☎ **818/792-7943.** Main courses $5–$11. DISC, MC, V. Sun–Thurs 7:30am–10pm, Fri–Sat 7:30am–midnight. CONTINENTAL.

Set back from the street in a quaint fountain courtyard, this cheery bakery is an especially popular place to read the morning paper over one of their tasty breakfasts like pumpkin pancakes or zesty omelets. The display counters are packed with cakes, muffins, scones, and other confections, all baked expressly for this shop. The rest of the menu is a mishmash of pastas, salads, and the like, borrowing heavily from Latin and Mediterranean cuisines. The Old Town Bakery is a great place to spy on local Pasadenans in their natural habitat.

Pasadena Baking Company / Mi Piace. 25–29 E. Colorado Blvd. (east of Fair Oaks Ave.), Old Pasadena. ☎ **818/796-9966** or 818/795-3131. Main courses $6–$15; bakery items under $3. AE, MC, V. Mon–Thurs 7am–11pm, Fri 7am–midnight, Sat 8am–midnight, Sun 8am–11pm. BAKERY/ITALIAN CAFE.

This little cafe holds just a handful of small tables, which spill out onto the sidewalk during nice weather (which is to say 90% of the time). The particularly large—and sweet-smelling—selection of fresh pastries, tarts, truffles, cakes, and candies are all proudly displayed. There's also an assortment of fresh breads and a fresh-fruit stand to accompany the breakfast and lunch menu.

Mi Piace is the adjoining casual trattoria, offering the usual pastas and northern Italian dishes done unusually well. The Baking Company commandeers the sidewalk tables during breakfast, but starting around 11:30am it's not unusual to see Pasadena locals enjoying an espresso with their dogs tethered to a table leg!

PASADENA AFTER DARK

Espresso Bar. 1039 E. Green St. (near Catalina). ☎ **818/577-9113.**

This simply named coffeehouse has been around so long that it almost seems as though Pasadena grew up around it. It was formerly hidden down a hard-to-find alleyway, but its new location is on Green Street's Antique Row—outside Old Town but close to Pasadena City College. Open-mike nights are popular with beat poets and singers, and bands play on Friday and Saturday nights to an eclectic crowd lounging on the hodgepodge of dingy furniture typical of Espresso Bar's Greenwich Village ambience. There's a spacious upstairs loft, and a beverage menu with some exotic entries like steamed milk with molasses. Coffee drinks and baked goodies run $1 to $4. No credit cards. Open Monday to Thursday from 9am to 1am, Friday and Saturday from 9am to 2am, and on Sunday from noon to midnight.

Gordon Biersch Brewery & Restaurant. In the One Colorado Mall, 41 Hugus Alley (between Colorado and Fair Oaks blvds.). ☎ **818/449-0052** or 818/449-0067.

The Pasadena branch of the Northern California chain is one of the most successful brewpubs in Southern California. The wood-and-brick interior is large and noisy, and the food woefully uneven, but the house Pilsner and dark Bavarian-style brews are great and the atmosphere upbeat. Go for drinks and an appetizer, then head to a real restaurant for dinner. Open Sunday to Wednesday from 11am to midnight and Thursday to Saturday from 11am to 1am.

The Ice House. 24 N. Mentor Ave. ☎ **818/577-1894,** or 818/577-9133 for the Annex.

Pasadena's best-known comedy and music club since 1960 claims to have launched the careers of Robin Williams, Steve Martin, David Letterman, and Lily Tomlin, among others. There are usually three acts nightly, with two shows on Friday and three shows on Saturday. The Ice House Annex presents blues, improvisational theater, and intimate performance art shows. Phone for the latest.

The Muse. 54 E. Colorado Blvd. (near Fair Oaks Blvd.), Pasadena. ☎ **818/588-1030.**

This nightclub in the core of Old Town will draw you in with its wild, Gaudí-esque bar furniture and decor—kind of like Toontown for the 21-and-over crowd (but generally not *too* much over!). In back are some pool tables, and there's dancing till 2am on Friday and Saturday.

Pasadena Playhouse. 35 S. El Molino Ave. (near Colorado Blvd.). ☎ **818/356-7529.**

One of the most highly acclaimed professional theaters in L.A., the Pasadena Playhouse was founded in 1917, is a registered historic landmark, and has served as the training ground for many theatrical, film, and television stars, including William Holden and Gene Hackman. Productions are staged both on the main theater's elaborate Spanish Colonial Revival stage and in a smaller theater on the second floor. Call to find out what's on.

2 Long Beach & the *Queen Mary*

21 Miles S of downtown L.A.

The fifth-largest incorporated city in California, Long Beach consists mostly of business and industrial areas interspersed with unremarkable neighborhoods. The city is best known as the permanent home of the former cruise liner *Queen Mary* (see "The *Queen Mary* & Other Port Attractions" and "Where to Stay," below) and for the annual Long Beach Grand Prix in mid-April, whose star-studded warm-up race sends the likes of young hipster Jason Priestly (*Beverly Hills, 90210*) and perennial racer Paul

Newman burning rubber through the streets of the city. Although Long Beach is too far away to be considered part of Los Angeles as a tourist destination, and it's not as attractive as most of the smaller coastal communities to either the north or south, the *Queen Mary* makes a trip here worthwhile.

ESSENTIALS

GETTING THERE   See Section 1 in Chapter 14 for airport and airline information. When driving from Los Angeles on either I-5 or I-405, take I-710 south; it follows the Los Angeles River on its path to the ocean and leads directly to both downtown Long Beach and the *Queen Mary* Seaport.

ORIENTATION   Most of seaside Long Beach is in vast San Pedro Harbor, L.A.'s busy industrial port. Terminal Island sits right in the middle. To the west across the pretty Vincent Thomas Bridge is the city of San Pedro, home to the nautical and touristy **Ports O' Call Village.** The *Queen Mary* is docked near the eastern end of Long Beach, looking over the actual "long beach" extending along peaceful, affluent Belmont Shore to tiny Long Beach Marina, home to charming Naples Island (see "The *Queen Mary* & Other Port Attractions," below).

VISITOR INFORMATION   Contact the **Long Beach Area Convention & Visitors Bureau**, One World Trade Center, Suite 300 (☎ **800/4LB-STAY** or 562/436-3645). There's a city-run Website at **http://www.ci.long-beach.ca.us,** which offers, in addition to business and government information, a section with tourism listings. For further information on the **Long Beach Grand Prix** call 562/981-2600 or visit their Website at **http://www.longbeachgp.com.**

THE *QUEEN MARY* & OTHER PORT ATTRACTIONS

Queen Mary. Pier J (at the end of I-710), Long Beach. ☎ **562/435-3511.** Admission $10 adults, $8 seniors 55 and over and military, $6 children 4–11, free for kids 3 and under. Daily 10am–6pm (last entry at 5:30pm), with extended summer hours. Charge for parking.

It's easy to dismiss the *Queen Mary* as a barnacle-laden tourist trap, but it *is* the only surviving example of this particular kind of 20th-century elegance and excess. From the staterooms paneled lavishly in now-extinct tropical hardwoods to the miles of hallway handrails made of once-pedestrian Bakelite and the perfectly preserved crew quarters which are an art deco homage, wonders never cease aboard this luxury liner. Stroll the teakwood decks with just a bit of imagination and you're back in 1936 on the maiden voyage from Southampton, England. Kiosk displays of photographs and memorabilia are everywhere, and the ship has been virtually unaltered since its heyday. Especially evocative is the first-class observation lounge, a Streamline Moderne masterpiece you might recognize from *Barton Fink, Beverly Hills, 90210,* and other shows. Regular admission includes a self-guided tour. For an additional $6 for adults or $3 for kids, you can take a behind-the-scenes guided tour of the ship, peppered with worthwhile anecdotes and details.

Gondola Getaway. Naples Island, Long Beach. ☎ **562/433-9595.** 1-hour cruise $55 for two. Daily 11am–11pm.

Since 1982 these authentic Venetian gondolas have been snaking around the man-made canals of Naples Island, under gracefully arched bridges and past the gardens of resort cottages. Feel free to bring your beverage of choice, for they send you out with a nice basket of bread, cheese, and salami plus wine glasses and a full ice bucket. Perhaps your traditionally clad oarsman will sing an Italian aria, or relate the many tales of marriage proposals by romance-minded passengers (some not-so-successful!).

Area Code Change Notice

Pleae note that, effective January 25, 1997, the area code for Long Beach, previously in the 310 area, will change to **562**. You will be able to dial 310 until July 26, 1997, after which you will have to use 562.

Shoreline Village. 407 Shoreline Dr. (at Pine Ave. across the channel from the *Queen Mary*). ☎ **562/435-2668,** or 562/432-3053 for information. Daily 10am–9pm (later in summer and on holidays).

If you've seen the real thing in New England you won't be overly impressed, but Long Beach likes to promote this cluster of shops, restaurants, and waterside cafés as a replica 19th-century seaport village. But our favorite surprise was an ornate merry-go-round hand-carved in 1906 by Charles Looff, master carousel maker who helped build The Pike, an old-fashioned seaside amusement park that stood on this spot in the 1930s. The 62 wooden carousel animals include not only horses but leaping camels, giraffes, and rams, all illuminated by glittering Austrian crystal; rides are $1.

The Tall Ship *Californian*. ☎ **800/432-2201** for reservations.

Literally the flagship of the Nautical Heritage Society, the *Californian* sails from Long Beach between late August and mid-April (it's based in Northern California during summer). At 145 feet long, this two-masted wooden cutter-class vessel offers barefooters the opportunity to help raise and lower eight sails, steer by compass, and generally experience the "romance of the high seas." Landlubbers will want to choose the 4-hour day sail for $75 ($113 for two), including lunch, while old salts can take 2-, 3-, or 4-day cruises out to Catalina or the Channel Islands at $140 per person per day. Overnight sails should be booked well in advance.

WHERE TO STAY

✪ **Hotel *Queen Mary*.** 1126 Queen's Hwy. (end of I-710), Long Beach, CA 90802-6390. ☎ **800/437-2934** or 562/435-3511 or 562/432-6964. Fax 562/437-4531. 365 rms, 17 suites. A/C TV TEL. $75–$160 double; from $350 suite. AE, DC, EU, MC, V. Charge for parking.

Although the *Queen Mary* is considered the most luxurious ocean liner ever to sail the Atlantic, with the largest rooms ever built aboard a ship, the quarters aren't exceptional when compared to those on terra firma today, nor are its amenities. The idea is to enjoy the novelty and charm of the original bathtub watercocks ("cold salt," "cold fresh," "hot salt," "hot fresh"). The ship's beautifully carved interior is a festival for the eye and fun to explore, plus the weekday rates are hard to beat. Three onboard restaurants are overpriced but convenient, and the original shopping arcade has a decidedly British feel (one shop sells great *Queen Mary* souvenirs). An elegant Sunday champagne brunch—complete with ice sculpture and harpist—is served in the ship's Grand Salon, and it's always worth having a cocktail in the art deco Observation Bar. If you're too young or too poor to have traveled on the old luxury liners, this is the perfect opportunity to experience the romance of an Atlantic crossing—and with no seasickness, cabin fever, or week of formal dinners.

WHERE TO DINE

Belmont Brewing Company. 25 39th Place (at the Belmont Pier), Long Beach. ☎ **562/433-3891.** Main courses $5–$11. AE, CB, DC, MC, V. Mon–Fri 11:30am–9:30pm, Sat–Sun 10:30am–10pm. (Bar, daily till midnight.) BREWPUB/AMERICAN.

This brewed-on-premises beer restaurant's outdoor patio has a million-dollar harbor view of the *Queen Mary*, fiery sunsets, and the pier's unusual chameleon streetlamps.

The five house brews include "Top Sail" (amber) and "Long Beach Crude" (porter). The menu consists of salads, sandwiches, pizzas, pasta, and happy hour appetizer favorites, including a deep-fried whole onion "flower" served with sweet-spicy dipping sauce.

Papadakis Taverna. 301 W. 6th St. (at Centre St.), San Pedro. ☎ **562/548-1186.** Reservations recommended. Main courses $8–$16. CB, DC, MC, V. Sun–Thurs 5–9pm, Fri–Sat 5–10pm. GREEK.

The food here rates higher than the ambience—even genial host John Papadakis's hand-kissing greeting doesn't soften the blunt lines and bright lights of this banquet room–like space decorated with equal parts Aegean murals and football art (in deference to Papadakis's glory days as a USC football legend). The waiters dance and sing loudly when they're not bringing plates of spanikopita (spinach-filled filo pastries) or thick, satisfying tsatziki (garlic-laced cucumber-and-yogurt spread) to your table. Servings are very generous, prices reasonable, and the wine list has something for everyone.

Parker's Lighthouse. 435 Shoreline Village Dr., Long Beach. ☎ **562/432-6500.** Reservations recommended on weekends. Lunch $6–$15; dinner $9–$27. AE, DC, DISC, MC, V. Mon–Thurs 11am–10pm, Fri 11am–11pm, Sat 3–11pm, Sun 3:30–9:30pm. SEAFOOD GRILL.

Built to look like a giant Cape Cod lighthouse, Parker's fits right into the Shoreline Village motif. It's actually kind of fun to wind upstairs to one of three dining levels, including the circular bar on the top floor which looks out over the harbor and the behemoth *Queen Mary*. The main dining room specializes in mesquite-fired fresh seafood, but also offers steaks and chicken.

3 Santa Catalina Island

22 miles W of mainland Los Angeles

Santa Catalina—which everyone calls simply Catalina—is a small, cove-fringed island famous for its laid-back inns, largely unspoiled landscape, and crystal-clear waters. Many devotees consider it Southern California's alternative to Capri or Malta. Because of its relative isolation, out-of-state tourists tend to ignore it; but those who do show up have plenty of elbow room to boat, fish, swim, scuba, and snorkel. There are miles of hiking and biking trails, plus golf, tennis, and horseback riding.

Catalina is so different from the mainland that it almost seems like a different country, remote and unspoiled. In 1915 the island was purchased by William Wrigley, Jr., the chewing gum manufacturer, in order to develop a fashionable pleasure resort. To publicize the new vacation land, Wrigley brought big-name bands to the Avalon Ballroom and moved the Chicago Cubs, which he owned, to the island for spring training. His marketing efforts succeeded, and this charming and tranquil retreat became—and still is—a favorite vacation resort for mainlanders.

Today about 86% of the island remains undeveloped, owned and preserved by the Santa Catalina Island Conservancy. Some of the specacular outlying areas can only be reached by arranged tour (see "Exploring the Island," below).

ESSENTIALS

GETTING THERE The most common way to get to and from the island is via the **Catalina Express** (☎ 562/519-1212), which operates up to 20 daily departures year round to Catalina from San Pedro and Long Beach. The trip takes about an hour. One-way fares from San Pedro are $17.75 for adults, $16 for seniors, $13 for children 2 to 11, and $1 for infants. Long Beach fares are about $2 higher for all except infants, who are still charged $1. The trip is an additional $1.80 if you travel to Two Harbors. The Catalina Express departs from the Sea/Air Terminal at Berth 95, Port of L.A. in San Pedro; from the Catalina Express port at the *Queen Mary* in Long Beach; and from the Catalina Express port at 161 N. Harbor Dr. in Redondo Beach. Call for information and reservations.

Note: Luggage on the Catalina Express is limited to 50 pounds per person; reservations are necessary for bicycles, surfboards, and dive tanks; and there are restrictions on transporting domestic pets. Call for information.

Catalina Cruises (☎ 800/CATALINA) also ferries passengers from Long Beach to Avalon Harbor—it has the best rates going (about $5 cheaper than above) because it runs monstrous 700-passenger boats which take longer to make the crossing (about 1 hour and 50 minutes). But it does offer twice-daily sailings during the high season, plus frequent runs to Twin Harbors. If you want to save money, particularly if you're staying overnight and don't have to maximize your island time, Catalina Cruises is the choice for you.

Island Express Helicopter Service, 900 Queens Way Dr., Long Beach (☎ 310/510-2525; fax 310/510-9671), flies from Long Beach or San Pedro to Catalina in about 15 minutes. They fly on demand between 8am and sunset year-round, charging $66 each way. If you just want a airborne tour of Catalina, they'll spend 10 to 30 minutes showing you island sights. There's a four-passenger minumum and the cost is $50 to $90 per person.

VISITOR INFORMATION   The **Catalina Island Chamber of Commerce and Visitor's Bureau,** (P.O. Box 217), Avalon, CA 90704 (☎ 310/510-1520; fax 310/510-7606), located on the Green Pleasure Pier, distributes brochures and information on island activities, including sightseeing tours, camping, hiking, fishing, and boating. It also offers information on hotels and boat and helicopter transport. Call for a free 100-page visitor's guide.

The Santa Catalina Island Company–run **Visitor's Information Center,** which is just across from the chamber of commerce, on Crescent Avenue (☎ 310/510-2000), handles hotel reservations, sightseeing tours, and other island activities.

There's also a colorful Internet site at **http://www.catalina.com** that offers current news from the *Catalina Islander* newspaper in addition to updated activities, events, and general information.

ORIENTATION   The picturesque town of Avalon is the island's only city. Named for a passage in Tennyson's *Idylls of the King,* Avalon is also the port of entry for the island. From the ferry dock you can wander along Crescent Avenue, the main road along the beachfront, and easily explore adjacent side streets.

Visitors are not allowed to drive cars on the island. There are only a limited number of autos permitted; most residents motor around in golf carts (many of the homes only have golf cart–sized driveways). But don't worry—you'll be able to get everywhere you want to go by renting a cart yourself or just hoofing it, which is what most visitors do.

Northwest of Avalon is the village of Two Harbors (see below), accessible only by boat or the most intrepid of hikers. Its twin bays are favored by pleasure yachts from L.A.'s various marinas, so there's more camaraderie and a less touristy ambience overall.

GETTING AROUND   If you want to explore the area around Avalon beyond where your feet can comfortably carry you, try renting a mountain bike or tandem from **Brown's Bikes,** 107 Pebbly Beach Rd., Avalon (☎ 310/510-0986), or even a gas-powered golf cart from **Cartopia,** 615 Crescent Ave., Avalon (☎ 310/510-2493), where rates are $30 per hour.

EXPLORING THE ISLAND

ORGANIZED TOURS The Santa Catalina Island Company's **Discovery Tours,** Avalon Harbor Pier (☎ **800/626-7489** or 310/510-TOUR), operates several motorcoach excursions that depart from the tour plaza in the center of town on Sumner Avenue.

The Skyline Drive Tour basically follows the perimeter of the island and takes about 1³/₄ hours. Trips leave several times a day from 11am to 3pm and cost $18 for adults, $16 for seniors, and $10 for children 3 to 11.

The Inland Motor Tour is more comprehensive; it includes some of the 66 square miles of preserve owned by the Santa Catalina Island Conservancy. You'll see El Rancho Escondido and probably have a chance to view buffalo, deer, goats, and boars. Tours, which take about 3³/₄ hours, leave at 9am; from June to October, they leave at other times as well. Tours are $29 for adults, $26 for seniors, and $16 for children 3 to 11; free for children 2 and under.

Other excursions offered by the company include the 40-minute Casino Tour, which explores Catalina's most famous landmark; the 50-minute Avalon Scenic Tour, a 9-mile introductory tour of the town; and the 1-hour Flying Fish Boat Trip, during which an occasional flying fish lands right on the boat.

Check with the Catalina Island Company for other tour offerings, as well as for information on multiple excursion packages.

VISITING TWO HARBORS If you want to get a better look at the rugged natural beauty of Catalina and escape the throngs of beachgoers, head over to Two Harbors, the quarter-mile "neck" at the island's northwest end that gets its name from the "twin harbors" on each side, known as the Isthmus and Cat Harbor. An excellent starting point for campers and hikers, Two Harbors offers just enough civilization for the less intrepid traveler.

The **Banning House Lodge** (☎ **310/510-7265**) is an 11-room bed-and-breakfast overlooking the Isthmus. The clapboard house was built in 1910 for Catalina's pre-Wrigley owners, and has seen duty as a girls' camp, army barracks, and on-location lodging for movie stars like Errol Flynn and Dorothy Lamour. The innkeepers are gracious, the atmosphere peaceful and isolated. Call from the pier and they'll even drive you up to the lodge.

Everyone eats at **Doug's Harbor Reef** (☎ **310/510-7265**), down on the beach. This nautical/South Seas–themed saloon/restaurant serves breakfast, lunch, and dinner, the latter being hearty steaks, ribs, swordfish, chicken teriyaki, and buffalo burgers in the summer. The house drink is sweet "buffalo milk," a potent concoction of vodka, crème de cacão, banana liqueur, milk, and whipped cream.

Avalon Casino and Catalina Island Museum. At the end of Crescent Ave. ☎ **310/510-2414.** Museum admission $1.50 adults, $1 seniors, 50¢ children 6–11, free for children 5 and under. Daily 10:30am–4pm.

The Avalon Casino is the most famous structure on the island, and one of its oldest. It was built in 1929 to house a ballroom and theater, but its massive circular rotunda topped with a red-tile roof is its most notable feature. The Avalon Casino is widely known for its beautiful art deco ballroom, which once hosted the Tommy Dorsey and Glen Miller orchestras and other top bands. You can see the inside of the building by attending a ballroom event or watching a film (the Casino is Avalon's primary movie theater). Otherwise, admission is by guided tour only, operated daily by the Santa Catalina Island Company (see "Organized Tours," above).

The Catalina Island Museum, located on the ground floor of the Casino, features exhibits on island history, archeology, and natural history—it also has a contour relief map of the island which can be helpful to anyone planning to venture into the interior.

SNORKELING, DIVING & KAYAKING

Snorkeling, scuba diving, and sea kayaking are among the main reasons mainlanders head to Catalina. Purists will prefer the less-spoiled waters of Two Harbors, but Avalon's many coves have plenty to offer as well. **Banana Boat Riders,** 107 Pebbly Beach Rd., Avalon (☎ **800/708-2262** or 310/510-1774), offers snorkel gear and sea kayak rentals, as well as half- and full-day excursions to Two Harbors and other island coves. **Catalina Divers Supply** (☎ **800/353-0330** or 310/510-0330) offers guided snorkel and scuba tours with certified instructors, in addition to gear rental, at three Avalon locations. **Descanso Beach Ocean Sports** (☎ **310/510-1226**) offers sea kayak and snorkel rentals with instruction, plus specialty expeditions and kids' programs.

At Two Harbors, sit-on-top beginner kayaks as well as advanced touring types can be rented at **Two Harbors Kayak Center** (☎ **310/510-7265**). They offer instruction and guided tours of the secluded coves on the northern end of the island.

WHERE TO STAY

Catalina's accommodations range from old-salt motels to yachting-set luxury. If you plan to stay overnight, be sure to reserve a room in advance, since most places fill up pretty quickly during the summer and holiday seasons. **Catalina Island Accommodations** (☎ **310/510-3000**) might be able to help you out in a pinch; it's a reservations service with updated information on the whole island. Here are three of the most noteworthy places to stay:

Catalina Island Inn. 125 Metropole (north of Crescent Ave.; P.O. Box 467), Avalon, CA 90704. ☎ **800/246-8134** or 310/510-1623. Fax 310/510-7218. 35 rms, 1 minisuite. TV TEL. May–Sept, and holidays and weekends year round, $89–$179 double; $189 minisuite. Oct–Apr weekdays, $45–$99 double; $155 minisuite. Rates include continental breakfast. AE, DISC, MC, V.

Innkeepers Martin and Bernadine Curtin provide clean, comfortable rooms simply furnished with a vaguely tropical motif. Many rooms have balconies with views of the harbor, and you can't beat the location right in the center of bustling Avalon.

✪ **The Inn on Mt. Ada.** 398 Wrigley Rd. (P.O. Box 2560), Avalon, CA 90704. ☎ **310/ 510-2030.** 6 rms, 2 suites. June–Oct, and Fri–Sun year-round, $320–$490 double; $490–$590 suite. Nov–May Mon–Thurs, $230–$370 double; $370–$470 suite. Rates include three meals. MC, V.

When William Wrigley, Jr., purchased Catalina Island in 1921, he built this remarkably ornate Georgian Colonial mansion as his summer vacation home. In 1985 several local residents signed a 30-year lease for the estate and lovingly transformed it into one of the finest small hotels in California. The opulent inn has several ground-floor salons, a fireplaced club room, a deep-seated formal library, and a wickered sunroom where tea, cookies, and fruit are always available. Once the master bedroom, the best guest room is the Grand Suite, fitted with a fireplace and a large private patio. Room 2 has a queen-size four-poster bed, a fireplace, and a sitting lounge with wingback chairs. Amenities include bathrobes. TVs are available on request, but there are no telephones in the rooms. A hearty full breakfast, a light deli-style lunch, and a beautiful multicourse dinner complemented by a limited wine selection are included in the tariff.

Zane Grey Pueblo Hotel. Off Chimes Tower Rd. (north of Hill St.; P.O. Box 216), Avalon, CA 90704. ☎ **800/378-3256** or 310/510-0966. 17 rms. Apr–Oct, $75–$125 double. Nov–Mar, $59 double. Rates include continental breakfast. AE, MC, V.

You'll have the most superb views on the island from this Shangri-la mountain retreat, the former home of novelist Zane Grey, who spent his last 20 years in Avalon.
He wrote many books here, including *Tales of Swordfish and Tuna,* which tells of his
fishing adventures off Catalina Island.

The hotel has teak beams that the novelist brought from Tahiti on one of his fishing trips. Most of the rooms also have large windows and ocean or mountain views.
They have all been renovated with new furniture, carpeting, and ceiling fans. An
outdoor patio has an excellent view. The original living room has a grand piano, a
fireplace, and a TV. The hotel also has a pool and sundeck, with chairs overlooking
Avalon and the ocean. Coffee is served all day, and there's a courtesy bus to town.

WHERE TO DINE

The Busy Bee. 306 Crescent Ave. (north of the Pleasure Pier). ☎ **310/510-1983.** Reservations not accepted. Main courses $7–$15. AE, CB, DC, DISC, MC, V. Summer, daily 8am–10pm;
winter, daily 8am–8pm. AMERICAN.

The Busy Bee, an Avalon institution since 1923, is located right on the beach. The
fare is light-deli style. The extensive menu offers breakfast, lunch, and dinner at all
times. The restaurant grinds its own beef, cuts its own potatoes for french fries, and
makes its own salad dressings. Even if you're not hungry, come here for a drink—
it's Avalon's only waterfront bar.

El Galleon. 411 Crescent Ave. ☎ **310/510-1188.** Reservations recommended on weekends.
Main courses $11–$37 at dinner. AE, DISC, MC, V. Daily 11am–2:30pm and 5–10pm. (Bar, daily
10am–1:30am.) AMERICAN.

El Galleon is large, warm, and woody, complete with portholes, rigging, anchors,
wrought-iron chandeliers, oversize leather booths, and tables with red-leather captain's
chairs. There's additional balcony seating, plus outdoor café tables overlooking the
ocean harbor. Lunch and dinner feature seafood. Favorite dinner dishes include fresh
swordfish steak and broiled Catalina lobster tails in drawn butter. "Turf" main dishes
range from country-fried chicken to broiled rack of lamb with mint jelly.

Sand Trap. Avalon Canyon Rd. (north of Tremont St.). ☎ **310/510-1349.** Reservations not
accepted. Main courses $4–$12. No credit cards. Daily 7:30am–3:30pm. CALIFORNIA/
MEXICAN.

This local favorite is a great place to escape from the bayfront crowds. Enjoy breakfast, lunch, or snacks while overlooking the golf course. Specialties of the house
include delectable omelets served until noon and soft tacos served all day. Either can
be made with any number of fillings. Burgers, sandwiches, salads, and chili are also
served. Beer and wine are available.

4 Big Bear Lake & Lake Arrowhead

100 miles NE of Los Angeles

These two deep blue lakes lie close to one another in the San Bernardino Mountains,
and have long been a favorite weekend getaway for city-weary Angelenos. Both were
created in the early 20th century by damming what had been known as Little Bear
and Big Bear valleys. In addition to bringing power and water to the Inland Empire
communities below, they provide Southern California with a year-round alpine
playground.

Big Bear Lake has always been popular with skiers as well as avid boaters (it's
much larger than Arrowhead and equipment rentals abound). In the past decade the
area has been given a much-needed face-lift. Big Bear Boulevard was substantially
widened to handle high-season traffic, and downtown Big Bear Lake (the "Village")

was spiffed up without losing its woodsy charm. In addition to two excellent ski slopes less than 5 minutes from town (see "Winter Fun," below), you can enjoy the comforts of a real supermarket (there's even a KMart now) and several video-rental shops, all especially convenient when staying in a cabin! Most people choose Big Bear over Arrowhead because there's *so much* more to do—from boating and fishing to snow sports and mountain biking, hiking and horseback riding. The weather is nearly always perfect at this 7,000-foot-plus elevation. If you want proof, ask Caltech, which operates a solar observatory on the north shore to take advantage of nearly 300 days of sunshine per year.

Lake Arrowhead, on the other hand, has always been privately owned, as is immediately apparent from the affluence of the surrounding homes, many of which are gated estates rather than rustic mountain cabins. The lake and the private docks lining its shores are reserved for the exclusive use of homeowners, but visitors can enjoy Lake Arrowhead by boat tour (see "Organized Tours," below) or use of the summer-season beach clubs, a privilege included in nearly all private home rentals (see "Where to Stay at Lake Arrowhead," below). Reasons to choose a vacation at Lake Arrowhead? The roads up are less grueling than the winding ascent to Big Bear Lake, and being at a lower elevation, Arrowhead gets little snow (you can forget those pesky tire chains). It's very easy and cost-effective to rent a luxurious house from which to enjoy the spectacular scenery, crisp mountain air, and relaxed resort atmosphere—and if you do ski, the slopes are only a half-hour away.

ESSENTIALS

GETTING THERE   Lake Arrowhead is reached by taking Calif. 18 from San Bernardino. The last segment of this route takes you along the aptly named Rim of the World Highway, offering a breathtaking panoramic view out over the valley below (or alternatively, a big ditch of smog). Calif. 18 then continues east to Big Bear Lake, but to get to Big Bear Lake it's quicker to bypass Arrowhead by taking Calif. 330 from Redlands, which meets Calif. 18 in Running Springs. During heavy traffic periods it can be worthwhile to take scenic Calif. 38, which winds up from Redlands through mountain passes and valleys to approach Big Bear from the other side.

VISITOR INFORMATION   National ski tours, mountain bike races, and one of Southern California's largest Oktoberfest gatherings are just some of the many year-round events that may either entice or discourage you from visiting at the same time. Contact the **Big Bear Lake Resort Association,** 630 Bartlett Rd., Big Bear Lake Village (☎ 909/866-7000), for schedules and information. The association also provides information on sightseeing and lodging, will send you a free visitors guide, and is open 7 days a week. Visit their Website at **http://www.bigbear.com.**

In Lake Arrowhead, contact the **Lake Arrowhead Communities Chamber of Commerce** (☎ 909/337-3715, or 800/337-3716 for the Lodging Information Line; fax 909/336-1548). The visitor center, located in the Lake Arrowhead Village lower shopping center, is open Monday to Friday from 10am to 5pm and on Saturday from 10am to 3pm. Their Website is **http://www.apsm.com/lakearrow.**

ORIENTATION   The south shore of Big Bear Lake was the first resort area to be developed and remains the most densely populated. Calif. 18 passes first through the city of Big Bear Lake and its downtown Village; then, as Big Bear Boulevard, it continues east to Big Bear City, which is more residential and suburban. Calif. 38 traverses the north shore, home to pristine national forest and great hiking trails, as well as a couple of small marinas (see "Water Sports," below) and a lakefront bed-and-breakfast inn (see "Where to Stay in Big Bear Lake," below).

Big Bear Lake & Lake Arrowhead

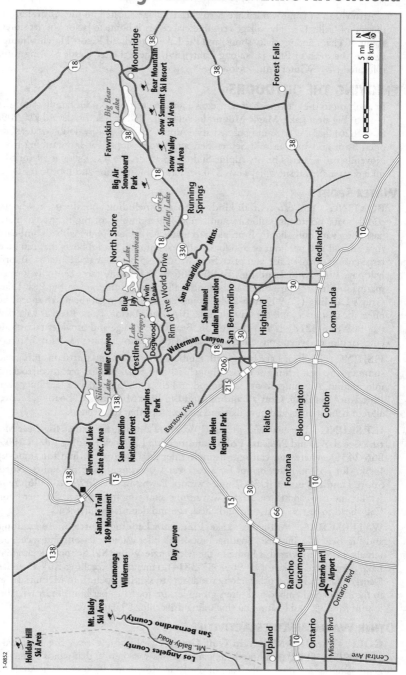

1-0852

Arrowhead's main town is Lake Arrowhead Village, located on the south shore at the end of Calif. 173. The village's commercial center is home to factory-outlet stores, about 40 chain and specialty shops, and the Lake Arrowhead Resort Hotel. Minutes away is the town of Blue Jay (along Calif. 189), where the Ice Castle Skating Rink is located (see "Winter Fun," below).

ENJOYING THE OUTDOORS

In addition to the activities below, there's a great recreation spot for families near the heart of Big Bear Lake: **Magic Mountain,** on Calif. 18 /Big Bear Boulevard (☎ **909/ 866-4626**), has a year-round bobsled-style Alpine Slide, a splashy double water slide open from mid-June to mid-September, and bunny slopes for snow tubing from November to Easter. The dry Alpine Slide is $3 a ride, the water slide is $1 (or $10 for a day pass), and snowplay costs $10 per day including tube and rope tow.

WATER SPORTS

BOATING   You can rent all kinds of boats—including speedboats, rowboats, paddleboats, pontoons, sailboats, and canoes—at a number of Big Bear Lake marinas. Rates vary only slightly from place to place: A 14-foot dinghy with an outboard runs around $10 per hour or $30 for a half day; pontoon (patio) boats that can hold large groups range in size and price from $25 to $45 per hour or $80 to $150 for a half day. **Pine Knot Landing** (☎ **909/866-BOAT**) is the most centrally located marina, behind the post office at the foot of Pine Knot Boulevard in Big Bear Lake. **Gray's Landing** (☎ **909/866-2443**) is just across the dam on the north shore and offers the best prices and the least attitude. **Big Bear Marina,** Paine Road at Lakeview (☎ **909/866-3218**), is also close to Big Bear Lake Village and provides take-along chicken dinners when you rent a pontoon boat for a sunset cruise ($75 for 3 hours).

FISHING   Big Bear Lake brims with rainbow trout, bass, and catfish in spring and summer, the best fishing seasons. Phone 310/590-5020 to hear recorded stocking information. A fishing license is required and costs $8.95 per day, $24.95 per year. **Pine Knot Landing, Gray's Landing,** and **Big Bear Marina** (see "Boating," above) all rent fishing boats and have bait and tackle shops that sell licenses.

JET SKIING   Personal Water Craft (PWCs) are available for rent at **Big Bear Marina** (see above) and **Pleasure Point Landing,** 603 Landlock Landing Rd. (☎ **909/ 866-2455**), where you can rent a single-rider SeaDoo (easier than the stand-up JetSki) for $35 an hour, or opt for a two-seat Waverunner ($55 per hour). **North Shore Landing,** on Calif. 38, 2 miles west of Fawnskin (☎ **909/868-4386**), rents JetSkis and two- and three-person Waverunners ranging from $55 to $65 per hour. Call ahead to reserve your craft and check age and deposit requirements.

WATERSKIING   At Big Bear Lake, **Pine Knot Landing, North Shore Landing,** and **Big Bear Marina** (see "Boating," above) all offer waterski lessons and speedboat rentals. Lake Arrowhead is home to the **McKenzie Water Ski School,** dockside in Lake Arrowhead Village (☎ **909/337-3814**), famous for teaching Kirk Douglas, George Hamilton, and other Hollywood stars to ski. It's open from Memorial Day to the end of September, and offers group lessons for $115 per hour, short refresher lessons for $35, and boat rental (including driver) for $95 an hour.

OTHER WARM WEATHER ACTIVITIES

GOLF   The **Bear Mountain Golf Course,** Goldmine Drive, Big Bear Lake (☎ **909/585-8002**), is a nine-hole, par-35, links-style course that winds through a gently sloping meadow at the base of the Bear Mountain Ski Resort. The course is open daily from April to November. Greens fees are $17 and $23 for 9 and 18 holes, respectively. Both riding carts and pull carts are available. Phone for tee times.

HIKING   Hikers will love the San Bernardino National Forest. The gray squirrel is a popular native; you may see them scurrying around gathering acorns or material for their nest. You can sometimes spot deer, coyotes, and American bald eagles, which come here with their young during winter months. The black-crowned stellar jay and the talkative red, white, and black acorn woodpecker are the most common of the great variety of birds in this pine forest.

Stop in at the **Big Bear Ranger Station** on Calif. 38, 3 miles east of Fawnskin on Big Bear Lake's north shore (☎ **909/866-3437**). There you can pick up free trail maps, as well as other information on the area's plants, animals, and geology. The best trail for a short mountain hike is the **Woodland Trail,** which begins near the ranger station. The best long hike is the **Pacific Crest Trail,** which travels 39 miles through the mountains above Big Bear and Arrowhead lakes. The most convenient trailhead is located at Cougar Crest, half a mile west of the Big Bear Ranger Station.

The best place to begin a hike in Lake Arrowhead is at the **Arrowhead Ranger Station,** located in the town of Skyforest on Calif. 18 (☎ **909/337-2444**), a quarter-mile east of the Lake Arrowhead turn-off (Calif. 173). The staff will provide you with maps and information on the best area trails, which range from easy to difficult. The **Enchanted Loop Trail,** near the town of Blue Jay, is an easy half-hour hike. The **Heaps Peak Arboretum Trail** winds through a grove of redwoods; the trailhead is located on the north side of Calif. 18, half a mile east of Santa's Village.

The area is home to a **National Children's Forest,** a 20-acre area developed so that children, the wheelchair-bound, and the visually impaired could enjoy nature. To get to the Children's Forest from Lake Arrowhead, take Calif. 330 to Calif. 18 east, past Deer Lick Station; when you reach a road marked IN96 (only open in the summer season), turn right and go 3 miles.

HORSEBACK RIDING   Horses are permitted on all the mountain trails through the national forest. **Magic Mountain Stables,** 40355 Big Bear Blvd., City of Big Bear Lake (☎ **909/878-HORSE**), offers 1- and 2-hour guided rides for $20 per hour, and 1¹/₂-hour sunset rides for $30. The stables are open daily from May to December. Phone for reservations. **Baldwin Lake Stables,** southeast of Big Bear City (☎ **909/ 585-6482**), also conducts hourly, lunch, and sunset specialty rides in addition to offering lessons.

MOUNTAIN BIKING   Big Bear Lake has become a mountain-bicycling center, with most of the action around the **Snow Summit Ski Area** (see "Winter Fun," below), where a $7 lift ticket will take you and your bike to a scenic web of trails, fire roads, and meadows at about 8,000 feet. Call its Summer Activities Hotline at 909/866-4621. The lake's north shore is also a popular biking destination; the Forest Service Ranger Stations (see "Hiking," above) have maps to the historic Gold Rush–era Holcomb Valley and the 2-mile Alpine Pedal Path (an easy lakeside ride).

Big Bear Bikes, 41810 Big Bear Blvd. (☎ **909/866-4565**), rents mountain bikes for $6 an hour or $21 for 4 hours. **Bear Valley Bikes,** 40298 Big Bear Blvd. (☎ **909/866-8000**), rents bikes and offers free lessons on Sunday. **Team Big Bear** is located at the base of Snow Summit (☎ **909/866-4565**); it rents bicycles and provides detailed maps and guides for all Big Bear area trails.

At Lake Arrowhead, bicycles are permitted on all hiking trails and backroads except the Pacific Crest Trail (see the local ranger station for an area map), and gear can be rented from **Above & Beyond Sports,** 32877 Calif. 18, Running Springs (☎ **909/867-5517**).

WINTER FUN

SKIING & SNOWBOARDING   When the L.A. basin gets wintertime rain, skiers everywhere rejoice, for they know snow is falling up in the mountains. The last few seasons have seen abundant natural snowfall at Big Bear, augmented by sophisticated snowmaking equipment, which also compensates during drier years. While the slopes can't compare with those in Utah or Colorado, they do offer diversity, difficulty, and convenience.

✪ **Snow Summit** at Big Bear Lake (☎ **909/866-5766**) is the skier's choice, especially since they installed their second high-speed quad express from the 7,000-foot base to the 8,200-foot summit. Another nice feature is green (easy) runs *even* from the summit, so beginners can also enjoy the Summit Haus lodge and breathtaking lake views from the top. Advanced risk-takers will appreciate three *double-*black-diamond runs. Lift tickets range from $30 to $42. The resort offers midweek, beginner, half-day, night, and family specials, as well as ski and snowboard instruction. Hey, you can even ski free on your birthday here! Other helpful Snow Summit phone numbers include advance lift ticket sales (☎ 909/866-5841), the ski school (☎ 909/866-4546), and a snow report (☎ 310/390-1498 in L.A. County). Or you can visit the facility's Website at **http://www.bigbear.com/summit.**

The **Bear Mountain Ski Resort** at Big Bear Lake (☎ **909/585-2519,** or 213/683-8100 in L.A. for a snow report) is smaller than the other two, but experts flock to the double-black-diamond "Geronimo" run from the 8,805-foot Bear Peak. Natural terrain skiers and snowboarders will enjoy legal access to off-trail canyons, but the limited beginner slopes and kids' areas get pretty crowded in season. One high-speed quad express rises from the 7,140-foot base to 8,440-foot Goldmine Mountain; most runs from there are intermediate. Bear Mountain has a ski school, abundant dining facilities, and a well-stocked ski shop.

The **Snow Valley Ski Resort** in Arrowhead, midway between Arrowhead and Big Bear (☎ **800/680-SNOW** or 909/867-2751), has improved its snowmaking and facilities to be competitive with the other two major ski areas, and is the primary choice of skiers staying at Arrowhead. From a base elevation of 6,800 feet, Snow Valley's 13 chair lifts (including 5 triples) can take you from the beginner runs all the way up to black-diamond challenges at the 7,898-foot peak. Lift tickets cost $35 to $40 for adults; children's programs, night skiing, and lesson packages are available. Snow Valley's Internet address is **http://www.aminews.com/snowvalley.**

The **Big Air Snowboard Park** in Green Valley (☎ **909/867-2338**)—take Green Valley Lake Road from Arrowbear—is the answer to a snowboarder's dream. Absolutely no skiers are allowed on Big Air's 50 rideable acres full of hits, bonks, spines, and more. Use the rope tow or take the high-speed chair to untouched forest full of natural hits. It offers equipment rentals, lessons, and package deals. All-day passes are $24 for adults, $18 for kids 12 and under; half-day passes are $20 and $14, respectively.

ICE SKATING   The **Blue Jay Ice Castle,** at North Bay Road and Calif. 189 (☎ **909/33-SKATE**), near Lake Arrowhead Village, is a training site for world champion Michelle Kwan, and boasts Olympic gold medalist Robin Cousins on its staff. Several public sessions each day—as well as hockey, broomball, group lessons, and book-in-advance private parties—give nonpros a chance to enjoy this impeccably groomed "outdoor" rink (it's open on three sides to the scenery and fresh air).

ORGANIZED TOURS

LAKE TOURS   The *Big Bear Queen* (☎ 909/866-3218), a midget Mississippi-style paddlewheeler, cruises Big Bear Lake on 90-minute tours daily from late April to November. The boat departs from Big Bear Marina (at the end of Paine Avenue). Tours are $9.50 for adults, $8 for seniors 65 and older, and $5 for children 3 to 12. Call for reservations and information on the special Sunday brunch, champagne sunset, and dinner cruises. And 50-minute tours of Lake Arrowhead are offered year-round on the *Arrowhead Queen* (☎ 909/336-6992), a sister ship that departs hourly each day between 10am and 6pm from Lake Arrowhead Village. Tours cost $9.50 for adults, $8.50 for seniors, and $6.50 for children 2 to 12. This is about the only way for visitors to really see this alpine jewel, unless you know a resident with a boat.

FOREST TOURS   Big Bear Jeep Tours (☎ 909/878-JEEP) journeys into Big Bear Lake's backcountry, including historic Holcomb Valley, relic of the Gold Rush, plus the panoramic viewpoint Butler Peak. These off-road adventures range in length from 2 to 4$^1/_2$ hours, and from $38 to $80 per person. Bring your own snack though because, although the guide carries ample water, the longer excursions have short but appetite-building hikes scheduled into the intinerary. Phone for reservations, particularly on weekends and holidays.

WHERE TO STAY AT BIG BEAR LAKE

Vacation rentals are plentiful around the Big Bear area, from cabins to condos to private homes. Some can accommodate up to 20 people and can be rented on a weekly or monthly basis. The oldest realtor, with seven area offices and a wide range of rental properties, is **Spencer Real Estate** (☎ 800/237-3725 or 909/866-7591). The **Village Reservation Service** (☎ 909/866-8583 or 909/585-5850) can arrange for everything from Jacuzzi condos to lakefront homes; or call the **Big Bear Lake Resort Association** (☎ 909/866-7000) for general information and referrals on all types of lodging.

Grey Squirrel Resort. 39372 Big Bear Blvd., Big Bear Lake, CA 92315. ☎ **909/866-4335.** Fax 909/866-6271. 18 cabins. TV TEL. $75–$95 one-bedroom cabin; $99–$125 two-bedroom cabin; $125–$275 three-bedroom cabin. Value rates available; higher rates on holidays. AE, DISC, MC, V.

This is the most attractive of the many cabin cluster–type motels near the city of Big Bear Lake, offering a wide range of rustic cabins, most with fireplace and kitchen. They're adequately, if not attractively, furnished—the appeal here is the flexibility and privacy it gives long-term or large parties. A heated pool is enclosed in winter, and there is an indoor spa, a fire pit and barbecues, volleyball and basketball courts, laundry facilities, and completely equipped kitchens. Pets are welcome for a $5 daily surcharge.

Janet Kay's Bed & Breakfast. 695 Paine Rd., Big Bear Lake, CA 92315. ☎ **800/243-7031** or 909/866-6800. 19 rms and suites. TV TEL. $59–$175 double or suite. Rates include full breakfast and afternoon tea with snacks. AE, DISC, MC, V.

This large, colonial-style inn within walking distance of Big Bear Lake Village is more comfortable than the standard hotel but less personal than most true B&Bs. Still, it offers a centrally located alternative and spacious, comfortable rooms each decorated to a theme (Victorian, jungle, garden, etc.). All have Jacuzzis; some have terraces and/or fireplaces. The hotel offers winter ski and summer fun packages.

Windy Point Inn. 39015 North Shore Dr., Fawnskin, CA 92333. ☎ **909/866-2746.** 2 rms, 1 suite. $105–$225 double. Rates include full breakfast and afternoon hors d'oeuvres. AE, DISC, MC, V.

A contemporary home on the scenic north shore, the Windy Point is the only shorefront B&B in Big Bear, and two rooms have a spectacular view of the sunrise over the lake. Hosts Val and Kent Jessler's attention to detail is impeccable—if you're tired of knotty pine and Victorian frills, this is a grown-up place for you. There's an outdoor Jacuzzi, a romantic master suite, private whirlpools in two rooms, fireplaces in all units, a casual sunken living room with floor-to-ceiling windows overlooking the lake, and a custom gourmet breakfast served on the deck in summertime. The city of Big Bear Lake is only a 10-minute drive across the dam.

WHERE TO STAY AT LAKE ARROWHEAD

There are far more private homes than tourist accommodations in Arrowhead (many residents even live here full-time and commute down to Redlands or San Bernardino). On the other hand, rental properties abound, from cozy cottages to palatial mansions, and many can be surprisingly economical for families or other groups. Two of the largest agencies are **Arrowhead Cabin Rentals** (☎ 800/244-5138 or 909/337-2403) and **Arrowhead Mountain Resorts Rentals** (☎ 800/743-0865 or 909/337-4413). **The Forrester Homes of Lake Arrowhead** (☎ 800/587-5576 or 909/845-1004) is worth a call; they represent only six private homes but have a warm, personal touch.

Overnight guests enjoy some resident lake privileges—be sure to ask when you reserve.

Chateau du Lac. 911 Hospital Rd. (near Calif. 173), Lake Arrowhead, CA 92352. ☎ **909/337-6488.** 5 rms. TV TEL. $135–$240 double. Rates include full breakfast and afternoon tea. AE, DISC, MC, V.

The Chateau du Lac is one of the newest inns in the area. It enjoys an enviable location, directly on Lake Arrowhead about 3 miles from the village. The 6,000-square-foot clapboard, stone, and brick chateau has more than 100 windows that provide spectacular views. The best—and most expensive—room is aptly named Lake View; it features a private balcony overlooking the lake, a fireplace, beamed ceilings, and a large bathroom with a Jacuzzi and double sinks.

Lake Arrowhead Resort. 27984 Calif. 189, Lake Arrowhead, CA 92352. ☎ **800/800-6792** or 909/336-1511. Fax 909/336-1378. 261 rms and suites. A/C MINIBAR TV TEL. $125–$305 double; $255–$395 suite. AE, CB, DC, MC, V.

This sprawling resort has been upgraded somewhat since it was part of the Hilton chain, but location is still its most outstanding feature, coupled with service and facilities unavailable anywhere else in the mountains. Situated on the lakeshore adjacent to Lake Arrowhead Village, the hotel has its own beach, plus docks ideal for fishing. The rooms are fitted with good-quality, bulk-purchased contemporary furnishings, and most have balconies, king-size beds, and fireplaces. The suites, some in private cottages, are equipped with full kitchens and whirlpool tubs.

The hotel offers a casual restaurant serving all meals (and room service), plus the elegant Seasons, which has only limited hours off-season. Facilities include a fully equipped health club, a heated outdoor pool and whirlpool, racquetball courts, massage, and a video arcade. A full program of supervised children's activities is offered on weekends year-round; it includes fishing, arts and crafts, nature hikes, and T-shirt painting. Be sure to inquire about auto-club membership discounts.

Pine Rose Cabins. 25994 Calif. 189, Twin Peaks, CA 92391. ☎ **800/429-PINE** or 909/337-2341. 15 cabins. $69–$159 cabin for up to four people; $700 five-bedroom lodge. AE, MC, V.

The only place of its kind in Lake Arrowhead, Pine Rose Cabins is a good choice for families. Situated on 5 forested acres about 3 miles from the lake, the wonderful, free-standing cabins offer lots of privacy. Innkeepers Tricia and David Dufour have 15 cabins, ranging in size from romantic studios to a large five-bedroom lodge; each is decorated in a different theme. The Indian cabin has a tepeelike bed; the bed in Wild Bill's cabin is covered like a wagon. One- and two-bedroom units have a fully stocked kitchen and a separate living area. There's a large heated swimming pool on the premises, plus swing sets, croquet, tetherball, and Ping-Pong. Ski packages are offered in season.

WHERE TO DINE AT BIG BEAR LAKE
EXPENSIVE

Blue Whale Lakeside. 350 Alden Rd. (2 blocks east of Pine Knot Blvd.), Big Bear Lake. ☎ **909/866-5771.** Reservations recommended. Main courses $10–$22. AE, MC, V. Daily 4–9pm. SEAFOOD/STEAK.

This nautically themed restaurant has great views of Big Bear Lake from every table. Fresh fish and lobsters are delivered three times a week, and the broiled steaks and roasted poultry are imaginatively prepared. A guitar/piano combo entertains while you dine. Tail of the Whale is the adjoining lounge and oyster bar; it's open and serving lunch Thursday to Sunday from 11am and has its own dancing and entertainment, clambakes, and beach parties in the summer.

The Captain's Anchorage. Moonridge Way at Big Bear Blvd., Big Bear Lake. ☎ **909/866-3997.** Reservations recommended. Full dinners $10–$23. AE, MC, V. Sun–Thurs 4:30–9pm, Fri–Sat 4:30–10pm. STEAK/SEAFOOD.

Historic and rustic, this knotty-pine restaurant has been serving fine steaks, prime rib, seafood, and lobster since 1947. Inside, the dark, nautical decor and fire-warmed bar will hit the spot on blustery winter nights. It's got one of those mile-long soup-and-salad bars, plus some great early-bird and weeknight bargain specials.

MODERATE

Madlon's. 829 W. Big Bear Blvd., Big Bear City. ☎ **909/585-3762.** Reservations required. Main courses $8–$16. AE, MC, V. Mon, Wed–Fri 8am-3pm and 5–9pm, Sat–Sun 8am–3pm. Winter hours may vary. AMERICAN/CONTINENTAL.

One of the few non-retro-fare dining rooms at the mountain resorts, Madlon's brings a bit of European flair to this fairy-tale cottage with a tulip-shaped white picket fence. A variety of creative croissant sandwiches at lunch are complemented by dinner selections like black-pepper filet mignon with mushroom-and-brandy sauce, and lemon-pepper–marinated chicken breast over pasta, all of which is prepared with a sophisticated touch.

INEXPENSIVE

Old Country Inn. 41126 Big Bear Blvd., Big Bear Lake. ☎ **909/866-5600.** Main courses $5–$14. AE, DC, DISC, MC, V. Mon–Fri 7am–9pm, Sat–Sun 7am–10pm. DINER/GERMAN.

The Old Country Inn has long been a favorite for hearty pre-ski breakfasts and stick-to-your-ribs old-world dinners. The restaurant is casual and welcoming; the adjacent cocktail lounge, raucous on weekends. At breakfast enjoy German apple pancakes or colossal omelets, while salads, sandwiches, and burgers are lunch choices. At lunch or dinner feast on Weiner schnitzel, sauerbraten, and other gravy-topped German standards, along with grilled steaks and chicken.

Paoli's Italian Country Kitchen. At Pine Knot Blvd. and Village Dr., Big Bear Lake. ☎ **909/866-2020.** Pizza $11–$17; pasta and entrees $7–$15. MC, V. Mon–Thurs 10:30am–10pm, Fri 10:30am–midnight, Sat 8am–midnight, Sun 8am–10pm. ITALIAN.

You can't beat Paoli's for authentic thin-crust pizzas, tangy antipasto, and saucy lasagnes. They've augmented their traditional menu with a few trendy touches, like pesto, primavera, and the absence of politically incorrect veal, but Paoli's will always be a checked-tablecloth/woven-chianti-bottle kind of place. As such, it's perfect in Big Bear.

WHERE TO DINE AT LAKE ARROWHEAD

Surprisingly for an affluent residential community, there aren't many dining options around Lake Arrowhead. But not surprisingly, what there is tends to run to pricey elegance—elegant for a rustic mountain resort, that is. Although there are both a California/continental restaurant and a casual family eatery in the Lake Arrowhead Resort (see "Where to Stay," above), you might want to venture out to some of the locals' choices. These include the **Chef's Inn & Tavern,** 29020 Oak Terrace, Cedar Glen (☎ 909/336-4488), a moderate to expensive continental restaurant in a turn-of-the-century former bordello; the **Antler's Inn,** 26125 Calif. 189, Twin Peaks (☎ 909/337-4020), serving prime rib, seafood, and buffalo in a historic log lodge; the **Royal Oak,** 27187 Calif. 189, Blue Jay Village (☎ 909/337-6018), an expensive American steakhouse with a pub; and **Belgian Waffle Works,** dockside at Lake Arrowhead Village (☎ 909/337-5222), an inexpensive coffee shop with Victorian decor known for its generous, crispy waffles with tasty toppings.

5 Disneyland & Other Anaheim Area Attractions

27 miles SE of downtown Los Angeles

The sleepy Orange County town of Anaheim grew up around Disneyland, the West's most famous theme park. Now, even beyond this Happiest Place on Earth, the city and its neighboring communities are kid-central: Otherwise unspectacular, sprawling suburbs have become a playground of family-oriented hotels, restaurants, and unabashedly tourist-oriented attractions. Among the nearby draws are Knott's Berry Farm, another family-oriented theme park, in nearby Buena Park. At the other end of the scale is the Richard Nixon Library and Birthplace, a surprisingly compelling presidential library and museum, just 7 miles northeast of Disneyland in Yorba Linda.

ESSENTIALS

GETTING THERE **Los Angeles International Airport (LAX)** is located about 30 minutes from Anaheim via I-5 south (see Section 1 in Chapter 14). If you're heading directly to Anaheim and want to avoid Los Angeles altogether, try to land at the **John Wayne International Airport** in Irvine (☎ 714/252-5200), Orange County's largest airport. It's about 15 miles from Disneyland. The airport is served by Alaska, American, Continental, Delta, Northwest, TWA, and United airlines. Check to see if your hotel has a free shuttle to and from either airport, or call one of the following commercial shuttle services (fares are generally $10 one-way from John Wayne or $12 from LAX): **L.A. Xpress** (☎ 800/I-ARRIVE); **Prime Time** (☎ 800/262-7433); or **SuperShuttle** (☎ 714/517-6600). Car-rental agencies located at the John Wayne Airport include **Budget** (☎ 800/221-1203) and **Hertz** (☎ 800/654-3131).

VISITOR INFORMATION The **Anaheim/Orange County Visitor and Convention Bureau,** at 800 W. Katella Ave. (P.O. Box 4270), Anaheim, CA 92803 (☎ 714/999-8999), can fill you in on area activities and shopping shuttles. It's located just inside the Convention Center (across the street from Disneyland), next to the dramatic cantilevered arena, and welcomes visitors Monday to Friday from

8:30am to 5:30pm. The **Buena Park Convention and Visitors Office,** 6280 Manchester Blvd., Suite 103 (☎ **800/541-3953** or 714/562-3560), will provide specialized information on its area, including Knott's Berry Farm.

DISNEYLAND

Disney was the originator of the mega-theme park. Opened in 1955, Disneyland remains unsurpassed. Despite constant threats from pretenders to the crown, Disneyland and its sibling park, Walt Disney World outside Orlando, Florida, remain the kings of the theme parks. At no other park is fantasy elevated to an art form. Nowhere else is as fresh and fantastic every time you walk through the gates, whether you're 6 or 60—and no matter how many times you've done it before. There's nothing like Disney Magic.

The park stays on the cutting edge by continually updating and expanding, while still maintaining the hallmarks that make it the world's top amusement park (a term coined by Walt Disney himself). Look for the most recent Disney additions during your visit—Toontown, an interactive cartoon area added in 1993, and 1995's Indiana Jones Adventure, a high-tech thrill that's not to be missed—no matter how long you have to wait in line. Also look for live-action musical extravaganzas based on Disney's most recent animated features, *The Lion King, Pocahontas,* and *The Hunchback of Notre Dame.* It was "lights out" in 1996 for the Main Street Electrical Parade's 20-year run, but at press time plans were already in the works for a completely new nighttime spectacular.

GETTING THERE   Disneyland is located at 1313 Harbor Blvd. in Anaheim. It's about an hour's drive from downtown Los Angeles. Take I-5 south to the well-marked Harbor Boulevard exit.

ADMISSION, HOURS & INFORMATION   Admission to the park, including unlimited rides and all festivities and entertainment, is $34 for adults and children 12 and over, $30 for seniors 60 and over, and $26 for children 3 to 11; children under 3 enter free. Parking is $6. Also, 2- and 3-day passes are available; in addition, many area accommodations offer lodging packages that include one or more days' park admission.

Disneyland is open every day of the year, but operating hours vary, so we recommend that you call for information that applies to the specific day(s) of your visit (☎ **714/781-4565** or 213/626-8605, ext. 4565). Generally speaking, the park is open from 9 or 10am to 6 or 7pm on weekdays, fall through spring; and from 8 or 9am to midnight or 1am on weekends, holidays, and during winter, spring, or summer vacation periods.

If you've never been to Disneyland before and would like to get a copy of their *Souvenir Guide* to orient yourself to the park before you go, write to **Disneyland Guest Relations,** P.O. Box 3232, Anaheim, CA 92803. Or pick up a copy of *The Unofficial Guide to Disneyland* (Macmillan Travel) at your local bookstore.

DISNEY TIPS   Disneyland is busiest from mid-June to mid-September, and on weekends and holidays year-round. Peak hours are from noon to 5pm; visit the most popular rides before and after these hours, and you'll cut your waiting times substantially. If you plan on arriving during a busy time, purchase your tickets in advance and get a jump on the crowds at the ticket counters.

Disneyland's attendance falls dramatically during the winter, so the park offers discounted (about 25% off) admission to Southern California residents who may purchase up to six tickets per ZIP Code verification. If you'll be visiting the park with someone who lives here, be sure to take advantage of this money-saving opportunity.

Disneyland

Big Thunder Mountain **8**
Circlevision **13**
Haunted Mansion **5**
Indiana Jones Adventure **3**
It's A Small World **10**
Jungle Cruise **1**
King Arthur Carousel **9**
Matterhorn Bobsleds **11**

Pirates of the Caribbean **4**
Space Mountain **15**
Splash Mountain **6**
Star Tours **14**
Submarine Voyage **12**
Swiss Family Treehouse **2**
Tom Sawyer Island **7**

Frontierland's Rivers of America

Frontierland **8**

Critter Country **6**

Tom Sawyer Island **7**

New Orleans Square

Adventureland **4 2 3 1**

Disneyland Hotel

Picnic Area

Group Sales

Ticket Booths

Disabled Parking

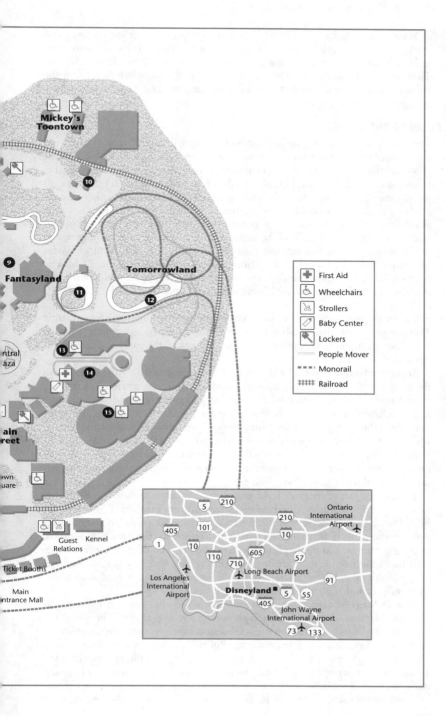

Mickey's
Toontown

10

9
Fantasyland
11
Tomorrowland
12

ntral
aza
13
14
15

ain
reet

wn
uare

Guest Kennel
Relations

Ticket Booths

Main
ntrance Mall

First Aid
Wheelchairs
Strollers
Baby Center
Lockers
People Mover
Monorail
Railroad

5 210
405 101 210 Ontario International Airport
1 10 10
110 710 605 57
Los Angeles International Airport
Long Beach Airport
Disneyland 5 55
405 91
John Wayne International Airport
73 133

Many visitors tackle Disneyland systematically, beginning at the entrance and working their way clockwise around the park. But a better plan of attack is to arrive early and run to the most popular rides first—the Indiana Jones Adventure, Star Tours, Space Mountain, Big Thunder Mountain Railroad, Splash Mountain, the Haunted Mansion, and Pirates of the Caribbean. Lines for these rides can last an hour or more in the middle of the day.

TOURING THE PARK

The Disneyland complex is divided into several themed "lands," each of which has a number of rides and attractions that are, more or less, related to that land's theme.

Main Street U.S.A., at the park's entrance, is a cinematic version of turn-of-the-century small-town America. This whitewashed Rockwellian fantasy is lined with gift shops, candy stores, a soda fountain, and a silent theater that continuously runs early Mickey Mouse films. You'll find the practical things you might need here too, such as stroller rentals and storage lockers. Because there are no rides here, it's best to tour Main Street during the middle of the afternoon, when lines for rides are longest, and in the evening, when you can rest your feet in the theater that features "Great Moments with Mr. Lincoln," a patriotic (and Audio-Animatronic™) look at America's 16th president. There's always something happening on Main Street; stop in at the information booth to the left of the main entrance for a schedule of the day's events.

You might start your day by circumnavigating the park by train. An authentic 19th-century steam engine pulls open-air cars around the park's perimeter. Board at the Main Street Depot and take a complete turn around the park, or disembark at any one of the lands.

Adventureland is inspired by the most exotic regions of Asia, Africa, India, and the South Pacific. There are several popular rides here. This is where you'll find the Swiss Family Treehouse. On the Jungle Cruise, passengers board a large authentic-looking Mississippi River paddleboat and float along an Amazon-like river. En route, the boat is threatened by Audio-Animatronic™ wild animals and hostile natives, while a tour guide entertains with a running patter. A spear's throw away is the Enchanted Tiki Room, one of the most sedate attractions in Adventureland. Inside, you can sit down and watch a 20-minute musical comedy featuring electronically animated tropical birds, flowers, and "tiki gods."

The Indiana Jones Adventure is Adventureland's newest ride. Based on the Steven Spielberg series of films, this ride takes adventurers into the Temple of the Forbidden Eye, in joltingly realistic all-terrain vehicles. Riders follow Indy and experience the perils of bubbling lava pits, whizzing arrows, fire-breathing serpents, collapsing bridges, and the familiar cinematic tumbling boulder (this effect is *very* realistic in the front seats!). Disney "imagineers" reached new heights with the design of this ride's line which, take our word for it, has so much detail throughout its twisting path that 30 minutes or more simply flies by.

New Orleans Square, a large, grassy, gas lamp–dotted green, is home to the Haunted Mansion, the most high-tech ghost house we've ever seen. The spookiness has been toned down so kids won't get nightmares anymore, so the events inside are as funny as they are scary. Even more fanciful is Pirates of the Caribbean, one of Disneyland's most popular rides. Here, visitors float on boats through mock underground caves, entering an enchanting world of swashbuckling, rum-running, and buried treasure. Even in the middle of the afternoon you can dine by the cool moonlight and to the sound of crickets in the Blue Bayou Restaurant, the best eatery in the land.

Critter Country is supposed to be an ode to the backwoods—a sort of Frontierland without those pesky settlers. Little kids like to sing along with the Audio-Animatronic™ critters in the musical Country Bear Jamboree show. Older kids and grownups head straight for Splash Mountain, one of the largest water flume rides in the world. Loosely based on the Disney movie *Song of the South,* the ride is lined with about 100 characters who won't stop singing "Zip-A-Dee-Doo-Dah." Be prepared to get wet, especially if someone sizable is in the front seat of your log-shaped boat.

Frontierland gets its inspiration from 19th-century America. It's full of dense "forests" and broad "rivers" inhabited by hearty-looking (but, luckily, not-smelling) "pioneers." You can take a raft to Tom Sawyer's Island, a do-it-yourself play island with balancing rocks, caves, and a rope bridge, and board the Big Thunder Mountain Railroad, a runaway roller coaster that races through a deserted 1870s gold mine. You'll also find a petting zoo and an Abe Lincoln–style log cabin here; both are great for exploring with the little ones.

On Saturday, Sunday, holidays, and vacation periods, head to Frontierland's Rivers of America after dark to see the FANTASMIC! show—a mix of magic, music, live performers, and sensational special effects. Just as he did in *The Sorcerer's Apprentice,* Mickey Mouse appears and uses his magical powers to create giant water fountains, enormous flowers, and fantasy creatures. There's plenty of pyrotechnics, lasers, and fog, as well as a 45-foot-tall dragon that breathes fire and sets the water of the Rivers of America aflame. Cool!

Mickey's Toontown, opened in 1993, is a colorful, wacky, whimsical world inspired by the *Roger Rabbit* films. This is a gag-filled land populated by toons. There are several rides here, including Roger Rabbit's CarToonSpin, but these take a backseat to Toontown itself—a trippy smile-inducing world without a straight line or right angle in sight. This is a great place to talk with Mickey, Minnie, Goofy, Roger Rabbit, and the rest of your favorite toons. You can even visit their "houses" here. Mickey's red-shingled house and movie barn is filled with props from some of his greatest cartoons.

Fantasyland has a storybook theme and is the catch-all "land" for all the stuff that doesn't quite seem to fit anywhere else. Most of the rides here are geared to the under-6 set, including the King Arthur Carousel, Dumbo the Flying Elephant ride, and the Casey Jr. Circus Train, but some, like Mr. Toad's Wild Ride and Peter Pan's Flight, grownups have an irrational attachment to as well. You'll also find Alice in Wonderland, Snow White's Scary Adventures, Pinocchio's Daring Journey, and more in Fantasyland. The most lauded attraction is It's a Small World, a slow-moving indoor river ride through a saccharine nightmare of all the world's children singing the song everybody loves to hate. For a different kind of thrill, try the Matterhorn Bobsleds, a zippy roller coaster through chilled caverns and drifting fog banks. It's one of the park's most popular rides.

Tomorrowland may now seem a bit dated, but it still offers some of the park's best attractions. Space Mountain, a pitch-black indoor roller coaster, is one of Disneyland's best rides. Star Tours, the original Disney/George Lucas joint venture, is a 40-passenger StarSpeeder that encounters a spaceload of misadventures on the way to the Moon of Endor, achieved with wired seats and video effects (not for the queasy); the line can last an hour or more, but it's worth the wait. In addition to all this, you can take a dive in a submarine and soar in a rocket jet in Tomorrowland; there's also a huge video arcade.

The "lands" themselves are only half the adventure. Other joys include roaming Disney characters, penny arcades, restaurants and snack bars galore, summer fireworks, mariachi and ragtime bands, parades, shops, marching bands, and much more.

Disney Dossier

Believe it or not, the Happiest Place on Earth keeps more than a few skeletons—as well as some just plain interesting facts—in its closet. Did you know that:

- Disneyland was carved out of orange groves, and the original plans called for carefully chosen individual trees to be left standing and included in the park's landscaping. On groundbreaking day, July 21, 1954, each tree in the orchard was marked with a ribbon—red to be cut and green to be spared. But the bull-dozer operator went through and mowed down *every* tree indiscriminately . . . no one had foreseen his color-blindness.

- Disneyland designers utilized forced perspective in the construction of many of the park's structures to give the illusion of height and dramatic proportions while keeping the park a manageable size. The buildings on Main Street U.S.A., for example, are actually 90% scale on the first floor, 80% on the second, and so forth. The stones on Sleeping Beauty Castle are carved in diminishing scale from the bottom to the top, giving it the illusion of towering height.

- The faces of the Pirates of the Caribbean were modeled after some of the early staff of Walt Disney Imagineering, who also lent their names to the second-floor "businesses" along Main Street U.S.A.

- Walt Disney maintained two apartments inside Disneyland. His private apart-ment above the Town Square Fire Station has been kept just as it was when he lived there.

- The elaborately carved horses on Fantasyland's King Arthur Carousel are between 100 and 120 years old; Walt Disney found them lying neglected in storage at Coney Island in New York, and brought them home to be carefully cleaned and restored.

- It's a Small World was touted at its opening as "mingling the waters of the oceans and seas around the world with Small World's Seven Seaways." This was more than a publicity hoax—records from that time show such charges as $21.86 for a shipment of sea water from the Caribbean.

- The peaceful demeanor of Disneyland was broken during the summer of 1970 by a group of radical Vietnam protesters who invaded the park. They seized Tom Sawyer Island and raised the Viet Cong flag over the fort before being expelled by riot specialists.

- Indiana Jones: Temple of the Forbidden Eye, Disneyland's newest attraction, won't be experienced the same way by any two groups of riders. Like a sophisti-cated computer game, the course is programmed with so many variables in the action that there are 160,000 possible combinations of events.

Oh, yeah—there's also the storybook Sleeping Beauty Castle . . . can you spot the evil witch peering from one of the top windows?

KNOTT'S BERRY FARM

Cynics say that Knott's Berry Farm is for people who aren't smart enough to find Disneyland. Well, there's no doubt that visitors should tour Disney first, but it's worth staying in a hotel nearby so you can play at Knott's during your stay.

Like Disneyland, Knott's Berry Farm is not without its historical merit. Rudolph Boysen crossed a loganberry with a raspberry, calling the resulting hybrid the "boysenberry." In 1933 Buena Park farmer Walter Knott planted the boysenberry, thus launching Knott's berry farm on 10 acres of leased land. When things got tough during the Great Depression, Mrs. Knott set up a roadside stand, selling pies, preserves, and home-cooked chicken dinners. Within a year she was selling 90 meals a day. Lines became so long that Walter decided to create an Old West Ghost Town as a diversion for waiting customers.

The Knott family now owns the farm that surrounds the world-famous Chicken Dinner Restaurant, an eatery serving over a million fried meals a year. And Knott's Berry Farm is the nation's third-most-attended family entertainment complex (after the two Disney parks, of course).

During the last half of October locals flock to Knott's Berry Farm. Why? Because the entire park is revamped as "Knott's *Scary* Farm"—the ordinary attractions are made spooky and haunted, every grassy area is transformed into a graveyard or gallows, and even the already-scary rides get special surprise extras, like costumed ghouls who grab your arm in the middle of a roller-coaster ride!

GETTING THERE   Knott's Berry Farm is located at 8039 Beach Blvd. in Buena Park. It's about an hour's drive from downtown Los Angeles and about a 5-minute ride north on I-5 from Disneyland. From I-5 or Calif. 91, exit south onto Beach Boulevard. The park is located about half a mile south of Calif. 91.

ADMISSION, HOURS & INFORMATION   Admission to the park, including unlimited access to all rides, shows, and attractions, is $29 for adults and children 12 and over, $19 for seniors 60 and over and children 3 to 11, and free for children under 3. Admission is $14 for everyone after 4pm. Like Disneyland, Knott's offers discounted admission during off-season for Southern California residents, so if you're bringing local friends or family members along, be sure to take advantage of the bargain. Also like Disneyland, Knott's Berry Farm's hours vary from week to week, so you should call about the day you plan to visit. Generally speaking, the park is open during the summer every day from 9am to midnight. The rest of the year, it opens at 10am and closes at 6 or 8pm, except Saturday when it stays open till 10pm. Knott's is closed Christmas Day. Special hours and prices are in effect during Knott's Scary Farm in late October.

For recorded information, call **714/220-5200.**

Touring the Park

Knott's Berry Farm still maintains its original Old West motif. It's divided into five "Old Time Adventures" areas:

Old West Ghost Town, the original attraction, is a collection of refurbished 19th-century buildings that have been relocated from actual deserted Old West towns. Here, you can pan for gold, ride aboard an authentic stagecoach, ride rickety train cars through the Calico Mine, get held up aboard the Denver and Rio Grande Calico Railroad, and hiss at the villain during a melodrama in the Birdcage Theater.

Fiesta Village has a south-of-the-border theme that means festive markets, strolling mariachis, and wild rides like Montezooma's Revenge and Jaguar!, a roller coaster that includes two heart-in-the-mouth drops and a loop that turns you upside down.

The Roaring '20s Amusement Area contains Sky Tower, a parachute jump/drop with a 20-story free-fall. Other white-knuckle rides include XK-1, an excellent flight simulator "piloted" by the riders; and Boomerang, a state-of-the-art roller coaster that turns riders upside down six times in less than a minute. Kingdom of the Dinosaurs features extremely realistic *Jurassic Park*–like creatures. It's quite a thrill, but it may scare the little kids.

Wild Water Wilderness is a $10-million, 3¹/₂-acre attraction styled like a turn-of-the-century California wilderness park. The top ride here is a white-water adventure called Bigfoot Rapids, featuring a long stretch of artificial rapids; it's the longest ride of its kind in the world.

Camp Snoopy will probably be the youngsters' favorite area. It's meant to re-create a wilderness camp in the picturesque High Sierra. Its 6 rustic acres are the playgrounds of Charles Schulz's beloved beagle and his pals, Charlie Brown and Lucy, who greet guests and pose for pictures. The rides here, including Beary Tales Playhouse, are tailor made for the 6-and-under set.

Thunder Falls, Knott's newest area, contains Mystery Lodge, a truly amazing high-tech, trick-of-the-eye attraction based on the legends of local Native Americans. Don't miss this wonderful theater piece.

Stage shows and special activities are scheduled throughout the day. Pick up a schedule at the ticket booth.

ATTRACTIONS BEYOND THE THEME PARKS

To locate these attractions, see the map "Anaheim Area Attractions & the Orange Coast," in Section 6 of this chapter.

Arrowhead Pond of Anaheim. 2695 E. Katella Ave. (at Douglas Rd.). ☎ **714/704-2500.**

This contemporary salmon and green-glass arena's whimsical name is outdone only by that of its resident NHL team . . . the Mighty Ducks! In addition to hockey, the rink also presents ice show extravaganzas like *Disney on Ice,* featuring skaters costumed as characters in Disney feature films. Call for events schedule and ticket information.

Crystal Cathedral. 12141 Lewis St., Garden Grove. ☎ **714/971-4000.**

This angular, mirror-sheathed church (think the movie Superman's Fortress of Solitude), otherwise known as the Garden Grove Community Church, is a shocking architectural oddity, with nine-story-high doors and a vast, open interior that's shaped like a four-pointed star. Opened in 1980, it's the pulpit for televangelist Robert Schuller, who broadcasts sermons and hymns of praise on radio and television to an international audience of millions. Each Sunday an overflow crowd listens to the service blaring from loudspeakers into the parking lot. Annual Christmas and Easter pageants feature live animals, floating "angels," and other theatrics. A $5-million stainless-steel carillon, which began ringing in 1991, has prompted some of the cathedral's neighbors to complain that they want less joyful noise and more peace on earth.

Medieval Times Dinner and Tournament. 7662 Beach Blvd., Buena Park. ☎ **800/899-6600** or 714/521-4740. Admission $33–$36 adults, $23–$26 children 12 and under. Shows Mon–Thurs at 7pm, Fri at 6:30 and 8:45pm, Sat at 6 and 8:15pm, Sun at 5 and 7:15pm. Call for reservations (be sure to inquire about auto-club discounts).

Guests crowd around long wooden tables and enjoy a four-course banquet of roast chicken, ribs, herbed potatoes, and pastries—all eaten with your hands in medieval fashion, of course. More than 1,100 people can fit into the castle, where sword fights, jousting tournaments, and various feats of skill are performed by colorfully costumed actors, including fake knights on real horses. It's kind of ridiculous, but kids of all ages love it. *A word of warning:* the horses (and horseplay) kick up lots of dirt, so if you have any allergies to dust or animal dander, keep an eye on the nearest exit.

Movieland Wax Museum. 7711 Beach Blvd. (Calif. 39), Buena Park. ☎ **714/522-1155.** Admission $12.95 adults, $10.55 seniors, $6.95 children 4–11, free for children 3 and under. Daily

9am–7pm. Discount combination admission includes Ripley's Believe It Or Not! Museum (across the street).

At this goofy museum, located 1 block north of Knott's Berry Farm in Buena Park, you can see wax-molded figures of all your favorite film stars, from Bela Lugosi in *Dracula* and Marilyn Monroe in *Gentlemen Prefer Blondes,* to Leslie Nielsen in the *Naked Gun* movies. "America's Sweetheart," Mary Pickford, dedicated the museum on May 4, 1962; it has risen steadily in popularity ever since, with new stars added yearly, taking their place next to the time-tested favorites. The museum was created by film addict Allen Parkinson, who saw to it that some of the most memorable scenes in motion pictures were re-created in exacting detail in wax. In the seemingly unrelated Chamber of Horrors, you almost expect the torture victims to scream "tourist trap!" Discount combination admission tickets include the new **Ripley's Believe It Or Not! Museum** across the street—grown-ups yawn but young kids marvel at the "astounding" facts presented in a sensational manner.

Richard Nixon Library and Birthplace. 18001 Yorba Linda Blvd., Yorba Linda. ☎ **714/ 993-5075.** Fax 714/528-0544. Admission $5.95 adults, $3.95 seniors, $2 children 8–11, free for children 7 and under. Mon–Sat 10am–5pm, Sun 11am–5pm.

Although he was the most vilified U.S. President in modern history, there has always been a warm place in the hearts of Orange County locals for Richard Nixon. This presidential library, located in Nixon's boyhood town, celebrates the roots, life, and legacy of America's 37th President. The 9-acre site contains the modest farmhouse where Nixon was born, manicured flower gardens, a modern museum containing presidential archives, and the final resting place of both Nixon and his wife, Pat.

Displays include videos of the famous Nixon-Kennedy TV debates, an impressive life-size statuary summit of world leaders, gifts of state (including a gun from Elvis Presley), and exhibits on China and Russia. There's also an exhibit of the late Pat Nixon's sparkling First Lady gowns. There's a 12-foot-high graffiti-covered chunk of the Berlin Wall, symbolizing the defeat of Communism, but hardly a mention of Nixon's leading role in the anti-Communist "witch hunts" of the 1950s. There are exhibits on Vietnam, yet no mention of Nixon's illegal expansion of that war into neighboring Cambodia. Only the Watergate Gallery is relatively forthright, where visitors can listen to actual White House tapes and view a montage of the President's last day in the White House.

WHERE TO STAY
VERY EXPENSIVE

✪ **Disneyland Hotel.** 1150 W. Cerritos Ave. (west of the Disneyland parking lot), Anaheim, CA 92802. ☎ **714/778-6600.** Fax 714/965-6597. 1,136 rms, 62 suites. A/C MINIBAR TV TEL. $155–$250 double; from $425 suite. AE, MC, V. Parking $10.

The "Official Hotel of the Magic Kingdom," attached to Disneyland via a monorail system that runs right to the hotel, is the perfect place to stay if you're doing the park. You'll be able to return to your room anytime you need to during the day, whether it's to take a much-needed nap or to change your soaked shorts after your Splash Mountain Adventure. Best of all, hotel guests get to enter the park early almost every day and enjoy the major rides before the lines form. The amount of time varies from day to day, but usually you can enter 1¹/₂ hours early. Call ahead to check the schedule for your specific day.

The theme hotel is a wild attraction unto itself. The rooms aren't fancy, but they're comfortably and attractively furnished like a good-quality business hotel. Many rooms feature framed reproductions of rare Disney conceptual art, and the Disney Channel is free on TV, naturally. The beautifully landscaped hotel is an all-inclusive resort, offering six restaurants, five cocktail lounges, every kind of service desk imaginable, a "wharfside" bazaar, a walk-under waterfall, and even an artificial white-sand beach. Disneyland has also just taken over the adjoining Pacific Hotel, whose Asian tranquility (including a fine and pricey Japanese restaurant) brings a slightly higher tariff.

When you're planning your trip, inquire with the hotel about multiday packages that allow you to take on the park at your own pace.

Dining/Entertainment: The best restaurant is Stromboli's, an Italian/American eatery that serves all the pasta staples. Kids love Goofy's Kitchen, where the family can enjoy breakfast and dinner with the Disney characters.

Services: Concierge, room service, shoeshine, laundry, nightly turndown, babysitting, express checkout.

Facilities: Three large heated outdoor pools, complete health club, putting green, shuffleboard and croquet courts, sundeck, special children's programs, beauty salon, 20 shops and boutiques.

Sheraton Anaheim Hotel. 1015 W. Ball Rd. (at I-5), Anaheim, CA 92802. ☎ **800/ 325-3535** or 714/778-1700. Fax 714/535-3889. 500 rms, 26 suites. A/C MINIBAR TV TEL. $90–$190 double; $220–$280 suite. AE, CB, DC, MC, V. Free parking; shuttle to Disneyland.

This hotel rises to the festive theme-park occasion with its fanciful English Tudor architecture, a castle that lures business conventions, Disney-bound families, and area high-school proms equally successfully. The public areas are quiet and elegant— intimate gardens with fountains and koi ponds, plush lobby and lounges—which can be a pleasing touch after a frantic day at the amusement park. The rooms are modern and unusually spacious, but otherwise not distinctive; a large swimming pool is located in the center of the complex, surrounded by attractive landscaping.

Dining/Entertainment: The Garden Court Bistro offers indoor and outdoor ambience, while the California Deli is open from 6am to midnight and serves standard delicatessan fare. There's also a wood and tapestry cocktail lounge.

Services: Concierge, room service, overnight shoeshine, laundry services, nightly turndown.

Facilities: Heated outdoor pool, sundeck, gift shop.

MODERATE

Anaheim Plaza Hotel. 1700 S. Harbor Blvd., Anaheim, CA 92802. ☎ **800/228-1357** or 714/772-5900. Fax 714/772-8386. 300 rms and suites. A/C TV TEL. $79–$119 double; from $175 suite. AE, DC, DISC, MC, V. Free parking; shuttle to Disneyland.

You can easily cross the street to Disneyland's main gate, or you can take advantage of the Anaheim Plaza's free shuttle to the park. Once you return, however, you'll appreciate the way this 30-year-old hotel's clever design shuts out the noisy world. In fact, the seven two-story garden buildings remind us of 1960s Waikiki more than busy Anaheim. The Olympic-size heated outdoor pool and whirlpool are unfortunately surrounded by Astroturf, but the new management was doing a total room renovation in 1996 so there's always hope. They won't change a thing about the light-filled modern lobby, nor the friendly rates. The hotel will still offer room service from the casual Cafe in the lobby, plus laundry valet and coin-operated laundry.

Buena Park Hotel. 7675 Crescent Ave. (at Grand), Buena Park, CA 90620. ☎ **800/ 422-4444** or 714/995-1111. Fax 714/828-8590. 350 rms and suites. A/C TV TEL. $89–$99 double; $175–$250 suite. AE, DC, DISC, MC, V. Free parking; shuttle to Disneyland.

Within easy walking distance of Knott's Berry Farm, the Buena Park Hotel also offers a free shuttle to Disneyland just 7 miles away. The pristine lobby has the look of a business-oriented hotel, and that it is. But vacationers can also benefit from the elevated level of service designed for the business traveler. Be sure to inquire about

Executive Club rates as well as Knott's or Disneyland package deals. The rooms in the nine-story tower are tastefully decorated, and facilities and services include room service, a charming heated outdoor pool and spa, two restaurants and a 1950s-1960s dance club, and rental-car desk.

Candy Cane Inn. 1747 S. Harbor Blvd., Anaheim, CA 92802. ☎ **800/345-7057** or 714/774-5284. Fax 714/772-5462. 173 rms. A/C TV TEL. $70–$84 double. Rates include breakfast. AE, DC, DISC, MC, V. Free parking; shuttle to Disneyland.

Take your standard U-shaped motel court with outdoor corridors, spruce it up with cobblestone drive- and walkways, old-time streetlamps, and flowering vines engulf-ing the balconies of attractively painted rooms, and you have the Candy Cane. The face-lift worked, making this motel near Disneyland's main gate a real treat for the stylish bargain hunter. The guest rooms are decorated in bright floral motifs with comfortable furnishings, including queen-size beds and a separate dressing and vanity area. Complimentary breakfast is served in the courtyard, where you can also splash around in a heated pool, spa, or kids' wading pool.

Howard Johnson Hotel. 1380 S. Harbor Blvd., Anaheim, CA 92802. ☎ **800/422-4228** or 714/776-6120. Fax 714/533-3578. 320 rms. A/C TV TEL. $64–$94 double. AE, CB, DC, DISC, MC, V. Free parking.

This hotel occupies an enviable location, directly opposite Disneyland, and a cute San Francisco trolley car runs to and from the park every 30 minutes. The rooms are divided among several low-profile buildings, all with balconies opening onto a cen-tral garden with two heated pools for adults and one for children. Garden paths lead under eucalyptus and olive trees to a splashing circular fountain. During the sum-mer you can see the nightly fireworks display at Disneyland from the upper balco-nies of the parkside rooms. Try to avoid the rooms in the back buildings, for they get some freeway noise. Services and facilities include in-room movies and cable, room service from the attached Coco's Restaurant, gift shop, games room, laundry service plus coin-laundry room, airport shuttle, and family lodging/Disney admission packages. We think it's pretty classy for a HoJo's.

Inn at the Park. 1855 S. Harbor Blvd. (south of Katella Ave.), Anaheim, CA 92802. ☎ **800/421-6662** or 714/750-1811. Fax 714/971-3626. 500 rms. A/C TV TEL. $120–$145 double. AE, DC, DISC, MC, V. Free parking; shuttle to Disneyland.

Although the inn is in the Anaheim Convention Center Complex (across the street from Disneyland) and draws primarily a business crowd, there's much to appeal to the leisure traveler. The contemporary and confortable rooms in the 12-story tower all have balconies overlooking either Disneyland or the hotel's luxurious pool area, which includes a large heated pool, deluxe spa, attractive sundeck, and snack/cocktail-bar gazebo. The hotel offers guest laundry and valet, an activities desk, room service, and a gift shop, plus the Old West frontier-themed Overland Stage Restau-rant, serving up steak and seafood plus a few colorful game selections.

Jolly Roger Hotel. 640 W. Katella Ave. (west of Harbor Blvd.), Anaheim, CA 92802. ☎ **800/446-1555** or 714/772-7621. Fax 714/772-2308. 225 rms, 11 suites. A/C TV TEL. $65–$118 double; $78–$185 suite. AE, DC, DISC, MC, V. Free parking; shuttle to Disneyland.

The only thing still sporting a buccaneer theme here is the adjoining Jolly Roger Restaurant, and that's just fine. The comfortable but blandly furnished rooms are in either an older, two-story L-shaped motel or two newer five-story annexes. We pre-fer the older units for their quiet and also for the palm-shaded heated pool in the cen-ter of it all. Across the driveway is the swashbuckling restaurant where dinner will set you back a few doubloons. The all-day coffee shop is more reasonable, and there's nightly entertainment and dancing in the lounge. Conveniently located across the street from Disneyland, the Jolly Roger also has meeting and banquet rooms, plus a second pool, a spa, beauty salon, and gift shop.

INEXPENSIVE

Best Western Anaheim Stardust. 1057 W. Ball Rd., Anaheim, CA 92802. ☎ 800/222-3639 or 714/774-7600. Fax 714/535-6953. 103 rms, 18 suites. A/C TV TEL. $58–$70 double; $95 suite. Rates include full breakfast. AE, DC, DISC, MC, V. Free parking.

Located on the back side of Disneyland, this modest hotel will appeal to the budget-conscious traveler who isn't willing to sacrifice absolutely everything. All rooms have a refrigerator and microwave, breakfast is served in a refurbished train dining car, and you can relax by the large outdoor heated pool and spa while doing wash in the laundry room. The large family suites will accommodate virtually any brood, and shuttles run regularly to the park.

Colony Inn. 7800 Crescent Ave. (west of Beach Blvd.), Buena Park, CA 90620. ☎ 800/98-COLONY or 714/527-2201. Fax 714/826-3826. 130 rms and suites. A/C TV TEL. $49–$98 double or suite. AE, MC, V. Free parking.

Although it's composed of two modest U-shaped motels, the recently refurbished Colony Inn has a lot to offer. It's the closest lodging to Knott's Berry Farm's south entrance and is just 10 minutes away from Disneyland. They cheerfully offer discount coupons for Knott's and other nearby attractions, as well as complimentary coffee and doughnuts to jump-start your morning. The rooms are spacious (doubles sleep up to four people, and suites sleep up to eight) and comfortably outfitted with conservatively styled furnishings. There are two pools, two wading pools for kids, two saunas, and a coin-operated laundry on the premises.

Travelodge Apollo Inn. 1741 S. West St. (north of Katella Ave.), Anaheim, CA 92802. ☎ 800/826-1616 or 714/772-9750. Fax 714/772-5842. 136 rms. A/C TV TEL. $52–$75 double. AE, DC, DISC, MC, V. Free parking.

There are several Travelodges surrounding Disneyland, all superbly located and functional. The Apollo Inn, while still your run-of-the-mill motel, provides such distinctive touches as refrigerators in all rooms, available VCR and video rentals, elevators—and the convenience of being next door to the Disneyland Hotel's monorail stop, so you can bypass the main gate flurry and whiz directly into the park. The Apollo has a heated pool, spa, saunas, and children's wading pool; plus Vern's coffee shop dressed up like a 1950s diner.

WHERE TO DINE

Inland Orange County isn't known for its restaurants, most of which are branches of reliable California or national chains you'll easily recognize. We've listed a few intriguing options, but if you're visiting the area just for the day, you'll probably eat inside the theme parks; there are plenty of restaurants to choose from at both Disneyland and Knott's Berry Farm. At Disneyland, in the Créole-themed **Blue Bayou,** you can sit under the stars inside the Pirates of the Caribbean ride—no matter what time of day it is. At Knott's, try the fried chicken dinners and boysenberry pies at Mrs. Knott's historic **Chicken Dinner Restaurant.** For the most unusual dinner you've ever had with the kids, go to **Medieval Times** (see "Attractions Beyond the Theme Parks," above).

EXPENSIVE

Chanteclair. 18912 MacArthur Blvd. (opposite John Wayne Airport), Irvine. ☎ 714/752-8001. Reservations required. Main courses $15–$24. AE, CB, DC, MC, V. Mon–Fri 11am–3pm and 6–11pm, Sat 6–11pm. CONTINENTAL/FRENCH.

Chanteclair is expensive and a little difficult to reach, but it's worth seeking out. Designed in the style of a provincial French inn, the rambling stucco structure is built around a central garden court and houses several dining and drinking areas, each with its own unique ambience. The antique-furnished restaurant has five fireplaces. At lunch you might order grilled lamb chops with herb-and-garlic sauce, chicken-and-mushroom crêpes, or Cajun charred ahi. Dinner is a worthwhile splurge that might begin with a lobster bisque with brandy or Beluga caviar with blinis. For a main dish, we recommend the rack of lamb with thyme sauce and roasted garlic.

Mr. Stox. 1105 E. Katella Ave. (east of Harbor Blvd.), Anaheim. ☎ **714/634-2994.** Reservations recommended on weekends. Main courses $12–$23. AE, DC, MC, V. Mon–Fri 11am–2:30pm and 5:30–10pm, Sat 5:30–10pm, Sun 5–9pm. AMERICAN.

Hearty steaks and fresh seafood are served in an early California manor-house setting here at Mr. Stox. Specialties include roast prime rib and mesquite-broiled fish, veal, and lamb. Chef Scott Raczek particularly excels at reduction sauces and innovative herbal preparations. Sandwiches and salads are also available. The homemade breads and desserts, such as chocolate-mousse cake, are unexpectedly good. Mr. Stox has an enormous and reknowned wine cellar, and there's live entertainment every night.

MODERATE

Felix Continental Cafe. 36 Plaza Sq. (at the corner of Chapman and Glassell), Orange. ☎ **714/633-5842.** Reservations recommended for dinner. Main courses $6–$14. AE, DC, MC, V. Mon–Thurs 7am–9pm, Fri 7am–10pm, Sat 8am–10pm, Sun 8am–9pm. CUBAN/SPANISH.

If you like the re-created Main Street in the Magic Kingdom, then you'll love the historic 1886 town square in the city of Orange, on view from the cozy sidewalk tables outside the Felix Continental Cafe. Dining on traditional Cuban specialties and watching traffic spin around the magnificent fountain and rosebushes of the plaza evokes old Havana or Madrid rather than the cookie-cutter Orange County communities just blocks away. The food receives glowing praise from restaurant reviewers and loyal locals alike.

Peppers Restaurant and Nightclub. 12361 Chapman Ave. (west of Harbor Blvd.), Garden Grove. ☎ **714/740-1333.** Reservations recommended on weekends. Main courses $9–$14. AE, CB, DC, DISC, MC, V. Mon–Thurs 11am–10pm, Fri–Sat 11am–11pm, Sun 10am–10pm. CALIFORNIA/MEXICAN.

This colorful Californian/Mexican-themed restaurant just south of Disneyland looks like a partying kind of place, and it doesn't disappoint. The varied menu features mesquite-broiled dishes and fresh seafood daily. Mexican specialties include lots of variations of tacos and burritos, but the grilled meats and fish are best, especially Pepper's signature King Fajitas with crab legs or lobster tails. Dancing is available nightly to Top 40 hits starting at 9pm, and Monday nights a Mexican group plays live music. There's a free shuttle to and from six area hotels between 6pm and the nightclub closing time of 2am.

Renata's Caffè Italiano. 227 E. Chapman Ave. (at Grand), Orange. ☎ **714/771-4740.** Reservations recommended for dinner. Main courses $8–$15. AE, MC, V. Mon–Thurs 11am–9pm, Fri 11am–10pm, Sat–Sun 4–10pm. Closed Sun in summer. ITALIAN.

Near Felix Cafe in the historic plaza district, owner Renata Cerchiari draws a steady stream of regulars with good if not great contemporary Italian specialties. We found the charming patio dining in this small-town atmosphere a welcome change from Orange County's frantic pace (particularly if you're staying by the amusement parks), and the wide selection of appetizers and pasta dishes more authentic and reasonably priced than anywhere else, although the creamy Caesar salad wins higher marks than the disappointing cannolli.

INEXPENSIVE

Belisle's Restaurant. 12001 Harbor Blvd. (at Chapman), Garden Grove. ☎ **714/750-6560.** Main courses $3–$23. MC, V. Sun–Thurs 7am–midnight, Fri–Sat 7am–2am. AMERICAN.

Harvey Belisle's modest pink cottage has been doling out "Texas-size" portions of diner-style food since before Disneyland opened in 1955. This is the place to bring a ravenous football team, or just your hollow-legged teenage boys. Portions are enormous, we can't say that enough; from the four-egg omelettes accompanied by mountains of hash browns to the 12-oz. chicken fried steak to a chocolate eclair the size of a log, we think Paul Bunyan would feel right at home. Just say "fill 'er up"!

6 The Orange Coast

Whatever you do, don't say "Orange County." The mere name evokes images of smoggy industrial parks, cookie-cutter housing developments, and the staunch Republicanism that prevail behind the so-called orange curtain.

We're talking instead about the Orange Coast, one of Southern California's best-kept secrets, a string of seaside jewels that have been compared with the French Riviera or the Costa del Sol. Here, 42 miles of beaches offer pristine stretches of sand, tide pools teeming with marine life, ecological preserves, charming secluded coves, quaint pleasure-boat harbors, and legendary surfers atop breaking waves. Whether your bare feet want to stroll a funky wooden boardwalk or your gold card gravitates toward a yacht club, you've come to the right place.

ESSENTIALS

GETTING THERE See Section 1 of Chapter 14 for airport and airline information. By car from Los Angeles, take I-5 or I-495 south. The scenic, shore-hugging Pacific Coast Highway (Calif. 1, or just PCH to the locals) links the Orange Coast communities from Seal Beach in the north to Capistrano Beach just south of Dana Point, where it merges with I-5. To reach the beach communities directly, take the following freeway exits: **Seal Beach,** Seal Beach Boulevard from I-405; **Huntington Beach,** Beach Boulevard / Calif. 39 from either I-405 or I-5; **Newport Beach,** Calif. 55 from either I-405 or I-5; **Laguna Beach,** Calif. 133 from I-5; **San Juan Capistrano,** Ortega Highway / Calif. 74 from I-5; and **Dana Point,** Pacific Coast Highway / Calif. 1 from I-5.

VISITOR INFORMATION The **Seal Beach Chamber of Commerce,** 201 8th St., at Central (☎ 310/799-0179), is open Monday to Friday from 10am to 2pm.

The **Huntington Beach Conference & Visitors Bureau,** 101 Main St., Suite A2 (☎ 800/SAY-OCEAN or 714/969-3492; fax 714/969-5592), makes up for being *really* hard to find by genially offering tons of information, enthusiasm, and personal anecdotes. They're at the corner of PCH and Main Street—from the rear parking lot take the elevator to the second floor. Open Monday to Friday from 8:30am to noon and 1:30pm to 5pm. Their Internet Website is at **http://www.imark.com/hbcvb.**

The **Newport Beach Conference & Visitors Bureau,** 3300 W. Coast Hwy. (☎ 800/94-COAST or 714/722-1611; fax 714/722-1612), distributes brochures, sample menus, a calendar of events, and their free and very helpful Visitor's Guide. Call or stop in Monday to Friday from 8am to 5pm. The Internet Website is at **http://www.newport.lib.ca.us/default.htm.**

Anaheim Area Attractions & the Orange Coast

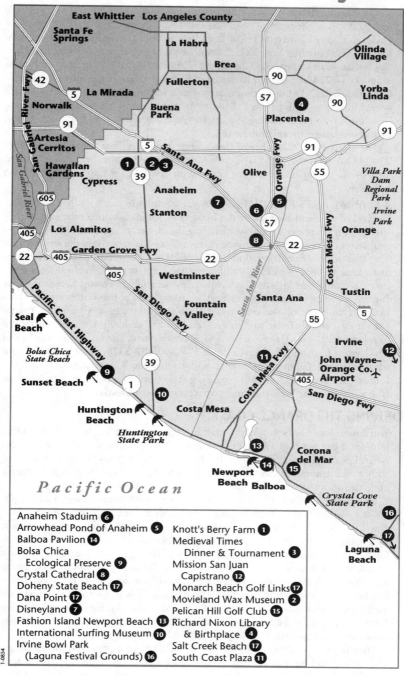

Anaheim Staduim 6
Arrowhead Pond of Anaheim 5
Balboa Pavilion 14
Bolsa Chica
  Ecological Preserve 9
Crystal Cathedral 8
Doheny State Beach 17
Dana Point 17
Disneyland 7
Fashion Island Newport Beach 13
International Surfing Museum 10
Irvine Bowl Park
  (Laguna Festival Grounds) 16

Knott's Berry Farm 1
Medieval Times
  Dinner & Tournament 3
Mission San Juan
  Capistrano 12
Monarch Beach Golf Links 17
Movieland Wax Museum 2
Pelican Hill Golf Club 15
Richard Nixon Library
  & Birthplace 4
Salt Creek Beach 17
South Coast Plaza 11

1-0854

The **Laguna Beach Visitors Bureau,** 252 Broadway (☎ **800/877-1115** or 714/497-9229), is in the heart of town and distributes lodging, dining, and art gallery guides. It's open Monday to Friday from 9am to 5pm and on Saturday from 10am to 4pm. Their Internet Website is at **http://www.orangecounty.com/lagunabeach.**

The **San Juan Capistrano Chamber of Commerce,** 31931 Camino Capistrano, Suite D (☎ **714/493-4700**), is located in El Adobe Plaza at the corner of Camino Capistrano and Del Abispo, conveniently within walking distance of the mission. It's open Monday to Friday from 8:30am to 4pm, and prints a sepia-toned "Walking Tour Guide" to historic sites. The Internet Website with lots of helpful links is at **http://www.sanjuancapistrano.com.**

The **Dana Point Chamber of Commerce,** 24681 La Plaza, Suite 120 (☎ **800/290-DANA** or 714/496-1555), is open Monday to Friday from 9am to 4:30pm and carries some restaurant and lodging information as well as a comprehensive recreation brochure.

A SPECIAL ARTS FESTIVAL   A 60-year tradition in arts-friendly Laguna, the **Festival of Arts and Pageant of the Masters** is held each summer throughout July and August. It's pretty large now, including the formerly "alternative" Sawdust Festival across the street and the unique Pageant of the Masters. Amid the artists exhibiting (and selling) original works in every medium, local volunteers perform a series of *tableaux vivants,* re-creating well-known paintings by posing perfectly still in accurate costumes and elaborate makeup against carefully re-created backdrops. The Pageant is one-of-a-kind, creating an extraordinary sense of two-dimentionality. Musical entertainment ranging from jazz ensembles to ethnic groups perform throughout the day, and there are workshops for adults and children, plus demonstrations of printmaking, *raku* (Japanese pottery), and other arts. The festival grounds are at 650 Laguna Canyon Rd., Laguna Beach (☎ **800/487-3378,** or 714/494-1145 for advance tickets). Grounds admission is $3 for adults and $2 for seniors and students. Pageant tickets cost $15 to $40, depending on performance night and seat location. Check it out on the Web at **http://www.coolsville.com/festival.**

DRIVING THE ORANGE COAST

You'll most likely be exploring the coast by car, so we cover the beach communities in order, from north to south. Keep in mind, however, that if you're traveling between Los Angeles and San Diego, the Pacific Coast Highway (Calif. 1) is a splendidly scenic detour that adds less than an hour to the commute. So pick out a couple of destinations and go for it.

Seal Beach, on the border between Los Angeles and Orange Counties and neighbor to Long Beach's Naples harbor, is geographically isolated both by the adjacent U.S. Naval Weapons Station and the self-contained Leisure World retirement community. As a result, the charming beach town appears untouched by modern development— Orange County's answer to small-town America. Taking a stroll down Main Street is a walk back in time which culminates in the Seal Beach Pier. Although there are no longer clusters of the sunbathing, squalking seals that gave the town its name, old-timers fish hopefully, lovers stroll swooningly, and families cavort by the seaside, perhaps capping off the afternoon with an old-fashioned double dip from **Main Street Ice Cream & Yogurt,** at the corner of Main Street and Ocean Avenue, where the walls are decorated with sepia-toned photographs of Seal Beach's yesteryear.

Huntington Beach is probably the largest Orange Coast city; it stretches quite a ways inland and has seen the most urbanization. To some extent this has changed the old boardwalk and pier to a modern outdoor mall where cliques of gang kids co-exist with families and the surfers who continue to flock here, for Huntington is legendary in surf lore. Hawaiian surfer Duke Kahanamoka brought the sport here in the 1920s, and some say the breaks around the pier and Bolsa Chica are the best in California. The world's top wave-riders flock to Huntington each August for the rowdy but professional **U.S. Open of Surfing** (call 310/286-3700 for information). If you'll be around during Christmastime, try to see the gaily decorated marina homes and boats in Huntington Harbour by taking the **Cruise of Lights,** a 45-minute narrated sail through and around the harbor islands. The festivities generally last from mid-December until Christmas; call 714/840-7542 for schedules and ticket information.

The name **Newport Beach** conjures comparisons to Rhode Island's Newport, where the well-to-do enjoy seaside living with all the creature comforts. That's the way it is here too, but on a less grandiose scale. From the million-dollar Cape Cod–style cottages on sunny Balboa Island in the bay, to elegant shopping complexes like Fashion Island (surrounded by ultra-manicured country club lawns) and South Coast Plaza (an *über*-mall with valet parking, car detailing, limo service, and concierge), this is where fashionable socialites, right-wing celebrities, and business mavens can all be found. Alternatively, you could explore **Balboa** peninsula's historic Pavilion and old-fashioned pier or board a passenger ferry to Catalina Island.

Laguna Beach, whose breathtaking geography is marked by bold elevated head-lands, coastal bluffs, and pocket coves, is known as an artists' enclave, but the truth is that Laguna has became so *in* (read: expensive) that it drove most of the true bo-hemians *out.* Their legacy remains with the annual **Festival of the Arts and Pageant of the Masters** (see "A Special Art Festival," below), as well as a proliferation of art galleries intermingling with high-priced boutiques along the town's cozy streets. In warm weather Laguna Beach has an overwhelming Mediterranean-island ambience, which makes *everyone* feel beautifully, idly rich.

San Juan Capistrano, nestled in the verdant headlands just inland of Dana Point, is defined by Spanish missions and its loyal flock of swallows. The "mission" archi-tecture is authentic, and history abounds here. Consider San Juan Capistrano a com-pact, life-size diorama illustrating the evolution of a small western town from Spanish mission era to secular rancho period, into statehood and the 20th century. Ironically, Mission San Juan Capistrano (see "Seeing the Sights," below) is once again the cen-ter of the community, just as the founding friars intended 200 years ago.

Dana Point, the last town south, has been called a "marina development in search of a soul." Overlooking the harbor stands a monument to 19th-century author Richard Henry Dana, who gave his name to the area and described it in *Two Years Before the Mast.* Activities generally center around yachting and Dana Point's jewel of a harbor. Nautical themes are everywhere; particularly charming are the series of streets named for old-fashioned shipboard lights, a rainbow that includes "Street of the Amber Lantern", ". . . the Violet Lantern," ". . . the Golden Lantern," and so on. Bordering the harbor is Doheny State Beach (see "Beaches & Nature Preserves," below), which wrote the book on seaside park and camping facilities.

ENJOYING THE OUTDOORS
BEACHES & NATURE PRESERVES

The **Bolsa Chica Ecological Reserve,** in Huntington Beach (☎ **714/897-7003**), is a 300-acre restored urban salt marsh that's a haven to more than 200 bird species, as well as a wide variety of protected plants and animals. Naturalists come to spot herons and egrets as well as California horn snails, jackknife clams, sea sponges, com-mon jellyfish, and shore crabs. An easy 1 1/2-mile loop trail begins from a parking lot on the Pacific Coast Highway (Calif. 1) a mile south of Warner Boulevard; docents lead a narrated walk the first Saturday of every month. The trail heads inland, over Inner Bolsa Bay and up Bolsa Chica bluffs. It then loops back toward the ocean over a dike that separates the Inner and Outer Bolsa bays and traverses a coastal sand dune system. This beautiful hike is a terrific afternoon adventure. The Bolsa Chica Conservancy has been working since 1978 on reclaiming the wetlands from oil companies that began drilling here 70 years ago. It's an ongoing process, and you can still see those "seesaw" drills dotting the outer areas of the reserve. Although Bolsa Chica State Beach across the road has superb facilities, fantastic surfing, and well-equipped campsites, you might find that the hulking offshore oil rigs spoil the view.

Huntington City Beach, adjacent to Huntington Pier, is a haven for volleyball players and surfers; dense crowds abound, but at least so do amenities like outdoor showers, beach rentals, and rest rooms. Just south of the city beach is 3-mile-long **Huntington State Beach.** Both popular beaches have lifeguards and concession stands seasonally. The state beach also has rest rooms, showers, barbecue pits, and a waterfront bike path. The main entrance is on Beach Boulevard, and there are access points all along the Pacific Coast Highway (Calif. 1).

Newport Beach runs for about 5 miles and includes both Newport and Balboa piers. There are outdoor showers, rest rooms, volleyball nets, and a vintage boardwalk that just may make you feel as though you've stepped 50 years back in time. **Balboa Bike and Beach Stuff** (☎ **714/723-1516**), at the corner of Balboa and Palm near the pier, can rent you a variety of items, from pier fishing poles to bikes, beach umbrellas, and bodyboards. The **Southwind Kayak Center,** 2801 W. Pacific Coast Hwy. (☎ **800/768-8494** or 714/261-0200), rents sea kayaks for use in the bay or open ocean at rates of $8 to $10 per hour; instructional classes are available on weekends only. They also conduct bird-watching kayak expeditions into the Upper Newport Bay Ecological Reserve at rates of $40 to $65.

Crystal Cove State Park, which covers 3 miles of coastline between Corona del Mar and Laguna Beach, and then extends up into the hills around El Moro Canyon, is a good alternative to the more popular beaches for you seekers of solitude. There are, however, lifeguards and rest rooms. The beach is a winding sandy strip, backed with grassy terraces; high tide sometimes sections it into coves. The entire area offshore is an underwater nature preserve. There are four entrances, including Pelican Point and El Moro Canyon. For more information call 714/494-3539 or 714/848-1566.

Salt Creek Beach Park lies below the palatial Ritz-Carlton Laguna Niguel; guests who tire of the pristine swimming pool venture down the staircase on Ritz Carlton Drive to wiggle their toes in the sand. The setting is marvelous, wide white-sand beaches looking out toward Catalina Island (why do you think the Ritz-Carlton built here?). There are lifeguards, rest rooms, a snack bar, and convenient parking near the hotel.

Doheny State Beach in Dana Point has long been known as a premier surfing spot and camping site. Just south of lovely Dana Point Marina (enter off Del Abispo Street), Doheny has the friendly vibe of beach parties in days gone by: Tree-shaded lawns give way to wide beaches, and picnicking and beach camping are encouraged. There are 121 sites for both tents and RVs, plus a state-run visitors center featuring several small aquariums of sea and tidepool life. For more information and camping availability, call 714/492-0802.

BIKING

Bicycling is the most popular beach activity up and down the coast. A slower-paced alternative to driving, it allows you to enjoy the clean fresh air and notice smaller details of these laid-back beach towns and harbors. Bikes and safety equipment are available for rent at **Zack's Too,** Pacific Coast Highway at Beach Boulevard, Huntington Beach (☎ 714/536-2696); **Balboa Bike & Beach Stuff,** 601 Balboa Blvd., Newport Beach (☎ 714/723-1516); **Laguna Beach Cyclery,** 240 Thalia St. (☎ 714/494-1522); and **Dana Point Bicycle,** 34155 Pacific Coast Hwy. (☎ 714/661-8356).

GOLF

Many golf course architects have used the geography of the Orange Coast to its full advantage, molding challenging and scenic courses from the rolling bluffs. Two beautiful courses open to the public are the **Monarch Beach Golf Links,** 23841 Stonehill Dr., Dana Point (☎ 714/240-8247), and the **Pelican Hill Golf Club,** 22651 Pelican Hill Rd. South, Newport Beach (☎ 714/760-0707). Both offer holes with breathtaking views of the ocean (remember, the break is always toward the water!)

SEEING THE SIGHTS

International Surfing Museum. 411 Olive Ave., Huntington Beach. ☎ **714/960-3483.** Admission $2 adults, $1 students, free for kids 5 and under. Mid-June to late Sept, daily noon–5pm; the rest of year, Wed–Sun noon–5pm.

Nostalgic Gidgets and Moondoggies shouldn't miss this monument to this laid-back sport that has become synonymous with California beaches. There are gargantuan longboards from the sport's early days, memorabilia of Duke Kahanamoka and the other surfing greats represented on the "Walk of Fame" near Huntington Pier, and a gift shop where a copy of the "Surfin'ary" can help you bone up on your surfer slang even if you can't hang 10.

Balboa Pavilion. 400 Main St., Balboa, Newport Beach. ☎ **714/673-5245.** From Calif. 1, turn south onto Newport Blvd. (which becomes Balboa Blvd. on the peninsula); turn left at Main St.

This historic cupola-topped structure, a California Historical Landmark, was built in 1905 as a bathhouse for swimmers in ankle-length bathing costumes. Later during the Big Band era, dancers rocked the Pavilion doing the "Balboa Hop." Now it serves as the terminal for Catalina Island passenger service, harbor and whale-watching cruises, and fishing charters. The surrounding boardwalk is the Balboa Fun Zone, a collection of carnival rides, game arcades, and vendors of hot dogs and cotton candy. For Newport Harbor or Catalina cruise information, call 714/673-5245; for sportfishing and whale-watching information, call 714/673-1434.

Balboa Island

The charm of this pretty little neighborhood isn't diminished by knowing that the island was man-made—and it certainly hasn't affected the price of real estate. Tiny clapboard cottages in the island's center and modern houses with two-story windows and private docks along the perimeter make a colorful and romantic picture. You can drive onto the island on Jamboree Road to the north, or take the three-car ferry from Balboa Peninsula (about $1 per vehicle). It's generally more fun to park and take the ferry as a pedestrian, since the tiny alleys they call streets are more suitable for strolling, there usually are crowds, and parking spaces are scarce. Marine Avenue, the main commercial street, is lined with small shops and cafés that evoke a New England fishing village. Refreshing shaved ices sold by sidewalk vendors will relieve the heat of summer.

Mission San Juan Capistrano. Ortega Hwy. (Calif. 74), San Juan Capistrano. ☎ **714/248-2049.** Admission $4 adults, $3 children and seniors. Daily 8:30am–5pm. Closed Good Friday, Thanksgiving, and Christmas.

The seventh of the 21 California coastal missions, Mission San Juan Capistrano is continually being restored, a mix of old ruins and working buildings that are home to small museum collections and various adobe rooms that are as quaint as they are interesting. The intimate mission chapel with its ornate baroque altar is still regularly used for religious services, and the mission complex is the center of the community, hosting performing arts, children's programs, and other cultural events year-round.

This mission is best known for its swallows, which are said to return to nest each year at their favorite sanctuary. According to legend, the birds wing their way back to the mission annually on March 19, St. Joseph's Day, arriving here at dawn; they are said to take flight again on October 23, after bidding the mission farewell. In reality, however, you can probably see the well-fed birds here any day of the week, winter or summer.

SHOPPING

Just as the communities along the coast range from casually barefoot summer playgrounds to meticulously groomed yacht-clubby enclaves, so does the shopping scene stretch to both ends of the spectrum. Seal Beach, indifferent to tourists, has charming low-tech shops designed to service the year-round residents, while Huntington Beach offers a plethora of surf and water-sport shops, reflecting its sporty nature. Both Huntington and Balboa have more than their share of T-shirt and souvenir stands, while tony Newport Beach has been called "Beverly Hills south" because of the many European designer boutiques and high-priced shops there. Corona del Mar, immediately south of Newport Beach on Calif. 1, is more like "Pasadena south," with branches of stylish but affordable L.A. boutiques sharing several fun blocks with local boutiques and services. Laguna Beach is art gallery intensive; there are too many to list, but most are along the Pacific Coast Highway or Ocean, Forest, and Park avenues. Reflecting a wide range of artistic media, their wares can also come from all over the country—try to purchase the work of local artists unavailable elsewhere. There's little shopping in Dana Point and mostly mission-themed souvenirs in San Juan Capistrano.

Shoppers from all over the Southland flock to the two excellent malls listed below. If that isn't to your taste, a drive along the Pacific Coast Highway will yield many other opportunities for browsing and souvenir purchases.

Fashion Island Newport Beach. 401 Newport Center Dr., Newport Beach. ☎ **714/721-2000.**

Not an island at all, this shopping center is located next to the harbor and is designed to resemble an open-air Mediterranean village. A pretty upscale village, that is, with tiled streets and plazas dotted with strolling pull-cart vendors and lined with upscale stores and boutiques, including Neiman-Marcus and Macy's department stores as well as Baywatch (they sell timepieces) and other specialty shops. Open Monday to Friday from 10am to 9pm, on Saturday from 10am to 7pm, and on Sunday from 11am to 6pm.

✪ **South Coast Plaza.** 3333 Bristol St. (at I-405), Costa Mesa. ☎ **800/782-8888** or 714/435-2000.

South Coast Plaza is one of the most upscale shopping complexes in the world, and it's so big that it's a day's adventure unto itself. This beautifully designed center is home to some of fashion's most prominent boutiques, including Emporio Armani, Chanel, Alfred Dunhill, and Coach; beautiful branches of the nation's top department stores such as Saks Fifth Avenue and Nordstrom; and outposts of the best high-end specialty shops like Williams Sonoma, L.A. Eyeworks, and Rizzoli Booksellers.

The mall is home to many impressive works of art, including a 1.6-acre environmental sculpture by Isamu Noguchi. In between shoe-store browsing or sale-rack pillaging, you can stroll along the sculpture garden path, climb its hill, listen to its rushing water, cross its bubbling stream, and wonder at the sculpture's striking geometric forms from the garden benches. Not the usual rest in the food court, is it?

Speaking of food, here you won't find Hot-Dog-on-a-Stick among the 40 or so restaurants scattered throughout. Wolfgang Puck Cafe, Morton's of Chicago, Ghiradelli Soda Fountain, Planet Hollywood, and Scott's Seafood Grill lure the hungry away from Del Taco and McDonald's. Open Monday to Friday from 10am to 9pm, on Saturday from 10am to 7pm, and on Sunday from 11am to 6:30pm.

WHERE TO STAY
VERY EXPENSIVE

Four Seasons Hotel Newport Beach. 690 Newport Center Dr., Newport Beach, CA 92660. ☎ **800/332-3442** or 714/759-0808. Fax 714/760-8073. 221 rms, 64 suites. A/C MINIBAR TV TEL. $260–$300 double; from $350 suite. AE, DC, MC, V. Valet parking $13.50.

This polished and professional member of the world-class Four Seasons group gets the highest marks for its comprehensive facilities and impeccable service. The guest rooms, conservatively designed in inoffensive beiges, have lovely touches like terry robes, oversize closets, and marble baths. Most have small balconies, even though the Newport skyline is nothing special to look at. Butlers are on call around the clock. Because of their larger size, rooms with two double beds are the hotel's best value. Guests are encouraged to bring their pets; doggie biscuits and food are always available.

Dining/Entertainment: The Pavilion Restaurant, serving California-French cuisine, is popular with locals at lunch. The poolside Cabana Cafe enjoys a nice garden setting. Afternoon tea and evening cocktails are served in the Gardens Cafe and Lounge.

Services: Concierge, room service (24 hours), overnight laundry and shoeshine, nightly turndown, complimentary transportation to/from the John Wayne Airport.

Facilities: Large heated outdoor pool, small fitness club, Jacuzzi, sundeck, two outdoor lighted tennis courts, business center, gift shop.

☺ Ritz-Carlton Laguna Niguel. 1 Ritz-Carlton Dr., Dana Point, CA 92629. ☎ **800/241-3333** or 714/240-2000. Fax 714/240-1061. 393 rms and suites. A/C MINIBAR TV TEL. $215–$485 double; $500–$1,100 suite. Children 12 and under stay free in parents' room. Weekday and special packages available. AE, DC, DISC, MC, V. Parking $15.

The Old World meets the Pacific Rim at this glorious hotel, majestically set among terraces and fountained gardens on a 150-foot-high bluff above a 2-mile-long beach. There's a beautiful limestone fireplace in the elegant, silk-lined lobby, and lush foliage abounds throughout the interior. A ravishingly arched lounge is perfect for watching the sun set over the Pacific. The service, in Ritz-Carlton style, is unassuming and impeccable. Some guests, however, might find the hotel's palatial airs out of keeping with the beachy location.

The spacious rooms are outfitted with sumptuous furnishings and fabrics; despite their generous size, however, some are overfurnished to the point of being cramped. All rooms come with a terrace, and some even have fireplaces. The most expensive rooms overlook the blue Pacific below. All come with three phones (with voice-mail), a refrigerator, a shoe polisher, and a safe. The Italian marble bathrooms are equipped with double vanities, hair dryers, and bathrobes.

Dining/Entertainment: The Dining Room is the most elegant of the hotel's four restaurants, offering continental/French cuisine served by a knowledgeable staff. The gracious setting features subdued lighting, European chandeliers, and original paintings. Dine by the numbers, choosing from two- to seven-course prix-fixe dinners with matching wines from the formidable cellar. There's also a clubby lounge for nightcaps and five bars (two with nightly entertainment).

Service: Room service (on Rosenthal china, no less), twice-daily maid service (they'll even stick a bookmark in the appropriate page of your *TV Guide*), masseur, baby-sitting, children's programs, regular shuttle to/from the beach and the golf course; the two staffers for every room are generally alert in responding to requests.

Facilities: Beach with lifeguard, games room, lawn games, sauna, steam room, whirlpool, beauty salon, day-care center, 24-hour business center, car-rental desk; first-rate sports facilities include a smart fitness center with unisex steam rooms and a public golf course designed by Robert Trent Jones II.

EXPENSIVE

Surf and Sand Hotel. 1555 S. Coast Hwy. (south of Laguna Canyon Rd.), Laguna Beach, CA 92651. ☎ **800/524-8621** or 714/497-4477. 155 rms, 2 penthouses. MINIBAR TV TEL. Apr–Oct, $200–$275 double; from $475 penthouse. Nov–Mar, $190–$240 double; from $375 penthouse. AE, CB, DC, DISC, MC.

The fanciest hotel in Laguna Beach has come a long way since it started life in 1937 as a modest little hostelry with just 13 units. Still occupying the same fantastic oceanside location, it now features dozens of top-of-the-line luxurious rooms that, despite their standard size, feel enormously decadent. Done entirely in white—from walls to linens to furnishings—they're very bright and beachy, and every one has a private balcony with an ocean view, a marble bath, and plush robes; some have whirlpool tubs. Try to get a deluxe corner room.

Dining/Entertainment: Splashes Restaurant (see "Where to Dine," below) serves three meals daily in a beautiful oceanfront setting. Towers offers contemporary northern Italian cuisine for dinner. Because the windows don't open, a sound system was installed to pipe in the sounds of the surf below.

Services: Concierge, room service, dry cleaning, overnight laundry, complimentary morning newspaper, nightly turndown.

Facilities: Heated outdoor pool, gift shop, salon, boutique.

MODERATE

Blue Lantern Inn. 34343 Street of the Blue Lantern, Dana Point, CA 92629. ☎ **800/950-1236** or 714/661-1304. Fax 714/496-1483. 29 rms. A/C TV TEL. $125–$275 double. Rates include full breakfast. AE, MC, V.

A newly constructed three-story New England–style gray clapboard inn, the Blue Lantern is a pleasant cross between romantic B&B and sophisticated small hotel. Almost all the rooms, which are decorated with reproduction traditional furniture and plush bedding, have a balcony or deck overlooking the harbor. All have a fireplace and Jacuzzi tub. Have your breakfast here in private (clad perhaps in the fluffy robe provided), or choose to go downstairs to the sunny dining room which also serves complimentary afternoon tea. There's an exercise room and a cozy lounge with menus for many area restaurants. The friendly staff welcomes you with home-baked cookies at the front desk.

Doryman's Inn Bed & Breakfast. 2102 W. Ocean Front, Newport Beach, CA 92663. ☎ **800/634-3303** or 714/675-7300. 8 rms, 2 suites. A/C TV TEL. $135–$230 double; from $185 suite. Rates include breakfast. AE, MC, V.

The Doryman's rooms are both luxurious and romantic, making this one of the nicest B&Bs to be found anywhere. The rooms are outfitted with French and American antiques, floral textiles, beveled mirrors, and cozy furnishings. Every room has a working fireplace and a sunken marble tub (some have Jacuzzi jets). King- or queen-size beds, lots of plants, and good ocean views round out the decor. The Doryman's location, directly on the Newport Beach Pier Promenade, is also enviable, though some may find it a bit too close to the action. Breakfast includes fresh pastries and fruit, brown eggs, yogurt, cheeses, and international coffees and teas.

Vacation Village. 647 S. Coast Hwy., Laguna Beach, CA 92651. ☎ **800/843-6895** or 714/494-8566. Fax 714/494-1386. 100 rms, 38 suites and apts. TV. $80–$155 double; from $175 suite. AE, CB, DC, DISC, MC, V.

Vacation Village has something for everyone. This cluster of seven oceanfront and near-the-ocean motels offers rooms, studios, suites, and apartments. Most of the accommodations are standard motel fare: bed, TV, table, basic bath. The best rooms are oceanfront in a four-story structure overlooking the Village's private beach. Umbrellas and backrests for beachgoers are available in summer. There's a restaurant on the premises, and facilities include a private beach, two pools, and a whirlpool.

WHERE TO DINE
EXPENSIVE

Splashes Restaurant and Bar. In the Surf and Sand Hotel, 1555 S. Coast Hwy., Laguna Beach. ☎ **714/497-4477.** Reservations recommended. Main courses $16–$22. DC, DISC, MC, V. Daily 7am–10pm. MEDITERRANEAN.

Splashes is truly stunning. Almost directly on the surf, this light and bright restaurant basks in sunlight and the calming crash of the waves. At dinner, a basket of fresh-baked crusty bread prefaces a long list of appetizers that might include wild-mushroom ravioli with lobster sauce or sautéed Louisiana shrimp with red chiles and lemon. Gourmet pizzas also make great starters; they come topped with interesting combinations like grilled lamb, roasted fennel, artichokes, mushrooms, and feta cheese. Main courses change daily and might offer baked striped bass and braised duck in a cabernet.

MODERATE

Five Feet. 328 Glenneyre, Laguna Beach. ☎ **714/497-4955.** Reservations recommended on weekends. Main courses $14–$24. AE, MC, V. Sun–Thurs 5–10pm, Fri 11:30am–2:30pm and 5–11pm, Sat 5–11pm. CALIFORNIA/ASIAN.

Chef/proprietor Michael Kang has created one of the area's most innovative and interesting restaurants, combining the best in Californian cuisine with Asian technique and ingredients. If the atmosphere were as good as the food, Five Feet would be one of the best restaurants in California. Main courses run the gamut from tea-smoked filet mignon topped with Roquefort cheese and candied walnuts to a hot Thai-style mixed grill of veal, beef, lamb, and chicken stir-fried with sweet peppers, onions, and mushrooms in curry-mint sauce. Unfortunately, the dining room's gray-concrete walls aren't much to look at, and the exposed vents on an airplane hangar–scale wooden ceiling just look unfinished, not trendy industrial. Fortunately, this unspectacular decor is brightened by an exceedingly friendly staff and unparalleled food.

Harbor Grille. 34499 Street of the Golden Lantern, Dana Point. ☎ **714/240-1416.** Reservations suggested on weekends. Main courses $8–$18. AE, DC, MC, V. Mon–Sat 11:30am–10pm, Sun 9am–10pm. SEAFOOD.

In a business/commercial mall right in the center of the pretty Dana Point Marina, the Harbor Grille is enthusiastically recommended by locals for mesquite-broiled, ocean-fresh seafood. Hawaiian mahi-mahi with a mango-chutney baste is on the menu, along with Pacific swordfish, grilled shark steaks, and teriyaki chicken.

Las Brisas. 361 Cliff Dr. (off the PCH north of Laguna Canyon), Laguna Beach. ☎ **714/ 497-5434.** Reservations recommended. Main courses $8–$17. AE, MC, V. Mon–Sat 8am– 10:30pm, Sun 9am–10:30pm. MEXICAN.

Boasting a breathtaking view of the Pacific, Las Brisas is popular for sunset drinks and alfresco appetizers—so much so that it can get pretty crowded during the summer months. Affordable during lunch but pricey at dinner, the menu consists mostly of seafood recipes from the Mexican Riviera. Even the standard enchiladas and tacos get a zesty update with crab or lobster meat and fresh herbs. Calamari steak is sauteed with bell peppers, capers, and herbs in a garlic-butter sauce, and king salmon is mesquite broiled and served with a creamy lime sauce. Although a bit on the touristy side, Las Brisas can be a fun part of the Laguna Beach experience.

Twin Palms. 630 Newport Center Dr., Newport Beach. ☎ **714/721-8288.** Reservations suggested. Main courses $9–$17. AE, CB, DC, MC, V. Sun–Wed 11:30am–10pm, Thurs–Sat 11:30am–1am. MEDITERRANEAN/FRENCH.

Opened in late 1995, this sibling restaurant to one of Pasadena's most popular eateries seems to be leading the Newport Beach pack as well. From the famous original started by, among others, movie star Kevin Costner, comes the high-tented, palm-accented, huge circuslike space that is Twin Palms's trademark. Amid this festival atmosphere you can enjoy the French "comfort food" original chef Michael Roberts created as a backlash against pricey haute cuisine. Favorites include juicy, roasted sage-infused pork and honey-glazed coriander-scented duck from the rotisserie grill, as well as the popular salt cod mashed potato brandade appetizer. Sautéed dishes and salads are not as successful, but Twin Palms has brought its traditional Sunday "Gospel Brunch" to the new location.

INEXPENSIVE

El Adobe de Capistrano. 31891 Camino Capistrano (near the mission), San Juan Capistrano. ☎ **714/493-1163** or 714/830-8620. Dinner $8–$15; lunch $5–$10. AE, DISC, MC, V. Mon–Thurs 11:30am–10pm, Fri–Sat 11:30am–11pm, Sun 10:30am–2:30pm and 4–10pm. CLASSIC MEXICAN.

This restaurant is housed in a historic landmark 1778 Spanish adobe near San Juan Capistrano's main attraction, the mission. It's understandably touristy, but there's some interesting history inside, like the enclosed lobby that was originally a dirt pathway between two buildings. A former dungeon jail cell makes a fine wine cellar, and El Adobe proudly offers a menu combination named "the President's Choice" after Richard Nixon, who visited often from his Summer White House at the shore nearby. Hot plates overflow with cheesy combinations featuring chiles rellenos, tamales, and enchiladas topped with rich, red sauce. Dinner selections also include steak and seafood.

Ruby's. 1 Balboa Pier, Balboa. ☎ **714/675-7829.** Most items under $5. AE, MC, V. Sun–Thurs 7am–10pm, Fri–Sat 7am–11pm. AMERICAN DINER.

With their trademark red-and-white hamburger-stand decor sprouting up all over the Southland, Ruby's is fast becoming a local institution. Housed in a former baithouse, the Balboa Pier Ruby's is the original, and several others can be found on or near the end of Orange Coast piers, including Seal Beach, Huntington, and Laguna. Ruby's sells nostalgia and food in equal measure. The hamburgers, fries, milkshakes, and flavored sodas are reasonably priced, and the fun, kid-friendly atmosphere really suits the surroundings.

The Southern California Desert

by Stephanie Avnet

To the casual observer, Southern California's desert seems like a desolate place—nothing but vast landscapes baking under a relentless sun. Its splendor is subtle, letting each traveler discover its beauty in his or her own time. For some it will be the surprising lushness of unique varieties of trees, flowering cacti, fragrant shrubs, and other plants—many of them found only here—that have adapted ingeniously to the harsh climate. The unique Joshua Tree, majestic to some and ugly to others, thrives in the upper Mojave Desert. Each spring the ground throughout the Lancaster area is carpeted with brilliant golds and oranges of the poppy, California's state flower. Like the autumn leaves in New England, the poppies along Calif. 14 draw seasonal tourists in droves.

If it looks as if nothing except insects could survive here, look again: You're bound to see the speedy roadrunner or a tiny gecko dart across your path. Close your eyes and listen for the cry of a hawk or an owl. Check the ground for coyote or bobcat tracks. Notice the sparkle of fish in the streams running through flourishing palm oases. Road signs near Barstow warn of desert tortoise crossing. The tortoise is just one of the many endangered species found only here. Fortunately, most of the Southern California desert's flora and fauna is protected by the federal government in a wildlife sanctuary.

Or perhaps the beauty you seek is that of personal renewal surrounded by the spectacular desert landscape. Whether it's in the shadow of purple-tinged mountains, amid otherworldly rock formations, or beside a sparkling swimming pool, you'll find as much or as little to occupy your time as you desire. Destinations range from gloriously untouched national parks to ultra-luxurious resorts—and it's a rare day when the sun doesn't shine out here.

1 En Route to the Palm Springs Resorts

If you're making the drive from Los Angeles via I-10, the first hour or more will be spent just, well, getting out of the L.A. metropolitan sprawl. Soon you'll leave the Inland Empire auto plazas behind, sail past the last of the bedroom community shopping malls, and edge ever closer to the (if you're lucky) snow-capped San Bernardino and San Jacinto mountain ranges. (Coming from San Diego via I-15, the areas discussed below are east of the junction with I-10.)

Antiquing is a very popular pastime in Southern California (we're not talking Louis XIV here, though; mostly late 19th- and early 20th-century stuff), and there will be some great opportunities to stop and poke around. What used to be a ramshackle string of junk shops along the I-10 service road in **Yucaipa** is now a respectable "antique row" worth exiting the freeway for. Farther along I-10 lies **Beaumont,** touting itself as "City of Antiques," for it holds almost a dozen (at last count) mall-style antiques and collectibles emporiums.

If all this sifting through tchotchkes makes you hungry, how about some kitschy roadside dining? Although their fare is coffee-shop standard, don't tell the enthusiastic gingham- and overall-clad service staff at **The Farm House** in **Banning** (signs will direct you off the freeway). From the giant rooster and rusty agricultural implements out front to the proudly framed photos of Banning's heyday as "Stagecoach Town U.S.A.," this is just the kind of place you'd expect the rural Kiwanis Club to meet each week, and a far sight more interesting than the Denny's next door.

Or, as the horse- and silo-dotted fields give way to pale, dry desert, keep your eyes peeled for the dinosaurs that stand guard over the **Wheel Inn Restaurant** in **Cabazon.** That's right, a four-story-tall brontosaurus and his *Tyrannosaurus rex* pal. They were built in the 1960s by Claude K. Bell, a sketch artist and sculptor at Knott's Berry Farm with a way-before-his-time dream of an entire dinosaur amusement park. These two behomoths were all he completed. You can stop and climb up into the belly of the larger one, where you'll find a remarkably spacious gift shop selling dinosaur toys, books, and souvenirs.

Cabazon is also the home of **Hadley's Orchards,** a fixture on this stretch of road since 1931. They're always packed with folks shopping for dates, dried fruits, nuts, honey, preserves, and other regional products. A snack bar serves the date shake so beloved in this region, and gift packs of tasty treats to carry home (for more about the date mystique, see "Exploring the Area" in Section 2, later in this chapter). Nearby, you'll either love or hate the **Desert Hills Factory Stores**. Southern California's largest outlet mall contains over 100 stores, the most intriguing of which is Barney's New York, presenting a nice opportunity to pick up designer threads at a fraction of the cost.

Soon after leaving Cabazon you'll enter the **San Gorgonio Pass.** Be prepared for an awesome and otherworldly sight—never-ending windmill fields which harness the powerful force of the wind gusting through this passage, converting it to electricity for air conditioners throughout the Coachella Valley. The Calif. 111 turnoff leads you past the Albert Frey–designed "hyperbolic paraboloid" gas station at Tramway Road, which for 30 years has served as the unofficial gateway to Palm Springs—and symbol that you've arrived!

2 The Palm Springs Desert Resorts

Palm Springs had been known for years as a golf course–studded retirement mecca annually invaded by raucous herds of libidinous college kids at spring break. Well, the city of Palm Springs has been quietly changing its image and attracting a whole new crowd. Former mayor (now U.S. Congressman) Sonny Bono's revolutionary "anti-thong" ordinance in 1991 put a lightning-quick halt to the spring break migration by eliminating public display of the bare co-ed derrière, and the upscale fairway-condo crowd has been sticking to the tony outlying resort cities of Rancho Mirage, Palm Desert, Indian Wells, and La Quinta.

These days, there are no billboards allowed in Palm Springs itself, all the palm trees in the center of town are appealingly backlit at night, and you won't see the word

---

Area Code Change Notice

Please note that, effective March 22, 1997, the area code for the Southern California desert areas is scheduled to changed to **760.** You will be able to dial 619 until September 27, 1997, after which you will have to use 760.

"motel" on any establishment. Senior citizens are everywhere, dressed to the nines in brightly colored leisure suits and keeping alive the retro-kitsch establishments from the days when Elvis, Liberace, and Sinatra made the balmy desert a *swingin'* place. But they're not alone: Baby boomers and yuppies nostalgic for the kidney-shaped swimming pools and backyard luaus of the Eisenhower/Kennedy glory years are buying ranch-style vacation homes and restoring them to their 1950s splendor. Hollywood's young glitterati are returning, too. Today the city fancies itself a cross between a European Riviera–style destination and a good ol' American small town combining *Jetsons*-ish architecture and the crushed-velvet vibe of piano bars with the colors and attitude of a laid-back Aegean island village. One thing hasn't changed: Swimming, sunbathing, golfing, and playing tennis are still the primary pastimes in this convenient little oasis.

An important presence in Palm Springs has little to do with socialites and Americana, for the Agua Caliente band of Cahuilla Indians settled in this area 1,000 years before the first golf ball was ever teed up. Recognizing the beauty and spirituality of this wide-open space, they lived a simple life around the natural mineral springs on the desert floor, migrating into the cool canyons during the hot summer months. Under a treaty with the railroad companies and the U.S. government, the tribe owns half the land on which Palm Springs is built and actively works to preserve Native American heritage. It's easy to learn about the American Indians during your visit, and it will definitely add to your appreciation of this part of California.

ESSENTIALS

GETTING THERE   Several airlines service the **Palm Springs Regional Airport,** 3400 E. Tahquitz Canyon Way (☎ **619/323-8161**), including **Alaska Airlines** (☎ 800/426-0333), **America West** (☎ 800/235-9292), **American** (☎ 800/433-7300), **Delta/Skywest** (☎ 800/453-9417), **United** (☎ 800/241-6522), and **USAir** (☎ 800/428-4322). Flights from Los Angeles International Airport (see Section 1 in Chapter 14) take about 40 minutes.

If you're driving from Los Angeles, take I-10 to the Calif. 111 turnoff to Palm Springs. You'll breeze into town on North Palm Canyon Drive, the main thoroughfare. The trip from downtown Los Angeles takes about 2 hours. If you're driving from San Diego, take I-15 north to I-10 east; it's 135 miles.

VISITOR INFORMATION   Be sure to pick up *Palm Springs Life* magazine's free monthly **"Desert Guide."** It contains tons of visitor information including a comprehensive calendar of events. Copies are distributed in hotels and newsstands and by the **Palm Springs Desert Resorts Convention & Visitors Bureau,** in the Atrium Design Centre, 69-930 Calif. 111, Suite 201, Rancho Mirage, CA 92270 (☎ **800/417-3529,** or 619/770-9000). The bureau's office staff can help with maps, brochures, and advice Monday to Friday from 8:30am to 5pm. They also operate a **24-hour information line** (☎ **619/770-1992**), and an Internet site at **http://www.desert-resorts.com.**

The **Palm Springs Visitors Information Center,** 2781 N. Palm Canyon Dr. (☎ **800/34-SPRINGS;** fax 619/323-3021), offers maps, brochures, advice, souvenirs, and a free hotel reservation service. The office is open Monday to Sunday from 9am to 5pm and on Sunday from 8am to 4pm.

ORIENTATION   The commercial downtown area of Palm Springs stretches about half a mile along North Palm Canyon Drive between Alejo and Ramon streets. The street is one-way through the heart of town, but its other-way counterpart is Indian Canyon Drive, 1 block east. The mountains lie directly west and south, while the rest of Palm Springs is laid out in a grid to the southeast. Palm Canyon forks into South Palm Canyon (leading to the Indian Canyons) and East Palm Canyon (the continuation of Calif. 111) traversing the resort towns of Cathedral City, Rancho Mirage, Palm Desert, Indian Wells, and La Quinta before looping up to rejoin I-10 at Indio. Desert Hot Springs is north of Palm Springs, straight up Gene Autry Trail. Tahquitz Canyon Way creates North Palm Canyon's primary intersection, tracking a straight line between the airport and the heart of town.

ENJOYING THE OUTDOORS
GOLF
The Palm Springs desert resorts are world-famous meccas for golfers (see the "Fairways & Five-Irons, Desert Style" box in this chapter). There are 85 public, semiprivate, and private courses in the area, and if you're the kind who starts polishing your irons the moment you begin planning your vacation, you're best off staying at one of the valley's many golf resorts, where you can enjoy the proximity of your hotel's facilities as well as economically smart package deals that can give you a taste of country club membership. If, on the other hand, you'd like to fit a round of golf into an otherwise varied trip and you aren't staying at a hotel with its own links, there are courses at all levels open to the general public, mostly in Palm Springs. Call ahead to see which will rent clubs or other equipment to the spontaneous player.

Beginners will enjoy **Tommy Jacobs' Bel-Air Greens,** 1001 El Cielo, Palm Springs (☎ 619/322-6062), a scenic 9-hole, par-32 executive course that has some water and sandtrap challenges but also allows for a few confidence-boosting successes. Generally flat fairways and mature trees characterize the relatively short (3,350 yards) course. The complex also offers an 18-hole miniature golf course. Greens fees range from $23 to $27.

Slightly more intermediate amateurs will want to check out the **Tahquitz Creek Golf Resort,** 1885 Golf Club Dr., Palm Springs (☎ 619/328-1005), whose two diverse courses both appeal to mid-handicappers. The "Legend's" wide, water-free holes will appeal to anyone frustrated by the "target" courses popular with many architects, while the new Ted Robinson–designed "Resort" course offers all those accuracy-testing bells and whistles more common to lavish private clubs. Greens fees range from $35 to $85, depending on day and cart rental.

The **Palm Springs Country Club,** 2500 Whitewater Club Dr. (☎ 619/ 323-8625), is the oldest public-access golf course within the city of Palm Springs, and is especially popular with budget-conscious golfers, as greens fees are only $40 to $50, including the required cart. The challenge of bunkers and rough can be amplified by the oft-blowing wind along the 5,885 yards of this unusually laid-out course.

The ♦ **Westin Mission Hills Resort Course,** Dinah Shore and Bob Hope drives, Rancho Mirage (☎ 619/328-3198), is somewhat more forgiving than most of legendary architect Pete Dye's courses, but don't play the back tees unless you've got a consistent 220-yard drive and won't be fazed by the Dye-trademark giant sand bunkers and elevated greens. Water only comes into play on four holes, and the scenery

The Palm Springs Desert Resorts

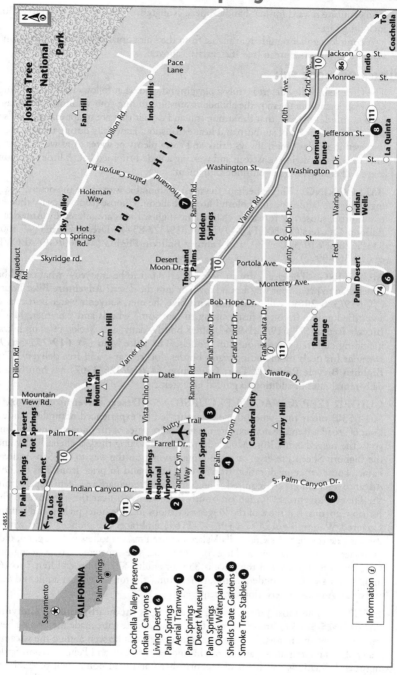

Coachella Valley Preserve **7**
Indian Canyons **5**
Living Desert **6**
Palm Springs
Aerial Tramway **1**
Palm Springs
Desert Museum **2**
Palm Springs
Oasis Waterpark **3**
Sheilds Date Gardens **8**
Smoke Tree Stables **4**

Information ⓘ

is an exquisite reward for low-handicappers. Nonguest greens fees are $120 to $130, including cart.

A complete golfer's guide is available from the Palm Springs Desert Resorts Convention & Visitors Bureau (see "Essentials," above).

OTHER OUTDOOR FUN

The Coachella Valley desert is truly a playground, and what follows is but a sampling of the opportunities to enjoy the abundant sunshine during your vacation here. Please keep in mind, however, that the strong sun and dry air that are so appealing can also sneak up in the form of sunburn and heat exhaustion. Especially during the summer, but even in milder times, always drink and carry plenty of water. And we shouldn't have to advise bringing sunscreen and wearing a wide-brimmed hat. A little common sense will ensure hours of outdoor enjoyment!

BALLOONING   This is perhaps the most memorable way to see the desert: floating above the landscape in a colorful hot-air balloon. Choose from specialty themes like sunrise, sunset, or romantic champagne flights. Rides are offered by **American Balloon Charters** (☎ 800/FLY-OVER or 619/327-8544), **Dream Flights** (☎ 800/933-5628 or 619/321-5154), and **Fantasy Balloon Flights** (☎ 800/GO-ABOVE or 619/568-0997).

BICYCLING   The clean, dry air here just cries out to be enjoyed—what could be better than to pedal your way around town or into the desert? **Adventure Bike Tours** (☎ 619/328-2089) will outfit you with bike, helmet, souvenir water bottle, and a certified guide. If you're just looking to rent some wheels and a helmet, **Mac's Bicycle Rental** (☎ 619/321-9444) offers hourly, daily, and weekly rates on bikes, including children's and mountain models. **The Bike Man** (☎ 619/771-3619) sweetens his deals by including water bottles, locks, maps, and free delivery. The **Bighorn Bicycle Rental & Tour Company** (☎ 619/325-3367) has hourly and daily rental rates in addition to guided bike treks.

GUIDED JEEP & WAGON EXCURSIONS   **Desert Adventures** (☎ 619/864-6530) offers four-wheel-drive eco-tours led by experienced naturalist guides. Your off-road adventure may explore the lush palm oases of the ancestral Indian Canyons, the rugged Santa Rosa Mountain roads overlooking the Coachella Valley and the Bighorn Sheep Preserve, or picturesque ravines on the way to the San Andreas Fault. Tours range in duration from 2 to 4 hours and in price from $60 to $99. Advance reservations are required. The company's trademark red Jeeps depart from the Desert Adventures Ranch on South Palm Canyon near the entrance to the Indian Canyons, but most of the longer excursions include hotel pickup and return. **Covered Wagon Tours** (☎ 619/347-2161) embraces the pioneer spirit with a 2-hour ride through the Coachella Valley Nature Preserve followed by a good, old-fashioned barbecue cookout and live country music. They operate 7 days a week from October to mid-May, and the price is $55 for adults, $27.50 for children 7 to 16, and free for kids 6 and under. Without the "grub," the tour is $40 per adult and $20 per child. Advance reservations are required.

HIKING   The most popular spot for hiking is the nearby **Indian Canyons** (☎ 619/325-5673 for information). The Agua Caliente tribe made their home here centuries ago, and remnants of their simple lifestyle can be seen among the streams, waterfalls, and astounding palm groves in Andreas, Murray, and Palm canyons. Striking rock formations and herds of bighorn sheep and wild ponies will probably be more appealing than the "Trading Post" in Palm Canyon, but it does sell detailed trail maps. This is Indian land, and the Tribal Council charges admission of $6 per

Fairways & Five-Irons, Desert Style

Two hours outside of Los Angeles in the Coachella Valley, strung like ripe dates from I-10, lie the resort cities of Palm Springs, Rancho Mirage, Palm Desert, Indian Wells, and La Quinta. This all-season golfer's paradise boasts over 80 courses, their lush fairways and velvety greens incongruously carved from the arid desert scruff. Both public and resort/semiprivate courses range in difficulty to accommodate low-handicappers and weekend duffers alike, and every imaginable service is available nearby.

If you'd like to sharpen your game, all the principal clubs have resident pros, and there are several schools and clinics, including the **Indian Wells Golf School** at Indian Wells Resort (☎ 800/241-5782 or 619/346-4653), the **Golf Center at Palm Desert** (☎ 619/779-1877), and the **Leadbetter Golf Academy** at PGA West in La Quinta (☎ 800/424-3542 or 619/564-0777). If you're looking to pick up new equipment or some stylish attire, try **Nevada Bob's Discount Golf** in Palm Springs (☎ 619/324-0196) and Indian Wells (☎ 619/346-6166), the **Roger Dunn Golf Shop** in Palm Desert (☎ 619/345-3133) and Cathedral City (☎ 619/324-1160), and **Lady Golf** in Rancho Mirage (☎ 619/773-4949).

Many fine resorts offer generous golf packages, among them **Marriott's Desert Springs Resort** in Palm Desert (☎ 619/341-2211), **Marriott's Rancho Las Palmas** in Rancho Mirage (☎ 619/568-2727), the **Hyatt Grand Champions** in Indian Wells (☎ 619/341-1000), **La Quinta Resort & Club** in La Quinta (☎ 619/346-2904), and the **Estrella Inn** (☎ 800/237-3687 or 619/320-4417). Tee times at many courses cannot be booked more than a few days in advance for nonguests, but several companies are able to make arrangements several months earlier, and even construct a custom package for you with accommodations, golf, meals, and other extras. Among them are **Golf a la Carte** (☎ 619/324-5012; fax 619/321-1242; e-mail glfalacart@aol.com) and **Palm Springs Golf and Tours** (☎ 800/PS-GOLF-1 or 619/346-3331; fax 619/346-4473).

For the nonplaying spectator (or anyone longing to see the pros make it look *so* easy) there are dozens of golf tournaments year round, including many celebrity and pro-am events in addition to regular PGA, LPGA, and Senior Tour stops. February brings the PGA Tour **Bob Hope Chrysler Classic** at the Bermuda Dunes Country Club and the **Frank Sinatra Celebrity Invitational** at Marriott's Desert Springs Resort & Spa. In March, catch the LPGA Tour **Nabisco Dinah Shore** at the Mission Hills Country Club, then in April the Senior PGA **Liberty Mutual Legends of Golf** comes to PGA West. November brings two of the desert's longest-running charity events, the **22st Annual Frostig Center/Chris Korman Celebrity Tournament** at the Westin Mission Hills, and the 24-year-old **Billy Barty/7Up Celebrity Golf Classic** at the Mesquite Country Club in Palm Springs. Also in November, check out the wacky **Palm Desert Golf Cart Parade** along El Paseo.

For more information you can call the Palm Springs Desert Resorts Convention and Visitors Bureau (☎ 800/41-RELAX or 619/770-9000). The bureau also maintains an Activities Hotline (☎ 619/770-1992).

adult, with discounts for seniors, children, students, and military. The canyons are closed to visitors from late June to early September.

Ten miles east of Palm Springs is the 13,000-acre **Coachella Valley Preserve** (☎ **619/343-1234**), which is open daily from sunrise to sunset. There are springs, mesas, both hiking and riding trails, the Thousand Palms Oasis, a visitor center, and picnic areas. If you're heading up to Joshua Tree National Park, consider stopping at the **Big Morongo Canyon Preserve** (☎ 619/363-7190), which was once an Indian village and later a cattle ranch. It's open for visitors Wednesday to Sunday from 7:30am. The park's high water table makes it a magnet for birds and other wildlife; the lush springs and streams are an unexpected desert treat.

HORSEBACK RIDING   Equestrians from novice to advanced can experience the natural solitude and quiet of the desert on horseback at **Smoke Tree Stables** (☎ 619/327-1372). Located south of downtown and ideal for exploring the nearby Indian Canyon trails, Smoke Tree offers guided rides for $25 per hour. But don't expect your posse leader to be primed with facts on the nature you'll encounter— this is strictly a do-it-yourself experience.

SKYDIVING   **Parachutes over Palm Springs** (☎ 800/535-5867 or 619/345-8321)—the name says it all! Their tandem skydiving system allows even the most timid beginner the opportunity to experience the exhilaration of a 30-second freefall followed by the serenity of a parachute descent while enjoying the panoramic beauty of the desert. You're harnessed to your instructor for the entire jump, and you can even take home a videotaped record of your bravery. The single-jump rate is $169; ask about group rates for two or more. The company operates from the Bermuda Dunes Airport 7 days a week November to April. Advance reservations are required.

TENNIS   Virtually all the larger hotels and resorts have tennis courts, but if you choose the intimate B&B option you might want to play at the **Tennis Center,** 1300 Baristo Rd., Palm Springs (☎ 619/320-0020), which has nine courts and offers day and evening clinics for adults, juniors, and seniors, as well as ball machines for solo practice. USPTA pros are on hand.

If you'd like to play for free, the night-lighted courts at **Palm Springs High School,** 2248 E. Ramon Rd., are open to the public on weekends, holidays, and during the summer. There are also eight free night-lighted courts in beautiful **Ruth Hardy Park** at Tamarisk and Caballero streets.

A FAMILY WATER PARK   **Palm Springs Oasis Waterpark,** off I-10 south on Gene Autry Trail between Ramon Road and East Palm Canyon Drive (☎ 619/325-7873), is a water playground with 13 water slides, body- and boardsurfing, an inner-tube ride, beach volleyball, and more. Dressing rooms, lockers, and private beach cabanas (with food service) are available. Admission is $16.95 for visitors over 60 inches tall, $11.50 for 40 to 60 inches, and free for kids under 40 inches ($9.95 for seniors). The park is open mid-March to Labor Day, daily from 11am to 6pm, plus weekends through all of October.

EXPLORING THE AREA

Haven't seen any celebrities wandering the streets? You may want to hook up with **Celebrity Tours,** located on East Palm Canyon Drive at Gene Autry Trail (☎ 619/770-2700). Advance reservations are required for their 1- and 2¹/₂-hour tours of Palm Springs, which include some history and lore but mostly the opportunity to gawk at the homes of movie stars and celebrities. The longer tours take in the estates of surrounding Rancho Mirage and Palm Desert, "playground of the international elite."

Palm Springs Desert Museum. 101 Museum Dr. (just west of the Palm Canyon/Tahquitz intersection), Palm Springs. ☎ 619/325-7186. Admission $5 adults, $4 military and seniors 62 and over, $2 children 6–17, free for children 5 and under, free for everyone the first Fri of every month. Tues–Thurs and Sat–Sun 10am–4pm, Fri 10am–8pm.

This well-endowed museum combines world-class western and Native American art collections, the natural history of the desert, and an outstanding anthropology department, primarily representing the local Cahuilla tribe. Traditional Indian life as it was conducted for centuries before the white presence is illustrated by tools, baskets, and other relics. Check local schedules to find out about (usually excellent) visiting exhibits; plays, lectures, and other events are presented in the museum's Annenberg Theater.

The Living Desert Wildlife and Botanical Park. 47-900 Portola Ave., Palm Desert. ☎ 619/346-5694. Admission $7 adults, $6 seniors 62 and over, $3.50 children 3–12, free for kids under 2. Daily 9am–5pm (last admission 4:30pm); call for summer schedule. Closed Aug and Christmas Day.

This 1,200-acre desert reserve, museum, zoo, and educational center is designed to acquaint visitors with the unique habitats that make up the Southern California deserts. You can walk or take a tram tour through sectors that re-create life in several distinctive desert zones. See and learn about a dizzying variety of plants, insects, and wildlife, including bighorn sheep, mountain lions, rattlesnakes, lizards, owls, golden eagles, and the ubiquitous roadrunner.

Palm Springs Aerial Tramway. Tramway Rd. off Calif. 111, Palm Springs. ☎ 619/325-1391. Tickets $17 adults, $14 seniors, $11 children 5–12, free for kids 4 and under; Ride 'n' Dine combination (available after 2:30pm, dinner served after 4pm), $21 adults, $14 children. Mon–Fri 10am–8pm, Sat–Sun 8am–8pm (closes 1 hour later during daylight saving time).

To gain a bird's-eye perspective on the Coachella Valley, take this 14-minute ascent up $2^{1}/_{2}$ miles to the top of Mt. San Jacinto. The whole experience has a fabulous 1960s feel, from the original Swiss funicular equipment to the scratchy recording broadcast during the trip up (often drowned out by the periodic squeals of white-knuckled passengers). There's a whole other world once you arrive: alpine scenery, a ski lodge–flavored restaurant and gift shop, and temperatures typically 40°F cooler than the desert floor. The most dramatic contrast is during the winter when the mountaintop is a snowy wonderland, irresistible to hikers and bundled-up kids with saucers. The excursion might not be worth the expense during the rest of the year. Guided mule rides and cross-country ski equipment are available at the top.

✪ **Shields Date Gardens.** 80225 Calif. 111, Indio. ☎ 619/347-0996. Free admission. Daily 8am–6pm.

In a splendid display of wishful thinking and clever engineering, the Coachella Valley has grown into a rich agricultural region, known internationally for grapefruit, figs, and grapes—but mostly for dates. The fascination of 1920s entrepreneurs with Arabian lore fueled by the Sahara-like conditions of the desert around Indio led to the planting of date palm groves. Started with just a few parent trees imported from the Middle East, the groves now produce 95% of the world's date crop. The trees are hand-pollinated by farmers, a process detailed in *The Romance and Sex Life of the Date,* a film running continuously (its racy title is the best part). Also housed in the splendid 1930s Moderne building is a lunch counter (date shake anyone?) and store selling an endless variety of dates and related goodies.

SHOPPING

Downtown Palm Springs revolves around **North Palm Canyon Drive,** and many art galleries, souvenir shops, and restaurants are located here, along with a couple of large-scale hotels and shopping centers. This wide, one-way boulevard is designed for pedestrian enjoyment, with many businesses set back from the street itself—don't be shy about poking around the little courtyards you'll encounter. On Thursday night from 6 to 10pm the blocks between Amado and Baristo roads are transformed into **VillageFest,** a street fair tradition celebrating its fifth anniversary. Handmade crafts vendors and aromatic food booths compete for your attention with wacky street performers and even-wackier locals shopping at the mouth-watering fresh produce stalls.

The northern section of Palm Canyon is becoming known for vintage collectibles and is being touted as the **"Antique and Heritage Gallery District."** The plain truth is that, as the older residents of Palm Springs say good-bye to this life, consignment and estate-sale companies are becoming better stocked than ever before. Check out **John's Resale Furnishings,** in the Village Attic, 849 N. Palm Canyon Dr. (☎ 619/320-6165) if you're interested in reliving the '50s in all their fabulous glory; it's one of the best places to see well-preserved relics from Palm Springs' heyday of development.

Down in Palm Desert lies the delicious excess of **El Paseo** (the name of the avenue), a glitzy cornucopia of high-rent boutiques, salons, and upscale eateries reminiscent of Rodeo Drive in Beverly Hills, along with a dozen or more major shopping malls just like back home. **Factory-outlet shopping** is 20 minutes away in Cabazon (see Section 1, "En Route to the Palm Springs Resorts," earlier in this chapter).

Bloomsbury Books. 555 S. Sunrise Way no. 105 (at Ramon Rd.). ☎ **619/325-3862.**

Opened in September 1995, Bloomsbury is a treat to browse through, and proprieter Brad Confer is hard at work compiling an impressive array of out-of-print books and signed and rare editions, all reasonably priced and in great condition. Bloomsbury is especially strong in gay-lesbian literature (including rare early magazines and foreign publications) that's meticulously organized by topic. Every section is cleverly decorated with related memorabilia and noteworthy selections. Located in an ugly strip mall several blocks from the center of town, this treasure is well worth the detour. Open Monday to Saturday from 11am to 9pm.

Celebrity Bookstore. 170 E. Tahquitz Canyon (half a block east of Palm Canyon Dr.). ☎ **800/320-6575** or 619/320-6575.

Owner Darrell Meeks is the resident expert on local publications. If it's Palm Springs history or literature you seek, visit his appealingly cluttered bookshop or stroll by the tables he sets up for VillageFest each week (in front of the Hollywood Stars Diner). Open Monday to Saturday from 9am to 8pm and on Sunday from 9am to 4pm.

Patsy's. 4121 E. Palm Canyon Dr. ☎ **619/324-8825.**

Looking for a simply fabulous sequined evening frock, some blindingly tacky golf pants, gabardine leisure suits, or other retro-garb? Patsy's is a consignment shop filled with entire wardrobes (some are from the local rich and famous) and frequented by young hipsters and cabaret costumers. She's open Wednesday to Saturday from 10am to 4:30pm and on Sunday from noon to 4:30pm.

GAY LIFE IN PALM SPRINGS

Don't think the local chamber of commerce doesn't recognize that the Palm Springs area is one of the current top three American destinations for gay travelers. After just a short while in town it's easy to tell how the gay tourism dollar is courted as agressively as straight spending. Real estate agents cater to gay shoppers for vacation properties, and entire condo communities are marketed toward the gay resident. Advertisements for these and scores of other proudly gay-owned businesses can be found in *The Bottom Line,* the desert's free biweekly magazine of articles, events, and community guides for the gay reader, available at hotels, newsstands, and select merchants.

Throughout the year events are held that transcend the gay community to include everyone. In March the **Desert AIDS Walk** benefits the Desert AIDS Project, while the world's largest organized gathering of lesbians coincides with the Nabisco Dinah Shore Golf Tournament.

Be sure to visit **Between the Pages Bookstore,** on Arenas Road east of Indian Canyon (☎ **619/320-7158**). Besides offering an extensive selection of gay- and lesbian-oriented books and videos, you'll find a wealth of free brochures and guides in the adjacent espresso bar, which also serves as the lobby for the **Between the Pages Playhouse.** This short block of Arenas is home to a score of gay establishments, including **Streetbar** (☎ **619/320-1266**), a neighborhood gathering spot for tourists and locals alike.

Just a few blocks away is a cozy neighborhood of modest homes and small hotels, concentrated on Warm Sands Drive south of Ramon. Known simply as **"Warm Sands,"** this area holds the very nicest "private resorts"—mostly discreet and gated B&B-style inns. Locals recommend the co-ed **El Mirasol Villas** (☎ **800/327-2985** or 619/326-5913) and the all-male **Warm Sands Villas** (☎ **619/323-3006**). Near the center of town lies the historic **Harlow Club Hotel,** 175 E. El Alameda (☎ **800/ 223-4073** or 619/320-4333), where men enjoy luxury haciendas amid lush gardens. The **Bee Charmer Inn,** 1600 E. Palm Canyon (☎ **619/778-5883**), caters to a female clientele, as does the party-atmosphere **Delilah's Enclave,** 641 San Lorenzo Rd. (☎ **800/621-6973** or 619/325-5269).

Gay nightlife is everywhere in the Valley, and especially raucous on holiday weekends. Pick up the *The Bottom Line* for the latest restaurant, nightclub, theater, and special events listings.

WHERE TO STAY

The city of Palm Springs offers a wide range of accomodations—we particularly like the B&B-type inns that are becoming more prevalent as new owners renovate the many fabulous 40- to 60-year-old cottage complexes in the wind-shielded "Tennis Club" area west of Palm Canyon Drive. The other desert resort cities have little diversity in lodgings, consisting mostly of sprawling resort complexes, many boasting world-class golf, tennis, or spa facilities and multiple on-site restaurants. Most are destinations in and of themselves, offering abundant activity options for the whole family (including a whole lot of relaxing and being pampered), so if you're looking for a good base from which to shop or sightsee, Palm Springs is your best bet. Regardless of your choice, remember that the rates given below are for high season (winter, generally October to May). During the hotter summer months, tariffs literally plummet, and it's common to find $300 rooms going for $89 or less as part of off-season packages. Even in season, midweek and golf packages are common, so always ask about them when making your reservation.

PALM SPRINGS

Expensive

Ingleside Inn. 200 W. Ramon Rd. (at Belardo Rd.), Palm Springs, CA 92264. ☎ **800/ 772-6655** or 619/325-0046. Fax 619/325-0710. 29 rms, 16 suites. A/C MINIBAR TV TEL. $75–$235 double; $205–$285 minisuite; $135–$265 villa; from $295 full suite. Rates include continental breakfast. AE, DISC, MC, V. Free valet parking.

Once the 1920s estate of the Humphrey Birge family, manufacturers of the Pierce Arrow automobile, this hideaway offers some of the most charming rooms in town. Each guest room and suite is uniquely decorated with antiques—perhaps a canopied bed or a 15th-century vestment chest. Many rooms have wood-burning fireplaces; all have in-room whirlpools and steam baths.

There's an old-world charm here that's matched by fine service. The Ingleside is hardly low-key, however, for they are quick to mention in brochures, on wall plaques, and other places that celebrities such as Elizabeth Taylor, Howard Hughes, John Wayne, Bette Davis, Salvador Dalí, John Travolta, and Goldie Hawn have stayed here (the celebrity watching is still first-rate). They also like to boast of the inn's *two* appearances on *Lifestyles of the Rich & Famous*.

Dining/Entertainment: Melvyn's is the expensive continental dining room, and the adjacent piano bar and lounge attract a fancy, old-money crowd. Frank and Barbara Sinatra hosted a dinner here on the eve of their wedding.

Services: Concierge, room service, in-room massage, complimentary limousine service.

Facilities: Large heated outdoor pool, Jacuzzi, sundeck, croquet, shuffleboard, business center, car-rental desk, tour desk, boutiques.

La Mancha Villas, Spa & Court Club. 444 Avenida Caballeros, Palm Springs, CA 92262. ☎ **800/64-PRIVACY** or 619/323-1773. 54 suites and villas. A/C TV TEL. $115–$195 suite for two; $175–$695 villa. AE, DC, DISC, MC, V. Free parking.

The security-gated entry makes La Mancha look like a private community, and it was designed that way. Once inside, though, a warmly respectful staff and quiet elegance will pamper you the same way it has the countless celebs who've lent their names to the brochure. The service distinguishes La Mancha from the other resorts, not its modern but unoriginal furnishings. Fruit baskets welcome guests to the quarters, most of them suites with TVs and phones in every room, and VCRs (they'll even provide Nintendo for the kids). Many guests opt for the countless pleasures of the villas, which have private pools, fireplaces, and wet bars. Scores of bicycles and a private fleet of rental cars stand ready should you want to venture the half mile into town, and there's a spa and fitness center—how about a massage on your personal patio?

Dining: In keeping with the La Mancha theme, the aptly named Don Quixote Dining Room is open for breakfast, lunch, and dinner.

Services: Concierge, room service (limited), valet, laundry (for units without their own washer/dryer), morning newspaper, evening turndown, courtesy airport limo.

Facilities: Heated outdoor pool with Jacuzzi, spa and fitness center (fee for massage, fitness classes, personal trainer, or salon services), seven tennis courts (four lighted for night play), two paddle tennis courts (one lighted), three croquet lawns (one lighted), two practice greens, gift shop, conference rooms, video rental.

Moderate

Estrella Inn. 415 S. Belardo Rd. (south of Tahquitz Way), Palm Springs, CA 92262. ☎ **619/320-4117.** Fax 619/323-3303. 37 rms, 25 cottages. A/C TV TEL. $120–$150 double; $160–$200 one-bedroom cottage; $200–$300 two-bedroom cottage. Rates include continental breakfast. Monthly rates available. AE, CB, DC, MC, V. Free parking.

One of the best moderately priced establishments here, the Estrella Inn is located on a quiet, secluded street that seems to be miles from everywhere, even though it's just a block from the center of town. Clark Gable and Carole Lombard often trysted at this 1930s property, which was recently restored to its early Hollywood charm. The rooms vary widely in size from very small quarters to cottages with decks, wet bars, full kitchens, and fireplaces. There are two swimming pools and a children's pool, two Jacuzzis, an outdoor barbecue, and a lawn and court games area. They also offer attractive golf packages that include play at one of several nearby courses.

✪ **Korakia Pensione.** 257 S. Patencio Rd., Palm Springs, CA 92262. ☎ **619/864-6411.** 12 rms and suites. $79–$169 double or suite. No credit cards. Rates include breakfast. Free parking.

If you can work within the Korakia's rigid deposit-cancellation policy and tolerate the lackadaisical staff, you're in for a special stay at this Greek/Moroccan oasis just a few blocks from Palm Canyon Drive. The simply furnished rooms and unbelievably spacious suites are peaceful and private, surrounded by flagstone courtyards and flowering gardens. Eight have kitchens, while five sport fireplaces. This former artist's villa from the 1920s draws a fashionable international crowd of artists, writers, and musicians. All beds are blessed with thick feather duvets, while the windows are shaded by flowing white canvas draperies in the Mediterranean style. Add a sumptuous breakfast served in your room or poolside (*korakia* is Greek for "crow," and a tile mosaic example graces the pool bottom). This unusual B&B shapes up as a pleasant and cost-efficient treat.

Spa Hotel & Casino. 100 N. Indian Canyon Dr., Palm Springs, CA 92263. ☎ **800/854-1279** or 619/325-1461. Fax 619/325-3344. 230 rms, 20 suites. A/C MINIBAR TV TEL. $129–$194 double. Rates include continental breakfast. AE, CB, DC, MC, V. Free parking.

Located on the Indian-owned parcel of land containing the original mineral springs for which Palm Springs was named, this is one of the more unusual choices in town. The Cahuilla claimed that the springs had magical powers to cure illness, and today's travelers still come here to pamper both body and soul by "taking the waters." There are three pools on the premises. One is a conventional outdoor swimming pool; the other two are filled from the underground natural springs brimming with revitalizing minerals. Inside the hotel's extensive spa are private sunken marble swirlpools fed by the springs, and after your bath you can avail yourself of the many other pampering treatments offered. The spa recently opened the adjoining Vegas-style Casino, featuring the familiar hush of card gaming tables and clanging of video poker and slot machines. Other hotel facilities include a fitness center, steam room, concierge, car-rental desk, two restaurants, and two bars.

Villa Royale. 1620 Indian Trail (off East Palm Canyon), Palm Springs, CA 92264. ☎ **800/245-2314** or 619/327-2314. Fax 619/322-3794. 31 rms and suites. A/C TV TEL. $75–$165 double; $150–$225 suite. Rates include breakfast. Additional person $25 extra. AE, MC, V. Free parking.

Located 5 minutes from the hustle and bustle of downtown Palm Springs, this bed-and-breakfast evokes a European cluster of villas, complete with climbing bougainvillea and rooms filled with international antiques and artwork. The main building was once home to Olympic and silver screen ice skater Sonya Henie. The present owner, Bob Lee, later commandeered and combined two adjacent apartment buildings. The guest rooms vary widely in quality, so you might find that the trade-off for quiet seclusion is a small, dark room in back. Some rooms and suites, on the other hand, are spacious and have fireplaces and/or private patios with spas. Continental breakfast is served in an intimate garden setting surrounding the main pool. At lunch and dinner this patio becomes the Europa Restaurant, serving slightly pricey but inventive continental fare. Europa is heavily advertised as a "romantic" dining spot, but you'd better bring your own romantic distraction, since the service can sometimes be frustratingly leisurely.

Inexpensive
Casa Cody. 175 S. Cahuilla Rd. (between Tahquitz Way and Arenas Rd.), Palm Springs, CA 92262. ☎ **619/320-9346.** 17 rms, studio suites, and villas. A/C TV TEL. $55–$69 double; $69–$115 studio suite; $115–$135 one-bedroom villa; $165–$185 two-bedroom villa. Rates include continental breakfast. AE, DISC, MC, V.

Once owned by "Wild" Bill Cody's niece, this 1920s *casa* with a double courtyard (each with swimming pool) has been restored to fine condition, sporting a vaguely southwestern decor and peaceful grounds marked by large lawns and mature, blossoming fruit trees. You'll feel more like a houseguest than a hotel client at the Casa Cody. It's located in the primarily residential "Tennis Club" area of town, a couple easy blocks from Palm Canyon Drive. Many units here have fireplaces and full-size kitchens. Breakfast is served poolside, as is complimentary wine and cheese on Saturday afternoon.

Orchid Tree Inn. 261 S. Belardo Rd. (at Baristo Rd.), Palm Springs, CA 92262. ☎ **800/ 733-3435** or 619/325-2791. Fax 619/325-3855. 40 rms and suites, 1 two-bedroom bungalow. A/C TV TEL. $95–$110 double; $100–$155 suite; $290 bungalow. AE, MC, V.

Although it's billed as a "1930s desert garden retreat," both the interior and exterior of the Orchid Tree bear many marks (like contemporary sliding glass doors) of a 1970s remodeling. If you're not too picky about authenticity, however, the Orchid Tree's beautifully landscaped, sprawling grounds and three swimming pools, complemented by two outdoor whirlpools, make this a good choice in the genuinely historic "Tennis Club" area near the heart of town. Flowering shrubs, mature citrus trees, and other foliage surrounding the red-tile-roofed one- and two-story buildings make for pleasant and private accommodations, 30 of which have kitchens. An added treat are the multitudes of twittering hummingbirds, sparrows, and quail drawn by the bird feeders and baths that abound.

RANCHO MIRAGE

Marriott's Rancho Las Palmas Resort & Country Club. 41000 Bob Hope Dr., Rancho Mirage, CA 92270. ☎ **800/I-LUV-SUN** or 619/568-2727. Fax 619/568-5845. 450 rms, 22 suites. A/C MINIBAR TV TEL. $175–$250 double; $250–$280 suite. AE, MC, V.

The early California charm of this relaxing Spanish hacienda makes Rancho Las Palmas one of the less pretentious luxury resorts in the desert. Dedicated golfers come to play on the adjoining country club's 27 holes of golf, and tennis buffs flock to the 25 hotel courts (3 of them red clay). The rooms are arranged in a complex of low-rise, tile-roofed structures, and the public areas have an easygoing elegance, filled with flower-laden stone fountains, smooth terra-cotta–tile floors, and rough-hewn wood trim. All rooms have a balcony or patio.

Dining/Entertainment: The Marriott's four restaurants range from casual patio dining to dressy dinner fare, and Miguel's Lounge offers cocktails, snacks, and music in a cantina setting.

Services: Room service, laundry service, baby-sitting.

Facilities: Golf and tennis pro shops, two swimming pools with adjacent whirlpools, fully equipped free fitness center.

Ritz-Carlton Rancho Mirage. 68-900 Frank Sinatra Dr., Rancho Mirage, CA 92270. ☎ **800/ 241-3333** or 619/321-8282. Fax 619/321-6928. 240 rms and suites. A/C MINIBAR TV TEL. $260–$395 double; from $650 suite. Additional person $25 extra; children 9 and under stay free in parents' room. AE, MC, V. Indoor valet parking $12.

This desert resort is situated on a spectacular mountain bluff, which provides a breathtaking setting but can make you feel disconnected from the community below. It's a bit too clubby and formal, and the service a little stuffy, for this relaxed desert location. The accommodations themselves, all with terraces, sport the tasteful elegance that's the hallmark of Ritz-Carlton hotels, and feature the usual Ritz touches like hair dryers, movie channels, refrigerators, and bathrobes. If you have a taste for posh luxury and want to get away from it all, this might be the place for you.

Dining/Entertainment: There are three restaurants, including the Club Grill, which serves regional American fare in a sophisticated ambience created by crystal chandeliers, fine china, and piano music playing softly in the background. Jackets are required for men. There's also a bar with live entertainment.

Services: Concierge, room service, twice-daily maid service, dry cleaning/laundry, baby-sitting, children's program, masseur.

Facilities: Swimming pool (the only chilled pool in Palm Springs), 10 tennis courts, compact but well-equipped fitness center, whirlpool, spa, sauna, games room, volleyball, basketball, car-rental desk, business center.

Westin Mission Hills Resort. Dinah Shore Dr. and Bob Hope Dr., Rancho Mirage, CA 92270. ☎ **800/999-8284** or 619/770-2132. Fax 619/321-2955. 512 rms and suites. A/C MINIBAR TV TEL. $239–$299 double; from $390 suite. Additional person $25 extra. Children 17 and under stay free in parents' room. AE, MC, V. Free valet and self-parking.

Designed to resemble a Moroccan palace surrounded by pools, waterfalls, and lush gardens, this self-contained resort stands on 360 acres. It's an excellent choice for families and for travelers who take their golf game seriously.

The rooms are a bit bland when compared to the spectacular exterior of the hotel, but do have views of the mountains and golf course. They all have terraces, and come with coffeemakers, hair dryers, movie channels, voice-mail, and bathrobes. Pets are accepted.

Dining/Entertainment: The dining options include Bella Vista, an atrium dining room serving California cuisine. There are also three bars, two of which offer live entertainment.

Services: Concierge, room service, twice-daily maid service, dry cleaning/laundry, masseur, baby-sitting. The fully staffed activities center for children offers educational instruction about the flora, fauna, and history of the desert.

Facilities: Renowned championship golf course, seven tennis courts, three swimming pools, fitness center, games room, lawn games, spa, steam room, whirlpool, beauty salon, bikes and bike trails, running track, car-rental desk, business center.

PALM DESERT

Marriott's Desert Springs Spa & Resort. 74885 Country Club Dr., Palm Desert, CA 92260. ☎ **800/228-9290** or 619/341-2211. Fax 619/341-1872. 833 rms, 51 suites. A/C MINIBAR TV TEL. $210–$295 double; from $575 suite. Children 17 and under stay free in parents' room. AE, CB, DC, DISC, MC, V.

A tourist attraction in its own right, Marriott's Desert Springs Resort is worth a peek even if you're not lucky enough to stay here. Most of the resort's guests are attracted by its excellent golf and tennis facilities. The huge, luxurious, and full-service spa is an added perk, offering massages, facials, aerobics classes, and supervised weight training. Visitors enter this artificial desert oasis via a sweeping palm tree–lined road wending its way past a small pond that's home to a gaggle of pink flamingos. Once inside, guests are greeted by a shaded marble lobby "rain forest" replete with interior moat and the squawk of tropical birds. Canopied water taxis congregate here, ready to float guests to their rooms.

While the rooms here are not as fancy as the lobby would lead you to believe, they're exceedingly comfortable, decorated with muted pastels and contemporary furnishings. All have terraces with views of the golf course and the San Jacinto Mountains. Most units have large baths, and are outfitted with hair dryers, ironing boards and irons, and separate tubs. The suites have large sitting/dining areas furnished with Murphy beds.

Dining/Entertainment: There are six restaurants, four snack bars, and two lounges, one of which features live entertainment. The poolside snacks are remarkably tasty.

Services: Concierge, room service, twice-daily maid service, masseur, overnight laundry, baby-sitting, special children's programs.

Facilities: Four heated outdoor pools, sunbathing "beach" with volleyball court, full-service spa and health club with aerobic classes, three outdoor Jacuzzis, sundecks, two 18-hole golf courses, putting green, driving range, 20 tennis courts (hard, clay, and grass; seven lighted), jogging trail, games room, car-rental desk, tour desk, Jose Eber beauty salon.

LA QUINTA

✪ **La Quinta Resort & Club.** 49-499 Eisenhower Dr., La Quinta, CA 92253. ☎ **800/ 854-1271**, 800/472-4316 in California, or 619/564-4111. Fax 619/564-5758. 640 rms and suites. A/C MINIBAR TV TEL. $200–$255 double; from $650 suite. Additional person $15 extra; children 17 and under stay free in parents' room. AE, MC, V.

A luxury resort set amid citrus trees, towering palms, cacti, and desert flowers at the base of the rocky Santa Rosa Mountains, La Quinta is *the* place to be if you're serious about your golf or tennis game. All rooms are in comfortable single-story, Spanish-style casitas scattered throughout the grounds. Each has a private patio and access to one of two dozen small pools, enhancing the feeling of privacy at this retreat. All accommodations come with two phones, movie channels, and refrigerators; some have fireplaces or their own Jacuzzis. Pets are accepted.

Dining/Entertainment: The tranquil lounge-library in the unaltered original hacienda hearkens back to the early days of the resort, when Clark Gable, Greta Garbo, Frank Capra, and other luminaries chose La Quinta as their hideaway. There are three restaurants, including Montanas with outstanding Mediterranean fare, and three bars (two with entertainment).

Services: Concierge, room service, dry cleaning, laundry, twice-daily maid service, masseur, children's program, baby-sitting.

Facilities: The resort is renowned for its five championship golf courses and 30 tennis courts. There's a large main swimming pool, plus 24 smaller pools and dozens of whirlpools; a fitness center; bicycles; car-rental desk; a business center; and a beauty salon

DESERT HOT SPRINGS

✪ **Two Bunch Palms.** 67-425 Two Bunch Palm Trail, Desert Hot Springs, CA 92240. ☎ **800/ 472-4334** or 619/329-8791. Fax 619/329-1317. 40 rms, suites, and efficiencies; 4 cottages/ villas. A/C TV TEL. $110–$232 double; $220–$375 suite or efficiency; $252–$570 cottage or villa. Rates include breakfast. AE, MC, V. Closed Aug.

Posh yet intimate, this spiritual sanctuary in Desert Hot Springs has been drawing weary city dwellers with its healing mineral springs since Chicago mobster Al Capone hid out here in the 1930s. Two Bunch Palms later became a playground for the movie community, but today it's a friendly and informal haven offering renowned spa services, quiet bungalows nestled on lush grounds, and trademark pools of steaming mineral water. All accommodations have terraces and such thoughtful extras as coffeemakers, hair dryers, and refrigerators, and some units have fireplaces or their own Jacuzzis. Surrounding Desert Hot Springs offers little incentive to leave this sybaritic paradise; you'll probably eat your meals at the unremarkable but health-conscious Casino Dining Room; legions of return guests will attest that the outstanding spa treatments (nine varieties of massage, mud baths, body wraps, facials, salt glo, etc.) and therapeutic waters are what make the luxury of Two Bunch Palms worth the price. The staff offers discreet, excellent service, and other amenities include a swimming pool, bicycles, two tennis courts, a fitness center, and private sunning bins.

WHERE TO DINE
PALM SPRINGS

You can get rid of the caffeine shakes in Palm Springs at **Lalajava,** 300 N. Palm Canyon Dr., at the corner of Amado (☎ **619/325-3494**). The cheerful staff will help you navigate their extensive menu of coffee items, which run the gamut from steaming hot cappuccinos to blended ice mochas, including flavored lattes, mochas, and cocoas. Nibble on a fresh muffin or bagel spread with plain or honey-walnut cream cheese, and you'll be well prepared for your day.

Expensive

✪ **Palmie.** 276 N. Palm Canyon Dr. (across from the Hyatt). ☎ **619/320-3375.** Reservations recommended. Main courses $15–$22. AE, MC, V. Mon–Fri 11am–2pm and 5:30–9:30pm, Sat 5:30–9:30pm. CLASSIC FRENCH.

You can't see Palmie from the street, and once you're seated inside its softly lit, lattice-enclosed dining patio, you won't see the bustle outside anymore, either. Art deco posters of French seaside resorts abound, transporting you to the cozy bistro of owners Martine and Alain Clerc. Chef Alain sends out dishes of traditional French masterpieces such as bubbling cheese soufflé, green lentil salad dotted with pancetta, steak au poivre rich with cognac sauce, and lobster raviolis garnished with caviar; in fact, every carefully garnished plate is a work of art. To the charming background strains of French chanteuses, hostess/manager Martine circulates between tables, determined that visitors should enjoy their meals as much as the loyal regulars she greets by name. Forget your cardiologist for one night and don't leave without sampling dessert: Our favorite is the trio of petite crème brûlées, flavored with ginger, vanilla, and Kahlúa.

Moderate

La Provence. 254 N. Palm Canyon Dr. (upstairs from an arcade). ☎ **619/416-4418.** Reservations recommended. Main courses $10–$21. AE, DC, DISC, MC, V. Thurs–Tues 5:30–10:30pm. COUNTRY FRENCH.

A favorite of erudite locals and recommended by knowledgeable innkeepers, the casually elegant La Provence eschews heavy traditional French cream sauces in favor of carefully married herbs and spices. The second-story terrace filled with tables sets a lovely mood on balmy desert evenings, whether or not it "subtly infuses the diner with an elevated sense of tranquillity" as the restaurant pretentiously promises. The menu offers some expected items (escargots in mushroom caps, bouillabaisse, steak au poivre) as well as inventive pastas like wild-mushroom raviolis in a sun-dried tomato and sweet-onion sauce. Like Palmie, La Provence is run by French expatriates who've brought their culinary expertise to the desert.

Las Casuelas Terraza. 222 S. Palm Canyon Dr. ☎ **619/325-2794.** Reservations recommended on weekends. Main courses $7–$13. AE, DC, DISC, MC, V. Mon–Thurs 11am–10pm, Fri–Sat 11am–11pm, Sun 10am–10pm. CLASSIC MEXICAN.

The original Las Casuelas is still open, a tiny storefront several blocks from this popular *terraza* (terrace) offspring, but the bougainvillea-draped front patio here is a much better place to people-watch over Mexican standards like quesadillas, enchiladas, and mountainous nachos washed down with equally super-size margaritas. Inside, the action heats up with live music and raucous happy-hour crowds. During hot weather the patio and even sidewalk passersby are cooled by the restaurant's well-placed misters, making this a perfect late-afternoon or early-evening choice.

Livreri's. 350 Indian Canyon Dr. (between Tahquitz Way and Ramon Rd.). ☎ **619/327-1419.** Reservations recommended. Pizza, pasta, and main courses $8–$24. AE, MC, V. Wed–Mon 4:30–10pm. CLASSIC ITALIAN.

The Livreri family came to the desert from Long Island, New York, in the mid-1970s and began preparing traditional Italian cuisine served in generous portions: steaming pastas, cheesy pizzas, and garlicky seafood specialties. It's not the glamorous, old-money Sinatra spot (for that, try Dominick's or Alberto's in Rancho Mirage), but it's conveniently located and satisfying. Separate rooms hold a long, leather-upholstered bar and the "Celebrity Room," where a retirement-age crowd gathers to enjoy dinner-theater performances of Broadway showtunes.

Inexpensive

Big Weenys. 238 N. Palm Canyon Dr. ☎ **619/416-0766.** Hot dogs and sandwiches $2.50–$6.25. MC, V. Mon–Fri 9:30am–9pm, Sat–Sun 9:30am–10pm. WIENERS.

Feed your inner adolescent with the double entendres abundant at this surprisingly varied hot dog shop. The "big weeny" is fine-quality meat, though, and equivalent in mass to three or four state-fair standards. Or choose the "normal," "long," or "teeny weeny." For the culinary adventurer, they offer designer sausages such as chicken and jalapeño, Italian antelope, and smoked pheasant. Which of the 11 available toppings would *you* choose for an alligator or kangaroo wiener?

🟢 **Edgardo's Café Veracruz.** 233 S. Indian Canyon (between Arenas and Baristo). ☎ **619/864-1551.** Reservations recommended. Main courses $3.50–$15. DISC, MC, V. Mon–Fri 11am–3pm and 5–10pm, Sat–Sun 8am–1pm (brunch). REGIONAL CENTRAL MEXICAN.

The pleasant but humble ambience at Edgardo's is a welcome change from touristy Palm Springs, and is the perfect backdrop for its expert menu of authentic Mayan, Huasteco, and Aztec cuisine. The dark interior boasts an array of colorful masks and artwork from Central and South America, but the postage-stamp-sized front patio with a trickling fountain is the best place to sample Edgardo's tangy quesadillas, desert cactus salad, and traditional poblano chiles rellenos—perhaps even a oyster/tequila shooter from the oyster bar!

Hollywood Stars Diner. 103 S. Palm Canyon Dr. (at Tahquitz Canyon). ☎ **619/416-1555.** Reservations not accepted. Most items under $10. MC, V. Daily 8am–9pm. AMERICAN.

Centrally located and flashy, this diner offers great people-watching from its expansive patio seating while serving up reliably tasty blue-plate specials and soda fountain treats. If you can't get into the superior but often-packed Louise's, you'll do fine to cross the street to the Hollywood Stars Diner.

Lincoln View Café. 278 N. Palm Canyon Dr. (in back of the courtyard). ☎ **619/327-6365.** Breakfast $2–$7; salads and sandwiches $4–$6; coffee drinks $1.25–$3.75. AE, DC, DISC, MC, V. Daily 7:30am–5:30pm. CAFE/BAKERY.

Tucked into the same quiet courtyard as Palmie (see above), this tasteful purveyor of coffee specialties, baked treats, and light meals is named for the unlikely "historic" view of Abraham Lincoln. Okay, it's not quite Mt. Rushmore, but the city makes the most of it. Use the purple scope outside the cafe's entrance to help fix your gaze on Lincoln's profile, formed in the scraggy hillside beyond the skyline. Enjoy live jazz here on the weekends.

Louise's Pantry. 124 S. Palm Canyon Dr. ☎ **619/325-5124.** Reservations not accepted. Most items under $10. MC, V. Daily 7am–8:30pm. AMERICAN.

A real old-fashioned diner, Louise's has been a fixture in Palm Springs since it opened as a drugstore lunch counter in 1945. Locals line up for the very few booths (expect a wait during mealtimes) to enjoy premium-quality comfort foods such as Cobb salad,

Rueben and French dip sandwiches, chicken and dumplings, hearty breakfasts with biscuits and gravy, and tasty fresh-baked pies. There's another branch in Palm Desert in the Town Center Plaza, Fred Waring Drive and Town Center Way (☎ 619/346-1315).

Mykonos. 139 Andreas (just off Palm Canyon). ☎ **619/322-0223.** Reservations not accepted. Most items under $10. MC, V. Wed–Mon 11am–10pm. GREEK.

Sit at the simple, candlelit tables in this off-street brick courtyard with locals who've been enjoying authentic Greek specialties at this family-run spot for 9 years. Mykonos is super-casual (vinyl tablecloths, that sort of thing) and decorated in white and blue like its Aegean namesake, but it's a pleasant treat in a town of mostly mediocre retro-diner fare. Traditional lamb shanks over rice, dolmades (stuffed grape leaves), salad tangy with crumbled feta cheese, and sweet, sticky baklava are among their best items.

RANCHO MIRAGE

The Chart House. 69934 Calif. 111 (between Country Club and Frank Sinatra drs.). ☎ **619/324-5613.** Reservations not accepted. Full dinners $13–$25. AE, DISC, MC, V. Mon–Fri 5–10pm, Sat 4:30–11pm, Sun 4:30–10pm. STEAKS/SEAFOOD.

Looking like a giant alien crustacean partially embedded in the earth, this traditional steakhouse is a treasure of wild 1960s architecture. You've seen this menu before—fine steaks, prime rib and seafood, endless salad bar, oversize baked potatoes—but the Chart House prepares each meal superbly, and the surreal setting makes it worth the expenditure.

LA QUINTA

La Quinta Cliffhouse. 78-250 Calif. 111. ☎ **619/360-5991.** Reservations recommended. Main courses $14–$27. AE, DC, MC, V. Mon 5:30–9:30pm, Tues–Fri noon–2pm and 5:30–9:30pm, Sat 5:30–9:30pm, Sun (in fall only) 10am–2pm. REGIONAL AMERICAN.

King of its own little hill on the east side of Calif. 111, La Quinta Cliffhouse successfully combines high-quality cuisine with a lovely setting. The stairs leading to the restaurant's entrance wind through a rocky waterfall. Try to get a table on the outdoor terrace or near a window to enjoy the Cliffhouse's best-known nonculinary draw: breathtaking sunsets virtually every night of the year. The entirely à la carte menu ensures that you'll pay handsomely for your dinner, but plenty of regulars attest to its worth. A large steamed artichoke served with drawn butter is a popular appetizer pick, perhaps followed by fresh mahi mahi prepared with soy and ginger and topped with razor-thin stir-fried vegetables. Aged filet mignon, pork ribs, and several chicken selections keep the grill busy. The bar offers a great early-bird dinner.

PALM DESERT

Max's Opera Cafe. 73-030 El Paseo (Monterey at Calif. 111). ☎ **619/776-6635.** Reservations not accepted. Salads and sandwiches $9–$11; main courses $12–$19 at dinner. AE, DC, DISC, MC, V. Mon–Thurs 11:30am–10pm, Fri 11:30am–11pm, Sat 11am–11pm, Sun 11am–10pm. DELI.

There's plenty of schmaltz at this upscale deli in the Beverly Hills of the desert, from the "secret recipe" of the "Matzoh Ball Queen" to cute menu Sinatra-isms like "Luck Be a Latke Tonight." The robust overstuffed pastrami sandwich falls just shy of New York–deli authenticity, but after 7pm nightly the place swings to opera and showtunes performed by the service staff!

THE DESERT RESORTS AFTER DARK

Every month a different club or disco is the hot spot in the Springs, and the best way to tap into the trend is by consulting *The Desert Guide*, *The Bottom Line* (see "Gay

Life in Palm Springs," above), or one of the many other free newsletters available from area hotels and merchants. **VillageFest** (see "Shopping," above) turns Palm Canyon Drive into an outdoor party each Thursday night. Here are a few more of the enduring arts and entertainment attractions around the desert resorts:

Cactus Corral. 67-501 Calif. 111, Cathedral City. ☎ **619/321-8558.**

Billing itself as "the Coachella Valley's Country Music Nightclub," the Cactus Corral has stood the test of time with billiards, a sports bar, and live country bands, plus firewater and good, greasy grub. Early in the evening they offer western-style dance lessons. Open limited summer days 6pm to 2pm; call ahead for exact days.

The Fabulous Palm Springs Follies. At the Plaza Theatre, 128 S. Palm Canyon Dr., Palm Springs. ☎ **619/327-0225.** Tickets $25–$37.

This vaudeville-style show filled with lively production numbers is celebrating its 5th year of running in the historic Plaza Theatre in the heart of Palm Springs. With a cast of energetic retired showgirls, singers, dancers, and comedians, the revue has been enormously popular around town. Call for show schedule.

McCallum Theatre for the Performing Arts. 73-000 Fred Waring Dr., Palm Desert. ☎ **619/340-ARTS.**

For urban sophisticates who move to the Palm Springs desert, the McCallum Theatre offers the only cultural high road around. Frequent symphony performances with visiting virtuosos such as conductor Seiji Ozawa or violinist Itzhak Perlman, musicals like Tommy Tune's *Grease,* and pop performers like the Captain and Tennille or the Ink Spots are among the theater's recent offerings. Call for upcoming event information.

Touché Restaurant & Nightclub. 42-250 Bob Hope Dr., Rancho Mirage. ☎ **619/773-1111.**

Run by the same team who keep Melvyn's piano lounge (at the Ingleside Inn) one of the desert's "in" spots for the old-money/celebrity set, Touché offers dining and dancing in the old style, and hip devotees of the "cocktail nation" movement can be seen swinging alongside perfectly coiffed retirees. Open Wednesday to Sunday from 6:30pm.

3 Joshua Tree National Park

by John McKinney

John McKinney is an award-winning nature writer, conservationist, and hiking columnist for the *Los Angeles Times* who has authored six guides to the West, including *Walking the West* (HarperCollins West) with Cheri Rae.

For many visitors to Joshua Tree National Park, the trees themselves are not only the essence but the whole of their park experience. The park is much more than a tableau of twisted yucca, however, for it beckons the explorer with a diversity of desert environments, including sand dunes, native palm oases, cactus gardens, and jumbles of jumbo granite.

The Joshua trees' distribution defines the very boundaries of the Mojave Desert. Here in their namesake national park, they reach the southernmost limit of their range.

Sometimes known as the "in between" desert because of its location between the Mojave and the Colorado deserts, the parkland shares characteristics of each. The mountainous, Joshua tree–studded Mojave Desert is relatively cooler, wetter, and higher; it forms the northern and western parts of the park. Hotter, drier, lower, and characterized by a wide variety of desert flora including ironwood, smoketree, and native California fan palms, the Colorado Desert comprises the southern and eastern sections of the park. Cacti, especially cholla and ocotillo, thrive in the more southerly Colorado Desert (a part of the larger Sonoran Desert).

During the 1920s a worldwide fascination with the desert emerged, and cactus gardens were very much in vogue. Entrepreneurs hauled truckloads of desert plants into Los Angeles for quick sale or export. The Mojave was in danger of being picked clean of its cacti, yucca, and ocotillo. Wealthy socialite Minerva Hoyt organized the International Desert Conservation League to halt this destructive practice. Almost single-handedly, she successfully lobbied for the establishment of Joshua Tree National Monument in 1936.

In 1994, under provisions of the federal California Desert Protection Act, Joshua Tree was "upgraded" to national park status and expanded by a 250,000 acres.

The Joshua tree is said to have been given its name by early Mormon settlers traveling west. The tree's upraised limbs and bearded appearance reminded them of the prophet Joshua leading them to the promised land.

Other observers were not so kind. Explorer John C. Frémont called it "the most repulsive tree in the vegetable kingdom." Nature writer Charles Francis Saunders opined: "The trees themselves were as grotesque as the creations of a bad dream; the shaggy trunks and limbs were twisted and seemed writhing as though in pain, and dagger-pointed leaves were clenched in bristling fists of inhospitality."

Despite its harsh appearance, the Joshua tree belongs to the lily family. Like lilies and other flowers, it must be pollinated in order to reproduce. The Tegeticula moth does the job for the Joshua tree, which in turn provides seeds for the newly hatched larvae of the moth. Long ago, during the evolutionary history of the Mojave Desert, the Joshua tree and the moth joined together to produce a partnership that continues to this day.

The trees grow at the foot of mountain slopes and capture the surface and groundwater draining from higher elevations. Once in a while you'll see a Joshua tree clumsily embrace one of its fellows but, generally, its water requirements keep it distant from other trees. Pale yellow, lilylike flowers festoon the limbs of the Joshuas when they bloom (depending on rainfall) in March, April, or May.

JUST THE FACTS

No restaurants, lodging, gas stations, or stores are found within Joshua Tree National Park. In fact, water is only available at four park locations: Cottonwood Springs, the Blackrock Canyon Campground, the Indian Cove Ranger Station, and the Oasis Visitors Center. Yucca Valley has lots of restaurants and every fast-food franchise imaginable.

ACCESS POINTS   From metropolitan Los Angeles, the usual route to the Oasis Visitor Center in Joshua Tree National Park is via I-10 to its intersection with Calif. 62 (some 45 miles east of San Bernardino). Calif. 62 leads north and east for about 43 miles to the town of Twentynine Palms. From the town, follow the park signs a short distance to the visitor center.

VISITOR CENTERS   In addition to the main Oasis Visitor Center at the Twentynine Palms entrance, there is Cottonwood at the south entrance, and Black Rock Canyon, located at the campground southeast of Yucca Valley.

The Oasis Visitor Center is open daily (except Christmas) from 8am to 4:30pm. Check here for a schedule of ranger-guided walks and evening interpretive programs.

Ask about the weekend tours of the Desert Queen Ranch, once a working ranch and now part of the park.

CONTACT INFORMATION   For information, contact the Superintendent, Joshua Tree National Park, 74485 National Park Dr., Twentynine Palms, CA 92277 (☎ 619/367-7511).

SEEING THE HIGHLIGHTS

An excellent first stop is the main **Oasis Visitor Center,** located alongside the Oasis of Mara, also known as the Twentynine Palms Oasis. For many generations the native Serrano tribe lived at this "place of little springs and much grass." Get maps, books, and the latest in road, trail, and weather conditions before beginning your tour.

Two paved roads explore the heart of the park. The first loops through the high northwest section, visiting Queen and Lost Horse valleys, as well as the awesome boulder piles at Jumbo Rocks and Wonderland of Rocks. The second angles northwest-southeast across the park and crosses both the Mojave Desert Joshua tree woodland and the cactus gardens of the Colorado Desert.

From the Oasis Visitor Center, drive south to **Jumbo Rocks,** which captures the complete essence of the park: a vast array of rock formations, a Joshua tree forest, the yucca-dotted desert open and wide. Check out Skull Rock (one of the many rocks in the area that appear to resemble humans, dinosaurs, monsters, cathedrals, and castles) via a 1¹/₂-mile-long nature trail that provides an introduction to the park's flora, wildlife, and geology.

In Queen Valley, just west of Jumbo Rocks, is the signed beginning of **Geology Tour Road,** a rough dirt road (four-wheel-drive recommended) extending 18 miles into the heart of the park. Motorists get close-up looks at the considerable erosive forces that shaped this land, forming the flattest of desert playas, or dry lake beds, as well as massive heaps of boulders that tower over the valley floor. Geology Tour Road also delivers a Joshua tree woodland, a historic spring, abandoned mines, and some fascinating Native American petroglyphs.

Farther west of Jumbo Rocks is **Indian Cave,** typical of the kind of shelter sought by the nomadic Cahuilla and Serrano clans that traveled this desert land. A number of bedrock mortars found in the cave suggest its use as a work site by its aboriginal inhabitants. A 4-mile round-trip trail climbs through a lunar landscape of rocks and Joshua trees to the top of 5,470-foot Ryan Mountain. Your reward for making this climb is one of the park's best panoramic views.

At Cap Rock Junction, the paved park road swings north toward the **Wonderland of Rocks,** 12 square miles of massive jumbled granite. This curious maze of stone hides groves of Joshua trees, trackless washes, and several small pools of water.

The easiest, and certainly the safest, way to explore the Wonderland is to follow the 1¹/₄-mile **Barker Dam Loop Trail.** The first part of the journey is on a nature trail that interprets botanical highlights; the second part visits some Native petroglyphs and a little lake created a century ago by cattle ranchers.

From Cap Rock Junction, dirt Keys View Road dead-ends at mile-high **Keys View.** From the crest of the Little San Bernardino Mountains, enjoy grand desert views that encompass both the highest (Mt. San Gorgonio) and lowest (Salton Sea) points in Southern California.

Pinto Basin Road tours the Colorado Desert side of the park. The **Cholla Cactus Garden** preserves an unusually thick concentration of cholla, often called teddybear cactus because of the soft, fluffy appearance of its spines. Don't be deceived; the spines stick in the skin with only the lightest touch.

This Is Our Life: The Roy Rogers & Dale Evans Museum

Passing through Victorville, it's tough to miss a log fort visible from I-15, with the words "Roy Rogers and Dale Evans Museum" emblazoned on the side, Las Vegas style—larger than life, brightly lit, embellished with stars.

Fans of cowboy lore, western movies, or country music can all tell you the museum is legendary for being the final resting place of Roy's faithful horse Trigger, which he had stuffed and mounted. For company, Trigger has Buttermilk (Dale's golden horse), Bullet (their canine companion), and a veritable Noah's Ark of taxidermy—Roy's trophies from safaris in every corner of the globe.

These are among the many surprises awaiting visitors to the museum, a glorified attic containing the relics and souvenirs of two lifetimes. The displays are folksy, accented by tags saying "my first cowboy boots" (bronzed, of course), "the 1923 Dodge I came to California in, in 1930," and other personal remarks. But because of Roy and Dale's wealth, years of travel, varied interests, and an apparent inability to throw anything away, this museum truly has something for everyone. Some of the highlights are:

- Beautifully arranged cases commemorating each of Roy and Dale's three children who died in childhood. On display are photos, toys, letters, and report cards, as well as the inspirational books written in tribute by Dale Evans Rogers after each of their deaths. The Rogerses' many living children and grandchildren are also well represented; in fact, by the end of your visit you might feel as if you know the whole family personally!

- Gifts from the couple's fans all over the world, including a pair of stitched samplers framed near the entrance, containing poetic tributes both epic and homespun.

- Every piece of Roy Rogers and/or Dale Evans merchandise from over the years: comic books, breakfast cereal boxes, fan club items, war effort promotions, and more. See the 1950s-era "den/playroom" filled with vintage furniture and littered with dozens of Roy and Dale toys, storybooks, dolls, model horses, and board games.

- Roy's personal collection of western memorabilia from his role models—real-life and movie cowboys—includes Tom Mix's director's chair, Buck Jones's saddle, Hoot Gibson's piano, and last but not least, an autographed picture of Lee Majors (remember him in *The Big Valley?*).

The museum is open daily from 9am to 5pm except Thanksgiving and Christmas. For more information call **619/243-4547.**

Pinto Basin is, to say the least, forbidding: a barren lowland surrounded by austere mountains and punctuated by trackless sand dunes. Nevertheless, some 2,000 to 4,000 years ago a hardy group of Native Americans managed to live here by forging some specialized tools; so unique were these ancients that anthropologists describe them as "Pinto Man." Try to imagine how even the most primitive people could have survived in the harsh environs of Pinto Basin as you enjoy a mellow stroll to a group of low sand dunes.

HIKING, ROCK CLIMBING & MOUNTAIN BIKING

HIKING The national park holds a couple of California's loveliest palm oases. The **Fortynine Palms Oasis Trail** (3 miles round-trip) winds up and over a hot rocky crest to the dripping springs, pools, and the blessed shade of palms and cottonwoods.

Cottonwood Spring, near the south end of the park, is a little palm- and cottonwood-shaded oasis that attracts desert birds and birdwatchers. From Cottonwood Campground, a 3-mile round-trip trail leads to the old Mastodon Gold Mine, then climbs behemoth-looking Mastodon Peak for a view from Mt. San Jacinto above Palm Springs to the Salton Sea.

The **Lost Palms Oasis Trail** (8 miles round-trip) visits the park's premier palm grove.

The **Black Rock Canyon Trail** (6 miles round-trip) follows a classic desert wash, then ascends to the crest of the Little San Bernardino Mountains at Warren Peak. The desert and mountain views from the peak are stunning.

The **Lost Horse Mine Trail** (3¹/₂ miles round-trip) visits one of the area's most successful gold mines, and offers a close-up look back into a colorful era, and some fine views into the heart of the park.

ROCK CLIMBING From Hidden Valley to the Wonderland of Rocks, the park has emerged as one of the world's premier rock-climbing destinations. The park offers some 3,000 climbing routes, ranging from the easiest of bouldering to some of the sport's most difficult technical climbs. During the November to May climbing season, the superstars of the sport from Europe, Japan, and America can be seen surmounting flared chimneys and difficult jam cracks.

MOUNTAIN BIKING Although they're not encouraged by park officials, mountain bikes are a good tool for touring Joshua Tree. Much of the park is designated wilderness, meaning that mountain bikes are limited to roads; they'll damage the fragile ecosystem if you venture off the beaten track. Try the 18-mile **Geology Tour Road.** Hammer out the miles on the rarely traveled, rough washboard roads in **Hidden Valley** and **Queen Valley.**

CAMPING & ACCOMMODATIONS

Nine campgrounds scattered throughout the park offer pleasant though often spartan accommodations, with just picnic tables and pit toilets for the most part. Only two— **Black Rock Canyon** and **Cottonwood**—have water.

If you're staying in the Palm Springs area, it's entirely possible to make a day trip to the national park. But if you'd like to stay close by and spend more time here, Twentynine Palms and Yucca Valley, just outside the north boundary of the national park on Calif. 62, offer budget to moderate lodging. In Twentynine Palms is the 71-room **Best Western Gardens Motel** (☎ 619/367-9141). In Yucca Valley is the **Yucca Inn** (☎ 619/365-3311). For a complete listing of Yucca Valley lodging, contact the **Yucca Valley Chamber of Commerce,** 56300 Twentynine Palms Hwy., Yucca Valley, CA 92284 (☎ 619/365-6323).

4 Mojave National Preserve

by John McKinney

Two decades of park politicking finally ended in 1994 when President Clinton signed into law the California Desert Protection Act that transferred the East Mojave National Scenic Area, previously administered by the U.S. Bureau of Land Management, to the National Park Service and established the new Mojave National Preserve. Thus far the Mojave's elevated status has not attracted hordes of sightseers.

To most Americans, the East Mojave is that vast, bleak, interminable stretch of desert to be crossed as quickly as possible while driving I-15 from L.A. to Las

Vegas. Few realize that I-15 is the northern boundary of what desert rats have long considered the crown jewel of the California desert.

With few campgrounds and even fewer motels—without even a visitor center—this land is a hard one to get to know. But it's an easy one to get to like. Its 1.4 million acres include the world's largest Joshua tree forest, wild burros and grazing cattle, spectacular canyons and volcanic formations, nationally honored scenic backroads and footpaths to historic mining sites, tabletop mesas, and a dozen mountain ranges.

JUST THE FACTS

GETTING THERE I-15, the major route taken between the Southern California metropolis and the state line by Las Vegas–bound travelers, extends along the northern boundary of Mojave National Preserve. I-40 is the southern access route to the East Mojave.

WHEN TO GO Spring is a splendid time (autumn is another) to visit this desert. From March to May the temperatures are mild, the Joshua trees are in bloom, and the lower Kelso Dunes are bedecked with yellow and white desert primrose and pink sand verbena.

REGULATIONS Most National Park Service regulations apply, but certain land uses permitted in Mojave National Preserve that would not be found in the more pristine national parks include cattle grazing, mining, and hunting.

SEEING THE HIGHLIGHTS

One of the preserve's spectacular sights is the **Kelso Dunes,** the most extensive dune field in the West. The 45-square-mile formation of magnificently sculpted sand is famous for its "booming": Visitors' footsteps cause mini-avalanches and the dunes to go "sha-boom-sha-boom-sha-boom." Geologists speculate that the extreme dryness of the East Mojave Desert, combined with the wind-polished, rounded nature of the individual sand grains, has something to do with their musicality. Sometimes the low rumbling sound resembles a Tibetan gong; other times it sounds like a 1950s doo-wop musical group.

From atop the Kelso Dunes is a stunning view: the Kelso Mountains to the north, the Bristol Mountains to the southwest, the Granite Mountains to the south, the Providence Mountains to the east. Everywhere you look there are mountain ranges, small and large, from the jagged, red-colored spirelike Castle Peaks to the flattopped Table Mountain. In fact, despite evidence to the contrary—most notably the stunning Kelso Dunes—the East Mojave is really a desert of mountains, not sand.

A 10-mile drive from the Kelso Dunes is **Kelso Depot,** built by the Union Pacific in 1924. The Spanish Revival–style structure was designed with a red-tile roof, graceful arches, and a brick platform. Train passengers and visitors ate meals in a restaurant nicknamed "The Beanery." The depot continued to be open for freight train crew use through the mid-1980s, although it ceased to be a railroad stop for passengers after World War II. The National Park Service is considering refurbishing the building for use as the preserve's visitor center.

Another preserve highlight is **Cima Dome,** a 75-square-mile chunk of uplifted volcanic rock. A geological rarity, Cima has been called the most symmetrical natural dome in the United States. Another distinctive feature of the dome is its handsome rock outcroppings—the same type found in Joshua Tree National Park to the south, and a lure for rock climbers and hikers.

On and around Cima Dome grows the world's largest and densest **Joshua tree forest.** Botanists say Cima's Joshuas are more symmetrical than their cousins elsewhere in the Mojave. The dramatic colors of the sky at sunset provide a breath-taking backdrop for Cima's Joshua trees, some more than 25 feet tall and several hundred years old.

A half-hour drive from the Joshuas bring you to the tiny, blink-and-you'll-miss-it **Nipton,** located in the northeast corner of the preserve a few miles from the California-Nevada state line. The town consists of a few houses, a general store, and the Hotel Nipton, a southwestern-style bed-and-breakfast.

Jerry Freeman, a former hard-rock miner who purchased the entire town in 1984, says hotel occupancy is up 80% since the East Mojave became a national preserve. He and his wife, Roxanne, moved from the famous sands of Malibu to the abandoned ghost town and have gradually brought it back to life.

While you can see the lights of Vegas (50 miles away) from Nipton, this is testimonial to the clarity of the desert sky, not Nipton's proximity to civilization. The opalescent light, and the spectacular sunrises and sunsets in the East Mojave, are grand. And for city dwellers all too accustomed to viewing murky night skies, gazing at the Milky Way on display is a revelation. This is a place where shooting stars and constellations appear with startling clarity and the nearby New York Mountains seem sprinkled with stardust.

Hole-in-the-Wall and Mid Hills are the centerpieces of Mojave National Preserve. Both locales offer diverse desert scenery, fine campgrounds, and the feeling of being in the middle of nowhere, though in fact they're located right in the middle of the preserve.

Linking the two sites is the preserve's best drive. In 1989 **Wildhorse Canyon Road,** which loops from Mid Hills Campground to Hole-in-the-Wall Campground, was declared the nation's first official "Back Country Byway," an honor federal agencies bestow upon America's most scenic backroads. The 11-mile, horseshoe-shaped road crosses wide-open country dotted with cholla and, in season, delicate purple, yellow, and red wildflowers. Dramatic volcanic slopes and flattop mesas tower over the low desert. I stopped to scramble among large pinyon pine trees and lichen-covered granite rocks and to visit a "Devil's Garden," a grouping of several types of cactus interspersed with boulders.

Mile-high **Mid Hills,** so named because of its location halfway between the Providence and New York mountains, recalls the Great Basin Desert topography of Nevada and Utah. Mid Hills Campground offers a grand observation point from which to gaze out at the coffee-with-cream-colored Pinto Mountains to the north and the rolling Kelso Dunes shining on the western horizon.

Hole-in-the-Wall is the kind of place Butch Cassidy and the Sundance Kid would have chosen as a hideout. This twisted maze of rocks called rhyolite is a form of crystallized red lava rock. A series of iron rings aids descent into Hole-in-the-Wall; they're not particularly difficult for those who are reasonably agile and take their time.

Kelso Dunes, the Joshua trees, a night at Nipton, Hole-in-the-Wall, and Mid Hills—the heart of the new preserve can be viewed in a weekend. But you'll need a week just to see all the major sights, and maybe a lifetime to really get to know the East Mojave. And right now, without much in the way of services, the traveler to this desert must be well prepared and self-reliant. For many, this is what makes a trip to the East Mojave an adventure.

If Mojave National Preserve attracts you, you'll want to return again and again to see the wonders of this desert, including **Caruthers Canyon,** a "botanical island" of pinyon pine and juniper woodland, and **Ivanpah Valley,** which supports the largest desert tortoise population in the California Desert. You'll want to climb atop enormous volcanic cinder cones, then with flashlights crawl through narrow lava tubes; explore the ruins of Fort Piute and wonder about the lonely life of the soldiers stationed there and marvel at the ruts carved into rock by the wheels of pioneer wagon trains; and guess at the meaning of the petroglyphs left behind by the Native Americans who roamed this land long ago.

Just west of the preserve is **Afton Canyon,** often called the Grand Canyon of the Mojave. Afton Canyon is a geological wonderland sculpted by the Mojave River, a dramatic 8-mile-long, narrow gorge with some sheer walls that rise 600 feet above the canyon floor.

Afton Canyon is one of the few places where the Mojave River runs year round. The dependable source of water supports a variety of plants, including cottonwoods, willows, rabbit bush, smoketrees, and grasses.

HIKING & MOUNTAIN BIKING

HIKING   The climb to the top of the Kelso Dunes is 3 miles round-trip. A cool, inviting, pinyon pine–juniper woodland is explored by the **Caruthers Canyon Trail** (3 miles round-trip).

The longest pathway is the 8-mile (one-way) **Mid Hills to Hole-in-the-Wall Trail,** a grand tour of basin and range tabletop mesas, large pinyon trees, and colorful cactus. If you're not up for a long day hike, the three-quarter-mile trip from Hole-in-the-Wall Campground to Banshee Canyon and the 5-mile jaunt to Wildhorse Canyon offer some easier alternatives.

MOUNTAIN BIKING   Opportunities are as extensive as the preserve's hundreds of miles of lonesome dirt roads. The 140-mile-long historic **Mojave Road,** a rough four-wheel-drive route, visits many of the most scenic areas in the East Mojave; sections of this road make excellent bike tours. Prepare well—the Mojave Road and other dirt roads are rugged routes through desert wilderness.

CAMPING

The **Mid Hills Campground** is located in a pinyon pine–juniper woodland and offers outstanding views. This mile-high camp is the coolest in the East Mojave. Nearby **Hole-in-the-Wall Campground** is perched above two dramatic canyons.

The **Afton Canyon Campground,** 33 miles east of Barstow, can easily be reached via the Afton exit off I-15 and a well-graded 3-mile dirt road.

One of the highlights of the East Mojave Desert is camping in the open desert all by your lonesome, but certain rules apply. Call the California Desert Information Center for suggestions.

NEARBY TOWNS WITH TOURIST SERVICES

BARSTOW   The **California Desert Information Center,** 831 Barstow Rd., Barstow (☎ 619/255-8760), is a logical first stop for any desert tour. Maps, brochures, information about area camping, lodging, and desert attractions, and a selection of guidebooks are available. Nature exhibits, as well as personable National Park Service and U.S. Bureau of Land Management staff are on hand to help the visitor get oriented. Open daily from 9am to 5pm.

Barstow has a great many restaurants and motels. Call the **Barstow Chamber of Commerce** (☎ 619/256-8617) for suggestions.

BAKER   Accommodations and food are available in this small desert town, a good point to fill up your gas tank and purchase supplies before entering Mojave National Preserve. Check out the world's tallest thermometer in front of the new **Desert Visitor Center,** which provides information about Mojave National Preserve, Death Valley National Park, and surrounding U.S. Bureau of Land Management lands.

The **Bun Boy Coffee Shop** is open 24 hours. For a tasty surprise, stop at the **Mad Greek Restaurant.** Order a Greek salad, a souvlaki, or zucchini sticks, and marvel at your good fortune—imagine finding such tasty food and pleasant surroundings in the middle of nowhere.

Inexpensive lodging can be secured at a couple of motels, including the **Bun Boy Motel** (☎ 619/733-4363).

NIPTON   This tiny town boasts a general store and the **Hotel Nipton** (☎ 619/856-2335), a B&B with a sitting room, two bathrooms down the hall, and four guest rooms, each going for $45 a night. Nipton is located on Nipton Road, a few miles from I-15 near the Nevada state line.

STATELINE   The aptly named town on the California-Nevada border features **Whiskey Pete's** (☎ 702/382-4388), a casino-hotel-restaurant-truckstop in ersatz Wild West decor; it boasts of "Nevada's loosest slots." Pete's sister, the Prima Donna Casino and Hotel, also vies for your attention.

5 Death Valley National Park

by John McKinney

Entering Death Valley at Towne Pass, Calif. 190 crests the rolling Panamint Range and descends into Emigrant Wash. Along the road is a new sign: DEATH VALLEY NATIONAL PARK.

Park? Death Valley National Park? The Forty-niners, whose suffering gave the valley its name, would have howled at the notion. "Death Valley National Park" seems a contradiction in terms, an oxymoron of the great outdoors. To them, other four-letter words would have been more appropriate: gold, mine, heat, lost, dead. And the four-letter words shouted by teamsters who drove the 20-mule-team borax wagons need not be repeated.

Visitors to Death Valley have long linked the Creator with the place—not as a heavenly spot, but as the closest place to Hell on earth. It's been called the land that God forgot, a land God made in anger.

Mountains stand naked, unadorned. The bitter waters of saline lakes evaporate into bizarre, razor-sharp crystal formations. Jagged canyons jab deep into the earth. Ovenlike heat, frigid cold, and the driest air imaginable combine to make this one of the most inhospitable locations in the world.

In Death Valley, the forces of the earth are exposed to view with dramatic clarity: A sudden fault and a sink became a lake. The water evaporated, leaving behind borax and, above all, fantastic scenery. Although Death Valley is called a valley, in actuality it is not. Valleys are carved by rivers, but Death Valley is what geologists call a graben. Here a block of the earth's crust has dropped down along fault lines in relation to its mountain walls.

At **Racetrack Playa,** a dry lake bed, visitors puzzle over rocks that weigh as much as a quarter of a ton and yet move mysteriously across the mud floor, leaving trails as a record of their movement. Research suggests that a combination of powerful winds and rain may skid the rocks over slick clay.

Badwater, at 282 feet below sea level the lowest point in the Western Hemisphere, is also one of the hottest places in the world, with regularly recorded summer temperatures of 120° Fahrenheit.

Death Valley is raw, bare earth, the way it must have looked before life began. Just looking out on the landscape, it's impossible to know what year—what century—it is.

Today's visitor to Death Valley drives in air-conditioned comfort, stays in comfortable hotel rooms or well-maintained campgrounds, orders meals and provisions at park concessions, even quaffs a cold beer at the local saloon. He or she may take a swim in the Olympic-size pool, tour a Moorish castle, shop for souvenirs, and enjoy the desert landscape while hiking along a nature trail with a park ranger.

It hasn't always been so.

Americans looking for gold in California's mountains in 1849 were forced to cross the burning sands to avoid severe snowstorms in the nearby Sierra Nevada. Some perished along the way, and the land became known as Death Valley.

Many of Death Valley's topographical features are associated with hellish images—the Funeral Mountains, Furnace Creek, Dante's View, Coffin Peak, and the Devil's Golf Course. But it can be a place of serenity.

In one of his last official acts, President Herbert Hoover signed a proclamation designating Death Valley as a national monument on February 11, 1933. With the stroke of a pen he not only authorized the protection of a vast and wondrous land, but helped to transform one of the earth's least hospitable spots into a popular tourist destination.

The naming of Death Valley National Monument came at a time when Americans began to discover the romance of the desert. Land that had previously been considered hideously devoid of life was now celebrated for its spare beauty; places that had once been feared for their harshness were now admired for their uniqueness.

Death Valley National Park became the largest national park outside Alaska, with over 3.3 million acres, when President Clinton signed the California Desert Protection Act of 1994. Numerous parts of the mountain ranges surrounding Death Valley, as well as two other large valleys—Eureka and Saline—were added to the park.

This land may as well be a national park because it cannot be settled and will never be tamed. The urbanization of other parts of the Mojave notwithstanding, this is a land that will never see suburbs or shopping centers. It's too naked, too harsh. It's a land that meets you face to face on its own terms—and it always wins. Formerly rich mining sites stand empty. Once-bustling towns silently crumble into dust. Broken slabs of asphalt mark where roads have been demolished by powerful flash floods.

Death Valley is an alien land, so apart from the rest of America that it may just as well be located on Mars. But this harsh land attracts visitors, more than a million a year, from all over the world. During the winter months, much of the visitation is by retired snowbirds camping in their motorhomes or trailers. But during the summer months you're more likely to hear visitors speaking German, French, and Japanese.

JUST THE FACTS

The **Death Valley Visitor Center** at Furnace Creek, 15 miles inside eastern park boundary on Calif. 190 (☎ **619/786-3244**), offers well-done interpretive exhibits and an hourly slide program. Ask at the information desk for ranger-led nature walks and evening naturalist programs. Visitor center hours are daily 8am to 7pm in the winter, daily 8am to 5pm in the summer. For information, before you go, contact the Superintendent, Death Valley National Park, Death Valley, CA 92328 (☎ **619/786-2331**).

Perhaps the most scenic entry to the park is via Calif. 190, east from Calif. 395 through Towne Pass. Another scenic drive to the park is by way of Calif. 127 and Calif. 190 from Baker.

SEEING THE HIGHLIGHTS

A good first stop after checking in at the main park visitor center in Furnace Creek is the **Harmony Borax Works**—a rock-salt landscape as tortured as you'll ever find. Death Valley prospectors called borax "white gold," and though it wasn't exactly a glamorous substance, it was a profitable one. From 1883 to 1888 more than 20 million pounds of borax were transported from the Harmony Borax Works. A short trail with interpretive signs leads past the ruins of the old borax refinery and some outlying buildings.

Transport of the borax was the stuff of legends, too. The famous 20-mule teams hauled the huge loaded wagons 165 miles to the rail station at Mojave. (To learn more about this colorful era, visit the Borax Museum at Furnace Creek Ranch and the park visitor center, also located in Furnace Creek.)

Salt Creek is the home of the **Salt Creek pupfish,** found nowhere else on earth. This little fish, which has made some amazing adaptations to survive in this arid land, can be glimpsed from a wooden boardwalk nature trail. In spring a million pupfish might be wriggling in the creek; but by summer's end only a few thousand remain.

Before sunrise, photographers set up their tripods at **Zabriskie Point** and aim their cameras down at the pale mudstone hills of Golden Canyon and the great valley beyond. The panoramic view of Golden Canyon is magnificent, but don't miss getting right into the canyon itself—only possible by hitting the trail.

Another grand park vista is seen at **Dante's View.** From this 5,475-foot viewpoint in the Black Mountains, one can see the Funeral Mountains, Greenwater Valley, and the shimmering Death Valley floor backed by the high Panamint Mountains.

A 14-square-mile field of dunes and some bizarre geology are some of the attractions of a visit to the **Stove Pipe Wells** area. Death Valley's dunes lie between Towne Pass on the west and Daylight Pass to the east; there's quite a sand-laden draft between the two passes. The sand in the dunes is actually tiny pieces of rock, most of them quartz fragments.

Those surreal corn stalks you see across Calif. 190 from the dunes are actually clumps of arrowweed. The **Devil's Cornstalks** are perched on wind- and water-eroded pedestals.

Mosaic Canyon, located near Stovepipe Wells, displays mosaics of water-polished white, gray, and black rock. Nature has cemented the canyon's stream gravels into mosaics large and small. It's easy to imagine you've entered an art gallery when you view the mosaics on the canyon walls; not only are nature's works of art on display, but the long, narrow, white marble walls of the canyon seem quite "gallery"-like.

Scotty's Castle, the Mediterranean-to-the-max mega-hacienda in the northern part of the park, is unabashedly Death Valley's premier tourist attraction. Visitors are wowed by the elaborate Spanish tiles, well-crafted furnishings, and innovative construction that included solar water heating. Even more compelling is the colorful history of this villa in remote Grapevine Canyon, brought to life by park rangers dressed in 1930s period clothing. Don't be surprised if the castle cook or a friend of Scotty's gives you a special insight into castle life.

Construction of the "castle"—more officially, Death Valley Ranch—began in 1924. It was to be a winter retreat for eccentric Chicago millionaire Albert Johnson. The insurance tycoon's unlikely friendship with prospector/cowboy/spinner-of-tall-tales Walter Scott put the $2.3-million structure on the map and captured the public's imagination. Scotty greeted visitors and told them fanciful stories from the early hard-rock-mining days of Death Valley.

The 1-hour walking tour of Scotty's Castle is excellent, both for its inside look at the mansion and for what it reveals about the eccentricities of Johnson and Scotty. Tours fill up quickly; arrive early for the first available spots (there's a small fee). A snack bar and gift shop make the wait more comfortable. To learn more about the castle grounds, pick up the pamphlet, "A Walking Tour of Scotty's Castle," which leads you on an exploration from stable to swimming pool, from bunkhouse to powerhouse.

Near Scotty's Castle is **Ubehebe Crater.** It's known as an explosion crater—one look and you'll know why. When hot magma rose from the depths of the earth to meet the ground water, the resultant steam blasted out a crater and scattered cinders.

To the native Shoshone of Death Valley, the crater was known as Temp-pin-tta Wo' sah, "Basket in the Rock"—an apt description indeed. Half a mile in diameter, Ubehebe is not the only basket around; to the south is Little Hebe Crater and a cluster of smaller craters.

HIKING & MOUNTAIN BIKING

HIKING The **Keane Wonder Mine Trail** (2 miles round-trip) climbs very steeply to a historic mine and terrific valley view.

Golden Canyon (5 miles round-trip) explores a colorful canyon and climbs to one of the park's grandest vistas at Zabriskie Point. The first mile of the Golden Canyon Trail is a self-guided interpretive trail. At the end of the nature trail, the path branches. One fork heads for Red Cathedral, also called Red Cliffs. The red color is essentially iron oxide (rust) produced by the weathering of rocks with high iron content. Enjoy the grand view of the valley, framed by the badlands just below and the Panamint Mountains to the west.

The **Telescope Peak Trail** (14 miles round-trip) is an all-day trek to the 11,049-foot summit, where as one pioneer declared: "You can see so far, it's just like looking through a telescope." Snow-covered during the winter, the peak is best climbed from May to November. Nearby **Wildrose Peak** (8½ miles round-trip) also offers an awesome panorama with somewhat less effort.

The **Eureka Valley Dunes,** newly added to the national park, offer free-form hiking. California's highest at nearly 700 feet tall, they're a delight to roam.

MOUNTAIN BIKING Because most (94%) of the park is federally designated wilderness, cycling is allowed only on roads used by automobiles. Cycling is not allowed on hiking trails.

Good routes for bikers include Racetrack (28 miles, mainly level), Greenwater Valley (30 miles, mostly level), Cottonwood Canyon (20 miles), and West Side Road (40 miles, fairly level with some washboard sections). Artists Drive is 8 miles long, paved, with some steep uphills. A favorite is Titus Canyon (28 miles on a hilly road—it's highly recommended that you make this a one-way descent).

CAMPING & ACCOMMODATIONS

The park's nine campgrounds are located at elevations ranging from below sea level to 8,000 feet. In Furnace Creek, Sunset offers 1,000 spaces with water and flush toilets. Furnace Creek Campground has 200 similarly appointed spaces. Stovepipe Wells has 200 spaces with water and flush toilets.

The **Furnace Creek Ranch** (☎ **619/786-2345**) has 225 no-frills cottage units with air-conditioning and showers. The swimming pool is a popular hangout for tired lodgers. Nearby are a coffee shop, cafeteria, steakhouse, Mexican restaurant, and general store. The **Furnace Creek Inn** (☎ **619/786-2345**), an elegant resort, boasts

67 deluxe rooms with a formal dining room, heated pool, golf, and tennis courts. **Stove Pipe Wells Village** (☎ **619/786-2387**) has 74 modest rooms with air-conditioning and showers.

Because accommodations in Death Valley are both limited and expensive, consider spending a night at one of the two gateway towns: **Lone Pine** on the west side of the park, and **Baker** on the south. **Beatty, Nevada,** which has inexpensive lodging, is only a 20-mile drive from the park's eastern boundary. The restored **Amargosa Hotel** (☎ **619/852-4441**) in Death Valley Junction offers 14 rooms in a historic, out-of-the-way place.

San Diego & Environs   17

by Elizabeth Hansen

San Diego is best known for its benign climate and bodacious beaches, but our hometown has much more to offer than sunny skies, offshore breezes, and miles of clean sand. The sixth-largest city in the United States, San Diego is home to top-notch tourist attractions, a wide variety of dining and lodging options, and some of the country's best regional theater. If it's been a while since your last visit, you'll notice the changes right away: our avant-garde architecture is readily apparent (but happily we've managed to preserve our small-town ambience). Welcome! You're going to have a great time.

1 Orientation

ARRIVING

BY PLANE   San Diego International Airport, 3707 N. Harbor Dr. (☎ **619/231-7361**), locally known as Lindbergh Field, is just 3 miles from downtown. Most of the major domestic carriers fly here, including **Alaska Airlines** (☎ 800/426-0333), **American** (☎ 800/433-7300), **America West** (☎ 800/235-9292), **Continental** (☎ 800/525-0280), **Delta** (☎ 800/221-1212), **Northwest** (☎ 800/447-4747), **Southwest** (☎ 800/435-9792), **TWA** (☎ 619/295-7009), United (☎ 800/241-6522), and **USAir** (☎ 800/428-4322, or 619/574-6233). International carriers include **British Airways** (☎ 800/247-9297) and **Aeromexico** (☎ **800/ 237-6639**).

Lindbergh Field consists of three adjacent airport terminals: "East," "West," and the "Commuter Terminal." San Diego Transit's bus no. 2 stops at the center traffic aisle of the East Terminal and at the intersection of Harbor Island and Windship Lane at the Commuter Terminal. The no. 2 bus runs weekdays every 20 minutes from 5:30am to midnight (every 30 minutes on weekends); the fare is $1.50. The bus connects the airport with downtown, stopping at Broadway and 4th Avenue. At Broadway and 1st Avenue is the **Transit Store** (☎ 619/233-3004), where the staff can answer your transit questions and provide free route maps to help you get where you're going.

Several shuttles run regularly from the airport to downtown hotels. They charge about $5, and you'll see designated areas outside each terminal.

Taxis line up outside both terminals and charge about $8 to take you to a downtown location.

Several major car-rental companies operate at the airport, including **Avis** (☎ 800/331-1212), **Budget** (☎ 800/527-0700), **Dollar** (☎ 800/800-4000), **Hertz** (☎ 800/654-3131), and **National** (☎ 800/CAR-RENT). If you're driving into the city from the airport, take Harbor Drive south to Broadway, the main east-west thoroughfare, and turn left.

BY CAR   From Los Angeles, you'll enter San Diego via coastal route I-5. From points northeast of the city, you'll come down on I-15 (link up with I-8 west and Calif. 163 south to drive into downtown). From the east, you'll come in on I-8, connecting with Calif. 163 south (Calif. 163 turns into 10th Avenue). The freeways are well marked, pointing the way to downtown streets.

BY TRAIN   Amtrak (☎ 800/USA-RAIL) trains connect San Diego to Los Angeles and the rest of the country. Trains pull into San Diego's pretty mission-style Santa Fe Station, 1850 Kettner Blvd. (at Broadway), within walking distance of many downtown hotels and 1¹/₂ blocks from the Embarcadero.

VISITOR INFORMATION

San Diego's excellent **International Visitors Information Center,** 11 Horton Plaza, at 1st Avenue and F Street (☎ **619/236-1212**), offers a free San Diego visitors guide. The center employs a multilingual staff and sells street maps, phone cards, and the Annual Major Events Calendar. Here you can get the Visitor Value Pack, which is full of money-saving coupons. The office is open Monday to Saturday from 8:30am to 5pm; June to August it's also open on Sunday from 11am to 5pm. Cybernauts can access the Visitors Guide on the San Diego Convention & Visitors Bureau's homepage at **http://www.sandiego.org.**

Traveler's Aid (☎ **619/231-7361**) has booths at both the East and the West Terminal of the airport and at the San Diego Cruise Terminal, B Street Pier.

Specialized visitor information outlets include the **Balboa Park Visitors Center,** 1549 El Prado (☎ 619/239-0512); **Coronado Visitor Information Center,** 1111 Orange Ave., Suite A, Coronado (☎ 800/622-8300 or 619/437-8788); **Old Town Visitor Information Center,** 4002 Wallace St. (☎ 619/220-5422); and the **Mission Bay Visitors Information Center,** 2688 E. Mission Bay Drive, San Diego (☎ 619/276-8200).

The **North County Convention & Visitors Bureau,** 720 N. Broadway, Escondido (☎ **800/848-3336** 24 hours, or 619/745-4741), can provide information on La Jolla and excursion areas in San Diego County, including Escondido, Julian, and Anza-Borrego State Park.

To find out what's on at the theater and who's playing in the clubs during your visit, pick up a copy of *The Reader,* a free weekly newspaper available all over the city. There's also a Thursday entertainment supplement called "Night & Day" in the *San Diego Union-Tribune.*

CITY LAYOUT

San Diego is more a chain of separate neighborhoods than a single cohesive city, but each is well defined and relatively compact. The street system is straightforward, so getting around is fairly easy.

MAIN ARTERIES & STREETS   Interstate 5 is the most important thoroughfare in San Diego, connecting the city's divergent parts with one another and the entire region with the rest of the state. Access to the Coronado Bay Bridge is via I-5.

Downtown, Broadway is the main street; in the heart of the central business district it's intersected by 4th and 5th avenues (running south and north respectively). Harbor Drive, hugging the waterfront, connects downtown with the airport to the north and the Convention Center to the south.

FINDING AN ADDRESS   It's easy to find an address when you're downtown. Avenues run north-south and are numbered from 1 to 12. Streets run east-west and are lettered A to L. If the address is 411 Market St., for example, you'll find it between 4th and 5th avenues on Market Street. Most downtown streets are one-way.

Outside the city center, street names get a little more complex, but most are laid out in a grid.

Harbor Drive runs along the Embarcadero, or waterfront, connecting downtown with the airport. I-5 doglegs around the city center and runs south to the U.S.–Mexico border and north to Old Town, Mission Bay, and La Jolla. Balboa Park is most easily accessible via 12th Avenue, which becomes Park Boulevard.

NEIGHBORHOODS IN BRIEF

Downtown   Business travelers will definitely want to stay in this area, which encompasses Horton Plaza, the Gaslamp Quarter, the Embarcadero, Seaport Village, and the Convention Center. San Diego's dining and entertainment heart is the **Gaslamp Quarter,** a 16-square-block Victorian-style National Historic District, bordered by 4th and 5th avenues between Broadway and Market Street. **Horton Plaza,** immediately north of the Gaslamp Quarter, is a colorful 6-block shopping mall that's a major attraction in itself. **Seaport Village,** a themed shopping/dining area just south of the Embarcadero, is sandwiched between a waterfront walkway and Harbor Drive.

Old Town   Northwest of downtown, San Diego's first commercial center was designated a state historic park in 1968 and now operates primarily as a tourist attraction. The region encompasses the Old Town State Historic Park, Presidio Park, Heritage Park, a couple of museums, and restaurants that are popular with visitors seeking Mexican fare and huge margaritas.

Hillcrest/Uptown   These two adjacent neighborhoods offer a slightly funky dining and nightlife scene. Hillcrest is the center of San Diego's gay community. Hillcrest and Uptown lie near Balboa Park, which comprises more than 1,400 acres northeast of downtown and contains the San Diego Zoo and numerous museums. The park is the city's cultural center and a recreational paradise.

Mission Bay/Pacific Beach   A playground for swimmers, boaters, and sun-seekers, this is one of your options for hitting the beach. It's also home to Sea World, one of San Diego's top attractions. The area between Mission Bay and the Pacific Ocean is one of the city's most colorful regions, known for its nightlife and hip, casual dining. The boardwalk runs from South Mission Beach through Pacific Beach and is popular for inline skating, biking, and sunset watching.

La Jolla   About 12 miles north of downtown San Diego, La Jolla is one of the prettiest parcels of San Diego County. For over half a century wealthy seniors and successful professionals have chosen to live in La Jolla because of its rugged coastline, lush plantings, good restaurants, beautiful homes, great beaches, and proximity to the city. La Jolla still retains its "old-money" image despite its openness to adventurous yuppies, emigrants from various foreign countries, and retirees from the Midwest. The University of California San Diego and the Museum of Contemporary Art are here.

The San Diego Area at a Glance

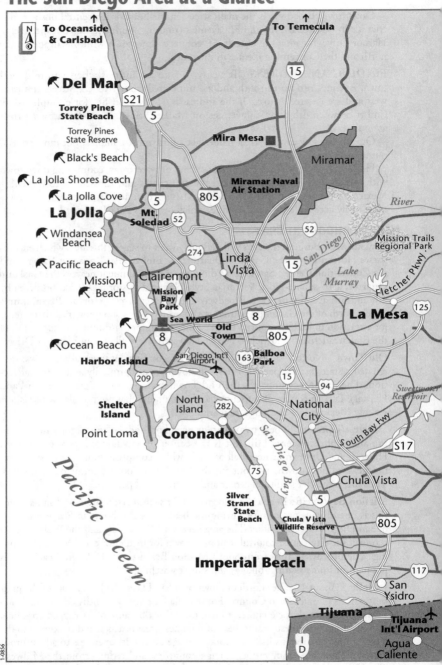

N

To Oceanside
& Carlsbad

To Temecula

15

Del Mar

S21

Torrey Pines
State Beach

5

Mira Mesa

Torrey Pines
State Reserve

Miramar

Black's Beach

La Jolla Shores Beach

Miramar Naval
Air Station

La Jolla Cove

5

805

River

La Jolla

Mt.
Soledad

52

52

Mission Trails
Regional Park

Windansea
Beach

274

San Diego

Fletcher Pkwy

Pacific Beach

Linda
Vista

15

Lake
Murray

Clairemont

Mission
Beach

Mission
Bay
Park

Sea World

8

La Mesa

125

Old
Town

805

Ocean Beach

8

San Diego Int'l
Airport

163

Balboa
Park

Harbor Island

209

15

94

Sweetwater
Reservoir

Shelter
Island

North
Island

282

National
City

South Bay Fwy

S17

Point Loma

Coronado

San Diego Bay

Chula Vista

75

5

Silver
Strand
State
Beach

Chula Vista
Wildlife Reserve

805

Pacific Ocean

Imperial Beach

117

San
Ysidro

Tijuana

Tijuana
Int'l Airport

I
D

Agua
Caliente

1-0856

586

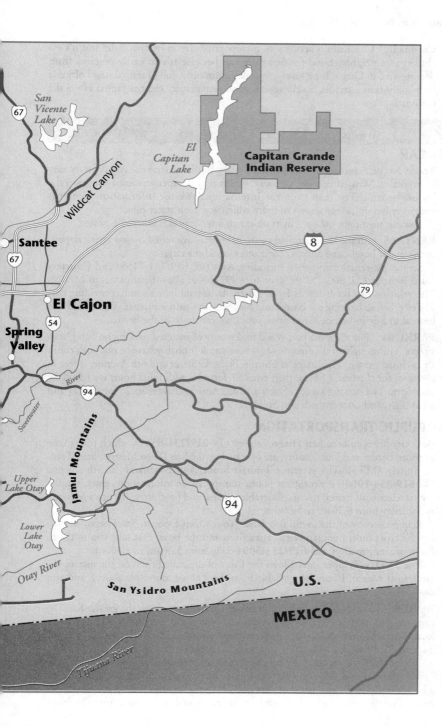

Coronado   Coronado is actually an incorporated city in its own right, but it's included as a neighborhood for our purposes because it's so easily reached from downtown San Diego. It's a lovely, upscale community, full of retired naval officers; here you'll find a terrific beach, several good restaurants, and the famed Hotel del Coronado.

2 Getting Around

BY CAR

Traffic has been getting heavier in recent years, but in general the city is pretty easy to negotiate. Many streets run one-way, which may hamper you until you learn the lay of the land. The map from the International Visitor Information Center is extremely helpful, since arrows indicate which way each street runs.

You can turn right on a red light unless an intersection is otherwise posted.

RENTALS   All the large national car-rental firms have rental outlets at the airport, in the major hotels, and at other locations around the city.

Several car-rental companies, including **Avis** (☎ 619/231-7155) and **Courtesy Auto Rentals** (☎ 800/252-9756 or 619/497-4800) allow their cars into Mexico. The vehicles may be driven as far as Ensenada, several hours south, providing that you stop before crossing the border and buy Mexican auto insurance. You would also be wise to buy insurance if you drive your own car south of the border.

PARKING   For the most part you'll find plenty of metered parking on San Diego streets. Things tighten up downtown, where you'll probably have to put your car in an enclosed garage. The garage at Horton Plaza, G Street and 4th Avenue, is free to shoppers for the first 3 hours, then costs $1 for each additional hour; it's free daily after 5pm. The parking lot at G Street and 6th Avenue charges $3.25 for the day and $3 at night and on weekends and holidays.

BY PUBLIC TRANSPORTATION

Both city buses and the **San Diego Trolley** (☎ **619/231-8549**), which runs to the Mexican border and East County, are operated by the San Diego Metropolitan Transit System (MTS). The system's **Transit Store,** 449 Broadway, at 5th Avenue (☎ **619/234-1060**), is a complete public-transportation information center, supplying travelers with passes, tokens, timetables, maps, and brochures. It's open Monday to Saturday from 8:30am to 5:30pm.

Request a copy of the useful brochure "Your Open Door to San Diego," detailing the city's most popular tourist attractions and the buses that take you to them. For route information, call **619/233-3004** daily from 5:30am to 8:30pm.

The $5 **Day-Tripper pass** allows for 1 day of unlimited rides on the metropolitan transit system. Passes are available from the Transit Store (see above), and you can also get a 4-day pass for $15.

BY BUS   The city bus system encompasses over 100 routes in the greater San Diego area. Bus stops are marked by rectangular blue signs, every other block or so on local routes. More than 20 bus routes traverse downtown, including nos. 2, 7, 9, 29, 34, and 35. Local fare is $1.50. Express buses charge fares that range from $1.75 to $3. Exact change is required ($1 bills are accepted). Most buses run every half hour.

Transfers are available at no extra charge as long as you continue your journey on a bus or trolley with an equal or lower fare (if it's higher, you simply pay the difference). Transfers must be used within an hour and should be obtained from the driver when boarding.

BY TROLLEY The San Diego Trolley system runs south to the Mexican border (a 40-minute trip) and east to the city of Santee. Downtown, trolleys run along C Street and stop at the Santa Fe Station, 3rd Avenue (Civic Center), 5th Avenue, 12th Avenue (City College), Seaport Village, and the Convention Center.

Trolleys operate on a self-service fare-collection system; riders purchase tickets from machines in stations before boarding. The machines list fares for each destination and dispense change. Tickets are valid for 2 hours from the time of purchase in one direction only. Fare inspectors board trains at random to check tickets. The bright-red trains run every 15 minutes and stop for only 30 seconds at each stop. To board, push the lighted green button beside the doors; to exit, push the lighted white button.

Trolley travel within the downtown area costs only $1; the fare to the Mexican border is $1.75. Children under 5 ride free; seniors and riders with disabilities pay only 75¢. For recorded trolley information call 619/231-8549. To talk to a live body you can call 619/235-3004 daily from 5:30am to 8:30pm.

BY FERRY & WATER TAXI There's regularly scheduled **ferry service** between San Diego and Coronado (☎ **619/234-4111** for information). It's a 15-minute ride. Ferries leave from the Broadway Pier on the hour from 9am to 9pm Sunday to Thursday and from 9am to 10pm on Friday and Saturday. They return from the Old Ferry Landing in Coronado to San Diego every hour on the half hour from 9:30am to 9:30pm Sunday to Thursday and from 9:30am to 10:30pm on Friday and Saturday. The fare is $2 one-way (50¢ extra if you bring your bike). Purchase tickets in advance at the Harbor Excursion kiosk on the pier in San Diego or at the Old Ferry Landing in Coronado. **Water taxis** (☎ **619/235-TAXI**) will take you anywhere you want to go on San Diego Bay for $5.

BY TAXI

Cab companies don't have standardized rates, except from the airport into town, which costs $1.80 per mile. Taxis may be hailed in the street, but you'll be lucky if you can find one; phone for a guaranteed pickup. Companies include **Orange Cab** (☎ 619/291-3333), **San Diego Cab** (☎ 619/226-TAXI), and **Yellow Cab** (☎ 619/234-6161). The **Coronado Cab Company** (☎ 619/435-6211) serves Coronado. In our part of town, use **La Jolla Cab** (☎ 619/453-4222).

BY TOUR TROLLEY

The **Old Town Trolley,** 4040 Twiggs St. (☎ **619/298-8687**), is not a trolley at all; it's a privately operated open-air tour bus that travels in a continuous loop around the city, stopping at sightseeing highlights. It stops at more than a dozen places around the city, and you can hop on and off as many times as you please during one entire loop (but once you've completed the circuit, you can't go around again). A nonstop tour takes 90 minutes and is accompanied by a fast-moving live commentary on city history and sights. Major stops include Old Town, Presidio Park, Bazaar del Mundo, Balboa Park, the San Diego Zoo, the Embarcadero, Seaport Village, and the Gaslamp Quarter. Tours operate daily from 9am to 5pm in summer, to 4pm the rest of the year; they cost $17 for adults and $8 for children 6 to 12; kids 5 and under ride free.

BY BICYCLE

San Diego is great for bikers; it's relatively flat and many roads have designated bike lanes. If you didn't bring your own wheels, you can rent from **Penny-farthing's,** 314 G St. in the Gaslamp Quarter (☎ 619/233-7696), or **Hamel's Action Sports Center,** 704 Ventura Place, off Mission Boulevard. at the roller coaster in North Mission Beach (☎ 619/488-5050). In Coronado, there's **Bikes & Beyond** at the Old Ferry Landing (☎ 619/435-7180).

If a bus stop has a bike-route sign attached (not all of them do), you can place your bike on the bus's bike rack for free while you ride. The San Diego Trolley also allows bikes on board for free during certain hours. You just need a bike permit, which is available for $4 from the **Transit Store**, 102 Broadway, at first Ave. (☎ 619/234-1060). Bikes can also be brought aboard the San Diego–Coronado ferry.

FAST FACTS: San Diego

American Express   A convenient downtown office is at 258 Broadway (☎ 619/234-4455), open Monday to Friday from 9am to 5pm.

Dentists/Doctors   For dental referrals, contact the San Diego County Dental Society at 800/201-0244 or call 800/DENTIST. Hotel Docs (☎ 619/275-2663) is a 24-hour network of physicians, dentists, optometrists, chiropractors, and podiatrists who'll come to your hotel room within 45 minutes of your call. They accept credit/charge cards and their services are covered by most insurance policies.

Emergencies   For police, fire, highway patrol, or life-threatening medical emergencies, dial **911** from any phone. No coins are required.

Hospitals   Mercy Hospital, 4077 5th Ave. (☎ 619/294-8111), has the best-located downtown emergency room. Coronado Hospital, 250 Prospect Place (☎ 619/435-6251), is a good pick in Coronado. In La Jolla, bring your bruises to Scripps Memorial, 9888 Genesee Ave. (☎ 619/457-4123).

Information   See "Visitor Information" in "Orientation," earlier in this chapter.

Newspapers/Magazines   The *San Diego Union-Tribune* is published daily, and its informative entertainment section, "Night & Day," is in the Thursday edition. *The Reader*, published weekly (on Thursday), is more alternative and offers dining and entertainment information, too. *San Diego* magazine is also filled with extensive entertainment and dining listings. The free *San Diego This Week* has restaurant listings and information about shopping, attractions, nightlife, and the latest goings-on about town.

Police   In an emergency, dial 911 from any phone. No coins are needed. For other matters, contact the downtown precinct, 1401 Broadway (☎ 619/531-2000).

Post Office   The main post office, 2535 Midway Dr., San Diego, CA 92110 (☎ 800/333-8777), is between Barnett Avenue and Rosecrans Street. It's open to 1am Monday to Friday. A convenient downtown branch is at 815 E St. (open Monday to Friday from 8:30am to 5pm and on Saturday from 8:30am to noon).

Safety   As cities go, San Diego is pretty safe. But use particular caution on beaches after dark (romantic as they may seem), and stay on designated walkways and away from secluded areas in Balboa Park—night or day. In the Gaslamp Quarter, stay west of 5th Avenue.

Taxes   A 7.75% sales tax is added on at the register for all goods and services purchased in San Diego. The city hotel tax is 10.5%.

Transit Information   Public transportation is operated by San Diego Regional Transit (☎ 619/233-3004). See "Getting Around," earlier in this chapter, for complete information.

Useful Telephone Numbers   Time (☎ 619/853-1212); local highway conditions (☎ 800/427-7623).

Weather   For local weather information and surf reports call 619/289-1212.

3 Accommodations

Remember to factor in the city's 10.5% hotel tax. Rates tend to be higher in summer (especially true of beach hotels) and when there's a big convention in town.

Mission Valley/Hotel Circle, north of Balboa Park and east of Mission Bay, consists of cheek-to-jowl motels on either side of I-8. As awful as this sounds, the area is popular with budget-minded visitors. Harbor Island and Shelter Island—minutes from the airport and downtown—are two man-made peninsulas that command excellent views. Coronado is a bit out of the way from everything else, but that's part of the charm of staying on this "island." La Jolla offers some lovely lodging alternatives, as do the beach areas—Mission Bay and Pacific Beach.

Note: For good prices in all accommodation categories, contact **San Diego Hotel Reservations** (☎ 800/SAVE-CASH or 619/627-9300), which has an Internet site at **http://www.savecash.com.** For information on 30 bed-and-breakfasts in the San Diego area, send $3.95 for a 20-page directory to **B&B Resources,** P.O. Box 3292, San Diego, CA 92163 (☎ **800/619-7666** or 619/297-3130).

Since there's not enough space here give you complete accommodations coverage, you might want to check out *Frommer's San Diego,* which offers many more options. Note that some hostelries also provide information on the Internet at **http://www.infopost.com/sandiego/hotels/index.html.**

DOWNTOWN
VERY EXPENSIVE

✪ **Hyatt Regency San Diego.** 1 Market Place, San Diego, CA 92101. ☎ **800/233-1234** or 619/232-1234. Fax 619/239-5678. 819 rms, 56 suites. A/C MINIBAR TV TEL. $159–$245 double; from $325 suite. Additional person $25 extra; children 11 and under stay free in parents' room. Packages and special weekend rates available. AE, DC, DISC, MC, V. Valet parking $13, self-parking $9. Bus: 1. Trolley: Seaport Village.

The Hyatt Regency enjoys a convenient position on San Diego Bay, within walking distance of the Gaslamp Quarter, Seaport Village, and the Convention Center, and its rooms have terrific views. The impressive high-rise features a contemporary three-story lobby of green marble and Italian limestone topped by an additional three floors of meeting space. The rooms are pretty much what you'd expect from a Hyatt—attractive, kind of an updated 18th-century English-style decor and high-standard amenities. You can rent videos, and rooms offer voice-mail. Spacious two-bedroom suites are located on the top floors and feature walk-in closets, whirlpool tubs, and minikitchens. There's a club floor, and 50% of all rooms are designated non-smoking.

Dining/Entertainment: Sally's, a rather formal seafood restaurant, attracts locals as well as guests. There are two other less formal spots (all three offer alfresco dining) and two bars (including one with a spectacular 40th-floor view).

Services: Concierge, room service (24 hours), dry cleaning, laundry, shoeshine, newspaper delivery, in-room massage, twice-daily maid service, baby-sitting, express checkout, valet parking, courtesy car.

Facilities: Movie channels, heated outdoor pool, state-of-the-art health club/spa, whirlpool, four tennis courts, boat/bicycle rental, water-sports rental, business center, conference rooms, car-rental desk, beauty salon, gift shop.

✪ **San Diego Marriott Marina.** 333 W. Harbor Dr. (at Front St.), San Diego, CA 92101-7700. ☎ **800/228-9290** or 619/234-1500. Fax 619/234-8678. 1,355 rms, 50 suites. A/C MINIBAR TV TEL. $220–$225 double; from $330 suite. Children 17 and under stay free in parents' room. AARP discount and honeymoon and other packages available. AE, CB, DC, DISC, MC, V. Valet parking $13, self-parking $9. Bus: 1. Trolley: Convention Center.

Located right on the waterfront, this striking modern hotel has a 446-slip marina and lush grounds. Many rooms have balconies with breathtaking water views, and when you tire of the view, you can rent videos. The Marriott has a great location, just a short walk from Seaport Village, the Embarcadero, the Convention Center, and the Gaslamp Quarter.

Dining/Entertainment: There are several restaurants; our favorite is the Yacht Club, a popular place for informal dining and dancing on the waterfront.

Services: Concierge, room service (24 hours), dry cleaning/laundry service, newspaper delivery, secretarial services, express checkout, valet parking.

Facilities: VCR, in-room movies, two outdoor pools (including one with a waterfall), fitness center, daily aerobics classes, two whirlpools, sauna, six lighted tennis courts, bicycle and boat rentals, games room, spa, business center with secretarial services, conference rooms, self-service laundry, car-rental desk, tour desk, hair salon, shops.

EXPENSIVE

⑤ **Clarion Hotel Bay View San Diego.** 660 K St. (at 6th Ave.), San Diego, CA 92101. ☎ **800/766-0234** or 619/696-0234. Fax 619/231-8199. 312 rms and suites. A/C TV TEL. $109–$139 double; $149–$169 suite. Additional person $10 extra; children 17 and under stay free in parents' room. AE, CB, DC, DISC, MC, V. Parking $8 per day. Bus: 1. Trolley: Gaslamp/Convention Center.

This newish entry on the San Diego hotel scene provides an economical alternative for those attending meetings at the Convention Center—it's very nearly as close as the Marriott and the Hyatt, but considerably less expensive. The Clarion is also close to the Gaslamp Quarter and an excellent choice for those who plan to enjoy the nightlife here and want to avoid walking far late at night. All quarters are spacious, bright, and modern, and more than half offer views of San Diego Bay and the Coronado Bridge. All rooms have sliding-glass doors which provide ample fresh air, and many have minibars. In-room safes are standard, as are tub/shower combinations; and 80% of the rooms are reserved for nonsmokers.

The carpeted rooftop sundeck offers a great view as well as a Jacuzzi, sauna, workout room, and video arcade.

Dining/Entertainment: The 6th & K Cafe is just off the marble-floored lobby. Breakfast, lunch, and dinner are served 7 days a week. There's a big-screen TV in the bar, and karaoke is popular on Friday and Saturday nights.

Services: Concierge, room service (6am–10pm), dry cleaning/laundry, express checkout.

Facilities: In-room pay-per-view movies, workout room with Nautilus equipment, Jacuzzi, sauna, sundeck, video games room, conference rooms, coin-operated washer and dryer, in-room touch-screen TVs (can be used for express checkout, ordering breakfast, and retrieving voice-mail messages).

Horton Grand. 311 Island Ave. (at 3rd Ave.), San Diego, CA 92101. ☎ **800/542-1886** or 619/544-1886. Fax 619/544-0058. 108 rms, 24 mini-suites. TV TEL. $119–$139–$1799 double; from $189 suite. Children 15 and under stay free in parents' room. Weekend and special packages available. AE, CB, DC, MC, V. Valet parking $8 overnight with unlimited in/out privileges. Bus: 1. Trolley: Convention Center.

A cross between an elegant hotel and a charming B&B, the Horton Grand combines two hotels dating from 1886—the Horton Grand and the Brooklyn Hotel, which for a time was the Kahle Saddlery Shop. Both were saved from demolition, moved to this spot, and connected by an airy atrium lobby filled with white wicker. The facade with its graceful bay windows is original.

Each room is unique but contains antiques, a gas fireplace (on a timer so you can fall asleep in front of it), and a comfortable queen-size bed; even the baths, complete with toilet and pedestal sink, are genteel. The rooms overlook either the city or the fig tree–filled courtyard. Each suite has a microwave, a minibar, two TVs and telephones, a sofa bed, and a computer modem hookup. This is an old hotel, and sounds carry more than they might in a modern one, so if you're a light sleeper request a room with no neighbors above or adjacent.

Dining/Entertainment: Ida Bailey's restaurant, named for the well-loved madam whose establishment used to stand on this spot, is open for breakfast, lunch, and dinner. It opens onto the hotel's courtyard, which is used for Sunday brunch on warm days. Afternoon tea is served in the Palace Bar Tuesday to Saturday from 2:30 to 5pm; jazz is featured on Friday and Saturday evening. Historical guided tours are available on Wednesday at 3pm.

Service: Room service (7am–10pm), dry cleaning/laundry, express checkout, valet parking, courtesy car, free coffee in lobby 5–7am daily.

Facilities: Access to nearby pool and weight room, conference rooms.

MODERATE

In addition to the hotels described below, there's also an **Embassy Suites** at 601 Pacific Hwy. (☎ 800/EMBASSY or 619/239-2400), and the **Holiday Inn on the Bay,** 1355 N. Harbor Drive (☎ 800/HOLIDAY or 619/232-3861).

Best Western Bayside Inn. 555 W. Ash St. (at Columbia St.), San Diego, CA 92101. ☎ **800/ 341-1818** or 619/233-7500. Fax 619/239-8060. 122 rms. A/C TV TEL. $85–$105 double, $95–$115 double with harbor view. Rates include continental breakfast. Children 11 and under stay free in parents' room. Weekend rates (except in summer) and packages available. AE, AM (Amoco), CB, DC, DISC, ER, MC, V. Free covered parking. Bus: 5 or 105. Trolley: C St and Kettner.

The friendly, accommodating staff and stunning city and harbor views of this quiet, unassuming hotel may very well please you. It's an easy walk to the Embarcadero (it should be called Bayview rather than Bayside), a bit farther to Horton Plaza, 4 blocks to the trolley stop, 5 blocks to the train station. The hotel has comfortable rooms decorated in restful colors, with king- or queen-size beds as well as balconies overlooking the bay or downtown; all were remodeled in 1993. The lobby, glass-enclosed on the street side, is sunny and inviting.

The hotel's restaurant, the Bayside Bar & Grill, serves breakfast, lunch, and dinner; the bar has a 50-inch TV. Good restaurants and bars are nearby and meals are available from room service. Complimentary airport transportation is provided, as are cable TV, in-room movies, an outdoor pool, and a Jacuzzi.

INEXPENSIVE

Ⓢ La Pensione. 1700 India St. (at Date St.), San Diego, CA 92101. ☎ **619/236-8000.** Fax 619/236-8088. 80 rms. TV TEL. $44–$70 double. Packages available. AE, CB, DC, MC, V. Free daily parking, or $10 per week. Bus: 5 or 105. Trolley: County Center/Little Italy.

This place has a lot going for it: modernity, cleanliness, remarkable value, a quiet location within walking distance of the central business district, a friendly staff, and parking, which is a premium for small hotels in San Diego. The lobby is small but inviting, and the rooms, while not overly large, make the most of their space and leave you with area to move around. Each room offers a tub/shower combination, ceiling fan, wet bar, microwave, and small refrigerator. Quarters are cleaned once a week for weekly guests, daily for those who stay a shorter period.

La Pensione is built around a courtyard and feels like a small European hotel. It has two restaurants: Caffè Italia, which offers sandwiches and salads, as well as Sunday brunch and jazz on Friday and Saturday, and the Indigo Grill, which serves southwestern fare. There's also a self-service laundry on the premises. The fourth floor is for nonsmokers. One reader complained about noise filtering up to his room from the restaurants on the ground level; other readers have raved about this property.

La Pensione has a similarly priced sibling hotel of the same name at 1654 Columbia St. between Cedar and Date streets (☎ 619/232-3400), which is rented by the week or month only; however, there's no parking. Both properties are centrally located and within walking distance of eateries (mostly Italian) and nightspots.

HILLCREST/UPTOWN

☉ Sommerset Suites Hotel. 606 Washington St. (at 5th Ave.), San Diego, CA 92103. ☎ **800/962-9665**, 800/356-1787 in California or 619/692-5200. Fax 619/299-6065. 80 suites. A/C TV TEL. $90 studio suite; $160 one-bedroom suite; $180 executive suite. Rates include large continental breakfast. Children 11 and under stay free in parents' room. AE, CB, DC, DISC, MC, V. Free covered parking. Bus: 16 or 25. Take the Washington St. exit off I-5.

A terrific bargain, this is a good choice for those who find traditional hotels too impersonal. The staff is friendly and helpful, and in the late afternoon they serve complimentary snacks, soda, beer, and wine in the cozy guest lounge. The poolside patio, set up for barbecues, encourages impromptu gatherings and picnics among guests. Your options here include studio, one-bedroom, and executive suites. All are tastefully furnished and have in-room safes and fully equipped modern kitchens (including dishwashers in the executive suites), large closets, and balconies. Even the studios are spacious.

Services include a concierge; laundry and dry cleaning; baby-sitting; courtesy van service (7am to 9pm) to the airport, Sea World, the zoo, and other attractions within a 5-mile radius; video rentals; and two-line phones and voice-mail. Rollaway beds and cribs are available. Facilities include a small heated outdoor pool, a Jacuzzi, a rooftop sundeck, gas barbecue grills, a snack room, and a coin-operated laundry. Non-smoking rooms are available.

HARBOR ISLAND & SHELTER ISLAND

Humphrey's Half Moon Inn. 2303 Shelter Island Dr., San Diego, CA 92106. ☎ **800/345-9995** or 619/224-3411. Fax 619/224-3478. 182 rms and suites. A/C TV TEL. $99–$159 double; from $110 suite. Children 17 and under stay free in parent's room. AE, CB, DC, DISC, MC, V. Free parking.

Humphrey's Half Moon Inn is a favorite choice for families. The grounds are lovely, with palm trees, tropical flowers, and a pond. Though this place is a little worn around the edges, each room is very attractive, with Hawaiian decor created by bamboo and rattan furnishings. Also included are free in-room coffee, refrigerators, a complimentary movie channel, free newspaper delivery, and free transportation to the airport or the Amtrak station. There are heated pools for adults and children, a whirlpool, table tennis, a washer/dryer, bicycles, and room for lawn games.

MISSION VALLEY/HOTEL CIRCLE

In addition to the places described below, you might also be interested in the **Best Western Hanalei Hotel,** 2270 Hotel Circle North (☎ **800/882-0858** or 619/ 297-1101).

Comfort Inn & Suites. 2485 Hotel Circle Pl., San Diego, CA 92108. ☎ **800/647-1903** or 619/291-7700. Fax 619/297-6179. 200 rms. A/C TV TEL. $69–$99 double. Rates include continental breakfast. Additional person $10 extra; children 17 and under stay free in parent's room. AE, CB, DC, DISC, MC, V. Free parking.

This well-priced modern motel at the western end of Hotel Circle is a high-rise, complete with box balconies and a small free-form pool. It underwent a complete refurbishment in 1996, and all rooms are large and comfortably furnished with king- or queen-size beds, plus baths with separate dressing areas. Higher-priced rooms have whirlpool baths, individual refrigerators, and terraces. No-smoking rooms are available. There's a heated outdoor pool and Jacuzzi, a car-rental desk, a games room, and a washer/dryer. Tennis courts are across the street, as is an 11-hole golf course (yes, *11* holes).

Town & Country. 500 Hotel Circle North, San Diego, CA 92108. ☎ **800/77-ATLAS** or 619/ 291-7131. Fax 619/291-3584. 1,000 rms and suites. A/C MINIBAR TV TEL. $135–$175 double; from $200 a suite. Additional person $20 extra; children 17 and under stay free in parents' room. Lower rates off-season. AE, MC, V. Parking $5.

Town & Country is one of the largest hotels in San Diego—so it's only natural that it caters to conventioneers. However, it's also a nice choice for independent travelers. The always-bustling property is something of a "city within a city." The rooms are outfitted with comfortable furnishings, though the baths are rather small. A high standard of service includes nightly turndown and morning newspaper delivery. Nonsmoking rooms are available. The hotel has four heated outdoor pools, lovely gardens, five restaurants, and a country-music saloon hosting live local bands several nights a week.

MISSION BAY/PACIFIC BEACH
VERY EXPENSIVE

Hilton Beach & Tennis Resort. 1775 E. Mission Bay Dr., San Diego, CA 92109. ☎ **800/ 962-6307** in California, Arizona, and Nevada, 800/445-8667 elsewhere in the U.S. or 619/ 276-4010. Fax 619/275-7991. 357 rms, 8 suites. A/C MINIBAR TV TEL. $175–$230 double; from $325 suite. Additional person $20 extra; children 17 and under stay free in parents' room. Lower rates off-season. AE, CB, DC, DISC, MC, V. Free parking. Take I-5 to the Sea World Dr. exit and turn north on East Mission Bay Dr.

Completely renovated in 1995, this handsome resort occupies 18 acres on the east side of Mission Bay and is a handy quarter mile from the Visitor Information Center. This Mediterranean-style resort with terra-cotta roofs offers pleasant rooms in sand and sea-green tones, with TVs hidden in armoires. All quarters have ceiling fans, and a balcony or terrace, a king-size bed or two queen-size beds, a refrigerator, a coffeemaker, an iron and ironing board, a hair dryer, and a makeup mirror. The baths are elegant, with shells surrounding the sconce-flanked mirrors. Even the standard rooms are spacious, and many are interconnecting. The staff is friendly and helpful here, and the shops are fun for browsing in between lolling by the pool, biking along the bay, and taking tennis lessons. Sea World is across the bay, and the ocean is 5 miles to the west.

Dining/Entertainment: Cafe Picante is open for all meals 7 days a week and offers casual fare and atmosphere. The Cavatappi restaurant serves Italian cuisine nightly. You can dine and drink at Fundidos, which overlooks Mission Bay. Cocktails are also served in the Lobby Bar and at the poolside Banana Cabana.

Services: Concierge, room service (7am–11pm), dry cleaning/laundry service, baby-sitting, supervision for children weekends and in summer, free airport transportation.

Facilities: In-room movies, Olympic-size pool, children's wading pool, four Jacuzzis, sauna, weight-training room, five lighted tennis courts, pro shop, water sports, scuba diving, bike and jogging trails, putting green, arts and crafts for kids, children's playground, business center, bike and boat rental, yacht charters, massage, game arcade, meeting rooms, launderette, hair salon, shops, voice-mail messages.

EXPENSIVE

✪ Catamaran Resort Hotel. 3999 Mission Blvd. (4 blocks south of Grand Ave.), San Diego, CA 92109. ☎ **800/288-0770,** 800/233-8172 in Canada or 619/488-1081. Fax 619/488-1387. 160 rms, 100 studios, 50 suites. A/C TV TEL. $140–$195 double; from $265 suite. Children 17 and under stay free in parents' room. AE, DISC, MC, V. Valet parking $7, self-parking $5. Take the Grand/Garnet exit off I-5 and go west on Grand Ave., then south on Mission Blvd.

The Catamaran is beautifully situated on Mission Bay, with its own beach, lots of water-sports facilities, and lovely grounds. The Polynesian-style decor includes a 15-foot interior waterfall, lush foliage, squawking parrots, and plenty of island artifacts, like a full-size dugout canoe in the lobby. The guest rooms are divided between a 13-story tower and six two-story bungalows. Each continues the tropics theme and opens onto a balcony or patio. Tower rooms have memorable views of the bay, the skyline, La Jolla, and Point Loma, but the bungalow units are far more intimate. Non-smoking rooms are available; pets are allowed.

Dining/Entertainment: The Atoll Restaurant offers indoor and outdoor seating. The lively Cannibal Bar has bands and videos; there's a cover for nonguests. Moray's, its counterpoint, is an intimate, crowded piano bar.

Services: Concierge, room service (until 11pm), dry cleaning/laundry service, nightly turndown, baby-sitting, secretarial services, express checkout, valet parking.

Facilities: Kitchenettes, movie channels, outdoor heated pool, whirlpool spa, beach, sundeck, health club, water-sports concessions, jogging track, bike rental, children's program during the summer, business center, conference rooms, car-rental desk, tour desk, gift shop.

✪ Crystal Pier Hotel. 4500 Ocean Blvd., San Diego, CA 92109. ☎ **800/748-5894** or 619/483-6983. 26 cottages for up to four people. TV. Mid-June to mid-Sept, $145–$225 cottage. Mid-Sept to mid-June, $95–$190 cottage. Three-day minimum in summer; weekly and monthly rates available. DISC, MC, V. Free parking. Take I-5 to the Grand/Garnet exit and follow Garnet to the pier.

This historic hotel, which dates from 1927, offers a unique opportunity to sleep *over* the water. Built on a private pier jutting into the ocean in the center of Pacific Beach, 20 older cottages date from 1936, while 6 more were added in 1992. The management recently did a great job of remodeling 12 of the older cottages, but try not to get one of the untouched units. All quarters have a living room, bedroom, kitchenette, and private deck. The quietest units are farthest out on the pier, away from the noise of the boardwalk. Boogie boards, fishing poles, beach chairs, and umbrellas are available.

To make a reservation, call between 8am and 8pm, when the office is open.

(✢) Family-Friendly Hotels

The Beach Cottages *(see p. 597)* Kids enjoy the informality and the terrific location near the beach.

Humphrey's Half Moon Inn *(see p. 595)* A great value, with lovely tropical grounds and a lighthearted Hawaiian theme that kids will enjoy. A washer/dryer is an added convenience for parents.

Hilton Beach & Tennis Resort *(see p. 595)* This bay-front hostelry has myriad sports and recreational facilities and plenty of space for active offspring. The tranquil water of the bay is more inviting for small children than the sometimes-itimidating waves at the ocean.

Hotel del Coronado *(see p. 601)* In addition to a beautiful beach, the hotel offers special supervised children's programs led by experienced counselors.

Loews Coronado Bay Resort *(see p. 601)* The Commodore Kids Club, for children 4 to 12, is a terrific supervised program with arts and crafts projects, nature hikes, beach games, and evening events.

◎ Pacific Terrace Inn. 610 Diamond St., San Diego, CA 92109. ☎ **800/344-3370** or 619/581-3500. Fax 619/274-3341. 65 rms, 8 suites. A/C MINIBAR TV TEL. $175–$205 double, $185–$215 double with kitchenette; from $275 suite. Rates include continental breakfast. Additional person $10 extra. AE, CB, DC, DISC, MC, V. Free security parking. Bus: 34 or 34A. Take I-5 to the Grand/Garnet exit and follow either Grand or Garnet west to Mission Blvd., turn north, then left (west) onto Diamond; it's at end of the street on the right.

This is a wonderful choice along the Pacific Beach boardwalk. It's attractive and upscale, and it's quieter than the other nearby beachfront properties. The guest rooms are large and comfortable, and have balconies or terraces, refrigerators, wall safes, hair dryers, cotton robes, vanities with separate sinks, and voice-mail. Forty rooms have kitchens. Third-story rooms have particularly nice views, and the suites have large baths with Jacuzzis. There's popcorn, coffee, and lemonade set out for guests in the Caribbean Room.

Services: Valet dry cleaning/laundry service, complimentary copy of *USA Today* delivered daily.

Facilities: Kitchenettes, outdoor heated pool facing the ocean, Jacuzzi, beach, conference rooms, coin-operated laundry.

MODERATE

The Beach Cottages. 4255 Ocean Blvd. (a block south of Grand Ave.), San Diego, CA 92109. ☎ **619/483-7440.** Fax 619/273-9365. 28 rms, 12 studios, 18 apts, 17 cottages, 3 suites. TV TEL. Summer, $90–$110 double; $120 studio for up to four; $145–$185 apt for up to six; $140–$175 cottage for up to six; $220–$240 two-bedroom suite for up to six. Lower rates rest of year. Weekly rates available except in summer. AE, CB, DC, DISC, MC, V. Free parking. Take I-5 to the Grand/Garnet exit, then go west on Grand Ave. and left on Mission Blvd.

The Beach Cottages are particularly suited for young couples and families who want to stay directly on the beach. It's within walking distance of shops and restaurants and has barbecue grills, shuffleboard courts, table tennis, and a laundry. In addition to regular motel rooms, the hotel offers cottages, apartments, studios, and suites; all accommodations except the motel rooms have fully equipped kitchens. The rustic cottages, which are literally sandside, contain either one or two bedrooms and sleep up to six; each has a private patio with tables, chairs, and recliners. The other units are outfitted with more contemporary interiors, but they're farther from the waves.

Guests gather in a lovely patio courtyard with plant-filled trellises, or head straight for the beach.

To make a reservation, call between 9am and 9pm, when the office is open.

✪ **Ocean Park Inn.** 710 Grand Ave., San Diego, CA 92109. ☎ **800/231-7735** or 619/483-5858. Fax 619/274-0823. 73 rms, 4 suites. A/C TV TEL. Summer, $99–$149 double; from $159 suite. Rates include continental breakfast. Lower rates rest of the year. AE, DC, DISC, MC, V. Free indoor parking. Take the Grand/Garnet exit off I-5 and follow Grand Ave. to the ocean.

On Pacific Beach's lively, circuslike beach path, this three-story standout is visually appealing both inside and out. Behind the hotel's modern Spanish-Mediterranean facade is a sharply designed marble lobby that gives way to the less splendid but completely comfortable guest rooms. The accommodations are contemporary but bland; all units have terraces and refrigerators. The most expensive rooms have oceanfront balconies but can be a bit noisy. "King suites" are extra large and have Roman tubs; some also have kitchenettes. Hotel facilities include a sundeck, a heated pool, an outdoor Jacuzzi, vending machines, and a coin laundry.

INEXPENSIVE

Surfer Motor Lodge. 711 Pacific Beach Dr. (at Mission Blvd.), San Diego, CA 92109. ☎ **800/787-3373** or 619/483-7070. Fax 619/274-1670. 52 rms. TV TEL. Summer, $89–$122 double. Winter, $69–$90 double. Weekly rates offered in winter. AE, DC, MC, V. Free parking.

This high-rise motel has acceptable rooms and a heated outdoor pool. It's not remarkable, but it does offer relatively low-cost accommodations right on the beach. Almost all the rooms have balconies and ocean views and are cooled by ocean breezes. Fans are also available. In addition to standard doubles, there are kitchenette units, one-bedroom units that can sleep up to four, and family units that can sleep up to six. There are self-serve laundry facilities on the premises. The hotel can arrange fishing and golf outings.

CAMPING

Campland on the Bay. 2211 Pacific Beach Dr., San Diego, CA 92109-5699. ☎ **800/4BAYFUN** 619/581-4200 or 619/581-4212 (24 hours). 600 hookup sites. Summer, $26–$52 site for up to four people. Off-season, $19–$37 site for up to four people. Lowest-priced sites don't have hookups. Senior rates available. MC, V. Take I-5 to the Grand/Garnet exit, follow Grand to Olney, turn left, and turn left again onto Pacific Beach Dr.

This family-oriented bayside campground draws RVs, campers (with or without vans), and boaters. Conveniently located nearby are parks, a beach, bird sanctuary, and dog walk. Other facilities include pools, a Jacuzzi, catamaran and windsurfer rentals and lessons, bike and boat rentals, a games room, a café, a market, and a laundry. Sea World is 5 minutes away.

LA JOLLA
VERY EXPENSIVE

La Valencia Hotel. 1132 Prospect St. (at Herschel Ave.), La Jolla, CA 92037. ☎ **800/451-0772** or 619/454-0771. Fax 619/456-3921. 90 rms, 13 suites. A/C MINIBAR TV TEL. $170–$200 standard double, $340–$370 full ocean-view double; from $400 suite. Children 11 and under stay free in parents' room. AE, DC, DISC, MC, V. Valet parking $8. Take the Ardath Rd. exit off I-5 north or the La Jolla Village Dr. west exit off I-5 south; then take Torrey Pines Rd. to Prospect Pl. and turn right (Prospect Pl. becomes Prospect St.).

La Valencia is a gracious Spanish-colonial resort that delights the senses at every turn. Overlooking the ocean, it's a beauty, from the colonnaded entrance with a vine-covered trellis to the lush gardens surrounding the large pool to the exquisite mosaic tile work within. Old-world charm, outstanding personal service, and the impressive location have made it a haven for celebrities and entertainers, dating all the way back to Greta Garbo and Charlie Chaplin. At the back of the hotel, garden terraces open toward the ocean.

The guest rooms are decorated with European antique reproductions and offer fine-quality linens. Amenities include terry robes, oversize towels, and bathroom phones. The ocean-view rooms have fantastic vistas. The bungalows are not air-conditioned.

Dining/Entertainment: The elegant rooftop Sky Room serves French cuisine in a romantic setting; the Mediterranean Room and Patio serves California cuisine either indoors or on a patio. There's also the legendary Whaling Bar & Grill (where Ginger Rogers and Charlton Heston once hung out) and the adjoining Café La Rue. Piano music is offered in the lobby lounge Monday to Saturday from 6 to 10pm and refreshments are served on the adjoining ocean-view terrace on request.

Services: Concierge, room service (24 hours), dry cleaning/laundry service, morning newspaper, nightly turndown, in-room massage, twice-daily maid service, baby-sitting, secretarial services, express checkout, valet parking.

Facilities: Kitchenettes, VCR, video rental, a free-form heated pool (edged with a lawn, flowering trees, shrubs, and a flagstone sundeck), mini health club, Jacuzzi, sauna, putting green, shuffleboard, access to tennis courts, conference rooms.

EXPENSIVE

There's also the spectacularly sited **Sheraton Grande Torrey Pines,** 10950 N. Torrey Pines Rd., La Jolla, CA 92037 (☎ **800/762-6160** or 619/558-1500), perched on a bluff above the Pacific and adjacent to the renowned Torrey Pines Golf Course.

✪ **Colonial Inn.** 910 Prospect St., La Jolla, CA 92037. ☎ **619/454-2181** or 800/826-1278. Fax 619/454-5679. 64 rms, 11 suites. TV TEL. $150 double with village view, $175–$210 double with ocean view; from $230 suite. Children 17 and under stay free in parents' room. Lower rates off-season. AE, CB, DC, MC, V. Valet parking $5. Take the Ardath Rd. exit off I-5 north or the La Jolla Village Dr. west exit off I-5 south; then take Torrey Pines Rd. to Prospect Pl. and turn right (Prospect Pl. becomes Prospect St.).

An outstanding choice, the Colonial Inn offers old-world atmosphere, tasteful decor, and spacious rooms enhanced by traditional furnishings and elegant fabrics. The property was built in 1913, and stands 1 block from the ocean and just down the street from the more expensive La Valencia. Guests who choose to stay here instead of at "La V" will sacrifice air-conditioning for a ceiling fan in each room, but will gain elbow room (and save money). The inn, originally an apartment hotel, has oversize closets and feels more homey. Refrigerators and terry robes available on request.

Dining/Entertainment: The bar in Putnam's was once a drugstore soda-fountain; today it's a popular watering hole. A large spray of fresh flowers is the focal point in the lounge, where guests gather in front of the fireplace for drinks. The restaurant serves excellent California cuisine.

Services: Room service (24 hours), dry cleaning/laundry, turndown service on request, baby-sitting, valet parking, complimentary shoeshine. Walking tours of La Jolla depart from the hotel at 11am Thursday to Saturday or other times by appointment. Airport transportation is available for $9 one-way.

Facilities: Heated outdoor pool (set in a landscaped garden and open from sunup to sundown), conference rooms, car-rental desk.

Sea Lodge. 8110 Camino del Oro (at Avenida de la Playa), La Jolla, CA 92037. ☎ **800/237-5211** or 619/459-8271. Fax 619/456-9346. 128 rms, 8 suites. TV TEL. $176–$373 double; $427 suite. Children 11 and under stay free in parents' room. Lower rates off-season. AE, CB,

DC, DISC, MC, V. Free covered parking. Take the Ardath Rd. exit off I-5 north or the La Jolla Village Dr. west exit off I-5 south; then take La Jolla Shores Dr., turn west onto Avenida de la Playa, and then north (right) on Camino del Oro.

This three-story sunset-colored hotel is sited right on mile-long La Jolla Shores Beach. The large rooms are in a long, low stucco building with a terra-cotta–tile roof and highlighted by fountains, attractive landscaping, open-air walkways, ceramic tile, graceful arches, and Mexican antiques—like the 200-year-old cathedral doors leading into the main dining room. The third-floor rooms—our favorites—have high sloped barnwood ceilings. Almost all rooms have ocean views. Each has a balcony or patio, and some have kitchens.

Dining/Entertainment: The Shores restaurant, open for breakfast, lunch, and dinner daily, features indoor and patio seating. Ocean views are available from every table, and seafood is the specialty.

Services: Concierge, room service.

Facilities: Heated outdoor pool, children's pool, sauna, tennis and volleyball courts, tour desk, complimentary underground parking.

MODERATE

There's also the **Radisson Hotel La Jolla,** 3299 Holiday Court, La Jolla, CA 92037 (☎ 800/333-3333 or 619/453-5500), the **Residence Inn by Marriott,** 8901 Gilman Drive, La Jolla, CA 92037 (☎ 800/331-3131 or 619/587-1770), and a less expensive choice, the **La Jolla TraveLodge,** 1141 Silverado St., La Jolla, CA 92037 (☎ 800/578-7878 or 619/454-0791).

Bed & Breakfast Inn at La Jolla. 7753 Draper Ave. (near Prospect St.), La Jolla, CA 92037. ☎ **619/456-2066.** Fax 619/456-0510. 16 rms. A/C $85–$225 double. Rates include continental breakfast. MC, V. Limited free parking. Take the Ardath Rd. exit off I-5 north or the La Jolla Village Dr. west exit off I-5 south; then take Torrey Pines Rd. to Prospect Pl. and turn right; after Prospect Pl. becomes Prospect St., turn left on Draper and the inn is nestled between the La Jolla Women's Club and La Jolla Prebyterian Church.

In 1913 architect Irving Gill designed this rambling house in his innovative "cubist" style. Across from the Museum of Contemporary Art and the Recreation Center (which has tennis and basketball courts), the inn features unique cottage-style rooms in two wings. Each beautifully kept accommodation contains a king- or queen-size bed or twin beds, and is graced with fresh flowers. Some rooms have fireplaces; telephones are available on request. It's fun to stroll from the garden to the sundeck to the sitting room, where you can enjoy complimentary wine and cheese in the afternoon. The hosts neither accept children under 12 nor allow smoking.

✪ Empress Hotel of La Jolla. 7766 Fay Ave. (at Silverado), La Jolla, CA 92037. ☎ **800/525-6552** or 619/454-3001. Fax 619/454-6387. 73 rms and suites. A/C TV TEL. $109–$135 double; $250 Jacuzzi suite. Rates include continental breakfast. Additional person $10 extra; children 17 and under stay free in parents' room. Lower off-season and long-stay rates. AE, DC, DISC, MC, V. Valet parking $5. Take the Ardath Rd. exit off I-5 north or the La Jolla Village Dr. west exit off I-5 south; then take Torrey Pines Rd. to Girard, turn right, and then left on Silverado to Fay.

The Empress Hotel offers spacious quarters with traditional furnishings a block or two away from La Jolla's main drag. It's definitely quieter here than at the Colonial Inn or the Prospect Park Inn.

All rooms come equipped with hair dryers, coffeemakers, and terry robes. The four Empress Rooms have a sitting area with a full-size sofa sleeper. While these rooms have only a microwave, four suites have complete cooking facilities. Two suites come equipped with a grand piano. The top two floors in this five-story building have partial ocean views. We like the European ambience, marble bathrooms with large mirrors, and tasteful decor. Room service comes from the award-winning Manhattan Restaurant located on the ground floor.

CORONADO
VERY EXPENSIVE

✪ **Hotel del Coronado.** 1500 Orange Ave., San Diego, CA 92118. ☎ **800/468-3533** or 619/522-8000. Fax 619/522-8238. 700 rms. and suites. A/C MINIBAR TV TEL. $179 standard double, $209 deluxe double, $269–$289 ocean-view double, $349–$399 oceanfront double; from $499 suite. Children 17 and under stay free in parents' room. Packages available. AE, CB, DC, DISC, MC, V. Parking $10. From I-5 take the Coronado Bridge and turn left onto Orange Ave.

Opened in 1888 and designated a National Historic Landmark in 1977, this is one of the state's grand old hotels. The "Hotel Del," as it's affectionately known, is the last of California's extravagant seaside hotels. Here the duke of Windsor met his duchess, and Marilyn Monroe frolicked in *Some Like It Hot*. This monument to Victorian grandeur boasts tall cupolas, red turrets, gingerbread trim, and grounds that occupy 33 acres. The rooms run the gamut from compact to extravagant, and all are packed with antique charm. Most contain custom-made furnishings. The best rooms have balconies fronting the ocean and large windows that take in one of the city's finest white-sand beaches. The Del is near an 18-hole golf course. Non-smoking rooms are available.

Dining/Entertainment: Each of the Del's nine restaurants and lounges has its own special charm. Our favorite is the alfresco Ocean Terrace, the only outside restaurant in Coronado with a beach view. The newly renovated Prince of Wales Grill has garnered numerous rave reviews for both cuisine and atmosphere. The Palm Court overlooks the Garden Patio, where afternoon tea is served on Sunday. Traditionalists still flock to the Crown Room, which has remained unchanged since the turn of the century; it serves one of the city's finest Sunday brunches. There's music and dancing nightly in the Ocean Terrace Lounge, and piano music in the Palm Court Bar.

Services: Concierge, room service (24 hours), dry cleaning/laundry service, nightly turndown, in-room massage, baby-sitting, secretarial services, express checkout, valet parking, special activities for children, guided tours of the hotel for $10.

Facilities: Movie channels, two outdoor pools, beach, state-of-the-art health spa, Jacuzzi, sauna, sundeck, six night-lit championship tennis courts, water-sports equipment rentals, bicycle rentals, games room, children's center, business center, conference rooms, car-rental desk, tour desk, beauty salon, shopping arcade.

✪ **Loews Coronado Bay Resort.** 4000 Coronado Bay Rd., Coronado, CA 92118. ☎ **800/23-LOEWS** or 619/424-4000. Fax 619/424-4400. 400 rms, 37 suites; 4 cabanas. A/C MINIBAR TV TEL. $195–$245 double; $395 suite; $495 cabana. Additional person $20 extra; children 17 and under stay free in parents' room. Romance and tennis packages available. AE, CB, DC, DISC, MC, V. Valet parking $11, self-parking (under cover) $9. Take I-5 to the Coronado Bridge; go left onto Orange Ave. and continue 6¹/₂ miles down Silver Strand Hwy.; then make a left at Coronado Bay Rd., the entrance to the resort.

This lovely hideaway occupies a secluded 15-acre peninsula, 30 minutes from the airport and 4¹/₂ miles from downtown Coronado. Your room will overlook the hotel's private 80-slip marina (boat rentals and sailing lessons available) and the San Diego skyline. Each room is very well appointed with elegant furnishings and large marble bathrooms; extras include terrycloth robes and in-room safes. A private pedestrian underpass leads to nearby Silver Strand Beach.

Dining/Entertainment: Azzura Point serves up California cuisine and a memorable view, while the more casual RRR's has both indoor and outdoor seating. Guests also enjoy a lounge, a poolside bar and grill, and a gourmet market.

Services: Concierge, room service (24 hours), laundry/valet, newspaper delivery, evening turndown, in-room massage, twice-daily maid service, baby-sitting, secretarial service, express checkout, valet parking. The hotel's Commodore Kids Club, for children 4 to 12, offers supervised activities daily, and on weekend evenings as well (for an extra fee).

Facilities: VCRs, video rentals, three outdoor swimming pools, fitness center (with equipment, saunas, steam room, and whirlpools), massage, large sundeck, hydro spas, five night-lit tennis courts and pro shop, water sports; bicycle, inline skate, and

Scenes from the "Hotel Del"

Coronado was still a wilderness frequented only by hunters and fisherman when two businessmen dreamt they could capitalize on the coming Santa Fe Railroad by opening a grand hotel. Today's wood-paneled Lobby Shop was the "ladies' salon" when the Hotel del Coronado opened in 1888, sparing women the discomfort of the main lobby, where men often displayed the day's catch—rabbits, fish, quail, and other gamey prizes.

Believed to be the world's largest surviving wooden structure, the "Hotel Del" is built of timber carefully chosen to resist termites, and it maintained its own fire equipment and water supply for many years. Its revolutionary lighting system was personally installed by its creator, Thomas A. Edison, in 1887. The earliest guests were so unaccustomed to this modern convenience that instructional cards were discreetly placed near the fixtures, advising "do not attempt to light with a match."

The Hotel del Coronado is proud of its colorful past—as is made clear in the lower-level History Gallery, filled with memorabilia. There you'll learn the story of Kate Morgan, whose body was found in 1892 on the present site of the tennis courts and whose ghost still walks the halls. And you might be surprised to learn that author L. Frank Baum, a frequent guest, designed the Crown Dining Room's elegant crown-shaped chandeliers. He wrote several of his beloved Oz series in the Coronado, and many think he modeled the Emerald City's geometric spires after the Del's conical turrets.

The hotel's first visiting monarch was Hawaii's last king, Kalakaua, who spent Christmas here during the 1890s. But the best-known royal guest was Edward, prince of Wales (later Edward VIII, then duke of Windsor), who came to the hotel in April 1920, the first British royal to visit California. Of the many lavish social affairs held during his stay, at least two were attended by a Coronado navy wife, Mrs. Wallis Spencer, who later remarried and become Wallis Simpson. She was officially introduced to the prince 15 years later in London, but there's much speculation as to whether their love affair, which culminated in his abdicating the throne of England so he could marry her, might've begun at the romantic Del.

America's own "royalty" came often to the hotel. San Diego's beloved son, Charles Lindbergh, was feted here in 1927 following his historic solo flight across the Atlantic, and Hollywood stars like Mary Pickford, Greta Garbo, Charlie Chaplin, and Esther Williams have flocked to the Del since the early days of pictures. The first movie filmed here was *The Flying Fleet* (1927) starring Ramon Navarro, but the most famous is surely Billy Wilder's 1958 *Some Like It Hot*. Long-time hotel staffers remember seeing stars Marilyn Monroe, Tony Curtis, and Jack Lemmon romping on the beach during shooting.

—*Stephanie Avnet*

water-sports rentals; marina; business center, faxes in suites; meeting space; washer and dryer; car-rental desk; beauty salon; boutiques.

EXPENSIVE

Glorietta Bay Inn. 1630 Glorietta Blvd. (near Orange Ave.), Coronado, CA 92118. ☎ **800/ 283-9383** or 619/435-3101. Fax 619/435-6182. 81 rms, 17 suites. A/C TV TEL. Mansion, $145–$155 double; $165–$179 suite; $279–$299 penthouse suite. Annex, $79–$89 economy double; $109–$139 contemporary double; $139–$179 family suite with kitchen. AE, DC, DISC, MC, V. Free parking. Take I-5 to the Coronado Bridge, and turn left on Orange Ave.; after 2 miles, turn left onto Glorietta Blvd.; it's across the street from the Hotel del Coronado.

Once the summer mansion of 19th-century multimillionaire sugar baron John Spreckels, former owner of the Hotel del Coronado, the Glorietta Bay Inn is a beautifully restored 1908 house surrounded by lush gardens, with intricate moldings and a fine brass-and-marble staircase leading to the well-appointed rooms. The rooms in the original mansion have a nice Victorian style; those in the less charming annex are contemporary, with bright furnishings and large windows overlooking Glorietta Bay. The hotel is within walking distance (1 block) of the beach. There's a heated pool, a spa pool, bike rentals, and a guest laundry. Free morning coffee is offered, and continental breakfast is available for a charge.

INEXPENSIVE

Ⓢ **El Cordova Hotel.** 1351 Orange Ave. (at Adella St.), Coronado, CA 92118. ☎ **800/ 229-2032** or 619/435-4131. Fax 619/435-0632. 14 rms, 26 suites. TV TEL. $75–$95 double; $85–$105 studio with kitchen; $110–$140 one-bedroom suite; $135–$170 two-bedroom suite. Children 11 and under stay free in parents' room. Weekly and monthly rates available off-season. AE, DC, DISC, MC, V. No off-street parking. Take I-5 to the Coronado Bridge, and turn left onto Orange Ave.

Entering the El Cordova is like stepping into a village south of the border. Colorful little shops and an atmospheric Mexican restaurant are woven into this property, which was built as a mansion in 1902 and converted into a hotel in 1930. The Spanish-style low-rise is located across a busy street from the beachfront Hotel del Coronado. The lobby has a quarry-tile floor and hacienda-style furnishings, and this decor is carried out in the comfortable rooms and suites. Each room is slightly different from the next. The best accommodations are the suites, with oak floors and bay windows. Several come with kitchenettes, which like the baths and stairways are decorated with handcrafted Mexican designs. About half the rooms offer air-conditioning. El Cordova is a good family choice; you're welcome to bring the kids and even the family dog. All the family activity does increase the noise level at times, however, so if you're looking for a really quiet retreat, the El Cordova probably isn't for you. If you do decide to give it a try, reserve well in advance. In addition to Miguel's Cocina, there's a heated pool, a barbecue area with a picnic table, and a coin-op laundry.

4 Dining

What follows is only a sampling of San Diego's dining scene. For a greater selection of reviews, see *Frommer's San Diego.*

DOWNTOWN

EXPENSIVE

Anthony's Star of the Sea Room. 1360 Harbor Dr. (at Ash St.). ☎ **619/232-7408.** Reservations suggested. Main courses $19.50–$38.50. AE, CB, DC, DISC, MC, V. Daily 5:30–10:30pm. Valet parking $5. SEAFOOD.

For as long as I've lived in San Diego—which is a long time—this Anthony's has been the poshest place in town. This is not to say that it's always offered the best meals, but it's been the standard-setter for traditional, upmarket dining. Today it continues to attract folks for whom only the finest will do—although they no longer have to wear a necktie in order to be seated (jackets are still required for men, however). Should you decide to splurge, you can try chef Jonathan Pflueger's sole admiral, stuffed with shellfish; the mixed grill of salmon, swordfish, and halibut, with a triad of sauces; or the sautéed frogs' legs flamed tableside with aged cognac. Filet mignon is available for landlubbers. The restaurant is handsomely decorated, and its location adjacent to the three-masted *Star of India* in the San Diego Harbor means unmatched harbor views. Candlelight adds to the glow. Service is polished (the waiters have all worked here forever) and portions are huge. Don't confuse this spot with the mini-chain of Anthony's seafood cafes—the same family owns them, but the resemblance stops there.

Dobsons's. 956 Broadway Circle (between Broadway and Horton Plaza). ☎ **619/231-6771.** Fax 619/696-0861. Reservations recommended. Main courses $15–$24. AE, CB, DC, MC, V. Mon–Wed 11:30am–10pm, Thurs–Fri 11:30am–11pm, Sat 5:30–11pm. Valet parking (after 5pm) $3. CONTINENTAL.

This place has long attracted the city's political movers and shakers. Owner Paul Dobson or his wife, Carol, often greet diners at the door. The menu changes twice daily and includes popular dishes such as mussel bisque; confit of Muscovy duck leg with horseradish cream; risotto with rock shrimp, calamari, prawn, sun-dried tomatoes, and asparagus; and for lunch, Dobson's famous 8-ounce "Bar Room Burger" or Cobb salad. There's a good wine list, including a nice selection of wines by the glass. Downstairs there's a handsome wooden bar adorned with the brass nameplates of frequent customers; the bar stays open till midnight.

MODERATE

✪ **Croce's Restaurant and Jazz Bar.** 802 5th Ave. (at F St.). ☎ **619/233-4355.** Fax 619/232-9836. Reservations recommended. Main courses $13.50–$18. AE, DC, DISC, MC, V. Daily 7:30am–3pm and 4pm–midnight. Valet parking $5 with validation. AMERICAN.

This very popular jazz restaurant/bar is named after the late musician Jim Croce and is owned by his wife, Ingrid. You might think the food would be an afterthought to the scene here, but that's not the case. The menu runs the gamut from casual breakfast and lunch fare to salmon baked in puff pastry, served with wild spinach hollandaise, and grilled breast of chicken with figs and goat cheese, served with a peach and caramelized-onion chutney. The above-mentioned salmon is one of our favorite dishes in San Diego. In addition to the main restaurant, there's Ingrid's Cantina & Sidewalk Cafe next door for southwestern cuisine, and Upstairs at Croce's for cocktails, coffee, and desserts. Two adjacent nightspots, the Jazz Bar and the Top Hat, serve up jazz and R&B; if you have dinner in the restaurants, you won't have to pay the cover charge. See "San Diego After Dark," later in this chapter, for more information.

Dakota Grill & Spirits. 901 5th Ave. (at E. St.). ☎ **619/234-5554.** Reservations required. Main courses $9–$18. AE, DC, DISC, MC, V. Mon–Thurs 11:30am–2:30pm and 5–10pm, Fri 11:30am–2:30pm and 5–11pm, Sat 5–11pm, Sun 5–9pm. Valet parking $5, self-parking $7. AMERICAN/SOUTHWEST.

This pretty glass-wrapped Gaslamp Quarter eatery is San Diego's most upscale Southwest restaurant. Its succulent mesquite-grilled chicken, meats, and seafood are consistently excellent and very fairly priced, and the portions are large. Our vote goes to the shrimp tasso (sautéed with Tasso Cajun ham and sweet peas in an ancho-chile cream). The atmosphere is casual but polished, and the service is unpolished but attentive. For good value, award-winning Dakota is definitely worth a letter home.

Planet Hollywood. 197 Horton Plaza. ☎ **619/702-STAR.** Reservations not accepted. Main courses $6.50–$14. AE, DC, MC, V. Daily 11am–2am. Parking Horton Plaza Garage (3 hours free with validation). Bus: 1, 2, 3, 25, 34, or 34A. Trolley: America Plaza. CALIFORNIA/AMERICAN.

Folks stand in line for a turn to eat at this 19th member of the chain and ogle the myriad movie memorabilia, including the Audio-Animatronic™ owl from *Indiana Jones & the Temple of Doom,* Roddy McDowell's costume from *Planet of the Apes,* and a submachine gun from *Die Hard.* This is a noisy, friendly, thoroughly enjoyable place understandably popular with families. Menu items include pizza, pasta, burgers, sandwiches, salads, and a handful of light California cuisine choices. Kids can sip on the likes of "Home Alone," an "E.T.," or a "Predator." If you don't relish standing in line, be there at 11am when they open, between 2 and 5pm, or after 9pm.

INEXPENSIVE

Filippi's Pizza Grotto. 1747 India St. (between Date and Fir sts. in Little Italy). ☎ **619/232-5095.** Fax 619/695-8591. Reservations accepted. Main courses $4.75–$12.50. AE, DC, DISC, MC, V. Mon–Sat 11am–11pm, Sun 11am–10pm. Free parking. Trolley: America Plaza. ITALIAN.

This is one of those down-home Italian places, right down to the chianti bottles lining the dining areas. It's been around since the 1950s, and has given birth to a dozen spin-off locations throughout the city. You enter through an Italian deli that will stir your hunger pangs with a selection of cheeses, pastas, wines, and salamis. Choose from 15 pizzas and the requisite pasta dishes. Kids will feel right at home here.

Galaxy Grill. Horton Plaza (top level). ☎ **619/234-7211.** Reservations not accepted. Main courses $3.50–$6.50. AE, DISC, MC, V. Mon–Thurs 11am–9pm, Fri–Sat 11am–10pm, Sun 11am–8pm. 3 hours' free parking with validation. Trolley: America Plaza. AMERICAN/DINER.

The waitresses in 1950s garb serve up good old-fashioned burgers, shakes, tuna melts, cherry Cokes, and the like. Can you remember the last time you had a cherry Coke, or got two tunes on the jukebox for a quarter?

Kansas City Barbecue. 610 W. Market St. ☎ **619/231-9680.** Reservations accepted only for large parties. Main courses $9–$16. MC, V. Daily 11am–1am. Trolley: Seaport Village. AMERICAN.

Scenes from *Top Gun* were filmed at this old-fashioned honky-tonk barbecue joint. The walls are cluttered with county fair memorabilia and license plates. The barbecue is done right, slow-cooked over an open fire and served with white bread and your choice of cole slaw, beans, fries, extra-large and flaky onion rings, potato salad, or corn on the cob.

ⓢ Mandarin House. 2604 5th Ave. (at Maple). ☎ **619/232-1101.** Reservations accepted. Most main courses $6.50–$10. AE, DC, MC, V. Mon–Thurs 11am–10pm, Fri 11am–11pm, Sat noon–11pm, Sun 2–10pm. CHINESE.

This is the most popular Chinese restaurant in San Diego and winner of many awards. Our favorite dish is the kung pao chicken, which is hot and spicy in the traditional Szechuan style and laced with lots of peanuts. The Peking duck (the most expensive item on the menu) also comes with pancakes. If you expect the usual Chinese-red decor, you'll be surprised by the pleasant sea-foam-and-peach color scheme. Mandarin House also has locations in La Jolla and Pacific Beach.

ⓢ Old Spaghetti Factory. 5th Ave. and K St. ☎ **619/233-4323.** Reservations not necessary. Main courses $4.25–$8. DISC, MC, V. Mon–Thurs 11:30am–10pm, Fri 11:30am–10pm, Sat–Sun noon–10pm. Trolley: Gaslamp Quarter. ITALIAN.

A family restaurant with a Victorian atmosphere, this place allows you and your kids to dine in a trolley car that's been converted into a dining room. The main courses—mostly old standbys such as lasagne and spaghetti—come with lots of extras, such as salad, sourdough bread, ice cream, and coffee or tea with refills. The word is out about what a great deal this place offers, so there's always a wait. There's a small play area for kids.

HILLCREST/UPTOWN

Celadon. 3628 5th Ave. (between Brooks and Pennsylvania). ☎ **619/295-8800.** Reservations recommended on weekends. Main courses $8.50–$14.50. AE, MC, V. Mon–Fri 11:30am–2pm and 5–10pm, Sat 5–10pm. THAI.

With its pink stucco exterior, Celadon is easy to spot. Inside you'll discover a very pretty interior done in pinks and greens, with Thai artifacts lining the walls. The lemongrass beef is outstanding, as are the sautéed scallops in "burnt" sauce with a touch of garlic and onions.

Kung Food. 2949 5th Ave. (between Palm and Quince). ☎ **619/298-7302,** or 619/298-9232 for deli/take-out. Reservations not accepted. Main courses $6.50–$9.50. DISC, MC, V. Mon–Thurs 11:30am–9pm, Fri 11:30am–10pm, Sat 8:30am–10pm, Sun 8:30am–9pm. VEGETARIAN.

San Diego's best-known vegetarian eatery offers an extensive menu created from natural ingredients—no meat products, no bleached flours, no sugar, and lots of low-fat choices. But that doesn't mean the food is boring or bland. The menu includes Greek spinach pie, tofu vegetable enchiladas, lentil-walnut loaf, and garden burgers. There's indoor and outdoor seating, and soothing music sets the scene. Beer and wine are served. No smoking.

Liaison. 2202 4th Ave. (at Ivy). ☎ **619/234-5540.** Reservations recommended. Main courses $9.50–$18.75. AE, CB, DC, DISC, MC, V. Tues–Sat 5–10:30pm, Sun 10am–3pm and 5–10:30pm. FRENCH.

This cozy little cafe, with its stone walls, candlelit tables, and copper pots and pans, will take you back to the French countryside. Your main course might be a selection such as roast duck à l'orange, or coquilles St-Jacques. The lunch menu features salads, pastas (such as homemade crab ravioli in lobster sauce), and three fresh fish dishes daily. You can't leave without having a Grand Marnier chocolate or amaretto soufflé for two, at $5 per person. Ooh la la!

OLD TOWN

EXPENSIVE

Cafe Pacifica. 2414 San Diego Ave. ☎ **619/291-6666.** Reservations recommended. Main courses $11–$18. AE, CB, DC, DISC, MC, V. Tues–Fri 11:30am–2pm and 5:30–10pm, Sat–Mon 5:30–10pm. Valet parking free at lunch, $4 at dinner. CALIFORNIA.

Excellent fresh fish, grilled over mesquite, keeps visitors happy and locals returning. The setting is slightly formal and charming, with tiny twinkling lights overhead and candles adorning the tables. On our last visit I started with the Dungeness crab salad, an intriguing combination of flavors that included papaya, avocado, and endive. Then I moved on to the Hawaiian ahi with shiitake mushrooms and ginger butter. The menu changes daily but always offers excellent dishes like pan-fried catfish, shrimp tacos, and perfect crab cakes—crunchy outside, moist inside.

Casa de Bandini. Opposite Old Town Plaza, Old Town. ☎ **619/297-8211.** Reservations not accepted. Main courses $6.50–$14. AE, CB, DC, MC, V. Mon–Thurs 11am–9:30pm, Fri–Sat 11am–10pm, Sun 10am–9:30pm. Bus: 4 or 5/105. MEXICAN.

As much an Old Town tradition as the mariachi music that's played here on weekends, this lively restaurant—with its appealing balcony and courtyard—fills the nooks and crannies of an adobe hacienda built in 1823 for Juan Bandini, once a merchant and politician in these parts. Later, with a second floor added, it became a hotel. Today it's the scene of many a happy repast over dishes like crab enchiladas, chicken-and-avocado salad, crab brochette with mild green chiles, and jumbo cod filet with sautéed vegetables. Some of the dishes are gourmet Mexican, others simple south-of-the-border fare; you'll never run short of refried beans, guacamole, or jumbo margaritas. It's the house itself that makes the restaurant extra special.

INEXPENSIVE

La Piñata. 2836 Juan St. ☎ **619/297-1631.** Reservations recommended on weekends. Main courses $5–$11. MC, V. Sun–Thurs 11am–9pm, Fri–Sat 11am–9:30pm. Free parking. MEXICAN.

The brightly colored Mexican toys that give this restaurant its name hang from the ceiling in this cozy, friendly spot. It's slightly out of the way, but a pleasant alternative to the larger, somewhat noisy tourist emporiums, and it has a small outdoor patio for alfresco dining. La Piñata is an all-around winner: It's attractive, the food is always good, the prices are moderate, and the service is pleasant and prompt. Familiar Mexican dishes like fajitas, tacos, and tostadas are well prepared and usually preceded by a complimentary cheese quesadilla. Good margaritas are served in glasses the size of a small bird bath.

Old Town Mexican Cafe. 2489 San Diego Ave. ☎ **619/297-4330.** Reservations accepted only for parties of 10 or more. Main courses $7.50–$11.50. AE, DISC, MC, V. Daily 7am–11pm. MEXICAN.

A fun margarita bar and homemade tortillas are the primary draws of this boisterous Mexican restaurant that's popular with both families and couples. (Expect a wait.) It's nothing fancy; the food speaks for itself. All the south-of-the-border standards are available—tacos, burritos, fajitas, and the like—served with excellent salsa. You'll see the staff in the window facing the street making each day's fresh tortillas by hand. Check out the Mexican-style rotisserie pork ribs.

MISSION BAY/PACIFIC BEACH

The Atoll. In the Catamaran Resort Hotel, 3999 Mission Blvd. ☎ **619/539-8635.** Reservations recommended for Sun brunch. Main courses $8–$20. AE, CB, DC, DISC, MC, V. Sun–Thurs 6:30am–10pm, Fri–Sat 6:30am–11pm. Valet parking $7, free self-parking with validation. CALIFORNIA.

You can dine at a wrought-iron table on the waterfront patio here and take in the view of Mission Bay, or inside, where the interior is made elegant by rattan chairs, crisp tablecloths, and Villeroy and Boch china. We'd start with the spicy crab cakes with lime and ginger-butter sauce, then move on to the broiled lamb chops. If you're looking for something light and simple, though, there are selections like club sandwiches to keep you happy. The service is friendly and polished.

Firehouse Beach Cafe. 722 Grand Ave. ☎ **619/272-1999.** Reservations recommended on weekends. Main courses $8–$12. AE, CB, DC, DISC, MC, V. Sun–Thurs 7am–9pm, Fri–Sat 7am–10pm. Free parking. AMERICAN.

This casual place is always packed (though not oppressively so), and if you're lucky, you can get an umbrella table on the upstairs deck with an ocean view. The locals love eating breakfast here—the omelets are especially popular. The kitchen turns out one of the best burgers in San Diego, in addition to perennial favorites like taco salad, fish and chips, and lasagne. A patio bar overlooking the ocean was added in 1996.

⊕ Family-Friendly Restaurants

Galaxy Grill *(see p. 605)* How could burgers, shakes, and an old-time jukebox let you down?

Old Spaghetti Factory *(see p. 605)* The service staff here make kids feel especially welcome, and the ambience is definitely family-friendly. Kids get their own toys, and there's a special play area for them.

Planet Hollywood *(see p. 605)* This noisy, friendly place is popular with families thanks to the more than 300 pieces of movie memorabilia that hang from the walls and ceiling, and the great casual food.

The Green Flash. 701 Thomas Ave. (at Mission Blvd.). ☎ **619/270-7715.** Reservations recommended. Main courses $10–$25. AE, DC, DISC, MC, V. Mon–Thurs 8am–9:30pm, Fri 8am–10pm, Sat 7:30am–10pm, Sun 7:30am–9:30pm. Bus: 34 or 34A. SEAFOOD/ INTERNATIONAL.

You can spend as much or as little as you choose in this oceanfront place, which has a menu to match a variety of budgets and hankerings. It's known for its fresh fish, but you may also order steaks and prime rib, steak-and-seafood combos, chicken dishes, or burgers. Or simply make a meal of appetizers: fresh oysters, steamed clams, shrimp cocktail, and ceviche. Salads and sandwiches are available at lunch, and there are sunset dinner specials Sunday to Thursday from 5 to 7pm for $9.95. The outdoor tables here are prime real estate, especially when the sky begins to blush. The ambience couldn't be livelier. Ask your service person to explain how the restaurant got its name.

Ichiban. 1441 Garnet Ave. ☎ **619/270-5755.** Reservations not accepted. Sushi $4–$9. No credit cards. Mon–Sat 11am–2:30pm and 5–9:30pm, Saun 5–9:30pm. JAPANESE.

Trendy 20-somethings have claimed this budget sushi shop as their own, and for good reason. The fish is morning fresh, the service is excellent, and the crowd is always lively. While the dining room is decidedly downscale, the unstudied casual atmosphere is one of the main attractions. Diners order at the counter and are then served at a table. In addition to sushi, there's chicken teriyaki, ginger chicken, mixed fried seafood, vegetable sukiyaki, and fried salmon. Japanese beer and sake are served.

LA JOLLA

Most of La Jolla's top restaurants are clustered along Prospect Street and Pearl Street in the village.

VERY EXPENSIVE

✪ **George's at the Cove.** 1250 Prospect St. ☎ **619/454-4244.** Reservations recommended. Main courses $16.50–$39.50. AE, DC, DISC, MC, V. Mon–Thurs 11:30am–10pm, Fri–Sat 11:30am–11pm, Sun 11am–10pm. CALIFORNIA.

This popular local restaurant gets raves for its seafood dishes, creative pastas, ocean view, and great sunsets in summer. For lunch, you can go light with a soup and salad or have one of the many seafood dishes. For dinner, start with the house specialty smoked chicken soup and proceed to the rack of lamb; sautéed venison chops with yam cakes; steak; or mixed grill of shrimp, king salmon, and swordfish with three sauces. On a recent visit, I was disappointed with the chocolate soufflé-cake dessert— chocoholics might do better getting a fix across the street at the Rocky Mountain

Chocolate Factory. Owner George Hauer, whom you might meet Tuesday to Saturday, started out as a waiter in Pacific Beach and became a legend in San Diego's restaurant business. Upstairs, the more casual Café Bar and George's Ocean Terrace have indoor and outdoor seating overlooking La Jolla Cove and offer light fare of sandwiches, soups, salads, and pastas, as well as lower prices. Valet parking is available for $3 during the day, $4 at night.

EXPENSIVE

Putnam's Restaurant & Bar. In the Colonial Inn, 910 Prospect St. ☎ **619/454-2181.** Reservations recommended. Main courses $12–$21. AE, DC, MC, V. Mon–Thurs 7–10am, 11am–2:30pm, and 5–10pm; Fri 7–10am, 11am–2:30pm, and 5–11pm; Sat 7am–2:30pm and 5–11pm, Sun 7am–2:30pm and 5–10pm. Valet parking $5. NEW AMERICAN/CALIFORNIA.

When the Colonial Inn was completed in 1928 it housed a drugstore named Putnam's, known in La Jolla as "Putty's." Gregory Peck's father was the pharmacist, and locals flocked there to buy their sundries and enjoy a soda. Today that corner of the hotel is the site of Putnam's Restaurant, which retains an elegant, old world atmosphere, complete with polished terrazzo floors, gleaming woodwork, brass fixtures, crisp white tablecloths, and fresh flowers. The dinner menu changes seasonally, but often contains grilled farm-raised chicken with honey-onion marmalade, grilled marinated duck breast with golden tomato curry sauce, grilled Atlantic salmon filet, and roasted rack of lamb with mustard-herb crust.

Top o' the Cove. 1216 Prospect St. ☎ **619/454-7779.** Fax 619/454-3783. Reservations recommended on weekends. Main courses $25–$30; Sun brunch $18.50. AE, DC, MC, V. Daily 11:30am–10:30pm. Valet parking $5. CONTINENTAL.

This restaurant, in a historic cottage with fig trees out front, has fireplaces glowing on chilly evenings, an intimate piano bar, and a gazebo and patio for dining on balmy days—perfect for Sunday brunch with champagne, fruit, pastries, one of 10 main dishes, and coffee or tea. Lunch is on the light side—creative salads, fettuccine dishes, or a tenderloin burger on a sourdough bun. Dinner is romantic and more lavish, with fish, duck, veal, lamb, and venison prepared and served elegantly, and jackets suggested for men. A computerized wine list keeps track of the 10,000-plus bottles in the cellar. The less expensive upstairs bar/bistro is open until midnight. Proprietor and community dynamo Ron Zappardino heads a stellar staff.

MODERATE

✪ **The Cottage.** 7702 Fay Ave. (at Kline). ☎ **619/454-8409.** Reservations accepted for dinner only. Breakfast and lunch $5–$7; main courses $7–$12 at dinner. MC, V. June–Sept, daily 7:30am–3pm and 4–9pm; Oct–May, daily 7:30am–3pm. LIGHT FARE.

This turn-of-the-century Cottage, on a sunny corner in downtown La Jolla, is light and airy inside, with booths and tables under a skylight. Outside there's a welcoming white fence, trellis, and large brick patio. You can start the day with farm-fresh eggs most any style, granola and fresh fruit, oatmeal pancakes, Belgian waffles, or a vegetable frittata. The dinner menu (summer only) features California bistro cuisine. The Cottage bakery makes *wonderful* desserts, pastries, and bread (with the exception of focaccia). There's no smoking inside or out.

INEXPENSIVE

✪ **Brockton Villa.** 1235 Coast Blvd. (across from the La Jolla Cove). ☎ **619/454-7393.** Reservations accepted for Sun brunch (call by Thurs). Breakfast $4–7.25; main courses $8–$14 at dinner. AE, DISC, MC, V. Mon–Wed 8am–5pm, Thurs–Sun 8am–9pm (later in summer). Validated parking in Coast Walk Shopping Center. CALIFORNIA.

Located in a beach cottage dating from 1894, Brockton Villa offers good food, a great view of the La Jolla Cove, and charming historic surroundings. The blue-and-white bungalow has a wooden floor that's appropriately worn and perhaps not entirely level. Diners can sit inside, outside on the patio, or on a semi-enclosed porch. Our favorite dinner is the basil ravioli with saffron shrimp sauce, and our lunch choice is Shari's turkey meatloaf sandwich on toasted sourdough bread with spicy tomato mint chutney. For breakfast I have difficulty choosing between homemade granola, "coast toast" (French toast that resembles a soufflé), and Greek steamers (three eggs steam scrambled using the espresso machine and mixed with feta, tomato, and basil). There's no smoking allowed, and no access for people with disabilities.

S D'Lish. 7514 Girard Ave. (at Pearl St.). ☎ **619/459-8118.** Reservations accepted. Main courses $6–$9. AE, DC, DISC, MC, V. Sun–Thurs 11:30am–10pm, Fri–Sat 11:30am–11pm. Free off-street parking. CONTEMPORARY ITALIAN.

This is the place for one of those trendy wood-fired pizzas with designer toppings you wouldn't have imagined a decade ago. Our favorite is the Greek grilled chicken, but I also like the pizza with shrimp, mozzarella, Roma tomatoes, kalamata olives, sun-dried tomatoes, pesto sauce, and pine nuts. The salads make it painless to feel virtuous when ordering. There are also good pasta dishes, especially the shrimp-scallop angel hair, one of many heart-healthy choices. *Here's a hot tip:* Don't sit upstairs when the weather's warm.

CORONADO

Bay Beach Cafe. 1201 1st St. (in the Ferry Landing Marketplace). ☎ **619/435-4900.** Reservations recommended for dinner on weekends. Main courses $9–$17. AE, DISC, MC, V. Daily 7am–10:30pm. Free parking. AMERICAN/SEAFOOD.

You can't beat the views at the Bay Beach Cafe: the San Diego skyline across the water. Dine indoors or alfresco, and choose from items such as daily fresh fish specials, vegetarian pasta, and roasted free-range chicken with wild-mushroom sauce. There's also a bar menu featuring sandwiches and burgers.

S Mandarin Cafe. In Coronado Plaza, 1330 Orange Ave., second floor. ☎ **619/435-2771.** Reservations not accepted. Main courses $5.75–$12.50. AE, MC, V. Mon–Thurs 11:30am–10pm, Fri 11:30am–11pm, Sat 3–11pm, Sun 1–10pm. Free parking with validation. MANDARIN/ SZECHUAN.

Located within steps of the beach, this is a local favorite, a reliable standby for those times when nothing but Chinese food will satisfy the munchies. House favorites are the honey shrimp and the sizzling seafood noodles. The kitchen will hold the MSG, sugar, and salt on request.

✪ Primavera. 932 Orange Ave. ☎ **619/435-0454.** Reservations recommended. Main courses $11–$20. AE, DC, DISC, MC, V. Mon–Fri 11am–2:30pm and 5–10:30pm, Sat–Sun 5–10:30pm. Free parking. NORTHERN ITALIAN.

The lovely dining room at Primavera is the setting for delicious, creatively prepared Italian dishes. One of the most popular appetizers is bagna caoda primavera (grilled eggplant, roasted red peppers, sun-dried tomatoes, Montrachet, and parmesan cheese, with bagna caoda sauce). Main courses include angel-hair pasta with mushrooms, garlic, prosciutto, capers, anchovies, and herbs; osso buco; and chicken breast with eggplant, mozzarella cheese, mushrooms, and wine sauce. For dessert, I can't resist the homemade tiramisù. This is the best restaurant in Coronado, but the last time I dined here the service felt slightly robotic.

5 Beaches

San Diego County is blessed with 70 miles of sandy coastline and more than 30 beaches that attract surfers, snorkelers, swimmers, and sunbathers. In summer the beaches teem with locals and visitors alike. The rest of the year they're popular places to walk and jog, and surfers don wet suits to pursue their passion.

The following are some of San Diego's most accessible beaches, each with its own personality and devotees. If you're interested in others, *The California Coastal Access Handbook,* published by the California Coastal Commission, is helpful. All California beaches are public to the mean high-tide line. If you plan to poke around in tidepools, get a tide chart, available free or for a nominal charge from many surf and diving shops, including **Emerald City Surf Shop,** at 118 Orange Ave., Coronado, (☎ 619/435-6677); and **San Diego Divers Supply,** at 5701 La Jolla Boulevard., La Jolla (☎ 619/459/2691).

OCEAN BEACH Near the pier off I-8 and Sunset Cliffs Blvd., this is surfers' and sunset lovers' heaven and the stuff Beach Boys songs are made of. Not far away are Dog Beach, where four-legged beach lovers roam unleashed, and Garbage Beach, another surfing spot (don't worry—it doesn't live up to its name).

MISSION BAY PARK In this 4,600-acre aquatic playground you'll discover 27 miles of bayfront, 17 miles of oceanfront beaches, picnic areas, children's playgrounds, and paths for biking, roller skating, and jogging. The bay lends itself to windsurfing, sailing, jet skiing, waterskiing, and fishing. There are dozens of access points; one of the most popular is off I-5 at Clairemont Dr., where there's a visitor information center.

PACIFIC BEACH Here you'll find a popular beach and boardwalk for meeting friends, grabbing a bite to eat, jogging, biking, or inline skating. It runs along Ocean Blvd. (just west of Mission Blvd.), north of Pacific Beach Dr.

MISSION BEACH Surfing is popular year round here. The long beach and boardwalk extend from Pacific Beach Dr. south to Belmont Park and beyond to the jetty.

BONITA COVE, MARINER'S POINT & MISSION POINT Facing Mission Bay in South Mission Beach, these spots are perfect for families, with calm waters, grassy areas for picnicking, and playground equipment.

WINDANSEA One of California's finest surfing beaches, this area along Neptune Street in La Jolla achieved cult status in 1968 when the serious surfers who rode its waves were the subject of Tom Wolfe's book *The Pump House Gang.* Hang around for the usually memorable sunset.

LA JOLLA COVE The protected, calm waters here—praised as the clearest along the California coast—attract swimmers, snorkelers, scuba divers, and families on outings. There's a small sandy beach and on the cliffs above, the Ellen Browning Scripps Park. The cove's "look but don't touch" policy protects the colorful Garibaldi, California's state fish, plus other marine life, including abalone, octopus, and lobster. The unique Underwater Park stretches from here to the northern end of Torrey Pines State Reserve and incorporates kelp forests, artificial reefs, two deep submarine canyons, and tidal pools.

LA JOLLA SHORES BEACH A mile-long flat stretch of beach, it's popular for jogging, swimming, and body and board surfing for beginners. Families often come here, where lifeguards are on duty year round.

BLACK'S BEACH   The area's unofficial nude beach, it lies between La Jolla Shores Beach and Torrey Pines State Beach. Below some steep cliffs, it's out of the way and not easy to reach. To get here, take North Torrey Pines Road, park at the Glider Port, and walk from there. *Note:* Though the water is shallow and pleasant for wading, this area is known for its rip currents.

DEL MAR   After a visit to the famous fairgrounds that host the Del Mar Thoroughbred Club, you may want to make tracks for the beach, a long stretch of sand backed by grassy cliffs and a playground area. Del Mar is about 15 miles from downtown San Diego.

NORTHERN SAN DIEGO COUNTY   Those inclined to venture even farther north in San Diego County won't be disappointed. The Pacific Coast Highway (Calif. 1) leads to some inviting beaches, such as these in Encinitas: peaceful Boneyards Beach, Swami's Beach for surfing, and Moonlight Beach, popular with families and volleyball buffs. Farthest north in this beach-blessed county is Oceanside, which has one of the West Coast's longest wooden piers and several popular surfing areas.

CORONADO BEACH   Lovely, wide, and sparkling white, this romantic beach is conducive to strolling and lingering, especially in late afternoon. It fronts Ocean Blvd. and is especially pretty in front of the Hotel del Coronado. The islands visible from here, but 18 miles away, are named Los Coronados, and they belong to Mexico.

IMPERIAL BEACH   Half an hour south of San Diego by car or trolley and only a few minutes from the Mexican border lies Imperial Beach. Besides being popular with surfers, it hosts the annual U.S. Open Sandcastle Competition in July, with world-class sand creations ranging from sea scenes to dragons to dinosaurs.

6 Ménagerie à Trois: The Zoo, Wild Animal Park & Sea World

✪ **San Diego Zoo.** 2920 Zoo Dr., Balboa Park. ☎ **619/234-3153** or 619/231-1515. Admission $15 adults, $6 children 3–11. AE, DISC, MC, V. July–Labor Day, daily 9am–9pm; the rest of the year, daily 9am–4pm. Bus: 7A or 7B.

More than 3,500 animals reside at this world-famous zoo, founded in 1916 with a handful of animals originally brought here for the 1915–16 Panama-California International Exposition. Many of the buildings you see in surrounding Balboa Park were built for the Exposition. The zoo's founder was Dr. Harry Wegeforth, a local physician and lifelong animal lover, who once braved the fury of an injured tiger in order to toss needed medicine into its mouth while it was roaring.

In the early days of the zoo, "Dr. Harry" would take native southwestern animals like rattlesnakes and sea lions to trade around the world for more exotic species; this tradition is carried on today. In September 1996, the Zoo received two giant pandas from the People's Republic of China. Shi Shi, a 16-year-old male, and Bai Yun, a 5-year-old female, live in a posh panda-minum that cost the zoo over $1 million. The pandas are expected to be at the zoo for 12 years.

The zoo is also a botanical garden, representing over 6,500 species of flora from many climate zones, all installed to help simulate native environments for the animals that live here. In fact, some say the plants are actually worth more than the animals.

It's famous for its rare and exotic species: cuddly koalas from Australia, long-billed kiwis from New Zealand, wild Przewalski's horses from Mongolia, lowland gorillas from Africa, and giant tortoises from the Galapagos. The usual lions, elephants, giraffes, and tigers are present too, not to mention a great number of tropical birds. Most of the animals are housed in barless, moated enclosures that resemble their natural habitats. These habitats include African Kopje, Tiger River, Sun Bear Forest, Scripps Aviary, Flamingo Lagoon (renovated in 1996), Gorilla Tropics, and Hippo Beach. New polar bear, wombat, and okapi exhibits opened in 1996.

The zoo offers two types of bus tours—both provide a narrated overview and you see 75% of the park. You can choose the 35-minute guided bus tour—where you get on the bus and complete a circuit around the zoo (the cost is $4 for adults and $3 for kids 3 to 11). Or you might opt to take the Kangaroo Bus, which for $8 for adults and $5 for children provides unlimited use; you can get on and off the bus as many times as you desire at any of the eight stops and even complete the circuit more than once. Alternatively, you can get an aerial perspective via the Skyfari which costs $1 per person each way. Packages are available that include zoo admission, bus tour, and Skyfari Tramway.

The Children's Zoo is scaled to a youngster's viewpoint. There's a nursery with baby animals and a petting area where kids can cuddle up to sheep, goats, and the like.

For a preview, the Zoo has an Internet home page at **http.//www.sandiegozoo.org.**

Sea World. 1720 S. Shores Rd., Mission Bay. ☎ **619/226-3901.** Admission $29.95 adults, $25.45 seniors 55 and older, $21.95 children 3–11, free for children 2 and under. DISC, MC, V. Parking $5 per car, $2 per motorcycle, and $7 per RV. Mid-June to Aug, daily 9am–11pm; the rest of the year, daily 10am–5pm. Bus: 9 or 81. Exit I-5 west onto Sea World Dr.

Sea World is one of the best-promoted attractions in California. The 150-acre, multi-million-dollar aquatic playground is a zoo and showplace for marine mammals, made politically correct with a nominally "educational" atmosphere. Several successive 4-ton black-and-white killer whales have functioned as the park's mascot, all named Shamu. At its heart, Sea World is a family entertainment center where the performers are dolphins, otters, sea lions, walruses, and seals. Shows are presented continuously throughout the day, while visitors rotate to various theaters to watch the performances.

The 2-acre hands-on park called Shamu's Happy Harbor encourages kids to handle everything, including a pretend pirate ship, with plenty of netted towers, tube crawls, slides, and chances to get wet. The newest attractions are Baywatch at Sea World, a waterski show named for the popular TV show; Bermuda Triangle, an adventure ride; and Shamu Backstage, which makes it possible for visitors to get up close and personal with killer whales.

The Dolphin Interaction Program creates an opportunity for people to interact with bottlenose dolphins. Although this program does not allow swimming with the dolphins, it gives you the opportunity to wade waist-deep into the water and plenty of time to stroke the mammals and give commands like the trainers. This 2-hour program (1 hour of education and instruction, 15 minutes of wetsuit fitting, and 45 minutes of interaction in the water with the dolphins) costs $125 per person ($95 per person for SeaWorld members). Space is limited to eight people per day, so advance reservations are required. Participants must be 13 years old or older.

Although Sea World is best known as Shamu's home, the facility also plays an important role in rescuing and rehabilitating animals found beached along the San Diego coast—more than 300 seals, sea lions, marine birds, and dolphins in a recent year. Sea World also helps out with injured marine species in other parts of the world, such as the oil-soaked victims of the *Exxon Valdez* disaster in Alaska. You might like to take a guided tour of the park and get an insiders view for $6 per adult and $5 per child.

San Diego Attractions

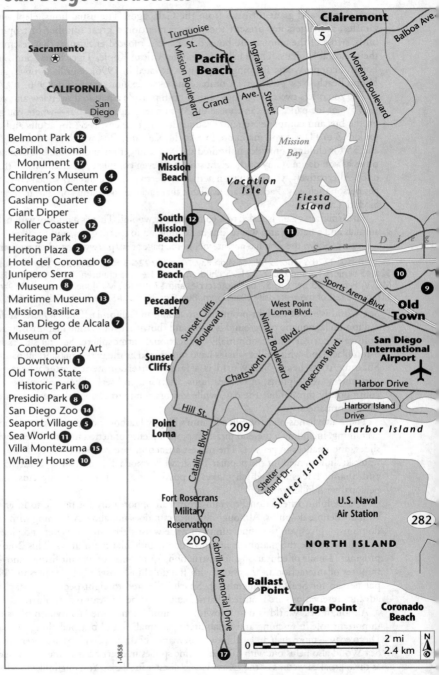

Belmont Park 12
Cabrillo National
    Monument 17
Children's Museum 4
Convention Center 6
Gaslamp Quarter 3
Giant Dipper
    Roller Coaster 12
Heritage Park 9
Horton Plaza 2
Hotel del Coronado 16
Junípero Serra
    Museum 8
Maritime Museum 13
Mission Basilica
    San Diego de Alcala 7
Museum of
    Contemporary Art
    Downtown 1
Old Town State
    Historic Park 10
Presidio Park 8
San Diego Zoo 14
Seaport Village 5
Sea World 11
Villa Montezuma 15
Whaley House 10

CALIFORNIA
Sacramento
San Diego

Clairemont
Turquoise St.
Pacific Beach
Balboa Ave.
Mission Boulevard
Ingraham Street
Morena Boulevard
Grand Ave.
Mission Bay
North Mission Beach
Vacation Isle
Fiesta Island
South Mission Beach
Ocean Beach
Pescadero Beach
Sports Arena Blvd.
Old Town
West Point Loma Blvd.
Sunset Cliffs Boulevard
Nimitz Boulevard
Rosecrans Blvd.
San Diego International Airport
Sunset Cliffs
Chatsworth
Harbor Drive
Harbor Island Drive
Harbor Island
Hill St.
Point Loma
Catalina Blvd.
Shelter Island Dr.
Shelter Island
U.S. Naval Air Station
Fort Rosecrans Military Reservation
Cabrillo Memorial Drive
NORTH ISLAND
Ballast Point
Zuniga Point
Coronado Beach
0   2 mi
    2.4 km
N

1-0858

Downtown

Date Street
Cedar Street
Beech Street
Ash Street
A Street
B Street
C Street
Broadway
Date Street

Drive
Highway
Harbor
Pacific
Kettner Blvd.
State Street
Union Street
Front Street

4th Ave.
5th Ave.
6th Ave.
7th Ave.
8th Ave.
9th Ave.
10th Ave.
11th Ave.

E Street
F Street
G Street

❶

❷

❸

Market Street

❹

❺

Harbor Dr.

1st Ave.
2nd Ave.
3rd Ave.

❻

**Gaslamp
Quarter**

Island Avenue
J Street
K Street

Vista Rd.
Linda
Friars Rd.
River

❼

8

❽

**Hillcrest/
Uptown**

Pacific Hwy.

5

163

1st Ave.
5th Ave.

**Balboa
Park**

❶❹

Park Blvd.

805

15

94

Ash Street
Broadway

SAN DIEGO

❶❸

❶❺

Ave.
Euclid

3rd St.
4th St.
Orange Ave.

San Diego–Coronado
Bay Bridge (Toll)

National
Ave.

Logan
Ave.

Division St.

**National
City**

8th St.

❶❻

Silver

75

805

✪ **Wild Animal Park.** 15500 San Pasqual Valley Rd., Escondido (30 miles north of San Diego). ☎ **619/747-8702.** Admission $18.95 adults, $11.95 children 3–11, free for children 2 and under. AE, DISC, MC, V. Daily 9am–4pm, with extended hours in summer. Parking $3 per vehicle. Take I-15 to Via Rancho Pkwy. and follow the signs from there for about 3 miles.

Many zoos could learn a lesson from the Wild Animal Park: Over 3,000 animals, many of them endangered species, roam freely over 2,200 acres, while the humans are enclosed. This living arrangement encourages breeding colonies, so it's not surprising that more than 75 white rhinoceroses were have been born here. Several species of other animals that had vanished from the wilds have been reintroduced to their natural habitats from stocks bred here. The park is also is a botanical preserve with more than two million plants, including 300 endangered species.

The best way to see the animals is by riding the 5-mile monorail (included in the price of admission); for the best views sit on the right side. During the 50-minute ride, as you pass through areas resembling Africa and Asia you'll learn interesting tidbits—did you know that rhinos are susceptible to sunburn and mosquito bites? Trains leave every 20 minutes; you can watch informative videos while you wait in the stations. On the 1³/4-mile Kilimanjaro hiking trail, you'll see tigers, elephants, and cheetahs close up, as well as the Australian rain forest and views of East Africa.

Photo tours take place May to September on Wednesday, Thursday, Saturday, and Sunday, costing $60 or $85 depending on the tour. Stroller and wheelchair rentals are available. Take a jacket along; it can get cold in the open-air monorail. Local public transportation will get you here, but it takes three buses and 3¹/2 hours. Gray Line offers a 7-hour tour for $40 for adults and $24 for kids, including admission and transportation (for more information, call 619/491-0011).

7 Exploring the Area

BALBOA PARK

Balboa Park is one of the nation's largest, loveliest, and most important municipal greenbelts. This is no simple city park: It boasts walkways, gardens, historical buildings, a couple of restaurants, an ornate pavilion with one of the world's largest outdoor organs, and the world-famous San Diego Zoo (see above). Stroll along **El Prado,** the park's main street, and admire the distinctive Spanish-Mediterranean buildings, which house an amazing array of museums.

Entry to the park is free, but most of its museums have admission charges and varying open hours. A free tram will transport you around the park. Below are the highlights:

✪ **Aerospace Museum and International Aerospace Hall of Fame** (☎ 619/234-8291): Great achievers and achievements in the history of aviation and aerospace are celebrated by this superb collection of historical aircraft and related artifacts, including art, models, dioramas, and films.

Museum of Art (☎ 619/232-7931): The impressive painting and sculpture collections here include outstanding Italian Renaissance and Dutch and Spanish baroque art. Exhibits in the ground-floor Grant-Munger Gallery include works by Monet, Toulouse-Lautrec, Renoir, Pissarro, and Van Gogh. Upstairs in the Fitch Gallery is El Greco's *Penitent St. Peter,* and in the Gluck Gallery hangs Modigliani's *Boy with Blue Eyes* and Braque's *Coquelicots.*

✪ **Museum of Photographic Arts** (☎ 619/239-5262): One of the finest museums in the city, the Museum of Photographic Arts occupies an imitation Spanish baroque building that served as part of Charles Foster Kane's Xanadu in the film *Citizen Kane.* The museum displays a wide range of historic and contemporary work and has made a commitment to issue-oriented photography.

Balboa Park

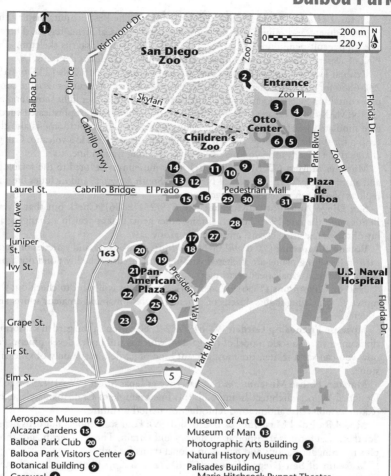

Aerospace Museum 🅩
Alcazar Gardens 🅕
Balboa Park Club 🅪
Balboa Park Visitors Center 🅭
Botanical Building 🅱
Carousel 🅐
Casa de Balboa 🅰
   Hall of Champions Sports Museum
   Museum of Photographic Arts
   Museum of San Diego History
   Model Railroad Museum
Casa del Prado 🅱
Federal Building 🅫
Hall of Nations 🅜
House of Charm
   Mingei International
     Museum of World Folk Art
   San Diego Art Institure 🅖
House of Pacific Relations
 International Cottages 🅝
Japanese Friendship Garden 🅮
Marston House 🅐
Municipal Museum 🅩

Museum of Art 🅛
Museum of Man 🅓
Photographic Arts Building 🅔
Natural History Museum 🅖
Palisades Building
   Marie Hitchcock Puppet Theater
   Recital Hall 🅪
Reuben H. Fleet Space Theater
 & Science Center 🅫
San Diego Automotive Museum 🅪
San Diego Miniature Railroad 🅒
San Diego Zoo 🅑
Sculpture Garden 🅛
Simon Edison Centre for the Performing Arts 🅝
   Old Globe Theatre
   Cassius Carter Centre Stage
   Lowell Davies Festival Theatre
Spanish Village Art Center 🅕
Spreckels Organ Pavilion 🅪
Starlight Bowl 🅪
Timken Museum of Art 🅚
United Nations Building 🅜

1-0859

617

Natural History Museum (☎ 619/232-3821): The best exhibits display the plants, animals, and minerals of the San Diego and Baja California region. There's also a Foucault pendulum, a seismograph, and a life-size Allosaurus skeleton. The Hall of Desert Ecology features a discovery lab, with living desert denizens.

Reuben H. Fleet Space Theater and Science Center (☎ 619/238-1233, or 619/232-6866 for advance ticket sales): Easily the park's busiest museum, this large complex contains a Science Center with 65 hands-on exhibits, a laser light show, and an OMNIMAX movie theater with a 76-foot screen. In the theater, sophisticated effects give simulated journeys an incredible feeling of reality. The giant dome is also the setting for thrilling travelogs and voyages under the sea and inside a volcano. Call to charge tickets in advance; you may save yourself a long wait in line.

Museum of Man (☎ 619/239-2001): This museum is devoted to the sociology and anthropology of the peoples of North and South America, and includes life-size replicas of a dozen varieties of *Homo sapiens*.

San Diego Automotive Museum (☎ 619/231-2886): Check out that classic Bentley and the rare 1948 Tucker, among other gems that appear in a changing array of shows featuring classic, antique, and exotic cars.

Botanical Museum (☎ 619/235-1100): More than a thousand varieties of tropical and flowering plants are sheltered within this structure. The lily pond out front attracts the occasional street performer.

Hall of Champions (☎ 619/234-2544): Sports fans will want to check out this museum, which highlights dozens of different professional and amateur sports and athletes.

Japanese Friendship Garden (☎ 619/232-2780): Stop in the garden's information center to see a scale model of the garden, which is still under development. For now you can see a sekitei, the most ancient kind of garden, made only of sand and stone.

Marston House Museum, on Balboa Drive at Upas Street (☎ 619/232-6203): Designed by local architect Irving Gill, this fine example of Craftsman-style architecture exhibits fine antique and reproduction period furniture.

Model Railroad Museum (☎ 619/696-0199): Four scale-model railroads depict Southern California's transportation history and terrain. There's a terrific gift shop, plus multimedia exhibits and hands-on Lionel trains for kids.

Museum of San Diego History (☎ 619/232-6203): Photographs and other changing exhibits tell the city's story.

Sprekels Organ Pavilion (☎ 619/226-0819): The ornate pavilion houses a fantastic organ with more than 4,000 individual pipes. Free Sunday concerts are given at 2pm.

Timken Museum of Art (☎ 619/239-5548): On display here is the Putnam Foundation's collection of American and European paintings, including works by Boucher, Rembrandt, and Brueghel. The private gallery also exhibits a rare collection of Russian icons and 19th-century American paintings.

MORE ATTRACTIONS IN & AROUND SAN DIEGO

✪ **Cabrillo National Monument.** 1800 Cabrillo Memorial Dr., Point Loma. ☎ **619/557-5450.** Admission $4 per vehicle, $2 for walk-ins, free for seniors 62 and over (with a National Parks Service Golden Age Passport) and children 16 and under. Daily 9am–5:15pm. Follow I-5 or I-8 to Rosecrans St. (Calif. 209), which leads to Point Loma and the monument via Catalina Blvd.

Enjoy stunning views while you're learning about California history at this monument commemorating Juan Rodríguez Cabrillo, the European discoverer of America's west coast. At the restored Old Point Loma Lighthouse, visitors are treated to a sweeping vista of the ocean, bays, islands, mountains, valleys, and plains that make up San Diego. From mid-December to February the lighthouse is a good vantage point for watching the migration of the Pacific gray whales. National Park rangers offer free 30-minute films about the monument daily from 10am to 4pm, and there are tidepools that beg for exploration. A free film about the whale migration is shown during winter.

Children's Museum of San Diego. 200 W. Island Ave. ☎ **619/233-8792.** Admission $5 ($2.50 for seniors), free for children under 2. Tues–Sat 10am–4:30pm, Sun 11am–4:30pm. Trolley: Convention Center stop; the museum is a block away.

This interactive museum encourages hands-on participation. It provides ongoing supervised activities, as well as a monthly special celebration, with changing exhibits every month. A big draw for kids 2 to 10 is the indoor and outdoor art studio. There's also a theater with costumes for budding actors to don.

Maritime Museum. 1306 N. Harbor Dr. ☎ **619/234-9153.** Admission (to all three ships) $5 adults, $4 seniors and children 13–17, $2 children 6–12. DISC, MC, V. Daily 9am–8pm. Bus: 4, 9, 29, 34, 34A, or 35.

This nautical museum consists of three restored historic vessels docked downtown at the Embarcadero. *The Berkeley,* a propeller-driven ferry launched in 1898, participated in the evacuation of San Francisco after the Great Earthquake and fire of 1906. *The Medea,* a steam yacht built in Scotland in 1904, was used in both world wars. *The Star of India,* launched in 1863, is the oldest square-rigged merchant vessel still afloat. Each vessel can be boarded and explored. April to October you can even watch movies on the deck.

☉ Museum of Contemporary Art, Downtown (MCA). 1001 Kettner Blvd. (at Broadway). ☎ **619/234-1001.** Admission $4 adults; $2 students, military with ID, and seniors; 50¢ children 5–12, free for kids 4 and under, free for everyone the first Tues of each month. AE, MC, V. Tues–Thurs and Sat–Sun 10:30am–5:30pm, Fri 10:30am–8pm. Parking $2 with validation at America Plaza Complex. Trolley: America Plaza.

Two large galleries and two smaller ones present changing exhibitions of distinguished contemporary artists. Lectures and tours for adults and children are offered.

Villa Montezuma. 1925 K St. (at 20th Ave.). ☎ **619/239-2211.** Admission $3 adults ($5 in combination with Marston House), free for children 12 and under. MC, V. Sat–Sun noon–4:30pm; in Dec, Thurs–Sun noon–4:30pm. Bus: 3, 3A, 4, 5, 16, or 105 to Market and Imperial sts.

Just east of downtown, this stunning mansion was built in 1887 for then internationally acclaimed musician and author Jesse Shepard. Lush with Victoriana, it features stained-glass windows depicting Mozart, Beethoven, Sappho, Rubens, St. Cecilia (patron saint of musicians), and other notables. The San Diego Historical Society painstakingly restored the house, on the National Register of Historic Places, and furnished it with period pieces. Unfortunately, the neighborhood is not as fashionable as the house, but it's safe to park your car here in the daytime. If you love Victorian houses, don't miss this one for its quirkiness.

OLD TOWN & BEYOND: A LOOK AT CALIFORNIA'S BEGINNINGS

The birthplace of San Diego—indeed, of California—Old Town brings back to life Mexican California, which existed here until the mid-1800s. You can get to Old Town on the trolley. Free walking tours leave daily at 2pm from the visitor center at **Old Town State Historic Park** (☎ 619/220-5422), located at the head of the pedestrian walkway that's the continuation of San Diego Avenue. Admission to the center, open daily from 10am to 5pm, is free. Among the highlights are the following:

Heritage Park. 2455 Heritage Park Row (corner of Juan and Harney sts.), Old Town. ☎ **619/ 694-3049.** Free admission. Daily 9:30am–3pm. Tours ($10, including tea) Tues–Sun 2:30–5pm. Bus: 4 or 5/105.

This small 7.8-acre park is filled with seven original 19th-century houses moved here from other places and given new uses, among them a bed-and-breakfast inn, a doll shop, and a gift shop.

Junípero Serra Museum. 2727 Presidio Dr., Presidio Park, Old Town. ☎ **619/297-3258.** Admission $3 adults, free for children 12 and under. MC, V. Tues–Sat 10am–4:30pm, Sun noon– 4:30pm. Take I-8 to the Taylor St. exit, turn right on Taylor, then left on Presidio Dr., or take bus a bus to the intersection of Taylor and Juan sts. and walk uphill.

Perched on a hill above Old Town, the stately mission-style building overlooks the spot where California began. Here in 1769 the first mission and first nonnative settlement on the west coast of the United States and Canada were founded. Inside, the museum's exhibits introduce visitors to California's origins, and to the Native American, Spanish, and Mexican peoples who first called this place home. On display are their belongings, from cannons to cookware. The mission remained San Diego's only settlement until the 1820s, when families began to move down the hill into what is now known as Old Town. Watch an ongoing archeological dig uncover more of the items used by early settlers.

The museum is located in **Presidio Park,** called the "Plymouth Rock of the Pacific." The large cross in the park was made from floor tile from the Presidio ruins. Sculptor Arthur Puntnam made the statues of Father Serra, founder of the missions in California, and the Native American. Climb up to Inspiration Point for a sweeping view of the area.

Mission Basilica San Diego de Alcala. 10818 San Diego Mission Rd., Mission Valley. ☎ **619/281-8449.** Admission $2 adults, $1 seniors and students, 50¢ children 12 and under. Daily 9am–5pm; mass daily at 7am and 5:30pm. Bus: 6, 16, 25, 43, or 81. Take I-8 to Mission Gorge Rd. to Twain Ave.

Established in 1769, this was the first link in a chain of 21 missions founded by Spanish missionary Junípero Serra. In 1774 the mission was moved to its present site for agricultural reasons and to separate Native American converts from a fortress that included the original building. A few bricks belonging to the original mission can be seen in Presidio Park in Old Town. Mass is said regularly in this still-active Catholic parish.

Whaley House. 2482 San Diego Ave. ☎ **619/298-2482.** Admission $4 adults, $3 seniors 65 and over, $2 children 5–16. Daily 10am–5pm.

In 1856 this striking two-story house (the first one in these parts) just outside Old Town State Historic Park was built for Thomas Whaley and his family. Whaley was a New Yorker who arrived here via San Francisco, where he had been lured by the Gold Rush. The house is one of only two authenticated haunted houses in California, and 10,000 schoolchildren come here each year to see for themselves. Exhibits include a life mask of Abraham Lincoln, one of only six made; the spinet piano used in the movie *Gone with the Wind;* and the concert piano that accompanied Swedish soprano Jenny Lind on her final U.S. tour in 1852. Director June Reading will make you feel at home, in spite of the ghost.

LA JOLLA

Some folks just enjoy driving around La Jolla, taking in the sea views and the 360° vista from the top of **Mount Soledad.** However, our community also offers other attractions, including **Torrey Pines State Reserve** (☎ 619/755-2063), which has hiking trails with wonderful ocean views and a chance to see the rare torrey pine. Access is via North Torrey Pines Road. The trails are free of charge; parking costs $4 per car, $3 for seniors.

✪ **Museum of Contemporary Art, San Diego.** 700 Prospect St. ☎ **619/454-3541.** Admission $4 adults; $2 students, military with ID, and seniors; free for children 11 and under; free for everyone the first Tues of each month. Take the Ardath Rd. exit off I-5 north or the La Jolla Village Dr. West exit off I-5 south; take Torrey Pines Rd. to Prospect Pl. and turn right; Prospect Pl. becomes Prospect St.

Focusing primarily on work produced since 1950, the museum is known internationally for its permanent collection and thought-provoking exhibitions. It reopened in March 1996 after being closed for 2 years while it underwent a major renovation and expansion. The ocean views from the galleries are gorgeous.

Stephen Birch Aquarium-Museum. At the Scripps Institution of Oceanography, 2300 Expedition Way. ☎ **619/534-3474** for a recording. Admission $6.50 adults, $5.50 seniors, $4.50 students, $3.50 children 3–12. AE, MC, V. Daily 9am–pm. Take I-5 to La Jolla Village Dr. West, which turns into North Torrey Pines Rd., then turn left at Expedition Way. Parking $3.

Part of the Scripps Institution of Oceanography, a branch of the University of California San Diego, the Aquarium-Museum offers close-up views of the Pacific Ocean in 33 marine-life tanks. The giant kelp forest is particularly impressive. World renowned for its oceanic research, Scripps offers visitors a chance to view its marine aquarium and artificial outdoor tidepools. The museum has interpretive exhibits on the current and historical research done at the institution, which has been in existence since 1903. In 1997 the Aquarium will highlight the Year of the Reef with special exhibits and programs.

Stuart Collection. At the University of California San Diego (UCSD). ☎ **619/534-2117.** Free admission. From La Jolla, take Torrey Pines Rd. to La Jolla Village Dr., turn right, go 2 blocks to Gilman Dr., and turn left onto the campus; in about a block the information booth will be visible on the right.

The Stuart Collection is a work in progress on a large scale. The still-growing collection consists of site-related sculptures by leading contemporary artists placed throughout the 1,200-acre UCSD campus. Among the 12 diverse sculptures on view are Niki de Saint-Phalle's *Sun God,* a jubilant 14-foot fiberglass bird on a 15-foot concrete base, nicknamed "Big Bird" and made an unofficial mascot by the students. Pick up a brochure and map with marked sculpture locations from the information booth at the Northview Drive or Gilman Drive entrance to the campus.

MISSION BAY/PACIFIC BEACH

Giant Dipper Roller Coaster. 3146 Mission Blvd. ☎ **619/488-1549.** Summer, Sun–Mon and Thurs 11am–8pm, Tues–Wed 11am–9pm, Fri–Sat 11am–10pm. Closes earlier the rest of the year. Admission: Park, free; ride on Giant Dipper, $2.50. Take I-5 to the Sea World exit, and follow West Mission Bay Dr. to Belmont Park.

A local landmark for 70 years, the Giant Dipper is one of two surviving fixtures from the original Belmont Amusement Park (the other is the Plunge indoor swimming pool). After sitting dormant for 15 years, this vintage wooden roller coaster, with over 2,600 feet of track and 13 hills, underwent an extensive restoration and reopened in

1991. You can also ride on the Giant Dipper's neighbor, the Liberty Carousel ($1), or the newer rides: Tilt-a-Whirl, Crazy Sub, Thunder Boats, and Baja Buggies. You might like to participate in the Dive-In Movies shown at the Plunge (☎ 619/488-3110). Viewers float on rafts in 91° water and watch water-related movies projected onto the wall. *Jaws* is a perennial favorite.

8 Outdoor Activities & Spectator Sports

OUTDOOR ACTIVITIES

For coverage of San Diego's best beaches, see Section 5, earlier in this chapter.

BALLOONING For a bird's-eye glimpse of the area at sunrise or sunset, followed by champagne and hors d'oeuvres, contact **A Skysurfer Balloon Company** (☎ 619/481-6800), **Pacific Horizon Balloon Tours** (☎ 800/244-1790), or—our favorite—**California Dreamin** (☎ 800/748-5959). The balloon rides provide sweeping vistas of the Southern California coast, rambling estates, and golf courses.

BIKING & MOUNTAIN BIKING Mission Bay and Coronado, especially, are good for leisurely bike rides. The boardwalk in Pacific Beach and Mission Beach can get very crowded, especially on weekends. Most major thoroughfares offer a bike lane. Just remember to wear a helmet—it's the law. For information on bike rentals, see Section 2, "Getting Around," earlier in this chapter.

For a downhill thrill of a lifetime, take the **Palomar Plunge.** From the top of Palomar Mountain to its base, you'll experience, courtesy of gravity, a 5,000-foot vertical drop stretched out over 16 miles. Or try the **Desert Descent,** a 12-mile, 3,700-foot descent down the Montezuma Valley Grade to the desert floor, followed by a tour of the visitor center and a delicious lunch. **Gravity Activated Sports** (☎ 800/985-4427 or 619/742-2294) supplies the mountain bike, helmet, gloves, souvenir photo, and T-shirt.

Adventure Bike Tours, based at the Hyatt (☎ **619/234-1500,** ext. 6514) offers a "Bay to Breakers" bike ride which starts in downtown San Diego and includes Coronado. The cost of $39 covers bikes, helmets, the ferry, and guiding.

Backroads Bicycle Touring (☎ **800/BIKE-TRIP** or 415/527-1555) offers cycling packages to San Diego.

BOATING **Club Nautico,** a concession at the San Diego Marriott Marina, 333 W. Harbor Dr. (☎ **619/233-9311;** fax 619/689-2363), provides guests and nonguests an exhilarating way to see the bay by the hour, half day, or full day in 20- to 27-foot offshore powerboats. Rentals start at $89 per hour. They rent Waverunners as well and allow their boats to be taken into the ocean, and also provide diving, waterskiing, and fishing packages.

Seaforth Boat Rental, 1641 Quivira Rd., Mission Bay (☎ **619/223-1681**), has a wide variety of fishing boats for bay and ocean, powerboats for $50 to $90 per hour, and 14- to 27-foot sailboats for $20 to $45 per hour, with half-day and full-day rates. Canoes, pedalboats, kayaks, and rowboats are available for those who prefer a slower pace. If you don't want to go out on the water, they also rent bicycles and equipment with which you could fish off the Municipal Pier (see "Fishing," below). **Downtown Boat Rental,** at the Marriott, 33 W. Harbour Drive (☎ **619/239-2628**), has similar rentals.

Coronado Boat Rental, 1715 Strand Way, in Coronado (☎ **619/437-1514**), has powerboats renting for $65 to $90 per hour, with half- and full-day rates; 14- to 30-foot sailboats for $25 to $40 per hour; and jet skis, skiboats, canoes, pedalboats, kayaks, fishing skiffs, and charter boats.

La Jolla

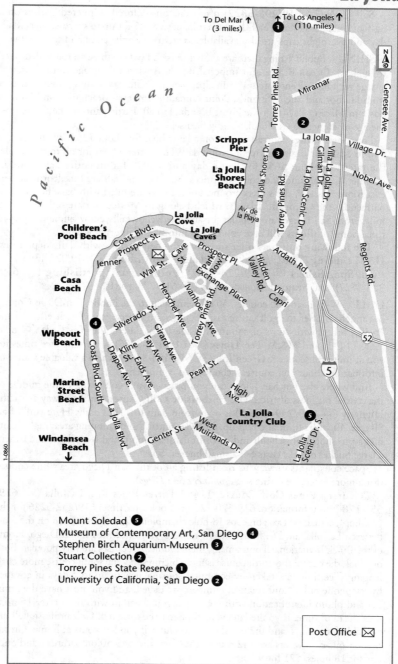

To Del Mar ↑
(3 miles)

To Los Angeles ↑
(110 miles)

1

N
↑

Pacific Ocean

Torrey Pines Rd.

Miramar

Genesee Ave.

2

La Jolla

Village Dr.

Villa La Jolla Dr.

Gilman Dr.

Nobel Ave.

Scripps
Pier

La Jolla Shores Dr.

3

La Jolla
Shores
Beach

Torrey Pines Rd.

La Jolla Scenic Dr. N.

Regents Rd.

Av. de
la Playa

Children's
Pool Beach

La Jolla
Cove

La Jolla
Caves

Coast Blvd.

Prospect St.

Cave
St.

Prospect Pl.

Ardath Rd.

Jenner

Wall St.

Park
Row

Exchange Place

Hidden
Valley Rd.

Via
Capri

Casa
Beach

Herschel Ave.

Ivanhoe Ave.

Torrey Pines Rd.

52

4

Silverado St.

Girard Ave.

Wipeout
Beach

Coast Blvd. South

Kline
St.

Fay Ave.

Eads Ave.

5

Marine
Street
Beach

Draper Ave.

Pearl St.

High
Ave.

La Jolla
Country Club

5

Windansea
Beach
↓

La Jolla Blvd.

Genter St.

West
Muirlands Dr.

La Jolla Scenic Dr. S.

1-0860

Mount Soledad **5**
Museum of Contemporary Art, San Diego **4**
Stephen Birch Aquarium-Museum **3**
Stuart Collection **2**
Torrey Pines State Reserve **1**
University of California, San Diego **2**

Post Office ✉

Sail USA (☎ **619/298-6822**) offers custom-tailored skippered cruises on a 34-foot Catalina sloop. A half-day bay cruise costs $275 for up to six passengers. Full-day and overnight trips are also available, as are trips up the coast and to Catalina.

FISHING   Public fishing piers are at Shelter Island (where there's a statue dedicated to anglers), Ocean Beach, and Imperial Beach. Anglers of any age can fish free of charge without a license off any municipal pier in California. Fishing charters depart from Harbor and Shelter islands, Point Loma, the Imperial Beach pier, and Quivira Basin in Mission Bay (near the Hyatt Islandia Hotel). Participants in these trips over the age of 16 need a California fishing license.

For **sportfishing,** you can go out on a large boat for about $25 for half a day or $40 to $100 for three-quarters to a full day. To charter a boat for up to six people, the rates run about $550 for half a day and $1,000 for an entire day, more in summer. Call around and compare prices. Summer and fall are excellent times for excursions. Locally, the waters around Point Loma are filled with bass, bonita, and barracuda; the Coronado Islands, which belong to Mexico but are only about 18 miles from San Diego, are popular for abalone, yellowtail, yellow fin, and big-eyed tuna. Some outfitters will take you farther into Baja California waters.

The following outfitters offer short or extended outings with daily departures: **H&M Landing** (☎ 619/222-1144), **Islandia Sportfishing** (☎ 619/222-1164), **Lee Palm Sportfishers** (☎ 619/224-3857), **Point Loma Sportfishing** (☎ 619/223-1627), and **Seaforth Boat Rentals** (☎ 619/223-1681).

GOLF   With nearly 80 courses, 50 of them open to the public, San Diego County has much to offer the golf enthusiast. Courses are diverse, some with vistas of the Pacific, others with views of country hillsides or of desert. **Par-Tee Golf** (☎ 800/PAR-TEE-1) and **M&M Tee Times** (☎ 619/456-8366) can arrange tee times for you at most golf courses. **Greenlink** (☎ 619/456-8346) is also a valuable source of information about golf courses, schools, and equipment.

And where else but San Diego can you practice your golf swing in the middle of the central business district? The **Harborside Golf Center,** on Broadway at Pacific Highway (☎ **619/239-GOLF**) is open from 8am to 11pm daily. Here you'll find 80 tees, 40 with automatic pop-up; a USGA putting and chipping area; night lighting; a pro shop; golf school; and golf simulators. Club rental is available at $1 each; a large bucket of balls costs $6; a small bucket, $3.

Space constraints prevent us from listing all of the San Diego area's fine courses (for a more extensive listing see *Frommer's San Diego*).

✪ **Torrey Pines Golf Course,** 11480 Torrey Pines Rd., La Jolla (☎ **619/552-1784** for information, 619/570-1234 to book a tee time, 619/452-3226 for the pro shop), actually is two gorgeous 18-hole championship courses located on the coast between La Jolla and Del Mar, only 15 minutes from downtown San Diego. Home of the Buick Invitational Tournament, these municipal courses are very popular. Both overlook the ocean; the north course is more picturesque, the south course more challenging. Tee times are taken by computer starting at 5am up to 7 days in advance by telephone only. Confirmation numbers are issued, and you must have the number and photo identification with you when you check in with the starter 15 minutes ahead of time. If you're late, your time may be forfeited. Golf professionals are available for lessons, and the pro shop rents clubs, if you left yours at home. Greens fees for out-of-towners are $42 during the week and $49.50 on Saturday and Sunday for 18 holes, $21 for 9 holes.

The ✪ **Coronado Municipal Golf Course,** 2000 Visalia Row, Coronado (☎ **619/435-3121**), is the first sight that welcomes you as you cross the Coronado

Bay Bridge (the course is off to the left). It's an 18-hole, par-72 course overlooking Glorietta Bay, and there's a coffee shop, pro shop, and driving range. Two-day prior reservations are strongly recommended; call anytime after 7am. Greens fees are $20 for 18 holes, $10 after 4pm.

HIKING   The **Sierra Club** sponsors regular hikes in the San Diego area, and nonmembers are welcome to participate. There's always a Wednesday mountain hike, usually in the Cuyamaca Mountains, though sometimes in the Lagunas; there are evening and day hikes as well. Most are free. For a recorded message of upcoming hikes, call 619/299-1744, box no. 4000, or call the office (☎ **619/ 299-1743**) Monday to Friday from noon to 5pm and on Saturday from 10am to 4pm.

The Bayside Trail near **Cabrillo National Monument** is popular because hikers can stop and look in the tidepools. Drive to the monument and follow the signs to the trail. **Mission Trails Regional Park,** 8 miles northeast of downtown, offers a glimpse of what San Diego looked like before development. Located between Calif. 52 and I-8 and east of I-15, rugged hills, valleys, and open areas provide a quick escape from urban hustle-bustle. A visitor and interpretive center (☎ **619/668-3275**) is open daily from 9am to 5pm. Access is via Mission Gorge Road. Torrey Pines State Park in La Jolla is another great spot for hiking.

HORSEBACK RIDING   Hosts Earl and Liz Hammond at **Holidays on Horseback** (☎ **619/445-3997**), located 40 miles east of San Diego in Descanso, offer halfand full-day outings, as well as overnight camping trips, through Cuyamaca Rancho State Park. Riders pass through beautiful scenery that includes native chaparral, live oak, and manzanita. A 4-hour ride with a picnic lunch on the trail costs $60, and a 1¹/₂-hour ride is $25.

IN-LINE SKATING   Gliding around San Diego, especially the Mission Bay area, on in-line skates is as much a Southern California experience as sailing or surfing. In Mission Beach, rent a pair of regular or in-line skates from **Skates Plus,** 3830 Mission Blvd. (☎ 619/488-PLUS), or **Hamel's Action Sports Center,** 704 Ventura Place, off Mission Blvd. at the roller coaster (☎ 619/488-5050); and in Pacific Beach, at **Pacific Beach Sun & Sea,** 4539 Ocean Blvd. (☎ 619/483-6613). In Coronado, go to **Mike's Bikes,** at 1343 Orange Ave. (☎ 619/435-7744); or **Bikes & Beyond,** 1201 1st St. and at the Ferry Landing (☎ 619/435-7180).

SCUBA DIVING & SNORKELING   The **San Diego–La Jolla Underwater Park,** especially the La Jolla Cove, is the best spot for scuba and snorkeling. For more information, see Section 5, "Beaches," earlier in this chapter. The **Underwater Pumpkin Carving Contest,** held at Halloween, is a fun local event. For information phone 619/565-6054.

TENNIS   There are 1,200 public and private tennis courts in San Diego. Public courts are located throughout the city, including the **La Jolla Recreation Center** (☎ 619/295-9278) and **Morley Field** (☎ 619/459-9950) in Balboa Park.

SPECTATOR SPORTS

BASEBALL   The National League **San Diego Padres** play April to September at San Diego Jack Murphy Stadium, 9449 Friars Rd., in Mission Valley (☎ **619/ 283-4494** for schedules and information, 619/29-PADRES for tickets). The Padres Express bus costs $5 round-trip and picks up fans at several locations throughout the city, beginning 2 hours before home games on Friday, Saturday, and Sunday (call 619/233-3004 for bus information).

FOOTBALL   San Diego's professional football team, the **San Diego Chargers,** made it all the way to the 1995 Super Bowl before losing to their in-state rivals, the San Francisco 49ers. And in 1998 San Diego will host the Super Bowl. The Chargers play their home games at San Diego Jack Murphy Stadium, 9449 Friars Rd., Mission Valley (☎ **619/280-2121**). The season runs from August to December. The Chargers Express bus costs $5 round-trip and picks up passengers at several locations throughout the city, beginning 2 hours before all home games (call 619/233-3004 for bus information).

GOLF TOURNAMENTS   San Diego hosts some of the country's most important golf tournaments, including the **Mercedes Championships,** held at La Costa Resort in Carlsbad in early January (call 800/918-4653 for tickets and information). Another popular event is the **Buick Invitational of California,** held every February at Torrey Pines Golf Course in La Jolla (☎ 800/888-BUICK or 619/281-4653). The **HGH Pro-Am Golf Classic** is held at Carlton Oaks Country Club every September (☎ 619/448-8500).

HORSE RACING   Live thoroughbred racing takes place at the **Del Mar Racetrack** (☎ **619/755-1141** for information, 619/792-4242 for tickets) from late July to mid-September every year. Post time is 2pm for the nine-race program; there's no racing on Tuesday. Reserved seating in both the Clubhouse and Grandstand costs $4 per person, in addition to admission charges of $6 for the Clubhouse and $3 for the Grandstand. Seating is also available in the members-only Turf Club (if you are or know a member).

Bing Crosby and Pat O'Brien founded the track in 1937, and it has been frequented by stars ever since. Del Mar's 1993 season marked the opening of a new $80-million grandstand, built in the Spanish mission style of the original structure. The new grandstand features more seats, better race viewing, and a centrally located scenic paddock.

RODEOS   In the outlying areas of the county you can watch bull riding, bronco busting, and calf roping several times a year. In April there's **Lakeside Western Days,** which features seven major rodeo events as well as food and entertainment; for information call 619/561-1031 or 619/561-4331. The **Ramona Rodeo,** held in May, is one of the country's top 50 rodeos; for information call 619/789-1484. The **KSON Country Fest Rodeo,** held in Lakeside every June, features bands, music and a full-scale rodeo; for information call 619/299-1240.

SANDCASTLE COMPETITIONS   Sandcastle enthusiasts will want to attend the 2-day **Annual U.S. Open Sandcastle Competition** at the pier in Imperial Beach in July. On Saturday there's a parade and children's castle contest at 2pm, but Sunday is the main event. For information call 619/424-6663. A similar event is held in October: the **Ocean Beach Sandcastle Event and Family Fun Carnival.** For information call 619/226-8613.

TENNIS TOURNAMENTS   San Diego hosts some major tennis tournaments, including the **Toshiba Tennis Classic,** held at the La Costa Resort & Spa in Carlsbad. In 1997 this professional women's tennis tournament is tentatively scheduled to be held July 28 to August 3. For tickets and information call 619/438-LOVE.

9 Great Shopping Areas

Shops in San Diego tend to stay open late. Expect to find the welcome mat out until 9pm on weeknights, 8pm on Saturday, and 6pm and sometimes 8pm on Sunday. In addition to the specific shopping clusters listed below, you might like to check out the local malls: **Fashion Valley,** 352 Fashion Valley Rd. (☎ 619/297-3381); **Mission Valley,** 1640 Camino del Rio North (☎ 619/296-6375); and **University Towne Center,** 4545 La Jolla Village Drive, San Diego (☎ 619/546-8858).

Bazaar del Mundo. 2754 Calhoun St., in Old Town State Historic Park. ☎ **619/296-3161.** Bus: 4 or 5/105. Trolley: Old Town.

Always festive, the central courtyard here vibrates with folkloric music, mariachis, and a splashing fountain. Shops are pricey, but feature one-of-a-kind folk art, home furnishings, clothing, and textiles from Mexico and South America. You'll find a top-notch bookstore called Libros, with a large kids' selection. If you're pooped, collapse at Casa de Pico and enjoy one of their bathtub-size margaritas.

The Ferry Landing Market Place. 1201 1st St. (at B Ave.), Coronado. ☎ **619/435-8895.** Take I-5 to the Coronado Bay Bridge, to B Ave., and turn right. Bus: 901. Ferry: From Broadway Pier.

The entrance is impressive—turreted red rooftops with jaunty blue flags that draw closer as the ferry to Coronado pulls into the slip. Then a stroll up the pier and you're in the midst of shops filled with gifts, imported and designer fashions, jewelry, and crafts. You can get a quick bite to eat or have a leisurely dinner with a view, wander along landscaped walkways, or laze on a friendly beach or grassy bank.

✪ **Horton Plaza.** 324 Horton Plaza. ☎ **619/238-1596.** Bus: 2, 7, 9, 29, 34, or 35. Trolley: City Center.

The Disneyland of shopping malls, Horton Plaza is almost as much a San Diego attraction as Sea World or the Zoo, partly for its unusual eclectic designs and colors. It's right in the heart of San Diego; in fact, it *is* the heart of the revitalized city center, bounded by Broadway, 1st and 4th avenues, and G Street. Covering 6½ city blocks, this multilevel center has 140 specialty shops, including art galleries, clothing and shoe stores, several fun shops for kids, bookstores, a seven-screen cinema, three major department stores, and a variety of restaurants and short-order eateries. The plaza is purposefully designed for meandering, so expect to take some wrong turns and make some delightful discoveries (or stay close to the escalator, which you can pick up at the front of the plaza beside Long's Pharmacy, or take the elevator beside Nordstrom). Among the favorite shops here are Horton Toy & Doll, for inexpensive toys for kids and great gag gifts for adults. Horton Plaza usually has free entertainment daily from noon to 2pm. Parking is free the first 3 hours with validation, $1 per half hour thereafter; parking levels are confusing, and temporarily losing your car is part of the Horton Plaza experience.

La Jolla. Prospect St. and Girard Ave. Bus: 34 or 34A.

"The village," as it is still referred to by long-time locals, has become sort of a cross between Rodeo Drive and a shopping mall. A few of the old-time stores remain—Warwick's (books and stationery), Burns Drugs, John Cole's Book Shop, Meanley Hardware—but these are outnumbered by the glossy newcomers. Look for Ann Taylor, Armani Exchange, Banana Republic, The Gap, Georgiou, Mondi, Polo Ralph Lauren, Port International, Sigi's Boutique, Talbots (a personal favorite of ours), and Tina's Boutique. You can park on the street, but watch your time. The local parking enforcement officers are slightly overzealous.

The Paladion. 777 Front St. (opposite Horton Plaza between 1st Ave. and G St.). ☎ **619/232-1627.** Bus: 2, 7, 9, 29, 34, or 35. Trolley: Civic Center.

The posh Paladion brought world-class shopping to downtown San Diego when it opened early in 1992, with tony tenants like Alfred Dunhill, Cartier, Tiffany & Co., H. Stern, Bernini, Gianni Versace, and Salvatore Ferragamo. Sadly, the timing couldn't have been worse from the developer's point of view. The combined devaluation of the Mexican peso and the economic downturn of San Diego caused many of the original businesses in this center to close for lack of customers. As we go to press the fate of the Paladion is uncertain; discussions include the addition of theaters and mid-priced shops. The Ivy Court, on the ground level, a lovely spot for coffee, a light lunch, or cocktails—all with piano music as a backdrop. There's also a rooftop Italian restaurant called Bice, a French-Caribbean restaurant called Alizé, and even free valet parking and concierge service.

Seaport Village. 849 W. Harbor Dr. (at Kettner Blvd.). ☎ **619/235-4014,** or 619/235-4013 for events information. Two hours' free parking with validation; $1 per half hour thereafter. Bus: 7. Trolley: Seaport Village.

This 14-acre ersatz village snuggled alongside San Diego Bay was built to resemble a small Cape Cod community, but the 75 shops are very much the Southern California cutesy variety. Favorites include the Tile Shop; the Seasick Giraffe for resort wear; and the Upstart Crow bookshop/coffeehouse with the Crow's Nest children's bookstore inside. Be sure to see the 1890 carousel imported from Coney Island, New York.

FARMERS' MARKETS

Farmers' Markets throughout San Diego County sell fresh local fruits, vegetables, and flowers, as well as specialty items such as raw apple cider (in the fall), macadamia nuts, and rhubarb pies.

Sunday: El Cajon at "The Boulevard" at Marlborough (3 blocks east of 40th Street), 10am to 2pm.

Tuesday: Coronado at the Old Ferry Landing, corner of 1st Street and B Avenue, 2:30 to 6pm; Escondido at Grand Avenue and Broadway, 3 to 7pm.

Wednesday: North County Market in Escondido at 3660 Sunset Drive (across from North County Fair), 9am to noon; Ocean Beach at the 4900 block of Newport Avenue (west of Sunset Cliffs Boulevard.), 4 to 8pm; Carlsbad, on Roosevelt Street between Grand Avenue and Carlsbad Village Drive, 3 to 6pm.

Thursday: Downtown Oceanside at the corner of North Hill and 3rd Street, 9am to 12:30pm; Mission Valley at Hazard Center, Friars Road at Calif. 163, 3 to 6:30pm; Chula Vista at 3rd Avenue and E Street, 3 to 6pm.

Friday: Rancho Bernardo at the Bernardo Winery, 13330 Paseo del Verano Norte, 9am to noon; La Mesa, at 8500 Allison St. (east of Spring Street), 3 to 6pm.

Saturday: Pacific Beach at Promenade Mall, Mission Boulevard. between Reed and Pacific Beach Drive, 8am to noon; Vista, at the corner of Eucalyptus and Escondido Avenue (City Hall parking lot), 8am-11am. Poway in Old Poway Park, corner of Midland and Temple, 8am to 11am; Del Mar, in the City Hall Parking Lot, at the corner of El Camino del Mar and 10th Street, 1 to 4pm; Carlsbad, in the parking lot north of Andersen's Pea Soup, 2 to 5pm.

10 San Diego After Dark

San Diego is hardly the wild 'n' crazy nightlife capital of America, but pockets of lively after-dark entertainment *do* exist around the city. On the more sedate side of things, we offer wonderful and varied live theater experiences. This isn't just civic pride speaking—both the Old Globe and La Jolla Playhouse have won Tonys for "best regional theater."

For a rundown of the latest performances, gallery openings, and other events in the city, check the listings in "Night and Day," the Thursday entertainment section of the *San Diego Union-Tribune,* or *The Reader,* San Diego's free alternative newspaper, published weekly on Thursday. For what's happening at the gay clubs, get the weekly *San Diego Gay & Lesbian Times.* The *San Diego Performing Arts Guide,* produced every 2 months by the San Diego Theatre Foundation, is also very helpful. You can pick one up at the Times Art Tix booth.

THE PERFORMING ARTS

Half-price tickets to theater, music, and dance events are available at the **Times Arts Tix** booth, in Horton Plaza Park, at Broadway and 3rd Avenue. Park in the Horton Plaza parking garage and have your parking validated or pause at the curb nearby. The kiosk is open Tuesday to Saturday from 10am to 7pm. Half-price tickets for Sunday performances are sold on Saturday. Only cash payments are accepted. For a daily listing of half-price offerings, call **619/497-5000.** Full-price advance tickets are also sold; the kiosk doubles as a Ticketmaster outlet, selling tickets to concerts throughout California.

THEATER

The **Gaslamp Quarter Theatre Company,** at 444 4th Ave. (☎ **619/232-9608** or 619/234-9583), stages contemporary productions in the 250-seat Hahn Cosmopolitan Theatre.

The **San Diego Repertory Theatre** offers professional, culturally diverse productions of contemporary and classic dramas, comedys, and musicals at the Lyceum Theatre, 79 Horton Plaza (☎ **619/235-8025** or 619/231-3586; fax 619/235-0939). Its annual *A Christmas Carol* is a perennial favorite.

Founded in 1948, the **San Diego Junior Theatre,** at Balboa Park's Casa del Prado Theatre (☎ **619/239-8355;** fax 619/239-5048), is the country's oldest continuously producing children's theater, providing training and performance opportunities for children and teenagers 4 to 18. Students act and technically crew five main stage shows each year.

In Coronado, **Lamb's Players Theatre,** at 1142 Orange Ave. (☎ **619/437-0600;** fax 619/437-6053), is a professional repertory company whose season runs from February to December. Shows take place in their 340-seat theater in Coronado's historic Spreckels building, where no seat is more than seven rows from the stage.

✪ **Old Globe Theatre.** Balboa Park. ☎ **619/239-2255** or 619/23-GLOBE for 24-hour hotline. Tickets $28.50–$39 (previews $22); seniors and students $25 matinees, $29 weeknights. Bus: 7 or 25.

Near the entrance to Balboa Park and just behind the Museum of Man, this Tony Award–winning theater, fashioned after Shakespeare's, has produced the revival of *Damn Yankees,* and has billed such notable performers as John Goodman, Marsha Mason, Cliff Robertson, Jon Voight, and Christopher Walken.

The 581-seat Old Globe is part of the Simon Edison Centre for the Performing Arts, which also includes the 245-seat Cassius Carter Centre Stage and the 620-seat open-air Lowell Davies Festival Theatre, and mounts a dozen plays a year on the three stages between January and October. Tours are offered Saturday and Sunday at 11am and cost $3 ($1 for students, seniors, and military). The box office is open Tuesday to Sunday from noon to 8:30pm.

✪ **La Jolla Playhouse.** La Jolla Village Dr. and Torrey Pines Rd., La Jolla. ☎ **619/550-1010.**
Winner of the 1993 Tony Award for outstanding American regional theater, the La
Jolla Playhouse stages six productions each year in its 500-seat Mandell Weiss Theater and 400-seat Mandell Weiss Forum on the campus of UCSD. Performances are
held May to November. Playhouse audiences cheered The Who's Tommy, and Matthew Broderick in How to Succeed in Business Without Really Trying before they
went on to Broadway fame and fortune. The original La Jolla Playhouse was founded
by Gregory Peck, Dorothy McGuire, and Mel Ferrer in 1947 and closed in 1964.
This stellar reincarnation emerged on the theatrical scene in 1983. The box office is
open Monday from noon to 6pm, and Tuesday to Sunday from noon to 8pm. Each
show designates one Saturday matinee as a "pay-what-you-can performance." Re-
duced-price "Public Rush" tickets are available 10 minutes before curtain, subject to
availability. Tickets run $19 to $39. Self-parking is $3.

OPERA & CLASSICAL MUSIC

The **San Diego Opera** performs at the Civic Theater, 202 C St. (☎ **619/232-7636**),
and often showcases international stars. The 1997 season, January to May, will in-
clude Carmen, The Italian Girl in Algiers, The Conquistadore (world première), La
Traviata, and Turandot. Plácido Domingo will be featured in concert on April 10.
The box office is located across the plaza from the theater and is open Monday to
Friday from 9am to 5pm. Tickets run $25 to $100. Student and senior discounts and
$17 standing-room tickets are available an hour before the performance.

The future of **San Diego's Symphony,** whose home is Copley Symphony Hall,
750 B St. (☎ **619/699-4205**), is up in the air. In early 1996 it was announced that
the symphony would play no more because of financial problems. Now it appears that
a civic-minded angel may rescue them. Should the symphony play again, they'll probably be led by Israeli-born conductor Yoav Talmi. Call to find out.

MOVIES SAN DIEGO STYLE

In addition to the usual multiplex theaters, San Diegans like to watch movies in
some unusual situations. **Movies Before the Mast** are shown on a special "screensail"
April to October aboard the Star of India, all of them nautical in genre such as Black
Beard the Pirate and Hook. Call 619/234-9153 for the schedule.

In August you can view a mix of classic and current films free of charge from a
blanket or chair on the beach during the **Sunset Cinema Film Festival.** Films are
projected on screens mounted on floating barges from San Diego to Imperial Beach.
Call 619/454-7373 for details.

Dive-In Movies are shown at the Plunge (☎ **619/488-3110**), an indoor
swimming pool in Mission Beach. Viewers float on rafts in 91° water and watch
water-related movies projected onto the wall. Jaws is a perennial favorite.

The San Diego Symphony, Copley Symphony Hall, 750 B St. (☎ **619/
699-4205**), accompanies **silent movies** during a film series in its winter concert season, October to May.

THE CLUB & MUSIC SCENE

Clubs come and go, so your best bet for finding the latest, hottest spot is to stroll
through the Gaslamp Quarter. The current favorites are **Johnny Loves,** 664 5th Ave.
(☎ 619/595-0123), which endears itself to an over-30 crowd; **Club 66,** at 901 5th
Ave. (☎ 619/234-4166), which has a Route 66 motif and caters to those aged 25
to 45; **E Street Alley,** on the north side of E Street between 4th and 5th Aves.
(☎ 619/231-9200), which is a dressier club; **Ole Madrid,** 751 5th Ave. (☎ 619/
557-0146), the destination of choice for Europhiles; **Dick's Last Resort,** 345 4th

Ave., with entrances on both 4th and 5th aves. (☎ 619/231-9100), popular with the college crowd; and **Buffalo Joe's Saloon,** 600 5th Ave. (☎ 619/236-1616), a country-western nightclub. Cover charges vary from nil to $10, depending on who's playing and the night of the week.

Fans of alternative music might enjoy the **Casbah,** 2501 Kettner Boulevard. (☎ 619/232-4355), where breakthrough bands are the norm, or **Bodies,** 528 F St. (☎ 619/236-8988), where live original music is played nightly.

If you're under 21, **SOMA Live,** 5305 Metro St., Mission Bay (☎ 619/239-SOMA), is the place for you. This concert venue in a warehouselike building has hosted Courtney Love, Social Distortion, and Faith No More.

From May to October a series of contemporary concerts takes place outdoors at **Humphrey's,** 2241 Shelter Island Drive, San Diego (☎ 619/523-1010). During the 1996 season Ray Charles, Willie Nelson, and Wayne Newton were just three of the popular performers who appeared here. For the 1997 schedule, call or check their Web site: **http://user.aol.com/humconcert.**

Videos and live bands (sometimes local, sometimes nationally known) take center stage in the **Cannibal Bar,** in the Catamaran Hotel, 3999 Mission Boulevard. (☎ 619/539-8650). Open Wednesday to Sunday till about 2am; weekend cover charges range from $3 to $15.

The nautical theme and waterfront location, with a curving window wall looking onto the marina, make **The Yacht Club,** in the San Diego Marriott Marina, 333 W. Harbor Drive (☎ 619/234-1500), a comfortable spot. There's live dance music nightly, with appetizers and light fare available until 11pm, along with a dinner menu served from 5 to 11pm. A band plays 5 nights a week, a DJ 2 nights at 9pm. No cover, no drink minimum.

COMEDY

Top L.A. comics regularly visit the **Comedy Store,** 916 Pearl St., La Jolla (☎ **619/454-9176**). Monday and Tuesday are amateur nights; the acts improve as the week progresses. Showtime is 8pm Sunday to Thursday, 8 and 10:30pm on Friday and Saturday. The cover is $8 to $10, with a two-drink minimum.

JAZZ & BLUES

Croce's. 802 5th Ave. (at F St.). ☎ **619/233-4355.** No cover to either Croce's Jazz Bar or Croce's Top Hat if you have dinner at Croce's Restaurant or Ingrid's Cantina. Cover $3–$7 for regional bands, $10–$18 for national acts. Minimum at both bars $5.

There's traditional jazz every night in Croce's Jazz Bar and rhythm and blues at Croce's Top Hat, both named after the late musician Jim Croce and owned by his wife, Ingrid. Jim Croce's son, A.J., an accomplished musician in his own right, sometimes performs. Jazz holds sway in the Jazz Bar and drifts easily into the adjoining restaurant (see "Where to Dine," above); it opens nightly at 5pm and music starts at 8:30pm. Next door, in Croce's Top Hat, balcony seating overlooks the stage; it's open daily, with music starting at 9pm.

BIG BAND

Hotel del Coronado. 1500 Orange Ave., Coronado. ☎ **619/435-6611.** Cover $15 without dinner.

The West Coast's most glorious Victorian hotel kicks up its heels on Sunday nights, when it's swing time in the Crown Room. Besides the music and dancing, the architecturally memorable room makes the trip here worthwhile. Prices are $24.95 with buffet dinner.

THE BAR & COFFEEHOUSE SCENE

The **Top o' The Cove,** 1216 Prospect St. in La Jolla (☎ 619/454-7779), is an intimate setting, where the pianist plays old favorites, and leans heavily toward Gershwin. Nab the corner table next to the piano. On nice evenings, the music is piped to the patio, another idyllic spot to sit and sip. Valet parking is $5.

BREWPUBS

Karl Strauss' Old Columbia Brewery, at 1157 Columbia St. (☎ 619/234-BREWS), opened several years ago and started something of a microbrewery trend in San Diego. Strauss named his brews after local attractions—Gaslamp Gold Ale, Red Trolley Ale, Black's Beach Extra Dark, Star of India Pale Ale—but he brought the recipes from the old-world. Want to try them all and still be able to walk? You can order a Taster Series, 4 ounces of eight different brews for only $5.95. Old Columbia serves great beer and hearty American fare. Hours are 11:30am to 10pm Sunday through Thursday and 11:30am to midnight Friday and Saturday.

While an upscale crowd of "suits" gathers at Karl's place, **R.J.'s Riptide Brewery,** at 5th and K in the Gaslamp Quarter (☎ 619/231-7700), attracts a sports-happy bunch who appreciate the pub's big-screen TV. The copper-clad brewing tanks take center stage here, with the large U-shaped bar curving around them. R.J.'s produces top-fermented English-, German-, Irish-, and Belgium-style ales, stouts, and porters (no lagers). This is an upbeat, light-hearted place, where the slogan is *Save the Ales.*

In contrast, the **La Jolla Brewing Company,** 7536 Fay Ave., La Jolla (☎ 619/456-BREW), feels more like a neighborhood pub. The wood floor is appropriately worn, and pool and darts are played in the back room. Brewmaster John Atwater makes his handcrafted beers from his own recipes and names them after local spots. John offers TVs for sports fans and serves meals such as Baja fish tacos, brewhouse pasta, and a "cheeseburger in paradise."

COFFEEHOUSES

Pannikin Hillcrest, 523 University Ave., Hillcrest (☎ 619/295-1600), is a laid-back place to enjoy your latte or espresso. The desserts are rich, and the art on the wall is the work of local artists. Open Sunday to Thursday from 6am to 11pm and on Friday and Saturday from 6am to midnight.

Upstart Crow, on the central plaza at Seaport Village (☎ 619/232-4855), is a coffeehouse/bookstore where tables and chairs fill cozy spaces surrounded by books. The selection of books, coffees, and desserts is scrumptious. And coffee refills are only 25¢. Open Sunday to Thursday from 9am to 10pm (until 11pm in summer), Friday and Saturday from 9am to 11pm.

Centrally located in the Gaslamp Quarter and particularly popular with students, **Cafe Lulu,** 419 F St. near 4th Avenue (☎ 619/238-0114), is open worknights till 2am, until 4am on Friday and Saturday. Light fare at this sparsely decorated coffeehouse runs the gamut from Brie or pizza baguettes to bagels to croissants to quiche to lasagne. Drinkwise, the emphasis is on coffees, but you can also get teas, natural sodas, Aqua Libra, sarsaparilla, and beer or wine by the glass or bottle. No credit cards.

In La Jolla, try the **Wall Street Cafe,** at 1044 Wall St., between Girard and Herschel avenues (☎ 619/551-1044), which was once a bank (the old vault contains the rest rooms). Live entertainment, such as light jazz or a mellow guitar, makes this a particularly popular place on Friday and Saturday nights.

GAY & LESBIAN HANGOUTS

The Flame. 3780 Park Blvd. ☎ **619/295-4163.** Cover $2 Sun–Fri, $3 Sat.

The Flame has a large dance floor and two bars, including a video bar open Tuesday to Saturday. A different style of music is played every night of the week: Tuesday is "Boys Night Out"; Wednesday is "Trash Disco"; on Saturday top-40s dance music is played; Sunday night there's Latin music. The Flame is open daily till 2am.

Kickers/Hamburger Mary's. 308 University Ave. (between 3rd and 4th aves.). ☎ **619/491-0400.** No cover.

Kickers is a foot-stomping, gay-owned and -operated bar with an adjacent outdoor restaurant, Hamburger Mary's. The atmosphere is relaxed and informal, and no western garb is expected (the waiters are likely to be in shorts). If you're unschooled in the art of country-western dancing, just show up on Monday and Friday for lessons from 7 to 8:30pm, then put what you've learned to the test for the rest of the evening. Beginner classes are taught Monday and Tuesday, tougher moves the rest of the week. There's line dancing, too. Before, during, or after an evening at Kickers, head outside to the patio and Hamburger Mary's for a burger or sandwich and a chance to catch your breath. This place, which is equally popular among men and women, is a definite kick. Open daily till 2am.

Rich's. 1051 University Ave. (between 10th and 11th aves.). ☎ **619/295-2195,** or 619/497-4588 for upcoming events. Cover $4–$5 Thurs–Sat; Sun, none before 9pm, $3 after 9pm.

This popular club/dance space welcomes primarily gay men 21 and older. Sunday is popular for Tea and Me, when there's no cover between 7 and 9pm, and Thursday for Club Hedonism, with techno tunes and more. On Friday and Saturday nights, go-go dancers and high-energy music set the tone for the night. Always check the events hotline, since the schedules can change. Open Thursday to Sunday till 2am.

11 North County Beach Towns

Picturesque beach towns, each poised over a stretch of sand, dot the coast of San Diego County from Del Mar to Oceanside. These make great day-trip destinations for sunworshippers and surfers.

Getting there is easy: Del Mar is only 18 miles north of downtown San Diego; Carlsbad, about 33; and Oceanside, approximately 36. If you're driving, follow I-5 north: You'll find freeway exits for Del Mar, Solana Beach, Cardiff by the Sea, Encinitas, Leucadia, Carlsbad, and Oceanside. The farthest point, Oceanside, will take you about 45 minutes. The other choice by car is to wander up the coast road—known variously along the way as Camino del Mar, the Pacific Coast Highway, Old U.S. 101, and County Highway S21.

Amtrak and the Coaster provide service to Carlsbad and Oceanside, and Amtrak also stops in Solana Beach, a few minutes north of Del Mar. Check with Amtrak (☎ 800/USA-RAIL), the Coaster (☎ 800/COASTER), or the local tourist information offices about schedules.

The **San Diego North County Convention & Visitors Bureau** (☎ **800/848-3336**) is also a good information source.

DEL MAR

Less than 20 miles up the coast from San Diego lies Del Mar, a community with just over 5,000 inhabitants in a 2-square-mile municipality. The town has adamantly

Area Code Change Notice

Note that, effective March 22, 1997, the telephone area code for the North County beach towns is scheduled to change to **760.** You can continue to dial 619 until September 27, 1997, after which you will have to use 760.

maintained its independence, eschewing incorporation into the city of San Diego. Sometimes known as "the people's republic of Del Mar," this community was one of the nation's first to ban smoking. The upscale folks who live here grin and bear it during the summer racing season when the Del Mar Thoroughbred Club attracts droves of out-of-towners.

Del Mar Beach connects with **Torrey Pines Beach,** providing miles of sand for walking; swimmers congregate north of Jake's seaside restaurant, surfers go south. On the **Del Mar Beach,** Powerhouse Park has picnic tables and a children's playground. On the cliff above it overlooking the ocean is **Seagrove Park,** the scene of free concerts in July and August (☎ 619/755-9313).

The town is best known for the **Del Mar Thoroughbred Club,** a racetrack founded in 1937 by Bing Crosby and Pat O'Brien. Thoroughbred racing still takes place here from late July to mid-September. The new grandstand seats 14,300, and like the 1937 original is in Spanish mission style. In addition to the Del Mar Thoroughbred Club, the Fairgrounds also host the **Del Mar Fair,** one of the country's largest, during the last 2 weeks in June, culminating on the Fourth of July.

On Camino del Mar in the town center, the stylish **Del Mar Plaza** has well-selected shops and a variety of restaurants, as well as jazz concerts in summer. **Esmeralda Books & Coffee** on the upper level provides food and food for thought. Parking is under the plaza.

For more information about Del Mar, contact or visit the **Del Mar Chamber of Commerce Visitor Information Center,** 1104 Camino del Mar, Del Mar, CA 92014 (☎ **619/793-5292).**

WHERE TO STAY

Expensive

L'Auberge Del Mar Resort and Spa. 1540 Camino del Mar, Del Mar, CA 92014. ☎ **800/553-1336** or 619/259-1515. Fax 619/755-4940. 120 rms, 8 suites. A/C MINIBAR TV TEL. $189-$349 double; from $500 suite. Packages available. AE, DC, MC, V. Valet parking $8, self-parking $6.

L'Auberge stands on the site of the old Del Mar Hotel—midway between the beach and the shops and dining spots in Del Mar Plaza. The resort retains an exclusive air, and the lobby is reminiscent of the old hotel's, with a fireplace that's an exact replica. The rooms feature private balconies or terraces, sitting areas, marble baths and vanities, and traditional furnishings. About half have ocean views, some offer fireplaces, and some have ceiling fans. Most are no-smoking.

Dining/Entertainment: The 15th Street Grille and Terrace serves all meals. There are 3 hours of free music and dancing in the lobby on Friday and Saturday nights, and you can pop into Durante's Pub most anytime.

Services: Concierge, room service (6:30am–10pm), laundry/dry cleaning, complimentary newspaper, in-room massage, baby-sitting, secretarial services, express

North County Beach Towns

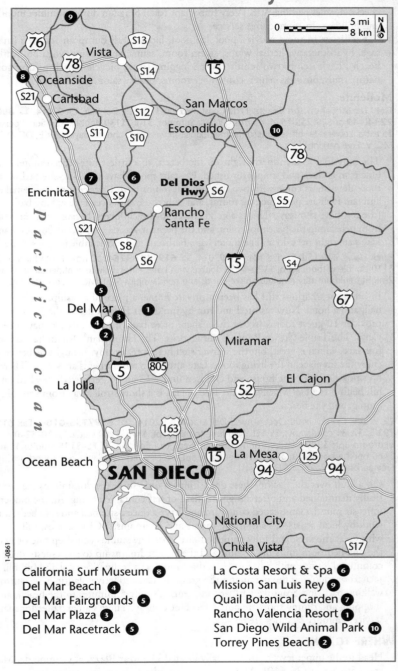

0 | 5 mi
0 | 8 km

N

Pacific Ocean

76

78 Vista
S13

S14

15

8 Oceanside

S21 Carlsbad

San Marcos

5 S11 Escondido 10

S12

S10 78

7 6 Del Dios Hwy S6

Encinitas S9 S5

S21 Rancho Santa Fe

S8

S6 15 S4

5 67

Del Mar 1

4 3 Miramar

2

5 805

La Jolla

52 El Cajon

163

8

Ocean Beach SAN DIEGO 15 La Mesa 125 94

94

National City

1-0861 Chula Vista S17

California Surf Museum 8   La Costa Resort & Spa 6
Del Mar Beach 4   Mission San Luis Rey 9
Del Mar Fairgrounds 5   Quail Botanical Garden 7
Del Mar Plaza 3   Rancho Valencia Resort 1
Del Mar Racetrack 5   San Diego Wild Animal Park 10
                               Torrey Pines Beach 2

checkout, valet parking, VIK (Very Important Kids) program during summer months and holidays, in-room coffee service.

Facilities: In-room movies, pool, lap pool, Jacuzzi, full European-style spa (massage, hydrotherapy, herbal wraps, steam room, sauna, spa cuisine, yoga on nearby beach), health club, two tennis courts, jogging track, bicycle rental, nearby golf, nature trails, business center, conference rooms, beauty salon, gift shops.

Moderate

Del Mar Motel on the Beach. 1702 Coast Blvd. (at 17th St.), Del Mar, CA 92014. ☎ **800/ 223-8449** or 619/755-1534. 45 rms. TV TEL. Summer, $100–$130 double. Additional person $5 extra. Lower rates off-season; sometimes higher on weekends and holidays. AE, CB, DC, DISC, MC, V. Free parking.

The only Del Mar property right on the beach, this little white-stucco motel with blue trim is clean and simply furnished. Upstairs rooms have one king-size bed, while those downstairs come with two doubles. All rooms have a refrigerator, coffeemaker, and fan. Half are non-smoking rooms, and only those with ocean views have bathtubs (the rest have showers). This is a good choice for beach lovers, because you can walk from here along the beach for miles, and the popular seaside restaurants Poseidon and Jake's are right next door. The motel has a barbecue and picnic table for guests' use.

Rock Haus. 410 15th St., Del Mar, CA 92014. ☎ **619/481-3764.** 10 rms, 4 with bath. $90– $110 double without bath; $120–$150 double with bath. Rates include continental breakfast. 2-night minimum stay required on weekends and holidays July–Sept. MC, V. Free parking.

In other incarnations this has been a private home, a place of worship, a gambling hall, and a hotel. Now restored and run by innkeeper Doris Lucero, the Rock Haus provides 10 guest rooms (six of them share three baths); most quarters have ocean views. The Triple Crown Room is our favorite. The Huntsman's Room has its own fireplace, which is great, but the shower stall here is really tiny. It might be better to enjoy the fireplace in the living room. Late-afternoon refreshments are served. There's no smoking inside the house and children under 13 aren't permitted. Perched on a hill behind the Del Mar Plaza, the Rock Haus is a short stroll away from shopping, dining, and the beach.

✪ **Wave Crest.** 1400 Ocean Ave., Del Mar, CA 92014. ☎ **619/755-0100.** Fax 619/ 793-8232. 31 condo apts. TV TEL. Mid-June to mid-Sept, $175–$200 studio; $210–$240 one-bedroom apt; $300 two-bedroom apt. Mid-Sept to mid-June, $115–$135 studio; $140– $160 one-bedroom apt; $195 two-bedroom apt. Weekly rates available year-round. MC, V. Free parking.

On a bluff over the Pacific, these gray-shingled time-share condominiums are beautifully maintained and offer a high standard of self-contained living. All the modern units surround a landscaped courtyard and have a queen-size bed and sofa beds, artwork by local artists, TVs in living rooms and bedrooms, VCRs, stereos, full baths with great showers, and fully equipped kitchens. The studios can sleep one or two, the one-bedroom units up to four, and the two-bedrooms up to six. Guests share a communal lounge with a fireplace, wetbar, and TV; a really nice pool and bubbling Jacuzzi overlooking the ocean and the grounds have attractive plantings. A clifftop walking path and Seagrove Park are adjacent. It's only 5 minutes to the beach, and shopping and dining spots are only a few blocks away. There's an extra fee for maid service. Laundry facilities are on site.

WHERE TO DINE

Head to the upper level of the centrally located **Del Mar Plaza,** at Camino del Mar and 15th Street (☎ 619/792-1555), and consider **Il Fornaio Cucina Italiana** for excellent Italian cuisine; **Epazote** for Mexican, Tex-Mex, and southwestern fare; or **Pacifica Del Mar** for outstanding seafood. Kids like to eat at **Johnny Rockets,** an old-fashioned diner on the lower level. Down on the beach, **Jake's** and **Poseidon** are both good for California cuisine and sunset views; Jake's has a Sunday champagne brunch, and Poseidon's club sandwich and grilled chicken salad are wonderful. The racetrack crowd congregates at **Bully's,** 1404 Camino del Mar (☎ **619/755-1660**), for Bully Burgers, prime rib, and crab legs.

CARLSBAD

Fifteen miles north of Del Mar and 33 miles from downtown San Diego (a 45-minute drive), the pretty beach community of Carlsbad provides many reasons to linger: good swimming and surfing beaches (with a mile-long two-tiered beach walk that's accessible for travelers with disabilities), three lagoons perfect for walks or birdwatching, landscaped streets, memorable restaurants, and an abundance of antiques and gift shops.

There's a small-town atmosphere—the population is 63,000, but it actually feels smaller than Del Mar. You won't see any high-rise buildings (and none are on the drawing board). The town extends a warm welcome to travelers in the recycled train depot (1887) that's now home to the **Visitors Information Center** (☎ **619/ 434-6093**).

Carlsbad was named for Karlsbad, Bohemia, because of the similar mineral (some say curative) waters they both produced, but the town's once-famous artesian well has long been plugged up. You can picnic in small **Florence Magee Park;** while there, peek into tiny **St. Michael's by the Sea** Episcopal Church (1894); the original organ is to the right.

In spring, visit the 200 acres of cultivated flower fields that transform the hills south of town into a startling rainbow from March to May; in winter, witness a profusion of poinsettias here. The latest Flower Fields information is available at 619/431-0352 or on the Internet at **http://www.flowerflds@aol.com.** You can also see 3,000 varieties of flowers, plants, and trees year round at the serene, 30-acre **Quail Botanical Garden** in nearby Encinitas (☎ **619/436-3036**), open daily from 8am to 5pm.

WHERE TO STAY

Beach Terrace Inn. 2775 Ocean St., Carlsbad, CA 92003. ☎ **800/622-3224** in California, 800/433-5415 elsewhere in the U.S., or 619/729-5951. Fax 619/729-1078. 41 rms, 5 suites. A/C TV TEL. Summer, $108–$219 double; from $139 suite. Winter, $97–$177 double; from $117 suite. Rates include continental breakfast. Additional person $10 extra. AE, CB, DC, DISC, ER, MC, V. Free parking.

Carlsbad's only beachside hostelry (others are across the road or a little farther away), this Best Western property has a helpful staff, a living room–like lobby, and rooms and an outdoor pool with ocean views. The rooms, though not elegant, are extra large, and some have balconies, fireplaces, and kitchenettes; the suites have separate living rooms and bedrooms. VCRs and films are available at the front desk. This place is good for families. You can walk everywhere from here, and there's street parking as well as carports.

La Costa Resort and Spa. Costa del Mar Rd., Carlsbad, CA 92009. ☎ **800/854-5000** or 619/438-9111. Fax 619/931-7585. 478 rms and suites. A/C TV TEL. $245–$420 double; $395–$2,100 suite. Golf, spa, and tennis packages available. AE, CB, DC, DISC, MC, V. Valet parking $10 overnight, self-parking free.

La Costa Resort boasts two championship 18-hole golf courses (home of the annual Mercedes Championships); a 21-court racquet club comprising 2 grass, 4 clay, and 15 composite courts (home of the WTA Toshiba Tennis Classic); resident tennis pro Pancho Segura (who has coached Jimmy Connors and Andre Agassi); an extensive spa with a multitude of treatments available; and five restaurants. These amenities are spread over 450 landscaped acres. The attractive accommodations offer all the bells and whistles you'd expect at this price level. The big advantage is that travel partners can do their own things during the day (golf, tennis, or the spa) and still rendezvous for dinner. However, this resort—built in the mid-1960s—isn't looking as fresh as it once did.

✪ **Pelican Cove Inn.** 320 Walnut Ave., Carlsbad, CA 92008. ☎ **619/434-5995.** 8 rms. $85–$175 double. Rates include full breakfast. Additional person $15 extra. AE, MC, V. Free parking. Complimentary transfer from Oceanside train station or Palomar Airport.

This Cape Cod–style hideaway near the beach combines romance with luxury— down to the bedcovers, which resemble clouds more than comforters. All rooms have fireplaces and private entrances; two have spa tubs. You can lounge or have breakfast in the garden with a gazebo and a sundeck. Hosts Kris and Nancy Nayudu can provide beach towels and chairs or prepare a wonderful picnic basket (with 24-hour notice) that you can enjoy on the lovely local beaches or parks. All guest rooms are non-smoking.

Tamarack Beach Resort. 3200 Carlsbad Blvd., Carlsbad, CA 92008. ☎ **800/334-2199** or 619/729-3500. Fax 619/434-5942. 23 rms, 54 condo apts. A/C TV TEL. $115–$150 double; $155–$260 condo apt. Children 11 and under stay free in parents' room. Weekly rates available. AE, MC, V. Free security parking.

This resort property's rooms, across the street from the beach, are restfully decorated in tropical colors and wicker furniture, with small refrigerators, coffee making facilities, and VCRs (movies are complimentary). The fully equipped condos (including washer/dryer) are available on a daily or weekly basis. The pretty Tamarack also has a pleasant lobby, a heated pool in a sunny courtyard, two Jacuzzis, exercise facilities, valet services, barbecue grills, and a good restaurant, Dini's by the Sea, which is popular with locals.

WHERE TO DINE

Local favorites include **Branci's Caldo Pomodoro,** 2907 State St. (☎ 619/720-9998); **Neiman's,** 2978 Carlsbad Boulevard. (☎ 619/729-4131); and ❸ **Tip Top Meats,** 6118 Paseo del Norte (☎ 619/438-2620).

OCEANSIDE

The most northerly town in San Diego County (actually it's a city of 100,000) and 36 miles from San Diego, Oceanside claims almost 4 miles of beach and one of the West Coast's longest wooden piers (a tram does nothing but transport people 1,600 feet from the street to the end and back for 25¢ one-way). The restaurant at the end of the pier is a great place for lunch over the ocean. The beach, the pier, and a well-tended recreational area with playground equipment and an outdoor amphitheater are within easy walking distance of the train station. The small **California Surf Museum,** across from the pier, at 308 Pacific St. (☎ 619/721-6876), is open Monday, Thursday, and Friday from 10am to 4pm, and on Saturday and Sunday from 10am to 4pm.

Try not to miss **Mission San Luis Rey** (☎ 619/757-3651), a few miles inland. Founded in 1798, it's the largest of California's 21 missions. There's a small charge to tour the mission's impressive church, exhibits, grounds, and cemetery. You might recognize it as the backdrop for several Zorro movies. To get there, take Mission Drive to Rancho del Oro Avenue; toe mission is on the left-hand side.

For an information packet about Oceanside and its attractions, send a check for $3 to the **Oceanside Chamber of Commerce,** P.O. Box 1578, Oceanside, CA 92051 (☎ **619/722-1534**).

A SIDE TRIP INLAND: RANCHO SANTE FE

The coastal and inland sections of North San Diego County are as different as night and day. Beaches and laid-back villages where work seems to be the curse of the surfing class characterize the coast, while inland you'll find beautiful barren hills, citrus groves, and conservative communities where agriculture plays an important role.

Rancho Santa Fe is located about 27 miles north of downtown San Diego, and from there the Del Dios Highway (S6) leads to Escondido, almost 32 miles from the city. San Marcos, Vista, and Fallbrook are even farther north. Nearly 70 miles away is Palomar Mountain in the Cleveland National Forest, which spills over the border into Riverside County. The **San Diego North County Convention & Visitors Bureau** (☎ **800/848-3336**) can answer all your questions.

Certainly one of the county's loveliest communities, exclusive Rancho Santa Fe was once the property of the Santa Fe Railroad, and the eucalyptus trees it grew there still create a stately atmosphere. The Del Dios Highway (S6) is the scenic route to Escondido and the Wild Animal Park. This road affords views of Lake Hodges, as well as glimpses of expansive estates, some of the most expensive in the country.

WHERE TO STAY

✪ **Rancho Valencia Resort.** 5921 Valencia Circle (P.O. Box 9126), Rancho Santa Fe, CA 92067. ☎ **800/548-3664** or 619/756-1123. Fax 619/756-0165. 43 suites in 21 casitas. MINIBAR TV TEL. $360–900 suite. Tennis, golf, and romance packages available. AE, CB, DC, MC, V. Free valet and self-parking.

If you need pampering and relaxation or a romantic getaway, read on. A member of Relais et Châteaux and Preferred Hotels, this sun-baked Spanish- and Mediterranean-style resort sits on 40 acres overlooking the San Diequito Valley and the rolling hills of Rancho Santa Fe. Small and intimate, the resort is far removed from the fast pace of the real world, even though it's only a short way from I-5 and only 6 miles inland from Del Mar. Imagine having your own casita with cathedral ceilings, terra-cotta tiles, Berber carpets, wood-burning fireplace, ceiling fans, oversize tiled bath, walk-in closet, patio, and private terrace. To boot, spa treatments and massages can be given in the casita itself. Fresh-squeezed juice and a newspaper are left outside your door in the morning, and coffeemaking equipment is available. Those who actually do venture outside their casita will discover grounds filled with 2,000 citrus trees, bougainvillea, and air sweetened by flowers and birdsong.

There's a lap pool; a large, secluded pool; three Jacuzzis; and a fitness room. Those more athletically inclined can take advantage of the 18 tennis courts and tennis clinics with a four-to-one student/teacher ratio. You also might check out the championship croquet lawn, or play a round of golf at private courses adjacent to the resort. Bikes for adults and kids are available at no extra charge, and there are plenty of hiking trails to enjoy. I highly recommend this place, and I don't think you'll be disappointed. You can visit Rancho Valencia on the Internet via their home page at **http://www.infopost.com/valencia/index.html.**

Dining/Entertainment: The pretty dining room serves three Mediterranean-California meals a day, with a cellist or guitarist on Friday and Saturday nights; there's dancing under the stars on Thursday nights in July and August. The Clintons dined here while they were in town. Tea and cocktails are served in La Sala, from which there's a great view of the hot-air balloons at sunset.

Services: Concierge, room service (24 hours), laundry/dry cleaning, complimentary morning paper and fresh orange juice, in-room massage, twice-daily maid service, evening turndown, baby-sitting, secretarial services, valet parking, airport transportation from San Diego's Lindbergh Field.

Facilities: Two cable TVs and VCRs in each suite; video rentals; in-room safes; two pools; three Jacuzzis; unlimited use of 18 hard-turf tennis courts, tennis clinics, and match arranging; regulation croquet court; golf privileges at four nearby private golf clubs; fitness room; bicycles; massage rooms.

12 Julian: Apples, Pies & A Slice of Small-Town California

A trip 60 miles northeast of San Diego to Julian (pop. 1,500) is a trip back in time. The old gold-mining town, now best known for its apples, has some good eateries and a handful of cute B&Bs, but its popularity is based on the fact that it provides a chance for city-weary folks to get away from it all. However, when it's sunny in San Diego it may be snowing in Julian, perched 4,235 feet above sea level.

Before you leave, try Julian's apple pies; whether the best pies come from Mom's Pies, Mrs. Glad's Bakery, or the Julian Pie Company is a toss-up. It's fun to sample all of them and decide for yourself.

ESSENTIALS

AREA CODE On March 22, 1997, the area code in Julian will change from 619 to **760.**

GETTING THERE The 90-minute drive from San Diego can be made via Calif. 78 or I-8 to Calif. 79. I suggest taking one route going and the other coming back, since Calif. 79 winds through scenic Rancho Cuyamaca State Park, while Calif. 78 traverses open country and farmland.

If you come by Calif. 78, you'll pass the mission church of **Santa Ysabel** (1812), where there's a tiny museum and a large Native American cemetery, on your right, as well as **Dudley's Bakery,** off to the left at the junction with Calif. 79 and just 7 miles from Julian. The bakery, here since 1963, is known for its breads, from raisin date nut to jalapeño, and on weekends 5,000 to 6,000 loaves come out of the ovens. Dudley's is open Wednesday to Sunday from 8am to 5pm.

VISITOR INFORMATION Town maps and flyers for accommodations are available from the Town Hall, on Main Street at Washington Street. The town has a **24-hour hotline** (☎ 619/765-0707) to provide information on lodging, dining, shopping, activities, upcoming events, weather, and road conditions. For a brochure on what to see and do, contact the **Julian Chamber of Commerce** (☎ 619/765-1857). The **Julian Arts Guild** (☎ 619/765-0560) can answer questions about the Fine Arts Show.

EXPLORING THE TOWN

It's fun to learn about the town and surrounding area by visiting the **Julian Cider Mill,** which moved in about 20 years ago when a service station moved out. The father-and-son team of Turk and Fred Slaughter run this actual mill where you can see cider being made. Homemade peanut butter is ground on the premises too, and in the spring a glass-enclosed beehive bustles with activity. Because the town is relatively near to both desert and sea (either is within 1 1/2 hours' drive), Julian honey is particularly good. It's hard not to feel like a kid in this store filled with jawbreakers, preserves, nuts, trail mix, and easy conversation around a potbelly stove.

On the right as you come into town is the **Julian Pioneer Museum,** at 4th and Washington streets (☎ **619/765-0227**), housed in an old brewery and open Tuesday to Sunday from 10am to 4pm April to November, weekends and holidays December to March. Here you can learn about some of the old-timers buried up the hill in the Haven of Rest Cemetery.

The **Eagle & High Peak Mines** (☎ **619/765-0036**), 6 blocks from Main Street via C Street, operate daily from 9am to 4pm but only for educational reasons, since the gold is long gone.

It's fun to dart in and out of the little shops in Julian. Our favorites are the **Julian Farms Antiques Shop,** 2818 Washington St. (☎ 619/765-0250), for gifts and patio accessories, and **Warm Hearth,** 2125 Main St. (☎ 619/765-1022), for gifts, cassettes, and wood-burning stoves, if you're in the market for one. **Applewood,** next door to Julian Farms Antiques, is also very good.

You can mix culture with barbecue at the **Pine Hills Dinner Theater** on Friday and Saturday nights at Pine Hills Lodge, a few miles from Julian off Pine Hills Road (☎ **619/765-1100**). The rustic lodge opened its doors on July 4, 1912; in 1980 Dave and Donna Goodman bought it and opened the 96-seat dinner theater, which has staged almost 70 productions, among them *I'm Not Rappaport* and *Last of the Red-Hot Lovers.* The dinner buffet of delicious baby back pork ribs or barbecued chicken starts promptly at 7pm; give them 24-hour notice and you can get a vegetarian plate. Showtime is at 8pm, and the price for the dinner and the theater is $28.50; for the show alone it's $14.50. The playhouse was built in 1926 as a gym for boxing champion Jack Dempsey when he was training for his fight against Gene Tunney.

To hear some music—folk or piano or maybe the strains of a hammered dulcimer—head out to the **Wynola Coffee Company** (☎ 619/765-2023), in a big red barn just over 3 miles south of town on Calif. 78; it'll be on the left. The musicians are on hand only on Saturday from 7pm, and people of all ages come to this local hangout with its mismatched tables and chairs to hear them and indulge in dessert and coffee. The cover is about $3.

Country Carriages (☎ 619/765-1471) will show you the sights and give you a spin down a country lane in a horse-drawn wagon for $20 per couple or around the town for $5 per adult, $2 per child. Hop on in front of or catercorner to the drugstore; the ride lasts half an hour.

Special events here have special appeal, especially Julian's popular fall apple harvest starting in mid-September and continuing for an entire month (it used to be only one weekend, but the traffic in town got way out of hand). The annual wildflower show lasts for a week in early May. There's also a Spring Fine Arts Show in May. And the annual weed show, a tradition since 1961, is usually held the last few weeks in August or the beginning of September.

EXPLORING THE COUNTRYSIDE

If there's something about being in the country that makes you want to hop in the car and drive down one rural road after another, Julian is an ideal starting point. You'll pass rolling hills, country stores, rambling houses, and fruit stands and come upon towns with names like Ramona, Ballena, and Wynola.

One of our favorite short drives is along the road leading to the **Menghini Winery** (☎ 619/765-2072), owned and run by Toni and Michael Menghini; it's 2 miles out on Farmer's Road (follow it west out of town until you see the winery sign, then bear to the left down the hill). The winery is usually open on Monday, Friday, Saturday, and Sunday from 10am to 4pm, daily in October and December, or call for an appointment. The grapes come from Ramona and Temecula, and the local favorite wine is Julian Blossom. The tanks are right in the tasting room, and the wines are sold only locally, for $7 to $10 per bottle. You may enjoy your purchase right away in the picnic area in the apple orchard.

If you don't make it to the desert this trip, at least take a moment to gaze out at it and the Salton Sea from **Inspiration Point,** just 1¹/₂ miles south of Julian on Calif. 79, opposite Pinecroft Park. **Lake Cuyamaca** (pronounced *Kwee*-yah-*mack*-ah), 10 miles south on Calif. 79, offers boating, fishing (bass, trout, and crappie), and recreational vehicle camping on a first-come, first-served basis. Its facilities are open from sunrise to sunset daily (☎ 619/765-0515 or 619/447-8123). There are motorboat and rowboat rentals, a 3¹/₂-mile hiking trail around the lake, and a charge for fishing ($4.50 for adults, $2.50 for children 8 to 15). A restaurant with a deck and adjoining store overlook the lake.

For a different way to tour, try **Llama Trek** (☎ 800/LAMAPAK or 619/765-1890; fax 619/765-1512). Trips include rural neighborhoods, a historic gold mine, mountain and lake views, and apple orchards. They even conduct a trek to the local winery. Rates vary from $55 to $75 per person and include lunch (the winery trek also includes wine tasting).

WHERE TO STAY

🏠 **Julian Farms Lodging.** 2818 Washington St., Julian, CA 92036. ☎ **619/765-0250.** 4 attached cottages, 1 cabin. TV. $69 double; $99 cabin. Additional person $5 extra. AE, MC, V.

Driving into town, you'll find it easy to pass right by this little place on the left. That would be a shame because the yellow cottages with blue shutters and a grape arbor in front make the perfect secret hideaway. Three of the cottages have a double bed and a daybed in a single room; one has two double beds in two rooms and is perfect for families. All have small private baths with showers, hot pots, country antiques, goose-down comforters, and a split of Julian Blossom wine. A nearby cabin has a queen-size bed and a sitting area. You can pick all the grapes you want and eat them in the vine-covered gazebo. It's just down the hill from Main Street. Reserve 3 to 4 months ahead for weekends. Smoking is permitted outside only.

Julian Hotel. Main St. and B St. (P.O. Box 1856), Julian, CA 92036. ☎ **619/765-0201.** 15 rms, 3 with bath; 2 cottages. $72–$90 double without bath; $82–$110 double with bath; $125–$160 cottage. Rates include full breakfast. AE, MC, V.

The Julian Hotel has been putting a roof over travelers' heads since the days when the Butterfield stagecoach stopped across the street. A potbelly stove still sits in the parlor, along with an upright piano that arrived from Philadelphia via Cape Horn. The hotel's original owners, Albert and Margaret Robinson, were former slaves; their photograph hangs on the parlor wall. There are a dozen rooms in the original part of the house—with "necessary rooms" at the end of the hall—and each room is decorated in a variation of a Victorian theme. Another three rooms (with bath) were added off the front porch in 1920. One of the cottages, the Honeymoon House, features a Franklin (freestanding) fireplace and an old-fashioned tub. The cottages book up 2 months in advance. The hotel's generous breakfast menu includes apple-filled pancakes and omelets. Coffee, tea, cakes, and cookies are served in the parlor at 5pm.

❂ Orchard Hill Country Inn. 2502 Washington St. (at 2nd St.; P.O. Box 425), Julian, CA 92036-0425. ☎ **619/765-1700.** Fax 619/765-0290. 10 rms, 12 suites. A/C MINIBAR TV TEL. $140–$195 double. Rates include full breakfast and afternoon hors d'oeuvres. Additional person $25 extra. 2-night minimum stay if including Fri or Sat. Deposit required. Midweek discounts available. AE, MC, V. Limited free parking.

Darrell and Pat Straube offer the most upscale lodging in Julian—a two-story lodge and four 1928 California Craftsman-style cottages on a hill with a panoramic view that includes the historic townsite. Ten guest rooms, a guests-only dining room, and a "great room" with a massive stone fireplace are in the lodge; 12 suites are in cottages over 3 acres of grounds. All quarters feature attractive furnishings including plantation shutters. Suite amenities include fireplaces, whirlpool tubs, wet bars, VCRs, books, videos, games, and wraparound porches. Breakfast can be delivered to suite occupants.

BED & BREAKFASTS

For a list and a description of a dozen interesting B&Bs, contact the **Julian Bed & Breakfast Guild,** P.O. Box 1711, Julian, CA 92036 (☎ **619/765-1555** daily from 9am to 9pm). All members are within a few miles of the town center.

Our favorites are the **Julian White House** (☎ 800/WHT-HOUS or 619/ 765-1764) and the **Artists' Loft** (☎ 619/765-0765).

CAMPING

Cuyamaca Rancho State Park is 11 miles from Julian, and a new camp store and interpretive center are located a mile from the entrance. It's another 2 miles to a little museum and park headquarters where you can stock up on maps, information, and even books to help you identify local flora and fauna. The park has more than 100 miles of trails, and you can see Mexico from Cuyamaca Peak (6,512 feet).

Campsites are set in the midst of trees and scrubs; each one has a table and fire ring. Reserve a spot in **Paso Picacho** or **Green Valley Campground,** both with about 80 sites (☎ **800/444-PARK** for reservations, or 619/765-0755 for park information only). The camping fee is $14 in summer, $12 off-season, or $5 for day use only. They book up fast on weekends from Easter to Thanksgiving, so plan ahead. Park headquarters is open Monday to Friday from 8am to 5pm.

WHERE TO DINE

Julian Cafe. Main St. ☎ **619/765-2712.** Menu items $2.50–$9. MC, V. Mon–Fri 8am– 7:30pm, Sat–Sun 7am–8pm. AMERICAN.

A tasty, filling chicken pie is the specialty here; buy it at lunch for $6.95 or pay $8.95 for the full dinner. Mashed potatoes come the old-fashioned way, smothered in country gravy. Other home-cooked offerings include fried chicken, liver and onions, meatloaf dinner, and a hot vegetable plate. This is a good place to bring kids; the waitresses are friendly and service is quick, even when it's packed.

Julian Fondue and Cheesecake Company. 1921 Main St. ☎ **619/765-2817.** Reservations recommended. Classic Swiss fondue $10.50 per serving. No credit cards. Fri–Sat noon–9pm, Sun (and Mon holidays) noon–7pm. SWISS.

You'll know you're in the right place when you see the red-and-white Swiss flag. Proprietor John Nyffenegger is proud of his heritage—and his grandfather, uncle, and cousin who were cheesemakers should be proud of him, too. John's fondue is made in the Bernese style with imported emmenthaler, gruyère, and some raclette cheeses, as well as garlic, spices, and a blend of six Napa Valley wines. Chocolate fondue is available for dessert. There's no liquor license here, but you're welcome to bring your own wine and pay a small corkage fee. Couples who dine here will learn about the

600-year-old tradition that says if she drops her bread in the cheese, he gets a kiss, but if he drops his bread, he buys another bottle of wine for them to share. Either way, I figure he's going to get that kiss.

13 Anza-Borrego Desert State Park

The vast, striking landscapes of Anza-Borrego comprise the largest state park in the Lower 48 states. Most visitors come during the spring **wildflower season,** when a colorful carpet of flowers blankets the desert floor and climbs into the surrounding hills and mountains. Call the Wildflower Hotline at 619/767-4684 to find out what's blooming during your trip.

JUST THE FACTS

Anza-Borrego Desert State Park (☎ **619/767-4205** or 619/767-5311) is open from October to May, daily from 9am to 5pm; June to September, on Saturday, Sunday, and holidays from 9am to 5pm.

The park lies about 90 miles northeast of San Diego or 150 miles southwest of Los Angeles between I-10 and I-8. It's reached by Calif. 78 and Calif. 79 from the east and by I-8 from the south.

Information on the park is available from the **Borrego Springs Chamber of Commerce** (☎ 619/767-5555); the **California Desert Tourism Association** (☎ 619/328-9256); and the **Julian Chamber of Commerce** (☎ 619/765-1857).

Note: The telephone area code here will change from 619 to **760** in March 1997.

SEEING THE HIGHLIGHTS

At the **visitors center,** you're introduced to the park and desert with a 15-minute slide show and exhibits that cover the local ecosystem and the history of the Native Americans who once lived here. Hiking maps are on sale here as well.

Hikers can choose from more than 100 miles of designated trails. About 35 miles are part of the **Pacific Crest Trail** that goes from Mexico to Canada. Register at the visitors center before setting out. If you don't want to attempt a serious hike, there are a number of shorter **nature trails.** The **Borrego Palm Canyon Trail** starts at the main campground and will take you to a grove of California fan palms, the largest palm species in North America, and a year-round stream, one of the 25 oases in the park. Brochures are available at the visitors center for a number of these nature trails.

A few hundred rare bighorn sheep live in the park's rough, rocky terrain, and other animal residents include rabbits, desert mice, the chuckwalla (the largest lizard in the park), coyotes, mule deer, and bobcats.

Horseback trails surround the park's Vernon Whitaker horse camp. One trail ascends 12 miles to the top of the mountains for a spectacular vista. Riders may use all the dirt roads in the park, but not the nature or hiking trails.

CAMPING

There are two developed campgrounds in the park. **Borrego Palm Canyon Campground** has 52 full-hookup sites (fees are $16 to $22) and 65 multi-use sites without hookups ($10 to $16). Another 27 multi-use nonhookup sites are situated at **Tamarisk Grove** ($10 to $16). All the park's nonhookup sites have shade ramadas.

You and your horse can stay at the park's **Vernon Whitaker horse camp.** All 10 campsites can hold up to eight people and have corrals for four horses. Reservations for the campgrounds and horse camp are made through Destinet

(☎ 800/444-PARK). Payment can be made with MasterCard, Visa, or personal check. The horse camp is the hub of many miles of riding trails.

Bow Willow is a primitive camping site off S2. It has picnic tables and portable toilet facilities. Once you're out of the developed areas of the park, you can camp just about anywhere along its 500 miles of primitive roads. Only two restrictions apply: First, you must keep your vehicle within one car length of the road so as not to damage the fragile plant life. Second, you can't camp near a watering hole or spring, as it scares away the wildlife.

WHERE TO STAY NEARBY IN BORREGO SPRINGS

The nearby town of Borrego Springs, just down the road from the visitors center, offers tourist services, including restaurants, shops, and motels, plus one very special accommodation:

✪ **La Casa del Zorro.** 3845 Yaqui Pass Rd., Borrego Springs, CA 92004. ☎ **800/824-1884** or 619/767-5323. Fax 619/767-5963. 79 rms and suites, 19 cottages/villas. A/C TV TEL. $85–$100 double; from $125 suite; from $150 cottage/villa. Children 11 and under stay free in parents' room. Lower summer and midweek rates. Special packages available. AE, DC, DISC, MC, V.

This is a beautiful oasis in the desert, surrounded by more than 500,000 acres of the unforgettable scenery of Anza-Borrego State Park. Each room is accented with pieces that reflect the early California heritage of Borrego Spring, and comes with thoughtful touches such as bathrobes, hair dryers, and coffeemakers. Some units have terraces, fireplaces, or Jacuzzis. The resort's facilities include three swimming pools, bicycles, six tennis courts, a fitness center, a whirlpool, and a beauty salon. There's a restaurant on the premises, as well as a bar that offers live entertainment.

14 Temecula: San Diego's Wine Country

Located in Riverside County, 60 miles north of San Diego, Temecula is known for its wineries and the excellent vintages they produce. The name of the town is pronounced Te-*mec*-u-la, a Native American word meaning "where the sun shines through the mist." It's the only town on California's west coast that still goes by its aboriginal name, and if you gaze out over the vineyards early in the morning or in the middle of the afternoon, the name still holds true. The region was used as the setting for Helen Hunt Jackson's novel *Ramona*, first published in 1884.

Temecula has a couple of unique claims to fame. Granite from its quarries (most of which closed down in 1915, when reinforced concrete became popular) constitutes most of the street curbs in San Francisco. The last person sentenced to death by hanging in California was Temecula's blacksmith, John McNeil, who killed his wife in 1936.

When you turn onto Rancho California Road, all you'll see at first is new construction, but soon the vineyards come into view and the countryside turns natural again—a relief after the onslaught of progress, something relatively new to this area. Back in 1968, one vintner recalls, "if you heard a car come down Rancho California Road, you'd go to the window to see who could possibly be lost way out here."

Temecula's microclimate, allowing grapes to flourish, is due to a notch in the coastal mountains called Rainbow Gap, which lets breezes blow through from the ocean, 22 miles away. They result both in temperatures that are 8°F to 10°F cooler than on the coast, and it has a longer growing season; this lets grapes ripen more slowly. Most vineyards here are more than 1,400 feet above sea level.

ESSENTIALS

To get there, travel north from San Diego on I-15 for 50 miles; when the Temecula Valley comes into view, it'll take your breath away. To reach the vineyards (they're well marked), head east on Rancho California Road.

For information on accommodations and maps and brochures on Old Town Temecula and the vineyards, contact the **Temecula Valley Chamber of Commerce,** 27450 Ynez Rd., Suite 104, Temecula, CA 92591 (☎ **909/676-5090**), or visit their homepage at **http://www.temecula.org**. The **Temecula Valley Vintners Association,** P.O. Box 1601, Temecula, CA 92593-1601 (☎ **909/699-3626**), is another good source, especially about the vineyards.

EXPLORING THE AREA
VISITING THE WINERIES

Temecula is not as well known for its wines as Napa or Sonoma because those wine-producing regions have been at it 100 years longer. Franciscan missionaries planted the first grapevines here in the early 1800s, but the land ended up being used primarily for cattle raising on the 87,000-acre Vail Ranch from 1904 until 1964, when the ranch was sold. Grapevines began to take root in the receptive soil again in 1968, and the first Temecula wines were produced in 1971.

Today there are 11 wineries in the region, most of them strung side by side for a couple of miles along Rancho California Road, producing white, red, and rosé wines. Most of them are not sold outside of California or the West, although some have made it as far as the White House.

Since the wineries in Temecula are smaller than their counterparts in Northern California, and are mostly family-owned and -operated, you're more likely to meet and talk with the vinters when you come to their property. You're not likely to be there alone, however; 300 to 400 people can show up on the weekends.

Harvest time is usually mid-August to September, and visitors are welcome then and all the year through to tour, taste, and stock up. In addition, half a dozen local companies offer balloon rides over the vineyards, an unforgettable sight. Two that have been around for about 20 years are **DAE Flights** (☎ **909/676-3902**) and **Sunrise Balloons** (☎ **800/548-9912**).

THORNTON   As you drive along Rancho California Road, you'll first come to the **Thornton Winery** (☎ **909/699-0099**), housed in a striking stone building with a waterfall and sloping lawn in front and a herb garden in back. Today Thornton produces Culbertson sparkling wine, à la méthode champenoise, as well as Brindiamo premium varietal wines. The gift shop sells a nice range of wine-related items. There's a champagne bar with a jukebox where drinks are about $5 a glass, or you can pay $6 to taste two champagnes and two still wines. Open daily from 10am to 5pm, with the bar opening at noon. There are tours on Saturday and Sunday. Café Champagne, the vineyard's award-winning restaurant, is open for lunch and dinner and serves California cuisine (see "Where to Dine," below). The winery hosts jazz concerts in from April to October.

CALLAWAY   Across the road from Thronton is **Callaway** (☎ **909/676-4001**), in a long, low white building with brown trim, set in grounds lush with 2,500 rose bushes and orange trees. Producing wine here since 1974—nine labels in all, mostly whites—it offers the most in-depth tour. There's a $3 charge to sample four different wines; you get to keep the glass. The large gift shop features not only the Callaway vintages, but also gift baskets, books on wine, aprons, cups, and T-shirts. A vine-covered picnic area overlooks the vineyards (if you didn't come prepared to dine alfresco, there's a market 4 miles down the road). Open daily from 10:30am to 5pm, with free tours Monday to Friday at 11am, 1pm, and 3pm, on the hour from 11am to 4pm weekends. Closed New Year's Day, Easter, Thanksgiving, and Christmas.

MOUNT PALOMAR   Turn off the main road and follow the blacktop up and over the hill to the **Mount Palomar Winery** (☎ 909/676-5047), where tastings of four wines of your choice cost $2, including the souvenir glass. Outside, 60 tables are available for picnicking, some on a spot overlooking the property belonging to the vineyard. From the winery, you can gaze out at Mt. San Jacinto and, behind it, Mt. San Gorgonio, the highest mountain in Southern California. Deli snacks are always available, and a full-service deli operates Friday to Sunday. Open October to March, daily from 10am to 5pm; April to September, daily from 10am to 6pm. Free tours are given Monday to Friday at 1:30 and 3:30pm, and on Saturday and Sunday at 11:30am, 1:30pm, and 3:30pm. Try to come before 1pm on weekends, when people may stand five deep for tastings, so popular are Mount Palomar's reisling and chardonnay, along with their port and cream sherry.

CILURZO   Turn off on Calle Contento to the **Cilurzo Vineyard & Winery** (☎ 909/676-5250), whose owner, Vince Cilurzo, may be better known in some circles in Los Angeles as the man who has lighted the TV game show *Jeopardy!* for many years (he still does so a couple of days a week). Out here he's known as a vintner who established this 52-acre vineyard in 1968 and started producing wines in 1978. One of the most popular Cilurzo labels is the Petite Sirah, which, Vince claims, can be served with anything from tomato sauce to curry. Unlike many other Temecula wineries, this one has no bar for tastings; instead, visitors sit in chairs and Vince Cilurzo or his wife, Audrey, serves them. A tasting of five or six wines costs $1, refundable with a purchase. Photos on the wall at the back of the tasting room capture moments from Vince's star-studded career. A picnic area overlooks the pond. Open daily from 9:30am to 4:45pm.

MAURICE CARRIE   Last on Rancho California Road we come to **Maurice Carrie** (☎ 909/676-1711), in a large two-story pseudo-southern building with veranda and gazebo—a "Victorian farmhouse," owner Maurice Van Roekel likes to call it. She and her husband, Budd, came here to retire, but soon were producing red and white wines instead. Four of their wines are named after their grandchildren. The property has a wine boutique, a resident cat named Butterscotch, and a lovely oak bar trimmed with black and white tiles that draws a good afternoon crowd. The boutique sells wine and champagne glasses and insulated wine coolers, among other items. A deli section carries juice, crackers, and cold wine. Tastings available. Open daily from 10am to 5pm.

A WALKING TOUR OF OLD TOWN TEMECULA

A wonderful, eccentric counterpoint to the vineyards is the old part of the city of Temecula, preserved as it was in the 1890s—western storefronts and all. It lies 4 miles west of the vineyards off Rancho California Road, stretches along 6 short blocks, and has a reputation as an antique hunter's haven.

Park at the south end of town near the Swing Inn Café or Butterfield Plaza and walk north along Main Street to 6th Street and back, going up one side of the street and back on the other. Take time to read the plaques on the old buildings along the way. Be forewarned that Temecula has become a traffic-clogged town, and you'll hear the drone of cars most everywhere, even on the golf course.

One of our favorite spots in town, partly for the name, is the **Swing Inn Café,** at 28676 Front St. (see "Where to Dine," below), where a sign claims that the cafe's been in existence since 1927. I asked my waitress if that was true. "Look around," she said. "Some of our customers have been here that long."

Continue along the same side of Front Street as the Swing Inn Café 1 block to Main Street to visit the **Temecula Valley Museum,** at 41950 Main St. On the right (unless it has moved to Sam Hicks Park by the time you pass through), the museum houses Native American artifacts from the area that are more than 1,000 years old, along with memorabilia from 1846 to the 1940s, and a model of the town from 1914. The museum, which is open Wednesday to Sunday from 11am to 4pm and by appointment, will eventually move into a new, three-times-larger space at Sam Hicks Park, across from the post office on Moreno Drive (☎ 909/676-0021).

For antiques, check out **Ronnie's House,** Front Street at 5th Street (☎ 909/ 676-4229). While a number of the "antiques" stores in the town sell more of what I'd call "collectibles," Ronnie has the real thing—all more than 100 years old. She's originally from Brooklyn, New York, and has had her store here since 1980. A lot of the items come from back East and beyond.

At Front and 6th streets, turn right and walk a short block to **Sam Hicks Park,** home to the "They Passed This Way" Monument and the Old St. Catherine's Church, which dates from the early 1920s and is now part of the Temecula Valley Museum, which will relocate to the park.

Cross Front Street and walk back down the west side of the street. At Front and 6th streets is the **Chaparral Antique Mall,** with more than 70 dealers under one roof (☎ 909/676-0070). Down at Front and Main streets stands the **First National Bank,** which was built in 1912 and managed to stay open during the Great Depression, gaining it the nickname the "Pawn Shop." The bank finally closed in 1941 and the building now houses a Mexican restaurant. For many years its second floor was the town's community center and dance hall.

Nearby are two plunderable antiques malls: **Morgan's Antiques** (☎ 909/ 676-2722), in a brick building dating from 1891 that for 60 years was Burnham's Store, the mainstay of local ranchers, and beside it, the **Temecula Trading Post** (☎ 909/676-5759). Across the street stands the Old Welty/Temecula Hotel, built in 1882, the year the railroad came to Temecula; it burned and was rebuilt in 1891 and now is a private residence. Check out the store beside it, **Country Seller and Friends** (☎ 909/676-2322), which sells furniture and antiques.

At the southwest corner of Main and Front streets, the **Welty Building,** which dates from the 1880s, now houses a deli but it used to be a gym where Jack Dempsey worked out.

A NATURE PRESERVE

For an outing in more than 3,000 acres of unspoiled terrain, take I-15 north to Clinton Keith Road and drive west on it for about 5 miles to get to the **Santa Rosa Plateau Ecological Reserve,** owned and maintained by the Nature Conservancy (☎ 909/677-6951). Here walking trails, coyotes, hawks, migrating birds, and maybe even an eagle or two await you.

WHERE TO STAY

Butterfield Inn Motel. 28718 Front St., Temecula, CA 92390. ☎ **909/676-4833.** Fax 909/ 676-2019. 39 rms. A/C TV TEL. $45–$89 double weekends, $55–$94 double weekdays. Additional person $5 extra. AE, DISC, MC, V. Take I-15 north to Rancho California Rd. West to Front St.

Within walking distance of Old Town Temecula shops, this motel (it's not really an inn) has an Old West facade, rooms with double or king-size beds, a small, unheated outdoor pool, and a Jacuzzi. There's complimentary coffee in the lobby in the morning. It's easy to imagine the Butterfield stagecoach pulling up any moment.

Loma Vista. 33350 La Serena Way, Temecula, CA 92591. ☎ **909/676-7047.** 6 rms. A/C. $95–$135 double weekends, $75–$115 double weekdays. Rates include full champagne breakfast. DISC, MC, V. Take I-15 to Rancho California Rd. East; the inn is on the left just beyond Callaway Vineyard.

Montana natives Betty and Dick Ryan came here from Los Angeles in 1988 and designed and built this tile-roofed, mission-style house for their bed-and-breakfast inn. Perfectly named, it sits on a hill (*loma* in Spanish) overlooking the best vista around. From the living room, you can look out at the Callaway Vineyard and the Santa Ana Mountains. All the guest rooms have full private bath and a queen- or king-size bed. Four have private wisteria-covered balconies; of these, favorites are Sauvignon Blanc, with southwestern furnishings made of white pine and a four-poster queen-size bed; and Fumé Blanc, in California garden style with white wicker. Besides complimentary fruit and a decanter of sherry in each room, free wine and cheese are served by the fire at 6pm. A spa bubbles away on the back patio, while the front patio, a great place just to wile away the hours, has a fire pit. The property is a real oasis, with 85 rosebushes, rununculas, daisies, Australian tea bushes, and 325 grapefruit trees. The resident dog is a dalmatian named Casey. Old Town Temecula is 5 miles away.

✪ Temecula Creek Inn. 44501 Rainbow Canyon Rd., Temecula, CA 92592. ☎ **800/962-7335** or 909/694-1000. Fax 714/676-3422. 70 rms, 10 junior suites. A/C MINIBAR TV TEL. Sun–Thurs, $115–$130 double; $145–$150 junior suite. Fri–Sat, $135–$130 double; $165–$170 junior suite. Golf and wine-country packages available. AE, DC, DISC, MC, V. From San Diego, take I-15 north to Exit 79 (Indio); turn right off the exit ramp and proceed to Pala Rd.; turn right, go over a little bridge, then take an immediate right onto Rainbow Canyon Rd. for half a mile.

This is a great spot for golfers and is a convenient location for visiting the wineries. Magnolia trees line the walkway from the resort's lobby to the restaurant. The pleasant lobby includes adobe walls, a leather couch, Native American artifacts, and a fireplace. The rooms, in five two-story buildings, all have restful views, as well as Native American–inspired furnishings that creatively combine art, muted colors, and textures. Most of the furnishings were custom designed or selected especially for the rooms from local antiques shops to evoke the region's Native American, Spanish, and western heritage. The junior suites are oversize corner rooms with two queen-size beds or a king-size bed, sitting areas, in-room safes, two balconies, and floor-to-ceiling windows. The TV is cleverly hidden under a piece of sculpture. If you're not allergic to feathers, you'll enjoy the down pillows. There are no porters, but you can drive up close to many of the rooms.

Dining/Entertainment: The Temet Grill (see "Where to Dine," below) is outstanding, from the service to the California wine country cuisine to the view beyond the dramatic window wall; breakfast, lunch, dinner, and Sunday brunch are offered. There's live music nightly in the lounge adjoining the restaurant. Food and cocktail service are available poolside.

Services: Laundry/dry cleaning, complimentary newspaper in lobby.

Facilities: Hair dryer and magnifying mirror in baths, coffee and tea in room (including beans and a grinder), in-room safe, cribs. Outdoor pool, spa, barbecue under live oaks, 27 holes of golf, driving range, volleyball, croquet, two tennis courts, golf and tennis pro shop, meeting rooms.

WHERE TO DINE

Baily Wine Country Cafe. In Miller's Outpost shopping center, 27644 Ynez Rd. (at Rancho California Rd.). ☎ **909/676-9567.** Reservations recommended, especially on weekends. Main courses $8.75–$19. AE, CB, DC, MC, V. Sun–Thurs 11:30am–9pm, Fri–Sat 11:30am–9:30pm. CALIFORNIA/CONTINENTAL.

If you aren't interested in winery tours and tastings, just come here. Baily's has the largest selection of Temecula Valley wines anywhere, including those from the Baily family's own winery on Rancho California Road. To show them off to best advantage, the cafe's chef has concocted some mouth-watering dishes, which change every few months. At lunch, try the penne with roasted garlic, fresh vegetables, and tomato sauce made chunky with Italian sausage, or better yet, a southwestern-style grilled cheese sandwich with cilantro (a regional prize winner). At night, consider such appetizers as crab cakes with roasted red-bell-pepper sauce and mixed greens. For a main course, choose from the likes of southwestern pork tenderloin with garlic mashed potatoes, salmon Wellington with cucumber and papaya relish and fresh vegetables, or chicken ravioli in a basil pesto. Finish off the meal with Carol Baily's white-chocolate cheesecake, a top choice with local diners. If you're in luck, the Baily family, who are always in evidence at the cafe, will be hosting one of their celebrated Dinners in the Wine Cellar. Smoking is allowed on the patio but not inside the restaurant. They can provide picnics to go with 24 hours' notice. The restaurant is to your right and up the hill after you enter the shopping center.

❁ **Cafe Champagne.** Thornton Winery, 32575 Rancho California Rd. ☎ **909/699-0088.** Reservations recommended. Main courses $13–$21. AE, MC, V. Daily 11am–9pm. CALIFORNIA.

The toast of the Temecula wine country, this bistro and cafe features tasty dishes specially created to be served with nine Thornton champagnes. The wine list also features other Temecula and California labels. Featuring California cuisine at its best, the lunch and dinner menus offer appetizers like warm brie en croûte with honey-walnut sauce, crab-and-shrimp strudel, and smoked salmon carpaccio. Among the entrees are angel-hair pasta primavera or with seafood, mesquite-grilled tuna, and baked pecan chicken. The list of mesquite-grilled entrees expands at dinner, and at lunch tempting lighter fare includes hearty salads and sandwiches filled with mesquite-grilled hamburger, steak, or chicken. The setting, overlooking the vineyard, is sublime. It's a small place, so do reserve ahead. If you have a high regard for really good food, you'll like it here.

Temet Grill. In the Temecula Creek Inn, 44501 Rainbow Canyon Rd. ☎ **909/676-5631.** Reservations recommended. Main courses $15.50–$19.50. AE, DC, DISC, MC, V. Mon–Sat 6:30am–10pm, Sun 6am–10pm. CALIFORNIA/SOUTHWESTERN.

The very attractive dining room has five striking chandeliers, Native American artifacts in glass cases, and floor-to-ceiling picture windows overlooking the golf course. The menu changes frequently, but you might find such specialties of the house as grilled tortilla pizza or grilled chiles rellenos with chipotle salsa. Creatively presented main courses might include roasted sea bass in a five-spice crust, sautéed or grilled chicken breast with beer-mustard and chipotle hollandaise, or grilled swordfish or steak. The wine list emphasizes California vintages, along with some from Oregon and Washington and a few French champagnes.

TEMECULA AFTER DARK

Any time of year for a fun evening out in Old Town Temecula, indulge in a little bit of country-western dancing at **The Temecula Stampede,** 28721 Front St., opposite the Butterfield Inn (☎ **909/695-1760**). This may be California's biggest saloon/dance hall, with 4,000 square feet incorporating dance areas for two-steppers, swing dancers, and line dancers. There's room left for eight pool tables, tables and chairs, and two impressive bars, one 110 feet long and the other 60 feet long. It's open Tuesday to Sunday from 6pm, with dance lessons given on Tuesday and Thursday nights. Live bands are on hand from 8:30pm until 2am Thursday to Saturday nights, when there's a $5 cover; otherwise, there's a DJ. Devotees range in age from the minimum of 21 to 80-plus, most decked out in western garb. Weekends are crowded. The entrance is at the back of the building.

On a spring or fall afternoon, head over to the **Thornton Winery** to hear jazz (see "Visiting the Wineries," above). There's an admission charge.

Index